**W9-DDL-135**

# CRITICAL SURVEY
## OF
# SHORT FICTION
### Fourth Edition

# CRITICAL SURVEY
# OF
# SHORT FICTION
## Fourth Edition

## Volume 4
### American Writers

J. D. Salinger - Paul Yoon

Appendixes - Indexes

*Editor*

### Charles E. May

California State University, Long Beach

Kishwaukee College Library
21193 Malta Rd.
Malta, IL 60150-9699

SALEM PRESS

Ipswich, Massachusetts    Hackensack, New Jersey

*Cover Photo:* Philip Roth © (Hulton Archive/Getty Images)

Copyright © 1981, 1987, 1993, 2001, 2012, Salem Press, A Division of EBSCO Publishing, Inc.

All rights in this book are reserved. No part of this work may be used or reproduced in any manner whatsoever or transmitted in any form or by any means, electronic or mechanical, including photocopy, recording, or any information storage and retrieval system, without written permission from the copyright owner. For information, contact the publisher, EBSCO Publishing, 10 Estes Street, Ipswich, MA 01938.

Some of the essays in this work, which have been updated, originally appeared in the following Salem Press publications, *Critical Survey of Short Fiction* (1981), *Critical Survey of Short Fiction, Supplement* (1987), *Critical Survey of Short Fiction, Revised Edition*, (1993; preceding volumes edited by Frank N. Magill), *Critical Survey of Short Fiction, Second Revised Edition* (2001; edited by Charles E. May).

The paper used in these volumes conforms to the American National Standard for Permanence of Paper for Printed Library Materials, X39.48-1992 (R1997).

LIBRARY OF CONGRESS CATALOGING-IN-PUBLICATION DATA

Critical survey of short fiction / editor, Charles E. May. -- 4th ed.
    p. cm.
Includes bibliographical references and index.
ISBN 978-1-58765-789-4 (set : alk. paper) -- ISBN 978-1-58765-790-0 (set, american : alk. paper) --
ISBN 978-1-58765-791-7 (vol. 1, american : alk. paper) -- ISBN 978-1-58765-792-4 (vol. 2, american : alk. paper) --
ISBN 978-1-58765-793-1 (vol. 3, american : alk. paper) -- ISBN 978-1-58765-794-8 (vol. 4, american : alk. paper) --
ISBN 978-1-58765-795-5 (set, british : alk. paper) -- ISBN 978-1-58765-796-2 (vol. 1, british : alk. paper) --
ISBN 978-1-58765-797-9 (vol. 2, british : alk. paper) -- ISBN 978-1-58765-798-6 (european : alk. paper) --
ISBN 978-1-58765-799-3 (world : alk. paper) -- ISBN 978-1-58765-800-6 (topical essays : alk. paper) --
ISBN 978-1-58765-803-7 (cumulative index : alk. paper)

1. Short story. 2. Short story--Bio-bibliography. I. May, Charles E. (Charles Edward), 1941-
PN3321.C7 2011
809.3'1--dc23

    2011026000

First Printing

PRINTED IN THE UNITED STATES OF AMERICA

# CONTENTS

# CONTRIBUTORS

Randy L. Abbott
*University of Evansville*

Michael Adams
*CUNY Graduate Center*

Patrick Adcock
*Henderson State University*

Thomas P. Adler
*Purdue University*

A. Owen Aldridge
*University of Illinois*

Charmaine Allmon-Mosby
*Western Kentucky University*

Emily Alward
*College of Southern Nevada*

Andrew J. Angyal
*Elon University*

Jacob M. Appel
*The Mount Sinai Medical School*

Gerald S. Argetsinger
*Rochester Institute of Technology*

Karen L. Arnold
*Columbia, Maryland*

Marilyn Arnold
*Brigham Young University*

Leonard R. N. Ashley
*Brooklyn College, City University of New York*

Bryan Aubrey
*Fairfield, Iowa*

Stephen Aubrey
*Brooklyn College*

Edmund August
*McKendree College*

Jane L. Ball
*Wilberforce University*

David Barratt
*Montreat College*

Melissa E. Barth
*Appalachian State University*

Martha Bayless
*University of Oregon*

Alvin K. Benson
*Utah Valley University*

Stephen Benz
*Barry University*

Margaret Boe Birns
*New York University*

Nicholas Birns
*Eugene Lang College, The New School*

Elizabeth Blakesley
*Washington State University Libraries*

Richard Bleiler
*University of Connecticut*

Lynn Z. Bloom
*University of Connecticut*

Julia B. Boken
*Indiana University, Southeast*

Jo-Ellen Lipman Boon
*Buena Park, California*

William Boyle
*University of Mississippi*

Virginia Brackett
*Park University*

Harold Branam
*Savannah State University*

Gerhard Brand
*California State University, Los Angeles*

Alan Brown
*Livingston University*

Mary Hanford Bruce
*Monmouth College*

Carl Brucker
*Arkansas Tech University*

John C. Buchanan
*Original Contributor*

Stefan Buchenberger
*Kanagawa University*

Louis J. Budd
*Original Contributor*

Rebecca R. Butler
*Dalton College*

Susan Butterworth
*Salem State College*

Edmund J. Campion
*University of Tennessee, Knoxville*

Larry A. Carlson
*Original Contributor*

Amee Carmines
*Hampton University*

Thomas Gregory Carpenter
*Lipscomb University*

John Carr
*Original Contributor*

Warren J. Carson
*University of South Carolina, Spartanburg*

Mary LeDonne Cassidy
*South Carolina State University*

Thomas J. Cassidy
*South Carolina State University*

Hal Charles
*Eastern Kentucky University*

C. L. Chua
*California State University, Fresno*

David W. Cole
*University of Wisconsin Colleges*

Laurie Coleman
*Original Contributor*

Richard Hauer Costa
*Texas A&M University*

Ailsa Cox
*Edge Hill University*

Lisa-Anne Culp
*Nuclear Regulatory Commission*

Heidi K. Czerwiec
*Univeristy of North Dakota*

Dolores A. D'Angelo
*American University*

Anita Price Davis
*Converse College*

Frank Day
*Clemson University*

Danielle A. DeFoe
*Sierra College*

Bill Delaney
*San Diego, California*

Joan DelFattore
*University of Delaware*

Kathryn Zabelle Derounian
*University of Arkansas-Little Rock*

Joseph Dewey
*University of Pittsburgh*

Marcia B. Dinneen
*Bridgewater State University*

Thomas Du Bose
*Louisiana State University-Shreveport*

Stefan Dziemianowicz
*Bloomfield, New Jersey*

Wilton Eckley
*Colorado School of Mines*

K Edgington
*Towson University*

Robert P. Ellis
*Northborough Historical Society*

Sonia Erlich
*Lesley University*

Thomas L. Erskine
*Salisbury University*

Christopher Estep
*Original Contributor*

Walter Evans
*Augusta College*

Jack Ewing
*Boise, Idaho*

Kevin Eyster
*Madonna University*

Nettie Farris
*University of Louisville*

Howard Faulkner
*Original Contributor*

James Feast
*Baruch College*

Thomas R. Feller
*Nashville, Tennessee*

John W. Fiero
*University of Louisiana
  at Lafayette*

Edward Fiorelli
*St. John's University*

Rebecca Hendrick Flannagan
*Rrancis Marion University*

James K. Folsom
*Original Contributor*

Ben Forkner
*Original Contributor*

Joseph Francavilla
*Columbus State University*

Timothy C. Frazer
*Western Illinois University*

Kathy Ruth Frazier
*Original Contributor*

Tom Frazier
*Cumberland College*

Rachel E. Frier
*Rockville, Maryland*

Terri Frongia
*Santa Rosa Junior College*

Miriam Fuchs
*University of Hawaii-Manoa*

Jean C. Fulton
*Landmark College*

Louis Gallo
*Radford University*

Ann Davison Garbett
*Averett University*

Marshall Bruce Gentry
*Georgia College & State University*

Jill B. Gidmark
*University of Minnesota*

M. Carmen Gomez-Galisteo
*Esne-Universidad Camilo
Jose Cela*

Linda S. Gordon
*Worcester State College*

Julian Grajewski
*Tuscon, Arizona*

Charles A. Gramlich
*Xavier University of Louisiana*

James L. Green
*Arizona State University*

Glenda I. Griffin
*Sam Houston State University*

John L. Grigsby
*Appalachian Research & Defense
Fund of Kentucky, Inc.*

William E. Grim
*Ohio University*

Elsie Galbreath Haley
*Metropolitan State College of Denver*

David Mike Hamilton
*Original Contributor*

Katherine Hanley
*St. Bernard's School of Theology
and Ministry*

Michele Hardy
*Prince George's Community
 College*

Betsy Harfst
*Kishwaukee College*

Alan C. Haslam
*Sierra College*

CJ Hauser
*Brooklyn College*

Peter B. Heller
*Manhattan College*

Terry Heller
*Coe College*

Diane Andrews Henningfeld
*Adrian College*

DeWitt Henry
*Emerson College*

Cheryl Herr
*Original Contributor*

Allen Hibbard
*Middle Tennessee State Univer-
sity*

Cynthia Packard Hill
*University of Massachusetts at
Amherst*

Jane Hill
*Original Contributor*

Nika Hoffman
*Crossroads School for
Arts & Sciences*

William Hoffman
*Fort Myers, Florida*

Hal Holladay
*Simon's Rock College of Bard*

Kimberley M. Holloway
*King College*

Gregory D. Horn
*Southwest Virginia Commmunity
College*

Sylvia Huete
*Original Contributor*

Edward Huffstetler
*Bridgewater College*

Theodore C. Humphrey
*California State Polytechnic Uni-
versity, Pomona*

Robert Jacobs
*Central Washington University*

Shakuntala Jayaswal
*University of New Haven*

Clarence O. Johnson
*Joplin, Missouri*

Eunice Pedersen Johnston
*North Dakota State University*

Theresa Kanoza
*Lincoln Land Community College*

William P. Keen
*Washington & Jefferson College*

Fiona Kelleghan
*South Miami, Florida*

Cassandra Kircher
*Elon College*

Paula Kopacz
*Eastern Kentucky University*

Uma Kukathas
*Seattle, Washingtom*

Rebecca Kuzins
*Pasadena, California*

Marvin Lachman
*Santa Fe, New Mexico*

Thomas D. Lane
*Original Contributor*

John Lang
*Emory & Henry College*

Carlota Larrea
*Pennsylvania State University*

Donald F. Larsson
*Mankato State University*

William Laskowski
*Jamestown College*

Norman Lavers
*Arkansas State University*

David Layton
*University of California, Santa Barbar*

Allen Learst
*Oklahome State University*

James Ward Lee
*University of North Texas*

Katy L. Leedy
*Marquette University*

Leon Lewis
*Appalachian State University*

Elizabeth Johnston Lipscomb
*Randolph-Macon Women's College*

Douglas Long
*Pasadena, California*

Michael Loudon
*Eastern Illinois University*

Robert M. Luscher
*University of Nebraska at Kearney*

Carol J. Luther
*Pellissippi State Community College*

R. C. Lutz
*CII Group*

Laurie Lykken
*Century College*

Andrew F. Macdonald
*Loyola University*

Joanne McCarthy
*Tacoma Washington*

Richard D. McGhee
*Arkansas State University*

S. Thomas Mack
*University of South Carolina-Aiken*

Victoria E. McLure
*Texas Tech University*

Robert J. McNutt
*University of Tennessee at Chattanooga*

Bryant Mangum
*Original Contributor*

Barry Mann
*Alliance Theatre*

Mary E. Markland
*Argosy University*

Patricia Marks
*Valdosta State College*

Wythe Marschall
*Brooklyn College*

Karen M. Cleveland Marwick
*Hemel Hempstead, Hertfordshire, England*

Charles E. May
*California State University, Long Beach*

Laurence W. Mazzeno
*Alvernia College*

Patrick Meanor
*SUNY College at Oneonta*

Martha Meek
*Original Contributor*

Ann A. Merrill
*Emory University*

Robert W. Millett
*Original Contributor*

Christian H. Moe
*Southern Illinois University at Carbondale*

Robert A. Morace
*Daemen College*

Christina Murphy
*Original Contributor*

Earl Paulus Murphy
*Harris-Stowe State College*

John M. Muste
*Ohio State University*

Donna B. Nalley
*South University*

Keith Neilson
*California State University, Fullerton*

William Nelles
*University of Massachusetts-Dartmouth*

John Nizalowski
*Mesa State College*

Martha Nochimson
*Mercy College*

Emma Coburn Norris
*Troy State University*

Bruce Olsen
*Austin Peay State University*

Brian L. Olson
*Kalamazoo Valley Community College*

James Norman O'Neill
*Bryant College*

Keri L. Overall
*University of South Carolina*

Janet Taylor Palmer
*Caldwell Community College & Technical Institute*

Sally B. Palmer
*South Dakota School of Mines & Technology*

Robert J. Paradowski
*Rochester Institute of Technology*

David B. Parsell
*Furman University*

Susie Paul
*Auburn University, Montgomery*

Leslie A. Pearl
*San Diego, California*

David Peck
*Laguna Beach, California*

William Peden
*University of Missouri-Columbia*

Chapel Louise Petty
*Blackwell, Oklahoma*

Susan L. Piepke
*Bridgewater College*

Constance Pierce
*Original Contributor*

Mary Ellen Pitts
*Rhodes College*

Victoria Price
*Lamar University*

Jere Real
*Lynchburg, Virginia*

Peter J. Reed
*University of Minnesota*

Rosemary M. Canfield Reisman
*Sonoma, California*

Martha E. Rhynes
*Oklahoma East Central University*

James Curry Robison
*Original Contributor*

Mary Rohrberger
*New Orleans, Louisiana*

Douglas Rollins
*Dawson College*

Carl Rollyson
*Baruch College, CUNY*

Paul Rosefeldt
*Delgado Community College*

Ruth Rosenberg
*Brooklyn, New York*

Irene Struthers Rush
*Boise, Idaho*

David Sadkin
*Hamburg, New York*

David N. Samuelson
*California State University, Long Beach*

Elizabeth D. Schafer
*Loachapoka, Alabama*

Barbara Kitt Seidman
*Linfield College*

D. Dean Shackelford
*Concord College*

M. K. Shaddix
*Dublin University*

Allen Shepherd
*Original Contributor*

Nancy E. Sherrod
*Georgia Southern University*

Thelma J. Shinn
*Arizona State University*

R. Baird Shuman
*University of Illinois at Urbana-Champaign*

Paul Siegrist
*Fort Hays State University*

Charles L. P. Silet
*Iowa State University*

Karin A. Silet
*University of Wisconsin-Madison*

Genevieve Slomski
*New Britain, Connecticut*

Roger Smith
*Portland, Oregon*

Ira Smolensky
*Monmouth College*

Katherine Snipes
*Spokane, Washington*

Sandra Whipple Spanier
*Original Contributor*

Brian Stableford
*Reading, United Kingdom*

John Stark
*Original Contributor*

Joshua Stein
*Los Medanos College*

Karen F. Stein
*University of Rhode Island*

Judith L. Steininger
*Milwaukee School of Engineering*

Ingo R. Stoehr
*Kilgore College*

Louise M. Stone
*Bloomsburg University*

William B. Stone
*Chicago, Illinois*

Theresa L. Stowell
*Adrian College*

Gerald H. Strauss
*Bloomsburg University*

Ryan D. Stryffeler
*Western Nevada College*

W. J. Stuckey
*Purdue University*

Catherine Swanson
*Austin, Texas*

Philip A. Tapley
*Louisiana College*

Terry Theodore
*University of North Carolina at Wilmington*

Maxine S. Theodoulou
*The Union Institute*

David J. Thieneman
*Original Contributor*

Lou Thompson
*Texas Woman's University*

Michael Trussler
*University of Regina*

Richard Tuerk
*Texas A&M University-Commerce*

Scott Vander Ploeg
*Madisonville Community College*

Dennis Vannatta
*University of Arkansas at Little Rock*

Jaquelyn W. Walsh
*McNeese State University*

Shawncey Webb
*Taylor University*

James Michael Welsh
*Salisbury State University*

James Whitlark
*Texas Tech University*

Barbara Wiedemann
*Auburn University at Montgomery*

Albert Wilhelm

*Tennessee Technological University*

Donna Glee Williams

*North Carolina Center for the Advancement of Teaching*

Patricia A. R. Williams

*Original Contributor*

Judith Barton Williamson

*Sauk Valley Community College*

Michael Witkoski

*University of South Carolina*

Jennifer L. Wyatt

*Civic Memorial High School*

Scott D. Yarbrough

*Charleston Southern University*

Mary F. Yudin

*State College, Pennsylvania*

Hasan Zia

*Original Contributor*

Gay Pitman Zieger

*Santa Fe College*

# COMPLETE LIST OF CONTENTS

## American Volume 1

## American Volume 2

## American Volume 3

## American Volume 4

# KEY TO PRONUNCIATION

To help users of the *Critical Survey of Short Fiction* pronounce unfamiliar names of profiled writers correctly, phonetic spellings using the character symbols listed below appear in parentheses immediately after the first mention of the writer's name in the narrative text. Stressed syllables are indicated in capital letters, and syllables are separated by hyphens.

## *VOWEL SOUNDS*
### *Symbol: Spelled (Pronounced)*

a:   answer (AN-suhr), laugh (laf), sample (SAM-puhl), that (that)

ah:   father (FAH-thur), hospital (HAHS-pih-tuhl)

aw:   awful (AW-fuhl), caught (kawt)

ay:   blaze (blayz), fade (fayd), waiter (WAYT-ur), weigh (way)

eh:   bed (behd), head (hehd), said (sehd)

ee:   believe (bee-LEEV), cedar (SEE-dur), leader (LEED-ur), liter (LEE-tur)

ew:   boot (bewt), lose (lewz)

i:   buy (bi), height (hit), lie (li), surprise (sur-PRIZ)

ih:   bitter (BIH-tur), pill (pihl)

o:   cotton (KO-tuhn), hot (hot)

oh:   below (bee-LOH), coat (koht), note (noht), wholesome (HOHL-suhm)

oo:   good (good), look (look)

ow:   couch (kowch), how (how)

oy:   boy (boy), coin (koyn)

uh:   about (uh-BOWT), butter (BUH-tuhr), enough (ee-NUHF), other (UH-thur)

## *CONSONANT SOUNDS*
### *Symbol: Spelled (Pronounced)*

ch:   beach (beech), chimp (chihmp)

g:   beg (behg), disguise (dihs-GIZ), get (geht)

j:   digit (DIH-juht), edge (ehj), jet (jeht)

k:   cat (kat), kitten (KIH-tuhn), hex (hehks)

s:   cellar (SEHL-ur), save (sayv), scent (sehnt)

sh:   champagne (sham-PAYN), issue (IH-shew), shop (shop)

ur:   birth (burth), disturb (dihs-TURB), earth (urth), letter (LEH-tur)

y:   useful (YEWS-fuhl), young (yuhng)

z:   business (BIHZ-nehs), zest (zehst)

zh:   vision (VIH-zhuhn)

# S

## J. D. SALINGER

**Born:** New York, New York; January 1, 1919
**Died:** Cornish, New Hampshire; January 27, 2010

PRINCIPAL SHORT FICTION

*Nine Stories,* 1953

*Franny and Zooey,* 1961

*"Raise High the Roof Beam, Carpenters"* and
*"Seymour: An Introduction,"* 1963

OTHER LITERARY FORMS

The most famous work of J. D. Salinger (SAL-ihn-jur), besides his short stories, is the novel *The Catcher in the Rye* (1951), which influenced a generation of readers and is still considered a classic.

ACHIEVEMENTS

The precise and powerful creation of J. D. Salinger's characters, especially Holden Caulfield and the Glass family, has led them to become part of American folklore. Salinger's ironic fiction and enigmatic personality captured the imagination of post-World War II critics and students. His authorized books were published over the course of twelve years, from 1951 to 1963, yet his works still remain steadily in print in many languages throughout the world.

Salinger received a number of awards in his career. "This Sandwich Has No Mayonnaise" was selected as one of the distinguished short stories published in American magazines for 1945 and was later included in *The Best Short Stories 1946*. "Just Before the War with the Eskimos" was reprinted in *Prize Stories of 1949*. "A Girl I Know" was selected for *The Best American Short Stories 1949*. "For Esmé--with Love and Squalor" was selected as one of the distinguished short stories published in American magazines in 1950 and is included in *Prize Stories of 1950*. The novel *The Catcher in the Rye* was a Book-of-the-Month Club selection for 1951.

Critic Martin Green remarked that Salinger was not so much a writer who depicted life as one who celebrated it, an accurate characterization of the humor and love in his work. Ultimately, the most serious charge against him is that his output was too small.

BIOGRAPHY

Jerome David Salinger was the second child--his sister, Doris, was born eight years before him--and only son of Sol and Miriam Jillich Salinger, a Jewish father and a Christian mother. His father was a successful importer of hams and cheeses. Salinger was a serious child who kept mostly to himself. His IQ test score was above average, and his grades at public schools in the upper West Side of Manhattan were in the "B" range. Socially, his experiences at summer camp were more successful than in the Manhattan public schools. At Camp Wigwam in Harrison, Maine, he was voted at age eleven "the most popular actor of 1930."

In 1934, Salinger entered Valley Forge Military Academy in Pennsylvania, a school resembling Pencey Prep in *The Catcher in the Rye*. Salinger, however, was more successful at Valley Forge than Holden had been at Pencey, and in June, 1936, Valley Forge gave him his only diploma. He was literary editor of the academy yearbook and wrote a poem that was set to music and sung at the school.

In 1937, he enrolled in summer school at New York University but left for Austria and Poland to try working in his father's meat import business. In 1938, after returning to the United States, he briefly attended Ursinus College in Collegeville, Pennsylvania. There, he wrote a column, "Skipped Diploma," which featured film reviews for the college newspaper. In 1939, he signed up for a short-story course at Columbia

University, given by Whit Burnett, editor of *Story* magazine. In 1940, his first short story, "The Young Folks," was published in the March/April issue of *Story* magazine, and he was paid twenty-five dollars for it.

The story "Go See Eddie" was published in the December issue of the University of Kansas City *Review*. In 1941, "The Hang of It" appeared in *Collier's* and "The Heart of a Broken Story" in *Esquire*. Salinger sold his first story about Holden Caulfield to *The New Yorker*, but publication was delayed until 1946 because of the United States' entry into World War II.

In 1942, Salinger was drafted. He used his weekend passes to hide in a hotel room and write. He attended Officers, First Sergeants, and Instructors School of the Signal Corps. He engaged in a brief romantic correspondence with Oona O'Neill, daughter of the playwright Eugene O'Neill and later to be the wife of Charles Chaplin. In 1943, he was stationed in Nashville, Tennessee, with the rank of staff sergeant and transferred to the Army Counter-Intelligence Corps. During this time, "The Varioni Brothers" became his first story published in *The Saturday Evening Post*. He received counterintelligence training in Devonshire, England. During the war, he landed on Utah Beach in Normandy as part of the D-Day invasion force and participated in five campaigns. It was during this period that he met war correspondent Ernest Hemingway.

In 1945, Salinger was discharged from the Army. He continued to publish stories, including two stories with material later to be used in *The Catcher in the Rye*. In 1948, he began a long, exclusive association with *The New Yorker* with "A Perfect Day for Bananafish," the first story about Seymour Glass. Early in 1950, Salinger began studying Advaita Vedanta, an Eastern religious philosophy, in New York City. In 1951, *The Catcher in the Rye* was published, and in 1953, he moved to Cornish, New Hampshire, where he would live until his death on January 27, 2010.

In the following years, several of his stories were published in *The New Yorker*, including "Franny," "Raise High the Roof Beam, Carpenters," "Zooey," "Seymour: An Introduction," and "Hapworth 16, 1924." Salinger married Claire Douglas on February 17, 1955. A daughter, Margaret Ann, was born in 1955,

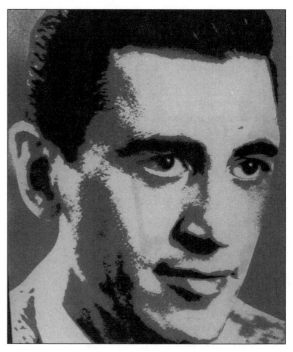

*J. D. Salinger* (D.C. Public Library)

and a son, Matthew, in 1960. Salinger was divorced from his wife in 1967. In 1987, Matthew Salinger starred in a made-for-television film. In the mid-1980's, Salinger, known to be a reclusive person, became the center of public attention when he protested the publication of an unauthorized biography by Ian Hamilton. The suit led to the rewriting of Hamilton's biography, which was published in 1988.

ANALYSIS

The main characters of J. D. Salinger, neurotic and sensitive people, search unsuccessfully for love in a metropolitan setting. They see the phoniness, egotism, and hypocrisy around them. There is a failure of communication between people: between husbands and wives, between soldiers in wartime, between roommates in schools. A sense of loss, especially the loss of a sibling, recurs frequently. Many of his stories have wartime settings and involve characters who have served in World War II. Some of these characters cannot adjust to the military, some have unhappy marital relationships, and others are unsuccessful in both areas. The love for children occurs frequently in his stories--for example, the love for Esmé, Phoebe, and Sybil. Like William Wordsworth, Salinger appreciates childhood innocence. Children have a wisdom and a spontaneity that is lost in the distractions and temptations of adult life.

Salinger's early stories contain elements foreshadowing his later work. Many of these stories are concerned with adolescents. In "The Young Folks," however, the adolescents resemble the insensitive schoolmates of Holden Caulfield more than they resemble Holden himself. Salinger demonstrates his admirable ear for teenage dialogue in these stories.

The reader sees how often members of the Glass family are present in the stories or novelettes. Looking back at Salinger's early works, one sees how these selections can be related to events in the actual life of Salinger, as well as how they contain characters who are part of the Glass family saga.

### "FOR ESMÉ--WITH LOVE AND SQUALOR"

An early example is the character of Sergeant X in "For Esmé--with Love and Squalor," from the collection *Nine Stories*. The time and setting of this story tie it into the experiences of Salinger abroad during World War II. At the same time, Sergeant X is Seymour Glass. The reader is shown the egotism of the wife and mother-in-law of Sergeant X, who write selfish civilian letters to the American soldier about to be landed in France, requesting German knitting wool and complaining about the service at Shrafft's restaurant in Manhattan.

This behavior is the same as that of the insensitive wife of "A Perfect Day for Bananafish" and that of the wife and mother-in-law of "Raise High the Roof Beam, Carpenters." The only person who offers love to Sergeant X is the brave British orphan Esmé, who sings with a voice like a bird and offers him the wristwatch of her deceased father. Esmé is too proper a British noblewoman to kiss Sergeant X, but she drags her five-year-old brother, Charles, back into the tearoom to kiss the soldier good-bye and even invites him to her wedding, five years later. Esmé's love restores Sergeant X from the breakdown that he suffered from the war. The gestures of love from Esmé lead to Sergeant X finally being able to go to sleep, a sign of recovery in the Glass family.

The love of Esmé is contrasted to the squalor of the other people around Seymour. His wife, "a breathtakingly levelheaded girl," discourages Sergeant X from attending the wedding of Esmé because his mother-in-law will be visiting at the same time (another selfish reason). The "squalor" that is contrasted to the pure, noble love of Esmé is also exemplified in the letter of the older brother of Sergeant X, who requests "a couple of bayonets or swastikas" as souvenirs for his children. Sergeant X tears up his brother's letter and throws the pieces into a wastebasket into which he later vomits. He cannot so easily escape the squalor of the "photogenic" Corporal Z, from whom readers learn that Sergeant X had been released from a hospital after a nervous breakdown. Corporal Clay, the jeep-mate of Sergeant X, personifies even more the squalor that Sergeant X is "getting better acquainted with," in one form or another. Clay has been "brutal," "cruel," and "dirty" by unnecessarily shooting a cat and constantly dwelling upon the incident.

Clay has a name that represents earth and dirt. He is obtuse and insensitive. He is contrasted to the spirituality, sensitivity, and love expressed by Esmé. Clay brings news of the officious character Bulling, who forces underlings to travel at inconvenient hours to impress them with his authority, and of Clay's girlfriend Loretta, a psychology major who blames the breakdown of Sergeant X not on wartime experiences but on lifelong instability, yet excuses Clay's sadistic killing of the cat as "temporary insanity." The killing of the cat is similar to Hemingway's killing a chicken in the presence of Salinger when the two men met overseas. The love of Esmé redeems and rejuvenates Sergeant X from his private hell in this well-written and moving story.

### "UNCLE WIGGILY IN CONNECTICUT"

References to other members of the Glass family tie other stories to the saga of the Glass children. Eloise, the Connecticut housewife in "Uncle Wiggily in Connecticut," had been in love with a soldier named "Walt." Walt was one of the twin brothers in the Glass family. He had been killed during the war not in battle but in a senseless accident. The central characters in the story are Eloise, a frustrated housewife, living trapped in a wealthy Connecticut home with a man she does not love and her memories of the soldier Walt whom she had loved dearly; and Ramona, her young daughter. Salinger himself was living in Connecticut at the time when he wrote this story.

Ramona may lack the nobility and capacity to show affection that Esmé had, yet she is an imaginative child, with abilities that her mother does not understand or appreciate. Ramona compensates for her loneliness by creating imaginary friends, such as "Jimmy Jimmer-eeno." This imaginative spontaneity in Ramona is in danger of being stifled by Eloise. Once when drunk, Eloise frightens her daughter by waking her up during the night after seeing her sleeping on one side of the bed to leave space for her new playmate, "Mickey Mic-keranno." Eloise herself was comforted by memories of her old beloved Walt but did not permit Ramona to also have an imaginary companion. The suburban mother suddenly realizes what has happened to her and begins to cry, as does her frightened daughter. All El-oise has left is the small comfort of her memories of Walt. She now realizes that she had been trying to force Ramona to give up her fantasies about imaginary boy-friends too. In this Salinger story, there is again a con-trast between the "nice" world of love that Eloise re-members she once had and the rude, "squalid" Connecticut world in which she is currently living.

### THE GLASS FAMILY CYCLE

The Glass Family Cycle writings of Salinger can be best discussed by dividing them into three sections: his early writings, his great classic works, and the Glass family cycle. The later works of Salinger are more con-cerned with religion than the earlier ones. Most of these later works deal with members of the Glass family, char-acters who have elements in common with Salinger him-self. They are sensitive and introspective, they hate pho-niness, and they have great verbal skill. They are also interested in mystical religion. "Glass" is an appropriate name for the family. Glass is a clear substance through which a person can see to acquire further knowledge and enlightenment, yet glass is also extremely fragile and breakable and therefore could apply to the nervous break-downs or near breakdowns of members of the family. The Glass family also attempts to reach enlightenment through the methods of Zen Buddhism. Professor Daisetz Suzuki of Columbia University, whose work is said to have influenced Salinger, commented that

the basic idea of Zen is to come in touch with the inner workings of our being, and to do this in the most direct way possible, without resorting to any-thing external or superadded. . . . Zen is the ultimate fact of all philosophy and religion.

What Seymour, Zooey, and Franny Glass want to do is to come in touch with the inner workings of their being in order to achieve nonintellectual enlighten-ment. With all religions at their fingertips, the Glass siblings use anything Zen-like, and it is their compara-tive success or failure in this enterprise that forms the basic conflict in their stories. In "Raise High the Roof Beam, Carpenters," the point made is that Seymour, who has achieved the satori, or Zen enlightenment, is considered abnormal by the world and loved and ad-mired only by his siblings. He is despised by other people who cannot comprehend his behavior. The maid of honor at the wedding that Seymour failed to attend describes him as a schizoid and a latent homosexual. His brother Buddy, the only Glass family member at-tending the wedding, is forced to defend his brother by himself. After enduring all the misinformed verbal at-tacks on his brother, Buddy replies: "I said that not one God-damn person, of all the patronizing, fourth-rate critics and column writers, had ever seen him for what he really was. A poet, for God's sake. And I mean a *poet*."

The central figure around whom all the stories of the Glass family revolve is Seymour, Seymour alive, Sey-mour quoted by Zooey, and the memory of Seymour when he is no longer physically alive. Once the Zen experience is understood by the reader, the meaning of earlier stories about the Glass siblings becomes more intelligible as contributing to Salinger's goal in his later stories. Zen is a process of reducing and emptying all the opinions and values that one has learned and that one has been conditioned to that interfere with one's perceptions.

### "A PERFECT DAY FOR BANANAFISH"

The first Glass story, "A Perfect Day for Banan-afish," is a kind of koan (paradox), one whose meaning the Glass children will be mediating upon for years to come. Seymour is the Bananafish. He has taken in so much from outside himself, knowledge and sensations, and he is so stuffed that he cannot free himself and climb out of the banana hole.

Seymour, in this first story, is married to Muriel and lives in a world of martinis and phony conversations in Miami Beach. He discovers that Muriel looks like Charlotte, the girl at whom he threw a stone in his earlier life because her physical loveliness was distracting him from his spiritual quest. He cannot communicate with his wife either. Muriel Fedder was aptly named because her presence serves as a "fetter" to Seymour. The only one with whom he *can* communicate is Sybil, the young child who is still so uncorrupted by the opinions and values of the world that her clear perceptions give her the status of the mythological Sybil.

Seymour has found, unfortunately, that Muriel Fedder Glass will not serve, teach, or strengthen him, as Seymour's diary entry before his marriage had indicated: "Marriage partners are to serve each other. Elevate, help, teach, strengthen each other, but above all, serve." Boo Boo Glass wrote a more admiring tribute to Seymour on the bathroom mirror than one senses from Muriel. Muriel is found reading a *Reader's Digest* article, "Sex Is Fun--or Hell." Marriage to Muriel has turned out not to be a spiritually enlightening experience. The only move that Seymour can make in his spiritual quest is to empty himself totally of all the opinions, values, and drives, of all sensations that distract and hinder him in achieving his spiritual goal. He is best able to move forward in his search by committing suicide and becoming pure spirit. Critic Warren French wrote, "When Muriel then subsequently fails to live up to his expectations of a spouse, he realizes the futility of continuing a life that promises no further spiritual development."

The critic Ann Marple noted that

> Salinger's first full-length novel, *The Catcher in the Rye*, emerged after scattered fragments concerning his characters appeared over a seven-year span. For some time now it has been evident that Salinger's second novel may be developing in the same way.

Salinger wrote of *Franny and Zooey*: "Both stories are early, critical entries in a narrative series I am doing about a family of settlers in 20th Century New York,

the Glasses." The remaining stories deal with Zen Buddhism and the effort to achieve a Zen-inspired awakening. They continue to deal with Seymour Glass and his influence on his siblings. In addition, the work of Salinger becomes increasingly experimental as he continues to write.

### "FRANNY" AND "ZOOEY"

When "Franny" was first published in the January 29, 1955, issue of *The New Yorker*, no mention was made that Franny was a member of the Glass family. All the reader knows is that Franny is visiting her boyfriend Lane for a football weekend at an Ivy League college. Lane is an insensitive pseudointellectual who brags about his successful term paper on Gustave Flaubert as he consumes frogs' legs. Lane is not interested in the religious book *The Way of the Pilgrim* that Franny describes to him or in hearing about the Jesus prayer that has a tremendous mystical effect on the entire outlook of the person who is praying. The luncheon continues, with Lane finishing the snails and frogs' legs that he had ordered. The contrast has deepened between the mystical spirituality of Franny and Lane's interest in satisfying his physical appetites. The reader is shocked at the part of the story when Franny faints. She is apparently suffering from morning sickness. The implication is that Lane is the father of her unborn child.

Almost two and a half years pass before the title character is identified as Franny Glass. "Zooey" was published in the May 4, 1957, issue of *The New Yorker*. It continued the story of Franny Glass, the youngest of the siblings of Seymour Glass. It is made clear in this story that Franny was not pregnant in the earlier story but was suffering from a nervous breakdown as a result of her unsuccessful attempt to achieve spiritual enlightenment. In "Zooey," her brother identifies the book that Franny is carrying to their mother as *The Pilgrim Continues His Way*, a sequel to the other book, both of which she had gotten from Seymour's old room. Zooey cannot console his sister at first. Franny is crying uncontrollably. Zooey finally goes into the room that had been occupied previously by Seymour and Buddy. Zooey attempts to impersonate Buddy when he calls Franny on the telephone, but Franny eventually recognizes the voice of the caller. Zooey is finally able to convince his sister that the mystical experience she should strive for is not of seeing Christ directly but that of seeing Christ through ordinary people. "There isn't anyone anywhere who isn't Seymour's Fat Lady," who is really "Christ himself, buddy." Reassured by the words of her brother, Franny can finally fall asleep.

In "Franny," as in many other Salinger short stories, character is revealed through a series of actions under stress, and the purpose of the story is reached at the moment of epiphany, an artistic technique formulated by James Joyce, in which a character achieves a sudden perception of truth. In "Franny," Salinger uses the theatrical tricks of a telephone in an empty room and of one person impersonating another. He often uses the bathroom of the Glass apartment as a place where important messages are left, important discussions are conducted, important documents are read. It is on the bathroom cabinet mirror that Boo Boo Glass leaves the epithalamium prayer for her brother on his wedding day, from which the title of the story "Raise High the Roof Beams, Carpenters" is taken. The Glass bathroom is almost a sacred temple. Bessie Glass, in the "Zooey" portion of *Franny and Zooey*, goes in there to discuss with Zooey how to deal with Franny's nervous breakdown. Buddy closes the bathroom door of the apartment he had shared with Seymour to read the diary of Seymour on his wedding day. He reads that Seymour is so happy that he cannot attend his wedding on that date (although he subsequently elopes with Muriel Fedder). The reader sees in *Franny and Zooey* the role Seymour played in the lives of his youngest brother and sister, the influence he had over them and their religious education. The reader sees in "Franny" a spiritual crisis in her efforts to retain her spiritual integrity, to live a spiritual life in an egotistical, materialistic society, a society personified by Lane Coutell.

"Franny" can be considered as a prologue to "Zooey," which carries the reader deeply into the history of the Glass family. The last five pieces that Salinger published in *The New Yorker* could constitute some form of a larger whole. The narrative possibly could constitute parts of two uncompleted chronicles. One order in which the stories could be read is with Buddy as the narrator, the order in which they were published (this is the order in which Buddy claims to have written them); the other order is the one suggested by the chronology of events in the stories. Arranged one way, the stories focus on Buddy and his struggle to understand Seymour by writing about him; arranged the other way, the stories focus on the quest of Seymour for God. Salinger for many years had been a devoted student of Advaita Vedanta Hinduism, and the teachings of Seymour Glass reflect this study.

If one focuses on Seymour Glass, his spiritual quest, and how this quest is reflected in the behavior and beliefs of his siblings, one sees as a result an unfinished history of the Glass family. Salinger announced, in one of his rare statements about his intentions, on the dust jacket of a later book, that he had "several new Glass family stories coming along," but, by the close of the century, only "Hapworth 16, 1924" had appeared in 1965. Readers see in this story the presence of Seymour, a presence that is evident in the four stories published after that time.

These four stories became more experimental in literary technique and are also involved with the Eastern mystical religious beliefs studied by Salinger and promoted by his character Seymour Glass. One interpretation of the stories that deal with Seymour (that of Eberhard Alsen) is that together these selections constitute a modernist hagiography, the account of the life and martyrdom of a churchless saint. "Raise High the Roof Beam, Carpenters" is the first story to be published after "Franny" and the first to introduce all the members of the Glass family. "Zooey" continues the account of specific events introduced in "Franny," and the reader learns that the behavior of Franny is influenced by two books of Eastern religion that she found in the old room of Seymour. In "Zooey" the name of Seymour is evoked when Franny wants to talk to him. In "Raise High the Roof Beam, Carpenters," the reader learns what Seymour has written in his diary, although Seymour is not physically present. In "Seymour: An Introduction," the reader is offered a much wider range of what he said and wrote, conveyed by his brother Buddy. In "Hapworth 16, 1924," which appeared in *The New Yorker* on June 19, 1965, Buddy, now at age forty-six, tries to trace the origins of the saintliness of his older brother in a letter that Seymour wrote home from Camp Simon Hapworth in Maine when he was seven. In giving the reader the exact letter, Buddy provides the reader with a full example of how things are seen from the point of view of Seymour and introduces the reader to the sensitivity and psychic powers that foreshadow his spirituality. The reader sees the incredibly precocious mind of Seymour, who reflects on the nature of pain and asks his parents to send him some books by Leo Tolstoy, Swami Vivekananda of India, Charles Dickens, George Eliot, William Makepeace Thackeray, Jane Austen, and Frederick Porter Smith.

### "SEYMOUR: AN INTRODUCTION" AND "HAPWORTH 16, 1924"

In these last two works, "Seymour: An Introduction" and "Hapworth 16, 1924," the reader sees Seymour Glass more closely than anywhere before. The reader perceives the brilliance of Seymour, his spirituality, his poetic ability, and his capacity for love. With the character of Seymour, Salinger is trying to create a modern-day saint.

Salinger's last works received mixed critical reception. Some critics believed that Salinger had lost the artistic ability he had showed during his classic period. His characters write, and others subsequently read, long, tedious letters filled with phrases in parentheses and attempts at wit. Buddy describes "Zooey" as "a sort of prose home movie." Some critics criticized these last works, calling "Zooey" the longest and dullest short story ever to appear in *The New Yorker*, but others recognized that Salinger was no longer trying to please conventional readers but, influenced by his many years of studying Eastern religious philosophy, was ridding himself of conventional forms and methods accepted by western society. In his later years, Salinger continued to become increasingly innovative and experimental in his writing techniques.

OTHER MAJOR WORKS

LONG FICTION: *The Catcher in the Rye*, 1951.

BIBLIOGRAPHY

Alexander, Paul. *Salinger: A Biography.* New York: Renaissance Books, 2000. An attempt to explain Salinger's reclusiveness, which Alexander relates to themes in his fiction.

Alsen, Eberhard. *A Reader's Guide to J. D. Salinger.* Westport, Conn.: Greenwood Press, 2003. Provides introductory overviews and analyses of all Salinger's work, as well as useful indexes and appendices.

Bloom, Harold, ed. *J. D. Salinger.* New ed. New York: Bloom's Literary Criticism, 2008. Collection of previously published essays about Salinger's writings. Three of the pieces pertain to the short fiction: "*Nine Stories*: J. D. Salinger's Linked Mysteries," by Ruth Prigozy, "Keeping It in the Family: The Novellas of J. D. Salinger," by David Seed, and "'Along This Road Goes No One': Salinger's 'Teddy' and the Failure of Love," by Anthony Kaufman.

French, Warren. *J. D. Salinger, Revisited.* Boston: Twayne, 1988. One of the most helpful and informative books on Salinger. French, who has written an earlier book on Salinger, explains here how he changed his perspective on some of Salinger's works. In addition to offering a useful chronology and bibliography, French discusses the New Hampshire area, where Salinger and French have lived. French also makes enlightening comparisons of the stories to films. Includes notes, references, and index.

Gardner, James. "J. D. Salinger, Fashion Victim." *National Review* 49 (April 7, 1997): 51-52. Contends that Salinger is intensely different from what American culture has become since the public last heard from him; the adolescent challenge to the falsity of one's elders that inspired *The Catcher in the Rye* has become the most established kind of conformity. Analyzes the reasons for the outdatedness of Salinger's last story, "Hapworth 16, 1924."

Gelfant, Blanche H., ed. *The Columbia Companion to the Twentieth-Century American Short Story.* New York: Columbia University Press, 2000. Includes a chapter in which Salinger's short stories are analyzed.

Grunwald, Henry Anatole. *Salinger: A Critical and Personal Portrait.* New York: Harper & Row, 1962. This collection of articles about Salinger contains a biographical sketch by Jack Skow of *Time* magazine (September 15, 1961). Also includes a long introduction by Grunwald, who became senior editor of

*Time*, and articles by such well-known Salinger critics as Ihab Hassan and Joseph Blotner. The postscripts contain a select catalog of the early stories and a discussion of the language of *The Catcher in the Rye*.

Laser, Marvin, and Norman Furman, eds. *Studies in J. D. Salinger: Reviews, Essays, and Critiques of "The Catcher in the Rye," and Other Fiction*. New York: Odyssey Press, 1963. In addition to discussing the publishing history and early reviews of *The Catcher in the Rye*, this book also provides a collection of some of the most important criticism of the shorter fiction.

Maynard, Joyce. *At Home in the World: A Memoir*. New York: Picador, 1998. Reveals many details of Salinger's private life, which he struggled to suppress. A good source for biographical information.

Purcell, William F. "Narrative Voice in J. D. Salinger's 'Both Parties Concerned' and 'I'm Crazy.'" *Studies in Short Fiction* 33 (Spring, 1996): 278-280. Argues that "I'm Crazy" lacks the essential characteristic of *skaz* narrative that communicates the illusion of spontaneous speech.

Salinger, Margaret A. *Dream Catcher: A Memoir*. Washington Square Press, 2000. Salinger's daughter describes her experience growing up in the shadow of her famous yet reclusive father.

Silverberg, Mark. "A Bouquet of Empty Brackets: Author-Function and the Search for J. D. Salinger." *Dalhousie Review* 75 (Summer/Fall, 1995): 222-246. Examines the consequences of Salinger's "disappearance" from the literary scene and looks at the obsessive desire to find him. Explores how Salinger's characters and name have been freed from his person and re-created in various fictional and nonfictional contexts, concluding that while Salinger may have disappeared, his name and creations remain.

Slawenski, Kenneth. *J. D. Salinger: A Life Raised High*. Hebden Bridge, England: Pomona Books, 2010. A lengthy, detailed biography, the product of more than seven years of research, written by the creator of an authoritative Salinger Web site.

*Linda S. Gordon*

---

# JAMES SALTER

**Born:** Passaic, New Jersey; June 10, 1925

PRINCIPAL SHORT FICTION
*Dusk, and Other Stories,* 1988
*Last Night,* 2005

OTHER LITERARY FORMS

James Salter (SAHL-tur) is known primarily for his longer fiction, including *The Hunters* (1957), *The Arm of Flesh* (1961), *A Sport and a Pastime* (1967), *Light Years* (1975), *Solo Faces* (1979), and *Cassada* (2000), a revision of *The Arm of Flesh*. Salter's fiction is described as "literary"; he does not write in genres nor could his novels be described as best-seller types. In many ways, he is a writer's writer, one whose prose style is distinguished by its elegance and grace.

For many years, Salter worked as a screenwriter, with many of his screenplays realized by famous directors, including *The Appointment* (1969), directed by Sidney Lumet, and *Downhill Racer* (1969), directed by Michael Ritchie. Salter also directed one of his own scripts, *Three* (1969). For many years his screenplays supplied Salter with an income that supported his other writing. In addition to the Hollywood film work, Salter made documentaries for the production company he formed with a television writer Lane Slate. Their first effort was never completed, but they did produce one on college football, *Team, Team, Team*, which won a prize at the Venice Film Festival in 1961. They also filmed a multipart series on the circus for Public Broadcasting Service and one on contemporary painters for Columbia Broadcasting System.

Salter's writing experiences have been varied and include a privately printed poem to New York City, *Still Such* (1992); several small-run editions of his short fiction; a book on food, written with his wife, Kay, that includes reminiscences and receipts, *Life Is Meals: A Food Lover's Book of Days* (2006); and two collections of stories. Salter also has done travel writing, *Tasting Paris: An Intimate Guide* (1996) and his collected travel pieces, *There and Then: The Travel Writing of James Salter* (2005). He also wrote an autobiography, *Burning the Days: Recollections* (1997), and a collection of letters, *Memorable Days: The Selected Letters of James Salter and Robert Phelps* (2010).

In addition, Salter has written a portrait of his alma mater, the military academy *West Point* (2001); contributed to a book on flying, *Gods of Tin: The Flying Years* (2004); and provided introductions to reissues of books by others, including the foreword to a 2000 edition of Irwin Shaw's *The Young Lions* (1932) and the afterword to a 2010 edition of Evan S. Connell's *Mrs. Bridge* (1959).

ACHIEVEMENTS

Although James Salter's novels have never sold especially well, they uniformly have been well received, usually garnering good reviews from the major literary outlets. He also has managed to pursue his writing at a fairly steady pace. Most of his longer fiction and the Hollywood work came before the mid-1970's; his shorter fiction appeared in the 1980's and 1990's, a decade that also saw him doing more journalism, for such magazines as *Esquire*, *Vogue*, *Gentleman's Quarterly*, *The New York Times*, and *Life*. Since the 1990's he has worked on the reminiscences, the food book, and the second collection of stories.

In 1982, Salter received the American Academy and Institute of Arts and Letters Award. In 1998, he was awarded the Edith Wharton Citation of Merit from the New York State Writers Institute and in that same year the John Steinbeck Award. Salter's short fiction was included in the *O. Henry Prize Stories* in 1970, 1972, 1974, and 1984. He had stories in *The Best American Short Stories* in 1984 and *American Short Story Masterpieces* in 1987. In 1992, his story collection *Dusk*

won the PEN/Faulkner Award. Salter has taught at or been a writer-in-residence at the University of Alabama, Vassar, the University of Houston, Williams College, and the Iowa Writers' Workshop.

BIOGRAPHY

James Salter was born James Arnold Horowitz on June 10, 1925, in Passaic, New Jersey. His father, George, was an engineer, West Point graduate, and real estate agent in New York City, whose career would fluctuate throughout his life. His mother, Mildred Scheff, was a housewife. Salter was an only child, and soon after his birth the family moved to Manhattan's East Side, near the Metropolitan Museum of Art. Salter went to local schools, to Horace Mann, and was planning to attend Stanford or the Massachusetts Institute of Technology when an appointment to West Point came through. In order to please his father, Salter went off to the U.S. military academy. At first chafing under the discipline, Salter settled in and, soon after his graduation in 1945, began training as a pilot in the Air Force. He missed the final months of combat in World War II but remained stationed in the Pacific. In 1952, he flew a hundred missions during the Korean conflict.

In 1950, he made his first trip to Europe and Paris, and the next year he married Ann Altemus; they had four children, one of whom died in a freak accident. During the 1950's, the growing family lived primarily abroad during various military deployments, where Salter served in a fighter squadron. The publication of his first novel, *The Hunters*, prompted him not only to change his name, because of military regulations, but also to resign his commission, although he was recalled during the Berlin crisis. The change from Horowitz to Salter erased whatever residual Jewishness he retained, although religion was never important in his life or history. The family then moved back to New York.

During the 1960's, he published two more novels, one of which, *The Arm of Flesh*, he largely disowned and later rewrote as *Cassada*. He also did film work, initially in Hollywood and later with his own documentary film company. In the 1970's, he divorced and began living with Kay Eldredge, also a writer, with whom he had a son, and he published his forth novel. The 1980's were a time for many literary projects, especially short stories, and a time to begin to collect recognition through awards and teaching stints. Salter later married Eldredge, taught, and published his remembrances and a selection of his correspondence. He and his wife settled on Long Island and continue to make occasional trips to Aspen, Colorado.

## ANALYSIS

James Salter has been known as a writer's writer, someone who has made a reputation based not on productivity or popularity or sales but someone for whom the crafting of the sentences and the choosing of the words are of paramount importance. Salter's short fiction therefore is of some importance as examples of his prose. Because of the restrictions imposed by their length, short stories demand compression and a delicate balance of language often missing in longer literary works. It is such precision that Salter brings to his writing.

Much of Salter's short fiction has autobiographical elements. For example, "Lost Sons" is a story about a reunion at West Point, which is Salter's alma mater, and "The Cinema" is about a film shoot, something Salter could have witnessed. Many of the stories reflect Salter's experiences abroad as a traveler, on a military assignment, or during the times he and his family lived there. Some of the stories are about writers and the art and act of writing, the failures and frustrations of working to create with language. Most of Salter's fiction is about human relationships--as friends, as lovers, as spouses, as colleagues--and the difficulties and the betrayals that strain them. Salter is the poet of memory, loss, the past.

Salter's short fiction has appeared in such periodicals as *The Paris Review*, *Grand Street*, *Esquire*, *Carolina Quarterly*, *Zoetrope*, and *The New Yorker*. He also has contributed stories to collections such as *Flight Patterns: A Century of Stories About Flying* (2009) and "Charisma" (2010) for the Atlantic Fiction for Kindle Short Story. His short fiction has been collected in two volumes: *Dusk, and Other Stories* (1988) and *Last Night* (2005).

Salter is a lyric writer, whose prose is often elegiac; he writes of memory suffused with nostalgia. Marriages break up, parents age, children mature;

*James Salter* (Getty Images)

sometimes the characters come to a realization or recognition of something, sometimes not. Each story is a marvel of texture, sensuality, and nuance, which carries the plot. Salter's tales are mostly character studies that focus on the seemingly inconsequential, diurnal events of lives; they often reach no real conclusion or definitive ending.

The structures of Salter's stories are episodic, rather like a film; they consist of scenes or sequences, which connect as often through proximity or imagery or rhetoric as through chronology or plot development. These stories read like edited films with jump cuts, overlapping dialogue, and a fractured time line. The cohesion in the unfolding text is made in the reader's mind, creating the story and teasing out the meaning of the prose. The endings of the stories frequently are enigmatic; they seem suspended, not quite complete, open-ended, demanding a closure that simply is not there. This is a technique that compels reader involvement often missing from routine short stories. Because of these characteristics, Salter's stories are squarely "modernist," a literary tradition that puts more emphasis on the writer's personal style than on plot conventions. It is a style with open endings, disjunctive structure, complex temporal sequencing, and precise, evocative use of language.

### "AM STRANDE VON TANGER"

This is a story in which virtually nothing happens, very much like those of Anton Chekhov. It is a mood piece about three characters living a rather dissolute life in Barcelona, Spain, where they eat, sleep, make love, go the beach, and ponder the meaning of it all. Clearly, this is not a fiction about action or the importance of events; it is a piece about atmosphere, tone, or mood. The leisurely pacing, the languid, drifting emptiness of the lives of the characters, the seeming futility of it all make the story's meaning. This is a perfect example of Salter's ability to craft significance from the language alone, relying only minimally on the events or characters of the fiction.

### "VIA NEGATIVA"

This story begins with a snapshot of a minor writer and proceeds to dissect with surgical skill his life, his work habits, and his failure. This is a story about the art of writing, and in it Salter is unsparing in his portrayal of a man coddled by the women around him, who smother him as they nurture him; they are the graces of inaction and ennui. This writer lives literally in a world of make believe, of hopes, and of unrealized dreams. Unfortunately, it is a world he is largely responsible for through his inaction. Like a character in an existentialist novel, something by Albert Camus, the writer is immobilized, unable to act.

### "PALM COURT"

Many of the male figures who inhabit Salter's stories are types who seem immobilized by love, relationships, and women. Arthur, the central character in "Palm Court," is one of those. In the past, he had a love affair with Noreen, who left him for another man; years later, she returns to his life, only to have Arthur reject her. This in spite of the fact that he is not married and seems not to have had another serious relationship. These diffident gentlemen characters of Salter appear to long for affection and companionship, and yet they frequently put up stumbling blocks to relationships. They are curiously withdrawn and at times do cruel things to their partners. Salter,

however, does not judge them, and they come off in the fiction more pitiful than monstrous.

Salter's short prose is distinguished by its polish and elegance and his ability to create the precise image or gesture to sum up any scene or character. The stories are often elliptical and fragmentary but not incomplete. Salter is devastating in his observations of what is often called "Cheeverland," after the work of John Cheever, who wrote so brilliantly about the upper middle class and their haunts in suburbia and the city. Salter is largely nonjudgmental about the foibles and failings of his creations. Salter's stories are among the most remarkable of his generation.

OTHER MAJOR WORKS

LONG FICTION: *The Hunters*, 1957; *The Arm of Flesh*, 1961. revised 2000 (as *Cassada*); *A Sport and a Pastime*, 1967; *Light Years*, 1975; *Solo Faces*, 1975.

NONFICTION: *Tasting Paris: An Intimate Guide*, 1996 (with Kay Eldredge); *Burning the Days: Recollections*, 1997; *West Point*, 2001 (with Marcia Lippman); *Gods of Tin: The Flying Years*, 2004; *There and Then: The Travel Writing of James Salter*, 2005; *Life Is Meals; A Food Lover's Book of Days*, 2006 (with Kay Salter); *Memorable Days: The Selected Letters of James Salter and Robert Phelps*, 2010.

POETRY: *Still Such*, 1992.

SCREENPLAYS: *The Appointment*, 1969; *Downhill Racer*, 1969; *Three*, 1969; *Threshold*, 1981.

BIBLIOGRAPHY

Baker, Charles. "James Salter 1925-        " In *American Writers: A Collection of Literary Biographies: Supplement IX: Nelson Algren to David Wagoner*, edited by Jay Parini. New York: Scribner's, 2002. This encyclopedia essay provides a comprehensive overview of Salter's life and career, with a bibliography of primary and secondary works.

Burke, Robert. "Interview with James Salter." *Bloomsbury Review* 8 (May/June 1988): 3. Burke conducts one of the earliest and best of the interviews with Salter.

Cocchiarale, Michael. "'The Most Direct Way': James Salter's *Solo Faces* and the Escape from Modern Sport." *Aethlon: The Journal of Sport Literature* 22, no. 1 (Fall, 2004), 117-123. Cocchiarale examines the role of mountaineering in Salter's novel *Solo Faces*.

Dowie, William. *James Salter*. New York: Twayne, 1998. The first full-length book on Salter, with chapters on his life story and his work up to the publication date.

Hirsch, Edward, "James Salter: Art of Fiction CXXXIII," *The Paris Review* 127 (Summer, 1993): 54-100. A superb interview with Salter.

Kahn, Ed, and John Boe. "'The Things You Remember': An Interview with James Salter." *Writing on the Edge* 16, no. 2 (Spring, 2006): 82-95. Salter discusses his writing and the art of fiction.

Miller, Margaret Winchell. "Glimpses of a Secular Holy Land: The Novels of James Salter." *Hollins Critic* 19, no. 1 (1982): 1-13. In this early analysis of Salter's prose, Miller comments on the Salter's poetic ear and his obsession with human desire.

Morawetz, Thomas. "Lawyers and Introspection." In *Law and Literature*, edited by Michael Freeman, Andrew E. D. Lewis, and Anthony Julius. Oxford, England: Oxford University Press, 1999. The essays in this collection examine legal issues. Includes James Salter's "American Express" and short stories by Ward Just and Cynthia Ozick.

Myers, Jeffrey. "James Salter's 'Am Strande von Tanger.'" *Notes on Contemporary Literature* 38, no. 4 (September, 2008): 2-5. Myers discusses in some depth Salter's short story.

Pope, Dan. "Dan Pope Talks with James Salter." In *The Believer Book of Writers Talking to Writers*, edited by Vendela Vida. San Francisco: Believer, 2005. Pope, a short-story writer, interviews Salter, offering insight into his work.

*Charles L. P. Silet*

---

# WILLIAM SAROYAN

**Born:** Fresno, California; August 31, 1908
**Died:** Fresno, California; May 18, 1981

PRINCIPAL SHORT FICTION

*The Daring Young Man on the Flying Trapeze, and Other Stories,* 1934
*Inhale and Exhale,* 1936
*Three Times Three,* 1936
*Little Children,* 1937
*The Gay and Melancholy Flux: Short Stories,* 1937
*Love, Here Is My Hat, and Other Short Romances,* 1938
*The Trouble with Tigers,* 1938
*Peace, It's Wonderful,* 1939
*Three Fragments and a Story,* 1939
*My Name Is Aram,* 1940
*Saroyan's Fables,* 1941
*The Insurance Salesman, and Other Stories,* 1941
*Forty-Eight Saroyan Stories,* 1942

*Dear Baby,* 1944
*Some Day I'll Be a Millionaire: Thirty-Four More Great Stories,* 1944
*The Saroyan Special: Selected Stories,* 1948
*The Fiscal Hoboes,* 1949
*The Assyrian, and Other Stories,* 1950
*The Whole Voyald, and Other Stories,* 1956
*William Saroyan Reader,* 1958
*Love,* 1959
*After Thirty Years: The Daring Young Man on the Flying Trapeze,* 1964
*Best Stories of William Saroyan,* 1964
*The Tooth and My Father,* 1974
*The Man with the Heart in the Highlands, and Other Early Stories,* 1989

OTHER LITERARY FORMS

William Saroyan (suh-ROY-uhn) was a prolific writer whose works included novels, plays, and several autobiographical memoirs. Among his most famous plays are *My Heart's in the Highlands* (pr., pb. 1939) and *The Time of Your Life* (pr., pb. 1939). The latter was awarded the Pulitzer Prize in 1939, but Saroyan rejected it because he "did not believe in official patronage of art." His screenplay, *The Human Comedy* (1943), was one of the most popular wartime films and was later revised into a successful novel. Saroyan's talents also extended to songwriting, his most famous song being "Come Ona My House." His last work, *My Name Is Saroyan*, a potpourri of stories, verse, play fragments, and memoirs, was published posthumously in 1983.

### ACHIEVEMENTS

William Saroyan's reputation rests mainly on his pre-World War II plays and fictional sketches that embraced an upbeat, optimistic, and happy view of people during a period of deep economic depression and increasing political upheaval. His immense popularity and critical acclaim in the United States declined after the war, though in Europe, notably France and Italy, his reputation has remained high. His plays and fiction have been translated into several languages.

Although highly diversified in technique, Saroyan's best works all bear an irrepressible faith in the goodness of the human spirit. His unique, multifaceted style has been emulated by other writers who lack his sanguine outlook and control of craft. Occasional flashes of brilliance partially restored Saroyan's reputation after World War II, and his memoir *Obituaries* (1979) was nominated for the American Book Award. Saroyan's greatest and most influential works, however, belong to his early, experimental period.

### BIOGRAPHY

William Stonehill Saroyan was born in Fresno, California, in 1908. His father, who died when William was two, was a minister turned grape farmer; upon his death, young Saroyan spent seven years in an orphanage, after which his family was reunited. He worked at many odd jobs, including a stint as a telegraph operator, spending most of his time in Fresno and San Francisco. His first short stories began to appear in 1934 and found instant success. In his first year as a writer his work appeared in the O'Brien volume of *The Best Short Stories*, and he published what is still

his best-received volume of short stories, *The Daring Young Man on the Flying Trapeze, and Other Stories*. Thereafter he produced an amazingly prolific stream of short stories, plays, novels, and memoirs. Saroyan was twice married to Carol Marcus, with whom he had two children. In 1959, after his second divorce, he declared himself a tax exile and went to live in Europe. He returned in 1961 to teach at Purdue University and later returned to live in Fresno. He was actively writing right up to his death from cancer in 1981.

### ANALYSIS

While William Saroyan cultivated his prose to evoke the effect of a "tradition of carelessness," of effortless and sometimes apparently formless ruminations and evocations, he was in reality an accomplished and conscious stylist whose influences are varied and whose total effect is far more subtle than the seemingly "breezy" surface might at first suggest. His concern for the lonely and poor--ethnic outsiders, barflies, working girls, children--and their need for love and connectedness in the face of real privation

*William Saroyan* (Library of Congress)

recalls Sherwood Anderson. All of Saroyan's best work was drawn from his own life, although the central character must be regarded as a persona, no matter how apparently connected to the author. In this aspect, and in his powerful and economical capacity to evoke locale and mood, Saroyan is in the tradition of Thomas Wolfe. The empathetic controlling consciousness and adventurous experiments with "formless form" also place Saroyan in the tradition that includes Walt Whitman and Gertrude Stein. It might also be noted that Saroyan's work shows the influence of Anton Chekhov in his use of seemingly "plotless" situations which nevertheless reveal some essential moment in the characters' lives and philosophical insight into the human condition.

Certainly, while the tone of Saroyan's stories evolves from the richly comic to the stoical to the sadly elegiac mood of his later work, his ethos stands counter to that of the naturalists and the ideologically programmatic writers of the 1930's, the period during which he produced some of his best work. Often his stories portray the world from the perspective of children, whose instinctual embrace of life echoes the author's philosophy. Saroyan wrote,

> If you will remember that living people are as good as dead, you will be able to perceive much that is very funny in their conduct that you might never have thought of perceiving if you did not believe that they were as good as dead.

Both the tone and outlook of that statement are paradigmatic.

### "THE DARING YOUNG MAN ON THE FLYING TRAPEZE"

The title story of his first and most enduring collection, "The Daring Young Man on the Flying Trapeze," is still one of the most ambitious stylistic exercises of the Saroyan canon and an embodiment of the first phase of his career. The impressionistic style uses a welter of literary allusions in a stream-of-consciousness technique to portray the inner mind of an educated but destitute writer during the Depression who is literally starving to death as his mind remains lucid and aggressively inquiring. The poignant contrast between the failing body and the illuminated mind might evoke pity and compassion on the part of the reader, but somehow Saroyan also invokes respect and acceptance.

The story begins with the random associated thoughts of the half-dreaming writer which reveal both the chaos of the present era-- ". . . hush the queen, the king, Karl Franz, black Titanic, Mr. Chaplin weeping, Stalin, Hitler, a multitude of Jews . . ." --and the young protagonist's literary erudition: ". . . Flaubert and Guy de Maupassant, a wordless rhyme of early meaning, Finlandia, mathematics highly polished and slick as green onions to the teeth, Jerusalem, the path to paradox."

Upon awakening, the writer plunges into "the trivial truth of reality." He is starving, and there is no work. He ironically contemplates starvation as he combines the food in a restaurant into a mental still life; yet without a shred of self-pity, and with great dignity in spite of a clerk's philistine and patronizing attitude, he attempts to obtain a job at an employment agency where the only skill which the writer can offer to a pragmatic world is the ability to type. He is relieved when there is no work because he can now devote his remaining energies to writing a literary last will and testament, an "Apology for Permission to Live."

He drinks copious amounts of water to fill his empty belly, steals some writing paper from the Y.M.C.A. (Young Men's Christian Association), and repairs to his empty apartment to compose his manifesto. Before beginning to write, he polishes his last remaining coin--a penny (he has sold his books for food, an act of which he feels ashamed)--and savors the "absurd act." As he contemplates the words on the coin which boast of unity, trust in God, and liberty, he becomes drowsy, and he takes final leave of the world with an inner act of grace and dignity reminiscent of the daring young man of the title. His last conscious act of thought is the notion that he ought to have given the coin to a child:

> A child could buy any number of things with a penny. Then swiftly, neatly, with the grace of the young man on the trapeze he was gone from his body. . . . The city burned. The herded crowd rioted. The earth circled away, and knowing that he did so, he turned his lost face to the empty sky and became dreamless, unalive, perfect.

The story embodies Saroyan's control of his materials and the sensitive and ironic understatement for which he is famous. While the stories written during the Depression express bitterness about the situation, Saroyan eschews political solutions of any particular stripe and emphasizes the dignity of the individual and his tenacious connection to the forces of life and survival with grace and good humor.

## MY NAME IS ARAM

Another collection which gained worldwide fame is the series of interconnected stories which form the book *My Name is Aram*. Told through the eyes of the title character, a young boy in the milieu of Armenian Fresno, the collection reveals the characteristics of the stories of the middle part of Saroyan's career and foreshadows the direction taken in his later work. The reader sees childlike adults and children imbued with the burdens of adulthood. Throughout, the collection explores the often contradictory claims of emotional, poetic, and instinctive needs and the claims of reality. The author's vision is dualistic. Some of the stories show a happy symbiosis between the poetic and the rational needs of his characters; others portray the conflicting demands unresolved. Even in the latter case, however, his characters cheerfully accept their fate, not with a stoicism so much as with a recognition that such a condition is a necessity to life and does not preclude savoring the moments of beauty which occur even in the midst of squalor or hardship.

### "THE SUMMER OF THE BEAUTIFUL WHITE HORSE"

The first aspect of the mature and late phase of Saroyan's writing is aptly illustrated by the story "The Summer of the Beautiful White Horse." Typical of Saroyan's boyhood reminiscences, this tale concerns the seven-year-old Aram Garoghlanian and his slightly older cousin Mourad, who "borrow" a horse from their neighbor's barn and keep him for months at an abandoned farm, enjoying clandestine early morning rides. The owner of the horse, John Byro, complains to the boys' uncle Khosrove, a Saroyan eccentric who responds, "It's no harm. What is the loss of a horse? Haven't we all lost the homeland? What is this crying over a horse?" When the owner complains that he must walk, the uncle reminds him that he has two legs. When Byro laments that the horse had cost him sixty dollars,

the uncle retorts, "I spit on money." Byro's loss of an agent to pull his surrey brings a roar of "Pay no attention to it!"

Uncle Khosrove's attitude is typical of the charming impracticality of many of Saroyan's characters. When the boys at last secretly return the animal, the farmer is merely thankful that it has been returned and makes no attempt to find out who had stolen it. He marvels that the horse is in better condition than when it had been stolen. The story charmingly resolves the conflicting demands of the poetic and the practical (in favor of the poetic).

### "POMEGRANATE TREES"

"Pomegranate Trees" illustrates the darker and more elegiac side of the later Saroyan canon. Uncle Melik purchases some arid desert land which he intends to farm. The land is obviously impossible to render productive; yet the uncle persists in tilling the soil, planting his crops, and beating back the encroaching cactus while holding little dialogues with Aram and the prairie dogs. He decides against all reason to produce pomegranate trees, since he associates the fruit with his Assyrian past, but the trees are stunted, and the fruit yield is merely enough to fill a few boxes. When the meager harvest fails to bring a high enough price to suit Melik, he has the fruit sent back to him at still more expense. For the uncle, the enterprise has nothing to do with agriculture. "It was all pure aesthetics. . . . My uncle just liked the idea of planting trees and watching them grow."

The real world of unpaid bills intrudes, however, and the man loses the land. Three years later Aram and his uncle revisit the land which had given Melik such quixotic pleasure. The trees have died and the desert has reclaimed the land: "The place was exactly the way it had been all the years of the world." Aram and his uncle walk around the dead orchard and drive back to town. "We didn't say anything because there was such an awful lot to say, and no language to say it in."

There is nominal defeat, yet the still wistfully remembered joy in attempting the impossible for its own sake is a counterweight to the sadness of the finality of the experience. Such a resonance is at the heart of Saroyan's ethos, expressed in countless stories which have made him a popular favorite and which are beginning to elicit a high critical acclaim.

OTHER MAJOR WORKS

LONG FICTION: *The Human Comedy*, 1943; *The Adventures of Wesley Jackson*, 1946; *Rock Wagram*, 1951; *Tracy's Tiger*, 1951; *The Laughing Matter*, 1953 (reprinted as *The Secret Story*, 1954); *Mama I Love You*, 1956; *Papa You're Crazy*, 1957; *Boys and Girls Together*, 1963; *One Day in the Afternoon of the World*, 1964.

PLAYS: *My Heart's in the Highlands*, pr., pb. 1939; *The Time of Your Life*, pr., pb. 1939; *The Hungerers: A Short Play*, pb. 1939, pr. 1945; *Love's Old Sweet Song*, pr., pb. 1940; *Subway Circus*, pb. 1940; *The Ping-Pong Game*, pb. 1940 (one-act); *Three Plays: My Heart's in the Highlands, The Time of Your Life, Love's Old Sweet Song*, pb. 1940; *The Beautiful People*, pr. 1940, pb. 1941; *The Great American Goof*, pr. 1940, pb. 1942; *Across the Board on Tomorrow Morning*, pr., pb. 1941; *Jim Dandy*, pr., pb. 1941; *Three Plays: The Beautiful People, Sweeney in the Trees, Across the Board on Tomorrow Morning*, pb. 1941; *Hello Out There*, pr. 1941, pb. 1942 (one-act); *Razzle Dazzle*, pb. 1942 (collection); *Talking to You*, pr., pb. 1942; *Talking to You*, pr., pb. 1942; *Get Away Old Man*, pr. 1943, pb. 1944; *Sam Ego's House*, pr. 1947, pb. 1949; *A Decent Birth, a Happy Funeral*, pb. 1949; *Don't Go Away Mad*, pr., pb. 1949; *The Slaughter of the Innocents*, pb. 1952, pr. 1957; *The Cave Dwellers*, pr. 1957, pb. 1958; *Once Around the Block*, pb. 1959; *Sam the Highest Jumper of Them All: Or, The London Comedy*, pr. 1960, pb. 1961; *Settled Out of Court*, pr. 1960, pb. 1962; *The Dogs: Or, The Paris Comedy, and Two Other Plays*, pb. 1969; *An Armenian Trilogy*, pb. 1986 (includes *Armenians, Bitlis*, and *Haratch*); *Warsaw Visitor and Tales from the Vienna Streets: The Last Two Plays of William Saroyan*, pb. 1991.

SCREENPLAY: *The Human Comedy*, 1943.

NONFICTION: *Harlem as Seen by Hirschfield*, 1941; *Hilltop Russians in San Francisco*, 1941; *Why Abstract?*, 1945 (with Henry Miller and Hilaire Hiler); *The Twin Adventures: The Adventures of William Saroyan*, 1950; *The Bicycle Rider in Beverly Hills*, 1952; *Here Comes, There Goes, You Know Who*, 1961; *A Note on Hilaire Hiler*, 1962; *Not Dying*, 1963; *Short Drive, Sweet Chariot*, 1966; *Look at Us*, 1967; *I Used to Believe I Had Forever: Now I'm Not So Sure*, 1968; *Letters from 74 Rue Taitbout*, 1969; *Days of Life and Death and Escape to the Moon*, 1970; *Places Where I've Done Time*, 1972; *Sons Come and Go, Mothers Hang in Forever*, 1976; *Chance Meetings*, 1978; *Obituaries*, 1979; *Births*, 1983.

CHILDREN'S LITERATURE: *Me*, 1963; *Horsey Gorsey and the Frog*, 1968; *The Circus*, 1986.

MISCELLANEOUS: *My Name Is Saroyan*, 1983 (stories, verse, play fragments, and memoirs); *The New Saroyan Reader*, 1984 (Brian Darwent, editor).

BIBLIOGRAPHY

Balakian, Nona. *The World of William Saroyan*. Lewisburg, Ohio: Bucknell University Press, 1998. Balakian, formerly a staff writer for *The New York Times Book Review*, knew Saroyan personally in his last years, and her observations of him color her assessment of his later works. She viewed it as her mission to resurrect his reputation and restore him to his place among the finest of twentieth century American writers. She traces his evolution from ethnic writer to master of the short story, to playwright, and finally to existentialist.

Dyer, Brenda. "Stories About Stories: Teaching Narrative Using William Saroyan's 'My Grandmother Lucy Tells a Story Without a Beginning, a Middle, or an End.'" In *Short Stories in the Classroom*, edited by Carole L. Hamilton and Peter Kratzke. Urbana, Ill.: National Council of Teachers of English, 1999. Offers some suggestions for teaching Saroyan's story as a tale about storytelling; argues that the story provides tools that empower and enrich when taught this way.

Floan, Howard R. *William Saroyan*. New York: Twayne, 1966. Floan's study remains one of the best extensive critical monographs on Saroyan's work. It focuses on Saroyan's early literature, glossing over the post-World War II period as less productive and durable. Contains a valuable annotated bibliography through 1964.

Foster, Edward Halsey. *William Saroyan*. Boise, Idaho: Boise State University Press, 1984. A condensed but helpful survey stressing Saroyan's unique voice. Draws parallels between Saroyan's work and that of the Beat generation.

_____. *William Saroyan: A Study of the Short Fiction*. New York: Twayne, 1991. An introduction to Saroyan's short stories that discusses his use of the oral tradition, his Armenian heritage, and his usual themes and experimental techniques. Includes Saroyan's own comments on his fiction, as well as previously published essays by other critics.

Gelfant, Blanche H., ed. *The Columbia Companion to the Twentieth-Century American Short Story*. New York: Columbia University Press, 2000. Includes a chapter in which Saroyan's short stories are analyzed.

Haslam, Gerald W. "William Saroyan." In *A Literary History of the American West*, edited by Thomas J. Lyon et al. Fort Worth: Texas Christian University, 1987. A good introductory essay. Haslam focuses on Saroyan's post-World War II decline in popularity and its cause. Includes a select bibliography.

_____. "William Saroyan and San Francisco: Emergence of a Genius (Self-Proclaimed)." In *San Francisco in Fiction: Essays in a Regional Literature*, edited by David Fine and Paul Skenazy. Albuquerque: University of New Mexico Press, 1995. Discusses the influence of San Francisco in a number of Saroyan's stories. Suggests that his stylistic triumph in "The Daring Young Man on the Flying Trapeze" is to force the readers to become cocreators in the story.

Keyishian, Harry, ed. *Critical Essays on William Saroyan*. New York: G. K. Hall, 1995. A collection of essays on Saroyan, from early reviews to critical articles. Helpful essays to a study of Saroyan's short stories are Edward Halsey Foster's discussion of Saroyan's relationship to Gertrude Stein and Walter Shear's essay on Saroyan's ethnicity.

Kherdian, David. *A Bibliography of William Saroyan, 1934-1964*. San Francisco: R. Beachman, 1965. Although in need of updating, this volume is a thorough and indispensable bibliographical guide to both primary and secondary works.

Lee, Lawrence, and Barry Gifford. *Saroyan: A Biography*. New York: Harper & Row, 1984. Lee and Gifford's study is rich with anecdotes and segments of interviews with Saroyan's family, friends, and associates. Supplemented by a chronology and a bibliography.

Leggett, John. *A Daring Young Man*. New York: Alfred A. Knopf, 2003. Leggett relies heavily on Saroyan's journals to produce a sustained glimpse of the author that is neither admiring nor forgiving.

*David Sadkin*
*Updated by John W. Fiero*

# GEORGE SAUNDERS

**Born:** Amarillo, Texas; December 2, 1958

PRINCIPAL SHORT FICTION

*CivilWarLand in Bad Decline,* 1996
*Pastoralia,* 2000
*In Persuasion Nation,* 2006

OTHER LITERARY FORMS

George Saunders (SAWN-durs) has worked almost completely in the short-fiction genre, although he has stretched the field in some ways. At times, he has dabbled in nonfiction. In 2000, he wrote *The Very Persistent Gappers of Frip*, a short novella (ostensibly for children) that was illustrated by artist Lane Smith. The book became a best seller. He published an independent novella, *The Brief and Frightening Reign of Phil*, in 2005; alternate European editions of *In Persuasion Nation* added *The Brief and Frightening Reign of Phil* to the collection and went by that title. He published a limited edition of a chapbook of essays in 2006 titled *A Bee Stung Me, So I Killed the Fish*. In 2007, he published a collection of essays titled *The Braindead Megaphone;* several of the essays were travelogues written by Saunders about trips to places such as Dubai.

## Achievements

George Saunders won a National Magazine Award for "The Four Hundred-Pound CEO" (in 1994), "Bounty" (1996), "The Barber's Unhappiness" (1999), and "The Red Bow" (2004). His first two collections, *CivilWarLand in Bad Decline* and *Pastoralia*, were *New York Times* Notable Books of the Year. *CivilWarLand in Bad Decline* also was a PEN/Hemingway Fiction Award finalist. He was chosen by *The New Yorker* as one of the Twenty Best Writers Under Forty in 1999. He has won an O. Henry Award (for "Pastoralia") and the World Fantasy Award for Best Short Fiction (for "CommComm"). In 2006, he won the illustrious MacArthur "genius" grant and a Guggenheim Fellowship. His third collection, *Persuasion Nation*, won an Academy Award from the American Academy of Arts and Letters in 2009.

## Biography

George Saunders was born in Amarillo, Texas, in 1958, but he was raised in Chicago, Illinois. Initially determined to be an engineer or scientist, he attended the Colorado School of Mines, graduating with a degree in geophysical engineering in 1981. He went to work in that capacity for a geological survey firm, spending brief periods in places as diverse as Malaysia, Thailand, and Russia, and Sumatra.

In 1986, he returned to college, partaking in the creative-writing program at Syracuse University. He married Paula Redick in 1987, and the first of his two daughters was born in 1988 (the second followed in 1990). After earning his M.A. from Syracuse, he worked for Radian International as a technical writer and engineer until 1996. While at Radian, he wrote and published the stories that would make up the collection *CivilWarLand in Bad Decline.* Two of the stories in the collection (the title story and "Bounty") won National Magazine Awards, and the book received sterling reviews. Soon he was hired to teach in the M.F.A. program in creative writing at Syracuse. His work continued to be published in prestigious venues, such as *Harper's* and *The New Yorker*, and in 2006 Saunders garnered two great laurels for his writing: a MacArthur Foundation grant and a Guggenheim Fellowship. Saunders settled in Syracuse, New York, with his wife

and two daughters. He was a Visiting Writer at Wesleyan University and Hope College in 2010, and he participated in Wesleyan's Distinguished Writers Series and Hope's Visiting Writers Series.

## Analysis

George Saunders emerged in the mid-1990's in the second wave of a generation of postmodern writers who took the literary world by storm. Often considered alongside such writers as David Foster Wallace, author of *Infinite Jest* (1996) and *Brief Interviews with Hideous Men* (1999), and Rick Moody, author of *The Ice Storm* (1994), Saunders gained immediate notice for his work's satirical take on the American scene and for his singular and unique voice. The odd twists and turns of his plots also have drawn attention. Like Wallace and Moody, Saunders is known for a particularly satirical vision of the contemporary era, and, like them, he primarily is a stylist, although his fictive voice is not as dense as Moody's or as baroque as Wallace's. Saunders's characters are surprisingly forthcoming to other characters, telling them things that real people would probably prefer to keep secret. At the same time, dialogue rarely is sparse and perfunctory. Characters rarely speak in one-line, straightforward rejoinders, but rather in expository paragraphs.

Saunders made his mark in contemporary fiction by publishing a number of stories (while still largely undiscovered) in the two preeminent fiction venues of recent years, *The New Yorker* and *Harper's*. From the beginning of his career, the interests, obsessions, and recurring tropes that appear in and often define his fiction were on full display. Saunders's vision is extraordinarily consistent, so that many of his stories are less distinctly original in terms of their relationship to each other and are instead variations on a theme. Foremost among these recurring tropes are his settings. Often in Saunders's stories, the present is a near future when things that the reader always thought would go wrong have gone wrong. Although dystopian in nature, these futures are close enough to the reader's time to be horribly and eerily familiar. In essence, in these worlds slightly different, but not terribly different, from the reader's own, things have fallen apart and the center is not holding. "Pastoralia," for example (from the collection with the same title), is set in a near future when corporations sustain their employees and people not employed by corporations are in serious danger of starving or being harmed. "Bounty" is in a similar near future, when radiation poisoning has caused mutation among many people and where the regular government has fallen apart.

Saunders also is intrigued by theme parks and attractions. "CivilWarLand in Bad Decline," "Bounty," and "Downtrodden Mary's Failed Campaign of Terror" (all from *CivilWarLand in Bad Decline*) and "Pastoralia" (from the collection of the same title) are all set at least partially inside attractions. Similarly, "Jon" and "CommComm" from *Persuasion Nation* deal with characters isolated into subcommunities. The frequent use of theme parks--and thus the frequent creation of characters who exist as spectacles first and people second--perhaps demonstrates a tacit assertion that Americans, as a people, have so separated themselves from fellowship and so estranged themselves that most of their pleasures are vicarious rather than actual. At the same time, other humans mean little to them. They are like characters in a film or video game, to be exploited for fun or profit and not deserving of our empathy.

Although Saunders's stories are not particularly evocative of the Latin American Magical Realists such as Gabriel Garcia Márquez or Jorge Luis Borges, there are certain similarities in that a number of Saunders's stories feature ghosts or other unexplained phenomena. As in the stories by Garcia Márquez and other Magical Realists, ghosts or supernatural phenomena are not the purpose of the plot or narrative (as in ghost stories or gothic tales); rather, they serve the overall thematic tapestry of the piece. Both "CivilWarLand in Bad Decline" and "Sea Oak" (from *Pastoralia)* feature ghosts.

Another difficult-to-quantify trait of Saunders's fiction is the consistent portrayal of a struggle between the diametrically opposed modes of self-centeredness on one side and of empathy and compassion on the other. Characters in stories such as "Sea Oak" and "The Four Hundred-Pound CEO" struggle to maintain their humanity--which is at least partly defined by their ability to empathize and feel the pain and needs of other people--while everyone around them opts for

*George Saunders*
(Time & Life Pictures/Getty Images)

selfishness and self-indulgence.

Above Saunders's stylistic idiosyncrasies are his courage in his writing and his willingness to touch repeatedly upon such familiar shores. The use of the familiar over and over opens him up to criticism, and yet for the most part Saunders's stories stand up as individual accomplishments. Still, when read one after another in collections, a certain sameness or repetitiveness arises that can tire a reader. Taken as a whole, however, the variations on the theme convey points more richly than singly different stories would.

### CIVILWARLAND IN BAD DECLINE

*CivilWarLand in Bad Decline* is Saunders's first and perhaps most successful collection of stories. "Bounty," a short novella or long short story and the final story of the book, demonstrates many of Saunders's common interests and tropes. "Bounty" is set in a near future dystopia where (despite the apparent existence of a federal government) life seems more or less feudal; the citizens of this United States are segregated between "Flawed" people who have obvious genetic mutations (the narrator of "Bounty," Cole, has claws instead of toes and his sister has a tiny vestigial tail, while other mutants lack teeth, have too many, and so on) and Normals. The Flawed of America are denied their human rights. Initially, the narrator and his sister work in a castle theme park, pretending to be members of a medieval society for the entertainment of wealthy clients. When his sister is sold to a wealthy client, the narrator leaves to find her, despite the dangers of the journey. "Bounty" demonstrates the human capacity to hate those who are different but shows the redemptive power of love.

The title story is also set in an attraction; "CivilWarLand" is, unfortunately, losing ground, even as its narrator tries to keep both his angry boss and his impatient wife happy. He is friendly with a family of ghosts, the McKinnons, who haunt the land of the attraction and tell him enough about life in the Civil War era to help him out. The park is attacked constantly by roving gangs, however, and before long the park's owner overreacts and hires a psychopathic veteran to keep the peace, which he does by killing an innocent boy. In his attempts to help people, the narrator is destined to become a victim. The ghosts, in a sense, are the ultimate spectators, even as their lives serve as the basis for spectacle. Others refuse to engage, caught up in their own problems.

"The Four Hundred-Pound CEO" offers a similar conundrum. Jeffrey, the obese narrator, has great sympathy for other people in his life, but none of these characters treats him with any sympathy. When he finally stands up against his bully of a boss and fights back, Jeffrey is temporarily empowered, and in that brief time he does his best to make others happy. As is usually the case in Saunders's world, however, Jeffrey's victories are brief and fleeting.

### Pastoralia

Saunders's second collection is similar to the first in many ways. The title story is a short novella (or a longer short story), and again Saunders makes use of dystopian near futures and similar themes of isolation, selfishness, and empathy. The title story tells of a man who works in an attraction that highlights different times in history. He works in "prehistory" with his partner Janet, where as caveman and cavewoman they search for bugs and roast and eat goats. Janet cannot

stay in character, but the narrator must keep his job to support his wife and sick child. Over and over again, Saunders's characters are victims of their economic circumstances. Even as they become more and more isolated by their world and their jobs, the narrator realizes that he must reach out to others. This need for helping others is best demonstrated in "The Falls," about a man named Morse, walking home from work along a river, wrapped in a world of his own worries and fears. In contrast, he walks by another man, Cummings, who is sure of his supremacy in all things. However, when the two see young girls in danger in a canoe on the river, headed toward the deadly falls, it is Morse who acts, flinging his body into the river, despite his great fear.

In "Sea Oak," a young man is again at the whim of economic circumstances and has to work at a job he finds loathsome--erotic dancing and stripping--to support his sisters and Aunt Bernie. Their apartment complex is "Sea Oak," and it is in a bad neighborhood. Things seem to get worse when Aunt Bernie dies, but they become even more complicated when she rises from the dead, full of orders and invective, intent upon straightening out everyone's life.

### In Persuasion Nation

Saunders's third collection reflects the same interests and style of his first two. Although there are no theme parks in the stories, "Jon" tells of young people raised in an ultraconsumerist society as an enclave of perfect focus-group participants, who achieve a kind of reality-show cult status in the culture as "assessors" of everything they interact with in their lives. Just as the theme parks in "CivilWarLand" and "Pastoralia" reflect the isolation of modern lives divorced from reality, so, too, does the need to consume and demonstrate worth through consumption. The title story takes the forms of several commercials interlocked as a psychedelic fairy tale, again questioning the American mania with consumption. The final story in the collection, "CommComm," deals with another powerful corporation in control of its employees; in this case, the company styles itself as a "Center for Terror," suggesting that in the age of terror the obsession with it has become just another form of consumerism.

OTHER MAJOR WORKS

LONG FICTION: *The Brief and Frightening Reign of Phil*, 2005

NONFICTION: *A Bee Stung Me, So I Killed the Fish (Notes from the Homeland, 2003-2006)*, 2006; *The Braindead Megaphone: Essays*, 2007.

CHILDREN'S LITERATURE: *The Very Persistent Gappers of Frip*, 2000 (illustrations by Lane Smith).

BIBLIOGRAPHY

Hansen, Joseph. "An Interview with George Saunders." *Denver Quarterly* 40, no. 2 (2005): 43-49. Hansen's interview with Saunders discusses Saunders's use of satire and his frequent tackling of consumerism in his fiction.

Larimer, Kevin. "George Saunders: The Very Persistent Mapper of Happenstance." *Poets and Writers* 28, no. 4 (July/August, 2000): 34-40. An interview with Saunders that discusses some of his abiding interests and how his life experiences are translated into fiction.

Siegal, Nina. "George Saunders, Satirist." *The Progressive* 70, no. 6 (June, 2006): 38-40. An excellent brief overview of Saunders's work.

Tanner, Ron. *"CivilWarLand in Bad Decline."* *Studies in Short Fiction* 35, no. 1 (Winter, 1998): 94-97. A review that offers a good introduction to Saunders's work.

*Scott D. Yarbrough*

# JOHN SAYLES

**Born:** Schenectady, New York; September 28, 1950

PRINCIPAL SHORT FICTION

*The Anarchists' Convention,* 1979

*Dillinger in Hollywood: New and Selected Short Stories,* 2004

OTHER LITERARY FORMS

John Sayles (salz) is best known as a director, screenwriter, and actor, but he also has written short stories and published three novels: *The Pride of the Bimbos* (1975); *Union Dues* (1977), which was nominated for both the National Book Award and the National Book Critics Circle Award; and *Los Gusanos* (the worms, 1991). His fourth novel, *Some Time in the Sun*, was scheduled to be released in 2011. With Gavin Smith, he published *Sayles on Sayles* (1998), in which he discusses his career and his films. In addition, his *Thinking in Pictures: The Making of the Movie "Matewan,"* which concerns his directing this mining film, was published in 1987.

ACHIEVEMENTS

John Sayles's stories "I-80 Nebraska, m.490-m.205" (1975) and "Breed" (1977) won O. Henry Awards. He has directed about twenty feature films and in 1983 received a John D. and Catherine T. MacArthur Foundation ("genius") Award: a grant of thirty thousand dollars per year for five years, tax-free.

BIOGRAPHY

John Thomas Sayles was born in Schenectady, New York, on September 28, 1950, and attended Mount Pleasant High School in Schenectady, earning letters in basketball, baseball, track, and football. After being turned down by the U.S. Army, in 1968 Sayles enrolled at Williams College, where he took creative writing classes and acted in dramatic productions. Following his graduation in 1972, he worked in a variety of jobs, including one in a meatpacking plant, and hitchhiked thousands of miles. In 1975, he published his first novel, *The Pride of the Bimbos*, and won an O. Henry Award for "I-80 Nebraska, m.490-m.205." In 1977, he published his second novel, *Union Dues*, and began writing for filmmaker Roger Corman's New World Pictures. *The Return of the Secaucus Seven* (1979), his first feature film, was a critical and financial success;

and in the same year he published his first collection of short stories, *The Anarchists' Convention*. Aside from writing and staging his one-act plays in 1981, the rest of his career has primarily been devoted to working in films as an actor, screenplay writer, editor, and director. Two of his screenplays, *Alligator* (1980) and *Wild Thing* (1987), are based on his short stories. In 1991, he published his third novel, *Los Gusanos*, but Sayles is primarily a filmmaker rather than a fiction writer.

### Analysis

John Sayles's fiction is in the realist tradition of Theodore Dreiser and James T. Farrell in its economic determinism. However, as in the fiction of Stephen Crane, that determinism is tempered by occasional passages of sentimentality and romanticism. Though his blue-collar workers are often depicted as victims of their environment, they are resilient and resourceful victims. Like Crane, Sayles, especially in the Brian McNeil stories, focuses on the initiation of a young man on a quest for identity and manhood. In that quest,

*John Sayles* (AP Photo/Krista Niles, File)

Sayles's characters encounter a variety of misfits, people on the margins of society. Sayles's narratives are relatively straightforward, with the exception of "Tan," which uses flashbacks to juxtapose present and past, and "Schiffman's Ape," which uses flashbacks and provides parallels between scientific observations and the scientists' lives.

These narratives, with the exception of the somewhat surreal "I-80 Nebraska, m.790-m.205," which uses a cinematic sound montage of short citizens band (CB) radio messages to heighten tension, are recounted in an efficient, plain style without rhetorical flourishes. Sayles has a fetish for technical details, especially when the subject is something he has experienced, and the wealth of details engages the reader. Much of the fiction, especially the Brian McNeil stories, seems closely tied to Sayles's own life. Partly because of the somewhat "autobiographical" nature of the content, Sayles is compassionate about his characters, even when they are seriously flawed.

### "At the Anarchists' Convention"

"At the Anarchists' Convention" is an ironic title, for anarchy is antithetical to organization, especially as manifested in a meeting with name tags, place cards, and committees. Leo, the elderly narrator, recounts the events that culminate in a confrontation with hotel management, which has also booked a Rotary Club, full of "gin and boosterism," into the Elizabethan Room, an ironic venue for anarchists. Leo, in love with Sophie and jealous of Brickman's relationship with her some forty years ago, reminisces with old left-wing colleagues about past political battles and even manages a eulogy about Brickman, now deceased. When the hotel manager informs the aging leftists that they must vacate the room, they barricade the doors, link arms, and sing "We Shall Not Be Moved." In his exhilaration, Leo holds Sophie's hand and thinks that if Brinkman, his old rival, were here, "we'd show this bastard the Wrath of the People."

### "Schiffman's Ape"

In "Schiffman's Ape" Warden, an associate professor, and Lisa, his graduate assistant and wife, study Esau, a rare Schiffman ape in the ape's natural habitat. In the course of the story Sayles neatly parallels Warden's recorded observations of Esau's sexual activity with the fading relationship between the two academics. The parallel is comically reinforced by a native legend, fabricated by Sayles, about the creator separating twin brothers into men and apes. Warden, whose name suggests his tendency to imprison others, is a patriarchal, macho, control-oriented person who magnanimously "forgives" Lisa for saving Esau, when he himself was ready to intervene. He also has a double standard for sexual infidelity, condemning hers while dismissing his own as trivial. As Lisa becomes increasingly disenchanted with Warden, Esau experiences difficulty having sex with female Schiffman apes, all of this recorded by Warden. Warden observes Esau giving up his pursuit of a female and resorting to masturbation just before Lisa and he observe Esau drown without either intervening. Esau's death is the death of their relationship.

### "TAN"

Sayles's story begins with Con Tinh Tan sitting in a waiting room and quickly flashes back to Tan as a thirteen-year-old girl in Vietnam in 1963. Her first experience with Americans is ostensibly positive because the American dentist fixes her teeth and improves her appearance, but she believes that the "American had taken her face." The rest of the story details the other things that are taken from her as a result of American interference in Southeast Asia. Soon after her father's imprisonment and death, she sees a monk set himself on fire and die, and when she moves to her uncle's house, he rapes her during the Tet offensive. After the Communists take her uncle away, she is on the streets. At age twenty, she is "befriended" by Sergeant Plunkett, who gives her food for sex and gets her pregnant. Dr. Yin, who performs the abortion, also implants opium in her breasts; and Plunkett sends her to America, where he promises to meet her. When Plunkett does not appear, she decides to have the implants removed. She is surprised to find out that the surgeon who is to do the surgery is Dr. Yin, who has been "expecting" her. When Tan loses her identity through two operations designed to "improve her" and is sexually exploited, she becomes both the real and the symbolic victim of western exploitation.

### "I-80 NEBRASKA, M. 490-M. 205"

On a section of Interstate 80 a rebel trucker named Ryder P. Moses leads his pursuers, fellow truckers obsessed with finding him, on a chase that ends with his deliberately driving his tractor-trailer into the concrete support of an overpass. Moses, whose name ironically suggests he is a leader of the people, becomes a phantom driver, a legend on westbound 80, which Sayles describes as "an insomniac world of lights passing lights to the music of the Citizens Band." While the narrator occasionally comments on the action, the narrative is primarily a series of citizens band conversations by truckers and Moses, who is "breaking every trucker commandment." The gossip about him is as erroneous and widespread as are the suppositions about the identity of the Great Gatsby. Moses, who identifies himself as the Paul Bunyan of Interstate 80, scares and thrills the other truckers with a monologue induced by drugs and devoted to condemning American culture. Just before he crashes, Moses says, "Going west. Good night and happy motoring," a bitter echo of a 1960's advertisement for Esso gasoline and an ironic farewell to a world gone bad.

### THE ANARCHISTS' CONVENTION

The six stories that comprise the second part of Sayles's collection of short stories are linked by Brian McNeil, a high school basketball player who drops out of school and hitchhikes across the United States. The stories, which may have been intended as episodes in a picaresque novel, take Brian from high school sexual initiation ("Bad Dogs") and basketball success ("Hoop") to California, where he sees his future ("Golden State"). Brian's story, which closely resembles Sayles's early life, includes a short farewell to his mother ("Buffalo") before he leaves. In "Fission" Brian encounters an obese drug-dealing woman whose family farm has been lost to agribusiness and a mad recluse whose fear of missiles has led him to build an underground bomb shelter for his promiscuous daughter and himself. Farther west in Wyoming, Brian meets Cody Sprague, whose futile entrepreneurial efforts cast some doubt on the American Dream, and a group of Native Americans, whose plight reflects their treatment by white America ("Breed"). Finally in "Golden State," Sayles ironically uses the familiar term for California to suggest that what Brian finds on the Pacific beach is not golden at all. When Brian, whose alcoholic father had praised the Pacific, gets to the city by the sea, he sees coins in a pool. Almost destitute, he dives into the pool only to discover that the pool is too deep and the illusory money is beyond his reach. The theme of illusion resurfaces when he meets two alcoholics at the beach: Cervantes (an allusion to Don Quixote's failed idealistic quester) and Daniel Boone (an allusion to the idealistic pioneer whose quest ended at the Alamo). When Brian leaves them and returns to the pool, he finds Stuffy, another alcoholic attracted to illusory money, dead by drowning. In a sense, Brian sees himself in the pool.

OTHER MAJOR WORKS

LONG FICTION: *The Pride of the Bimbos*, 1975; *Union Dues*, 1977; *Los Gusanos*, 1991.

PLAYS: *New Hope for the Dead*, pr. 1981; *Turnbuckle*, pr. 1981.

SCREENPLAYS: *Piranha*, 1978; *The Lady in Red*, 1979; *Alligator*, 1980 (adaptation of a short story by Sayles and Frank Ray Perilli); *Battle Beyond the Stars*, 1980; *Return of the Secaucus Seven*, 1980; *The Howling*, 1981 (with Terence H. Winkless; adaptation of Gary Brandner's novel); *The Challenge*, 1982 (with Richard Maxwell); *Baby, It's You*, 1983 (adaptation of Amy Robinson's short story); *Enormous Changes at the Last Minute*, 1983 (with Susan Rice; adaptation of Grace Paley's short stories); *Lianna*, 1983; *The Brother from Another Planet*, 1984; *The Clan of the Cave Bear*, 1986 (adaptation of Jean Auel's novel); *Matewan*, 1987; *Wild Thing*, 1987 (adaptation of a short story by Sayles and Larry Stamper); *Eight Men Out*, 1988 (adaptation of Eliot Asinof's book); *Breaking In*, 1989; *City of Hope*, 1991; *Passion Fish*, 1992; *Men of War*, 1994 (with Ethan Reiff and Cyrus Voris); *The Secret of Roan Inish*, 1994; *Lone Star*, 1996; *Men with Guns*, 1997; *Limbo*, 1999; *Sunshine State*, 2002; *Casa de los Babys*, 2003; *Silver City, and Other Screenplays*, 2004.

TELEPLAYS: *A Perfect Match*, 1980; *Unnatural Causes*, 1986; *Shannon's Deal*, 1989 (pilot and two episodes).

NONFICTION: *Thinking in Pictures: The Making of the Movie "Matewan,"* 1987; *Sayles on Sayles*, 1998 (with Gavin Smith).

BIBLIOGRAPHY

Bourjaily, Vance. "A Revivalism of Realism." *The New York Times Book Review* (April 1, 1979): 15, 33. Lengthy review of *The Anarchists' Convention*, stressing Sayles's links to the realism of Theodore Dreiser and James T. Farrell, tempered by a limited amount of optimism. Bourjaily also points out Sayles's fascination with the technical details of particular kinds of work, usually jobs Sayles had at one point in his life.

Butscher, Edward. "Books in Brief: *The Anarchists' Convention*." *Saturday Review* 6 (April 28, 1979): 46. Butscher suggests that Sayles's tendency toward sentimentality, caused by his sympathy for his lower-class characters, occasionally interferes with his ability to translate "acute psychological insights into viable fiction."

Epps, Garrett. "Tales of the Working Class." *The Washington Post Book World*, April 29, 1979, p. M5. Epps focuses on the blue-collar workers in Sayles's fiction and praises his "unerring ear for American speech." According to Epps, Sayles presents keen observations about America in the 1970's and succeeds in depicting characters without caricature or sentiment.

Molyneaux, Gerard. *John Sayles: An Unauthorized Biography of the Pioneering Indie Filmmaker*. Los Angles: Renaissance Books, 2000. Molyneaux focuses his biography on Sayles's work as an independent filmmaker, describing how he finances and directs his motion pictures. However, he also discusses the novels and short stories and provides insight into Sayles's life and character.

Ryan, Jack. *John Sayles, Flmmaker: A Critical Study and Filmography*. 2d ed. Jefferson, N.C.: McFarland, 2010. Like most books about Sayles, this one focuses on his films. However, the first chapter, "A Storyteller: From Literature to Film," discusses Sayles's fiction.

Sayles, John. *John Sayles: Interviews*. Edited by Diane Carson. Jackson: University Press of Mississippi, 1999. Carson's questions are primarily about Sayles's films, but there are scattered references to the stories through the book. The book contains an invaluable four-page chronology of Sayles's life and career.

Smith, Gavin, ed. *Sayles on Sayles*. London: Faber and Faber, 1998. An extended interview by Smith, who tends to focus on Sayles's films, but who also elicits some comments by Sayles about *The Anarchists' Convention* and the two stories "Breed" and "Hoop"

(in which he compares basketball to jazz) that were adapted to film. Sayles compares the stories in *The Anarchists' Convention* to an album, with each picture or story having its own "emotion and rhythm."

*Thomas L. Erskine*

---

# DELMORE SCHWARTZ

**Born:** Brooklyn, New York; December 8, 1913
**Died:** New York, New York; July 11, 1966

PRINCIPAL SHORT FICTION

*In Dreams Begin Responsibilities,* 1938 (includes poetry and prose)
*The World Is a Wedding,* 1948
*Successful Love, and Other Stories,* 1961

OTHER LITERARY FORMS

Besides being an author of short fiction, Delmore Schwartz (shwarts) was a poet, playwright, critic, editor, and prolific letter writer.

ACHIEVEMENTS

Delmore Schwartz's merit as both poet and short-story writer has been widely recognized. Along with his contemporaries John Berryman, Robert Lowell, and Randall Jarrell, Schwartz can be seen as a representative literary figure who poignantly lived and wrote about his personal struggles, which were also the struggles of a generation of American writers.

Schwartz's stories deal, above all, with the problems associated with creating a Jewish identity in the United States. Schwartz obsessively depicts the son's relation to his parents and a pre-American past. In the face of the twin burdens of an active intellect and a Jewish past, the son/hero is overwhelmed by a profound sense of alienation.

Doubtless these qualities, which made Schwartz a legend, were what attracted Saul Bellow sufficiently to create a fictionalized version of Schwartz in *Humboldt's Gift* (1975). Ultimately, Schwartz's life might be seen in the wider context of American literature. His negotiation of, and escape from, the trappings of mainstream American society are akin to those of Huckleberry Finn and Nick Adams.

BIOGRAPHY

From earliest youth, Delmore Schwartz's entire identity was shaped by his expectation that he would become a great American writer. Tied in with this grandiose fantasy was the anticipation of inheriting great wealth. Although his father had been a millionaire, the crash of the stock market in 1929 eroded much of his fortune, and a dishonest executor dissipated the remaining funds. Schwartz, however, continued to hope for his legacy until as late as 1946. His childhood was much damaged by his parents' arguments. When Delmore was nine, in 1923, his father left, but his mother resisted a divorce until 1927.

Schwartz attended the University of Wisconsin and then transferred to New York University, where he received his B.A. in 1935. That same year he finally received a few thousand dollars from his father's estate and enrolled in Harvard University graduate school in philosophy, having to leave school in March, 1937, however, because of debts. From 1940 to 1947 Schwartz taught at Harvard as a Briggs-Copeland Fellow. Schwartz's first marriage to Gertrude Buckman on June 14, 1938, ended in divorce. On June 10, 1949, he married Elizabeth Pollet. Schwartz was a frequent contributor to *Partisan Review*, of which he was an editor from 1946 to 1955. Later, from 1962 to 1966, he taught at Princeton and Syracuse Universities. He died at fifty-two without having fulfilled his great early promise. A paranoid failure, he was destroyed by drugs, drink, and many shock treatments.

ANALYSIS

Delmore Schwartz's place in American literature is unique and problematic. His life, as well as his modest literary production, which includes thirty-five poems, a verse play, short stories, and other works, has continued to fascinate a select group of critics and writers. The republication of Schwartz's stories, *In Dreams Begin Responsibilities*, by New Directions in 1978, and the appearance of Schwartz's letters and journals have helped solidify his position and shed light on his career. Critics have dwelt on the importance of Schwartz's Jewish heritage and have also tried to stress how American are his concerns.

### "IN DREAMS BEGIN RESPONSIBILITIES"

The character of Schwartz's work can be felt in "In Dreams Begin Responsibilities." Published when the writer was twenty-five, the story, like practically everything else he wrote, is distinctly autobiographical. The story is divided into six parts. It opens on a Sunday afternoon, June 12, 1909, in Brooklyn, as his father is courting his mother. They take the streetcar to Coney Island to inhale the sea air from the boardwalk and to watch the strollers promenade in their Sunday clothes. They ride the merry-go-round and snatch at the brass ring. Later they eat dinner, while his father boasts of all the money he will make, and then proposes. His mother begins to cry because this is what she has wanted him to say ever since she met him. They have their picture taken, but the photographer corrects their pose so many times that his father becomes impatient; his smile becomes a grimace, hers "bright and false." Then they argue about having their fortune told, and in terrible anger, he strides out of the booth. The story of his parents' courtship is narrated by their child, who watches it as if it were a film, reacts to the scenes being portrayed on the screen, and is threatened with expulsion from the theater by the rest of the audience who object to his interruptions. Finally the usher reprimands him, seizing his arm and dragging him away. He awakens on the morning of his twenty-first birthday, a bleak, snowy, wintry day.

The undisguised autobiographical elements of this story are the use of Schwartz's actual birthday, December 8, which took place four years after this mismatched couple was married; the use of his real mother's name, Rose; the grouping of his real relatives around the dinner table; and the depiction of his father's financial ambitions. To a certain extent, the cinematic presentation could also be considered autobiographical since Schwartz was a lifelong film addict. Saul Bellow, in his fictionalized version of Schwartz's life, shows him as an aficionado of old films and portrays him as acting out scenes from the films he doted on, quoting from them, and even scripting one collaboratively and composing a scenario for another.

The psychological implications of this perspective are frightening. The author on his birthday night five times tries to interrupt the film which will end in his conception. Once he freezes a frame into a still shot. Three times he actually leaves his seat because he cannot endure what is coming, but he returns in horrified fascination to watch it being relentlessly played out to the end, except that he is forcibly expelled from the theater for having created such commotion with his outcries. He awakens in the cold present of his own manhood to the recognition that this has been an anxiety dream. To have wished his parents not to marry is to have wished his own extinction. To suffer such fears of dissolution, as Schwartz did nightly, is to suffer from insomnia, a condition for which Schwartz was famous. He dreaded sleep because it meant losing control. Much of his erudition resulted from the thousands of books he read at night to fend off his terrors, taking fistfuls of Benzedrine tablets to stay awake.

The Brechtian alienation effect of interrupting the narrative flow in each of the sections of the story is an authorial strategy which makes the experience of the reader conform to the experience of the author, who is also the narrator. It is a perfect narcissistic mirroring technique: The content reflects the form, which reflects the theme; the home film being replayed on the dream screen reflects a past in which he could not have participated in any other guise because he had not yet been born. The youth must reconstruct the images of his parents' youth, as well as images of their parents, from faded images in old-fashioned clothes on family photographs.

The story opens in the subjunctive mood, "I feel as if I were in a motion picture theater," then shifts into the indicative. The author's use of the present tense throughout to describe things in the distant past has a curious effect; if all the verbs were changed to their past-tense forms, this story would become a simple retrospective narrative. Their obtrusive presentness makes the artificiality more conspicuous. This is not a story intended to entertain; it is instead a series of obsessive images which relentlessly thrust themselves upon the dream screen and which can no more be stopped than the paralyzed dreamer can obliterate the visions that insist upon playing themselves out in his consciousness.

The first interruption is posed as a break in the film. Just at the point when his mother's father is indicating his doubts about the contemplated engagement, "something happens to the film." The audience protests by clapping vigorously until it is fixed. Instead of going on, however, it replays the same scene again, and once more the grandfather critically watches the prospective husband of his eldest daughter, worried about his character. This is both effective literary technique and valid psychology. The reiterated episode foreshadows the imminent disaster. To the narrator, the recurrent scene is a way of coping with his own sense of foreboding. The father is awkward and uneasy. The narrator, totally identified with him, "stirs uneasily also, slouched in the hard chair of the theater," and at the end of this second section, he begins to weep.

The third section is based on a contrast of perceptions, and it ends like an incremental repetition with another gush of tears while the old lady sitting next to him pats him consolingly on the shoulder and says, "There, there, all of this is only a movie, young man, only a movie." Because he knows that it is not, however, he stumbles out over the feet in his row to hide his uncontrollable grief in the men's room. The double irony of the film's being real, while the old lady seeking to assure him of its unreality is herself unreal, augments the solipsism which the story so terrifyingly expresses. The narrator's parents feel no "danger"; they are "unaware"; they stare at the ocean "absently." Overhead the sun's lighting strikes and strikes, but neither of them is at all aware of it. The unborn son, watching their "indifference" to the ocean's force, harshness, and fierceness, is shocked. "I stare at the terrible sun which breaks up sight, and the fatal,

merciless, passionate ocean . . . and finally shocked by the indifference of my father and mother, I burst out weeping once more." He is as divorced from them, in the intensity of his perceptions, as they are from each other and from the miracles of nature. Their reactions are stereotyped and superficial; they look at the bathing suits and buy peanuts. He sees the "terrifying sun and the terrifying ocean."

The fourth part begins: "When I return, feeling as if I had awakened in the morning sick for lack of sleep, several hours have apparently passed and my parents are riding on the merry-go-round." Their mechanical revolution in endless cycles is an appropriate metaphor for the meaningless rounds of their lives. When his father proposes in the restaurant, the son stands up and screams: "Don't do it. It's not too late to change your minds, both of you. Nothing good will come of it, only remorse, hatred, scandal, and two children whose characters are monstrous." The entire audience glares at him, the usher approaches brandishing his flashlight, and the old lady tries to tug him back down into his seat; because he cannot bear to see what is happening, he shuts his eyes. The irony of his behavior is that shutting his eyes cannot obliterate the pictures because he is already dreaming them with his eyes shut. No amount of protest can stop the film that is unreeling in the theater of his mind, and there is nowhere that he can go to escape it.

The fifth episode is a tour de force. The photographer who wants to fix a beautiful image of his parents and cannot find a way of posing them so that the picture will be "right" is the artistic son. He wants to "fix" them forever in his word picture as the shapers and reflectors of his identity, but he is frustrated by their inadequacies from defining them permanently. The print that emerges from the photographer's dedicated efforts is patently false. The writer that emerges from their doomed conjunction is condemned to uncertain and fluctuating ego boundaries.

In the sixth part, a terrible quarrel arises in the fortune-teller's booth. Enraged, the father stalks out yanking at the mother's arm, but she stubbornly refuses to budge, so he strides away. The son, in terrible fear, screams "What are they doing?" The ensuing passage mirrors both the actions and the words of the preceding one.

The usher has seized my arm and is dragging me away, and as he does so, he says: 'What are *you* doing? Don't you know that you can't do whatever you want to do? Why should a young man like you, with your whole life before you, get hysterical like this?'

As the usher drags him through the lobby of the theater into the cold light, he awakens into the bleak winter morning of his twenty-first birthday. His fortune has been foretold; it is a cold and bleak one with which he enters chronological maturity, aware that he will never attain the emotional maturity which this day should mark.

### "America! America!"

The protagonist of another story, "America! America!," is Shenandoah Fish. This name is one of a number of self-mocking ones that Schwartz invented for his personae. He felt sharply the incongruity of his Latinate first name and his Hebraic surname, so all his fictional surrogates have equally incongruous names. His alter egos are Shenandoah Fish, Marquis Fane, Richmond Rose, Berthold Cannon, Maximilian Rinehart, Cornelius Schmidt, and Hershey Green. In "America! America!" an author, unable to write, listens to his mother's monologue about the Bauman family. He is troubled by his loss of fluency, feeling it as "a loss, or a lapse of identity." Because he feels real only when he is working, he asks anxiously, "Who am I?" As he listens to the story about the insurance agent and his family whom his mother had known for thirty years, he wonders whether

> its cruelty lay in his mother's tongue or in his own mind. And his own thoughts which had to do with his own life, and seemed to have nothing to do with these human beings, began to trouble him.

As his mother drones on about the sons, Sydney and Dick, who were never able to make a living even in a land where everyone who is willing to work hard enough can get rich, he listens with irony and contempt. His mother interrupts her ironing to tell him that it is late afternoon and time he got dressed. As he changes from his pajamas, he stares in the mirror, thinking that no one truly sees himself as he is: "I do not see myself. I do not know myself. I cannot look at myself truly."

His mother's representation of the Baumans becomes a metaphor for the writer's handling of his subject. Her summation of the theme of the story she has just told is that the Bauman sons were spoiled by having had too pleasant a family life. They were so indulged that they became indolent and lost the will and the aggressiveness necessary for success. He feels that her judgment is external, merely gossip, and that the story would be very different if seen from the inside. As he stares at the mirror, he realizes that she has stirred up his self-contempt with her tale of waste and failure. He becomes aware that he is defending his own rationalizations; her story with its abstractions, its outlines, has exhausted him. While he had listened to it at such a distance, it remained a caricature, but as he enters into it, it becomes a self-criticism. The Baumans, who had seemed so remote from his concerns, now merge with his own ruined life, and the scorn with which he had fended them off stares back at him from the mirror. The accusation reflected there is that his own indolence and lassitude are equal to those of the Baumans', whose story has only aggravated his anxiety about lacking the volition to work, and this last scene answers the question he had asked in the first. In this story about telling a story, the cruelty is not in his mother's tongue but rather is engendered in his own mind.

### Other major works

PLAY: *Shenandoah*, pb. 1941.

POETRY: *Genesis, Book I*, 1943; *Vaudeville for a Princess, and Other Poems*, 1950; *Summer Knowledge*, 1959; *Last and Lost Poems of Delmore Schwartz*, 1979 (Robert Phillips, editor).

NONFICTION: *Selected Essays of Delmore Schwartz*, 1970; *Letters of Delmore Schwartz*, 1984; *Portrait of Delmore: Journals and Notes of Delmore Schwartz, 1939-1959*, 1986; *The Ego Is Always at the Wheel: Bagatelles*, 1986..

CHILDREN'S LITERATURE: *"I Am Cherry Alive," the Little Girl Sang*, 1958.

MISCELLANEOUS: *Screeno: Stories and Poems*, 2001.

### Bibliography

Ashbery, John. *The Heavy Bear: Delmore Schwartz's Life Versus His Poetry--A Lecture Delivered at the*

*Sixty-seventh General Meeting of the English Literary Society of Japan on 21st May 1995*. Tokyo: English Literary Society of Japan, 1996. Ashbery, himself a poet, compares and contrasts Schwartz's life and work.

Atlas, James. *Delmore Schwartz: The Life of an American Poet*. 1977. Reprint.San Diego, Calif.: Harcourt Brace Jovanovich, 2000. A comprehensive biography that attempts to cut through Schwartz's poses and personae. Contains extracts of his poems illustrating his development as a poet and discusses his short fiction.

Bawer, Bruce. *The Middle Generation: The Lives and Poetry of Delmore Schwartz, Randall Jarrell, John Berryman, Robert Lowell*. Hamden, Conn.: Archon Books, 1986. Bawer persuasively argues that these poets "shared an affliction." His particularly useful study, integrating biographical detail with literary analysis, teases out the important thematic threads connecting these late modern writers: rocky childhoods, quests for love and faith, and disillusionment in maturity.

Gelfant, Blanche H., ed. *The Columbia Companion to the Twentieth-Century American Short Story*. New York: Columbia University Press, 2000. Includes a chapter in which Schwartz's short stories are analyzed.

Goldman, Mark. "Reflections in a Mirror: On Two Stories by Delmore Schwartz." *Studies in American Jewish Literature* 2 (1982): 86-97. In his discussion of two stories, "America! America!" and "The Child Is the Meaning of Life," Goldman focuses on Schwartz's obsession with personal history and identity, relations between children and parents, and determinism.

Howe, Irving. Foreword to *In Dreams Begin Responsibilities*. New York: New Directions, 1978. Howe's introduction, appreciative and sensitive, is a good place to start with Schwartz. He concisely guides the reader through the development of Schwartz's work, noting salient elements of stories and placing them historically.

Malin, Irving. *Jews and Americans*. Carbondale: southern Illinois University Press, 1965. Malin discusses the writings of Schwartz, along with those of Karl Shapiro, Isaac Rosenfeld, Leslie Fiedler, Saul Bellow, Bernard Malamud, and Philip Roth, to determine the shared "Jewishness" of their works.

McDougall, Richard. *Delmore Schwartz*. New York: Twayne, 1974. Provides an overview of Schwartz's writing career, placing emphasis on the theme of alienation and relating it to Schwartz's status as poet and Jew in modern times.

New, Elisa. "Reconsidering Delmore Schwartz." *Prooftexts: A Journal of Jewish Literary History* 5, no. 3 (September, 1985): 245-262. New suggests that the Jewish American heroes in Schwartz's stories "map out danger zones of intergenerational paralysis where we languish in the throes of a cultural adolescence that will not let us stop selling ourselves as Americans, hawking our goods, both material and intellectual."

Ozick, Cynthia. "Delmore Schwartz: The Willed Abortion of the Self." In *The Din in the Head: Essays*. Boston: Houghton Mifflin, 2006. Ozick provides her critical assessment of Schwartz's poetry and short fiction, comparing their themes and language. She analyzes "In Dreams Begin Responsibilities" and several other short stories.

Schreier, Benjamin. "Jew Historicism: Delmore Schwartz and Overdetermination." *Prooftexts* 27, no. 3 (Fall, 2007): 500-530. Schreier uses "In Dreams Begin Responsibilities" to argue that Schwartz finds "experience alienating precisely in the expectation that it recover a legible reality." He discusses Schwartz's insistence that "the ideal imaginative investments made in experiences--investments that are presumed to render reality emotionally and ethically useful--on the contrary put reality at an irretrievable remove."

Schwartz, Delmore. *Delmore Schwartz and James Laughlin: Selected Letters*. Edited by Robert Phillips. New York: W. W. Norton, 1993. This collection of letters provides insight into Schwartz's character.

Waldhorn, Arthur, and Hilda K. Waldhorn, eds. *The Rite of Becoming: Stories and Studies of Adolescence*. Cleveland, Ohio: World Publishing, 1977. An extended analysis of "In Dreams Begin Responsibilities," focusing on how the story embodies Sigmund Freud's idea that dreams are wish fulfillments.

*Ruth Rosenberg*
*Updated by Allen Hibbard*

# LYNNE SHARON SCHWARTZ

**Born:** Brooklyn, New York; March 19, 1939

PRINCIPAL SHORT FICTION

*Acquainted with the Night, and Other Stories,* 1984
*The Melting Pot, and Other Subversive Stories,* 1987
*Referred Pain, and Other Stories,* 2003

OTHER LITERARY FORMS

Lynne Sharon Schwartz (lihn SHAR-uhn swohrtz) has published several novels, including *Rough Strife* (1980), *Balancing Acts* (1981), *Disturbances in the Field* (1983), *Leaving Brooklyn* (1989), *The Fatigue Artist* (1995), *In the Family Way: An Urban Comedy* (1999), and *The Writing on the Wall* (2005). She has also written much poetry and nonfiction. Other publications include a children's book, *The Four Questions* (1989), and a memoir, *Ruined by Reading: A Life in Books* (1996). In 2002, her collection of poetry *In Solitary* was released, and in 2009 her memoir *Not Now, Voyager* came out. She also edited in 2010 *The Emergence of Memory: Conversations with W. G. Sebald.*

ACHIEVEMENTS

Lynne Sharon Schwartz's awards for her short fiction include the James Henle Award (1974) and the Lamport Foundation Award (1977). Her work has been included in *The Best American Short Stories 1978, The Best American Short Stories 1979, Prize Stories: The O. Henry Awards* (1979), and *Imagining America* (1992).

BIOGRAPHY

Lynne Sharon Schwartz was born in Brooklyn, New York, on March 19, 1939. She married Harry Schwartz, a city planner, on December 22, 1957; they had two children, Rachel Eve and Miranda Ruth. Lynne Sharon

Schwartz attended Barnard College, earning a B.A. in 1959, and Bryn Mawr College, earning an M.A. in 1961, followed by further graduate study at New York University, 1967-1972. She left the program without completing her dissertation, deciding instead to devote her time to writing. She worked from 1961 to 1963 as an associate editor for *Writer Magazine* and as a writer for a civil rights-fair housing organization, Operation Open City (1965-1967). From 1970 to 1975, she lectured at Hunter College of the City University of New York and taught fiction workshops at the University of Iowa (1982-1983), Columbia University (1983-1985), Boston University (1984-1985), Rice University (1987), University of California, Irvine (1991), and University of Hawaii, Manoa (1994).

Schwartz's stories, poems, articles, translations, and reviews have appeared in literary journals and popular magazines, including *The North American Review, Salmagundi, Michigan Quarterly Review, Prairie Schooner, The Sewanee Review, The Hudson Review, The Ontario Review, Harper's, The New York Times Book Review, The Washington Post Book World, Ploughshares, Redbook,* and *The Chicago Review.*

ANALYSIS

Lynne Sharon Schwartz's short stories and novels often focus on fear, especially of loss: of love, of spouse, of children, of looks and physical capacities, of mind and personhood. Most but not all of her principal characters are females, who strive mightily to avoid loss of one sort or another and then often to survive its inevitability. In the short story "Do Something About It," for instance (published in May/June, 1995, in *The North American Review*), her central figure struggles to come to terms with the senseless death of her husband, a reporter who has been killed in a police raid in the Bronx. An earlier story, "What I Did for Love," develops a similar theme of a woman trying to survive the unimaginable death of her husband; in this story she is also tries to protect her daughter from the realities of death, first of guinea pigs, then of Carl, husband and father. One cannot change the world much, especially the fundamental reality of death and loss.

Many of Schwartz's works of fiction appear to have close connections to events within her own life. "The Last Frontier," for example, utilizes as its inciting event the fire that took place in her New York City apartment building (owned by Columbia University) and that in 1985 engendered her first nonfiction work, *We Are Talking About Homes: A Great University Against Its Neighbors*. "Two Portraits of Rembrandt" is in some measure a tribute to her father, as she writes in *Ruined by Reading*. "The Wrath-Bearing Tree," in *Acquainted with the Night, and Other Stories*, would appear to stem in part from the death of her father, a lawyer, in a hospital. Certainly her fictional pieces develop from the close observation of ordinary life around her, its pains and its pleasures, its obsessive and irrational fears, and its real losses. As she argues in her discussion in *Ruined by Reading* of Henry James's *The Awkward Age* (1898-1899), his characters "simply didn't care enough about ordinary human fulfillments--love, sex, work--to be credible." Schwartz's characters care very much about "ordinary human fulfillments," and that is the compelling charm of her fiction.

### ACQUAINTED WITH THE NIGHT, AND OTHER STORIES

In this 1984 collection of sixteen stories, all of which were previously published elsewhere, Schwartz explores in a variety of voices a number of painful issues: the death of a parent; the nature of marriage; the effects of the mental illness of a child on a relationship; the difficulties of breaking the social barriers between races of the same class; the strategies one employs to deal with loss, whether of identity or of a life partner; the births and deaths of relationships; the adaptations of immigrants. The more satisfying stories offer technically clever and effective beginnings and endings, as well as a strongly realized narrative voice, whatever the technical narrative point of view.

"The Age of Analysis" takes a sharply satiric look at the vogue for psychoanalytical "talk therapy." In the story, a happily married professional couple, both of whom are therapists, find themselves incapable of dealing with their son, Paul, who is, from an early age, prone to

temper tantrums and destructive fits. Thus, they engage first a child psychiatrist and then, in the natural course of things, a specialist in adolescent psychology to treat him. The regular long talk sessions, however, do little to instill in Paul maturity, wisdom, control, understanding, or limits. Thus, when Paul's father makes an apparently sudden decision to leave his wife and son for a young client because he "needs to find his space," Paul is outraged, especially because his father takes the Steinway piano, and Paul "acts out" even more violently than before, finally attempting suicide by slicing one wrist in front of his parents, brought together to talk about the father's wishes for a new life. Paul's dramatic gesture breaks through their psychobabble and results in his being rushed to the hospital by his guilt-stricken parents, who promise to do anything and everything for poor Paul.

"The Middle Classes" focuses on the consequences of the social changes in a middle-class Brooklyn neighborhood during the 1950's and 1960's, when growing numbers of African Americans moved into the middle class and hence changed what had been a Jewish middle-class neighborhood into a black middle-class neighborhood. The story explores retrospectively the narrator's deepening understanding of the nature of race relations by focusing on a time in her life when her family employed a talented black pianist to provide her advanced piano lessons. She grows attached to Mr. Simmons, an excellent teacher, who is willing to pronounce "awful" as "beautiful," and they consequently enjoy a "mutually appreciative" relationship. She is somehow offended that her parents go out of their way to develop a middle-class relationship with Mr. Simmons, perhaps because friendship with a black man is for them a new and strange phenomenon, one that erodes the prejudices of ignorance.

### THE MELTING POT, AND OTHER SUBVERSIVE STORIES

A growing control over tone and material characterizes the eleven stories in *The Melting Pot, and Other Subversive Stories*. The title story examines a deliciously complex relationship between Rita and Sanjay. The daughter of a Jewish man and a Mexican immigrant, Rita has been reared by her very conservative Jewish grandparents in New York City because her mother killed her father and is serving time in prison. Rita is involved in a relationship with Sanjay, a recently widowed Hindu twice her age, who wants to marry her. The complexities of love, marriage, and relationships in this new land play out wonderfully in this deftly constructed story.

"So You're Going to Have a New Body" appeared first in *Mother Jones* magazine. Its wryly ironic tone and feminist attack on the facile (and arrogant) attitudes of many male gynecologists are tempered by Schwartz's humor in this first-person account of a woman who undergoes a hysterectomy and removal of ovaries or so-called female castration. Urged to ask her doctor all about it because he can help, the protagonist feels betrayed by the condescending attitude and behavior of both her doctor and his staff, resolving during her exit exam never again to permit any male doctor to treat her.

"The Last Frontier" first appeared in the publication *Witness*. In it, George Madison, his wife, Louise, and their three children, immigrants from Saint Thomas, struggle to find a home in New York City after a fire in their first apartment building has left them homeless. Despite being employed, George and Louise are unable to find an apartment because of the lack of affordable public housing and a stubborn prejudice against blacks, but George is resourceful and determined "to take care of his family." The family "homesteads" in a building that wholesales household furnishings and maintains display rooms that look like "a regular house" without, however, the third wall. George's initiative and buoyant attitude sustains the family on this urban frontier, in direct contrast to the generally hostile attitude of New Yorkers and the necessity of packing up before the store's employees arrive--and being careful to leave no trace. The story makes a powerful argument about human resourcefulness and homelessness.

"What I Did for Love" chronicles the efforts of Chris to cope with the changes brought to her life and her relationship with Carl, her husband. Former political radicals of the 1960's, they have changed: Their youthful ambitions to change the "power structure and [make] the world a better place" have been altered by the birth of their daughter, Martine. Carl drives a cab; Chris works as an X-ray technician. As their daughter grows up, they turn their attention to making her life the best they can, in a familiar switch from lofty enterprises to rearing one's child. Schwartz cleverly structures the story around four guinea pigs, sequential pets of Martine, despite Chris's aversion to such animals. The unexpected death of Carl, alone in his cab, causes Chris to redouble her efforts to protect Martine, which include sending her to camp again and making every possible effort to care for Rusty, "a one-eyed guinea pig who is going to live out his four-to-six-year life span no matter what it takes, in the middle of the journey of my life. . . ."

## REFERRED PAIN, AND OTHER STORIES

The opening story in *Referred Pain, and Other Stories*, "Heat," seems energized by the writer's compulsion to explore some mysterious encounter, obsession, disruption, or awareness in an intense and precise way. A woman has a secret passion for an older man she watches grow ill and weak. Nothing really happens except that, at his wife's request, the woman gives the man a haircut. However, it is enough to communicate desire that cannot be spoken, opportunity that must be missed, and passion that is always a puzzle.

After such a promising start, it is disappointing that most of the other eleven stories here seem merely professional pastimes. The title story is a novelistic exercise about a man named Koslowski who cracks a tooth on an olive pit, which then leads to a never-ending series of excruciating encounters with dentists, periodontists, endodontists, oral surgeons, and other purveyors of pain that goes on so absurdly and agonizingly long that the whole thing is just, well, painful. Schwartz probably means something Kafka-esque in all this business of ground-down molars, piercing root canals, mouth-filling bridgework, and oversized implants. A "referred pain," the reader is told, is a pain that originates from some other place than where it is felt. That must mean something. The poor throbbing, whining Koslowski constantly compares his experiences to those of his persecuted parents during World War II and the horror stories his girlfriend tells him about rape victims in Bosnia. The problem with physical pain is that it is so difficult to communicate; one can only multiply it, which Schwartz does for some seventy pages.

"Twisted Tales" is a set of five parables that begin in the traditional way: There once was a woman who could not abide clutter; there was a man who never wanted to go to sleep; a certain woman never felt comfortable speaking her native tongue. However, a fable, to be truly irresistible, has to have some charm, some terror, some awe, some significance. Do not expect any Borgesian scintillation here--just a writer having a little harmless fictional fun. "The Stone Master" is an inconclusive parable about a man, a writer it appears, who wanders into a parallel universe, or a mirror town, or an ideal replica, or some such fantasy concoction. "Deadly Nightshade" is about the first woman to dare to eat the forbidden tomato and thus become a "Prometheus of the vegetable world." Even the somewhat realistic fictions here, such as "By a Dimming Light" and "Francesca," arguably stronger than the abortive fables, seem more like writerly busy work, turning on facile premises and spinning out simplistic contrasts. More a novelist, Schwartz seems to forget that the short story is too fine a form to be fiddled with while waiting for a novel to gather enough wool to become a loose, baggy monster.

## OTHER MAJOR WORKS

LONG FICTION: *Rough Strife*, 1980; *Balancing Acts*, 1981; *Disturbances in the Field*, 1983; *Leaving Brooklyn*, 1989; *The Fatigue Artist*, 1995; *In the Family Way: An Urban Comedy*, 1999; *The Writing on the Wall*, 2005.

POETRY: *In Solitary*, 2002.

NONFICTION: *We Are Talking About Homes: A Great University Against Its Neighbors*, 1985; *Ruined by Reading: A Life in Books*, 1996; *Face to Face: A Reader in the World*, 2000; *Not Now, Voyager: A Memoir*, 2009.

TRANSLATION: *Smoke over Birkenau*, 1991.

CHILDREN'S LITERATURE: *The Four Questions*, 1989.

EDITED TEXT: *The Emergence of Memory: Conversations with W. G. Sebald*, 2007.

MISCELLANEOUS: *A Lynne Sharon Schwartz Reader: Selected Prose and Poetry*, 1992.

## BIBLIOGRAPHY

Burke, Kathleen. Review of *Ruined by Reading*, by Lynne Sharon Schwartz. *Smithsonian* 27 (December, 1996): 137. Summarizes the book as a celebration of reading.

Hulbert, Ann. *Acquainted with the Night, and Other Stories*, by Lynne Sharon Schwartz. *The New York Times Book Review*, August 26, 1984, p. 9. Only the title story sustains the "wry tone and . . . spiritual struggle" that mark her best novels.

Klass, Perri. Review of *The Melting Pot, and Other Subversive Stories*, by Lynne Sharon Schwartz. *New York Times Book Review*, October 11, 1987, p. 15. Focuses on "What I Did for Love," "The Sound of Velcro," "Killing the Bees," and "The Melting Pot."

Mano, D. Keith. Review of *Acquainted with the Night, and Other Stories*, by Lynne Sharon Schwartz. *National Review* 37 (February 22, 1985): 48-49. Argues that Schwartz's stories are often perceptive, smooth, and careful, but reflect exactly the state of short fiction today, which Mano finds generally "elitist, condescending, narrow, 'caring,' and relatively unimaginative."

Mellard, James M. "Resisting the Melting Pot: The Jewish Back-Story in the Fiction of Lynne Sharon Schwartz." In *Daughters of Valor: Contemporary Jewish American Women Writers*, edited by Jay Halio and Ben Siegel. Newark: University of Delaware Press, 1997. Argues that although Schwartz seeks to capture the "value and power of the American 'melting pot'" in her fiction, an ethnic "back story" about origins underlies it and is implicit in the details, if absent from the surfaces of, both her novels and her short stories. Analyzes in detail "Opiate of the People" and "The Melting Pot."

Schwartz, Lynne Sharon. Interview by Wendy Smith. *Publishers Weekly* 226 (August 3, 1984): 68-69. In an interview on the publication of *Acquainted with the Night, and Other Stories* Schwartz reveals some relationships among her three early novels and her short fiction.

*Theodore C. Humphrey*
*Updated by Charles E. May*

# BOB SHACOCHIS

**Born:** West Pittston, Pennsylvania;
September 9, 1951

PRINCIPAL SHORT FICTION
*Easy in the Islands,* 1985
*The Next New World,* 1989

OTHER LITERARY FORMS

While Bob Shacochis (shuh-KOH-chihs) has distinguished himself in both fiction and nonfiction, he is primarily known as a journalist. He has been a contributing editor at *Harper's* and *Outside* magazines, and for some years he wrote the "Dining In" column for *Gentlemen's Quarterly*. An assignment at *Harper's* resulted in *The Immaculate Invasion* (1999), covering the U.S. response to the Haitian uprising against Jean-Bertrand Aristide in 1994, and his culinary columns were collected in *Domesticity: A Gastronomic Interpretation of Love* (1994). He also wrote the Introduction to Sara Nickles's *Drinking, Smoking, and Screwing: Great Writers on Good Times* (1994) and the Foreword for C. Peter Ripley's *Conversations with Cuba* (2001).

ACHIEVEMENTS

Bob Shacochis won a literary fellowship from the National Endowment for the Arts in 1982 and awards from both Yaddo and the Bread Loaf Writers' Conference. In 1982, he was named the best new fiction contributor by *Playboy* magazine for "Lord Short Shoe Wants the Monkey"; in 1985, he won a Pushcart Prize for his story "Hot Day on the Gold Coast"; in 1986, he won a Best Stories from the South Award for "Where Pelham Fell." He received the American Book Award for First Fiction from the Association of American Publishers in 1985 for *Easy in the Islands*, and his novel *Swimming in the Volcano* (1994) was nominated for the National Book Award. He also has been honored by the American Academy and Institute of Arts and Letters with a Rome Prize for Literature.

BIOGRAPHY

Robert G. Shacochis grew up in McLean, Virginia, outside of Washington, D.C., and earned a B.A. at the University of Missouri in 1973. He served in the Peace Corps on various islands in the Caribbean in 1975 and 1976, and later he was a reporter for Palm Beach's *Evening Times*. He went back for his M.F.A. degree at the University of Iowa Writers' Workshop in 1982. He has been associated with both *Harper's* and *Outside* magazines for some years, and he has taken writing assignments around the world. He has taught creative writing at Florida State University in Tallahassee for some years.

ANALYSIS

Most of Bob Shacochis's fiction appeared in the 1980's and early 1990's, and he is known both as a fiction writer of the Caribbean region and of the American South. The stories in his first collection, *Easy in the Islands*, take place almost exclusively in the Caribbean, while several in his second are set on Caribbean islands, but more take place in Florida, North Carolina, Virginia, and even London, England. Likewise, of the nine stories in his first collection, five first appeared either in *Playboy* or *Esquire*. Shacochis was understandably seen, in his early career, as a men's or outdoor writer, in the tradition of Ernest Hemingway and later of Peter Matthiessen and Jim Harrison. The stories in Shacochis's second collection, however, appeared in a wider range of journals (such as *Harper's*) and revealed a deeper exploration of both history and the complexity of human emotions. Shacochis's stories are distinguished by fresh, poetic language and often by unique, idiosyncratic, first-person narrators.

## EASY IN THE ISLANDS

*Easy in the Islands* is a collection of nine stories linked by location and a feeling for Caribbean island life. Seriocomic in tone, the stories are best in their evocation of the color and the music of the Caribbean islands, whether Barbados, Jamaica, or St. Vincent, and many capture the distinctive pidgin English of island speakers. Most of the stories focus on the interplay between mainland and island culture, as visitors from the United States, both tourists and expatriates, wrestle with the "enigma" (Shacochis's epigraph is from Joseph Conrad's 1899 novel *Heart of Darkness*) of island life, trying to figure out if it is "inviting" or "savage." Often, in the fiction of Shacochis, it is both. The weakest stories in this first collection show only minimal interaction between white and native life and focus on romantic voyages: Both "Dead Reckoning" and "The Heart's Advantage," for example, describe American men so driven to sail the Caribbean that they fail to appreciate the women who accompany them.

The last three stories in the collection are connected through the central character of Bowen, an American archaeologist studying island culture and learning from its customs and folkways. In the strongest of these three, "The Pelican," Bowen tries to kill a wounded bird the natives have caught for food, but can't complete the deed with his knife dulled by digging for pottery shards. The bird is finally dispatched by a young islander wielding a stone. The tools of civilization, Shacochis suggests symbolically, are not always effective. In the coda to the story, the boy offers to sharpen Bowen's knife with the same stone.

The dominant tone in the collection is comic: "Redemption Songs" (a reference to the Jamaican reggae singer Bob Marley) describes two island natives, Glasford and Fish, trying to foment revolution with spray-paint cans, only to end up in a bungled, slapstick robbery of American tourists. In "Hot Day on the Gold Coast," Weber is pursued by the police for jogging through Palm Beach streets in his boxer shorts, jumps from a bridge, and swims to a nearby boat to escape, only to find a boatload of Haitian refugees waiting to land. Again, a story with political overtones is undercut by comic conclusions. In the title story, Tillman keeps his dead mother's corpse in the walk-in freezer of the rundown "Rosehill Plantation" hotel he has inherited from his father, until Tillman can figure out a way to circumvent the island authorities, who want to turn her death from old age into a murder mystery. Tillman's conclusion that "life on the island had a certain fullness, that it was . . . authentic in the most elemental ways" is bolstered by narrative language that is often poetic and metaphorical and by images that can be both violent and seriocomic.

## "LORD SHORT SHOE WANTS THE MONKEY"

In perhaps the best story in Shacochis's first collection, and the story that earned him the title of best new fiction contributor to *Playboy* in 1982, a popular calypso singer is trying to buy a live prop for his recent political hit, "Dis Country Need a Monkey," and is even willing to trade his sultry singer and lover Melandra Goodnight to the American who owns the animal. After a night of drinking on the terrace outside a Bridgetown, Barbados, jazz bar, the bargain is struck, but the American Harter is now too drunk to realize that the singer is making love to him in front of many of the bar's patrons, and he learns a hard lesson. "'Monkey,' she hisses, pointing at Harter. 'Womahn,' she says, jerking a thumb at herself." Harter will undoubtedly become the subject of the next Lord Short Shoe calypso hit. Even the comic lesson may be less significant than the atmosphere Shacochis creates, a Caribbean night dripping with music and sexual tension. The story found its ideal home in *Playboy*.

## THE NEXT NEW WORLD

Shacochis's second collection of short stories showed a clear growth in range of subject and depth of feeling. The eight stories were set in new locales and the characters and plots revealed a further exploration of history and human emotion. The first story in the collection, "Les Femmes Creoles: A Fairy Story," is set in Haiti in 1923, at the end of the American occupation of that island nation, and tells of two spinster sisters hiding out in their abandoned plantation and awaiting imagined lovers. The story is both comic and surreal, and by the end it becomes a true fairy tale. (In an author's note, Shacochis acknowledges that he lifted the first line of the story from Richard Hughes's magical 1928 children's novel, *A High Wind in Jamaica*.) "Where Pelham Fell," the best story in the collection, focuses on two men, one white and one African American, haunted by ghosts from the Civil War in northern Virginia. "The Trapdoor" is set at an Elizabethan London theater during a performance of William Shakespeare's *Hamlet, Prince of Denmark* (pr. c. 1600-1601, pb. 1603), and includes actors and historical figures in its cast of characters. Other stories show a wider range of human emotion, from "Stolen Kiss," a sketch about a caretaker painting a beach house in Delaware and imagining how the imprint of a kiss has been left on a porch post, through "Celebrations of the New World," a slapstick comedy of two wildly different families coming together for a party with both comic and melancholic results, and "Hidalgos," in which old friends reunite after the death of one's wife and try to come to grips with their loss. The range of style and tone is equally broad, from romantic, even sentimental emotions, as in "Hidalgos," to the quirky narration of violent events that make up "I Ate Her Heart," to the provincial, gossipy first-person narration of "Squirrelly's Grouper," set on Hatteras Island, on the Outer Banks of North Carolina.

### "Where Pelham Fell"

It is understandable why "Where Pelham Fell" won the first Best Stories from the South Award in 1986, but what the award fails to indicate is the depth of feeling probed in the story. The action takes place near Culpepper, in northern Virginia, where Colonel Taylor Coates (a World War II veteran) and his wife, Dippy Barrington Coates, are slipping into old age. Prohibited from driving, the colonel does it anyway, searching the Virginia countryside for Civil War battle sites; the colonel is haunted by such figures as the Confederate John Mosby ("The Gray Ghost"), head of the First Virginia Cavalry. Lost looking for the spot where Major John Pelham, an artillery officer who served in the Confederate cavalry under J. E. B. Stuart, fell at the Battle of Kelly's Ford, Colonel Coates's car gets stuck on the property of President Trass, an African American, who

sees Coates as a savior: Four generations of the Trass family have been holding two burlap sacks full of human bones from soldiers who fell nearby in the Civil War. Trass sees Coates as sent by providence "to relieve the Trass clan of the macabre burden they had accepted as their own for more than a hundred years." Coates takes the bones home and becomes an amateur forensic scientist, putting them together with the accompanying belt buckles and cartridges to try to identify the soldiers, whose ancient memory he should be honoring. Meanwhile, his wife tries to take care of their antebellum brick farmhouse and her wandering husband. Like William Faulkner, Eudora Welty, Reynolds Price, and other southern writers, Shacochis explores the ways in which contemporary southern life is haunted by ghosts of its own storied past.

### Other major works

LONG FICTION: *Swimming in the Volcano*, 1993.

NONFICTION: *Domesticity: A Gastronomic Interpretation of Love*, 1994; *The Immaculate Invasion*, 1999.

### Bibliography

Basuch, Richard. "Stepping Through the Trapdoor." *The New York Times Book Review*, February 19, 1989, p. 10. Review of Shacochis's second collection of short stories.

Hitchcock, Bert. "Bob Shachocis." In *Contemporary Fiction Writers of the South: A Bio-Bibliographical Sourcebook*, edited by Joseph M. Fiora and Robert Bain, Westport, Conn.: Greenwood, 1993. A useful summary of the themes of Shacochis's short fiction and reviews of his two collections of stories.

Jardim, Keith. "Bob Shacochis: American Writer in Caribbean Light." The Observer, November 4, 2010. Long interview with Shacochis that mentions his his skill at portraying the expatriate experience.

*David Peck*

# IRWIN SHAW

**Born:** New York, New York; February 27, 1913
**Died:** Davos, Switzerland; May 16, 1984

PRINCIPAL SHORT FICTION

*Sailor off the Bremen, and Other Stories,* 1939
*Welcome to the City, and Other Stories,* 1942
*Act of Faith, and Other Stories,* 1946
*Mixed Company,* 1950
*Tip on a Dead Jockey, and Other Stories,* 1957
*Love on a Dark Street,* 1965
*Retreat, and Other Stories,* 1970
*God Was Here, but He Left Early,* 1973
*Short Stories: Five Decades,* 1978

OTHER LITERARY FORMS

Irwin Shaw wrote novels, plays, screenplays, nonfiction books, articles, and short stories. His novels *The Young Lions* (1948) and *Rich Man, Poor Man* (1970) and his plays *Bury the Dead* (pr., pb. 1936) and *Sons and Soldiers* (pr. 1943, pb. 1944) are well known and received critical acclaim. "Out of the Fog," "Act of Faith," "Tip on a Dead Jockey," *Two Weeks in Another Town* (1960), and *The Young Lions* have been filmed. *Rich Man, Poor Man* was the television miniseries believed by some critics to have launched America's novel-to-miniseries craze.

ACHIEVEMENTS

Irwin Shaw's forty-six-year roller coaster ride with American critics began in 1935 when Brooks Atkinson wrote of Shaw's first play, "What *Waiting for Lefty* was for Clifford Odets, *Bury the Dead* is to Irwin Shaw." Within the next four years *The New Yorker* and other top magazines published some of Shaw's best short stories, including "The Girls in Their Summer Dresses," "Second Mortgage," and the title story of his first book of short stories, *Sailor off the "Bremen," and Other Stories.* His first novel, *The Young Lions,* was

hailed by some critics as the best novel to emerge from World War II, comparable to Ernest Hemingway's *A Farewell to Arms* (1929). Not all of his novels were so well received; *Lucy Crown* (1956) was branded a soap opera. In 1970, however, *Rich Man, Poor Man* put him back on the favored son list. Critics who praised and critics who panned his novels did so by comparing them to Shaw's own brilliant short stories.

BIOGRAPHY

Irwin Shaw began professional writing for *The New Republic* after graduating from Brooklyn College. He worked as a drama critic and teacher of creative writing before serving in the Army from 1942 to 1945, and during the war he spent time in Africa, England, France, and Germany. He was a member of the Author's Guild, Dramatist's Guild, and Screen Writer's Guild, and he received a National Institute of Arts and Letters grant in 1946. He was married and had one son. In 1951 he moved to Europe. In his later years, Shaw lived in Switzerland but spent his summers in Southampton, New York. On May 16, 1984, Irwin Shaw died, the result of a heart attack, in a hospital in Davos, Switzerland. He was seventy-one.

ANALYSIS

Irwin Shaw's stories appeared in many respected magazines and are frequently anthologized in collections of short fiction. War, crime, financial disaster, adultery, and moral sterility provide major conflicts as Shaw presents a wide range of human emotions. "Sailor off the Bremen," "The Eighty-Yard Run," "Tip on a Dead Jockey," and "The Girls in Their Summer Dresses" are well-known examples of his narrative sophistication.

### "SAILOR OFF THE BREMEN"

In "Sailor off the Bremen," a story of naïve revenge, an American football player learns the identity of the Nazi who disfigured his brother's face. Charley, arrogant and angry in his strength, overrules his injured brother's objections to ensnaring and punishing the offender. A series of discussions between Charley, Ernest the disfigured brother, and their friends and family develops a plot suggesting various perspectives on violence.

In a scene that takes place at the brothers' kitchen table, Ernest, Preminger, and Stryker, new members of the Communist Party, disregard violence as a means for change. However, Charley and Ernest's wife, Sally, want satisfaction for their loved one's suffering. In the course of their arguments, even the strongest Communist of the three, Preminger, admits that aside from party leanings, the Nazi ought to be punished for his cruelty not merely to Ernest but to others he has sent to concentration camps. Then Stryker, although he is usually anxious and timid, agrees to help effect the revenge because he is Ernest's friend. Finally Ernest himself is resigned.

Shaw handles characterization by focusing on suggestive details that reveal much about each of the men: Ernest's face twitches almost uncontrollably; his blind eye is concealed with a dark patch. Charley's muscular hands are cleat-marked from the previous week's game. Stryker, a dentist who is attempting to replace Ernest's teeth, has a dry, raspy voice filled with doubt. Preminger, an officer aboard the *Bremen*, is cool and confident; he looks like a midwestern college boy despite his profession of espionage. In the background, Sally, patient and hospitable, performs kitchen duties as the men discuss their plans.

Once the decision is made, the pace quickens. Preminger identifies the Nazi, Lueger, so that Sally, Charley, and Stryker will recognize him as they watch separately from another deck of the *Bremen*. Sally manages to arrange a date with Lueger, who is well known for his affairs with women. On the appointed evening, they see a film, stop for a drink, and then continue along the street past a corner where Charley and Stryker are waiting.

Sally escapes when Stryker asks directions of Lueger, giving Charley the opportunity to land the first blow. In a brutal climactic scene, Stryker stands guard while Charley knocks Lueger unconscious and beats him until he has lost an eye and many teeth. Sobbing and cursing, Charley continues to beat Lueger until he is satisfied that Lueger will suffer serious injury permanently. Stryker and Charley then leave the Nazi lying in a pool of his own blood. Later, in the hospital, Preminger identifies Lueger for a questioning detective but denies any knowledge that Lueger had enemies. The eye-for-an-eye theme of the story raises questions concerning violence and morality; clearly the social and political context makes immediate answers impossible.

### "The Eighty-Yard Run"

"The Eighty-Yard Run" presents another kind of social dilemma. Christian Darling, a former midwestern college football player, recalls the practice run he made that changed his football career and won for him the daughter of a wealthy manufacturer. Admired by the coaches, the students, and his wife Louise, he appeared successful through college and afterward, when he began to manage accounts for Louise's father in New York. As Christian muses over the long run and the intervening years, he struggles to accept the fact that he could not cope with the social and intellectual changes of the 1920's and 1930's.

*Irwin Shaw* (AP Photo/George Brich)

Louise's father, a maker of inks, had survived the initial crash and waited until 1933 to commit suicide, leaving only debts and unbought ink behind. Christian turned to alcohol, and Louise began working for a women's magazine. Their apartment became a showcase for the sophisticated intellectuals of New York. Unable to understand the new art or the philosophies of the new breed, Christian lost Louise's respect. Although he had attempted a succession of jobs, he had never done well at any of them, until he was hired, for his collegiate appearance, as a traveling representative for a tailoring firm. Now as Christian reflects, he realizes that while he travels, Louise dines with new, more sophisticated men and makes the social contacts that are now so important to her. Not since the eighty-yard practice run has he had any hope of his own success. Christian, visiting his old practice field, reenacts the eighty-yard run when he thinks the field is deserted. Recalling his own ease and grace at that moment, he executes perfectly the movements of fifteen years before, only to discover with embarrassment that a young couple is watching him. He leaves the field with sweat beginning to break out across his face. His situation is fixed in space and time; the story presents the effects of social and economic changes in American life as they are experienced by a particular, although representative, man.

### "TIP ON A DEAD JOCKEY"

"Tip on a Dead Jockey" spotlights the lives of American expatriate flyers in Paris after the war. When Lloyd Barber, out of work and living in a shabby Parisian hotel, learns from a friend's wife that her husband, Jimmy, has disappeared for more than a month, he realizes that Jimmy must have accepted a smuggling job he himself had refused because of its risks. In this story, like "The Eighty-Yard Run," flashbacks indicate the contrast between past security and present struggle. Barber recalls, for example, the youthful beauty of Jimmy's wife, now evidencing poverty and anguish. He gives her what he can spare of his cash and reassures her that he will try to locate Jimmy.

Barber himself is depressed and lonely; he has no job but amuses himself occasionally by going to the races, where he met Bert Smith who had offered him twenty-five thousand dollars for two flights between Egypt and France, an offer which must now account for Jimmy's disappearance. Barber searches the bars and restaurants of Paris in an attempt to locate Smith, a wealthy and educated European who had entertained him for weeks before revealing his intent to use Barber to smuggle money into France.

Barber's initial contact with Smith had been most profitable. As Barber continues his search through the streets of Paris, he recalls that Smith's tips on winning horses had paid off generously for the first two weeks of their acquaintanceship. On their last afternoon together at the track, however, perhaps the afternoon he decided against the smuggling job, Smith had recommended betting on a horse which fell, killing its jockey, an event Barber accepted as a bad omen. Barber had immediately refused Smith's offer and returned flight maps Smith had given him. That evening, preparing to dine alone, Barber had stumbled onto Smith and Jimmy, talking casually about racing, and Barber had thought nothing of it, underestimating Jimmy's financial need and gullibility.

Barber's search is unsuccessful. He returns to his room to find that Jimmy's wife has left a message requesting that he meet her at a nearby bar. There he finds her with Jimmy, suntanned and thin, eagerly spending the earnings of his crime. The couple asks him to go with them to dinner at an expensive restaurant, but Barber, despite his relief that Jimmy is safely home, only feels lonelier as he witnesses their happy reunion. He returns to his hotel room where a collection of letters reminds him of the emptiness of his own life: His former wife wants to know what to do with an old army pistol she found in a trunk belonging to him; his mother wants him to stop being foolish and come home to a regular job; a woman he does not love wants him to come and stay with her in a villa near Eze; none of the letters makes him feel less isolated. Finally, there is a letter from a boy who had flown as his waist-gunner during the war, and this letter, more than the rest, reminds him of the emptiness of expatriate life in Europe. The lonely hotel room, the evening chill, and the memory of Jimmy's reunion with his wife converge on Barber as he concludes that Europe is not the place for him, however adventurous he may have been in the past.

## "THE GIRLS IN THEIR SUMMER DRESSES"

"The Girls in Their Summer Dresses" is a famous example of Shaw's skill in portraying urban life with little more than an anecdote. Michael and Frances, a young married couple, walk along Fifth Avenue in New York City on a Sunday afternoon. They decide to spend the day alone, enjoying the city, instead of visiting friends in the country as they had planned, but the husband's habit of girl-watching leads to an angry confrontation in which the beautiful women of New York become a symbol of the freedom and sexual vitality his wife resents. As a Japanese waiter cheerfully serves them drinks just after breakfast in a small bar, the husband admits his fascination with the variety of women passing daily along New York streets. Their expensive clothing, their health, and their beauty draw him like a magnet, especially as he approaches middle age.

As Frances sobs into her handkerchief, Michael finds courage to celebrate the wonderful experience of observing women, richly dressed in furs in winter or in summer dresses in warm weather. Although he reassures Frances that she is a good wife, she believes that he only wants his freedom, and he cannot convince her of his loyalty because he is not convinced of it himself. They decide to spend the rest of the day with friends after all, and as Frances walks across the bar to make a phone call, Michael cannot help admiring her figure, her legs, just as he admires the features of strangers passing along the street. Their situation is a modern one, appropriately symbolized by New York women reflecting the economic vitality of the urban setting. Although Shaw frequently stops at the surface of the modern lifestyle, his portraits of modern men and women effectively suggest the conflicts below apparent comfort and success.

## OTHER MAJOR WORKS

LONG FICTION: *The Young Lions*, 1948; *The Troubled Air*, 1951; *Lucy Crown*, 1956; *Two Weeks in Another Town*, 1960; *Voices of a Summer Day*, 1965; *Rich Man, Poor Man*, 1970; *Evening in Byzantium*, 1973; *Nightwork*, 1975; *Beggarman, Thief*, 1977; *The Top of the Hill*, 1979; *Bread upon the Waters*, 1981; *Acceptable Losses*, 1982.

PLAYS: *Bury the Dead*, pr., pb. 1936; *Siege*, pr. 1937; *Quiet City*, pr. 1939; *The Gentle People: A Brooklyn Fable*, pr., pb. 1939; *Retreat to Pleasure*, pr. 1940; *Sons and Soldiers*, pr. 1943, pb. 1944; *The Assassin*, pr. 1945, pb. 1946; *The Survivors*, pr., pb. 1948 (with Peter Viertel); *Children from Their Games*, pb. 1962, pr. 1963; *A Choice of Wars*, pr. 1967; *I, Shaw*, pr. 1986 (2 one-acts; *The Shy and the Lonely* and *Sailor off the Bremen*).

SCREENPLAYS: *The Big Game*, 1936; *Commandos Strike at Dawn*, 1942; *Talk of the Town*, 1942 (with Sidney Buchman); *The Hard Way*, 1942 (with Daniel Fuchs); *Take One False Step*, 1949 (with Chester Erskine); *I Want You*, 1951; *Act of Love*, 1953; *Fire Down Below*, 1957; *Desire Under the Elms*, 1958; *This Angry Age*, 1958 (with Rene Clement); *The Big Gamble*, 1961; *In the French Style*, 1963; *Survival*, 1968.

NONFICTION: *Report on Israel*, 1950 (with Robert Capa); *In the Company of Dolphins*, 1964; *Paris! Paris!*, 1977; *Paris/Magnum: Photographs, 1935-1981*, 1981.

## BIBLIOGRAPHY

Eisinger, Chester E. *Fiction of the Forties*. Chicago: University of Chicago Press, 1963. In the section titled "Irwin Shaw: The Popular Ideas of the Old Liberalism," Eisinger both praises and condemns Shaw for his treatment of racial and social prejudice in the four volumes of short stories he produced between 1939 and 1950.

Giles, James R. "Interview with Irwin Shaw." *Resources for American Literary Study* 18 (1992): 1-21. Shaw discusses his experiences writing for films, his reaction to being a "popular" writer, his blacklisting, and his opinion of Ernest Hemingway. Contends "Act of Faith" is an "angry" story.

_____. *Irwin Shaw*. Boston: Twayne, 1983. An introductory overview to Shaw's life and works aimed at students and general readers.

_____. *Irwin Shaw: A Study of the Short Fiction*. Boston: Twayne, 1991. Examines Shaw's short stories.

Parini, Jay, ed. *David Budbill to Bruce Weigl*. Supplement 19 of *American Writers: A Collection of Literary Biographies*. Farmington Hills, Mich.: Thomson Gale, 2010. Includes an providing an overview of Shaw's life, literary career, and works.

Reynolds, Fred. "Irwin Shaw's 'The Eighty-Yard Run.'" *The Explicator* 49 (Winter, 1991): 121-123. Interprets the story as a case study in psychoneurosis in which the protagonist exhibits three symptoms of arrested development: sexual confusion, Oedipal relationships, and neurotic fixation on the past.

Shaw, Irwin. "The Art of Fiction IV." *The Paris Review* 1 (1953): 26-49. In this interview, Shaw discusses all the different literary forms he explored. Beginning with his earliest efforts as a script writer for the radio series *Dick Tracy*, he lays out many of his theories and techniques as playwright, novelist, and screenwriter. Of the short stories he says "The form . . . is so free as to escape restrictions to any theory."

_____. "The Art of Fiction IV, Continued." *The Paris Review* 21 (Spring, 1979): 248-262. This interview is an update of the one conducted twenty-six years earlier. Shaw discusses being an expatriate writer, how he feels he has mellowed, and how dramatically his lifestyle changed when he gave up writing for the theater.

Shnayerson, Michael. *Irwin Shaw: A Biography*. New York: Putnam, 1989. An objective biography focusing on Shaw's life, literary career, and character, without deep analysis of his works. Charts Shaw's development as a serious writer and how his literary reputation declined as his life overwhelmed him.

Startt, William. "Irwin Shaw: An Extended Talent." *Midwest Quarterly* 2 (1961): 325-337. In comparing Shaw's short stories to his novels, Startt credits the shorter works with projecting more "immediacy" and a greater sense of "reality." Shaw is compared favorably with Ernest Hemingway.

Werlock, Abby H. P., and James P. Werlock, eds. *The Facts On File Companion to the American Short Story*. 2d ed. New York: Facts On File, 2010. Contains a brief entry about Shaw that provides a biography, plot synopses, character sketches, and analyses of some of his short stories.

*Chapel Louise Petty*
*Updated by Edmund August*

---

# SAM SHEPARD

**Born:** Fort Sheridan, Illinois; November 5, 1943

PRINCIPAL SHORT FICTION

*Hawk Moon: A Book of Short Stories, Poems, and Monologues,* 1973
*Motel Chronicles,* 1982 (includes short fiction, poetry, and journals)
*Cruising Paradise,* 1996
*Great Dream of Heaven,* 2002
*Day out of Days,* 2010

OTHER LITERARY FORMS

Sam Shepard is known primarily as a playwright, and he is an actor and a screenwriter. His first nine plays were one-act dramas, such as *Cowboys*, produced Off-Off Broadway in 1964, and *Icarus's Mother* (1965). In 1967, his first two-act play, *La Turista*, appeared, followed by more than twenty one- and two-act dramas during the 1960's and 1970's. *True West*, one of his best-known plays, appeared in 1980, and *Fool for Love* made its debut in 1983. Another well-known play, *A Lie of the Mind*, was first produced in 1985. *Simpatico* was published in 1994, and in 2000 Shepard directed his play *The Late Henry Moss*. Shepard has written several screenplays, and many of his plays have been published in collections.

ACHIEVEMENTS

Sam Shepard may be the most influential American playwright of his time, encapsulating the vision of the American West as it is imagined and experienced. Fragmented, unstructured, and violent, his writings, powered by his genius for dialogue, have come to epitomize American western thought and culture. Many of his plays have received Obie

Awards for best plays of the Off-Broadway season. These include *Chicago* (1965), *Icarus's Mother*, *Red Cross* (1966), and *La Turista*. Subsequent Obies were given for *Melodrama Play* (1966), *Forensic and the Navigators* (1967), *The Tooth of Crime* (1972), and *Action* (1974). In 1977, he received the Obie for *Curse of the Starving Class* (1976); in 1979, he received the Obie for *Buried Child* (1978); in 1984, he received the Obie for *Fool for Love* (1983). Subsequent Obie-winning plays were *A Lie of the Mind* (1985), *The Late Henry Moss* (2000), and *The God of Hell* (2004).

Shepard received grants from the University of Minnesota in 1966, from the Rockefeller Foundation and Yale University in 1967, and from the Guggenheim Foundation in 1968 and 1971. In 1974, he received the National Institute and American Academy Award for Literature, followed in 1975 by the Brandeis University Creative Arts Award. He was awarded the Pulitzer Prize for drama in 1979 for *Buried Child. Paris, Texas* received the Golden Palm Award from the Cannes Film Festival in 1984, and *A Lie of the Mind* garnered the New York Drama Critics' Circle Award in 1986. In 1992, Shepard received the Gold Medal for Drama from the American Academy of Arts and Letters, and in 1994 he was inducted into the Theatre Hall of Fame. His story collection *Great Dream of Heaven* was a finalist for the W. H. Smith Literary Award. He was named the 2010 Janet Weis Fellow in Contemporary Letters at Bucknell University. Shepard also was nominated by the Academy of Motion Picture Arts and Sciences for best supporting actor in 1984 for playing Chuck Yeager in *The Right Stuff* (1983).

BIOGRAPHY

Samuel Shepard Rogers was born on November 5, 1943, in Fort Sheridan, Illinois, the first of three children. His father was a World War II veteran and Army officer, and his mother was a high school teacher. After moving around among Army bases, the family settled on an avocado farm in Duarte, California, where Shepard worked as a stable hand on a horse ranch, played the drums, and began writing and acting. His father's violent alcoholism became an element in many of Shepard's plays and stories. After graduating from high school in 1960, Shepard attended Mount San Antonio Junior College briefly to study agriculture, then left to join a Christian traveling theater group, ending up in New York City to work in food service at a jazz club, while writing his first one-act plays under the encouragement of Ralph Cook, an Off-Off Broadway company founder. Shepard also became involved in rock music, playing drums and guitar with the Holy Modal Rounders from 1968 to 1971.

Shepard's first plays were well received, and he rapidly began to write more of them, incorporating into the fragmented, collagelike, imaginative, and offbeat works his interest in jazz and rock-and-roll riffs. He also began writing screenplays. Shepard married actress O-Lan Jones Dark in 1969, and they had a son, Jesse Mojo Shepard. The family moved to London in 1971, partly to escape Shepard's destructive involvement with women and illegal drugs, and partly to enhance his involvement in rock music. He continued to write and produce award-winning plays, which began slowly to move from experimental to traditional forms. In 1974, Shepard returned to the United States, settling in San Francisco as a playwright for the Magic Theater. While writing plays, he also was involved with Bob Dylan's traveling band, which inspired Shepard's book *Rolling Thunder Logbook* (2004). He also began his film-acting career in 1978, but his primary success was as an award-winning playwright.

The 1980's saw Shepard becoming more involved as a film actor and branching out into directing. He met actress Jessica Lange, subsequently ending his marriage and becoming Lange's companion. The couple have a son and a daughter. While garnering many awards for his plays, Shepard began focusing more on his acting roles than on his writing. In the 1990's and 2000's, he gained greater recognition as an actor, and in 2010 he began moving into television. Shepard settled on a cattle ranch in Minnesota, where he has continued to write, to act, and to indulge his lifelong interests in horses, rodeo, and polo.

ANALYSIS

Sam Shepard's stories seem not to be collections of random writings of indeterminate genre: journal entries, memoirs, free-form poems, dialogues, stream-of-consciousness musings, and other miscellaneous jottings. They range in length from a paragraph to several pages and are accompanied in one collection, *Motel Chronicles*, by black-and-white photographs of the author and unidentified people in typically rural, bleak, and arid western settings. Many of the stories are written in the first person and evoke images of Shepard, in settings from his own experience. The story's narrator invariably is male, frequently alone, and often a traveler on the American plains.

The unstructured, pastichelike character of Shepard's short-story collections reflects the overall fragmented style for which the author is celebrated in his avant-garde plays and screenplays. Images appear, then disappear; non sequiturs abound; characters erupt into anger or violence and then abruptly subside. The effect adds to the recurring themes of dislocation, aimlessness, confusion, and isolation. The most effective stories contain dialogue, as might be expected from a playwright whose specialty is terse, revealing and realistic dialogue. Some of the topics and messages seem banal, some extraordinarily insightful. The thoughts, memories, and experiences presented almost all are centered on the problems of a disconnected lower-class loner, separated from his moorings, who is searching, frequently cluelessly, for meaning.

Shepard's stories, like his other works, tend to focus on the image of the American West: both its mythical past and its impersonal, mechanized present. His characters most often are caught between the two, part of neither yet yearning for identity. The stories' personae live or travel in the rural West, where they strive to find a place for themselves. The theme of broken family relationships, particularly abusive fathers, is a common one. Low-paying menial jobs, inclement weather, drinking, and the impossibility of sustaining relationships with women abound. The prevailing tone is melancholy mixed with nostalgia.

Occasionally the bizarre and inexplicable will jar readers' sensibilities, such as in the story in which a traveler passes a severed human head along the

*Sam Shepard* (Carlo Allegri/Getty Images)

highway. The mystic head then speaks to the traveler, imploring him to pick it up and carry it. In another story, a wounded hawk rescued by a well-meaning traveler turns in its panic into a terrifying monster in her car, upending the urn containing her mother's ashes. Other stories seem mysteriously open-ended. The erratic and the unpredictable, the surprising and the grotesque, contrast with the the mundane and the dispirited. Through all this, the prose is terse and gritty, and the description restrained and condensed.

MOTEL CHRONICLES

The fragmented, stream-of-consciousness entries in the collection *Motel Chronicles* are untitled, and most are autobiographical. In one short entry, the narrator recalls trying as a teenager to imitate Burt Lancaster, practicing his Lancaster smile on his schoolmates with unsatisfying results. Convinced that he looks like Burt, he has forgotten his physical defects, so he stops grinning and goes back to his "empty" face. In one paragraph, this story manages to convey both the appeal of cinema and acting to the adolescent (escape from his own persona) and the ironic pathos of his conviction

Critical Survey of Short Fiction

that real life is "empty" (only pretense has substance).

Another entry in this volume, an autobiographical poem, recalls the period early in Shepard's life when his family was stationed on Guam. In a series of vivid images, he shows his mother carrying him on one hip and a pistol on the other. He also comes across a Japanese skull, with ants crawling out of a bullethole. The juxtaposition of life and death images, connected by the object of the gun, expresses the surreality of war as well as the vulnerability of family relationships to violence, a theme that is explored over and over again in Shepard's writings, as he works out the implications of alcoholic violence by his father.

### "CRUISING PARADISE"

This story, for which Shepard's 1996 collection is named, is narrated by a friend of a racetrack employee named Crewlaw, whose father has died in a cigarette-caused motel fire. Crewlaw is obsessed with finding the burned mattress upon which his father died. The story details how the two men obtain the mattress, load it on top of their car, throw it into an aqueduct, and set it afire. They then go for beer to the house of Crewlaw's aunt, an old termagant, who, while watching television and smoking, hurls abuse at her nephew, telling him he is going to be just like his old man.

Continuing the themes of father-son enmity and familial conflict, "Cruising Paradise" shows the blind obsession of a son with punishing his dead abusive father by reenacting his death symbolically. Ironically, this could also represent Shepard himself, continuing to punish his own dead father in his plays, so many of which shows parental violence and estrangement. Further ironies in the story appear in the scene with the aunt, suggesting unwitting similarities between those who point the finger and those who are incriminated by them. Paradise is mockingly presented as the idyllic lemon and orange groves through which the men drive to Aunt Mellie's squalid house of hate, amid the concrete towers of the gravel plant. Like so many of Shepard's characters, the narrator and his friend, uncomprehending yet intent on their own motivations and purposes, only briefly glimpse the ephemeral dream that eludes their lives, played out in a geographical setting whose beauty has been ruined by similarly ignorant men pursuing their own dreams.

### "GREAT DREAM OF HEAVEN"

In this title story of the 2002 anthology, two old Stetson-wearing South Dakota widowers, living together for twelve years in a cinderblock bungalow in the southern California desert, have an unspoken rivalry about who can get up earlier in the morning. Momentarily winning this rivalry, in fact, provides Sherman with the greatest joy he can remember since a transcendent boyhood dream. The two find pleasure in their uneventful, habitual life, crowned by their daily walk down the highway to Denny's for coffee, poured by a kindly waitress named Faye. One morning Sherman awakes alone; Dean has already gone down to Denny's, and Faye is not there. Sherman learns that Dean had awakened at 3 a.m. and gone to visit Faye during her new graveyard shift. Sherman returns to the bungalow, packs his suitcase, and leaves without a word.

Again, in this story, the reader sees blighted contentment and unrealized dreams, caused by uncomprehending men who only seek limited versions of pleasure. As is common with Shepard's characters, inept handling of relationships with women causes much of their pain, and longing for the opposite sex draws them inevitably toward conflict. Unable, as consummate taciturn western cowboys, to communicate their feelings to each other, the characters then lose what little happiness they had previously enjoyed and return to their customary solitary and miserable state.

OTHER MAJOR WORKS

PLAYS: *Cowboys*, pr. 1964 (one-act); *Up to Thursday*, pr. 1964; *The Rock Garden*, pr. 1964, pb. 1972 (one-act); *Chicago*, pr. 1965; *Dog*, pr. 1965; *Rocking Chair*, pr. 1965; *Icarus's Mother*, pr. 1965, pb. 1967; *4-H Club*, pr. 1965, pb. 1971; *Fourteen Hundred Thousand*, pr. 1966, pb. 1967; *Melodrama Play*, pr. 1966, pb. 1967; *Red Cross*, pr. 1966, pb. 1967; *La Turista*, pr. 1967, pb. 1968; *Forensic and the Navigators*, pr. 1967, pb. 1969; *Cowboys #2*, pr. 1967, pb. 1971; *The Unseen Hand*, pr., pb. 1969; *Shaved Splits*, pr. 1969, pb. 1971; *Operation Sidewinder*, pb. 1969, pr. 1970; *The Holy Ghostly*, pr. 1970, pb. 1971; *Back Bog Beast Bait*, pr., pb. 1971; *Cowboy Mouth*, pr., pb. 1971 (with Patti Smith); *The Mad Dog Blues*, pr. 1971, pb. 1972; *Nightwalk*, pr., pb. 1972 (with

Megan Terry and Jean-Claude van Itallie); *The Tooth of Crime*, pr. 1972, pb. 1974; *Action*, pr. 1974; *Geography of a Horse Dreamer*, pr., pb. 1974; *Little Ocean*, pr. 1974; *Killer's Head*, pr. 1975, pb. 1976; *The Sad Lament of Pecos Bill on the Eve of Killing His Wife*, pr. 1975, pb. 1983; *Angel City*, pr., pb. 1976; *Suicide in B Flat*, pr. 1976, pb. 1979; *Curse of the Starving Class*, pb. 1976, pr. 1977; *Buried Child*, pr. 1978, pb. 1979; *Seduced*, pr. 1978, pb. 1979; *Tongues*, pr. 1978, pb. 1981; *Savage/Love*, pr. 1979, pb. 1981; *True West*, pr. 1980, pb. 1981; *Seven Plays*, pb. 1981; *Fool for Love*, 1983; *A Lie of the Mind*, pr. 1985, pb. 1986; *States of Shock*, pr. 1991, pb. 1992; *Simpatico*, pr. 1994, pb. 1995; *When the World Was Green*, pr. 1996, pb. 2002 (with Joseph Chaikin); *Plays*, pb. 1996-1997 (3 volumes); *Eyes for Consuela*, pr. 1998, pb. 2002; *The Late Henry Moss*, pr. 2000, pb. 2002; *The God of Hell*, pr. 2004, pb. 2005; *Kicking a Dead Horse*, pr. 2007.

SCREENPLAYS: *Me and My Brother*, 1967 (with Robert Frank); *Zabriskie Point*, 1969 (wht Michelangelo Antonioni); *Ringaleevio*, 1971; *Renaldo and Clara*, 1978 (with Bob Dylan); *Paris, Texas*, 1984 (with L. M. Kit Carson); *Far North*, 1988; *Silent Tongue*, 1994; *Don't Come Knocking*, 2005.

TELEPLAYS: *True West*, 2002; *See You in My Dreams*, 2004.

NONFICTION: *Rolling Thunder Logbook*, 1977.

BIBLIOGRAPHY

Bottoms, Stephen J. *The Theatre of Sam Shepard: States of Crisis.* Cambridge, England: Cambridge University Press, 1998. This volume examines Shepard's work by comparing it to contemporary sociopolitical conditions extant at the time the various plays were written.

DeRose, David J. *Sam Shepard.* New York: Twayne, 1992. DeRose studies Shepard's theatrical elements and intentions, examining his plays for a sense of the unfixed.

Hart, Lynda. *Sam Shepard's Metaphorical Stages.* Westport, Conn.: Greenwood, 1987. Attempts to present a unified vision of Shepard's drama as mirroring the major movements of drama in the twentieth century. Analyzes ten plays in chronological order.

Oumano, Ellen. *Sam Shepard: The Life and Work of an American Dreamer.* New York: St. Martin's, 1986. Mainly a biography and personality analysis, with literary criticism tracing influences of Shepard's early life on his work.

Shewey, Don. *Sam Shepard.* New York: Da Capo Press, 1985. This is a biography, with quotes from Shepard, that correlates stages of his life and career with titles of his plays.

*Sally B. Palmer*

---

# LESLIE MARMON SILKO

**Born:** Albuquerque, New Mexico; March 5, 1948

PRINCIPAL SHORT FICTION

*Storyteller,* 1981 (includes poetry and prose)
*Yellow Woman,* 1993

OTHER LITERARY FORMS

Leslie Marmon Silko is known most widely for her novels, including *Ceremony* (1977), *Almanac of the Dead* (1991), and *Gardens in the Dunes* (1999). An early collection of poetry, *Laguna Woman* (1974),

established her as an important young Native American writer, and most of the lyric and narrative poems in that book are integrated with the autobiographical writings and short stories that make up *Storyteller*. With Frank Chin, Silko has also adapted one of her short stories into a one-act play of the same title, *Lullaby*, which was first performed in 1976. In addition. Silko has written screenplays; in one, she adapted a Laguna Pueblo myth, "Estoyehmuut and the Kunideeyah" (arrowboy and the destroyers), for television production in 1978. Earlier, she wrote a screenplay for Jack Beck and Marlon Brando that depicted, from a Native American viewpoint, the expedition of

Francisco Vásquez de Coronado in 1540; the script was sent to Hollywood in 1977 but was not produced.

Several of Silko's critical essays and interviews provide useful insights into her short fiction, as does her correspondence with the poet James Wright, which is collected in *The Delicacy and Strength of Lace: Letters Between Leslie Marmon Silko and James A. Wright* (1986); a second edition of this book appeared in 2009. Two particularly useful essays are "An Old-Time Indian Attack Conducted in Two Parts," published in *The Remembered Earth: An Anthology of Contemporary Native American Literature* (1979), and "Language and Literature from a Pueblo Indian Perspective," published in *English Literature: Opening Up the Canon* (1981). Silko's interviews often supply autobiographical and cultural contexts that enhance the understanding of her work; among the most insightful is the videotape *Running on the Edge of the Rainbow: Laguna Stories and Poems* (1978), which shows Silko reading from her work and is interspersed with her commentary on Laguna culture. Her nonfiction works include *Sacred Water: Narratives and Pictures* (1993), *Yellow Woman and a Beauty of the Spirit: Essays on Native American Life Today* (1996), and an autobiography, *The Turquoise Ledge: A Memoir* (2010). A collection of Silko's work and related material is housed at the University of Arizona library in Tucson.

## Achievements

Leslie Marmon Silko, along with Louise Erdrich, N. Scott Momaday, Simon Ortiz, James Welch, and Sherman Alexie, is regarded by critics as among the best of the more than fifty Native American writers with significant publications to have emerged since the mid-1960's. Formal recognition of Silko's fiction came quite early in her career. Her story "Lullaby" was included in *The Best American Short Stories 1975*, and "Yellow Woman" was included in *Two Hundred Years of Great American Short Stories* (1975), published to commemorate the American bicentennial. In 1974, she won the *Chicago Review* Poetry Award, and in 1977 she won the Pushcart Prize for poetry. She has also been awarded major grants from the National Endowment for the Humanities and the National Endowment

for the Arts for her work in film and in fiction. In 1981, Silko received a five-year fellowship from the John D. and Catherine T. MacArthur Foundation, permitting her the freedom to pursue whatever interests she wished to develop. She received the *Boston Globe* prize for nonfiction in 1986, the New Mexico Endowment for the Humanities Living Cultural Treasure award in 1988, and a Lila Wallace-*Reader's Digest* Fund writers award in 1991.

## Biography

Leslie Marmon Silko was born in Albuquerque, New Mexico, on March 5, 1948, the descendant of Laguna, Mexican, and Anglo-American peoples. Silko's mixed ancestry is documented in *Storyteller*, in which she recounts the stories of white Protestant brothers Walter Gunn Marmon and Robert G. Marmon, her great-grandfather, who, with his older brother, settled in New Mexico at Laguna as a trader, having migrated west from Ohio in 1872. Her great-grandmother Marie, or A'mooh, married Robert Marmon, and her grandmother Lillie was a Model A automobile mechanic. Both were well educated and well informed about both Anglo and Laguna lifestyles. Growing up in one of the Marmon family houses at Old Laguna, in western New Mexico, Silko inherited from these women and from Susie Marmon, the sister-in-law of Silko's grandfather Hank Marmon, a treasury of Laguna stories, both mythological and historical. Indeed, "Aunt Susie" is created in *Storyteller* as Silko's source for many of the traditional stories that shaped her childhood.

Silko's early years were spent in activities that neither completely included her in nor fully excluded her from the Laguna community. She participated in clan activities but not to the same extent as the full-bloods; she helped prepare for ceremonial dances, but she did not dance herself. Attending the local day school of the Bureau of Indian Affairs, she was prohibited from using the Keresan language which her great-grandmother had begun teaching her. She had her own horse at eight, and she helped herd cattle on the family ranch; at thirteen, she had her own rifle and joined in the annual deer hunts. From the fifth grade on, Silko commuted to schools in Albuquerque. After high school, she entered the University of New Mexico, also in

Albuquerque, and, in 1969, she was graduated summa cum laude from the English department's honors program. After three semesters in the American Indian Law Program at the same university, Silko decided to pursue a career in writing and teaching. For the next two years, she taught English at Navajo Community College in Tsaile, Arizona. She spent the following two years in Ketchikan, Alaska, where she wrote *Ceremony*. She returned to teach in the University of New Mexico's English department for another two years before she moved, in 1980, to Tucson, where she became a professor of English at the University of Arizona for a few years. In addition, Silko has held writing residencies in fiction at several universities and has been invited for lectures and readings at schools from New York to California.

More recently, Silko returned to bookmaking, an art she enjoyed as a child, with the production of *Sacred Water: Narratives and Pictures*, a collection of autobiographical vignettes. On facing pages, Silko juxtaposes verbal pictures with graphic images. Under her own imprint, Flood Plain Press, she has personally assembled, numbered, and bound every copy by hand.

## ANALYSIS

While she is well read in the canonical tradition of Anglo-American writing, having delighted particularly, at an early age, in Edgar Allan Poe, John Steinbeck, William Faulkner, and Flannery O'Connor, and, later in college, William Shakespeare and John Milton, Leslie Marmon Silko brings to her own work the sensibility and many of the structures inherent in the Laguna oral tradition, creating, for example, a subtext of revisioned Laguna mythology to the more conventional aspects of her novel *Ceremony*. Although, in a manner similar to that of other American writers drawing upon an ethnic heritage, Silko chooses to place her work in the context of Laguna culture, her work appeals to diverse readers for its insights not only into the marginal status of many nonwhite Americans but also into the universal celebration of the reciprocity between land and culture.

Silko's short fiction is "told" in the context of her personal experience in Laguna Pueblo and serves as a written extension, continuation, and revitalization of Laguna oral tradition. Blurring the genre of the short story with historical anecdotes, family history, letters, cultural legacies, photographs, and lyric and narrative poems, *Storyteller* includes most of Silko's published short stories and poems. While the stories certainly stand on their own, and, indeed, many of them are included in various anthologies, Silko's matrix of thick description, conveying the mood of events, as well as describing them, testifies to the essential role of storytelling in Pueblo identity, giving the people access to the mythic and historic past and relating a continuing wisdom--about the land, its animals, its plants, and the human condition--as an integral part of the natural process. About her collection, Silko has said,

> I see *Storyteller* as a statement about storytelling and the relationship of the people, my family and my background to the storytelling--a personal statement done in the style of the storytelling tradition, i.e., using stories themselves to explain the dimensions of the process.

### "LULLABY"

In unifying the past and the present to illuminate the kinship of land and people, Silko's story "Lullaby," a pastoral elegy, evokes both beauty and loss. Set north of the Laguna Reservation, the story traces the life of an old Navajo couple, Chato and Ayah, from whose point of view the story is told by an omniscient narrator. While Ayah sits in the snow, presiding over her husband's death, she recalls various episodes in her own life just as if she were sharing in Chato's last memories. She is wrapped in an old Army blanket that was sent to her by her son Jimmie, who was killed while serving in the Army. She recalls, however, her own mother's beautifully woven rugs, themselves symbolic of stories, on the hand loom outside her childhood hogan. Again contrasting the past with the present, Ayah gazes at her black rubber overshoes and remembers the high buckskin leggings of her childhood as they hung, drying, from the ceiling beams of the family hogan.

What Ayah remembers of the past seems better than what she has at present--and it was--but she does not escape into nostalgia for the old ways. Ayah recalls events and things as they were, for they have brought her to the present moment of her husband's death. She remembers Jimmie's birth and the day the Army officials came to tell Chato of his death. She remembers how doctors from the Bureau of Indian Affairs came to take her children Danny and Ella to Colorado for the treatment of tuberculosis, which had killed her other children. Despite their good intentions, the white doctors frightened Ayah and her children into the hills after she had unknowingly signed over her custody of the children to them. When the doctors returned with reservation policemen, Chato let them take the children, leaving Ayah powerless in her protest that she wanted first to try the medicine men. Chato had taught her to sign her name, but he had not taught her English. She remembers the months of refuge in her hatred of Chato for teaching her to sign her name, and thus to sign away her children, and how she fled to the same hill where she had earlier fled with her children. She remembers, too, Chato's pride during his years as a cattle hand and how, after he broke his leg in a fall from a horse, the white rancher fired him and evicted them from the gray boxcar shack that he had provided for the couple.

As Ayah recalls these losses, she also recalls the peacefulness of her own mother, as if she were rejoining her mother, in contrast to the alienation of her own children from her after they had been away from home and learned to speak English, forgetting their native Navajo and regarding their mother as strangely backward in her ways. Now, with Chato reduced to alcoholism, senility, and incontinence, the old couple lives in the hogan of Ayah's childhood, and her routine is interrupted only by her treks to Azzie's bar to retrieve her husband. Ayah now sleeps with Chato, as she had not since the loss of Danny and Ella, because only her body will keep him warm. Fused with the heat of her body is the heat of her memory, as Ayah recalls how the elders warned against learning English: It would endanger them.

Ayah's recollection is presumably in Navajo, though Silko writes in English: The language is the story of her life and her relationship with the land on which she lived it. Place dominates her values; an arroyo and a cow path evoke precise memories, yet the evocation of her life culminates in her decision to allow Chato to freeze to death rather than see him suffer through the

last days of his degradation. She wraps him in Jimmie's blanket and sings a lullaby to him which her grandmother and her mother had sung before her:

> The earth is your mother,
> she holds you.
> The sky is your father,
> he protects you.
> Sleep . . .
> We are together always
> There never was a time
> when this
> was not so.

Ayah's closing song in the story joins birth with death, land with life, and past with present. Through her story, Ayah creates an event that supersedes the oppression of the white rancher, the stares of patrons at the Mexican bar, the rejection of her acculturated children, and the apparent diminution of traditional ways: The story continues the timeless necessity of the people to join their land with the sacredness of their language.

### "STORYTELLER"

In the title story of her collection *Storyteller*, an arctic allegory set in Alaska, Silko focuses even more emphatically on the power of the story to create and to sustain the life of a people. By shifting from Laguna characters to Navajo characters and, finally, by using an Eskimo context, Silko stresses the universality of storytelling among peoples who codify the world through an oral tradition. "Storyteller" seeks to explore the ramifications of divergent ways of seeing the world (or hearing it), and, at the same time, the story models the process of the oral tradition: It is not a Yupik story so much as it is one that is written as if it were a Yupik story.

"Storyteller," like "Lullaby," begins in medias res, as do many stories in any oral tradition. It, too, is told from the point of view of a woman, but the Eskimo protagonist is a young girl, anonymous though universal as the storyteller. She is in jail for killing a "Gussuck" (a derogatory term for a white person) storekeeper. According to Anglo law and logic, however, the girl is innocent. Through juxtaposed flashbacks, Silko's omniscient narrator reconstructs the events that have led to the girl's imprisonment. Moving away from the familiarity of a Pueblo context, Silko sets the story in Inuit country on the Kuskokwim River near Bethel, where she spent two months while she was in Alaska; she brings, then, her own attentiveness to the land to her fashioning of the story about attentiveness to storytelling. The imprisoned girl grew up with an old couple who lived in a shack outside the village, and she was nurtured by the stories of her grandmother. Although the girl had attended a Gussuck school, she was sent home for refusing to assimilate, having been whipped for her resistance to speaking English. Sexually abused by the old man, the girl takes the place of her grandmother in the old man's bed after her death. Before the grandmother's death, however, the girl had learned about the death of her parents, who had been poisoned with bad liquor by a trader who was never taken to court for the crime. Her grandmother had not told her the complete story, leaving much of it ambiguous and unfinished. While the girl witnesses the destruction of village life by oil drillers and listens to her "grandfather" ramble on and on, telling a story of a polar bear stalking a hunter, she recalls her grandmother's last words: "It will take a long time, but the story must be told. There must not be any lies." The girl believes that the "story" refers to the old man's bear story, but, in fact, it is the story which the girl herself will act out after the grandmother's death.

Bored by sex with the old man, the girl begins sleeping with oil drillers, discovering that they are as bestial as the old man, who sleeps in a urine-soaked bed with dried fish while he adds to his story throughout the winter. When she is about to have sex with a red-haired oil driller, he tapes a pornographic picture of a woman mounted by a dog to the wall above the bed, and then in turn mounts the girl. When she tells the old man about it, he expresses no surprise, claiming that the Gussucks have "behaved like desperate people" in their efforts to develop the frozen tundra. Using her sexuality to comprehend the strange ways of the Gussucks, the girl stalks her parents' killer as the old man's bear stalks the hunter. The Gussucks, seemingly incapable of grasping the old man's story, fail in their attention to the frozen landscape; they do not see or hear the place, the people, or the cold, blue bear of the story.

That failure to grasp the analogy of the bear story to the impending freeze of winter is what finally permits the girl to avenge the death of her parents. She lures the "storeman" from his store, which doubles as a bar, to the partially frozen river. Knowing how to breathe through her mitten in order to protect her lungs and wrapped in her grandmother's wolf-hide parka, the girl testifies mutely to the wisdom of her grandmother's stories. She knows where it is safe to tread on the ice and where it is not--she hears the river beneath her and can interpret the creaking of the ice. The storekeeper, taunted by her body, which is symbolic itself of her repository of knowledge for survival, chases her out onto the ice, trying to catch her by taking a single line to where she stands on the ice in the middle of the river. Without mittens and parka and oblivious to the warning sounds from below the ice, the storeman ignores the girl's tracks that mark a path of safety and crashes through the thin ice, drowning in the freezing river. He has had many possessions, but he lacked a story, a narrative thread, that would have saved him.

When the state police question her, the girl confesses: "He lied to them. He told them it was safe to drink. But I will not lie. . . . I killed him, . . . but I don't lie." When her court-appointed attorney urges her to recant, saying, "It was an accident. He was running after you and he fell through the ice. That's all you have to say in court," the girl, disregarding the testimony of children who witnessed the man's death, insists: "I will not change the story, not even to escape this place and go home. I intended that he die. The story must be told as it is." Later, at home under a female trooper's guard, the girl watches as the old man dies, still telling his story even as it evokes the death of the hunter; his spirit passes into the girl, who will now continue the story of the bear's conquest of the man.

Now the storyteller herself, the girl, has fused or merged with her story: The story has taken revenge on both the storeman and the old man, her first seducer, through her actions, namely the telling of the stories. The story, then, does not end but returns to itself, the bear turning to face the hunter on the ice, just as the myth of natural revenge turns the story against the storeman and the seductive power of the story turns against the storyteller, the old man. However, even as a new storyteller, the girl/the story has no beginning and no end: It continues as long as the people and the land continue. Indeed, the story's survival is the survival of the people; ironically, the girl's story will provide the lawyer with a plea of insanity, ensuring the survival of the story and the storyteller despite the degradation involved in charging her with madness.

### "YELLOW WOMAN"

Silko's most celebrated story, the frequently anthologized "Yellow Woman," uses a classic Laguna legend as a structural frame for an account of a contemporary woman, whose narration recognizes parallels with a mythic figure while maintaining a wary distance from full participation in a powerful myth. From a mundane modern community where her life is drab and undistinguished, the unnamed narrator recounts a temporary excursion into the hills beyond the Pueblo village with a charismatic, confident man, a stranger whose origins and actions--while mysterious and compelling--are also dangerous and destabilizing, a crucial part of his appeal.

The beginning of the story, located in an immediate present, emphasizes the physical reality of the experience in order to establish the tangibility of the woman's adventure. "My thigh clung to his with dampness," the woman reports, before describing the impressive mountain landscape which implies a linkage between the power of the man and a supportive energy flow in the natural world surrounding the pueblo. Struck by the strangeness of the man and by his address to her as "Yellow Woman," the familiar figure from the Laguna folk tradition, she asks "Who are you?"--a query that is never completely answered and which informs the narrative as a thematic expression of the woman's awakening desire to explore a destiny that transcends the limits of her life.

The man, whose name, Silva, is an echo of the author's and the Spanish word for "collection" or "anthology," is both a representation of the *ka'tsina* or Mountain Spirit, which functions as a guiding deity for the Laguna nation, and a man of an exciting moment in the woman's life. The story recalls various abduction tales across cultures, but both characters are exercising choices that respect and respond to the other person's preferences. As the narration continues, the woman's

thoughts move between the life she has left and to which she will inevitably return and the vivid, unfolding action of passion and fulfillment. Just as she continually questions her relation to the myth, asserting "I will see someone, eventually I will see someone, and then I will be certain that he is only a man--some man from nearby--and I will be sure that I am not Yellow Woman," her willingness to respond to what she calls "the same tricks" underscores her pleasure and excitement in seeing herself involved in an incident so that ". . . someday they will talk about us, and they will say 'Those two lived long ago when things like that happened.'"

In the conclusion of the narrative, Silva is challenged by a white man with a "young fat face," the intrusive authority of the dominant world dramatized by his dismissal of Silva as a thief and cattle rustler. In accordance with the heroic dimension of the myth, Silva, his eyes "ancient and dark," sends the woman toward safety, where, from a distance she hears "four hollow explosions that remind me of deer hunting," another connection to ancient tribal practice. Realizing that she does not have "very far to walk" to return home, the power of the adventure retreating into memory as she thinks of the mountains already "too far away now," she reenters her ordinary life, where "my mother was telling my grandmother how to fix Jell-O and my husband, Al, was playing with the baby." The significance of the story which she has lived and which she will eventually tell is epitomized by her concluding remark that she wishes her "old Grandpa" was still alive "to hear my story because it was the Yellow Woman stories he liked to tell best," an acknowledgment of her participation in a living tradition and an indication of her awareness of the importance of storytelling as a vital means of preserving and shaping cultural identity.

While Silko's stories are about the characterization of individuals, of a culture, of the land's significance to a people and their values, and of discrimination against a people, they are most fundamentally about the oral tradition that constitutes the people's means of achieving identity. Storytelling for Silko is not merely an entertaining activity reminiscent of past glories but an essential activity that informs and sustains the vitality of present cultures, shaping them toward survival and bestowing meaning for the future. The people, simply put, are their stories: If the stories are lost, the people are lost.

OTHER MAJOR WORKS

LONG FICTION: *Ceremony*, 1977; *Almanac of the Dead*, 1991; *Gardens in the Dunes*, 1999.

PLAY: *Lullaby*, pr. 1976 (with Frank Chin).

POETRY: *Laguna Woman*, 1974.

NONFICTION: *The Delicacy and Strength of Lace: Letters Between Leslie Marmon Silko and James Wright*, 1986; *Sacred Water: Narratives and Pictures*, 1993; *Yellow Woman and a Beauty of the Spirit: Essays on Native American Life Today*, 1996; *Conversations with Leslie Marmon Silko*, 2000 (Ellen L. Arnold, editor); *The Delicacy and Strength of Lace: Letters Between Leslie Marmon Silko and James Wright*, 2009 (Anne Wright, editor); *The Turquoise Ledge: A Memoir*, 2010.

BIBLIOGRAPHY

Fitz, Brewster E. "The Silence of the Bears: Leslie Marmon Silko's Writerly Act of Spiritual Storytelling." In *The Postmodern Short Story: Forms and Issues*, edited by Farhat Iftekharrudin et al., under the auspices of the Society for the Study of the Short Story. Westport, Conn.: Praeger, 2003. A critical reading of *Storyteller*.

_____. *Silko: Writing Storyteller and Medicine Woman*. Norman: University of Oklahoma Press, 2004. Analyzes Silko's short stories and novels, arguing that her storytelling is informed less by oral Laguna culture than by the Marmon family tradition. Describes how Silko's work reflects the conflict between the spoken and written forms of storytelling.

Gelfant, Blanche H., ed. *The Columbia Companion to the Twentieth-Century American Short Story*. New York: Columbia University Press, 2000. Includes a chapter in which Silko's short stories are analyzed.

Jaskoski, Helen. "From the Time Immemorial: Native American Traditions in Contemporary Short Fiction." In *Since Flannery O'Connor: Essays on the Contemporary American Short Story*, edited by Loren Logsdon and Charles W. Mayer. Macomb: western Illinois University Press, 1987. Suggests

that the narrator of "Yellow Woman" experiences the wish fulfillment of Romantic novels, playing out in a dreamlike state the fantasy of an encounter with a masterful stranger with no sense of guilt or consequence.

_____. *Leslie Marmon Silko: A Study of the Short Fiction*. New York: Twayne, 1998. A thorough critical study of Silko's short fiction, touching upon the roles of women, Native Americans, and the Southwest as they figure in her work. Includes a bibliography and an index.

Krumholz, Linda J. "'To Understand This World Differently': Reading and Subversion in Leslie Marmon Silko's *Storyteller*." *Ariel* 25 (January, 1994): 89-113. Discusses the role of the reader in Silko's *Storyteller*. Argues that one of the central ways in which Silko challenges the representation of Native Americans is to contest their relegation to the past and to break down the oral/written distinction used to support the past/present (them/us) dichotomy.

Krupat, Arnold. "The Dialogic of Silko's *Storyteller*." In *Narrative Chance: Postmodern Discourse on Native American Indian Literature*, edited by Gerald Vizenor. Albuquerque: University of New Mexico Press, 1989. Analyzes *Storyteller* from the perspective of Mikhail Bakhtin and Native American autobiography.

Morel, Pauline. "Storytelling and Myth as a Means of Identification, Subversion, and Survival in Leslie Marmon Silko's 'Yellow Woman' and 'Tony's Story.'" In *Interdisciplinary and Cross-Cultural Narratives in North America*, edited by Mark Cronlund Anderson and Irene Maria F. Blayer. New York: Peter Lang, 2005. An analysis of Silko's use of myth and storytelling in two of her short stories.

Nakadate, Neil. "Leslie Marmon Silko." In *A Reader's Companion to the Short Story in English*, edited by Erin Fallon, et al., under the auspices of the Society for the Study of the Short Story. Westport, Conn.: Greenwood Press, 2001. Aimed at the general reader, this essay provides a brief biography of Silko followed by an analysis of her short fiction.

Palmer, Linda. "Healing Ceremonies: Native American Stories of Cultural Survival." In *Ethnicity and the American Short Story*, edited by Julie Brown. New

York: Garland, 1997. Shows how the structure, image, and theme of Silko's story "Lullaby," from *Storyteller*, exemplifies the recurring Native American theme of ceremony, song, story, and memory as a means of cultural survival against the dominant society.

Ramirez, Susan Berry Brill de. "Storytellers and Their Listener-Readers in Silko's 'Storytelling' and 'Storyteller.'" *The American Indian Quarterly* 21 (Summer, 1997): 333-335. Discusses the role of the listener-reader in American Indian literature. Examines the "transformational" relationship between a storyteller and listener-readers in Silko's stories "Storyteller" and "Storytelling."

Salyer, Gregory. *Leslie Marmon Silko*. New York: Twayne, 1997. A critical study of Silko's work, including examinations of the depictions of women and the Laguna Indians in her fiction. Includes a bibliography and an index.

Seyersted, Per. *Leslie Marmon Silko*. Boise, Idaho: Boise State University, 1980. A solid critical study of Silko's work. Includes a bibliography.

Silko, Leslie Marmon. *Conversations with Leslie Marmon Silko*. Edited by Ellen L. Arnold. Jackson: University Press of Mississippi, 2000. A compilation of sixteen interviews, in which Silko discusses her life experiences, creative processes, political views, and the sources of her inspiration, among other topics.

_____. "Interview." *Short Story*, n.s. 2 (Fall, 1994): 91-95. Silko explains the process by which her fiction is written, her fiction's sources in the storytelling traditions of her ethnic background, and how and why she began writing.

_____. "The Man to Seed Rain Clouds." In *The Art of the Short Story*, edited by Dana Gioia and R.S. Gwynn. New York: Pearson Longman, 2006. In addition to this short story, this volume also includes Silko's commentary on this story, a brief biography, and the editors' analysis of her work and its place within the literary tradition.

Wiget, Andrew. *Native American Literature*. Boston: Twayne, 1985. Offers an overview analysis of *Ceremony* and compares the novel to N. Scott Momaday's *House Made of Dawn* (1968), maintaining that the novel sets the human struggle against mythic Native American legends. Argues that the novel explores the death of, or threats to, traditional Native American values and ways. Also examines *Storyteller*, contending that Silko successfully uses the possibilities afforded her by Native American myths and the persona of the storyteller figure to do more than provide local color: Instead, Silko uses these references to develop her characters and plot. Provides a useful but brief bibliography.

*Michael Loudon*
*Updated by Melissa E. Barth and Leon Lewis*

# MARISA SILVER

**Born:** Shaker Heights, Ohio; April 23, 1960

PRINCIPAL SHORT FICTION
  *Babe in Paradise,* 2001
  *Alone with You,* 2010

OTHER LITERARY FORMS

Marisa Silver wrote the screenplay for the feature film *Old Enough* (1984), which she also directed. It won the Grand Jury Prize at the Sundance Film Festival and was distributed by Orion. In addition to her short-story collections, she has published two novels, *No Direction Home* (2005) and *The God of War* (2008).

ACHIEVEMENTS

*Babe in Paradise* was a *New York Times* Notable Book of the Year and a *Los Angeles Times* Book of the Year. Her stories also have been featured in the *Best American Short Stories* and the *O. Henry Prize Stories* collections.

BIOGRAPHY

Born in Shaker Heights, Ohio, Marisa Silver is the daughter of Raphael and Joan Micklin Silver. The middle child, Marisa Silver has two sisters, Rina and Claudia. Both of her parents work in film: her father as a producer, and her mother as a screenwriter and director. Rina is also a film producer. The family moved from Cleveland to New York when Silver was seven years old. She attended the Brearley School and then studied at Harvard, although she did not complete her degree, leaving after two years for an opportunity to codirect a documentary film for Public Broadcasting Service. Before turning to writing fiction, Silver worked as a director, with feature films *Vital Signs* (1990) and *Permanent Record* (1988) among her accomplishments. While working on her first stories,

Silver studied in the low-residency M.F.A. program at Warren Wilson College. In an interview with Derek Alger, she praised the value of the program to her growth as a writer, noting that no one can teach someone to write, but that one can learn how to read. She is married to director and screenwriter Ken Kwapis; together they directed the film *He Said, She Said* (1991). Silver and Kwapis had two sons and settled in Los Angeles.

ANALYSIS

Marisa Silver sets all of her works in Los Angeles, but her setting is not the glamorous Los Angeles so often portrayed in the media. Many reviewers mention this, noting that her characters are surviving on the edge, the fringes, or the margins of the city. Bernard Cooper puts it more colorfully, stating that Silver's Los Angeles "bears as much relationship to the 'paradise' of the title as a cactus does to a Christmas tree."

Jeff Zaleski writes that many of Silver's stories feature "painfully real characters and strikingly inventive writing," but that often the stories leads "to a dead end." That may be the point that Silver is making: that people struggle and that life does not change radically. Cooper praises Silver's stories for not being "melodramatic or numbing," noting that the "onslaught of misery retains its sting in story after story."

*Babe in Paradise* features nine stories, three of which focus on the same character, Babe Ellis. The other stories vary widely in character and plot, but all of them address similar themes of dealing with loss, making difficult choices, and trying to find a place in the world. From the couple dealing with the death of their infant son to the couple that stumbles into the pornography business, Silver's characters are interesting, flawed people, dealing with the worst sorts of things life can bring.

### "Babe in Paradise"

The opening story of the collection introduces sixteen-year-old Babe Ellis. When asked what her real name is, she responds that her birth certificate reads "Baby Girl Ellis." "My mother couldn't think of anything better," she says. "I can choose my own name whenever I want. She doesn't want the responsibility." Babe has grown up all over the United States with her mother Delia, who suffers from mental illness. As the story begins, Babe and Delia are attempting to keep their roof wet during a wildfire. Babe asks her mother why they are going to so much trouble for a rental. Her mother replies that they paid first month, last month, and a deposit on the apartment; she considers that to be all of her savings.

Babe is having a sexual relationship with the man who staffs the Goodwill donations trailer, which also serves as the site of their trysts. She first meets him when she drops off a bag of items (including snow boots from when they lived in St. Louis) on her way to school. Although she finds him the "ugliest man she'd ever seen," with acne scars that Silver describes as "unpitying souvenirs of childhood," she accepts his invitation to join him in the trailer within minutes of meeting him.

When Babe and Delia are evacuated because of the fire, they end up in a shelter. Annoyed with her mother for unpacking their belonging there, Babe leaves to visit the Goodwill trailer. While she is gone, some of their possessions are stolen, including all their photographs. Babe is angry and becomes more so when her mother tries to placate her. By the time they return home, they find that they have been unlucky in the fire's "random game of chance," which burned some houses and spared others. They find a few odds and ends of their belongings, and Babe sees her mother "simply defeated," no longer pretty but just the "ghost of someone pretty." Babe herself feels like "just one more object, stranded in this ruined world."

### "Thief"

A woman and her disabled son return home and interrupt a burglary. Billy immediately grabs the phone to call 911, but he keeps getting a busy signal. While trying to leave the house in case the burglar is still there, the mother spots someone in the bushes. A young woman has twisted her ankle trying to escape and has been abandoned by her partner and accomplice, who had all the stolen goods. The foiled burglar is none other than Babe. Billy, who has been in a wheelchair since he was old enough to walk, is attracted to Babe and pities her, insisting that he and mother help her. The trio returns to the living room, where the mother questions Babe about her motives, Babe tries to call her partner-in-crime for a ride and then falls asleep, while Billy and his mother discuss what to do. She ends up cooking dinner and promising Babe a ride to the clinic to get her ankle checked. After cleaning up from dinner, the mother discovers Babe and Billy having sex in his bedroom. Although this is not out of the ordinary for Babe, it is for Billy. Mother and son eventually take Babe home to the motel where she is living with her mother. Babe casually says, "See you later," but Billy presses the issue, telling her that "people say that all the time, but it's usually not true." Babe looks vulnerable for a moment, then hardens again, walking away with a flippant retort, "See you never." Months later, Billy's mother sees Babe working as a cashier and notices she is wearing one of the mother's stolen bracelets. Back in the parking lot, Billy's mother reflects on the cycles of life, the transient nature of things, as she thinks about Billy, away at college, and the changes in her life because she is not taking care of him every day.

### "The Passenger"

The final story of the collection takes place a few years later, when Babe is twenty-three and working as a limousine driver. She describes her relationship with the dispatcher Ruthanne. Although they have never met in person, she is the person Babe talks to the most often. Babe saw Ruthanne's jacket once, though: a red jacket with an appliquéd dog. "Normally," Babe notes, "someone who would wear that jacket would have nothing to say to me, and so, in a sense, not meeting has brought us closer." She has "a few friends left over from high school," but their evenings out have become less frequent because they find themselves staring into their drinks, "because facing each other is like looking into a mirror in bad lighting." Interwoven throughout the story are details about her mother, who has attempted suicide several times and is now living in the desert with a spiritual group.

Assigned to pick up a Chinese couple at the airport, Babe is driving them to their destination in the suburbs. Because of an accident on the freeway, they are delayed, and when a police officer approaches the car, the couple becomes nervous and flees, leaving behind a suitcase. Babe opens the case to discover a baby hidden inside, with an oxygen tank. She takes the infant to the emergency room, where she is hassled by various doctors, nurses, and social workers, who do not quite believe her at first. As Babe notes in the beginning of the story, "I have a ring in my nose and a ring in my navel, and people make assumptions about me."

After publishing two novels, Silver returned to the short story form in 2010 with *Alone with You*, a collection of eight stories. When asked why, Silver responded that she loves "dealing with the issue of compression in stories" and the challenge of telling a story "with as few moves as possible." Many of these stories focus on relationships between mothers and daughters. One reviewer notes that Silver concentrates on the "complexity of people's closest relationships and the ambivalence they feel for those they love best." Ron Carlson finds that the women in these stories are "visit[ing] their lives trying to find a home."

### "THE VISITOR"

When Candy begins working at a Veterans Administration hospital as a nurse's aide, she is warned to not look at the injuries but focus on the wounded soldiers' faces. Candy finds that she isn't disgusted or embarrassed; she finds the injuries "frankly interesting," seeing similarities to her grandmother's work as a seamstress. She overhears some of her coworkers talking about her, saying she has no heart. "Well," thinks Candy, having "no heart was better than no brain." Candy lives with her grandmother; her mother, deceased, was an addict who would visit occasionally and sneak out with items she could pawn. When she took the sewing machine, Candy's grandmother finally changed the locks.

At work, Candy is drawn to a badly wounded young man who has lost both legs and one arm. He refuses to speak; she sees a notation about elective muteness on his chart. Candy takes this as a challenge and begins tormenting him in minor ways, staring at him, refusing to speak herself, once pinching him on the arm. As

Taylor Antrim notes, Silver "makes such hostility comprehensible, even human, by incrementally revealing the source of Candy's own grief and bottled rage." Candy is left alone to assist him, and she almost leaves him lying there until someone returns, but she decides to do what needs to be done, and she does it with care and compassion. When he looks at her this time, she sees "the arrow of his hatred for her and for everything that had happened to him bending back on itself and aiming straight into his own heart."

### "THREE GIRLS"

At age seventeen, Connie takes care of her younger sisters, Jean and Paula, the family pet, and most of the household chores. Their parents are both professors at the local college, and they are also both alcoholics. Late one winter night, the doorbell rings, and a family, a couple with three daughters, is on the doorstep. They explain that their car is stuck, they cannot get cell phone service, and they ask to use a phone to call for assistance. Connie's father is loath to let them in, but Connie's mother sees an opportunity for an instant party and pulls them inside, refusing to let them go back out to wait in their car after the phone calls are made. Connie sees that the woman and her daughters are uncomfortable, but she does not understand. She hears one of the girls being told that she will have to wait. "Didn't the woman think they had a bathroom?" Connie wonders. When neither of the men will accept an invitation to dance, Connie's mother pulls her up. Connie thinks that the girls like her dancing, and it is not until Jean yells at Connie to stop that she realizes the girls are not smiling, they are trying hard not to laugh at her. Connie looks to Jean for comfort, but the bond between them has been broken somehow, and Connie realizes that "she wouldn't know Jean when they were older, that when Jean left the family, she would leave Connie, too, because Connie would remind her of things she didn't want to remember."

### "NIGHT TRAIN TO FRANKFURT"

Dorothy has chosen to receive an experimental treatment for her cancer. She asks her daughter to accompany her to Germany, where "they were going to boil Dorothy's blood. Take it out, heat it, put it back in. The cancer would be gone." Although the daughter, Helen, is worried that her mother has been duped by the clinic's advertising, with its statistics and testimonials, Helen understands and flies to Germany with her mother. During the train ride to the clinic location, there is a scene in which Helen offers to read to Dorothy, telling her mother that she has copies of *Vogue* and *People* and a volume of Pablo Neruda's poetry. Her mother reacts badly, and when Helen protests that Dorothy loves Neruda, Dorothy asks, "Are we searching for my epitaph?" Helen tries to defend herself, but "the truth was that she *had* thought about what to read at her mother's funeral and had made the private decision that it would be Neruda." Helen and Dorothy have a number of substantial conversations during the trip, and when they arrive at the clinic, Dorothy is overwhelmed and seems to panic. Before Helen can put her arm around her mother to lead her in, "Dorothy drew herself up, somehow guided back to herself by her daughter's confidence, and started forward on her own."

OTHER MAJOR WORKS

LONG FICTION: *No Direction Home*, 2005; *The God of War*, 2008

SCREENPLAY: *Old Enough*, 1984

BIBLIOGRAPHY

Antrim, Taylor. "Crucible of Pain." *New York Times Book Review*, June 6, 2010, p. 35. Review of the *Alone with You* collection, which provides analysis of Silver's writing

Carlson, Ron. "*Alone with You: Stories*." *Los Angeles Times*, April 11, 2010. Review of the collection, describing a breathtaking moment and the longing and loneliness that infuse Silver's stories.

Uhlin, David. "*Babe in Paradise* by Marisa Silver." *The Atlantic* (July/August, 2001): 163. Review of Silver's collection, calling it "powerful and heartfelt."

Werris, Wendy. "Silver Linings." *Publishers Weekly* (February 22, 2010): 36. Provides many insights about Silver's style, process, and influences.

Zaleski, Jeff. "City of Angels." *The New York Times Book Review*, August 26, 2001, p. 25. This review of *Babe in Paradise* notes Silver's "considerable gifts" in embroiling her characters in trouble that comes "thick and fast."

*Elizabeth Blakesley*

---

# WILLIAM GILMORE SIMMS

**Born:** Charleston, South Carolina; April 17, 1806
**Died:** Charleston, South Carolina; June 11, 1870

PRINCIPAL SHORT FICTION

*The Book of My Lady,* 1833
*Carl Werner,* 1838
*The Wigwam and the Cabin,* 1845
*Southward Ho!,* 1854
*Tales of the South,* 1996 (Mary Ann Wimsatt, editor)

OTHER LITERARY FORMS

William Gilmore Simms was one of the most versatile and prolific writers of his day; his more than eighty volumes include novels, short stories, poetry, plays, literary criticism, essays, biographies, and histories. Simms was also highly respected in his time as a magazine and newspaper editor.

ACHIEVEMENTS

The enormous literary output of William Gilmore Simms places him among the foremost writers of the early nineteenth century in the United States; indeed, he was the most important writer in the South at the time. His many novels are mostly historical romances in the tradition of Sir Walter Scott and James Fenimore Cooper, but they use southern settings, dialects, and heroes as their subject. His best-known novel, *The Yemassee: A Romance of Carolina* (1835), deals with the issue of Native American dispossession, a theme also common to Cooper. Simms's short stories are often told in the tall-tale mode, which was later popularized by the Southwest humorists. In addition to his fiction, Simms wrote a number of volumes of poetry and several plays, which, like the novels, have patriotic settings and subjects. His nonfiction works include histories, biographies, and several important essays of literary criticism, one of which details the difference between romance and novel. Though often noted for the quantity rather than the quality of his work, Simms occupies an important position in American letters.

BIOGRAPHY

William Gilmore Simms was the son of an Irish immigrant tradesman. His mother died when he was two, and Simms was left in the care of his maternal grandmother when his father moved to Tennessee and later to Mississippi. Simms's formal schooling amounted to less than six years, and he was largely self-educated. At the age of twelve, he was apprenticed to a druggist but later left that trade to study law. In 1827, he was admitted to the bar in Charleston. His marriage to Anna Malcolm Giles in 1826 ended with her death in 1832.

Simms's literary talents became manifest very early in his life. At nineteen, he edited the literary journal, *The Album* (1825), and at this time began publishing collections of his poetry. In 1828, he cofounded and edited *The Southern Literary Gazette*. He ventured into journalism as the editor of a daily newspaper, the Charleston *City Gazette*, from 1830 until its bankruptcy in 1832. Between 1833 and 1835, he published four novels, *Martin Faber: The Story of a Criminal* (1833), *Guy Rivers: A Tale of Georgia* (1834), *The Yemassee*, and *The Partisan: A Tale of the Revolution* (1835), and established his reputation as a significant voice in American fiction.

In 1836, Simms married Chevilette Roach and moved to her father's seven-thousand-acre plantation, "Woodlands." His newly acquired wealth freed him to pursue his literary career more fully and to venture into new avenues, such as serving from 1844 to 1846 as a representative to the South Carolina legislature. His marriage to Roach lasted until her death in 1863, and the couple had fourteen children. During the period from 1836 to 1860, in addition to his many literary productions, Simms was active in the editing of several

magazines, including *The southern and western Monthly Magazine* (1845), *The southern Quarterly Review* (1849-1855), and *Russell's Magazine* (1857-1860), which he helped Paul Hamilton Hayne to edit. Simms's fortunes were ruined by the Civil War; in 1865, "Woodlands" was burned by stragglers from William Tecumseh Sherman's army. Reduced to poverty, Simms spent the final years of his life editing newspapers and writing to support himself and his children. He died in Charleston on June 11, 1870.

ANALYSIS

William Gilmore Simms is often viewed as the successor to Sir Walter Scott in the fostering of Romanticism. Simms was fond of asserting that his works should be viewed as romances, filled with sweeps of the imagination, bold characterization, and clearly defined moral stances. His literary works, considered as a whole, can be viewed as an epic of the South; in the epic, there are realistic elements to be sure, but Simms was interested in realism only when it served his more consuming passion for creating works of originality

*William Gilmore Simms* (Getty Images)

and vitality that portrayed the South as it was and as it aspired to be ideally. Simms's writings, too, can be associated with regionalism and the local-color movement in American letters, for he borrowed richly from the traditions and mores of his region to capture a sense of a spirit and a time.

### "HOW SHARP SNAFFLES GOT HIS CAPITAL AND HIS WIFE"

"How Sharp Snaffles Got His Capital and His Wife," published posthumously in *Harper's New Monthly Magazine* in October, 1870, is a short story which demonstrates at a high level of quality Simms's particular and fanciful interest in local color and southern tall-tale humor. In early winter, a group of seven hunters, four professionals and three amateurs, gather around the campfire on a Saturday night after a week of hunting in the "Balsam Range" of mountains in North Carolina. Saturday night is dedicated among the professional hunters to what is called "The Lying Camp," in which mountaineers engaged in a camp hunt, which sometimes lasts for weeks at a time, are encouraged to tell "long yarns" about their adventures and the wild experiences of their professional lives. The hunter who actually inclines to exaggeration in such a situation is allowed to deal in "all the extravagances of invention; nay, he is *required* to do so." To be literal or to confine oneself to details of fact is a finable offense. The hunter is, however, required to exhibit a certain degree of art in his invented tales, "and thus he frequently rises into a certain realm of fiction, the ingenuities of which are made to compensate for the exaggerations, as they do in the 'Arabian Nights' and other Oriental romances."

The tale for the evening is told, in dialect fashion, by Sharp Snaffles to the "Jedge," the narrator of the story. Sharp tells the tale of how fourteen years ago he was in love with Merry Ann Hopson and sought to marry her. When Sharp appears at Squire Hopson's house and announces his intentions, the squire tells Sharp that he does not have the types of possessions, or capital, that would attract a woman or that would enable her to live in style. Sharp knows he must get himself some capital, but he cannot figure out how, although he spends half the night thinking and figuring.

The next day, Sharp sees a flock of wild geese landing on a lake. Sharp calculates that there must be forty thousand geese on the lake and considers that he could get fifty cents a head for them if he could get them to the markets in Spartanburg and Greenville. His plan is to spread a huge net across the lake, and, after the geese have landed, at a key moment pull both ends of the net in quickly and catch all the geese. The plan works perfectly, except for the fact that after reeling all the geese in, Sharp wraps the rope around his left arm and his right thigh rather than tying it to the tree in front of him. As if of one mind and body, the geese lift from the lake and carry Sharp for several miles until they hit a tree and land in its branches. Suddenly the branch on which Sharp is sitting gives way and throws him backward into the tree trunk, which is hollow and filled with honey. In the midst of his prayers for deliverance, a huge bear begins to lower himself down, bottom end first, to get to the honey. Sharp sees his chance and grabs hold of the bear's ankle; the bear is so frightened he claws his way out of the tree, taking Sharp with him. When they get to the top, Sharp pushes the bear out of the tree; the bear falls and breaks his neck.

Safely out of the tree, Sharp realizes the potential capital available to him in the bear, the geese, and the honey. When all of his dealings are done, he has sold twenty-seven thousand geese for $1,350, the bear's hide, meat, grease, and marrow for $100, and two thousand gallons of honey for $1,400. His wealth accumulated, Sharp then sets about the business of establishing himself as a man of capital by buying a 160-acre farm with a good house on it, furniture, and a mule for working his land. The rest of his money he has converted to gold and silver coins and loads up his pockets and his saddlebags.

As he prepares to go to Squire Hopson's, Sharp tells his friend, Columbus Mills, of the squire's talk about capital. Columbus tells Sharp that the squire has no room to talk; the squire owes Columbus a 350-dollar-note on which he has not paid a cent in three years and on which Columbus is holding the mortgage to the squire's farm as security. Sharp asks Columbus if he will sell him the squire's mortgage for the face value of the note, and Columbus agrees. Dressed in his best new outfit, Sharp then goes to Squire Hopson's house; on the way, he meets Merry Ann and tells her that they are going to be married that evening. Merry Ann thinks that he has gone slightly crazy but agrees to follow along after him and see what happens.

The squire receives Sharp coldly, but he is impressed by Sharp's rich clothing and his fancy new appearance. Sharp states that he has come on business and brings up the issue of the debt to Columbus Mills. The squire tells Sharp to tell Columbus he will pay him soon, and Sharp says that the squire misunderstands Sharp's mission. The note, and consequently the mortgage, now belong to him, and, since he plans to be married this evening, he wants the squire to move out so that Sharp and his new bride can move in in the morning. The only way the squire can acquire any capital now and save his farm is to allow Sharp to marry Merry Ann. At first the squire protests, but when Sharp shows him the gold and silver coins in his saddlebags and his pockets he finally gives in and agrees to the wedding. Sharp fetches Parson Stovall, and the wedding is performed that evening, exactly as Sharp had promised Merry Ann. Thirteen years later, Sharp tells the Judge at the conclusion of his tale that he and Merry Ann have a happy marriage, nine beautiful children, and more capital than Sharp ever imagined.

### "GRAYLING"

Simms's passion for the wonderful and the mysterious is exemplified by "Grayling," a story which Edgar Allan Poe admired and which begins with the lamentation that the world has become so matter-of-fact lately that "we can no longer get a ghost story, either for love or money." To break the hold which "that cold-blooded demon called Science" has upon "all that concerns the romantic," the narrator proposes to tell a story that he heard as a boy from his grandmother and that involves ghosts and many things wondrous.

Set in the Carolinas in the period immediately following the Revolutionary War, the tale is of the murder of Major Lionel Spencer by Sandy Macnab. Macnab has learned that Spencer is to sail from Charleston to England to claim a large inheritance. All the Major need do to secure the estate is prove that he is Lionel Spencer. With the intention of impersonating Spencer in England, Macnab follows the Major, murders him, and throws his body in the bay.

James Grayling, a close friend of Major Spencer and an army comrade with whom Spencer camped the night before he was murdered, learns that Spencer has neither reached the tavern in the next town on his journey nor been seen on the road. While searching for Spencer, Grayling sees the ghost of Major Spencer, which tells Grayling that Macnab has murdered him and hidden his body in the bay. The murderer, Spencer is sure, is on his way to Charleston to sail for England. Spencer pleads with Grayling to have Macnab brought to justice, and Grayling hurriedly sets out to avenge his friend's murder.

In Charleston, Grayling's search eventually uncovers Macnab, hiding under the alias of Macleod. Macleod protests his innocence, but his guilty behavior leads the sheriff to arrest Macleod as the murderer.

Macleod secures a lawyer who files a writ of habeas corpus, and the judge states the case against Macleod would be stronger if the body was discovered and the murder actually proven. Grayling sets out to search the bay area, and he eventually finds Spencer's body. Macnab, alias Macleod, is found guilty and hanged.

Here ends the grandmother's tale; the narrator's father, however, suspicious of such irrationalities, tells his son the ghost was an invention of Grayling's mind and that all the supposed mysterious happenings of the tale can be accounted for by natural laws. Grayling was a bold, imaginative man. When he learned his friend had not made it to the tavern, he thought of Macnab traveling along the same road and became suspicious of foul play. He also was aware that Macnab knew Spencer was on his way to England to prove his identity and claim a large fortune. The spot where the "ghost" appeared was simply one which had already struck Grayling's keen intelligence as a perfect place for an ambush; these thoughts were in his mind as he sat down to rest by the tree. Falling asleep--or so the father contends--Grayling sees a "ghost"; you will note, however, the father states, that, although Spencer told Grayling he had been murdered by Macnab, he did not tell him how or by which weapons. Neither does he reveal which wounds he has suffered. To ride to Charleston and discover the murderer onboard the very ship Major Spencer would have sailed upon for England required no great or superior logical deduction from Grayling. "The whole story," the father tells the son, "is one of strong probabilities which happened to be verified." The son hears his father "with great patience to the end," noting that the father "had taken a great deal of pains to destroy one of my greatest sources of pleasure." The son, however, chooses to believe in ghosts and to reject his father's philosophy, saying that "it was more easy to believe the one than to comprehend the other."

### "The Snake of the Cabin"

Both "How Sharp Snaffles Got His Capital and His Wife" and "Grayling" demonstrate Simms's penchant for stories which unmask villains, reward the just and virtuous, and show the eventual triumph of good over evil. A similar pattern can be seen in the story "The Snake of the Cabin," which focuses upon the mysterious death of Ellen Ramsay, a young woman of health and vigor who faded rapidly into sickness and death barely a year after her marriage to Edward Stanton. At her funeral, her spurned lover, Robert Anderson, appears and accuses Stanton of using slander and witchcraft to steal Ellen away from him. Stanton is enraged, and the men have to be separated before a fight ensues. Anderson keeps up a steady vigil at Ellen's grave for several months, until he himself dies, presumably of a broken heart. Upon his death, it is discovered that he has carved matching headstones for his grave and Ellen's. Stanton, however, is adamant that the headstone is not to be erected over his wife's grave.

The tale is narrated by Mr. Atkins to a stranger who has appeared upon the scene and made inquiries about Edward Stanton. Hearing the details of the story, he tells Atkins that he has proof against Stanton which will end his claim to Ellen's estate and thus save her father, John Ramsay, the pain of having to sell several of his slaves to pay Stanton his share. The stranger is taken to Mr. Ramsay's house, where Stanton is engaged in an argument with Ramsay over how he is to receive his share of his wife's estate. The stranger listens for a while, then asks Stanton to which wife he is referring. Stanton, obviously flustered, responds that he is talking about Ellen Ramsay. The stranger responds that he thinks not, since Stanton has recently married three women in different parts of the country and claimed shares of their estates. Stanton shouts that

the stranger can prove none of these charges, and the stranger reveals papers he has carried with him that substantiate his claims. Stanton is confused and shaken, and those present conclude that his behavior and the legal papers at hand reveal his guilt. The stranger unmasks himself as Henry Lamar of Georgia, the cousin and once the betrothed of a girl Stanton married and later wronged. Lamar tells Stanton he has no claim against Ellen Ramsay's estate and warns him to be out of town within forty-eight hours or Lamar will have him prosecuted.

Later that evening, Abraham, one of the slaves Stanton wanted Ramsay to sell, comes up to Ellen's brother, Jack Ramsay, and shows him a twenty-dollar bill, asking him if it is genuine. Ramsay tells him it is not and asks him where he got it. Abraham responds that he got it from Mr. Stanton, who gave Abraham twenty dollars to convince the slaves to run away with him and achieve their freedom in the North. Ramsay decides that they will hatch a plot to seize Stanton at once, and he tells Abraham to round up Lamar, Atkins, and several others to disguise themselves as the Negro slaves and meet Stanton later that night at the designated spot. The men wait for Stanton in the woods, and when he appears, they move to capture him. He escapes and runs down the path, only to be tripped up by Abraham. In trying to escape once more, Stanton shoots at Abraham and wounds him in the arm. Abraham falls, however, and lands upon Stanton's knife, driving the blade deep into Stanton's side and killing him. For his virtuous conduct in revealing Stanton's plot to Jack Ramsay and in aiding in Stanton's capture, Abraham is provided for by the Ramsay family and becomes the official recounter of the tale of Stanton's efforts to attain gain by evil and devious means. The moral of the story is presented by Lamar, who states that evil is not an exclusive possession of the wealthy or the powerful; "the same snake, or one very much like it, winds his way into the wigwam and the cabin--and the poor silly country girl is as frequently the victim, as the dashing lady of the city and city fashions."

Simms's writings are often regarded as frivolous and criticized for their heavy Romanticism and simplistic conceptions of morality. Those who find

Simms's works to be insubstantial often charge him with being a dated historical writer, one whose works must fade in significance and interest as quickly as the era they depicted passes into history and into memory. While there is some obvious merit to these charges against Simms, it cannot be denied that Simms never aspired to be anything more than a recorder of his era and its particular charms and peculiarities. More than any other writer of the Old South he achieved that aim, and his collected works remain the most sensitive, insightful, and imaginative record of the formative years of southern culture.

OTHER MAJOR WORKS

LONG FICTION: *Martin Faber: The Story of a Criminal*, 1833; *Guy Rivers: A Tale of Georgia*, 1834; *The Partisan: A Tale of the Revolution*, 1835; *The Yemassee: A Romance of Carolina*, 1835; *Mellichampe: A Legend of the Santee*, 1836; *Pelayo: A Story of the Goth*, 1838; *Richard Hurdis: Or, The Avenger of Blood, a Tale of Alabama*, 1838; *The Damsel of Darien*, 1839; *Border Beagles: A Tale of Mississippi*, 1840; *Confession: Or, The Blind Heart*, 1841; *The Kinsmen: Or, The Black Riders of the Congaree*, 1841 (revised as *The Scout*, 1854); *Beauchampe: Or, The Kentucky Tragedy, a Tale of Passion*, 1842; *Count Julian: Or, The Last Days of the Goth, a Historical Romance*, 1845; *Helen Halsey: Or, The Swamp State of Conelachita, a Tale of the Borders*, 1845; *The Lily and the Totem: Or, The Huguenots in Florida*, 1850; *Katharine Walton: Or, The Rebel of Dorchester*, 1851; *The Sword and the Distaff: Or, "Fair, Fat and Forty,"* 1852 (revised as *Woodcraft*, 1854); *Vasconselos: A Romance of the New World*, 1853; *The Forayers: Or, The Raid of the Dog-Days*, 1855; *Charlemont: Or, The Pride of the Village*, 1856; *Eutaw: A Sequel to the Forayers*, 1856; *The Cassique of Kiawah: A Colonial Romance*, 1859.

PLAY: *Michael Bonham: Or, The Fall of Bexar, a Tale of Texas*, pb. 1852.

POETRY: *Monody on the Death of Gen. Charles Cotesworth Pinckney*, 1825; *Early Lays*, 1827; *Lyrical, and Other Poems*, 1827; *The Vision of Cortes*, 1829; *The Tri-Color*, 1830; *Atalantis: A Story of the Sea*, 1832; *Areytos: Or, Songs of the South*, 1846; *Poems Descriptive, Dramatic, Legendary and Contemplative*, 1853.

NONFICTION: *The History of South Carolina*, 1840; *The Geography of South Carolina*, 1843; *The Life of Francis Marion*, 1844; *Views and Reviews in American Literature, History and Fiction*, 1845; *The Life of Captain John Smith*, 1846; *The Life of Chevalier Bayard*, 1847; *The Life of Nathanael Greene*, 1849; *South-Carolina in the Revolutionary War*, 1853; *Sack and Destruction of the City of Columbia, S. C.*, 1865; *The Letters of William Gilmore Simms*, 1952-1982 (six volumes; Mary C. Simms Oliphant, Alfred Taylor Odell, and T. C. Duncan Eaves, editors).

MISCELLANEOUS: *The Centennial Edition of the Writings of William Gilmore Simms*, 1969-1975 (sixteen volumes; John C. Guilds and James B. Meriwether, editors); *The Simms Reader: Selections from the Writings of William Gilmore Simms*, 2001 (John Caldwell Guilds, editor).

BIBLIOGRAPHY

Butterworth, Keen, and James E. Kibler, Jr. *William Gilmore Simms: A Reference Guide*. Boston: G. K. Hall, 1980. This thorough bibliography lists all writings about Simms in chronological order from 1825 to 1979. The lengthy introduction gives general background information, and the index provides an efficient means of locating books and articles on specific topics relating to Simms.

Current-Garcia, Eugene. *The American Short Story Before 1850: A Critical History*. Boston: Twayne, 1985. Current-Garcia gives a useful overview of early nineteenth century American short fiction, including a chapter on "Simms and the southern Frontier Humorists." Several bibliographies are also included.

Guilds, John Caldwell, ed. *"Long Years of Neglect": The Work and Reputation of William Gilmore Simms*. Fayetteville: University of Arkansas Press, 1988. The twelve essays in this collection address Simms as novelist, poet, historical philosopher, humorist, lecturer, and literary critic. Mary Ann Wimsatt's essay on "The Evolution of Simms' Backwoods Humor" deals particularly with Simms's short fiction.

_____. *Simms: A Literary Life*. Fayetteville: University of Arkansas Press, 1992. The first critical biography of Simms to appear in one hundred years,

Guilds's book proceeds in a chronological fashion and emphasizes Simms's accomplishments as a novelist. Features five appendixes, including a useful list of Simms's writings appearing in book form.

Guilds, John Caldwell, and Caroline Collins, eds. *William Gilmore Simms and the American Frontier*. Athens: University of Georgia, 1997. Focuses on Simms's depiction of the frontier.

Johanyak, Debra. "William Gilmore Simms: Deviant Paradigms of southern Womanhood?" *The Mississippi Quarterly* 46 (Fall, 1993): 573-588. Discusses the portrayal of women in Simms's fiction. Argues that even though intellectual, independent, or masculinized women are repeatedly destroyed by seducers in Simms's work, readers are encouraged to view these women as deviant and as contributing to their own downfall.

Mayfield, John. "'The Soul of a Man': William Gilmore Simms and the Myths of southern Manhood." *Journal of the Early Republic* 15 (Fall, 1995): 477-500. An examination of southern men in Simms's fiction. Argues that both as literary figures and as paradigms Simms's characters are failures because they are stereotypes with little to offer. Explores Simms's use of masks, deceit, representation, and misrepresentation, as well as his introduction of the romantic rogue to reveal a subtext that provides a more realistic portrait of southern manhood.

Newton, David W. "'It Is Genius Only Which Can Make Ghosts': Narrative Design and the Art of Storytelling in Simms's 'Grayling: Or, Murder Will Out.'" *Studies in the Literary Imagination* 42, no. 2 (Spring, 2009): 59-82. An in-depth analysis of Simms's short story "Grayling," describing the complexity and sophistication of its narrative structure and its storytelling techniques. Reviews the story's publication history and critical reception. Notes that Edgar Allan Poe considered this story one of the best ghost stories he had ever read.

Perkins, Laura Ganus. "An Unsung Literary Legacy: William Gilmore Simm's African-American Characters." *Studies in the Literary Imagination* 42, no. 1 (Spring, 2009): 83-95. Argues that Simm's depiction of African American characters appears to contradict his professed beliefs in the inferiority of black people. Discusses Simms's story "Maize in Milk," demonstrating how both its white and black characters are influenced by Simm's ideas about the benefits of slavery.

Romine, Scott. "The Capital Comedy of William Gilmore Simms's 'Sharp Snaffles.'" *southern Quarterly* 41, no. 2 (Winter, 2003): 11. Examines the "subliterary status" in American literature of "How Sharp Snaffles Got His Capital and Wife." Discusses the origin of the story; explores Simms's use of metaphors for social interactions surrounding marriage, status, and social obligations; analyzes the story's style.

Simms, William Gilmore. *Backwoods Tales: Paddy McGann, Sharp Snaffles, and Bill Bauldy*. Introduction by Keen Butterworth. Fayetteville: University of Arkansas Press, 2010. Reprints three comic tales that Simms wrote late in his career. In his introduction, Butterworth states that these are the "three best examples" of Simms's comic writing, and he traces the comedic elements in all of Simms's works.

Watson, Charles S. *From Nationalism to Secessionism: The Changing Fiction of William Gilmore Simms*. Westport, Conn.: Greenwood Press, 1993. Examines Simms's political and social views. Includes bibliography and index.

Wimsatt, Mary Ann. *The Major Fiction of William Gilmore Simms: Cultural Traditions and Literary Forms*. Baton Rouge: Louisiana State University Press, 1989. Although Wimsatt focuses primarily on Simms's novels, this study is one of the most useful discussions of Simms's work as it reevaluates many of the misconceptions and dismissive attitudes about his fiction. Wimsatt makes use of biographical as well as historical information, and she discusses Simms's novels within the context of twentieth century critical formulations about the romance genre.

*Christina Murphy*
*Updated by Ann A. Merrill*

# HELEN SIMPSON

**Born:** Bristol, England; March 2, 1957

PRINCIPAL SHORT FICTION

*Flesh and Grass,* 1990 (novella)
*Four Bare Legs in a Bed, and Other Stories,* 1990
*Dear George, and Other Stories,* 1995
*Hey Yeah Right Get a Life,* 2000 (pb. in U.S. as *Getting a Life,* 2001)
*Constitutional,* 2005 (pb. in U.S. as *In the Driver's Seat,* 2007)
*In-Flight Entertainment,* 2010

OTHER LITERARY FORMS

Readers may sample Helen Simpson's style as a journalist in *The London Ritz Book of Afternoon Tea: The Art and Pleasures of Taking Tea* (1986) and *The London Ritz Book of English Breakfasts* (1988). Following the publication of *Four Bare Legs in a Bed, Flesh and Grass* was paired with Ruth Rendell's *The Strawberry Tree* as the first volume of a series from the feminist publisher Pandora under the general heading of *Unguarded Hours* (1990). *Flesh and Grass* is a mischievous black comedy about gourmet chefs, butchery, and militant vegetarianism. While the pairing of Simpson with a best-selling crime writer did not presage a career as a writer of suspense, the novella does reveal a link between her early food writing and the later fiction. Simpson also has written song lyrics for the jazz composers Kate and Mike Westbrook and adapted her story "Good Friday, 1663" as a libretto for their opera of the same name.

ACHIEVEMENTS

Following the success of *Four Bare Legs in a Bed,* Simpson became the first *Sunday Times* Young Writer of the Year. In 1991, she received the prestigious Somerset Maugham Award, which, like the

*Sunday Times* award, is given to a writer under the age of thirty-five. Youth also was on her side in 1993, when she was named as one of *Granta* magazine's Best of Young British Novelists, in a list including, among others, Kazuo Ishiguro, A. L. Kennedy, and Jeanette Winterson. Unlike the other nineteen authors on the list, she has resisted the pressure to publish a full-length novel. Indeed, she is the only significant contemporary British writer who bases a successful mainstream career entirely on short fiction. Other awards include the Hawthornden Prize for *Hey Yeah Right Get a Life* and the E. M. Forster Award from the American Academy of Arts and Letters in 2002.

BIOGRAPHY

Brought up in an unfashionable North London suburb with schoolteacher parents, Helen Simpson claims to have fabricated a more picturesque autobiography for her entry to a *Vogue* talent competition, inventing a bucolic lifestyle in a Yorkshire market garden. Success in the *Vogue* contest resulted ultimately in a job as a staff writer on the magazine, interrupting her Ph.D. research on Restoration farce. Both Simpson's undergraduate degree and her postgraduate work took place at Oxford University, where, at the age of twenty, she was the winner of a short-story competition in the student magazine *Isis*. Although she abandoned academic research, Simpson's literary background is evident in the numerous intertextual references in her work. Soon after publishing her story "The Bed" in *Vogue*, Simpson was taken on by a leading literary agent, Pat Kavanagh. Kavanagh's belief in literary values, her support of the short-story form, and her influence among publishers are key factors in the blossoming of Simpson's career. Simpson got married, had two children, and settled in London.

ANALYSIS

Helen Simpson excels at the witty, well-made story, combining tight dramatic structure with striking imagery. While her stories tackle large-scale themes, including the exigences of mortality, the gender war, and the planet's finite resources, they are characterized by a preference for the comic mode. Her protagonists may embody the postfeminist dilemma, but they never descend to victimhood. She is best known for those stories in *Getting a Life* and *In the Driver's Seat*, which chronicle the ambivalence felt by educated women whose autonomy is compromised by motherhood. In England, acclaim for her technical mastery of short-story form has been tempered, in some quarters, by a perception that her material is limited by this domestic milieu. Nonetheless, Simpson is unchallenged as the most significant British short-story writer since Angela Carter, and one whose work is influenced consciously by a range of women writers, including Colette, Alice Munro, and, crucially, Katherine Mansfield. Like Mansfield, Simpson has an ear for spoken language, especially children's voices. Her use of heightened imagery is another link with Mansfield; sensual pleasures, especially food and sex, are described with great relish. She also, like Mansfield, makes use of vivid natural imagery. A suburban garden or a touch of morning frost introduces a note of transcendence into the mundanities of everyday existence. Later, her evocations of the natural order acquired extra intensity through the prism of climate change, which became a major preoccupation in Simpson's work.

Since *Four Bare Legs in a Bed*, Simpson's collections have been published about every five years, the individual stories appearing in magazines and anthologies and broadcast on British Broadcasting Corporation radio. Most, though not all, of the stories are told from a female perspective, the lives of her protagonists broadly following the stages of Simpson's own life. While not directly autobiographical, the five collections may be regarded as an organic cycle, charting the experiences of her generation.

### FOUR BARE LEGS IN A BED

Simpson's debut collection takes a wry view of sex, relationships, and family life. "The Bed," Simpson's first published story, is a monologue about a woman who cannot resist buying a luxurious bed. Her boyfriend Tom is infuriated by this outrageous extravagance, until he, too, is seduced by its sensory pleasures. While the erotic delights of the bed reinvigorate Tom, fueling his energy in his job, they have a narcotic effect on the narrator, who loses all interest in the drab office routine. The story celebrates hedonism, ending with the couple making love on Christmas morning; however, taken in the context of the other stories in the collection, it reads more ambiguously.

"An Interesting Condition" describes the blunt and often gruesome reality of the antenatal clinic, a world that is almost the opposite to the soft furnishings department described in "The Bed." Pregnant women are made to sit on foam cushions, rather than chairs, so as to stretch their pelvic joints. In a surreal touch, a midwife is knitting a model of the uterus in pink wool. The protagonist, Alice, dreams about her changing body; dreams are described at greater length in "The Bed" and in the title story. There is a sense that the characters in the "bed" stories almost literally are sleepwalking into the rude awakening of pregnancy and motherhood.

"Labour" reconstructs childbirth as a five-act drama, with choruses of midwives speaking in iambic pentameter and other *dramatis personae*, including the uterus, the placenta, and the goddess of childbirth. Her appearance at the end of the "play" recalls the court masques of the seventeenth century, and Simpson's interest in this period is also reflected in "Good Friday, 1663." This story, later adapted as a jazz opera, is a skilled pastiche, based on Simpson's familiarity with the age of Samuel Pepys. It interweaves extracts from a grisly Easter sermon with the thoughts of a young wife in the congregation. Her present condition, heavily pregnant and yoked to a boorish husband, is contrasted with memories of the pleasure gardens at Vauxhall and a fateful dalliance with a London gallant. The juxtaposition of the sermon with her monologue suggests a rereading of the rhetoric of Calvinist theology. The equation of the womb with the tomb is more than a verbal trope for a woman facing the distinct possibility of death in childbirth. As in the contemporary stories, the fancies, dreams, and pleasures of the girl yield to an inexorable physical reality, but while the contemporary stories tip the balance toward the comic, "Good Friday, 1663" is an overtly tragic reworking of Restoration drama.

"Christmas Jezebels" is another historical story, using a modern idiom to describe fourth century sisters and would-be courtesans; "Give Me Daughters Any Day" explores intergenerational tensions among the women in a family.

### DEAR GEORGE

Although *Dear George* is the least well known of Simpson's collections, it contains several key stories, including "Heavy Weather" and "To Her Unready Boyfriend." The themes begun in *Four Bare Legs in a Bed* are developed further; while sex, pregnancy, and unexpected transformation are the central concerns of the first collection, the focus moves in the second collection toward early motherhood and marital disharmony. In the title story, the teenage protagonist is disgusted by the thought of her mother breastfeeding the new baby and by the whole idea of someone her mother's age procreating. The young girl is supposed to be writing an essay on William Shakespeare, but in fact she is daydreaming and drafting silly letters. "Dear George" serves as a prelude to the collection, evoking the aimlessness, arrogance, and unsuspecting innocence of youth. "Bed and Breakfast" and "When in Rome" both shift viewpoints between a couple on holiday together, exploring both unspoken and surface tensions between the man and the woman.

### GETTING A LIFE

Like *Dear George*, *Getting a Life* begins with what Jay McInerney has called an "overture," articulating a teenager's repugnance at the spectacle of mother and baby. "Golden Apples" (published in England as "Lentils and Lilies") is a more nuanced and structurally complex story than "Dear George"; as a consequence, its ironies resonate with greater emotional depth. This volume is Simpson's most popular collection and the most widely studied. As a collection, it achieves a remarkable cohesion, and, technically, it marks a rise in confidence and ambition. Many readers have recognized their experience in stories such as "Café Society," in which two exhausted mothers' attempts at a civilized conversation over coffee are thwarted, inevitably, by a fractious toddler.

"Golden Apples" initiates a mini-cycle, incorporating the title story, "Getting a Life," "Burns and the Bankers," and the final piece, "Hurrah for the Hols." These four interconnecting stories shift perspectives among a young girl, a woman who juggles family life and a high-powered career, and a stay-at-home mother of three children all under four years of age. Jade, the carefree teenager in "Golden Apples," is the daughter of Nicola Beamount, the corporate lawyer in "Burns and the Bankers," a woman who, superficially at least, has the best of both worlds. Jade makes a brief reappearance as the babysitter in the title story, which, at thirty-nine pages, is one of the longest Simpson has written. At the center of this story is Dorrie, the harassed stay-at-home mother.

"Getting a Life" is set on Dorrie's wedding anniversary, describing what is, for the most part, a typical day, leading to the anticlimax of a celebratory meal at a restaurant. Dorrie is never off duty; she is entirely bound, practically and psychologically, by the maternal role, and when she comes back from her night out with her husband, she is obliged to bathe her little boy, who has been sick in the night. The story ends with an epiphany. Dorrie is, finally, alone, standing at the kitchen window, rinsing the linen. The passage is violent, even masochistic. Dorrie visualizes her former, autonomous self as a ghost on the other side of the window, smashing the glass and, in an image that evokes *Wuthering Heights* (1847), dragging her wrists across the sharp edges.

"Hurrah for the Hols" also ends with an epiphany, but the mood this time is one of reconciliation. While the story is unsparing in its depiction of a chaotic seaside holiday, Dorrie and her husband appear more closely bonded, sharing a dry sense of humor in the battle of wills. Even in the earlier story, the children are described with great affection, and it is clear that Dorrie's attitude toward her role is not entirely negative. There is complicity between mother and child. The final story, and hence the collection, affirm the maternal drive through the urge to comfort a child in distress, an image that recurs in *In the Driver's Seat*.

Simpson's extensive use of dialogue in her work adds to the dramatic qualities of her stories. Theatrical imagery, spectacle, and display are foregrounded in "Burns and the Bankers" and "Opera," which satirize corporate hospitality, revealing the boorishness, infantilism and venality of the "greed is good" years. "Millennium Blues" strikes an apocalyptic chord, which becomes increasingly evident in Simpson's recent stories.

### IN THE DRIVER'S SEAT

The British title, *Constitutional*, sums up the broad themes of circularity, cycles, and repetition linking this collection. A "constitutional" is a recreational stroll, with no particular goal. In the story of that title, it is a circular walk that maps out the story, as the narrator considers the muddled life cycles of human beings at the start of the new millennium; on the verge of menopause, she finds herself pregnant just at the point when she is contemplating her mortality after the death of a friend. The theme of mortality recurs in "Every Third Thought" and "If I'm Spared," both of them darkly comic responses to cancer. In "If I'm Spared," a philandering journalist is stopped in his tracks by a cancer scare, but, in another story with a circular structure, eventually returns to his old ways. "Early One Morning" describes the school run: a round trip through the urban traffic, covering a short distance in a long time, punctuated by the thoughts of the mother at the wheel and comments from the young passengers. The seasonal cycle represents another aspect of circularity; "The Year's Midnight" is set at a public swimming pool on the winter equinox, a transitional time before the New Year. The protagonist, like so many others in this collection, is also in a transitional phase between youth and old age. However, the key figure in this story is a howling child, whom she is drawn to protect. The title is taken from John Donne's poem "A Nocturnal upon St. Lucy's Day"; "Every Third Thought" is derived from Shakespeare's *The Tempest* (1611). "In the Driver's Seat" and "Up at a Villa" are included in the U.S. edition only, appearing again in the British edition of *In-Flight Entertainment*.

### IN-FLIGHT ENTERTAINMENT

With *In-Flight Entertainment*, Simpson's work moves in two new directions. She addresses the issue of global warming, and she experiments with generic styles and structures. "Diary of an Interesting Year" uses the diary form to paint an apocalyptic vision of what life on Earth will be like for someone born in 2010 by the time she reaches thirty. "The Festival of the Immortals" fills

a literary festival with sessions from canonical authors, including a master class on keeping a notebook with Samuel Taylor Coleridge and Mansfield. "Charm for a Friend with a Lump" is what the title suggests. Formal experimentation is not unheard of in previous collections, nor is the introduction of fantastical elements (see "The Green Room" in *In the Driver's Seat*), but the playful variations of style in this collection, combined with the use of satire and comic irony, help to compensate for any didactic tendencies. Indeed, in several of the stories, including "Diary of an Interesting Year," the protagonist expresses resistance to being preached at by prophets of ecological doom. Both the title story and "The Tipping Point" question the morality of frequent air travel. The latter story was written as a radio commission for the Shakespearean actor Alan Howard.

### OTHER MAJOR WORKS

NONFICTION: *The London Ritz Book of Afternoon Tea: The Art and Pleasures of Taking Tea*, 1986; *The London Ritz Book of English Breakfasts*, 1988.

### BIBLIOGRAPHY

Cox, Ailsa. "Helen Simpson's 'Opera.'" *Journal of the Short Story in English* 51 (2008): 137-148. A reading of the story, looking at the intertextual relationship with Christoph Gluck's opera *Orfeo ed Euridice* (1762) and Simpson's debt to Restoration comedy.

Lepaludier, Laurent. "Theatricality in the Short Story: Staging the Word?" *Journal of the Short Story in English* 51 (2008): 17-28. A general introduction to theatricality in the short story, illustrated with a discussion of Simpson's work.

McInerney, Jay. "Honey, I Loathe the Kids." *The New York Times*, June 17, 2001. There are many reviews of Simpson's work, but this short piece is especially striking because it applies Frank O'Connor's concept of "submerged populations" to the the characters in *Getting a Life*.

Ward, Amanda Eyre. "Helen Simpson." *The Believer* 47 (September 2007): 67-72 Interview of Simpson that discusses the politics of being considered a "domestic" writer.

*Ailsa Cox*

# MONA SIMPSON

**Born:** Green Bay, Wisconsin; June 14, 1957
**Also Known As:** Mona Jandali

PRINCIPAL SHORT FICTION

*"What My Mother Knew,"* 1982
*"Approximations,"* 1983
*"The Day He Left,"* 1983
*"Lawns,"* 1984
*"You Leave Them,"* 1985
*"Victory Mills,"* 1989
*"I Am Here to Tell You It Can Be Done,"* 1990

OTHER LITERARY FORMS

Mona Simpson has published five novels in addition to her short stories. Her first novel, *Anywhere but Here* (1986), explores the complex relationship between mother and daughter; the second novel, *The Lost Father* (1991), continues the story as Mayan Stevenson searches for her missing father. In *A Regular Guy* (1996), Simpson examines the relationship between a geneticist-tycoon and the illegitimate daughter he abandoned. *Off Keck Road* (2000) is the story of a woman who comes of age in her fifties. *My Hollywood* (2010) recounts how a Philippine nanny stabilizes the rocky marriage of a Los Angeles-based couple.

ACHIEVEMENTS

Mona Simpson's short stories have been selected for *Twenty Under Thirty* and the annual *The Best American Short Stories*. She was chosen as one of *Granta*'s Best Young American Novelists. In 1986, she received a National Endowment for the Arts grant and a monetary award from the Whiting Foundation; in 1988, she won a John Simon Guggenheim Memorial Foundation Fellowship and a Hodder Fellowship from Princeton University. She is also the recipient of a Lila Wallace *Reader's Digest* Prize, a *Chicago Tribune* Heartland Prize, and a Literature Award from the American Academy of Arts and Letters.

BIOGRAPHY

Mona Elizabeth Simpson was born in Green Bay, Wisconsin, on June 14, 1957. Her mother's great-grandparents had emigrated from Germany in the nineteenth century and settled in Sheboygan, Wisconsin. Her grandmother moved to Green Bay, where she and her husband raised mink and ran a photo engraving business and gas stations. Simpson's father, originally from Syria, was a college professor; her mother was a speech therapist. As a child, Simpson attended the same school as the children of the Green Bay Packers. After her father abandoned the family, her mother moved to Beverly Hills, California, with Mona and her older brother.

Following graduation from Beverly Hills High School, Simpson earned a B.A. from the University of California at Berkeley in 1979. She worked as a reporter for newspapers in the San Francisco area until 1981, when she won a scholarship to the graduate program in writing at Columbia University in New York City; there she earned an M.F.A. in 1983. She was accepted into Yaddo, the writers' colony at Saratoga Springs, New York, where she was able to devote her time to writing. She married Richard Appel, a public prosecutor, who later became a writer for the television series *The Simpsons*; they would have a son, Gabriel. She taught a writing workshop in the graduate program at New York University, worked as a writing instructor at Bard College, and served as senior editor of *The Paris Review*.

ANALYSIS

Mona Simpson has earned a reputation as a writer who explores the relationships of members of families who struggle in the aftermath of divorce or other situations in which the father leaves the family. She writes about unusual family structures and problems that exist in relationships between parents and children. Her writing is filled with insights into these troubled families as she describes domestic scenes in realistic detail. She depicts her characters' experiences with vivid images and stark details. Although the stories are not autobiographical in content, she draws on her own family background for feelings and insights.

In her work, Simpson combines the minimalist style of Ann Beattie with Anne Tyler's insights into family life. She portrays characters involved in real-life situations who have faced heartbreaking crises yet have found the courage to go on with their lives. Her female protagonists emerge with scars inflicted on them by incompetent or indifferent parents and manage to survive, even thrive. As she tells her stories from the first-person point of view, her young narrators show the pain they have suffered, the longing for a normal family, and finally their acceptance of their lives.

The theme of the lost father dominates Simpson's short fiction. Whether the men die, divorce their spouses, or abandon their families, in one way or another the women are left to care for themselves and their children. The mothers are often inept or poorly equipped for the responsibilities of parenting, forcing the young narrators to strike out on their own to create lives for themselves.

### "What My Mother Knew"

Emily, the narrator of "What My Mother Knew," is a young woman living in New York, struggling to establish an acting career. At her mother's request, she and her brother and sister have flown to California for a visit. After her father died when Emily was a baby, her mother, Elena Hanson, struggled to support herself and her children. Her mother has always dreamed of having a beautiful home, but she could never afford one. Now, at age fifty-nine, she tells her children that she has a surprise for them and drives them to her home in Pacific Heights, a place where Emily says the rich people live. She thinks that the brick house on the hill is the most beautiful house she has ever seen.

When her children question her, Elena admits that she has leased the house for only one year. As she enjoys the view of the Golden Gate Bridge, Emily admires the music and furnishings and can see that her

mother has made every attempt to create a beautiful home for this reunion. As they raise their glasses in a toast, Emily sees the secret in her mother's eyes: She is dying, and this is her last attempt to create the illusion of a happy family life. In a flashback, Emily remembers that when she was twelve years old she was looking through her mother's dresser and found evidence that her mother had been selling her blood for money. Emily finally recognizes how difficult life has always been for her mother, and the two women share an embrace of love and understanding.

### "Approximations"

Melinda, the story's protagonist, lives alone with her mother, Carol, and has no real memories of her father. In the opening paragraph of "Approximations," Melinda, a midwestern teenager, imagines a scene in which her parents are dancing. She has cultivated this fantasy over a period of years, ever since she was four years old and learned that the man in a family photograph was her father. When Melinda finally meets her father, a waiter in Las Vegas, she is disappointed by his obvious lack of interest in her. When Carol marries Jerry, an ice-skating professional, Melinda at first refuses to accept him as a substitute father. As their relationship grows, however, Melinda replaces her dream of reunion with her father with the sense of security and stability that Jerry offers. Simpson's story recounts how a girl grows from childhood to adolescence with an absent father and a vain, immature mother who drifts along refusing to face reality. Through her use of flashbacks and vivid images, Simpson describes how the girl learns to accept the "approximations" that make up the realities of her life and to survive in spite of the indifference and incompetence of her parents.

### "The Day He Left"

A wife and mother trying to survive after her husband leaves her is a common theme in Simpson's fiction, and here again the reader hears this story from the first-person point of view as the wife narrates the story. "The Day He Left" centers on the day a young woman's husband, Steven, leaves her and her daughter, Laura. The couple have lived together for nine years, but Steven has chosen to leave his wife and child to pursue a homosexual relationship; although he has remained on good terms with his family and plans to continue seeing his daughter, Steven wants a different life. The situation is difficult for the wife to accept because she still loves him, and they get along well together. She struggles to save the marriage, but after Steven leaves, she decides to focus her attention on making a life for herself and her daughter.

**"LAWNS"**

"Lawns" was included in *The Best American Short Stories 1986*, edited by Raymond Carver. First published in the *Iowa Review*, "Lawns" is the story of Jenny, a college freshman, who opens the narrative with the sentence, "I steal." Working in the mail room of her dormitory provides her with the opportunity to steal money, presents, and letters addressed to other students. On her first day on the Berkeley campus, she sees a young man, Glenn, riding a lawn mower. She sees him again that evening, the two begin spending time together, and soon she is in love. Jenny is troubled by a secret that she does not want to share with Glenn, and it influences their relationship. Through a series of flashbacks, it becomes clear that Jenny has suffered years of molestation from her father. She finally tells her mother, and her mother forces Jenny's father to leave and visits Jenny on campus to provide support. When Jenny tells her secret to Glenn, the relationship ends, and she feels that her father has cost her everything she wants from life. It is Lauren, Jenny's roommate, who finally offers the sympathy and understanding Jenny needs to go on with her life.

**"VICTORY MILLS"**

"Victory Mills" is included in *Louder Than Words* (1989), a collection of short fiction by twenty-two writers who each contributed a previously unpublished story, the profits from which were donated to organizations fighting hunger, homelessness, and illiteracy. This story follows the lives of three high school friends as they move away from their hometown of Victory Mills to pursue careers in New York City: Katy, the daughter of a woman who works at the mill and a father who has abandoned the family; Tray, the handsome young man she loves; and Alex, a homosexual who has been having an affair with Whipple, an antiques dealer. Although she is a bright student, Katy is not accepted into the college of her choice and opts instead for a career as an actress. She and Alex, a graduate student,

*Mona Simpson* (AP Photo/Tom Keller)

share an apartment, and Tray plays in a band. Disappointed when Tray marries Betsy, his high school girlfriend, Katy marries and has a child. As Katy becomes more famous as an actress, the three friends drift apart. Alex and Katy are reunited at the funeral of Katy's mother, June. In looking through some old papers, Katy finds a letter from her mother that shows she had her heart broken by a man named Rudy. When asked about the letter, Whipple admits that he was the man with whom June had been in love. Told from the points of view of Katy and Alex, the story alternates between the two narrators.

OTHER MAJOR WORKS

LONG FICTION: *Anywhere but Here*, 1986; *The Lost Father*, 1991; *A Regular Guy*, 1996; *Off Keck Road*, 2000; *My Hollywood*, 2010.

BIBLIOGRAPHY

Bing, Jonathan, "Mona Simpson: Return of the Prodigal Father." *Publishers Weekly*, 243 (November 4, 1996): 50. Notes that Simpson's three novels all center on daughters neglected by incompetent parents. In the interview, Simpson says that she considers herself a minimalist and cites Raymond Carver as a writer who has influenced her work. In speaking of her own parents, Simpson says that the feelings and themes in *The Lost Father* were close to her life, but not the details.

Blinkhorn, Lois. "Mona Simpson." *Writer* 114, no. 7 (July, 2001): 26. A profile of Simpson, written after the publication of her novel *Off Keck Road*. Discusses her family and career, the themes of her novels, and her writing style.

Graham, Judith, ed. "Mona Simpson." In *Current Biography Yearbook*. New York: H. W. Wilson, 1993. Provides biographical information about Simpson's family life, education, and early career. Includes brief synopses of her novels, *Anywhere but Here* and *The Lost Father*. Describes her work as marked by striking imagery and shrewd insights into family relationships. Although much of her work seems drawn from her family history, Simpson is quoted as denying that her writing is autobiographical: "It's definitely not a memoir."

McGee, Celia. "Writing for the Crowds, and Avoiding Them." *The New York Times*, July 29, 2010, p.1 An interview and profile of Simpson, in which McGee accompanies Simpson to the Museum of Modern Art to view an exhibition of paintings by Henri Matisse.

Mona (Elizabeth) Simpson. In *Contemporary Literary Criticism*. Vol. 44. Detroit: Gale, 1987. Describes Simpson's first novel, *Anywhere but Here*, as an exploration of the mother-daughter relationship and a blend of family and social themes. Includes reviews of this novel from a number of sources. In her comments to *Current Biography Yearbook* Simpson says that she wrote the first draft in one summer but spent several months revising it. The article includes an excerpt from the novel.

Simpson, Mona. "Thirteen Maxims for Novelists: A Bestselling Author Offers Words of Wisdom on Everything from Committing to Your Craft to Evaluating Criticism." *Writer* 112, no. 10 (October, 2009): 24. Reprints an article that previously appeared in 1992, in which Simpson advises would-be fiction writers about the significance of personal decision making, the need to maintain a writing routine, and the importance of reading their work aloud.

*Judith Barton Williamson*

# JULIA SLAVIN

**Born:** Maryland; 1960

OTHER LITERARY FORMS

PRINCIPAL SHORT FICTION

*The Woman Who Cut Off Her Leg at the Maidstone Club,* 1999

OTHER LITERARY FORMS

In addition to her short-story collection, Julia Slavin has also published a novel, *Carnivore Diet*, (2005).

ACHIEVEMENTS

Julia Slavin's short stories have appeared in a number of well-respected literary journals. She won a Pushcart Prize and the Frederick Exley Fiction Award, both in 1999.

BIOGRAPHY

Julia Slavin grew up in Bethesda, Maryland, among four older brothers. In a *Washington Post* interview, she said that she was "a complete washout at school. I had one of those diseases with initials that when I was growing up just meant screwing up." Her parents influenced her writing career in different ways. Her father, a psychologist, taught her about the unconscious mind and the role of dreams, while her mother gave her a love of language.

Salvin graduated from college with a degree in art history, although her career goal was to go to New York and be a playwright. A few days in New York demonstrated to her how difficult it would be to make a living in this way. She took a job at American Broadcasting Company (ABC) television, where she finally became the producer of *Prime Time Live*. After ten years in New York, she decided to return to writing. She, her husband, and her two daughters moved to Chevy Chase, Maryland, in 1992. She met with success almost immediately, placing several stories in respected literary journals. The appearance of *The Woman Who Cut Off Her Leg at the Maidstone Club* marked her first book-length publication.

ANALYSIS

Julia Slavin's stories are quirky and hip, revealing a quick wit and close attention to the language. Often, Slavin seems to select an image, metaphor, or slang phrase and follow it to its logical (or illogical) conclusion. In so doing, her writing at times resembles Donald Barthelme's surreal flights of fancy. Slavin's language is generally straightforward and uncomplicated, in keeping with her suburban settings. This down-to-earth language, however, contrasts with the sometimes absurd, sometimes fantastic situations in which she places her characters. Thematically, Slavin's stories run more deeply than the humorous and quirky situations might suggest. Indeed, these little stories often embody complex psychological issues and fears. Using figurative language as a starting place, Slavin constructs stories that behave in ways similar to dreams by revealing the inner workings of the human psyche.

With their ironic twists, smooth exteriors, and multilayered interiors, these stories fit comfortably into the postmodern style, revealing and concealing simultaneously. The title story in *The Woman Who Cut Off Her Leg at the Maidstone Club*, in particular seems to poke fun at itself and at a whole social class, maintaining ironic distance from its subject, a common tactic in many postmodern works. At yet other moments, Slavin seems to be aligning herself with the Magical Realists of the late twentieth century; certainly the story "Blight" brings the writer Laura Esquival to mind. Other reviewers compare Slavin's work to that of John Updike or Don DeLillo. In the final analysis, the stories generally work well, leading the reader through the sometimes amusing, sometimes surreal, sometimes horrendous landscapes of the twentieth century. What Slavin's stories share is a concern with the big issues in life: How can individuals ever understand each other? How can people protect each other from harm? How can an individual not be alone in a world that is frequently cruel?

### "SWALLOWED WHOLE"

The opening story in the collection *The Woman Who Cut Off Her Leg at the Maidstone Club*, "Swallowed Whole" takes a common off-color expression and expands it to an absurd degree. The humor in the story depends on the double meaning of "swallowing a man." Slavin commented in an article in *The Washington Post* that the story had its roots in her own fantasy concerning her lawn boy. However, under the humor is a darker subtext concerning fear of pregnancy and miscarriage. In the story, a thirtyish suburban housewife named Sally engages in what starts out as a flirtation with her lawn boy, Chris. Before the story travels more than a few paragraphs, Sally and Chris have engaged in a "deep" kiss, a kiss so deep that Sally ends up swallowing Chris whole. Chris resides in Sally's abdomen for weeks, the two of them carrying on a bizarre internal affair. At the end of the story, Sally awakens to bloody sheets and the sound of Chris's lawn mower outside. The ending forces the reader back into the story to reread the clues that Slavin strews along the way.

The feelings of movement in Sally's abdomen, her ongoing problems with vomiting, and the odd fantasies in which she engages all suggest that what Sally is experiencing is not some fantastic encounter with her lawn boy. Rather, these all point to a pregnancy. Sally's concern that her "affair" with Chris is distracting her from her husband also highlights another common fear during pregnancy--that the new baby will interfere with the normal functioning of the couple, particularly the couple's sex life. When Sally says that she drinks a household cleanser to rid herself of Chris, it is difficult to determine if this is the common pregnancy fantasy of wishing to rid oneself of the fetus or if Sally truly does ingest large amounts of cleanser. In any event, when she rouses herself, she finds that her sheets are bloody and that Chris has left her body, clearly a signal that what she has really experienced is a miscarriage. Again, Slavin's images are so dreamlike that is difficult to separate the fantasies within fantasies. It is possible

that Sally dreams the bloody sheets, just as she has dreamed having Chris in her belly; such blood-filled dreams are also common during pregnancy. In any event, Slavin has craftily woven these common pregnancy images and fantasies with the controlling metaphor, swallowing a man.

### "BABYPROOFING"

In the story "Babyproofing," Slavin once again uses a common expression and carries it to the extreme. At the same time, she also uncovers one of the deepest fears young parents can have--that something will happen to their child as the result of their own carelessness. As the story opens, a young couple has put themselves into the hands of Mitzy Baker, the owner of a company that will come into a home and render it completely harmless to a child. By the time Mitzy is finished with the house, however, all the couple's belongings have disappeared, to be replaced with thick foam padding. Even the trees in the yard have been removed. Perhaps the most disturbing removal of all, however, is the removal of the husband as a safety hazard. By the end of the story, the husband forces his way back into his transformed house to find his wife and child sitting on the floor. Surprisingly, the family is not unhappy with the results of the babyproofing. Walter says,

> The three of us sit on the cushy floor, covered with Mitzy Baker's foam padding. . . . Caroline can drag herself up on her toys and fall and not feel a thing. . . . Tomorrow we can wake up and relax, finally. Tonight we can sleep without dreaming.

Slavin identifies a number of common fears and fantasies in this story. Certainly, most new parents consider extreme and extravagant ways of keeping their child safe. Moreover, what father has not felt slightly superfluous in the flurry of activity that overtakes a new family when the baby comes home? Slavin's ending also points to the sacrifice young parents are willing to make; while they may be willing to take risks with their own lives, they will sacrifice their own freedoms and individuality for the sake of protecting their child. In so doing, Slavin demonstrates that the instinctual protection of the young still overrides postmodern individuality.

## "DENTOPHILIA"

A beautiful woman named Helen, much beloved by her husband, begins to sprout teeth all over her body. This is the unlikely situation in the short story "Dentophilia." In this case, Slavin takes the mythological motif of the "vagina dentata" and gives it a contemporary twist. Psychologists claim that the motif of the vagina filled with teeth surfaces so frequently across cultures because it reveals deep, subconscious fears of castration and the dangers of sexual intercourse. The symbolic element of the story seems most clear after Helen's deciduous teeth all fall out and permanent teeth take their place, a process that roughly coincides with puberty in young women. Further, Helen tells the narrator that her "wisdom teeth" have erupted "down there." Clearly, the juxtaposition of the words "wisdom" and "teeth," along with the indication that they have erupted in Helen's vagina, point to the notion of biblical wisdom, that of "knowing" one's spouse. After all, it was partaking of the fruit of the tree of knowledge that led to the expulsion from Eden. Thus, Slavin seems to be suggesting that sexual intercourse, which is a kind of wisdom, is not without dangers. For the couple in the story, Helen's dentition leads to her death, and the narrator is bereft, alone on a beach that resembles in its own way the lost paradise.

## "LIVES OF THE INVERTEBRATES"

An eight-pound lobster named Max, yet another creature with a bony exoskeleton, stars in another of Slavin's odd little stories. The narrator of the story soon renames Max "Gina," after discovering that he is really a she. The relationship between the narrator and Gina is nothing if not obsessive. Gina attacks a young zookeeper responsible for the invertebrates when she exhibits sexual interest in the narrator. In an odd twist, it seems that the narrator is not only obsessed with Gina but also identifies with her. He notes that they are about the same age. The narrator is metaphorically a "horny" creature, given his constant thoughts of sexual encounters; Gina is literally horny. Thus, although Gina is identified as female, she continues to behave like a male. Indeed, even the imagery that Slavin uses to describe Gina suggests something horrifically phallic about the creature. She is an invertebrate, yet she is hard and stiff, just as the human penis, a soft "invertebrate" most of the

time, becomes hard and stiff when preparing for sex. Even the attack on the invertebrate keeper resonates with sexual violence: "Gina, who'd been slack in my hands suddenly arched the front section of her body back . . . she lunged toward Katherine, scissoring through her upper lip with her cutter claw." Consequently, in spite of the sex change of the creature, in spite of the unlikeliness of the situation, Slavin is able to turn a flight of fantasy into a study of psychological fixation and obsession.

## OTHER MAJOR WORKS

LONG FICTION: *Carnivore Diet*, 2005.

## BIBLIOGRAPHY

Lewis, Nicole. "Outer Suburbia: Julia Slavin's Stories Chart Some Very Unfamiliar Territory." *The Washington Post*, September 15, 1999, p. C01. A feature article on Slavin and her short-story collection. Provides some useful background information on the writer, as well as comments from Slavin on the writing of the book.

Pakenham, Michael. "Debut Stories by Julia Slavin: Deliciously Insane." Review of *The Woman Who Cut Off Her Leg at the Maidstone Club*, by Julia Slavin. *The Baltimore Sun*, July 25, 1999, p. 10F. Another reviewer noting the fantastic, surreal, and dreamlike quality of the stories. Calls the book "wonderfully strong, delightfully readable stuff."

Reynolds, Susan Salter. "Voyage to the Future of Fiction." Review of *The Woman Who Cut Off Her Leg at the Maidstone Club*, by Julia Slavin. *Newsday*, July 18, 1999, p. B12. Reviews *The Woman Who Cut Off Her Leg at the Maidstone Club* in the context of contemporary fiction. Argues that the stories exhibit "a quietly desperate, normalized insanity that has a brave tradition in literature."

Rosenfeld, Lucinda. "Down and Dirty." *Harper's Bazaar* (July, 1999): 144. Rosenfeld traces male-female relationships in several works of contemporary fiction, including *The Woman Who Cut Off Her Leg at the Maidstone Club*. Suggests that Slavin's characters "find their internal malaise mirrored in the external world."

Taylor, Charles. "Nightmares on Elm Street." *The New York Times Book Review* (August 15, 1999): 7. Taylor comments on Slavin's notion of the grotesque and points out that her subject is the fear and anxiety of contemporary life.

Wittman, Juliet. "Storied Presents: Two Collections." Review of *The Woman Who Cut Off Her Leg at the Maidstone Club*, by Julia Slavin. *The Washington Post*, September 9, 1999, p. C2. Wittman calls Slavin "a major discovery." She notes the surreal, fantastic qualities of the stories and suggests that Slavin could be compared to Franz Kafka.

Zeidner, Lisa. "What Rough Beast: Review of *Carnivore Diet*, by Julia Slavin. *The York Times Book Review* (August 28, 2005): 18. Zeidner's review of Slavin's first novel points out the similarities in style and content between this novel and Slavin's short fiction.

*Diane Andrews Henningfeld*

---

# JANE SMILEY

**Born:** Los Angeles, California; September 26, 1949

PRINCIPAL SHORT FICTION

*The Age of Grief: A Novella and Stories,* 1987
*"Ordinary Love"* and *"Good Will": Two Novellas,* 1989

OTHER LITERARY FORMS

Jane Smiley has published several novels, as well as short fiction. In addition to studies of family life, she has experimented with several novelistic subgenres, including a murder thriller (*Duplicate Keys*, 1984) and a historical epic (*The Greenlanders*, 1988). With the publication of her academic satire *Moo* in 1995 and the 1998 picaresque novel *The All-True Travels and Adventures of Lidie Newton* (an exploration of the intersections of racism and violence in American history inspired in part by the 1993 Oklahoma City bombing), Smiley completed a self-imposed task of writing fiction in the four major literary modes: epic (*The Greenlanders*), tragedy (*A Thousand Acres*, 1991), comedy (*Moo*), and romance (*The All-True Travels and Adventures of Lidie Newton*). She subsequently published several other novels, including *Horse Heaven* (2000), *Good Faith* (2003) *Ten Days in the Hills* (2007), and *Private Life* (2010). Smiley has written nonfiction books, including *A Year at the Races: Reflections on Horses, Humans, Love, Money, and Luck* (2004), *Thirteen Ways of Looking at the Novel* (2005), and *The Man Who Invented the Computer: The Biography of John Atanasoff, Digital Pioneer* (2010). She has also published the young adult novels *The Georges and the Jewels* (2009) and *A Good Horse* (2010).

In 1996, Smiley found herself unwittingly at the center of an editorial firestorm when she published an essay in *Harper's* that challenged the canonized status of Mark Twain's *Adventures of Huckleberry Finn* (1884) by criticizing its moral dishonesty and aesthetic flaws, touting instead Harriet Beecher Stowe's *Uncle Tom's Cabin: Or, Life Among the Lowly* (1851-1852, serial; 1852, book) as an underappreciated realist and morally serious masterpiece.

ACHIEVEMENTS

Jane Smiley's short fiction, for which she received a Pushcart Prize in 1977 and O. Henry Awards in 1982, 1985, and 1988, has drawn consistent praise for its linguistic economy and incisive detail in the service of the complex mysteries of American family life. *The Age of Grief*, which signaled a new gathering of creative force in Smiley's writing, was nominated for the National Book Critics Circle Award. With *A Thousand Acres*, a novel retelling the family drama of William Shakespeare's *King Lear* (pr. c. 1605-1606, pb. 1608) in terms of an Iowa farm family, Smiley attained new levels of national and even international recognition, winning the Pulitzer Prize (1992) and the National Book Critics Circle Award for fiction (1991), in addition to a number of regional awards. In 2001, Smiley was inducted into the American Academy of Arts and Letters and in 2006, she received the PEN/USA Lifetime Achievement Award for Literature.

### BIOGRAPHY

Born to James LaVerne Smiley and Frances Graves Nuelle on September 26, 1949, during her father's military tour of duty in California, Jane Graves Smiley was transplanted at a young age to the Midwest and grew up in a suburb of St. Louis, Missouri. The daughter of a writer-mother, she attended Vassar College and received her B.A. in English in 1971; in composing her first novel as her senior thesis, she discovered that "this was for me, this creation of worlds." Smiley completed a master of fine arts degree at the University of Iowa in 1976, and she received an M.A. (1975) and a Ph.D. (1978) in medieval literature from the same institution. While earning her doctorate, she received a Fulbright Fellowship in 1976-1977 which allowed her to spend time in Iceland, where her study of Norse sagas laid the groundwork for her epic novel *The Greenlanders*.

In 1981, Smiley began teaching literature and creative writing as a member of the faculty of Iowa State University, where she became a full professor in 1989. In 1981 and 1987, she also served as visiting professor at the University of Iowa. Though awarded the title of distinguished professor in 1992, she left Iowa State in 1996 to become a full-time writer at a Northern California horse-breeding ranch she bought with the substantial earnings provided her from the book sales of and film rights to *A Thousand Acres*.

Smiley has commented that a childhood shadowed by the existence of the atomic bomb and an adolescence marked by the invention of "the Pill" have given her two major subjects: "sex and apocalypse." Her personal history indicates a familiarity with the challenges of family life. A first marriage to John Whiston in 1970, while she was still at Vassar, lasted until 1975. Her second marriage, to editor William Silag in 1978, produced daughters Phoebe and Lucy. A third marriage in 1987 to screenwriter Stephen Mark Mortensen led to the birth of son Axel James when Smiley was forty-three years old; the couple later divorced. Among her

avocations Smiley lists cooking, swimming, playing piano, quilting, and raising horses on her California ranch.

### ANALYSIS

David Leavitt has called Jane Smiley "the contemporary American master of the novella form," and she herself regards the novella's "more meditative" thematic concentration and streamlined plotting as particularly congenial to her artistic ends. Having begun her career as what she calls a "devoted modernist" preoccupied with the nihilistic anomie dramatized in the great literature of the early twentieth century, Smiley found herself losing that alienated edge when she first became pregnant. In trying to resolve the ensuing creative challenge that plagued her-- "Can mothers think and write?"--she discovered her true subject: the continually shifting dynamics of familial relationships. Her best work captures the intricate dance of need, love, retribution, and loss that entwines competing subjectivities within every family. Smiley has proved especially adept at writing the maternal experience into

*Jane Smiley* (Ulf Anderson/Getty Images)

literature, challenging the familiar cultural idealizations and caricatures of "mother love" produced by writers invariably engaging their subject from the position of the child; she regards her version of parenting as "a critique and correction" of both the child and the father's stories. Smiley's investigations are not limited to female protagonists, however. She regularly assumes male personas and argues that doing so is a less arduous imaginative feat for her than writing as a mother, since few viable models exist for the latter. Smiley's versatile experiments in character, voice, and plotline are well suited to short-fictional forms. The psychological immediacy she achieves bespeaks a compassionate interest in decent people caught at dramatic crossroads, where they must assess the compromises and delusions that have shaped their lives.

Although an extremely eclectic writer in terms of the range of projects she has completed, in her short fiction Smiley offers perhaps the purest distillation of her long-standing fascination with the domestic spaces individuals construct as assumed havens from the otherwise chaotic assaults of daily living--spaces inevitably disrupted, despite the best intentions of their decently bourgeois inhabitants, by their own convulsive desires. Smiley discovered early in her career that the critical contempt regularly directed toward such "feminine" domestic themes willfully ignored a rich dramatic venue into which she quickly moved and made her own (propelled not a little by her newly married status and plans to raise a family of her own). She explains that her writerly endeavors show a sustained interest

> in how people relate to the groups that they're in (whether those groups are families or communities), in how power is negotiated among people, in character idiosyncrasies, and in the relationship of power to love.

Smiley not only demonstrates her attunement to the mundane rhythms and speech of family life but also deftly captures the hunger for connection and empathy that the nuclear family promises to satisfy--doing so only to reveal its heartbreakingly predictable insufficiency. Loyalties abruptly give way to shattering betrayals, and love fails repeatedly to transcend the imperatives of sexual longing or personal doubt. Family members and childhood friends face the challenge of finding ways to survive their tortured devotions, a pattern critic Vivian Gornick in *The End of the Novel of Love* (1997) laments as evidence of the diminished belief in romantic love's transformative potential that has characterized fiction since the 1960's. Gornick fails, however, to recognize that Smiley's emotional realism is as firmly grounded in her medievalist training as in her contemporary worldview, both of which posit a tragic and incomprehensible universe in which the steady turn of the wheel of fortune insistently exposes the transitoriness of all earthly pursuits, pleasure as well as profit. Within that context the misery that fallible human beings inflict upon themselves and others--violence, sexual betrayal, greed, and envy--continually upends the most strenuous efforts to create social harmony, be it in the family or the community at large, and even love proves as likely to destroy as to create. In such a world, Smiley's most admirable characters are those who, despite their limitations and failures, stumble toward a personal vision of moral responsibility and communal obligation that both enables their survival and dignifies their self-awareness.

### THE AGE OF GRIEF

*The Age of Grief* is a loosely constructed volume. Consisting of five short stories and a novella, it presents an array of characters who range from active aggressors to passive victims in the contemporary battles for and against emotional commitment raging among adults not yet willing to see themselves in their parents' shoes. The stories evoke a cultural ambiance of fragmentation and insubstantiality through which the longed-for idyll of family life demolished in the volume's closing novella achieves its tragic incandescence.

Thus *The Age of Grief* breaks essentially into two parts: The short-story section examines family life through a series of characters on the periphery of domesticity. In "Lily" and "The Pleasure of Her Company," the female protagonists are admiring outsiders to the marriages they observe, and both find themselves unprepared for the destruction of their illusions. Their limited notions about the potential for sudden psychological violence within seemingly conventional contexts result in part from the absence of such entanglements in their own lives. Lily's emotional "virginity" permits the freedom she needs for her work as a poet but also leads her to meddle unwittingly in the heart of marital darkness, whose capacity for long-borne compromise and truce she disastrously misreads. Florence in "The Pleasure of Her Company" (one of Smiley's O. Henry Award-winning stories) is allowed a more graceful if ironically inflected exit. Faced with the dissolution of a marriage that she once regarded as ideal, she rejects the cynic's conclusion that all love is delusion and instead pursues her own blossoming relationship, believing that "it's worth finding out for yourself." Florence, unlike Lily, risks emotional involvement because the experience it will provide will be its own reward, despite clear evidence of its price.

Within this collection Smiley is most harshly disposed toward those who orchestrate their emotional destinies with the same professional calculation they apply to their stock portfolios, as does the female letter writer of "Jeffrey, Believe Me." Smiley caricatures the narcissistic self-gratification of upwardly mobile urbanites by making this protagonist so intent on satisfying her biological clock that she seduces a gay male friend to achieve pregnancy and then willfully resists personal responsibility for the other human beings she exploits. Her opposite in the volume is the male protagonist of "Long Distance," whose odyssey to join his brothers for the Christmas holidays prompts a reassessment of his callousness toward a Japanese woman with whom he has had an affair. Never having acknowledged the continual negotiations at the heart of family life, he now sees the moral bankruptcy in his self-serving flight from attachments.

Emotional stock-taking of this kind is central to Smiley's most deeply felt writing, and hence her narratives are often most effective when they enter the unmediated psychological terrain of the first person. Her characteristic tone, a laconic meditative stillness, emerges for the first time in *The Age of Grief* in "Dynamite," a piece in which the outsiders of the earlier stories give way to the hybrid insider/outsider Sandy, a woman in early middle age caught between lifelong conflicting impulses to connect and to disrupt. Oscillating between past and present, as well as between the discrete identities into which her life has split as a result of the radical politics that sent her underground for twenty years, she juggles a desire for the mother she feels she has never known with a restless urge "to do the most unthought-of thing, the itch to destroy what is made--the firm shape of my life, whether unhappy, as it was, or happy, as it is now." Memory and fantasy weave an elaborate web of old and new longings that explain her wild behavior swings and puncture the bourgeois stability that she seems, superficially, to covet. Sandy's paradoxes defy taming and make her representative of the struggle against self that is typical of Smiley's characters.

With *The Age of Grief*, Smiley moves full force into that theme, shifting the angle of vision from the aggressor to the victim of another family in crisis. By so doing she exposes the insufficiency of such categories to explain the emotional upheavals that beset "normality" from within its own preserve. The novella centers on dentist David Hurst, whose wife and professional partner in a busy dentistry practice suddenly falls in love with another man. At the center of the drama is David's struggle with his knowledge of his wife's affair and his choice to remain silent about it. Smiley is familiar not only with the routines of parenting small children but also with the social changes that have necessitated fathers becoming full participants in all the nuances of that routine. David is intimately involved in the daily lives--and illnesses--of his young daughters, aged seven, five, and two. The emotional tyranny of Leah, a toddler who insistently demands all her father's attention, mimics the jealous ownership of a lover and stands in bittersweet counterpoint to the waning love between her parents. Neither spouse can speak to the other of their estrangement, and in his anguish David concludes:

> I am thirty-five years old, and it seems to me that I have arrived at the age of grief. . . . It is not only that we know that love ends, children are stolen, parents die feeling that their lives have been meaningless. . . . It is more that the barriers between the circumstances of oneself and of the rest of the world have

broken down, after all--after all that schooling, all that care . . . it is the same cup of pain that every mortal drinks from.

The family moves to the end of dissolution as the obsession of David's wife, Dana, finally upends her carefully maintained schedule altogether and for the first time keeps her away from home for twenty-four hours. When she inexplicably reappears, the couple agree not to discuss what has led her to return. With a generosity of spirit--or failure of will--steeped in sadness, David offers by way of explanation his dearly bought insight that "marriage is a small container after all. . . . Two inner lives . . . burst out of it and out of it, cracking it, deforming it." Thus Smiley reveals the impossible burden placed on the emotional bonds of family and marriage and quietly ponders the challenge of learning to live with diminished faith in the future.

### ORDINARY LOVE

Each of the novellas constituting *"Ordinary Love" and "Good Will"* offers another sustained examination into the disruption of a once-idyllic household. While strikingly dissimilar in story line, atmospherics, and point of view, the two works together provide variations on a common theme: the loss of parental illusions about one's protective power and authority within the family circle and the compensatory wisdom of discovering the mysterious otherness and humanity of one's children.

The first-person narrator of *Ordinary Love*, a fifty-two-year-old divorced Iowan mother of five adult children, typifies Smiley's clear-eyed rejection of sentimental pieties about the heartland matriarch. Rachel Kinsella does indeed tend to the baking of cakes and spoiling of grandchildren as she awaits the homecoming of a long-absent son. Her story, however, matter-of-factly told in a voice both accepting and unrepentant, includes the jarring paradox of her having, years earlier, proudly borne five babies in five years with a doting, ambitious doctor husband, then inexplicably initiating an adulterous affair that ruptured the family idyll so completely that even her identical twin sons were separated in the ensuing custody battles. Rachel's history, an arc of emotional devastation and recovery, leads her in middle age to a maturity brought into being out of wildness, grief, and tenacity.

Rachel's perspective, however, is not self-serving. She admits the contradictions driving her emotional life: the allure of creating a timeless domestic haven free from the typical ravages of family life, her relief upon being freed from the marriage that lay as the cornerstone to that haven, and her "terror" upon entering the void left when her family collapsed and her children disappeared for a time from her life. Smiley plots Rachel's history as an arc of emotional loss and recovery, and in late middle age she is self-possessed and steady, a mature woman who, because she has consciously made herself anew out of wildness, grief, and perseverance, now possesses the strength to confront the ongoing costs of the past within the present.

The novella's present-tense drama, while inseparable from the rupture of twenty years earlier, involves Rachel's effort to manage the return of her son Michael from a two-year stint as a teacher in poverty-stricken India. In a family where each separation reprises the primal severance of mother from child and sibling from sibling, Michael's transformation overseas exposes once again the instability afflicting even the most fundamental human ties. Within this charged atmosphere, a series of confidences delivers a powerful lesson about the tantalizing impenetrability of each family member's private reality. Rachel tells her children for the first time of the love affair that upended their young lives; her elder daughter, Ellen, retaliates with a description of their neglect by a vengeful father who transplanted them to London; Michael reveals his destructive relationship with a married woman, which resulted in an abortion and the loss of the woman he really loved. The shock created by each of these "secrets" is multiple, and Rachel registers them all. Unlike her former husband, she struggles to subordinate the possessive assumptions of a parent and instead tries "to accept the mystery of my children, of the inexplicable ways they diverge from parental expectations, of how, however much you know or remember of them, they don't quite add up." She muses on the disruptive irrationality of human desire and realizes that Michael's new maturity reflects his own discovery of that fact. The real fruit of knowledge, she concedes, lies not simply in one's own suffering but in learning one's potential to inflict suffering on others, especially those one holds most dear. With a fatalism balanced against faith in the human capacity for renewal, Rachel squarely confronts the fact that she cannot spare her children life's bitterest lesson--the perverse and unrelenting hunger of the heart for what it cannot have and that given the destructive pressure of the inner life, a parent may unforgivably offer her children "the experience of perfect family happiness, and the certain knowledge that it could not last."

## Good Will

*Good Will* places its stark dramatic enactment of another adult's acquiring wisdom too late within a matrix of suspense about what is coming rather than through a melancholy retrospective about what has been. In placing a mother's story beside a father's, Smiley describes the first piece in this volume as "more feminine . . . things are hidden and revealed," while the second is "more masculine" and "linear." *Good Will* also shows Smiley's talent for exposing the tensions generated by the endless daily struggles for psychological control underlying even the smoothest family surfaces. Here the first-person narrator is Bob Miller, a Vietnam veteran who has systematically created a world for his nuclear family of three which exists parallel to, not within, mainstream American society. The novella opens eighteen years into his countercultural experiment, when the rearing of the child he and his wife Liz thought would complete their idyll begins instead to erode their illusory self-sufficiency.

Bob's considerable talents as a craftsman correspond to his principled determination to live by a moral code purged of the empty materialism of his time. Slowly, however, he reveals the contours of a personality whose virtues slip over into dogmatism and whose ingenuity is actually trained on keeping his loved ones within the range of his authority. The evidence of discord within Bob's self-willed paradise comes from the very people he believes to be his allies. Liz becomes a member of a fundamental religious community whose pull on her suggests the spiritual hunger she cannot satisfy through her marriage. More sinister and ultimately more devastating is the racist hostility conceived seemingly in a vacuum by their seven-year-old son for the African American newcomer whose affluent home life focuses the boy's rage at his own marginality. Tommy's

innocence of the world offers him no defense against the corrosive envy he conceives for Annabelle's possessions, and in coolly destroying them he forces his parents to confront their arrogance in assuming they have the right, much less the power, to direct Tommy's responses to the world.

Finally even Bob finds that he has not renounced the world as completely as he has assumed: Lydia Harris, Annabelle's mother and a professor of mathematics, whose specialty is the suggestive realm of probability, offers her own fascination for him. To compensate for Tommy's vandalism he does various odd jobs for her and becomes preoccupied with her home, her personality, her assessment of his life. To the degree that he feels drawn to the mother, he finds himself growing perversely angrier toward the daughter on whom she lavishes much affectionate concern. Like Tom, Bob struggles with the shock of seeing the limitations of his own meager existence so baldly exposed.

Bob's stubborn refusal to accept his family's dissatisfaction with their lives contributes to a steadily escalating tension, which climaxes in a catastrophe that unfolds with the surreal pacing of a dream. The drowning of Tommy's beloved pony, Sparkle, is closely followed by an arson fire that destroys the Harris home, and Tommy's complicity becomes increasingly undeniable. His real target is the father who has isolated him from the world of his peers and who has refused him his own choices in that world.

The spotlight Tommy casts on his parents puts in motion a grim social-services machinery that has all the inexorability of a Dreiserian tragedy. Demands for reparations by the insurance company force the sale of the Millers' homestead and the conversion of both parents to wage earners struggling simply to keep up with the expenses of apartment living. All three family members enter therapy and face the threat of further legal action for the "recklessness" that led them to live without the amenities that could have enabled interception of, and intervention in, the unfolding crisis. Bob's anguish takes the form of a metaphysical stoicism that his wife regards as more stubborn unwillingness to yield to processes beyond his control, but his thoughts reveal that he has conceded to the incoherence of modern life that his farm was an attempt to keep at bay:

Let us have fragments, I say. . . . if no wholes are made, then it seems to me that I can live in town well enough . . . and remember the vast, inhuman peace of the stars pouring across the night sky above the valley.

He rejects efforts to buffer the grinding truth of Eden's evanescence or of his own role as a worm at the very heart of that dream.

In her fictional preoccupation with the family, then, Smiley has decidedly not abandoned her early artistic attraction to the condition of modernist anomie that inspired her to become a writer. Rather, she has concentrated upon the innumerable ways in which the family, that bulwark against meaninglessness of middle-class American faith, dramatizes the unbridgeable chasm between an individual's simultaneous capacity for selflessness and self-love and the terrible grief to be had in experiencing that gap.

OTHER MAJOR WORKS

LONG FICTION: *Barn Blind*, 1980; *At Paradise Gate*, 1981; *Duplicate Keys*, 1984; *The Greenlanders*, 1988; *A Thousand Acres*, 1991; *Moo*, 1995; *The All-True Travels and Adventures of Lidie Newton*, 1998; *Horse Heaven*, 2000; *Good Faith*, 2003; *Ten Days in the Hills*, 2007; *Private Life*, 2010.

NONFICTION: *Catskill Crafts: Artisans of the Catskill Mountains*, 1988; *Charles Dickens*, 2002; *A Year at the Races: Reflections on Horses, Humans, Love, Money, and Luck*, 2004; *Thirteen Ways of Looking at the Novel*, 2005; *The Man Who Invented the Computer: The Biography of John Atanasoff, Digital Pioneer*, 2010.

CHILDREN'S LITERATURE: *The Georges and the Jewels*, 2009; *A Good Horse*, 2010.

EDITED TEXT: *Best New American Voices, 2006*, 2005.

BIBLIOGRAPHY

Bernays, Anne. "Toward More Perfect Unions." Review of *The Age of Grief*, by Jane Smiley. *The New York Times Book Review* (September 6, 1987): 12. Bernays praises Smiley's powerful use of short-fictional forms to examine the contours of troubled personal relationships. Most of the commentary is devoted to the "splendid" title novella, which offers "a poignant and rich meditation on the nature of love and change."

Carlson, Ron. "King Lear in Zebulon County." Review of *A Thousand Acres*, by Jane Smiley. *The New York Times Book Review* (November 3, 1991): 12. Carlson examines the ways in which Smiley adopts the terrain of *King Lear* to explore contemporary family dynamics in rural Iowa. He praises the novel's skill in conveying the interplay of factors--nature, business, community--that shape the farmer's life. He also cites the powerful impact of telling the tale through the eyes of the eldest daughter of the tyrant-father at the center of the tale.

Humphreys, Josephine. "Perfect Family Self-Destructs." Review of *"Ordinary Love" and "Good Will,"* by Jane Smiley. *The New York Times Book Review* (November 5, 1989): 1, 45. Calling the novella a fictional form "most closely resembling a troubled dream," Humphreys discusses Smiley's artistry in *"Ordinary Love" and "Good Will"* and praises her provocative investigations into the role of power, imagination, and desire in family life. Argues that the first piece in the collection explores the consequences of desire, while the second involves "imagination as an act of power," the two together elaborating "the myth of the family, told by two principals: an Eve and an Adam," both of whom achieve a "realized ignorance" as "one ancient form of wisdom."

Kakutani, Michiko. Review of *The Age of Grief*, by Jane Smiley. *The New York Times*, August 26, 1987, p. C21. This strong review examines each of the pieces in the collection and pays particular attention to the novella *The Age of Grief*, wherein Smiley proves her "talent for delineating the subtle ebb and flow of familial emotions" and her attunement for the multiple levels on which everyday communication operates in such close quarters--so much so that "we are left with a sense of having participated in her characters' lives."

Leavitt, David. "Of Harm's Way and Farm Ways." *Mother Jones* 14 (December, 1989): 44-45. Leavitt praises the probing power of *"Ordinary Love" and "Good Will,"* calling Smiley "one of our wisest writers" for her insight into the tragic center of her characters' most admirable dreams. He also cites her knowledgeable evocation of the real-world activities that fill their lives and her sensitivity to the physical landscape through which they move.

Nakadate, Neil. *Understanding Jane Smiley*. Rev. ed. Columbia: University of South Carolina Press, 2010. A close examination of Smiley's work, devoting a chapter each to *The Age of Grief* and *"Ordinary Love" and "Good Will."*

Smiley, Jane. "The Adventures of Jane Smiley." Interview by Katie Bacon. *Atlantic Unbound* (May 28, 1998). In this interview about the influences shaping *The All-True Travels and Adventures of Lidie Newton*, Smiley discusses her controversial 1996 *Harper's* essay comparing Twain's *Huckleberry Finn* unfavorably to Stowe's *Uncle Tom's Cabin*, her interest in the unresolved question of race in American life, her belief that all of her writing is on some level historical fiction, and her continually evolving perspective on the family drama as literary subject.

_____. "Cheltenham Festival: Talking About a Revolution, Feminism, Horses, Sex, and Slavery--Jane Smiley's Novels Are a Potent Mixture of All of Them." Interview by James Urquhart. *The Independent*, October 16, 1998. Even though it is plagued with factual errors, this 1998 interview with Smiley provides illuminating commentary on the ways feminism informs her perspective on the family as a "political system," "what it means to be a daughter," and her antiromantic sensibility.

_____. "A Conversation with Jane Smiley." Interview by Lewis Burke Frumkes. *The Writer* 112 (May, 1999): 20-22. Smiley discusses her work, her favorite contemporary writers, and her own writing habits.

_____. Interview by Matthew Rothschild. *Progressive* 71, no. 12 (December, 2007): 29-33. Focuses on Smiley's political opinions and her decision to write a blog for the *Huffington Post*. Smiley states that all of her novels are political and liberal.

_____. Interview by Marcelle Thiebaux. *Publishers Weekly* 233 (April 1, 1988): 65-66. Notes that in all her books, Smiley focuses on the theme of family life. Smiley discusses the research that goes into her writing.

*Barbara Kitt Seidman*

---

# LEE SMITH

**Born:** Grundy, Virginia; November 1, 1944

PRINCIPAL SHORT FICTION

*Cakewalk,* 1981

*Me and My Baby View the Eclipse: Stories by Lee Smith,* 1990

*The Christmas Letters: A Novella,* 1996

*News of the Spirit,* 1997

*Mrs. Darcy and the Blue-Eyed Stranger: New and Selected Stories,* 2010

OTHER LITERARY FORMS

Lee Smith's first published work was a novel, *The Last Day the Dogbushes Bloomed*. It was followed by the novels *Something in the Wind* (1971) and *Fancy Strut* (1973). After a seven-year hiatus, Smith brought out what has been called the first work of her second career, *Black Mountain Breakdown* (1980), which was followed by additional novels, including *Saving Grace* (1995), *The Last Girls* (2002), and *On Agate Hill* (2006). In 2010, she published her fourth short-fiction collection, *Mrs. Darcy and the Blue-Eyed Stranger: New and Selected Stories*, featuring a handful of new stories, as well as some previously published works.

ACHIEVEMENTS

Lee Smith received a Book-of-the-Month Club fellowship in 1967, O. Henry Awards in 1978 and 1980, a Sir Walter Raleigh Award in 1984, a North Carolina Award for Literature in 1985, a Lila Wallace-*Reader's Digest* Award in 1995, and an Award in Literature from the American Academy of Arts and Letters in 1999.

## Biography

Lee Smith was born on November 1, 1944, in Grundy, Virginia, a mining town in the southwestern part of the state. Her father, Ernest Lee Smith, was in business, running the local Ben Franklin store; her mother, Virginia Marshall Smith, was a teacher. An only child who was born to her parents late in their lives, Lee had a watchful and observant childhood, spending much of her time reading and writing.

Smith was educated at St. Catherine's School in Richmond, Virginia, and then studied in the well-known writing program at Hollins College. Her first novel, *The Last Day the Dogbushes Bloomed*, developed out of a senior writing project. It was published and earned her a Book-of-the-Month Club fellowship. In 1967, Smith was graduated from Hollins College and married the poet James E. Seay, the father of her two children. The marriage later ended in divorce.

From 1968 to 1969, Smith was in Tuscaloosa, Alabama, working as a reporter for the *Tuscaloosa News* and gathering the material that would appear in her third novel, *Fancy Strut*. In 1971, the year her second novel appeared, she began teaching seventh grade in Nashville, Tennessee; in 1974, after the publication of *Fancy Strut*, she moved to Durham, North Carolina, to teach language arts and continue writing.

By 1977, Smith was teaching creative writing at the University of North Carolina at Chapel Hill. After three of her books lost money for her publishers, however, her fourth novel was rejected, and other publishers followed suit. As years went by, Smith began to believe that her career as a writer was ending. She credits a new agent and a new editor, one who wished to work actively with her, for enabling her to begin writing again. The critics were impressed with *Black Mountain Breakdown*, the first book from Smith's second period.

In 1981, Smith joined the faculty of North Carolina State University at Raleigh. In 1985, she married Hal Crowther. Smith's growing importance can be seen in the increasing number of interviews with her, the articles about her work published each year, the full-length studies of her, and her major awards.

## Analysis

With the publication of *Black Mountain Breakdown*, Lee Smith was recognized as one of the outstanding southern writers of her generation; the novels and short stories that appeared after *Black Mountain Breakdown* have only strengthened this estimation. Like earlier southern writers, Smith has an eye for interesting characters and an ear for colorful speech, as well as both a sense of place and a sense of humor. Except when she reaches back into history, Smith's settings are the New South, and her characters are ordinary people, most of them trying to come to terms with their ordinary lives. Perhaps the quality for which Smith is most admired is her compassion; although she dramatizes her characters' limitations and often satirizes their pretensions, she respects them as human beings, who cope as best they can with the human condition, and she admires their individuality and singularity.

Smith's short stories are set primarily in the contemporary South of shopping malls and convenience stores, where dreams and hopes are defined not by tradition or faith but rather by the images on the television screen. Her protagonists are apparently ordinary people, who are not quite satisfied with their ordinary lives but have small chance of changing them because they have neither the opportunity nor the initiative that would enable them to move up in the world. Furthermore, because most of Smith's protagonists are women, many of whom have been betrayed and abandoned by men, they are especially vulnerable, both emotionally and socially. It is clear that Smith is realistic about the future of such characters, and perhaps, by extension, about life in general. One cannot, however, simply define her tone as pessimistic. There is too much comedy and gentle satire in Smith's works for that kind of assessment; furthermore, she emphasizes the courage of her characters, who despite defeat and disappointment refuse to give up on life.

### Cakewalk

It is interesting that of the fourteen stories in *Cakewalk*, thirteen are told through the eyes of women. This focus is typical of Smith's fiction. The point of view varies; frequently the writer uses first person, but sometimes third person with limited omniscience, which concentrates on the thoughts and activities of a single character and thus has much the same effect as first person. No matter which technique she chooses, Smith does not interfere with or comment on her characters but lets them reveal themselves in the words and rhythms of everyday speech.

For example, Mrs. Jolene B. Newhouse, the first-person narrator in "Between the Lines," seems to be speaking to the reader rather than writing her own story. She begins by explaining why her gossip column is called "Between the Lines," but it is soon clear that what Jolene really wants to do is to point out how superior both she and her newspaper column are. There are dozens of lines in the story that enable Smith to satirize Jolene's character--for example, all the smug self-evaluations: She has a sunny nature, she is naturally good, she is highly intelligent, she has always been a remarkable writer. There is also comedy of situation, such as the real story of Alma Goodnight, who has been hospitalized because her husband hit her with a rake and who now is getting her revenge, lying in luxury in a hospital bed while he suffers the torments of guilt. Clearly, Jolene is not so self-centered that she cannot see a situation as it really is. Her admirable grasp of reality is later illustrated when she describes her youngest daughter as an indecisive whiner. The realist Jolene, however, has a surprising depth to her character. She responds to the beauties of nature, which she describes in her column. Furthermore, she cherishes the memory of an almost mystical sexual encounter in the woods with a visiting evangelist. Perhaps because of her own experience, she has accepted her husband's frailty, along with all the mysterious human actions that are written "between the lines" of her column.

Another of Smith's first-person stories in *Cakewalk*, "Dear Phil Donahue," is told by a woman who, like Jolene, has broken the rules, but who, unlike Jolene, has not been able to control her own situation. Having married her high school sweetheart, twenty-eight-year-old Martha Rasnick is living the life she always expected to live. However, isolated with her babies, uncertain who she is and uncertain who her husband really is, she has a mental breakdown. When a mentally disturbed boy hides in her garage, she feeds him as if he were a stray cat and even comforts him. As a result, she is abandoned by both her husband and their supposed friends, and she has to tell her story to her only human contact, a television personality.

Many of Smith's characters are as isolated as Martha, but because of what might be interpreted either as an unwillingness to face reality or as a triumph of the human spirit, they refuse to give up hope. For example, the protagonist in "All the Days of Our Lives" is a mother of three who has been divorced by her husband because she ran off to Daytona Beach with an insurance claims adjuster, long since departed, and who now alternates between disappearing into the world of television and imagining her lost husband to be some ideal creature, instead of the perfectionist who actually drove her away. At the end of the story, however, she snaps out of her depression and makes some decisions, including a resolution to take another look at her neighbor, who obviously adores her and who might give her a new love or at least a new interest.

Similarly, in "Gulfport," a young girl who has been used, betrayed, and abandoned by a lover, who she had convinced herself was going to marry her, clings to some possibilities for the future. Her lover might come back to her, she thinks, or she might go for a walk with the young Mormon missionary, or she might take a job in a lounge. As long as there is life, there are possibilities; as long as there are possibilities, there is hope.

Like "All the Days of Our Lives" and "Gulfport," the title story of the collection, "Cakewalk," is told in the third person. However, the character whose thoughts are related, Stella Lambeth, is not really the protagonist. When she emphasizes her own superiority in the community and her elegance at the department store cosmetics counter and points out the deficiencies of her disorganized, cake-baking sister, it becomes clear which of the two is more capable of loving and of being loved. At the end of the story, a brief excursion into the thoughts of Stella's husband suggests that Stella's own world is not as secure as she believes it to be. Again, Smith ends with possibilities, leaving the future up to her characters.

Indeed, one of the major themes in Smith's stories is the fragility not only of life itself but also of a seemingly fixed pattern. Actually, it takes very little to change a life: a chance encounter, an impulse, a vivid memory, a sudden glimpse of happiness. The protagonist of "Heat Lightning," Geneva, comments on this fact, when, in the midst of cooking and mothering, she senses that a change is coming. In the past, this feeling foretold a major event in her life--the death of her father, the first glimpse of the man she was to marry, and the death of a baby she was carrying. As it turns out, the fourth prediction is as insignificant as heat lightning. Geneva takes the children to a carnival, grins at a carnival worker, and returns cheerfully to her husband.

An event so slight, however, might have had tragic results. In "Saint Paul," it is unclear whether Paul Honeycutt was destroyed by the fact that in his childhood he could not bring himself to declare his love for his young playmate or by the fact that she shattered his image of himself and of her by offering herself to him many years later. At any rate, at the end of the story, although the narrator has proceeded with her life, she realizes that Paul has become almost as important to her as she has always been to him. This suggestion that the world is ruled not by Providence but by chance is basic to Smith's clear-eyed realism. It is consistent with the fact that her characters do not ordinarily make significant choices. They do not act in accordance with some larger plan; instead, they look at the limited possibilities for their lives and then drift in one direction or another, directed by impulse, whim, or instinct.

### ME AND MY BABY VIEW THE ECLIPSE

The first story in Smith's second collection of short stories, *Me and My Baby View the Eclipse*, illustrates this kind of aimlessness. Again, the central character in this story, which is entitled "Bob, A Dog," is a wife deserted by her husband, who at thirty-nine has decided that he needs to make his life simpler and has left his family for a singles apartment complex and a young woman. His wife, Cheryl, a good-natured woman who has spent her life being agreeable to everyone, especially to men, cannot even bring herself to be angry with him. Meanwhile, she drifts. She sleeps with one man, then drops him; she refuses to sleep with another. The central problem in the story illustrates both Cheryl's kindness and her purposelessness. She has adopted a dog, who, not unlike her husband, is determined to run free. Despite all the trouble that Bob, the dog, causes her, Cheryl continues to love him and to forgive

him. At the end of the story, she considers the possibility that her husband will return to her; ironically, just at that point, Bob runs away.

Sometimes a Smith story will move not merely toward possibilities but toward love. "Life on the Moon" is the story of two cousins, the narrator, June, who stayed at home, lived by the rules, took care of her family, and has just been abandoned for a younger woman, and Lucie, who went away to college and made her own decisions. Even though June has not approved of Lucie, it is Lucie who persuades her to load the children in the car for a trip to Washington, and it is Lucie who enables June to see her marriage and her husband as they really were. The story ends with a scene of reconciliation between the cousins. Similarly, at the end of the title story, "Me and My Baby View the Eclipse," even though Sharon Shaw knows that she cannot continue her affair with her imaginative lover, Raymond Stewart, she also knows that she will never forget the magic he has brought into her life. Although they will part and she will once again be faithful to her dull husband, Sharon will always be grateful to Raymond, and, in her way, she will always love him.

Because in each of her stories Smith concentrates on a single point of view and because she so expertly imitates the rhythms of speech, reading her work is like listening to various individuals discussing their lives. Although Smith's comedy is delightful and her satire effective, her most memorable stories are those, such as "Between the Lines," "Cakewalk," "Life on the Moon," and "Me and My Baby View the Eclipse," which prove that ordinary people can sometimes break free of life's prisons through the power of emotional energy. Even if life is ruled by chance and people are ruled by impulse, Smith suggests that there can be relationships that make life worthwhile, that there can be memories that cast their spell over the years that follow. That is probably the most that human beings can expect out of life, but in Smith's stories, it can be enough.

### NEWS OF THE SPIRIT

Smith's third collection, *News of the Spirit*, continues to explore the themes which she introduced in her earlier work, while widening the range of experience of her characters and extending the segments of their lives that are covered. "This collection is all about storytelling," she has commented, "time, memories, and women trying to lead authentic lives," but she has also observed that at this point in her writing life, "It has become harder for me to stick to the classic short story format because I am really interested in the long haul." Two of the stories, "Blue Wedding" and "The southern Cross," maintain what Smith calls "the classic form . . . a story that covers a very short period in a character's life . . . emblematic of an entire life" while the others, particularly "Live Bottomless" and the title story, "are more like collapsed novels."

The initial selection, "The Bubba Stories," is a kind of recapitulation of Smith's earlier concerns and an extension beyond the boundaries of region and experience which have often contained her characters. The narrator, a writer in mid-career recalling her youth in a small southern town and her emergence into experience at college in the turbulence of the 1960's, demonstrates how background shapes character and then how character transcends (without discarding) background. Smith calls the story "very autobiographical" while also pointing out how many key elements are drawn from her imagination, illustrating the vital function that the imaginative capacity occupies in "the struggle to find an authentic voice." As the narrator tells her friends about her mythical brother, the thwarted fantasies of her own life are actualized in fiction as the character she has created takes over and takes off on an unplanned, unanticipated tangent of delight.

A mode of recollection also operates in "Live Bottomless," which, at a little more than one hundred pages, is the longest of the stories. The narrator recalls, beginning in 1958, her beloved father's family-shattering affair, which anticipates her own growth toward sexual awakening. The unexpected and exciting turns her life takes as she moves through adolescence, culminating in her idealistically romantic, almost desperate, attempt to bring her parents back together, leads to a conclusion that mixes Hollywood fantasy with the seemingly mundane to suggest the deeper dimensions of almost everything in the characters' lives.

"southern Cross" and "Happy Memories Club" are both extrapolations from incidents that Smith noticed almost obliquely, providing her with situations in which "ordinary people" are carried beyond familiar geographical and psychic regions. The narrator of "southern Cross" has refashioned herself from a small-town girl (Mayruth) into an international adventurer (Chanel Keen), able and ready to use every trick of style and beauty to hold her own with rapacious men on a Caribbean cruise. The narrator of the ironically titled "Happy Memories Club" is a retired English teacher, aging but still very lucid, fusing the past and present in a vivid tableau of memory and immediacy. Like the title story--an extended exposition of a character overcoming uncertainty by learning to treasure the things of her life that are valuable and energizing--they bring the "news of the spirit" which Smith defines as "what storytelling means to me," a way "we find our authentic selves over the course of our lives."

OTHER MAJOR WORKS

LONG FICTION: *The Last Day the Dogbushes Bloomed*, 1968; *Something in the Wind*, 1971; *Fancy Strut*, 1973; *Black Mountain Breakdown*, 1980; *Oral History*, 1983; *Family Linen*, 1985; *Fair and Tender Ladies*, 1988; *The Devil's Dream*, 1992; *Saving Grace*, 1995; *The Last Girls*, 2002; *On Agate Hill*, 2006.

NONFICTION: *Conversations with Lee Smith*, 2001 (Linda Tate, editor).

EDITED TEXT: *Sitting on the Courthouse Bench: An Oral History of Grundy, Virginia*, 2000.

BIBLIOGRAPHY

Buchanan, Harriette C. "Lee Smith: The Storyteller's Voice." In *southern Women Writers: The New Generation*, edited by Tonette Bond Inge. Tuscaloosa: University of Alabama Press, 1990. An introduction to Smith's life and art, focusing primarily on her novels. Claims that the irony that shows the difference between Smith's humanism and the narrow, judgmental views of her characters can best be seen in her short stories.

Canin, Ethan. "The Courage of Their Foolishness." Review of *Me and My Baby View the Eclipse*, by Lee Smith. *The New York Times Book Review* (February 11, 1990): 11. A brief but perceptive summary of Smith's themes, her strengths, and her weaknesses. Although it deals specifically with the short-story collection cited, this essay is an excellent introduction to Smith's fiction as a whole.

Cook, Linda Byrd. *Dancing in the Flames: Spiritual Journey in the Novels of Lee Smith*. Jefferson, N.C.: McFarland, 2009. Examines all of Smith's novels to date, focusing on how they reflect her personal search toward spiritual reconciliation. Describes how Smith "retrieves" sexual, maternal, and feminine divine power in her fiction.

Guralnick, Peter. "The Storyteller's Tale." *Los Angeles Times Magazine* (May 21, 1995): 15. Biographical sketch of Smith's childhood in West Virginia and her college career at Hollins College; includes quotations from Smith about the influences on her literary career, what motivates her writing, and what most fascinates her about the South.

Hill, Dorothy Combs. *Lee Smith*. New York: Twayne, 1992. An introductory overview and critical study of Smith's work.

Jones, Anne Goodwyn. "The World of Lee Smith." In *Women Writers of the Contemporary South*, edited by Peggy Whitman Prenshaw. Jackson: University Press of Mississippi, 1984. An incisive exploration of the relation between the spoken and written word in Smith's fiction, which makes classification of her work according to the tenets of contemporary criticism extremely difficult, while richly rewarding her readers. The stories in *Cakewalk* are analyzed separately and in relation to the novels.

MacKethan, Lucinda H. "Artists and Beauticians: Balance in Lee Smith's Fiction." *The southern Literary Journal* 15 (Fall, 1982): 3-14. This important article discusses the problem of attaining a balance in life, which is involved in every choice Smith's characters make. Also looks at Smith's own attempts to achieve artistic balance, primarily through alterations in tone and variations in point of view.

Ostwalt, Conrad. "Witches and Jesus: Lee Smith's Appalachian Religion." *The southern Literary Journal* 31 (Fall, 1998): 98-118. Discusses the dual religious consciousness in Smith's fiction: traditional religions that try to go beyond the Appalachian landscape and an elemental, supernatural force bound up with nature.

Parrish, Nancy C. *Lee Smith, Annie Dillard, and the Hollins Group: A Genesis of Writers*. Baton Rouge: Louisiana State University Press, 1998. Describes the importance of Smith's literary development at Hollins College during the 1960's. Discusses a number of Smith's early short stories, such as "The Wading House," "The Red Parts," and "Fatback Season," and how they experiment with themes and techniques that she develops in her novels.

Smith, Lee "A Spiritual Journey: An Interview with Lee Smith." Interview by Lynda Byrd Cook. *southern Quarterly* 47, no. 1 (Fall, 2009): 74-103. A lengthy interview, in which Smith discusses her religious experiences and religious passions, the difference between organized religion and spirituality, and her characters' connections between mental instability and spirituality.

_____. "When Craft and Storytelling Come Together: Award-Winning Fiction Writer Lee Smith Builds on Her southern Traditions in Bringing Characters and Settings to Life." Interview by Elfried Abbe. *Writer* 122, no. 4 (April, 2009): 18-21. Smith discusses how her storytelling has been influenced by Appalachian oral tradition, her opinions on the use of first- and third-person narratives, and her use of prewriting exercises.

Smith, Virginia A. "Luminous Halos and Lawn Chairs: Lee Smith's *Me and My Baby View the Eclipse*." *The southern Review* 27 (Spring, 1991): 479-485. Argues that the stories in this collection have a repeated pattern, which takes the characters from darkness to moments of illumination, occurring primarily through the power of love. Stresses Smith's sensitivity to the experiences of women.

Teem, William M., IV. "Let Us Now Praise the Other: Women in Lee Smith's Short Fiction." *Studies in Literary Imagination* 28 (Fall, 1994): 63-73. Discusses the means by which Smith's female characters in her short stories deal with the conflicts that result from clashes between rural culture and urban values.

Walsh, William J. "Lee Smith." In *Speak So I Shall Know Thee: Interviews with southern Writers*. Jefferson, N.C.: McFarland, 1990. In this interview, conducted in November, 1987, Smith comments on her development as a writer, her experience with editors and publishers, her methods of research, and her evaluation of her own work, as well as on various opinions and biographical details.

Wesley, Debbie. "A New Way of Looking at an Old Story: Lee Smith's Portrait of Female Creativity." *The southern Literary Journal* 30 (Fall, 1997): 88-101. Discusses Smith's female characters, who refuse to conform to traditional stereotypes and bring

meaning and order to their communities. Argues that what makes her protagonists artists is the fellowship they create and the rituals they maintain.

*Rosemary M. Canfield Reisman*
*Updated by Leon Lewis*

---

# SUSAN SONTAG

**Born:** New York, New York; January 16, 1933
**Died:** New York, New York; December 28, 2004
**Also Known As:** Susan Rosenblatt

## PRINCIPAL SHORT FICTION

*I, Etcetera,* 1978

## OTHER LITERARY FORMS

In addition to her short stories, Susan Sontag wrote four published four novels: *The Benefactor* (1963), *Death Kit* (1967), *The Volcano Lover* (1992), and *In America* (2000); she also published a play, *Alice in Bed* (1993), and was the author of several screenplays. Sontag is perhaps best known as a cultural critic and essayist, and she published many nonfiction works, including *Against Interpretation, and Other Essays* (1966), *Styles of Radical Will* (1969), *On Photography* (1977), *Illness as Metaphor* (1978), *Under the Sign of Saturn* (1980), *AIDS and Its Metaphors* (1989), *Where the Stress Falls* (2001), and *Regarding the Pain of Others* (2003).

## ACHIEVEMENTS

Susan Sontag was the recipient of many awards and honorary degrees, including the Arts and Letters Award of the American Academy of Arts and Letters, the 1977 National Book Critics Circle Award for Criticism for *On Photography*, and the 2000 National Book Award for her novel *In America.* She also received a John D. and Catherine T. MacArthur Foundation Fellowship (1990); the Malparte Prize from Italy (1992); the Commandeur de l'Ordre des Arts et des Lettres from France (1999); the Jerusalem Prize (2001), awarded to a writer

whose work explores the freedom of the individual in society; the Peace Prize of the German Book Trade (2003); and the Prince of Asturias Award for Literature (2003).

## BIOGRAPHY

Born Susan Rosenblatt in New York City on January 16, 1933, Sontag, her younger sister, and their mother moved to Tucson, Arizona, in 1939, shortly after her father died. Sontag attended local schools in Tucson. Her mother remarried in 1945. The family moved to southern California, where Sontag took her stepfather's last name and attended North Hollywood High School.

A precocious student, Sontag graduated from high school at the age of fifteen. After spending a semester at the University of California at Berkeley, she transferred to the University of Chicago, earning a B.A. degree in two years and marrying Philip Rieff, a sociology professor. The couple moved to Cambridge, Massachusetts, where Sontag began work on a graduate degree at Harvard University and Rieff taught at Brandeis University. After a year of study abroad at Oxford University and the Sorbonne, Sontag returned to the United States in 1959, divorcing Rieff and taking custody of their son, born in 1952.

In New York City, Sontag taught at Columbia University and other schools while writing her first novel. It was the publication of her essays, however, that brought her recognition as a new young critic with provocative ideas. She quickly established herself as a cultural commentator and independent intellectual. She quit teaching in 1964 and made her living as a writer, lecturer, and filmmaker. Sontag died of myelodysplastic syndrome in 2004 at the age of seventy-one.

ANALYSIS

Susan Sontag's fiction has often been linked with that of the French New Novel, advocated and practiced by Alain Robbe-Grillet and Nathalie Sarraute. These novelists rejected the conventions of realistic fiction; they did not create lifelike characters and compelling plots. Rather, they wanted to promulgate a view of literature as a contrivance, a calculated construction of an independent world. Literature did not imitate reality; literature created its own reality, its own reason for being.

Sontag found the New Novelists compelling because the American fiction of the 1950's seemed stale. Novelists seemed to have nothing new to say about their environment or about the form of fiction itself. A good example of Sontag's effort to create a new kind of fiction is her story "American Spirits," collected in *I, Etcetera*. Essentially the story is a satire about the boredom of American middle-class life. Instead of documenting the life of realistic characters, Sontag turns her fiction into an allegory, naming her main character "Miss Flatface," a name that suggests a person with no dimension, a person who lacks a rounded, enriching life. Miss Flatface forsakes her family and embarks on a flamboyant life with Mr. Obscenity.

By making her characters types or symbols of "American Spirits" Sontag attempts to broaden the focus of American fiction, making it less concerned with the minute particulars of individual lives and more perceptive about the broad patterns of cultural behavior. Miss Flatface, for example, is looking for thrills, entertainment, and a sense of destiny that is continuously alluded to in the story as Sontag mentions such classic American strivers as Benjamin Franklin, Abraham Lincoln, and John F. Kennedy.

Sontag's fiction is often about the narrator's or writer's dilemma: How to be creative, how to find the proper structure for a story, a story which is often an account of the writer's own perceptions. Thus Sontag's stories tend to be autobiographical. "Project for a Trip to China," for example, reads like a diary of her feelings about her father and mother, and "Baby," she admitted in interviews, is partly a

*Susan Sontag* (Library of Congress)

reminiscence of how she and her husband responded as parents of their son David.

"PROJECT FOR A TRIP TO CHINA"

The lead story in *I, Etcetera* deals with the narrator's anticipation of a journey that will take her, for the first time, to the land where her father died. Rather than presenting a narrative of her feelings about her father, the narrator jots down her earliest memories involved with hearing about China from her mother, who brought back souvenirs from her stays in the country with her husband. The narrator tries to re-create her sense of China, of her father, of her family, from these tokens of the past. Ultimately she concludes that the real "trip" is the one she has taken in her imagination, for as she says at the end of her story, "Perhaps I will write the book about my trip to China before I go."

This final sentence provides the clue of what Sontag is most interested in as a writer: how she can transform the raw materials of life into a story. "Project for a Trip to China" is unique in her collection because it reads like the listing of the raw materials themselves, the fragments that she tries to fuse into fiction.

## "DEBRIEFING"

The second story in *I, Etcetera* reads more like a continuous narrative. The narrator mourns the loss of her best friend, Julia, an intense thinker who troubles herself about the meaning of existence. Is life coherent? If not, then all is chaos and meaninglessness. However, if everything in life that happens is meant to happen, then everything is determined, and there is not much reason to assert oneself--and not much reason, in Julia's case, to go on living. The narrator, also a serious thinker, nevertheless tries to humor Julia out of the black moods that isolate her from the world. The narrator points out that some questions just cannot be answered and do not bear thinking about.

Once a question is asked, however, it is difficult not to want an answer. This is as true for the narrator as it is for Julia. Thus the narrator weaves into her reminiscence the stories of several women named Doris. Each Doris leads a separate life, yet elements of their stories suggest that they may be linked in ways the narrator cannot understand. The narrator's inability to understand is linked to the fact that Julia (as the end of the story reveals) commits suicide. The narrator is as powerless to prevent Julia's death as she is to understand how the stories of the different Dorises are linked.

The term "debriefing," which refers to questioning or interrogating someone to extract information, serves as an ironic title for the story. The narrator tries to explore what the story of Julia, of the different Dorises means, but the interrogation does not result in knowledge; rather, the knowledge obtained is about the heartbreaking ambiguity of life and the difficulty of warding off despair.

## "THE DUMMY"

The fourth story in *I, Etcetera*, coming after "American Spirits," "The Dummy" is another version of Sontag's playing with the idea of shifting identities. The narrator, who does not name himself, is like Miss Flatface in "American Spirits," bored with his middle-class family life. To relieve himself of his responsibilities at home and at work, he employs a dummy who is an exact copy of himself and who is able to do everything the narrator does. The trouble is that the dummy falls in love with a woman at the narrator's office and demands precisely the sort of freedom that the narrator coveted

for himself in employing the dummy in the first place. The narrator's solution is to employ yet a second dummy who seems better suited to the job.

Given the story's title, it seems appropriate to ask who is the "dummy." Obviously it is the replacement self the narrator employs, but is it also the narrator? Is he as happy with his solution, as he suggests at the end of the story, or is he rationalizing? In other words, the form of the story expresses the narrator's seeming complacency about using a dummy, yet the form also leaves open the possibility that perhaps the narrator is a dummy for fooling himself into thinking he has found a happy solution to his problems. Certainly the narrator's final words seem too pat, too self-satisfied, to be believed without qualification, for he congratulates himself for "having solved in so equitable and responsible a manner the problems of this one poor short life that was allotted me." However, his vaunted freedom seems to consist in not much more than allowing himself to lead an indolent life and to affect a "shabby appearance." What exactly has he accomplished?

## "BABY"

The sixth story in *I, Etcetera*, concerns an unnamed couple's worries about their precocious son. They are bringing him up to be a genius, but they are concerned about his willful nature. They want him to be independent, yet they want him under their control. These parents are, in short, befuddled by their contradictions, and they have come to a psychiatrist for help in sorting out how they should bring up their baby.

The entire story is told through the words of the two frustrated parents. The psychiatrist's advice is alluded to in their responses. Like their child, they behave in contradictory fashion. That is, they come seeking advice but they reject it almost as soon as the psychiatrist offers it. Just as they try to shape their son's responses, they try to manipulate the psychiatrist.

"Baby" is about the tyranny of family life and about the power relationships that infest the parent-child relationship. It is also, on a simpler level, an account of anxious parents who mean well and yet do devastating things to their child. Like the other stories in *I, Etcetera*, "Baby" is not realistic. It does not give characters names or spend much time describing settings. However, the story deals with real issues in the same way that a dream or a fantasy does. Thus, when the parents tell the psychiatrist that they have begun cutting off their son's limbs, they are expressing the desire to hobble a child, to keep him a "baby," that parents can sometimes express in less extreme forms.

OTHER MAJOR WORKS

LONG FICTION: *The Benefactor*, 1963; *Death Kit*, 1967; *The Volcano Lover*, 1992; *In America*, 2000.

PLAY: *Alice in Bed: A Play in Eight Scenes*, pb. 1993.

SCREENPLAYS: *Duet for Cannibals*, 1969; *Brother Carl*, 1972; *Promised Lands*, 1974; *Unguided Tour*, 1983.

NONFICTION: *Against Interpretation, and Other Essays*, 1966; *Trip to Hanoi*, 1968 (journalism); *Styles of Radical Will*, 1969; *On Photography*, 1977; *Illness as Metaphor*, 1978; *Under the Sign of Saturn*, 1980; *AIDS and Its Metaphors*, 1989; *Conversations with Susan Sontag*, 1995 (Leland Poague, editor); *Where the Stress Falls*, 2001; *Regarding the Pain of Others*, 2003; *At the Same Time: Essays and Speeches*, 2007 (Paolo Dilonardo and Anne Jump, editors); *Reborn: Journals and Notebooks, 1947-1964*, 2008 (David Rieff, editor).

EDITED TEXTS: *Selected Writings*, 1976 (by Antonin Artaud); *A Barthes Reader*, 1982; *Homo Poeticus: Essays and Interviews*, 1995 (by Danilo Kiš).

MISCELLANEOUS: *A Susan Sontag Reader*, 1982.

BIBLIOGRAPHY

Bruss, Elizabeth W. *Beautiful Theories: The Spectacle of Discourse in Contemporary Criticism*. Baltimore, Md.: The Johns Hopkins University Press, 1982. A thorough exploration of Sontag's essays and screenplays, with discussions of her theory of literature that contribute greatly to an understanding of the aims of her short fiction.

Ching, Barbara, and Jennifer A. Wagner-Lawlor, eds. *The Scandal of Susan Sontag*. New York: Columbia University Press, 2009. Although the majority of the essays in this collection focus on Sontag's role as a cultural critic, essayist, and political activist, Wagner-Lawlor's piece analyzes "Romances of Community in Sontag's Later Fiction." The book does provide an understanding of Sontag's cultural sensibilities which can help in explicating her short fiction.

Kennedy, Liam. *Susan Sontag: Mind as Passion*. Manchester, England: Manchester University Press, 1995. A detailed study of Sontag's career. Kennedy is especially insightful about the intellectual influences on Sontag's writing. His book includes discussions of individual stories.

Liddelow, Eden. "Speaking for Yourself: Susan Sontag and the Melancholy Aesthetic." In *After Electra: Rage, Grief, and Hope in Twentieth-Century Fiction*. Melbourne, Victoria.: Australian Scholarly, 2002. Examines how several women writers portray the struggle inherent in a child's separation from its mother. Argues that Sontag depicts this conflict as a "melancholy aesthetic" that starts from her view that the self is a "text which must be deciphered."

Meyer, Sara. "Susan Sontag's 'Archaeology of Longings.'" *Texas Studies in Literature and Language* 49, no. 1 (Spring, 2007): 45-63. Analyzes two of Sontag's travel stories, "Project for a Trip to China" and "Unguided Tour." Argues that in the former, Sontag symbolizes going to an exotic destination as a means of redefining oneself and seeking renewal. "Unguided Tour," according to Meyer, is on the surface about tourism, but challenges readers because it lacks a clear meaning for its textual twists.

Platizky, Roger. "Sontag's 'The Way We Live Now.'" *Explicator* 65, no. 1 (Fall, 2006): 53-56. Focuses on the symbolism of the names of the characters in this story. Although neither the protagonist's name nor the disease from which he is dying is ever mentioned, his illness is understood to be acquired immunodeficiency syndrome (AIDS). Also discusses the significance of the fact that the twenty-six other characters in the story are each named for a letter of the alphabet, from Aileen to Zack.

Poague, Leland, ed. *Conversations with Susan Sontag*. Jackson: University Press of Mississippi, 1995. An indispensable guide to Sontag's writing. Not only do her interviews contain many illuminating remarks about her short fiction, but also Poague's introduction and chronology provide the best introduction to Sontag's work as a whole.

Rollyson, Carl. *Reading Susan Sontag: A Critical Introduction to Her Work*. Chicago: Ivan R. Dee, 2001. Provides a chronological overview of

Sontag's life and analyses of her works. Devotes one chapter to an examination of *I, Etcetera.*

Rollyson, Carl, and Lisa O. Paddock. *Susan Sontag: The Making of an Icon.* New York: W. W. Norton, 2000. The first, and unauthorized, biography of Sontag, chronicling her life and works. Especially good at describing how she became a literary celebrity and how her books were marketed to project her image, as well as her ideas.

Sayres, Sohnya. *Susan Sontag: The Elegiac Modernist.* New York: Routledge, 1990. Sayres's introduction and biographical chapter provide significant insight into the background of Sontag's short fiction. Sayres

also discusses individual stories, but her jargon will prove difficult to the beginning student of Sontag's work.

Vidal, Gore. *United States Essays 1952-1992.* New York: Random House, 1993. Contains essays on the French New Novel and on Sontag's second novel, *Death Kit.* Although Vidal does not discuss Sontag's short fiction, his lucid explanation of the New Novel and of Sontag's theory of fiction provide an excellent framework for studying the stories in *I, Etcetera.*

*Carl Rollyson*

---

# ELIZABETH SPENCER

**Born:** Carrollton, Mississippi; July 19, 1921

PRINCIPAL SHORT FICTION

*Knights and Dragons,* 1965
*Ship Island, and Other Stories,* 1968
*Marilee: Three Stories,* 1981
*The Stories of Elizabeth Spencer,* 1981
*Jack of Diamonds, and Other Stories,* 1988
*On the Gulf,* 1991
*The southern Woman: New and Selected Fiction,* 2001

OTHER LITERARY FORMS

In addition to numerous short stories published in periodicals, as well as in book-length collections, Elizabeth Spencer has produced several novels and novellas, including her best-known work, *The Light in the Piazza* (1960), which was adapted for a film released in 1962 and a musical play that debuted in Seattle, Washington, in 2003 and was staged in New York City in 2005. She has also written the novels *The Salt Line* (1984) and *The Night Travellers* (1991) and a memoir, *Landscapes of the Heart: A Memoir* (1998).

ACHIEVEMENTS

Elizabeth Spencer's artistic achievement has garnered her many awards, including a Women's Democratic Committee Award (1949), a recognition award from the National Institute of Arts and Letters (1952), a John Simon Guggenheim Memorial Foundation Fellowship (1953), the Richard and Hinda Rosenthal Foundation Award from the American Academy of Arts and Letters (1957), a McGraw-Hill fiction award (1960), the Henry H. Bellamann Foundation Award for creative writing (1968), an Award of Merit Medal for the short story from the American Academy of Arts and Letters (1983), the Salem Award for Literature (1992), the John Dos Passos Award for fiction (1992), the North Carolina Governor's Award for Literature (1994), the Corrington Award for Literature (1997), and the Richard Wright Award for Literature (1997). She was also a Kenyon College Fellow in Fiction (1957), a Bryn Mawr College Donnelly Fellow (1962), and a National Endowment for the Arts grantee in literature (1983), as well as a Senior Arts Award grantee by the National Endowment for the Arts (1988). In the twenty-first century, Spencer continued to be honored for her works, receiving the Cleanth Brooks Medal for Achievement by the Fellowship of southern Writers (2001), the Thomas Wolfe Award for Literature from the University of North Carolina, Chapel Hill, and the

Morgan Foundation (2002), the William Faulkner Medal for Literary Excellence (2002), the Governor's Award for Achievement in Literature from the Mississippi Arts Commission (2006), the PEN/Malamud Award for Short Fiction (2007), and the Lifetime Achievement Award of the Mississippi Institute of Arts and Letters (2009).

## Biography

Elizabeth Spencer was born on July 19, 1921, in Carrollton, Mississippi, the daughter of Mary J. McCain Spencer and James L. Spencer, a businessman. Both her mother and her father's families had lived in northern Mississippi for almost a century. Spencer's childhood was almost ideal for a writer. Her mother and her mother's family gave her a passion for books, and her father gave her a love of nature. During long summer visits to the McCain plantation, she developed an appreciation of the land. Meanwhile, like the character in her short stories who she says she most resembles, the intensely curious Marilee Summerall, Spencer was storing local legends and gossip. She would never lack material for her fiction, and even as a child she had begun to write.

After graduating from her local high school, Spencer attended Belhaven College, a Presbyterian girls' school in Jackson, Mississippi. There, she edited a newspaper, won awards for fiction and poetry, and became a friend of Eudora Welty, who lived across the street from the college. Welty comments in her foreword to *The Stories of Elizabeth Spencer* that there was a seriousness and determination about Spencer that convinced Welty that she would indeed become a writer. After receiving her B.A., Spencer went to Vanderbilt University in Nashville, Tennessee, carrying with her a partially completed novel. While there, she encountered the scholar and writer Donald Davidson, who later helped her get a book contract for her first novel at the publishing firm Dodd, Mead. In 1948, the novel was published under the title *Fire in the Morning*.

After receiving her M.A. from Vanderbilt University in 1943, Spencer taught English at Northwest Mississippi Junior College in Senatobia and at Ward-Belmont College in Nashville. She also worked for a year as a reporter at the Nashville *Tennessean*. In 1948, she

went to the University of Mississippi to teach creative writing while she worked on her second novel, *This Crooked Way* (1952). After this novel was published, Spencer was given an award by the National Institute of Arts and Letters, which enabled her to spend a summer in New York. In 1953, she went to Italy on a John Simon Guggenheim Memorial Foundation Fellowship. There, Spencer met and married an Englishman from Cornwall, John Arthur Blackwood Rusher, a language school director.

After five years in Italy, Spencer and Rusher moved to Montreal, Canada, where he had been offered a position. That city was to be their home for twenty-eight years. For most of that time, Spencer worked full time at her writing, publishing novels, novellas, and short stories at regular intervals. In 1976, however, she began to teach creative writing courses and conduct workshops at Concordia University in Montreal. In 1986, Spencer and her husband moved to Chapel Hill, North Carolina. There, she continued to write, while also teaching courses in creative writing at the University of North Carolina.

## Analysis

Elizabeth Spencer established herself as one of the major fiction writers of the southern Renaissance, a writer whose subjects and preoccupations have kept pace with the times through which she has lived, while her style has remained unique. Throughout her career, Spencer has been particularly interested in the influence of memory, the sense of place, and the power of tradition in the life of the individual. Although in theme and complexity she reminds critics of fellow Mississippian William Faulkner and in subtlety of Henry James, no comparisons do justice to Spencer's art, for, as her readers inevitably realize, the voice in Spencer's fiction is unmistakably her own.

In terms of tone, Spencer's fiction might be described as a combination of disciplined detachment from her subject matter and passionate attachment to her southern roots, to lush, semitropical natural settings, to the rich language of born storytellers, and to the conviction that the past dwells in the present. Spencer is much admired for her craftsmanship, which enables her to handle complexities of time, memory, and imagination so deftly that the shifts of focus are almost imperceptible. It is this combination of intellectual power and disciplined skill that ensures Spencer permanent recognition as one of the important writers of her generation.

For the subject matter of her novels and novellas, Spencer often chooses issues tied to a particular place and time; for example, *The Voice at the Back Door* (1956) deals with changing attitudes toward race after World War II; *The Salt Line* (1984) describes the transformation of the Mississippi Gulf Coast after Hurricane Camille; and *The Night Travellers* (1991) examines the ongoing plight of Vietnam War activists. In most of Spencer's short stories, however, the narrative is less clearly dependent on a particular time in history. Instead, Spencer concentrates on a brief period in an individual's life, when that person comes to recognize some need or some truth.

The themes of Spencer's short stories remain constant from her earliest works to her later ones. One of these themes pits the demands for social conformity, often expressed in the family, against an individual's need for freedom; similarly, the conflict may be internalized, with the individual torn between two desires, one for security, the other for independence. A related theme is the search for identity, particularly by women, whose enslavement to conformity has been especially evident in the conservative South. In addition, there is always a moral element in a Spencer story; to her, evil is very real, and her characters make difficult choices between good and evil. Spencer also recognizes, however, the fact that fate, or chance, can restrict those choices. Finally, as a writer, she is conscious of the importance of imagination and memory as a part of life; these human faculties can torment or liberate her characters.

### "THE LITTLE BROWN GIRL"

The imagination dominates the earliest story in *The Stories of Elizabeth Spencer*, "The Little Brown Girl." The story is told in the third person, but the point of view is limited to that of the seven-year-old white girl, Maybeth, who is charmed by a black man, Jim Williams, who works for her father. Maybeth loves Jim's stories, some of which she knows he invented. She chooses, however, to believe that he has a little girl who is going to come and play with her. Even though her parents tell her that Jim is not telling the truth, and even though she half knows it, Maybeth lets herself think about the little girl and even gives Jim her own birthday money, supposedly to buy the little girl a dress. Prompted by Jim, she even sees a glimpse of her playmate in the yellow dress. At this point, frightened, Maybeth runs home to her mother's arms. What Spencer leaves unstated is the source of Maybeth's fear. Is it the fact that she can be so deceived by a friend, or is it that her imagination can be prompted to see the unseen? Obviously, Maybeth is too young to analyze her own reactions. Even with adult protagonists, Spencer frequently ends her short stories with this kind of uncertainty, which leaves room for the reader's interpretation.

### "FIRST DARK"

"First Dark" and "A southern Landscape" illustrate the conflict between conformity and independence, the security to be found in family and home and the freedom to be experienced when one escapes. In "First Dark," Frances Harvey is surprised to find her elderly mother urging her marriage to Tommy Beavers, whose family background is distinctly inferior to that of the Harveys. In fact, Mrs. Harvey evidently commits suicide to make sure that she will not stand in the way of the marriage. What both Frances and Tommy know, however, is that the house in which Mrs. Harvey expected them to live would possess them and stifle them. At the end of the story, Tommy insists that Frances leave with him, and she chooses to do so.

### "A SOUTHERN LANDSCAPE"

However, in "A southern Landscape," the earliest of the Marilee Summerall stories, Spencer reveals her very real appreciation of those things that never change, symbolized by Windsor, an antebellum mansion in ruins, and by Foster Hamilton, whom Marilee is dating. Like the mansion, Foster has grace. He so admires Marilee's mother, his ideal of southern womanhood, that simply the suggestion of her presence can shock him into instant sobriety. Foster, too, is already in ruins, joyfully addicted to drink. Years later, when she tells the story, Marilee rejoices that some things have not changed, among them the mansion Windsor, the heavenward-pointing hand on a Presbyterian church, and

Foster's addiction. Obviously, Spencer is not arguing for alcoholism; her point, instead, has to do with permanence: "I feel the need of a land, of a sure terrain, of a sort of permanent landscape of the heart." Spencer does realize that this sense of a sure terrain may be one of the fringe benefits that comes with an assured place in society, such as that which is given at birth to a Harvey or a Summerall. Tommy Beavers knows that if he stays in the Harvey house, it will possess and govern him; he will become less than nothing.

### "SHIP ISLAND"

Similarly, in "Ship Island: The Story of a Mermaid," one of the stories to which Spencer frequently refers, Nancy Lewis is painfully aware that she is, and always will be, an outsider in Mississippi Gulf Coast society. Her family has no money, no background, and no taste. Nancy is accepted by the young aristocrats only because one of them has chosen to sponsor her, and, even then, she must watch every word she says, every move she makes. As the story progresses, Nancy rebels against her own denial of her self. The subtitle, "The Story of a Mermaid," suggests that Nancy will die if she attempts to live outside her own natural element, where she can be free. To save herself, she runs off to New Orleans with a couple of men she has met. The action is heroic and potentially tragic; certainly it could have caused Nancy's death. When she returns home, however, she knows that she can never become a part of Gulf Coast society. Therefore she need not worry about being tempted to do something that she knows is wrong: to deny her own self in order to become socially and financially secure.

### "KNIGHTS AND DRAGONS"

In an essay on Spencer, Elsa Nettels points out that, after the mid-1950's, the theme of women's search for their identity took on major importance in Spencer's fiction. The long short story "Knights and Dragons," which was expanded into a novella and published separately in 1965, is concerned with this issue. The title is significant: Trained from childhood to look for knights to rescue them from dragons, women often mistake selfish, destructive men for good, protective ones. Martha Ingram knows that the husband she divorced is determined to play psychological games with her, but she cannot resist reacting when he decides to pull her

strings, either with a letter from his lawyer or with carefully chosen clippings sent in the mail. Gordon Ingram is her dragon. When two other men help Martha to break free from Ingram's tyranny, she sees them as her chivalric knights, providentially appearing to protect their lady. Martha comes to understand, however, that life is not so simple. In their own benevolent way, these knights are as oppressive as her dragon husband. Like him, they demand the surrender of her identity; each has invented a role that she must play. That is the price of a knight's protection. At the end of the story, Martha realizes that she has freed herself from all roles. In a kind of death of the old self, she has become truly free.

### "THE BUFORDS"

Although Spencer never resorts to simplistic delineations of good and evil, it is obvious that she believes in those opposing forces. Even though Gordon Ingram's friends find him delightful, he is clearly motivated by malice in his attempt to destroy Martha. There is a difference, however, between malice such as his and simple nonconformity, which seeks to harm no one.

"The Bufords," for example, is the story of an unequal battle between a young schoolteacher and a large family of people who seem to live life simply for the joy of it. The teacher is determined to discipline the Buford children. Unable to make headway at school, she goes to see their parents. There, she discovers that the behavior that she has found outrageous is a source of pride to the rest of the family. The adults all find it wonderful that their offspring are the most irrepressible in school. The fact that there is no ill will in the Buford temperament, however, is shown by the warm hospitality that they offer the teacher. Although they do not understand her, they forgive her for lashing out at their children. Actually, they consider her, and her way of thinking, simply a bit exotic, as if she were a member of another species or of another society. At the end of the story, the well-meaning teacher realizes not only that she has been defeated by the family at whose table she has just been entertained but also that she has been adopted by them, as an interesting if peculiar pet, like their possum in a cage.

### "JEAN-PIERRE"

The sense of family, which is treated so comically in "The Bufords," is at the center of a very different narrative, set not in the Deep South but in Montreal. "Jean-Pierre" is a love story in which a Protestant, English-speaking woman and a Catholic, French-speaking man marry and then begin to understand each other. After the couple have been married almost a year, Jean-Pierre Courtois disappears without any explanation to his young wife. Courageously, she gets a job, endures her loneliness, and waits until he returns. In the meantime, she picks up bits and pieces of knowledge about him and his people, enough to know that, for some reason, he had to go to his home. When Jean-Pierre returns, his wife is waiting. Despite being tempted to leave him, she has remained faithful. At that point, then, he is ready to change his emotional address and to establish a new home with her.

### ON THE GULF

Four of the short stories from *On the Gulf*, including "Ship Island," were reprinted from *The Stories of Elizabeth Spencer*, and a fifth was first published elsewhere. These stories are brought together with a previously unpublished story ("A Fugitive's Wife") and an evocative introduction by Spencer. Illustrated by a series of pen-and-ink drawings made in the 1940's by Gulf Coast artist Walter Anderson, the collection exhibits Spencer's love for the Gulf Coast, as well as her love-hate relationship with the southern family. Although the title story is humorous, it links the collection thematically in its depiction of the desire of families to dictate the very thoughts of their children. In this brief tale, the family prepares for the annual visit of acquaintances from New Orleans, whom no one really likes. When young Mary Dee voices the opinion of all by wishing the Meades were gone before they have arrived, her mother rebukes her, "What are you trying to grow up to be?. . . . Stop listening to us! Stop hearing anything we say!"

In "The Legacy," by contrast, Dottie Almond attempts to escape the tyranny of her aunts by taking an inheritance and going to Miami, where she meets an exciting young man. For a while, she blends into his social group, but on discovering that he has a dark secret, she decides to return to the confining society she

had momentarily escaped. Mary's separation from her husband in the delicate "A Fugitive's Wife" is forced, and, though she attempts to reassure her husband that she and the baby are well, pain and loneliness pervade her being. In "Mr. McMillan," Aline and the late Mr. McMillan fulfill and resist the expectations their families place on them. Aline

> believed in self-knowledge, even though trying to find it in the bosom of a Mississippi family was like trying to find some object lost in a gigantic attic, when you really didn't know what you were looking for.

Like her, Mr. McMillan has come to New Orleans to lead life on his own terms. Upon his death he allows his family to bury him and then discover in his will that he wanted to be cremated and have one of his friends cast his ashes into the waters off Hawaii, where he had served during the war. As Aline relates the story of Mr. McMillan to her friend from Chicago, he senses her bitterness, which she attributes to her failure (whether to fulfill Mr. McMillan's wishes or her own is ambiguous).

The penultimate story, "Go South in the Winter," recounts the tale of an older wife vacationing alone and feeling a welcome detachment from life, when dreams of her son as a child intrude on her consciousness along with a radio announcement of a traffic accident that killed a man with the same last name as her son. Overcome by emotion, she cannot make the young couple who have befriended her understand that her son was not killed. When she is able to clear the situation up with them she feels ready to engage herself in society again.

Most of Spencer's short stories are essentially optimistic. Her characters have proven their courage by being willing to seek understanding, both of themselves and of their relationship to their families and their societies. Spencer's protagonists, armed with understanding and courage, are ready to seek their destinies.

### OTHER MAJOR WORKS

LONG FICTION: *Fire in the Morning*, 1948; *This Crooked Way*, 1952; *The Voice at the Back Door*, 1956;

*The Light in the Piazza*, 1960; *No Place for an Angel*, 1967; *The Snare*, 1972; *The Salt Line*, 1984; *The Night Travellers*, 1991.

NONFICTION: *Conversations with Elizabeth Spencer*, 1991 (Peggy Whitman Prenshaw); *Landscapes of the Heart: A Memoir*, 1998.

BIBLIOGRAPHY

Entzminger, Betina. "Emotional Distance as Narrative Strategy in Elizabeth Spencer's Fiction." *The Mississippi Quarterly* 49 (Winter, 1995/1996): 73-87. Discusses emotional detachment in Spencer's fiction. Argues that Spencer's female characters become separate and autonomous by repressing the emotion that traditionally binds them to their confining domestic roles. Maintains that Spencer involves the reader with the emotions that her characters hide from themselves.

Greene, Sally. "Mending Webs: The Challenge of Childhood in Elizabeth Spencer's Short Fiction." *Mississippi Quarterly* 49 (Winter, 1995/1996): 89-98. Argues that, as human relationships become more fragile in her fiction, Spencer repeatedly turns to the imaginative perspective of a child to mend and protect these relationships. However, because of social fragmentation, Spencer's children face increasingly difficult challenges in holding their world together.

Nettels, Elsa. "Elizabeth Spencer." In *southern Women Writers: The New Generation*, edited by Tonette Bond Inge. Tuscaloosa: University of Alabama Press, 1990. This insightful essay draws on biographical details, as well as on comments in a number of published interviews with Spencer, in order to trace the development of her art and thought. The extensive annotations and the list of interviews in the bibliography are particularly helpful.

Phillips, Robert. "Elizabeth Spencer." In *The Madness of Art: Interviews with Poets and Writers*. Syracuse, N.Y.: Syracuse University Press, 2003. Originally published in *The Paris Review*, Phillips's interview with Spencer focuses on her theories about writing and her personal approach to the practice of her craft.

Prenshaw, Peggy Whitman. *Elizabeth Spencer*. Boston: Twayne, 1985. An authoritative book-length study based on numerous interviews with the author and checked by her for factual accuracy. The novella *Knights and Dragons* and "Ship Island" are treated together; other short stories are discussed in another chapter. Contains a chronology and a helpful selected bibliography.

_____. "Surveying the Postage-Stamp Territory: Eudora Welty, Elizabeth Spencer, and Ellen Douglas." In *Faulkner and His Contemporaries*, edited by Joseph R. Urgo and Ann J. Abadie. Jackson: University Press of Mississippi, 2004. Examines William Faulkner's relationship to the three contemporary southern women writers, including Spencer.

Roberts, Terry. "Mermaids, Angels, and Free Women: The Heroines of Elizabeth Spencer's Fiction." In *Women Writers of the Contemporary South*, edited by Peggy Whitman Prenshaw. Jackson: University Press of Mississippi, 1984. Argues that in Spencer's later fiction, strong female heroines characteristically move from confusion through pain and dislocation to assertion of the self, courageously accepting the alienation that that implies.

_____. *Self and Community in the Fiction of Elizabeth Spencer*. Baton Rouge: Louisiana State University Press, 1994. Discusses a wide range of themes appearing in Spencer's fiction. Includes a bibliography and an index.

Seltzer, Catherine. *Elizabeth Spencer's Complicated Cartographies: Reimagining Home, the South, and southern Literary Production*. New York: Palgrave Macmillan, 2009. Examines Spencer's fiction to determine her place within the canon of southern literature. Describes how she challenges conventional notions of home, southern identity, and southern literary orthodoxies. Chapter 3 focuses on her collection *Jack of Diamonds, and Other Stories*.

Smith, Lee. "Return to Ship Island." *southern Review* 40, no. 1 (Winter, 2004): 153-157. Examines Spencer's fiction, providing biographical information and comparing her works to those of Eudora Welty. Analyzes Spencer's short story "Ship Island."

Spencer, Elizabeth. *Conversations with Elizabeth Spencer.* Edited by Peggy Whitman Prenshaw. Jackson: University Press of Mississippi, 1991. Interviews with Spencer about her writing and the representation of Mississippi in her work. Includes an index.

_____. "Elizabeth Spencer: The southern Writer Optimistically Explores the Almost Impenetrable Mysteries of the Human Heart." Interview by Amanda Smith. *Publishers Weekly* 234 (September 9, 1988): 111-112. This interview took place after Spencer's return to the South, where she established a permanent residence. Focuses on Spencer's assessment of her own relationship with the South. Includes perceptive comments by the author about the stories in the collection *Jack of Diamonds, and Other Stories.*

_____. "An Interview with Elizabeth Spencer." Interview by Betina Entzminger. *The Mississippi Quarterly* 47 (Fall, 1994): 599-618. Comments on the quality of detachment in *The Stories of Elizabeth Spencer* and on whether constantly writing in a hard, masculine style contributes to that detachment. Discusses Spencer's handling of women protagonists, her feelings of empathy with her characters, and individual characters in her fiction.

Welty, Eudora. Foreword to *The Stories of Elizabeth Spencer.* Garden City, N.Y.: Doubleday, 1981. Welty offers a brief but significant description of her first meeting with Spencer and the friendship that developed between the two writers. Welty's succinct evaluation of Spencer as a writer who is both part of the southern tradition and uniquely herself is essential reading for students.

Winchell, Mark Royden. "A Golden Ball of Thread: The Achievement of Elizabeth Spencer." *The Sewanee Review* 97 (Fall, 1989): 581-586. In this overview of Spencer's fiction, Winchell argues that its excellence can be explained, at least in part, by two facts: that moral issues and moral decisions are inherently complex and that real independence can be attained only by someone who recognizes and accepts every human being's need for a memory of home.

*Rosemary M. Canfield Reisman*
*Updated by Jaquelyn W. Walsh*

# JEAN STAFFORD

**Born:** Covina, California; July 1, 1915
**Died:** White Plains, New York; March 26, 1979

PRINCIPAL SHORT FICTION

*Children Are Bored on Sunday,* 1953
*Bad Characters,* 1964
*Selected Stories of Jean Stafford,* 1966
*The Collected Stories of Jean Stafford,* 1969

OTHER LITERARY FORMS

Jean Stafford's first three books were novels, *Boston Adventure* (1944), *The Mountain Lion* (1947), and *The Catherine Wheel* (1952). She also published juvenile fiction and a short, book-length interview with the mother of Lee Harvey Oswald, *A Mother in History* (1966).

ACHIEVEMENTS

Although critics suggest that her insightful, carefully crafted fiction deserves more attention, Stafford is generally considered to be a minor writer. Best known for her more than forty short stories, which, like her novels, are largely autobiographical, Jean Stafford investigates the complexities of human nature and explores the powerlessness of women in society as a major theme. Her treatment of women has generally been viewed as a metaphor for universal human alienation in modern society.

Stafford's reputation as a fiction writer was established with the publication of *Boston Adventure* in 1944, the same year she was awarded a prize by *Mademoiselle* magazine. Over the years, she received numerous other awards, including grants from the National Institute of Arts and Letters, the Guggenheim and Rockefeller Foundations, and the National Press

Club. She also received an O. Henry Memorial Award for her story "In the Zoo" in 1955 and the Pulitzer Prize for *The Collected Stories of Jean Stafford* in 1970.

## BIOGRAPHY

Although born in California, where she spent part of her childhood, Jean Stafford grew up in Colorado, attended the University of Colorado (A.M., 1936), and did postgraduate work at the University of Heidelberg. Her father, at one time a reporter, had written a number of western stories. After a year teaching at Stephens College in Missouri and then briefly at the Writers' Workshop in Iowa, Stafford decided to focus on her own writing and moved to Boston. There she married poet Robert Lowell in 1940; they were divorced in 1948. After a short marriage to Oliver Jensen in 1950, Stafford married again in 1959 to A. J. Liebling, critic and columnist for *The New Yorker*. After Liebling's death in 1963, Stafford withdrew from the New York literary world and made her home in Springs, Long Island. There she lived, becoming more and more reclusive, until her death in 1979.

## ANALYSIS

It is clear from a brief preface she wrote for *The Collected Stories of Jean Stafford* that Jean Stafford did not wish to be considered a regional writer. Her father and her mother's cousin had both written books about the West, but she had read neither before she began writing. Moreover, as soon as she could, she "hotfooted it across the Rocky Mountains and across the Atlantic Ocean" and came back to the West only for short periods. Her roots might therefore remain in Colorado, but the rest of her abided "in the South or the Midwest or New England or New York." The short stories in this collection, which span twenty-five years of her productive life, she grouped under headings that both insisted on the national and international character of her art and echoed universally known writers with whom she clearly wished to associate herself: Henry James, Mark Twain, Thomas Mann.

It is true, as one discovers from the stories themselves, that Stafford's fiction is not limited geographically but is set in such widely separated places as Colorado, Heidelberg, France, New York, and Boston; if,

therefore, one thinks of these stories as the result of social observation they do indeed have the broad national and international scope their author claimed for them. Her stories, however--and this may have been as apparent to Stafford as it has been to some of her critics--are not so much the result of observation and intellectual response as they are expressions of Stafford's personal view of life, a reflection of her own feeling of having been betrayed by family and friends. Her protagonists are often girls or young women, pitted against persons who feel themselves superior but are revealed to be morally, emotionally, or even physically corrupt. Although Stafford's fiction was all but forgotten at the time of her death, it has been rediscovered by a new generation of readers, mainly through the work of feminist scholars. This is ironic because Stafford herself did not embrace feminist views and, in fact, spoke harshly about aspects of the feminist movement.

The thirty stories in Stafford's *The Collected Stories of Jean Stafford* are unified by one pervasive theme, illness--physical, mental, and emotional--and the snobbery which she finds an accompaniment, the snobbery of aberrant behavior. Fascinated, repelled, and at times outraged by the way illness can be used to purchase power over vulnerable individuals, Stafford describes the various forms of this currency, the number of places where it can be spent, and the way it can be used by those of any age or sex willing to employ it. The emotional and physical invalids in these stories clearly think themselves superior to ordinary folk, and the tensions built up in these stories are often the result of conflicts between a protagonist (who usually appears to speak for the author) and neurotic individuals who think themselves justified in exploiting others. Sometimes there is an actual physical sickness--disease, old age--but the illness or psychological aberration frequently becomes a metaphor for moral corruption.

## "MAGGIE MERIWETHER'S RICH EXPERIENCE"

In "Maggie Meriwether's Rich Experience" the protagonist is a naïve young American woman from Tennessee visiting in France, where she has been invited to spend the weekend at a fashionable country house. There she discovers a crowd of titled Europeans, rich, overdressed, and eccentric, who look down their collective nose at the simple girl from the American South. The reader, who looks through the eyes of the young American, sees how stupid and arrogant these aristocrats are and understands Maggie's relief at escaping to Paris, where she telephones the older brother of her roommate at Sweet Briar College and spends the evening delighting in the wholesome provincialism of her southern American friends, regaling them with stories about her recent experience.

### "THE ECHO AND THE NEMESIS"

In "The Echo and the Nemesis" the combination of neurosis and snobbery becomes more convincingly sinister. The story is also set in Europe, in Heidelberg, Germany, but the two main characters are Americans. The protagonist, Sue, appears to be a rather unexceptional young woman from a family of ordinary means; the "invalid," Ramona, is an enormously fat girl from a very rich family (so she says), living permanently in Italy. Sue is at first impressed by Ramona's learning and by the stories she tells of her family's wealth, and the two girls become constant companions. At first the relationship, with frequent meetings in cafés, becomes routine, like another philosophy lecture or seminar in Friedrich Schiller, but then Ramona begins a series of revelations about herself and her family that embarrass, mystify, and then entrance Sue. Ramona reveals that she had a twin sister who died at an early age, a beautiful girl of whom there are many drawings and paintings, and whose room had been turned into a shrine. Ramona next reveals that she has come to Heidelberg not to study but to lose weight, and she enlists Sue's aid. Captivated by Ramona's stories about her loose-living family, Sue readily accepts an invitation to visit Ramona's brothers at a ski resort in Switzerland.

Thereafter Ramona begins to change. She misses lunches, fails to show up for appointments, and wildly indulges herself in food. When Sue makes inquiries about the coming trip and questions her about her doctor, Ramona snaps at her and, once, even slaps her face. Ramona tells Sue that Sue resembles her dead sister Martha and implies that the trip to Switzerland must therefore be called off, since Ramona's family would be too upset by the resemblance. Ramona's mysterious behavior is partially explained by Sue's discovery in Ramona's room of a photograph of a younger,

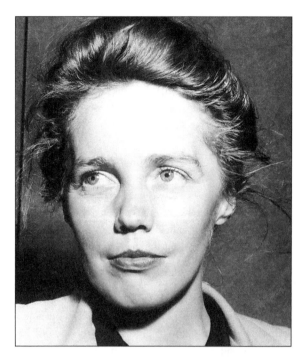

*Jean Stafford* (AP Photo)

thinner, and beautiful Ramona. In a final scene prior to Ramona's departure from Heidelberg, the revelation about her is made complete: Sue promises to remain her friend, and Ramona replies

> 'Oh, no, no, there would be nothing in it for you. Thank you just the same. I am exceptionally ill.' She spoke with pride, as if she were really saying, "I am exceptionally talented" or "I am exceptionally attractive." When Sue responds, "I'm sorry," Ramona snaps back, "I'm not sorry. It is for yourself that you should be sorry. You have such a trivial little life, poor girl. It's not your fault. Most people do.

### "THE BLEEDING HEART"

The neurotics in Stafford's stories are not always so aggressive and unappealing. In "The Bleeding Heart" an elderly dandy who is browbeaten by his invalid mother attempts to establish a "fatherly" relationship with a young Mexican girl who has come East and works as a secretary in a "discreet girl's boarding school." The girl is at first impressed with the old gentleman's aristocratic bearing and imagines she would like him for a stepfather, but when she visits his mother with a plant, a gift from the school, she is appalled by the odors, the repellent condition of the mother, and the disgusting behavior of a parrot. When the old man attempts to force his attentions on her, she turns on him and tells him to leave her alone. "Rose," he tells her, "All I am asking is a little pity."

### "THE LIBERATION"

A briefer summary of several other stories reveals how pervasive is this theme in Stafford's stories, both in the way characters are conceived and relationships established, and in the way the main action is resolved. In "The Liberation," an old couple, pathetic in their loneliness, try to prevent their young niece from marrying. At her announcement of her forthcoming marriage in Boston to a teacher at Harvard University (the story takes place in Colorado), the aunt, who "suffers" from chronic asthma, wrings her hands, and her uncle glares at her, and both are outraged at the idea of her marrying and going off to live somewhere else. The story takes a curious turn as word comes that the girl's fiancé has died of a heart attack. The girl is at first stunned and about to resign herself to remaining in Colorado, but her uncle and aunt try to "appropriate" her grief and bind her even faster to themselves. In a panic, without luggage, the girl flees for Boston and her emotional freedom from the "niggling hypochondriacs she had left behind."

### "THE HEALTHIEST GIRL IN TOWN"

"The Healthiest Girl in Town" also takes place in Colorado, where a girl, whose mother is a practical nurse in a town inhabited mainly by tuberculous patients and their families, is forced to become friends with two sisters because her mother nurses the girls' grandmother. At first the girl is impressed with the sisters (they also have illnesses) and their eastern pretentiousness and ashamed of her own good health, but then, after a quarrel with them, she proudly declares herself to be the healthiest girl in town.

### ABNORMALITIES AND NEUROSES

Two other easterners also proud of their abnormalities are a Boston spinster in "The Hope Chest" who delights in humiliating her maid and in tricking a boy who comes to her door selling Christmas wreaths into kissing her, and an elderly woman in "Life Is No Abyss" from a

rich and socially prominent Boston family whom she punishes by going to the poorhouse and allowing them to come and observe her in her impoverishment. "A Country Love Story" also deals with an invalid, in this instance a writer who neglects his wife and then accuses her of being unfaithful to him and so drives her to the brink of insanity. Other characters include a woman (in "The End of a Career") who devotes her life to looking beautiful and dies when her hands betray her age and a woman ("Beatrice Trublood's Story") who marries three times and each time selects the same brutal kind of husband.

"Bad Characters," which is perhaps Stafford's most amusing story, treats her usual theme comically. Here the neurotic invalid is cast as a vagabond girl with an appealing swagger, a female Huck Finn but without Huck's decency. She charms the daughter of a respectable family into shoplifting and, when the two are caught, feigns deaf-and-dumbness and allows the respectable girl (the protagonist) to bear the responsibility alone.

F. Scott Fitzgerald said that a writer has but one story to tell. Stafford tells hers in many different places, about people from rather different social levels, ages, education, and backgrounds: There is almost always an innocent charmed or somehow trapped by neurotic individuals from whom she finally escapes. Sometimes Stafford gives the stage to this neurotic individual and gradually peels away the mystery that always shrouds those who think themselves superior to others. This story holds up well in the retelling, for it is a universal and timeless theme.

### OTHER MAJOR WORKS

LONG FICTION: *Boston Adventure*, 1944; *The Mountain Lion*, 1947; *The Catherine Wheel*, 1952; *A Winter's Tale*, 1954 (novella in *New Short Novels*; with others).

NONFICTION: *A Mother in History*, 1966.

CHILDREN'S LITERATURE: *Arabian Nights: The Lion and the Carpenter, and Other Tales from the Arabian Nights, Retold*, 1959; *Elephi: The Cat with the High I.Q.*, 1962.

### BIBLIOGRAPHY

Austenfeld, Thomas Carl. "Memories of Heidelberg: Jean Stafford's Multiple Selves." In *American Women Writers and the Nazis: Ethics and Politics in Boyle,*

*Porter, Stafford, and Hellman.* Charlottesville: University Press of Virginia, 2001. Describes how Stafford's experiences as a postgraduate student in Heidelberg, Germany, in the 1930's made her aware of Nazism and how this awareness gave her writing an ethical dimension. Includes discussion of some of her short stories.

Avila, Wanda. *Jean Stafford: A Comprehensive Bibliography.* New York: Garland, 1983. Contains short summaries of 220 publications written by Stafford (books, stories, articles, essays, book and film reviews) and 428 critical works about her.

Gelfant, Blanche H., ed. *The Columbia Companion to the Twentieth-Century American Short Story.* New York: Columbia University Press, 2000. Includes a chapter in which Stafford's short stories are analyzed.

Goodman, Charlotte. *Jean Stafford: The Savage Heart.* Austin: University of Texas Press, 1990. This 390-page literary biography emphasizes the connections between Stafford's life and art, with their often contradictory demands. Drawing heavily from Stafford's letters, the book is well researched and makes interesting reading.

Hassel, Holly. "'Intellectual Loves Rube!' Class, Gender, and Alcohol in Jean Stafford's 'Children Are Bored on Sunday.'" *Women's Studies* 37, no. 7 (October, 2008): 815-832. Analyzes Stafford's short story "Children Are Bored on Sunday," discussing its depiction of gender and drinking.

Hulbert, Ann. *The Interior Castle: The Art and Life of Jean Stafford.* New York: A. A. Knopf, 1992. A vivid portrait of Stafford, describing the conflicts in her life and in her literary career.

Oates, Joyce Carol. "Domestic Gothic." *The New York Review of Books* 52, no. 14 (September 22, 2005): 62-64. A brief profile of Stafford, discussing her life and works, describing her literary style, and assessing her reputation in American literature.

_____. "The Interior Castle: The Art of Jean Stafford's Short Fiction." *Shenandoah* 30 (Spring, 1979): 61-64. Part of a memorial issue for Jean Stafford, this article looks closely at characters in some of Stafford's short stories. The issue also includes Stafford's last story, "Woden's Day," which was extracted from her unfinished novel *The Parliament of Women*; portions of Stafford's letters to friends; and essays and reminiscences.

Roberts, David. *Jean Stafford: A Biography.* Boston: Little, Brown, 1988. A comprehensive, 494-page biography, which connects the examination of loss and unhappiness in Stafford's fiction to the incidents in her own life. Includes photographs and a select bibliography of primary and secondary sources.

Rochette-Crawley, Susan. "'Enjoying the Conceit of Suddenness': An Analysis of Brevity, Context, and Textual 'Identity' in Jean Stafford's 'Caveat Emptor.'" *Short Story*, n.s. 2 (Spring, 1994): 69-78. A theoretical discussion of how brevity is a narrative strategy that disorients the reader's generic expectations, using Jean Stafford's story "Caveat Emptor" as an example of the short story's method of displacement.

Ryan, Maureen. *Innocence and Estrangement in the Fiction of Jean Stafford.* Baton Rouge: Louisiana State University Press, 1987. This detailed study of Stafford's themes and technique includes two chapters that focus on the feminine situations she creates in her short fiction. Supplemented by a bibliography.

Walsh, Mary Ellen Williams. *Jean Stafford.* Boston: Twayne, 1985. This extended critique examines Stafford's fiction from the perspective of the stages in women's lives: childhood, adolescence, young womanhood, maturity, and old age. It gives considerable attention to her stories, both collected and uncollected, and includes a chronology and select bibliography.

Wilson, Mary Ann. *Jean Stafford: A Study of the Short Fiction.* New York: Twayne, 1996. Discusses a representative sample of Stafford's stories under her own regional headings. Includes several comments about fiction writing by Stafford and brief comments on her fiction by a number of critics, including Joyce Carol Oates and Peter Taylor. Discusses such stories as "A Country Love Story" and "The Interior Castle," as well as many lesser-known stories.

*W. J. Stuckey*
*Updated by Jean C. Fulton*

# WILBUR DANIEL STEELE

**Born:** Greensboro, North Carolina; March 17, 1886
**Died:** Essex, Connecticut; May 26, 1970

PRINCIPAL SHORT FICTION

*Land's End, and Other Stories,* 1918
*The Shame Dance, and Other Stories,* 1923
*Urkey Island,* 1926
*The Man Who Saw Through Heaven, and Other Stories,* 1927
*Tower of Sand, and Other Stories,* 1929
*The Best Stories of Wilbur Daniel Steele,* 1946
*Full Cargo: More Stories,* 1951

OTHER LITERARY FORMS

Between 1914 and 1955, Wilbur Daniel Steele published ten novels, none of which achieved any critical success or extended life. Despite his early association with the Provincetown Players, his several attempts at writing plays came to nothing. Much of the popular success of Steele's short stories derived from his manipulation of the O. Henry ending, a knack that does not carry over to other genres.

ACHIEVEMENTS

Of Wilbur Daniel Steele's nearly two hundred published short stories, nine were included in the annual collection *The Best American Short Stories*, and eleven won various O. Henry story awards. One story, "How Beautiful with Shoes," was not only chosen for *The Best American Short Stories 1933* but also produced as a Broadway play in 1935.

BIOGRAPHY

Wilbur Daniel Steele was born on March 17, 1886, in Greensboro, North Carolina. His father, the Reverend Wilbur Fletcher Steele, taught the Bible at the University of Denver from 1892 until 1923, and the

young Wilbur received a bachelor's degree from that university before enrolling at the Boston Museum School of Fine Arts in 1907 and spending the next two years painting and etching in Paris and Italy. In 1913, Steele married the painter Margaret Thurston and moved from Greenwich Village to Provincetown, Massachusetts, where he apprenticed with such writers as Susan Glaspell and Eugene O'Neill, and where the couple's two sons, Thurston and Peter, were born. Margaret died in 1931, and in 1932 Steele married the actress Norma Mitchell and moved to Hamburg, Connecticut.

Wilbur Daniel Steele's first story, "On the Ebb Tide," was published in *Success Magazine* in 1910, and for the next two decades he published prolifically and traveled to many of the locales that appear in his fiction, including Bermuda, North Africa, the Caribbean, and the South Carolina coast. In 1932, he was awarded an honorary doctorate from the University of Denver. *The Best Stories of Wilbur Daniel Steele*, published in 1946, included most of the stories for which Steele would want to be remembered, and it was supplemented by *Full Cargo: More Stories* in 1951.

Steele moved to Old Lyme, Connecticut, in 1956, spent 1964 at Essex Rest Home in Connecticut, and in 1965 entered Highland Hall Convalescent Home in Essex, where he died in 1970.

ANALYSIS

Wilbur Daniel Steele enjoyed a long and highly successful career writing for *Harper's Magazine* and other popular periodicals. In stories that typically ran about twenty carefully plotted pages, he presented smooth, flowing narratives blessed with convincing dialogue that sometimes featured regional dialects. Commonly, Steele's tales feature endings that recall the plot switches of O. Henry, who shared Steele's birthplace of Greensboro, North Carolina. The great variety of settings compensates somewhat for the reader's eventual sense that a Steele story will lead to a contrived and often predictable ending. Of the twenty-four tales in *The Best Stories of Wilbur Daniel Steele*, four are set along the Massachusetts coast and feature Portuguese immigrants, one is set in the Caribbean, one in the South Pacific, three in North Africa, and two in the South Carolina coastal islands. The others take place in American locales that have no significant plot function.

Steele has had only negligible impact on literary history. He did not chronicle a period, as did Edgar Allan Poe. Steele's best stories create characters for whom the reader genuinely cares (for example, the wife and mother in "When Hell Froze" and the girl in "How Beautiful with Shoes"), but he seldom achieves the kind of convincing moral and psychological complexity of Nathaniel Hawthorne in "The Birthmark," Herman Melville in "Bartleby the Scrivener" or, much later, John Cheever. Steele was a graceful stylist, but he frequently lapsed into the kind of ethnic stereotyping and demeaning epithets that later generations would find offensive. In this respect, as in his sense of the taste of his audience, Steele was thoroughly a writer of his time.

### "THE SHAME DANCE"

"The Shame Dance," included in *The Best American Short Stories 1921*, is set on a tiny island in the South Pacific and reads a little like one of Joseph Conrad's stories set in the same region. The narrator, Cole, captains a trading schooner, and when he puts in at Taai he finds himself trapped in conversation with Signet, an American vagabond on board as a passenger. The man is a blatherer, borrowing cigarettes and chattering about making a lot of money in Manhattan. When Cole goes ashore, he is entertained by the de facto ruler of Taai, known only as "the Dutchman." They watch that evening an entertainment staged by three touring "Kanaka" men and a woman who is described as their common "wife." The husbands play a beguiling melody on primitive instruments while the wife performs the so-called Shame Dance, an extraordinarily erotic arabesque, which hypnotizes the Dutchman, the vagabond, and the narrator. Later, the Dutchman implants in the vagabond's mind the idea of killing the husbands, and then he imprisons the hapless murderer

and appropriates the woman. Cole returns thirteen days later to find the Dutchman apparently dead and Signet briefly ruling Taai before disappearing with the dancer.

Sitting in a bar in Honolulu sometime later, Cole hears a startling tune, which he recalls from the Shame Dance, and learns that it is an old melody called "Paragon Park" and the original music of the "Shimmie" dance. Moreover, his bar companion, a telegraph operator from Colorado, tells of being visited in his station one night by a woman in a horse blanket and a nearly insane man, who becomes distressed when he hears "Paragon Park" on the juke box. The distraught visitor exclaims, "Seas o' blood!" and he and the woman disappear. Later, Cole returns to the Marquesas Islands to find Signet "quite nude save for a loincloth," established with his dancer, and still fantasizing schemes to overwhelm Manhattan. "At last, despite the malignant thrusts and obstacles of destiny, this guttersnipe of Gotham had come to a certain estate."

### "WHEN HELL FROZE"

A farm wife, Addie Joslin, has devoted her eighteen years of married life to being a faithful helpmate to her husband John and a loving mother to her sons Ray, sixteen, and Frankie, four. Awaiting John and Ray's return from a business trip to New York one day, Addie chats innocently with a wandering tinker who plays some familiar harmonica tunes, and as he recites some trite lyrics about "Kiss me, kiss me, again . . . ," Frankie misinterprets the conversation, thinking that Addie has been kissing the stranger. The menfolk return that evening, and the next day Frankie tells Ray that Addie had kissed the vagrant with the harmonica. The upset Ray then confides to others in town. From this moment, everyone is against the innocent Addie: John and Ray reject her delicious meals, and John presents her with a can of lye water in which to wash her hands. Addie's responds, "You can leave it there till hell freezes over." When three local farmers confront Addie in the pasture, warning her against "unholy, un-Christian goings on," she rushes home to find the local minister preparing an orgy of prayer in which Addie is supposed to confess after John and Ray wash their hands in the lye water. After the defiant Addie has exiled herself in town for five months, everyone is emotionally exhausted, and Ray is ready to fight John to get Addie back. At this point Addie walks in, looking splendid in new clothes and bringing a harmonica for Frankie. When John asks if hell has frozen over, Addie replies, "Oh yes. Oh, long ago," and dips her hands in the lye can. The ending is happy, with buckwheat cakes all around and Addie dreaming of the green rye growing in the spring.

### "THE MAN WHO SAW THROUGH HEAVEN"

"The Man Who Saw Through Heaven" tells the story of the Reverend Hubert Diana whose contemplation of the immensities of space leads him to a more profound faith. On the night before the Reverend Diana is to embark from Boston for missionary work in East Africa, his whole vision of God changes during a visit to an observatory, where he is shocked by the immensities of space, especially when his astronomer-guide speculates that the opal ring on the Reverend's finger may contain universes that in the scale of the whole creation may be as the universe to the boundlessness of space. Because of his shocking public nakedness en route to East Africa, Diana has to be put ashore in Algiers, from which he escapes and wanders to East Africa, where the narrator and Mrs. Diana track him down months later. It seems that he has recapitulated the evolution of man in his own way. Following him from village to village, they find a trail of sculpted mud blobs that progress from low life forms through lizards to bulls, all executed "to give the Beast of the Infinite a name and a shape." The natives at his final village had named him "Father Witch." Diana's mud figure had become a recognizable man distinguished by a carefully molded finger bearing an opal ring. The ending is triumphant. When Mrs. Diana expresses her shock that the Reverend had "sunk to idolatry," the narrator explains: "To the bottom, yes. And come up its whole history again. And from here he walked out into the sunshine to kneel and talk with 'Our Father Witch--.'"

### "HOW BEAUTIFUL WITH SHOES"

Amarantha Doggett, a "broad-fleshed, slow-minded" farm girl called simply Mare, allows the attentions of her tobacco chewing yokel of a beau, not knowing anything more romantic until Humble Jewett, a deluded escapee from the nearby asylum, takes her hostage and quotes poetry to her. Jewett quotes Richard Lovelace: "Amarantha sweet and fair--/ Ah, braid no

more that golden hair," the Middle English lyric that ends "Christ, that my love were in my arms/ And I in my bed again," and "How beautiful are thy feet with shoes, O prince's daughter" from the Song of Solomon. Amarantha remains unharmed and is kept under duress only for a night before Humble Jewett dies from shotgun blasts, but despite her fright she has been moved in ways she does not understand by the only poetry and tenderness she will ever know in life. When her loutish lover later importunes her for a kiss, "She pushe[s] him to the door and through it with all her strength, and close[s] it in his face, and st[ands] with her weight against it, crying, 'Go 'way! Go 'way! Lea' me be!'" "How Beautiful with Shoes" anticipates Flannery O'Connor in some ways and is a story that many better-known authors would be glad to claim.

OTHER MAJOR WORKS

LONG FICTION: *Storm*, 1914; *Isles of the Blest*, 1924; *Taboo*, 1925; *Meat*, 1928; *Undertow*, 1930; *Sound of Rowlocks*, 1938; *That Girl from Memphis*, 1945; *Diamond Wedding*, 1950; *Their Town*, 1952; *The Way to the Gold*, 1955.

PLAYS: *The Giant's Stair*, pb. 1924; *The Terrible Woman, and Other One-Act Plays*, pb. 1925; *Post Road*, pr. 1934 (with Norma Mitchell).

BIBLIOGRAPHY

Bucco, Martin. *Wilbur Daniel Steele*. New York: Twayne, 1972. This volume in the Twayne series provides an introductory overview to Steele's life and work, as well as an indispensable bibliography. Seven chapters of summary and commentary discuss the seven collections of stories in chronological order.

Elser, Frank B. "Oh, Yes . . . Wilbur Daniel Steele." *The Bookman* 62 (February, 1926): 691-694. An interview that provides a good picture of Steele as a person and insight into his writing practices.

Gelb, Arthur, and Barbara Gelb. *O'Neill*. New York: Harper and Brothers, 1960. This biography of Eugene O'Neill describes the circumstances of life at Provincetown when Steele was there and alludes to Steele's friendship with O'Neill.

Mirrielees, Edith R. "The Best of Steele." A review of *The Best Stories of Wilbur Daniel Steele*, by Wilbur Daniel Steele. *The New York Times*, July 14, 1946, p. 5, 20. This review provides an overall assessment of Steele's work.

Peterson, Theodore. *Magazines in the Twentieth Century*. Urbana: University of Illinois Press, 1964. Does not treat Steele directly but explains the editorial policies of his publishers.

Williams, Blanche Colton. *Our Short Story Writers*. New York: Dodd, Mead, 1926. One chapter appraises Steele's work.

*Frank Day*

# WALLACE STEGNER

**Born:** Lake Mills, Iowa; February 18, 1909
**Died:** Santa Fe, New Mexico; April 13, 1993

PRINCIPAL SHORT FICTION

*The Women on the Wall,* 1950
*The City of the Living, and Other Stories,* 1956
*Collected Stories of Wallace Stegner,* 1990

OTHER LITERARY FORMS

Primarily a novelist and historian, Wallace Stegner (STEHG-nur) is the author of many novels, from *Remembering Laughter* (1937) to *Crossing to Safety* (1987); his best-known and perhaps his best novel, *The Big Rock Candy Mountain*, was published in 1943, and *Angle of Repose* (1971) was awarded the Pulitzer Prize. *Mormon Country*, his first book of nonfiction, was published in 1942; it was followed by approximately a dozen others, including *Beyond the Hundredth Meridian: John Wesley Powell and the Second Opening of the West* (1954), *The Sound of Mountain Water* (essays, 1969), and *The Uneasy Chair: A Biography of Bernard DeVoto* (1974). In addition, he edited many books, including *Great American Short Stories* (with Mary Stegner, 1957), numerous annual volumes of *Stanford Short Stories* (with Richard Scowcroft), and *The Letters of Bernard DeVoto* (1975).

In 1987, Stegner published the novel *Crossing to Safety*, which he said is "a sort of memoir . . . for Mary [his wife] and myself." A gentle and affectionate portrait of two very different academic couples, *Crossing to Safety* met with great critical and popular acclaim. In an offshoot to his long teaching career, Stegner published *On the Teaching of Creative Writing: Responses to a Series of Questions* in 1988.

ACHIEVEMENTS

Wallace Stegner's talent lay in his evocation of the West, which otherwise has been poorly documented in so-called westerns, whether they be films or novels. As writer Richard Etulain has noted, what gives Stegner's work "its essential character is a deep familiarity with American historical, cultural, and political terrain." Stegner's work reveals the many aspects that make up American culture, or Americana. In addition, it provides a basis for understanding modern life in the United States. His literary efforts in this pursuit to portray fast-disappearing cultural and geographic sections of the United States were recognized with the western History Association Prize in 1990.

Stegner received many awards and honors, including a Guggenheim Fellowship, a Rockefeller Fellowship, the Pulitzer Prize, a National Endowment for the Humanities Senior Fellowship, and an American Academy in Rome fellowship. In the spring of 1990, Stegner was given a lifetime achievement award by PEN USA Center West. In September of the same year, he was awarded a senior fellowship by the National Endowment for the Arts.

## BIOGRAPHY

Born in Iowa on his grandfather's farm, Wallace Earle Stegner moved with his family to East End, Saskatchewan at the age of five. He was educated in Utah, where he received an A.B. from the University of Utah in 1930; and in his native state, where he earned an M.A. in 1932 and a Ph.D. in 1935 from the University of Iowa. Although he was briefly enrolled at the University of California at Los Angeles, he never actually attended any classes--he did not like California and returned to Utah as soon as he could.

Stegner once commented that his subjects and themes, both in fiction and in nonfiction, "are mainly out of the American West, in which I grew up." He taught at various colleges and universities, primarily at Stanford University, where he was director of its creative writing program. Stegner coauthored books with both his wife, Mary, and his son, Page, but he stopped publishing short stories after 1960. He said that everything he wanted to write "somehow wanted to be long." His attention continued to remain focused on the environment, a concern that began after World War II but that probably dated back to his childhood, when, as he said, he was "imprinted by the prairies."

## ANALYSIS

Of the eighteen stories in *The Women on the Wall*, almost half are concerned with incidents in the life of Brucie, a young boy growing up in Saskatchewan in the later years of the second decade of the twentieth century. In these semirelated stories, strongly rooted in time and place, Wallace Stegner is in complete control of his material and writes with insight and understanding which never lapse into sentimentality. The Brucie stories revolve around relatively commonplace subjects: the trapping of a gopher, the slaughtering of a sow, a family picnic.

### "TWO RIVERS"

"Two Rivers," an O. Henry second-prize winner in 1942, is characteristic. The action is simple. Following an unhappy Fourth of July (the failure of the family's dilapidated Ford and the subsequent missed ball game in Chinook, the missed parade and fireworks, climaxed by the cuff on the ear from his father), the family set off for a picnic. Very little

actually happens in this effective account of family relations, but at the story's end the reader shares Brucie's quiet pleasure:

> The boy looked up at his father, his laughter bubbling up, everything wonderful, the day a swell day, his mother clapping hands in time to his father's fool singing (an impromptu song about "a kid and his name was Brucie").
>
> "Aw, for gosh sakes," he said, and ducked when his father pretended he was going to swat him one.

### "BEYOND THE GLASS MOUNTAIN"

In his stories about adults, Stegner's vision is considerably darker. Life was essentially good for a boy in 1917, he suggests; for an adult in the 1940's, it was likely to be just the opposite. "Beyond the Glass Mountain" (like "Two Rivers," the recipient of an O. Henry Award, second-prize, 1948) is characteristic. The narrative is structurally simple, uncluttered, and admirably economical: an account of a few moments during the reunion of two men who had been close friends during their college days. The narrator,

*Wallace Stegner* (Library of Congress)

"prepared . . . for nostalgia," finds his friend to be a pathetic alcoholic, irreparably damaged by the passing of time and a destructive marriage. (For the "love of God," he thinks, "Get rid of her. . . . She'll cheat on you. . . . She'll suck you dry like an old orange skin)."

"Beyond the Glass Mountain," "The View from the Balcony," "The Women on the Wall," and other stories similarly depict the encroachment of the always present scourges of humanity on lives that might or should be "ordinary" or "happy": the itch for domination, the dark shadow of emotional instability or insanity, the tyranny of sex, and the insecurity of the unloved.

### THE CITY OF THE LIVING, AND OTHER STORIES

The seven stories and one novella of *The City of the Living, and Other Stories* share in common with *The Women on the Wall* Stegner's thoroughly disciplined narrative skill and his unblinking understanding of his characters. These later stories are more varied than their predecessors, ranging as they do from a flea bag of a California pool hall during the American Depression ("The Blue-Winged Teal," the O. Henry Memorial Award first-prize winner in 1950); to Egypt ("The City of the Living"); to Salt Lake City ("Maiden in a Tower"); to the French Riviera ("Impasse"); to an unspecified snowswept rural landscape-with-figures piece ("The Traveler"); to life among the wealthy and not-so-beautiful people in southern California ("Field Guide to the western Birds").

Stegner is again at his best in his shorter, less complicated, pieces. "Maiden in a Tower," for example, is virtually without incident: The drama of the story is the evocation of the past. The narrator has driven from San Francisco to a funeral home in Salt Lake City where his aunt lies awaiting burial. By coincidence, the funeral home was, a quarter of a century ago, the setting of the narrator's first love, and it evokes in him memories of life in the Jazz Age and his infatuation with the girl who epitomized all the glamour, the folly, the joy of youth and love and aspiration of the past, a past as dead as the narrator's aunt and the corpse of another woman whom he contemplates in her coffin in what had been the enchanted tower of his youth. Thoroughly controlled, moving, and full of emotion which never degenerates into sentimentality, "Maiden in a Tower" is a

masterly piece, as is the title story "The City of the Living." This story provides a glimpse of a father and son during a few hours of almost unbearable crisis (the son is desperately ill in a hotel in Egypt); here, Stegner presents a brilliant picture of father-son relations; and the setting, with its contrast of luxury and poverty, sickness and health, is unforgettable. Stegner is equally effective in his other stories of the parent-child relations which furnish subject and theme for "The Blue-Winged Teal," "Impasse," and "The Volunteer."

The novella, "Field Guide to the western Birds," however, in spite of some memorable moments, seems rather too long for what it accomplishes, too predictable in its denouement. As social history, however, Stegner's creation of well-heeled intellectuals and pseudointellectuals, frauds, hangers-on and circuit riders of the "good and opulent life," narrated by a self-congratulatory retired literary agent, has about it the ring of permanence. As John Galsworthy said of his Forsytes, here are characters miraculously preserved, pickled in their own juices.

### OTHER MAJOR WORKS

LONG FICTION: *Remembering Laughter*, 1937; *The Potter's House*, 1938; *On a Darkling Plain*, 1940; *Fire and Ice*, 1941; *The Big Rock Candy Mountain*, 1943; *Second Growth*, 1947; *The Preacher and the Slave*, 1950; *A Shooting Star*, 1961; *All the Little Live Things*, 1967; *Angle of Repose*, 1971; *The Spectator Bird*, 1976; *Recapitulation*, 1979; *Joe Hill*, 1980; *Crossing to Safety*, 1987.

NONFICTION: *Mormon Country*, 1942; *One Nation*, 1945 (with the editors of *Look*); *Look at America: The Central Northwest*, 1947; *The Writer in America*, 1951; *Beyond the Hundredth Meridian: John Wesley Powell and the Second Opening of the West*, 1954; *Wolf Willow: A History, a Story, and a Memory of the Last Plains Frontier*, 1962; *The Gathering of Zion: The Story of the Mormon Trail*, 1964; *The Sound of Mountain Water*, 1969; *Ansel Adams: Images 1923-1974*, 1974; *The Uneasy Chair: A Biography of Bernard DeVoto*, 1974; *One Way to Spell Man*, 1982; *American Places*, 1983; *Conversations with Wallace Stegner on western History and Literature*, 1983; *The American West as Living Space*, 1987; *On the Teaching of*

*Creative Writing: Responses to a Series of Questions*, 1988 (Edward Connery Lathem, editor); *Where the Bluebird Sings to the Lemonade Springs: Living and Writing in the West*, 1992; *Marking the Sparrow's Fall: Wallace Stegner's American West*, 1998 (Page Stegner, editor); *Stealing Glances: Three Interviews with Wallace Stegner*, 1998 (James R. Hepworth, editor); *On Teaching and Writing Fiction*, 2002 (Lynn Stegner, editor); *The Selected Letters of Wallace Stegner*, 2007 (Page Stegner, editor).

EDITED TEXTS: *An Exposition Workshop*, 1939; *Readings for Citizens at War*, 1941; *Stanford Short Stories, 1946*, 1947 (with Richard Scowcroft); *The Writer's Art: A Collection of Short Stories*, 1950 (with Scowcroft and Boris Ilyin); *This Is Dinosaur: The Echo Park and Its Magic Rivers*, 1955; *Great American Short Stories*, 1957 (with Mary Stegner); *The Exploration of the Colorado River of the West*, 1957; *Selected American Prose: The Realistic Movement*, 1958; *Report on the Lands of the Arid Region of the United States*, 1962; *Modern Composition*, 1964 (four volumes); *The American Novel: From Cooper to Faulkner*, 1965; *Twenty Years of Stanford Short Stories*, 1966; *The Letters of Bernard DeVoto*, 1975.

BIBLIOGRAPHY

Arthur, Anthony, ed. *Critical Essays on Wallace Stegner*. Boston: G. K. Hall, 1982. Although not an exhaustive discussion of Stegner's works, these essays cover much of his most important writing, including his short fiction. Notes for further reference are included, as are primary and secondary bibliographical information and an index.

Benson, Jackson J. *Down by the Lemonade Springs: Essays on Wallace Stegner*. Reno: University of Nevada Press, 2001. These essays trace Stegner's development as a writer. One of the essays focuses on Stegner's short stories, while others discuss Stegner as an environmentalist, his friendship with poet Robert Frost, and his novels Angle of Reposeand *Crossing to Safety*.

_____. *Wallace Stegner: His Life and Work*. New York: Viking Press, 1996. A biography that argues against pigeonholing Stegner as a western writer. Focuses largely on the people and events that most influenced Stegner's art, including Robert Frost and Bernard DeVoto. Covers Stegner's teaching career and his influence on such writers as Ken Kesey, Edward Abbey, Wendell Berry, and Larry McMurty.

_____. *Wallace Stegner: A Study of the Short Fiction*. New York: Twayne, 1998. A comprehensive study that discusses Stegner's short fiction in relation to his life in Saskatchewan and his experiences as an adolescent and in college, the influence of Robert Frost on his stories, the stories as a preface to his novels, and the critical reception to his short fiction.

Burrows, Russell. "Wallace Stegner's Version of Pastoral: The Topic of Ecology in His Work." *western American Literature* 25 (May, 1990): 15-25. Stegner's environmentalist stance has had a definite impact on his work, and this article discusses Stegner's use of the pastoral setting in much of his fiction, both long and short. Includes bibliographical information and notes for further reference.

Colberg, Nancy. *Wallace Stegner: A Descriptive Bibliography*. Lewiston, Idaho: Confluence Press, 1990. Contains detailed descriptions of Stegner's works, from his very early writing to *The American West as Living Space*. Colberg also provides sections for other Stegner material, such as contributions to books and edited works. A short appendix that also serves as a secondary bibliography is a good resource for the original publication information for Stegner's individual short stories.

Cook-Lynn, Elizabeth. *Why I Can't Read Wallace Stegner, and Other Essays*. Madison: University of Wisconsin Press, 1996. In the title essay of this collection, Cook-Lynn, a Native American, argues with Stegner's view of Native American culture. She particularly takes issue with Stegner's claim that western history ended in 1890, the year of the massacre at Wounded Knee, and his unchallenged statement that the Plains Indians are done forever.

Fradkin, Philip L. *Wallace Stegner and the American West*. New York: Alfred A. Knopf, 2008. Fradkin, an environmental historian, analyzes the influence of the West on Stegner's life and works, from his childhood years in Saskatchewan to his later life in Utah and California. Explicates Stegner's writings about the effect of nature upon the human condition. Discusses Stegner's environmental work with Secretary of the Interior Stewart L. Udall and the Sierra Club.

Gelfant, Blanche H., ed. *The Columbia Companion to the Twentieth-Century American Short Story*. New York: Columbia University Press, 2000. Includes a chapter in which Stegner's short stories are analyzed.

Meine, Curt, ed. *Wallace Stegner and the Continental Vision: Essays on Literature, History, and Landscape*. Washington, D.C.: Island Press, 1997. A collection of papers presented at a 1996 symposium in Madison, Wisconsin. Includes essays on Stegner and the shaping of the modern West, the art of storytelling, history, environmentalism, politics, and bioregionalism.

Nelson, Nancy Owne. "Land Lessons in an 'Unhistoried' West: Wallace Stegner's California." In *San Francisco in Fiction: Essays in a Regional Literature*, edited by David Fine and Paul Skenazy. Albuquerque: University of New Mexico Press, 1995. Argues that Stegner's California experience from the 1940's to the 1970's helped to shape the environmental philosophy of his work. Discusses Stegner's preservationist position in several fictional and nonfictional works.

Rankin, Charles E., ed. *Wallace Stegner: Man and Writer*. Albuquerque: University of New Mexico Press, 1996. A collection of essays by various critics on Stegner's life and art. Most helpful for understanding Stegner's short fiction are the essays by Elliott West on "Storytelling and western Identity," Jackson J. Benson's "The Story of Wallace Stegner's Fiction," and William Bevis's "The Civic Style."

Robinson, Forrest G. *Wallace Stegner*. Boston: Twayne, 1977. A combination of biographical information on Stegner and interpretation and literary criticism of his work up to the mid-1970's. Robinson provides a chronology of Stegner's life and writings, as well as detailed bibliographical information, both primary and secondary. Supplemented by notes and an index.

Stegner, Wallace. "The Art of Fiction: An Interview with Wallace Stegner." Interview by James R. Hepworth. *The Paris Review* 115 (Summer, 1990): 58-90. Stegner talks about how he became a writer, as well as about writing in general. Although no references are included, this article is useful for the firsthand information it provides about Stegner through the interview process.

Stegner, Wallace, and Richard Etulain. *Conversations with Wallace Stegner*. Rev. ed. Salt Lake City: University of Utah Press, 1990. This edition is an expanded version of a book that first appeared in 1983, and the revised edition includes an interview section. In it, Stegner talks about all of his work up to *Crossing to Safety*. Includes biographical information in the form of answers to interview questions. Covers Stegner's view of the American literary West and the West in general, including aspects of western history and the wilderness areas of the West. References to individual short stories and to the collections can be found in the index.

Willrich, Patricia Rowe. "A Perspective on Wallace Stegner." *The Virginia Quarterly Review* 67 (Spring, 1991): 240-258. Covers the high points of Stegner's long career as a writer and scholar, giving both biographical details and information about his work. Good for an overview of, as well as for specifics on, Stegner's literary output.

Zahlan, Anne Ricketson. "Cities of the Living: Disease and the Traveller in the *Collected Stories* of Wallace Stegner." *Studies in Short Fiction* 29 (Fall, 1992): 509-515. Discusses a number of thematically complementary stories in which characters travel into or away from exile, attempt to recover the past, or explore new avenues in order to discover the self.

*William Peden*
*Updated by Jo-Ellen Lipman Boon*

# GERTRUDE STEIN

**Born:** Allegheny (now in Pittsburgh), Pennsylvania;
February 3, 1874
**Died:** Neuilly-sur-Seine, France; July 27, 1946

PRINCIPAL SHORT FICTION

*Three Lives,* 1909
*Tender Buttons: Objects, Food, Rooms,* 1914
*Mrs. Reynolds and Five Earlier Novelettes, 1931-
1942,* 1952
*As Fine as Melanctha,* 1954
*Painted Lace, and Other Pieces, 1914-1937,* 1955
*Alphabets and Birthdays,* 1957

OTHER LITERARY FORMS

It is difficult to classify Gertrude Stein's writings, because she radically upset the conventions of literary genres and because she worked in many different forms. Traditional generic labels simply do not describe individual works. Even when Stein names the genre in a work's title (*Ida, a Novel,* 1941, for example), the conventional form marks only how far Stein has digressed from the norm. Works such as *Ida, a Novel* and *Mrs. Reynolds and Five Earlier Novelettes* are Stein's version of the novel, while *The Autobiography of Alice B. Toklas* (1933) and *Operas and Plays* (pb. 1932), among other works, encourage comparison with other genres. Stein became famous in the United States with *The Autobiography of Alice B. Toklas,* and her success encouraged her to experiment further with the genre in *Everybody's Autobiography* (1937). Even when writing "autobiography," however, Stein did not adhere to conventional restrictions, using multiple viewpoints in the composite work. Similarly, although Stein wrote many plays, some of which have been performed, they do not follow dramatic conventions, for frequently they lack plot and character. Stein also wrote meditations and other quasi-philosophical and theoretical musings, and in numerous essays she attempted to explain her theories of composition and her notions of art. In addition, she experimented in verse and developed a special genre which she called portraits. Regardless of the form, however, the style is unmistakably Stein's and serves as a signature to all her works.

ACHIEVEMENTS

Gertrude Stein's greatest achievement was her wily and strong independence, which revealed itself as much in her lifestyle as in her work. She was a creative person with a strong personality, a gift for conversation, and a good ear, and her home became a center for the avant-garde circle of artists in Paris during the early 1900's. Perhaps this salon would not be so famous were it not for the fact that those associated with it were later accepted as the outstanding figures of the modern art world. In time, artists as different as Ernest Hemingway, Sherwood Anderson, Virgil Thomson, Guillaume Apollinaire, Henri Matisse, and Pablo Picasso became associated with Stein and were drawn into the discussions and activities that took place in her home. Among contemporaries she was recognized as a fascinating individual, a woman of strong opinions and definite views, a lively intelligence and vibrant mind; among the cultural historians who came later, she was acknowledged to be a person of enormous creative influence and an empowering force.

Stein's achievements were not limited to her role as a cultural catalyst, however, for she was a pioneering writer in her own right. Working from a sense that the present moment of consciousness is supreme, Stein increasingly radicalized her writing to focus on the here and now, on the mystery of consciousness, and ultimately on the enigma of language and words. This drive led Stein increasingly away from the conventions of language as commonly understood and practiced through the structures and preoccupations of genre, through the patterns and assumptions of syntax, and finally even through the basic referential quality of words. Repetition--of sounds and words themselves--became the hallmark of Stein's writing. Some contemporaries thought her experimental language to be foolish and childlike, but others hailed her efforts as truly pioneering literary breakthroughs. Most of the key terms in the criticism of modern literature have been applied to Stein at one time or another, including abstractionist, cubist, and minimalist. Indeed, most historians of the period agree that her work and her personality must be acknowledged before any serious discussion of any of these movements can proceed. However her work is defined, regardless of whether one likes or dislikes it, it has made a significant impact on the development of modern literature.

In addition to its variety and inventiveness, the sheer bulk of Stein's canon should not be overlooked as an accomplishment. Richard Bridgman's *Gertrude Stein in Pieces* (1970) lists nearly six hundred titles in the Stein bibliography, some very short pieces but others significantly longer. She was prolific, flexible, and varied--at her best in the unclassifiable writings that mingle verse, prose, and drama into a unique species of art that bears the imprint of Gertrude Stein alone.

Stein had the misfortune of living through two world wars. During the first she obtained a Ford van, which she drove for the American Fund for French Wounded. In 1922, she was awarded the Médaille de la Reconnaissance Française for wartime activities.

BIOGRAPHY

When Daniel Stein and Amelia Keyser were married in 1864, the seeds of Gertrude Stein's future independence were sown, for the couple had some unusual ideas about child rearing and family life. Perhaps most psychologically damaging to the children was the parents' firm decision to have five children--no more and no fewer. Consequently, Gertrude's beloved older brother Leo and she were conceived only after the deaths of two other Stein children. In *Everybody's Autobiography* Stein says that the situation made her and her brother feel "funny." Knowing that one's very existence depends on the deaths of others surely would have some psychological effect, and some biographers

attribute Stein's lifelong interest in identity to her knowledge of her parents' decision about family size.

Daniel Stein was apparently as quarrelsome and independent as his daughter was to become. Having operated a successful cloth and clothing business in Baltimore with his brothers, Daniel and another brother broke up the partnership by moving out to Pittsburgh to open a new business. When Daniel had earned enough money, he moved the family across the Ohio River to Allegheny, Pennsylvania, and it was there that Gertrude Stein was born in 1874. She was the last child the Steins were to have, completing the unit of five children. Michael Stein was the oldest child (born in 1865); Simon was next (1867); then came Bertha (1870) and Leo (1872). When Allegheny was hit with fire and flood, Daniel once again moved the family, this time to Austria, having decided that the older children needed the benefits of a European education.

The family went first to Gemünden and then to Vienna. Although not wealthy, they lived well and were able to afford a nurse, a tutor, a governess, and a full domestic staff. The children were exposed to music

*Gertrude Stein* (AP Photo)

and dancing lessons, and they enjoyed all the sights and activities of the upper middle class in Europe at the time. In his concern for the education of his children, Daniel resembled Henry James, whose educational theories also featured the advantages of the European experience to a developing mind. During this period, letters from Amelia and her sister Rachel Keyser, who accompanied the Steins, reveal that the baby was speaking German and experiencing an apparently contented, pampered, and protected infancy.

The roaming continued. In 1878, the family moved to Paris, and Stein got her first view of the city she would later make her home. When the Steins returned to the United States in 1879, they lived at first with the Keyser family in Baltimore, but Daniel was set on living in California. By 1880, the family had relocated to Oakland, where they stayed for some time (until 1891), long enough for Stein to develop an attachment to the place. It was Oakland that Stein always thought of as home.

The unsettled life of the Steins continued with the death of Amelia when Stein was fourteen. Three years later (in 1891), Daniel died, leaving Michael head of the family. He moved the family to San Francisco that year, but by the following year the family was dispersed--Michael and Simon remaining in San Francisco, Gertrude and her sister Bertha going back to Baltimore to live with their mother's sister, and Leo transferring from the University of California at Berkeley to Harvard University. In the fall of 1893, Gertrude Stein herself entered Harvard Annex (later renamed Radcliffe College), thus rejoining the brother to whom she had grown so attached. Their strong bond was to survive into adulthood, being broken only by Gertrude's lifelong commitment to Alice B. Toklas and her ascendancy in Parisian art circles.

Stein was at Harvard during a wonderful period in that institution's history. She had the good fortune to study under William James, whose theories of psychology intrigued the young woman and initiated a lifelong interest in questions of personality, identity, and consciousness. Stein's later attempts to present in her writing awareness of a continuing flux in the present, the immediacy of present existence, and the inclusiveness and randomness of consciousness can be

traced in part to James's influence. Stein's first publication came out during this Harvard period. "Normal Motor Automatism," co-authored with Leon M. Solomons, was published in *Psychological Review* in September, 1896. Although this essay was primarily Solomons's, Stein published her own work on the subject in the *Psychological Review* of May, 1898-- "Cultivated Motor Automatism: A Study of Character in Its Relation to Attention." Stein's early interest in automatic writing has led some readers to believe that the method directed her own subsequent writing, but that claim has been generally discredited. Harvard did more to focus her attention on the consciousness behind the work than on the techniques and strategies of the writing process.

The Harvard experience was not, however, completely successful. In the spring of 1897, Stein failed the Radcliffe Latin entrance examination and consequently was not awarded her bachelor's degree. Undaunted, in the fall of 1897 she entered the Johns Hopkins School of Medicine, and she received the Harvard degree in 1898, having been privately tutored in Latin so that she could pass the examination. It was William James who encouraged her to take the Harvard degree and to continue her education; Johns Hopkins seemed a likely choice both because it was funded to accept women into the program on a basis equal to men and because her brother Leo was studying there. The first two years of medical study went well, but after that, Stein complained of boredom and began to dislike her classes. In the end, she did not pass her final examinations and never took the degree. She had learned what she wanted to learn and had no interest in practicing medicine.

For some time, Stein had been spending her summers in Europe with Leo, so it seemed natural that they would settle in London in September, 1902. In February of the following year, Stein sailed back to the United States, this time staying in New York until rejoining Leo once again for summer travel. In the fall of 1903, they occupied the house at 27 rue de Fleurus, the address which was to become famous as an artistic mecca. *Things as They Are* (1950; originally known as *Q.E.D.*) was written there, although Stein then overlooked the work for some thirty years.

In 1904, Gertrude and Leo began purchasing paintings by men destined to become the leading figures of modern art. Having studied the great masters throughout the museums of Europe, the Steins were not automatically impressed with the world of modern art, yet something about Paul Cézanne's work struck Leo, and he took his sister to a gallery of his works. After the purchase of their first Cézanne, they were soon given freer rein to look among the canvases of the Paris art dealers. They purchased works by Honoré Daumier, Édouard Manet, Pierre-Auguste Renoir, Henri Toulouse-Lautrec, Paul Gauguin, and others. Thus Leo and Gertrude Stein laid out a new direction in their own cultural life and established a new model for American art collectors. People began to go to the rue de Fleurus address to see the paintings and then to talk about art and to socialize. The cultural center of modern art was born.

During this time, Stein was also writing. *The Making of Americans: Being a History of a Family's Progress* (1925) and *Three Lives* date to this period, *Three Lives* being published in 1909 as Stein's first book. Another important event of the period was Stein's meeting Alice Toklas in September, 1907; Toklas moved into the Stein household on rue de Fleurus early in 1909. Her presence hastened the deterioration of the relationship between Stein and her brother (he finally left in 1913) and facilitated Stein's writing, because Toklas learned to type and transcribed Stein's work. She was Stein's companion for the remainder of the writer's life.

In June, 1914, *Tender Buttons* was published. The work marks a significant movement on Stein's part toward abstractionism, as she focuses more on things than on people and blurs the distinction between poetry and prose. When war broke out, Stein and Toklas were house guests of the Alfred North Whiteheads in Lockridge, England, and they did not return to Paris until October of that year. In 1915, they left Paris for Spain, returning in 1916. In 1917, Stein obtained a Ford van from the United States, which she drove for the American Fund for French Wounded as a supply truck, and Stein's preoccupation with automobiles, especially Fords, began. She contributed to the war effort in France in various ways and in various areas of France, not returning to Paris "permanently" until May, 1919.

After the war, writing and socializing could once again begin in earnest. In 1922, she met Hemingway and became godmother to his son born the following year. Stein continued to write and began to give lectures during this period; she continued also to cultivate her interest in cars (she was now on her third) and in pet dogs. In 1930, *Lucy Church Amiably* was published, and in 1932, *The Autobiography of Alice B. Toklas* was written at Bilignin, France. It became a literary sensation in 1933, and it continues to be the most widely read and appreciated of all Stein's writings. Early in 1934, the first public performance of *Four Saints in Three Acts* (pb., pr. 1934) took place in Hartford, Connecticut. Performances in other cities soon followed, and Stein began a lecture tour in the United States that established her reputation.

When Paris was occupied in 1940, Stein was advised to leave, which she did, not returning until December, 1944. In the following year, she toured United States Army bases in occupied Germany and lectured in Belgium and elsewhere. In July, 1946, en route to a friend's summer house, Stein fell ill and was admitted to the American hospital at Neuilly-sur-Seine. On July 27, she died following an operation for cancer. Her brother Leo died a year later, almost to the day. Toklas, Gertrude Stein's dearest companion, survived another twenty-two years. A chapter in the history of modern art had come to an end.

ANALYSIS

Gertrude Stein's work has never been easily accessible to the reader. During her lifetime, her work was both ridiculed and celebrated, and indeed these two attitudes continue to prevail among Stein's readers. Historical distance has provided a supportive context for Stein's work, however. Now that readers can see Stein in a milieu of highly creative artists devoted to wrenching art from the restrictions of realism and verisimilitude, her work is more easily appreciated for the inroads it makes against conventions, although perhaps not more easily understood. Stein was a powerful initiator, a ruthless experimenter, and a bold and forthright manipulator of words.

## TENDER BUTTONS

Having already written *Things as They Are*, *Three Lives*, and *The Making of Americans*, Stein was in full command when she made the surprising innovations of *Tender Buttons*. The author herself always rated the work highly, considering it to be one of her most significant writings despite the ridicule and scorn it received from those who did not agree that it added a new dimension to literature. Prior to *Tender Buttons*, Stein had grown increasingly abstract in her writing. *Tender Buttons* marks something of a culmination in this progressing abstractionism, for here she produces a set of "still lifes," each of which sustains abstraction. The subject matter, too, has changed from her earlier writing. In *Tender Buttons*, Stein moves from people to things. The book is divided into three sections: "Objects," "Food," and "Rooms." While the divisions classify, the effect is still that of eclecticism, for no perceptible principles of order determine either the arrangement within each section or the sequencing of the sections themselves.

The title of *Tender Buttons* indicates some of the ironies of the collection. A button is something hard, concrete, and functional, while the word "tender" as an adjective suggests the opposite--something soft. "Tender" can also be a verb, and, in this sense, the collection is Stein's offering of discrete bits of prose. "Tender" may suggest an emotional state, but, if so, the emotion must emanate from the reader, for the hard little buttons of prose in *Tender Buttons* do not themselves develop an emotional state. In the title, as in the name of each passage within the work, Stein seems to be offering the reader something tangible, something realistic, but she does so only to challenge the reader's notions of reality and to tease the mind.

The verbal fragments in *Tender Buttons* reveal a variety of strategies, and it is the flexibility of language and idea that keeps one reading. Each entry is titled; "A Red Stamp," "A Plate," "Roastbeef," "Sugar," and "Oranges" are typical examples. Entries range in length from a single short line to the approximately twelve pages of the undivided section "Rooms." In some of the entries, the title shapes the suggestions and hints, while in others, the title seems to bear little or no relationship to what follows. Stein's prose does not describe the objects realistically, but rather opens the mind to the flow of thoughts that the title evokes. In these verbal fragments there is no logic and no sequence; sometimes an entry shows accretion, but no line of thought is developed. Indeed, even the logic of syntax is refused in favor of phrases and, ultimately, in favor of single words.

The work is abstract not only because it collects seemingly discrete verbal fragments but also because it seems to follow one of Stein's axioms about abstract painting: that a painting has its own existence, its own life. Aesthetic value does not derive from a work's referential quality but rather from itself. In modern painting, the focus is on the colors of the paint, the shapes, the textures, the forms. In *Tender Buttons*, the focus is on the words themselves, their sounds, juxtapositions, and the life that emanates from their unconventional arrangement. Stein recognized that words bring with them a whole series of associations that are different for each reader and uncontrollable by the artist, so she deliberately aimed to remove words from their usual contexts to reduce their associational qualities and to cause new associations to arise from novel juxtapositions. A reader of Stein's work must surrender selfhood to the text and accept the linguistic experience offered.

## "AS FINE AS MELANCTHA"

In naming volume 4 of the Yale edition of Stein's writings *As Fine as Melanctha*, the editors draw attention to one of Stein's short pieces of prose that takes the appearance of a short story but turns out to defy the conventions of that genre, just as Stein defies other literary conventions. "As Fine as Melanctha" was Stein's answer when requested to write something "as fine as 'Melanctha,'" one of the three pieces that constitute *Three Lives*; yet "As Fine as Melanctha" is radically different from the earlier work. The 1922 piece has no characters, no setting, no plot, and no chronology. The opening line announces that it is "a history of a moment," but a moment has no history. "As Fine as Melanctha" is a moment out of time, or rather many moments out of time, moments so common as to be timeless and timely simultaneously.

"As Fine as Melanctha" is a good example of Stein's perfected verbal strategies throughout the decade of the 1920's as she attempted to make immediate and alive the verbal moment. She ignores, for example, the rules of syntax, mingling phrases and clauses and sentences indiscriminately. The only punctuation mark in the piece is the period, and it closes sentence fragments and sentences alike. Even questions end in a period rather than the expected question mark. The effect is that syntax no longer aids communication; consequently, readers must release their fierce hold on sentence structure as a way to capture meaning. Where, however, can they turn in their drive to understand? The logical next step is the word itself; yet the reader is so accustomed to thinking of words as they relate to one another that when Stein violates expected word order, as well as the rules of syntax, the reader confronts the stunning reality that words themselves are empty. Since everything one knows is understood through context, the removal of context both in the larger areas of character development and plot and in the smaller areas of language renders the reading of "As Fine as Melanctha" something of an existential experience.

Reading Stein's work puts the reader in tension with the text--that is, when the sparks fly for those willing to accept the challenge. Repeatedly, and in a variety of ways, Stein makes language meaningless. One of the hallmarks of Stein's work is repetition. Repetition, however, does not contribute to communication by stressing meaning; instead, it reduces meaning. The following sentence from "As Fine as Melanctha" uses internal repetition: "I mean that it has been noticed again and again that abundance that in abundance that the need of abundance that there is therein a need of abundance and in this need it is a necessity that there is stock taking." A reader is grateful to emerge from the tangled web in the inner core of the sentence--repetition of "abundance," "need," and "need of abundance." The sentence seems to accumulate words that lose meaning in the process of being accumulated. Even the apparent meaning at the end vanishes in the light of "abundance." The repetition so confuses the reader that the end of the sentence seems to have meaning because it apparently follows normal English syntax, yet even

that meaning reduces itself to the redundancy of "stock taking" and "abundance." The reader is left with a single, uncontextualized word, systematically emptied of meaning and association.

There are other kinds of repetition in "As Fine as Melanctha." Repetitions of sounds as well as words prevail in a passage such as the following: "How dearly clearly merely is she me, how dearly clearly merely am I she. How dearly is she me how dearly is she me how dearly how very dearly am I she." The words "dearly," "clearly," "merely," "she," and "me" are repeated in varied arrangements that challenge syntax. The sounds of the words tend to flatten them, to make them anonymous. Repetition of the sound "erely" eventually is reduced to repetition of the "e" sound, as in "me." The sentence shows Stein's progressive reductionism: The meanings of different words are reduced to sounds; the repetition of multiple sounds is reduced to a single sound. Not only do the words become meaningless when repeated in such close proximity, but also characters become such close approximations of one another that identity is destroyed. Language here is subversive and destructive.

In another example, repetition is used to change syntax: "The difference between humming to-day yesterday and to-morrow is this, it always means more. The difference between humming to-day yesterday and to-morrow is this. It always means more." The reader yearns to believe that this variation of syntax is meaningful, because that is the way readers have been taught to read. Once again, however, the repetition is used to destroy meaning. When Stein's reader puts mind against text, the mind returns as a wet noodle, aware only of its own limpness. Such awareness, however, is knowledge of one's fleeting consciousness, and Stein's objective is achieved.

### "BRIM BEAUVAIS"

"Brim Beauvais" represents Stein's work during the decade of the 1930's, when she became increasingly minimalist. In this work, her paragraphs are shorter, most being only a single line, and formal sections come from division into chapters, although such divisions are useless. Many chapters have the same identifying label: For example, three sections are identified as "Chapter X"; two are "Chapter Ten." Furthermore, the numbers are not always sequential. More confusion in the structure occurs through embedding. Several pages into "Brim Beauvais" appears the heading "Beauvais and His Wife: A Novel." There are labeled episodes within sections, although neither the chapter headings nor other labels contribute to communication. The work has a "Part II," but no Part I. All these devices are merely added to the verbal disruptions seen in her earlier work. Even the opening of "Brim Beauvais" suggests how much further Stein has gone in her developing abstractionism. The work begins with the single word "once." It functions elliptically to suggest the "once upon a time" opening of fairy tales. However, the second line truncates that suggestion. "Always excited to say twice" forces readers to understand "once" in a numerical framework and thus to count something they do not know; similarly, the adjective "excited" describes a person not yet introduced. Stein is a master at invoking emptiness. Like the cubists, she presented a part without feeling it necessary to fill in or even suggest the surrounding whole. She believed that the mind partakes of the world through fragments, not through complete systems, and that her writing was an open window on this process.

### ALPHABETS AND BIRTHDAYS

By the winter of 1940, another war had begun in Europe, and Stein was finding it difficult to carry on any sustained writing project. "To Do: A Book of Alphabets and Birthdays" (published in 1957 as *Alphabets and Birthdays*) provided a structure while allowing for the intermittent composition that met Stein's needs during this period. The structure was provided by the alphabet, which Stein marched progressively through, assigning four names to each letter and creating episodes, events, and nonsense rhymes around each. The work has the fantastic actions and situations that children love, and Stein had children in mind when she wrote it. However, some publishers have insisted that the work is really more appropriate for adults than for children. If so, it must be adults who are young at heart, for the work has a delightful lightness, a happy flippancy, and a joy of language that emerges from repetition of sounds and words. The alphabet book shows Stein's skill at duplicating the rhythms and sounds of conversation and thoughts as people silently talk to themselves. Stein's ear for speech has often been noted, and here the speech of conversation conveys a swiftness and easy familiarity that make the work especially pleasant to read. At the same time, it remains true to the developing minimalism throughout Stein's career, for the letter is a reduction of the word.

Stein adhered to her principles throughout her life, always finding new ways to bring the meaning of her craft to the reader's awareness--even if this meant shocking the reader out of the lethargy of language. When she began to attract more people than her brother, Leo's support deteriorated and he claimed to find her work silly. His evaluation is shared by many. Stein is not a writer for all readers. Indeed, she tends to attract only coterie groups. Because her work is amenable to literary critics practicing deconstruction, however, and because the feminist movement has brought lesbian relationships into the open and searches out the quiet subversions such a lifestyle encouraged, both the work of Gertrude Stein and the writer herself have been looked at anew. The new reader and the returning reader alike will find Stein's work ever fresh, ever varying, ever innovative, and ever shocking, and for that reason alone it will always have enthusiastic readers somewhere, someplace.

OTHER MAJOR WORKS

LONG FICTION: *The Making of Americans: Being a History of a Family's Progress*, 1925, abridged 1934; *Lucy Church Amiably*, 1930; *A Long Gay Book*, 1932; *Ida, a Novel*, 1941; *Brewsie and Willie*, 1946; *Blood on the Dining-Room Floor*, 1948; *Things as They Are*, 1950 (originally known as *Q.E.D.*); *A Novel of Thank You*, 1958.

PLAYS: *Geography and Plays*, pb. 1922; *Operas and Plays*, pb. 1932; *Four Saints in Three Acts*, pr., pb. 1934; *In Savoy: Or, Yes Is for a Very Young Man (A Play of the Resistance in France)*, pr., pb. 1946; *The Mother of Us All*, pr. 1947; *Last Operas and Plays*, pb. 1949; *In a Garden: An Opera in One Act*, pb. 1951; *Lucretia Borgia*, pb. 1968; *Selected Operas and Plays*, pb. 1970.

POETRY: *Before the Flowers of Friendship Faded Friendship Faded*, 1931; *Two (Hitherto Unpublished) Poems*, 1948; *Bee Time Vine, and Other Pieces,*

*1913-1927*, 1953; *Stanzas in Meditation, and Other Poems, 1929-1933*, 1956.

NONFICTION: *Composition as Explanation*, 1926; *How to Write*, 1931; *Matisse, Picasso, and Gertrude Stein, with Two Shorter Stories*, 1933; *The Autobiography of Alice B. Toklas*, 1933; *Portraits and Prayers*, 1934; *Lectures in America*, 1935; *Narration: Four Lectures*, 1935; *The Geographical History of America*, 1936; *Everybody's Autobiography*, 1937; *Picasso*, 1938; *Paris, France*, 1940; *What Are Masterpieces?*, 1940; *Wars I Have Seen*, 1945; *Four in America*, 1947; *Reflections on the Atomic Bomb*, 1973; *How Writing Is Written*, 1974; *The Letters of Gertrude Stein and Thornton Wilder*, 1996 (Edward Burns and Ulla E. Dydo, editors); *Baby Precious Always Shines: Selected Love Notes Between Gertrude Stein and Alice B. Toklas*, 1999 (Kay Turner, editor); *The Letters of Gertrude Stein and Virgil Thomson: Composition as Conversation*, 2010.

CHILDREN'S LITERATURE: *The World Is Round*, 1939.

MISCELLANEOUS: *The Gertrude Stein First Reader and Three Plays*, 1946; *The Yale Edition of the Unpublished Writings of Gertrude Stein*, 1951-1958 (eight volumes; Carl Van Vechten, editor); *Selected Writings of Gertrude Stein*, 1962; *The Yale Gertrude Stein*, 1980.

BIBLIOGRAPHY

Bowers, Jane Palatini. *Gertrude Stein*. New York: St. Martin's Press, 1993. A succinct, feminist-oriented introduction to Stein, with separate chapters on the short fiction, novels, and plays. Includes notes and bibliography.

Bridgman, Richard. *Gertrude Stein in Pieces*. New York: Oxford University Press, 1970. The first detailed, chronological study of all Stein's work. Bridgman's approach is primarily psychobiological; he locates Stein's experimentalism in pathology rather than intention, seeing guilty evasiveness about lesbian sexuality as the crucial impetus for her avant-garde writing.

Brinnin, John Malcom. *The Third Rose: Gertrude Stein and Her World*. Boston: Little, Brown, 1959. Aside from its significant biographical value, this study contains provocative comments on Stein's writing, twentieth century painting, and modern intellectual and artistic movements. Includes a useful bibliography.

Curnutt, Kirk, ed. *The Critical Response to Gertrude Stein*. Westport, Conn.: Greenwood Press, 2000. While including quintessential pieces on Stein by Carl Van Vechten, William Carlos Williams, and Katherine Anne Porter, this guide to her critical reception also includes previously obscure estimations from contemporaries, such as H. L. Mencken, Mina Loy, and Conrad Aiken.

DeKoven, Marianne. *A Different Language: Gertrude Stein's Experimental Writing*. Madison: University of Wisconsin Press, 1983. DeKoven's feminist study focuses on Stein's experimental work published after *Three Lives* and before *The Autobiography of Alice B. Toklas*. She argues that this period of Stein's writing is important not so much because of its influence on other writers but because of its attempt to redefine patriarchal language and provide alternatives to conventional modes of signification.

Detloff, Madelyn. "Stein's Shame." In *The Persistence of Modernism: Loss and Mourning in the Twentieth Century*. New York: Cambridge University Press, 2009. Argues that some aspects of literary modernism, particularly its depiction of loss, retribution, and desire, remain pertinent in the twenty-first century. Analyzes works by Stein and other writers to prove this thesis.

Hoffman, Michael J. *Critical Essays on Gertrude Stein*. Boston: G. K. Hall, 1986. A collection of reviews and essays, most of which appeared during and immediately after Stein's long career in letters. Diverse forms of literary analysis, such as New Criticism, structuralism, feminism, and deconstruction, are represented. Among the contributors are Lisa Ruddick, Marianne DeKoven, Wendy Steiner, Catharine R. Stimpson, Donald Sutherland, Allegra Stewart, Sherwood Anderson, Marianne Moore, William Carlos Williams, B. F. Skinner, Katherine Anne Porter, Edmund Wilson, and W. H. Auden.

_____. *The Development of Abstractionism in the Writings of Gertrude Stein*. 1956. Reprint. Philadelphia: University of Pennsylvania Press, 1965. In the first version of this book, Hoffman traces the progressive development of abstractionism in Stein's early writing (1903-1913), focusing on the varieties of abstractionism manifesting themselves in each work. In his subsequent study, published almost a decade later, Hoffman again focuses on the abstract, refining his earlier definition of Stein's abstractionism as a "leaving-out" of stylistic and thematic elements normally appearing in the major works of American and European literature. This second study, covering the period from 1902-1946, stresses the ways in which Stein progressively abstracted from her writing most of the traditional elements of fictional prose narrative.

Knapp, Bettina. *Gertrude Stein*. New York: Continuum, 1990. A general introduction to Stein's life and art. Discusses her stylistic breakthrough in the stories in *Three Lives*, focusing on repetition and the use of the continuous present. Devotes a long chapter to *Tender Buttons* as one of Stein's most innovative and esoteric works; discusses the nonreferential nature of language in the fragments.

Murphy, Margueritte S. *A Tradition of Subversion: The Prose Poem in English from Wilde to Ashbery*. Amherst: University of Massachusetts Press, 1992. Devotes a chapter to *Tender Buttons*. Argues that Stein borrowed her genre from painting. Discusses the experimental nature of Stein's prose poems in the collections.

Neuman, Shirley, and Ira B. Nadel, eds. *Gertrude Stein and the Making of Literature*. Boston: Northeastern University Press, 1988. A collection of essays on Stein from a variety of theoretical perspectives that attempt to "reread" her work in the 1970's and 1980's. Includes essays on Stein and the modernist canon, her relationship to American art and to Henry James, and her experimental collection of prose fragments, *Tender Buttons*.

Ruddick, Lisa. *Reading Gertrude Stein: Body, Text, Gnosis*. Ithaca, N.Y.: Cornell University Press, 1990. Examines the cultural and psychosocial contexts of "Melanctha," *The Making of Americans, G.M.P.* (Stein's abbreviated title for the work she also called *Matisse, Picasso, and Gertrude Stein*), and *Tender Buttons*--works that Ruddick argues have a creative momentum rarely achieved in Stein's later experimental works because all four are serial acts of self-definition. Ruddick's study combines poststructuralism with a humanist understanding of the artistic process; she sees *Tender Buttons* as Stein's work of genius because it orients the reader ethically rather than disorienting the reader in the play of language.

Stein, Gertrude. *Three Lives and Q. E. D.: Authoritative Texts, Contexts, Criticism*. Edited by Marianne DeKoven. New York: W. W. Norton, 2006. In addition to the texts of *Three Lives* and *Q. E. D.*, this book features a biography of Stein and information about the intellectual context of these works. It also features nineteen chronologically organized critical essays that analyze these works from the perspectives of feminism, queer studies, the interrelation of race and sexuality, primitivism, and eugenics.

Sutherland, Donald. *Gertrude Stein: A Biography of Her Work*. Westport, Conn.: Greenwood Press, 1951. The first substantial critical book on Stein's writing, this work treats Stein's radical works as an illustration of her own modernist philosophy and aesthetics. Includes a useful appendix, which catalogs Stein's writing according to stylistic periods.

Watson, Dana Cairns. *Gertrude Stein and the Essence of What Happens*. Nashville, Tenn.: Vanderbilt University Press, 2005. Focuses on Stein's fascination with conversation and how that is reflected in her works. Argues that Stein's works "entangle" silent reading and social speaking to "build communities of meaning." Devotes a chapter to an analysis of *Tender Buttons*.

*Paula Kopacz*
*Updated by Cassandra Kircher*

# JOHN STEINBECK

**Born:** Salinas, California; February 27, 1902
**Died:** New York, New York; December 20, 1968

PRINCIPAL SHORT FICTION

*The Pastures of Heaven,* 1932
*Saint Katy the Virgin,* 1936
*The Long Valley,* 1938

OTHER LITERARY FORMS

Besides two volumes of short fiction, John Steinbeck produced numerous novels, among which is his masterpiece, *The Grapes of Wrath* (1939). He also authored several screenplays and three dramas, two of which were based on his novels, *Of Mice and Men* (1937) and *The Moon Is Down* (1942). Among his nonfiction are several travel books and a collection of war sketches. His last work was a translation of Sir Thomas Malory's Arthurian stories. A volume of letters was published posthumously.

ACHIEVEMENTS

John Steinbeck assumes an important place in American literature chiefly for his powerful and deft portrayal of the common people--the migrant worker, the ranch hand, and the laborer--whose capacity for survival surpassed the attempts of economic and corporate forces to defeat them. His novels, especially, render the human condition with sensitivity and lyrical grace. His work often shows a versatility unrivaled among his contemporaries. The comic, the tragic, the whimsical, and the naturalistic all merge in such a way as to make Steinbeck one of the United States' most popular writers, one whose art form is particularly suited to the cinema. Many of his books have been turned into successful films. Though much of Steinbeck's best work was written in the 1930's, he is not only a propagandist of the Great Depression era

but also a writer who is deeply concerned with the dignity of human beings. A human being as an individual may pass away, but human beings as a group, humankind as a species, is immortal. As Ma Joad remarked in the final pages of The Grapes of Wrath: "We're the people. We go on."

BIOGRAPHY

The Salinas Valley, where John Steinbeck was born, lies about a hundred miles south of San Francisco. It is a fertile, temperate trough between two mountain ranges and encompasses some of central California's most picturesque areas, notably Pacific Grove and the serenity of Monterey Bay. Such a landscape was at the heart of Steinbeck's boyhood experience and forms a crucial link with the characteristics of the writer's work. The son of a mill owner and a schoolteacher, Steinbeck grew up in Salinas, a small railroad town just entering the twentieth century, a town not quite pastoral yet not quite industrial, whose people were farmers and ranchers and shopkeepers but whose location and natural resources were quickly making it an agricultural and mercantile hub. This unique duality of the Salinas Valley--the long valley of Steinbeck's fiction--became a formative agent in the quality of Steinbeck's work, stories at once gently romantic and mythic as they were also realistic and proletarian. His early reading was evidence of his growing dualism. The realistic novels of Gustave Flaubert and Thomas Hardy were supplemented by his readings in Greek and Roman mythology, the Bible, and especially Sir Thomas Malory's *Le Morte d'Arthur* (1485), the first book given to him as a child and the last to serve as a source for his fiction. (His retelling of the King Arthur stories, *The Acts of King Arthur and His Noble Knights*, was published posthumously in 1976).

By the time Steinbeck entered Salinas High School in 1915, he was a widely read young man, tall, with rugged good looks and a desire to write. At seventeen, he entered Stanford University, already convinced that he was going to be a writer. Like many creative artists before and since, Steinbeck found the discipline of the college curriculum too irksome. Though he enjoyed reading contemporary European and American writers, such as Theodore Dreiser and Sinclair Lewis, he was uninterested in much else and took a leave of absence after two years. For the next few years, he worked in the San Francisco area as a clerk and a field hand on a ranch, gaining the invaluable experience of ranch life and ranch hands that was to figure in such works as *Of Mice and Men* and *The Long Valley*.

He returned to Stanford University briefly as an English major but finally left in 1925 without a degree. He had written two stories for the *Stanford Spectator*, one a satire on college life and the other a bizarre tale about a strangely inarticulate woman and her marriage to a migrant worker who kept horses' heads in a rain barrel. The story is insignificant but interesting for its odd mixture of the real and the whimsical, a characteristic typical of much of Steinbeck's mature work.

*John Steinbeck* (AP Photo/File)

Steinbeck was in New York during the late 1920's, working as a construction worker on the original Madison Square Garden by day and writing stories by night. Unsuccessful, he returned to California, married, and settled in his family's cottage in Pacific Grove. He wrote constantly, and in 1929, his first novel, *Cup of Gold*, was published. This thinly fictionalized account of the pirate Henry Morgan was both an artistic and a financial failure. *The Pastures of Heaven*, Steinbeck's second book, was a collection of short stories about the people of an almost mythically beautiful valley. Influenced by Sherwood Anderson's *Winesburg, Ohio* (1919), published a decade earlier, neither it nor his next novel, *To a God Unknown* (1933), brought Steinbeck much critical or popular success.

His apprenticeship, however, was over. Beginning in 1935 with the publication of *Tortilla Flat*, Steinbeck was to produce half a dozen books over the next ten years, works that were to establish his reputation as a writer of power and versatility. *Tortilla Flat* was followed by *In Dubious Battle* (1936), regarded by some as one of the best strike novels ever written. *Of Mice and Men* was followed by *The Long Valley*, containing his best short stories. His masterpiece, on which he had been working for three years, was published as *The Grapes of Wrath* in 1939.

During World War II, Steinbeck wrote propaganda scripts for the U.S. Army and published *The Moon Is Down*, a short novel set in Nazi-occupied Norway. His postwar work showed a marked decline. Aside from the massive *East of Eden* (1952), the works of this period are characterized by a bland whimsy. *Cannery Row* (1945) is generally recognized as the novel that signaled the beginning of Steinbeck's decline. Throughout the 1950's and 1960's, Steinbeck, then a national celebrity, continued to produce a variety of fiction, novels such as *Sweet Thursday* (1954), *The Short Reign of Pippen IV* (1957), and *The Winter of Our Discontent* (1961). They are works of minor importance and show little of the narrative strength that won for Steinbeck the Nobel Prize in Literature in 1962.

His last years were spent quietly in New York City and on Long Island. By then he had become an honored American writer. In 1963, he was selected as honorary consultant in American literature for the Library of

Congress. He was elected to the National Arts Council in 1966. Steinbeck died peacefully in his sleep on December 20, 1968.

ANALYSIS

The qualities that most characterize the work of John Steinbeck are a supple narrative style, a versatility of subject matter, and an almost mystical sympathy for the common human being. His fiction is peopled with men and women somehow shoaled from society's mainstream yet possessed of a vision that is itself a source of strength. His characteristic narrative method is to portray these people with an unerring mixture of realism and romance.

Though the Great Depression is the central social focus of his best work, his characters respond to those social forces not only in terms of realistic confrontation but also in the form of a romantic, intuitive escape. His characters become not so much victims of social or economic failure but celebrants of a life force beyond society and economics. The best of Steinbeck's work maintains this tension--developed by a narrative tone--between the world of harsh reality and the world of animal-like freedom. Even in a late novel such as *East of Eden*, his best books behind him, Steinbeck symbolically construed this duality in the reference to the two mountain ranges that defined the territory of his narrator's childhood, the "sunny" flowered slopes of the Gabilans to the east and the dark, brooding peaks of the Santa Lucias to the west.

THE PASTURES OF HEAVEN

Nowhere is this duality--the tension between realism and romance--more evident than in Steinbeck's earliest short stories, those forming his first major work, *The Pastures of Heaven*. Structurally the book shows the influence of Anderson's *Winesburg, Ohio*, a series of short stories, each independent but each connected by the locale and the theme of psychic isolation.

Using the frame narrative of Winesburg as a model, *The Pastures of Heaven* deals with the lives of a number of characters living in the peaceful, idyllic valley in the hills beyond Monterey. Secluded like some medieval bower or enchanted castle, the place evokes images of romance and peace. For all the outward tranquillity, however, the valley cannot remain isolated from the real world of economic hardship and violence.

The Munroe farm, for example, is cursed, and the curse executes itself on all the characters who come into contact with the Munroes. The theme of this collection of short stories is the conflict inherent in the tension between the characters' desire to live in the peaceful valley and their own human weaknesses, which prevent them from fulfilling their desires. Put in another way, the stories form a latter-day Garden of Eden myth. The land is beautiful, fruitful, prosperous; but the people of the land are thwarted by the serpent of human frailty.

Though some of the characters are spiritual kin to the "grotesques of Anderson's famous collection," they are markedly different in their attempts to reconcile their romantic intuition with the reality of social convention. Tularecito, for example, is all instinct. Though an idiot, he possesses great strength and an intuitive ability to draw. The title of the story, "The Legend of Tularecito," suggests that, like a legend, Tularecito is a child of romance. In his contradictory nature, he is the archetype of all the characters in the collection. Foreshadowing the half-witted giant Lenny, in *Of Mice and Men*, Tularecito brings destruction on himself when he attacks Bert Munroe and is sent to a state asylum outside the valley. His punishment is not physical death, as in Lenny's case, but banishment from the valley, from Eden. Tularecito has come into contact with the reality of social convention and is defeated. Intuition is thwarted in the interest of social stability.

The conflict between an idyllic life, communing with nature, and the demands of middle-class respectability is the focus of another story, "Junius Maltby." Like prelapsarian man, Junius lives innocently off the land. Reminiscent of the *paisanos*, such as Danny and Mac in later novels such as *Tortilla Flat* and *Cannery Row*, Junius is shiftless and, by society's standards, an irresponsible dreamer. Like Tularecito, Junius is intuitive, instinctual, indifferent to the economic imperatives of being a farmer, and casually indecorous in his personal appearance. To Mrs. Munroe, Junius's life of the imagination is a threat. Junius is forced to abandon his farm and to leave the valley. There is no place for the poor and the romantic in Eden.

### "THE CHRYSANTHEMUMS"

The garden as instinct, as the life of the spirit, is a prominent image in two stories in a later collection. Published in 1938, *The Long Valley* contains some of Steinbeck's most brilliant work in the genre of short fiction. In "The Chrysanthemums," Steinbeck presents the figure of Eliza Allen, a woman whose romantic gentleness conflicts with the brusque matter-of-factness of her husband and the deceitful cunning of a tinker. The story reveals a skillful meshing of character and setting, of symbol and theme. The garden is at once the chief setting and abiding symbol that define Eliza's character and her predicament as a woman.

Dressed in a man's clothing, Eliza is working in her garden when the story opens. Already the contrast is clear between Eliza's sensitive nature and the manlike indifference of her dress, her husband and life on the ranch, bathed in "the cold greyflannel fog of winter." Eliza's only emotional outlet, her only contact with a deeper life-pulse, is her growing of chrysanthemums, symbolic of both her sexual need and her recognition of the dominance in her nature of the life of the instinct. Like the virgin queen Elizabeth, Eliza has no children and her mannish ways merely disguise her sensitivity, a sensitivity that her husband Henry does not understand.

When a tinker stops his wagon at the ranch, looking for pots to repair, Eliza at first has no work for him, but when he praises her chrysanthemums, implying an understanding of her nature, Eliza gives him the flowers in a pot. That night, on their way to town for dinner and--the husband teases--to the prizefights, Eliza sees the discarded flowers on the road and realizes that the tinker had deceived her. Like her husband, the tinker did not really understand her; he had merely used her to his own advantage. At the end of the story, Eliza cries quietly, "like an old woman."

### "THE WHITE QUAIL"

Still another story in the collection presents the image of the garden as both physical and psychic landscape. The garden that Mary Tiller tends in "The White Quail," however, is symbolic not of a healthy life of the spirit but of self-love and egotism. Mary's happiness with her garden, complete when she sees a white quail in it one night, is at the expense of her love for her husband. Harry is shut out of her love, often forced to sleep alone, though he virtually idolizes her. Mary's garden is her dream of an ordered, nonthreatening and nonsexual existence. In a sense, Mary "quails" before a life of passion or the body. When a cat one day wanders into the garden, Mary is fearful of its potential as a predator and demands that Harry shoot it. Inexplicably, he shoots the quail; in destroying Mary's dream, he has brought his wife back to the real world, to a sexuality that she had refused to admit.

### "FLIGHT"

A story of maturity and death is the much-praised "Flight." Opening amid the rocky crags of the Torres farm, the story centers on Pepe, the oldest son of the widow Torres. A tall, lazy youth, Pepe has inherited his father's knife and yearns for the day when he will become, like his father, a man. Sent into Monterey on an errand, Pepe is insulted by a townsman and kills the man with his knife. Returning, he bids his mother good-bye and, armed with his father's rifle and horse, leaves his home to flee into the mountains. Gradually, he loses his rifle, then his horse. Now alone, he faces the threat of natural forces and the human pursuers. In the end, he is shot by one of the unseen "dark watchers."

Significantly, Pepe relies more on his own strength and courage as he flees deeper into the wild mountain passes; as he leaves his childhood behind, however, he also approaches his own death. Pepe's journey has become not only a physical escape from society's retribution but also a symbolic pilgrimage toward manhood and a redemptive death.

OTHER MAJOR WORKS

LONG FICTION: *Cup of Gold*, 1929; *To a God Unknown*, 1933; *Tortilla Flat*, 1935; *In Dubious Battle*, 1936; *Of Mice and Men*, 1937; *The Red Pony*, 1937, enlarged 1945; *The Grapes of Wrath*, 1939; *The Moon Is Down*, 1942; *Cannery Row*, 1945; *The Pearl*, 1945 (serial), 1947 (book); *The Wayward Bus*, 1947; *Burning Bright*, 1950; *East of Eden*, 1952; *Sweet Thursday*, 1954; *The Short Reign of Pippin IV*, 1957; *The Winter of Our Discontent*, 1961.

PLAYS: *Of Mice and Men*, pr., pb. 1937; *The Moon Is Down*, pr. 1942; *Burning Bright*, pb. 1951.

SCREENPLAYS: *The Forgotten Village*, 1941; *Lifeboat*, 1944; *A Medal for Benny*, 1945; *The Pearl*, 1945; *The Red Pony*, 1949; *Viva Zapata!*, 1952.

NONFICTION: *Their Blood Is Strong*, 1938; *Sea of Cortez: A Leisurely Journal of Travel and Research*, 1941 (with Edward F. Ricketts); *The Forgotten Village*, 1941; *Bombs Away*, 1942; *A Russian Journal*, 1948 (with Robert Capa); *Once There Was a War*, 1958; *Travels with Charley: In Search of America*, 1962; *Letters to Alicia*, 1965; *America and Americans*, 1966; *Journal of a Novel*, 1969; *Steinbeck: A Life in Letters*, 1975 (Elaine Steinbeck and Robert Wallsten, editors); *Steinbeck and Covici: The Story of a Friendship*, 1979 (Thomas Fensch, editor); *America and Americans, and Selected Nonfiction*, 2002 (Susan Shillinglaw and Jackson J. Benson, editors).

TRANSLATION: *The Acts of King Arthur and His Noble Knights*, 1976.

## BIBLIOGRAPHY

Astro, Richard, and Tetsumaro Hayashi, eds. *Steinbeck: The Man and His Work*. Corvallis: Oregon State University Press, 1971. One of the first full-length works published after Steinbeck's death, this superb collection of essays presents opinions which regard Steinbeck as everything from a mere proletarian novelist to an artist with a deep vision of humankind's essential dignity.

Benson, Jackson D. *The True Adventures of John Steinbeck, Writer*. New York: Viking Press, 1984. This biography emphasizes Steinbeck's rebellion against critical conventions and his attempts to keep his private life separate from his role as public figure. Benson sees Steinbeck as a critical anomaly, embarrassed and frustrated by his growing critical and popular success.

Burkhead, Cynthia. *Student Companion to John Steinbeck*. Westport, Conn.: Greenwood Press, 2002. An introductory overview, with information on Steinbeck's life, his career and contributions to American literature, and analyses of his works. One chapter is devoted to a discussion of his short stories.

Fontenrose, Joseph. *John Steinbeck: An Introduction and Interpretation*. New York: Holt, Rinehart and Winston, 1963. A good introduction, this book discusses some of the symbolism inherent in much of Steinbeck's fiction and contains some insightful observations on Steinbeck's concept of the "group-man"--that is, the individual as a unit in the larger sociobiological organism.

French, Warren. *John Steinbeck's Fiction Revisited*. New York: Twayne, 1994. The chapter on *The Long Valley* in this revision of French's earlier Twayne book on Steinbeck provides brief discussions of the major stories, including "Flight" and "The Chrysanthemums."

Gelfant, Blanche H., ed. *The Columbia Companion to the Twentieth-Century American Short Story*. New York: Columbia University Press, 2000. Includes a chapter in which Steinbeck's short stories are analyzed.

George, Stephen K., ed. *John Steinbeck: A Centennial Tribute*. New York: Praeger, 2002. A collection of reminiscences from Steinbeck's family and friends, as well as wide-ranging critical assessments of his works.

Hayashi, Tetsumaro, ed. *Steinbeck's Short Stories in "The Long Valley": Essays in Criticism*. Muncie, Ind.: Steinbeck Research Institution, 1991. A collection of new critical essays on the stories in *The Long Valley* (excluding *The Red Pony*), from a variety of critical perspectives.

Heavilin, Barbara A., ed. *A John Steinbeck Reader: Essays in Honor of Stephen K. George*. Lanham, Md.: Scarecrow Press, 2009. These essays examine Steinbeck's aesthetics, ethics, political opinions, and views on war, among other subjects, with two focusing on his fiction: "It's All in Your Head: Transforming Heavenly and Hellish Settings in Steinbeck's *The Pastures of Heaven*," by Michael J. Meyer, and Charlotte Cook Hadella's comparison of Steinbeck's "The White Quail" with Eudora Welty's "A Curtain of Green."

Hughes, R. S. *John Steinbeck: A Study of the Short Fiction*. New York: Twayne, 1989. A general introduction to Steinbeck's short fiction, focusing primarily on critical reception to the stories. Also includes some autobiographical statements on short-story writing, as well as four essays on Steinbeck's stories by other critics.

Johnson, Claudia Durst, ed. *Understanding "Of Mice and Men," "The Red Pony," and "The Pearl": A Student Casebook to Issues, Sources, and Historical Documents*. Westport, Conn.: Greenwood Press, 1997. Contains historical, social, and political materials as a context for Steinbeck's three novellas. Places the novellas within the contexts of California and the West, land ownership, the male worker, homelessness, and oppression of the poor in Mexico.

McCarthy, Paul. *John Steinbeck*. New York: Frederick Ungar, 1980. Though much of this study is a recapitulation of earlier critical views, the book has the virtues of clarity and brevity and contains a fairly thorough bibliography.

Noble, Don, ed. *Critical Insights: John Steinbeck*. Pasadena, Calif.: Salem Press, 2011. Collection of reprinted and original essays, including articles describing the social and historical contexts of Steinbeck's works, evaluating his relationship with literary naturalism, and providing an ecofeminist reading of the stories in *The Long Valley*. Also includes a biography, a chronology listing major events in Steinbeck's life, a complete list of his works, and a bibliography listing resources for further research.

_____. *The Steinbeck Question: New Essays in Criticism*. Troy, N.Y.: Whitston, 1993. A collection of essays on most of Steinbeck's work, including three that are especially important for a study of his short fiction: "The Art of Story Writing," by Robert S. Hughes, Jr., "Steinbeck's Cloistered Women," by Charlotte Cook Hadella, and "The Snake," by Michael J. Meyer."

Parini, Jay. *John Steinbeck: A Biography*. New York: Henry Holt, 1995. Offers psychological interpretations of the effect of Steinbeck's childhood on his works and sociological interpretations of his fiction. Parini crticizes Steinbeck for his politically incorrect gender and social views and his "blindness" to the political reality of the Vietnam War.

Steinbeck, Elaine, and Robert Wallsten. *Steinbeck: A Life in Letters*. New York: Viking Press, 1975. An indispensable source for the Steinbeck scholar, this collection of letters written by Steinbeck between 1929 and his death forty years later shows a writer both well read and well disciplined. Those letters to his friend and publisher, Pascal Covici, shed light on the writer's working methods and are particularly revealing.

Timmerman, John H. *The Dramatic Landscape of Steinbeck's Short Stories*. Norman: University of Oklahoma Press, 1990. A formalist interpretation of Steinbeck's stories, focusing on style, tone, imagery, and character. Provides close readings of such frequently anthologized stories as "The Chrysanthemums" and "Flight," as well as such stories as "Johnny Bear" and "The Short-Short Story of Mankind."

*Edward Fiorelli*

# RICHARD G. STERN

**Born:** New York, New York; February 25, 1928

PRINCIPAL SHORT FICTION

*Teeth, Dying, and Other Matters*, 1964
*1968: A Short Novel, an Urban Idyll, Five Stories,
    and Two Trade Notes*, 1970
*Packages*, 1980
*Noble Rot: Stories, 1949-1988*, 1989
*Shares, and Other Fictions*, 1992
*Almonds to Zhoof: Collected Stories*, 2005

OTHER LITERARY FORMS

Richard G. Stern is best known as a novelist. He has also written literary criticism, both of his work and of that of others, as well as autobiographical sketches and a play. A new collection of his short fiction, *Almonds to Zhoof*, appeared in 2005 and contains forty-nine short stories and novellas written from 1949 through the twenty-first century.

ACHIEVEMENTS

Richard G. Stern has written numerous volumes of prose. His novels have received wide critical acclaim from reviewers, including Saul Bellow, Joan Didion, and Bernard Malamud, yet none has been widely read, and few have received attention from professional literary critics. His first novel, *Golk* (1960), was hailed as one of the best fictive accounts of the early days of television and the ways in which it intrudes into the lives of people who work in the medium and those who watch it. He has received numerous awards for his work, including a Longwood Award (1960), a Friends of Literature Award (1963), a Rockefeller Foundation grant (1965), an American Academy and Institute of Arts and Letters grant (1968), a National Endowment for the Arts grant (1969), a John Simon Guggenheim Memorial Foundation Fellowship (1973-1974), a Carl Sandburg Award from the Friends of the Chicago Public

Library (1979), an American Academy and Institute of Arts and Letters Award of Merit Medal (1985), and a Heartland Award for best work of nonfiction (1995). In 1965, his novel *Stitch* (1965) was selected as an American Library Association book of the year, and in 1989 his short-story collection *Noble Rot* was named the *Chicago Sun-Times* book of the year.

BIOGRAPHY

Richard Gustave Stern was born in New York City on February 25, 1928, the son of German-Jewish immigrants. He married Gay Clark in 1950 and was divorced in 1972; he married his second wife, Alane Rollings, in 1985. He has four children.

Stern received his B.A. degree from the University of North Carolina at Chapel Hill in 1947, graduating with Phi Beta Kappa honors. After graduation, he worked at a department store in Indiana, at a Florida radio station, and at Paramount International Films in New York. He earned his M.A. degree from Harvard University in 1949, writing the Bowdoin Prize essay on the poet John Crowe Ransom. He was a lecturer at Collège Jules Ferry in Versailles, France, from 1949 to 1950, a lecturer at the University of Heidelberg in Germany from 1950 to 1951, and an educational adviser for the U.S. Army from 1951 to 1952. While teaching at the University of Heidelberg, he worked nights as a cable clerk with the American occupation army. He received his Ph.D. from the University of Iowa in 1954. From 1954 to 1955, he was an instructor at Connecticut College in New London, Connecticut.

In 1956, Stern became an assistant professor of English at the University of Chicago, where he continued to teach until his retirement in 2004. He became an associate professor in 1962 and a full professor in 1965; in 1991, he was named the Helen A. Regenstein Professor of English. He has been a visiting lecturer at the University of Venice (1962-1963), the University of California at Santa Barbara (1964, 1968), the State

University of New York at Buffalo (1966), Harvard University (1969), the University of Nice (1970), and the University of Urbino (1977).

In one of his autobiographical sketches, he describes his elation at having his first important story accepted in 1952 for *The Kenyon Review* by Ransom, who was the subject of Stern's prize-winning essay. This acceptance occurred in the same year that he went to Iowa to begin work on his Ph.D. Following this first publication, Stern contributed numerous stories and essays to literary magazines, including *The Kenyon Review, The Antioch Review, Commentary, The Atlantic, Harper's, The Hudson Review, Partisan Review, The Paris Review, Encounter, Transatlantic Review, TriQuarterly*, and *western Review*.

In 1957, he met Saul Bellow, a former colleague at the University of Chicago, who became his friend and who greatly influenced his ideas about writing and about the writer's life. Bellow, Stern has said, showed him that one could be a Jew and still be a great American novelist.

ANALYSIS

Saul Bellow has been known to wonder aloud why Richard G. Stern's work is not more popular. Like many other discerning reviewers, Bellow notes the excellence of Stern's novels and short stories and their lack of readers. The answer to Bellow's question probably lies in the kinds of demands that Stern makes on his readers. According to Stern, his early writing was done under the influence of *Understanding Fiction* (1945), a highly influential textbook-anthology edited by Robert Penn Warren and Cleanth Brooks. Under the influence of Brooks and Warren, Stern tried to achieve what he calls a polished style, to integrate the materials in his stories, and "to suspend the meaning of the story in action as 'naturally' as orange bits in jello." Between 1952 and 1954, he said, he wrote about ten stories following these principles, but he became dissatisfied with what he was producing and, in 1957, stopped working on short stories, interrupted work on what became his second published novel, *Europe: Or, Up and Down with Schreiber and Baggish* (1961), and started working on what became his first published novel, *Golk*.

Like Bellow's writing, Stern's work tends to be highly erudite and allusive; in fact, it tends to be even more erudite and allusive than Bellow's. To understand Stern's stories fully, readers must be familiar with a large body of western literature. They must also be at least slightly familiar with several languages, including French, German, and Italian. In some stories, he demands that his readers be familiar with such topics as Eastern and western European history, anatomy, and the history of philosophy.

Stern is at his best as a humorist. He is sometimes classified as a black humorist and even a satirist, but his works tend to reflect more love for humankind than those of most black humorists and satirists. Stern's short stories provide a mirror of the absurdity of the human situation at the same time that they display not only a tolerance of human foibles but also a love for humankind. A consummate craftsman, he admits to polishing his works by revising them again and again. The resulting stories are worth the time and effort he puts into them, and they are certainly worth the time and effort the reader must expend to appreciate them.

### "GOOD MORROW, SWINE"

Even in many of his short works of humorous fiction, Stern makes inordinate demands on his readers. Most of his best short works are collected in *Noble Rot*, a book that can serve as an excellent introduction to Stern's techniques as a story writer. His extremely short story "Good Morrow, Swine," for example, is included in the collection. This early work is hilarious, yet to comprehend the jokes in it one must recognize the allusions in the title and be able to understand at least a bit of French, since most of the jokes within the story depend on recognizing French mistranslations of English phrases. In the story, Mr. Perkins constantly misinforms his young male students about the meanings of English words, quotations, and everyday expressions.

### "VENI, VIDI . . . WENDT"

Similarly, in "Veni, Vidi . . . Wendt," a long short story that Stern calls a short novel and which was collected in *1968*, he writes a comic study of Jeffrey Charles Wendt, a composer of operas to which no one listens and who desires to have his operas listened to by no one. This story is set in the same year as the assassinations of Martin Luther King, Jr., and Robert F. Kennedy and the Democratic Convention in Chicago that nominated Hubert H. Humphrey while young people rioted in the streets. Although Wendt, who has been called a modern Nero, is aware of these events, he largely ignores them, concentrating instead on writing an opera based on the life of Horace Walpole and trying to satisfy his own sexual lust and desire so as to show his superiority to his colleagues. Wendt and his wife and children are spending the summer in Santa Barbara, California. In the course of the story, he rediscovers his love for his wife and children.

Still, to understand the humor in "Veni, Vidi . . . Wendt," the reader must bring something to the story. The title itself alludes to Julius Caesar's famous words "Veni, Vidi, Vici" ("I came, I saw, I conquered"), which Caesar used to report to the Roman senate about his Pontic victory. Wendt, however, does not conquer. He came, he saw, and through a terrible pun, he left (Wendt-went). Even the Latin pronunciation of the letter "v" as "w" and the German pronunciation of the letter "w" as "v" seem part of the joke involved in the story's title.

The irony of comparing Wendt to Caesar becomes greater when one compares Caesar's amorous conquests to Wendt's. In his Egyptian conquest, achieved shortly before his Pontic one, Caesar also won Cleopatra. Comparing Caesar's conquest to Wendt's one amorous conquest in "Veni, Vidi . . . Wendt" produces more humor. Unlike Caesar, Wendt finds that he can ultimately take no pride in his dalliance, even though the woman with whom he has an affair is Patricia Davidov, the beautiful wife of a musicologist whom Wendt abhors. In the course of his first assignation with Patricia, he wonders whether there is no mouthwash in the Davidov household. Shortly thereafter, he finds himself exhausted by his extramarital affair and extremely anxious for it to end. No Caesar, Wendt runs from the affair back to his home in Chicago, feeling only relief that he has escaped from the demanding Patricia. The writing throughout the story is similarly allusive and erudite.

For a reader able or willing to make a way through Stern's short stories, the rewards are great. At his best, he is wildly comic, illustrating the absurdity of the human situation in humorous scene after humorous scene in stories such as "Good Morrow, Swine," "Veni, Vidi . . . Wendt," "Packages," "Milius and Melanie," and "A Recital for the Pope."

### "ARRANGEMENTS AT THE GULF"

In fact, Stern is often classified as a writer of the absurd. He can write good, slightly sentimental fiction in works such as "Arrangements at the Gulf." In it, Mr. Lomax, an old man, wants to die away from his family in Lake Forest, Illinois, but with his bachelor friend Granville, whom he sees every other summer on the Florida Gulf Coast. During the summers in between, Granville goes to California. The arrangements of the title involve seeing to it that Granville will go to the Gulf Coast every summer so that he can be present when Mr. Lomax dies.

### "DOUBLE CHARLEY" AND "A COUNTERFACTUAL PROPOSAL"

Many of Stern's stories involve the kinds of reversals found in "Arrangements at the Gulf." In one, "Double Charley," Charley Rangel discovers that his girlfriend, Agnes, slept with his partner in songwriting, Charley Schmitter, when he asks Olive, Schmitter's wife, to allow Agnes to visit Schmitter's grave. In another, "A Counterfactual Proposal" (collected in *Teeth, Dying, and Other Matters* and in *Almonds to Zhoof: Collected Stories*), after years of longing for a beautiful woman, Patchell finally is able to get Twyla K. Diggs into bed with him. Diggs is a student at the college where Patchell teaches. Shortly after they go to bed, they are discovered by Diggs's roommate and landlady. Immediately after the discovery, Patchell confronts the college president, Miss Emory, and succeeds in persuading her to give him a year's research grant, which he will use to go to France to study at the Bibliothéque Nationale. He also enlists Miss Emory's aid in getting Diggs's father to agree to send her to the Sorbonne for the year.

### "WISSLER REMEMBERS"

In "Wissler Remembers," a fairly sentimental story, an aging teacher recalls the students he has taught over the years and the love that he has felt for all of them. In this work, too, Stern shows the absurdity of the human situation. "Wissler Remembers" also has its humorous moments, especially when Wissler recalls that, while teaching at the Collége Jules Ferry in Versailles, France, where Stern himself taught, Wissler assigned his students the task of translating back into English a poem for which he supplied the French translation. Anyone who could come within twelve words of the original would, Wissler announced, get a present. The poem itself is a French version of Robert Frost's "Stopping by Woods on a Snowy Evening," and the student translation that Wissler recalls is hilarious. However, the reader must understand enough French to recognize the original poem in order to see how hilarious the student version is.

### "A Recital for the Pope"

Critics have recognized in Stern's novels a unique mixture of what they call the language of the street and of the library. This same mixture of colloquialisms and book language pervades his tales. Story after story in *Noble Rot* and in *Shares, and Other Fictions* exemplifies this mixture. At the same time, the actions in the stories often echo this mixture by placing grotesque characters in extremely formal situations. "A Recital for the Pope," for example, begins like a history textbook, describing magnificent old buildings in Rome, but quickly places in that setting a violinist, Yerva Grbisz, who tortures horrible tunes out of the violin and refuses to use deodorant or practice other elements of hygiene. Yerva has a brief audience with the pope, after which she and others pose for a picture with the pontiff. As they pose, she tells the pope that she wants to play her violin for him. He says that he would love for her to do so. She then plays execrable music, which he claims to enjoy very much.

### "La Pourriture Noble"

Similarly, "La Pourriture Noble" (meaning "noble rot," from which the collection gets its title) shows Dennis Sellinbon climbing up some very expensive curtains in a very elegant apartment at which he is attending a party. Readers never discover any reasonable explanation for Dennis's actions but cannot help laughing when they hear the excuse that Dennis makes up to get himself released from the mental ward to which he has had himself committed.

### "Dying"

Another story in the collection that deserves special attention is "Dying," in which F. Dorfman Dreben, through repeated entreaties, gets Professor Bly, a plant physiologist who has published a volume of poetry, to write a poem to be entered into a competition, the winner of which will receive $250, and have the poem inscribed on Dreben's mother's tombstone. Dreben's persistence leads Bly to understand that his poem will be the only one in the contest. At first, Bly is uninterested. Then, however, he decides to use the money for a trip, so he quickly conceives of, writes, and sends what he considers a good poem to Dreben, requesting that Dreben send the prize by return mail. After not hearing from Dreben, Bly, while in bed with his girlfriend, calls Dreben to find out why he has not received his check. As it turns out, there were two other contestants, a yearbook editor and a friend of Dreben's sister. The yearbook editor won first prize, the sister's friend won second, and Bly, Dreben says, won honorable mention.

### "Aurelia Frequenzia Reveals the Heart and Mind of the Man of Destiny"

In one of Stern's uncollected tales, "Aurelia Frequenzia Reveals the Heart and Mind of the Man of Destiny" (*The Paris Review*, 1976), Frequenzia writes the transcript of several interviews presented as though they are one interview with Tao Thinh, once ruler of Annam, which the reader quickly recognizes as a thinly disguised version of Vietnam. In the story, Stern shows the basic similarity between Frequenzia and Thinh, even though she claims to hate him and all for which he stands. She especially hates his having worked beside colonial powers--the French and Americans--while claiming to be a patriot, and his having enriched himself at the expense of his country. However, the reader quickly discovers that Frequenzia and Thinh lust for each other. Actually, the transcript reveals far more about Frequenzia than it does about either the heart or mind of Thinh.

### Shares, and Other Fictions

"Veni, Vidi . . . Wendt" is included in *Shares, and Other Fictions* and fits nicely into the stories there, for at the center of the stories lies the family with all of its problems. In "The Degradation of Tenderness" Stern treats the family of a psychotherapist named Charlie who used his children as case studies. In two articles, "The Father as Clinical Observer I, II," he "dismantled his children," but he could not understand the anger with which his children reacted to the articles. The children saw them as an indication of a lack of real tenderness or love; they saw them as a degradation of tenderness. In turn, Anna, the narrator, is a childless psychotherapist who apparently was Charlie's mistress and claims to feel affection for the children; she explains the father-child interactions in psychoanalytic terms, ironically converting the whole family into a case study. Thus, she indicates her own lack of or unwillingness to deal with real emotion and her similarity to Charlie. Anna's psychoanalytic jargon becomes a means of dehumanizing the children, Charlie, and Anna herself.

The title story, "Shares: A Novel in Ten Pieces," as its subtitle indicates, is a series of stories or "pieces." In it Stern explores the Share family, focusing on George and Robert, two brothers. George remains unmarried and childless. A successful shoe salesman who eventually owns his own stores, he founds the Share Museum, which gives a grant each year for a woman to travel to Europe with George, but she has to be his mistress. Robert becomes a lawyer, a deputy Secretary of State, marries, and has two children, a boy, Reg, and a girl, Obie. Robert's ability to compromise works well in his job, and he is a faithful husband and tries to be a good father. His children do not, however, respect his work and see his compromises as doing more harm than good. Obie writes him letters in which she tells him how he should be running the nation's affairs, and Reg tends to fail at all he tries, blaming his father for his problems. Using money his father gives him, Reg travels to Venice, meets and begins a relationship with his uncle's current lover, and starts a business taking people on balloon flights over Venice. At first, the business is extremely successful, but a tragedy occurs, and Reg is again a failure.

The final story in the collection, "In a Word, Trowbridge," treats the problems involved in having "a famous name." Charlotte, daughter of a well-known artist, dwells on the verbal abuse she suffered as a child, especially from her mother. She does not begin really to live until she is mugged. Then, she and her mother are reunited, she sees that her mother really cares about her, and she is able to recognize that having a famous parent is not such a burden after all.

## OTHER MAJOR WORKS

LONG FICTION: *Golk*, 1960; *Europe: Or, Up and Down with Schreiber and Baggish*, 1961; *In Any Case*, 1962 (also known as *The Chaleur Network*, 1981); *Stitch*, 1965; *Other Men's Daughters*, 1973; *Natural Shocks*, 1978; *A Father's Words*, 1986; *Pacific Tremors*, 2001.

PLAY: *The Gamesman's Island*, pb. 1964.

NONFICTION: *One Person and Another: On Writers and Writing*, 1993; *A Sistermony*, 1995; *Still on Call*, 2010.

EDITED TEXTS: *Honey and Wax: The Powers and Pleasures of Narrative*, 1966; *American Poetry of the Fifties*, 1967.

MISCELLANEOUS: *The Books in Fred Hampton's Apartment*, 1973; *The Invention of the Real*, 1982; *The Position of the Body*, 1986; *What Is What Was*, 2002.

## BIBLIOGRAPHY

Allen, Bruce. "The Writer Who Never Was . . . and Still Is." Review of *Almonds to Zhoof: Collected Stories*, by Richard G. Stern. *Sewanee Review* 116, no. 1 (Winter, 2008): xx-xxii. A generally admiring review of the collection, featuring a discussion of Stern's subject matter and writing style and analyses of some of the individual stories.

Cavell, Marsha. "Visions of Battlements." *Partisan Review* 38, no. 1 (1971): 117-121. Cavell reviews four books in this article, including *1968*, by Stern. She discusses "Veni, Vidi . . . Wendt" and "East, West . . . Midwest" from Stern's collection, describing him as a satirist whose writing is "at once gentle and biting."

Fishman, Boris. "Burgher King." Review of *Almonds to Zhoof: Collected Stories*, by Richard G. Stern. *New Republic* 233, no. 16 (October 17, 2005): 41-44. Although Fishman calls Stern the "best American fiction writer of whom you have never heard," he concludes that the "major ingredients of Stern's fiction--expansive language, compressed content, erudition as a means to emotional liberation--coexist uneasily."

Harris, Mark. *Saul Bellow: Drumlin Woodchuck*. Athens: University of Georgia Press, 1980. Although this book is primarily a study of Stern's friend, Saul Bellow, it is dedicated to Stern and refers to him throughout the book, with particularly intensive treatment in Chapters 2 and 3. Discusses Stern's friendships with Bellow, Philip Roth, and Mark Harris and recognizes the difficulty most readers have with Stern's work.

Izzo, David Garrett. *The Writings of Richard Stern: The Education of an Intellectual Everyman.* Jefferson, N.C.: McFarland, 2001. A literary biography, discussing the major themes in Stern's fiction and his use of fictionalized autobiography. Analyzes all of his novels and short stories through 2001.

Rogers, Bernard. Foreword to *Golk.* Chicago: University of Chicago Press, 1987. This introduction to the Phoenix reprint of Stern's first novel treats his fiction in general, especially his novels. It traces through Stern's novels four of his major themes: adapting to change, handling moral responsibility, dealing with problems of fatherhood and domestic life, and handling power. It also discusses his distinctive narrative voice.

Schiffler, James. *Richard Stern.* New York: Twayne, 1993. The first book-length critical study of Stern. Includes a brief overview of his life, a survey of his novels and short stories, and discussions of his style and themes. Chapter 5 is primarily on the theme of the "comedy of failure" in his short stories.

Stern, Richard G. "Conversation with Richard Stern." Interview by Milton Rosenberg and Elliot Anderson. *Chicago Review* 31 (Winter, 1980): 98-108. This article is an edited transcript of an interview that took place on WGN radio. In it, Stern traces what he calls the change in his writing from creating stories drawn from the external world to creating ones drawn from inside himself. He also briefly discusses the works of several other contemporary American writers, including John Barth, Donald Barthelme, John Gardner, Truman Capote, and Irving Wallace.

_____. Interview by Molly McQuade. *Publishers Weekly* 235 (January 20, 1989): 126-128. This interview appeared after the publication of Stern's collection of short stories *Noble Rot.* It briefly traces his life, literary career, and career as a university professor. Includes a photograph of Stern.

*Richard Tuerk*

# JAMES STILL

**Born:** Double Creek, Alabama; July 16, 1906
**Died:** Hazard, Kentucky; April 28, 2001

PRINCIPAL SHORT FICTION
  *On Troublesome Creek,* 1941
  *Pattern of a Man, and Other Stories,* 1976
  *The Run for the Elbertas,* 1980

OTHER LITERARY FORMS

Best known for his novel *River of Earth* (1940, 1968, 1978), James Still also wrote critically acclaimed poetry: *Hounds on the Mountain* (1937), *River of Earth*, 1983, *The Wolfpen Poems* (1986), and *From the Mountain, from the Valley: New and Collected Poems* (2001). Specifically for young readers were *Sporty Creek* (1977), *Jack and the Wonder Beans* (1977), *An Appalachian Mother Goose* (1998), and *Way Down Yonder on Troublesome Creek: Appalachian Riddles and Rusties* (1974). Still's adult nonfiction includes *The Wolfpen Notebooks: A Record of Appalachian Life* (1991) and the autobiographical *James Still: Portrait of the Artist as a Boy in Alabama* (1998).

ACHIEVEMENTS

James Still's stories were included in several volumes of *O. Henry Memorial Prize Stories* (1937, 1936, 1939, 1941). He received two Guggenheim Fellowships, the Appalachian Treasure Award, and the first Milner Award. *River of Earth* won the southern Authors Award from the southern Women's National Democratic Organization; the American Academy of Arts and Letters presented him with its Fiction Award and the Marjorie Peabody Waite Award. Kentucky's governor appointed Still the Commonwealth's first poet laureate (1995-1996). The University of Kentucky Library awarded him its Medallion for Intellectual Excellence, and Berea College honored him with its Weatherford Award. In 1997, the Fellowship of southern Writers created the James Still Award for Writing About the Appalachian South.

BIOGRAPHY

The sixth of nine children, James Still was born on a farm in Double Creek, Alabama. From early childhood, he declared he would be a writer and an editor. After high school graduation, he enrolled in Lincoln Memorial University (LMU) in Harrogate, Tennessee, where, like many of his classmates, he worked on campus to pay tuition. One job, as library janitor, allowed him to spend many nights reading in the library. Financially unable to return to LMU for his junior year, he hitchhiked and rode the rails, searching for a job. An LMU professor arranged for a wealthy sponsor to pay Still's expenses and later send him to Vanderbilt University for an M.A. in English and the University of Illinois for a B.S. in Library Science.

In 1932, Still began working as librarian (initially unpaid) at the Hindman Settlement School (Knott County, Kentucky). His stories and poems about the farmers and miners of Appalachia increasingly were accepted for publication in national magazines, so in 1939 he quit his job and became a full-time writer. Except for service in Africa with the Army Air Force during World War II, he remained in Hindman, settling in a 150-year-old log cabin. Later, from 1952 to 1962, Still was again librarian for the Hindman Settlement School and then taught English at Morehead State University, from 1962 to 1971. Then he retired to spend his time writing stories and poems for both young people and adults.

Although Still gave lectures and readings worldwide, he devoted his life and his career to Appalachian Kentucky, always returning to his cabin on Wolfpen Creek. Still chronicled the traditional lifestyle of farmers and miners being displaced by harsh economic conditions, but even more important to him was the education of young people in the region. From the early days, when he hand-carried boxes of books to area schools, organized baseball teams, and sponsored Boy Scout troops, to his later teaching at the Hindman Settlement School and at Morehead State, to his guest lectures at a number of Kentucky colleges and universities, Still repeatedly emphasized the importance of education, especially reading, for the future of individuals and the region as a whole. Thus, although his countless awards could have gained him a number of prestigious and financially rewarding positions elsewhere, he chose to remain in eastern Kentucky. His collected papers are located at Berea College, Morehead State University, and the University of Kentucky.

## ANALYSIS

Having lived in Knott County most of his life, James Still possessed an intimate knowledge of the landscape, the language, the economic conditions, the people, and their social activities, such as hog-killing and sorghum-making. Though he expressed doubt that his neighbors read his books, many of those neighbors insisted that he had portrayed faithfully the physical and social geography of the region with his vivid accounts of the rugged valleys, the steep and rocky trails, and the patches of quicksand. Readers can visualize the locations because of his specific sensory imagery, and some readers seem convinced they could go immediately to the farms and mines where Still's characters live.

Equally credible is the language Still used in his narrative frameworks and the words his characters speak. Linguistic scholars have repeatedly observed that--unlike local colorists, who used multiple misspellings to convey a sense of dialect--Still used archaic word forms, such as holp (help), hit (it), pizen (poison), quare (strange), tuck (took), and sun-ball (sun). He also used folk idioms, such as tator holed (saved), hold your tater (be patient), tight as Dick's hatband (stingy), and saving as a squirrel (very frugal). When a character says he "can hear everything but the truth and the meat a-frying," Still's readers understand his meaning and accept him as a true Appalachian character.

## ADOLESCENT BOY NARRATOR

Much of Still's fiction involves family stories told by adolescent or preadolescent boys, often as first-person narrators. The families are struggling economically. While fathers attempt to support their families by mining, farming, trading, or hunting and trapping, mothers hold their families together fiscally and emotionally, insisting that they save their money and hold on to their family traditions. As the entire family moves from one home and job site to another (as in "The Moving" and "The Burning of the Waters"), the mothers are the cohesive force, who not only "make do" with limited resources but also provide the children with security and a unifying sense of family purpose. Female children prepare themselves for this role. Elvy (in "Mrs. Razor") claims her imaginary husband has left her and stolen her children; she refuses to eat until her father drives six miles toward the family's "Nowhere Place" to rescue the children. Though readers may be amused by Elvy's demands, the story reflects a serious problem, and Elvy's siblings not only believe her tale but also are distressed by it.

Girls play a small role in most Still stories. Aside from Elvy, only Nezzie (in "The Nest") and Peep Eye (in "The Stir-Off") interact significantly with the main characters. With the exception of the mother figures, adult women are likely to be treated humorously. Maybelle (in "Maybelle Upshaw") is the largest woman the narrator has ever seen, and the carnival manager agrees, offering her a place in his sideshow, though his men have to dismantle the narrator's front door to get her out. Similarly, the widow Sula Basham (in "The Moving") is the butt of the town's jokes until she hits the principal joker with her fist; as the young male narrator looks back, he sees that joker kneeling before her, cringing in fear. Aunt Besh (in "A Master Time") is another comic character who nonetheless is humored by the community because of her age and the many generations of local citizens she delivered during her years as midwife.

The boys in Still's stories are of two types: Some are responsible sons and brothers, while others are pranksters and sometimes rascals or cheats. Although a few, such as the narrator of "Snail Pie," are self-centered, most of the first-person narrators attempt to help their families. The narrator of "Locust Summer" agrees to show the traveling "medicine" salesman a patch of ratsbane in exchange for a tonic to help his mother, his little brother, and the family horse. Likewise, in "Journey to the Forks," the same narrator takes responsibility for leading his brother and sister to their new school. In contrast, a recurring trickster character is Godey Spurlock. In "A Ride on the Short Dog," with his friend Mal, he incites trouble on a small local bus, banging together the heads of two other passengers and forcing the first-person narrator to fight him until eventually Godey appears to be seriously injured. Godey and Mal appear again in "The Run for the Elbertas," where they cheat and bedevil their employer, who eventually outsmarts them and gains revenge.

### PAIN AND DEATH

Still does not avoid heart-wrenching elements such as pain and death. Clebe (in "One Leg Gone to Judgment") tells an essentially humorous story about the funeral conducted for his amputated leg, but when he muses about how much he misses that leg, the tone becomes much more serious. Loss and disappointment are part of everyday life, as livestock die and crops fail. Human deaths occur frequently and often at the same time as births. Thus, the household in "Locust Summer" is experiencing the deaths of an adored child and a beloved grandmother at the same time a baby is being born. Young Nezzie Hargis ("The Nest") is sent alone on the mountain trail to her aunt's house, but, unable to find that path or the path back home, she wanders all day and night, until finally making herself a nest in a clump of broomsage, where she freezes to death. Becoming young again at the age of 103, Uncle Mize Hardburly (in "Brother to Methuselum") finally decides to remarry, only to die as his bride-to-be is driving up to the house. Death is treated even more ironically in "The Scrape," in which the narrator referees a fight between two men courting the same girl; although he says he begged them to stop, both wind up dead and the narrator has a clear field to pursue the girl.

### HUMOR

Humor is important in Still's stories. In "A Master Time," the hard work of hog killing is followed by the men's drinking and their resounding defeat by the women in a snowball fight. Politics is another subject of humor. Crafton Rowan (in "Pattern of a Man"), who is running for the office of county jailer, claims to be "the pattern of a man to elect." In a series of letters between May 17 and August 11, Crafton uses flattery, bribery, and eventually insults in attempts to gain the political support of his neighbor, at the same time revealing the negative side of his character. Likewise, the first-person narrator of "Encounter on Keg Branch" attempts to defend himself against a lawsuit, only to demonstrate that he actually has not dealt honorably with his common-law wife or her sister. Preachers, too, are customary subjects of humor. The preacher, Jerb Powell (in "The Sharp Tack"), berates Talt Evarts, a returned soldier, for claiming to have visited the Holy Land. After four letters denouncing Talt as a liar, Powell finally understands Evarts is not claiming to have visited heaven, and the two are reconciled.

### EDUCATION

Often schools are the center of the community. Mace Crownover (in "The Fun Fox") builds a new school in his area and coerces his neighbors into providing a playground and buying the necessary sports equipment. Similarly, in "School Butter," when the local schoolteacher refuses to order new textbooks for the students, Uncle Jolly Middleton, a well-known local prankster, creates a diversion so all the old, damaged textbooks can be dumped in the well. The overall goal, though, is to provide education that will eliminate situations such as that of Jabe and Shridy, who cannot read the letter from their new daughter-in-law.

### FUNDAMENTAL VALUES

Overall, the harsh economic environment of Knott County leads residents to prize fundamental values, such as courage, honor, neighborliness, and generosity. Thus, Gid Buckheart accepts his daughter's suitor when that young man not only proves his courage by confronting Gid directly but also shows his endurance by continuing to shake hands, even though Gid is known for his crushing grip. Riar Thomas (in "The Run for the Elbertas") displays a somewhat different type of honor, as he refuses to cheat either his employees or the farmer who sells him the peaches. The father in "Snail Pie" considers it a breach of honor to evict his stepfather, though the old man's stories are disrupting family meals, and the narrator of "Mabel

Upshaw" continues to provide a home for his wife's sister-in-law because one cannot turn away kinfolk. The Crownover family (in "The Proud Walkers") are similarly generous to their new neighbors, building a hearth-fire to welcome them and helping them plant their crops. The Jarretts, too, invite their neighbors to share the bounty of their crops ("A Master Time"). Metaphorically, Still also has shared the bounty of his mountain harvest with readers widely separated in time and place.

OTHER MAJOR WORKS

LONG FICTION: *River of Earth*, 1940, 1968, 1978

POETRY: *Hounds on the Mountain*, 1937; *River of Earth*, 1983; *The Wolfpen Poems*, 1986; *From the Mountain, from the Valley: New and Collected Poems*, 2001.

PLAY: *Searching for Eden: The Diaries of Adam and Eve*, pr., pb. 2006.

NONFICTION: *The Man in the Bushes: The Notebooks of James Still, 1935-1987*, 1988; *The Wolfpen Notebooks: A Record of Appalachian Life*, 1991; *James Still: Portrait of the Artist as a Boy in Alabama*, 1998.

CHILDREN'S LITERATURE: *Way Down Yonder on Troublesome Creek: Appalachian Riddles and Rusties*, 1974; *Jack and the Wonder Beans*, 1977; *Sporty Creek: A Novel About an Appalachian Boyhood*, 1977; *An Appalachian Mother Goose*, 1998.

EDITED TEXT: *The Wolfpen Rusties: Appalachian Riddles and Gee-Haw Whimmy-Diddles*, 1975

BIBLIOGRAPHY

Cadle, Dean. "Pattern of a Writer: Attitudes of James Still." *Appalachian Journal* 15, no. 2 (1988): 104-143. Discussion of Still's technique of blending traditional and folk elements.

Chappell, Fred. "'Menfolk Are Heathens': Cruelty in the Short Stories." In *James Still: Critical Essays on the Dean of Appalachian Literature*, edited by Ted Olson and Kathy H. Olson. Jefferson, N.C.: McFarland, 2007. Discussion of gender's effect on cultural attitudes.

_____. "The Seamless Vision of James Still." *Appalachian Journal* 8, no. 3 (1981): 196-202. Analysis of Still as literary artist and cultural historian.

Crumb, Claude Lafie. *River of Words: James Still's Literary Legacy*. Nicholasville, Ky.: Wind, 2007. Discussion of Still's persona, analysis of individual stories, and assessment of his place in the canon.

Glaser, Joe. "'Slick as a Dogwood Hoe Handle': Craft in the Short Stories." In *James Still: Critical Essays on the Dean of Appalachian Literature*, edited by Ted Olson and Kathy H. Olson. Jefferson, N.C.: McFarland, 2007. Analysis of parallels between Still's technique and traditional techniques in English literature.

Miller, Jim Wayne. Introduction to *The Wolfpen Poems--James Still*. Frankfort, Ky.: Berea College Press, 1986. Discussion of Still's unique combination of the oral tradition and sophisticated literary elements of theme, language, and imagery.

*Charmaine Allmon-Mosby*

# FRANK R. STOCKTON

**Born:** Philadelphia, Pennsylvania; April 5, 1834
**Died:** Washington, D.C.; April 20, 1902
**Also known as:** John Lewees; Paul Fort

PRINCIPAL SHORT FICTION

*The Floating Prince, and Other Fairy Tales,* 1881
*Ting-a-Ling Tales,* 1882
*The Lady, or the Tiger?, and Other Stories,* 1884
*A Christmas Wreck, and Other Stories,* 1886
*Amos Kilbright: His Adscititious Experiences, with Other Stories,* 1888
*The Stories of the Three Burglars,* 1889 (mystery and detective)
*The Rudder Grangers Abroad, and Other Stories,* 1891
*The Clock of Rondaine, and Other Stories,* 1892
*The Watchmaker's Wife, and Other Stories,* 1893
*Fanciful Tales,* 1894
*A Chosen Few,* 1895
*New Jersey: From the Discovery of the Scheyichbi to Recent Times,* 1896
*Stories of New Jersey,* 1896 (also known as *New Jersey*)
*A Story-Teller's Pack,* 1897
*Afield and Afloat,* 1900
*John Gayther's Garden and the Stories Told Therein,* 1902
*The Magic Egg, and Other Stories,* 1907
*Stories of the Spanish Main,* 1913
*Best Short Stories,* 1957

OTHER LITERARY FORMS

Frank R. Stockton (STAHK-tuhn) wrote many articles for periodicals; he was on the staffs of *Hearth and Home* and *The Century Illustrated Monthly Magazine,* and he was assistant editor of *St. Nicholas* from the time he was thirty-nine until forty-seven. He began as a juvenile writer, and some of his children's stories are still popular, particularly "The Bee Man of Orn," illustrated by Maurice Sendak. Of his many adult novels, the best loved was *Rudder Grange* (1879), for which the public demanded two sequels, *The Rudder Grangers Abroad, and Other Stories* and *Pomona's Travels* (1894).

ACHIEVEMENTS

A prolific writer, Frank R. Stockton is grouped with Mark Twain and Joel Chandler Harris as one of the finest humorists of the last quarter of the nineteenth century. He was widely admired during his lifetime, especially for his short stories, and was perhaps the first American science-fiction novelist. Nevertheless, Stockton's name is all but unknown to the modern reader. The choice presented in his most popular story-- "The Lady or the Tiger?"--may be familiar to some today, but the story itself--which has been cited as a predecessor of modern recreative fiction--essentially has been forgotten.

It has been suggested that Stockton led the way for other more well-known authors. His novel *What Might Have Been Expected* (1874) was a forerunner of Twain's *The Adventures of Tom Sawyer* (1876) and *Adventures of Huckleberry Finn* (1884); Stockton's portrayal of ordinary middle-class life in the 1880's preceded James Thurber's stories of the 1940's. Stockton's experiments with narrative technique inspired Gertrude Stein's approach in her *The Autobiography of Alice B. Toklas* (1933), and his political satire "The Governor-General" (1898) is remarkably similar to Leonard Patrick O'Connor Wibberley's 1950's best seller *The Mouse That Roared* (1955).

BIOGRAPHY

Francis Richard Stockton was a descendant of American pioneers, one of whom, Richard Stockton, was a signer of the Declaration of Independence. The third son of nine children, Frank R. Stockton was expected to become a doctor. Instead, upon graduating from high school, he studied wood engraving, at which he was proficient enough to support himself until he was thirty-two, when he decided to become a journalist. Until 1880, he specialized in children's stories; then he began writing for adults, although the tone and the situations were not much different from his earlier works. He completed more than a dozen novels, comedies, satires, scientific speculations, and whimsies.

## ANALYSIS

Because the masses read Stockton mainly for escape, it was easy for them to miss the underlying thought and sophistication in much of his work. Simply because he was so popular with the general public, Stockton has tended to be ignored by scholars and critics.

### "THE MAGIC EGG"

In "The Magic Egg," Stockton successfully employed a narrative device as old as *The Arabian Nights' Entertainments:* the frame story. The enclosed tale is about a magic show put on by Herbert Loring for a few carefully invited friends. The first part of the exhibition is a slide show projected on the screen of what Loring calls "fireworks," a kind of kaleidoscope arrangement of pieces of colored glass, which form, by means of mirrors and lights, into fascinating patterns. After half an hour of this, the host brings out a table upon which he places a box containing an egg. When he touches the egg with a wand, it hatches into a downy chick that continues to grow until it is an enormous cock. Flapping its wings, the cock ascends to a chair placed upon the table for that purpose, its weight nearly tipping it over. The audience stands, cheers, and becomes extremely excited. Then the magician reverses the growth process and the bird grows smaller and smaller until it enters the egg again, is put back into the box, and the host leaves the stage.

The frame narrative tells how the audience assembled at the Unicorn Club by invitation at three o'clock on a January afternoon has to wait fifteen minutes, because Loring sees that two reserved seats in the front row have not yet been filled. Because the audience is becoming restless, Loring decides to

begin, even though someone important has not yet arrived. A few minutes after the fireworks part of the show, Edith Starr, who had been betrothed to Herbert Loring a month before, enters unobtrusively; not wishing to disturb the proceedings to find her front-row reserved seat, she sits in the back behind two large gentlemen who completely conceal her person. Her mother had had a headache so she stayed with her until she fell asleep and then came alone to "see what she could."

At this point the narration changes from omniscient to first person, as the magician describes what is happening in a long monologue of six and a half pages, which concludes the frame story. Elated with his success, Loring uses a metaphor in which he becomes the rooster that he produced. He feels as if he "could fly to the top of that steeple, and flap and crow until all the world heard me." Since the crowing cock who lords it over the hen yard is soon to be deflated, the emblem of masculine power is thus used as ironic foreshadowing, as well as summing up what preceded.

*Frank R. Stockton* (Library of Congress)

Herbert and Edith meet in her library. He has been in the habit of calling on her every night, so this is part of the acknowledged routine of the engaged lover. The remainder of the action is unfolded in dialogue. She says that she saw the audience wild with excitement. She, however, saw no chick, nor any full-grown fowl, no box, no wand, and no embroidered cloth. Nothing was what he said it was. "Everything was a sham and a delusion; every word you spoke was untrue. And yet everybody in the theatre, excepting you and me, saw all the things that you said were on the stage." Loring explains that he had hypnotized the audience with the revolving pieces of colored glass by which he had forced them to strain their eyes upward for half an hour in order to induce hypnotic sleep. He had been careful to invite only "impressionable subjects." When he was absolutely sure that they were under his influence, he proceeded to test his hypnotic powers with the illusion, which they believed they saw.

"Did you intend that I should also be put under that spell?" she asks, indignant that he would have considered taking away her reason and judgment and making her "a mere tool of his will." She now understands that "nothing was real, not even the little pine table--not even the man!" She says a final good-bye to him, never to see him again, because she wants nothing further to do with a man who would cloud her perceptions, subject her intellect to his own, and force her to believe a lie. As the rejected suitor leaves, he says, "And this is what came out of the magic egg!"

This is an inverted fairy tale. The normal formulaic plot would have ended in a marriage whose happy ending was achieved by the use of magical objects. Instead, the magic object here leads to the dissolution of the happy ending because the "princess" has a mind of her own; she is a strong-willed woman who refuses to submit to male domination. The second important aspect of the story is that it is a metaphor for the art of storytelling. The speaker, with his words alone, hypnotizes his audience into suspending their disbelief. His power over them is like that of a magician, and Stockton, whose enthusiastic public followed his legerdemain through more than a dozen novels, must have at times confronted the ambiguities of his position. The blank page must have seemed the white shell of a magic egg which he alone could "crack" to release wonders that lasted only as long as he was relating them and then, when the cover was closed, went back to being only an object.

### "HIS WIFE'S DECEASED SISTER"

"His Wife's Deceased Sister" is a charming tale built on the interrelations between life and literature and on the paradox that failure results from too-great success. A newly married author in the elation of his honeymoon writes a moving story. He has supported himself quite adequately up to that time with his fictions, but this story is a masterpiece. The problem is that everything he writes afterward is rejected because it would disappoint the public for not being on the same level that they have come to expect from him. The author then meets a pauper who earlier had the same paradoxical experience of having been ruined by the success of one story. Depressed by his visit to the pauper's room, where the pauper sleeps on newspapers and lives by grinding heads on pins, the author consults his editor, saying he faces similar ruin. They hit on the device of an assumed name.

Once more the author is making a good, steady income when a son is born. In his first joy of fatherhood, he composes a story that is even superior to "His Wife's Deceased Sister." He places it in a tin box with the edges soldered together, which he hides in the attic with instructions to throw away the key to the solid lock he has purchased for it. The underlying assumption is that great fiction is inspired by happy events in life, which contradicts the Freudian notion that art sublimates suffering. The problem with the plot is that readers may think they have a better solution to the author's problem. Why not publish the story under his real name? The spark for "His Wife's Deceased Sister" is clearly Stockton's own experience with "The Lady or the Tiger?"--which made him a cult figure--and subsequent publication problems that ensued. Although Stockton's work generally expressed admiration for the middle class, with all its weaknesses, he could also be satirical and interpreted on many levels. In this story, the main character chooses to relegate his masterpiece to oblivion rather than again subject himself to the upheaval of public adulation.

## "THE LADY OR THE TIGER?"

"The Lady or the Tiger?" is one of the most famous short stories of the nineteenth century, creating so much controversy when it was first published that Stockton was bombarded with letters and accosted at parties by readers frustrated at his refusal to provide a definitive ending. The plot of the story is straightforward. The semibarbaric king of an unnamed country establishes what he considers to be a completely fair method of justice. When someone is accused of a crime, he is placed in a large arena with two identical doors. Behind one is a beautiful woman; behind the other is a ferocious tiger. He is free to choose whichever one he wishes. If he chooses the woman, they are married and live happily ever after. If he chooses the tiger, he is devoured. The two possible culminations of the game played by the semibarbaric king are the conventional alternative endings of comedy or tragedy--marriage or death.

However, in this particular enactment of the king's justice, the accused one is a young man who has broken the law by secretly seeing the king's daughter. When he is placed in the arena and told to choose one of the doors, he knows that the princess must have discovered which door hides the beautiful woman and which hides the tiger. When she gives him a signal as to which door to open, he unhesitatingly goes to one of the doors. At that point, Stockton ends the story and asks the reader to guess which door. The fact that this particular story "ends" before it ends, giving the reader the freedom to choose a conclusion, is a game on Stockton's part to exploit the reader's need to "close" a story, to see true justice enacted.

Stockton urges readers to close the story not by choosing what they want to come out of the doors, but rather in the way readers always achieve closure--by looking back at the plot, the tone, and the thematic motifs to determine the story's thematic "end." Since the story makes quite clear that the semibarbaric nature of the king's daughter consists of her being both ladylike and tigerish, what readers are really asked to decide is which aspect of the princess dominates at the end--her lady side or her tigerish jealous side. The reader closes the story in all its openness by determining the pattern and tone of the story. Because the presentation of what goes on in the princess's mind makes quite clear which side that is, the reader is not so free to choose as it first appears. Even though the story leaves little doubt that the tiger pounces out at the end (for the princess has more tiger in her personality than lady), most readers feel tricked or cheated that Stockton leaves the final choice ostensibly open. "The Lady or the Tiger?" is almost solely a story of technique; its content is a pretext for the self-conscious game it plays with the conventions of narrative endings.

## OTHER MAJOR WORKS

LONG FICTION: *What Might Have Been Expected*, 1874; *Rudder Grange*, 1879; *A Jolly Fellowship*, 1880; *The Story of Viteau*, 1884; *The Transferred Ghost*, 1884; *The Casting Away of Mrs. Lecks and Mrs. Aleshine*, 1886; *The Late Mrs. Null*, 1886; *The Hundredth Man*, 1887; *The Dusantes: A Sequel to "The Casting Away of Mrs. Lecks and Mrs. Aleshine,"* 1888; *Personally Conducted*, 1889; *The Great War Syndicate*, 1889; *Ardis Claverden*, 1890; *The House of Martha*, 1891; *The Squirrel Inn*, 1891; *Pomona's Travels*, 1894; *The Adventures of Captain Horn*, 1895; *Captain Chap: Or, The Rolling Stones*, 1896; *Mrs. Cliff's Yacht*, 1896; *The Buccaneers and Pirates of Our Coasts*, 1898; *The Girl at Cobhurst*, 1898; *The Great Stone of Sardis: A Novel*, 1898; *The Associate Hermits*, 1899; *The Vizier of the Two-Horned Alexander*, 1899; *The Young Master of Hyson Hall*, 1899; *A Bicycle of Cathay: A Novel*, 1900; *Kate Bonnet: The Romance of a Pirate's Daughter*, 1902; *The Captain's Toll-Gate*, 1903; *The Lost Dryad*, 1912; *The Poor Count's Christmas*, 1927.

NONFICTION: *A Northern Voice Calling for the Dissolution of the Union of the United States of America*, 1860; *The Home: Where It Should Be and What to Put in It*, 1872.

CHILDREN'S LITERATURE: *Ting-a-Ling*, 1870; *Roundabout Rambles in Lands of Fact and Fancy*, 1872; *Tales Out of School*, 1875; *The Bee-Man of Orn, and Other Fanciful Tales*, 1887; *The Queen's Museum, and Other Fanciful Tales*, 1906.

MISCELLANEOUS: *The Novels and Stories of Frank R. Stockton*, 1899-1904 (twenty-three volumes).

BIBLIOGRAPHY

Golemba, Henry L. *Frank R. Stockton*. Boston: Twayne, 1981. Part of Twayne's United States Authors series, this extended examination of Stockton and his art includes a chronological investigation of Stockton's works. Golemba also suggests reasons for Stockton's neglect, in relation not only to the works themselves but also to the history of publishing and literary criticism over the last hundred years. The 182-page volume contains a select bibliography of primary and secondary sources.

Griffin, Martin I. J. *Frank R. Stockton*. Philadelphia: University of Pennsylvania Press, 1939. This biography gathers together details of Stockton's life--many taken from original sources--and shows the relationship between his life and his works. In the discussion of Stockton's work, however, plot summary dominates over critical interpretation. Includes a bibliography.

Howells, William Dean. "Stockton's Stories." *The Atlantic Monthly* 59 (January, 1887): 130-132. Citing particular Stockton stories, Howells discusses Stockton's influence on the short-story form, analyzing characteristics of both the author and the form that make them such a good match. This article, along with three others Howells wrote during Stockton's lifetime, provides some of the best criticism of Stockton's art.

Johnson, Robert U. *Remembered Yesterdays*. Boston: Little, Brown, 1923. This memoir by a former editor in chief of *The Century Illustrated Monthly Magazine* includes information about many men and women memorable in the fields of letters and publishing. His short chapter on Stockton, entitled "A Joyful Humorist," gives a feeling for the man through personal recollections and anecdotes.

May, Charles. *The Short Story: The Reality of Artifice*. New York: Twayne, 1995. Brief comment on Stockton's best-known story-- "The Lady or the Tiger?"--as a so-called trick-ending story; suggests the story is not as open-ended as it is often claimed to be.

Vedder, Henry C. *American Writers of Today*. Boston: Silver Burdett, 1894. This analysis of American writers includes a twelve-page chapter on Stockton and his work. Although obviously dated and considering works only to the early 1890's, the chapter offers interesting insights and a flavor of the times in which Stockton wrote. Vedder gives considerable attention to Stockton's originality and droll humor.

*Ruth Rosenberg; Jean C. Fulton*
*Updated by Charles E. May*

# ROBERT STONE

**Born:** Brooklyn, New York; August 21, 1937

PRINCIPAL SHORT FICTION

*Bear and His Daughter,* 1997
*Fun with Problems,* 2010

OTHER LITERARY FORMS

Robert Stone is best known as an award-winning novelist, but he also wrote the screenplay adaptations of his first two novels, *A Hall of Mirrors* (1967) and *Dog Soldiers* (1974), entitled *WUSA* (1970) and *Who'll Stop the Rain* (1978), respectively. He has also written the novel *Damascus Gate* (1998) and contributed dozens of literary and social essays, travel pieces, and political commentaries to leading journals, and he edited (with Katrina Kenison) *The Best American Short Stories 1992*. In 2008, Stone published his memoir *Prime Green: Remembering the Sixties*. His novel *Bay of Souls* appeared in 2003.

ACHIEVEMENTS

Robert Stone was awarded the William Faulkner Foundation First Novel Award in 1967 and won a John Simon Guggenheim Memorial Foundation Fellowship in 1971. *Dog Soldiers* won the National Book Award in 1975; *A Flag for Sunrise* (1981) was a finalist for that award and for the Pulitzer Prize in Letters in 1982. He has been the recipient of numerous other awards, including a National Endowment for the Humanities Fellowship in 1982 and the Mildred and Harold Strauss Living Award in 1987.

## BIOGRAPHY

Robert Anthony Stone's life has mirrored the colorful lives so frequently portrayed in his stories and novels. After Catholic school and a stint in the U.S. Navy (1955 to 1958), Stone and his wife (who married in 1959) traveled and worked at various odd jobs. (Their daughter Deirdre was born in a charity hospital in New Orleans.) In New York, Stone supported his growing family--a son, Ian, was born in 1964--as an advertising copywriter, wrote his first novel, and soon won a Wallace Stegner writing fellowship at Stanford University. Since his first novel, Stone has been able to support himself with his writing, supplemented by fellowships and teaching positions. (He has taught at Princeton and Harvard Universities, among other schools.) Largely self-educated (he spent less than a year at New York University), Stone has commented extensively on a wide range of political topics and has engaged in a number of public literary controversies.

## ANALYSIS

Robert Stone has published a number of short stories and the short-story collections *Bear and His Daughter* and *Fun with Problems*. Many of his stories have been reprinted in other collections, however, and in the annual publication *The Best American Short Stories*.

Stone's fictional world does not look appealing initially. His stories deal with violent and troubling events: abortion, drug dealing, alcoholism, the effects of war. However, there is a moral vein running beneath the surface of these stories--even when the world they reflect seems without moral structure--and many of his characters are desperately seeking freedom from their demons. One of Stone's themes seems to be the consequences of early actions and the need for mercy and forgiveness--of self as well as of others. Stone's characters are sometimes mad, often brutal--the surface of his stories has constant tension--but they are often

seeking spiritual transcendence. His writing is spare, he renders dialogue beautifully, and it is easy for readers to identify with his characters, in spite of their troubled lives.

## BEAR AND HIS DAUGHTER

Robert Stone has published more than a dozen short stories over the course of his career, and his collection *Bear and His Daughter* brings together six stories written over some thirty years with a previously unpublished title novella. The collection includes "Helping," which was also reprinted in *The Best American Stories 1988*, and "Under the Pitons," which appeared in *The Best American Stories 1997*. The remaining five stories are equally strong and represent Stone's fictional style at its best. Stone is a realist who captures contemporary American life in its starkest, often most brutal moments. In his minimalist style Stone often reads like Raymond Carver, but in his deeper ethnical concerns he resembles such British novelists as Joseph Conrad and Graham Greene.

### "MISERERE"

"Miserere" leads off the *Bear and His Daughter* collection, and it is a powerful story of contemporary American life and a ready example of Stone's fictional style. Mary Urquhart, a librarian in a decaying northern New Jersey city, receives a call as she finishes work one night from her friend Camille Innaurato. Mary drives to Camille's house, as Mary has done on earlier occasions. Camille's brother is a policeman who recovers fetuses disposed of by abortion clinics and brings them to Camille, who then enlists Mary and Mary's priest friend, Father Hooke, to inter the fetuses in a Catholic rite. On this cold night, when they arrive at Father Hooke's rectory, however, they learn that he has changed his mind and will not perform the service."'I think women have a right,'" he announces. There is an ugly scene in which Mary reduces Father Hooke to tears, and he accuses the women of violence and cruelty. They drive to a second priest, Monsignor Danilo, who performs the ceremony, but it is an unsatisfactory experience for Mary.

The title of the story comes from the Latin prayer "Agnus Dei, qui tollis peccate mundi,/ Miserere nobis" ("Lamb of God, who takest away the sins of the world,/ Have mercy on us"). In the argument with Father

Hooke, readers learn that thirteen years earlier Mary lost her husband and three children in a skating accident when the ice on a frozen lake gave way, and the four fetuses before the altar remind readers of that tragedy. After recovering from alcoholism and then converting to Catholicism, Mary became a rabid antiabortionist, but her rage at life simmers just beneath the taut surface of this story. The prayer that closes the short story, "Have mercy on us," applies to all the flawed characters here.

### "ABSENCE OF MERCY"

"Absence of Mercy" is another story of violence--and mercy. Mackay is a young man in his late twenties, working to support his wife and baby. The greatest impact on his life, it is clear, came from his brief stay in an orphanage, where he was placed in the 1940's, when his mother was institutionalized. He survived the violence and "absence of mercy" at St. Michael's and during his years in the U.S. Navy, and he is working his way up to middle-class respectability when he reads that a friend from the orphanage, also a young married man, was killed in a New York City subway trying to be a good Samaritan. The murder haunts Mackay, for somehow the violence of his childhood has reached out to touch him again.

A year later on a nearby subway platform, Mackay tries to intervene when a crazed man attacks an old woman. The woman escapes, but Mackay and the man fall into a struggle on the platform. Mackay finally gets away, but the attacker yells for help, and the crowd sees Mackay as the criminal. Mackay will survive, Stone implies, but "he wondered just how far he would run and where it was that he thought to go." His childhood violence and "absence of mercy" have followed him, in the upside-down moral order that seems to describe this world. There are no easy ethical answers here.

### "HELPING"

"Helping" is one of Stone's best-known stories and has been anthologized several times and included in *The Best American Stories 1988*. Elliot--and all Stone's male protagonists seem to be known by their last names--has been sober for some eighteen months, until his client Blankenship comes into the office at the state hospital where Elliot is a counselor. Blankenship has not been to Vietnam, while Elliot has, but Blankenship appropriates Elliot's experience, even his dreams of that awful war. Elliot's anger soon gives way to anxiety, and he ends up drinking and driving home with a bottle. When Elliot's wife Grace returns from her own nightmarish day to discover the drunken Elliot, she announces she is not going to stay with him this time. Grace works for a service that helps battered children and has lost a battered child to parents in a court case, so both partners have been unable to help others. When the child's father, Vopotik, calls to abuse her verbally, Elliot invites him over and gets out his shotgun. He awakens the next morning in the chair by the window, where he has been waiting for Vopotik, and goes outside with the gun. Standing in a snow-covered field, he sees his wife in their bedroom window and hopes for some sign of forgiveness from her. The story ends on this ambiguous note. Will Elliot recover? Will his wife stay and help him? In the universe of Stone's stories, anxiety, desperation, and rage dominate, and mercy can never be taken for granted.

### "UNDER THE PITONS"

"Under the Pitons" was included in *The Best American Stories 1997* and is a tale of adventure that could have been written by Ernest Hemingway. The story covers several days as a motley crew of one-time drug dealers sails from St. Vincent to Martinique in the Caribbean. Blessington is aboard to pilot the *Sans Regret*, but it is his French partner Freyincet who has set up the dope deal. Along for the ride are the women Marie and Gillian. The four had picked up the dope in St. Vincent some days ago and must deliver it to Martinique. When Marie becomes sick, Freyincet insists they anchor off the southwest coast of St. Lucia, under the shadow of the Pitons, twin peaks whose name means "stakes." The stakes here are high, and all four will lose. Two pirates come out to the boat, and Freyincet scares them off with a shotgun. The four smugglers go swimming in the clear Caribbean water, suddenly realize they have forgotten to put down the ladder, and, when they discover that the pirates have cut their ropes, are unable to keep up with the drifting boat. Blessington tries to save Gillian, but she is too stoned to help herself and eventually drowns. Blessington makes it to shore and sees what may be one of the other two near the stranded boat, but he heads off into the jungle and to the imagined comfort of an Irish bar in the island town of Soufriere. Gillian goes down singing "Praise God, from whom all blessings flow," but there is little to praise in this tale of drugs and mistakes. All the characters believed they could make easy money and escape without consequences-- "without regret," as the boat's name declares--but that is impossible in the world Stone creates.

### "BEAR AND HIS DAUGHTER"

The title story of Stone's collection of short fiction is a grim and gripping tale. "Bear" is William Small, a famous poet who is doing a western tour of readings, when he stops to visit his daughter Rowan, a ranger at a national park in Nevada. His last tour ended in disaster, and this one seems headed the same way. On the night that readers are introduced to him, Small is kicked out of a casino after getting drunk. When he finds his daughter, she has been taking crystal methedrine all day, and the two of them drink wine and talk about their failed and fragmented lives. Both are haunted by their sexual relations in the past, and Rowan is filled with a rage that the drugs and alcohol only fuel. Small has been trying all day to remember a poem about returning salmon he wrote for her years earlier. After she shoots her father and then kills herself--in a natural cavern where she claims Indian sacrifices were once made--her boyfriend finds the poem. The story is completed, like the troubled lives of these two, but there is little else to salvage.

### FUN WITH PROBLEMS

The central theme that runs through many of Stone's stories in this collection is the enactment of retribution against a successful man who is not a nice guy. The obvious example is the story "From the Lowlands," in which a man named Leroy, who has somewhat ruthlessly made a lot of money in the Silicon Valley technology boom, travels, with "little sense of sin," to a vacation home he has built in the mountains.

When he stops in the local post office and sees a wanted poster for a murderer named Alan Ladd and later sees a construction worker whose brutal face reminds Leroy of the poster, he becomes unsettled by the coincidence and begins to notice what he takes to be portents of evil and disaster. When he breaks an egg in a frying pan, he sees a bright spot of blood and thinks it

looks like a skull. The signs and portents he has seen are fulfilled when a panther with a skull-like face shows up by his pool.

The title story is about an aging attorney with the public defender's office named Peter Matthews, another of Stone's gratuitously mean guys, but one who this time escapes retribution. Visiting a young burglar who he thinks the police are trying to railroad him into making a confession, Matthews meets a young psychologist named Amy Littlefield. When Matthews takes the young woman for a drink, he learns that she has a second career in Off-Broadway plays and does not drink because it makes her forget her lines. However, Matthews, who is bored and lonely and whose attraction to the woman is "sensual, sexual, and mean," the way he wants it, flatters her and gets her to drink margaritas, stopping at a liquor store for more tequila when he takes her home. As she gets drunk, he senses her weakness and her need for abasement, and he slaps her on the bottom "as hard as she might reasonably require," after which they go to bed. The next morning when she cries, he shrugs and walks away, saying nothing. Matthews's attitude, typical of many of the men in these stories, is best expressed by his ex-wife, who once told him that he did not even care if he had sex with a woman as long as he could make her unhappy.

The shortest story in the collection and the most carefully written is "Honeymoon," in which a man, on his honeymoon in the Caribbean, calls his ex-wife to tell her how lonely he is. When he tells her he wants to come home, the ex-wife hangs up on him, reminding him that he was the one who wanted to leave. Later, when the man and his bride go deep sea diving, he takes off his oxygen tank and drops it. As he sinks in the water, he watches the desired form of his bride swim above him. Because of its shortness, the result is a tight little tale about the basic mystery of the difference between love and desire, the kind of universal mystery that the short-story form handles best.

OTHER MAJOR WORKS

LONG FICTION: *A Hall of Mirrors*, 1967; *Dog Soldiers*, 1974; *A Flag for Sunrise*, 1981; *Children of Light*, 1986; *Outerbridge Reach*, 1992; *Damascus Gate*, 1998; *Bay of Souls*, 2003.

SCREENPLAYS: *WUSA*, 1970; *Who'll Stop the Rain*, 1978 (with Judith Roscoe).

NONFICTION: *Prime Green: Remembering the Sixties*, 2007.

EDITED TEXT: *The Best American Short Stories*, 1992.

BIBLIOGRAPHY

Bonetti, Kay, et al., eds. *Conversations with American Novelists*. Columbia: University of Missouri Press, 1997. Stone talks about his early stories in this far-ranging 1982 interview.

Finn, James. "The Moral Vision of Robert Stone: Transcendent in the Muck of History." *Commonweal* 119 (November 5, 1993): 9-14. Although focused on the novels, this article in a *Commonweal* series on contemporary Catholic writers of fiction identifies the peculiarly moral strain of Stone's writing.

Parks, John G. "Unfit Survivors: The Failed and Lost Pilgrims in the Fiction of Robert Stone." *CEA Critic* 53 (Fall, 1990): 52-57. Examines the characters of Stone's fiction.

Solotaroff, Robert. *Robert Stone*. New York: Twayne, 1994. In this first full-length study of Stone's fiction, Solotaroff's final chapter, "The Stories and the Nonfiction," is a trenchant treatment of Stone's work, with analyses of "Helping" and "Absence of Mercy," as well as two other stories from *Bear and His Daughter*, "Porque No Tiene, Porque Le Falta" and "Aquarius Obscured."

*David Peck*
*Updated by Charles E. May*

---

# SUSAN STRAIGHT

**Born:** Riverside, California; October 19, 1960

PRINCIPAL SHORT FICTION

*Aquaboogie: A Novel in Stories,* 1991
"Mines," 2002
"El Ojo de Agua," 2006
"The Golden Gopher," 2007

OTHER LITERARY FORMS

Susan Straight has appropriated characters and settings from her short fiction into several novels, beginning with incorporating literary elements from *Aquaboogie: A Novel in Stories* (1991) in *I Been in Sorrow's Kitchen and Licked Out All the Pots* (1992). Straight's later novels, especially *Blacker Than a Thousand Midnights* (1994), *A Million Nightingales* (2006), and *Take One Candle Light a Room* (2010), include imagery and themes associated with her short stories. Straight has also written nonfiction essays and book reviews for anthologies and print and online periodicals. She read the text for the compact disc recording *An Introduction to*

*"The Grapes of Wrath" by John Steinbeck: Audio Guide* (2006) produced for the National Endowment for the Arts' the Big Read program. Straight also has created children's literature.

ACHIEVEMENTS

In 1991, Susan Straight's first book, *Aquaboogie: A Novel in Stories*, won the Milkweed National Fiction Prize. She received a 1997 Guggenheim Fellowship. Straight was selected as the 1999 Lannan Foundation Award winner. In 2001, her novel *Highwire Moon* was a finalist for the National Book Award in fiction. The Commonwealth Club presented that novel its Gold Medal for Fiction the following year. Straight's short story "Mines" received a 2003 Pushcart Prize in fiction and was included in *The Best American Short Stories* that year. The 2005 edition of *The Best American Short Stories* designated Straight's short fiction "Bridge Work" a distinguished story. In 2006, Straight's novel *A Million Nightingales* was a finalist for the *Los Angeles Times* Book Prize and southern California Booksellers' Award. The next year, her overall writing was honored with the 2007 Lannan Award for Fiction, and her story "El Ojo de Agua" received the O. Henry Prize. The Mystery Writers of America presented Straight a 2008 Edgar Award for Best Short Story for "The Golden Gopher." In 2010, Straight was selected as the first Inlandia Literary Laureate.

## BIOGRAPHY

Susan Straight was born on October 19, 1960, in Riverside, California, to salesman Richard Straight and Gabrielle Gertrude Leu, an office worker. When Susan Straight was three, her father left the family, and her mother later married John Watson. Straight attended Riverside public schools. While a North High School student, Straight read O. Henry Prize stories, which inspired her. Bold, resourceful female protagonists in *Anne of Green Gables* (1908), *A Tree Grows in Brooklyn* (1943), *and Sula* (1973) also impacted her as a writer.

At sixteen, Straight took a creative-writing course at Riverside Community College (RCC). After high school graduation, she enrolled at the University of Southern California. She majored in journalism, contributing to the campus newspaper *The Daily Trojan*. Straight completed her bachelor of arts degree in 1981. That year she published her initial op-ed in the *Los Angeles Herald Examiner*, describing area businesses' racism during a recession.

After a writing professor suggested that Straight seek a master of fine arts degree, she secured a fellowship from the University of Massachusetts at Amherst, where her mentors included Julius Lester, Jay Neugeboren, and James Baldwin. Straight married Dwayne Sims on August 20, 1983. She listened to her in-laws' stories, telling why their families migrated from southern states to California. Creating short fiction mostly set in her California hometown, Straight completed her M.F.A. in 1984.

Straight accepted a position as a teacher at RCC. In 1988, she began teaching creative writing at the University of California, Riverside (UCR). Straight also presented creative-writing workshops to California Youth Authority inmates. She submitted her short fiction to literary journals, resulting in *TriQuarterly* editor Reginald Gibbons accepting "The Box," which was published in the fall, 1988, issue. "Buddah" appeared in the next issue. Awarded a *Poets and Writers* grant, Straight read her work at a Minneapolis, Minnesota, event where Milkweed Editions editor Emilie Buchwald encouraged her to compete for that press's literary prize.

In 1992, Straight was promoted to professor at UCR. Straight's picture book *Bear E. Bear* (1995) depicted her family's domestic life. After the couple's 1996 divorce, Straight's former husband often visited their three daughters, Gaila, Delphine, and Rosette. His family remained prominent figures in Straight's life, influencing her literary work. She incorporated aspects of their memories about often overlooked aspects of African American history in her fiction. Straight chaired UCR's Department of Creative Writing and with a colleague established its M.F.A. program in 2002. She served as a National Book Award judge in 2004.

Straight's fiction has been published in numerous journals, such as *Ontario Review*, *Story*, and *Ploughshares*. Her nonfiction has appeared in newspapers and periodicals, including the *Los Angeles Times*, *Harper's*, and *The Nation*. She wrote the introduction for *Inlandia: A Literary Journey Through California's Inland Empire* (2006) and the afterword for a *Little Women* (2004) edition. Anthologies containing Straight's essays include *Race, an Anthology in the First Person* (1997), *Unnatural Disaster: The Nation on Hurricane Katrina* (2006), and *Bound to Last: Thirty Writers on Their Most Cherished Book* (2010).

## ANALYSIS

History frames Susan Straight's fiction, in which modern characters are bound by memories and secrets perpetuated by atrocities their ancestors experienced. She intertwines factual and fictional details to create her primary setting, Rio Seco, California, based on her hometown. Straight populates her stories with working-class characters, mostly African Americans. Her characters undergo transitions as they endure violence and hostilities, which force them to flee their homes, suffer losses, or face abandonment. They are sometimes overwhelmed by their suspicions, distrust, and desire for vengeance. Themes of survival and resilience emphasize many characters' strengths when they encounter bigotry and elude predators.

Straight chronicles generations of families, revealing how they are connected by loyalty, tradition, culture, and place. Characters often feel responsible for members of their communities, whether kin or neighbors, and help feed, secure employment for, protect, defend, and nurture them. She emphasizes self-sufficient, resourceful protagonists. Identity is an essential theme because people's perceptions of other characters often result in unfair judgments and restrictions. Straight's use of slang and vernacular expressions reinforces the unyielding honesty of her depictions and speaks for those who exist on the periphery. Her writing is blunt, intense, and unapologetic, countering stereotypes and assumptions about racial and socioeconomic groups. Although her fictional worlds are frequently brutal and oppressed by crime and drugs, some characters choose hope and kindness over submission to addiction and fear.

### AQUABOOGIE: A NOVEL IN STORIES

Tenacity shapes characters in the fourteen short-fiction pieces in *Aquaboogie: A Novel in Stories*. The introductory epigraph, an excerpt from "Aqua Boogie" song lyrics, refers to dancing and rhythm, creating a metaphor that unites this collection's stories. This epigraph suggests people endure by adapting to adverse circumstances to avoid succumbing to those struggles. Although characters experience varied settings and conflicts, many exemplify the beauty of becoming strong as the ugliness of turmoil, hate, and deprivation surrounds them.

Art empowers characters. Their imaginations provide lifelines to escape racism, crime, gangs, and other threats. Color symbolizes elements significant to each story, such as death approaching in "Back" because of a character's black lung disease. In "Aquaboogie," Nacho, a college janitor, embraces an employment benefit permitting him to enroll tuition-free in one class each academic term, choosing to study art. While performing unsavory tasks, which are the antithesis to beauty, he endures racist insults from white coworkers. Nacho utilizes his artistic skills to attack his tormentors by recognizing their weaknesses and creating specific images to taunt each man.

His father Floyd considers Nacho's artistic endeavors wasted time in "Hollow." Floyd represents the necessity of physical labor to earn money versus Nacho's need to create art for solace, emphasizing the juxtaposition of practical versus aesthetic compensation. Despite Floyd's contempt for traditional art, he has innate artistic sensibilities, expressing appreciation for the attractive appearance of smoothly poured cement.

Characters demonstrate that art is not confined to canvases. In "Esther's," the protagonist reveals her creativity through her cooking. Her unique combination of ingredients parallels artists choosing techniques and media to portray their visions. Esther names her variation Quiche Esther, much like artists' signatures on artwork. She also expresses her artistic nature by stylishly braiding hair.

Grief-stricken Shawan in "The Box" relies on her radio for healing after gang members shoot her friend V-Roy. Feeling powerless in her lawless environment, she gains some control by playing music. Shawan protects the radio when a gunman tries to steal it. She borrows V-Roy's car, crashing it and synchronizing stations on the car's stereo with her radio as rescuers rush to save Shawan.

### "MINES"

Duty and accountability motivate Clarette, a guard at a juvenile detention facility, in "Mines," which explores how gender and generational roles influence characters' choices and reactions to adversity, greed, and success. The title suggests militaristic and materialistic imagery, which develops characterizations. Clarette tolerates the demands of her risky job because of the benefits, particularly the health insurance for her asthmatic daughter, and because of the consistent income it offers, enabling her to secure belongings for sustenance, physical and emotional. Her husband Ray resents the time Clarette invests in work. Their elementary-school-age children, Ray, Jr., and Danae, do not appreciate their mother's sacrifices to ensure they have access to luxuries they crave.

Clarette finds most of her wards, including her nephew Alfonso, distasteful, internally criticizing their tattoos, some of them obscenities, and shaved heads. She resents how the teenage boys, including Alfonso, sass and curse her and laments their limited options, choosing delinquency instead of military employment, like previous generations. The materialistic Alfonso justifies his unlawful behavior as his way to acquire possessions easily and at a young age, ridiculing Clarette for working. Clarette monitors the inmates, always vigilant for potential fights between gang members, especially in the laundry area, which parallels her focus on domestic chores, such as washing clothes, at home after work.

Overwhelming responsibilities and worries at work and home exacerbate Clarette's exhaustion and constant pain. She itemizes the costs of objects and how many hours she has to work to afford them. Ray abandons Clarette, enraged by her interest in buying a five-hundred-dollar upright piano. He takes their son to have his hair shaved in a style resembling the boys that Clarette guards, intensifying her fears that her son might reject the lifestyle she has cultivated carefully in favor of becoming a thug like Alfonso. She confines her hair in braids. During a brawl, Clarette boldly intervenes. The braid yanked from her scalp symbolizes her separation from people who attempt to intimidate and control her.

### "El Ojo de Agua"

Water plays multiple roles in "El Ojo de Agua," draining the essence of settings and characters and witnessing their torment. As an elderly man, Gustave recalls memories from his childhood in Bayou Becasse during the 1927 flood, which inundated parts of Louisiana. Gustave's mother, her ankle puffy from a sting obtained in the sugarcane fields, drowns in her bed as the river rises. Gustave seeks shelter on a levee when land around him is submerged in floodwaters. The theme of survival dominates as African American sugarcane laborers and their families form a community on the levee, huddling together for warmth while waiting for rescuers. A mother named Net grasps her children, including her three-year-old son Enrique, to her body to prevent the water from pulling them away.

White soldiers guard the group, which consists mostly of women and children because the men are taken to reinforce a levee protecting a plantation. They try to seize Gustave, but Net grabs him, like a safety net, saying Gustave is too young. Gustave watches floodwater transport bodies, human and animal, past

him, foreshadowing tragedy. People wrap human corpses in blankets because they cannot bury them. Hunger torments the refugees. Although the racist guards forbid people to scavenge livestock drifting onto the levee, Gustave kills a pig. When guards see Net cooking the hog, they shoot her. As she floats away in the river, Gustave feeds Enrique meat and they become family.

In his Rio Seco home, adult Gustave mourns the loss of his daughter Glorette to her drug addiction, drifting away like the flood victims. Gustave's apartment parallels the Louisiana levee as he waits for his grandson Victor to call. Gustave frets about Victor's safety and worries he is hungry. Gustave views his daughter's body at Enrique's home, then accompanies Sidney Chabert to a taqueira called El Ojo de Agua, translated as "water's eye," where Sidney had found her corpse. The men agree not to report Glorette's death, realizing police, like the levee guards, will be apathetic about her loss. Gustave prepares for Glorette's clandestine burial, assuring her dignity denied the dead the flood washed away.

### "The Golden Gopher"

Solitude haunts characters as they cope with loss and comprehend their sense of belonging to place and people in "The Golden Gopher," which is told from FX (Fantine Xavierine) Antoine's perspective. Antoine, a successful travel writer, is devastated when she learns her cousin Glorette's body has been discovered, abandoned in a shopping cart in an alley. Shocked by the murder of the woman she once considered her best friend, Antoine is determined to find the elusive Grady Jackson, who had loved Glorette, despite her rejecting him for a flashy musician, Sere Dakar. As Antoine walks from her Los Feliz home to downtown Los Angeles, she recalls how she hid as a teenager in a car Grady stole, intending to drive Glorette from Rio Seco to Los Angeles. Unable to find Glorette, Grady drove to Los Angeles anyway and was shocked when Antoine revealed her presence. The pair walked twenty-two miles when the car ran out of fuel. Since then, walking has comforted Antoine, symbolizing freedom and purpose to her.

Antoine's memories trouble her. She remembers how Glorette's beauty enchanted men, who preyed on her vulnerabilities and contributed to Glorette becoming a crack addict. Antoine arrives at the Golden Gopher, a bar where Grady's sister Hattie works; Antoine hopes Hattie can tell her where to find Grady. The Golden Gopher confronts Antoine with the despair of the disheveled homeless, who lurk outside that bar. She is startled by the presence of film crews and affluent celebrities temporarily attracted to the refurbished tavern as an "in" place to patronize.

Antoine unintentionally disrupts Hattie and Grady's routine, in which Hattie provides him food, severing their well-established source of mutual support, emotional and nutritional. Hattie, who has reinvented herself as Gloria, is furious. Antoine is horrified by Grady's revelations of the fate of Dakar after he abandoned Glorette and their son Victor, admitting to stashing Dakar's body in a landfill. She watches Grady walk away, vanishing before Hattie also disappears. Guilt confounds Antoine as she considers the privileges and entitlements she has enjoyed, which enable her autonomy and advancement in contrast to Grady, Hattie, and Glorette being confined by limited options and decisions, with movement being equated with escape.

OTHER MAJOR WORKS

LONG FICTION: *I Been in Sorrow's Kitchen and Licked Out All the Pots*, 1992; *Blacker Than a Thousand Midnights*, 1994; *The Gettin Place*, 1996; *Highwire Moon*, 2001; *A Million Nightingales*, 2006; *Take One Candle Light a Room*, 2010.

CHILDREN'S LITERATURE: *Bear E. Bear*, 1995 (illustrated by Marisabina Russo); *The Hallway Light at Night*, 1999; *The Friskative Dog*, 2007.

BIBLIOGRAPHY

Coffey, Michael. "Susan Straight: Her Hard-Won Lyrical Vision Issues from Inside America's Urban Cauldron." *Publishers Weekly* 241, no. 27 (July 4, 1994): 41-42. Provides biographical details and quotations from Straight discussing her early short-fiction accomplishments.

Furman, Laura, ed. *The O. Henry Prize Stories 2007: The Best Stories of the Year*. New York: Anchor Books/Random House, 2007. Straight's author profile explains her inspiration for "El Ojo de Agua," which is printed in this anthology.

Hamilton, Denise, ed. *Los Angeles Noir*. New York: Akashic Books, 2007. Contains "The Golden Gopher" and author information accompanied by Straight's photograph; comments that this story's characters are also featured in her trilogy.

Michener, Christian. "Dancing Under Water: Art and Survival in Susan Straight's 'Aquaboogie.'" *The Midwest Quarterly* 36, no. 1 (Autumn, 1994): 9-18. Examines the role of creativity in this collection's stories, analyzing how characters perceive artistry and embrace or reject it.

Mosley, Walter, and Katrina Kenison, eds. *The Best American Short Stories, 2003*. Boston: Houghton Mifflin, 2003. Straight's story "Mines" is supplemented by her statement specifying her diverse associations with prisons.

Phillips, Gary, ed. *Orange County Noir*. New York: Akashic Books, 2010. Includes Straight's short story "Bee Canyon," in which a California Highway Patrolman conceals his murderous vigilantism, just as Grady admits to having committed in "The Golden Gopher."

Reid, E. Shelley. "Beyond Morrison and Walker: Looking Good and Looking Forward in Contemporary Black Women's Stories." *African American Review* 34, no. 2 (Summer, 2000): 313-328. Addresses how Straight's comprehension and respect for her in-laws' and neighbors' stories empowers her authentic literary depictions of African American experiences.

Tobar, Hector. "'The Weirdness of the City': Hopes and Desperation Collide in Susan Straight's New L.A. Novel." *Los Angeles Times*, December 10, 2010, p. 2. Describes Straight's visit to the Golden Gopher, telling how that bar, places in surrounding areas, and interactions with people impact her fiction.

*Elizabeth D. Schafer*

# Elizabeth Strout

**Born:** Portland, Maine; January 6, 1956

Principal short fiction

*"A Different Road,"* 2008
*"Toads and Snakes,"* 2008
*"English Lesson: A Memoir,"* 2009
*Olive Kitteridge,* 2008

Other literary forms

Elizabeth Strout (strowt) is a prolific writer in many genres, having written journal articles, magazine articles, and screen scripts. Her work has appeared in such mainstream publications as *The New Yorker, Seventeen*, and *Redbook*.

Achievements

In 1999, Elizabeth Strout received the *Chicago Tribune* Heartland Award and the *Los Angeles Times* Book Award for First Fiction for *Amy and Isabelle* (1998). *Amy and Isabelle* was short-listed for the 2000 Orange Prize and nominated for the 2000 PEN/Faulkner Award for Fiction. It also was made into a television film starring Elizabeth Shue and was produced by Oprah Winfrey Studios. Strout won a Fall Semester National Endowment for the Humanities at Colgate University and taught creative writing at both the introductory and the advanced level. In 2009, Strout won the Pulitzer Prize in Fiction for *Olive Kitteridge*.

Biography

Elizabeth Strout was the first of two children born to a university science professor and a high school English teacher, Richard and Beverly Strout. The Strouts lived in self-imposed isolation in small Maine and New Hampshire towns because of a sense that danger lurked outside the home and the children needed to be kept under close protective watch: no television, no newspapers, no dating, no hanging around with friends. Both parents came from generations of staunch New Englanders, who were tight-lipped, wedded to self-reliance, and suspicious of outsiders, sometimes viewing pleasure as an indulgence. Strout's father believed that if one could not say something nice about someone, one should not say anything at all. Elizabeth Strout once broached the subject to him of her mother's discontent at never having pursued a writing career, but he brushed aside his daughter's concerns, saying her mother seemed to have had a pretty good life. He was often distracted by his work but always greeted Strout heartily when she visited his laboratory at the university.

Strout had a particularly close bond with her mother. The two of them often sat at Woolworth's lunch counter, observing and eavesdropping on the people around them, making up life stories from overheard conversations. Strout would jot down notes in one of the many notebooks her mother had supplied, so that Strout could comment on what she had done on a given day, what the waitress looked like, how the shoe salesman had treated them. Strout's skill at observing and imagining complete lives from these snippets served her well with her fiction. She never lost the sense of fun that such exercises gave her, and they augmented her awareness of her environment. She claims to love cell phones, where one-sided conversations allow her to imagine the rest. At times, her isolation caused her to suffer loneliness, but she used her solitary moments, she said, to become acquainted with "the tree toads and pine needles and turtles and creeks and the coastline and collecting periwinkles [and to appreciate] the beauties of the physical world."

Strout hated high school and, with her mother's blessing, dropped out in her junior year. Even so, she was admitted to Bates College in Lewiston, Maine. After earning her bachelor of arts degree in 1977, she spent a year in Oxford, England. In 1982, she graduated with honors and received both a law degree from Syracuse University College of Law and a Certificate of Gerontology from Syracuse School of Social Work. In that year, she published her first story, "A Suicide's Daughter," in *Newsletters* magazine. In 1982, she married fellow law student Martin Feinman, with whom she had one child, Zorina. They were divorced in 2002.

Strout moved to New York City and continued writing stories and publishing in literary magazines and in *Redbook* and *Seventeen*. When not writing, she found employment as a pub worker, a house cleaner, a secretary, a cocktail waitress, an artist's model, an elderly abuse project worker, and a staff attorney in Legal Services in Syracuse. She soon realized that she was not cut out to be a member of the legal profession.

A self-confessed slow writer, she took nearly ten years to produce her first novel, *Amy and Isabelle*, joking that she needed three months just to clear her throat. She says she has to know her characters before she can commit them to paper, writing in longhand. She lives with them, wondering how they might react in certain situations and thinking about their motivations. She wants their responses to ring true. First drafts are rewritten many times. So dedicated is she to her craft that she hides manuscript pages around the house so she can come upon them by accident and read with a fresh eye. Her second novel, *Abide with Me* (2006), took seven years to write and *Olive Kitteridge* appeared nearly three years later.

In 1994, Strout became frustrated by a feeling that she was not yet authentic in her writing, so she enrolled in a stand-up comedy class and experienced the terror of presenting herself to strangers. For her final examination, she made fun of her roots and realized she had to get back home. Her subject had to be New England, for most of her material revolved around the eccentricities she found in that region of the country.

### ANALYSIS

Elizabeth Strout writes to be read and wants to feel in touch with her readers. She focuses on only what she thinks the reader wants to know. She cares about how sentences sound when they hit the ear. She tells stories and hopes readers will see themselves in her characters or plots or understand the world a little bit better. She does not preach or hope to convey messages, though troublesome issues abound in her novels and her short stories: divorce, infidelity, suicide, catastrophic illness, loneliness, accidental death, kidnapping, threatened murder, anorexia. These are depressing areas, but she deals with them in such a way that generosity of spirit or unqualified love allows hope, or at least the promise of hope, keep despair at bay.

### OLIVE KITTERIDGE

The central character in Strout's Pulitzer Prize-winning collection of interwoven short stories is the title character, a middle-aged woman with a toughness that is sometimes mistaken for meanness. Olive is a retired junior high school mathematics teacher in a small Maine coastal town, where everyone knows everyone else's business. Strout re-creates the New England mentality without stereotyping or exaggeration. She turns the image of quaint, picture-perfect gatherings for lobster bakes upside down. The beauty of the whitecaps and the tall trees and winding dirt roads is there, but Strout delves into the lives of the people, who are,

*Elizabeth Strout* (Time & Life Pictures/Getty Images)

characteristically, not given to disclosure of personal matters. The reader sees and feels the pain of betrayals, mental collapse, untimely deaths, and alienation. The book is divided into thirteen chapters, each of which could stand alone. Olive is in most of the stories but features in the narrative whether she makes an appearance or not.

Strout chose this decentralized approach to show the many facets of Olive's complex personality from varying points of view, so as not to overwhelm the reader with a linear approach. To be fair to Olive, musing that Olive would not have it any other way, Strout believed she needed to tell Olive's story in segments, with time in between to allow the reader to absorb the character. Presenting an unpleasant character can create problems for a writer, who hopes to give the reader characters he or she can identify with in some way. Strout handles the challenge deftly. Olive is unlikable but has some redeeming qualities: a tenderness, an intelligence, and a forthrightness that makes her incapable of artifice. Olive is a force of nature. She can be loving, but she is also short-tempered, one time berating her gentle, kind husband for dragging her to church. She says: "You, Mr. Head Deacon Claptrap Nice Guy, expect me to give up my Sunday mornings and go sit among a bunch of snotwots." In addition, she excoriates him when he spills ketchup. Henry can overlook the attacks because he knows and loves his wife. Though Olive is mightily impatient with the slow and the dumb and hates those who imagine they are neither, her heart overflows when her son seems to need her. People, through small kindnesses, maybe a smile or a polite response, make her feel hopeful. She thinks wistfully of a colleague who seems to "see" her, when she didn't even know she was invisible. She gets crushes because she needs to love.

*Olive Kitteridge* is paean to the people who prevail, who live to see the next day, picking up where they left off and doing as well as they can. In that sense, it is more uplifting than despairing. Strout shakes up the image of a quaint New England town by delving into the lives of its inhabitants. Though they are tight-lipped about personal matters, the reader sees lives torn apart, suffering, infidelity, murder, mental collapse, and suicide.

### "Pharmacy"

"Pharmacy" highlights gentle Henry and sets him up in contrast to his wife. He is loved in the community for his kindness. He is steady and reliable, and his opening of the pharmacy each morning seems to bring a peacefulness, a sense that all is right with the world. He develops a warm and loving relationship with a young employee, Denise, calling their one year together as coworkers the happiest of his life. He loves her but is a faithful man. The love is reciprocated, though Denise understands that he could not behave otherwise.

### "Incoming Tide"

This story involves Olive and two former students. One, a young man, Keith, has lost his will to live and intends to put an end to his suffering in a parking area on a rocky outcropping of land overlooking the ocean. While he sits in his car planning for his death, Olive knocks on the window. Before long, she is seated next to him, and they are sharing experiences with suicides and mental illnesses. Keith finds himself once again wanting to impress his teacher, because, even though she was scary, he liked her. While wishing that she would get out of the car so that he could get on with his death, he cannot give any indication that he wants her gone. They begin watching another student who has emerged from a shop where she works and is cutting flowers on the precipice. She either slips down the cliff or jumps, but Olive and Keith save her from drowning.

### "Piano Player"

Angela O'Meara has played the piano at the cocktail lounge for years, despite having stage-fright and needing alcoholic reinforcement. She is the sweetheart of the place, no one knowing of her torturous affair with a cad of a public official. She greets the bartender, the barmaid, a regular customer who was relieved from his position at the university because of alcoholism. She blows kisses and winks, smiles, brings happiness, and plays tunes that she knows her customers want to hear. Henry always delights in "Goodnight, Irene," and so she includes that song in her repertoire. She thinks that seeing him is like "moving into a warm pocket of air."

### "A Little Burst" and "Security"

These two stories deal with Henry and Olive's son Christopher, who faces what many teenagers do, both love and uneasiness with parents. Olive loves her son deeply, the strength of her feeling frightening her. All he sees is a domineering woman with a critical word at every turn, a woman who intimidates her students and insults the townspeople because she speaks her mind. Olive is a major force. She has exacting standards that few people can meet satisfactorily. Most cannot get beyond her gruff exterior and see the tender person at the core.

Christopher has no choice but to leave the area, but the break will be painful. He marries at thirty and moves away, with no intention of returning, even when his wife leaves him. Olive has to fight off her jealous impulses at having to share her boy with an undeserving woman. In a fit of childlike spite, she decorates his second wife's sweater with Magic Marker, steals her brassiere and one shoe, and stuffs them in the trash at a nearby Dunkin' Donuts. Olive has reverted to childlike spite because she doesn't feel she has an identity any longer. She is not a teacher, Henry will only need her as he grows ill, and Christopher has headed for safer ground.

### "A Different Road"

*Olive Kitteridge* reads like a novel, so skillful are the transitions from one chapter to the next. The only story that seems out of place is a long one, "A Different Road," in which Olive and Henry are held captive by bank robbers. Strout, interested in what came to be known as Stockholm Syndrome, when Patti Hearst was kidnaped and later joined forces with her captors, gives Olive a moment of pure love for the young, itchy, pimply-faced hostage-taker who holds life and death in his hands. This chapter serves as a climax, after which everything changes and heads downhill. Olive and Henry say things to each other that cannot be retracted.

### Other major works

LONG FICTION: *Amy and Isabelle*, 1998; *Abide with Me*, 2006.

### Bibliography

Bacon, Katie. *"Tight-Knit--Loose-Lipped."* The Atlantic (March, 2006). Excellent details about Strout's background and her approach to writing. Includes a discussion of her novel *Abide with Me*, which covers her writing style in general.

Strout, Elizabeth. "Introduction." *Ploughshares* 36, no. 1 (Spring, 2010). Strout, who edited this issue of *Ploughshares*, talks about her first encounter with a literary journal.

Thomas, Louis. "Elizabeth Strout's *Olive Kitteridge*." *The New York Times*, April 18, 2008. Review notes that the "stories combine the sustained, messy investigation of the novel with the flashing insight of the short story."

*Gay Pitman Zieger*

# JESSE STUART

**Born:** W-Hollow, near Riverton, Kentucky;
   August 8, 1907
**Died:** Ironton, Ohio; February 17, 1984

PRINCIPAL SHORT FICTION

*Head o' W-Hollow,* 1936
*Men of the Mountains,* 1941
*Tales from the Plum Grove Hills,* 1946
*Clearing in the Sky, and Other Stories,* 1950
*Plowshare in Heaven: Tales True and Tall from the
   Kentucky Hills,* 1958
*Save Every Lamb,* 1964
*My Land Has a Voice,* 1966
*Come Gentle Spring,* 1969
*Come Back to the Farm,* 1971
*Votes Before Breakfast,* 1974
*The Best-Loved Short Stories of Jesse Stuart,* 1982
*New Harvest: Forgotten Stories of Kentucky's Jesse
   Stuart,* 2003 (David R. Palmore, editor)

OTHER LITERARY FORMS

Although Jesse Stuart probably found the best outlet for his artistic expression in the short story, he published more than two thousand poems, a number of autobiographical works, six children's books, and nine novels, one of which was the best-selling *Taps for Private Tussie* (1943).

ACHIEVEMENTS

Through the vivid pictures that he presents in his stories of life in the Kentucky hill country, Jesse Stuart opened up significant veins of material for other writers who followed him. While not adding new dimensions to the short story, he did nevertheless produce many excellent examples in that genre.

Virtually all Stuart's stories deal with the hill country of eastern Kentucky, where generations ago people dropped off from the movement west to settle in the hills and hollows of what has come to be a part of Appalachia. The life depicted in these stories is hard, and the people who live it are fundamentally religious and close to the earth. A natural storyteller, Stuart captured not only the idiom of his characters but also the very essence of their relationship to one another and to the natural world around them. He does not take solely the realist's approach but blends in a strain of romantic optimism.

Although cast in what appears to be a realist mode, Stuart's stories often blend a romantic optimism with an exuberance for life that is sometimes expressed in comic juxtapositions that verge on the grotesque. A popular as well as prolific author, Stuart was named poet laureate of Kentucky in 1954, won an award for *Taps For Private Tussie* in 1943, and was nominated for a Pulitzer Prize in 1975 for *The World of Jesse Stuart: Selected Poems* (1975).

BIOGRAPHY

A native of Kentucky, Jesse Hilton Stuart was educated at Lincoln Memorial University. Following his graduation, he began a career as a writer and teacher. In these roles, he evinced a lifetime concern for educational reform and engaged in a lifelong struggle with the educational establishment. During his long career, he served as both teacher and administrator, and, after retiring from teaching to turn to full-time farming, writing, and lecturing, he never lost his passionate belief in the power of knowledge.

In 1939, after a courtship of seventeen years, Stuart married Naomi Deane Norris. They had one child, a daughter, Jessica Jane, born in 1942. During World War II, he served in the U.S. Navy, accepting disability in 1945. During subsequent years, though he traveled extensively, Stuart continued to live on the working farm in W-Hollow, the area where he was born and that he made famous through his poems, novels, and stories, many of which were published in *Esquire.*

He suffered the first of several heart attacks in 1954 but was able to return to normal activity. After a second stroke in 1982, however, he was unable to recover and remained more or less bedridden until his death two years later.

## ANALYSIS

America's southern highlands have long been viewed as an area removed from the influences of the "civilized" world; indeed, for more than a century they were. Rich in folklore and tradition, these highlands have provided stimulus to a vast number of writers as far back as William Gilmore Simms. The majority produced mostly second-rate novels and stories that relied on melodrama, sentimentality, and effusive description of natural setting to carry their plots. A few writers, however, have risen above that level to present the southern highlanders and their land in a more graphic and realistic light. Jesse Stuart was one such writer.

Once commenting that as a child he "read the landscape, the streams, the air, and the skies," Stuart had "plenty of time to grow up in a world that I loved more and more as I grew older." With his abiding love and respect for the people and the land of this picturesque region, Stuart, in a fashion matched by few American regional writers, brought the southern highlands into sharp focus for his readers. His short stories--the fictional form in which he was at his best--are a journey of exploration into the many aspects of life in the region. Using his home place of W-Hollow as a vantage point and springboard, Stuart treated various themes and motifs in his stories: religion, death, politics, folklore, sense of place, nature, and the code of the hills. While these themes are treated from a realistic stance, through all of them runs the romantic idea of the ever-renewing power of the earth, and many demonstrate an exuberant sense of humor, where the comic juxtaposition is the primary structural pattern.

## "DAWN OF REMEMBERED SPRING"

A story that clearly illustrates a blending of realism and romanticism is "Dawn of Remembered Spring." Like so many of Stuart's stories, this one has an autobiographical ring to it. The main character is Shan, a young boy who appears in a number of Stuart's stories. In this particular instance, Shan is being cautioned by his mother not to wade in the creek because of the danger of water moccasins. Just a few days prior, Roy Deer, another youngster, was bitten by a water moccasin and is now near death. To Shan's comment that all water moccasins ought to be killed, his mother agrees but adds, "They're in all these creeks around here. There's so many of them we can't kill 'em all." As idyllic as one side of life in W-Hollow may be, there is the ever-present factor of death, in this case symbolized by water moccasins.

Shan, however, is not to be deterred by his mother's warning, and, armed with a wild-plum club, he sets out wading the creek to kill as many water moccasins as he can. It is a suspenseful journey as Shan, frightened but determined, kills snake after snake. "This is what I like to do," he thinks. "I love to kill snakes." He wades up the creek all day, and when he steps out on the bank at four o'clock, he has killed fifty-three water moccasins. As he leaves the creek, he is afraid of the snakes he has killed and grips his club until his hands hurt, but he feels good that he has paid the snakes back for biting Roy Deer-- "who wasn't bothering the water moccasins that bit him. He was just crossing the creek at the foot-log and it jumped from the grass and bit him."

As he goes near home, Shan sees two copperhead snakes in a patch of sunlight. "Snakes," he cries, "snakes a-fightin' and they're not water moccasins! They're copperheads!" The snakes are wrapped around each other, looking into each other's eyes and touching each other's lips. Shan's Uncle Alf comes upon the scene and tells Shan that the snakes are not fighting but making love. A group of onlookers soon gathers, including Shan's mother, who asks him where he has been. "Killin' snakes," is his reply. To her statement that Roy Deer is dead, Shan says that he has paid the snakes back by killing fifty-three of them. At this point his mother, along with the rest who have gathered at the scene, is spellbound by the loving copperheads. She sends Shan to the house to get his father. As the boy goes, he notices that the snakes have done something to the people watching: "The wrinkled faces were as bright as the spring sunlight on the bluff; their eyes were shiny as the creek was in the noonday sunlight."

In "Dawn of Remembered Spring" Stuart has juxtaposed images of death and life; Shan has killed fifty-three snakes, and Roy Deer has died from his snake bite. The two copperheads making love remind the reader and the people watching that, cruel though nature may be at times, there is always the urge for life. The hate that demands revenge is somehow redeemed in the laughter that Shan hears from the group--a laughter "louder than the wild honeybees I had heard swarming over the shoemake, alderberry, and wild flox blossoms along the creek."

### "SYLVANIA IS DEAD"

In "Sylvania Is Dead" Stuart uses the death motif to bring out the prevalent stoicism of the highlanders, as well as their ability to see humor in a grotesque situation. The story opens as Bert Pratt and Lonnie Pennix are on their way to the funeral of the story's namesake. It is September, and nature is presented through images of death: "The backbone of the mountain was gray and hard as the bleached bone of a carcass. The buzzards floated in high circles and craned their necks." When

*Jesse Stuart* (Library of Congress)

the men reach Sylvania's cabin at the top of the mountain, they see a large crowd already gathered and buzzards circling low overhead. Lonnie pulls his pistol and shoots into the buzzards, scaring them away. When Skinny, Sylvania's husband, runs from the cabin scolding them for firing guns at such a sorrowful time, they respond that they were only trying to shoo away buzzards. Skinny says it is all right, for buzzards are a "perfect nuisance in a time like this."

The black humor in the story derives from Sylvania's size and her occupation. She weighs six hundred and fifty pounds; her husband, only about one hundred. Her occupation has been selling moonshine, and as one of the men digging her grave says, "I say we'll never miss Sylvania until she's gone. She's been a mother to all of us." Sylvania is so big that when she was caught "red handed" by the revenuers on one occasion, she simply laughed and said that even "if they could get her out of the house, they couldn't get her down the mountain."

Getting Sylvania out of the house is the big problem now. Building a coffin that takes six men to carry, they finally get Sylvania in it, but it will not go through the door. The only answer is to tear down the chimney. Before carrying the coffin out, however, the men stop for a drink from Sylvania's last barrel. "I patronized Sylvania in life and I'll patronize her in death," Bert says. The drinks from Sylvania's last barrel, combined with the sorrow at her death, make the crowd noisy. As the coffin is carried to the grave, there is laughing, talking, and crying, accompanied by another pistol shot at circling buzzards. Finally Sylvania is lowered to her rest, and, as Skinny is led back to his cabin, there are "words of condolence in the lazy wind's molesting the dry flaming leaves on the mountain."

The human drama played out at this mountaintop funeral is marked not predominantly by sorrow but by acceptance and humor. Sylvania was mother to them all in life, and it is only fitting that her "children" should see her to her grave. The humor in the story is not strained or out of place; on the contrary, the comedy underlines the grotesque element of human behavior as juxtaposed with the natural order. Humor is part of the hard life lived close to nature that is common to the people of Stuart's fictional world--as much a part as are Sylvania's moonshine and the buzzards circling overhead.

### "SUNDAY AFTERNOON HANGING"

In "Sunday Afternoon Hanging," Stuart again blends the comedy with grim realism, as an old man describes to his grandson what old-time hangings in Blakesburg, Kentucky, were like. Viewing the electric chair as a poor substitute for a hanging, he points out that at a hanging "everybody got to see it and laugh and faint, cuss or cry." Indeed, they would come from as far as forty miles for such an opportunity. As the old man relates one particular incident to his grandson, the reader is made aware of a combination of characteristics in the people Stuart writes about--violence, vengeance, fatalism, and a desire to escape the tedium of their daily lives.

The Sunday afternoon hanging that the old man describes is the result of the brutal murder of an elderly couple by five men--Tim and Jake Sixeymore, Freed Winslow, Dudley Toms, and Work Grubb. They are all sentenced to be hanged on the same day, and hundreds of people congregate to witness the affair. In contrast to the grisly vengeance to be exacted, the day is bright, with a June wind blowing and roses in bloom. Providing music for the event is a seven-piece band dressed in gaudy yellow pants with red sashes and green jackets. "It was the biggest thing we'd had in many a day," recalls the old man.

> Horses broke loose without riders on them and took out through the crowd among the barking dogs, running over them and the children. People didn't pay any attention to that. It was a hanging and people wanted to see every bit of it.

The procedure for the hanging is to have each man brought to the hanging standing on his coffin in a horse-drawn wagon. After a rousing number by the band and a confession from the condemned, the wagon is pulled away, leaving him "struggling for breath and glomming at the wind with his hands." When he is pronounced dead, the procedure begins for the next man. As each man is hanged, the gruesome scene becomes even more grotesque. The last to be hanged is Tim Sixeymore, and he is so large that he breaks six ropes before the execution is finally

carried out. His confession, reminiscent of the ballad "Sam Hall," begins, "Gentlemen bastards and sonofabitches. Women wenches and hussies and goddam you all." As the hanging is completed and the parents of the Sixeymores carry off their dead sons, the band plays softer music. The crowd breaks up, "getting acquainted and talking about the hanging, talking about their crops and the cattle and the doings of the Lord to the wicked people for their sins"; and so life goes on. The blending of the comic and the tragic in "Sunday Afternoon Hanging" is so subtle that one is not sure whether to be horrified at the terrible vengeance exacted amid frivolity and hatred or to laugh at the black humor apparent in the contradiction.

### "THE MOONSHINE WAR"

Whatever his feelings of admiration for the people about whom he wrote, Stuart was not blind to the aspect of their character that encourages a kind of macho violence. A number of his stories, for example, deal with feuding and selling moonshine, which, although they are usually thought of now in a more or less humorous vein, were in reality serious and often deadly activities. Fiercely proud, Stuart's characters consider such activities their own business and go about them in their own way, as shown in the story "The Moonshine War."

Combining moonshine and feuding, this story is narrated by Chris Candell, whose father in earlier days was one of four moonshine sellers in Greenwood County, Kentucky. With the help of his three sons, Charlie, Zeke, and Chris, he sold moonshine for twenty years before his wife prevailed upon him to lay his sins on the mourner's bench in the Methodist Church and give up "the business." Shortly after, the federal agents close in on the other three families that are still moonshining--the Whaleys, the Fortners, and the Luttrells--sending members from each to prison for varying terms.

When Willie Fortner is released because of his youth, he returns to Greenwood County, vowing revenge on the other families because he thinks that they helped the federal agents to discover his father's still. Two weeks later Jarwin Whaley is found stabbed to death. In quick succession, two more deaths by stabbing occur, of Lucretia Luttrell and Charlie Candell,

Chris's brother. There is no real evidence to connect these crimes to Willie Fortner, and, although he is arrested, he is acquitted, moving Zeke Candell to say, "Damn this circumstantial evidence stuff! We've got to take the law into our own hands." Before the Candells can do anything, however, Willie Fortner is killed in an auto wreck, the only one of five in the car who dies in the crash. Chris's father, obviously attributing Willie's death to the Lord, says that "we'll have peace. The knife killings are over."

Stuart does not condemn any of the actions in "The Moonshine War," but, as in all his stories, he accepts the characteristics of his highland ancestors. Indeed, in another story, "My Father Is an Educated Man," he says of the fiercely independent men of his family now sleeping in the Virginia, West Virginia, and Kentucky mountains, "Though I belong to them, they would not claim me since I have had my chance and unlike them I have not killed one of my enemies." The code of conduct that arises from such a life view may be a combination of savagery, civility, and moral contradiction, but it attests the belief of the highlander that he is master of his own destiny.

### SAVE EVERY LAMB

For those wishing to see another side of Stuart's writing, there is the volume of stories entitled *Save Every Lamb*. Virtually all the stories in this volume are autobiographical in background and have nature themes. In them Stuart harks back to another era--a time "when everybody in the country lived by digging his livelihood from the ground." It was a time when humans were in tune with the natural world about them and were better for it. "My once wonderful world has changed into a world that gives me great unhappiness," Stuart says in the introduction to *Save Every Lamb*. For the moment, at least, Stuart in these stories takes the reader back with him to that wonderful world of his youth.

In all his stories Stuart writes with an easy, almost folksy, style. Avoiding experimentation and deep symbolism, he holds his readers by paying close attention to detail and by painting starkly graphic scenes as he brings to life the characters and settings of W-Hollow. As a regionalist, Stuart draws constantly on his background in his stories, with the result that his style is underlined by an autobiographical bias, which contributes strongly to the sense of immediacy that marks all his work. Just as William Faulkner has his microcosm of the universe in Yoknapatawpha County, so too does Stuart in W-Hollow, and the American literarychronicle is the richer for it.

### OTHER MAJOR WORKS

LONG FICTION: *Trees of Heaven*, 1940; *Taps for Private Tussie*, 1943; *Foretaste of Glory*, 1946; *Hie to the Hunters*, 1950; *The Good Spirit of Laurel Ridge*, 1953; *Daughter of the Legend*, 1965; *Mr. Gallion's School*, 1967; *The Land Beyond the River*, 1973; *Cradle of the Copperheads*, 1988.

POETRY: *Harvest of Youth*, 1930; *Man with a Bull-Tongue Plow*, 1934; *Album of Destiny*, 1944; *Kentucky Is My Land*, 1952; *Hold April*, 1962; *The World of Jesse Stuart: Selected Poems*, 1975.

NONFICTION: *Beyond Dark Hills*, 1938; *The Thread That Runs So True*, 1949; *The Year of My Rebirth*, 1956; *God's Oddling*, 1960; *To Teach, To Love*, 1970; *My World*, 1975; *Lost Sandstones and Lonely Skies, and Other Essays*, 1979; *The Kingdom Within: A Spiritual Autobiography*, 1979; *If I Were Seventeen Again, and Other Essays*, 1980; *Jesse Stuart on Education*, 1992 (J. R. LeMaster, editor).

CHILDREN'S LITERATURE: *Mongrel Mettle: The Autobiography of a Dog*, 1944; *The Beatinest Boy*, 1953; *A Penny's Worth of Character*, 1954; *Red Mule*, 1955; *The Rightful Owner*, 1960; *Andy Finds a Way*, 1961.

### BIBLIOGRAPHY
Blair, Everetta Love. *Jesse Stuart: His Life and Works*. Columbia: University of South Carolina Press, 1967. Blair opens with a brief account of Stuart's life and background. Subsequent chapters survey his poetry, short stories, novels, and other accomplishments. General discussions provide insight into particular works and overall trends.

Foster, Ruel E. *Jesse Stuart*. New York: Twayne, 1968. One of the earliest, and, with a few exceptions, one of the best of the critical studies. Contains biographical information, as well as extensive critiques on Stuart's work up to the date of publication.

Kohler, Dayton. "Jesse Stuart and James Still: Mountain Regionalists." In *An American Vein: Critical Readings in Appalachian Literature*, edited by Danny L. Miller, Sharon Hatfield, and Gurney Norman. Athens: Ohio University Press, 2005. Compares and contrasts the works of Stuart and Still, two writers who have "given shape and life" to Appalachia. Discusses both Stuart's short stories and novels. Another essay in this collection compares Stuart's poetry with that of Ezra Pound.

Le Master, J. R. ed. *Jesse Stuart: Selected Criticism*. St. Petersburg, Fla.: Valkyrie Press, 1978. A collection of previously published articles by different scholars that offers an excellent introduction to Stuart's work.

Le Master, J. R., and Mary Washington Clark, eds. *Jesse Stuart: Essays on His Work*. Lexington: University Press of Kentucky, 1977. These essays, written specifically for this volume, provide critical perspectives on different facets and genres of Stuart's work, including poetry, short fiction, and novels, as well as his humor and use of folklore. The editors indicate that a primary purpose of this collection is to bring into sharper focus Stuart's use of multiple perspectives.

Lowe, Jimmy. *Jesse Stuart: The Boy from the Dark Hills*. Edited by Jerry A. Herndon, James M. Gifford, and Chuck D. Charles. Ashland, Ky.: Jesse Stuart Foundation, 1990. A solid, updated biography of Stuart.

Pennington, Lee. *The Dark Hills of Jesse Stuart*. Cincinnati: Harvest Press, 1967. Pennington discusses Stuart's system of symbolism as it emerges in his early poetry and later through his novels. Argues that Stuart is far more than a regionalist; rather, he is an important creative writer and spokesman not only for a region but also for all humankind.

Richardson, H. Edward. *Jesse: The Biography of an American Writer--Jesse Hilton Stuart*. New York: McGraw-Hill, 1984. This inclusive study, printed in the year of Stuart's death, is sensitively written, and it offers invaluable reading for anyone with more than a passing interest in Stuart's life and work. Includes some photographs.

Thompson, Edgar H. "A Cure for the Malaise of the Dislocated southerner: The Writing of Jesse Stuart." *Journal of the Appalachian Studies Association* 3 (1991): 146-151. A good survey of Stuart's work, emphasizing his regional heritage.

Towles, Donald B. "Twenty Stories from Jesse Stuart." *The Courier-Journal*, September 20, 1998, p. O51. A review of *Tales from the Plum Grove Hills*. Surveys the themes and subjects of the stories and comments on their use of Eastern Kentucky dialect.

Ward, William S. *A Literary History of Kentucky*. Knoxville: University of Tennessee Press, 1988. Includes a biographical-critical discussion of Stuart's work, pointing out that Stuart deals with people as individuals rather than in sociological terms. Argues that a principal source of his success with the short story was the zest with which he carried a story through in a flood of detail.

Weaks-Baxter, Mary. "Jesse Stuart: 'A Farmer Singing at the Plow.'" In *Reclaiming the American Farmer: The Reinvention of a Regional Mythology in Twentieth-Century southern Writing*. Baton Rouge: Louisiana State University Press, 2006. Although the essay focuses on the poems in *Man with a Bull-Tongue Plow* and the nonfiction work *Beyond Dark Hills*, many of the comments about these works can pertain to Stuart's short fiction. The chapter also provides an overview of Stuart's literary career and his contribution to American literature.

*Wilton Eckley*
*Updated by Mary Rohrberger*

# THEODORE STURGEON

**Born:** Staten Island, New York; February 26, 1918
**Died:** Eugene, Oregon; May 8, 1985
**Also known as:** Ellery Queen; Billy Watson; E. Hunter Waldo; E. Waldo Hunter; Frederick R. Ewing

PRINCIPAL SHORT FICTION

*Without Sorcery: Thirteen Tales,* 1948 (also known as *Not Without Sorcery*)
*E Pluribus Unicorn,* 1953
*A Way Home: Stories of Science Fiction and Fantasy,* 1955 (also known as *Thunder and Roses*)
*Caviar,* 1955
*A Touch of Strange,* 1958
*Aliens 4,* 1959
*Beyond,* 1960
*Sturgeon in Orbit,* 1964
*. . . And My Fear Is Great/Baby Is Three,* 1965
*The Joyous Invasions,* 1965
*Starshine,* 1966
*Sturgeon Is Alive and Well,* 1971
*The Worlds of Theodore Sturgeon,* 1972
*Sturgeon's West,* 1973 (with Don Ward)
*To Here and the Easel,* 1973
*Case and the Dreamer, and Other Stories,* 1974
*Visions and Venturers,* 1978
*Maturity: Three Stories,* 1979
*The Stars Are the Styx,* 1979
*The Golden Helix,* 1980
*Slow Sculpture,* 1982
*Alien Cargo,* 1984
*Pruzy's Pot,* 1986
*A Touch of Sturgeon,* 1987
*To Marry Medusa,* 1987
*The [Widget], the [Wadget], and Boff,* 1989
*The Complete Stories of Theodore Sturgeon,* 1994-2009 (eleven volumes; Paul Williams, editor)

OTHER LITERARY FORMS

It seems as though no literary form was wrong for Theodore Sturgeon (STUR-juhn). He wrote newspaper stories in the late 1930's, book and film reviews in the 1950's, and for twenty years after that, radio and television scripts, and a wide variety of fiction. He also published a coauthored western novel, a (pseudonymous) historical romance, a psychological vampire novel, a film novelization, and five highly acclaimed science-fiction novels.

ACHIEVEMENTS

Theodore Sturgeon's name is one of those most cited in lists of the writers of science-fiction's golden age. Many consider him the best golden-age author, mainly because he concentrated less on scientific hardware and more on character interaction than did his contemporaries. A moralistic and romantic writer, his major themes were tolerance for otherness of all kinds and concern for the environment before these became fashionable opinions. He was among the first American science-fiction writers to write plausibly about sex, homosexuality, race, and religion. Sturgeon was sometimes accused of writing pornography by those who prefer their science fiction in the standard starched-collar Puritan mode. In reality, Sturgeon was among the first to turn American science fiction into a fiction for mature, thinking adults, as his influence on writers such as Ray Bradbury and Samuel R. Delany attests. He received several awards nominations and won three awards: the International Fantasy Award in 1954, for *More Than Human* (1953), and the science-fiction Hugo and Nebula awards in 1970, for "Slow Sculpture." The University of Kansas presents an annual science-fiction short-story award in his name.

BIOGRAPHY

Born Edward Hamilton Waldo, Theodore Sturgeon led one of those archetypal writer's lives, roaming the world and holding many different kinds of jobs. In 1929, his name was officially changed to Theodore Sturgeon. As a child, he wanted to be a circus performer, even gaining an athletic scholarship to Temple University, but his career in gymnastics was stopped by rheumatic fever. As an adult, he sold newspapers; collected garbage; sailed the seas as an engine-room wiper; worked as a musician, a ghostwriter, and a literary agent; operated a bulldozer and a gas station; and held several door-to-door sales positions. During World War II, he worked building airstrips and later writing technical manuals. Married five times, usually to younger women, he fathered six children. Strugeon died in Eugene, Oregon, on May 8, 1985.

ANALYSIS

In a commercial literature devoted to galaxy-spanning concepts of paper-thin consistency, mechanical characters of whatever origin (human, alien, metal, or chemical), and wooden verbal expression, Theodore Sturgeon was an anomaly as early as 1939, when his stories began appearing in science-fiction magazines. A writer more of fantasy than of science fiction, whose predilection for words over machines was immediately apparent, Sturgeon was concerned with specific fantasies less for themselves than as means to the end of writing about human beings and human problems. Unlike those of so many of his colleagues, his tales usually take place in small, circumscribed locations, where love and healing can overshadow lesser, more conventional marvels and wonders.

Although style has always been somewhat suspect in science fiction, Sturgeon (along with Alfred Bester and Ray Bradbury) fought a rear-guard action throughout his career. His example speaks louder than theory about the importance of words, especially in terms of the planned resonance of images and the conscious manipulation of symbols to invite emotional responses to his romantic, even utopian view of the relationship between human beings and their technologies. Viewing "science" as "wisdom," he wrote of the search for wholeness, often without the aid of conventional means of attaining knowledge. He was antimachine in a way but more opposed to people's self-enslavement to mechanical procedures, be they metal or mental. Illustration of these themes calls

forth as often as not a kind of fantasy that bears a close relationship to magic, events being caused by words and gestures. His is not a "science" that tediously accumulates and interprets observations of the world as it can be measured with instruments fashioned by and limited to the rational capacities of human beings.

There is no typical Sturgeon story, so varied is his surface subject matter, which includes many traditional science-fiction "inventions" and "discoveries," with space travel, planetary exploration, matter transmission, cloning, alien contact, and paranormal powers among them. Sturgeon's stories usually speculate on love and sex in terms often considered radical for their market.

Sturgeon sold some remarkable "horror" stories in his early years of writing, such as "It," told from the point of view of a putrescent monster as dead as it is alive, and "Bianca's Hands," about a man in love with, and eventually strangled by, the hands of a girl who has the mind of an idiot. In "Killdozer," he created a masterpiece of contemporary terror in which two members of an eight-man construction crew on a deserted Pacific island barely withstand and defeat a malevolent alien consciousness which has taken possession of one of their bulldozers. The television motion picture made from this story did not do it justice.

**"MICROCOSMIC GOD"**

The most anthologized of Strugeon's early pieces is "Microcosmic God," whose popularity he resented because its relatively clumsy handling and apparently ruthless attitude toward certain life-forms are uncharacteristic of his best work and his own self-image.

Primarily narrative, what dialogue there is being rather stiff and self-conscious, "Microcosmic God" is somewhat of a self-parody, with its protagonist Mister Kidder and his antagonist a stereotyped grasping banker named Conant who seeks to exploit Kidder's discoveries so as to take over the world. Almost lost in the reader's obvious antipathy to Conant's manipulation of human beings is its direct parallel to Kidder's even more ruthless manipulation of the tiny conscious beings whose evolution he has accelerated purely to satisfy his own curiosity.

Explicitly science fictional, the story is not rooted in practical experience, unlike the details of construction machinery that make "Killdozer" so dramatically convincing. Instead Kidder's literal creation of an entire race for experimental purposes is couched in more theoretical and conceptual detail. The story's headlong pace races past problems in verisimilitude, in keeping with the simplistic morality of good (Kidder) versus evil (Conant), but intrusive commentary by the narrator reminds the reader sporadically that this is a fable, even if it does not specifically single out Kidder for censure.

Characterizing Kidder only minimally--both men are comic-book figures--the story shows his impatience with other people, with orthodox science (he claims no academic degrees), and with practical applications for his findings. In Conant, his alter ego, the reader sees explicitly the potential for abuse in his work, which reflects back on Kidder's own amorality. A god to his creatures, Kidder is a stand-in not for the "mad scientist" whose image Sturgeon specifically disavows, but for the shortsighted tinkerer, representing all those who endeavor by mechanical means to improve the lot of human beings. The danger within the story is that, when Kidder dies, the creatures will conquer the world; the real threat to which the story points is that the misapplication of science to means or ends in the real world will do the same.

### IRRESPONSIBILITY VERSUS HEROISM

Irresponsibility is also the theme of "Mewhu's Jet," in which an alien visitor with fabulous technological powers turns out to be a young child; of "The Sky Was Full of Ships," in which a naïve meddler unwittingly calls to Earth a menacing alien fleet; and of "Maturity," in which that quality is disavowed as the ripeness immediately preceding death. Sturgeon, however, was also concerned with the other side of the coin. In "Thunder and Roses," the beautiful Starr Anthim tries, in a nuclear-devastated America, to prevent late retaliation that might wipe out all human civilization. In "Saucer of Loneliness," another girl preserves the message given her by a miniature flying saucer, which assuages her despair with the knowledge that loneliness is shared. In "The Skills of Xanadu," an entire planet's people have overcome dependence on ugly machine technology and achieved a utopian state which is both dynamic and transferable.

Communication is central to these stories, as it is to "Bulkhead," in which the "partner" assigned to a space pilot with whom he has an intense love-hate relationship turns out to be another part of himself, part of a schizophrenic condition deliberately induced by his employers for his own good. In the classic novella, *Baby Is Three*, centerpiece of the award-winning novel *More than Human*, a "gestalt" being, composed of adolescent parapsychological misfits, fights to define its identity, which the last section of the novel will provide with maturity, responsibility, even community. Although this is arguably Sturgeon's best story, the novel to which it is converted is too well known to require analysis here of one of its parts.

The many ways that love and sex connect fascinated Sturgeon as early as "Bianca's Hands," but several provocative variations on this theme occupied him in the 1950's. *Venus Plus X* (1960) hypothesized physiological bisexuality in a "utopian" community on Earth. *Some of Your Blood* (1961) is a psychological case study of physiological vampirism. In "Affair with a Green Monkey," a psychologist obsessed with adjustment confuses gentleness with homosexuality, completely misjudging a humanoid alien whose sexual equipment would put to shame the best-endowed pornographic film star.

### "THE WORLD WELL LOST"

Sturgeon's best treatment of "aberrant" sexuality is probably "The World Well Lost." Again attacking the obsession with normality of America in the 1950's, Sturgeon describes a future world enchanted by the love for each other and for things earthly of a couple of unexpected alien visitors, before their home world requests the return of the "loverbirds." Having once sent an ambassador to Earth and found it wanting, the planet Dirbanu has stonewalled further contact attempts until this time, when humans' intolerance at being kept out prompts them to sacrifice the fugitives in quest of anticipated interplanetary relations. The "prison ship," however, is crewed by two men whose perfect record results from a complementariness unrecognized by Rootes and unspoken by Grunty. Discovery of the aliens' telepathic powers threatens the tongue-tied Grunty, whose threat to kill them is countered by two things: the fact that Dirbanu wants them dead, and the reason why.

Dirbanu females are so different in appearance from males that all human beings look to them to be of the same sex and just as repulsive as the two fugitive "lover-birds." Acknowledging their homosexuality, the alien prisoners recognize the same propensity in their captors. Rootes's tales of heterosexual exploits are repetitive and hollow-sounding, while Grunty suffers consciously from an involuntary attraction to his partner which he can never voice, despite all the poetry that swirls within his mind. Grunty lets the prisoners escape in a lifeboat which will isolate them for years before, if ever, they reach planet-fall. Although Rootes berates Grunty, Dirbanu is grateful for the presumed deaths. The residents of this planet still will have nothing to do with Earth, however, and their bigotry strikes a sympathetic chord in Rootes, as presumably it would back home. For all the "space opera" trappings, the tenuous coincidences, and the dated attitude toward homosexuality--even contextually, it seems inconsistent with an Earth that pursues, the reader is told, many other euphoric and aphrodisiac thrills--the story evokes with minimal sentimentality a love that literally "cannot speak its name" and the pathetic intolerance that will not let it.

### "THE MAN WHO LOST THE SEA"

In contrast to such a plot-laden construct, "The Man Who Lost the Sea" is as near to stream-of-consciousness style as market considerations would allow. Exploring the senses, hallucinatory experiences, and memories of the first astronaut to reach Mars alive, the story weaves past and present, childhood and adulthood, mechanical and psychological drives into a haunting impression of a time which might prove as traumatic and epoch-making as the emergence of the first air-breathers out of the sea of life's origin on Earth. As shifting point of view and chronology represent the man's dazed mental and emotional state, Sturgeon only gradually reveals the nature of the man's predicament (his ship has crashed and there is no way back), until the emotional shock of simultaneous gain and loss has prepared the way for the triumphant irony of the protagonist's dying exultation: "We made it!"

### "SLOW SCULPTURE"

Sturgeon's rather few stories of the 1960's and 1970's continued to deal with love and responsibility, especially healing, but often in a talky mode. His greatest success in that period is "Slow Sculpture," which first appeared in *Galaxy* magazine in 1970 and was named best story of that year by science-fiction fans and readers alike. (This novelette subsequently was included in the short-fiction collection *Sturgeon Is Alive and Well* and published separately in 1982). "Slow Sculpture" is a loving exploration of how an unnamed "man" and a "girl" come tentatively to know each other, although the specific means are entwined with science-fiction and fantasy motifs as the two people are with each other and with the fifteen-foot bonsai tree that grows in this garden. Like other Sturgeon protagonists, the man is a polymath, credentialed in law and in two kinds of engineering, who in this instance practices medicine without a license.

The girl believes that the man's cure for her cancer works, and readers are similarly asked to take this on faith, since establishment means and methods are deliberately eschewed, and the "technology" that the man uses is more obscured than revealed by the metaphorical language with which he describes it. There are some appropriate "special effects," suggesting the interrelatedness of house and garden, house and mountain, man and tree, matter and energy, mind and body. The medium and the message, however, are primarily communication, in conversation which may be more expressive than it is true to life, but which is far from stilted. The speeches, moreover, are contextually true, since the man, whatever his healing powers for others, fends off the girl's involvement with him, her own halting attempts to connect with the anger, fear, and frustration in him at the world's resistance to all he has offered to better it.

Throughout the story, the dominant symbol is the bonsai, which resists "instruction" because it knows how it should grow and achieves its form by compromising between its essential nature and the manipulation to which it is subjected, not by its "owner" but by its "companion." As in many of Sturgeon's works, but never more appropriately than here, the prose itself is "sculptured," reminding the reader that the magic of fantasy resides less in the act than in the telling of it.

Sturgeon's stories are in some ways "hopelessly romantic," conjuring impossible cures and utopian solutions, even when they are not projected long ahead and far away. Like the best science fiction, they lead the reader back to the present, not to external realities but rather to emotional confrontations with human problems, situations, and characters. Although readers may detach themselves from the ostensible subjects, removed from the here and now, the situation of the writer, often as a stand-in for the reader-as-dreamer, is frequently apparent, sometimes intensely personal. For all their variety, Sturgeon's stories betray an almost obsessive concern for wholeness and healing, for communication and tolerance of the misfit, and often for "September-June" relationships between "men" and "girls." That his work maintained and even increased its popularity as he wrote less and less suggests that he mined a vein of ore rich in its appeal to women as well as men, and to the adolescent in everyone. Almost despite their paraphernalia of science fiction and fantasy, Sturgeon's modern-day fairy tales communicate what his characters continually try to communicate: the truth of emotion and the magic of words.

OTHER MAJOR WORKS

LONG FICTION: *The Dreaming Jewels*, 1950 (also known as *The Synthetic Man*, 1957); *More Than Human*, 1953; *I, Libertine*, 1956 (as Frederick R. Ewing; with Jean Shepherd); *The King and Four Queens*, 1956; *The Cosmic Rape*, 1958; *Venus Plus X*, 1960; *Some of Your Blood*, 1961; *Voyage to the Bottom of the Sea*, 1961; *Alien Cargo*, 1984; *Godbody*, 1986.

PLAYS: *It Should Be Beautiful*, pr. 1963; *Psychosis: Unclassified*, pr. 1977 (adaptation of his novel *Some of Your Blood*).

TELEPLAYS: *Mewhu's Jet*, 1950's; *Ordeal in Space*, 1950's; *The Adaptive Ultimate*, 1950's; *The Sound Machine*, 1950's; *They Came to Bagdad*, 1950's; *Dead Dames Don't Dial*, 1959; "Shore Leave," 1966 (episode of television series *Star Trek*); "Amok Time," 1967 (episode of television series *Star Trek*); *Killdozer!*, 1974; *The Pylon Express*, 1975-1976.

RADIO PLAYS: *Incident at Switchpath*, 1950; *The Stars Are the Styx*, 1953; *Mr. ostello, Hero*, 1956; *Saucer of Loneliness*, 1957; *More than Human*, 1967 (adaptation of his novel).

NONFICTION: *Argyll: A Memoir*, 1993.

BIBLIOGRAPHY

Delany, Samuel. "Sturgeon." In *Starboard Wine: More Notes on the Language of Science Fiction.* Pleasantville, N.Y.: Dragon Press, 1984. Delany is not only one of science fiction's best authors but also is one of its best critics, particularly in analysis of style. Here Delany explores some of the nuances of Sturgeon's language and the "realism" of Sturgeon's stories.

Diskin, Lahna. *Theodore Sturgeon.* Mercer Island, Wash.: Starmont House, 1981. The first book-length study of Sturgeon's fiction, this volume focuses primarily on his most famous science-fiction works.

Malzberg, Barry N. "Grandson of the True and the Terrible." In *The Engines of the Night.* Garden City, N.Y.: Doubleday, 1982. A brief but poignant evaluation of Sturgeon's importance in the history of science fiction.

McGuirk, Carol. "Science Fiction's Renegade Becomings." *Science Fiction Studies* 35, no. 2 (July, 2008): 281-307. Gilles Deleuze and Félix Guattari in the 1980's argued that many science-fiction plots were about "becomings," such as human beings becoming-animal, -alien, -machine, or -child; these "becomings" were "antimemories" that challenged the presumption of human superiority. McGuirk uses their theory, as well as concepts about the relation of cognition to language, to analyze science fiction by Sturgeon and several other writers.

Moskowitz, Sam. "Theodore Sturgeon." In *Seekers of Tomorrow: Masters of Modern Science Fiction.* Westport, Conn.: Hyperion Press, 1966. This essay is a good general introduction to Sturgeon in terms of his place in science-fiction history and in what makes him "unique."

Sackmary, Regina. "An Ideal of Three: The Art of Theodore Sturgeon." In *Critical Encounters*, edited by Dick Riley. New York: Frederick Ungar, 1978. Sackmary discusses the motif of threes in Sturgeon's fiction as his symbol for unity.

Sallis, James. "*A Saucer of Loneliness: Selected Stories.*" *Fantasy and Science Fiction*, 100, no. 4 (April, 2001). A review of this short-story collection, volume 7 in the eleven-volume *The Complete Stories of Theodore Sturgeon*. Sallis, who credits Sturgeon for his own decision to become a writer, describes why he admires Sturgeon's work by analyzing stories in the collection.

Stephensen-Payne, Phil, and Gordon Benson, Jr. *Theodore Sturgeon, Sculptor of Love and Hate: A Working Bibliography*. San Bernardino, Calif.: Borgo Press, 1992. Part of the Galactic Central Bibliographies for the Avid Reader series, this is a helpful tool for students of Sturgeon.

Streitfield, David. "Science Fiction and Fantasy." *The Washington Post*, March 7, 1999, p. XO8. Discusses the renaissance of interest in Sturgeon, with the reissue of his novel *More Than Human* and his short-fiction collection *To Marry Medusa* in paperback, as well as a multivolume compilation of his short stories. Discusses briefly the story "Scars" and the unfinished "Quietly."

Westfall, Gary. "Sturgeon's Fallacy." *Extrapolation* 38 (Winter, 1997): 255-277. Takes issue with so-called Sturgeon's Law--that ninety percent of everything, especially science fiction, is worthless. Analyzes the output of science fiction in the twentieth century and argues that science fiction is a worthwhile form of writing.

*David N. Samuelson*
*Updated by David Layton*

# T

## ELIZABETH TALLENT

**Born:** Washington, D.C.; August 8, 1954

PRINCIPAL SHORT FICTION

*In Constant Flight,* 1983
*Time with Children,* 1987
*Honey,* 1993

OTHER LITERARY FORMS

In addition to her short fiction, Elizabeth Tallent is the author of the novel *Museum Pieces* (1985) and book of literary criticism, *Married Men and Magic Tricks: John Updike's Erotic Heroes* (1982).

ACHIEVEMENTS

Elizabeth Tallent's first story, "Ice," was selected for *The Best American Short Stories 1981*; "The Evolution of Birds of Paradise" was included in 1984's *Prize Stories: The O. Henry Awards*; "Prowler" was selected for *The Best American Short Stories 1990*; "Tabriz" received the 2008 Pushcart Prize Award. She was awarded a National Endowment for the Arts Fellowship in 1993. Tallent became head of Stanford University's creative writing program in 1994, and she subsequently has won honors for her teaching. In 2007, she received Stanford's Phi Beta Kappa Teaching Award; in 2008, she was the recipient of the Excellence in Teaching Award from the Northern California Chapter of Phi Beta Kappa; and in 2009, she received Stanford's Dean's Award for Distinguished Teaching.

BIOGRAPHY

Elizabeth Ann Tallent was born on August 8, 1954, in Washington, D.C., where her father worked for the government as an expert on agriculture. She spent most of her childhood in the Midwest, and she received a B.A. degree in anthropology at Illinois State University at Normal in 1975. Although accepted for graduate school in anthropology at the University of New Mexico at Taos, Tallent and her husband settled in Santa Fe, New Mexico, instead.

Her first story, "Ice," published in *The New Yorker* in 1980, received enough attention that writer Leonard Michaels invited her to a writers' workshop in Berkeley, California. Tallent gave readings with the important fiction trio, Raymond Carver, Richard Ford, andTobias Wolff, throughout England in 1985. The next year she taught writing at the University of California at Irvine and then the following year at the University of Nevada at Reno. In 1989, she was invited to teach in the prestigious University of Iowa Writers' Workshop. She accepted a full-time teaching position at the University of California at Davis in 1990, and four years later she joined the English department faculty of Stanford University.

ANALYSIS

Elizabeth Tallent's stories have been praised by many of her reviewers for the same reasons that they have been criticized by others: her precise detail, her metaphoric plots, her highly polished structure, and her elegant style--all characteristics that have changed little over the course of her writing career. Frequently, Tallent's critics charge, her stories are simply too geometrically structured and predictable, and her language is too mannered and forced. However, all Tallent's critics seem to agree that her understanding of the complexities that arise from broken marriages and reconstituted families is artistically acute.

Like her most obvious literary inspiration, John Updike, about whom she has written a critical book, Tallent creates stories that at first seem straightforwardly realistic and transparent, like chapters out of a domestic novel, but which, on closer reading, are recognized as tightly structured, symbolic stories in which no matter how loosely related and tangential events seem to be, they all inevitably come together by the end.

## "PROWLER"

The story's conflict begins when Dennis's former wife Christie returns from Europe after breaking up with her most recent boyfriend, and Dennis decides not to let their thirteen-year-old son Andy spend the summer with her because she has ignored the boy for the past year. The first event that contributes to changing Dennis's mind is Andy's getting a tattoo of a skeleton on a motorcycle, telling his father, "It's my body"--a realization which astonishes Dennis.

However, the most important event that changes Dennis's mind occurs when he enters Christie's apartment while she is not home. Dennis knows he is an intruder and feels an "amazed apprehension of his own wrongdoing," but he is fascinated by this glimpse into the life of a woman no longer his wife. He is even more enthralled when he lies down in a bedroom meant for Andy, for he knows there are things in it that Andy would like. Dennis dreams a dream he feels was meant for Andy about the boy and his mother cutting animals from construction paper when he was young, and "what he's seen won't let go easily." As a result of his "prowler" experience, Dennis takes Andy to his mother a few days later, although he can give her only a wave that means "I can't explain it."

"Prowler" is fairly typical of many of Tallent's stories. Dennis's refusing his former wife visitation rights for the summer is only a conventional motivation to make possible Dennis's dual realization. The tattoo then makes possible Dennis's realization that Andy is a separate entity, since it allows Andy to say that his body is his own and since it is a permanent change that cannot be undone. The more extended epiphany occurs when Dennis lies down on the bed in the room his former wife has prepared for Andy and sees that his son would like how she has prepared it, realizing that his former wife knows her son well and loves him. His knowledge that his son does not "belong" to him and that the boy has both a mother and a father makes him change his mind about the visitation.

## "ICE"

Although the "ice" of the title of this story derives from the fact that the central figure is a young woman

who skates in a traveling ice show with a man dressed as a bear, this is counterpointed by her memory of her grandmother, who slipped on icy stairs and died while trying to avoid being confined because of her delusions. A second counterpoint to the young woman's story is the family Abyssinian cat who spontaneously aborts her kittens and then eats her mother's prize roses.

There is no plot conflict in the story except the mother's distress that her daughter works at a carnival-like job and the girl's desire for more "artistic" skating. The girl's lover, Ben, a photographer, has left the show for Los Angeles but writes to the man who skates as the dancing bear to say that he is sorry he left. Images of the girl skating on the ice with the dancing bear dominate the story. She understands that the appeal of the bear is that he seems like a "clumsy, blotchy human being" who courts her with elegance while she skates in carefully circumscribed arcs, the light shining in her blond hair. The story ends with the girl crying while skating in the circle of the bear's shaggy arms.

Thematically, the story brings together several images of female fantasy and fear. The predominant image is the Goldilocks fantasy of the blond girl skating with the bear--an objectification of a childlike female wish fulfillment, which brings young girls to her performances. However, this is juxtaposed against images of the cat refusing to have offspring, the mother for whom roses are her entire life, and the grandmother who dies trying to avoid the final humiliation of being shut up in a room because of delusions. At the end, when the bear whispers in the young woman's ear-- "You know, don't you, that you are not yourself"--the girl, in fact, does not know who she is.

## "NO ONE'S A MYSTERY"

Although this is one of Tallent's shortest stories--less than four pages--it is a favorite anthology piece because of its tight compression and its focus on a single, highly suggestive scene. The central character is a young woman who is having an affair with Jack, a married man, who has just given her a five-year diary for her eighteenth birthday. The story centers on their driving around in his pickup when he sees his wife's Cadillac coming toward them and pushes her down on the floorboards. After the wife's car passes, Jack tells the girl that, although tonight she will write in the diary that she cannot imagine loving anyone more than she does him, in a year she will wonder what she ever saw in him.

She responds, however, that in one year she will write that Jack will be home any minute and that she does not know if she can wait until after their fancy dinner to make love to him; in two years, she will write that he will be home soon and little Jack is hungry for supper; and in three years she will write that her breasts are sore from nursing their little girl whose breath smells like vanilla. This brief story, which consists mostly of dialogue, ends when Jack says he likes her story better but believes his; he tells her that in her heart of hearts she believes his story also and, reflecting the bittersweetness of the relationship, that the little girl's breath would have a bittersweet smell. In its one brief encounter, the story quite poignantly captures the girl's unrealistic fantasies and the dead-end nature of the affair.

### "HONEY"

In the title story of Tallent's 1993 collection, she returns to characters introduced in her earlier book, *Time with Children*: Hart, a math teacher in New Mexico; Hannah, his first wife; Kevin, his son; Cao, his second wife; and Mercedes, his mother-in-law. The story begins with Mercedes flying into Albuquerque from her apartment in Brooklyn to be with Cao for the birth of her first child.

The story centers on old wounds that refuse to heal. Kevin, whose girlfriend committed suicide in "Black Dress," another story in the collection, is sullen because of his loss and his anxiety that the new baby will force him out. Mercedes fears that her daughter's marriage is not strong and harbors old rancor about her dead husband's infidelities. Hart continues to feel guiltily aligned with his first wife, Hannah, and emotionally unfaithful to Cao because he does not want the new baby.

Tallent heals all these old hurts by the end of the story in symbolically significant ways. When Mercedes tends to Kevin's mosquito bites and urges him to give up his own thoughts of suicide, she makes peace with her own demons by assuring Kevin that time will heal and everyone eventually stops feeling his or her

hurt. At the same time in another room, Cao assures Hart that her mother likes him, simultaneously reminding herself not to become the isolated mystery that her mother always was. The story ends with Hart and Cao making love in an effort to start the contractions for their overdue baby.

### OTHER MAJOR WORKS

LONG FICTION: *Museum Pieces*, 1985.

NONFICTION: *Married Men and Magic Tricks: John Updike's Erotic Heroes*, 1982.

### BIBLIOGRAPHY

Broyard, Anatole. "In Constant Flight." Review of *In Constant Flight*, by Elizabeth Tallent. *The New York Times*, April 29, 1983, p. C29. In this review of Tallent's first collection, Broyard is concerned that she tries too hard to divorce her characters from the ordinary. He says her characters often seem to be on the brink of an epiphany, but when they have one their emotions are unidentifiable.

Elder, Richard. "Extraordinary Tales from Ordinary Lives." *Los Angeles Times*, November 11, 1993, p. E6. Discusses Tallent's basic themes and typical characters. Comments on her subjects of broken marriages, family ties, shuffled children, and blind and aggressive men. Discusses the story "Prowler" as a compendium of her most typical elements.

Gelfant, Blanche H., ed. *The Columbia Companion to the Twentieth-Century American Short Story*. New York: Columbia University Press, 2000. Includes a chapter in which Tallent's short stories are analyzed.

Gilbert, Matthew. "Tallent Lights Up a Troubled Terrain." *The Boston Globe*, January 21, 1994, p. 73. Argues that Tallent is able to make everything her characters do mirror their emotional states. Says her plots are metaphorical and her style is graceful and incisive, but that occasionally the elegance of her stories gets in the way. Suggests that the stories in *Honey*, a kind of sequel to *Time with Children*, show thematic strides, for more is at stake in them.

Kakutani, Michiko. "Families Bound by Ties That Stifle." *The New York Times*, December 10, 1993, p. C29. Discusses how the stories in *Honey* continue the sagas of characters created in Tallent's earlier collection, *Time with Children*. Argues that although in terms of technique the stories are beautifully assembled and meticulously controlled, their emotional dilemmas reflect a stultifying sameness.

Milton, Edith. "What Changes and What Doesn't." *The New York Times Book Review*, August 14, 1983, p. 12. Praises the control and technical perfection of Tallent's stories in *In Constant Flight*, but criticizes Tallent for constantly reaching for surprise. Maintains that the eleven stories seem like variations on a single theme, each one filled with paradox and the unexpected.

Parini, Jay. "Torn Between Two Exes." Review of *Honey*, by Elizabeth Tallent. *The New York Times*, November 7, 1993, p. 11. A review of *Honey* which argues that language rather than plot is what interests Tallent most. Compares her work to that of John Updike; says she can summon up the sensations of everyday life concretely but that she sometimes seems to strain for effect.

Tallent, Elizabeth. "Prowler." In *Twelve Short Stories and Their Making*, edited by Paul Mandelbaum. New York: Persea Books, 2005. The twelve stories in this book have been selected to illustrate various aspects of the craft of short-story writing. Tallent's story "Prowler" demonstrates character development, and in addition to the story itself, the volume includes Tallent's comments on "Prowler," its characters, and other elements of the story.

Yagoda, Ben. "No Tense Like the Present." *The New York Times Book Review* 91: 1. Discusses the use of present tense by Tallent and other contemporary fiction writers; argues that the present tense can remind readers that the story is an artifice or emphasize the narrator's alienation from the events described. Claims that in much contemporary fiction, the present tense suggests that, in a meaningless age, expounding on meaning is not appropriate.

*Charles E. May*

---

# AMY TAN

**Born:** Oakland, California; February 19, 1952

PRINCIPAL SHORT FICTION
*The Joy Luck Club,* 1989

OTHER LITERARY FORMS

Amy Tan is best known for her novels. Her first book, *The Joy Luck Club*, is considered a novel, as well as a short-story collection, and she and Ronald Bass cowrote the screenplay for the film adaptation released in 1993. Her other novels are *The Kitchen God's Wife* (1991), *The Hundred Secret Senses* (1995), *The Bonesetter's Daughter* (2001), and *Saving Fish from Drowning* (2005). Tan also published two children's books, *The Moon Lady* (1992) and *The Chinese Siamese Cat* (1994), and a nonfiction book, *The Opposite of Fate: A Book of Musings* (2003). Her essays include "The Language of Discretion" and "Mother Tongue."

ACHIEVEMENTS

*The Joy Luck Club* received numerous honors, including the Bay Area Book Reviewers Award and the Commonwealth Gold Award and was a finalist for the National Book Award, the National Book Critics Circle Award, and the *Los Angeles Times* Fiction Prize. The National Endowment for the Arts chose *The Joy Luck Club* for its 2007 "Big Read" Program. Both *The Kitchen God's Wife* and *The Opposite of Fate* were *Booklist* editor's choice books; *The Hundred Secret Senses* was a finalist for the Orange Prize; *The Bonesetter's Daughter* was nominated for the Orange Prize and IMPAC Dublin Award; and *Saving Fish from Drowning* was nominated for the IMPAC Dublin Award. Tan's essay "Mother Tongue" was included in *Best American Essays of 1991*, edited by Joyce Carol Oates. Tan wrote the libretto for *The Bonesetter's Daughter*, an opera with music by Stewart Wallace, which had its world premiere with the San Francisco Opera in September, 2008.

## BIOGRAPHY

Amy Ruth Tan was born in Oakland, California, on February 19, 1952, the middle child and only daughter of John Yuehhan and Daisy Tu Ching Tan, who had emigrated from China. Her father was an electrical engineer in China, but he became a minister in the United States. The family moved frequently, finally settling in Santa Clara, California. After the death of her husband and older son when Amy was fifteen years old, Daisy took the family to Switzerland and enrolled her children in schools there, but she returned to California in 1969.

Tan's parents hoped she would become a physician and concert pianist. She began a premedical course of study but switched to English and linguistics, much to her mother's dismay. She received her B.A. in 1973 and her M.A. in 1974 from San Jose State University. She attended the University of California, Berkeley, from 1974 to 1976, beginning studies toward a doctorate. In 1974, she married Louis M. DeMattei, a tax attorney; they settled in San Francisco.

Tan was a language consultant, a reporter, a managing editor, and a freelance technical writer before she turned to fiction writing. She joined a writing workshop in 1985 and submitted a story about a Chinese American chess prodigy. The revised version was first published in a small literary magazine and reprinted in *Seventeen* magazine as "Rules of the Game." When Tan learned that the story had appeared in Italy and had been translated without her knowledge, she obtained an agent, Sandra Dijkstra, to help handle publication. Although Tan had written only three stories at that time, Dijkstra encouraged her to write a book. At her suggestion, Tan submitted an outline for a book of stories and then went on a trip to China with her mother. On her return, she learned that her proposal had been accepted by G. P. Putnam's Sons.

## ANALYSIS

Amy Tan's voice is an important one among a group of "hyphenated Americans" (such as African Americans and Asian Americans) who describe the experiences of members of ethnic minority groups. Her short fiction is grounded in a Chinese tradition of "talk story" (*gong gu tsai*), a folk art form by which characters pass on values and teach important lessons through narrative. Other writers, such as Maxine Hong Kingston, employ a similar narrative strategy.

A central theme of Tan's stories is the conflict faced by Chinese Americans who find themselves alienated both from their American milieu and from their Chinese parents and heritage. Other themes include storytelling, memory, and the complex relationships between mother and daughter, husband and wife, and sisters. By using narrators from two generations, Tan explores the relationships between past and present. Her stories juxtapose the points of view of characters (husband and wife, mother and daughter, sisters) who struggle with each other, misunderstand each other, and grow distant from each other. Like Tan, other ethnic writers, such as Louise Erdrich, use multiple voices to retell stories describing the evolution of a cultural history.

Tan's stories derive from her own experience as a Chinese American and from stories of Chinese life her mother told her. They reflect her early conflicts with her strongly opinionated mother and her growing

*Amy Tan* (AP photo/Joe Tabacca)

understanding and appreciation of her mother's past and her strength in adapting to her new country. Daisy's early life, about which Tan gradually learned, was difficult and dramatic. Daisy's mother, Jing-mei (Amy Tan's maternal grandmother), was forced to become the concubine of a wealthy man after her husband's death. Spurned by her family and treated cruelly by the man's wives, she committed suicide. Her tragic life became the basis of Tan's story "Magpies," retold by An-mei Hsu in *The Joy Luck Club*. Daisy was raised by relatives and married to a brutal man. After her father's death, Tan learned that her mother had been married in China and left behind three daughters. This story became part of *The Joy Luck Club* and *The Kitchen God's Wife*.

Tan insists that, like all writers, she writes from her own experience and is not representative of any ethnic group. She acknowledges her rich Chinese background and combines it with typically American themes of love, marriage, and freedom of choice. Her first-person style is also an American feature.

### THE JOY LUCK CLUB

Although critics call it a novel, Tan wrote *The Joy Luck Club* as a collection of sixteen short stories told by the club members and their daughters. Each chapter is a complete unit, and five of them have been published separately in short-story anthologies. Other writers, such as the American authors Sherwood Anderson (*Winesburg, Ohio*, 1919*)* and Gloria Naylor (*The Women of Brewster Place*, 1982*)*, and the CanadianMargaret Laurence (*A Bird in the House*, 1970), have built linked story collections around themes or groups of characters.

The framework for *The Joy Luck Club* is formed by members of a mah-jongg club, immigrants from China, who tell stories of their lives in China and their families in the United States. The first and fourth sections are the mothers' stories; the second and third are the daughters' stories. Through this device of multiple narrators, the conflicts and struggles of the two generations are presented through the contrasting stories. The mothers wish their daughters to succeed in American terms (to have professional careers, wealth, and status), but they also expect them to retain Chinese values (filial piety, cooking skills, and family loyalty). When

the daughters become Americanized, they are embarrassed by their mothers' old-fashioned ways, and their mothers are disappointed at the daughters' dismissal of tradition. Chasms of misunderstanding deepen between them.

Jing-mei (June) Woo forms a bridge between the generations; she tells her own stories in the daughters' sections and attempts to take her mother's part in the mothers' sections. Additionally, her trip to China forms a bridge between her family's past and present, and between China and America.

### "THE JOY LUCK CLUB"

The first story, "The Joy Luck Club," describes the founding of the club by Suyuan Woo to find comfort during the privations suffered in China during World War II. When the Japanese invaders approached, she fled, abandoning her twin daughters when she was too exhausted to travel any farther. She continued the Joy Luck Club in her new life in San Francisco, forming close friendships with three other women. After Suyuan's death, her daughter Jing-mei "June" is invited to take her place. June's uncertainty of how to behave there and her sketchy knowledge of her family history exemplify the tensions experienced by an American daughter of Chinese parents. The other women surprise June by revealing that news has finally arrived from the twin daughters Suyuan left in China. They present June with two plane tickets so that she and her father can visit her half sisters and tell them her mother's story. She is unsure of what to say, believing now that she really did not know her mother. The others are aghast, because in her they see the reflection of their daughters who are also ignorant of their mothers' stories, their past histories, their hopes and fears. They hasten to tell June what to praise about their mother: her kindness, intelligence, mindfulness of family, and "the excellent dishes she cooked." In the book's concluding chapter, June recounts her trip to China.

### "RULES OF THE GAME"

One of the daughters' stories, "Rules of the Game," describes the ambivalent relationship of Lindo Jong and her six-year-old daughter. Waverly Place Jong, named after the street on which the family lives, learns from her mother's "rules," or codes of behavior, to succeed as a competitive chess player. Her mother teaches her to "bite back your tongue" and to learn to bend with the wind. These techniques help her persuade her mother to let her play in chess tournaments and then help her to win games and advance in rank. However, her proud mother embarrasses Waverly by showing her off to the local shopkeepers. The tensions between mother and daughter are like another kind of chess game, a give and take, where the two struggle for power. The two are playing by different rules, Lindo by Chinese rules of behavior and filial obedience, Waverly by American rules of self-expression and independence.

### "Two KINDS"

Another daughter's story, "Two Kinds," is June's story of her mother's great expectations for her. Suyuan was certain that June could be anything she wanted to be; it was only a matter of discovering what it was. She decided that June would be a prodigy piano player and outdo Waverly Jong, but June rebelled against her mother and never paid attention to her lessons. After a disastrous recital, she stops playing the piano, which becomes a sore point between mother and daughter. On her thirtieth birthday, the piano becomes a symbol of her reconciliation with her mother, when Suyuan offers it to her.

### "BEST QUALITY"

"Best Quality" is June's story of a dinner party her mother gives. The old rivalries between June and Waverly continue, and Waverly's daughter and American fiancé behave in ways that are impolite in Chinese eyes. After the dinner Suyuan gives her daughter a jade necklace she has worn in hopes that it will guide her to find her "life's importance."

### "A PAIR OF TICKETS"

This is the concluding story of *The Joy Luck Club*. It recounts Jing-mei (June) Woo's trip to China to meet her half sisters, thus fulfilling the wish of her mother and the Joy Luck mothers and bringing the story cycle to a close, completing the themes of the first story. June learns from her father how Suyuan's twin daughters were found by an old school friend. He explains that her mother's name means "long-cherished wish" and that her own name Jing-mei means "something pure, essential, the best quality." When at last they meet the sisters, she acknowledges

her Chinese lineage: "I also see what part of me is Chinese. It is so obvious. It is my family. It is in our blood."

### OTHER MAJOR WORKS

LONG FICTION: *The Kitchen God's Wife*, 1991; *The Hundred Secret Senses*, 1995; *The Bonesetter's Daughter*, 2001; *Saving Fish from Drowning*, 2005.

SCREENPLAY: *The Joy Luck Club*, 1993 (adaptation of her novel; with Ronald Bass).

NONFICTION: "The Language of Discretion," 1990 (in *The State of the Language*, Christopher Ricks and Leonard Michaels, editors); *The Opposite of Fate: A Book of Musings*, 2003.

CHILDREN'S LITERATURE: *The Moon Lady*, 1992; *The Chinese Siamese Cat*, 1994.

### BIBLIOGRAPHY

Benanni, Ben, ed. *Paintbrush: A Journal of Poetry and Translation* 22 (Autumn, 1995). A special issue of the journal focusing on Tan and on *The Joy Luck Club* in particular. It includes articles on mothers and daughters, memory and forgetting.

Bloom, Harold, ed. *Amy Tan's "The Joy Luck Club."* New ed. New York: Bloom's Literary Criticism, 2009. Collection of essays examining various aspects of the book, including its depiction of mother-daughter relationships, its storytelling, and the role of mah-johngg and of traditional Chinese beliefs in the work.

Cooperman, Jeannette Batz. *The Broom Closet: Secret Meanings of Domesticity in Postfeminist Novels by Louise Erdrich, Mary Gordan, Toni Morrison, Marge Piercy, Jane Smiley, and Amy Tan*. New York: Peter Lang, 1999. A study of the role of traditionally feminine concerns, such as marriage and family, in the works of these postfeminist writers.

Dong, Lan. *Reading Amy Tan*. Santa Barbara, Calif.: Greenwood Press, 2009. Aimed at high school students, this book provides a biography of Tan, discusses her writing career, relates her life to her work, and describes the narrative structure in her writing. One chapter is devoted to an examination of "Amy Tan and the Novel and Short Story," while another chapter analyzes *The Joy Luck Club*.

Ellfson, Elias. "Amy Tan." In *A Reader's Companion to the Short Story in English*, edited by Erin Fallon, et al., under the auspices of the Society for the Study of the Short Story. Westport, Conn.: Greenwood Press, 2001. Aimed at the general reader, this essay provides a brief biography of Tan followed by an analysis of her short fiction.

Evans, Robert C., ed. *Critical Insights: "The Joy Luck Club," by Amy Tan*. Pasadena, Calif.: Salem Press, 2010. A collection of new and reprinted essays about the book, including discussions of its critical reception, its cultural and historical contexts, its depiction of mother-daughter relationships, and a feminist analysis of the work. Also features a biography of Tan, two interviews with her, a chronology of her life, a list of her works, and a bibliography.

Huh, Joonok. *Interconnected Mothers and Daughters in Amy Tan's "The Joy Luck Club."* Tucson, Ariz.: Southwest Institute for Research on Women, 1992.

Examines the mother- adult child relationship in the book. Includes a bibliography.

Huntley, E. D. *Amy Tan: A Critical Companion*. Westport, Conn.: Greenwood Press, 1998. Discusses Tan's biography and analyzes her novels in the context of Asian American literature. Examines major themes, such as the crone figure, food, clothing, language, biculturalism, and mothers and daughters. Includes a useful bibliography.

Snodgrass, Mary Ellen. *Amy Tan: A Literary Companion*. Jefferson, N.C.: McFarland, 2004. Replete with tools for further research, including study questions, an extensive bibliography, and a glossary of Chinese terms found in Tan's works, Snodgrass presents a readable, engaging introduction to both Tan's life and works.

*Karen F. Stein*

---

# BARRY TARGAN

**Born:** Atlantic City, New Jersey; November 30, 1932

PRINCIPAL SHORT FICTION

*Harry Belten and the Mendelssohn
    Violin Concerto,* 1975
*Surviving Adverse Seasons: Stories,* 1979
*Falling Free,* 1989

OTHER LITERARY FORMS

Barry Targan is the author of the poetry collections *Let the Wild Rumpus Start: Poems* (1971) and *Thoreau Stalks the Land Disguised as a Father: Poems* (1975) and of the novels *Kingdoms: A Novel* (1980), *The Tangerine Tango Equation: Or, How I Discovered Sex, Deception, and a New Theory of Physics in Three Short Months* (1990), and *The Ark of the Marindor* (1998).

ACHIEVEMENTS

Barry Targan won the 1975 University of Iowa Short Fiction Award for *Harry Belten and the Mendelssohn Violin Concerto*, the Associated Writing Programs Award for *Kingdoms* in 1980, and the Saxifrage Award for *Surviving Adverse Seasons* in 1981. He received a National Endowment for the Arts Grant in 1983. Several of his stories have appeared in *Prize Stories: The O. Henry Awards* and *The Best American Short Stories* and have won Pushcart Prizes.

BIOGRAPHY

Barry Targan was born in Atlantic City, New Jersey, on November 30, 1932, to Albert Targan, a grocer, and Blanche Simmons Targan. He received his B.A. degree with a major in English from Rutgers University in 1954 and an M.A. degree from the University of Chicago in 1955. He then served in the U.S. Army for two years. He married Arleen Shanken, an artist, in 1958, with whom he had two children. Targan received a Ph.D. degree in English from Brandeis University in

1962 and started a teaching career at Syracuse University. He has taught at the State University of New York at Cortland, Skidmore College, and, beginning in 1978, at the State University of New York at Binghamton. He later retired from teaching, and in 2010 he was living in Greenwich Village, New York.

## ANALYSIS

There is a determined optimism at the heart of many of Barry Targan's stories, perhaps best summed up in the title of one of his collections, *Surviving Adverse Seasons*. His middle-aged male characters are possessed of a quiet integrity that makes them survivors regardless of the adversity they face. Integrity is an important element in Targan's writing; he has spoken of his awe of great authors who write with honor and authenticity, feeling that to write with such "integrity . . . was one of the finest things a human being could do with a life."

Targan's characters are often driven by a passionate engagement in a meaningful action, a deep-seated desire and commitment to give oneself wholly to a task, craft, or art. Many of his characters, without the aid of dogma or social rules, develop and abide by their own quiet codes of conduct, and they manage to succeed in spite of the odds against them. As a result, the reader is irresistibly aligned with these men, for it is clear that they are honestly engaged in doing the best they can under adverse circumstances.

### "HARRY BELTEN AND THE MENDELSSOHN VIOLIN CONCERTO"

Targan's best-known story, anthologized several times, is the most representative expression of his central theme--one's passionate and honest devotion to a creative act. Harry Belten is a middle-aged man who has worked in a hardware store in a small town in southwest New York for thirty-two years. A reliable man whose "life had closed in upon him quickly," Harry has but one interest other than his family and his work--the violin, which, with modest lessons, he started learning how to play in 1941. More than two decades later, Harry has decided to take more serious professional lessons and to stage his own concert--renting a hall and paying for an orchestra--even though he and everyone else know he is not a concert-caliber violinist.

Among the pieces he plans to play at the concert is the Felix Mendelssohn *Violin Concerto*, a particularly difficult piece that Harry has been studying for the past eighteen years. Although his wife tells him they can ill afford the concert and people kid him and try to discourage him, Harry is determined. When the orchestra he has hired tries to cancel, he fights them for breach of contract and wins. When his family insists he see a psychiatrist, he agrees and successfully convinces the doctor that he should give the concert. He even manages to get his professional teacher, who has doubted him from the beginning, to fully support him.

The success of Targan's story depends on the irresistibility of Harry Belten himself, whose quiet and dignified determination, humility, and courage put the reader so much on his side that at the end of the story, when he is ready to play the Mendelssohn piece, the reader waits breathlessly, fingers crossed, silently cheering him on. The tension is at its highest when one of Harry's strings loses the exact tautness needed, forcing him to try to play all the notes on that one string slightly off while playing the notes on the other three strings correctly.

Although Harry plays the worst finale to the Mendelssohn concerto ever played with a real orchestra before a live audience, it is enough to make his teacher almost weep with pride. When Harry's family and friends cheer and shout for an "encore," Harry tunes his violin and plays one encore and then another. It is one of the most delightfully fulfilling conclusions in modern short fiction.

### "DOMINION"

Highly praised and often anthologized, "Dominion" is another Targan story that focuses on the integrity and honest courage of one man. When the central character, Morton Poverman, is driven to bankruptcy by the embezzlement of his partner, he simply forgives him and begins again with what little he has left, working long hours, doing practically everything by himself. When his son Robert, a senior in high school, offers to help, Poverman generously tells the boy to stick to his school and extracurricular activities.

The son, who has been accepted into Yale University, Cornell University, and the State University of New York at Binghamton, is the most serious source of heartache for Morton when the boy says he is considering not going to college and joining a religious cult instead. Poverman quietly begins an understated effort to save his son from what he considers a mistake by going to the headquarters of the cult, a branch of a large corporate religious entity, and declaring his own interest in their message to their smooth-talking representatives.

When Poverman begins attending the discussion meetings of the group, his son, formerly an active participant, withdraws, accusing his father of not being sincere. When the cult leaders try to get Poverman to stop attending, he challenges them and asks to receive further instruction. The climax of the story occurs when Poverman stands up at a meeting and declares himself for Jesus. Although he is doubted by the leaders, the young people accept this avowal with such enthusiasm that they have no choice but to receive Poverman into their organization. However, when Poverman stands in the midst of the group and repeats their codes--that he is an infection of evil, that he has made the world foul with his pride, that he is a bad man stained with sin--his son, knowing that these things are not true, tearfully urges him to stop. The story ends with Poverman telling his son not to worry, while he advances "upon his Hosts in dubious battle. And f[ights]. Not without glory."

It is another wonderfully fulfilling Targan conclusion, for Poverman has not only defeated his foes but also done so by means of the very virtues of love, forgiveness, and honesty that they espouse--values that he naturally and unselfconsciously possesses without their rituals, codes, or dogma. It is not just that Poverman has outsmarted the slick businessmen who run the cult, although that is cause enough for the reader's pleasure, it is that Poverman is a true religious man in the most basic sense of that word, courageously willing to abase himself for the sake of his son.

### "FALLING FREE"

Although Frank Higgins, the protagonist of this story, is relatively rootless and has broken the law by organizing bullfights in Texas, he is not the morally lax, down-and-out drifter encountered in the stories of a number of other American short-story writers of the 1970's and 1980's, such as Richard Ford, Barry Hannah, Richard Bausch, and Lee K. Abbott. The defining event in Higgins's life occurred when, as a nineteen-year-old soldier engaged in an airborne experiment, he jumped out of a C-47 at twenty-five thousand feet over Texas and "was seized by a nearly unutterable intention to possess what from this height appeared to be the boundlessly offered." Seeing the world below him as a "vast continent of possibility," Higgins has spent his life in one unsuccessful get-rich scheme after another--from selling cars to panning for gold--for his experience has left him "unmoored, untethered by vicissitude, necessity, or even dreams."

Having been ordered out of the state by the Texas Rangers, Higgins and his wife Miranda, who is ill, have decided to return to southern California to a poor carob tree orchard they own. However, their plans are altered by a burnt-out wheel bearing and the arrival of a hitchhiker who offers to help in exchange for a ride to El Paso. It is soon clear that the hitchhiker, who calls himself Joe Smith, has something to hide, although Higgins, feeling a sympathetic identification with Smith, thinks the young man lacks menace, the "hanging tangle of danger."

The story, however, does take a menacing turn when Miranda worsens; she desperately needs to get to El Paso for medication and notices that Smith has a gun. In a parallel to Higgins's own search for gold, success, and ultimate possibility after his youthful "free fall," Smith reveals that he has a million dollars worth of cocaine in his backpack smuggled out of Mexico. The situation worsens when Smith insists that they head south through rough country, endangering Miranda's life. Although Higgins knows that Smith has been broken by exactly what he has always believed-- "that he was a potentate, and that any rock he held in his hand was a jewel"--he also knows that whereas at twenty-five thousand feet he had "fallen free," for Smith it is too late.

The story comes to a head when Higgins gets his rifle and Smith points his gun at him and pulls the trigger, only to have nothing happen because he did not take off the safety. At this point, Higgins fires and shoots Smith through the head. The postlude of the story has Higgins and Miranda at the carob orchard on the coast of southern California, with Higgins thinking of the sea voyages they and Smith could have taken, out to where they were only "imagined images of places." However, Miranda holds him to earth with a squeeze of the hand.

OTHER MAJOR WORKS

LONG FICTION: *Kingdoms: A Novel*, 1980; *The Tangerine Tango Equation: Or, How I Discovered Sex, Deception, and a New Theory of Physics in Three Short Months*, 1990; *The Ark of the Marindor*, 1998.

POETRY: *Let the Wild Rumpus Start: Poems*, 1971; *Thoreau Stalks the Land Disguised as a Father: Poems*, 1975.

BIBLIOGRAPHY

"Barry Targan." In *Contemporary Authors*. New Revision Series 71, Detroit: Gale Research, 1999. A brief biographical survey of Targan's literary career. Summarizes critical reception of Targan's work and comments on his novel *The Ark of the Marindor*.

Clements, Arthur L. "Barry Targan." In *American Short-Story Writers Since World War. Vol. 130 in Dictionary of Literary Biography*. In a rare general discussion of Targan's fiction, Clements comments on some of the general themes and characters in *Harry Belten and the Mendelssohn Violin Concerto*, *Surviving Adverse Seasons*, and *Falling Free*. Argues that Targan works within the realistic tradition and often focuses on the theme of engaging in life with as much honesty, skill, love, and devotion as one can muster.

Evanier, David. "Storytellers." *The New York Times*, July 27, 1980, p. 18. A review of *Surviving Adverse Seasons*. Discusses "Kingdoms," which Evanier says is the best story in the collection. Says Targan's stories embody a tug of war between his abstract turn of mind and his concrete gifts as a story writer. Maintains that Targan needs to be less ponderous and more immediate and responsible.

Kardos, Michael. "MR Lost Classic." *Missouri Review* 27, no. 1 (Spring, 2004): 186-188. Kardos reviews the collection *Harry Belten and the Mendelssohn Violin Concerto*, at that time approaching its thirty-year anniversary. He maintains that the collection "continues to resonate for many reasons: its innovative storylines, unforgettable characters, page-by-page liveliness . . . but most of all, perhaps, for its generous spirit."

Lotozo, Elis. "Life: Want to Make Something of It?" Review of *Falling Free*, by Barry Targan. *The New York Times*, March 3, 1990, p. 24. Lotozo calls the stories passionate arguments with and love songs to a world that offers "no guarantees, only opportunities, and vicissitudes." Comments on the three stories in which aging men confront the choices they have made with their lives.

Morgan, Speer. "The Plot Thickens." *St. Louis Post-Dispatch*, September 9, 1998, p. E3. Maintains that *The Ark of the Marindor* is reminiscent of a Joseph Conrad novel, complete with compelling incident. Argues that the real story of this "beautifully crafted novel" is the protagonist's growing understanding of the bearing of her life.

Sweeney, Aoibheann. "Bermuda Triangle." Review of *The Ark of the Marindor*, by Barry Targan. *The New York Times*, June 14, 1998, p. 14. Maintains that Targan's work focuses on the theme of self-discovery; argues that what saves the book is the sensual descriptions of sailing rather than the dizzying pace of the plot and the page-turning Hollywood machinery of suspense.

*Charles E. May*

# PETER TAYLOR

**Born:** Trenton, Tennessee; January 8, 1917
**Died:** Charlottesville, Virginia; November 2, 1994

PRINCIPAL SHORT FICTION

*A Long Fourth, and Other Stories,* 1948
*The Widows of Thornton,* 1954
*Happy Families Are All Alike,* 1959
*Miss Leonora When Last Seen and Fifteen Other Stories,* 1963
*The Collected Stories of Peter Taylor,* 1968
*In the Miro District, and Other Stories,* 1977
*The Old Forest, and Other Stories,* 1985
*The Oracle at Stoneleigh Court,* 1993

OTHER LITERARY FORMS

In addition to his short fiction, Peter Taylor published the novels *A Woman of Means* (1950), *A Summons to Memphis* (1986), and *In the Tennessee Country* (1994), as well as plays. Several of his plays were performed at Kenyon College, and three of them have been published separately; a collection of seven dramas was also published in 1973. In addition, Taylor was one of three editors of a memorial volume, *Randall Jarrell, 1914-1965* (1967).

ACHIEVEMENTS

The publication of *The Collected Stories of Peter Taylor* brought general acknowledgment that Taylor was one of the most skillful practitioners of the modern short story in the United States. While his reputation prior to that volume had for the most part been limited to a fairly small circle of enthusiastic readers, the list of his awards indicates the respect in which he was always held by his peers. Taylor was honored twelve different times by inclusion in the annual volume of *The Best American Short Stories* and was included six times in the *O. Henry Award Stories*.

He was awarded a John Simon Guggenheim Memorial Foundation Fellowship (1950), a National Institute of Arts and Letters grant (1952), a Fulbright Fellowship (1955), first prize from the O. Henry Memorial Awards (1959), an Ohioana Book Award (1960), a Ford Foundation Fellowship (1961), a Rockefeller Foundation grant (1964), second prize from the *Partisan Review-Dial* and a National Institute of Arts and Letters gold medal (1979), a Ritz Paris Hemingway Award and the PEN/Faulkner Award (1986), and a Pulitzer Prize (1987).

While acknowledging his admiration for the work of Anton Chekhov, Ivan Turgenev, and Henry James, Taylor put his own unique mark on the short story. Much of his fiction is set in the South, recalling the work of William Faulkner and Flannery O'Connor, but he is less concerned with violence and moral themes than either of those writers, concentrating instead on social relationships and the inevitability of betrayal in the interactions between men and women.

BIOGRAPHY

Peter Matthew Hillsman Taylor grew up in middle-class circumstances in border states. His family moved to Nashville when he was seven, spent several years in St. Louis, and settled in Memphis when he was fifteen. Expected to follow his father and older brother into the practice of law, Taylor chose early to try to make his career as a writer. He studied with the poet Allen Tate. After a brief enrollment at Vanderbilt University, he preferred to follow the poet, editor, and teacher John Crowe Ransom to Kenyon College in Ohio. At Kenyon College, he was befriended by the poet and critic Randall Jarrell and shared a room with the poet Robert Lowell.

After service in the United States Army during World War II, Taylor took up teaching as a profession. Between 1945 and 1963, he held faculty appointments at Indiana State University and Ohio State University, and on three different occasions he was appointed to teaching positions at the University of North Carolina at Greensboro. In 1967, he accepted a professorship at the University of Virginia, where he remained until his retirement in 1984.

Success as a short-story writer came fairly early in his career. Prestigious magazines, such as *The southern Review* and *The New Republic*, published some of his stories written while he was still in college, and his first recognition in *Best American Short Stories* came in 1941, just after his graduation from Kenyon College. By 1948, his work was appearing in *The New Yorker*, which over the next three decades would publish more than two dozen of his works. Popular success, however, waited until the publication of *A Summons to Memphis* in 1986. The novel was a best seller and won for Taylor the Pulitzer Prize for fiction. One scholar has hypothesized that Taylor saw this as a means of gaining validation for his short stories, the genre he considered more demanding of real artistry. Taylor died on November 2, 1994, in Charlottesville, Virginia.

ANALYSIS

The art of Peter Taylor is ironic and subtle. In a typical story, the narrator or point-of-view character is an observer, perhaps a member of a community who remembers someone or something in the town's past that is puzzling or strange, or a character whose understanding of his or her life falls short of reality. In tone, the stories are deceptively simple and straightforward, masking their complex ironies in seemingly ordinary actions. Taylor does not experiment with form or structure in the manner of a Jorge Luis Borges or a Robert Coover, but his stories are not always about commonplace experience; the grotesque plays a major role in such stories as "The Fancy Woman" and "Venus, Cupid, Folly, and Time."

Low-keyed and rarely involving violent action, the stories are more complex in their effect than at first appears, often revealing more about the narrator or the society than about the character being described. Their settings are often in small towns or minor cities in the upper South, Tennessee or Missouri, places such as those where Taylor lived as a boy and young man. Familial relationships, including those between husband and wife, are often central. Racial and economic matters enter into many of the stories, but such major social issues are generally depicted in the context of the social interactions of ordinary people. Nevertheless, Taylor provides considerable insight into the effects of the radical changes that affected the South in the 1960's and 1970's.

"DEAN OF MEN"

Betrayal is a recurrent theme in Taylor's short fiction, and it is no accident that the story he chose to place first in *The Collected Stories of Peter Taylor* is the relatively late "Dean of Men," a recital of the history of the men in a family. The narrator, an older man and a successful academic, tries in the story to explain to his son the background of his career and his divorce from his first wife, the son's mother. The story unfolds by an examination of the past, in which the narrator's grandfather is revealed to have been a successful politician, governor of his state, and then United States senator. Younger men in his party convinced him to give up his Senate seat and run for governor again to save the party from a man he despised, and he agreed. It turned out that the plan was intended to get him out of his Senate seat. As a result, the grandfather gave up politics in disgust and lived out his life as an embittered man.

The narrator's father was similarly betrayed by a man he had known all his life, who had installed the father on the board of a bank. During the Great Depression of the 1930's, the friend promised to come from New York to explain doubtful investments he had made, but he never arrived, and the father was left holding the bag. In his turn, the narrator, as a young instructor in a small college, was used by other faculty members to block an appointment they all feared, but when the move was avenged by its target, the young man was left to suffer the consequences alone. In the aftermath, he left to take another job, but his wife did not go with him; both later remarried.

The story is the narrator's attempt to explain his life to the son who grew up without him. What the narrator is unaware of is the decline in the importance and stature of his family through the generations; his achievements and his place in life, of which he is unduly proud, are notably less important than those of his father, which were in turn significantly less than those of the grandfather. The entire family's history is flawed by the men's lack of initiative, their acceptance of what others do to them. This lack of self-knowledge on the part of a narrator will characterize Taylor's first-person fictions as late as "The Captain's Son."

### "A SPINSTER'S TALE"

The narrator or central figure's ignorance of her or his own attitudes is present from the beginning of Taylor's career, as evidenced in his first published story, "A Spinster's Tale," a study of sexual repression. Taylor's only explicit investigation of sexual deviance would come much later, in "The Instruction of a Mistress," although "Venus, Cupid, Folly, and Time" contains strong overtones of incest. In "A Spinster's Tale," the narrator, the spinster of the title, is a woman whose youth was blighted by her fear of an old drunk who often passed the house in which she lived with her father and brother. As she tells the story, it is clear that her fear of "Mr. Speed" is a transference of her inadmissible attraction to her older brother, who also drinks, often and to excess. She is unaware that her irrational fear is really fear of any kind of departure from the

*Peter Taylor* (Bettmann/CORBIS)

most repressed kinds of behavior. In the old man, drunkenness is revolting; in her brother, she fears it only because her dead mother had told the young man that he would go to hell if he continued, but her brother's antic behavior when drunk exercises an attraction on her that she struggles to deny. In her old age, she still has revealing dreams laden with sexual implications. The betrayal in this story, of which she is only dimly aware, is the narrator's calling the police to haul away Mr. Speed when he stumbles onto their lawn during a driving rainstorm. She acknowledges late in life that she had acted "with courage, but without wisdom."

### "WHAT YOU HEAR FROM 'EM?"

Betrayal of one kind or another seems to be inevitable in the relations between races, especially as those relations undergo the changes brought about by the Civil Rights movement and the push for integration. Since most of Taylor's stories are set in the South of the 1930's and 1940's, those relations are often between masters and servants, but that will change in the later tales. "What You Hear from 'Em?" is written from the point of view of an old black servant, Aunt Munsie, who lives in retirement, raising pigs and dogs and a few chickens. Her only real interest is in the lives of the two white men she reared when their mother died, and the question she addresses to people she meets in her daily rounds asks when they will return to the small town where she still lives. Their visits to her, bringing wives and children and eventually grandchildren, do not matter to Aunt Munsie; things will not be right until they again live in Thornton, a Nashville suburb. The betrayal is by the two men. Worried by her refusal to acknowledge automobiles or traffic rules as she goes through town collecting slop for her pigs, they arrange for an ordinance to be enacted that will forbid pig farming within the town limits. Aunt Munsie knows what they have done; she sells her pigs and loses her individuality, becoming a kind of parody of an old former servant.

### "A WIFE OF NASHVILLE"

A different kind of betrayal and a different kind of response occur in another early story, "A Wife of Nashville." On the surface, this is a story about a marriage between John R. and Helen Ruth Lovell, in some ways a typical southern couple. He has succeeded in the insurance business, but he has spent much of his time over the years with other businessmen, hunting and traveling. Helen Ruth, as a result, has been occupied with rearing her children, and her chief companions over the years have been the black women who have cooked and cleaned for her: Jane Blackemore, when they were first married; Carrie, during the time their two younger boys were born; Sarah, who at the age of sixty-eight left for Chicago and a new marriage; and Jess, hired during the Depression and the most durable and helpful of them all.

"A Wife of Nashville," however, is only partly about the marriage and the rearing of a family. It becomes clear as the story develops that Helen Ruth's genuine emotional life has increasingly been centered on her relationships with her servants and that they have been an integral part of the family. Jess, who does not drive a car herself, is essential to the boys' learning to drive, a symbol of their adulthood. In the end, she concocts a scene to explain her leaving the family; Helen Ruth knows that the explanation is false and that Jess and a friend are leaving Nashville for what they think is a more glamorous life in California. The husband and sons are shocked and resentful at the way they think Helen Ruth has been treated by Jess; Helen Ruth herself, however, rejects their sympathy and refuses to share their anger. It is clear that she wishes she had a means of escape, even one as improbable as that taken by Jess and her friend. On another level, it is clear also that she, unlike the men in the family, recognizes the social changes that are under way, changes that will alter the ways in which the races will survive. Other stories having to do with difficult marital relations were written throughout Taylor's career and include the early "Cookie," "Reservations," and "The Elect."

### "MISS LEONORA WHEN LAST SEEN"

Perhaps the story most typical of Taylor's work, and one of the most powerful, is the one he chose to conclude *The Collected Stories of Peter Taylor*, "Miss Leonora When Last Seen." Narrated by one of the middling successful men who populate this fiction, a small-town druggist, the story operates on several levels. It encompasses the narrator's sadness at having to carry bad news to the woman who was his teacher and who had encouraged him to aspire to greater things than he was able to achieve. At the same time, it is a

story about a town's revenge on Miss Leonora's family, the wealthiest and most powerful residents of the town; over the years, they had prevented every "improvement" that might have brought business and "progress" to Thomasville, using their influence to keep out the railroad, the asylum, and other projects that would have changed the town. Most of them moved away, but they retained the home place, and they continued to exercise their influence. Now the town has decided to condemn the old manor house in which Miss Leonora lives so as to build a new high school. The irony that Miss Leonora had been a superb teacher in the old school is not lost on the narrator.

More important, "Miss Leonora When Last Seen" shows the mixed blessings and curses of the old ways and of the changes that are coming to the "New South." The old ways were autocratic and sometimes unfair, and they depended upon a servant class descended from slaves, such as the blacks who still live on Miss Leonora's place. Modernity, however, may not be much of an improvement; the new high school is being pushed as a final attempt to avoid the supposed horrors of racial integration. The narrator is caught between these times and has nothing to look to for support.

While these elements are at work, and the narrator is showing his own lack of understanding of Miss Leonora, the story presents a picture of an eccentric but fascinating individual who has lived in Thomasville all her life, teaching, trying to inspire the young men who were her favorites to achievement, and living close to the blacks who still reside on the family property, which she has inherited. In her retirement, Miss Leonora has taken to traveling by car, driving always at night in an open convertible, wearing one of two strange costumes, and stopping at "tourist homes," which were the motels of the time. Informed of the town's decision, she has taken to the road. Postcards come from surrounding states, but "She seems to be orbiting her native state of Tennessee." There is no sign that she will ever return; the old ways are indeed dead, and those who lived in the old way are anachronisms.

### "THE OLD FOREST"

"The Old Forest" is a good example of Taylor's interest in the tensions between the old and new South. The story's action takes place in Memphis in 1937, although the story is told more than forty years later by Nat, the central character. Nat relates how in the 1930's a young man in Memphis, even if he was engaged, might continue to go out with the bright young women he and his friends jokingly called "demimondaines." These were intelligent young women who had good jobs, read good books, and attended concerts and plays. Nevertheless, they were not quite in the social class of Nat and his friends. The two groups went out for their mutual amusement without expecting long-term commitments, either sexual or matrimonial. Young men like Nat intended to marry duller girls of their own class who lived by the standards of the Memphis Country Club. Nat says that the demimondaines were at least two generations ahead of themselves in their sexual freedom, for although they did not usually sleep with Nat and his friends, they often entered sexual relationships with men they truly loved.

Although Nat is already working for his father's cotton firm, he is also studying Latin in a lackadaisical way at the local college. His family ridicules his interest in Horace's *Odes*, but he enjoys the distinction it brings him among his friends, even though he is nearly failing the course. This particular Saturday, about a week before Nat's December wedding to Caroline Braxton, he invites Lee Ann Deehart, his "other" girl, to come out to the college with him while he studies for a test. On snow-packed roads in the primeval forest near the Mississippi, they have a car accident. Nat is slightly hurt and hardly notices that Lee Ann has climbed out of the car and disappeared in the snow and virgin forest. When she does not return to her boardinghouse that evening, Nat knows he must confess the affair to Caroline, who is surprisingly understanding and agrees that he must find her.

Lee Ann's friends know where she is, but Nat soon realizes that she is deliberately hiding from him, and he fears the scandal when the story hits the newspapers. Especially he fears that Caroline will break off their engagement. In the end, Caroline is the one who finds Lee Ann and discovers her motives for hiding, motives which ironically involve her own fear of publicity and the identification of her family.

Throughout, Nat contrasts the Memphis of 1937 with the present Memphis and the two sorts of girls represented by Lee Ann and Caroline. Typically, Taylor invites the reader to take a slightly different view from Nat's. For all her supposed dullness, Caroline uses real intelligence in finding Lee Ann and real compassion in responding to her crisis. Moreover, ten years later she supports Nat's decision to leave the cotton business for a career teaching college. Caroline's own analysis of what happened, however, is straight from the old forest of Memphis convention. She has not set herself free, she says, like Lee Ann, so in protecting Nat she has protected for herself "the power of a woman in a man's world," the only power she can claim.

OTHER MAJOR WORKS

LONG FICTION: *A Woman of Means*, 1950; *A Summons to Memphis*, 1986; *In the Tennessee Country*, 1994.

PLAYS: *Tennessee Day in Saint Louis: A Comedy*, pr. 1956; *A Stand in the Mountains*, pb. 1965; *Presences: Seven Dramatic Pieces*, pb. 1973.

NONFICTION: *Conversations with Peter Taylor*, 1987 (Hubert H. McAlexander, editor).

EDITED TEXT: *Randall Jarrell, 1914-1965*, 1967 (with Robert Lowell and Robert Penn Warren).

BIBLIOGRAPHY

Baumbach, Jonathan. *Modern and Contemporaries: New Masters of the Short Story*. New York: Random House, 1968. Includes a brief analysis of Taylor's place in the development of the post-World War II short story.

Beck, Charlotte H. "Peter Taylor and the Fugitives: Surrogate Fathers, Foster Son." In *The Fugitive Legacy: A Critical History*. Baton Rouge: Louisiana State University Press, 2001. Analyzes the influence of the Nashville Fugitives, a group of prominent authors and literary critics that included John Crowe Ransom, Allen Tate, Robert Penn Warren, and Donald Davidson. The chapter on Taylor assesses the impact of this group on Taylor's work.

Gelfant, Blanche H., ed. *The Columbia Companion to the Twentieth-Century American Short Story*. New York: Columbia University Press, 2000. Includes a chapter in which Taylor's short stories are analyzed.

Kramer, Victor A., Patricia A. Bailey, Carol G. Dana, and Carl H. Griffin. *Andrew Lytle, Walker Percy, Peter Taylor: A Reference Guide*. Boston: G. K. Hall, 1983. One of the later and most complete bibliographies of Taylor's work and the reviews and criticism it received.

McAlexander, Hubert H. *Peter Taylor: A Writer's Life*. Baton Rouge: Louisiana State University Press, 2001. A biography written with the close cooperation of its subject. In fact, McAlexander, who edited *Conversations with Peter Taylor* and a collection of essays on the writer, was hand-picked by Taylor, and his portrait is admiring.

Oates, Joyce Carol. "Realism of Distance, Realism of Immediacy." *The southern Review* 7 (Winter, 1971): 295-313. A novelist's sensitive appreciation of other writers, including Taylor.

Robinson, Clayton. "Peter Taylor." In *Literature of Tennessee*, edited by Ray Will-banks. Rome, Ga.: Mercer University Press, 1984. Relates Taylor's fiction to his early years and explains his mother's influence on his techniques and subject matter.

Robinson, David M. *World of Relations: The Achievement of Peter Taylor*. Lexington: University Press of Kentucky, 1998. Robinson demonstrates how Taylor's fiction expresses the writer's concern with family relationships and with shifts in southern culture. Includes an extensive analysis of Taylor's final two works, *The Oracle at Stoneleigh Court* and *In the Tennessee Country*.

Robison, James C. *Peter Taylor: A Study of the Short Fiction*. Boston: Twayne, 1987. This volume not only is the only extended study of Taylor's short stories but also contains two interviews with the author, as well as essays by a number of critics. Robison's comments are occasionally wide of the mark, but he is an earnest and generally intelligent reader of Taylor's work. Essential reading.

Samarco, C. Vincent. "Taylor's 'The Old Forest.'" *The Explicator* 57 (Fall, 1998): 51-53. Argues that the car accident represents a collision between Nat Ramsey's pursuit of knowledge and the history of his upbringing within the narrow walls of privilege.

Shear, Walter. "Peter Taylor: Imagining the Social Self." In *The Feeling of Being: Sensibility in Postwar American Fiction*. New York: Peter Lang, 2002. Analyzes works by Taylor and other American writers to demonstrate how the anxieties and skepticism of the Cold War resulted in the growth of an intensely personal fiction, in which the characters must make their way in a new world of abundance and disorientation.

Stephens, C. Ralph, and Lynda B. Salamon, eds. *The Craft of Peter Taylor*. Tuscaloosa: University of Alabama Press, 1995. A collection of essays on Taylor's work, including discussions of his poetics, his focus on place, his relationship to the Agrarians, his treatment of absence, his role in American pastoralism, and such stories as "The Other Times," "The Old Forest," and "The Hand of Emmagene."

Taylor, Peter. "Interview with Peter Taylor." Interview by J. H. E. Paine. *Journal of the Short Story in English* 9 (Fall, 1987): 14-35. An extended interview with Taylor, dealing with his techniques and influences.

*John M. Muste*
*Updated by Ann Davison Garbett*

# JEAN THOMPSON

**Born:** Chicago, Illinois; January 3, 1950

PRINCIPAL SHORT FICTION

*The Gasoline Wars,* 1979
*Little Face, and Other Stories,* 1984
*Who Do You Love,* 1999
*Throw Like a Girl,* 2007
*Do Not Deny Me,* 2009

OTHER LITERARY FORMS

Jean Thompson has written novels, including *City Boy* (2004), *Wide Blue Yonder* (2002), *The Woman Driver* (1985), and *My Wisdom* (1982).

ACHIEVEMENTS

Jean Thompson has garnered awards from many sources, including a Guggenheim Fellowship and a fellowship from the National Endowment for the Arts. Her stories have appeared in the most selective venues, including *Best American Short Stories*, *The Pushcart Prize* anthology, and magazines such as *The New Yorker* and *Story*. The collection *Who Do You Love* was a finalist for the National Book Award.

BIOGRAPHY

Jean Thompson was born in Chicago and spent her childhood in Chicago, Louisville, Kentucky, and Memphis, Tennessee. She has described herself as a voracious and precocious reader from a young age, although she did not take herself seriously as a writer until her twenties. She earned a B.A. from the University of Illinois in 1971, followed by an M.F.A. from Ohio's Bowling Green State University in 1973. She began to teach at the University of Illinois in 1973. Her first collection, *The Gasoline Wars*, was published by the University of Illinois Press in 1979, followed by the novel *My Wisdom* in 1982, the collection *Little Face,*

*and Other Stories* in 1984, and the novel *The Woman Driver* in 1985. After some years in which no book-length fiction appeared, the widely acclaimed collection *Who Do You Love* was published in 1999 and earned Thompson a nomination for the National Book Award. Three years later she returned to the novel form with *Wide Blue Yonder* (2002) and *City Boy* (2004). Her two subsequent collections, *Throw Like a Girl* (2007) and *Do Not Deny Me* (2009), also garnered wide praise. Thompson has continued to teach at the University of Illinois and at writers' conferences; she also tutors Spanish speakers in English.

ANALYSIS

Jean Thompson's work centers on relationships, most often those between men and women, with a particular sensitivity to the way in which women can find themselves trapped and and tempted by despair. The weight of these themes is tempered by Thompson's facility for language and for satire, so that her fiction often has an edgy, dark humor to its insights.

THE GASOLINE WARS

*The Gasoline Wars* is so titled because a number of its ten stories involve cars, the staple and catalyst of so much that happens in small-town relationships. Thompson surveys the ignition of characters' hopes with a knowing eye, and the collection moves from battered wives, as in "The People of Color," to those who, as in "Dry Spring," are merely taking their first steps into the territory of disappointment.

LITTLE FACE, AND OTHER STORIES

*Little Face, and Other Stories*, Thompson's second collection, was published in 1984. Again Thompson examines the ways in which people hunger for intimacy and yet find it elusive. The title story traces the awakening of a young girl involved with an older student; others involve the deftly observed splintering of relationships between friends, lovers, and couples. Although some critics found the collection disappointing after Thompson's widely praised debut in *The Gasoline Wars*, the stories show a continuing interest in the circumstances and grief of women, themes which came to fruition in Thompson's subsequent collection, *Who Do You Love*.

### WHO DO YOU LOVE

*Who Do You Love* showcases some of Thompson's finest and most haunting work, much of it focused on love and its sorrows. In the title story, an emotionally isolated social worker confronts, or fails to confront, a series of situations that underline her despair, from romance gone awry to her relationship to other afflicted souls. The whole is set against a sound track of the song "Who Do You Love," its lack of a question mark mirroring the protagonist's failure to question her world. The other stories in the volume similarly throw their characters' isolation into sharp relief, from their hopes to their moments of recognition and reaction.

### THROW LIKE A GIRL

*Throw Like a Girl* is an astute, even acidic look at the gender wars and the situations in which women find themselves. In the powerful title story, one college friend visits another, and the two end up hurling pieces of broken sidewalk at a surly boyfriend, whose feeble retort is "You throw like a girl!" Although the friends view the boyfriend with lofty hilarity, the real and more sobering quandaries of adult womanhood also are starkly on view. The partner of the surly boyfriend will end up divorced and dying alone of that eminently female ailment, breast cancer. The collection surveys the circumstances of girls and women, the ways in which a sharp-eyed recognition of one's restricted options does not expand those options and how men in particular so often prove themselves limited in the face of women's need and hunger.

### DO NOT DENY ME

This collection of stories often depicts tired people holding despair at bay, their endurance observed with a keen eye for the details of everyday stoicism. In "Soldiers of Spiritos," an old English professor who feels his obsolescence keenly dreams of writing a science-fiction novel, *Soldiers of Spiritos*, which unwittingly will mirror his own despair in epic terms. He finds, however, that real inspiration springs from an encounter with an undergraduate with her own troubles. In the title story, a young woman whose boyfriend has died explores the possibility of being reconnected through a medium and ultimately turns her back on easy answers. Thompson's characters make few large advances in their lives, but Thompson shows how their small moments of truth hold back the tide of despair.

### OTHER MAJOR WORKS

LONG FICTION: *My Wisdom*, 1982; *The Woman Driver*, 1985; *Wide Blue Yonder*, 2002; *City Boy*, 2004.

### BIBLIOGRAPHY

Painter, Pamela. "The Art and Architecture of the Double Ending." In *Open Book: Essays from the Vermont College Postgraduate Writers Conference*. Newcastle-upon-Tyne, England: Cambridge Scholars Press, 2006. An analysis of Thompson's story "Mercy" and Alice Munro's "Post and Beam."

Ruback, Max. "Entanglements of the Heart--Jean Thompson's Stories Begin with a Basic Question: Why Is Happiness So Elusive?" *The Writer* 115, no. 2 (February, 2002): 39-42. Thompson discusses what she tries to instill in her writing students, her own process and influences, the idea underlying *Wide Blue Yonder*, and the current demand for short fiction.

Telkulve, Susan. "The Way of Stories: Interview with Jean Thompson." In *The Muse upon My Shoulder: Discussions of the Creative Process*, edited by Sylvia Skaggs McTague. Madison, N.J.: Fairleigh Dickinson University Press, 2004. An illuminating interview in which Thompson speaks of her sources and early career and comments on a number of her stories, among them "Who Do You Love."

*Martha Bayless*

# JAMES THURBER

**Born:** Columbus, Ohio; December 8, 1894
**Died:** New York, New York; November 2, 1961

PRINCIPAL SHORT FICTION

*Is Sex Necessary? Or, Why We Feel the Way We Do,*
    1929 (with E. B. White)
*The Owl in the Attic, and Other Perplexities,* 1931
*The Seal in the Bedroom, and Other Predicaments,*
    1932
*My Life and Hard Times,* 1933
*The Middle-Aged Man on the Flying Trapeze,* 1935
*Let Your Mind Alone!, and Other More or Less*
    *Inspirational Pieces,* 1937
*The Last Flower: A Parable in Pictures,* 1939
*Fables for Our Time and Famous Poems Illustrated,*
    1940
*My World--And Welcome to It!,* 1942
*The Great Quillow,* 1944
*The Thurber Carnival,* 1945
*The White Deer,* 1945
*The Beast in Me, and Other Animals: A New*
    *Collection of Pieces and Drawings About Human*
    *Beings and Less Alarming Creatures,* 1948
*The Thirteen Clocks,* 1950
*Thurber Country: A New Collection of Pieces About*
    *Males and Females, Mainly of Our Own Species,*
    1953
*Further Fables for Our Time,* 1956
*Alarms and Diversions,* 1957
*The Wonderful O,* 1957
*Lanterns and Lances,* 1961
*Credos and Curios,* 1962

OTHER LITERARY FORMS

The more than twenty published volumes of James Thurber (THUR-bur) include plays, stories, sketches, essays, verse, fables, fairy tales for adults, reminiscences, biography, drawings, and cartoons.

ACHIEVEMENTS

James Thurber's writings are widely known and admired in English-speaking countries and his drawings have a world following. He has been compared with James Joyce in his command of and playfulness with English, and he invites comparison with most of his contemporaries, many of whom he parodies at least once in his works. He greatly admired Henry James, referring to him often in his works and parodying him masterfully several times, for example, in "Something to Say." While Thurber is best known as a humorist, often with the implication that he need not be taken seriously as an artist, his literary reputation has grown steadily. His short story "The Secret Life of Walter Mitty" became an instant classic after it appeared in 1939 and was subsequently reprinted in *Reader's Digest*. After his death in 1961, several major studies and a volume in the Twentieth Century Views series have appeared, all arguing that Thurber should rank with the best American artists in several fields, including the short story. In 1980, "The Greatest Man in the World" was chosen for dramatization in the American Short Story series of the Public Broadcasting Service. Thurber received numerous awards for his work, including honorary degrees from Kenyon College (1950), Williams College (1957), and Yale University (1953), as well as the Antoinette Perry Award for the revue *A Thurber Carnival* (pr. 1960). His drawings were included in art shows worldwide. He became the first American after Mark Twain to be invited to *Punch*'s Wednesday Luncheon, attending this event in 1958.

BIOGRAPHY

On December 8, 1894, James Grover Thurber was born in Columbus, Ohio, where he spent his childhood except for a two-year stay in Washington, D.C. In Columbus, he absorbed the midwestern regional values that remained important to him all of his life: a liberal idealism, a conservative respect for the family, a belief in the agrarian virtues of industry and independence, and a healthy skepticism about the human potential for perfecting anything. He lost his left eye in a childhood accident that eventually led to almost complete blindness forty years later. He attended but did not graduate from Ohio State University, where he met Elliott Nugent, who was crucial in helping and encouraging Thurber to write. Thurber began his writing career as a journalist, earning his living primarily as a reporter in Ohio and France before he joined *The New Yorker* in 1927. There his friendship with E. B. White provided opportunities for him to perfect and publish the stories he had been working on since college. Within five years of beginning at *The New Yorker*, he became one of the best-known humorists in America. He married Althea Adams on May 20, 1922, and they had one daughter before their divorce in 1935. He married Helen Wismer on June 25, 1935. Despite impaired vision that seriously interfered with his work, beginning in the early 1940's, Thurber nevertheless continued writing, though he gave up drawing in 1951. He published more than twenty volumes in his lifetime and left many works uncollected at his death. He died of pneumonia on November 2, 1961, a month after suffering a stroke.

ANALYSIS

James Thurber is best known as the author of humorous sketches, stories, and reminiscences dealing with urban bourgeois American life. To discuss Thurber as an artist in the short-story form is difficult, however, because of the variety of things he wrote that might legitimately be labeled short stories. His essays frequently employ stories and are "fictional" in recognizable ways. His "memoirs" in *My Life and Hard Times* are clearly fictionalized. Many of his first-person autobiographical sketches are known to be "fact" rather than fiction only through careful biographical research. As a result, most of his writings can be treated as short fiction. Thurber seemed to prefer to work on the borderlines between conventional forms.

There is disagreement among critics as to the drift of the attitudes and themes reflected in Thurber's work. The poles are well represented by Richard C. Tobias on the one hand and the team of Walter Blair and Hamlin Hill on the other. Tobias argues that Thurber comically celebrates the life of the mind: "Thurber's victory is a freedom within law that delights and surprises." Blair and Hill, in *America's Humor* (1978), see Thurber as a sort of black humorist laughing at his own destruction,

a humorist bedeviled by neuroses, cowed before the insignificant things in his world, and indifferent to the cosmic ones. He loses and loses and loses his combats with machines, women, and animals until defeat becomes permanent.

While Tobias sees women as vital forces in Thurber's work, Hill and Blair see Thurber as essentially a misogynist bewailing the end of the ideal of male freedom best portrayed in 1950's Western films and pathetically reflected in the fantasies of Walter Mitty. In fact, it seems that critics' opinions regarding Thurber's attitudes about most subjects vary from one text to the next, but certain themes seem to remain consistent. His weak male characters do hate strong women, but the males are often weak because they accept the world in which their secret fantasies are necessary and, therefore, leave their women no choice but to try to hold things together. When a woman's strength becomes arrogance, as in "The Catbird Seat" and "The Unicorn in the Garden," the man often defeats her with the active power of his imagination. Characterizing Thurber as a romantic, Robert Morsberger lists some themes he sees pervading Thurber's writing: a perception of the oppression of technocracy and of the arrogance of popular scientism especially in their hostility to imagination; an antirational but not anti-intellectual approach to modern life; a belief in the power of the imagination to preserve human value in the face of contemporary forms of alienation; and a frequent use of fear and fantasy to overcome the dullness of his characters' (and readers') lives.

"THE SECRET LIFE OF WALTER MITTY"

"The Secret Life of Walter Mitty" is Thurber's best-known work of short fiction. Its protagonist, the milquetoast Walter Mitty, lives in a reverie consisting of situations in which he is a hero: commander of a navy hydroplane, surgeon, trial witness, bomber pilot, and condemned martyr. The dream is clearly an escape from the external life which humiliatingly interrupts it: his wife's mothering; the arrogant competence of a parking attendant and policeman; and the humiliating errands of removing tire chains, buying overshoes, and asking for puppy biscuits. In his dreams, he is Lord Jim, the misunderstood hero, "inscrutable to the last"; in his daily life he is a middle-aged husband enmeshed in a web of the humdrum. Tobias sees Mitty as ultimately triumphant over dreary reality. Blair and Hill see him as gradually losing grip of the real world and slipping into psychosis. Whether liberated or defeated by his imagination, Mitty is clearly incompetent and needs the mothering his wife gives him. Often described as an immoral and malicious woman, she is actually just the wife he needs and deserves; she seems to exist as a replacement ego to keep him from catching his death of cold as he somnambulates.

The story's artfulness is readily apparent in the precise choice and arrangement of details, such as sounds, objects, and images that connect fantasy and reality. The technical devices are virtually the same as those used by William Faulkner and Joyce to indicate shifts in levels of awareness in their "free-association internal monologues." Mitty has become a representative figure in modern culture, like T. S. Eliot's Prufrock and Faulkner's Quentin Compson, although perhaps more widely known. While many of Thurber's stories are similar to this one in theme and form, they are astonishingly diverse in subject, situation, and range of technique.

### "THE BLACK MAGIC OF BARNEY HALLER"

Another large group of Thurber stories might be characterized as fictionalized autobiography. One of the best of these sketches is "The Black Magic of Barney Haller" in *The Middle-Aged Man on the Flying Trapeze*. In this story, "Thurber" exorcises his hired man, a Teuton whom lightning and thunder always follow and who mutters imprecations such as "Bime by I go hunt grotches in de voods," and "We go to the garrick now and become warbs." The narrator becomes convinced that despite his stable and solid appearance, Barney is a necromancer who will transform reality with his incantations. At any moment, Barney will reveal his true devilish from and change "Thurber" into a warb or conjure up a grotch. It does not comfort him to

*James Thurber* (Library of Congress)

learn the probable prosaic meanings of Haller's spells, even to see the crotches placed under the heavy peach tree branches. At the end of the story, he feels regret that the only man he knows who could remove the wasps from his garret has departed.

The humor of these incidents is clear, and a humorous meaning emerges from them. The narrator would rather hide in *Swann's Way*, reading about a man who creates himself, but he feels threatened by the external supernatural power of another person's language to re-create the world. He first attempts exorcism with Robert Frost, well known for having successfully disposed of a hired man. He quotes "The Pasture" in an attempt to make the obscure clear, but succeeds only in throwing a fear that mirrors his own into Barney. This gives "Thurber" his clue; in the next attempt he borrows from Lewis Carroll and the American braggart tradition, asserting his own superior power as a magician of words, "Did you happen to know that the mome rath never lived that could outgrabe me?" The man with the superior control of language, the man of superior imagination, really is in control; he *can* become a playing card at will to frighten off black magicians. This story is typical of Thurber in its revelation of the fantastic in the commonplace, its flights of language play, and its concern for the relations among reality, self, imagination, and language.

### "THE MOTH AND THE STAR"

Also an author of fables, Thurber published two collections of fables. "The Moth and the Star" is a typical and often anthologized example. A moth spends a long life trying to reach a star, defying his disappointed parents' wish that he aspire normally to get himself scorched on a street lamp. Having outlived his family, he gains in old age "a deep and lasting pleasure" from the illusion that he has actually reached the distant star: "Moral: Who flies afar from the sphere of our sorrow is here today and here tomorrow." The moth and the star suggest images in Henry David Thoreau's *Walden: Or, Life in the Woods* (1854). The aspiring idealist who rejects the suicidal life of material accumulation and devotes himself to some perfect work ultimately conquers time and enriches life whether or not he produces any valuable object. Because the moth, like the artist of Kouroo, succeeds and is happy, this story seems more optimistic than *The Great Gatsby*. Many of Thurber's fables are more cynical or more whimsical, but all are rich in meaning and pleasure, like "The Moth and the Star."

Critics and scholars have noted ways in which Thurber's career and writings offer a parallel point of view similar to that of Percy Bysshe Shelley's *A Defence of Poetry* (1840). While "The Secret Life of Walter Mitty" and *Further Fables for Our Time* may be seen as affirming the view of modern life as a wasteland, the fairy tales suggest that the ash heap of modern culture is escapable. It seems especially significant that the mode of escape is represented in tales of magic in remote settings.

### THE WHITE DEER

*The White Deer* opens in the third period in King Clode's memory of waiting for the depleted game of his hunting grounds to replenish. The story develops in triads, the central one being the three perilous tasks set for the three sons of King Clode to determine which shall claim the hand of the fair princess who materializes when the king and his sons corner the fleet white deer in the enchanted forest. The sons complete their tasks simultaneously, but, in the meantime, King Clode determines that the nameless Princess is not a disenchanted woman but an enchanted deer. When the returned sons are told of this, Thag and Gallow refuse her. If denied love three times, she would be a deer forever, but Jorn accepts her: "What you have been, you are not, and what you are, you will forever be. I place this trophy in the hands of love. . . . You hold my heart." This acceptance transforms her into a new and lovelier princess, Rosanore of the Northland, and the April fragrance of lilacs fills the air suggesting direct opposition to the opening of Eliot's *The Waste Land:* "April is the cruellest month, breeding/ Lilacs out of the dead land." As King Clode later sees the full wisdom and beauty of Rosanore, he repeats, "I blow my horn in waste land." Echoes of Eliot show up repeatedly in the fairy tales, but the greater emphasis falls on the powers of love and imagination, which in this fairy world inevitably blossom in beauty and happiness.

The cast of secondary characters and the perilous labors provide opportunities to characterize wittily the world in need of magic. There is an incompetent palace wizard, as opposed to the true wizards of the forest, an astronomer-turned-clockmaker who envisions encroaching darkness ("It's darker than you think"), and a royal recorder who descends into mad legalese when the Princess's spell proves to be without precedent. Gallow's labor is especially interesting because he must make his way through a vanity fair bureaucracy in order to conquer a sham dragon, a task that tests his purse and persistence more than his love. This task allows a satire of the commercial values of modern culture. Each of the fairy tales contains similar delights as well as bizarre and beautiful flights of language: the Sphinz asks Jorn, "What is whirly?/ What is curly?/ Tell me, what is pearly early?" and in a trice, Jorn replies, "Gigs are whirly,/ Cues are curly/ and the dew is pearly early."

OTHER MAJOR WORKS

PLAYS: *The Male Animal*, pr., pb. 1940 (with Elliott Nugent); *Many Moons*, pb. 1943; *A Thurber Carnival*, pr. 1960 (revue).

NONFICTION: *The Thurber Album*, 1952; *The Years with Ross*, 1959; *Selected Letters of James Thurber*, 1982; *The Thurber Letters: The Wit, Wisdom, and Surprising Life of James Thurber*, 2003 (Harrison Kinney and Rosemary A. Thurber, editors).

BIBLIOGRAPHY

Bernstein, Burton. *Thurber: A Biography*. New York: Dodd, Mead, 1975. This authorized biography, written with the cooperation of Thurber's widow, provides a thorough survey of Thurber's life and career.

Bowden, Edwin T. *James Thurber: A Bibliography*. Columbus: Ohio State University Press, 1968. A complete listing of Thurber's published writings and drawings.

Fensch, Thomas. *The Man Who Was Walter Mitty: The Life and Work of James Thurber*. The Woodlands, Tex.: New Century Books, 2000. Fensch's biography relates Thurber to his fictional creations. Discusses how Thurber's writing was influenced by his domineering mother and by his colleagues E. B. White and Harold Ross.

Gelfant, Blanche H., ed. *The Columbia Companion to the Twentieth-Century American Short Story*. New York: Columbia University Press, 2000. Includes a chapter in which Thurber's short stories are analyzed.

Gottlieb, Robert. "The Years with Thurber." *The New Yorker* 79, no. 25 (September 8, 2003): 84-90. A profile of Thurber, providing biographical information and an overview of his career. Discusses his writing style, influences, and contemporaries.

Grauer, Neil A. *Remember Laughter: A Life of James Thurber*. Lincoln: University of Nebraska Press, 1994. A biography that examines the context of Thurber's work. Provides an interesting discussion of the background to the writing of "The Secret Life of Walter Mitty" and its reception when first published in *The New Yorker*.

Holmes, Charles S. *The Clocks of Columbus: The Literary Career of James Thurber*. New York: Atheneum, 1972. This literary biography devotes special attention to the relations between Thurber's Ohio background and his works. Supplemented by drawings, photographs, and a bibliography.

_____, ed. *Thurber: A Collection of Critical Essays*. Englewood Cliffs, N.J.: Prentice-Hall, 1974. A useful collection of twenty-five critical and biographical essays, as well as a chronology and a brief annotated bibliography.

Kaufman, Anthony. "'Things Close In': Dissolution and Misanthropy in 'The Secret Life of Walter Mitty.'" *Studies in American Fiction* 22 (Spring, 1994): 93-104. Discusses dissolution and misanthropy in the story. Argues that Mitty's withdrawal is symptomatic not of mild-mannered exasperation with a trivial world but of anger. Concludes that Mitty is the misanthrope demystified and made middle class the suburban man who, unable to imagine or afford the drama of a retreat into the wilderness, retreats inward.

Kenney, Catherine McGehee. *Thurber's Anatomy of Confusion*. Hamden, Conn.: Archon Books, 1984. A survey of Thurber's creative world, including analyses of his most characteristic works. Discusses *Fables for Our Time* and such stories as "The Greatest Man in the World" and "The Secret Life of Walter Mitty." Argues that the latter examines the impotent world of modern urban America, embodying all the elements of Thurber's fictional world.

Kinney, Harrison. *James Thurber: His Life and Times*. New York: Henry Holt, 1995. A biography that focuses largely on Thurber's relationship to the development of *The New Yorker* magazine. Discusses how Thurber made use of overheard conversation, wordplay, and literary allusions in his stories. Examines Thurber's obsession with the war between the sexes in his prose and cartoons.

Long, Robert Emmet. *James Thurber*. New York: Continuum, 1988. This biographical and critical study divides Thurber's works into drawings, fiction, autobiography, fables, fairy tales, and occasional pieces, devoting a chapter to each. Complemented by a bibliography.

Marshall, Gregory. "Ethics of Narrative in a Practical Vein Once More: Invitations to Misogyny in James Thurber's 'The Catbird Seat.'" In *Shaped by Stories: The Ethical Power of Narratives*. Notre Dame, Ind.: University of Notre Dame Press, 2009. Marshall argues that human beings are obsessed with narratives. He analyzes Thurber's short story "The Catbird Seat" and fiction by other writers to determine the ethical implications of these narratives for their readers.

Morsberger, Robert E. *James Thurber*. New York: Twayne, 1964. Morsberger sketches Thurber's life and then analyzes his works, looking at his contributions to various art forms and his characteristic themes. Contains a chronology of Thurber's life and a brief annotated bibliography.

Tobias, Richard Clark. *The Art of James Thurber*. Athens: Ohio University Press, 1970. Tobias studies Thurber's themes and worldview, with special attention to his methods and techniques of creating humor.

Updike, John. "Libido Lite." *The New York Review of Books* 51, no. 18 (November 18, 2004): 30-31. A review of Thurber and E. B. White's book *Is Sex Necessary?*

*Terry Heller*

# CHRISTOPHER TILGHMAN

**Born:** Boston, Massachusetts; September 5, 1946

PRINCIPAL SHORT FICTION

*In a Father's Place,* 1990

*The Way People Run,* 1999

OTHER LITERARY FORMS

In addition to his collections of short stories, Christopher Tilghman (TIHL-mehn) is the author of the novels *Mason's Retreat* (1996) and *Roads of the Heart* (2004).

ACHIEVEMENTS

Christopher Tilghman won a thirty thousand dollar Whiting Writers Award, given to "emerging writers of exceptional talent and promise," for *In a Father's Place*. He has also received a John Simon Guggenheim Memorial Foundation Fellowship and an Ingram Merrill Foundation Award.

BIOGRAPHY

Christopher Tilghman was born in Boston, Massachusetts, in 1946, the son of an executive for the publishing house Houghton Mifflin. He attended Fesenden School and St. Paul's Academy and received his B.A. from Yale University in 1968; during the summers while he was in college he worked in Montana. After graduation, Tilghman joined the U.S.

Navy. Three years later he moved to New England, took on freelance corporate writing, and built a house in rural northern Vermont, all the while writing fiction. His first public recognition came with his collection of stories *In a Father's Place*, which was featured on the cover of *The New York Times Book Review* in May, 1990. After teaching at Boston's Emerson College in the 1990s and participating in writing conferences, Tilghman taught in the writing program at the University of Virginia, eventually obtaining a tenured position there.

ANALYSIS

Christopher Tilghman's first book, *In a Father's Place*, filled with fictions that are like the later stories of Raymond Carver, fictions that Carver's mentor, John Gardner, champion of "moral fiction," would have endorsed wholeheartedly, marks the end of the so-called minimalism of the 1980's. Rather than challenging the foundations of Western culture, as absurdist stories of the 1960's did, or laying bare the basic mystery of individual human experience, as minimalist stories of the 1970's did, Tilghman's stories represent straightforward storytelling, firmly grounded in the conservative values most other contemporary short stories challenge. His second collection, *The Way People Run*, focuses on some of the same characters and many of the same longings for a lost center that his first collection does.

Tilghman holds up a set of basic American values of family and commitment against the rebellion of the 1960's, the deconstruction of the 1970's, and the "me" generation of the 1980's. Whether Tilghman's stories represent a general reaction against the self-reflexive and minimalist short fiction of the 1960's, 1970's, and 1980's, or whether they simply express one writer's personal convictions about the importance of traditional values, Tilghman is clearly more interested in moral truths and values than aesthetic ones.

### "ON THE RIVERSHORE"

This is not a story in which the fairly straightforward values of working-class men, landed gentry, and God-fearing women are questioned, probed, examined, or put to the test. A Chesapeake Bay fisherman kills a young man for annoying his daughter and gets help disposing of the body from friends who agree with him that the boy was basically no good. The story is told by a twelve-year-old boy who is the only witness to the killing by his own father of the troublemaker Tommie Todman. Instead of being placed in a wrenching conflict by this horror, the boy recites a litany of Tommie's offenses. As a man in the story says, Tommie has no family and no one cares what happens to him--all of which seems to justify sinking the boy's body in deep water with heavy blocks because that is what is best for the community. The story is not cold-blooded or heartless; it is simply coldly reasonable about what is of value and what is not.

### "HOLE IN THE DAY"

In this story, when Lonnie, a young wife in her twenties, finds out she is pregnant a fifth time--in spite of the fact that she is aging early and has told her husband she wants no more children--she decides to take it no longer and heads out across the midwestern plains to escape. The story, however, focuses on her husband Grant, who drops off three of the kids with family and friends and departs in his old pickup with the youngest, a baby of two years, in search of Lonnie. Never does he consider the individual needs of his wife; he only wants to find her so she can return to him. When he does find her, somehow she instantly realizes that she wants nothing else but Grant and her babies, although that decision has not been motivated by anything in the story except the general value system of home, family, and commitment that underlies Tilghman's fictional universe.

### "IN A FATHER'S PLACE"

One of the best stories in Tilghman's first collection is the title piece, for it is the most ambitious and potentially the most complex, even though ultimately it too asserts rather than questions the solid values of family and property on which the other stories are based. The story centers on Dan, an elderly patriarch of an old Chesapeake Bay family, who tries to come to terms with his children, Nick, who is writing a novel, and Rachel, who is planning to move to the state of Washington. Although Dan is worried about missing Rachel, his primary concern is with Nick, who has brought a strong-minded and domineering girlfriend, Patty Keith, home with him.

The primary metaphor for the conflict between the values of family and land represented by Dan and the iconoclastic vales of Patty Keith is Patty's urging Nick to write a novel influenced by her own interest in deconstructionist philosopher and literary critic Jacques Derrida. Patty is always reading Derrida during the visit (although Dan doubts she is really getting very far in the book) and tells Dan that the novel Nick is writing is intended to "deconstruct" his family. When Dan asks if she means "destroy," she condescendingly replies that "deconstruct" is a complicated literary term.

However, it is not such a complicated literary term as Tilghman uses it. The conflict here is basically and simply between the solidity of the old historical traditions and the threat to those traditions by modernist and postmodernist thought. In the end, the traditional wins out by the simple measure of the old patriarch kicking the interloper out of his house. With Patty sent away with Derrida under her arm, Dan wonders if Nick will also leave, never to return. Still, as he looks over his life, he feels a tide of joy rising over his mistakes and triumphs. Thus the story ends not only with the triumph of the traditional but also with the unquestioning celebration of that triumph.

### "LOOSE REINS" AND "ROOM FOR MISTAKES"

These two stories focus on Hal, who, after being raised on a ranch in Montana, becomes a well-to-do banker in the Northeast. In the first story, from *In a Father's Place*, he returns home two years after his father's death, when his mother marries one of the ranch hands. What the story is really about is Hal's having to come to terms with the realization that his father never really had time for him and that the old ranch hand, Roy, the living embodiment of the instinctive values of the "natural," is his true spiritual father.

"Room for Mistakes," from *The Way People Run*, is also a return-home-for-realization story; this time Hal is middle-aged, and the occasion is the death of his mother. He nostalgically remembers the pastoral simplicity of his childhood, rhapsodizes about the hope for renewal in the heart of America, and considers following the "dream-pull back to boyhood" by staying in Montana, although his mother's will has denied him the ranch. There is some vacillating indecision at the end of both of these stories--about whether to affirm or deny the father in the first one and whether to embrace and desert the land in the second--but there is no irony about the nostalgic pull of the past or the romantic allure of place in either of them. At the end of the story, Roy affirms the hope of the title, telling Hal that there is "room for mistakes" living naturally on the land, for there are "mercies" all though it.

### "THE WAY PEOPLE RUN"

In many ways the title story of Tilghman's second collection, perhaps because it is less straightforward than most of the other stories, is the purest and most thoughtful example of his use of the short-story genre. Barry, the protagonist is driving east across the country, on the way home to face his wife, his child, and numerous unpaid and unpayable bills. Stopping at a run-down western town on the plains, he becomes fascinated with the pull of permanence and place.

The center of this magnetism is a beat-up café where he has a casual conversation with the waitress, but the simple act of returning to the restaurant and having her remember what kind of beer he drinks makes him feel "utterly, extravagantly at home." Later, when she offers to rent him a spare bedroom, he puts his wife, child, and responsibilities out of his mind, and, against all reason, rents the room. By the time he and the waitress have sex, he has become so infatuated with the idea of being "at home" in the small town that, when the waitress talks about his leaving, he talks about finding a place and staying. Whether this is a momentary hallucinatory reaction or whether it is a realistic possibility is the culminating ambiguity that refuses to

be as simple and straightforward as many of Tilghman's fictions. The story ends with a haunting metaphor: a deserted school bus on the side of the road that makes Barry stop on his way out of town. In the final image, he stands on the vast "ownerless domain" of the prairie, wondering if this is the way such things happen, "the way people run."

### OTHER MAJOR WORKS

LONG FICTION: *Mason's Retreat*, 1996; *Roads of the Heart*, 2004.

### BIBLIOGRAPHY

Arana-Ward, Marie. "Christopher Tilghman." *The Washington Post*. June 16, 1996, p. X10. An interview/biographical sketch in which Tilghman talks about growing up surrounded by a sense of family and history. Tilghman also discusses his education, his stint in the Navy, and his long apprenticeship trying to learn to write.

Elder, Richard. "The Flash and Fragility of Revolt." *Los Angeles Times Book Review*, April 29, 1990, 3. Elder says that Tilghman's characters in *In a Father's Place* are value-seekers who care a lot and prize their caring. He discusses several of the stories, particularly "Hole in the Day," in which Elder says that Tilghman does what only a true storyteller can do--make the impossible inevitable.

Gilbert, Matthew. "Flight from the Sad Past Toward Epiphany." *The Boston Globe*. May 23, 1999, p. D2. A review of *The Way People Run* that argues that Tilghman creates a world that is both organic and spiritual, where men are interconnected with the family members from whom they run. Notes that once again Tilghman focuses on people who are facing unwanted feelings as they revisit a family home, but that more than those in his first collection these stories showcase his intuitive sense of the speed at which human feeling moves.

Hulbert, Ann. "*In a Father's Place*." *The New Republic* 202 (June 4, 1990): 40. An extensive and detailed review of *In A Father's Place* that praises the stories for their transcendent impulse that returns the characters to the world in their epiphanies rather than taking them away from it. Discusses the importance of place, plot, and history in the stories.

Kakutani, Michiko. "Going Home Again and Finding You Can't." *The New York Times*. April 3, 1990, p. C17. A review of *In a Father's Place* that calls Tilghman a gifted new writer and the book a radiant new collection. Discusses Tilghman's theme of a man or woman returning to a family home, tracing the hold that childhood memories and a familial past exert on them. Says that Tilghman has the ability to compress a characters's life into a couple of pages and to delineate the complexities and complications of familial love.

Lyons, Bonnie, and Bill Oliver. "Places and Visions." *Literary Review* 38 (Winter, 1995): 244-56. A detailed, extensive interview with Tilghman in which he discusses the relationship between his fiction and his own family, the importance of place in his stories, and the need for compassionate empathy to be a good writer. Tilghman says that one reason he writes is to grapple with the "holy mysteries," those things that do not make sense but seem to be always present. He affirms his preference for old-fashioned, nineteenth century storytelling with a strong plot.

Payne, Doug. "Small Stories, Big Windows." *The San Diego Union- Tribune*. May 16, 1999, p. B8. A review of *The Way People Run* that argues that Tilghman focuses on family history, individual careers, and the influence of community in the expansive way readers usually associate with novels. Claims that Tilghman does not so much sum up as let dramatic moments resonate with ordinary experiences over the long run.

Smith, Linell. "Writing Home: Since His First Book, Author Christopher Tilghman Has Looked Toward His Family's Ancestral Farm on the Eastern Shore for Comfort and Inspiration." *Baltimore Sun*, November 8, 2004, p. 1C. A profile of Tilghman, providing details of his biography and literary career. Points out similarities between his personal life and the plot of his second novel *Roads of the Heart*.

Tilghman, Christopher. "Interview: Christopher Tilghman Discusses His New Novel, *Roads of the Heart*." Interview by Brian Naylor. *Weekend All Things Considered*, August 1, 2004, p. 1. The transcript of an interview that aired on National Public Radio (NPR), in which Tilghman discusses the process of writing his second novel.

*Charles E. May*

# JEAN TOOMER

**Born:** Washington, D.C.; December 26, 1894
**Died:** Doylestown, Pennsylvania; March 30, 1967
**Also known as:** Eugene Pinchback Toomer

PRINCIPAL SHORT FICTION

*Cane,* 1923 (prose and poetry)
*"Mr. Costyve Duditch,"* 1928
*"York Beach,"* 1929
*The Wayward and the Seeking,* 1980 (prose and poetry; Darwin T. Turner, editor)

OTHER LITERARY FORMS

All of Jean Toomer's best fiction appears in *Cane,* which also includes fifteen poems. Toomer later wrote fragments of an autobiography and several essays, the most important of which are found in *Essentials: Definitions and Aphorisms* (1931).

ACHIEVEMENTS

Jean Toomer's *Cane,* published in 1923, is considered to be one of the masterpieces of experimental fiction and one of the most important and relevant evocations of African American life in the twentieth century. Toomer's book was rediscovered in the late 1960's after it was reprinted in 1967. *Cane* is represented in most anthologies of American literature, guaranteeing the author a distinguished place in American literary history.

BIOGRAPHY

Born Nathan Eugene Toomer in Washington, D.C., on December 26, 1894, Jean Toomer received his education at the University of Wisconsin and the City College of New York. He began writing and was published in the little magazines of his time before moving to the South to become a schoolteacher in rural Georgia, an experience which he uses as source material in "Kabnis," the final part of *Cane.* Married twice to whites, Toomer was often equivocal about his blackness, partially because of his involvement in Unitism, the philosophy of George Ivanovitch Gurdjieff. Toomer's later essays and stories expound his version of the philosophy and are often weakened by an excess of mystery and a deficiency of manners. In later life, he lived among the Quakers in Pennsylvania. Toomer died in 1967.

ANALYSIS

Divided into three parts, Jean Toomer's *Cane* consists of short stories, sketches, poems, and a novella. The first section focuses on women; the second on relationships between men and women; and the third on one man. Although capable of being read discretely, these works achieve their full power when read together, coalescing to create a novel, unified by theme and symbol.

### CANE

Like all Toomer's work, *Cane* describes characters who have, within their buried lives, a dream that seeks expression and fulfillment; *Cane* is a record of the destruction of those dreams. Sometimes the dreams explode, the fire within manifesting itself violently; more often, however, the world implodes within the dreamer's mind. These failures have external causes--the inadequacy or refusal of society to allow expression, the restrictions by what Toomer calls the herd--and internal ones--the fears and divisions within the dreamers themselves, as they struggle unsuccessfully to unite will and mind, passion and intellect, what Toomer in the later story, "York Beach," calls the wish for brilliant experience and the wish for difficult experience.

The one limitation on the otherwise thoroughgoing romanticism of this vision is Toomer's rigorous separation of humankind into those who dream and are worth bothering about, and those who do not. While the struggle of Toomer's characters is for unity, it is to unify themselves or to find union with one other dreamer, never to merge with man in general. Like Kabnis, many find their true identity in recognizing their differences, uniqueness, and superiority. At the end of "York Beach," the protagonist tells his listeners that the best government would be an empire ruled by one who recognized his own greatness.

Toomer's dreamers find themselves in the first and third sections of *Cane* in a southern society which, although poor in compassion and understanding, is rich in supportive imagery. In the second part, set in the North, that imagery is also absent, so the return of the protagonist to the South in part 3 is logical, since the North has not provided a nurturing setting. Although the return may be a plunge back into hell, it is also a journey to an underground where Kabnis attains the vision that sets him free.

The imagery is unified by a common theme: ascent. Kabnis says, "But its the soul of me that needs the risin," and all the imagery portrays the buried life smoldering within, fighting upward, seeking release. The dominant image of the book, the one that supplies the title, is the rising sap of the sugarcane. Cane whispers enigmatic messages to the characters, and it is to cane fields that people seeking escape and release flee. Sap rises, too, in pines, which also whisper and sing; and at the mill of part 1, wood burns, its smoke rising. The moon in "Blood-Burning Moon" is said to "sink upward," an oxymoronic yoking that implies the difficulty of "the risin" in this book.

A second pattern of imagery is that of flowing blood or water, although generally in the pessimistic *Cane*, water is not abundant. In "November Cotton Flower," dead birds are found in the wells, and when water is present, the characters, threatened by the life it represents, often fear it. Rhobert, in a sketch of that name, wears a diver's helmet to protect him from water, life which is being drawn off. Dreams denied, blood flows more freely than water.

### "ESTHER"

"Esther," the most successful story in *Cane*, comes early and embodies many of the book's major themes. It opens with a series of four sentences describing Esther as a girl of nine. In each, the first clause compliments her beauty, the second takes the praise away; the first clauses of each are progressively less strong.

Esther represents the destruction of potential by a combination of inner and outer forces. On the outside there is her father, "the richest colored man in town," who reduces Esther to a drab and obsequious life behind a counter in his dry goods store. "Her hair thins. It looks like the dull silk on puny corn ears." Then there is King Barlo, a black giant, who has a vision in the corner of town known as the Spittoon. There, while townspeople gather to watch (and black and white preachers find momentary unity in working out ways to rid themselves of one who threatens their power), Barlo sees a strong black man arise. While the man's head is in the clouds, however, "little white-ant biddies come and tie his feet to chains." The herd in Barlo's vision, as in Toomer's, may destroy the dreamer.

Many, however, are affected by what Barlo has seen, none more so than Esther, who decides that she loves him. The fire begins to burn within. As she stands dreaming in her store, the sun on the windows across the street reflect her inner fire, and, wanting to make it real, Esther calls the fire department. For the next

*Jean Toomer* (Bettmann/CORBIS)

eighteen years, Esther, the saddest of all Toomer's women, lives only on dreams, inventing a baby, conceived, she thinks, immaculately. Sometimes, like many of his characters, sensing that life may be too much for her, knowing that "emptiness is a thing that grows by being moved," she tries not to dream, sets her mind against dreaming, but the dreams continue.

At the end of the story, Esther, then twenty-seven, decides to visit Barlo, who has returned to town. She finds the object of her dream in a room full of prostitutes; what rises is only the fumes of liquor. "Conception with a drunken man must be a mighty sin," she thinks, and, when she attempts to return to reality, she, like many Toomer characters, finds that the world has overwhelmed her. Crushed from without, she has neither life nor dreams. "There is no air, no street, and the town has completely disappeared."

### "BLOOD-BURNING MOON"

So, too, in "Blood-Burning Moon," Toomer's most widely anthologized short story and also from the woman-centered first section of *Cane*, is the main character destroyed emotionally. Here, however, the destructive force is primarily internal. Among the most conventional of Toomer's stories, "Blood-Burning Moon" has both a carefully delineated plot and a familiar one at that: a love triangle. What shows creative invention is the way Toomer manages the reader's feelings about the woman whom two men love. Both men are stereotypes. Bob Stone is white and repulsively so. Divided within himself and content to be, he makes his mind consciously white and approaches Louisa "as a master should." The black, Tom Burwell, is a stereotype too: Having dreams, he expresses his love sincerely, but inarticulately; when denied or threatened, he expresses himself violently.

The first two sections open with rhythmic sentences beginning with the word "up"; Louisa sings songs against the omen the rising moon portends, seeking charms and spells, but refusing the simple act of choosing between the two men. Because Louisa does not choose, the story comes to its inevitable violent climax and the death of both men. There is more, however: When Louisa is last seen, she has also been destroyed, mentally, if not physically. She sings again to the full moon as an omen, hoping that people will join

her, hoping that Tom Burwell will come; but her choice is too late. Burwell is dead, and the lateness of her decision marks the end of her dreams. Like Esther, she is separated from even appropriate mental contact with the world that is.

### CANE, SECTION 2

Barlo's vision in "Esther," then, is accurate but incomplete as a description of what happens to Toomer's protagonists. While it is true that the herd will often destroy the dreamer, it is just as likely that the dreamer, from inaction, fear, and division, will destroy himself. The four stories of section 2 all focus on pairs of dreamers who can isolate themselves from the rest of society but who cannot get their dreams to merge. In "Avey" it is the man who, focused on his own dreams, refuses to listen to and accept the value of Avey's. In "Bona and Paul," Paul, a black man, takes Bona away from the dance, not, as everyone assumes, to make love to her, but to know her; in the end, knowing another human being is denied him because Bona assumes she already knows him, "a priori," as he has said. Knowing he is black, she "knows" that he will be passionate. When he is interested in knowledge before passion, she discovers that to know a priori is not to know at all and flees him, denying his dream of knowing her.

In "Theater" the divided main character, sitting half in light, half in shadow, watches another dreamer, the dancer on stage, Dorris. She is dreaming of him, but although "mind pulls him upward into dream," suspicion is stronger than desire, and by the end of the story John has moved wholly into shadow. When Dorris looks at him, "She finds it a dead thing in the shadow which is his dream." Likewise, in "Box Seat" Muriel is torn between the dreamer Dan, who stands with one hand lying on the wall, feeling from below the house the deep underground rumbling of the subway, literal buried life, and Mrs. Pribby, the landlady, rattling her newspaper, its thin noise contrasting with the powerful below-ground sound. Muriel chooses respectability. At the theater, to which Dan has followed her, she is repelled by a dwarf who offers her a rose; Dan rises to his feet to proclaim that Jesus was once a leper. This last, insistent image, suggesting the maimed sources of beauty that Muriel is too timid to accept, also indicates the overexplicit inflation of claims that damages some of Toomer's fiction. Although in *Cane* most of the stories are under control, some seem rather too sketchy; "Box Seat," however, foreshadows the fault that mars all of Toomer's later fiction: the sacrifice of dramatic ideas in favor of, often pallid, philosophical ones.

### "KABNIS"

The last and longest story in *Cane* integrates the themes, making explicit the nature of the destructive forces. The story is "Kabnis," and the force is sin, a word contained backward in Kabnis's name. It is the story of a black man out of place in the rural South, threatened not so much by whites as by his own people, by his environment, and by his sense of himself.

As the story opens, Kabnis is trying to sleep, but he is not allowed this source of dream; instead, chickens and rats, nature itself, keep him awake. He wants to curse it, wants it to be consistent in its ugliness, but he also senses the beauty of nature, and because that perception prevents him from hating it entirely, he feels that even beauty is a curse. Intimidated by nature, Kabnis is also attacked by society, by the local black church, where the shouting acclamations of faith torture Kabnis, and by the black school superintendent who fires him for drinking. As in "Box Seat," the protagonist is thus caught between expressions of life, which are too strong for him, and its repression, which traps him. Kabnis, like Rhobert, is a man drowning, trying vainly to avoid the source of life. From this low point, for the only time in the book, Toomer describes the way up, and Kabnis gains enough strength to throw off his oppression.

He has three friends: Halsey, an educated black who has been playing Uncle Tom; Layman, a preacher, whose low voice suggests a canebrake; and Lewis, a doppelgänger who suggests a version of what a stronger Kabnis might have become and who drops out of the story when Kabnis does indeed become stronger. Once fired, Kabnis takes up residence with Halsey, a Vulcan-like blacksmith who gives him work repairing implements, work for which Kabnis is ill-suited. In his basement, however, Halsey has his own buried life, an old man, Father John, and in the climactic scene, the three men descend into the underground for a dark night of the soul, for the Walpurgisnacht on which Kabnis confronts his own demons. Prefiguring the descents in

such black fiction as Richard Wright's "Man Who Lived Underground" and Ralph Ellison's *Invisible Man* (1952), this is likewise a descent during which the values of the world above, met on unfamiliar terrain, are rethought. It is a night of debauchery, but also the night when the destructive illusions and fears of the men are exposed.

Father John represents those fears; when he speaks, his message is sin. Kabnis knows, and for the first time can say, that because of sin the old man has never seen the beauty of the world. Kabnis has, and as he says, "No eyes that have seen beauty ever lose their sight." Kabnis then proclaims a new role for himself: If he is not a blacksmith, he may be, having known beauty, a wordsmith. "I've been shapin words after a design that branded here. Know whats here? M soul." If sin is what is done against the soul and if the soul of Kabnis is what needs the rising, then, as Kabnis says, the world has conspired against him. Now, however, Kabnis acknowledges and confronts that conspiracy, no longer fearing it or Father John. Exhausted by his effort, Kabnis sinks back, but Halsey's sister, Carrie K, does indeed carry K (Kabnis); she lifts Kabnis up, and together they ascend the stairs into the daylight, as the risen sun sings a "birth-song" down the streets of the town.

The end is not unequivocally optimistic: It is too small and too tentative a note in this large catalog of the defeated and destroyed. *Cane* does, however, suggest finally that as destructive as dreams may be, once people have seen beauty, if they can free themselves from repression, from sin, they may re-create themselves. "Kabnis is me," wrote Toomer to writer Waldo Frank, and he had more in mind than just his use of his experiences. For what Toomer has done in *Cane* is to chart the varieties of sin that society has inflicted upon and, more important, since individuals are always more interesting than society to Toomer, that people have inflicted upon themselves. Wholeness is the aim, a wholeness that breaks down barriers between mind and will, man and woman, object and subject, and that allows the potential of dreams to be fulfilled. That the wholeness is so difficult to achieve is the substance of Toomer's short fiction; that Toomer achieves it, both for a character in "Kabnis" and more permanently in his only successful work, a book uniting fiction and poetry, songs and narration, images of fire and water, of descent and ascent, is his testimony that wholeness can be achieved by those who dream of it.

OTHER MAJOR WORKS

PLAY: *Balo*, pb. 1927.

POETRY: "Banking Coal," 1922; "Blue Meridian," 1936; *The Collected Poems of Jean Toomer*, 1988.

NONFICTION: "Race Problems and Modern Society," 1929; "Winter on Earth," 1929; *Essentials: Definitions and Aphorisms*, 1931; "The Flavor of Man," 1949; *Jean Toomer: Selected Essays and Literary Criticism*, 1996 (Robert B. Jones, editor); *The Letters of Jean Toomer, 1919-1924*, 2006 (Mark Whalan, editor); *Brother Mine: The Correspondence of Jean Toomer and Waldo Frank*, 2010 (Kathleen Pfeiffer, editor).

MISCELLANEOUS: *A Jean Toomer Reader: Selected Unpublished Writings*, 1993 (Frederik L. Rusch, editor).

BIBLIOGRAPHY

Bone, Robert. *Down Home: A History of Afro-American Short Fiction from Its Beginnings to the End of the Harlem Renaissance*. New York: Capricorn Books, 1975. Argues that the theater in Toomer's story "The Theater" is an emblem of the two-way, reciprocal relationship of life and art, for there is an osmotic relationship between the life outside and the show inside. "Art-as-transfiguration" is Toomer's theme here; he is concerned with the death of experience and its rebirth as art.

Byrd, Rudolph. *Jean Toomer's Years with Gurdijieff: Portrait of an Artist, 1923-1936*. Athens: University of Georgia Press, 1990. A good introduction to Toomer's years of studying orientalism and the mystical philosophy of George Ivanovitch Gurdjieff. Byrd indicates that, although Toomer was an African American writer, his concerns were primarily spiritual and philosophical rather than social and ethnic. A fascinating account of one part of Toomer's life.

_____. "Was He There with Them?" In *The Harlem Renaissance: Reevaluations*. New York: Garland, 1989. Examines Toomer's tenuous relationship with the writers of the Harlem Renaissance. Argues that while Toomer identified with many of the issues and social concerns being addressed by African American writers, his style, techniques, and philosophy made him something of an outsider and gave him a unique position among the major African American writers of the 1920's.

Fabre, Geneviève, and Michel Feith, eds. *Jean Toomer and the Harlem Renaissance*. New Brunswick, N.J.: Rutgers University Press, 2001. A collection of essays that examine Toomer's works, placing him among his contemporaries in America and in Europe. Several of the essays analyze *Cane*, discussing the work in relation to modernism and race in interwar America and its depiction of "the politics of passing," preaching and dreaming, and the myth of belonging.

Ford, Karen Jackson. *Split-Gut Song: Jean Toomer and the Poetics of Modernity*. Tuscaloosa: University of Alabama Press, 2005. Analyzes *Cane* and some of Toomer's other works to describe how his experiments in literary form changed the modern depiction of race.

Griffin, John Chandler. *Biography of American Author Jean Toomer, 1894-1967*. Lewiston, N.Y.: Edwin Mellen Press, 2002. Comprehensive biography of Toomer that focuses on his life, including his relationships with writer Waldo Frank and Armenian mystic George Ivanovitch Gurdjieff.

Hajek, Friederike. "The Change of Literary Authority in the Harlem Renaissance: Jean Toomer's *Cane*." In *The Black Columbiad: Defining Moments in African American Literature and Culture*, edited by Werner Sollos and Maria Diedrich. Cambridge, Mass.: Harvard University Press, 1994. Argues that one of the main unifying elements in *Cane* is the concept of changing authority, which occurs in three phrases corresponding to the three sections of the text. Maintains that the work is a swan song for a dying folk culture and a birth chant for a new black aesthetic.

Jones, Robert B. Introduction to *The Collected Poems of Jean Toomer*. Edited by Robert B. Jones and Margery Toomer Latimer. Chapel Hill: University of North Carolina Press, 1988. Although this book is not about Toomer's fiction, the introduction gives an excellent account of Toomer's life and work within the context of the various phases of his writing and philosophical studies. In addition, it discusses the authors and poets who influenced Toomer's life and writings.

Kerman, Cynthia. *The Lives of Jean Toomer: A Hunger for Wholeness*. Baton Rouge: Louisiana State University Press, 1988. Recounts the various stages of Toomer's life and his attempts to find spiritual guidance and revelation throughout his lifetime. An interesting account of a fascinating life.

Moore, Lewis D. "Kabnis and the Reality of Hope: Jean Toomer's *Cane*." *North Dakota Quarterly* 54 (Spring, 1986): 30-39. Discusses the elements of "hope" within the context of the characters in *Cane*. In particular, Moore indicates that despite the repressive aspects of the society in which they live, Toomer's characters are redeemed and indeed triumph over that society by virtue of the positive aspects of their humanity.

Scruggs, Charles, and Lee VanDemarr. *Jean Toomer and the Terrors of American History*. Philadelphia: University of Pennsylvania Press, 1998. Provides a critical evaluation of *Cane* and other works by Toomer. Includes a biography and an index.

Taylor, Paul Beekman. *Shadows of Heaven*. York Beach, Maine.: S. Weiser, 1998. Examines the lives and works of Toomer, George Ivanovitch Gurdjieff, and A. R. Orage.

Wagner-Martin, Linda. "Toomer's *Cane* as Narrative Sequence." In *Modern American Short Story Sequences*, edited by J. Gerald Kennedy. Cambridge, England: Cambridge University Press, 1995. Discusses *Cane* as a modernist tour de force of mixed genre. Examines "Blood-Burning Moon" as Toomer's ideal fictional construct, providing insight into the structural and thematic radicalism of the collection.

Whalan, Mark. *Race, Manhood, and Modernism in America: The Short Story Cycles of Sherwood Anderson and Jean Toomer*. Knoxville: University of Tennessee Press, 2007. Compares the works of Toomer with Sherwood Anderson, focusing on *Cane* and on Anderson's story cycle *Winesberg, Ohio*. Describes how Toomer conceived a new type of manhood that altered traditional concepts of racial identity. Compares Anderson, Toomer, and writer Waldo Frank's depictions of the South.

*Howard Faulkner*
*Updated by Earl Paulus Murphy*

# WELLS TOWER

**Born:** Vancouver, Canada; April 14, 1973

PRINCIPAL SHORT FICTION
*Everything Ravaged, Everything Burned,* 2009

## OTHER LITERARY FORMS

In addition to his short fiction, Wells Tower is well known as the author of numerous long-form nonfiction essays, in which he immerses himself in various subcultures, such as young Republicans, traveling carnival workers, homeless soccer players, and professional miniature golf players. These essays have been published in *Harper's, The Washington Post Magazine, Outside, The Believer*, and other notable magazines.

## ACHIEVEMENTS

Since the beginning of his career, Wells Tower has been recognized as a promising American voice. The first story Tower ever wrote, "The Brown Coast," was awarded the 2002 Plimpton (Discovery) Prize by *The Paris Review.* Tower's first collection, *Everything Ravaged, Everything Burned,* was a finalist for the Story Prize and was named one of the ten best books of 2009 by *The New York Times.* Following its publication, *The Village Voice* crowned Tower the Best Young Writer of 2009.

In 2010, Tower was included on *The New Yorker's* "Twenty under Forty," a list of promising fiction writers under the age of forty, and presented with the New York Public Library's Young Lions Fiction award, an annual prize for an American writer younger than age forty. Tower also has won two Pushcart Prizes (for "Everything Ravaged, Everything Burned" in 2004 and "Retreat" in 2009) and a Henfield Foundation Award. Tower's story "Raw Water" (originally published in *McSweeney's*) was included in the 2010 edition of *Best American Short Stories.* He was the 2010-2011 David S. Ferriero Fellow at the New York Public Library.

## BIOGRAPHY

Wells Tower was born in Vancouver, Canada, on April 14, 1973, but he was raised in Chapel Hill, North Carolina. He was named after Wells Kerr, a legendary dean of students at Phillips Exeter Academy. His father is a Duke economics professor, and his mother is a high school Latin teacher. Tower calls the area he grew up in the "exurbs," a well-do-to progressive town in an isolated rural area. Tower attended Chapel Hill High School and received a B.A. in anthropology and sociology from Wesleyan University in 1996. Following his graduation from Wesleyan, Tower played lead guitar for Hellbender, a punk band he formed with several high school friends, and he worked a series of odd jobs in Louisiana, Maryland, Oregon, and Maine before returning to North Carolina, where he began freelancing for independent weekly newspapers.

Tower later was hired as the night manager of *DoubleTake*, a now-defunct literature and photography magazine once affiliated with the Center for Documentary Studies at Duke. Although Tower describes his initial position as little more than a glorified night watchman, he began writing press releases for the magazine and was eventually put in charge of its Web site. When *DoubleTake* was relocated to Boston, Tower followed one of its former editors, David Rowell, to *The Washington Post Magazine*, where, despite having no journalism experience, Tower convinced Rowell to assign him long-form reported pieces.

In 2000, Tower enrolled in the M.F.A. program at Columbia University, where he studied with Ben Marcus. In the fall of 2001, Tower published his first story, "Down in the Valley," in *The Paris Review* while still enrolled at Columbia. Another story, "The Brown Coast," was subsequently published in the spring, 2002, issue of *The Paris Review*, where it was awarded the 2002 Plimpton (Discovery) Prize.

However, following his graduation from Columbia, Tower decided to return to journalism. Although some of Tower's short stories were published in various publications, his focus for the next few years was journalism for *The Washington Post Magazine, Harper's*, and *Outside*. In 2007, Tower decided to return to fiction (though he has continued to write nonfiction). His first short-story collection, *Everything Ravaged, Everything Burned*, was published in 2009 to great acclaim. Since then, Tower has been recognized as one of the most promising young writers in the United States. In 2009, Tower settled in Brooklyn, dividing his time between New York and Chapel Hill.

ANALYSIS

Much of Wells Tower's short fiction concerns the experiences of the American blue-collar worker. Tower's protagonists are frequently men, who are down on their luck and fleeing the disappointments of middle age: broken marriages, unsatisfying jobs. Everything about the world of Tower's stories is faded and worn, from the character's hopes to the furniture in their houses. Working within the southern gothic tradition of such writers as Barry Hannah and Larry Brown, Tower often writes about class conflicts, his blue-collar antiheroes frequently clashing with more refined and progressive antagonists. Nearly obsolete relics, Tower's characters are searching constantly for a bit of hope, tranquillity, stability, or peace in the desolation of their lives.

In their search, Tower mines the emotional power of their uncomfortable conversations, strained relationships, and the sudden acts of violence that plague their lives. A recurring theme in Tower's work is difficulties between fathers and sons and between brothers, relationships where both males circle each other in primal (and often Oedipal) competition. Resisting theses and psychoanalyzing, Tower populates his character's interior lives with detailed descriptions of their tools and practices. Nearly crippled by their lives, it is clear that these are men and women who take pride in their work but find little solace in it.

Though Tower rarely offers his protagonists the peace and contentment they are searching for, his stories frequently feature epiphanic views of nature,

reminders that the world is much larger and more wonderful than previously imagined. Avoiding sentimentality, Tower tends to focus his sharp eye on the uncanny and the grotesque elements of nature. Tower's descriptions of the natural world are not always beautiful, but they are consistently wondrous, offering his characters what they need the most: a sense of their place in the world. In the process, Tower offers a panoramic view of America in all its splendor and disappointment.

**"THE BROWN COAST"**

In the first story Tower ever wrote, while he was still a graduate student at Columbia University, his fascination with the curdled middle class is already present. The middle-aged protagonist finds himself adrift after a string of bad luck events and poor decisions. Retreating to his uncle's cottage on a brown, unhappy island off the coast of Florida, Bob finds solace in filling an empty aquarium with the sea life he comes across on the island. Watching the tropical fish swim, he finds a sense of calm his life has been missing. This contentment, however, cannot last; at the conclusion of the story a

*Wells Tower* (Getty Images)

poisonous sea cucumber mistakenly is put into the aquarium with the fish. Surveying the menagerie floating on the surface of the tank the next morning, Bob begins to feel an affinity to the sea cucumber; they both can't help but poison everything they touch.

This sense of failure and desperation is a motif that runs through many of Tower's stories. His characters are rarely cruel or hateful people, they don't mean to ruin lives. Nevertheless, they consistently do the wrong thing. In "The Brown Coast," the trouble begins after the death of Bob's father. Overwhelmed by anger and confusion, Bob builds a faulty staircase and promptly is fired from his carpentry job after the homeowner is seriously injured. Already preoccupied by his worries, Bob then rear-ends a lawyer, who sues him for more money than Bob inherited from his father. Desperate, Bob eventually seeks comfort in an ultimately joyless affair that his wife discovers when she sees a woman's footprint on the windshield of his car. In short order, Bob has lost his father, his job, his inheritance, and his wife. Even though the reader can see where Bob has gone wrong, the poor choices he has made, Bob cannot. He seems almost helpless, convinced that every choice he makes will make matters only worse.

### "RETREAT"

Stephen and Matthew, the two estranged brothers at the center of "Retreat," have a similar inability to understand how they are responsible for the sad lives they are living. Matthew, the older brother, is twice divorced and living in an isolated mountain cabin in Maine, while Stephen, the younger brother, is a struggling musician living in near poverty in Oregon, his only companion a dying collie he must help urinate by performing the Heimlich maneuver on it nightly. When Matthew drunkenly invites Stephen to stay at his cabin for the weekend, the two brothers find themselves descending into an infantile display of sibling rivalry, each refusing to take responsibility for their strained relationship. What should have been a weekend of understanding and bonding instead quickly becomes a competition for the attention and respect of Matthew's outdoorsman neighbor. The story ends with Matthew forcing himself to eat the diseased meat of a moose he had shot earlier in the day, refusing to allow his minor victory against his

brother to be spoiled. Again, as in "The Brown Coast," the reader is left with a protagonist confronting a real symbol of his inner decay and ruin.

When "Retreat" was originally published in *McSweeney's* in 2007, Tower had written the story from the point of view of Stephen. Revising it for *Everything Ravaged, Everything Burned*, Tower shifted the point of view to the older brother, Matthew. While the plot of the story is more or less unchanged, by shifting the perspective from the more sympathetic brother to the less sympathetic brother, Tower's revision provides a new depth to his story. By hearing the story from Matthew's point of view, the reader is able to better empathize with Matthew, who came off as crass and unlikable in the original version. For a true understanding of the story, it is essential to read both versions; only then does the true picture of the brothers unfold.

### "ON THE SHOW"

Much of Tower's work exhibits his considerable skill as a journalist. "On the Show" is one such example. Drawn from the notes Tower took when he went undercover as a "carny" in a 2000 article for *The Washington Post Magazine*, Tower manages to transform his personal experience into a multifaceted account of a traveling carnival from several diverse points of view. Centering on the sexual assault of a young boy, Tower moves among two single parents on a first date, the gargantuan operator of a ride known as the Pirate and his lecherous assistant, a newly homeless young man just joining "the show," and the judge of the livestock competition. Weaving these narratives together, Tower provides a singular portrait of one night at a traveling carnival. Much larger and more ambitious in scope than any of the other stories collected in *Everything Ravaged, Everything Burned*, "On the Show" demonstrates Tower's talent for creating entire worlds in his fiction. Though Tower's consistent themes of working-class disappointment still populate the story, Tower structures the story as a mystery. It is not until the end of the story that the reader learns the identity of the young boy's assailant; once revealed, Tower makes readers confront their prejudices and assumptions about the divide between "carny folk" and the rest of us.

## "EVERYTHING RAVAGED, EVERYTHING BURNED"

Although Tower primarily writes realist stories with commonplace characters set in a recognizable present, one of his best-known and most celebrated stories, "Everything Ravaged, Everything Burned," concerns the comical trials of a group of aging Vikings. Goaded out of their quiet retirements and convinced to participate in one final raid of a distant land, they meditate on the implications of their violent pasts. As the battle begins, the middle-aged warriors find themselves disillusioned by warfare and horrified by the bloodlust of the younger men they have brought with them. As the town is razed around them, the older Vikings abandon the battle, taking advantage of the hospitality of the local peasants. The next day, with nothing to show for their efforts, the Vikings agree to row back to their homeland, eager to return to their families and retire, hoping that this will be the end of their lives as warriors.

Although this story is unique within Tower's fiction for its setting and its absurdist tone, it is nonetheless true to Tower's concerns. At its heart, "Everything Ravaged, Everything Burned" is another of Tower's stories about luckless men yearning for a simplicity they are unlikely to achieve. The aging Vikings of "Everything Ravaged, Everything Burned" yearn for the same sort of quiet stability for which Tower's blue-collar protagonists frequently search.

While "Everything Ravaged, Everything Burned" is set in the distant past, the concerns Tower expresses are immediate and current. The reader cannot help but read the prosecution of the Iraq War into the Viking warriors' disastrous raid. Watching Djarf, the blood-lusting leader, send his fellow warriors on a meaningless battle based on faulty intelligence, what emerges is a trenchant message about American imperialism and its effect on the common soldier.

OTHER MAJOR WORKS

NONFICTION: "Light: The Sky Kind," 2003; "Hotel: Adonis Palace," 2003; "Bird-dogging the Bush Vote," 2005; "The Restoration," 2005; "The Kids Are Far Right," 2006; "The Thing with Feathers," 2006; "Under the God Gun," 2006; "Meltdown," 2008; "Own Goal," 2010.

BIBLIOGRAPHY

Eisenberg, Deborah. "The World We Live In." *The New York Review of Books* 59, no. 9 (May 28, 2009): 22-24. Emphasizes how the sparseness and humor of Tower's stories manage to elevate ordinary stories to the level of literature.

Konisberg, Eric. "Witness to Luckless Lives on the Periphery." *The New York Times*, April 11, 2009, p. C1. Explores Tower's blue-collar background and how it has influenced the subject matter of his stories.

White, Edmund. "Hard Times." *The New York Times Book Review*, March 29 2009, p. BR1. Argues that Tower's dialogue and description function to bring out the strangeness inherent in realist narratives.

*Stephen Aubrey*

# Mark Twain

**Born:** Florida, Missouri; November 30, 1835
**Died:** Redding, Connecticut; April 21, 1910
**Also Known As:** Samuel Langhorne Clemens

### Principal short fiction

*The Celebrated Jumping Frog of Calaveras County, and Other Sketches,* 1867

*Mark Twain's (Burlesque) Autobiography and First Romance,* 1871

*Mark Twain's Sketches: New and Old,* 1875

*Punch, Brothers, Punch! and Other Sketches,* 1878

*The Stolen White Elephant, and Other Stories,* 1882

*Merry Tales,* 1892

*The £1,000,000 Bank-Note, and Other New Stories,* 1893

*The Man That Corrupted Hadleyburg, and Other Stories and Essays,* 1900

*King Leopold's Soliloquy: A Defense of His Congo Rule,* 1905

*The $30,000 Bequest, and Other Stories,* 1906

*The Curious Republic of Gondour, and Other Whimsical Sketches,* 1919

*The Complete Short Stories of Mark Twain,* 1957 (Charles Neider, editor)

*Letters from the Earth,* 1962

*Selected Shorter Writings of Mark Twain,* 1962

*Mark Twain's Satires and Burlesques,* 1967 (Franklin R. Rogers, editor)

*Mark Twains's Which Was the Dream? and Other Symbolic Writings of the Later Years,* 1967 (John S. Tuckey, editor)

*Mark Twain's Hannibal, Huck and Tom,* 1969 (Walter Blair, editor)

*Mark Twain's Fables of Man,* 1972 (Tuckey, editor)

*Life as I Find It,* 1977 (Neider, editor)

*Early Tales and Sketches,* 1979-1981 (two volumes; Edgar Marquess Branch and Robert H. Hirst, editors)

*A Murder, a Mystery, and a Marriage,* 2001 (Roy Blount, Jr., editor)

### Other literary forms

As a professional writer who felt the need for a large income, Mark Twain published more than thirty books and left many uncollected pieces and manuscripts. He tried every genre, including drama, and even wrote some poetry that is seldom read. His royalties came mostly from books sold door-to-door, especially five travel volumes. For more than forty years, he occasionally sold material, usually humorous sketches, to magazines and newspapers. He also composed philosophical dialogues, moral fables, and maxims, as well as essays on a range of subjects which were weighted more toward the social and cultural than the belletristic but which were nevertheless often controversial. Posterity prefers his two famous novels about boyhood along the banks of the Mississippi, *The Adventures of Tom Sawyer* (1876) and *Adventures of Huckleberry Finn* (1884), although Twain also tried historical fiction, the detective story, and quasi-scientific fantasy.

### Achievements

Certainly one of the United States' most beloved and most frequently quoted writers, Mark Twain earned that honor by creating an original and nearly inimitable style that is thoroughly American. Although Twain tried nearly every genre from historical fiction to poetry to quasi-scientific fantasy, his novels about boyhood on the Mississippi, *The Adventures of Tom Sawyer* and *Adventures of Huckleberry Finn*, are the works that permanently wove Twain's celebrity status into the fabric of American culture. During his own lifetime, Twain received numerous honors including an M.A., soon followed by an LL.D., from Yale University. The

University of Missouri granted him another doctorate in 1902. His proudest moment, however, was in 1907, when the University of Oxford awarded him an honorary LL.D. He was so proud of his scarlet doctor's gown that he wore it to his daughter's wedding.

BIOGRAPHY

Mark Twain was born Samuel Langhorne Clemens in Florida, Missouri, in 1835. After his education was cut short by the death of a stern father who had more ambition than success, at the age of eleven Twain was apprenticed to a newspaper office, which, except for the money earned from four years of piloting on the Mississippi, supplied most of his income until 1868. Then, he quickly won eminence as a lecturer and author before his marriage to wealthy Olivia Langdon in 1870 led to a memorably comfortable and active family life which included three daughters. Although always looking to his writing for income, he increasingly devoted energy to business affairs and investments until his publishing house declared bankruptcy in 1894. After his world lecture tour of 1895-1896, he became one of the most admired figures of his time and continued to earn honors until his death in 1910.

ANALYSIS

Many readers find Mark Twain most successful in briefer works, including his narratives, because they were not padded to fit some extraneous standard of length. His best stories are narrated by first-person speakers who are seemingly artless, often so convincingly that critics cannot agree concerning the extent to which their ingenuousness is the result of Twain's self-conscious craft. While deeply divided himself, Twain seldom created introspectively complex characters or narrators who are unreliable in the Conradian manner. Rather, just as Twain alternated between polarities of attitude, his characters tend to embody some extreme, unitary state either of villainy or (especially with young women) of unshakable virtue. As a consequence, they seldom interact with other people effectively. Except when adapting a plot taken from oral tradition, Twain does better with patently artificial situations, which his genius for suggesting authentic speech make plausible enough. In spite of their faults, Twain's stories

*Mark Twain* (Library of Congress)

captivate the reader with their irresistible humor, their unique style, and their spirited characters who transfigure the humdrum with striking perceptions.

"THE CELEBRATED JUMPING FROG OF CALAVERAS COUNTY"

"The Celebrated Jumping Frog of Calaveras County" is generally regarded as Twain's most distinctive story, although some readers may prefer the bluejay yarn related by Jim Baker, which turns subtly on the psyche of its narrator, or Jim Blaine's digressions on his grandfather's old ram, which reach a more physical comedy while evolving into an absurdly tall tale. In "The Celebrated Jumping Frog of Calaveras County," Jim Smiley's eagerness to bet on anything in the mining camp may strain belief, but it is relatively plausible that another gambler could weigh down Smiley's frog, Daniel Webster, with quail-shot and thus win forty dollars with an untrained frog. Most attempts to find profundity in this folk anecdote involve the few enveloping sentences attributed to an outsider, who may represent the literate easterner being gulled by Simon Wheeler's seeming inability to stick to his point.

The skill of the story can be more conclusively identified, from the deft humanizing of animals to the rising power and aptness of the imagery. Especially adroit is the deadpan manner of Wheeler, who never betrays whether he himself appreciates the humor and the symmetry of his meanderings. Twain's use of the oral style is nowhere better represented than in "The Celebrated Jumping Frog of Calaveras County," which exemplifies the principles of the author's essay "How to Tell a Story."

### "A True Story"

In 1874, Twain assured the sober *Atlantic Monthly* that his short story "A True Story" was not humorous, although in fact it has his characteristic sparkle and hearty tone. Having been encouraged by the contemporary appeal for local color, Twain quickly developed a narrator with a heavy dialect and a favorite folk saying that allows a now-grown son to recognize his mother after a separation of thirteen years. While she, in turn, finds scars confirming their relationship on his wrist and head, this conventional plot gains resonance from Rachel's report of how her husband and seven children had once been separated at a slave auction in Richmond. Contemporaries praised "A True Story" for its naturalness, testimony that Twain was creating more lifelike black characters than any other author by allowing them greater dignity, as Rachel is quick to insist that slave families cared for one another just as deeply as any white families. Her stirringly recounted memories challenged the legend of the Old South even before that legend reached its widest vogue, and her spirit matched her "mighty" body so graphically that "A True Story" must get credit for much more craftsmanship than is admitted by its subtitle, "Repeated Word for Word as I Heard It."

### "The Facts Concerning the Recent Carnival of Crime in Connecticut"

In "The Facts Concerning the Recent Carnival of Crime in Connecticut," in which Twain again uses first-person narration with a flawless touch for emphasizing the right word or syllable, the main character closely resembles the author in age, experience, habits, and tastes. Of more significance is the fact that the story projects Twain's lifelong struggles with, and even against, his conscience. Here the conscience admits to being the "most pitiless enemy" of its host, whom it is supposed to "improve" but only tyrannizes with gusto while refusing to praise the host for anything. It makes the blunder, however, of materializing as a two-foot dwarf covered with "fuzzy greenish mold" who torments the narrator with intimate knowledge of and contemptuous judgments on his behavior. When beloved Aunty Mary arrives to scold him once more for his addiction to tobacco, his conscience grows so torpid that he can gleefully seize and destroy it beyond any chance of rebirth. Through vivid yet realistic detail, "The Facts Concerning the Recent Carnival of Crime in Connecticut" dramatizes common musings about shame and guilt along with the yearnings some persons feel for release from them. If it maintains too comic a tone to preach nihilism or amorality, it leaves readers inclined to view conscience less as a divine agent than as part of psychic dynamics.

### "The £1,000,000 Bank-Note"

The shopworn texture of "The £1,000,000 Bank-Note" reveals Twain's genius for using the vernacular at a low ebb. Narrated by the protagonist, this improbable tale is set in motion by two brothers who disagree over what would happen if some penniless individual were loaned a five-million-dollar bill for thirty days. To solve their argument, they engage in an experiment with a Yankee, Henry Adams, a stockbroker's clerk stranded in London. Coincidence thickens when, having managed by the tenth day of the experiment to get invited to dinner by an American minister, Adams unknowingly meets the stepdaughter of one of the brothers and woos and wins her that very night. Having just as nimbly gained a celebrity that makes every merchant eager to extend unlimited credit, he endorses a sale of Nevada stocks that enables him to show his future father-in-law that he has banked a million dollars of his own. The overall effect is cheerfully melodramatic and appeals to fantasies about windfalls of money; the reader can share Adams's pleasure in the surprise and awe he arouses by pulling his banknote out of a tattered pocket. It can be argued that the story indicts a society in which the mere show of wealth can so quickly raise one's standing, but Twain probably meant Adams to deserve respect for his enterprise and shrewdness when his chance came.

## "THE MAN THAT CORRUPTED HADLEYBURG"

"The Man That Corrupted Hadleyburg" is one of the most penetrating of Twain's stories. It achieves unusual depth of character and, perhaps by giving up the first-person narrator, a firm objectivity that lets theme develop through dialogue and incident. It proceeds with such flair that only a third or fourth reading uncovers thin links in a supposedly inescapable chain of events planned for revenge by an outsider who had been insulted in Hadleyburg, a town smugly proud of its reputation for honesty.

The stealthy stranger leaves a sack of counterfeit gold coins which are to be handed over to the fictitious resident who once gave a needy stranger twenty dollars and can prove it by recalling his words at the time. Next, the avenger sends nineteen leading citizens a letter which tells each of them how to claim the gold, supposedly amounting to forty thousand dollars. During an uproarious town meeting studded with vignettes of local characters, both starchy and plebeian, eighteen identical claims are read aloud; the nineteenth, however, from elderly Edward Richards, is suppressed by the chairman, who overestimates how Richards once saved him from the community's unjust anger. Rewarded by the stranger and made a hero, Richards is actually tormented to death, both by pangs of conscience and by fear of exposure. Hadleyburg, however, has learned a lesson in humility and moral realism and shortens its motto from the Lord's Prayer to run: "Lead Us into Temptation."

"The Man That Corrupted Hadleyburg" exhibits Twain's narrative and stylistic strengths and also dramatizes several of his persistent themes, such as skepticism about orthodox religion, ambivalence toward the conscience but contempt for rationalizing away deserved guilt, and attraction to mechanistic ideas. The story raises profound questions which can never be settled. The most useful criticism asks whether the story's determinism is kept consistent and uppermost--or, more specifically, whether the reform of Hadleyburg can follow within the patterns already laid out. The ethical values behind the story's action and ironic tone imply that people can in fact choose to behave more admirably.

In printing the story, *Harper's Monthly* may well have seen a Christian meliorism, a lesson against self-righteous piety that abandons true charity. The revised motto may warn that the young, instead of being sheltered, should be educated to cope with fallible human nature. More broadly, the story seems to show that the conscience can be trained into a constructive force by honestly confronting the drives for pleasure and self-approval that sway everyone.

Many of these same themes reappear in quasi supernatural sketches, such as "Extract from Captain Stormfield's Visit to Heaven." Twain never tired of toying with biblical characters, particularly Adam and Eve, or with parodies of Sunday-school lessons. He likewise parodied most other genres, even those which he himself used seriously. In his most serious moods he preached openly against cruelty to animals in "A Dog's Tale" and "A Horse's Tale," supported social or political causes, and always came back to moral choices, as in "Was It Heaven or Hell?" or "The $30,000 Bequest." Notably weak in self-criticism, he had a tireless imagination capable of daringly unusual perspectives, a supreme gift of humor darkened by brooding over the enigmas of life, and an ethical habit of thought that expressed itself most tellingly through character and narrative.

## OTHER MAJOR WORKS

LONG FICTION: *The Gilded Age*, 1873 (with Charles Dudley Warner); *The Adventures of Tom Sawyer*, 1876; *The Prince and the Pauper*, 1881; *Adventures of Huckleberry Finn*, 1884; *A Connecticut Yankee in King Arthur's Court*, 1889; *The American Claimant*, 1892; *The Tragedy of Pudd'nhead Wilson*, 1894; *Tom Sawyer Abroad*, 1894; *Personal Recollections of Joan of Arc*, 1896; *Tom Sawyer, Detective*, 1896; *A Double-Barrelled Detective Story*, 1902; *Extracts from Adam's Diary*, 1904; *A Horse's Tale*, 1906; *Eve's Diary, Translated from the Original Ms*, 1906; *Extract from Captain Stormfield's Visit to Heaven*, 1909; *The Mysterious Stranger*, 1916 (revised as *The Chronicle of Young Satan*, 1969, by Albert Bigelow Paine and Frederick A. Duneka); *Report from Paradise*, 1952 (Dixon Wecter, editor); *Simon Wheeler, Detective*, 1963; *Mark Twain's Mysterious Stranger Manuscripts*, 1969 (William M. Gibson, editor).

PLAYS: *Colonel Sellers*, pr., pb. 1874 (adaptation of his novel *The Gilded Age*); *Ah Sin*, pr. 1877 (with Bret Harte); *Is He Dead?: A Comedy in Three Acts*, pb. 2003 (Shelley Fisher Fishkin, editor).

NONFICTION: *The Innocents Abroad*, 1869; *Roughing It*, 1872; *A Tramp Abroad*, 1880; *Life on the Mississippi*, 1883; *Following the Equator*, 1897 (also known as *More Tramp Abroad*); *How to Tell a Story, and Other Essays*, 1897; *My Début as a Literary Person*, 1903; *What Is Man?*, 1906; *Christian Science*, 1907; *Is Shakespeare Dead?*, 1909; *Mark Twain's Speeches*, 1910 (Albert Bigelow Paine, editor); *Europe and Elsewhere*, 1923 (Paine, editor); *Mark Twain's Autobiography*, 1924 (two volumes; Paine, editor); *Mark Twain's Notebook*, 1935 (Paine, editor); *Letters from the Sandwich Islands, Written for the Sacramento Union*, 1937 (G. Ezra Dane, editor); *Mark Twain in Eruption*, 1940 (Bernard De Voto, editor); *Mark Twain's Travels with Mr. Brown*, 1940 (Franklin Walker and Dane, editors); *Mark Twain to Mrs. Fairbanks*, 1949 (Wecter, editor); *The Love Letters of Mark Twain*, 1949 (Dixon Wecter, editor); *Mark Twain of the Enterprise: Newspaper Articles and Other Documents, 1862-1864*, 1957 (Henry Nash Smith and Frederick Anderson, editors); *Traveling with the Innocents Abroad: Mark Twain's Original Reports from Europe and the Holy Land*, 1958 (letters; Daniel Morley McKeithan, editor; letters); *Mark Twain-Howells Letters: The Correspondence of Samuel L. Clemens and William D. Howells, 1872-1910*, 1960 (Smith and William M. Gibson, editors); *The Autobiography of Mark Twain*, 1961 (Neider, editor); *Mark Twain's Letters to His Publishers, 1867-1894*, 1967 (Hamlin Hill, editor); *Clemens of the Call: Mark Twain in San Francisco*, 1969 (Edgar M. Branch, editor); *Mark Twain's Correspondence with Henry Huttleston Rogers, 1893-1909*, 1969 (Lewis Leary, editor); *A Pen Warmed-Up in Hell: Mark Twain in Protest*, 1972; *Mark Twain's Notebooks and Journals*, 1975-1979 (three volumes); *Mark Twain Speaking*, 1976 (Paul Fatout, editor); *Mark Twain Speaks for Himself*, 1978 (Fatout, editor); *Mark Twain's Letters*, 1988-2002 (six volumes; Branch, et al, editors); *Mark Twain's Own Autobiography: The Chapters from the "North American Review,"* 1990 (Michael J. Kiskis, editor); *Mark Twain's Aquarium: The Samuel Clemens Angelfish Correspondence, 1905-1910*, 1991 (John Cooley, editor); *The Bible According to Mark Twain: Writings on Heaven, Eden, and the Flood*, 1995 (Howard G. Baetzhold and Joseph B. McCullough, editors); *Mark Twain: The Complete Interviews*, 2006; *Autobiography of Mark Twain, Volume 1*, 2010 (Harriet Elinor Smith, editor).

MISCELLANEOUS: *The Writings of Mark Twain*, 1922-1925 (thirty-seven volumes); *The Portable Mark Twain*, 1946 (Bernard De Voto, editor); *Collected Tales, Sketches, Speeches, and Essays, 1853-1891*, 1992 (Louis J. Budd, editor); *Collected Tales, Sketches, Speeches, and Essays, 1891-1910*, 1992 (Budd, editor); *Who Is Mark Twain?*, 2009.

BIBLIOGRAPHY

Briden, Earl F. "Twainian Pedagogy and the No-Account Lessons of 'Hadleyburg.'" *Studies in Short Fiction* 28 (Spring, 1991): 125-234. Argues that within the context of Twain's skepticism about man's capacity for moral education "The Man That Corrupted Hadleyburg" is not a story about a town's redemptive lessons of sin but rather an exposé about humanity's inability to learn morality from either theory or practice, abstract principle or moral pedagogy.

Fishkin, Shelley Fisher. *Lighting Out for the Territory: Reflections on Mark Twain and American Culture*. New York: Oxford University Press, 1996. A broad survey of Twain's influence on modern culture, including the many writers who have acknowledged their indebtedness to him. Discusses Twain's use of Hannibal, Missouri, in his writings. Charts his transformation from a southern racist to a committed antiracist.

Krause, Sydney J. "The Art and Satire of Twain's 'Jumping Frog Story.'" *American Quarterly* 41 (1964): 562-576. Argues the story has at least eight levels of story interest, with each having multiple sides. The story is a moral satire on the simplicity of Jim Smiley, but Simon Wheeler, a foil for Smiley, represents the revenge of the West for the trick of the easterner. The satire is made more complicated by Wheeler's joke on Twain. Thus, Twain has the same relationship to Wheeler that Smiley has to the stranger.

Lauber, John. *The Inventions of Mark Twain*. New York: Hill & Wang, 1990. Very well written and often humorous, this biography reveals Twain as an extremely complex, self-contradictory individual. Includes an annotated bibliography.

Messent, Peter B. *The Short Works of Mark Twain: A Critical Study*. Philadelphia: University of Pennsylvania Press, 2001. An analysis of seven short-story collections that were published from 1867 through 1906, examining the collections as a whole and individual stories alongside the novels to trace Twain's changing use of forms, themes, and types of humor. Messent contradicts critics who claim that Twain had little to do with assembling his short-story collections, arguing that publication histories and primary documents reveal that Twain played a considerable role in the collections' publication.

Powers, Ron. *Mark Twain: A Life*. New York: Free Press, 2005. A massive, engrossing biography which examines not only Twain's life and work but also his context. Includes bibliography and index.

Rasmussen, R. Kent. *Critical Companion to Mark Twain*. New York: Facts On File, 2007. Revised and much expanded edition of *Mark Twain A to Z* (1995), which covered virtually every character, theme, place, and biographical fact relating to Twain and contained a comprehensive chronology. Among new features in this retitled edition are lengthy critical essays on Twain's major works, an extensive annotated bibliography, and a glossary of unusual words in Twain's writings. Indexed.

_____, ed. *Critical Insights: Mark Twain*. Pasadena, Calif.: Salem Press, 2011. A collection of new, classic, and contemporary essays on Twain's life and works. Includes a biography, a survey of Twain's critical reception, and analyses of his writings in the travel and science-fiction genres.

Scofield, Martin. "New Territories: Bret Harte and Mark Twain." In *The Cambridge Introduction to the American Short Story*. New York: Cambridge University Press, 2006. Analyzes some of Twain's short stories and discusses his place in the development of American short fiction.

Sloane, David E. E. "Mark Twain and the American Comic Short Story." In *A Companion to the American Short Story*, edited by Alfred Bendixen and James Nagel. Malden, Mass.: Wiley-Blackwell, 2010. Provides an overview of Twain's short fiction and its place within the development of the American short story. Sloane maintains that Twain's work is the "high water mark of the comic short story."

Twain, Mark. *Mark Twain: The Complete Interviews*. Edited by Gary Scharnhorst. Tuscaloosa: University of Alabama Press, 2006. A collection of interviews with Twain dating from 1871 to 1910, presented in chronological order. The interviews paint a vivid picture of Twain, bringing to life his speech patterns and idiosyncracies, his likes and dislikes, and his philosophies on life and writing. Editor Gary Scharnhorst makes the book easily accessible to those unfamiliar with Twain by providing annotations to clarify the historical and biographical references.

Wagenknecht, Edward. *Mark Twain: The Man and His Work*. 3d ed. Norman: University of Oklahoma Press, 1967. A thorough revision of the 1935 work in which Wagenknecht considers the vast historical and critical study conducted between 1935 and 1960. He has modified many of his original ideas, notably his belief that Mark Twain was "The Divine Amateur"; the original chapter with that title has been rewritten and renamed "The Man of Letters."

Wonham, Henry B. *Mark Twain and the Art of the Tall Tale*. New York: Oxford University Press, 1993. Discusses how Twain used the tall-tale conventions of interpretive play, dramatic encounters, and the folk community. Focuses on the relationship between storyteller and audience in Twain's fiction.

_____. "Mark Twain and the Short Fiction." In *A Companion to Mark Twain*, edited by Peter B. Messent and Louis J. Budd. Malden, Mass.: Blackwell, 2005. An overview of the short fiction, commenting on the variety of forms, themes, and characters and the use of humor in these works.

*Louis J. Budd*
*Updated by Leslie A. Pearl*

# Anne Tyler

**Born:** Minneapolis, Minnesota; October 25, 1941

Principal short fiction

*"The Common Courtesies,"* 1968
*"Who Would Want a Little Boy?,"* 1968
*"With All Flags Flying,"* 1971
*"The Bride in the Boatyard,"* 1972
*"Spending,"* 1973
*"The Base-Metal Egg,"* 1973
*"Half-Truths and Semi-Miracles,"* 1974
*"A Knack for Languages,"* 1975
*"Some Sign That I Ever Made You Happy,"* 1975
*"The Geologist's Maid,"* 1975
*"Your Place Is Empty,"* 1976
*"Average Waves in Unprotected Waters,"* 1977
*"Foot-Footing On,"* 1977
*"Holding Things Together,"* 1977
*"Uncle Ahmad,"* 1977
*"Under the Bosom Tree,"* 1977
*"Linguistics,"* 1978
*"Laps,"* 1981
*"The Country Cook,"* 1982
*"Teenage Wasteland,"* 1983
*"Rerun,"* 1988
*"A Woman Like a Fieldstone House,"* 1989
*"People Who Don't Know the Answers,"* 1991

Other literary forms

Anne Tyler has published more than a dozen novels, including *Searching for Caleb* (1976), *Earthly Possessions* (1977), *Morgan's Passing* (1980), *Dinner at the Homesick Restaurant* (1982), *The Accidental Tourist* (1985), *Breathing Lessons* (1988), *Saint Maybe* (1991), *Ladder of Years* (1995), *A Patchwork Planet* (1998), *Back When We Were Grownups* (2001), *The Amateur Marriage* (2004), *Digging to America* (2006), and *Noah's Compass* (2009). *The Accidental Tourist* was

adapted for a film released n 1988, and *Breathing Lessons* and *Saint Maybe* were adapted for television's *Hallmark Hall of Fame* in 1994 and 1998, respectively. Tyler has published many nonfiction articles and essays about writing and writers, and her numerous book reviews have appeared in national periodicals. She has also written the children's books *Tumble Tower* (1993) and *Timothy Tugbottom Says No!* (2005), both of which were illustrated by her daughter Mitra Modarressi.

Achievements

While she was a student at Duke University, Anne Tyler won the Anne Flexner Award for creative writing; in 1966, she won the *Mademoiselle* magazine award for showing promise as a writer. Since then, she has been the recipient of many other honors: She received O. Henry Awards for the short stories "Common Courtesies" and "With All Flags Flying" (1969 and 1972, respectively), a citation from the American Academy of Arts and Letters for her novel *Earthly Possessions* (1977), and the Janet Heidinger Kafka Prize for *Morgan's Passing* (1980). In 1982, Tyler was nominated for the Pulitzer Prize for her novel *Dinner at the Homesick Restaurant*, which won a PEN/Faulkner Award for fiction. *The Accidental Tourist* received the National Book Critics Circle Award in 1985, and three years later the film version garnered four Academy Award nominations. In 1988, Tyler was a National Book Award finalist for *Breathing Lessons*, the novel for which she won the Pulitzer Prize for Literature in 1989. *Breathing Lessons*, *Saint Maybe*, and *Ladder of Years* were Book-of-the-Month Club selections.

Biography

When Anne Tyler was seven, her parents moved to Celo, a Quaker commune in North Carolina, so that they could raise their family in a quiet, isolated environment. Anne and her two brothers were schooled at home. Tyler became an avid reader, and her favorite book was *The Little House* (1942) by Virginia Lee Burton. Unable to support the family adequately at Celo, Tyler's parents moved to Raleigh in 1952, where her father worked as a research chemist, and her mother became a social worker. The Tylers were activists in the Civil Rights movement, opposed the death penalty, and, as Quaker pacifists, opposed U.S. involvement in war. With this background, it is surprising that Tyler's writing reveals no political or social ideology, other than her portrayal of the family as a basic unit in society.

Tyler attended high school in Raleigh, where Mrs. Peacock, her English teacher, taught literature with a dramatic flair and inspired Tyler's desire to become a writer. At sixteen, she entered Duke University on scholarship, majoring in Russian studies and literature, and graduated Phi Beta Kappa in 1961. At Duke, professors Reynolds Price and William Blackburn recognized her talent. Eudora Welty's conversational dialogue, southern settings, and gentle satire also influenced Tyler.

Tyler attended Columbia University but did not finish her master's degree. While working in the library at Duke University, she met Taghi Modarressi, an Iranian medical student, and married him in 1963. He completed his residency in child psychiatry at McGill University in Montreal. The Modarressis family then moved to Baltimore, Maryland, where they established a permanent home and had two daughters, Tezh and Mitra.

As a full-time wife and mother, Tyler wrote and published many short stories and book reviews. Always time oriented and well organized, she wrote when the children were napping or at school. Tyler says her early novels are flawed because normal family distractions interfered with her concentration while she was writing them. In 1970, her novels began to attract readers and critics, and by 1980, her reputation as a mature writer was secure.

Tyler maintains disciplined work methods. She begins writing after breakfast and continues for seven hours daily until late afternoon. She keeps a file of ideas, interesting people, and newspaper articles. Then she plans a story, using charts, pictures, and doodles. She imagines life inside her characters' skins, until

they come alive for her. Tyler writes early drafts in longhand because the flow of her pen stimulates creativity; she writes final drafts on a word processor. When she finishes a project, she rests and enjoys gardening and her family. Her two greatest fears are blindness and arthritis, diseases affecting the senses of sight and touch. As Tyler's skill and success as a novelist has grown, her prolific production of short stories and articles has declined. Tyler, now a widow, remains a resident of Baltimore.

ANALYSIS

Classified by critics as a southern writer, Anne Tyler focuses on modern families and their unique relationships. Her underlying theme is that time inexorably changes the direction of people's lives. The past determines the present and the present determines the future. Her stories show that life moves in generational cycles and that conflicts inevitably arise as time passes and settings change. Within families, the perspective of love evolves, children grow up and leave home, and death and grief sever connections. When a character's freedom is restricted by too many demands on energy or resources, the individual must make choices, adapt to changing circumstances, and endure insecurity and hardship before reaching a temporary equilibrium. Tyler says that life is a "web, crisscrossed by strings of love and need and worry." Her humanistic worldview focuses on individuals, isolated and unable to communicate complex emotions, such as love, grief, despair, or guilt. Missed connections, language, social class, age, religious beliefs, ethnicity, and other barriers prevent communication.

Tyler is always aware of the connection between the writer and the reader. What draws a reader are "concrete details, carefully layered to create complexity and depth, like real life." Characters must be individuals with unique qualities, and their dialogue must flow like conversation. Tyler often uses multiple points of view as a third-person observer. She says she is able to assume a convincing masculine persona in her narrative because most human experience has no particular gender. She makes effective use of flashbacks, in which a character's memory travels to the past and links it to the present and future.

## "Your Place Is Empty"

The idea for this story occurred when Tyler accompanied her husband, Taghi Modarressi, to Iran to meet his large family. Before the journey, Tyler, like the character Elizabeth, taught herself Persian and spoke it well enough to communicate on a surface level, but she soon discovered that mere words could not express complex emotions or overcome her feelings of being an outsider in a foreign culture.

The situation is reversed in "Your Place Is Empty." Mrs. Ardavi arrives in the United States for a six-month visit with her son Hassan, his American wife Elizabeth, and their small daughter. Hassan has lived in the United States for twelve years and is a successful doctor. Upon arrival at the airport, his mother does not recognize him. She reminds him that his place at home is still empty and urges him to return to Iran. Hassan has not forgotten his heritage, but he has changed, an underlying theme of the story.

Another theme shows how conflicts arise when people from different cultures cannot adapt. At first Elizabeth tries to make Mrs. Ardavi welcome, but soon language and culture become barriers to communication. As Mrs. Ardavi attempts to express her personality and infuse her son's home with Iranian customs, Elizabeth feels resentful and isolated, as if her freedom within her own home is restricted. Food preparation symbolizes their conflict. Elizabeth serves bacon, a taboo food for Mrs. Ardavi, who clutters Elizabeth's kitchen with spices and herbs, pots and pans, as she prepares Hassan's favorite lamb stew. She thinks that Elizabeth's meals are inadequate and that she is a negligent mother. Like an unsuccessful arbiter, Hassan stands between his mother and Elizabeth.

Tyler uses a narrative point of view that shifts between Mrs. Ardavi and Elizabeth. Insight into both women's personalities evokes reader sympathy, especially for Mrs. Ardavi. In flashbacks, she recalls her traditional Muslim girlhood; an arranged marriage to a man she never loved; his prolonged illness and death; grief over her oldest son's unhappy marriage and his untimely death; problems with the spoiled and pregnant wife of her youngest son; and the small comfort of "knowing her place" within the family circle of thirteen sisters who gossip and drink tea each afternoon.

Elizabeth expresses resentment at her mother-in-law's interference with icy silence, zealous housecleaning, and private complaints to Hassan. Realizing that the situation has reached an impasse, Hassan suggests that for the duration of her visit, Mrs. Ardavi move to a nearby apartment, away from the intimacy of his family. Unable to find "her place" in her son's American home, Mrs. Ardavi returns to Iran.

## "Average Waves in Unprotected Waters"

This story shows how the passage of time causes physical and emotional changes for Bet, a single mother, and Arnold, her mentally disabled son. Avery Blevins, Bet's "grim and cranky" husband, deserts her after a doctor diagnoses their baby as mentally retarded, the result of a fateful genetic error. Without family (her parents are dead), Bet supports herself and her child at a low-paying job. Arnold's increasingly wild tantrums force her to place him in a state hospital. Bet's landlady and longtime baby-sitter is a kindly woman, who has grown too old to control Arnold's aggressive behavior. His lack of response to her tears and special gift of cookies when he leaves indicates his infantile emotional level. On the train he enjoys watching the conductor scold a black woman for trying to ride without a ticket and cheers loudly as if they are actors in a television comedy. Arnold ignores the hospital setting and the nurse until his mother leaves. Then, like a small child, he screams loudly enough for Bet to hear him in the driveway as she climbs into a taxi. The train is late, so Bet dries her tears and watches strangers draping bunting on a speaker's stand in preparation for a ceremony dedicating the antiquated depot's restoration. She observes their actions while she waits for the train to take her life in a new direction.

Tyler describes how the passage of time erodes concrete objects and compares it to changing human relationships. The shabby boardinghouse has peeling layers of wallpaper, symbolic of passing time and the people who once lived there. Bet is worn down physically and emotionally by Arnold's hyperactive behavior, his short attention span, and his loud, incoherent speech. Marble steps at the mental hospital are worn down by the feet of caregivers and patients who have climbed them. The hospital dormitory is stripped of color and warmth. Only a small, crooked clown picture indicates that children might live there. The nurse disengages emotionally when Bet tries to tell her about Arnold's unique qualities. The train conductor, taxi driver, and station attendant are coldly impersonal, showing lack of empathy for Bet and Arnold. In the past, they have witnessed many arrivals and departures like Bet's and no longer respond to them.

The title "Average Waves in Unprotected Waters" indicates how the main characters, Bet and Arnold, adapt to "waves" in their lives. Bet faces disappointments and griefs, just as she once allowed "ordinary" breakers in the ocean to slam against her body, "as if staunchness were a virtue." The waves are not life-threatening; they are unhappy experiences to which she and Arnold must adapt in environments of "unprotected waters." Bet must endure life without family, goals, or resources, and Arnold must endure life in an impersonal mental hospital without his mother's love and protection.

### "TEENAGE WASTELAND"

Originally published in *Seventeen* magazine, this story shows how lack of communication between a troubled adolescent and his parents results in tragedy. Tyler's title, "Teenage Wasteland," comes from a popular song by the musical group The Who. Contributing factors to fifteen-year-old Donnie's "wasted" life include Daisy and Matt's inept parenting skills, a tutor's destructive influence, and Donnie's changing needs as an adolescent. Poor grades, petty thefts, smoking and drinking, and truancy are symptoms of Donnie's low self-esteem.

Tyler tells the story from a third-person point of view, limited to Daisy, a mother who agonizes over her guilt and inadequacies as a parent. Significantly, Matt, the father, does not get directly involved in guiding or disciplining his son. Neither parent is able to talk to Donnie about his personal problems. They focus on academic performance. At first, the parents make strict rules, and Daisy helps Donnie complete his assignments. However, her best efforts result in minimal improvement and cause major emotional storms.

Humiliated and unable to cope, Daisy takes Donnie to see Cal, a young counselor and tutor whose office is in his house, where other students lounge around, playing basketball and listening to rock music by The Who. Cal "marches to a different drummer" and encourages Donnie and other adolescents under his tutelage to rebel from "controlling" adults, like parents and school authorities. Accepting responsibility for one's actions, setting goals, and studying are not part of Cal's agenda. Donnie gradually withdraws from his family in favor of "hanging out" at Cal's with teenagers like himself.

Donnie is expelled from the private school he attends after authorities find beer and cigarettes in his locker, and his academic performance drops even lower. Instead of going home, he runs to Cal's. Donnie claims it was a "frame up," and Cal excuses the boy by saying that the school violated his civil rights. Angry and frustrated, Daisy takes Donnie home and enrolls him in public school, where he finishes the semester. Miserable and friendless, Donnie runs away, his youth wasted, and Daisy wonders what went wrong.

### "PEOPLE WHO DON'T KNOW THE ANSWERS"

This story, published in *The New Yorker*, is a revised chapter from Tyler's novel *Saint Maybe*. Doug Bedloe, a recently retired schoolteacher, realizes that no one has the final answers to life's mysteries. The passage of time changes everything. To fill the void in his life, he tries several boring and unproductive hobbies. Then he becomes interested in some foreign students who live across the street. Like actors in a comedy, they enjoy a casual lifestyle and are fascinated by American gadgets, music, language, and clothing, far different from the "real" life and family responsibilities they have known in distant lands.

Doug compares their experimental lifestyle to his own static existence. Seen through the foreigners' window screen, his house reminds him of a framed needlepoint picture, something "cozy, old-fashioned, stitched in place forever." However, Doug's family has changed. His wife Bee has become crippled with arthritis. Death has taken their oldest son Danny, whose children now live with them. Beastie, Doug's old dog and companion, is buried under the azalea. Adult siblings Ian and Claudia have gradually assumed family authority. Doug feels physically fit, but his life has no anchor. His past is gone, and he must somehow endure the present.

Ian invites his family to a picnic sponsored by the Church of the Second Chance, viewed by some as a cult, or "alternative religion." Brother Emmett and church members have helped Ian endure his overwhelming sense of guilt over Danny's accidental death and support his role as surrogate father to Danny's children. Doug acknowledges that sharing one's joys and sorrows would benefit him, but Bee remains cynical. Doug's past and the present reality make him feel split, like the foreigners' old car, parked half inside their garage with the faulty automatic door bisecting it.

OTHER MAJOR WORKS

LONG FICTION: *If Morning Ever Comes*, 1964; *The Tin Can Tree*, 1965; *A Slipping-Down Life*, 1970; *The Clock Winder*, 1972; *Celestial Navigation*, 1974; *Searching for Caleb*, 1976; *Earthly Possessions*, 1977; *Morgan's Passing*, 1980; *Dinner at the Homesick Restaurant*, 1982; *The Accidental Tourist*, 1985; *Breathing Lessons*, 1988; *Saint Maybe*, 1991; *Ladder of Years*, 1995; *A Patchwork Planet*, 1998; *Back When We Were Grownups*, 2001; *The Amateur Marriage*, 2004; *Digging to America*, 2006; *Noah's Compass*, 2009.

CHILDREN'S LITERATURE: *Tumble Tower*, 1993 (illustrations by Mitra Modarressi); *Timothy Tugbottom Says No!*, 2005 (illustrations by Mitra Modarressi).

BIBLIOGRAPHY

Bail, Paul. *Anne Tyler: A Critical Companion*. Westport, Conn.: Greenwood Press, 1998. Includes a biography, a discussion of the literary influences on Tyler, and individual chapters that analyze twelve of her novels. Examines how her novels fit into southern regional literature, women's literature, and popular culture, and provides feminist and multicultural critiques of her work. Bail also describes plots, characters, themes, literary devices, historical settings, and narrative points of view as they apply to individual novels. Concludes with an extensive bibliography.

Cahill, Susan, ed. *New Women and New Fiction: Short Stories Since the Sixties*. New York: New American Library, 1986. According to Cahill's introduction, this anthology, which includes Tyler's "Teenage Wasteland," contains stories written by unrecognized women geniuses who have created works of art. Their style is minimalist, their humor subtle, and their characters and settings transcend time. Cahill includes a brief biographical sketch of each author preceding her short story.

Croft, Robert W. *Anne Tyler: A Bio-bibliography*. Westport, Conn.: Greenwood Press, 1995. Features a four-chapter biography of Tyler: "A Setting Apart" concerns her childhood in a commune, teen years in Raleigh, college experience at Duke, and early writing; "The Only Way Out" refers to her feelings of isolation during her early marriage and motherhood and how writing her first novels and short stories kept her in touch with the real world; "Rich with Possibilities" refers to her life in Baltimore, the setting of most of her stories, her book reviews, and discussion of her middle-period novels; and "A Border Crossing" deals with Tyler's fame and recurring themes in her novels. Also includes an extensive bibliography, with a list of Tyler's papers at Duke University.

_____. *An Anne Tyler Companion*. Westport, Conn.: Greenwood Press, 1998. Provides alphabetically arranged entries on Tyler's works, characters, and the themes that figure prominently in her writings. The entries for her short stories contain extensive plot summaries. Includes a bibliography and appendixes of songs and places mentioned in her works.

Gomez-Vega, Ibis. "Intersecting Oppressions and the Emotional Paralysis of the Working Poor in Anne Tyler's 'Average Waves in Unprotected Waters.'" *southern Quarterly* 41, no. 3 (Spring, 2003): 109. An analysis of the story's content, focusing on the "emotional paralysis" of its characters. Describes Tyler as a writer and discusses feminist issues in her work.

Jansen, Henry. *Laughter Among the Ruins: Postmodern Comic Approaches to Suffering*. New York: P. Lang, 2001. Examines the works of Tyler and three other novelists in order to understand how a secularized Western society deals with suffering.

Kissel, Susan S. *Moving On: The Heroines of Shirley Ann Grau, Anne Tyler, and Gail Godwin*. Bowling Green, Ohio: Bowling Green State University Popular Press, 1996. Topics include Tyler's heroines and her identity as a southern writer. Includes a bibliography and an index.

Quiello, Rose. *Breakdowns and Breakthoughts: The Figure of the Hysteric in Contemporary Novels by Women*. New York: P. Lang, 1996. Discusses the work of Tyler, Margaret Drabble, and Kate O'Brien. Includes a bibliography and an index.

Town, Caren J. "'Three Meal a Day Aftermaths': Anne Tyler's Determined Adolescents." In *The New southern Girl: Female Adolescence in the Works of Twelve Women Authors*. Jefferson, N.C.: McFarland, 2004. Examines the female adolescent characters in Tyler's works, focusing on the novels *A Slipping-Down Life*, *The Clock Winder*, and *Dinner at the Homesick Restaurant*. Compares these young girls to the other characters in Tyler's fiction.

Tyler, Anne. Introduction to *The Best American Short Stories 1983*, edited by Shannon Ravenel. Houghton Mifflin, 1983. Tyler discusses qualities of memorable short stories, maintaining that they are a unique literary form and not shortened novels. They must include precise descriptive details, unforgettable characters, and a "moment of stillness . . . the frame through which the reader views all that happens." Plot action is the result of characters' personalities.

_____. Introduction to *Best of the South*, edited by Shannon Ravenel. Chapel Hill, N.C.: Algonquin Books, 1996. Tyler discusses the importance of settings and how they change over time. To illustrate, she describes the southern town, where she spent her teens, and compares it to Raleigh, North Carolina, in the 1990's. She comments on the "yeasty prose" of southern writing, with its musical quality and conversational tone, characters who are just as important as what happens, and the narrative point of view and dialogue with which southerners identify.

_____. "Still Just Writing." In *The Writer on Her Work: Contemporary Women Writers Reflect on Their Art and Situation*, edited by Janet Sternberg. New York: Norton, 1980. Tyler explains how she keeps her life balanced. Writing fiction draws her into an imaginary world, but being a wife and mother keeps her anchored to the real world of home and family. Writing novels takes much time and concentration, so she has gradually given up writing short stories; however, revised chapters from some of her novels appear in periodicals as short stories.

*Martha E. Rhynes*

# u

## JOHN UPDIKE

**Born:** Reading, Pennsylvania; March 18, 1932
**Died:** Danvers, Massachusetts; January 27, 2009

### PRINCIPAL SHORT FICTION

*The Same Door,* 1959

*Pigeon Feathers, and Other Stories,* 1962

*Olinger Stories: A Selection,* 1964

*The Music School,* 1966

*Museums and Women, and Other Stories,* 1972

*Problems, and Other Stories,* 1979

*Three Illuminations in the Life of an American Author,* 1979

*Too Far to Go: The Maples Stories,* 1979

*The Chaste Planet,* 1980

*Bech Is Back,* 1982

*The Beloved,* 1982

*Trust Me,* 1987

*Brother Grasshopper,* 1990 (limited edition)

*The Afterlife, and Other Stories,* 1994

*Licks of Love: Short Stories and a Sequel, "Rabbit Remembered,"* 2000

*The Complete Henry Bech: Twenty Stories,* 2001

*The Early Stories, 1953-1975,* 2003

*My Father's Tears, and Other Stories,* 2009

*The Maples Stories,* 2009

### OTHER LITERARY FORMS

A prolific and versatile writer, John Updike (UHP-dik) was an accomplished novelist, perhaps best known for his "Rabbit" tetralogy. He was also the author of *The Centaur* (1963), which fuses myth and realism in middle-class America; *Couples* (1968), which examines the social and sexual mores of a modern American town; *The Coup* (1978), in which the narrator recounts the history of an imaginary African nation; and the trilogy *A Month of Sundays* (1975), *Roger's Version* (1986), and *S.* (1988), which are creative reworkings of the situation of Nathaniel Hawthorne's *The Scarlet Letter* (1850). In 1984, Updike wrote the best-selling *The Witches of Eastwick*, which was adapted into a popular film; more than two decades later he took up the story of his three heroines again in *The Widows of Eastwick* (2008). His later novels include *Toward the End of Time* (1997), *Gertrude and Claudius* (2000), and *Terrorist* (2006). Updike also published many books of verse and a play (*Buchanan Dying,* 1974), and he wrote reviews and critical essays on literature, music, and painting for a few decades. His nonfiction works include *Hugging the Shore* (1983), *Odd Jobs* (1991), *More Matter: Essays and Criticism* (1999), and *Due Considerations: Essays and Criticism* (2007). He was also the author of a memoir, *Self-Consciousness* (1989).

### ACHIEVEMENTS

*The Centaur* won for John Updike the National Book Award in 1964. He was elected to the National Institute of Arts and Letters, the youngest man to receive the honor at that time. "The Bulgarian Poetess" won an O. Henry Award in 1966. *Rabbit Is Rich* (1981) won an American Book Award and a Pulitzer Prize, while Updike's nonfiction collection *Hugging the Shore* (1983) won the National Book Critics Circle Award. In 1991, *Rabbit at Rest* won a Pulitzer Prize, and the Howells Medal in 1995, recognizing it as the most significant work of fiction published in the previous five years. In 1996, Updike's *In the Beauty of the Lilies* (1996) won the Ambassador Book Award, and the next year Updike received the Campion Award. In 1998, he earned the Harvard Arts First Medal and the National Book Medal for Distinguished Contribution to American Letters. He received the National Humanities Medal in 2003. He was honored with the PEN/Faulkner Award in 2004 for *The Early Stories,*

*1953-1975*, and the Rea Award for the Short Story in 2006. In 2007, the American Academy of Arts and Letters bestowed on him its Gold Medal for Fiction.

## BIOGRAPHY

John Hoyer Updike was born in 1932, the only child of Wesley Updike, a cable splicer who lost his job in the Great Depression and had to support his family on a meager teacher's salary ($1,740 per year), and Linda Grace Updike, an aspiring writer. The family moved to Plowville from Shillington, Pennsylvania, in 1945 to live on the farm of John Updike's maternal grandparents. Updike recalls that a gift subscription at that time to *The New Yorker*, a Christmas present from an aunt, was a significant factor in his decision to become an artist. In high school, he drew for the school paper, wrote articles and poems, and demonstrated sufficient academic gifts to be awarded a full scholarship to Harvard University, which he entered in 1950.

At college, Updike majored in English, became editor of the prestigious Harvard *Lampoon*, and graduated with honors in 1954. That year, *The New Yorker* accepted a poem and a story, an event that Updike remembered as "the ecstatic breakthrough of my literary life." After graduation, Updike and his wife of one year, Mary Pennington, a fine arts major from Radcliffe, spent 1955 in Oxford, where Updike held a Knox Fellowship. When E. B. White offered him a job as a staff writer with *The New Yorker*, Updike accepted and spent the next two years contributing brief, witty pieces to the "Talk of the Town" section at the front of the magazine. During this time, he worked on the manuscript of a six-hundred-page book, which he decided not to publish because it had "too many of the traits of a first novel." When his second child was born, he believed that he needed a different setting in which to live and work (the literary world in New York seemed "unnutritious and interfering") and moved to Ipswich, Massachusetts. There he found "the space" to write "the Pennsylvania thing," which became the novel *The Poorhouse Fair* (1959), and his first collection of short stories, *The Same Door*.

Choosing to work in a rented office in downtown Ipswich, Updike began an extremely active literary career that would continue for several decades. The first book in the Rabbit series, *Rabbit, Run*, was published in 1960, the same year in which the last of Updike's four children was born. *Rabbit, Run* caught the attention of the reading public with its combination of sexual candor and social insight, but *The Centaur* was Updike's first real success with serious critics, winning the National Book Award in 1964. That same year, Updike was elected a member of the National Institute of Arts and Letters. During 1964 and 1965, Updike traveled in Eastern Europe, the source for his first story about Henry Bech ("The Bulgarian Poetess"), who became a kind of slightly displaced version of himself in the guise of a Jewish writer from New York. Further travels to Africa led to other Bech stories as well as *The Coup*, but Updike generally remained in Ipswich, involved in local affairs, writing constantly, and using the beach to find the sun, which was the only cure at that time for a serious case of psoriasis. The book that garnered national attention for Updike was *Couples* (1968), an exposé of modern suburban lifestyle that featured promiscuity and adultery. The book was on the best-seller list for a year. The second Rabbit book,

*John Updike* (AP Photo/Caleb Jones)

*Rabbit Redux*, was published in 1971, and short-story collections appeared regularly. In the late 1960's, Updike sold the screen rights to his novel *Couples* for a half million dollars (the film was not produced).

After fifteen years, Updike and his wife ended their marriage, and in 1974 he moved to Boston, returning to the North Shore area in 1976, the year before he married Martha Bernhard. In 1977, Updike published his fifth volume of verse, *Tossing and Turning*, from a major press. In 1979, two collections of short stories that he had written during the emotional turmoil of the last years of his marriage and its conclusion were issued as *Problems, and Other Stories* and *Too Far to Go*. The latter volume included all the stories about a couple named Maple whose lives were a literary transmutation of aspects of Updike's first marriage. Updike continued his energetic and inventive career through the 1980's, publishing *Rabbit Is Rich* in 1981, continuing his series of novels imaginatively derived from Hawthorne's *The Scarlet Letter*, completing the Rabbit series with *Rabbit at Rest* (1990) and collecting another nine hundred pages of essays in *Odd Jobs* (1991). In 1991, *Rabbit at Rest* won a Pulitzer Prize.

Updike died of cancer in 2009 in Danvers, Massachusetts, at age seventy-six. At his death he was eulogized as one of America's major writers.

### ANALYSIS

From the beginning of his career as a writer, John Updike demonstrated his strengths as a brilliant stylist and a master of mood and tone whose linguistic facility has sometimes overshadowed the dimensions of his vision of existence in the twentieth century. His treatment of some of the central themes of modern times--sexual and social politics, the nature of intimate relationships, the collapse of traditional values, the uncertainty of the human condition as the twentieth century drew to a close--is as revealing and compelling as that of any of his contemporaries. Although he was regarded mainly as a novelist, the short story may well have been his true métier, and his ability to use its compressed structure to generate intensity and offer succinct insight made his work a standard of success for writers of short fiction, an evolving example of the possibilities of innovation and invention in a traditional narrative form.

### THE SAME DOOR AND PIGEON FEATHERS, AND OTHER STORIES

Always eloquent about his aspirations and intentions--as he was about almost everything he observed--Updike remarked to Charles Thomas Samuels in an interview in 1968 that some of the themes of his work are "domestic fierceness within the middle class, sex and death as riddles for the thinking animal, social existence as sacrifice, unexpected pleasures and rewards, corruption as a kind of evolution," and that his work is "meditation, not pontification." In his short fiction, his meditations followed an arc of human development from the exuberance of youth to the unsettling revelations of maturity and on toward the uncertainties of old age, a "curve of sad time" (as he ruefully described the years from 1971 to 1978, when his first marriage failed). This span illuminates the range of experience of an extremely incisive, very well-educated, and stylistically brilliant man, who was able to reach beyond the limits of his interesting life to capture the ethos of an era.

Updike's artistic inclinations were nurtured by his sensitive, supportive parents, who recognized his gifts and his needs, while the struggles of his neighbors in rural Pennsylvania during the Great Depression left him with a strong sense of the value of community and the basis for communal cohesion in a reliable, loving family. At Harvard, his intellectual capabilities were celebrated and encouraged, and in his first job with *The New Yorker*, his ability to earn a living through his writing endowed his entire existence with an exhilaration that demanded expression in a kind of linguistic rapture. The 1950's marked the steepest incline in time's curve, and his first two collections, *The Same Door* and *Pigeon Feathers, and Other Stories*, while primarily covering his youth and adolescence in the town of Shillington (which he calls Olinger), are written from the perspective of the young man who overcame the limitations of an economically strained and culturally depleted milieu to marry happily, begin a family, and capitalize on his talents in the profession that he adored. There is no false sentimentality about Olinger or the narrowness of some its citizens. Updike always saw right through the fakery of the Chamber of Commerce manipulators who disguised their bigotry and anti-intellectualism with pitches to patriotism, but the young men in these stories often seem destined to overcome whatever obstacles they face to move toward the promise of some artistic or social reward.

In "Flight," a high school senior is forced to relinquish his interest in a classmate because of his mother's pressures and his social status, but the loss is balanced by his initial venture into individual freedom. "The Alligators" depicts a moment of embarrassed misperception, but in the context of the other stories, it is only a temporary setback, an example of awkwardness that might, upon reflection, contribute to the cultivation of a subtler sensibility. "The Happiest I've Been" epitomizes the author's attitude at a pivotal point in his life, poised between the familiar if mundane streets of his childhood and the infinite expanse of a world beyond, enjoying the lingering nostalgia he feels for home ground, which he can carry in memory as he moves on to a wider sphere of experience. These themes are rendered with a particular power in the often-anthologized "A & P" and in "Wife-Wooing," both from *Pigeon Feathers, and Other Stories.*

### "A & P"

As in many of his most effective stories, in "A & P" Updike found a voice of singular appropriateness for his narrative consciousness: Sammy, a boy of nineteen from a working-class background, who is working as a checkout clerk at the local A & P grocery store. The store stands for the assembly-line numbness that is part of the lockstep life that seems to be the likely destiny of all the young men in the town, and it serves as a means of supply for a nearby resort area. When three young women pass the boy's register, he is enchanted by "the queen," a girl who appears "more than pretty." When she is ordered to dress properly by the store manager on her next visit ("Girls, this isn't the beach"), Sammy feels compelled to deliver a declaration of passionate defense of their innocence. Frustrated by the incipient stodginess and puritanical repression of the entire town and moved by his heart-driven need to make some kind of chivalrous gesture, he finds that his only recourse is to mumble "I quit" as the girls leave the store.

Lengel, the aptly named manager-curmudgeon, speaking for unreasoning minor authority, uses several power trips to maintain his petty tyranny, but Sammy refuses to back down, even when Lengel presents the ultimate guilt ploy, "You don't want to do this to your Mom and Dad." This is an appeal to conformist quiescence, and Sammy, like most of Updike's protagonists, is susceptible to the possibility of hurting or disgracing his family in a small, gossip-ridden community. When Lengel warns him, "You'll feel this for the rest of your life," Sammy recognizes the validity of his threat but realizes that, if he backs down now, he will always back down in similar situations. Frightened and uncertain, he finds the resolve to maintain his integrity by carrying through his gesture of defiance. He knows that he will have to accept the consequences of his actions, but this is the true source of his real strength. Acknowledging that now "he felt how hard the world was going to be to me hereafter," his acceptance of the struggle is at the root of his ability to face challenges in the future. As if to ratify his decision, Lengel is described in the last paragraph reduced to Sammy's slot, "checking the sheep through," his visage "dark gray and his back stiff." If the reward for selling out is a life like Lengel's, then even an act that no one but its agent appreciates (the girls never notice their champion) is better than the defeat of submerging the self in the despair of denial.

### "WIFE-WOOING"

"Wife-Wooing" is the real reward for acting according to principle. If the A & P is the symbol of enclosure and the girl a figure for the wonder of the cosmos beyond, then marriage to a woman who incarnates the spirit of wonder contains the possibilities for paradise. The mood of ecstasy is established immediately by the narrator's declaration of devotion, "OH MY LOVE. Yes. Here we sit, on warm broad floorboards, before a fire. . . . " He is a man whose marriage, in its initial stages, is informed by what seems like an exponential progression of promise. Thus, although he has "won" his mate, he is impelled to continue to woo her as a testament to his continuing condition of bliss, of his exultation in the sensuality of the body's familiar but still mysterious terrain--its "absolute geography." The evocative description of the couple together--framed in images of light and warmth--is sufficient to convey the delight they share, but what makes the story noteworthy is Updike's employment and investigation of the erotics of language as a register of feeling. The mood of arousal becomes a kind of celebration of the words that describe it, so that it is the "irrefutably magical life language leads with itself" that becomes the substance of erotic interest.

Updike, typically, recalls Joyce, using Blazes Boylan's word "smackwarm" from "the legendary, imperfectly explored grottoes of *Ulysses*" to let loose a chain of linguistic associations beginning with a consideration of the root etymology of "woman"--the "wide w, the receptive o. Womb." Located in a characteristically masculine perspective (inevitable considering Updike's background and the historical context), the narrator envisions himself as a warrior-hunter in prehistoric times. In a brilliantly imaginative, affectionate parody of Anglo-Saxon alliterative verse, Updike continues to express the husband's exultation through the kind of linguistic overdrive that makes his mastery of styles the focus of admiration (and envy) of many of his peers.

Beneath the wordplay and the almost self-congratulatory cleverness, however, there is still another level of intent. Once the element of erotic power in language itself has been introduced, Updike is free to employ that language in an investigation of sensuality that strains at the bounds of what was acceptable in 1960. His purpose is to examine a marriage at the potentially dangerous seven-year point, to recall the sexual history of the couple, and to show how the lessons of mutual experience have enabled them to deepen their erotic understanding as the marriage progressed. Continuing to use language to chart the erogenous regions of the mind and body, Updike arranges a series of puns ("Oh cunning trick") so that the dual fascination of love--for wife, words--is expressed in intertwined images of passion. The story concludes with the husband leaving for work in the cold stone of a city of "heartless things," then returning to the eternal mystery of woman/wooing, where, as Robert Creeley's poem "The Wife" expresses it, he knows "two women/ and the one/ is tangible substance,/ flesh and bone," while "the other in my mind/ occurs."

### THE HENRY BECH STORIES

Updike's energetic involvement with the dimensions of life--the domestic and the artistic--crested on a curve of satisfaction for him as the 1950's drew to a close. The chaotic explosion of countercultural diversity that took place in the 1960's fractured the comforting coordinates of a world with which Updike had grown familiar, and he began to find himself in an adversarial position with both the confines of bourgeois social values and the sprawling uncertainty of a country in entropic transition. As a means of confronting this situation at a remove that would permit some aesthetic distance from his displeasure, Updike created Henry Bech, an urban, blocked Jewish writer seemingly the polar opposite of the urbane Updike but actually only a slight transmutation of his own sensibility. Bech is much more successful in managing the perils of the age than Harry Angstrom, who represents Updike's peevish squareness in *Rabbit Redux*, and the "interview" "Bech Meets Me" (November, 1971) is a jovial display of Updike's witty assessment of his problems and goals.

The individual Bech stories, beginning with "The Bulgarian Poetess" (from *The Music School*), which covers Updike's experiences on a trip to Eastern Europe sponsored by the State Department, generally work as separate entities, but they are linked sufficiently that there is a clear progression in *Bech: A Book*, while *Bech Is Back* seems closer to a novel than a collection of short fiction and *Bech at Bay* (1998) is classified as long fiction. Through the personae of Henry Bech and Rabbit Angstrom, among others, Updike maintained a distinct distance from the political and incipient personal turmoil that he was experiencing.

### THE MUSIC SCHOOL

In *The Music School*, the stories include fond recollections of a positive, recent past, as in "The Christian Roommates" (which "preserved" aspects of Updike's Harvard experience), or tentative excursions into the malaise of the times, as in the fascinating dissection of psychoanalytic methods offered by "My Lover Has Dirty Fingernails" and in the unusual venture into the possibilities of renewal in a natural setting of "The Hermit." In the last story, the prickly, idiosyncratic spirit of the New England individualist and environmentalist Henry David Thoreau is expressed as an urge to escape from the social realities of *success*--an essentially forlorn quest for a larger sense of life than "they" will permit and an attempt to explore the possibility of a mystical essence beyond the attainment of intellectual power.

### MUSEUMS AND WOMEN, AND OTHER STORIES

While Updike spoke admiringly of the "splendid leafiness" of Pennsylvania and could evoke the mood of Scotland's highland moors (as in "Macbech") with typical facility, his central subject has always been the nature of relationships. In *Museums and Women, and Other Stories*, he returned to the consequences of marked changes in the social climate and in his personal life that could not be avoided by fictional explorations of subsidiary concerns. The story "When Everyone Was Pregnant" is a paean to an old order passing into history, a celebration of years of relative pleasure and satisfaction that he calls "the Fifties" but which actually encompass the first half of the century."My Fifties," he labels them, positioning himself at the center of a benign cosmos, where tests were passed ("Entered them poor and left them comfortable. Entered them chaste and left them a father") and life was relatively uncomplicated. The paragraphs of the story are like a shorthand list of bounty ("Jobs, houses, spouses of our own"), and the entire era is cast in an aura of innocence, a prelude to a sudden shock of consciousness that utterly changed everything. The factors that caused the shift are never identified, leaving the narrator bewildered ("Now: our babies drive cars, push pot, shave, menstruate, riot for peace, eat macrobiotic"), but the alteration in perception is palpable and its ramifications ("Sarah looks away" after fifteen shared years) unavoidable.

The last section of *Museums and Women, and Other Stories* contains five stories under the subhead "The Maples." Updike eventually published seventeen stories about Richard and Joan Maple, a family with four children that might be said to approximate Updike's first marriage, in *Too Far to Go*, and the narrative thread that becomes apparent in the full collection is the transition from optimism and contentment to uncertainty and fracture. A story that registers the process of psychological displacement particularly well is the last one in *Museums and Women, and Other Stories*, "Sublimating," in which the Maples have decided to give up sex, which they have mistakenly identified as the "only sore point" in their marriage. Since nearly all that

Updike has written on the subject indicates that sex is at the heart of everything that matters in a relationship, the decision--as Updike assumed would be obvious to everyone but the parties involved--was a false solution that could only aggravate the problem. What becomes apparent as the story progresses is that everything in the relationship has become a pretext for disguising true feeling, but the desperation of the participants makes their methods of camouflage sympathetic and understandable.

Unable to accept that change in both parties has permanently altered their position, Richard and Joan repeat strategies that have previously revitalized their marriage, but nothing can be successful, since the actors no longer fit their roles. The procedures of the past cannot be recapitulated, and their efforts produce a series of empty rituals that leave the Maples exhausted and angry. Using external remedies for internal maladies (the purchase of an old farmhouse, impulsive acquisition of trivia), bantering about each other's lovers to reignite passion, turning their children into would-be allies, exchanging barbed, bitchy, and self-regarding comments, the Maples are more baffled than destructive, but both of them are aware that they will eventually have to confront the fact that they have no solution. Sublimation is ultimately suppression of truth, and Richard's description of the people in a pornographic film house on Forty-Second Street in Manhattan as perpetual spectators, who watch unseeing while meaningless acts of obscenity occur in the distance, stands as an emblem of stasis and nullity, a corollary to the paralysis that engulfs the couple. Joan's final comment on their current state, a pathetic observation about the "cleansing" aspects of their nonsensual behavior, brings the story to a conclusion that is warped with tension, a situation that Richard's comment, "we may be on to something," does nothing to relieve.

### PROBLEMS, AND OTHER STORIES

Updike's next collection, *Problems, and Other Stories*, contains a prefatory note that begins, "Seven years since my last short story collection? There must have been problems." The central problem has been the end of Updike's first marriage and the removal of the core of certainty that the domestic structure of his family provided. The unraveling of the threads that were woven through a lifetime of intelligent analysis and instinctual response called everything into question and opened a void that had been lurking near the surface of Updike's work. Updike was far too perceptive ever to assume that a stable family was possible for everyone or that it would provide answers for everything. From the start of the Rabbit tetralogy, the strains inherent in an ongoing marital arrangement were examined closely, but the dissolution of his own primary household drew several specific responses that expanded the range and depth of his short fiction. First, the sad facts of the separation and divorce were handled in the last Maple stories.

"Separating" recounts the parents' attempts to explain the situation to their children. It is written in bursts of lacerating dialogue, a conversation wrought in pain and doubt that concludes with a child posing the tormenting, unanswerable query *"Why?"* to Richard Maple. "Here Come the Maples" presents the ceremony of the divorce as a reverse marriage, complete with programmed statements forcing the couple to agree by saying "I do." The jaunty tone of the proceedings does not mask totally the looming cloud of uncertainty that covers the future.

Then, the artist turns toward his work for sustenance. In "From the Journal of a Leper," Updike projects his psychic condition into the life of a potter who is afflicted with a serious skin disease akin to his own. The fear of leprosy stands for all of his doubts before an unknown universe no longer relatively benign; his work provides some compensation but is intricately connected to his psychological stability; a woman with whom he is developing a relationship improves and complicates the situation. The story is open-ended, but in a harbinger of the direction Updike has begun to chart for his protagonists, the artist recognizes the necessity of standing alone, dependent ultimately on his own strength. The final words may be more of a self-directed exhortation than a summary of actuality, but they represent a discernible goal: "I am free, as other men. I am whole."

### "TRANSACTION"

The difficulties of freedom and the elusiveness of wholeness are explored in "Transaction," one of Updike's most powerful stories. In *The Paris Review* interview with Charles Thomas Samuels, Updike said:

> About sex in general, by all means let's have it in fiction, as detailed as needs be, but real, real in its social and psychological connections. Let's take coitus out of the closet and off the altar and put it on the continuum of human behavior.

The transaction of the title involves a man in his middle years, married but alone in a city labeled "NC," in December at a conference, who somewhat impulsively picks up a prostitute and takes her to his hotel room. What exactly he is seeking is not entirely clear, because the cold, mechanical city and the "raffish army of females" occupying the streets are as much threat as promise and his temporary liberty to act as he chooses is undercut by his feelings of isolation and loneliness. Regarding his actions as a version of an exploratory adventure in which he is curious about how he will react and tempted not only by lust but also by the desire to test his virility and validity in establishing a human connection with the girl, he is moving into unknown country, where his usual persuasive strategies have no relevance. The "odorless metal" of the room mocks his efforts to re-create the warmth of a home in an anonymous city, and the false bravado of other men around him reminds him of the insecurity that lies beneath the bluster. Even what he calls the "paid moral agent" of his imagination--that is, his mostly vestigial conscience--is summoned briefly only as a source of comforting certainty in the uncharted, shifting landscape he has entered.

The man's initial investment in the room and in purchasing some aspect of the girl's time does not permit him to exercise any influence on their transaction, a reminder that his generally successful life (marriage, money, status) counts for less than he had thought. The language of commerce that he has mastered does not contain a vocabulary for expressing his current feelings. Ruled by old habits, the preliminary stages of the transaction are a capsule courtship, but he finds that his solicitations are subject to scorn or rebuke. The girl wavers in his imagination between alluring innocence and forbidding authority, an amalgam of a dream lover who accepts him and an indifferent critic who reinforces the mechanical motif by calling his genitals "them" and prepares for their assignation "with the deliberateness of an insult or the routine of marriage." Although Updike uses his extensive abilities of description to render the physical attributes of the girl in vivid detail, she does not seem sexually attractive--an implicit comment on the failure of erotic potential when it is restricted to the external surface, as well as a subtle dig at the magazine *Oui* (a *Playboy* clone), where the story originally appeared. Without the spontaneity of mutual discovery, the transaction becomes clinical and antierotic, an unnatural or perverse use of human capability.

The man is aware of the inadequacy of his supplications. He has been using the strategies of commerce--a mix of supposedly ingratiating self-pity and cold calculation--and when these fail he tries false compliance, then bogus amiability. In desperation, because of a severe reduction in sexual potence, he begins to "make love" to her, and in a shift in tone that Updike handles with characteristic smoothness, the writing becomes lyrical as the man becomes fully involved, and the woman finally responds freely and openly. Old habits intrude, however, and the man's heightened virility causes a reversion to his familiar self. He stops producing pleasure and seeks it again as his due. His excitement has been transformed from authentic passion to calculation, the transaction back on its original terms. Both parties to the agreement have reached a level of satisfaction (he is a successful sexual athlete, and she has met the terms of the contract), and, when she offers to alter the original bargain in a mixture of self-interest and genuine generosity, he is unable to make a further break away from a lifetime of monetary measure. He contents himself with small gestures of quasi-gallantry that carry things back toward the original situation of customer and salesperson. Thus, the true cost of real freedom is gradually becoming apparent. He feels an urge to go beyond the transactional to the honestly emotional, but he is hindered by fear, and his instincts are frozen. The residue of the encounter is a dreadful shrinking of his sense of the universe. "She had made sex finite," he thinks, but in actuality, it is only his cramped view of his own possibilities that he sees.

### "TRUST ME"

"Transaction" marks the beginning of a phase of maturity in Updike's work in which recollection of an earlier time of certitude, confidence, and optimism is still possible, but in which a search for new modes of meaning is gradually taking precedence. "Deaths of Distant Friends," from *Trust Me*, which appeared in an anthology of *Best American Short Stories*, is a finely wrought philosophical meditation--exactly the sort of story cautious anthologists often include, a minor-key minirequiem for a grand past with only a twist of rue at the conclusion to relieve the sentimental mood. "The Egg Race," from *Problems, and Other Stories*, is somewhat more severe in its recollection of the past, and the origins of the problems of the present are traced with some tolerance of human need back to the narrator's father. The title story, "Trust Me," is closer to the mood of middle-life angst that informs many of the stories. Again, the narrator reconsiders the past in an effort to determine the cause of the emptiness of the present, but in his attempts to explain the failure of faith in his life, he reveals (to himself) that his parents did not trust each other, that his first wife did not trust the modern world, that his child did not trust him, that with his girlfriend he does not trust himself, and that with a psychotropic agent, he does not (or cannot) trust his senses so he ultimately cannot trust his perceptions. Logically, then, he cannot know, with surety, anything at all.

His predicament is a part of a larger vision of loss that directs many stories in the volume, as Updike's characters attempt to cope with a deterioration of faith that revives some of the earlier questions of a religious nature that formed an important dimension of Updike's writing in books such as *The Poorhouse Fair* or *A Month of Sundays*. The situation has changed somewhat, though, as the more traditional religious foundations that Updike seemed to trust earlier have become less specifically viable, even if the theological questions they posed still are important. The newfound or sensed freedom that is glimpsed carries a terrifying burden of singularity.

### "SLIPPAGE"

"Slippage" conveys this feeling through its metaphors of structural fragility. A "not quite slight earthquake" awakens a man who is "nauseated without knowing why." His wife, a much younger woman, is hidden under the covers, "like something dead on the road," an image of nullity. Blessed or cursed with a memory that "extended so much further back in time than hers," he feels she is preparing them prematurely for senility. At sixty, he sees his life as a series of not-quite-achieved plateaus. His work as a scholar was adequate but not all that it might have been, and his "late-capitalist liberal humanism" now seems passé. Even his delight in the sensual has been shaken, "though only thrice wed." Updike depicts him in his confusion as "a flake of consciousness lost within time's black shale" and extends the metaphor of infirmity to a loose molar and a feeling that his children are "a tiny, hard, slightly shrivelled core of disappointment." In the story's denouement, the man meets a woman at a party; she excites him, but it turns out that she is "quite mad," an ultimate betrayal of his instincts. At the close, he lies in bed again, anticipating another earth tremor and feeling its unsettling touch in his imagination.

### "THE CITY"

The aura of discouragement that "Slippage" projects is balanced by another of Updike's most forceful stories, "The City" (also from *Trust Me*). Recalling both "Transaction" with its portrayal of a business traveler alone in an urban wasteland and several later stories in which illness or disease disarms a man, "The City" places Carson, a "victim of middle-aged restlessness--the children grown, the long descent begun," in a hospital, where he must face a battery of tests to determine the cause of a vague stomach pain. Confronted by doctors, nurses, orderlies, other patients, and fellow sufferers, none of whom he knows, Carson is alone and helpless in an alien environment. The hospital works as a fitting figure for the absurdity and complexity of the postmodern world. The health professionals seem like another species, and Carson's physical pain is a symbol of his spiritual discomfort as he proceeds with the useless repetition of his life's requirements. From the nadir of a debilitating operation, Carson begins to overcome the indignity and unreality of his plight. He becomes fascinated with people who are unknown to him, like a beautiful black nurse whose unfathomable beauty expands the boundaries of his realm. He calls upon his lifelong training as a stoic

white Anglo-Saxon Prostestant (WASP) and determines not to make a fuss about his difficulties. He finds his "curiosity about the city revived" and develops a camaraderie with other patients, a community of the wounded. His removal from the flow of business life--he is a computer-parts salesman fluent in techno-babble--helps him regain an ironic perspective that enables him to regard his estranged daughter's ignorance of his crisis as "considerate and loving" because it contributes to the "essential solitude" he now enjoys.

In a poetic excursion into Carson's mind, Updike illustrates the tremendous satisfaction available to a person with an artistic imagination capable of finding meaning in any pattern of life's variety. Carson makes the necessary leap of faith required to "take again into himself the miracle of the world" and seizes his destiny from a mechanized, indifferent cosmos. In a reversal of the curve of decline that was the trajectory of Updike's thought from the problems of the early 1970's through the 1980's, Carson is depicted at the end of "The City" as a version of existential man who can, even amid doubt and uncertainty, find a way to be "free" and "whole"--at least as much as the postmodern world permits.

### THE AFTERLIFE, AND OTHER STORIES

The central character in many of the stories collected in *The Afterlife, and Other Stories* has a superficial autobiographical relationship to Updike, including having moved from the city to the country as a child and having desired to return to the city. In the award-winning "A Sandstone Farmhouse," Joey Robinson visits his mother's farmhouse and watches her die as the farmhouse deteriorates. After she dies, he discovers that the farmhouse was his true home: "He had always wanted to be where the action was, and what action there was, it turned out, had been back there." "The Other Side of the Street" involves a protagonist, Rentschler, returning to his childhood home and seeing it from a house across the street, where he goes to have some papers notarized. He discovers that one of his childhood friends still lives next door to the notary's house. As he leaves, he sees what used to be his house "lit up as if to welcome a visitor, a visitor, it seemed clear to him, long expected and much beloved." He thus experiences a kind of homecoming. The final story in the collection, "Grandparenting," is another tale in the Maple saga. Divorced and married to others, both Richard and Joan (now Vanderhaven) Maple are present when their daughter Judith has her first baby. In spite of the divorce, the Maples continue to function as a family.

Central to *The Afterlife, and Other Stories* is the family as seen from the perspective of an aging male. Story after story deals with people aging and dying. One story, "The Man Who Became a Soprano," treats a group who get together to play recorders. As members of the group begin to form liaisons that end in divorce, and some move away, the group itself agrees to play a concert for an elderly audience at the Congregational church. The concert is a success, but it signals the end of the recorder group.

"The Afterlife," the first story in the collection, focuses on Carter Billings. His and his wife Joan's best friends, the Egglestons, move to England. During the first night of a visit there, Carter awakens and, wandering through the hall, tumbles down the stairs. "Then something--some*one*, he felt--hit him a solid blow in the exact center of his chest," and he finds himself standing on a landing on the stairway. The next morning he decides that he actually bumped into the knob of a newel post. Nonetheless, after the experience his life seems charged with new feeling. It is as though he has had some kind of taste of the afterlife so that he is now "beyond" all earthly matters.

## MY FATHER'S TEARS, AND OTHER STORIES

The themes of the stories in *My Father's Tears, and Other Stories* are familiar: childhood, marriage and divorce, infidelity, and the quest to make sense of life and speculations about God and the afterlife. Most are set in either Pennsylvania or New England. Several are reminiscent of the earlier Olinger stories. "The Guardians," "The Walk with Elizanne," "The Laughter of the Gods," and "Kinderszenen" reflect on childhood from the perspective of an elderly man taking stock of his life. Perhaps the most poignant of these is "The Road Home," in which the protagonist, who fled rural Pennsylvania half a century earlier to escape what he then perceived as its suffocating atmosphere, finds when re-

turns that he is a stranger in the land of his boyhood.

## "VARIETIES OF RELIGIOUS EXPERIENCE"

Not all of Updike's fiction is autobiographical. One story that demonstrates Updike's ability to get outside himself is "Varieties of Religious Experience." In it Updike uses the attack on the World Trade Center on September 11, 2001, as a background for examining the lives of people forever affected by the tragedy: a businessman visiting his adult daughter who works near the Twin Towers, a stockbroker working on an upper floor when the planes hit, two Muslim extremists who are involved in the plot to attack icons of U.S. power, and a woman aboard Flight 93 as it is hijacked and then taken over by the passengers. Without ever saying so directly, Updike makes it clear that each one of these characters is forced to decide if God is present in his or her life and to act on that belief.

## "THE FULL GLASS"

One story that captures the spirit of reminiscence exceptionally well is "The Full Glass." The elderly protagonist of this first-person narrative begins by describing a nightly routine in which he sets out a full glass of water to use in taking his daily medications. Though he admits the practical reason for filling the glass early is to avoid having to manipulate the faucet, glass, and pills, there is another, more revealing cause for his ritual. It is "a small but distinct pleasure," he says, and "that healthy swig near the end of the day has gotten to be something important, *a tiny piece that fits in*." The autobiographical elements in this tale are oblique but unmistakable. The narrator, a transplanted Pennsylvanian living in New England, is a craftsman, a floor refinisher who works not with words but with wood. His "favorite moment in the floor-finishing business" occurs when he departs, "knowing that all that remained was for the polyurethane to dry, which would happen without me, *in my absence*." The parallel with readers' experiencing the beauty of a story in the writer's absence is too strong to be coincidental. In the final scene the narrator transforms the act of taking medicine into a philosophical commentary.

My life-prolonging pills cupped in my left hand, I lift the glass, its water sweetened by its brief wait on the marble sinktop. If I can read this strange old guy's mind aright, he's drinking a toast to the visible world, his impending disappearance from it be damned.

It is as if Updike himself is bidding his farewell to the world.

OTHER MAJOR WORKS

LONG FICTION: *The Poorhouse Fair*, 1959; *Rabbit, Run*, 1960; *The Centaur*, 1963; *Of the Farm*, 1965; *Couples*, 1968; *Bech: A Book*, 1970; *Rabbit Redux*, 1971; *A Month of Sundays*, 1975; *Marry Me: A Romance*, 1976; *The Coup*, 1978; *Rabbit Is Rich*, 1981; *The Witches of Eastwick*, 1984; *Roger's Version*, 1986; *S.*, 1988; *Rabbit at Rest*, 1990; *Memories of the Ford Administration*, 1992; *Brazil*, 1994; *In the Beauty of the Lilies*, 1996; *Toward the End of Time*, 1997; *Bech at Bay: A Quasi-Novel*, 1998; *Gertrude and Claudius*, 2000; *Seek My Face*, 2002; *Villages*, 2004; *Terrorist*, 2006; *The Widows of Eastwick*, 2008.

PLAYS: *Three Texts from Early Ipswich: A Pageant*, pb. 1968; *Buchanan Dying*, pb. 1974, pr. 1976.

POETRY: *The Carpentered Hen, and Other Tame Creatures*, 1958; *Telephone Poles, and Other Poems*, 1963; *Dog's Death*, 1965; *Verse*, 1965; *Bath After Sailing*, 1968; *The Angels*, 1968; *Midpoint, and Other Poems*, 1969; *Seventy Poems*, 1972; *Six Poems*, 1973; *Cunts (Upon Receiving the Swingers Life Club Membership Solicitation)*, 1974; *Query*, 1974; *Tossing and Turning*, 1977; *Sixteen Sonnets*, 1979; *Five Poems*, 1980; *Jester's Dozen*, 1984; *Facing Nature*, 1985; *Mites, and Other Poems in Miniature*, 1990; *Collected Poems, 1953-1993*, 1993; *A Helpful Alphabet of Friendly Objects*, 1995; *Americana, and Other Poems*, 2001; *Endpoint, and Other Poems*, 2009.

NONFICTION: *Assorted Prose*, 1965; *Picked-Up Pieces*, 1975; *Hugging the Shore: Essays and Criticism*, 1983; *Just Looking: Essays on Art*, 1989; *Self-Consciousness: Memoirs*, 1989; *Odd Jobs: Essays and Criticism*, 1991; *Golf Dreams: Writings on Golf*, 1996; *More Matter: Essays and Criticism*, 1999; *Still Looking: Essays on American Art*, 2005; *Due Considerations: Essays and Criticism*, 2007; *Updike in Cincinnati: A Literary Performance*, 2007.

EDITED TEXT: *The Best American Short Stories of the Century*, 2000.

BIBLIOGRAPHY

Detweiler, Robert. *John Updike*. Boston: Twayne, 1984. Within the confines of the Twayne series format, Detweiler supplies sound, thorough analysis of all Updike's work through the mid-1980's and provides a brief biography and a useful, annotated bibliography.

Gopnik, Adam. "John Updike." *The New Yorker*, February 9, 2009. A review of Updike's long and fruitful career at *The New Yorker*.

Greiner, Donald J. *The Other John Updike: Poems, Short Stories, Prose, Play*. Athens: Ohio University Press, 1981. While devoting a considerable amount of space to other critics, Greiner, who has written three books about Updike, here traces Updike's artistic development in his writing that both parallels and extends the themes of the novels.

Halford, Macy. "American Centaur: An Interview with John Updike." *The New Yorker* (October 28, 2009). In 1978, Updike spoke to the Writers' Association of Croatia in Zagreb, and he gave a lengthy interview to two professors of English at the University of Sarajevo. In an unusually frank question-and-answer session, finally translated into English, Updike talked about his favorite novelists, his writing habits, and where he places himself in literary tradition.

Haupt-Lehmann, Christopher. "John Updike, Tireless Chronicler of Small-Town America, Dies at Seventy-Six." *The New York Times*, January 27, 2009. Insightful coverage of Updike's career in an obituary salute.

Luscher, Robert M. *John Updike: A Study of the Short Fiction*. New York: Twayne, 1993. An introduction to Updike's short fiction, dealing with his lyrical technique, his experimentation with narrative structure, his use of the short-story cycle convention, and the relationship between his short fiction and his novels. Includes Updike's comments on his short fiction and previously published critical essays representing a variety of critical approaches.

Macnaughton, William R., ed. *Critical Essays on John Updike*. Boston: G. K. Hall, 1982. A comprehensive, eclectic collection, including essays by writers such as Alfred Kazin, Anthony Burgess, and Joyce Carol Oates, who provide reviews, and various

Updike experts, who have written original essays. Contains a survey of bibliographies and an assessment of criticism and scholarship.

Olster, Stacey, ed. *The Cambridge Companion to John Updike*. Cambridge, England: Cambridge University Press, 2006. An excellent collection of essays covering Updike's fiction from a variety of critical perspectives; commentary on the short stories is interspersed throughout discussions of Updike's themes and techniques.

Pritchard, William H. *Updike: America's Man of Letters*. South Royalton, Vt.: Steerforth Press, 2000. A comprehensive assessment of Updike's achievement in various literary genres; brief commentary on individual short stories is included in chapters describing Updike's methodology and his chief concerns as a writer.

Schiff, James A. *John Updike Revisited*. New York: Twayne, 1998. A general introduction surveying all of Updike's work but focusing on his fiction in the late 1990's. The chapter on the short story is relatively brief, with short analyses of such stories as "A & P" and "Separating."

*Leon Lewis; Richard Tuerk*
*Updated by Laurence W. Mazzeno*

# V

---

## HELENA MARÍA VIRAMONTES

**Born:** East Los Angeles, California;
  February 26, 1954

PRINCIPAL SHORT FICTION
  *The Moths, and Other Stories,* 1985
  *"Miss Clairol,"* 1987
  *"Tears on My Pillow,"* 1992
  *"The Jumping Bean,"* 1993

OTHER LITERARY FORMS

Helena María Viramontes (veer-eh-MON-tays) is the author of *Under the Feet of Jesus,* a novel that she dedicated to the memory of civil rights activist César Chávez, and the novel *Their Dogs Came with Them* (2007). The latter novel took seventeen years to complete and is about the gang conflicts and social problems in East Los Angeles. Viramontes and María Herrera-Sobek coedited two anthologies: *Chicana Creativity and Criticism: Creative Frontiers in American Literature* (1987, revised 1996) and *Chicana (W)rites: On Word and Film* (1995).

ACHIEVEMENTS

Helena María Viramontes won a National Endowment for the Arts grant in 1989 and received the John Dos Passos Prize for Literature for 1995; she was also the recipient of a Sundance Institute Fellowship and the Luis Leal Award. In 2007, Viramontes was named a 2007 USA Ford Fellow by United States Artists, an arts advocacy foundation that grants cash awards to artists.

BIOGRAPHY

Helena María Viramontes was born on February 26, 1954, in East Los Angeles, California, a location that has served as the setting for most of her short fiction. One of nine children in the family, she learned the value of work from an early age. Her father was a construction worker, her mother a homemaker. The Viramontes household was often filled with friends and relatives who had crossed the Mexican border looking for work. In her fiction Viramontes draws on the memories of the stories she heard from these immigrants. As a student at Immaculate Heart College, where she was one of only five Chicanas in her class, Viramontes worked twenty hours a week while carrying a full load of classes. She received a B.A. in 1975 with a major in English literature.

In 1977 her short story "Requiem for the Poor" won first prize for fiction in a contest sponsored by *Statement Magazine* of California State University, Los Angeles. In 1978 "The Broken Web" was the first-place winner, and in 1979 "Birthday" won first prize in the Chicano Literary Contest at the University of California at Irvine. "The Broken Web" and "Birthday" appear in her collection of short stories *The Moths, and Other Stories.*

Viramontes received an M.F.A. in the creative writing program of the University of California at Irvine. She became a professor of English at Cornell University in Ithaca, New York. She has served as editor of the cultural magazine *Chismearte* and coordinator of the Los Angeles Latino Writers Association.

ANALYSIS

In her short stories Helena María Viramontes provides a vision of Hispanic women in American society, presenting female characters whose lives are limited by the patriarchy of Hispanic society and the imposition of religious values. She provides a humanistic and caring approach to the poor and downtrodden women who inhabit the working-class world of her fiction. She deals with the issues of abortion, aging, death, immigration, divorce, and separation. The stories in *The Moths, and Other Stories* are arranged in the order of the stages in a woman's life, beginning with the story of a young girl in "The Moths" and moving on to stories of women in the later stage of life. "Snapshots," a story near the end of the collection, is about a divorced woman who feels that she has wasted her life in the mundane and demanding trivia of housework. "Neighbors" depicts an elderly woman, isolated and living in fear of the young men in the neighborhood.

### "THE MOTHS"

"The Moths" is the story of a young Chicana girl who finds a safe refuge in caring for her aging grandmother, her Abuelita. Constantly in trouble at home, fighting with her sisters, and receiving whippings, the rebellious fourteen-year-old girl finds a purpose for her life as she works with her grandmother to plant flowers and grow them in coffee cans. Viramontes describes in detail how the two women nurture the plants as they form a world of their own, away from the dominating force of the girl's father.

The story contains elements of the Magical Realism that characterizes much contemporary Third World American literature. When her more feminine sisters call her "Bull Hands" because her hands are too large and clumsy for the fine work of embroidery or crocheting, the girl feels her hands begin to grow. As her grandmother soothes the hands in a balm of dried moth wings and Vicks, the girl feels her hands shrink back to normal size. Another example of Magical Realism occurs at the end of the story, when the image of the moths is realized as they fly out of the dead grandmother's mouth.

The women exist in a world of wild lilies, jasmine, heliotrope, and cilantro, working with mayonnaise jars and coffee cans. The vines of chayotes wind around the pillars of the grandmother's house, climbing to the roof and creating the illusion that the house is "cradled" in vines, safe and protected. In her own home the girl's Apá, her father, forces her to go to church by banging on the table, threatening to beat her, and lashing out at her mother, her Amá. In one brief scene Viramontes is able to portray the brutal hold the father has on the family. In contrast to this household, the grandmother's house, devoid of a masculine presence, is a place of peace and growth. When the grandmother dies, the girl finds her, and she bathes her grandmother's body in a

ceremony. As she performs this ritual, the girl sees the old scars on the woman's back, evidence that she, too, had suffered beatings.

### "SNAPSHOTS"

As the story opens, Olga Ruiz, a woman whose husband has left her, reflects on her life and admits that it was the "small things in life" that made her happy: "ironing straight arrow creases" on her husband's work shirts and cashing in coupons. Now that she has reached middle age, she realizes that she has wasted her life in the pursuit of housework with nothing to show for all her efforts. Now that she is alone, a hopeless lethargy has set in, and she seems unable to cope with her new circumstances. Marge, her daughter, tries to get her involved with projects, pleading "Please. Mother. Knit. Do something."

As she pores over the snapshots in family albums, Olga sees that she has been "longing for a past that never actually existed." The title of the story refers to more than the actual snapshots. Olga sees snapshots as ghosts and feels "haunted by the frozen moments." She remembers her grandmother's fear that snapshots would steal a person's soul, and she recounts how her grandfather tried to take a family picture with his new camera; not knowing how to operate it, he took the film out and expected it to develop in the sunlight. As the story ends, Olga, fearing that her grandmother was right, decides that if she finds a picture of her grandmother, she will destroy it.

Viramontes paints a portrait of a woman who has devoted her life to being a good wife and mother, cooking, cleaning, taking care of others, and then in her middle years has been abandoned. Her husband has remarried, and her son-in-law is tired of her calls to her daughter, Marge. At one point he takes the phone away from Marge and says, "Mrs. Ruiz, why don't you leave us alone." A few minutes later, Dave, her former husband, calls and asks her to "leave the kids alone." After a lifetime of hard work, Olga has been left alone, feeling that her life was worthless.

### "NEIGHBORS"

"Neighbors," the last story in the collection, tells the story of Aura Rodriguez, an isolated seventy-three-year-old woman who lives in fear of the young men in her neighborhood, who have vowed to get even with her for calling the police on them. Realizing that she must take care of herself, she gets a gun and sits in a chair facing the door, ready to protect herself. This story opens with a description of a neighborhood that has "slowly metamorphosed into a graveyard." Aura believes in living within her own space and expects her neighbors to do the same.

In the words of Fierro, Aura's old neighbor, Viramontes repeats the metaphor of the graveyard that she used at the beginning of the story. Fierro remembers the quiet hills and old homes that existed before the government destroyed the houses and covered the land with "endless freeway" that "paved over his sacred ruins, his secrets, his graves . . . his memories." The story is filled with realistic details such as the description of Aura's "Ben Gay scented house slipper."

### "THE CARIBOO CAFÉ"

Conflict in Central America is the focus of "The Cariboo Café," in which a woman from El Salvador has suffered the loss of her child at the hands of government officials. Interwoven with the story of her grief is the story of the cook, who suffers from loneliness after losing his wife and son, and the terrified illegal immigrants who fear capture by the police. The woman from El Salvador, who has been mourning the loss of her small son for several years, mistakenly believes that one of the immigrants in the café is her son.

In the first segment of this three-part story, Sonya and her brother Macky, children of illegal immigrants, are frightened when they see a police officer seizing a man on the street. Trained to fear the police, the children run to the café for protection. In the second part, the narrator is the cook, who has shown immigration agents where the immigrants are hiding even though they have been regular customers. The narrator of the third part is the Salvadoran woman whose young son was taken by army officials. After numerous attempts to find her son, the woman moved across the Mexican border to the United States. In the final, violent confrontation when the police enter the café, the woman fights them, identifying them with the army officials who took her son. Viramontes tells this complex story through shifting points of view to reveal different perspectives as she shows the power of oppressive governments.

### OTHER MAJOR WORKS

LONG FICTION: *Under the Feet of Jesus*, 1995; *Their Dogs Came with Them*, 2007.

NONFICTION: "Nopalitos: The Making of Fiction," 1989; "Why I Write," 1995.

EDITED TEXTS: *Chicana Creativity and Criticism: Charting New Frontiers in American Literature*, 1987, revised 1996 (with María Herrera-Sobek); *Chicana (W)rites: On Word and Film*, 1995 (with Herrera-Sobek).

### BIBLIOGRAPHY

Gelfant, Blanche H., ed. *The Columbia Companion to the Twentieth-Century American Short Story*. New York: Columbia University Press, 2000. Includes a chapter in which Viramontes's short stories are analyzed.

Green, Carol Hurd, and Mary Grimley Mason. *American Women Writers*. New York: Continuum, 1994. Contains a brief biographical sketch of Viramontes, as well as an analysis of the short stories in *Moths*. Focuses on her portrayal of Chicana women with their strengths and weaknesses as they struggle with the restrictions placed on them because they are women; notes that many of the characters pay a price for rebelling against traditional values.

Mermann-Jozwiak, Elisabeth, and Nancy Sullivan. "You Carry the Border with You: Conversation with Helena María Viramontes ." In *Conversations with Mexican American Writers: Languages and Literatures in the Borderlands*. Jackson: University Press of Mississippi, 2009. Among other subjects, Viramontes discusses her short fiction and her choice of language in her work.

Richards, Judith. "Chicano Creativity and Criticism: New Frontiers in American Literature." *College Literature* 25 (Spring, 1998): 182. In this review of the anthology edited by Viramontes and María Herrera-Sobek, Richards argues that the book provides a good starting place for those who want to evaluate the Chicana literary movement. Points to the emergence of urban working-class women as protagonists, the frequent use of child and adolescent narrators, and autobiographical formats that focus on unresolved issues as characteristics of Chicana literature.

Saldívar-Hull, Sonia. "Helena María Viramontes." In *Chicano Writers: Second Series*. Vol. 122 in *Dictionary of Literary Biography*. Detroit: Gale Research, 1992. Summarizes and analyzes several stories from *Moths*, stressing the cultural and religious traditions that restrict women's lives. Discusses the patriarchal privileges that the father assumes in the story when he shouts at his daughter "'Tu eres mujer'" (you are a woman) in an attempt to control her. Calls "Snapshots" a "scathing critique of the politics of housework" and refers to the divorced Olga as "an alienated laborer whose value has decreased."

_____. "'I Hear the Women's Wails and I Know Them to Be My Own': From Mujer to Collective Identities in Helena María Viramontes's U.S. Third World." In *Feminism on the Border: Chicana Gender Politics and Literature*. Berkeley: University of California Press, 2000. An in-depth analysis of *The Moths, and Other Stories*, placing Viramontes's work within the broader context of Chicana border literature. Saldívar-Hull argues that for Viramontes, "aesthetics is a practice of political intervention carried out in literary form."

Sandoval, Anna Marie. "Acts of Daily Resistance in Urban and Rural Settings: The Fiction of Helena María Viramontes." In *Toward a Latina Feminism of the Americas: Repression and Resistance in Chicana and Mexicana Literature*. Austin: University of Texas Press, 2008. Examines works by Viramontes and other Latina writers who rebel against their traditional patriarchal culture and reject negative depictions of women.

Yarbo-Bejarano, Yvonne. *Introduction to "The Moths and Other Stories."* Houston, Tex.: Arte Público Press, 1995. Discusses Viramontes's portrayal of women characters who struggle against the restrictions placed on them by the Chicano culture, the church, and the men in their lives. Provides a brief analysis of each story in the collection, showing that the stories deal with problems Chicana women face at various stages of their lives. Notes that, although Viramontes addresses the problems of racial prejudice and economic struggles, the emphasis is on the cultural and social values that shape these women and suggests that most of stories involve the conflict between the female character and the man who represents an oppressive authority figure.

*Judith Barton Williamson*

---

# GERALD R. VIZENOR

**Born:** Minneapolis, Minnesota; October 22, 1934

PRINCIPAL SHORT FICTION

*Anishinabe Adisokan: Stories of the Ojibwa,* 1974
*Wordarrows: Indians and Whites in the New Fur Trade,* 1978
*Earthdivers: Tribal Narratives on Mixed Descent,* 1981
*Landfill Meditation: Crossblood Stories,* 1991
*Wordarrows: Native States of Literary Sovereignty,* 2003 (originally pb. as *Wordarrows: Indians and Whites in the New Fur Trade*)

OTHER LITERARY FORMS

Best known for his novels, especially *Griever: An American Monkey King in China* (1987), Gerald Vizenor has also published several volumes of poetry, many of them devoted to haiku. He also wrote the screenplay *Harold of Orange* (1984) and a number of nonfiction volumes, including *Manifest Manners: Postindian Warriors of Survivance* (1994) and *Postindian Conversations* (1999), which champion the Native American cause.

ACHIEVEMENTS

Gerald Vizenor has received many honors, including the New York Fiction Collective Award (1987), the American Book Award from the Before Columbus

Foundation (1988), an Artists Fellowship in Literature from the California Arts Council Literature Award (1989), the PEN/Oakland Book Award (1990), the Lifetime Achievement Award from the Native Writers' Circle of the Americas (2001), the Distinguished Achievement Award from the Western Literature Association (2005), and the Lifetime Achievement Award from the Society for the Study of the Multi-Ethnic Literature of the United States (2011). He has become a prominent voice in Native American literature despite the difficulty of his works. His academic recognition has included the J. Hill Professorship at the University of Minnesota, the David Burr Chair at the University of Oklahoma, and the Richard and Rhoda Goldman Distinguished Professorship at the University of California, Berkeley

## BIOGRAPHY

On October 22, 1934, Gerald Robert Vizenor was born to La Verne Peterson Vizenor and Clement Vizenor, who was murdered twenty months later. Thereafter, Gerald was reared partly by his father's Anishinaabe relatives. At age fifteen, he joined the National Guard and at eighteen the U.S. Army--an experience he found intellectually stimulating, particularly during his station in Japan. In 1955, at the end of his enlistment, he entered New York University, then transferred in 1956 to the University of Minnesota. He married Judith Horns in 1959 and graduated the year his son Robert was born in 1960. He began graduate work until his writings as social worker and activist won him a position as a reporter for the *Minneapolis Tribune* (1968-1969). From 1970 to 1971, he taught at Lake Forest College in Illinois; from 1971 to 1972, he directed the Indian Studies Program at Bemidji State University in Minnesota; in 1973, he attended Harvard University; and in 1974, he rejoined the *Tribune*'s editorial staff. His career continued in a similarly nomadic fashion. Particularly notable was his time spent teaching at Tianjin University in China, which inspired the writing of *Griever*. He subsequently taught at the University of California at Santa Cruz, the University of Oklahoma, the University of California at Berkeley, and the University of New Mexico. He was divorced in 1969 and remained single until his marriage to Laura Hall in 1981.

## ANALYSIS

Like much postcolonial literature, Gerald Vizenor's short fiction refuses to accept the science-based worldview of the Occident, instead employing a Magical Realism that fuses Native American religious beliefs with modern images. This was already the case in his early, relatively more conventional short narratives (including *Wordarrows*) and has subsequently led to even freer fantasy. He is also postcolonial in that his engagé position inclines toward satire, playful diatribes, and seemingly pedantic documentation that interweave the conventions of factual and fictional literature, enabling him to comment on actual events without letting their seriousness constrain his sense of humor.

He undermines the distinction between fact and fiction because it is based on the dichotomy of objective and subjective, which colonialism used to subordinate the supposedly superstitious emotionalism of "primitive" people to its own "objectivity." Similarly, colonialism (in the guise of the Bureau of Indian Affairs, for example) long tried to replace oral traditions with bureaucratic literacy, taught by a school system that

*Gerald R. Vizenor* (Christopher Felver/Corbis)

forbade the use of Native American languages. Despite a decreasing market for short fiction (except in poorly paid academic journals), Vizenor produced many brief works, a practice congruent with the oral tradition he seeks to preserve; his craftsmanship cannot be separated from his politics.

### "THE PSYCHOTAXIDERMIST"

This story is a self-reflexive account of a generation. Its narrator, Colonel Clement Beaulieu, is a persona of Vizenor, who combined the first name of his father with the last of his grandmother. Beaulieu recalls an anecdote about Newcrows, a shaman whose imagination could bring dead animals to life. In a satire of white society, the shaman is arrested for performing this miracle on a golf course. He then infests the prosecutor and judge with magical ticks, thereby ending the trial. In an epilogue, Beaulieu begins telling the story to a group of nuns, with its protagonist changed to Sister Isolde. The point is that oral narratives are altered for each audience. Only through such imaginative adaptation can the tales themselves become psychotaxidermists, not merely preserving past forms but reanimating them.

### WORDARROWS

The preface to this work compares the ancient use of arrows to the modern employment of words in the defense of the tribe. Most of the stories are vignettes from the time when Vizenor was executive director of the American Indian Employment and Guidance Center in Minneapolis. As he has acknowledged, some of these vignettes might seem racist, except for Vizenor's being a Native American. For instance, "Roman Downwind" portrays a teenager who barely passes his driving test on the third try, celebrates until he has exhausted his cash and family, then talks an agency into giving him enough money so he can meet a white woman and be comfortable for one more day. In "Marleen American Horse," such self-defeating behavior is diagnosed as the result of Native Americans' accepting colonial stereotypes, which produces guilt that leads to substance abuse and then to more guilt, in a vicious circle.

### "LANDFILL MEDITATION"

First published in a slightly different version in 1979, "Landfill Meditation" later became the title story in Vizenor's 1991 collection. The tale's importance derives from its primary image: society's treating Native Americans as garbage. Nose Charmer, a trickster able to profit from this racism, becomes rich by dumping toxic waste on wetlands he is trying to claim as sacred grounds. His story is being told "backward" by Clement Beaulieu--a pun on the stereotype of "backward" Native Americans. Another of Beaulieu's anecdotes concerns "Belladonna Winter Catcher." Her fatal flaw is a predilection for "terminal creeds," a phrase that Vizenor uses repeatedly to signify any humorless conception of life. The other Native Americans murder her, as they have poisoned many of those guilty of the same fault. After telling these loosely related parables, Beaulieu floats out the window, buoyed by his laughter.

### EARTHDIVERS

This collection takes its name from the widely distributed myth that dry land was created by divers who brought it from the bottom of the sea. To Vizenor, the situation of having to create the ground of one's existence particularly suits "mixedbloods," who are between cultures. In the preface, where he discusses this myth, Vizenor derides cultural critic Alan Dundes's Freudian interpretation, which Vizenor considers the quintessence of humorless, colonial reduction of Native American creativity to filth. Vizenor's stories celebrate trickster figures who manage, for a while at least, to find a place for themselves in the wasteland of urban civilization. In "The Chair of Tears," for example, academia is arrayed against the Native American Studies Department, whose chair must have publications and other credentials to please the establishment but quite the opposite to satisfy the radical students. Knowing that he has no safe ground on which to proceed, the seventh appointee makes a series of startling innovations, such as establishing a Department of Undecided Studies, likely, given student procrastination, to become the largest and potentially most powerful unit on campus. The volume concludes, however, not with the success of such mediating tricksters but with a group of stories about a collapse in racial relations because of unsuccessful attempts to halt the execution of a Native American.

### "LUMINOUS THIGHS: MYTHIC TROPISMS"

This story's protagonist, Griever de Hocus, is also the center of Vizenor's novels *Griever*, a surrealistic fictionalization of Vizenor's teaching at Tianjin University, and *The Trickster of Liberty: Tribal Heirs to a Wild Baronage* (1988), largely about Griever's family. Although Vizenor's persona in his earlier books, Clement Beaulieu, appears in episodes of a Magical Realist bent, he is a more transparent and believable version of Vizenor than Griever, who seeks to turn himself into myth as a defense against the urbanized world. This self-transformation involves "tropisms," a word previously used by writer Nathalie Sarraute, who defined them as the psychological patterns with which people jockey for control over one another. To her, these behaviors are futile, but to Vizenor they are "mythic," bestowing a sense of connection to primordial meaning.

"Luminous Thighs: Mythic Tropisms" opens with one of these mythic tropisms. To annoy the man next to him on a train, Griever tells a preposterous story about driving a novelist's car into a river so that the novelist, after being rumored to be dead, could have the pleasure of publicly declaring himself to be alive. This metaphor of rebirth through water, present in Griever's other discourses, is meant to unsettle anyone near him, since stereotypes left unsettled are likely to turn against him in a white society. The luminous thighs themselves are sexually unsettling because they are of an androgynous statue. They give a title not only to the story but also to a screenplay Griever hoped to film with actor Robert Redford (Vizenor worked at Redford's Sundance Institute). The story's digressive conclusion is a denunciation of Ruth Beebe Hill's novel *Hanta Yo* (1979), a book that pandered to the public's desire for myths and imposed humorless stereotypes on Native Americans. For Vizenor's tale to wander into a review of this novel is perhaps more unsettling than any of his previous expansions of the short-story genre.

OTHER MAJOR WORKS

LONG FICTION: *Darkness in Saint Louis Bearheart*, 1978, revised 1990 (as *Bearheart: The Heirship Chronicles*); *Griever: An American Monkey King in China*, 1987; *The Trickster of Liberty: Tribal Heirs to a Wild Baronage*, 1988; *The Heirs of Columbus*, 1991; *Dead Voices: Natural Agonies in the New World*, 1992; *Chancers*, 2000; *Hiroshima Bugi:*

*Atomu 57*, 2003; *Father Meme*, 2008; *Shrouds of White Earth*, 2010.

SCREENPLAY: *Harold of Orange*, 1984.

POETRY: *Matsushima: Pine Islands*, 1984 (originally pb. as four separate volumes of haiku during the 1960's); *Almost Ashore: Selected Poems*, 2006; *Bear Island: The War at Sugar Point*, 2006.

NONFICTION: *Thomas James White Hawk*, 1968; *The Everlasting Sky: New Voices from the People Named the Chippewa*, 1972; *Tribal Scenes and Ceremonies*, 1976; *Crossbloods: Bone Courts, Bingo, and Other Reports*, 1990; *Interior Landscapes: Autobiographical Myths and Metaphors*, 1990, 2d ed. 2009; *Manifest Manners: Postindian Warriors of Survivance*, 1994; *Fugitive Poses: Native American Indian Scenes of Absence and Presence*, 1998; *Postindian Conversations*, 1999; *Native Liberty: Natural Reason and Cultural Survivance*, 2009.

EDITED TEXTS: *Summer in the Spring: Ojibwe Lyric Poems and Tribal Stories*, 1981 (revised as *Summer in the Spring: Anishinaabe Lyric Poems and Stories*, 1993); *Native American Perspectives on Literature and History*, 1992 (with Alan R. Velie); *Narrative Chance: Postmodern Discourse on Native American Indian Literatures*, 1993; *Native American Literature: A Brief Introduction and Anthology*, 1995.

MISCELLANEOUS: *The People Named the Chippewa: Narrative Histories*, 1984; *Shadow Distance: A Gerald Vizenor Reader*, 1994.

BIBLIOGRAPHY

Barry, Nora Baker. "Postmodern Bears in the Texts of Gerald Vizenor." *MELUS* 27, no. 3 (Fall, 2002): 93-112. Countering the trend to discuss Vizenor's work by focusing on his trickster figures, Barry turns attention to his use of the mythologically important figure of the bear in his work, including in some of his short stories.

Blaeser, Kimberly, M. "Gerald Vizenor: Postindian Liberation." In *The Cambridge Companion to Native American Literature*, edited by Joy Porter and Kenneth M. Roemer. New York: Cambridge University Press, 2005. Provides a concise overview of Vizenor's works.

_____. *Gerald Vizenor: Writing in the Oral Tradition.* Norman: University of Oklahoma Press, 1996. Blaeser emphasizes Vizenor's own awareness of ironic contrasts between his eclecticism and his sense of continuity with the tribal past.

Haseltine, Patricia. "The Voices of Gerald Vizenor: Survival Through Transformation." *American Indian Quarterly* 9, no. 1 (Winter, 1985): 31. In discussing Vizenor's multiplicity, Haseltine suggests that one strata of it arises from dream vision experience.

Hume, Kathryn. "Gerald Vizenor's Metaphysics." Contemporary Literature 48, no. 4 (Winter, 2007): 580-612. Examines Vizenor's depiction of Native Americans, his exploration of metaphysical philosophy, and his writing style.

Isernhagen, Hartwig. *Momaday, Vizenor, Armstrong: Conversations on American Indian Writing.* Norman: University of Oklahoma Press, 1999. Although Vizenor has given many interviews, this book brings him into the context of N. Scott Momaday's works, which have been a major influence on Vizenor's.

Lee, A. Robert, ed. *Loosening the Seams: Interpretations of Gerald Vizenor.* Bowling Green, Ohio: Bowling Green State University Popular Press, 2000. Collection of essays examining Vizenor's works, including discussions of "crossblood strategies," "trickster discourse," and postmodernism in his writings and a comparison of his work with that of writer Ishmael Reed.

Madsen, Deborah L. *Understanding Gerald Vizenor.* Columbia: University of South Carolina Press, 2009. An introductory overview to Vizenor's work in all literary genres. Explores the themes, images, and stylistic devices of his writings.

Monsma, Bradley John. "'Active Readers . . . Obverse Tricksters': Trickster-Texts and Cross-Cultural Reading." *Modern Language Studies* 26 (Fall, 1996): 83-98. Monsma investigates to what extent Vizenor's use of the trickster theme expects both the readers and the author to be tricksters.

Owens, Louis, ed. *Studies in American Indian Literatures: The Journal of the Association for the Study of American Indian Literatures* 9 (Spring, 1997). This special issue devoted to Vizenor contains articles on his contrasts between tribal and legal identity; how he, Samuel Beckett, and John Bunyan use the past in comparable ways; his employment of Buddhist and wasteland imagery; and his changing poetic vision.

Vizenor, Gerald. "An Interview with Gerald Vizenor." Interview by Neal Bowers and Charles L. P. Silet. *MELUS* 8, no. 1 (1981): 41-49. Vizenor relates the multiplicity, constant change, deliberate provocation, even contradiction in his own works to the traditional function of oral tales as a vivid dialogue between performer and audience, an activity he calls "word cinema."

_____. "Mythic Rage and Laughter: An Interview with Gerald Vizenor." Interview by Dallas Miller. *Studies in American Indian Literatures: The Journal of the Association for the Study of American Indian Literatures* 7 (Spring, 1995): 77-96. Explores the twin poles of anger and laughter in Vizenor's writing.

_____. "On Thin Ice, You Might as Well Dance: An Interview with Gerald Vizenor." Interview by Larry McCaffery and Tom Marshall. *Some Other Fluency: Interviews with Innovative American Authors.* Philadelphia: University of Pennsylvania Press, 1996. Vizenor considers that the precariousness of his situation has spurred his artistry.

_____. "'I Defy Analysis': A Conversation with Gerald Vizenor." Interview by Rodney Simard, Lavonne Mason, and Ju Abner. *Studies in American Indian Literatures: The Journal of the Association for the Study of American Indian Literatures* 5 (Fall, 1993): 42-51. Vizenor protests against critics' attempts to classify him.

*James Whitlark*

# KURT VONNEGUT

**Born:** Indianapolis, Indiana; November 11, 1922
**Died:** New York, New York; April 11, 2007

PRINCIPAL SHORT FICTION

*Canary in a Cat House,* 1961
*Welcome to the Monkey House,* 1968
*Bagombo Snuff Box: Uncollected Short Fiction,*
  1999
*Look at the Birdie: Unpublished Short Fiction,* 2009
*While Mortals Sleep: Unpublished Short Fiction,*
  2011

OTHER LITERARY FORMS

Kurt Vonnegut (VAHN-eh-geht) published numerous volumes, including essays, short stories, the play *Happy Birthday, Wanda June* (1970) and the teleplay *Between Time and Timbuktu: Or, Prometheus-5, a Space Fantasy* (1972), and the novels on which his reputation is principally based. His best-known novels include *The Sirens of Titan* (1959), *Cat's Cradle* (1963), *Slaughterhouse-Five: Or, The Children's Crusade, a Duty-Dance with Death* (1969), and *Breakfast of Champions* (1973). In 1997, he published *Timequake.*

ACHIEVEMENTS

For many years, the popular success of the writing of Kurt Vonnegut exceeded critical recognition of his work. With his earlier work labeled as science fiction and published in paperback editions and popular magazines such as *Ladies' Home Journal* and *The Saturday Evening Post,* critical attention was delayed. In 1986, Vonnegut received the Bronze Medallion from Guild Hall.

BIOGRAPHY

Although not specifically an autobiographical writer, Kurt Vonnegut frequently drew on facts and incidents from his own life in his writing. The youngest in a family of three children, Vonnegut was born and reared in Indianapolis, Indiana. While serving in the Army as an infantry scout during World War II, he was taken prisoner by the Germans and interned at Dresden, Germany, at the time of the 1945 Allied firebombing of the city that cost 135,000 lives. He survived only through the ironic circumstance of being quartered in an underground meat locker. This episode contributed much toward his authorial distance: After returning to that meat locker forty-three years later in 1998, Vonnegut commented that he was one of the few who could recall the destruction of an Atlantis.

Although the destruction of Dresden became a recurring motif in Vonnegut's work, not until twenty-three years later could he bring himself to write the novel of his war experiences, *Slaughterhouse-Five.* After the war, Vonnegut worked in public relations for General Electric in Schenectady, New York (called "Ilium" in his fiction), before leaving in 1950 to devote himself full-time to his writing. In 1945, he married Jane Marie Cox, and they settled in Cape Cod, where they reared their own three children and the three children of Vonnegut's deceased sister, Alice. In 1972, Vonnegut moved to New York City and divorced Cox early in 1974. He married to the photographer Jill Krementz in November, 1979, and they adopted a daughter, Lily. Vonnegut died in New York City in 2007 at the age of eighty-four after sustaining brain injuries in a fall.

ANALYSIS

After the publication of his masterpiece, *Slaughterhouse-Five,* the work of Kurt Vonnegut received increasingly serious critical commentary. He emerged as a consistent commentator on American culture through the second half of the twentieth century. His short stories ranged from satiric visions of grotesque future societies, which were extensions of modern societies, and portrayals of ordinary people, which reasserted the stability of middle-class values. In his novels, the social satire predominated, and Vonnegut blended whimsical humor and something approaching despair as he exposed the foibles of American culture and a world verging on destruction through human thoughtlessness. As in the short stories, however, attention to an unheroic protagonist doing his or her best and to the value of "common human decency" persisted.

Best known for his novels, Vonnegut acknowledged the ancillary interest of short stories for him. In the preface to his collection of short stories *Welcome to the Monkey House*, he described the stories as "work I sold in order to finance the writing of the novels. Here one finds the fruits of Free Enterprise." Vonnegut's blunt comment, however, did not imply that the stories can be dismissed out of hand. The themes of the stories are the concerns of all his work. Again, in the preface to *Welcome to the Monkey House*, Vonnegut describes those concerns in a characteristically tough style. He recalls a letter his brother sent him shortly after bringing his firstborn home from the hospital: "Here I am," that letter began, "cleaning the shit off of practically everything." Of his sister, Vonnegut says that she died of cancer: "her dying words were 'No pain.' Those are good dying words. . . . I realize now that the two main themes of my novels were stated by my siblings: 'Here I am cleaning the shit off of practically everything' and 'No pain.'" These terms apply equally well to the themes of Vonnegut's short stories. His muckraking is frequently social satire; his concern is with the alleviation of human suffering.

Vonnegut's short stories generally fall into two broad categories: those that are science fiction, and those that are not. The science fiction characteristically pictures a future society controlled by government and technology, whose norms have made human life grotesque. The protagonist is often an outlaw who has found such norms or conventions intolerable.

In contrast, Vonnegut's stories that are not science fiction regularly affirm social norms. Ordinary life in these stories is simply not threatened by large-scale social evil. Some of these stories indeed depict the victims of society--refugees, displaced persons, juvenile delinquents--but primarily they show such people's efforts to recover or to establish conventional lives. It is within the context of conventional life that Vonnegut's protagonists can achieve those qualities that in his view give a person stability and a sense of worth. These are the qualities of modesty, consideration (which he often calls common human decency), humor, order, and pride in one's work. They are values interfered with, in the science-fiction stories, by governmental and technological controls.

Vonnegut resented any dismissal of his work merely because it was science fiction, a kind of writing he described as incorporating "technology in the human equation." In the novel *God Bless You, Mr. Rosewater* (1965), Eliot Rosewater speaks for Vonnegut when he delivers an impassioned, drunken, and impromptu defense of the genre before a convention of science-fiction writers:

> I love you sons of bitches. . . . You're all I read any more. . . . You're the only ones with guts enough to *really* care about the future, who *really* notice what machines do to us, what wars do to us, what cities do to us, what big, simple ideas do to us, what tremen-

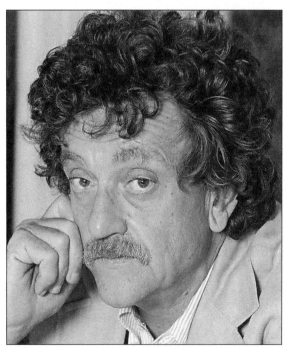

*Kurt Vonnegut* (AP Photo/Marty Reichenthal)

dous misunderstandings, mistakes, accidents and catastrophes do to us.

In Eliot Rosewater's opinion, society's "greatest prophet" is an obscure writer of science fiction named Kilgore Trout, a recurring character in Vonnegut's fiction. His masterpiece, the work for which he will be revered in the far future, is a book entitled *2BR02B*, a rephrasing of Hamlet's famous question.

### "WELCOME TO THE MONKEY HOUSE"

The story of *2BR02B*, in Vonnegut's précis, corresponds closely to his own short story, "Welcome to the Monkey House." Vonnegut writes of his fictional character, "Trout's favorite formula was to describe a perfectly hideous society, not unlike his own, and then, toward the end, to suggest ways in which it could be improved." The approach describes Vonnegut's writing as well. *2BR02B* predicates an America crippled by automation and overpopulation. Machines have taken over most jobs, leaving people idle and feeling "silly and pointless." The government's solution has been to encourage patriotic suicide. Ethical Suicide Parlors have been widely established, each identifiable by a purple roof and each located next to a Howard Johnson's restaurant (with an orange roof), where the prospective client is entitled to a free last meal.

This is also the world of "Welcome to the Monkey House." The story takes place in Cape Cod in an unspecified future time. Fourteen Kennedys, by now, have served as presidents of the United States or of the world. There is a world government; in fact, in this world, Vonnegut writes, "practically everything was the Government." Most people look twenty-two years old, thanks to the development of antiaging shots. The population of the world numbers seventeen billion people. For Vonnegut, the world's dilemma is the result of advanced technology combined with backward human attitudes. Suicide is voluntary, but everyone, under law, must use "ethical" birth control pills that, in fact, control not birth but sexuality. Their effect is to make people numb below the waist, depriving them not of the ability to reproduce, "which would have been unnatural and immoral," but rather of all pleasure in sex. "Thus did science and morals go hand in hand," Vonnegut ironically concludes.

The kind of morality that could produce these pills is exemplified in J. Edgar Nation, their inventor. Walking through the Grand Rapids Zoo with his eleven children one Easter, he had been so offended by the behavior of the animals that he promptly developed a pill "that would make monkeys in the springtime fit things for a Christian family to see." In the opinion of Billy the Poet, a renegade in this society, throughout history those people most eager "to tell everybody exactly how God Almighty wants things here on Earth" have been unaccountably terrified of human sexuality.

Billy the Poet's special campaign is to deflower hostesses in Ethical Suicide Parlors, who are all, as part of their qualifications for the job, "plump and rosy" virgins at least six feet tall. Their uniform is a purple body stocking "with nothing underneath" and black leather boots. In this world, only death is permitted to be seductive. Billy's modus operandi is to single out a hostess and send her some bawdy doggerel, calculated to offend (and to excite) narrow sensibilities. Nancy McLuhan, his present target, is more intrigued than she will admit to herself. Billy kidnaps her and takes her to his current hideout, the old Kennedy compound at Hyannis Port, now "a museum of how life had been lived in more expansive times. The museum was closed." The original lawn is now green cement; the harbor is blue cement. The whole of the compound is covered by an enormous plastic geodesic dome through which light can filter. The only "light" in which an earlier graciousness can now be seen is colored by the world's pervasive vulgarity. The current world president, named "Ma" Kennedy but not the "real thing," keeps a sign reading "Thimk!" on the wall of her office in the Taj Mahal.

Nancy's encounter with Billy is not the licentious orgy she expects but an approximation of an old-fashioned wedding night. Billy explains to her that most people only gradually develop a full appreciation of their sexuality. Embarrassed and confused, she tries conscientiously to resist her comprehension of his motives. As he leaves, Billy offers Nancy another poem, this time the famous sonnet by Elizabeth Barrett Browning that begins "How do I love thee? Let me count the ways." The implication is that sexuality is one dimension of human love sorely lacking in their world. Far from being obscene, that love pursues a larger "ideal Grace," in the words of the poem, wholly unavailable either to the vulgarity of "Ma" Kennedy or to the narrow-minded purity of J. Edgar Nation. Billy also leaves with Nancy a bottle of birth-control pills that will not hamper sexual enjoyment. On the label are printed the words "WELCOME TO THE MONKEY HOUSE." If Browning's poem risks sentimentality, the story ends in a comic readjustment of the reader's sense of proportion. Sex need not be humorless; the reader need not view himself and the human condition with the chilling seriousness and inflated self-importance of J. Edgar Nation. The reader is left with the impression that Nancy has begun her conversion. There is a measure of hope in this world where, as Billy assures her, the "movement is growing by leaps and bounds."

### "HARRISON BERGERON"

Governmental domination of private life is nearly total, however, in the world of "Harrison Bergeron," whose inhabitants are tortured and shackled as a matter of course, all in the name of equality. In the United States of 2081, equality of all persons has been mandated by the 211th, 212th, and 213th Amendments to the Constitution. People are not merely equal under the law, but "equal every which way." Those people of "abnormal" capacities must wear equalizing handicaps at all times. Hazel Bergeron is a person of average intelligence, which means that "she couldn't think about anything except in short bursts." Her husband, George, however, as a man of superior intelligence, has to wear a "mental handicap radio" in his ear, which broadcasts at twenty-second intervals strident noises designed to break his concentration: burglar alarms, sirens, an automobile collision, or a twenty-gun salute. A strong man as well, George wears "forty-seven pounds of bird shot in a canvas bag" padlocked around his neck.

Neither George nor his wife is able to recall that their fourteen-year-old son, Harrison, has just been arrested. They are watching on television a performance by ballerinas also weighted down with bird shot and masked to disguise their beauty. As a law-abiding couple, George and Hazel have only fleeting suspicions that the system is a bad one. If not for such handicaps, George says, "pretty soon we'd be right back to the dark ages again, with everybody competing against

everybody else." When the television announcer cannot deliver a news bulletin because he-- "like all announcers"--has a serious speech impediment, Hazel's response is a well-meaning platitude, "he tried. That's the big thing." A ballerina, disguising her "unfair" voice, reads the announcement for him: Harrison Bergeron, "a genius and an athlete," has escaped from jail.

Suddenly Harrison bursts into the television studio. A "walking junkyard," he wears tremendous earphones, thick glasses, three hundred pounds of scrap metal, a rubber ball on his nose, and black caps on his teeth. In this reductio ad absurdum of the ideal of equality, the technology is pointedly silly. "I am the Emperor!" Harrison cries and tears off his handicaps, revealing a man who "would have awed Thor, the god of thunder." Harrison is rival to the gods. A ballerina joins him as his empress. Freed of her restraints, she is "blindingly beautiful." Whatever the reader may perceive as ultimate human beauty, Harrison and the ballerina are that. Together the two of them dance in "an explosion of joy and grace" equally as fantastic as the shackles they have thrown off. They leap thirty feet to kiss the ceiling and hover midair to embrace each other, "neutralizing gravity with love and pure will." They have defied the laws of the land, the law of gravity, the laws of motion. They dance out the soaring aspiration of the human spirit, for a moment made triumphantly manifest.

The United States Handicapper General, ironically named Diana Moon Glampers, then breaks into the television studio and shoots them both. Her ruthless efficiency is in marked contrast to the bumbling capabilities of everyone else. The reader is suddenly aware that the idea of equality has been made an instrument of social control. Clearly some are allowed to be more equal than others. In their home, Harrison's parents are incapable of either grief or joy. They resume their passive, acquiescent lives, having forgotten the entire scene almost as soon as they witnessed it.

If the conventional life depicted in Vonnegut's work other than his science fiction has not been made this grotesque by technology and government, it is, nevertheless, also humdrum and uninspiring. These limitations, however, are more than compensated for by the fact that ordinary people feel useful, not superfluous, and they are capable of sustaining love. This dynamic is especially true of "Poor Little Rich Town," first published in *Collier's* and reprinted in *Bagombo Snuff Box*. In this story, an entire village rejects the wisdom of an efficiency expert, Newell Cady. The bonds of community love win over logic, because the townspeople do not want the postmistress to lose her job.

**"GO BACK TO YOUR PRECIOUS WIFE AND SON"**

In "Go Back to Your Precious Wife and Son" the narrator's occupation is selling and installing "aluminum combination storm windows and screens" and occasionally a bathtub enclosure. He marks as "the zenith of [his] career" an order for a glass door for a film star's bathtub specially fixed with a life-sized picture of the film star's face on it. He is comically intent on installing the enclosure and on doing the job well, even as the star's household disintegrates around him. Although this scene is funny, the narrator's pride in his mundane work is also the basis of stability in his life, a stability visibly lacking in the apparently glamorous life of Gloria Hilton, the film star. Also installing two windows for her, he says about them,

> The Fleetwood Trip-L-Trak is our first-line window, so there isn't anything quick or dirty about the way we put them up. . . . You can actually fill up a room equipped with Fleetwoods with water, fill it clear up to the ceiling, and it won't leak--not through the windows, anyway.

While the narrator is at work in the bathroom, Gloria is engaged in dismissing her fifth husband. She speaks to him, as she always speaks, in a series of fatuous clichés. She tells him, "You don't know the meaning of love," after earlier seducing him away from his family with the words, "Dare to be happy, my poor darling! Oh, darling, we were *made* for each other!" She had then promptly announced to the press that the two of them were moving to New Hampshire "to find ourselves." In the narrator's (and the reader's) only glimpse of Gloria, she is without makeup ("she hadn't even bothered to draw on eyebrows") and dressed in a bathrobe. He decides, "that woman wasn't any prettier than a used studio couch." Her actual commonplaceness and utter self-absorption are patent.

Her hapless fifth husband is a writer, George Murra, of whom she had expected no less than "the most beautiful scenario anybody in the history of literature has ever written for me." In the constant publicity and tempestuousness of their lives together, however, he has been unable to work at all. He had been lured by a hollow glamour, she by the possibility of greater self-glorification. The superficiality of their marriage is revealed in his references to her as "Miss Hilton," and her contemptuous parting words: "Go on back to your precious wife and your precious son."

In a long drinking session together after Gloria leaves, Murra describes to the narrator Murra's earlier dreams of breaking free from the petty marital squabbles, the financial worries, the drab responsibility and sameness of conventional life. The narrator momentarily and drunkenly succumbs to the appeal of the glamorous life; when he staggers home he immediately offends his wife. Murra is now repentant and nearly desperate for the forgiveness of his son, living at a nearby preparatory school. When the boy arrives to visit his father, it is apparent that the hurt and bitterness of his father's desertion have made the boy rigid with intolerant rectitude. The situation looks hopeless until the narrator (back to finish his job) suggests to Murra that he topple the boy from his pedestal with a kick in the pants. The gambit works, the family is reconciled, and the narrator returns home, having agreed to exchange bathtub doors with Murra. The narrator finds his own wife gone and his own son stuffily self-righteous; but his wife returns, her equanimity restored. The new bathtub enclosure with Gloria's face on it amuses his wife. She is exactly Gloria's height; when she showers, the film star's face on the door forms a "mask" for her. Gloria's glamour is all mask and pose; but his wife's good humor is genuine. The ordinary lives of the narrator and his wife have provided them with exactly what Gloria lacks and what Murra and his son need to recover: the saving grace of humor, tolerance, and a sense of proportion.

**BAGOMBO SNUFF BOX**

The 1999 publication of *Bagombo Snuff Box* presented again several of the previous stories, plus others that achieved magazine exposure in the 1950's and 1960's but had been forgotten. In the introduction to this volume, Vonnegut explains that his stories are "a bunch of Buddhist catnaps" designed to slow the pulse and breathing and allow one's troubles to fade away. He also provides his eight rules for writing stories. Only three of the twenty-three stories here could be construed as futuristic. The title story focuses on a braggart who attempts to win favor with a former wife by false exaggeration of the exotic snuffbox, which her son quickly identifies as a common item. As in Vonnegut's previous work, the high and mighty are deflated and the average person is ennobled.

George M. Helmholtz, a band director, is the qualified hero of three of these stories. Helmholtz appears to live only for music, and his reigning passion is the victory of his Lincoln High School Ten Square Band over its competition. He is preparing his bandsmen for a third consecutive victory, which will mean permanent possession of the state band festival trophy. However, unpredictable human emotions continue to interpose themselves between the bandmaster and his goal. In "The Boy Who Hated Girls," Helmholtz tries to understand the conflict Bert Higgens is experiencing between his commitment to his trumpet and to a girl named Charlotte. In "The No-Talent Kid," Helmholtz must deal with Walter Plummer, a clarinetist with a hugely inflated notion of his musical ability. In "Ambitious Sophomore," Helmholtz, a liberal spender, duels with Stewart Haley, Lincoln High's assistant principal, who is charged with overseeing the band's finances. Helmholtz is also a character in "A Song for Selma," found in *Look at the Birdie: Unpublished Short Fiction.*

In the most amusingly ironic story in the collection, "Der Arme Dolmetscher," the narrator-protagonist, a soldier during World War II, is made his unit's official interpreter because of the mistaken impression that he speaks German. On the last page, the Americans are captured, and the Germans have an interpreter who appears to lack proficiency in English.

The characters in most of the stories are recognizable members of the middle and upper middle class during the 1950's and early 1960's, among them, a real-estate salesman, plant owners, a postmistress, a farmer, a retired Army officer, investment counselors, a company cop, a jazz band leader, and an aluminum

storm window salesman. Each story is of a familiar type, since all were originally written for popular magazines. Only "Thanasphere" and "2BR02B" are clearly science fiction (or fantasy), but several others, while set in the 1950's, have touches of futurism. A few of the stories have surprise endings. There is a nice balance between tales of love thwarted and love realized. Despite the pessimism sometimes encountered in the author's work, this collection contains stories in which fate actually favors the deserving. In his "Coda to My Career as a Writer for Periodicals," Vonnegut appraised these early stories with a critical eye, but, he said, they taught him to write.

Vonnegut confessed that his editing of the stories sometimes amounted to a virtual revision. He was so upset by rereading three of the stories-- "The Powder-Blue Dragon," "The Boy Who Hated Girls," and "Hal Irwin's Magic Lamp"--that he almost completely rewrote each denouement. He expressed his gratitude that when he began, so many magazines were still publishing fiction and were willing to buy what in retrospect he considered clumsy work. He expatiated upon the middle westerner's persona. He observed that while the identities of Texans, Brooklynites, Californians, and southerners are so well established as to have become stereotypes, the Middle West is home to every ethnicity or blend thereof, making for a healthy mix of artists, ranging from the world-class to the merely competent. This authorial "coda" at the end of the volume argued for the importance of the "Middle West" of Ohio and Indiana.

Vonnegut's posthumously published *Look at the Birdie: Unpublished Short Fiction* (2009) is an interesting mix of three science-fiction stories, eleven that are not, and one that is a hybrid, and it contains twelve Vonnegut illustrations dated from 1994 through 2006. "Hall of Mirrors" is the story of K. Hollomon Weems, a murderous hypnotist. His powers seem great as he manipulates the detectives who have come to interrogate him, but his ironic death on the last page calls these powers into question. Harry Bowers, the protagonist of "Confido," has invented a talking box, a combination of confidante-adviser and household pet: thus Confido. Henry believes it will make him rich, but its advice appeals to the worst aspects of human nature. It ultimately must be buried beneath the hydrangeas. "The Nice Little People" features tiny extraterrestrials who have come to Earth in a spaceship resembling a paper knife. They develop a fondness for Lowell Swift, the diffident human who discovers them, a fondness that proves fatal to Madelaine, Lowell's unfaithful wife. "The Petrified Ants" tells of an ant society millions of years in the past, which was as highly developed as modern human society. Apparently, the totalitarian impulses of some of the ants (eerily comparable to what occurred in the Soviet Union, where the story is set) destroyed that society.

Three stories-- "Hello, Red," "Little Drops of Water," and "The Good Explainer"--have O. Henry-style surprise endings. The first deals with Red Mayo, a former merchant mariner, who believes his red-headed natural daughter, Nancy, has been raised by an oysterman, Eddie Scudder, as his own. In "Little Drops of Water," Ellen Sparks is jilted by Larry Whiteman, a famous singer and shameless womanizer. Ellen exacts her revenge in a clever campaign, the full nature of which is not revealed until the end of the story. In "The Good Explainer," Barbara Cunningham of Cincinnati, unable to conceive, directs her husband, Joe, to Dr. Leonard Abekian of Chicago, whom she represents as a renowned fertility specialist. When she joins the men in Dr. Abekian's office, she has a surprise for both of them.

"FUBAR," "Shout About It from the Housetops," "A Song for Selma," and "King and Queen of the Universe" are human-interest stories that largely emphasize the decency of common people. The text is peppered with the familiar Vonnegut exclamations, such as a single vowel followed by a long string of consonants.

"Ed Luby's Key Club," "The Honor of a Newsboy," and "Look at the Birdie" are crime stories, The last is an interesting choice as title story since it--a tale of photographic blackmail--is the shortest in the book. The first two are examples of how those on the right side can win out when a character is steadfast and honorable. Harve Elliot courageously fights a corrupt power structure when framed for a murder Ed Luby had committed; Elliot emerges triumphant. When Mark Crosby, a ten-year-old newsboy, restores his faith in his timid father, it ultimately brings a murderer, Earl Hedlund, to justice.

Despite the fact that most of Vonnegut's short stories are not science fiction and similarly applaud conventional life, the happy triumph of kindness and work seems contrary to the thrust of his novels. What he values remains the same, but the prospect of realizing those values becomes more desperate as the vision of normalcy recedes. The crises of the planet are too extreme and the capabilities of technology are too great for Vonnegut to imagine a benign society in the future that could foster those values.

Vonnegut's novels are often described as "black humor," wholly unlike the generous good humor of "Go Back to Your Precious Wife and Son." This is another label that annoyed the author ("just a convenient tag for reviewers"), but his description of black humor recalled his own lonely rebels whose cause is seriously overmatched by the monolithic enemy: "Black humorists' holy wanderers find nothing but junk and lies and idiocy wherever they go." Vonnegut said that the writer functions like the canaries coal miners took with them into the mines "to detect gas before men got sick." He must serve society as an early-warning system so that one can work to improve the human condition while one still may.

OTHER MAJOR WORKS

LONG FICTION: *Player Piano*, 1952; *The Sirens of Titan*, 1959; *Mother Night*, 1961; *Cat's Cradle*, 1963; *God Bless You, Mr. Rosewater: Or, Pearls Before Swine*, 1965; *Slaughterhouse-Five: Or, The Children's Crusade, a Duty-Dance with Death*, 1969; *Breakfast of Champions: Or, Goodbye Blue Monday*, 1973; *Slapstick: Or, Lonesome No More!*, 1976; *Jailbird*, 1979; *Deadeye Dick*, 1982; *Galápagos*, 1985; *Bluebeard*, 1987; *Hocus Pocus*, 1990; *Timequake*, 1997; *God Bless You, Dr. Kevorkian*, 1999 (novella).

CHILDREN'S LITERATURE: *Sun Moon Star*, 1980 (with Ivan Chermayeff).

PLAY: *Penelope*, pr. 1960, revised pr., pb. 1970 (as *Happy Birthday, Wanda June*).

TELEPLAY: *Between Time and Timbuktu: Or, Prometheus-5, a Space Fantasy*, 1972.

NONFICTION: *Wampeters, Foma, and Granfalloons (Opinions)*, 1974; *Palm Sunday: An Autobiographical Collage*, 1981; *Conversations with Kurt Vonnegut*, 1988; *Fates Worse than Death: An Autobiographical Collage of the 1980's*, 1991; *Like Shaking Hands with God: A Conversation About Writing*, 1999 (with Lee Stringer); *A Man Without a Country*, 2005; *Armageddon in Retrospect: And Other New and Unpublished Writings on War and Peace*, 2008.

BIBLIOGRAPHY

Barsamian, David. "Kurt Vonnegut." *The Progressive* 67, 6 (June, 2003): 35-38. Although Vonnegut's politics were not doctrinaire, his sympathies clearly lay with the progressive element. Illustrated with a portrait of the subject.

Broer, Lawrence R. *Sanity Plea: Schizophrenia in the Novels of Kurt Vonnegut*. Ann Arbor, Mich.: UMI Research Press, 1988. This volume focuses on the theme of social neurosis, with emphasis on schizophrenic behavior in the main characters of the novels through *Bluebeard*. The thesis has relevance to a number of the short stories and gives insight into the evolution of Vonnegut's fiction.

Giannone, Richard. *Vonnegut: A Preface to His Novels*. Port Washington, N.Y.: Kennikat, 1977. Treats the novels up to *Slapstick* and the play *Happy Birthday, Wanda June*, in the context of Vonnegut's life and times. Emphasizes developing themes and techniques connecting the novels, with chapters devoted to individual novels.

Hoppe, David. "Still Vonnegut . . . After All These Years." *Utne Reader* 117 (May/June 2003): 86-89. A tribute to the sustained quality of Vonnegut's fiction over five decades. Illustrated with a portrait of the subject.

Klinkowitz, Jerome. *"Slaughterhouse-Five": Reforming the Novel and the World*. Boston: Twayne, 1990. This book contains a thorough treatment of *Slaughterhouse-Five*. With care and insight, Klinkowitz debunks earlier, fatalistic interpretations of the novel. Features a comprehensive chronology, a thorough bibliography, and an index.

_____. *Vonnegut in Fact: The Public Spokesmanship of Personal Fiction*. Columbia: University of South Carolina Press, 1998. Klinkowitz makes a case for Vonnegut as a sort of redeemer of the novelistic form, after writers such as Philip Roth declared it dead. Klinkowitz traces Vonnegut's successful integration of autobiography and fiction in his body of work. Provides an extensive bibliography and an index.

Klinkowitz, Jerome, Julie Huffman-Klinkowitz, and Asa B. Pieratt, Jr. *Kurt Vonnegut, Jr.: A Comprehensive Bibliography*. Hamden, Conn.: Archon Books, 1987. An authoritative bibliography of works by and about Vonnegut. Lists Vonnegut's works in all their editions, including the short stories in their original places of publication, dramatic and cinematic adaptations, interviews, reviews, secondary sources, and dissertations.

Klinkowitz, Jerome, and David L. Lawler, eds. *Vonnegut in America: An Introduction to the Life and Work of Kurt Vonnegut*. New York: Delacorte Press, 1977. A collection of essays ranging from biography and an "album" of family photographs to Vonnegut as satirist, science-fiction writer, and short-story writer. Discusses his reputation in the Soviet Union and Europe. Contains an authoritative bibliography.

Klinkowitz, Jerome, and John Somer, eds. *The Vonnegut Statement*. New York: Delacorte Press, 1973. A collection of essays by various authors, which establishes the nature of Vonnegut's reputation at an important critical juncture. Analyzes his career from his college writing to the short fiction, and through the novels to *Slaughterhouse-Five*. Includes an interview and a bibliography. An important accounting of Vonnegut's career through its first two decades.

Merrill, Robert, ed. *Critical Essays on Kurt Vonnegut*. Boston: G. K. Hall, 1990. A comprehensive collection of essays on Vonnegut's works and career, which includes reviews, previously published essays, and articles commissioned for this work. The extensive introduction traces in detail Vonnegut's career and critical reception from the beginnings to 1990.

Nuwer, Hank. "Kurt Vonnegut Close Up." *The Saturday Evening Post* 258 (May/June, 1986): 38-39. A biographical sketch that discusses Vonnegut's writing career, noting that his work often deals with the subject of man's inability to cope with technology.

Rayner, Richard. "The Roots of Mr. Vonnegut." *Los Angeles Times*, January 30, 2011, p. E8. Review of *While Mortals Sleep* gives a good overview of his writing career, with a focus on his short fiction.

Reed, Peter J. *The Short Fiction of Kurt Vonnegut.* Westport, Conn.: Greenwood Press, 1997. A critical study of the author's short fiction. Includes a bibliography and an index.

Reed, Peter J., and Marc Leeds, eds. *The Vonnegut Chronicles: Interviews and Essays.* Westport, Conn.: Greenwood Press, 1996. Vonnegut discusses, among other topics, postmodernism and experimental fiction. Includes a bibliography and an index.

Schatt, Stanley. *Kurt Vonnegut, Jr.* Boston: Twayne, 1976. Discusses the first eight novels, with separate chapters on the short stories and on the plays.

Includes a chronology, a biography, and a bibliography up to 1975.

Stone, Brad. "Vonnegut's Last Stand." *Newsweek* 130 (September 29, 1997): 78. A biographical sketch that focuses on *Timequake*, which Vonnegut called his last book.

Vonnegut, Kurt, Jr. Interview by Wendy Smith. *Publishers Weekly* 228 (October 25, 1985): 68-69. Vonnegut discusses his writing career, censorship, and his work; notes that Vonnegut is an ardent foe of book censorship and has strong words for those who seek to limit the free speech of others.

West, Evan. "Favorite Sons." *Indianapolis Monthly* 28, no. 1 (September, 2004): 138-151. Although much of Vonnegut's fiction is set in the Northeast (where he lived for most of his life), Indianapolis continues proudly to claim him. Illustrated with a portrait of the subject.

*Martha Meek; Peter J. Reed and Scott Vander Ploeg*
*Updated by Patrick Adcock*

*W*

## KATE WALBERT

**Born:** New York, New York; August 13, 1961

OTHER LITERARY FORMS

Kate Walbert has written three novels, *The Gardens of Kyoto* (2001), *Our Kind* (2004), and *A Short History of Women* (2009). Though vastly different in plot, setting, and time frame, these novels are inhabited primarily by women characters, who experience great longing, unfulfillment, frustration, and melancholy in their search for identity and happiness. Both *The Gardens of Kyoto* and *A Short History of Women* grew out of characters and situations previously visited in short stories by Walbert and later were expanded and developed into long fiction.

Walbert also has written the plays *Year of the Woman* (1996) and *Elsewhere* (2009), which echo her fictional themes of women searching for autonomy and contentment in otherwise fragmented lives. *Year of the Woman,* the biographical story of Montana native Jeannette Rankin, the first woman elected to the United States Congress in 1917, has been produced by the Yale School of Drama and Villanova University. *Elsewhere,* produced at the Marin Theater in California, is a character study focusing on Nina, a woman whose life is undergoing extreme crisis, as she grieves her father's death, trains her ninth nanny, and helps her mother transition into remission from breast cancer. All of Walbert's plays and novels share a continuing thread expressed throughout her short fiction: women futilely seeking meaning, purpose, and themselves.

ACHIEVEMENTS

Although Kate Walbert initially received a plethora of rejections for her short fiction, her short stories were eventually published in *Ploughshares*, *Antioch Review*, *Ms.*, *The Paris Review*, *Fiction*, *DoubleTake*, and *The New York Times*. In 1986, Walbert was awarded a MacDowell Fellowship, followed in 1988 by a Yadoo Fellowship, allowing her to pursue her writing full time. In 1994, Walbert earned a grant from the Connecticut Commission on the Arts, and in 1998 Walbert was presented a National Endowment for the Arts Creative Writing Fellowship. In 1998, Walbert was chosen as a finalist for the National Magazine Award in Fiction, and her book of short stories, *Where She Went*, was chosen by *The New York Times* as a Notable Book of 1998. Walbert's short story "The Gardens of Kyoto" received both a Pushcart and an O. Henry Award in 2000, and in 2002 Walbert's novel *The Gardens of Kyoto* won the 2002 Connecticut Book Award in Fiction. Walbert was nominated as one of five National Book Award finalists in 2004 for her novel *Our Kind*, and in 2009 *The New York Times* Book Review chose Walbert's novel *A Short History of Women* as one of the ten best books of 2009.

BIOGRAPHY

Anne Katherine Walbert was born August 13, 1961, in New York to homemaker Donna Walbert and businessman J. T. Walbert. A Korean War veteran and executive for the DuPont Company, Kate Walbert's father was frequently transferred to manage operations in distant locales. His stories of the Korean War would later figure prominently in is daughter's fictional recounting of war in "The Gardens of Kyoto," a story transferred by Walbert from the Korean War to World War II. By the time Walbert was ten years old, her family had moved five times throughout the United States, and from 1963 to 1965 they lived in Kyoto, Japan. Walbert spoke Japanese fluently while attending preschool there, and her memories of living in Kyoto would later greatly influence her writing a short story and novel.

Although Walbert's family lived in American locations as diverse as New York, Delaware, Georgia, Pennsylvania, and Texas, they varied little socially, because Walbert's upper-middle-class family interacted within the sphere of country-club society wherever they lived. Walbert spent her childhood fascinated by the women of her mother's 1950's generation, eavesdropping on every detail of the latest gossip and scandal, as her mother and country-club lady friends played cards, drank, smoked, and talked. Walbert was mesmerized by the often shocking and unorthodox nature of the conversations of the seemingly conservative women of the country club, and she began writing to better understand what she overheard. After graduating from boarding school, Walbert entered Northwestern University in 1979, graduating with a bachelor's degree in English in 1983. Walbert attended graduate school at New York University, earning a master's degree in English in 1986.

In 1992, the year the media dubbed "the year of the woman" because of the inordinate number of women elected to the U.S. Congress that year, Walbert began her career as a playwright, traveling to Montana to research and write her first drama, *Year of the Woman*, a one-woman play profiling the life of Montana congresswoman Jeannette Rankin. On May 2, 1992, Walbert married Argentine architect Rafael Pelli, with whom she had two daughters. Walbert began to teach creative writing at Yale University and settled in New Haven, Connecticut, and New York City with her husband and daughters.

ANALYSIS

Kate Walbert's fiction follows very much in the tradition of Jane Austen and Virginia Woolf, exploring the intricacies and complexities of social constructs and constraints, especially as they influence the hopes, dreams, and ambitions of unfulfilled women. The myriad ways in which women's lives are thwarted by surrounding circumstances and their beleaguered attempts at validation are examined by Walbert in a painstaking manner, offering a poignant testament to

their fractured identities and broken aspirations. Walbert's language is sparse and precise, using meticulous details to convey vivid characters through subtle imagery and terse dialogue. Likewise, Walbert's authentic voice and lyrical prose create haunting stories of unforgettable women and their Sisyphean struggles.

### "ROCHESTER 1965"

Marion, suburban homemaker and mother, recounts in "Rochester 1965" her life as a company wife in the 1960's. Married to an efficiency-expert executive for an international corporation, Marion is forced to move at a moment's notice with her six-year-old daughter and husband whenever the company transfers him. Marion's life is an endless succession of anonymous towns, suburbs, houses, lawns, garages, and acquaintances. Upon arriving at each new destination, Marion canvasses her latest neighborhood, ringing doorbells, introducing herself to the other housewives, seeking out playmates for her young daughter.

Expecting the ritual to continue as it always has in previous cities, in Rochester, Marion unexpectedly encounters Dorothy, a suburban wife and mother like herself, but unlike any person Marion has ever known: elegant, sophisticated, worldly, refined, cosmopolitan, rarefied, exotic, and chic. Dorothy, daughter of missionaries, urbane and cultured, has traveled throughout the world prior to her marriage, is dressed immaculately in black silk, has household furnishings from Burma and other distant lands, serves cocktails at two o'clock in the afternoon on ornately carved foreign trays, and whisks Marion on an impromptu shopping adventure downtown. Marion feels as though she has been transported to another world, a realm of beauty, refinement, elegance, and grace. She admires Dorothy's exquisite style, her impeccable taste, and her transcendence over the mundane. Although trapped in a loveless marriage and a suffocating suburb, Dorothy has found a way to rise above her stultifying environment, Marion thinks, and she wishes to emulate Dorothy, someone whom she sees as a mirror image of her better self.

Several years later, after moving from Rochester to Norfolk, Marion is horrified to learn of Dorothy's death by suicide; she killed herself by breathing carbon monoxide fumes in her car while it idled in the garage. With a sudden shock, Marion realizes that the elegance, refinement, and sophistication that Dorothy had exuded were nothing more than a fragile veneer, an attempt to escape the numbing boredom, meaninglessness, and emptiness of her life by seeking refuge in a bastion of appearances. Marion reflects upon Dorothy's inability to survive, trapped in the suburban wasteland, even though Dorothy was someone whom Marion viewed as far superior to herself in every way. Marion recognizes herself in Dorothy and has profound fears and misgivings about her own fate, all while packing to move yet again to another imprisoning suburb in another anonymous town.

### "ITHACA 1992"

At age thirty-four and recently married, Rebecca grudgingly is reminded of her biological clock, but she has no desire just yet to be a wife or a mother. Almost immediately after marrying Tom, Rebecca asks him if it is possible to get the marriage annulled and then live together unmarried, in spite of the fact that both she and Tom love each other dearly. Rebecca fears becoming trapped as her mother, Marion, was, in a marriage that defines her identity and negates her free will. Rebecca values her freedom more than anything, and she seeks to escape the entrapment her mother experienced through virtually nonstop traveling throughout the world. Rebecca's mother had threatened for years to leave Rebecca and her father, so that she could travel alone to distant lands, but she never left home. Instead, Marion encourages Rebecca to travel the world and send postcards documenting her adventures, so that Marion can travel with her vicariously.

For almost all of her adult life, except for brief stints of boredom as an office worker and a student, Rebecca has traveled the globe randomly, dutifully sending her mother postcards from exotic locations, inventing romantic lovers and adventures that she knows will appeal to her mother's restless spirit. Rebecca, in turn, has become as isolated and trapped in her life of itinerancy as her mother is shackled by domesticity. Living the life of a gypsy, traveling everywhere and nowhere, in an attempt to run away from intimacy and constraint, Rebecca makes an intense effort to avoid her mother's confinement, which becomes its own special kind of prison.

After her mother's death, Rebecca is torn more than ever between her marriage to Tom and her need for independence. Leaving Tom a note, Rebecca spontaneously boards a flight for Ithaca, where tourist season is over, as it is the dead of winter, and Ithaca is in the throes of a blizzard. Skating alone on a frozen lake at the Blue Grottos, Rebecca pursues the unknown, herself, an identity and destiny that is not her mother's and not yet her own, but always just over the horizon, in the next exotic destination, the next great adventure.

### "A PLACE ON A LAKE 1966"

After Marion, suburban wife and homemaker, has a baby girl born with a heart defect who dies a short while later, Marion attempts suicide by overdosing on sleeping pills. Marion's husband sends her to a camp in the mountains of Virginia to recuperate, a retreat with cabins on a lake, run by a psychiatrist named Dr. Klein. While at the summer camp, Marion makes little or no progress with Dr. Klein in her analytical sessions; instead she learns to play a game of appeasement, by telling him what he wants to hear. Marion becomes more and more remote, further trapped inside herself, until her roommate, a virtual stranger named Mrs. Whitehead, awakens her in the middle of the night to ask her if she would like to accompany her for a swim.

Although initially alarmed, Marion agrees to accompany the elderly Mrs. Whitehead to the lake, where the two women remove their nightgowns and dive into the cold, deep water surrounded by darkness, mountains, loons, and pine trees. Marion feels cleansed, rejuvenated, and renewed in the frigid waters of the lake, and after swimming the two women sit naked on the dock, talking until sunrise. The year being 1966, it is long before the women's movement, and Marion and Mrs. Whitehead are awkward and unfamiliar with how to talk about themselves to each other. Nonetheless, the two women discuss their mutual suicide attempts, Mrs. Whitehead having first slashed her wrists and, after that failed, later slashed her throat.

In spite of being only brief acquaintances, the two women develop a bond and camaraderie based on mutual trust and respect, forged out of pain and loss. Both women achieve more healing and therapy by baring their wounds and scars to each other during one midnight swim at the lake than they have achieved during the entire treatment at the retreat. The women, in a sense, experience a rebirth at the lake. By shedding their skins (nightgowns), purifying themselves in the natural waters of the lake, and welcoming the dawn together on the dock, they begin a new day, a day in which women are on the verge of discovering that their greatest strength, support, and resources are to be found in each other. Artificial societal barriers previously have kept women separated from one another, each one isolated and hiding in her own anguish, but by revealing their deepest pain and vulnerabilities to each other, women can begin to heal and transform their lives.

### "Do Something"

Margaret, an elderly grandmother, is the daily lone protester at a remote Air Force base in Delaware, where transport planes land to unload the bodies of soldiers killed in the war in Iraq. Each day Margaret is arrested while photographing the caskets of the dead soldiers, and her film is destroyed. After Margaret bites one of the arresting soldiers at the military base, her protest, viewed by her daughter, Caroline, and her husband, Harry, as an absurd, quaint, and anachronistic exercise in futility, takes on a new level of urgency.

After her release from jail, Margaret arises again in the middle of the night to drive alone to the Air Force base. Her mind is consumed by thoughts of her son, James, who died of cancer; Margaret is grief stricken and tormented by the memories of him as a small child, a vibrant teenager, and a handsome young man. Margaret remembers that she originally found the Air Force base by accident, while driving aimlessly, listening to the radio, trying to drown out the painful memories of her son. Over time, Margaret has returned obsessively to the base, ostensibly protesting the war in Iraq by photographing the soldiers' coffins.

On this particular night, however, Margaret notes that she has not even brought her camera and reflects that the camera was never anything but a prop anyway. Margaret stands alone in the cold night, staring through a chain-link fence toward a remote watchtower, straining for a glimpse of the solitary young man behind the dark glass. Margaret wonders what he was like as a little boy, what kind of sandwiches he liked, if his mother tucked affectionate notes in his lunchbox. Margaret realizes that her trips to the Air Force base have

become a search for her dead son or someone reminiscent of her son. The dead and the living are so intermingled in Margaret's mind that the past and the present have become a blur. Margaret confusedly searches for her son, James, among the living and the dead at the Air Force base, in a desperate attempt to reunite with him. Through memory, the dead are always close at hand, influencing the living and subtly shaping their lives. Unable to find James or the man in the watchtower, Margaret returns to her car and drives home in the night.

### Other major works

LONG FICTION: *The Gardens of Kyoto*, 2001; *Our Kind*, 2004; *A Short History of Women*, 2009.

PLAYS: *Year of the Woman*, 1996; *Elsewhere*, 2009.

### Bibliography

Cohen, Leah Hager, "Feminine Mystique." *The New York Times*, June 12, 2009, p. BR1. In her review of *A Short History of Women*, Cohen discusses Walbert's remarkable talent for characterization, creating major and minor figures through exquisite details that encapsulate and define the character's essence, particularly the characters of women who speak from one century to the next in *A Short History of Women*.

Lee, Don. "*Where She Went.*" *Ploughshares* 24, nos. 2-3 (Fall, 1998). In his review of Walbert's book of short stories, *Where She Went*, Lee compares and contrasts the lives of the mother, Marion, and the daughter, Rebecca, juxtaposed in roles of suffocating suburban domesticity and carefree aimless wandering, creating in the book a dichotomy of two women, both lost and isolated.

Walbert, Kate, "*Charlotte's Web*." In *The Book That Changed My Life: Seventy-One Remarkable Writers Celebrate the Books That Matter Most to Them*, edited by Roxanne Coady and Joy Johannessen. New York: Penguin, 2006. Walbert explains how *Charlotte's Web*, by E. B. White, changed her life forever by inspiring her to want to be a writer. She observes that the language, structure, and style of *Charlotte's Web* are outstanding teachers for anyone who aspiring to write great fiction.

*Mary E. Markland*

# ALICE WALKER

**Born:** Eatonton, Georgia; February 9, 1944

PRINCIPAL SHORT FICTION

*In Love and Trouble: Stories of Black Women,* 1973
*You Can't Keep a Good Woman Down,* 1981
*The Complete Stories,* 1994
*Alice Walker Banned,* 1996 (stories and
commentary)
*The Way Forward Is with a Broken Heart,* 2000

OTHER LITERARY FORMS

Alice Walker is known for her achievements in both prose and poetry; in addition to her short-story collections, she has published several novels, volumes of poetry, collections of essays, and children's books. Her novels *The Third Life of Grange Copeland* (1970), *Meridian* (1976), *The Color Purple* (1982), *The Temple of My Familiar* (1989), *Possessing the Secret of Joy* (1992), and *By the Light of My Father's Smile* (1998) examine the struggles of African Americans, especially African American women, against destruction by a racist society. In 2004, she published the novel *Now Is the Time to Open Your Heart.* Her poetry is collected in *Once: Poems* (1968), *Five Poems* (1972), *Revolutionary Petunias, and Other Poems* (1973), *Good Night, Willie Lee, I'll See You in the Morning: Poems* (1979), *Horses Make a Landscape Look More Beautiful* (1984), and *Her Blue Body Everything We Know: Earthling Poems, 1965-1990 Complete* (1991). *In Search of Our Mothers' Gardens: Womanist Prose* (1983) is a collection of essays important to an understanding of Walker's purposes and methods as well as the writers influential on her fiction. A later collection of nonfiction prose is *Living by the Word: Selected Writings, 1973-1987* (1988). Walker also wrote *Langston Hughes: American Poet* (1974), *To Hell with Dying* (1988), and *Finding the Green Stone* (1991) for

children. The anthology she edited, *I Love Myself When I Am Laughing . . . and Then Again When I Am Looking Mean and Impressive: A Zora Neale Hurston Reader* (1979), did much to revive interest in the fiction of Zora Neale Hurston, the writer Walker considers one of the major influences on her fiction.

ACHIEVEMENTS

From the beginning of her career, Alice Walker has been an award-winning writer. Her first published essay-- "The Civil Rights Movement: What Good Was It?"--won first prize in *The American Scholar*'s annual essay contest in 1967. That same year she won a Merrill writing fellowship. Her first novel was written on a fellowship at the MacDowell Colony in New Hampshire. In 1972, she received a Ph.D. from Russell Sage College. *Revolutionary Petunias, and Other Poems* was nominated for a National Book Award and won the Lillian Smith Award of the Southern Regional Council in 1973. *In Love and Trouble* won the Richard and Hinda Rosenthal Award from the American Institute of Arts and Letters in 1974. *The Color Purple*, which remained on *The New York Times* list of best sellers for more than twenty-five weeks, was nominated for the National Book Critics Circle Award and won both an American Book Award and the Pulitzer Prize for Fiction. Walker's many honors include a National Endowment for the Arts grant in 1969 and 1977, a Radcliffe Institute Fellowship from 1971 to 1973, and a John Simon Guggenheim Memorial Foundation Fellowship in 1977-1978. In 1984, Walker received a Best Books for Young Adults citation from the American Library Association for *In Search of Our Mothers' Gardens.* She has also won the O. Henry Award (1986), the Langston Hughes Award (1989), the Nora Astorga Leadership Award (1989), the Fred Cody Award for lifetime achievement (1990), the Freedom to Write Award (1990), the California Governor's Arts Award (1994), and the Literary Ambassador Award (1998).

She has been inducted into the California Hall of Fame in the California Museum for History, Women, and the Arts (2006).

## BIOGRAPHY

Alice Malsenior Walker was born in Eatonton, Georgia, to sharecropper parents on February 9, 1944. She attended Spelman College in Atlanta on scholarship, transferring to Sarah Lawrence College in New York, from which she graduated in 1965. While working in the Civil Rights movement in Mississippi in the summer of 1966, she met Melvyn Rosenman Levanthal, an attorney, whom she married in 1967. After residing for seven years in Jackson, Mississippi, the couple returned to the East in 1974, where Walker served as a contributing editor to *Ms.* magazine. The two were divorced in 1976, sharing joint custody of a daughter, Rebecca. Walker cofounded a publishing house, Wild Trees Press, in Navarro, California. She has been a writer-in-residence and a teacher of black studies at Jackson State College (1968-1969), a lecturer in literature at Wellesley College and the University of Massachusetts at Boston (1972-1973), a distinguished writer in the African American Studies Department at the University of California, Berkeley (1982), and a Fannie Hurst Professor of Literature at Brandeis University (1982). She coproduced a 1992 film documentary, *Warrior Marks*, directed by Pratibha Parmar, a film she narrated and for which she wrote the script. It was based on her nonfiction book. Walker settled in Mendocino, California, where she has continued to write and to remain politically active.

## ANALYSIS

The heroism of black women in the face of turmoil of all kinds rings from Alice Walker's short stories like the refrain of a protest song. *In Love and Trouble* reveals the extremes of cruelty and violence to which poor black women are often subjected in their personal relationships, while the struggles in *You Can't Keep a Good Woman Down* reflect the social upheavals of the 1970's.

### IN LOVE AND TROUBLE

Such subjects and themes lend themselves to a kind of narrative that is filled with tension. The words "love" and "trouble," for example, in the title of the first collection, identify a connection that is both unexpected and inevitable. Each of the thirteen stories in this collection is a vivid confirmation that every kind of love known to woman brings its own kind of suffering. Walker is adept at pairing such elements, creating pronounced and revealing contrasts or intense conflicts. One such pair that appears in many of these short stories is a stylistic one and easy to see: the poetry and prose that alternate on the page. Another unusual combination at work throughout the short fiction may be called the lyrical and the sociological. Like protest songs, Walker's stories present a plea for justice, made more memorable by its poetic form. She breathes rhythmic, eloquent language into the most brutish and banal abuses.

These two elements--similarity of subject matter and the balance of highly charged contraries--produce a certain unity within each volume. Beyond this common ground, the stories have been arranged to convey a progression of interconnected pieces, whose circumstances and themes repeat, alternate, and overlap

*Alice Walker* (AP Photo)

rather like a musical composition. The first three stories of *In Love and Trouble*, for example, are about married love; the next two are about love between parent and child; the next three stories are about African American-white conflict; the fourth group are about religious expression; and the last three stories are about initiation. Other themes emerge and run through this five-set sequence, linking individual motifs and strengthening the whole. Jealousy is one of those motifs, along with the drive for self-respect, African American folkways, and flowers, in particular the rose and the black-eyed Susan.

Four stories suggest the breadth of Walker's imagination and narrative skills. "Roselily" strikes an anticipatory note of foreboding. "The Child Who Favored Daughter" is an equally representative selection, this time of the horrific destruction of the black woman. "The Revenge of Hannah Kemhuff" is as cool and clear as "The Child Who Favored Daughter" is dark and fevered. The narrator recounts a tale of Voodoo justice, specifically crediting Hurston, author of *Mules and Men* (1935). The final story in this collection, "To Hell with Dying," is an affirmative treatment of many themes Walker has developed elsewhere more darkly.

### "ROSELILY"

"Roselily" takes place on a front porch surrounded by a crowd of African American folk, in sight of Highway 61 in Mississippi, during the time it takes to perform a wedding ceremony. As the preacher intones the formal words, the bride's mind wanders among the people closest to her there--the bridegroom, the preacher, her parents, sisters, and children. The groom's religion is not the same as hers, and she knows that he disapproves of this gathering. She speculates uneasily about their future life together in Chicago, where she will wear a veil, sit on the women's side of his church, and have more babies. She is the mother of four children already but has never been married. He is giving her security, but he intends, she realizes, to remake her into the image he wants. Even the love he gives her causes her great sadness, because it makes her aware of how unloved she was before. At last, the ceremony over, they stand in the yard, greeting well-wishers, he completely alien, she overcome with anxiety. She squeezes his hand for reassurance but receives no answering signal from him.

Poetic and fairy-tale elements intensify the ambivalence felt by the bride in this magnetic mood piece. First, there are the ceremonial resonances of the words between the paragraphs of narrative, stately and solemn like a slow drumbeat. As these phrases alternate with Roselily's thoughts, a tension develops. At the words *"Dearly Beloved,"* a daydream of images begins to flow, and she sees herself as a small girl in her mother's fancy dress, struggling through "a bowl of quicksand soup"; the words *"we are gathered here"* suggest to her the image of cotton, waiting to be weighed, a Mississippi ruralness she knows the bridegroom finds repugnant; *"in the sight of God"* creates in her mind the image of God as a little black boy tugging at the preacher's coattail. Gradually, a sense of foreboding builds. At the words *"to join this man and this woman"* she imagines "ropes, chains, handcuffs, his religion." The bridegroom is her rescuer, like Prince Charming, and is ready to become her Pygmalion. Like Sleeping Beauty, Roselily is only dimly aware of exchanging one form of confinement, of enchantment, for another. At the end of the ceremony, she awakens to his passionate kiss and a terrible sense of being wrong.

### "THE CHILD WHO FAVORED DAUGHTER"

While "Roselily" is a subtle story of a quiet inner life, "The Child Who Favored Daughter" records the circumstances of a shocking assault. It begins, also, on a front porch. A father waits with a shotgun on a hot afternoon for his daughter to walk from the school bus through the front yard. He is holding in his hand a letter she had written to her white lover. Realizing what her father knows, the girl comes slowly down the dusty lane, pausing to study the black-eyed Susans. As his daughter approaches, the father is reminded of his sister, "Daughter," who also had a white lover. His intense love for his sister had turned to bitterness when she gave herself to a man by whom the brother felt enslaved; his bitterness poisoned all of his relationships with women thereafter. He confronts the girl on the porch with the words "White man's slut!"; he beats her with a stable harness and leaves her in the shed behind the house. The next morning, failing to make her deny the letter and struggling to suppress his "unnameable desire," he slashes off her breasts. As the story ends, he sits in a stupor on the front porch.

This story of perverted parental love and warring passions explores the destructive power of jealousy and denial. Its evil spell emanates from the father's unrepented and unacknowledged desire to possess his sister. He is haunted by her when he looks at his own daughter. Once again, a strongly lyrical style heightens the dominant tone, in this case, horror. Short lines of verse, like snatches of song interspersed with the narrative, contrast sharply in their suggestion of pure feeling with the tightly restrained prose. The daughter's motif associates her with the attraction of natural beauty: *Fire of earth/ Lure of flower smells/ The sun."* The father's theme sounds his particular resignation and doom: *"Memories of years/ Unknowable women--/ sisters/ spouses/ illusions of soul."* The resulting trance-like confrontation seems inevitable, the two moving through a pattern they do not control and do not understand.

### "THE REVENGE OF HANNAH KEMHUFF"

In "The Revenge of Hannah Kemhuff," a woman who has lost husband, children, and self-respect, all because a charity worker denied her food stamps, comes to the seer Tante Rosie for peace of mind. Tante Rosie assures the troubled woman that the combined powers of the Man-God and the Great Mother of Us All will destroy her enemy. Tante Rosie's apprentice, who narrates the story, teaches Mrs. Kemhuff the curse-prayer printed in Hurston's *Mules and Men*. Then the apprentice sets about to collect the necessary ingredients for the conjure: Sarah Sadler Holley's feces, water, nail parings. The apprentice's task seems to become almost impossible when her mentor tells her that these items must be gained directly from the victim herself. Nevertheless, with a plan in mind, the young woman approaches Mrs. Holley, tells her that she is learning the profession from Tante Rosie, and then asks Mrs. Holley to prove that she, as she claims, does not believe in "rootworking." It is only a short while until Mrs. Kemhuff dies, followed a few months later by Mrs. Holley, who had, after the visit of the apprentice, taken to her bedroom, eating her nails, saving her fallen hair, and collecting her excrement in plastic bags and barrels.

This is the first story in the collection in which the African American community comes into conflict with the white. It is a conflict of religious traditions and a strong statement in recognition of something profound in African folkways. Mrs. Holley failed Mrs. Kemhuff years before in the greatest of Christian virtues, that of charity. Mrs. Kemhuff, though now reconciled to her church, cannot find peace and seeks the even greater power of ancient conjure to restore her pride. Like other African American writers who have handled this subject, Walker first acknowledges that Voodoo is widely discounted as sheer superstition, but then her story argues away all rational objections. Mrs. Holley does not die as the result of hocus-pocus but because of her own radical belief, a belief in spite of herself. There is something else about this story that is different from those at the beginning of the collection. Instead of a dreamy or hypnotic action, alert characters speak and think purposefully, clearly, one strand of many evolving patterns that emerge as the stories are read in sequence.

### "TO HELL WITH DYING"

"To Hell with Dying" is the last story in the collection and a strong one. A more mellow love-and-trouble story than most preceding it, it features a male character who is not the villain of the piece. Mr. Sweet Little is a melancholy man whom the narrator has loved from childhood, when her father would bring the children to Mr. Sweet's bedside to rouse him from his depression with a shout: "To hell with dying! These children want Mr. Sweet!" Because the children were so successful in "revivaling" Mr. Sweet with their kisses and tickling and cajoling ways, they were not to learn for some time what death really meant. Years pass. Summoned from her doctoral studies in Massachusetts, the twenty-four-year-old narrator rushes to Mr. Sweet's bedside, where she cannot quite believe that she will not succeed. She does induce him to open his eyes, smile, and trace her hairline with his finger as he once did. Still, however, he dies. His legacy to her is the steel guitar on which he played away his blues all those years, that and her realization that he was her first love.

It is useful to recognize this story as an initiation story, like the two that precede it, "The Flowers" and "We Drink the Wine in France." Initiation stories usually involve, among other things, an unpleasant brush with reality, a new reality. A child, adolescent, or young adult faces an unfamiliar challenge and, if successful, emerges at a new level of maturity or increased status. Always, however, something is lost, something must be given up. As a small girl, the narrator remembers, she did not understand quite what was going on during their visits to the neighbor's shack. When she was somewhat older, she felt the weight of responsibility for the dying man's survival. At last, after she has lost her old friend, she is happy, realizing how important they were to each other. She has negotiated her initiation into the mysteries of love and death successfully, as, in truth, she had done already to the best of her ability at those earlier stages. This often-reprinted story is a culmination of the struggle between Death and Love for the lives of the girls and women, and really for all the African Americans of *In Love and Trouble*, a collection that well represents Walker's talent and demonstrates her vision of African Americans supporting and affirming one another in community.

### YOU CAN'T KEEP A GOOD WOMAN DOWN

*You Can't Keep a Good Woman Down* is Walker's salute to black women who are pushing ahead, those who have crossed some barriers and are in some sense champions. There are African American women who are songwriters, artists, writers, students in exclusive eastern schools; they are having abortions, teaching their men the meaning of pornography, coming to terms with the death of a father, on the one hand, or with the meaning of black men raping white women, on the other hand. Always, they are caught up short by the notions of whites. In other words, all the political, sexual, racial, and countercultural issues of the 1970's are in these stories, developed from what Walker calls the "womanist" point of view.

This set of stories, then, is somewhat more explicitly sociological than the first and somewhat less lyrical, and it is also more apparently autobiographical, but in a special sense. Walker is a champion, so her life is a natural, even an inescapable, source of material. Walker-the-artist plays with Walker-the-college-student and Walker-the-idealistic-teacher, as well as with some of the other roles she sees herself as having occupied during that decade of social upheaval. Once a writer's experience has become transformed within a fictive world, it becomes next to impossible to think of

the story's events as either simply autobiography or simply invention. The distinction has been deliberately blurred. Because Walker wants to unite her public and private worlds, her politics and her art, life as lived and life as imagined, these stories are interspersed with, instead of poetry, autobiographical parallels, journal entries, letters, and other expressions of her personality.

Three stories deserve special attention: "Nineteen Fifty-Five," "Fame," and "Source." To begin with, they serve as checkpoints for the collection's development, from the essentially simple and familiar to the increasingly complex and strange, from 1955 to 1980. Furthermore, these stories are independently memorable.

### "NINETEEN FIFTY-FIVE"

The opening story, "Nineteen Fifty-Five," is presented from the perspective of a middle-aged blues singer, Gracie Mae Still, whose signature song, recorded by a young white man named Traynor, brings him fame and fortune. Gracie Mae records her impressions of Traynor in a journal, beginning with their first meeting in 1955 and continuing until his death in 1977. Over the years, the rock-and-roll star (obviously meant to suggest Elvis Presley) stays in touch with the matronly musician, buying her lavish gifts--a white Cadillac, a mink coat, a house--and quizzing her on the real meaning of her song. From the Army, he writes to tell her that her song is very much in demand, and that everyone asks him what he thinks it means, really. As time goes by and his life disappoints him, he turns to the song, as if it were a touchstone that could give his life meaning. He even arranges an appearance for himself and Gracie Mae on the variety show hosted by Johnny Carson, with some half-developed notion of showing his fans what the real thing is and how he aspires to it. If he is searching for a shared experience of something true and moving with his audience, however, he is to be disappointed again. His fans applaud only briefly, out of politeness, for the originator of the song, the one who really gave it life, then squeal wildly for his imitation, without any recognition of what he wanted them to understand. That is the last time the two musicians see each other.

In part, this story is about the contribution that African American music made to the spirit of the times and how strangely whites transformed it. The white rock-and-roll singer, who seems as much in a daze as some of the women of *In Love and Trouble*, senses something superior in the original blues version, but he misplaces its value, looking for some meaning to life that can be rolled up in the nutshell of a lyric. In contrast to the bemused Traynor, Gracie Mae is a down-to-earth champion, and her dialect looks forward to Walker's masterful handling of dialect in *The Color Purple*. She repeatedly gives Traynor simple and sensible advice when he turns to her for help, and she has her own answer to the mystery of his emptiness: "Really, I think, some peoples advance *so* slowly."

### "FAME"

The champion of "Fame" is Andrea Clement White, and the events take place on one day, when she is being honored and confronted by her own fame. She is speaking to a television interviewer as the story begins. The old woman tells the young interviewer that to look at the world freshly and creatively, an artist simply cannot be famous. When reminded by the young woman that she, Andrea Clement White, is famous, she is somewhat at a loss. As the interview continues its predictable way, the novelist explaining once again that she writes about people, not their color, she uneasily asks herself why she does not "*feel* famous," why she feels as though she has not accomplished what she set out to do.

The highlight of the day is to be a luncheon in her honor, at which her former colleagues, the president, and specially invited dignitaries, as well as the generally detested former dean, will all applaud her life accomplishments (while raising money). All the while, the lady of the hour keeps a bitingly humorous commentary running in her mind. Her former students in attendance are "numbskulls," the professors are "mediocre." Out loud, she comments that the president is a bore. No matter how outrageous her behavior, she is forgiven because of her stature; when she eats her Rock Cornish hen with her hands, the entire assembly of five hundred follows suit. At last, however, the spleen and anxious bravado give way to something out of reach of the taint of fame: a child singing an anonymous slave

song. Recalled to her dignity, the honored guest is able to face her moment in the limelight stoically.

In this comic story of the aggravations and annoyances that beset the publicly recognized artist, Walker imagines herself as an aging novelist who does not suffer fools gladly. She puts the artist's inner world on paper so that something of her gift for storytelling and her habits of mind become visible. The stress of the occasion and being brought into forced contact with her former president and dean trigger her aggressive imagination, and her innate narrative gift takes over. She visualizes using her heavy award as a weapon against the repulsive, kissing dean, hearing him squeal, and briefly feels gleeful. The story, however, is something more than simply a comic portrait of the artist's foibles. When Andrea Clement White questions herself about her own sense of fame and admits her own doubts, she is searching for something certain, as Traynor was doing in "Nineteen Fifty-Five," though not so blindly. Like him, she is called out of the mundane by a meaningful song.

### "SOURCE"

The last story of *You Can't Keep a Good Woman Down* is "Source," which connects the social conscience of an antipoverty worker in Mississippi with the expanding consciousness of the alternative lifestyle as practiced on the West Coast. Two friends, Irene and Anastasia, had attended college together in New York. When funding for Irene's adult-education project was cut, she traveled to San Francisco for a change of scene, to be met by Anastasia, living on welfare with some friends named Calm, Peace, and their baby, Bliss, all under the guidance of a swami named Source. The two young women had been unable to find any common ground, Irene believing in collective action and Anastasia believing that people choose to suffer and that nothing can be changed. After walking out on a meeting with Source, Irene was asked to leave. Years later, the two meet again in Alaska, where Irene is lecturing to educators. Anastasia is now living with an Indian and passing for white. This time, the two women talk more directly, of color, of Anastasia's panic when she is alone, of her never being accepted as an African American because of her pale skin. Irene is brought to face her own part in this intolerance and to confess that her reliance on government funding was every bit as insecure as had been Anastasia's reliance on Source. Their friendship restored and deepened, the two women embrace.

The title of this story suggests a theme that runs throughout the entire collection, the search for a center, a source of strength, meaning, or truth. This source is important to the pioneer, but it can be a false lure. When Irene recognizes that she and Anastasia were both reaching out for something on which to depend, Irene states what might be taken as the guiding principle for the champion: *any* direction that is away from ourselves is the wrong direction." This final portrait of a good woman who cannot be kept down is a distinctively personal one. Women who are not distracted by external influences and who are true to themselves and able to open themselves to one another will triumph.

Walker's short fiction adds a new image to the pantheon of American folk heroes: the African American woman, in whatever walk of life, however crushed or blocked, still persevering. Even those who seem the most unaware, the most poorly equipped for the struggle, are persevering, because, in their integrity, they cannot do otherwise. The better equipped know themselves to be advocates. They shoulder their dedication seriously and cheerfully. They are the fortunate ones; they understand that what they do has meaning.

### "EVERYDAY USE"

One of the more widely anthologized of Walker's stories, "Everyday Use" addresses the issues of identity and true cultural awareness and attacks the "hyper-Africanism" much in vogue during the 1960's and 1970's as false and shallow. The occasion of the story is Dee's brief trip back to her home, ostensibly to visit with her mother and her sister, Maggie, who was left seriously scarred in a fire of suspicious origin that destroyed their home years earlier. Dee's real purpose, however, is to acquire some homemade quilts and other artifacts of her culture so that she can display them in her home as tokens of her "authenticity," her roots in the soil of rural Georgia. She wears a spectacular dashiki and wishes to be called by an "African" name; she is accompanied by a man who likewise affects "African" dress, hairstyle, naming tradition, and handshaking routines. Walker's tongue is firmly in her

cheek as she portrays these two characters in vivid contrast with Mama and Maggie, whose lives are simple, close to the earth, and genuine. Despite (or perhaps because of) Mama's sacrifices and hard work to send Dee off to acquire an education in the outside world, Dee reveals a fundamental selfishness and lack of understanding of her culture and family; her purposes thwarted, she leaves without the quilts in a cloud of dust and disdain. Mama and Maggie sit in their neat yard, its dirt surface carefully raked, enjoying the shade and their snuff together "until it was time to go in the house and go to bed."

Walker's control of style and tone is nowhere more certain than in this powerful and economical story. She shows that family, tradition, and strength are to be found in the items of everyday use that have survived the fires of prejudice, from whatever source, and illuminate the true meaning of family and love and forgiveness. Despite the truth of Dee's parting statement that "it really is a new day for us," Walker leaves no doubt that the promise of that new day will be dimmed if traditions are exploited rather than understood and cherished. Maggie, after all, learned how to quilt from her grandmother and her great aunt and thus has a much surer sense of her own identity than her sister.

### THE WAY FORWARD IS WITH A BROKEN HEART

This Walker collection of short stories was written from her own experiences and memories. It opens with a brief preface, which recounts her youthful marriage and time spent with the Civil Rights movement in Mississippi. The book begins with a missive, "To My Young Husband," and discusses their turbulent years together in an interracial marriage. This first segment of a seven-part collection is at times autobiographical, describing their meeting and the birth of their child, and at other times lyrical, describing their love for each other and what their union represented in those violence-prone years. The first section continues with six additional remembrances of the early days of their marriage and raising their daughter, initially referred to as "Our Child," later addressed by her name, Rebecca. The tone is reflective, as the writer selects isolated memories of incidents that affected her deeply, from the beggar at her door to being stopped while driving to the motion-picture theater by a white policeman. In the last part of this lengthy opening section, Walker introduces the characters of Rosa, Barbara, and Aunt Lily and the summer spent in Miami sharing stories.

Walker continues in subsequent sections to use vivid characters and situations to tell universal stories of love and loss in the African American community. In the second segment of the collection, she writes about "Orelia and John" and the successes and difficulties in their relationship. From the simple pleasure of using olive oil as a lotion to the challenges of remaining loyal in a long-distance relationship, Walker uses snapshot glimpses of a couple's struggle to protect their love as a device to comment on human relationships.

In the following five sections, Walker introduces additional characters, such as Anne, Jason, Auntie Fanny, and Miss Mary, and describes events in a couple's or a family's life that reflect a background of history or social change. Walker writes of taking hallucinogenic mushrooms, visiting an abandoned country home where a cousin was raped, and taking her aunts to see a pornographic film as a way of demonstrating the immense social changes that have taken place in her lifetime. Although the dialogue is sometimes humorous, the underlying tone is often disturbing.

In the final section, Walker closes with an epilogue, using the same title as the book. This section is again addressed to her former husband and is written in a thoughtful, often poignant tone as she reflects on the fact that they are no longer young but must not exist in the past. She closes with the hope that they can still find understanding of the world around them as well as peace. Their relationship provides the bookends for her stories and underscores the universal sense of love and loss which permeates this work of both autobiography and fiction.

## OTHER MAJOR WORKS

LONG FICTION: *The Third Life of Grange Copeland*, 1970; *Meridian*, 1976; *The Color Purple*, 1982; *The Temple of My Familiar*, 1989; *Possessing the Secret of Joy*, 1992; *By the Light of My Father's Smile*, 1998; *Now Is the Time to Open Your Heart*, 2004.

POETRY: *Once: Poems*, 1968; *Five Poems*, 1972; *Revolutionary Petunias, and Other Poems*, 1973; *Good Night, Willie Lee, I'll See You in the Morning: Poems*, 1979; *Horses Make a Landscape Look More Beautiful*, 1984; *Her Blue Body Everything We Know: Earthling Poems, 1965-1990 Complete*, 1991; *A Poem Traveled Down My Arm: Poems and Drawings*, 2003; *Absolute Trust in the Goodness of the Earth: New Poems*, 2003.

NONFICTION: *In Search of Our Mothers' Gardens: Womanist Prose*, 1983; *Living by the Word: Selected Writings, 1973-1987*, 1988; *Warrior Marks: Female Genital Mutilation and the Sexual Blinding of Women*, 1993 (with Pratibha Parmar); *The Same River Twice: Honoring the Difficult*, 1996; *Anything We Love Can Be Saved: A Writer's Activism*, 1997; *Sent by Earth: A Message from the Grandmother Spirit After the Attacks on the World Trade Center and Pentagon*, 2001; *We Are the Ones We Have Been Waiting For: Light in a Time of Darkness*, 2006; *Overcoming Speechlessness: A Poet Encounters the Horror in Rwanda, Eastern Congo, and Palestine/Israel*, 2010; *The World Has Changed: Conversations with Alice Walker*, 2010 (Rudolph P. Byrd, editor).

CHILDREN'S LITERATURE: *Langston Hughes: American Poet*, 1974; *To Hell with Dying*, 1988; *Finding the Green Stone*, 1991; *There Is a Flower at the Tip of My Nose Smelling Me*, 2006; *Why War Is Never a Good Idea*, 2007.

EDITED TEXT: *I Love Myself When I Am Laughing . . . and Then Again When I Am Looking Mean and Impressive: A Zora Neale Hurston Reader*, 1979.

## BIBLIOGRAPHY

Awkward, Michael. *Inspiriting Influences: Tradition, Revision, and Afro-American Women's Novels*. New York: Columbia University Press, 1989. Though dense, Awkward's book may be useful in placing Walker within the context of her African American literary heritage and in providing some possibilities for interpreting *The Color Purple* and for understanding the connections among Hurston, Jean Toomer, and Walker. The book is laden with critical jargon but nevertheless is important in placing Walker in context historically, thematically, and politically. Awkward emphasizes the creative spirit of African American females and their search for self in a nonpatriarchal community as themes of Walker's fiction. Endnotes may lead researchers to other useful materials on Walker's fiction as well as on works by and on other African American women.

Bates, Gerri. *Alice Walker: A Critical Companion.* Santa Barbara, Calif.: Greenwood Press, 2005. A comprehensive collection of criticism of all Walker's major works. Also provides autobiographical information and discusses her influence on other women writers of color.

Bauer, Margaret D. "Alice Walker: Another Southern Writer Criticizing Codes Not Put to 'Everyday Use.'" *Studies in Short Fiction* 29 (Spring, 1992): 143-151. Discusses parallels between Walker's *In Love and Trouble* and stories by William Faulkner, Katherine Anne Porter, Eudora Welty, and Flannery O'Connor. Argues that Walker, like these other southern writers, examines the tendency to support social and religious codes at the expense of individual fulfillment.

Bloom, Harold, ed. *Alice Walker.* New York: Chelsea House, 1989. An important collection of critical essays examining the fiction, poetry, and essays of Walker from a variety of perspectives. The fourteen essays, including Bloom's brief introduction, are arranged chronologically. Contains useful discussions of the first three novels, brief analyses of individual short stories, poems, and essays, and assessments of Walker's social and political views in connection with her works and other African American female authors. A chronology of Walker's life and a bibliography may be of assistance to the beginner.

Bloxham, Laura J. "Alice [Malsenior] Walker." In *Contemporary Fiction Writers of the South*, edited by Joseph M. Flora and Robert Bain. Westport, Conn.: Greenwood Press, 1993. A general introduction to Walker's "womanist" themes of oppression of African American women and change through affirmation of self. Provides a brief summary and critique of previous criticism of Walker's work.

Borgmeier, Raimund. "Alice Walker: 'Everyday Use.'" In *The African-American Short Story: 1970 to 1990*, edited by Wolfgang Karrer and Barbara Puschmann-Nalenz. Trier, Germany: Wissenschaftlicher Verlag Trier, 1993. A detailed discussion of the generic characteristics of one of Walker's best-known stories. Analyzes the tension between the typical unheard-of occurrence and everyday reality as well as the story's use of a central structural symbol.

Butler-Evans, Elliott. *Race, Gender, and Desire: Narrative Strategies in the Fiction of Toni Cade Bambara, Toni Morrison, and Alice Walker.* Philadelphia: Temple University Press, 1989. Focusing on the connections among gender, race, and desire, and their relationship to the narrative strategies in the fiction of these three writers, Butler-Evans argues that Walker's works are "structured by a complex ideological position" oscillating between "her identity as 'Black feminist' or 'woman-of-color' and a generalized feminist position in which race is subordinated." Useful discussions of Walker's first three novels are included. Although no attention is given to short fiction, the material helps explain the "womanist" position in all Walker's works. Includes somewhat lengthy endnotes and a bibliography.

Gates, Henry Louis, Jr., and K. A. Appiah. *Alice Walker: Critical Perspectives Past and Present.* New York: Amistad, 1993. An examination of African American women in Walker's work. Includes a bibliography and an index.

Gentry, Tony. *Alice Walker.* New York: Chelsea, 1993. Examines the life and work of Walker. Includes bibliographical references and index.

Harris, Melanie. *Gifts of Virtue, Alice Walker, and the Womanist Ethics.* Black Religion/Womanist Thought/Social Justice. New York: Palgrave Macmillan, 2010. The author examines spirituality in Walker's work. The book discusses Walker's work from the perspective of Womanist ethics.

McKay, Nellie. "Alice Walker's 'Advancing Luna-and Ida B. Wells': A Struggle Toward Sisterhood." In *Rape and Representation*, edited by Lynn A. Higgins and Brenda R. Silver. New York: Columbia University Press, 1991. Shows how the story allows readers to see that women's cross-racial relationships are controlled by systems of white male power. The story helps the reader understand why African American women fail to provide group support for feminists of the antirape movement in spite of their own historical oppression by rape.

Mills, Sara, Lynne Pearce, Sue Spaull, and Elaine Millard. *Feminist Readings, Feminists Reading*. Charlottesville: University Press of Virginia, 1989. Analyzes Walker as a feminist writer from a feminist perspective. The book devotes the discussion of Walker mostly to *The Color Purple*, which is interpreted as an example of "authentic realism" designed for a female audience and as part of a female tradition beginning in the nineteenth century. Walker is shown to be a part of the "self-conscious women's" revisionist tradition evident since the early 1980's. Contains endnotes and a bibliography, as well as a glossary of terms related to feminist literary criticism and to literary theory in general.

Petry, Alice Hall. "Walker: The Achievement of the Short Fiction." In *Alice Walker: Critical Perspectives Past and Present*, edited by Henry Louis Gates, Jr., and K. A. Appiah. New York: Amistad, 1993. A skeptical analysis of Walker's short fiction that contrasts the successful and focused achievement of *In Love and Trouble* with the less satisfying *You Can't Keep a Good Woman Down*. Petry argues that the latter collection suffers in many places from unfortunate unintentional humor, trite and clichéd writing, reductionism, and a confusion of genres that perhaps owes much to her being a "cross-generic writer."

Wade-Gayles, Gloria. "Black, Southern, Womanist: The Genius of Alice Walker." In *Southern Women Writers: The New Generation*, edited by Tonette Bond Inge. Tuscaloosa: University of Alabama Press, 1990. An excellent, thorough introduction to the life and literary career of Walker. Placing emphasis on Walker's voice as am African American southern woman throughout her works and arguing that Walker's commitment is to the spiritual wholeness of her people, Wade-Gayles examines several essays that are important to an understanding of Walker's fiction and beliefs, her first three novels, short-story collections, and her poetry. Supplemented by a bibliography of Walker's works, endnotes, and a useful secondary bibliography.

Walker, Alice, and Rudolph Byrd, eds. *The World Has Changed: Conversations with Alice Walker*. New York: New Press, 2010. A collection of conversations between Walker and other literary and cultural figures such as Gloria Steinem, Howard Zinn, William Ferris, and others. Each conversation takes place in a different period of her life, from 1973 until 2006. This gives a perspective on both her career and her personal development.

*Rebecca R. Butler; D. Dean Shackelford*
*and Theodore C. Humphrey*
*Updated by Dolores A. D'Angelo*

# DAVID FOSTER WALLACE

**Born:** Ithaca, New York; February 21, 1962
**Died:** Claremont, California; September 12, 2008

PRINCIPAL SHORT FICTION

*Girl with Curious Hair,* 1989
*Brief Interviews with Hideous Men,* 1999
*Oblivion,* 2004

OTHER LITERARY FORMS

David Foster Wallace published his first novel, *The Broom of the System* (1987), at age twenty-five. Based on his English B.A. thesis, it earned him critical admiration and respect, and he was hailed as the literary heir of post-postmodernism. However, his name became well known to critics and the general public only after the publication of his next novel, *Infinite Jest* (1996). It was almost immediately regarded as a cult novel and listed by *Time* as one of the best novels in English since 1923. *Infinite Jest,* more than one thousand pages long and with more than one hundred pages of endnotes, is set in the near future in the elite Enfield Tennis Academy and the Ennett House Drug and Alcohol Rehabilitation Center. Wallace uses these settings to establish parallels between both institutions, intended as symbols of modern society and the evils that beset people nowadays. The novel contains Wallace's characteristic combination of highbrow literature and popular culture.

Wallace also published several collections of essays. *A Supposedly Fun Thing I'll Never Do Again: Essays and Arguments* (1997) covers a variety of topics: the relationship between television and literature, and the Illinois State Fair. *Consider the Lobster* (2005) analyzes John McCain's 2000 campaign, the porn business, and September 11.

Wallace also wrote for a number of magazines, such as *GQ*, *Playboy*, *The New Yorker*, *Might*, or *The Paris Review*. His journalistic pieces follow the New Journalism initiated by Tom Wolfe but also include scholarly writing techniques and some elements taken from fiction writing. *Everything and More: A Compact History of Infinity* (2003), his study of Georg Cantor's mathematical theories, met with harsh reviews.

ACHIEVEMENTS

David Foster Wallace was the recipient of numerous awards and scholarships, including the MacArthur Foundation "genius" grant and the Whiting Writers' Award (1987), the John Traine Humor Prize (1988), the Illinois Art Council Award for Non-Fiction (1989), the Quality Paperback Book Club's New Voices Award for Fiction (1991), the Salon Book Award for Fiction (1996), the Lannan Literature Award for Fiction and the O. Henry Award. "Brief Interviews with Hideous Men No. 6," a story in *Brief Interviews with Hideous Men*, was awarded the Aga Khan Prize for Fiction.

BIOGRAPHY

The son of two professors, James Donald Wallace and Sally Foster, David Foster Wallace grew up in the university city of Champaign, Illinois. After graduating summa cum laude with honors from Amherst College with a degree in English and philosophy with a focus on modal logic and mathematics, Wallace enrolled in the philosophy program at Harvard University graduate school. However, he soon abandoned it, following a nervous breakdown, and decided to pursue a literary career instead. He then went on to earn a master of fine arts in creative writing from the University of Arizona in 1987.

Wallace taught at several universities. In 1991, he became adjunct professor of literature at Emerson College. The following year he accepted a post in the English Department of the Illinois State University. In

2002, he became the first Roy E. Disney Professor of Creative Writing and professor of writing at Pomona College in California.

Terribly shy and with a tendency toward suicide, Wallace fought depression for more than two decades, trying a number of antidepressant drugs and other treatments. He was found dead in his home by his wife on September 13, 2008. He had committed suicide by hanging, at the age of forty-six, the day before. He is survived by his wife, painter Karen L. Green, his parents, and his sister, Amy Wallace-Havens.

## ANALYSIS

Heralded as one of the most important voices in his generation, David Foster Wallace had difficulties coping with the stress of modern life and more than once expressed his amazement at people being able to survive to age thirty or fifty without killing themselves. In his writings he dealt with human experience at its worst, without concealing or disguising the ugliness and the pain of life. In his own words, "fiction's about what it is to be a f--king human being." Because of this understanding of the role of literature, Wallace was committed deeply to making of literature the mirror of human experience, not the site of formal experimentation merely for art's sake.

For Wallace, his fiction was a radical realist reflection of America at the turn of the century. He questioned the obvious, the things one takes for granted, because they may delude or mislead. For him, "the most obvious, impossible realities are often the ones that are hardest to see and talk about." A versatile writer, Wallace covered a vast array of topics in his literary production, looking at daily life in a different manner, minutely examining seemingly mundane and common occurrences that at first might seem too banal or trivial to deserve a thorough analysis.

His main concerns included what he perceived as the confusion inherent to American life, the sadness and isolation that mark modern life, and the inability to be understood. For Wallace, the perception of reality is biased by the media and technology, especially by television. The difficulties in communicating in the modern world, despite the technological advances that are supposed to facilitate communication and bridge distances, are central in many of his stories. Wallace was compared to William Gaddis, Thomas Pynchon, and John Irving. However, Wallace had a love-hate relationship with some writers: "If I have a real enemy, a patriarch for my patricide, it's probably (John) Barth and (Robert) Coover and (William) Burroughs, even (Vladimir) Nabokov and Pynchon." Wallace was regarded as the leading voice of American literature after postmodernism, the prophet who would show the way when postmodernism had been abandoned. David Ulin, the book editor of the *Los Angeles Times*, said that Wallace

> was one of the most influential and innovative writers of the last twenty years. . . . He is one of the main writers who brought ambition, a sense of play, a joy in storytelling, and an exuberant experimentalism of form back to the novel in the late 1980's and early 1990's. And he really restored the notion of the novel as a kind of canvas on which a writer can do anything.

Wallace's eclectic body of work is marked by experimentalism and a certain sense of dissatisfaction (if not bitterness) with postmodern society. His works are often peopled by addicts, symbolizing the decay and unease of capitalist society, since capitalism has created nothing but personal dissatisfaction. One of the most persistent topics in his short stories is the idea that capitalism has come to pervade every aspect of human interaction, corrupting the way people communicate with others. The extremely long sentences are a salient and easily recognizable feature of his works, and so are his extensive use of footnotes and endnotes, which explain his point of view about reality without marring the narrative flow of the text. Irony and dark humor convey philosophical issues, which are combined with the epic-comical elements of daily life. His works include slang, advertising, jargon from a number of areas, abbreviations, acronyms, colloquial language, and sometimes made-up words.

Wallace challenged a number of concepts and notions, including that of the short story; his stories are noted for their brevity, some of them of just two paragraphs long. His short stories at times read like interviews, therapy sessions, and encyclopedialike entries.

His great achievement is that he could appeal to a large readership while not compromising his innovative writing developments.

### BRIEF INTERVIEWS WITH HIDEOUS MEN

This collection of short stories is united by a woman who interviews several men described as hideous for a number of reasons: They are misogynistic, self-centered, and self-absorbed.

### "A RADICALLY CONDENSED HISTORY OF POSTINDUSTRIAL LIFE"

This seventy-three-word, two-paragraph short story captures the moment when two strangers, a man and a woman, are introduced by a common acquaintance. Despite its brevity, the story touches on a number of important concerns for Wallace--the human need for acceptance, the importance people give to appearances, the isolation of modern life, the need to keep good relationships, the need to belong and be well liked, and the small compromises people make for the sake of courtesy or social convention to be accepted.

### "THE DEPRESSED PERSON"

This story has been acclaimed as a painful and accurate portrayal of the feelings and thoughts of somebody suffering from clinical depression. The inability to properly articulate and transmit to others the symptoms and the infinite sadness that the depressed person is feeling is central to the story. "The depressed person was in terrible and unceasing pain, and the impossibility of sharing or articulating this pain was itself a component of the pain and a contributing factor in its essential horror," Wallace wrote. The detailed footnotes elaborate on depression, acquainting readers with the symptoms of this malady.

### "TRI-STAN: I SOLD SISSEE NAR TO ECKO"

Based on the myth of Narcissus in Ovid's *Metamorphoses* (c. 8 c.e.; English translation, 1567) and the Tristan and Isolde story of the Nibelungen saga, this story reads like a dictionary entry. It is also reminiscent of Hollywood-flavored television shows. Ovid the Obtuse, the narrator, transplants these mythical beings into actors playing in a television show.

### GIRL WITH CURIOUS HAIR

Wallace's main theme in this volume is the disparity between reality and appearances, how people relate to the world and try to discover the truth hidden by multiple layers of appearances, deceit, and disguises. It features a vast array of characters, ranging from fictional ones to real ones, such as historical and sports figures and television celebrities. For instance, Lyndon B. Johnson and his wife, Lady Bird, are the protagonists of "Lyndon."

The book also examines the role and value of poetry in modern life, whether poetry can be true or not, and whether poetry is an accurate reflection of the truth. Wallace makes use of metafiction to reflect on the state of contemporary fiction. The volume is heavily indebted to the literary techniques employed by Barth, Kurt Vonnegut, Donald Barthelme, and Pynchon.

### WESTWARD THE COURSE OF EMPIRE TAKES ITS WAY

This 150-page novella focuses on the differences between appearances and truth. It covers a variety of subjects, from seemingly insignificant topics to more transcendental ones. Set in a fictional Creative Writing Department in a Maryland college, the story analyzes the relationship between the professor teaching a workshop and his writer-to-be graduate students. Professor

*David Foster Wallace*
(Time & Life Pictures/Getty Images)

Ambrose, loved and hated by his students, a has-been, is a reference to a character in Barth's "Lost in the Funhouse," echoes of which can be perceived in this novella. Autobiographical elements and childhood memories can be perceived, as well as the author's personal opinion regarding the usefulness of creative-writing programs. The title comes from the name of a mural by Emanuel Gottlieb Leutze. Painted in 1861, it represented the notion of America's Manifest Destiny, one of the themes in this novella, along with consumption, literature, and the trap that postmodernism has created.

### "My Appearance"

This story again deals with the divergence between reality and appearances. Based on a real interview of actress Susan Saint James on the *Late Night with David Letterman* show, it first appeared in *Playboy* magazine under the title "Late Night."

### Oblivion

The complexity of *Oblivion* has made it difficult to understand and, consequently, the least read of Wallace's literary production. In *Oblivion*, Wallace attempted to reproduce faithfully how the mind works--in leaps, not in a logical sequence, as traditional fiction has it. To achieve this effect, the sequential narrative is not followed, which makes it harder to follow and to read. Massive sentences and colloquial language also are used.

Closure is not to be found at the end of the stories; the end is where the story finishes, but no conclusion is reached, leaving the reader feeling a sense of incompleteness or unease. There is a certain nightmarish quality since the book plays on the reader's deepest inner fears.

### "Good Old Neon"

In this story, a man who committed suicide "revives" to explain to the reader how he killed himself and what comes next after death. The suicide victim, Neal, is an advertising executive whose life is a fraud, according to his own parameters of truth and falsehood. The sequence of events leading to the protagonist's suicide conveys a desperate search for some attachment to other people.

Appearances play a major role in Neal's life, and his fraudulence stems from his necessity to appear as someone he is not. It is Neal's failure to cope with this fraudulence and his lies, which eventually leads him to take his own life. The failure of language to transmit feelings effectively and the inability to communicate are two central concerns in this story.

The author appears as a character in this story, David Wallace '81, whose reaction, once he learns of Neal's suicide, the narrator imagines.

### "Mister Squishy"

This story is set in an advertising agency, and what at first seems to be a targeted focus group for a market test of a new snack allows Wallace to digress on the divergence between reality and appearances. Statistical jargon is employed to convey how human life is reduced to figures, evidence of the pervasive influence of capitalism on daily life. The author discusses how capitalism has shaped everyone's life, forcing him or her to consume more and more so as to be perceived as part of society. Corporate life also comes under the author's analysis and criticism. Long sentences, often nonstandard from a grammatical point of view, and extremely long paragraphs make the story difficult to understand. Many of the topics dealt with here can be seen in other stories in the same collection, such as "Good Old Neon," "The Suffering Channel," and "Oblivion."

OTHER MAJOR WORKS

LONG FICTION: *The Broom of the System*, 1987; *Infinite Jest*, 1996.

NONFICTION: *A Supposedly Fun Thing I'll Never Do Again: Essays and Arguments*, 1997; *Signifying Rappers: Rap and Race in the Urban Present*, 1990 (with Mark Costello); *Up, Simba! Seven Days on the Trail of an Anticandidate*, 2000 (reprinted as *McCain's Promise: Aboard the Straight Talk Express with John McCain and a Whole Bunch of Actual Reporters, Thinking About Hope*, 2008); *Everything and More: A Compact History of Infinity*, 2003; *Consider the Lobster, and Other Essays*, 2005; *This Is Water: Some Thoughts, Delivered on a Significant Occasion, About Living a Compassionate Life*, 2009.

EDITED TEXT: *The Best American Essays 2007*, 2007

BIBLIOGRAPHY

Boswell, Marshall. *Understanding David Foster Wallace*. Columbia: University of South Carolina Press, 2003. Analyzes the author's life and works.

Eggers, Dave. "Interview with David Foster Wallace." *The Believer* (November, 2003). Wallace speaks about his writing method, the writing process, his interests, his political involvement, madness, and geniuses.

McCaffery, Larry. "An Interview with David Foster Wallace." *Review of Contemporary Fiction* (1993). Wallace speaks about the American people's relationship with television and the effect of this on fiction writing, the goal of literature, the lack of censorship or rules in contemporary literature constraining writers, mathematics, metafiction, serious fiction versus commercial entertainment, being a writer, Raymond Carver, and postmodernism.

*MODERNISM/modernity* 16, no. 1 (2009). "In Memoriam David Foster Wallace." Steven Moore, Dave Eggers, Kathleen Fitzpatrick, Marshall Boswell, Michael North, Stephen J. Burn, and Brendan Beirne write on the significance of Wallace's works.

Wallace, David Foster. "David Foster Wallace on Life and Work." *The Wall Street Journal*, September 19, 2008, p. W14. Adaptation of a speech given by Wallace at the 2005 graduation ceremony at Kenyon College.

_____. "E Unibus Pluram: Television and U.S. Fiction." *Review of Contemporary Fiction* 13, no. 2 (1993): 151-194. Analyzes the impact of television on the American people and the effect of this for fiction writers, the interrelationship between fiction and television, metafiction and metatelevision, and high and low culture.

_____. "Fictional Futures and the Conspicuously Young." *Review of Contemporary Fiction* 8, no. 3 (1988): 36-53. Analyzes the state of literature at the close of the 1980's, the impact of television on the reading audience and on writers, the existence of creative-writing programs, the role of television in shaping the understanding of reality, and popular culture in literature.

*M. Carmen Gomez-Galisteo*

# ROBERT PENN WARREN

**Born:** Guthrie, Kentucky; April 24, 1905
**Died:** West Wardsboro, near Stratton, Vermont; September 15, 1989

PRINCIPAL SHORT FICTION

*Blackberry Winter,* 1946
*The Circus in the Attic, and Other Stories,* 1947

OTHER LITERARY FORMS

In addition to his short fiction, Robert Penn Warren published ten novels, several volumes of poetry, plays, a biography, collections of critical essays, three historical essays, three influential textbooks, several children's books, two studies of race relations in America, a memoir, and several book-length treatises on literature.

He won a host of distinguished awards, including three Pulitzer Prizes, two for poetry and one for fiction. Three of his novels have been filmed, and one of them, *All the King's Men* (1946), has been adapted in operatic form.

ACHIEVEMENTS

Honored as a major American poet and novelist, Robert Penn Warren displayed uncommon versatility in significant contributions to almost every literary genre. His work has been translated worldwide, and his short stories are widely anthologized. While he is best known for his novel *All the King's Men*, which won the Pulitzer Prize, he was most prolific as a poet whose awards included two Pulitzer Prizes and an appointment as America's first poet laureate.

The subject of Warren's fiction, and much of his poetry, is southern rural life in the late nineteenth and early twentieth centuries. He reveals a rootedness in his subject and its values, a concern for moral issues, and a gift for dialogue and environmental detail that lends distinctiveness to his work. His short stories, for example, are set down in rich, vigorous style, and they delineate the flow of time, the influence of past on present, and the painful necessity of self-knowledge.

## BIOGRAPHY

Robert Penn Warren was educated at Guthrie High School and was graduated from Vanderbilt University in Nashville, Tennessee (B.A., 1925), where he was associated with the Fugitive Group of poets; he did graduate work at the University of California (M.A., 1927), Yale University, and Oxford, and as a Rhodes scholar (D.Litt., 1930). In 1930, he contributed an essay, "I'll Take My Stand," to the Agrarian symposium. Between 1935 and 1942, he was an editor of the *Southern Review* and was influential in the articulation and practice of the New Criticism. After an active career as a

*Robert Penn Warren* (©Washington Post; reproduced by permission of the D.C. Public Library)

professor of English at a number of American colleges and universities, he retired from Yale in 1973. His first marriage to Emma Brescia in 1930 ended in divorce in 1950. He and his second wife, the writer Eleanor Clark, herself a National Book Award winner, had one son and one daughter.

Warren won the Pulitzer Prize for Fiction in 1947, the Pulitzer Prize for Poetry in 1958 and 1979, and the National Book Award in 1958. From 1944 to 1945, he was the second occupant of the Chair of Poetry at the Library of Congress. In 1952, he was elected to the American Philosophical Society; in 1959, to the American Academy of Arts and Letters; and in 1972, to the American Academy of Arts and Sciences. In 1967, he received the Bollingen Prize in Poetry, and in 1970, the National Medal for Literature and the Van Wyck Brooks Award. In 1974, he was chosen to deliver the third Annual Jefferson Lecture in the Humanities. In 1975, he received the Emerson-Thoreau Award of the American Academy of Arts and Sciences; the next year he was given the Copernicus Award by the Academy of American Poets; and in 1977, he was awarded the Harriet Monroe Prize for Poetry. Other awards included the Shelley Memorial Prize and the Presidential Medal of Freedom. In 1986, Warren achieved the unique distinction of becoming the first poet laureate (by act of Congress) of the United States. Warren's life spanned almost the whole twentieth century. After producing a rich final harvest of work from the mid-1970's to the mid-1980's, he died in 1989 at age eighty-four at his summer residence in Vermont. He left to posterity a canon of outstanding creative effort.

## ANALYSIS

Many of Robert Penn Warren's stories feature an adult protagonist's introspective, guilty recollections of imperishable childhood events, of things done or left undone or simply witnessed with childish innocence.

### "BLACKBERRY WINTER"

"Blackberry Winter" (the literal reference is to an unseasonable, late spring cold snap) opens with a nine-year-old boy's unbroken, secure world, a small community permeated with the presence and warmth of protective loved ones. A vaguely sinister, city-clothed stranger happens by and is given a job burying drowned chicks and poults by the boy's mother. Later the boy watches with his father and neighboring farmers as a dead cow, the yoke still around her neck, bobs down a flooding creek past fields of ruined tobacco plants. Then the boy finds a somehow shocking heap of litter washed out from under the house of his father's black help. Dellie, who lives there, is sick in bed with "woman-mizry," and after calling him to her side, gives her son little Jebb a sudden, "awful" slap. Big Jebb predicts that the cold snap will go on and that everything and everyone will die, because the Lord is tired of sinful people.

Later on, when the boy's father explains that he cannot afford to hire any help now but offers the stranger fifty cents for a half day's work, the stranger curses the farm and leaves, followed by the curious boy, whom he also curses. "You don't stop following me and I cut yore throat, you little son-of-a-bitch." "But I did follow him," the narrator tells readers, "all the years." At the end of the story all the sureties of the boy's world have been threatened, and in the epilogue readers learn that the farm was soon lost, his parents died, and little Jebb has gone to prison. The narrator has learned that the essence of time is the passing away of things and people; he has been exposed to natural and moral evil.

### "When the Light Gets Green"

"When the Light Gets Green" (the reference is to a peculiar, ominous shade of greenish light just before a storm) recalls "Blackberry Winter" in its setting, characterization, and theme, as well as in its retrospective point of view. The story's first two sentences display the technique: "My grandfather had a long white beard and sat under the cedar tree. The beard, as a matter of fact, was not very long and not very white, only gray, but when I was a child. . . ." Grandfather Barden had served as a Confederate cavalry captain in the Civil War; he had been a hero, but now he is old and thin and his blue jeans hang off his shrunken hips and backside. During a bad hailstorm in the summer of 1914 which threatens his son-in-law's tobacco crop, the old man has a stroke and collapses, and later upstairs in his room he waits to die--unloved, as he believes. His is the necessarily uncomprehending and hopeless fight that love and pride wage against time and change. His

grandson, who visits him but cannot speak, suffers the guilt of having tried and failed both to feel and to communicate the impossible love the old man needed.

Mr. Barden, as readers learn in the epilogue, lived until 1918, by which time other catastrophes had intervened--the farm was sold, his son-in-law was fighting in France, where he would soon be killed, and his daughter was working in a store. "I got the letter about my grandfather, who died of the flu," the story concludes, "but I thought about four years back, and it didn't matter much." The now adult narrator is puzzled and shamed by his failure and betrayal of his grandfather. In the dual perspective of the story Warren infuses a self-condemnatory ambivalence toward the old man which gives to the narrative the quality of expiation.

### "Prime Leaf"

"Prime Leaf," Warren's first published story, derives from the Kentucky tobacco wars of the first decade of the twentieth century, in which tobacco farmers organized in an attempt to secure higher prices from the tobacco buyers. The focus of the story is upon contention within the Hardin family, most directly between Old Man Hardin and Big Thomas, his son, but also involving Thomas's wife and young son. Old Man Hardin leaves the farmers' association rather than support the use of force against those members who object to the association's price fixing. Big Thomas, whom he had originally convinced to join the association, refuses to resign immediately. Their reconciliation occurs only after Big Thomas wounds one of a party of barn-burning night riders raiding the Hardins' property. Big Thomas decides that he will wait at home for the sheriff, but his father urges him to ride into town to justice, and on the way Big Thomas is ambushed and killed. The opposition of father and son is a contest between idea and fact, between idealism and pragmatism. Old Man Hardin is a kind and morally upright man but is also notably detached, remote, and unyielding. To his idealism is opposed his son's stubborn practicality, born of hard experience.

In delineating the conflict of the two men, with its tragic and ironic outcome, Warren did not espouse the beliefs of either but focused on the incompleteness of each. Old Man Hardin, embodying the rocklike integrity of the gentleman-farmer tradition, places an unwise reliance on what he still--despite much evidence to the contrary--takes to be the due processes of law. He cannot save his son and is in a way responsible for his death. Big Thomas, firing at the night riders until his rifle jams, before yielding to his father, does not resolve in acceptable fashion the problem of ends and means.

### "THE CIRCUS IN THE ATTIC"

"The Circus in the Attic" is a long and crowded tale about the meaning--or apparent meaninglessness--of history. It features, appropriately enough, a would-be local historian, Bolton Lovehart, a frail, frustrated man of aristocratic antecedents, whose deepest desire is simply to be free and himself. The only child of a weak father and an almost cannibalistically possessive mother, Bolton as a boy makes several doomed gestures of resistance. To his mother's subsequent horror, he participates in a riverbank baptismal ceremony; later he runs off with a carnival but is immediately retrieved. During his first year at college his now widowed mother has a heart attack; such, at least, is her story, although she will not allow a specialist to examine her and treats her son's suggestion as treason. In any event, Bolton does not return to college and life closes in on him. He begins to see a young woman, but, realizing that Bolton's mother has the stronger hold, the woman deliberately seduces and then abandons him.

Establishing the context of local history back to the first white settlers, Warren provided a series of vivid and ironic vignettes, one of which distinguishes between the official, heroic, United Daughters of the Confederacy version of the Civil War battle of Bardsville and the half-comic, half-sordid truth of the unremarkable little affair. One of the heroes, Cash Perkins, full of liquor, climbed on the wrong horse, a particularly mean one, and was carried, helpless and roaring, directly into Yankee rifle range. The truth of the other memorialized hero, Seth Sykes, was somewhat more involved. He cared nothing for secession, said so publicly, and lost a stomp-and-gouge fight over it. Then he said he hoped the Yankees would come, which they soon did, to take his corn, for which they offered him a note. He would have none of it; he had offered them meat but not his corn. He resisted and was killed. Of the official, patriotic versions of these two deaths, Warren wrote, " . . . people always believe what truth they have to believe to go on being the way they are."

Bolton Lovehart's major resource and consolation is the painstaking creation of a tiny circus--complete with animals and clowns and trapeze artists and a lion tamer--which he carves in the attic office where he is supposedly composing his study of local history. Upon his mother's death (finally, she does have a heart attack), it appears that he may at last enter into a life of his own. Shortly before World War II, Bolton marries, finds a hero in his braggart stepson, a posthumous Medal of Honor winner, and becomes for a time in his reflected energy and glory a current affairs expert and historian of sorts. His wife, who has been unfaithful to him, is killed in an automobile crash, and then his stepson is taken from him. At last he returns to the creation of those small, inanimate, innocent, wooden objects whose world alone he cherishes, controls, and understands. Bolton Lovehart's is less a fully human life than a kind of pathetic facsimile. His study of Bardsville's past--and by extension, humans' study of history--seems to assert that historical causation and "truth" are unknowable, that all humans are equally unimportant, and that all people are trapped in their own dark compulsions.

Warren is commonly identified as a southern writer and associated with such other premier representatives of that area as William Faulkner and Eudora Welty. As long as "southern" is not equated with "regionalist" in the limiting sense of that term, the description is accurate if not very illuminating. In another sense, however, as is apparent in his short fiction, Warren was a provincial, at least insofar as he retained an attachment to and an awareness of generally humanistic values--moral, social, and theological--often regarded as a vital part of the region's heritage. Thus the frequently noticeable tension between stylistic understatement (apparent in passages quoted earlier) and thematic intensity characteristic of the stories seems a reflection of a pull between the old humanistic conception of human wholeness and a naturalistic belief in the fragmented and unintegrated nature of human experience.

Warren published his last short story, "The Circus in the Attic," in 1947; thereafter he published as stories fourteen prepublication excerpts from his novels. Although in his nearly twenty years as a short-story writer Warren produced some fine work, both the author and a good many of his readers have found his achievement in short fiction less satisfying than that in other genres, notably poetry and the novel.

Explanations for his limited success in and satisfaction with short fiction might start with the fact that when he wrote many of the stories collected in *The Circus in the Attic, and Other Stories*, he was a beginner, at least in fiction. It is also the case, as Warren conceded, that he wrote for the quick buck, which did not come. Most of the stories did not represent major efforts; as Arthur Miller has said of his own short stories, they were what came easier. Finally, and most importantly, the form itself seems to have inhibited Warren's natural talents and inclinations.

In writing stories in the 1930's and 1940's, Warren appears to have backed into what was for him an unhappy compromise; stories were neither long enough nor short enough, offered neither the satisfying extensive scope of the novel nor the demanding intensive concision of the poem. Short stories might occasionally serve as sketches for novels ("Prime Leaf," discussed earlier, is the prototype of Warren's first published novel, *Night Rider*, 1939), but Warren found that the overlap between the short story and the poem was bad for him, that stories consumed material that would otherwise have become poems. Thus he said, "Short stories are out for me."

Despite such demurs, however, Warren's achievement in the short story is that of a major talent. Warren's ear never failed him; the voices from the past and of the present always ring true. No one writing in his day had a better ear--one could almost say recollection, if one did not know Warren's age--for the voices of late nineteenth and early twentieth century America. His eyes were open to both the panorama and to the smallest evocative detail: from the trapper looking across the mountains to the West to the cracked and broken shoe of a tramp. He was intensely alive to the natural world. This is not to say simply that the natural backgrounds of the stories are vividly

realized and accurately observed, although Warren was here the equal of Ernest Hemingway or Faulkner, but that such observation and realization provide the bases for those effects characteristic of his stories, for the evocation of atmosphere, for tonal modulation, and for symbolic representation.

OTHER MAJOR WORKS

LONG FICTION: *Night Rider*, 1939; *At Heaven's Gate*, 1943; *All the King's Men*, 1946; *World Enough and Time: A Romantic Novel*, 1950; *Band of Angels*, 1955; *The Cave*, 1959; *Wilderness: A Tale of the Civil War*, 1961; *Flood: A Romance of Our Time*, 1964; *Meet Me in the Green Glen*, 1971; *A Place to Come To*, 1977.

PLAYS: *Proud Flesh*, pr. 1947; *All the King's Men*, pr. 1958 (adaptation of his novel).

POETRY: *Thirty-Six Poems*, 1935; *Eleven Poems on the Same Theme*, 1942; *Selected Poems, 1923-1943*, 1944; *Brother to Dragons: A Tale in Verse and Voices*, 1953; *Promises: Poems, 1954-1956*, 1957; *You, Emperors, and Others: Poems, 1957-1960*, 1960; *Selected Poems: New and Old, 1923-1966*, 1966; *Incarnations: Poems, 1966-1968*, 1968; *Audubon: A Vision*, 1969; *Or Else--Poem/Poems, 1968-1974*, 1974; *Selected Poems: 1923-1975*, 1976; *Now and Then: Poems, 1976-1978*, 1978; *Brother to Dragons: A New Version*, 1979; *Ballad of a Sweet Dream of Peace*, 1980 (with Bill Komodore); *Being Here: Poetry 1977-1980*, 1980; *Rumor Verified: Poems, 1979-1980*, 1981; *Chief Joseph of the Nez Percé*, 1983; *New and Selected Poems, 1923-1985*, 1985; *The Collected Poems of Robert Penn Warren*, 1998 (John Burt, editor).

NONFICTION: *John Brown: The Making of a Martyr*, 1929; *Modern Rhetoric*, 1949 (with Cleanth Brooks); *Segregation: The Inner Conflict in the South*, 1956; *Selected Essays*, 1958; *The Legacy of the Civil War: Meditations on the Centennial*, 1961; *Who Speaks for the Negro?*, 1965; *Democracy and Poetry*, 1975; *Portrait of a Father*, 1988; *New and Selected Essays*, 1989; *Cleanth Brooks and Robert Penn Warren: A Literary Correspondence*, 1998 (James A. Grimshaw, Jr., editor); *Selected Lettes of Robert Penn Warren*, 2000-2006 (four volumes; William Bedford Clark, editor).

EDITED TEXTS: *An Approach to Literature*, 1936 (with Cleanth Brooks and John Thibault Purser);

*Understanding Poetry: An Anthology for College Students*, 1938 (with Brooks); *Understanding Fiction*, 1943 (with Brooks); *Faulkner: A Collection of Critical Essays*, 1966; *Randall Jarrell, 1914-1965*, 1967 (with Robert Lowell and Peter Taylor); *American Literature: The Makers and the Making*, 1973 (with R. W. B. Lewis).

BIBLIOGRAPHY

Blotner, Joseph. *Robert Penn Warren: A Biography*. New York: Random House, 1997. Blotner's is the first of what will almost certainly be many biographies following Warren's death in 1989. Blotner began his work while Warren was still alive and had the good fortune to have the cooperation not only of his subject but also of the larger Warren family. Blotner's book is straightforward and chronological; it makes a good beginning to a study of Warren.

Bohner, Charles. *Robert Penn Warren*. 1962. Rev. ed. Boston: Twayne, 1981. This lucid survey encompasses details of Warren's literary career and an analysis of his major themes. Also charts the development of his art as evidenced in his novels and short fiction, his poetry (through *Being Here: Poetry 1977-1980*), and his major essays. Includes a detailed chronology and a valuable select bibliography.

Bradley, Patricia L. *Robert Penn Warren's Circus Aesthetic and the Southern Renaissance*. Knoxville: University of Tennessee Press, 2004. Analyzes the symbolism of the circus in selected works of American literature. For Warren and other southern writers, the conservatism of the circus complemented their representations of the mythic Old South and the cultural stagnation of their allegiance to this lost region. Bradley begins her examination by analyzing "The Circus in the Attic," demonstrating how Warren's use of the circus trope establishes a means by which to analyze not only this story but also his other works of fiction, poetry, essays, and criticism. She then analyzes the use of the circus and carnival motif in works by several southern writers, including Thomas Wolfe, William Faulkner, and Katherine Anne Porter, as well as works by Ralph Ellison and Toni Morrison.

Clark, William Bedford, ed. *Critical Essays on Robert Penn Warren*. Boston: G. K. Hall, 1981. A comprehensive collection of criticism by leading literary scholars who analyze Warren's major work as novelist, poet, biographer, and essayist. Among the contributors are Harold Bloom, Malcolm Cowley, Carlos Baker, John Crowe Ransom, and Randall Jarrell. The collection includes a valuable 1969 interview with Warren by Richard Sale.

Dietrich, Bryan. "Christ or Antichrist: Understanding Eight Words in 'Blackberry Winter.'" *Studies in Short Fiction* 29 (Spring, 1992): 215-220. Discusses the final line of the story, "But I did follow him, all the years," by analyzing and critiquing previous critical interpretations of the line and by providing a religious reading of the stranger as Antichrist. Suggests that the young protagonist of the story follows in the footsteps of disillusionment.

Ferriss, Lucy. "Sleeping with the Boss: Female Subjectivity in Robert Penn Warren's Fiction." *The Mississippi Quarterly* 48 (Winter, 1994/1995): 147-167. Part of a special issue on Warren, this article suggests a feminist reading of Warren's fiction, discussing significant women characters who have sexual liaisons with men of power and wealth. Argues that Warren's ability to risk the profound disruption of masculine authority either by admitting female "selves" or by exposing the self-other dialectic as unreliable demonstrates his faith in the continuing resilience of interpretation.

Gelfant, Blanche H., ed. *The Columbia Companion to the Twentieth-Century American Short Story*. New York: Columbia University Press, 2000. Includes a chapter in which Warren's short stories are analyzed.

Grimshaw, James A. *Understanding Robert Penn Warren*. Columbia: University of South Carolina Press, 2001. Although this introduction to Warren's work focuses on the novels, poems, and plays, Chapter 2 features an extended discussion of *Blackberry Winter*.

Justus, James H. *The Achievement of Robert Penn Warren*. Baton Rouge: Louisiana State University Press, 1981. A cogent study of Warren's writings with the premise that his works largely derive from the cultural circumstances of time and place in his career. The book is divided into four sections dealing, respectively, with Warren's themes, poetry, nonfiction prose, and novels.

Millichap, Joseph R. "Robert Penn Warren and Regionalism." *The Mississippi Quarterly* 48 (Winter, 1994/1995): 29-38. Discusses Warren's insistence that regional writing should aim at meanings that transcend mere parochialism. Notes Warren's constant effort to reshape his relationship to his regional roots.

Ruppersburg, Hugh. *Robert Penn Warren and the American Imagination.* Athens: University of Georgia Press, 1990. Ruppersburg considers the Warren opus an attempt to define a national identity. Subscribing to Warren's notion that he was not a historical writer, Ruppersburg attempts to place Warren in a contemporary context, emphasizing such modern American concerns as civil rights and nuclear warfare.

Warren, Robert Penn. *Conversations with Robert Penn Warren.* Edited by Gloria L. Cronin and Ben Siegel. Jackson: University Press of Mississippi, 2005. Reprints interviews conducted with Warren from the 1950's through the 1980's, including his conversations with Bill Moyers, C. Vann Woodward, Edwin Newman, and William Kennedy. Warren discusses his poetry, the uses of fiction in history, politics and the novel, and his views of the South, among other subjects.

*Allen Shepherd*
*Updated by Christian H. Moe*

---

# MARY YUKARI WATERS

**Born:** Kyoto, Japan; January 1, 1965

PRINCIPAL SHORT FICTION

*The Laws of Evening,* 2003
"The Caste System," 2006

OTHER LITERARY FORMS

Mary Yukari Waters published her novel *The Favorites* in 2009; it borrowed liberally from her previously published collection of short stories, *The Laws of Evening.* The novel echoes and expands upon many of the same settings, themes, conflicts, and characterizations, which were introduced by Waters in *The Laws of Evening,* especially characters and subplots first presented in the short story "The Way Love Works."

ACHIEVEMENTS

Although she did not begin writing until the age of thirty, when she enrolled in her first creative-writing extension class, Mary Yukari Waters built a steady and impressive national reputation as a short-fiction writer through her publications in literary journals, such as *Shenandoah, Glimmer Train, Manoa,* and *Zoetrope: All-Story.* Waters later earned a master of fine arts degree in creative writing from the University of California, Irvine. All of the short stories in *The Laws of Evening* were published individually in literary journals in the decade prior to 2003, when they were then compiled in the collection of short fiction. In 2002, Waters received a National Endowment for the Arts literature grant, and the short story "Seed" won a Pushcart award, appearing in *The Pushcart Book of Short Stories: The Best Stories from a Quarter-Century of the Pushcart Prize.* In 2002, two other short stories by Waters won awards: "Aftermath" was chosen to be published in *The Best American Short Stories, 2002,* and "Egg-Face" was included in *The O. Henry Prize Stories, 2002.* For the second year in a row, in 2003, Waters had the short story "Rationing" included in *The Best American Short Stories. The Laws of Evening* was selected by the *San Francisco Chronicle* as one of the best books of 2003, and in 2004 Waters received the Kiriyama Prize Notable Book Award for the collection of short stories. *The Laws of Evening,* Waters's debut collection of short fiction, also was a Book Sense 76 selection and a Discover Great New Writers Award selection.

BIOGRAPHY

Mary Yukari Waters was born January 1, 1965, in Kyoto, Japan. Her mother, a Kyoto housewife, and her father, an Irish American physicist, raised Waters in a small neighborhood, where she attended public school until the age of nine. Although biracial, Waters, an only child, bore no resemblance to her Japanese relatives, looking instead completely American. Caucasian children were extremely rare in Kyoto public schools at that time, and as a result Waters was singled out by her Asian classmates, severely teased, bullied, and persecuted as an outsider. Eventually, the anti-American discrimination toward Waters became so traumatic and destructive that, out of concern for their daughter's well-being, Waters's parents decided to leave Japan and move to the United States. When Waters was nine years old, the family moved to Red Bluff, California, a tiny rural community two hours north of Sacramento. Waters felt a huge sense of relief upon relocating to California; for the first time in her life, she was not pointed at, ostracized, or attacked, but was simply taken for granted because she looked like everyone else. Waters's first language was Japanese, and when she began school in California, her written and spoken English skills lagged far behind that of her peers. Both Waters's parents worked persistently with their daughter, tutoring her in English speech and grammar each day for years, until Waters finally caught up.

While attending college, Waters studied business, receiving a degree in economics, primarily because of its practicality. After graduation, Waters passed the examination to become certified public accountant (CPA). Soon thereafter she was hired by an international conglomerate, and Waters worked for the next decade as a CPA. When Waters was twenty years old, her mother, who was forty-five, died suddenly from a heart condition. Throughout their tenure in America, the Waters family had made regular visits back to Kyoto to visit Japanese relatives, particularly Waters's grandmother and her extended family. After the premature death of her mother, Waters became extremely close to her grandmother in Kyoto, who took on the role of surrogate mother for Waters.

Shortly before she turned thirty, Waters's father died, precipitating in her a profound personal crisis. Waters, who worked enormous amounts of overtime as an accountant, was unhappy, disillusioned, and unfulfilled in her work. Seeking to find an outlet other than work, she enrolled in a creative-writing extension class at University of California, Los Angeles. Waters had never written anything before the age of thirty, not even as a hobby. One creative-writing class led to another, and Waters met Tom Filer, who became her writing mentor for the next several years. Waters's writing culminated in her leaving accounting and graduating in 2002 with a master of fine arts degree in creative writing from University of California, Irvine. Waters's short stories were published piecemeal in literary magazines until 2003, when they were compiled in *The Laws of Evening*. Her novel *The Favorites* was published in 2009. Waters, who is single, settled in Los Angeles to teach creative writing in the M.F.A. program at University of California, Riverside and at Spalding University's Brief Residency M.F.A. program. Extended visits to Kyoto have continued to be frequent for Waters, who spends much time with her grandmother and other Japanese relatives in the same small neighborhood of Waters's childhood, the setting for all of Waters's fiction.

ANALYSIS

Mary Yukari Waters's fiction is centered in post-World War II Kyoto, Japan, and all of her characters are coming to terms, in various ways, with the aftermath of the war. The eleven short stories in *The Laws of Evening* reveal a Japan gripped in poverty, in spite of American occupation and rationing, and struggling to rise from the ashes after the devastating bombings. The inhabitants of Kyoto also are displaced culturally, torn between Japan's rich heritage of ritualistic formality and the jarring modernization thrust upon them by the Americans. Populated primarily by widows and orphans, the characters in Waters's fiction remember daily the husbands and fathers who died in the war. Grief, loss, and longing are persistent themes in all of Waters's writing, particularly insofar as Waters examines how ordinary people go on with their lives after horrific tragedy and suffering.

Memory plays a crucial role throughout Waters's writing, since much of what occurs in her stories is reflected in the characters' minds. Waters's stories are almost plotless, instead focusing on subtle character studies of people seemingly lost in time, juxtaposed between two worlds: Japan before the war and Japan after the war. Sensual details, especially those involving sounds, smells, and color, are deftly employed by Waters to trigger memories and transport her characters from one time to the next, forming a stream-of-consciousness reality. Waters's style is minimalistic, and her dialogue is sparse; what is not said in her stories is often as important as what is said. Much of what transpires between characters in Waters's fiction lies beneath the surface of their fixed facades, unspoken, unacknowledged, and unexpressed.

Women and their relationships with each other, particularly mother and daughter relationships, are a primary focus of Waters's writing. Through the lens of Japanese domesticity, Waters reveals an intricate world of beauty and charm, beset with modern challenges that threaten Japanese customs and confuse Japanese identity. The loss of self and the search for identity are especially poignant in Waters's writing, as evidenced in stories such as "The Caste System," in which biracial Sarah Rexford travels from America back to her childhood home of Kyoto to visit her mother's grave and her Aunt Kimiko. Wandering the streets of Kyoto, Sarah remembers the torment of her youth, being mercilessly ostracized and bullied because of her Caucasian appearance at a time when anti-American sentiments were prevalent in Japan. What is Japanese, what is American, and what is Japanese American? These questions confront the characters in Waters's fiction, as they traverse between cultures and time, seeking perennial truths and feeling universal joys and sorrows. Ultimately Waters's characters convey an internal landscape where race is indistinguishable, where pain, grief, loss, and yearning are experienced by all, regardless of the skin they inhabit.

### "AFTERMATH"

In "Aftermath," Makiko, a Japanese war widow, watches her son Toshi play the new American game of dodge ball in the park. She marvels at how quickly the players switch sides in this game, with no fixed

allegiance or loyalties. Although thankful the war is over, Makiko grieves the death of her husband and struggles to raise her seven-year-old son to remember his father and his proud Japanese heritage. That is made even more difficult by Japan's occupation and modernization by Americans. While Toshi eagerly embraces the new American games, foods, and customs, his mother resents the Americans' indoctrination of her son. Makiko reminds Toshi that these Americans are the same people who killed his father, a man of whom Toshi has but one memory: of being carried on his father's shoulders when Toshi was three years old. Trying to keep the father's memory alive, Makiko requires her son to pray before the altar containing his father's picture each night.

Later Makiko and her son attend Tanabata Night, an annual Japanese festival that Makiko remembers fondly from her own childhood. At first Makiko is shocked and disheartened to see the festival's shabby decorations, a reminder of Japan's poverty and defeat. However, after tasting the meager food procured through rationing and watching the sparkler fireworks, Makiko finds her spirits are lifted and she is filled with renewed hope, for her son, his future, and Japan. Makiko hopes that Toshi will remember Tanabata Night fondly when he is a man, along with his father, and she ponders the nature of memory, its randomness and uncertainty, making everyone vulnerable to forgetting the past.

"Aftermath" epitomizes Waters's depiction of Japanese characters caught up in the tumultuous years after the war, trying to rebuild their lives around an old Japan that is gone forever and forced to live in a modern world not of their own making. Torn between time, cultures, and loyalties, the remaining postwar widows and children must adapt to the new circumstances in which they find themselves, in their own way, preserving the fragments of their previous lives and surviving as best they can.

### "RATIONING"

In "Rationing," Waters provides one of her favorite character studies, the relationship in postwar Japan between parents and children, in this case, the relationship between father and son. The story traces the relationship of teenager Saburo and his aging academic father, as they share each other's physical space awkwardly and mutely down through the years, emotionally separated by formal boundaries of Japanese custom. Until Saburo is nineteen years old, his mother's cheerful small talk provides a socially acceptable buffer between Saburo and his father. Suddenly, however, when his mother is killed tragically, Saburo finds himself alone with his father in the hospital waiting room, gripped in terror at the prospect of reaching out and comforting him. Unable to bridge the gulf that divides the two men, a chasm of time and generations and culture, prewar and postwar, Saburo and his father clumsily remain emotional strangers.

When Saburo is thirty years old, his father is diagnosed with terminal cancer, and after surgery, Saburo tentatively touches his father's cold hand, arm, and shoulder while the old man lies sleeping. Saburo is shocked at the small, frail bones beneath his father's hospital gown. Who is this man? Was he always so vulnerable behind the stoic, stone-faced mask he had worn throughout Saburo's memory? Would he have needed and welcomed Saburo's comfort and emotional display? Saburo longs to tell his father how much he admires and loves him, more than anyone he has ever known, but when his father wakes up, Saburo is gripped by the same fear and panic of his childhood and is unable to speak. Waters's portrayal of a father and son who are deprived of each other and live vastly diminished lives because of Japanese formality and order is anguished and wrenching, and Waters's depiction of the masks which all people sometimes wear and hide behind is profound.

### "THE LAWS OF EVENING"

In this, the title short story of Waters's collection of short fiction, Sono, a Kyoto lady nearing eighty years old, is facing her own mortality. While her elderly friends and relatives occupy themselves by practicing the same principles of keeping busy and remaining socially active, "the laws of afternoon," which compel them to rush from one activity to the next, exactly as they did in the middle of their lives, Sono retreats to a bench at the temple grounds. Sono's first visit to the bench is accidental; she simply needed a place to rest after walking with a cane and feeling faint. While surrounded by the trees, crows, water, and Buddhas, Sono

finds herself increasingly drawn into the peaceful, serene world around her. She communes with nature, ever conscious of her waning physical strength, pondering her limbo in the physical world, and anticipating her final emergence into the unknown. Having long since honored the fiftieth anniversary of her husband and twin daughters' deaths in the war, Sono views the rushing hubbub of those around her from the perspective of one with nothing left to lose. Sono rejects her friends' denial of death as they continue to muffle their consciousness through frenetic busyness, and although not a religious person, she embraces the end of her life with calm and repose, clear eyed and watchful, waiting for her life's final mystery to unfold.

### OTHER MAJOR WORKS

LONG FICTION: *The Favorites*, 2009.

### BIBLIOGRAPHY

Johnson, Sarah Anne. "The Power of Revision: Using a Patient Process of Polishing Her Fiction and Letting It 'Ferment,' Mary Yukari Waters Has Crafted Emotionally Rich Stories That Capture the Aura of Another Era." *The Writer* 119, no. 8 (August, 2006): 20. Waters talks about the writing process and describes some of her writing techniques, such as how to write a good beginning and a good ending for a story. Waters says that she has learned from experience that two things are vital in her writing process. First, Waters says that she engages in innumerable revisions of her writing, too many to count. Second, Waters says that after writing a story, she always sets it aside before publishing, at least for six months, so that she can look at it and revise it later, from a fresh perspective.

Wachs, Stewart. "The Clarity of Double Vision: An Interview with Mary Yukari Waters." *Kyoto Journal* 56 (2004). Waters discusses her childhood, growing up biracial in Kyoto, Japan, and how being biracial affects her writing. Waters says that coming from two cultures is an advantage for a writer because it increases one's perspective. Waters emphasizes that when she was writing the stories that appear in *The Laws of Evening*, two primary issues were foremost in her mind:

exploring how people come to terms with loss and delving into the ways in which people use memory to cope with life.

Waters, Mary Yukari, and Edel Coffey. "Living Life After Loss." *Sunday Tribune*, April 27, 2003, p. 8. Waters discusses the death of her mother when Waters was twenty and the death of her father when Waters was nearly thirty, recounting how the loss of her parents when she was young precipitated a

personal crisis that led to Waters's writing. Waters explains that loss is a persistent theme in her writing because she is searching through her characters for ways in which people survive and go on living after loss. Waters acknowledges that writing about her grandmother's generation of loss in World War II helped Waters move forward after her parents' deaths.

*Mary E. Markland*

# JEROME WEIDMAN

**Born:** New York, New York; April 4, 1913
**Died:** New York, New York; October 6, 1998

PRINCIPAL SHORT FICTION

*The Horse That Could Whistle "Dixie," and Other Stories,* 1939
*The Captain's Tiger,* 1947
*A Dime a Throw,* 1957
*My Father Sits in the Dark, and Other Stories,* 1961
*Where the Sun Never Sets, and Other Stories,* 1964
*The Death of Dickie Draper, and Nine Other Stories,* 1965

OTHER LITERARY FORMS

The published works of Jerome Weidman (WID-muhn) include plays, essays, travelogues, more than twenty novels, autobiographical sketches, an autobiographical volume, and numerous short-story collections and uncollected short stories. He is probably best known for his dramatic scripts, including the musicals *Fiorello!* (pr. 1959, pb. 1960) and *Tenderloin* (pr. 1960, pb. 1961), written in collaboration with George Abbott, and a musical version of his first novel, *I Can Get It for You Wholesale* (1937), produced and published in 1962.

ACHIEVEMENTS

As a fiction writer, Jerome Weidman is known best for his unpleasant, sometimes brutal, portrayal of Jewish characters in novels such as *I Can Get It for You*

*Wholesale* and *What's in It for Me?* (1938), and in short stories such as "The Kinnehórrah," "Chutzbah," and "The Horse That Could Whistle 'Dixie.'" He portrays characters more sensitively in his novels *Fourth Street East: A Novel of the Way It Was* (1970) and *The Enemy Camp* (1958) and in his stories "My Father Sits in the Dark" and "Movable Feast." Many of the settings in his novels and short stories are drawn from the areas in which he grew up, New York's Lower East Side and the Bronx, and many of the activities his characters pursue are drawn from his own experiences as a child growing up in the slums and as an office boy, an accountant, a law student, and a writer. Weidman won a Pulitzer Prize in 1960 for his collaboration on *Fiorello!*

BIOGRAPHY

Educated in stints at City College, New York, 1931-1933; Washington Square College, 1933-1934; and New York University Law School, 1934-1937, Jerome Weidman married Elizabeth Ann Payne and had three children. He was cowinner of the Pulitzer Prize in drama and winner of the New York Drama Critics Circle Award and the Antionette Perry ("Tony") Award, all for *Fiorello!* in 1960. He was a member of the Authors Guild and Dramatists Guild of Authors League of America, of which he served as president from 1969 to 1974, and the Writers Guild of America West. Settling in the San Francisco area in the early 1990's, Weidman's work on a second autobiographical volume and short stories and sketches were also drawn from his

Lower East Side childhood and his young adulthood living in the Bronx. Weidman died in 1998 at the age of eighty-five.

ANALYSIS

While Jerome Weidman's novels, *I Can Get It for You Wholesale* and *What's in It for Me?*, are often neglected because of his brutally realistic treatment of unsavory Jewish characters, his short stories are frequently humorous, good-natured jabs at not only the Jewish community but also the world as a whole. His early stories, particularly those in *The Horse That Could Whistle "Dixie," and Other Stories* are remarkably well constructed and display the work of a writer who has a clear conception of what he portrays. His later work, often marred by hasty writing and commercialism, retains the same sense of humor, but it often lapses into the maudlin and into fits of bathos. Such flaws should be no surprise in the stories of a man who freely admits that his primary aim in writing is to make money.

Weidman draws extensively on his life as a child and young man trying to survive in the slums of New York, first on Fourth Street East and later in the Bronx. In fact, he claims that all of his short stories, even those with female protagonists, are more or less autobiographical. The people of Weidman's stories are almost universally playing the game of life, and Weidman's stories reflect the gamesmanship of their situations. The puzzles to be pieced together and the games to be played by Weidman's characters are the puzzles and games that all people have played at one time or another and, as such, Weidman's stories become something of a mirror of life. However, the mirror is faceted and reflects many pieces of a whole, and it is making those pieces reflect a steady image that is the challenge for the reader and for the characters alike.

### "MY FATHER SITS IN THE DARK"

It is the task, set for himself, of the youngster in "My Father Sits in the Dark" to "figure out" why his father, night after night, sits quietly alone in his darkened house. None of the conventional answers the young man sorts out seems to fit. The family is poor, but his father would not worry about money; he would not worry about the family's health, either.

It is not until the young man confronts his father in the dark kitchen of the house that the situation begins to make sense. His father is an immigrant. His home in Austria did not have electricity, which made him familiar with the dark, so dark now provides for him a comfortable, nostalgic feeling. When the son asks the father why he sits in the dark, his father replies that it helps him think. When asked what he thinks about, he replies, "Nothing." The implication is that the old man does not have to have a more rational reason to sit in the dark and that the son, with his rationalized, fabricated understanding of the situation, has come to an incomplete understanding, but an understanding nevertheless. The fact that Weidman is playing the conflicts of modern society against the idyllic Old World is evident, but he does not belabor the point; he only reveals the exultant son going back to bed after he finally accepts his father's explanation for sitting in the dark. The outcome makes both happy, but there is no real resolution for the reader.

*Jerome Weidman* (Library of Congress)

### "THREE-TWO PITCH"

The same sort of puzzle appears in "Three-Two Pitch." Harry Powell is a bright young graduate on a three-month internship with the office of the best public relations specialist in New York. Powell, from Cleveland, is considered a "hick," but he takes his father's advice to ingratiate himself with the secretary of the office so that he can succeed. His success is such that he is prepared to marry the secretary before the action begins. D. J., Powell's employer, has a yearly commitment to have lunch with his Cleveland high school teacher, Doc Hapfel, but this year, after making the arrangements, he gets "tied up" and tells Harry to meet Hapfel and begin without him. In the course of the lunch, during which Doc becomes drunker and drunker, a series of calls from D. J.'s office (from the secretary Powell is thinking of marrying) relate that D. J. will be later and later, and after every call, Doc seems to know, intuitively, what has been said--as if he were going through a familiar ritual. When Doc finally collapses and Powell is forced to cope with the situation, he begins to put the pieces together. The lunch happens every year; D. J. always sends his intern to lunch with Doc; D. J. is always tied up; he will always come later. Doc finally admits he has not seen D. J. for years, and when Powell discovers, fortuitously, that D. J. has not been in town all day, but is in Detroit, he realizes that he has been duped and used to pacify the expectations of an old man.

Weidman stresses the conflict between "hick" Cleveland and sophisticated New York, but the principal theme is the puzzle which Powell must put together. The pieces are the secretary, D. J., Doc Hapfel, and Harry Powell himself. Before Harry can solve the puzzle, he must assimilate all of the pieces and come to an understanding of the situation and of himself. When he does solve the puzzle, the solution is devastating. He understands he has no place in New York, that he has been used, and that his self-esteem has blinded him to all of these realities. Only by returning to Cleveland and entering law school, as his father counseled him to do at the start of the story, can Powell provide a definitive, if somewhat unsatisfactory, solution to the whole puzzle.

### "I KNEW WHAT I WAS DOING"

"I Knew What I Was Doing" presents life as more of a game than a puzzle, but the same unsavory undertone attaches itself to the outcome. Throughout the story, Myra, a fashion model, plays one potential escort against another until she works herself up from a mere stock clerk to a wealthy clothing buyer. By portraying her game of enticement and entrapment, Weidman shows her as a cold, calculating woman who succeeds at the game because she knows the rules so well. The irony of her role is that her chumps, the men in her life, fall so predictably within the rules of the game. One of them, however, nearly upsets the game plan when he falls in love with Myra and proposes marriage almost simultaneously with her conquest of the rich clothing buyer. She retains her composure, however, and tells this, the most ensnared chump, to "paste it [a marriage license] in your hat." Weidman's characters in this story are little more than pawns being played by the queen. Weidman is not particularly interested in character here but rather in the progress of the match. The story is, perhaps, the epitome of Weidman's depiction of game playing.

### "THE HORSE THAT COULD WHISTLE 'DIXIE'"

At the other end of the spectrum is "The Horse That Could Whistle 'Dixie.'" Rather than flat, featureless characters, Weidman gives readers a thoroughly reprehensible father playing the age-old game of growing up with his unwilling son. After watching many children ride the ponies at the zoo pony ride and sneering fatuously at those who only ride in the horse cart and not astride the beasts, the father drags the son to the ponies and forces him to ride. Despite the child's tearful entreaties and the sensible suggestions of the attendant, who can see that the child is terrified, the father forces the child to ride not once, but four times. At the end, the child is a "whipped, silent mass of tear-stained quivering fright" who has finally satisfied his father's sense of propriety. Here the game has no winner, no ending, and no understanding. The son does not understand the father's motives, the father does not understand the son's reluctance, and the crowd watching the events does not want to understand. This is the most undesirable of Weidman's games, in which a person is forced to play by someone else's rules.

From the gentle "My Father Sits in the Dark," to the savage "The Horse That Could Whistle 'Dixie,'" Weidman portrays, fabricates, and manipulates the games people play and the puzzles that they are. If readers are to understand the games and puzzles, they must abandon credulity and prepare themselves for the inconsistencies that the games-master builds into the game.

OTHER MAJOR WORKS

LONG FICTION: *I Can Get It for You Wholesale*, 1937; *What's in It for Me?*, 1938; *I'll Never Go There Anymore*, 1941; *The Lights Around the Shore*, 1943; *Too Early to Tell*, 1946; *The Price Is Right*, 1949; *The Hand of the Hunter*, 1951; *Give Me Your Love*, 1952; *The Third Angel*, 1953; *Your Daughter Iris*, 1955; *The Enemy Camp*, 1958; *Before You Go*, 1960; *The Sound of Bow Bells*, 1962; *Word of Mouth*, 1964; *Other People's Money*, 1967; *The Center of the Action*, 1969; *Fourth Street East: A Novel of the Way It Was*, 1970; *Last Respects*, 1972; *Tiffany Street*, 1974; *The Temple*, 1975; *Counselors-at-Law*, 1980.

PLAYS: *Fiorello!*, pr. 1959 (libretto with George Abbott; music and lyrics by Sheldon Harnick and Jerry Bock); *Tenderloin*, pr. 1960 (libretto with Abbott; music and lyrics by Harnick and Bock); *I Can Get It for You Wholesale*, pr. 1962 (libretto; music by Harold Rome; adaptation of his novel); *Cool Off!*, pr. 1964 (libretto; music by Howard Blackman); *Pousse-Café*, pr. 1966 (libretto; music by Duke Ellington); *Ivory Tower*, pr. 1968 (with James Yaffe); *Asterisk! A Comedy of Terrors*, pr., pb. 1969; *The Mother Lover*, pr. 1969.

SCREENPLAYS: *The Damned Don't Cry*, 1950 (with Harold Medford); *The Eddie Cantor Story*, 1953 (with Ted Sherdeman and Sidney Skolsky); *Slander*, 1957.

TELEPLAY: *The Reporter*, 1964 (series).

NONFICTION: *Letter of Credit*, 1940; *Traveler's Cheque*, 1954; *Back Talk*, 1963; *Praying for Rain*, 1986.

EDITED TEXTS: *A Somerset Maugham Sampler*, 1943; *Traveler's Cheque*, 1954; *The First College Bowl Question Book*, 1961 (with others).

BIBLIOGRAPHY

Bannon, Barbara A. "Authors and Editors." *Publishers Weekly* 196 (July 28, 1969): 13-15. Uses the publication of Weidman's novel *The Center of the Action* as a starting point for a treatment of his literary career. Discusses aspects of the relationship between Weidman's fiction and his life. Accompanied by a photograph of Weidman.

Barkham, John. "The Author." *Saturday Review* 45 (July 28, 1962): 38-39. This interview, concerning Weidman's fiction and theater work, accompanies a review of Weidman's novel *The Sound of Bow Bells*. Barkham's essay examines some of Weidman's ideas about the way stories should be written and discusses Weidman's daily schedule as a writer. A photograph of Weidman accompanies the review.

Hawtree, Christopher. "Chronicles of the Lower East Side." *The Guardian*, October 20, 1998, p. 22. A brief sketch of Weidman's life and literary career. Concludes with a comment on his story "Monsoon," which is compared to a story by Eudora Welty in its treatment of racism.

Liptzin, Sol. *The Jew in American Literature*. New York: Bloch, 1966. Discusses Weidman in the context of American literature. Liptzin briefly compares Weidman to Budd Schulberg in their treatment of "the Jewish go-getter" and of "unpleasant Jewish money-grubbers."

Sherman, Bernard. *The Invention of the Jew: Jewish-American Education Novels, 1916-1964*. New York: Yoseloff, 1969. Treats Weidman's *I Can Get It for You Wholesale* as a rogue-hero novel. Sherman places the work in a tradition beginning with *The Rise of David Levinsky*, by Abraham Cahan, and running through *Haunch, Paunch, and Jowl*, by Samuel Ornitz, and *What Makes Sammy Run*, by Budd Schulberg.

Weidman, Jerome. Interview by Lisa See. *Publishers Weekly* 230 (September 12, 1986): 72-73. Uses the publication of Weidman's autobiographical volume, *Praying for Rain*, as a point of departure for surveying his literary career. Weidman also discusses some of his ideas about composition. Includes a photograph of Weidman.

*Clarence O. Johnson*
*Updated by Richard Tuerk*

.

# EUDORA WELTY

**Born:** Jackson, Mississippi; April 13, 1909
**Died:** Jackson, Mississippi; July 23, 2001

PRINCIPAL SHORT FICTION

*A Curtain of Green, and Other Stories,* 1941
*The Wide Net, and Other Stories,* 1943
*The Golden Apples,* 1949
*Principal Short Stories,* 1950
*Selected Stories of Eudora Welty,* 1954
*The Bride of the Innisfallen, and Other Stories,* 1955
*Moon Lake, and Other Stories,* 1980
*The Collected Stories of Eudora Welty,* 1980
*Retreat,* 1981

OTHER LITERARY FORMS

In addition to her many short stories, Eudora (yoo-DOR-ah) Welty published novels, essays, reviews, an autobiography, a fantasy story for children, and a volume of photographs of Mississippi during the Depression, *One Time, One Place: Mississippi in the Depression, a Snapshot Album* (1971), taken during her stint as photographer and writer for the Works Progress Administration.

ACHIEVEMENTS

Eudora Welty possessed a distinctive voice in southern, and indeed in American, fiction. Her vibrant, compelling evocation of the Mississippi landscape, which was her most commonly used setting, led to comparisons between her work and that of other eminent southern writers, such as William Faulkner, Carson McCullers, and Flannery O'Connor. Welty's graceful, lyrical fiction, however, lacks the pessimism that characterizes much of established southern writing, and though her settings are distinctly southern, her themes are universal and do not focus on uniquely southern issues.

The honors and awards that Welty amassed throughout her long career are so many as to defy complete listing in a short space. Among her major achievements are four O. Henry Awards for her short stories (first prizes in 1942, 1943, and 1968, and a second prize in 1941), two Guggenheim Fellowships (1942, 1949), honorary lectureships at Smith College (1952) and the University of Cambridge (1955), election to the National Institute of Arts and Letters (1952) and to the American Academy of Arts and Letters (1971), honorary LL.D. degrees from the University of Wisconsin (1954) and Smith College (1956), a term as honorary consultant to the Library of Congress (1958-1961), the William Dean Howells Medal of the American Academy of Arts and Letters for *The Ponder Heart* (1954), the Gold Medal for Fiction of the National Institute of Arts and Letters (1972), the Pulitzer Prize in fiction (awarded in 1973 for her 1972 novel *The Optimist's Daughter*), the National Medal of Literature and Medal of Freedom (1981), the National Medal of Arts (1986), the naming of the Jackson Public Library in her honor (1986), and a Rea Award (1992).

BIOGRAPHY

Eudora Alice Welty was born on April 13, 1909, in Jackson, Mississippi. In the Welty household, reading was a favorite pastime, and Welty recalls in her autobiography, *One Writer's Beginnings* (1984), both being read to often as a young child and becoming a voracious reader herself. Her recollections of her early life are of a loving and protective family and of a close, gossip-prone community in which she developed her lifelong habit of watching, listening to, and observing closely everything around her. Her progressive and understanding parents encouraged her in her education, and in 1925, she enrolled at the Mississippi State College for Women. After two years there, she transferred to the University of Wisconsin and was graduated with a B.A. in English in 1929.

Welty subsequently studied advertising at the Columbia University Business School; her father had recommended to her that if she planned to be a writer, she would be well advised to have another skill to which she could turn in case of need. During the Depression, however, she had little success finding employment in the field of advertising. She returned to Mississippi and spent the next several years working variously as a writer for radio and as a society editor. In 1933, she began working for the Works Progress Administration, traveling throughout Mississippi, taking photographs, interviewing people, and writing newspaper articles. She later credited this experience with providing her with much material for her short stories, as well as sharpening her habit of observation. During these working years, she wrote short stories and occasionally traveled to New York in an effort to interest publishers in her work, with little success. Her first short story, "Death of a Traveling Salesman," was published in 1936 by a "little" magazine called *Manuscript*. Her ability as a writer soon attracted the attention of Robert Penn Warren and Cleanth Brooks, editors of *The Southern Review*, and over the next years her writing appeared in that magazine as well as in *The New Yorker*, *The Atlantic Monthly*, and *The Sewanee Review*.

Her first collection of short stories, *A Curtain of Green, and Other Stories*, appeared in 1941, with a preface by Katherine Anne Porter. Welty's reputation as an important southern writer was established with this first volume, and, at the urging of her editor and friend John Woodburn, who encouraged her to write a longer work of fiction, she followed it with her fabular novel *The Robber Bridegroom* in 1942. Thenceforth, she continued with a fairly steady output of fiction, and with each successive publication, her stature as a major American writer grew. Although fiction was her primary field, she wrote many essays and critical reviews and dabbled in the theater. In addition to stage adaptations of *The Robber Bridegroom* and *The Ponder Heart*, she collaborated on a musical (never produced) entitled *What Year Is This?* and wrote several short theatrical sketches. In 1984, her autobiography, *One Writer's Beginnings*, appeared and quickly became a best seller.

Welty spent most of her life living in, observing, and writing about Jackson and the Mississippi Delta country. Her frequent visits to New York and her travels in France, Italy, Ireland, and England (where she participated in a conference on American studies at the University of Cambridge in 1955) provided her with material for those few stories that are set outside her native Mississippi. From time to time, she lectured or taught but in general preferred the quiet and privacy of her lifelong home of Jackson. She died in Jackson on July 23, 2001, at the age of ninety-two.

ANALYSIS

Although some dominant themes and characteristics appear regularly in Eudora Welty's fiction, her work resists categorization. The majority of her stories are set in her beloved Mississippi Delta country, of which she paints a vivid and detailed picture, but she is equally comfortable evoking such diverse scenes as a northern city or a transatlantic ocean liner. Thematically, she concerns herself both with the importance of family and community relations and, paradoxically, with the strange solitariness of human experience. Elements of myth and symbol often appear in her work, but she uses them in shadowy, inexplicit ways. Perhaps the only constant in Welty's fiction is her unerring keenness of observation, both of physical landscape and in characterization, and her ability to create convincing psychological portraits of an immensely varied cast of characters.

"DEATH OF A TRAVELING SALESMAN"

One of her earliest stories, "Death of a Traveling Salesman," tells of a commercial traveler who loses his way in the hill country of Mississippi and accidentally drives his car into a ravine. At the nearest farm dwelling, the salesman finds a simple, taciturn couple who assist him with his car and give him a meal and a place to stay for the night. The unspoken warmth in the relationship of the couple is contrasted with the salesman's loneliness, and he repeatedly worries that they can hear the loud pounding of his heart, physically weakened from a recent illness and metaphorically empty of love. When he leaves their house in the morning, his heart pounds loudest of all as he carries his bags to his car; frantically he tries to stifle the sound and dies, his heart unheard by anyone but himself.

## "A WORN PATH"

Another relatively early story, "A Worn Path," recounts an ancient black woman's long and perilous journey on foot from her remote rural home to the nearest town. The frail old woman, called Phoenix, travels slowly and painfully through a sometimes hostile landscape, described in rich and abundant detail. She overcomes numerous obstacles with determination and good humor. Into the vivid, realistic description of the landscape and journey, Welty interweaves characteristically lyrical passages describing Phoenix's fatigue-induced hallucinations and confused imaginings. When Phoenix reaches the town, she goes to the doctor's office, and it is revealed that the purpose of her journey is to obtain medicine for her chronically ill grandson. A poignant scene at the story's close confirms the reader's suspicion of Phoenix's extreme poverty and suggests the likelihood that her beloved grandson will not live long; old Phoenix's dignity and courage in the face of such hardship, however, raise the story from pathos to a tribute to her resilience and strength of will. Like her mythical namesake, Phoenix triumphs over the forces that seek to destroy her.

*Eudora Welty* (AP Photo/AJC, Billy Downs)

## "WHY I LIVE AT THE P.O."

"Why I Live at the P.O." is a richly comic tale of family discord and personal alienation, told in the first person in idiomatic, naturalistic language that captures the sounds and patterns of a distinctive southern speech. It is one of the earliest examples of Welty's often-used narrative technique, what she calls the "monologue that takes possession of the speaker." The story recounts how Sister, the intelligent and ironic narrator, comes to fall out with her family over incidents arising from her younger sister Stella-Rondo's sudden reappearance in their small southern town, minus her husband and with a two-year-old "adopted" child in tow.

Welty's flair for comedy of situation is revealed as a series of bizarrely farcical episodes unfolds. Through the irritable Stella-Rondo's manipulative misrepresentations of fact and Sister's own indifference to causing offense, Sister earns the ire of her opinionated and influential grandfather Papa-Daddy, her gullible, partisan mother, and her short-tempered Uncle Rondo. Sister responds by removing all of her possessions from communal use in the home and taking up residence in the local post office, where she is postmistress. Inability to communicate is a recurrent theme in Welty's short fiction; in this case, it is treated with a controlled hilarity that is chiefly comic but that nevertheless reveals the pain of a family's disunity. This story is one of the best examples of Welty's gift for comic characterization, her gentle mockery of human foibles, and her ear for southern idiom and expression.

## "KEELA, THE OUTCAST INDIAN MAIDEN"

Although Welty disliked having the term "gothic" applied to her fiction, "Keela, the Outcast Indian Maiden" has a grotesque quality that characterizes much of southern gothic writing. Steve, a former circus sideshow barker, has enlisted the help of Max in finding a small, clubfooted black man who used to be exhibited in the sideshow as "Keela, the Outcast Indian Maiden." As a sideshow freak, he was forced to behave savagely and eat live chickens. Max has brought Steve to the home of Little Lee Roy, who is indeed the man Steve seeks.

As Little Lee Roy looks on, Steve tells Max the disgusting details of the sideshow act and explains how Little Lee Roy was ill treated by the circus until a kind spectator rescued the victim from his degrading existence. Although he persistently refers to Little Lee Roy as "it" and, unlike Max, refuses to address Little Lee Roy directly, Steve expresses guilt and regret over his role in Little Lee Roy's exploitation. There are subtle resonances of the South's troubled legacy in the way the obviously culpable Steve tries to diminish his role in this ugly episode of oppression by pleading ignorance. He claims that he never knew that the sideshow freak was a normal man and not the savage beast that he was displayed as being in the circus.

The simple-minded Little Lee Roy, however, reacts to these reminders of his bizarre past with uncomprehending glee; he seems to have forgotten the pain and unpleasantness of his life with the circus and remembers it only as a colorful adventure. Steve cannot expiate his guilt; he has nothing to offer Little Lee Roy to compensate him for his brutal treatment. He says awkwardly to Max, "Well, I was goin' to give him some money or somethin', I guess, if I ever found him, only now I ain't got any." After the white men's departure, Little Lee Roy's children return, but they hush him when he tries to tell them about the visitors who came to talk to him about "de old times when I use to be wid de circus." The ugly incidents have left no scar on their simple victim; rather, it is the victimizer who suffers an inescapable burden of guilt and shame.

### "THE WIDE NET"

"The Wide Net" is a fabular tale of the mysteries of human relationships and the potency of the natural world. Young William Wallace returns home from a night on the town to find a note from his pregnant wife saying that she has gone to drown herself in the river. William Wallace assembles a motley collection of men and boys to help him drag the river. The river's power as a symbol is apparent in the meaning that it holds for the many characters: To youngsters Grady and Brucie it is the grave of their drowned father; to the rough, carefree Malones, it is a fertile source of life, teeming with catfish to eat, eels to "rassle," and alligators to hunt; to the philosophical and somewhat bombastic Doc, it signifies that "the outside world is full of endurance." It is also,

the river-draggers discover, the home of the primeval "king of the snakes."

Throughout the story, Welty deliberately obscures the nature of William Wallace's relationship with his wife, the history behind her threat, and even whether William Wallace truly believes his wife has jumped in the river. Characteristically, Welty relies on subtle hints and expert manipulation of tone rather than on open exposition to suggest to her readers the underpinnings of the events that she describes. This deliberate vagueness surrounding the facts of the young couple's quarrel lends the story the quality of a fable or folktale. The young lover must undergo the test of dragging the great river, confronting the king of snakes, and experiencing a kind of baptism, both in the river and in the cleansing thunderstorm that drenches the searchers, before he is worthy of regaining his wife's love.

Like a fable, the story has an almost impossibly simple and happy ending. William Wallace returns from the river to find his welcoming wife waiting calmly at home. They have a brief, affectionate mock quarrel that does not specifically address the incident at all, and they retire hand in hand, leaving the reader to ponder the mystery of their bond.

### "LIVVIE"

"Livvie" has a lyrical, fabular quality similar to that of "The Wide Net." Livvie is a young black woman who lives with her elderly husband, Solomon, on a remote farm far up the old Natchez Trace. The strict old husband is fiercely protective of his young bride and does not allow her to venture from the yard or to talk with--or even see--other people. The inexperienced Livvie, however, is content in Solomon's comfortable house, and she takes loving care of him when his great age finally renders him bedridden. One day, a white woman comes to her door, selling cosmetics. Livvie is enchanted with the colors and scents of the cosmetics but is firm in her insistence that she has no money to buy them. When the saleswoman leaves, Livvie goes into the bedroom to gaze on her ancient, sleeping husband. Desire for wider experience and a more fulfilling life has been awakened in her, and as her husband sleeps, she disobeys his strictest command and wanders off down the Natchez Trace.

There, she comes upon a handsome, opulently dressed young man named Cash, whom she leads back to Solomon's house. When Solomon awakes and sees them, he is reproachful but resigned to her need for a younger man, asking God to forgive him for taking such a young girl away from other young people. Cash steals from the room, and as Livvie gazes on the frail, wasted body of Solomon, he dies. In a trancelike shock, Livvie drops Solomon's sterile, ticking watch; after momentary hesitation, she goes outside to join Cash in the bright light of springtime.

"Livvie" is almost like a fairy tale in its use of simple, universal devices. The beautiful young bride, the miserly old man who imprisons her, the strange caller who brings temptation, and the handsome youth who rescues the heroine are all familiar, timeless characters. Welty broadens the references of her story to include elements of myth and religion. Young Cash, emerging from the deep forest dressed in a bright green coat and green-plumed hat, could be the Green Man of folklore, a symbol of springtime regeneration and fertility. In contrasting youth with age and old with new, Welty subtly employs biblical references. Old Solomon thinks rather than feels but falls short of his Old Testament namesake in wisdom. Youthful Cash, redolent of spring, tells Livvie that he is "ready for Easter," the reference ostensibly being to his new finery but suggesting new life rising to vanquish death. The vague, dreamy impressionism of "Livvie," which relies on image and action rather than dialogue to tell the story (except in the scenes featuring the saleswoman), adds to this folktalelike quality.

### "A Still Moment"

In "A Still Moment," Welty uses historical characters to tell a mystically imaginative tale. Lorenzo Dow, the New England preacher, James Murrell, the outlaw, and John James Audubon, the naturalist and painter, were real people whom Welty places in a fictional situation. Dow rides with an inspired determination to his evening's destination, a camp meeting where he looks forward to a wholesale saving of souls. With single-minded passion, he visualizes souls and demons crowding before him in the dusky landscape. Dow's spiritual intensity is both compared and contrasted to the outlook of the outlaw Murrell, who shadows Dow along the Natchez Trace. Murrell considers his outlawry in a profoundly philosophical light, seeing each murder as a kind of ceremonial drawing out and solving of the unique "mystery" of each victim's being. Audubon, like Dow and Murrell, has a strange and driving intensity that sets him apart from other men. His passion is the natural world; by meticulously observing and recording it, he believes that he can move from his knowledge to an understanding of all things, including his own being.

The three men are brought together by chance in a clearing, each unaware of the others' identities. As they pause, a solitary white heron alights near them in the marsh. As the three men stare in wonder at the snowy creature, Welty identifies for the reader the strange similarity of these outwardly diverse men: "What each of them had wanted was simply *all*. To save all souls, to destroy all men, to see and record all life that filled this world." The simple and beautiful sight of the heron, however, causes these desires to ebb in each of them; they are transfixed and cleansed of desire. Welty uses the heron as a symbol of the purity and beauty of the natural world, which acts as a catalyst for her characters' self-discovery. Oddly, it is Audubon, the lover of nature, who breaks the spell. He reaches for his gun and shoots the bird, to add to his scientific collection. The magic of the moment is gone, and the lifeless body of the bird becomes a mere sum of its parts, a dull, insensate mass of feathers and flesh.

Audubon, his prize collected, continues on his way, and the horrified Dow hurries away toward his camp meeting, comforted by the vivid memory of the bird's strange beauty. The dangerous Murrell experiences an epiphanic moment of self-realization; the incident has reminded him poignantly of all men's separateness and innocence, a thought that reconfirms in him his desire to waylay and destroy. It is only through a brief but intense moment of shared feeling and experience that the men can recognize their essential loneliness. As in "The Wide Net" and "Livvie," the most important communication must be done without words.

## "MOON LAKE"

"Moon Lake" is from the collection *The Golden Apples*, the stories of which are nearly all set in or around the mythical community of Morgana, Mississippi, and feature a single, though extensive, cast of characters. Thematically, it shares with "A Still Moment" the sense of the paradoxical oneness and interconnectedness of the human condition. The story describes a sequence of events at a camp for girls at the lake of the story's title. The characteristically lushly detailed landscape is both beautiful and dangerous, a place where poisonous snakes may lurk in the blackberry brambles and where the lake is a site for adventure but also a brown-watered, bug-infested morass with thick mud and cypress roots that grasp at one's feet.

The story highlights the simultaneous attraction and repulsion of human connection. Antipathies abound among the group assembled at the lake: The lake's Boy Scout lifeguard, Loch, feels contempt for the crowd of young girls; the Morgana girls look down on the orphan girls as ragged thieves; rivalry and distrust crops up among individual girls. The sensitive Nina yearns for connection and freedom from connection at the same time; she envies the lonely independence of the orphans and wishes to be able to change from one persona to another at will, but at the same time she is drawn to Easter, the "leader" of the orphans, for her very qualities of separateness and disdain for friendship.

Nina and her friend Jinny Love follow Easter to a remote part of the lake in an unsuccessful attempt to cultivate her friendship, and when they return to where the others are swimming, Easter falls from the diving platform and nearly drowns. The near-drowning becomes a physical acting out of the story's theme, the fascinating and inescapable but frightening necessity of human connection. Without another's help, Easter would have died alone under the murky water, but Loch's lengthy efforts to resuscitate the apparently lifeless form of Easter disgust the other girls. The quasisexual rhythm of the resuscitation is made even more disturbing to the girls by its violence: Loch pummels Easter with his fists, and blood streams from her mudsmeared mouth as he flails away astride her. The distressing physical contact contrasts with the lack of any emotional connection during this scene. One orphan, a companion of Easter, speculates that if Easter dies, she gets her winter coat, and gradually the other girls grow bored with the spectacle and resent the interruption of their afternoon swim. Jinny Love's mother, appearing unexpectedly at the camp, is more concerned with the lewdness that she imputes to Loch's rhythmic motions than with Easter's condition and she barks at him, "Loch Morrison, get off that table and shame on you." Nina is the most keenly aware of the symbolic significance of the incident and of the peril of connection; she reflects that "Easter had come among them and had held herself untouchable and intact. For one little touch could smirch her, make her fall so far, so deep."

## "THE WHOLE WORLD KNOWS"

Another story from *The Golden Apples* is "The Whole World Knows," which features the adult Jinny Love Stark, whom readers have met as a child in "Moon Lake," and Ran McLain, who appears briefly in "Moon Lake" and other stories in this collection. The story addresses the inescapable net of personal and community relations and the potentially stifling and limiting nature of small-town life. Welty uses a monologue form similar to the one in "Why I Live at the P.O.," but in this story, told by Ran, the tone is lamenting and confessional rather than comically outraged.

Ran and Jinny are married but have separated, ostensibly over Jinny's infidelity. They both remain in the claustrophobically small town of Morgana, living in the same street and meeting occasionally in the town's bank, where Ran works alongside Jinny's lover, Woody Spights. On the surface, the story centers on Ran's developing relationship with a Maideen Sumrall, a foolish, chattering young country girl with whom he has taken up as a way of revenging himself on his wayward wife. The true focus, however, is on the causes of the deterioration of Ran's marriage to the lively, enthusiastic Jinny, revealed obliquely through other events in the story. The reasons for Jinny's initial infidelity are only hinted at; her irrepressibly joyous and wondering outlook is contrasted with Ran's heavy and brooding nature, indicating a fundamental incompatibility. Ran's careless and selfish use of Maideen, to whom he is attracted because she seems a young and "uncontaminated" version of Jinny, suggests a dark side to his nature that may be at the root of their estrangement. There is a vague suggestion, never clearly stated, that Ran may have been unfaithful to Jinny first. The merry, carefree Jinny baffles and infuriates Ran, and he fantasizes about violently murdering both Jinny and her lover, Woody. His true victim, however, is Maideen, the vulnerable opposite of the unflappable, independent Jinny. After Ran roughly consummates his shabby affair with the semi-willing Maideen, he wakes to find her sobbing like a child beside him. Readers learn in another story that Maideen eventually commits suicide. The story ends inconclusively, with neither Ran nor Jinny able or even entirely willing to escape from their shared past, the constricted community of Morgana being their all-knowing "whole world" of the story's title. As in "Moon Lake," true connection is a paradox, at once impossible, inescapable, desirable, and destructive.

### "WHERE IS THE VOICE COMING FROM?"

"Where Is the Voice Coming From?" was originally published in *The New Yorker*, and it remained uncollected until the appearance of the complete *The Collected Stories of Eudora Welty* in 1980. In it, Welty uses a fictional voice to express her views on the civil rights struggle in the South. The story, written in 1963 in response to the murder of Medgar Evers in Welty's hometown of Jackson, is told as a monologue by a southern white man whose ignorance and hate for African Americans is depicted as chillingly mundane. He tells how, enraged by black activism in the South, he determines to shoot a local civil rights leader. He drives to the man's home late on an unbearably hot summer night, waits calmly in hiding until the man appears, and then shoots him in cold blood. The callous self-righteousness of the killer and his unreasoning hate are frighteningly depicted when he mocks the body of his victim, saying

> Roland? There was only one way left for me to be ahead of you and stay ahead of you, by Dad, and I just taken it. . . . We ain't never now, never going to be equals and you know why? One of us is dead. What about that, Roland?

His justification for the murder is simple: "I done what I done for my own pure-D satisfaction." His only regret is that he cannot claim the credit for the killing.

Welty scatters subtle symbols throughout the story. The extremely hot weather, which torments the killer, reflects the social climate as the civil rights conflict reaches a kind of boiling point. To the killer, the street feels as hot under his feet as the barrel of his gun. Light and dark contrast in more than just the black and white skins of the characters: The stealthy killer arrives in a darkness that will cloak his crime and he finds light shining forth from the home of his prey, whose mission is to enlighten. When the killer shoots his victim, he sees that "something darker than him, like the wings of a bird, spread on his back and pulled him down."

Unlike most of Welty's fiction, "Where Is the Voice Coming From?" clearly espouses a particular viewpoint, and the reader is left with no doubt about the writer's intention in telling the story. The story, however, embodies the qualities that typify Welty's fiction: the focus on the interconnections of human society; the full, sharp characterization achieved in a minimum of space; the detailed description of the physical landscape that powerfully evokes a sense of place; the ear for speech and idiom; and the subtle, floating symbolism that insinuates rather than announces its meaning.

OTHER MAJOR WORKS

LONG FICTION: *The Robber Bridegroom*, 1942; *Delta Wedding*, 1946; *The Ponder Heart*, 1954; *Losing Battles*, 1970; *The Optimist's Daughter*, 1972.

NONFICTION: *Music from Spain*, 1948; *The Reading and Writing of Short Stories*, 1949; *Place in Fiction*, 1957; *Three Papers on Fiction*, 1962; *One Time, One Place: Mississippi in the Depression, a Snapshot Album*, 1971; *A Pageant of Birds*, 1974; *The Eye of the Story: Selected Essays and Reviews*, 1978; *Ida M'Toy*, 1979; *Miracles of Perception: The Art of Willa Cather*, 1980 (with Alfred Knopf and Yehudi Menuhin); *Conversations with Eudora Welty*, 1984 (Peggy Whitman Prenshaw, editor); *One Writer's Beginnings*, 1984; *Eudora Welty: Photographs*, 1989; *A Writer's Eye: Collected Book Reviews*, 1994 (Pearl Amelia McHaney, editor); *More Conversations with Eudora Welty*, 1996

(Prenshaw, editor); *Country Churchyards*, 2000; *On William Hollingsworth, Jr.*, 2002; *On Writing*, 2002 (includes essays originally pb. in *The Eye of the Story*); *On William Faulkner*, 2003; *Some Notes on River Country*, 2003.

CHILDREN'S LITERATURE: *The Shoe Bird*, 1964.

MISCELLANEOUS: *Stories, Essays, and Memoir*, 1998; *Early Escapades*, 2005 (Patti Carr Black, editor); *Occasions: Selected Writings*, 2009 (Pearl Amelia McHaney, editor).

BIBLIOGRAPHY

Arima, Hiroko. *Beyond and Alone! The Theme of Isolation in Selected Short Fiction of Kate Chopin, Katherine Anne Porter, and Eudora Welty*. Lanham, Md.: University Press of America, 2006. Examines the common theme of isolation in the short fiction of three southern women writers, describing both the gains and sufferings brought on by their female characters' alienation.

Bloom, Harold, ed. *Eudora Welty*. Updated ed. New York: Chelsea House, 2007. Collection of critical essays about Welty's works, including discussions of "A Worn Path," "Why I Live at the P.O.," *The Golden Apples*, and "The Bride of the Innisfallen." An essay by Robert Penn Warren examines "The Love and Separateness in Miss Welty," while other pieces address the "sense of place" in her writings and some of her novels.

Evans, Elizabeth. *Eudora Welty*. New York: Frederick Ungar, 1981. This accessible survey discusses both Welty's fiction and her essays and reviews. The brief literary biography of Welty in the opening chapter is useful and offers interesting information on her relationship with her publishers and editors in the early part of her long literary career.

Gelfant, Blanche H., ed. *The Columbia Companion to the Twentieth-Century American Short Story*. New York: Columbia University Press, 2000. Includes a chapter in which Welty's short stories are analyzed.

*Georgia Review* 53 (Spring, 1999). A special issue on Welty celebrating her ninetieth birthday, with articles by a number of writers, including Doris Betts, as well as a number of critics and admirers of Welty.

Kaplansky, Leslie A. "Cinematic Rhythms in the Short Fiction of Eudora Welty." *Studies in Short Fiction* 33 (Fall, 1996): 579-589. Discusses the influence of film technique on Welty's short fiction. Argues that in taking advantage of cinematic rhythm in her stories, Welty developed her mastery of technique and style.

Marrs, Suzanne. *Eudora Welty: A Biography*. Orlando, Fla.: Harcourt, 2005. Literary biography written by a longtime friend of Welty, who is also a scholar and the archivist of Welty's papers. Provides insight into Welty's life and writing and serves to refute some popular conceptions of the writer.

_____. *One Writer's Imagination: The Fiction of Eudora Welty*. Baton Rouge: Louisiana State University Press, 2002. A combination of critical analysis and memoir that discusses the effects of both close personal relationships and social and political events on Welty's imagination and writing. Devotes chapters to analyses of *A Curtain of Green*, "The Wide Net," *The Golden Apples*, and *The Bride of the Innisfallen*.

*Mississippi Quarterly* 50 (Fall, 1997). A special issue on Welty, with essays comparing her to William Faulkner, Edgar Allan Poe, and Nathaniel Hawthorne and discussions of the women in Welty's stories, her political thought, and her treatment of race and history.

Mortimer, Gail L. *Daughter of the Swan: Love and Knowledge in Eudora Welty's Fiction*. Athens: University of Georgia Press, 1994. Concentrates primarily on the short stories.

Prenshaw, Peggy Whitman, ed. *Conversations with Eudora Welty*. Jackson: University Press of Mississippi, 1984. A collection of interviews with Welty spanning the years 1942-1982. Welty talks frankly and revealingly with interviewers, such as William F. Buckley, Jr., and Alice Walker, about her fiction and her life, addressing such topics as her methods of writing, her southern background, her love of reading, and her admiration for the works of writers, such as William Faulkner, Elizabeth Bowen, and Katherine Anne Porter.

Scofield, Martin. "Katherine Anne Porter, Eudora Welty, and Flannery O'Connor." In *The Cambridge Introduction to the American Short Story*. New York: Cambridge University Press, 2006. An overview and analysis of short fiction by three southern women writers. Examines several stories from Welty's collection *A Curtain of Green*.

Vande Kieft, Ruth M. *Eudora Welty*. 1962. Rev. ed. Boston: Twayne, 1987. This comprehensive examination of Welty's fiction offers detailed explications of many of her works, as well as chapters on particular aspects of her writing, such as elements of comedy and her deliberate desire to "mystify" her readers.

Waldron, Ann. *Eudora Welty: A Writer's Life*. New York: Doubleday, 1998. The first full-length biography of Welty, but one that was done without her authorization or permission. Provides a great deal of detail about Welty's life and literary career but derives commentary about Welty's work from reviews and other previous criticism.

Westling, Louise. *Sacred Groves and Ravaged Gardens: The Fiction of Eudora Welty, Carson McCullers, and Flannery O'Connor*. Athens: University of Georgia Press, 1985. Westling examines Welty's fiction, along with the work of other eminent female southern writers, as part of a tradition of southern women's writing. Westling brings a feminist perspective to bear on such aspects of southern women's writing as myth, sexuality, and the symbolic power of place. Welty's fiction is analyzed as a feminine celebration of a matriarchal society in which women can find freedom and fulfillment outside the social strictures of traditional southern life.

Weston, Ruth D. "Eudora Welty and the Short Story: Theory and Practice." In *A Companion to the American Short Story*, edited by Alfred Bendixen and James Nagel. Malden, Mass.: Wiley-Blackwell, 2010. Offers an overview and critical examination of Welty's short fiction, examining many of the individual short stories.

_____. *Gothic Traditions and Narrative Techniques in the Fiction of Eudora Welty*. Baton Rouge: Louisiana State University Press, 1994. Discusses Welty's use of the gothic tradition in her fiction. Provides original readings of a number of Welty's short stories.

*Catherine Swanson*

# GLENWAY WESCOTT

**Born:** Kewaskum, Wisconsin; April 11, 1901
**Died:** Rosemont, New Jersey; February 22, 1987

PRINCIPAL SHORT FICTION

*. . . Like a Lover,* 1926
*Good-bye, Wisconsin,* 1928
*The Babe's Bed,* 1930
*The Pilgrim Hawk: A Love Story,* 1940 (novella)
*Twelve Fables of Aesop,* 1954

OTHER LITERARY FORMS

Glenway Wescott honed his writing skills early in his career by writing poetry: *The Bitterns: A Book of Twelve Poems* (1920) and *Natives of Rock: XX Poems,* *1921-1922* (1925). He went on to write three novels, *The Apple of the Eye* (1924), *The Grandmothers: A Family Portrait* (1927), and *Apartment in Athens* (1945), and two volumes of essays, *Fear and Trembling* (1932) and *Images of Truth: Remembrances and Criticism* (1962). Additional works include a hagiography entitled *A Calendar of Saints for Unbelievers* (1932) and a nonfiction volume, *The Best of All Possible Worlds: Journals, Letters, and Remembrances, 1914-1937* (1975).

ACHIEVEMENTS

Of all the expatriated Americans who were living in Europe during the 1920's, Glenway Wescott is most notable for the pursuit of his theme. Regardless of whether Wescott was writing about his native

Wisconsin or Europe, he always returned to his theme of returning home. In a sense, Wescott's single novella, three novels, and numerous short stories can be viewed as a journey in search of the source of the creative self.

Because Wescott stopped writing fiction at the age of forty-four, some critics have classified him as a writer who had the qualities needed for great achievement but who failed to live up to the promise of his early works. Although Wescott's body of work is relatively small, his technical achievements were significant. Not only was he a master of the carefully turned aphorism, but also he invented the technique of the participating narrator. Wescott may not be a major American writer, but he still ranks as one of the most distinctive prose stylists in twentieth century American fiction.

### Biography

Glenway Wescott's life is made up of two diametrically opposed phases. He was born on a farm in Kewaskum, Wisconsin, on April 11, 1901. Glenway was very close to his mother, who nurtured his interests in music, acting, and literature. He soon, however, proved to be a great disappointment to his father, Bruce Peters Wescott, because he hated the drudgery of farmwork. When Glenway was thirteen, his relationship with his father became openly hostile as the result of a minor incident, and he was shunted from relative to relative. During his last two years at Waukesha High School, Glenway lived with his father's brother, a preacher named William Samuel Wescott. His uncle's vast library opened an entirely new world to the young man, which he continued to explore in the literary society to which he belonged in high school.

By the time Wescott was sixteen, his experiences were no longer like those of other boys who had grown up on Wisconsin farms. After graduating from high school in 1917, Wescott went to Chicago. While he was living with the wealthy mother of his uncle's wife, Wescott attended the University of Chicago. His new experiences, like his previous ones on the farm in Wisconsin, were later to serve as material for his fiction. Wescott had no interest in a literary career when he first entered the university, but his distaste for required courses led him to enroll in several literature courses

during his first semester. His enthusiasm for literature soon led to his involvement in the university's newly formed Poetry Club. Through the imagistic poetry that he wrote as a college student, Wescott learned how to solidify an intense moment and to etch it into the consciousness with sharp imagery.

In 1918, Wescott went to New Mexico to recover from a failed homosexual relationship that had driven him to attempt suicide. Between 1918 and 1920, he began writing poetry based on his New Mexico experiences and published it in a volume entitled *The Bitterns*. Harriet Monroe was so impressed with Wescott's work that she hired him to work for *Poetry* magazine in 1921. It was also in 1921 that Wescott published his first short story, "Bad Han," which launched his career as a prose writer. Wescott's developing style was influenced by writers whom he met while working for the magazine, including Edwin Arlington Robinson.

It was during the summer of 1921 that Wescott traveled to Europe with his friend Monroe Wheeler. During the next eleven years, Wescott produced the fiction that established him as a midwestern prodigy. He became financially solvent following the publication in Europe of two novels, *The Apple of the Eye* and *The Grandmothers*, and a collection of short stories, *Good-bye, Wisconsin*. He was less successful with his two departures from fiction, *Fear and Trembling* and *A Calendar of Saints for Unbelievers*, both written in 1932.

Convinced that Europe had become a "rat trap" for him, Wescott returned to the United States in 1933 and settled in New York. While he was growing accustomed to living in the United States again, Wescott produced no fiction at all until 1940. In many ways, World War II shocked him into writing again. *The Pilgrim Hawk: A Love Story*, which continued to be his most popular work, changed the minds of those critics who believed that he had "written himself out." In 1945, he wrote *Apartment in Athens* in an attempt to convince his publisher that he was still a "valuable property."

Despite the success of *Apartment in Athens*, Wescott produced no more works of fiction, even though he did begin several projects. In 1962, a collection of essays entitled *Images of Truth* established him as one of the most influential critics in the United States because he was writing to the cultivated general reader, not to the most sophisticated and highbrow critics. Wescott's profiles of six writers whom he admired offered a memorable insight into how his own fiction writer's mind perceived the world. Although this, his final work, did not totally satisfy his faithful coterie of admirers, who had looked forward to the kind of a large complex novel that they believed he had the ability to write, it eloquently confirmed his faith in the literary life. It was a fitting end to the career of this melancholy yet tantalizing literary figure.

ANALYSIS

Glenway Wescott's short fiction employs many of the same themes and techniques that he used in his first two novels. The two major themes continue to be the self and love. A technical innovation that he first used in *The Grandmothers*, the participating narrator, also appears in his short fiction. His use of symbols is also similar to what he had done in his first two novels. The bird remained his favorite symbol and was usually placed at the center of the story. Except for *The Babe's Bed*, the short stories that appear after *Good-bye, Wisconsin* are inferior in quality and demonstrate how Wescott lost his enthusiasm for a literary form once he had mastered it. The next short form with which he experimented, the novella, perfected certain techniques of prose fiction that he used with mixed results in his short stories.

Wescott shaped a number of his early experiences into short stories in which he employed impressionistic techniques instead of the mere transcription of events.

**GOOD-BYE, WISCONSIN**

To a certain extent, the ten short stories and title essay in *Good-bye, Wisconsin* illustrate the reasons why Wescott could not stay in Wisconsin. They cannot, however, be dismissed simply as regional stories in that the universal truths of which they speak could be found anywhere.

Several of the stories that deal, in one way or another, with the search for the self illustrate the ways in which rural Wisconsin impedes that search. "The Sailor" goes beyond being a regional story in the way that it also includes the theme of love. Terrie, who is another of Wescott's expatriates, has joined the Navy to escape the depressing surroundings of rural Wisconsin.

*Glenway Wescott* (Library of Congress)

After spending some time in France, he recounts his adventures there to his brother, Riley. By the time Terrie has finished his narration, he has revealed that he has been severely traumatized by a failed love affair that he had with a French prostitute named Zizi. Riley, however, sees the stories as nothing more than tales of whiskey and women. Sensing Riley's lack of understanding, Terrie is filled with a thirst that cannot be quenched at home. Emotions such as the ones that Terrie encountered in Europe are foreign to Wisconsin.

Wisconsin serves primarily as the setting for a transition from innocence to experience in "In a Thicket." Lilly is a fifteen-year-old girl who lives with her senile grandfather in a house surrounded by a thicket. After hearing about a black convict who escaped the night before from a nearby prison, she stays up all night waiting for him to appear. When she finally sees him at the door, she stands transfixed until he walks away. The three-inch gash that she finds in the screen door the next morning symbolizes the figurative loss of her virginity. The sexual side of her nature has been awakened by the intruder, and she emerges from the thicket of her childhood into the world of the senses.

Like "In a Thicket," "The Whistling Swan" takes place in Wisconsin, but it focuses instead on the theme of love. Like Terrie in "The Sailor," the protagonist of "The Whistling Swan," Hubert Redd, is an expatriate. He is, however, closer to Wescott himself in that he is an artist, a composer, and a sophisticate who is aware of both the advantages and the drawbacks of living in Europe and the United States. He returns to his hometown in Wisconsin after his wealthy patrons withdraw their support on the grounds that he is immoral and untalented. The love that he feels for his childhood sweetheart complicates his life because it conflicts with his desire to return to Europe and resume his artistic pursuits. Redd's inner conflict is resolved when he impulsively shoots a swan and simultaneously kills that part of himself that draws him to Paris. The intentional ambiguity of the ending poses the possibility that he is sobbing not because he has killed the swan, but because he has destroyed the creative impulse that made him unhappy in Wisconsin.

"A Guilty Woman" traces a woman's progression from a type of love that enslaves to the type that liberates. Evelyn Crowe is a forty-five-year-old former convict who served six years in prison for murdering her lover, Bill Fisher. Fisher had been initially attracted to her because he relished the challenge of corrupting and abandoning an "old maid." Upon her release from prison, she is taken in by her friend Martha Colvin to live on her farm in Wisconsin. While living there, Evelyn is attracted to Martha's bachelor friend, Dr. John Bolton. She resists the romantic impulse that is building up inside her until she realizes that the passionless life to which she had returned was a form of pride. No longer content to be a self-sufficient spinster, she finally allows herself to fall in love. Wescott finds a kind of courage in Evelyn's flexibility, which he believed was discouraged by small-town America.

The short story that merited the most critical acclaim was "Like a Lover." Like Lilly in "In a Thicket," Alice Murray is an isolated girl who is mesmerized by a man, in this case, an older man named Hurst. Despite her mother's protests, she marries him. The assortment of whips and clubs that her husband keeps in the house,

however, terrifies her and drives her back to her mother's house. She remains in isolation for seven years until she learns that Hurst is to marry Mrs. Clayburn, a widow. Even though Mrs. Clayburn believes Alice's words of warning, she admits that she is unable to break the spell that he holds over her. For two months following Mrs. Clayburn's marriage, Alice is tormented by ominous nightmares that foretell the woman's murder. The story concludes with the appearance of Alice's friend, Mary Clifford, riding frantically from the Hurst farm, waving her arms. Shocked by what she knows has happened to the new Mrs. Hurst, Alice faints and falls backward on the porch. Ostensibly, "Like a Lover" exploits the same kind of scandalous material that Wescott used in "A Guilty Woman." The godlike power that the men in both stories have over women, however, illustrates Wescott's belief, discussed in depth four years later in *A Calendar of Saints for Unbelievers*, that the love for God is similar to the love for a man or a woman in that both forms of affection render a person completely helpless.

## The Babe's Bed

*The Babe's Bed*, which is a thirty-five-page short story published as a book in Paris, is, in a sense, a postscript to the introductory essay in *Good-bye, Wisconsin*. Both were written after Wescott returned to Wisconsin for a short visit and concern an expatriated American who compares the Midwest to Europe. In both works, Wisconsin and the United States in general are found to retard the development of the self.

The story is told from the limited point of view of a nameless bachelor who returns home. As in other stories by Wescott, dramatic tension is created through the narrator's conflicting impulses. The bachelor becomes so lost in fantasies involving his sister's baby that he becomes detached from reality. He begins by imagining that the baby is his and then convinces himself that his married sister is his mother. The climax occurs at the dinner table when the baby screams at being placed in the harness that serves as its bed. The baby's bed, which is the story's central symbol, bears a close resemblance to the mental web that has ensnared the bachelor. Before he attacks everyone at the table, he realizes that he has been living in a fantasy world and directs his anger toward himself before he can do any real harm to his loved ones.

## THE PILGRIM HAWK

With the publication of *The Pilgrim Hawk: A Love Story*, Wescott created what many critics have referred to as a genuine short masterpiece. This novella differs from most of Wescott's previous fiction in that it concerns expatriated Americans living in France instead of rural midwestern Americans. The story is retold in 1940 by the protagonist, Alwyn Tower, who interrupts his first-person narrative to comment on such matters as love, marriage, religion, alcoholism, and individual and artistic freedom. The events that he recalls took place during one day in May of 1928 or 1929 in France at the house of Alexandra Henry, a great friend of Tower. The story focuses on the arrival of Madeleine and Larry Cullen, a rich, handsome couple from Ireland who arrive unexpectedly with their chauffeur, Ricketts, and Madeleine Cullen's falcon, Lucy. For the most part, the action of the novella takes the form of a conversation among the four main characters.

As the Cullens chat about money and neighbors, it becomes clear that the hawk symbolizes the Cullens' relationship and the Cullens themselves. Madeleine resembles the feathered predator in the way she uses her charms to capture and hold her prey, Larry, who is too weak to escape the hold that she has on him. Both she and her husband, however, are hawklike in that they are prisoners of their own appetites. Although the hawk is consistent with the bird symbolism in Wescott's other stories and novels, it differs in the way it evolves, taking on different meanings in different situations.

Tower continues to attach symbolic meanings to the hawk until it comes to stand for himself and Alexandra as well. Eventually, he builds a tower of symbolic meanings that blinds him to the "petty" facts that constitute reality. The process continues until Cullen, in a drunken stupor, attempts to kill someone; Madeleine, who reports the event just before she and her husband leave for Paris, never makes it clear whether Larry tried to kill himself or Ricketts in a fit of jealous rage. This violent turn of events shocks Tower back to reality, enabling him to descend from the symbolic tower that he has constructed. He recognizes that the "whisper of the devil" is the fear that he has attached the wrong meanings to things in order to make life more meaningful.

OTHER MAJOR WORKS

LONG FICTION: *The Apple of the Eye*, 1924; *The Grandmothers: A Family Portrait*, 1927; *Apartment in Athens*, 1945.

PLAY: "The Dream of Audubon: Libretto of a Ballet in Three Scenes," pb. 1941.

POETRY: *The Bitterns: A Book of Twelve Poems*, 1920; *Natives of Rock: XX Poems, 1921-1922*, 1925.

NONFICTION: *Elizabeth Madox Roberts: A Personal Note*, 1930; *A Calendar of Saints for Unbelievers*, 1932; *Fear and Trembling*, 1932; *Images of Truth: Remembrances and Criticism*, 1962; *The Best of All Possible Worlds: Journals, Letters, and Remembrances, 1914-1937*, 1975; *Continual Lessons: The Journals of Glenway Wescott, 1937-1955*, 1990.

EDITED TEXTS: *The Maugham Reader*, 1950; *Principal short Novels of Colette*, 1951.

BIBLIOGRAPHY

Baker, Jennifer Jordan. "'In a Thicket': Glenway Wescott's Pastoral Vision." *Studies in Short Fiction* 31 (Spring, 1994): 95-187. Explores the paradox of the Midwest as both isolating and repressive, as well as simple and idyllic, in one of Wescott's best-known stories, "In a Thicket." Shows how Wescott treats this tension with narrative conventions and the narrative perspective of traditional pastoral.

Benfey, Christopher. "Bright Young Things." *The New York Times*, March 21, 1999, sec. 7, p. 9. A review of *When We Were There: The Travel Albums of George Platt Lynes, Monroe Wheeler, and Glenway Wescott*. Comments on Wescott's fussy style but claims that his novella *The Pilgrim Hawk* is a brilliant work that can stand comparison with William Faulkner or D. H. Lawrence. Argues that the central image of this novella comes from Wescott's relationship with George Platt Lynes.

Calisher, Hortense. "A Heart Laid Bare." *The Washington Post*, January 13, 1991, p. X5. In this review of Wescott's journals, *Continual Lessons*, Calisher provides a brief biographical sketch of Wescott. She argues that he was not a true original as a novelist, but rather he was a reporter of a nonfictive kind. She contends that the image readers will receive from Wescott's journals is of a writer not quite in the closet and not quite out of it.

Diamond, Daniel. *Delicious: A Memoir of Glenway Wescott*. Toronto: Sykes Press, 2008. Diamond, who was Wescott's secretary and assistant, fondly recalls the last years of the writer's life, discussing Wescott's daily affairs, writing, opinions, friends, engagement with literary society, and relationship with his partner Monroe Wheeler.

Johnson, Ira. *Glenway Wescott: The Paradox of Voice*. Port Washington, N.Y.: Kennikat Press, 1971. An incisive look into Wescott's career, explicating and criticizing each of Wescott's works in detail. Johnson demonstrates how each work reflects Wescott's development as a writer. Johnson does not, however, provide sufficient insight into Wescott's early life to qualify this book as a biographical study.

Rosco, Jerry. "An American Treasure: Glenway Wescott's *The Pilgrim Hawk*." *The Literary Review* 15 (Winter, 1988): 133-142. Rosco's analysis of Wescott's novella derives from information provided by Wescott himself during his last interview. Wescott's personal reflections regarding how he wrote the story and how he was influenced by W. Sommerset Maugham are particularly revealing.

_____. *Glenway Wescott Personally: A Biography*. Madison: University of Wisconsin Press, 2002. Rosco, who coedited a volume of Wescott's journals, describes how Wescott came to terms with his sexuality at a time when society strictly suppressed homosexuality. Among other subjects, he explains the reasons for Wescott's writer's block and discusses Wescott's relationship with his partner Monroe Wheeler and his close association with sex researcher Alfred Kinsey.

Rueckert, William H. *Glenway Wescott*. New York: Twayne: 1965. Rueckert attempts to revise Wescott's reputation as a man of letters who produced only one minor masterpiece. Although Rueckert's analysis is perceptive, he does not examine each work in enough depth to support his premise that Wescott is a major artist who deserves more attention.

Sontag, Susan. "Where the Stress Falls." *The New Yorker* 77, no. 1 (June 18, 2001-June 25, 2001): 152. Sontag reviews *The Pilgrim Hawk*, praising Wescott's skills as a novelist.

Wescott, Glenway. *Continual Lessons: The Journals of Glenway Wescott, 1937-1955*. Edited by Robert Phelps and Jerry Rosco. New York: Farrar, and Straus Giroux, 1990. Wescott's diaries provide a glimpse of his life.

*Alan Brown*

# JESSAMYN WEST

**Born:** North Vernon, Indiana; July 18, 1902
**Died:** Napa, California; February 23, 1984

PRINCIPAL SHORT FICTION

*The Friendly Persuasion,* 1945
*Cress Delahanty,* 1953
*Love, Death, and the Ladies' Drill Team,* 1955
*Except for Me and Thee: A Companion to the*
    *Friendly Persuasion,* 1969
*Crimson Ramblers of the World, Farewell,* 1970
*The Story of a Story, and Three Stories,* 1982
*Collected Stories of Jessamyn West,* 1986

OTHER LITERARY FORMS

Best known for her first collection of short stories, *The Friendly Persuasion*, Jessamyn (HEHS-ah-mihn) West also published eight novels during her long literary career, including *Leafy Rivers* (1967), set on the frontier in nineteenth century Ohio, and *South of the Angels* (1960), set, like many of her short stories, in Southern California. West also published an opera libretto based on the life of John James Audubon, *A Mirror for the Sky* (pb. 1948), and a collection of poems, *The Secret Look: Poems* (1974). Among her screenplays was that for the film *Friendly Persuasion* (1956), written in collaboration. Her autobiographical writings include an account of the production of that film, *To See the Dream* (1957); *Hide and Seek: A Continuing Journey* (1973), the story of her early life; *The Woman Said Yes: Encounters with Life and Death, Memoirs* (1976), dealing with her illness with tuberculosis and her sister's sickness and suicide; and *Double Discovery: A Journey* (1980), a travel diary. She edited *The Quaker Reader* in 1962.

ACHIEVEMENTS

Ever since the publication of her first book, Jessamyn West has had a large and loyal following. Critics praise her craftsmanship: her clear prose, her vivid realization of the natural setting, her historical accuracy, her effective creation of characters who are complex human beings beneath their seemingly simple surface. Her accomplishments have been recognized by the Indiana Authors' Day Award in 1957, the Thormod Monsen Award in 1958, and the Janet Kafka Prize in 1976, as well as by the awarding of honorary doctorates both in her native Midwest and in her longtime home, California. West's works are divided between the midwestern frontier of her family's past and the new frontier of twentieth century Southern California. The fact that her fiction is authentically regional does not limit her appeal, however, for her themes transcend local color, dealing as they do with survival as a moral and loving being in a difficult and dangerous world.

BIOGRAPHY

Jessamyn West was born in North Vernon, Indiana, on July 18, 1902. After moving with her parents to California, she completed her education at Fullerton High School, at Whittier College, where she received a B.A. in English in 1923, and at the University of California, Berkeley. Although she had published short stories based on her family's Quaker past, she did not collect them in a book until 1945; thus her first book appeared when she was forty-three years old. Later, she taught at numerous universities and at Bread Loaf Writers' Conference. Her last book, *The State of Stony Lonesome* (1984), was completed shortly before her death, on February 23, 1984, at her longtime home in Napa, California.

ANALYSIS

Jessamyn West's short stories fall into two categories: those which treat various episodes in the lives of a single family and are gathered in a single volume, and those which more conventionally are quite separate in plot and character, gathered in the customary collections. The books *The Friendly Persuasion, Except for Me and Thee: A Companion to the Friendly Persuasion*, and *Cress Delahanty* fall into the first category. Although some critics have called them novels, the sketches of which each volume is composed are obviously separate. The fact that an acknowledgment preceding *The Friendly Persuasion* refers to "stories in this book" which had been published in various magazines makes West's own assumptions clear. In the introduction to *Collected Stories of Jessamyn West*, Julian Muller calls those earlier volumes "novels," while admitting that the chapters could stand alone; consequently, he omits those sketches from his collection. A complete analysis of West's short fiction, however, must include the consideration of those works on an individual basis, even though a study of her long fiction might also include them.

The *Collected Stories of Jessamyn West* included all the stories from two previous volumes, *Love, Death, and the Ladies' Drill Team* and *Crimson Ramblers of the World, Farewell*, along with eight additional stories which Jessamyn West wished to have included. According to the editor, those stories which were omitted, West believed, needed revision.

### "99.6"

The focus in all West's work is a basic tension in human life. On the one hand, humans yearn to be free of restraints; on the other hand, they desire to love and to please the beloved, so they voluntarily accept limitations on their individuality. The beloved is not just their human partner: The term also suggests divinity, speaking to the spirit directly, in the Quaker tradition. Although social or religious groups may presume to judge the conduct of West's characters, the final judgment must be their own, guided by their separate and sacred consciences.

According to the editor of the *Collected Stories of Jessamyn West*, West's first published story was "99.6." Set in a tuberculosis sanatorium, the story reflects West's own experience. The protagonist, Marianne Kent, desperately watches her temperature, hoping for the change which would signal some improvement in her health. Aware of her own feverish condition, the consumption which is truly consuming her, she wishes that the nurse would help her with an illusion, with the suggestion that perhaps the heat she feels comes from warmer weather outside, not from her own fever. Although the obvious antagonists are Marianne Kent and her disease, at the conclusion of the brief story the protagonist turns to God, pleading with Him for some sign of hope, for some reduction from 99.6 degrees. Thus, the real struggle is a spiritual one. Mrs. Kent must accept what divinity permits.

### THE FRIENDLY PERSUASION

In *The Friendly Persuasion* stories, set in the nineteenth century among the Indiana Quakers of the Ohio River Valley, conscience is always a consideration. The Irish Quaker Jess Birdwell, a devout man but one who has a mind of his own, is married to Eliza Cope Birdwell, a stricter Quaker--in fact, a Quaker minister, who must consider the community's judgment of her as well as God's. "Music on the Muscatatuck" illustrates the stresses on the relationship between Jess and Eliza, which result from their differences in temperament and

*Jessamyn West* (Library of Congress)

convictions. After describing the natural beauty of the Birdwell farm, the comfort and plenty of their pretty home, the goodness of Eliza as a wife, and Jess's own prosperity, West sets the problem: Jess likes music; as a Quaker, he is supposed to have nothing to do with it.

Jess's temptation comes when, like Eve in the Garden, he is separated from his mate. On a business trip to Philadelphia, he meets an organ salesman; already seduced by his own love of music, he stops by the store. The result is inevitable: He orders an organ.

When Jess returns home, he cannot find the words to tell Eliza, who follows the Quaker teachings about music, what he has done. Unfortunately, when the organ arrives, Eliza makes a miscalculation about Jess's male pride: She commands him to choose between the organ and her. Jess moves the organ in the house, and Eliza is left in the snow, pondering her next course of action. Fortunately, Eliza knows the difference between her domain and that of the Lord. She compromises, and the organ goes in the attic. All goes well until a church committee comes to call just when the Birdwells' daughter Mattie has slipped up to the attic to play the organ. Surely God inspires Jess Birdwell in this crucial situation, for he prays and continues praying until the music stops. The committee concludes that angels have provided the accompaniment; Jess suspects that the Lord, who has kept him praying for so long, has made His statement. Just as Eliza is about to announce her triumph, however, the music once again comes from the attic, and Jess again responds.

The story is typical of West. The human beings involved live close to their natural setting; they are ordinary people, neither rich nor poor. Although they may disagree with one another and although they often have much to learn, they are usually basically good, and at the end of the story, some resolution of their conflict with one another and with their spiritual scruples is suggested. The tone is also typical. Perhaps one reason for West's popularity is that, in an age when many writers do not seem to like their own characters, and for good reason, she is honestly fond of hers. As a result, she laughs at their foibles and follies, their deficiencies in wisdom, and their mistakes in judgment without negating the fact of their basic goodness.

One of the endearing qualities of the Birdwell family is that, despite their strict religious convictions, they accept differences within the family; each member is expected, above all, to follow his or her own conscience. In the Civil War story "The Battle of Finney's Ford," what was supposed to be a fight against Morgan's raiders proves to be no fight at all, because Morgan's raiders change their route. In the meantime, however, the Birdwell boys must decide whether to fight. One of them, Joshua, says that he is willing to kill, if necessary; the other, Labe, will not join the town's defenders. Ironically, at the end of the story, Josh says that the reason he must fight is that he so dislikes fighting, while Labe admits that he must not fight because he truly enjoys fighting. Thus the real battle of Finney's Ford has been a battle of conscience for the boys and, for the parents, a struggle to let them make their own decisions. The slightness of the external plot, typical of many of West's stories, does not reduce the magnitude of the internal action. For Jess, Eliza, Josh, and Labe, there is a major spiritual battle; as usual, the element of love is present in the resolution of the conflict.

### CRESS DELAHANTY

Although *Cress Delahanty* is set in twentieth century California rather than nineteenth century Indiana, and although it lacks the specific Quaker religious background, the importance of the natural setting, the basic goodness of the characters, and the emphasis on spiritual problems are similar to the stories in *The Friendly Persuasion*. For example, "Fifteen: Spring" deals with Cress's selfish encounter with death, just as in the previous volume "The Meeting House" had followed Jess Birdwell through a similar crisis. In "Fifteen: Spring," Cress has developed a schoolgirl crush on a dying man, the father of sons her age. In her egotism, she wishes to be important to him, even to die in his place, if necessary, but after a visit to his home, after realizing that God is in charge, not Cress, she learns that she is not of major importance to her beloved, nor is her love of any help to him. Ironically, the final consolation comes from his wife, who recalls her own lost youth and, from her own tragic situation, finds pity for foolish Cress.

### "A Time of Learning"

Many of West's stories deal with young people who are being initiated into life. In *Love, Death, and the Ladies' Drill Team*, "A Time of Learning" describes the encounter of nineteen-year-old Emmett Maguire, a talented house and sign-painter, with his first love, Ivy Lish. Emmett loves the seemingly perfect girl with all of his heart. When he paints her picture, it is an act of total commitment. Unfortunately, Emmett must learn that the beloved is not always worthy of the emotion she inspires. As other men know, Ivy is consistently unfaithful. When Emmett learns that she has given his painting to another lover, his immediate impulse is toward revenge: He will paint her on the barn, as ugly as she has proved herself to be, for all to see. Then comes his spiritual crisis. Somehow, he finds, he cannot paint ugliness, or perhaps he cannot hate. When he paints a larger-than-life picture of her on the barn, he finally forgets about her in the joy of realizing that he is indeed a good painter. Thus, finally, his love of art is more important than her betrayal of him, and his wish to love defeats his temptation to hate.

### "Neighbors"

West clearly believes, however, that it is not just the young who must learn about life. One of the optimistic elements in her stories is the suggestion that life is learning itself. Because most of her major characters are willing to expand their consciousnesses, anxious to revise their judgments, they are appealing. Thus, in *Except for Me and Thee: A Companion to the Friendly Persuasion*, the Quaker preacher Eliza Birdwell, a stubborn woman with a strict conscience, must deal with the issue of fugitive slaves. In the long story "Neighbors," Eliza not only must decide whether to obey the law, as her religion dictates, by turning over the fugitive slaves who seek refuge with her or to hide them and defy the law of her country but also must come to terms with Jess's involvement in running slaves to freedom, at the risk of his life and his liberty. The decision is not easy, but in changing her mind about the law and in acquiescing to the demands of Jess's conscience, Eliza herself grows spiritually.

### Crimson Ramblers of the World, Farewell

Not all of West's stories have so hopeful a conclusion. In "The Condemned Librarian," from *Crimson Ramblers of the World, Farewell*, an embittered teacher, who believes that she has not been able to realize her dreams, consults a woman doctor who, against all odds, has risen from being a high school librarian to her present profession. Perversely, the teacher refuses to reveal her symptoms to the doctor, and, despite all of her efforts, the doctor fails to diagnose tuberculosis. As a result, the teacher nearly dies, but to her delight, the doctor must abandon her practice and go back to being a high school librarian. The title "The Condemned Librarian" makes it clear that hatred has, in this situation, had a great triumph, but ironically, the person most trapped is the bitter teacher, who must live with the knowledge that she herself is condemned. Although she feels happy thinking of the doctor's misery, she admits that the old magic is gone from her teaching. Clearly, by her spite she has corroded her own soul.

Other stories in this collection, however, end with understanding and reconciliation. For example, "Live Life Deeply" begins with the disappearance of fourteen-year-old Elspeth Courtney, who has turned up at the maternity ward of the local hospital. Her distraught father, pursuing her, discovers that she had been on Reservoir Hill early that morning, contemplating suicide because, as she confided to the troubled man she met there, a teacher she admired had made fun of her for a composition entitled "Live Life Deeply." The stranger had been worrying about his wife's cesarean section, while Ellie had been worrying about her humiliation. When the baby is born, the stranger's problem is solved. Then the new father solves Ellie's problem by pointing out that she wants to live life fully and that her pain is as much a part of a full life as the excitement and joy of the birth. Convinced, Ellie begins to plan her next composition, which will deal with her experiences in the maternity ward. Now that she understands that pain and joy are both a part of life and that both are necessary to make life interesting, she can move ahead, accepting even her setbacks.

In all of Jessamyn West's stories, whether the setting is the past or the present, Indiana or California, an individual, young or old, has the opportunity to grow spiritually. If, like the teacher in "The Condemned Librarian," one chooses to hate instead of to love or if one refuses to permit freedom of conscience to others, one's life will be miserable. Many ordinary people, however, live lives as meaningful and as exciting as those of Jess Birdwell, Cress Delahanty, and Elspeth Courtney. In her carefully crafted accounts of everyday life, Jessamyn West has revealed the drama of spiritual conflict in these later centuries as compellingly as did the productions of *Everyman* in medieval times.

OTHER MAJOR WORKS

LONG FICTION: *The Witch Diggers*, 1951; *Little Men*, 1954 (pb. in *Star: Short Novels*, Frederik Pohl, editor); *South of the Angels*, 1960; *A Matter of Time*, 1966; *Leafy Rivers*, 1967; *The Massacre at Fall Creek*, 1975; *The Life I Really Lived*, 1979; *The State of Stony Lonesome*, 1984.

PLAY: *A Mirror for the Sky*, pb. 1948 (libretto).

SCREENPLAY: *Friendly Persuasion*, 1956.

POETRY: *The Secret Look: Poems*, 1974.

NONFICTION: *To See the Dream*, 1957; *Love Is Not What You Think*, 1959; *Hide and Seek: A Continuing Journey*, 1973 (autobiography); *The Woman Said Yes: Encounters with Life and Death, Memoirs*, 1976; *Double Discovery: A Journey*, 1980.

EDITED TEXT: *The Quaker Reader*, 1962.

BIBLIOGRAPHY

Barron, James. "Jessamyn West, Author of Stories About Quakers in Indiana, Dies." *The New York Times*, February 24, 1984, p. B16. In this obituary of West, Barron briefly traces her personal and literary life and comments on her focus on Quakers.

Betts, Doris. "Skillful Styles from Two Storytellers." *Los Angeles Times*, February 26, 1987. A review of *Collected Stories of Jessamyn West*. Comments on her narrators as observers, her characters as eccentrics, and her animals as lovable.

Farmer, Ann Dahlstrom. *Jessamyn West: A Descriptive and Annotated Bibliography*. Lanham, Md.: Scarecrow, 1998. A helpful tool for students of West. Includes an index.

Neville, Susan. "Quaker Zen: On Jessamyn West's *The Friendly Persuasion*." In *Sailing the Inland Sea: On Writing, Literature, and Land*. Bloomington, Ind.: Quarry Books/Indiana University Press, 2007. A collection of essays about the consciousness of the Midwest, with the title referring to the region's vanished inland sea. Neville analyzes works by West and others whose writing reflects the "landlocked imagination." Her discussion of *The Friendly Persuasion* praises West's "lyrical gifts" and mystical heart.

Prescott, P.S. "The Massacre at Fall Creek." *Newsweek*, April 14, 1975, 86. According to Prescott, the ingredients in a "good old-fashioned novel" combine suspense, violence, and villainy with sentiment. West's novel *The Massacre at Fall Creek* is a concrete example of this genre. West's expertise, according to Prescott, extends not only to the "good old-fashioned novel" but also to other literary forms.

Shivers, Alfred S. *Jessamyn West*. Rev. ed. New York: Twayne, 1992. This biography of West probes the religious influences of her Quaker beliefs on her literary endeavors, thus providing an essential clue to her character and personality. Shivers incorporates his literary criticism of West's works with his account of her life.

Welty, Eudora. "A Search: Maddening and Infectious." *The New York Times Book Review*, January 14, 1951, 5. Welty discusses the characterizations and plot of *The Witch Diggers*, which she embeds in the metaphor of a game of charades. She states that both contain elements of the known and the unknown bound into a solvable puzzle so that this game is a clever metaphor for *The Witch Diggers*.

West, Jessamyn. *Double Discovery: A Journey*. New York: Harcourt Brace Jovanovich, 1976. West's own memoir incorporates her youthful letters and journals from her first trip abroad with her later rediscovery of that long-lost youthful self. This autobiography gives readers a glimpse of a woman's description of the development of her adult self.

_____. *The Woman Said Yes: Encounters with Life and Death*. New York: Harcourt Brace Jovanovich, 1980. West's account of her experiences as a survivor of tuberculosis is intermingled with an account of her mother's life. This amalgamation of two lives lets interested readers delve into another facet of West's intellectual and artistic development.

Yalom, Marilyn, and Margo B. Davis, eds. *Women Writers of the West Coast: Speaking of Their Lives and Careers*. Santa Barbara, Calif.: Capra Press, 1983. Jennifer Chapman's chapter discusses the role of religion--in this case, Quakerism--in West's life and work.

*Rosemary M. Canfield Reisman*
*Updated by Maxine S. Theodoulou*

---

# EDITH WHARTON

**Born:** New York, New York; January 24, 1862
**Died:** St.-Brice-sous-Forêt, France; August 11, 1937
**Also known as:** Edith Newbold Jones

PRINCIPAL SHORT FICTION

*The Greater Inclination*, 1899
*Crucial Instances*, 1901
*The Descent of Man*, 1904
*The Hermit and the Wild Woman*, 1908
*Tales of Men and Ghosts*, 1910
*Xingu, and Other Stories*, 1916
*Here and Beyond*, 1926
*Certain People*, 1930
*Human Nature*, 1933
*The World Over*, 1936
*Ghosts*, 1937
*The Collected Short Stories of Edith Wharton*, 1968
*Collected Stories, 1891-1910*, 2001 (Maureen Howard, editor)
*Collected Stories, 1911-1937*, 2001 (Maureen Howard, editor)

OTHER LITERARY FORMS

The prolific career of Edith Wharton (HWAWRT-uhn) includes the publication of novels, novellas, short stories, poetry, travel books, criticism, works on landscaping and interior decoration, a translation, an autobiography, and wartime pamphlets and journalism. Her novel *The Age of Innocence* (1920) was awarded the Pulitzer Prize in 1921. Several of her works have been adapted for the stage, including *The Age of Innocence* and the novels *Ethan Frome* (1911), *The House of Mirth* (1905), and *The Old Maid* (1924). The dramatization of *The Old Maid* was awarded the Pulitzer Prize for drama in 1935. Films based on Edith Wharton's works include *The Age of Innocence, The House of Mirth, The Glimpses of the Moon* (1922), and *The Old Maid*.

ACHIEVEMENTS

Edith Wharton's talent in affording her reader an elegant, well-constructed glance at upper-class New York and European society won for her high esteem from the earliest years of her career. The novel *The House of Mirth* was her first best seller and, along with *Ethan Frome* and *The Age of Innocence*, is considered to be one of her finest works. During World War I, Wharton served the Allied cause in Europe by organizing relief efforts and caring for Belgian orphans, work for which she was inducted into the French Legion of Honor in 1916 and the Order of Leopold (Belgium) in 1919. In the 1920's, Wharton's literary career in the United States flowered. In 1921, she became the first woman to receive the Pulitzer Prize, awarded to her for *The Age of Innocence*; in 1923, she also became the first female recipient of an honorary degree of doctor of letters from Yale University; in 1927, she was nominated for the Nobel Prize in Literature; in 1928, her novel *The Children* (1928) was the Book-of-the-Month Club selection for September. By 1930, Wharton was one of the most highly regarded American authors of the time and was elected to the American Academy of Arts and Letters. After Wharton's death in 1937, her fiction was not as widely read by the general public as it was during her lifetime. Feminist literary scholars, however, have reexamined Wharton's works for their unmistakable portrayal of women's lives in the early 1900's.

BIOGRAPHY

Edith Newbold Jones was born into the highest level of society. Like most girls of her generation and social class, she was educated at home. At the age of twenty-three she married a wealthy young man, Edward Wharton; they had no children. Wharton divided her time between writing and her duties as a society hostess. Her husband, emotionally unstable, suffered several nervous breakdowns, and in 1913, they were divorced. Wharton spent a great deal of time in Europe; after 1912 she returned to America only once, to accept the honorary degree of doctor of letters from Yale University in 1923. During World War I, Wharton was very active in war work in France for which she was made a Chevalier of the Legion of Honor in 1916. Realizing that after her death her friends would suppress much of her real personality in their accounts of her life, and wanting the truth to be told, Wharton willed her private papers to Yale University, with instructions that they were not to be published until 1968. These papers revealed a totally unexpected side of Wharton's character: passionate, impulsive, and vulnerable. This new view of the author has had a marked effect on subsequent interpretations of her work.

ANALYSIS

Because many of Edith Wharton's characters and themes resemble those of Henry James, her work has sometimes been regarded as a derivative of his. Each of these authors wrote a number of stories regarding such themes as the fate of the individual who challenges the standards of society, the effect of commercial success on an artist, the impact of European civilization on an American mentality, and the confrontation of a public personality with his or her own private self. In addition, both James and Wharton used ghost stories to present, in allegorical terms, internal experiences which would be difficult to dramatize in a purely realistic way. Wharton knew James and admired him as a friend and as a writer, and some of her early short stories--those in *The Greater Inclination* and *Crucial Instances*, for example--do resemble James's work. As she matured, however, Wharton developed an artistic viewpoint and a style which were distinctly her own. Her approach to the themes which she shared with James was much more direct than his: She took a more sweeping view of the action of a story and omitted the myriad details, qualifications, and explanations which characterize James's work.

It is not surprising that Wharton and James developed a number of parallel interests. Both writers moved in the same rather limited social circle and were exposed to the same values and to the same types of people. Not all their perceptions, however, were identical since Wharton's viewpoint was influenced by the limitations she experienced as a woman. She was therefore especially sensitive to such subtle forms of victimization as the narrowness of a woman's horizons in her society, which not only denied women the opportunity to develop their full potential but also burdened men with disproportionate responsibilities. This theme, which underlies some of her best novels--*The House of Mirth* is a good example--also appears in a number of her short stories, such as "The Rembrandt."

**"THE REMBRANDT"**

The narrator of "The Rembrandt" is a museum curator whose cousin, Eleanor Copt, frequently undertakes acts

*Edith Wharton* (Library of Congress)

of charity toward the unfortunate. These acts of charity, however, often take the form of persuading someone else to bear the brunt of the inconvenience and expense. As "The Rembrandt" opens, Eleanor persuades her cousin to accompany her to a rented room occupied by an elderly lady, the once-wealthy Mrs. Fontage. This widowed lady, who has suffered a number of financial misfortunes, has been reduced from living in palatial homes to now living in a dingy room. Even this small room soon will be too expensive for her unless she can sell the one art treasure she still possesses: an unsigned Rembrandt. The supposed Rembrandt, purchased under highly romantic circumstances during the Fontages' honeymoon in Europe, turns out to be valueless. The curator, however, is moved by the dignity and grace with which Mrs. Fontage faces her situation, and he cannot bring himself to tell her that the painting is worthless. He values it at a thousand dollars, reasoning that he himself cannot be expected to raise that much money. When he realizes that his cousin and Mrs. Fontage expect him to purchase the painting on behalf of the museum, he temporizes.

Meanwhile, Eleanor interests an admirer of hers, Mr. Jefferson Rose, in the painting. Although he cannot really spare the money, Rose decides to buy the painting as an act of charity and as an investment. Even after the curator confesses his lie to Rose, the young man is determined to relieve Mrs. Fontage's misery. The curator, reasoning that it is better to defraud an institution than an individual, purchases the painting for the museum. The only museum official who might question his decision is abroad, and the curator stores the painting in the museum cellar and forgets it. When the official, Crozier, returns, he asks the curator whether he really considers the painting valuable. The curator confesses what he has done and offers to buy the painting from the museum. Crozier then informs the curator that the members of the museum committee have already purchased the painting privately, and beg leave to present it to the curator in recognition of his kindness to Mrs. Fontage.

Despite its flaws in structure and its somewhat romantic view of the business world, "The Rembrandt" shows Wharton's concern with the relationship between helpless individuals and the society which produced them. Her portrait of Mrs. Fontage is especially revealing--she is a woman of dignity and breeding, whose pride and training sustain her in very difficult circumstances. That very breeding, however, cripples Mrs. Fontage because of the narrowness which accompanies it. She is entirely ignorant of the practical side of life, and, in the absence of a husband or some other head of the family, she is seriously handicapped in dealing with business matters. Furthermore, although she is intelligent and in good health, she is absolutely incapable of contributing to her own support. In this very early story, Wharton applauds the gentlemen who live up to the responsibility of caring for such women. Later, Wharton will censure the men and the women whose unthinking conformity to social stereotypes has deprived women like Mrs. Fontage of the ability to care for themselves and has placed a double burden on the men.

### "THE EYES"

As Wharton matured, her interest in victimization moved from the external world of society to the internal world of the individual mind. She recognized the fact that adjustment to life sometimes entails a compromise with one's private self which constitutes a betrayal. One of her most striking portrayals of that theme is in "The Eyes." This tale employs the framework of a ghost story to dramatize an internal experience. The story's aging protagonist, Andrew Culwin, has never become part of life, or allowed an involvement with another human being to threaten his absolute egotism. One evening, as his friends amuse themselves by telling tales of psychic events they have witnessed, Culwin offers to tell a story of his own. He explains that as a young man he once flirted with his naïve young cousin Alice, who responded with a seriousness which alarmed him. He immediately announced a trip to Europe; but, moved by the grace with which she accepted her disappointment, Culwin proposed to Alice and was accepted. He went to bed that evening feeling his self-centered bachelorhood giving way to a sense of righteousness and peace. Culwin awakened in the middle of the night, however, and saw in front of him a hideous pair of eyes. The eyes, which were sunken and old, had pouches of shriveled flesh beneath them and red-lined lids above them, and one of the lids drooped more than the other. These eyes remained in the room all night, and in the morning Culwin fled, without explanation, to a friend's house. There he slept undisturbed and made plans to return to Alice a few days later. Thereupon the eyes returned, and Culwin fled to Europe. He realized that he did not really want to marry Alice, and he devoted himself to a self-centered enjoyment of Europe.

After two years, a handsome young man arrived in Rome with a letter of introduction to Culwin from Alice. This young man, Gilbert Noyes, had been sent abroad by his family to test himself as a writer. Culwin knew that Noyes's writing was worthless, but he temporized in order to keep the handsome youth with him. He also pitied Noyes because of the dull clerk's job which waited for him at home. Finally, Culwin told Noyes that his work had merit, intending to support the young man himself if necessary. That night, the eyes reappeared; and Culwin felt, along with his revulsion, a disquieting sense of identity with the eyes, as if he would some day come to understand all about them. After a month, Culwin cruelly dismissed Noyes, who went home to his clerkship; Culwin took to drink and turned up years later in Hong Kong, fat and unshaven. The eyes then disappeared and never returned.

Culwin's listeners perceive what the reader perceives: The eyes that mock Culwin's rare attempts to transform his self-centered existence into a life of involvement with someone else are in fact his own eyes, looking at him from the future and mocking him with what he would become. The eyes also represent Culwin's lesser self, which would in time take over his entire personality. Even in his youth, this lesser self overshadows Culwin's more humane impulses with second thoughts of the effect these impulses are likely to have on his comfort and security. The story ends as Culwin, surprised by his friends' reaction to his story, catches sight of himself in a mirror and realizes the truth.

### "AFTER HOLBEIN"

Wharton's twin themes of social and self-victimization are joined most effectively in a later story which many readers consider her best: "After Holbein." The title refers to a series of woodcuts by Hans Holbein the Younger, entitled "The Dance of Death." They show the figure of death, represented by a skeleton, insinuating himself into the lives of various unsuspecting people. One of these engravings, entitled "Noblewoman," features a richly dressed man and woman following the figure of death.

The story begins with a description of an elderly gentleman, Anson Warley, who has been one of the most popular members of New York society for more than thirty years. In the first three pages of the story, the reader learns that Warley fought, long ago, a battle between his public image and his private self; the private self lost. Warley gradually stopped staying at home to read or meditate and found less and less time to talk quietly with intellectual friends or scholars. He became a purely public figure, a frequenter of hot, noisy, crowded rooms. His intellect gave itself entirely to the production of drawing-room witticisms, many of them barbed with sarcasm. On the evening that the story takes place, Warley finds himself reminded of one of these sallies of his. Some years earlier, Warley, who had been dodging the persistent invitations of a pompous and rather boring society hostess, finally told his circle of friends that the next time he received a card saying "Mrs. Jasper requests the pleasure," he would reply, "Mr. Warley declines the boredom." The remark was appreciated at the time by the friends who heard it; but in his old age Warley finds himself hoping that Mrs. Jasper never suffered the pain of hearing about it.

At this point in the story, Wharton shifts the scene to a mansion on Fifth Avenue, where a senile old woman prepares herself for an imaginary dinner party. She wears a grotesque purple wig and broad-toed orthopedic shoes under an ancient purple gown. She also insists on wearing her diamonds to what she believes will be another triumph of her skill as a hostess. This woman is the same Mrs. Jasper whom Warley has been avoiding for years. She is now in the care of an unsympathetic young nurse and three elderly servants. Periodically, the four employees go through the charade of preparing the house and Mrs. Jasper for the dinner parties which she imagines still take place there.

While Mrs. Jasper is being dressed for her illusory dinner party, Anson Warley is preparing to attend a real one. Despite his valet's protests concerning his health, Warley not only refuses to stay at home but also insists on walking up Fifth Avenue in the freezing winter night. Gradually he becomes confused and forgets his destination. Then he sees before him Mrs. Jasper's mansion, lighted for a dinner party, and in his confusion, he imagines he is to dine there. He arrives just as Mrs. Jasper's footman is reading aloud the list of guests whom Mrs. Jasper thinks she has invited.

When dinner is announced, Warley and Mrs. Jasper walk arm in arm, at a stately processional gait, to the table. The footman has set the table with heavy blue and white servants' dishes, and he has stuffed newspapers instead of orchids into the priceless Rose Dubarry porcelain dishes. He serves a plain meal and inexpensive wine in the empty dining room. Lost in the illusion, however, Warley and Mrs. Jasper imagine that they are consuming a gourmet meal at a luxuriously appointed table in the presence of a crowd of glittering guests. They go through a ritual of gestures and conversation which does indeed resemble the *danse macabre* for which the story is named. Finally, Mrs. Jasper leaves the table exhausted and makes her way upstairs to her uncomprehending and chuckling nurse. Warley, equally exhausted and equally convinced that he has attended a brilliant dinner party, steps out into the night and drops dead.

"After Holbein" is a powerful story primarily because of the contrasts it establishes. In the foreground are the wasted lives of Warley and Mrs. Jasper, each of whom has long given up all hope of originality or self-realization for the sake of being part of a nameless, gilded mass. The unsympathetic nurse, who teases Mrs. Jasper into tears, acts not from cruelty but from her inability to comprehend, in her own hopeful youth, the tragedy of Mrs. Jasper's situation. This nurse is contrasted with Mrs. Jasper's elderly maid, Lavinia, who conceals her own failing health out of loyalty to her mistress and who is moved to tears by Mrs. Jasper's plight. Even the essential horror of the story is intensified by the contrasting formality and restraint of its language and by the tight structuring which gives the plot the same momentum of inevitability as the movements of a formal dance.

Warley and Mrs. Jasper have been betrayed from within and from without. They have traded their private selves for public masks, and they have spent their lives among others who have made the same bargain. Lavinia's recollections suggest to the reader that Mrs. Jasper subordinated her role as mother to her role as hostess; her children, after being reared in that same world, have left her to the care of servants. Her friends are dead or bedridden, or they have forgotten her. She exists now, in a sense, as she has always existed: as a grotesque figure in a world of illusion.

Warley, too, has come to think of himself only in terms of his social reputation--he will not accept the reality of his age and infirmity. Thus, as he drags one leg during his icy walk along Fifth Avenue, he pictures a club smoking room in which one of his acquaintances will say, "Warley? Why, I saw him sprinting up Fifth Avenue the other night like a two-year-old; that night it was four or five below." Warley has convinced himself that whatever is said in club smoking rooms by men in good society is real. None of the acquaintances, however, to whom he has given his life is with him when he takes that final step; and it would not have mattered if anyone had been there. Warley is inevitably and irrevocably alone at last.

Wharton's eleven volumes of short stories, spanning thirty-eight years, record her growth in thought and in style. They offer the entertainment of seeing inside an exclusive social circle which was in many respects unique and which no longer exists as Wharton knew it. Some of Wharton's stories are trivial and some are repetitive; but her best stories depict, in the inhabitants of that exclusive social world, experiences and sensations which are universal.

OTHER MAJOR WORKS

LONG FICTION: *The Touchstone*, 1900; *The Valley of Decision*, 1902; *Sanctuary*, 1903; *The House of Mirth*, 1905; *Madame de Treymes*, 1907; *The Fruit of the Tree*, 1907; *Ethan Frome*, 1911; *The Reef*, 1912; *The Custom of the Country*, 1913; *Summer*, 1917; *The Marne*, 1918; *The Age of Innocence*, 1920; *The Glimpses of the Moon*, 1922; *A Son at the Front*, 1923; *Old New York*, 1924 (four volumes; includes *False Dawn*, *The Old Maid*, *The Spark* and *New Year's Day*); *The Mother's Recompense*, 1925; *Twilight Sleep*, 1927;

*The Children*, 1928; *Hudson River Bracketed*, 1929; *The Gods Arrive*, 1932; *The Buccaneers*, 1938.

POETRY: *Verses*, 1878; *Artemis to Actæon*, 1909; *Twelve Poems*, 1926; *Selected Poems*, 2005 (Louis Auchincloss, editor).

NONFICTION: *The Decoration of Houses*, 1897 (with Ogden Codman, Jr.); *Italian Villas and Their Gardens*, 1904; *Italian Backgrounds*, 1905; *A Motor-Flight Through France*, 1908; *Fighting France, from Dunkerque to Belfort*, 1915; *French Ways and Their Meaning*, 1919; *In Morocco*, 1920; *The Writing of Fiction*, 1925; *A Backward Glance*, 1934; *The Letters of Edith Wharton*, 1988; *The Uncollected Critical Writings*, 1997 (Frederick Wegener, editor); *Yrs. Ever Affly: The Correspondence of Edith Wharton and Louis Bromfield*, 2000 (Daniel Bratton, editor); *The Corresondence of Edith Wharton and Macmillan, 1901-1930*, 2007 (Shafquat Towheed, editor).

MISCELLANEOUS: *The Unpublished Writings of Edith Wharton*, 2009 (Laura Rattray, editor).

BIBLIOGRAPHY

Banta, Martha. "The Ghostly Gothic of Wharton's Everyday World." *American Literary Realism: 1870-1910* 27 (Fall, 1994): 1-10. An analysis of Wharton's ghost story "Afterward" and her novel *Ethan Frome* as illustrative of the nineteenth century craving for a circumscribed experience of the bizarre. Argues that Wharton's stories illustrate critic Walter Benjamin's concept of the threshold, for they embody a moment when dream is replaced by history.

Beer, Janet. *Kate Chopin, Edith Wharton, and Charlotte Perkins Gilman: Studies in Short Fiction*. London: Macmillan, 1997. Beer devotes two chapters to Wharton's short fiction, focusing primarily on the novellas in one chapter and the regional stories about New England in the other.

Bell, Millicent, ed. *The Cambridge Companion to Edith Wharton*. Cambridge, England: Cambridge University Press, 1995. Although many of the essays focus on Wharton's novels, Gloria C. Erlich's article examines "The Female Conscience in Wharton's Shorter Fiction," and two other essays discuss Wharton and the science of manners and Wharton and race. Includes a chronology of Wharton's life and publications and a bibliography.

Bendixen, Alfred, and Annette Zilversmit, eds. *Edith Wharton: New Critical Essays*. New York: Garland, 1992. Includes studies of individual works, as well as discussions of Wharton's treatment of female sexuality, modernism, language, and gothic borrowings. Also features an introduction and a concluding essay on future directions for Wharton criticism.

Benstock, Shari. *No Gifts from Chance: A Biography of Edith Wharton*. New York: Charles Scribner's Sons, 1994. Although Benstock applies a feminist perspective to Wharton's life, she does not claim that Wharton was a feminist. Using primary materials not previously available, she provides a detailed account of Wharton's early life. She also discusses Wharton's literary relationship with Henry James, whose work Wharton admired.

Campbell, Donna. "The Short Stories of Edith Wharton." In *A Companion to the American Short Story*, edited by Alfred Bendixen and James Nagel. Malden, Mass.: Wiley-Blackwell, 2010. Provides an overview of Wharton's short fiction and its place within the development of the American short story.

Farwell, Tricia M. *Love and Death in Edith Wharton's Fiction*. New York: Peter Lang, 2006. Examines Wharton's beliefs about the nature of love and how they reflect her philosophical views, namely those of Plato and Charles Darwin. Wharton's own shifting feelings on the role of love in human life are revealed in conjunction with the shifting role that love played for her fictional characters throughout her writing career. Although most of the book focuses on her novels, one chapter analyzes her short story "The Fullness of Life."

Fracasso, Evelyn E. *Edith Wharton's Prisoner of Consciousness: A Study of Theme and Technique in the Tales*. Westport, Conn.: Greenwood Press, 1994. Analyzes stories from three periods of Wharton's career. Focuses on her technique in treating the theme of imprisonment. Describes Wharton's characters as people trapped by love and marriage, imprisoned by the dictates of society, victimized by the demands of art and morality, and paralyzed by fear of the supernatural.

Gelfant, Blanche H., ed. *The Columbia Companion to the Twentieth-Century American Short Story*. New York: Columbia University Press, 2000. Includes a chapter in which Wharton's short stories are analyzed.

Haytock, Jennifer Anne. "'Unmediated Bonding Between Men': The Accumulation of Men in the Short Stories." In *Edith Wharton and the Conversations of Literary Modernism*. New York: Palgrave Macmillan, 2008. Although Wharton did not define herself as a modernist writer, Haytock, who here examines many of Wharton's works, concludes that these writings addressed many of the issues that were of concern to the modernists. Haytock's chapter on the short stories focuses on Wharton's depiction of men.

Lee, Hermione. *Edith Wharton*. New York: Knopf, 2007. An exhaustive study of Wharton's life from childhood through adulthood. Lee offers valuable insights and makes interesting analogies between Wharton's life and her fiction.

Lewis, R. W. B. *Edith Wharton: A Biography*. New York: Harper & Row, 1975. The definitive biography of Wharton. Uses the previously inaccessible papers of the Yale University collection to provide a meticulous portrait of the author.

McDowell, Margaret B. *Edith Wharton*. Boston: Twayne, 1975. A perceptive biography and analysis of Wharton's works. Chapter 6 discusses her most important short fiction.

Nevius, Blake. *Edith Wharton: A Study of Her Fiction*. Berkeley: University of California Press, 1961. Examines two recurrent themes in Wharton's fiction: the tension that arises between an individual's public and private selves, and the desire for individual freedom and the need to assume social responsibility.

Olin-Ammentorp, Julie. "'Not Precisely War Stories': Edith Wharton's Short Fiction from the Great War." *Studies in American Fiction* 23 (Autumn, 1995): 153-172. Argues that Wharton's war stories were not tales of action and heroism or of tedious hours in the trenches; instead, her stories were suggested by her experiences, observations, and reflections on the war and on the home front culture that it produced.

Pennell, Melissa McFarland. *Student Companion to Edith Wharton*. Westport, Conn.: Greenwood Press, 2003. Pennell's introductory overview of Wharton's life and works devotes a lengthy chapter to discussion of the short stories and another chapter to two novellas, *Madame de Treymes* and *The Old Maid*.

Scofield, Martin. "Charlotte Perkins Gilman, Kate Chopin, Willa Cather, and Edith Wharton." In *The Cambridge Introduction to the American Short Story*. New York: Cambridge University Press, 2006. Defines Wharton's place in the history of American short fiction and analyzes several of her short stories, including "After Holbein," "Bewitched," and "The Other Two."

Young, Judy Hale. "The Repudiation of Sisterhood in Edith Wharton's 'Pomegranate Seed.'" *Studies in Short Fiction* 33 (Winter, 1996): 1-11. Argues that the story is an indictment of the woman writer who perpetuates the state of noncommunication among women. Maintains the story is Wharton's antimanifesto of female writing; in it, she presents her notion of just what the woman who writes must not do.

*Joan DelFattore*
*Updated by Mary F. Yudin*

# E. B. WHITE

**Born:** Mount Vernon, New York; July 11, 1899
**Died:** North Brooklin, Maine; October 1, 1985

PRINCIPAL SHORT FICTION

*Is Sex Necessary? Or, Why We Feel the Way We Do,*
 1929 (with James Thurber)
*The Second Tree from the Corner,* 1954

OTHER LITERARY FORMS

Though best remembered for two children's books, *Stuart Little* (1945) and *Charlotte's Web* (1952), E. B. White was noted during his lifetime for humorous essays and light poetry. His phenomenally successful revision and expansion of William Strunk's textbook *The Elements of Style* (1959) is a publishing legend. In 1981, a miscellany, *Poems and Sketches of E. B. White,* was published.

ACHIEVEMENTS

E. B. White received numerous awards and honorary doctorates. He was awarded the National Institute of Arts and Letters Gold Medal for Essays and Criticism in 1960, the Presidential Medal of Freedom in 1963, the National Institute of Arts and Letters National Medal for Literature in 1971, and a Pulitzer Prize special citation in 1978.

BIOGRAPHY

Elwyn Brooks White was born in Mount Vernon, New York, on July 11, 1899. He graduated from Cornell University, where he had discovered his love for literature and served as editor-in-chief of the *Cornell Daily Sun*. The most important event in his career was being hired by *The New Yorker* in 1926. He was largely responsible for shaping this famous magazine's sophisticated tone with his prose and painstaking editing. At *The New Yorker* he met James Thurber, an important literary influence, and Katharine Sergeant Angell, his wife, collaborator, and inspiration until her death in 1977. Known to millions only as the author of *Stuart Little* and *Charlotte's Web*, White was one of America's finest essayists. Thurber, himself a perfectionist, praised "those silver and crystal sentences which have a ring like the ring of nobody else's sentences in the world." One of White's often quoted statements is: "The whole duty of a writer is to please and satisfy himself, and the true writer always plays to an audience of one." Fleeing the stress of New York City, this shy, retiring individualist spent much of his later life on a farm in Maine. He died on October 1, 1985.

ANALYSIS

E. B. White's most important literary influence was Henry David Thoreau, author of *Walden: Or, Life in the Woods* (1854), the only book White really cared about owning. The influence of Thoreau's subtle humor and individualistic philosophy can be seen in White's writing, including his short fiction. Like Thoreau, White believed that "the mass of men lead lives of quiet desperation," that most people spend their lives getting ready to live but never actually living. White's short stories usually deal with the quiet desperation of life in the big city, where human beings trapped in an unnatural environment are beset by stress and anxiety, often temporarily alleviated by alcohol, meaningless social activities, and unfulfilling work.

Whereas Thoreau wrote about the joy of living close to nature, White, as a *New Yorker* contributor, had to deal with the reverse side of the picture--the anomie of life in one of America's most crowded, most competitive cities. When he managed to effect a Thoreauvian escape from New York to the peace and quiet of Maine, White lost interest in writing short stories.

White, like Thoreau, never lost his sense of humor even when dealing with depressing subjects. Most characteristic of White's short stories is their strange mixture of humor and emotional distress. In this he resembles his friend and collaborator James Thurber, who defined humor as "emotional chaos remembered in tranquillity." Thurber was a major influence on White, just as White was a major influence on Thurber. White's stories would seem too morbid without their leavening of humor. White and Thurber were both admirers of Henry James, and that older writer's high literary standards and dedication to his craft are obviously reflected in White's short stories.

### "THE DOOR"

White's most frequently anthologized story, "The Door," is an interior monologue reminiscent of the stream-of-consciousness technique pioneered by James Joyce. White's harrowing but courageously humorous story concerns a lonely individual having a nervous breakdown. The only other character is an unnamed receptionist who says, "We could take your name and send it to you." Her unnerving--and ungrammatical--statement suggests that the protagonist, having lost his identity, must wait for someone to tell him who he is. He feels disoriented in a city whose friendly landmarks are being replaced by cold, forbidding modern buildings without character. He mentally equates the city with those cages in which psychologists condition laboratory rats to behave according to certain arbitrary rules, then drive them crazy by changing the rules. The protagonist goes on to reflect that he is not the only victim of "progress":

> . . . and I am not the only one either, he kept thinking--ask any doctor if I am. The doctors, they know how many there are, they even know where the trouble is only they don't like to tell you about the prefrontal lobe because that means making a hole in your skull and removing the work of centuries.

"The Door" is a very personal story. White tried psychotherapy after a nervous breakdown but was disappointed, as evidenced in another autobiographical story, "The Second Tree from the Corner." "The Door" also shows White's concern about the corruption of the English language through crass commercialism and

*E. B. White* (Getty Images)

general vulgarization of culture. He was appalled by the proliferation of ugly, newly coined words which this story mimics with his own coinages such as "flexsan," "duroid," and "thrutex." For White such perversions of language were symptomatic of the destruction of human values by the blind onrush of science and technology driven by avarice and consumerism.

### "THE SECOND TREE FROM THE CORNER"

White described this story as "the one where the fellow says goodbye to sanity." Here the nameless protagonist of "The Door" is called Trexler and has gotten past the receptionist into the psychiatrist's inner sanctum. The humor is contained in the contrast between materialistic doctor and idealistic patient. Little is accomplished during five sessions, until the psychiatrist asks, "What do you want?" Trexler puts the doctor on the defensive by asking the same question. The doctor thinks he knows what he wants: ". . . a wing on the small house I own in Westport. I want more money, and more leisure to do the things I want to do." Trexler refrains from asking, "And what are those things you want to do, Doctor?" The overworked psychiatrist has no idea what he really wants--and everyone is in the same boat. This insight ends psychotherapy. Outside, when Trexler notices the remarkable beauty of the second tree from the corner, he experiences an epiphany. Intentionally echoing the conclusion of Henry James's short story "The Beast in the Jungle," White writes:

> He felt content to be sick, unembarrassed at being afraid; and in the jungle of his fear he glimpsed (as he had so often glimpsed them before) the flashy tail feathers of the bird courage.

"The Second Tree from the Corner" is a humorous way of dramatizing Thoreau's painful truth that "most men lead lives of quiet desperation." White found contentment by moving from the bedlam of Manhattan to a farm in Maine. There he discovered what he really wanted: peace, quiet, and simplicity; work to occupy his hands; and a rational way of life close to nature.

### PREPOSTEROUS PARABLES

White wrote many satirical pieces he called "preposterous parables." "The Hour of Letdown" is a spinoff of countless jokes in which a man brings a talking dog into a saloon. Instead of a dog, the stranger brings a chess-playing machine, which has many human characteristics, including a thirst for rye whiskey. White was foretelling the future. Computers do not yet need alcoholic beverages, but they can now beat world chess champions. Intelligent machines are becoming indispensable to modern society, while displacing millions from jobs and creating new problems as fast as they help solve the old. Electronic engineers are experimenting with improvements to make computers superior to humans in more ways. At the end of the story the stranger leaves in his car with the machine driving. This may have seemed absurd in 1951, but computers now operate automobiles on freeways and perform better in stressful traffic conditions than their owners.

"The Morning of the Day They Did It" is narrated by a space orbiter who survived the nuclear holocaust that destroyed all life on earth. It might be described as a cautionary science-fiction story, warning readers what would happen if science and technology advanced faster than human moral and spiritual development. White advocated a democratic world government to create universal peace and prosperity.

In "Quo Vadimus" (Latin for "Where are we going?"), two strangers stop on a Manhattan sidewalk and begin an impromptu philosophical discussion in the midst of pedestrians rushing in both directions. It turns out that one man was hurrying to deliver a note regarding a petty change in a salesman's instruction book. The other confesses that he was on his way to the office to write an article about complexity, which nobody may have time to read. Both agree they have lost sight of what is essential and are trapped in lives of quiet desperation. The man planning to write the article predicts that modern life can only get more complicated. By implication, the scurrying pedestrians blindly jostling them on the sidewalk are all on equally trivial errands.

White's "Preposterous Parables," like most of his stories, have a common theme: Man is becoming dehumanized by his own inventions. Progress is a double-edged sword. Consumerism does not lead to happiness but to anxiety and wage slavery. The problems that troubled White during the relatively simple period when he was writing for *The New Yorker* continue to grow more ominous and perplexing in the new millennium.

### OTHER MAJOR WORKS

POETRY: *The Lady Is Cold*, 1929; *The Fox of Peapack, and Other Poems*, 1938.

NONFICTION: *Every Day Is Saturday*, 1934; *Farewell to Model T*, 1936; *Quo Vadimus? Or, The Case for the Bicycle*, 1939; *One Man's Meat*, 1942; *World Government and Peace: Selected Notes and Comment, 1943-1945*, 1945; *The Wild Flag*, 1946; *Here Is New York*, 1949; *The Elements of Style*, 1959, 2d edition 1972, 3d edition 1979, 4th edition 2000 (with William Strunk, Jr.), 50th anniversary edition 2009; *The Points of My Compass*, 1962; *The Egg Is All*, 1971; *Letters of E. B. White*, 1976 (revised 2006); *Essays of E. B. White*, 1977; *Writings from "The New Yorker," 1925-1976*, 1990.

CHILDREN'S LITERATURE: *Stuart Little*, 1945; *Charlotte's Web*, 1952; *The Trumpet of the Swan*, 1970.

EDITED TEXTS: *Ho-Hum: Newsbreaks from "The New Yorker,"* 1931; *Another Ho-Hum*, 1932; *A Subtreasury of American Humor*, 1941 (with Katherine Sergeant

White); *Onward and Upward in the Garden*, 1979 (by Katherine Sergeant White).

MISCELLANEOUS: *An E. B. White Reader*, 1966 (William W. Watt and Robert W. Bradford, editors); *Poems and Sketches of E. B. White*, 1981.

BIBLIOGRAPHY

Angell, Roger. "The Making of E. B. White." *The New York Times Book Review*, August 3, 1997, 27. White's stepson Angell, an editor and writer for *The New Yorker*, describes life on the Maine farm, White's need for independence and privacy, and his Thoreauvian love of nature and respect for honest manual labor. In spite of withdrawing from New York City, White kept informed and concerned about world events.

Elledge, Scott. *E. B. White: A Biography*. New York: W. W. Norton, 1984. This first full-length biography describes White's childhood, his years at Cornell University, his struggle to find himself as a writer, his friendships with humorist James Thurber and *New Yorker* editor Harold Ross, and his half-century marriage to Katharine Angell White. Analyzes the relationship between his life and his writings.

Mallonee, Barbara C. "Reading E. B. White: Perfect Pitch, Perfect Catch." *Georgia Review* 55, no. 2 (Summer, 2001): 232. An examination and critique of White's literary works. Compares his works with those of other litterateurs.

Root, Robert L., Jr. *E. B. White: The Emergence of an Essayist*. Iowa City: University of Iowa Press, 1999. Analyzes the "four fairly pronounced periods" in White's literary career, his painstaking method of writing and revising, and the influence of Henry David Thoreau, Michel Eyquem de Montaigne, and others. Focuses on White's dedication to his craft and developing technique as a prose stylist, with minimal attention to his personal life.

_____, ed. *Critical Essays on E. B. White*. C. K. Hall, 1994. Varying perspectives by prominent authors who are easy to read and worth knowing, including Diana Trilling, Joseph Wood Krutch, Irwin Edman, Malcolm Cowley, James Thurber, Clifton Fadiman, and John Updike. Contains discussions of "The Door," "The Second Tree from the Corner," and other stories.

Sampson, Edward C. *E. B. White*. Twayne's United States Authors series. New York: Twayne, 1974. This early study contains a wealth of valuable information in compressed form, including a chronology, a literary biography, an appraisal of White's significance, references, and selected bibliography.

Updike, John. "Introduction to a New Edition of the Letters of E. B. White." In *Due Considerations: Essays and Criticism*. New York: Alfred A. Knopf, 2007. Updike discusses White's prose style, his life, and his literary career.

_____. "Magnum Opus: At E. B. White's Centennial, Charlotte Spins On." *The New Yorker* 75 (July 12, 1999): 74-78. Updike, noted for his sensitive short stories, was strongly influenced by White's standards while working under him at *The New Yorker* early in Updike's career. In this tribute, Updike recounts personal memories and analyzes *Charlotte's Web* as White's "disguised autobiography."

*Bill Delaney*

## JOHN EDGAR WIDEMAN

**Born:** Washington, D.C.; June 14, 1941

PRINCIPAL SHORT FICTION

*Damballah,* 1981
*Fever: Twelve Stories,* 1989
*All Stories Are True,* 1992
*The Stories of John Edgar Wideman,* 1992
*God's Gym,* 2005
*Briefs: Stories for the Palm of the Mind,* 2010

OTHER LITERARY FORMS

John Edgar Wideman's career began officially in 1967 with the appearance of his first novel, *A Glance Away.* Since this first publication, he has repeatedly returned to the novelistic form in works such as *Hurry Home* (1970); *The Lynchers* (1973); *Hiding Place* (1981), intended as the middle volume of the Homewood Trilogy; *Sent for You Yesterday* (1983), the final volume in the trilogy; *Reuben* (1987); *Philadelphia Fire* (1990); *The Cattle Killing* (1996); and *Two Cities* (1998). Wideman's postmodernist novel *Fanon,* about a writer trying to write a novel about psychiatrist and revolutionary Frantz Fanon, appeared in 2008.

In addition, Wideman has written works of autobiographical nonfiction, such as *Brothers and Keepers* (1984), in which he compares his own life to that of his troubled younger brother, serving a lifetime jail sentence, and *Fatheralong: A Meditation on Fathers and Sons, Race, and Society* (1994). He has also published a basketball memoir and meditation entitled *Hoop Roots* (2001) and a travel memoir entitled *The Island: Martinique* (2003). Wideman has written regularly on African American topics for *The New York Times Book Review* and has published scholarly work on African American predecessors, such as Charles Waddell Chesnutt and W. E. B. Du Bois.

ACHIEVEMENTS

John Edgar Wideman has distinguished himself both as a strong contemporary voice within the African American literary tradition and as a serious scholar examining the legacy of his predecessors in that tradition. His early fictional technique reflects his aesthetic debt to Anglo-American narrative experimentation, ranging from the originators of the English novel in the eighteenth century to the great modernists of the twentieth century; racial concerns, while evident, did not predominate in his first works. With the 1980's, however, Wideman deliberately began exploring African American literary forms in accordance with his growing desire to reengage his own racial identity and reach out more directly to an African American readership. Accordingly, he published the three works that constitute the Homewood Trilogy as trade paperbacks rather than in initial hardcover in order to increase their accessibility. The trilogy's third volume, *Sent for You Yesterday,* received the PEN/Faulkner Award for Fiction for its innovative fusion of subject matter and novelistic technique. The traumatic experience of a brother's crime and punishment, which was an important source for the 1983 novel, also prompted the nonfictional *Brothers and Keepers,* in which Wideman's quest for forms adequate to the polyphonic character of the African American experience takes on great personal urgency; this autobiography was nominated for the National Book Award. Wideman has also received the John Dos Passos Award, the Lannan Literary Award, the John D. and Catherine T. MacArthur Foundation ("genius") Award, the Rea Award, and an honorary doctorate from the University of Pennsylvania. He edited *The Best American Short Stories 1996.*

BIOGRAPHY

John Edgar Wideman was the first of five children born to Bette French and Edgar Wideman. His youth was spent in the African American community of

Homewood, within the city of Pittsburgh, Pennsylvania, and his fiction draws heavily upon the experiences of his family across a century of Homewood history. As a youth, Wideman demonstrated the same blend of athletic and academic ambition that often distinguishes his fictional characters and dramatizes their divided allegiances. Upon graduation as Peabody High School valedictorian, Wideman received a Benjamin Franklin Scholarship to the University of Pennsylvania and subsequently played for its basketball team, hoping someday to be drafted by the National Basketball Association. Selected for the Philadelphia Big Five Basketball Hall of Fame and tapped for Phi Beta Kappa, Wideman also won a Rhodes Scholarship; upon completion of his B.A. at the University of Pennsylvania in 1963, he attended Oxford University, where, in 1966, he earned a B.Phil. as a Thouron Fellow. Having been an active writer since his undergraduate years, Wideman secured a Kent Fellowship from the University of Iowa Writers' Workshop in 1966. His first novel, *A Glance Away*, appeared in 1967, winning for him immediate attention as a significant new voice in contemporary American letters.

Alongside his creative endeavors, Wideman steadily pursued an academic career. In 1966, he accepted a teaching position at the University of Pennsylvania, where he later headed the African American studies program from 1971 to 1973 and rose to the rank of professor of English; he was also assistant basketball coach from 1968 to 1972. Academic appointments brought him to Howard University, the University of Wyoming at Laramie, and the University of Massachusetts at Amherst. The National Endowment for the Humanities in 1975 named him a Young Humanist Fellow; in 1976, the U.S. State Department selected him for a lecture tour of Europe and the Near East. That same year, he held a Phi Beta Kappa lectureship.

Wideman married Judith Ann Goldman in 1965, and the couple had three children: Daniel, Jacob, and Jamila. The family tragedy of his youngest brother, Rob, who was convicted in 1978 of armed robbery and murder, was grimly reiterated in 1988, when Wideman's son Jacob received a life sentence for the 1986 murder in Arizona of a teenage traveling companion.

In speaking about the formative influences upon his writing, Wideman asserts that his creative inclinations underwent a transformation upon his arrival as a new faculty member at the University of Pennsylvania, where students of color assumed him to be as well versed in the African American literary legacy as he was in the Anglo-American tradition. His responsiveness to their concerns prompted him not only to create the university's African American studies program but also to recover the cultural identity that he had self-consciously minimized in pursuit of the dominant culture's standards of academic excellence. His subsequent writing, fiction and nonfiction alike, repeatedly sounds the autobiographical theme of "coming home." Wideman not only dissects the obstacles that thwart such return but also espouses the belief that art can at least make possible a temporary reconciliation between past and present. By paralleling his own multigenerational family history and the community history of Homewood, Wideman fuses personal and collective memory to create a mythology of the human condition at once particular and universal.

*John Edgar Wideman* (Getty Images)

## ANALYSIS

John Edgar Wideman's avowed artistic end is the creation of characters whose rich inner lives testify to a "sense of themselves as spiritual beings" that challenges the deterministic simplicities often dominant in literary depictions of the African American sensibility. Like Richard Wright, Ralph Ellison, and James Baldwin before him, Wideman insistently links naturalistic detail to an existential quest for meaning and integrity that is complicated by the peculiar difficulties of sustaining one's humanity under the degradations of racism. While the material consequences of racist injustice are ever-present in his stories, Wideman makes clear that his most pressing concern is the threat posed to the souls of its victims. In turn, he suggests that the renewal of contemporary African American society, increasingly ravaged by hopelessness and self-destructiveness, lies in a self-conscious recovery of, and healing through, the cultural identity he so rigorously documents in his evocation of Homewood. Thus in Wideman's fiction the struggle of individual souls in an absurd and dehumanizing world does not unfold in a completely existential void; his characters move within a community whose past vitality derived from history, traditions, language, and relationships linking generations back beyond the darkness of slavery. The imaginative architecture that unifies the Homewood Trilogy employs interpenetrating plotlines, family trees, and community legends to make clear that Wideman's real subject is the communal survival once made possible by its citizens' heroic decency against great odds.

### DAMBALLAH

*Damballah*, the collection of twelve short stories that begins the trilogy, announces Wideman's intentions aesthetically as well as thematically. The fuguelike polyphony of voices achieved by bringing together separate narratives drawn from a wide spectrum of Homewood personalities and historical moments captures not only the community's diversity but also the power of oral culture in all its forms--speech, music, and storytelling--to nourish and sustain it in the midst of unrelenting racial hostility. In "The Chinaman," a narrative "I" identified elsewhere as John (and quite evidently an autobiographical presence) explains that the funeral of his maternal grandmother, Freeda, had reconnected him with old family legends that he had years earlier set aside as unworthy of serious literary treatment. Listening months later to his own mother describe Freeda's death and thereby complete a story he had been unable to finish alone, he concludes, "The shape of the story is the shape of my mother's voice." Wideman's narrator repeatedly explains that this text is a collaborative project in which narratives culled from the collective memory of his family are woven together through the mediating agency of his own consciousness to reveal a design that affirms the faith in human possibility now leaching away in the ruins that were once Homewood.

Wideman's preoccupation with the crisis of black men in modern America--a crisis vividly depicted in his own estrangement from his origins and his brother Rob's criminality and imprisonment--explains the placement of his maternal grandfather, John French, at the center of these stories. French's defiant courage, loyalty, quick wit, tough-minded devotion to his family, and acute survival instincts make him a model of masculine virtue for a new generation desperately in need of his example. He stands in seemingly obvious contrast to his equally talented but blighted grandson Tommy Lawson, the narrator's drug-addicted brother, whose crimes destroy his future and who is the counterbalancing focus of the last third of the collection. French lives on in Tommy's rebellious energy and probing mind, making the youth's current circumstances all the more tragic.

Wideman also records the voices of the strong women who have sustained the community throughout the crises surrounding their men and whose emotional anguish reflects the complex emotional dynamic between black men and women in his fiction. Freeda Hollinger French, the text's matriarch, proves herself capable of swift, violent intervention to safeguard her child or her husband in "Lizabeth: The Caterpillar Story." Lizabeth French Lawson actually gives birth to the narrator in "Daddy Garbage," within a story line juxtaposed to the grim discovery of another infant's frozen corpse and the moral imperative of the two old men who find it and insist upon a decent burial. As the future is denied to one child and extended to another, one perceives a subtle echo of the divergent paths Lizabeth's own sons will pursue in later years.

Wideman's sensitivity to the orality of African American culture leads him to seek linguistic approximations for the music and talk-story patterns at the heart of African American imaginative expression. His prose resonates with the jazz rhythms of African American vernacular and often quotes directly from the musical yoking of human misery and triumph in what is called the blues. In "The Songs of Reba Love Jackson," a successful gospel singer admits that her artistry expresses emotional nuances beyond the power of language alone: "Couldn't speak about some things. She could only sing them. Put her stories in the songs she had heard all her life so the songs became her stories." In the closing piece of the volume, "The Beginning of Homewood," the narrator creates a wall of sound from the voices he has unloosed in the preceding stories; writing to his brother Tommy in prison, he acknowledges that his real task as a writer has been to hear and synthesize those women's testimonials to the community's history of defeat and transcendence:

> The chorus wailing and then Reba Love Jackson soloing. I heard May singing and heard Mother Bess telling what she remembers and what she had heard about Sybela Owens. I was thinking the way Aunt May talks . . . her stories exist because of their parts and each part is a story worth telling . . . the voice seeks to recover everything, that the voice proclaims *nothing is lost*, that the listener is not passive but lives like everything else within the story.

Wideman's most immediate purpose here is to tell the story of the slave woman Sybela Owens who, together with her white master/lover, fled the South, settled on Bruston Hill, the symbolic navel of Homewood, and began the family line that has produced his own family. By embedding Sybela's story of physical and spiritual redemption within a mediation on his brother's grim circumstances, the narrator conveys the continued urgency of such issues for African Americans; he also engages in the metafictional self-reflexiveness that characterizes his generation of American writers as he muses over the act of writing and its problematic relationship to lived events. Wideman has even bigger aims with Sybela, however, for his imaginative energy also transforms her into a mythic female progenitor who becomes a thematic counterpart to the African slave Orion ("Ryan") introduced in the first (and title) story, "Damballah." Like Sybela, Orion resists the degradation of his circumstances, so much so that his unyielding integrity leads to his execution by enraged whites who accuse him of sexual crimes. Before his death, however, he inspires an American-born slave boy with the mysterious power of his native religious beliefs, having taught him to chant to Damballah, the "good serpent of the sky" and a paternal deity whose wisdom and benign oversight make of the cosmos one transcendent family. Despite Wideman's sophisticated postmodernist affinity for refracting illusions of "reality" through multiple conflicting subjectivities, he seeks, finally, an integrative vision in which the mythical and the historical coalesce to offer the hope of spiritual renewal.

## FEVER

While *Damballah* draws its cumulative power from its unifying narrative sensibility and its consistent focus upon the citizens past and present of Homewood, *Fever: Twelve Stories* demonstrates a much looser internal logic grounded in thematic rather than storytelling interlacings. Once again, Wideman uses the short story to escape the constraints of novelistic continuity and reconfigure--this time through unrelated voices--motifs that literally assume international proportions. His most striking theme correlates the historical catastrophes of American slavery, the Holocaust, and modern international terrorism, thereby suggesting a common pattern of scapegoating and racist antagonism that transcends the experience of any single group of victims.

"The Statue of Liberty" and "Valaida," for example, both demonstrate how episodes of interracial miscommunication and self-indulgent fantasizing about the imaginary "Other" continually compromise the possibility of real human engagement. Moreover, in the latter story, a Jewish Holocaust survivor relates to his black maid a story of the jazz performer, whose actions in a wartime concentration camp saved his life; the maid's droll response resists the intended empathy he has attempted to build between them: "Always thought it was just you people over there doing those terrible things to each other." In

"Hostages," an Israeli expatriate and daughter of Auschwitz survivors reflects on her first marriage to an Israeli Arab and her current marriage to a wealthy businessman who offers a prime target for Muslim terrorists; finally she sees herself as a hostage to the comfortable but isolated life she leads and meditates on the Talmudic lesson of the Lamed-Vov, or "God's hostages," predestined "sponges drawing mankind's suffering into themselves."

"Fever," the volume's title story--and one of its most accomplished--depicts the 1793 yellow fever epidemic in Philadelphia, a crisis attributed to African slaves brought up north from the Caribbean but in fact resulting from the internally bred corruption of the swamp-ridden city. A metaphor for the pervasive racial contagions of this ironically dubbed "City of Brotherly Love," the fever levels all distinctions of race, gender, and class even as it triggers responses affirming them. The story's protagonist, Richard Allen, is a minister exhausting himself in Christian service to dying whites and blacks alike. Eventually confronted by the angry monologue of an infected Jewish merchant unimpressed by his humanity, he too is told of the Lamed-Vov, the implication being that Allen has been arbitrarily selected "to suffer the reality humankind cannot bear," enduring an unimaginable and unrelieved burden of "earth, grief and misery." A nihilistic voice in the text, Abraham deconstructs Allen's faith and further magnifies the din of conflicting perspectives--past and present, conciliatory and confrontational--that make the story the touchstone of the volume's exploration of compassion as a limited but essential response to incomprehensible suffering, be its origins cosmic or human--or both.

Elsewhere, Wideman contrasts vision versus blindness ("Doc's Story" and "When It's Time to Go") to illustrate very different positionings by African Americans within the racially charged dominant culture through which they try to move. Wideman's attunement to the musical textures of African American culture again asserts itself, as does his interest in the drama of individuals alienated from their culture by their ambitions. "Surfiction" offers an exercise in postmodern pastiche that is both a self-conscious parody of the imaginative stasis to which contemporary critical and aesthetic practice can lead and a serious study of the ways in which human determination to communicate across the void poignantly subverts even the most sophisticated intellectual distancing devices. Finally, then, the reader of this volume is left musing on the cultural incompatibilities institutionalized by ideologies of difference--racial, gender, ethnic, nationalistic--and the heroic folly of the Richard Allens of the world, who resist them against all odds.

**ALL STORIES ARE TRUE**

Like Wideman's earlier stories, these stories experiment with an associative narrative technique and are also sometimes based on his family in Homewood. Whether set in Homewood or elsewhere, however, all these stories put the individual in the context of larger social conditions in America. The title story, which returns readers to Homewood and a visit by a middle-aged man to his mother, soon shifts scenes to the dehumanizing conditions of the modern American prison, where his brother fights endlessly to gain parole. For both his mother and his imprisoned brother, faith--whether Muslim or Christian--becomes a way to endure the harsh realities of their lives.

Another story of a mother and a wayward son is "Everybody Knew Bubba Riff," a free-form examination of the life and death of an aggressive young man named Bubba, whose indulgent mother and punitive stepfather cannot understand the reasons for his bad outcome. By story's end, the reader sees that the problem may have been less with his parents, however, than with the prevailing American myth of the empowered individual, which led Bubba to see himself as a footloose, free agent with no obligation or connection to his past or its traditions, whose only measure of manhood was in violence.

Another story, "Backseat," returns to Homewood and to Wideman's dying grandmother. In reviewing Martha Wideman's life, John Edgar Wideman discovers his grandmother's origins as an illegitimate child of a white man and sees that for her, sexuality was always part of larger issues, such as race, marriage, parenthood, male domination, and female subservience. This discovery of his grandmother's complicated sexual life contrasts with Wideman's own memories of shallow adolescent sexual adventures in the backseat of his car.

Other aspects of black life are explored in such stories as "Newborn Thrown in Trash and Dies," inspired by an article in *The New York Times*. This story adopts the perspective of an infant who has been thrown by its mother down a trash chute. As the baby hurtles past the floors, the narrative flashes forward to the various indignities and deprivations of contemporary inner-city life to which the child would have been exposed. Far from urban decay, the issue of racism nevertheless surfaces even in better circumstances. In such stories as "Signs," a young black woman in graduate school, on her way to a successful life, finds menacing notes addressed to her which make her realize that racial prejudice has not been eradicated in her privileged environment. Eventually the reader learns that the young woman has composed these signs of racial antagonism herself, suggesting that memories of racism are so ingrained that the individual may not be able to overcome them.

### GOD'S GYM

In the ten stories in *God's Gym*, Wideman often rejects linear narrative for a lyrical form of meditation and improvisation characteristic of jazz riff, a form that derives from the repetitive call-and-response patterns of West African music.

### "WEIGHT"

"Weight" is a touching extended eulogy, which both lyrically and lightheartedly explores a metaphor of the mother as a weightlifter, who should wear a T-shirt with the words "God's Gym," for she bears the burdens of her family and neighbors; it ends with the narrator son twisting his fingers into the brass handles of her coffin and lifting. Because Wideman is always concerned with the complex issues of the relationship between fiction to reality, he explores in this story the process by which he wrote it, recounting how his mother initially objected to the levity of the metaphor, complaining that he should be ashamed of himself for taking the Lord's name in vain by using the phrase "God's T-shirt." Admitting that the events in the story may not have happened exactly as he describes them, Wideman, always the artist, knows that what actually happened is sometimes less important than finding a good way to tell it. In "Weight," Wideman's way of telling the story of his mother is to explore the implications of a metaphor as he practices for her death, trying on for size a world without her.

### "WHAT WE CANNOT SPEAK ABOUT WE MUST PASS OVER IN SILENCE"

The longest and most memorable story in *God's Gym*, "What We Cannot Speak About We Must Pass over in Silence," reflects Wideman's recognition of the complexity of experience, which so often resists being captured by language. This story, chosen for *Best American Short Stories 2004*, begins with a fifty-seven-year-old man learning of the death of a casual friend whose son is in an Arizona prison. Although the death does not move the central character, he grieves to the point of tears for the man's son he has never seen, empathizing with him as one who has suddenly been cut off from his last living contact with the world outside prison walls. The story focuses on the central character's obsessive quest for the young man, which becomes a search for his own identity, for he realizes that when he looks in the mirror he sees a stranger, and he wonders how long he has been losing track of himself.

Navigating the labyrinthine, bureaucratic prison system in an effort to locate the boy, the central character enlists the help of a young female paralegal assistant named Suh Jung, with whom he begins a love affair. Finally locating the son, he writes to him to express his condolences, but the young man's only reply is that all he knew about his father until receiving the letter is that some man must have had sex with his mother. Still the man pursues his quest to meet the son. Pretending to be his father, he makes the trip to the Arizona prison, is searched, goes through various checkpoints, and finally arrives at the door to the visiting room, only to be told in the story's final paragraph that because of a computer error his visit has been cancelled. Such an ending is not as pessimistic as it sounds, for an actual meeting with the son would have been an inevitable disappointment, whereas the search has been a testimony to the human need to find both family and self.

### BRIEFS

Illustrating Wideman's constant efforts to challenge established genres, this collection of short meditations, lyrical narratives, sketches, descriptions, and anecdotes is difficult to classify. Most of the pieces are less than a page long; some are only a sentence or two. Wideman himself calls them short stories; critics have called them "microstories" or prose poems. In some ways, *Briefs* resembles a writer's notebook--jottings that reflect thoughts and experiences Wideman thinks he may someday use in a longer work. For example, in one piece entitled "Stories," Wideman ponders about writing a story about a man walking in the rain eating a banana, listing all the questions such an image raises.

Wideman's decision to digitally publish these "briefs" may reflect his desire to accommodate the short attention span encouraged by the Internet and new electronic reading devices. Whatever his motivation for this mélange, these pieces are quick reads that alternately elicit a knowing nod, a quiet chuckle, a sympathetic sadness, a puzzled look, or a provocative thought. They range from a description of hungry academics gobbling down free food, and a comic mock letter to the pop singer Madonna, to a meditation on the death of Martin Luther King, and a thought piece entitled "Art After Auschwitz" about looking at a horrifying old black-and-white photograph of persecution. They also include several meditations on writing, such as Wideman's lament that he is not the best writer in the world, and his sadness that even if he were the best writer in the world, he could not get his son out of prison.

OTHER MAJOR WORKS

LONG FICTION: *A Glance Away*, 1967; *Hurry Home*, 1970; *The Lynchers*, 1973; *Hiding Place*, 1981; *Sent for You Yesterday*, 1983; *The Homewood Trilogy*, 1985 (includes *Damballah*, 1981; *Hiding Place*, 1981; *Sent for You Yesterday*, 1983); *Reuben*, 1987; *Philadelphia Fire*, 1990; *The Cattle Killing*, 1996; *Two Cities*, 1998; *Fanon*, 2008.

NONFICTION: *Brothers and Keepers*, 1984; *Father-along: A Meditation on Fathers and Sons, Race and Society*, 1994; *Conversations with John Edgar Wideman*, 1998 (Bonnie TuSmith, editor); *Hoop Roots*, 2001; *The Island: Martinique*, 2003.

EDITED TEXTS: *Best American Short Stories 1996*, 1996 (with Katrina Kenison)*; My Soul Has Grown Deep: Classics of Early African-American Literature*, 2001; *Twenty: The Best of the Drue Heinz Literature Prize*, 2001.

BIBLIOGRAPHY

Bell, Bernard W. *The Afro-American Novel and Its Tradition*. Amherst: University of Massachusetts Press, 1987. Bell provides a short but incisive overview of Wideman's evolving concerns as an African American, as well as a postmodernist innovator. He also notes Wideman's evocative uses of history as an imaginative paradigm and identifies as his major theme "the conflict between [his protagonists'] ascribed and achieved identities as black men."

Bennion, John. "The Shape of Memory in John Edgar Wideman's *Sent for You Yesterday*." *Black American Literature Forum* 20 (1985): 143-150. While the sole analytic emphasis of this essay is the novel that closes the Homewood Trilogy, it nevertheless offers a useful introduction to major themes in Wideman's fiction.

Berben, Jacqueline. "Beyond Discourse: The Unspoken Versus Words in the Fiction of John Edgar Wideman." *Callaloo* 8 (1985): 525-534. Although this essay is primarily a study of the novel *Hiding Place*, the second volume in the Homewood Trilogy, Berben also discusses the mythic character of Homewood as it unfolds in *Damballah*. Berben's argument that Wideman regularly evaluates his characters according to their ability to deal with truth and break free from self-delusion offers useful insight into all Wideman's writing.

Byerman, Keith Eldon. *John Edgar Wideman: A Study of the Short Fiction*. New York: Twayne, 1998. A critical look at Wideman's short fiction, including interview material. Includes a bibliography and an index.

Coleman, James W. *Blackness and Modernism: The Literary Career of John Edgar Wideman*. Jackson: University Press of Mississippi, 1990. Coleman regards the personal pattern of Wideman's alienation from and return to Homewood as reiterated in his aesthetic movement "from an uncritical acceptance of the forms and themes of mainstream modernism . . . to a black voicing of modernism and postmodernism that is consistent with Afro-American perspectives." This book deals with all Wideman's work through 1989, includes a later interview with him, and appends a brief bibliography of critical sources.

Gysin, Fritz. "John Edgar Wideman: 'Fever.'" In *The African-American Short Story: 1970 to 1990*, edited by Wolfgang Karrer and Barbara Puschmann-Nalenz. Trier, Germany: Wissenschaftlicher Verlag, 1993. A detailed discussion of the title story of Wideman's 1989 collection. Provides historical background for the 1793 Philadelphia yellow fever epidemic and the part African American citizens played in fighting the epidemic. Analyzes the collage structure of the story and Wideman's use of formal narrative devices of compression, repetition, and telescoping of experiences.

Klein, Julia. "Darkness and Light." *Pages* (March/April, 2005): 62-63. Based on an interview with Wideman, this summary of his career includes remarks by Wideman on the stories in *God's Gym*. He says he used to think short stories were gimmicky until he began to realize that they had their own kind of "internal logic and their own beauty."

Mbalia, Doreatha D. *John Edgar Wideman: Reclaiming the African Personality*. Selinsgrove, Pa.: Susquehanna University Press, 1995. Discusses, among other topics, Wideman's narrative technique. Includes a bibliography and an index.

O'Brien, John, ed. *Interviews with Black Writers*. New York: Liveright, 1973. In this early interview, Wideman sets forth his interest in aesthetic experimentation at the expense of fictional realism, his penchant for fabulation, and the relationship between his racial subjects and his artistic choices in rendering them.

Samuels, Wilfred D. "Going Home: A Conversation with John Edgar Wideman." *Callaloo* 6 (1983): 40-59. Samuels asks Wideman to discuss his movement from a Eurocentric literary aesthetic to one grounded in African American culture, language, and art forms. Central to that shift has been his imaginative "return to Homewood" and his increasing preoccupation with the emotional complexity of growing up black and male in the United States.

TuSmith, Bonnie, ed. *Conversations with John Edgar Wideman*. Jackson: University Press of Mississippi, 1998. Includes nineteen interviews with Wideman conducted from 1963 to 1997, covering a wide range of topics about the sources of his fiction, his perspectives on race in America, his philosophic thought, and his writing technique.

Wideman, John Edgar. "John Edgar Wideman." In *Conversations with American Novelists*, edited by Kay Bonetti et al. Columbia: University of Missouri Press, 1997. In this interview by Bonetti, Wideman discusses the oral tales told to him by his aunt, which he developed into the stories in the Homewood Trilogy. He talks about the politics of writing in America, the risks writers have to take to write truthfully about themselves and those they love, and his fiction's concern with brotherhood and sisterhood.

*Barbara Kitt Seidman; Margaret Boe Birns*
*Updated by Charles E. May*

# MARIANNE WIGGINS

**Born:** Lancaster, Pennsylvania; November 8, 1947

PRINCIPAL SHORT FICTION

*Herself in Love, and Other Stories,* 1987
*Learning Urdu,* 1990
*Bet They'll Miss Us When We're Gone,* 1991

OTHER LITERARY FORMS

Marianne Wiggins has written the novels *Babe* (1975), *Went South* (1980), *Separate Checks* (1984), *John Dollar* (1989), *Eveless Eden* (1995), *Almost Heaven* (1998) *Evidence of Things Unseen* (2003), and *The Shadow Catcher* (2007).

ACHIEVEMENTS

Marianne Wiggins's works have produced considerable critical comment and recognition, earning her a reputation as an innovative and daring writer. In 1989, she received fiction grants from the National Endowment for the Arts and the Whiting Foundation; she also won the Janet Heidinger Kafka Prize for *John Dollar* (1989) and the Commonwealth Club Prize for fiction (2004). Wiggins was a finalist for both the 2004 Pulitzer Prize for Fiction and the 2004 National Book Award for *Evidence of Things Unseen* and a finalist for the 2008 National Book Critics Circle Award for Fiction for *The Shadow Catcher*.

BIOGRAPHY

Marianne Wiggins was born November 8, 1947, in Lancaster, Pennsylvania, the daughter of John Wiggins and Mary Klonis. Probably because she was born in the Amish region of Pennsylvania, Wiggins has always had a fascination with "utopian" communities. She considered her father the classic American "lost father"; an unsuccessful grocer and a farmer who lost his land, he eventually committed suicide. He was a stern and religious man who attended the church founded by his father. Wiggins's mother, rather paradoxically, was an exotic Greek woman whose family had immigrated to Virginia.

For the first years of Wiggins's life, she was reared as a fundamentalist Christian, and at age nine, she was baptized into the Greek Orthodox Church. She now professes no religion. Often ill as a child--she had hepatitis and later had a kidney removed--Wiggins spent much of her time reading. She first married at age seventeen to Brian Porzak, a film distributor, on June 6, 1965, and they had one child, Lara. Wiggins and Porzak were divorced in 1970, after which Wiggins had a brief career as a stockbroker, trying to support her daughter as a single parent.

On January 23, 1988, Wiggins married Salman Rushdie, a well-known author living in England. Their life together was thrown into disarray, however, with the publication of Rushdie's *The Satanic Verses* in 1988. With the ensuing uproar that this novel produced in the Islamic world and the subsequent death sentence issued by the Ayatollah Khomeini in Iran, Wiggins and Rushdie had to leave their London home and go into hiding, at times separately, and Wiggins had to cancel a tour promoting her novel *John Dollar*. This enforced exile undermined their relationship, and in 1991, Wiggins came out of hiding and acknowledged that the marriage had failed. That same year, her short-fiction collection *Bet They'll Miss Us When We're Gone*, which contains some of her most autobiographical work, was published.

ANALYSIS

Marianne Wiggins's work focuses largely on the decisions that women face, and make, throughout their lives. For example, most of the characters in Wiggins's *Herself in Love, and Other Stories* are women searching for the meaning of life. Through her skill of expression with the magic and mystery of words, Wiggins creates her own distinctive language and uses her originality and diversity to make eccentric characters and implausible plots seem believable. In addition, when writing a collection of stories, she challenges herself to write a better, more in-depth plot for each subsequent story. Her writing is based on the belief that "it's the role of writers to touch the nerve that otherwise, untouched, lulls [people] to complacency." She has stated that she writes about what she fears, a tenet that she believes is the underlying provocation in the role of the writer.

### "KAFKAS"

Perhaps one of Wiggins's greatest fears is that of going mad. In "Kafkas," the mental condition of a young woman with a doctorate (presumably in philosophy) deteriorates noticeably while searching for a man by the last name of Kafka who will discuss philosophy with her. She goes about her search by calling information in major cities throughout the United States and asking for all the listings of male Kafkas. She then calls each one, looking for her soulmate, explaining that she is searching for a husband who can give her the name Fran Kafka.

When her sister, Dina, discovers (by way of a seven-hundred-dollar telephone bill) what Fran is doing, she confronts Fran. It becomes clear at this point, however, that regardless of whether this project started off as a mere amusement, it has become very serious indeed. When Dina tells Fran that she must leave, Fran replies that she cannot: "They'll kill me, Dina. Can't you hear them? There are Indians out there."

### "GREEN PARK"

Similarly, an undercurrent of violence and madness runs through "Green Park," in which a woman takes back her married lover, who had left her for his wife, only to plan a way of avenging her previous hurts. The power of the story lies in the chilling way in which the main character never lets on to her lover the pain and rage that she is feeling.

As her lover carefully shaves her legs, the main character thinks to herself about what it would be like if he cut her. The reader is held in thrall, waiting for the slip that will lead to the

red ribbon, a bright racine vine in the water, a shimmering curtain, her blood, unfurling itself like a shoot, turning the water not crimson or brilliant, but soft pink and pearly and rose.

His comment that he "gardened like hell to forget" her leads to her thought that there is "an instant when she might have said that he's cut her."

### "AMONG THE IMPRESSIONISTS"

"Among the Impressionists" also speaks about lost love, although it is love of a much more fleeting, imaginary kind. Lucy is an elderly woman who fantasizes during her daily trip to the National Gallery (the story is set in London) that she meets a different artist (and sometimes more than one) each day. One day, it is Edgar Degas; another, it is Camille Pissarro. To each artist whom she meets, Lucy tells him--or her, for Lucy often meets Mary Cassatt--that she is meeting her lover.

Lucy's rendezvous, however, is nothing more than a pathetic re-creation of a one-time meeting with a young man whom she dismissed rather abruptly, being too shy to converse with him. Her missed chance has left her, fifty years later, worn down by "haunting regrets." As a love story, "Among the Impressionists" is extremely tragic: a life wasted on a memory. Wiggins finishes the story with Lucy's description to Édouard Manet of what she and her lover do each day when they meet:

> We look at each other. We stare and we stare until the edges of the things around us start to grow invisible. . . . Until the world itself begins to grow invisible, until the only thing we see is what exists between two lovers.

With this fantasy, Lucy has been able to insulate herself from the disappointments of her life, unlike the character Fran, in "Kafkas," who is becoming separated from reality in a much more painful way. Fran stares at her sister, although she is "looking less at Dina than at the *distance* that the walls define, the way they seem to form a ring around their voices."

### BET THEY'LL MISS US WHEN WE'RE GONE

In *Bet They'll Miss Us When We're Gone*, one of Wiggins's greatest fears is of being left alone. This volume of fiction, set mostly in the United States but also in London, Wales, Amsterdam, and Spain, is a collection of thirteen articulate, remarkably realized stories that portray Wiggins's original, challenging, and eloquent style. Wiggins's ability to move through myriad different perspectives, to use a convincing voice through very different characters, and to manipulate language in a surprising, sometimes shocking manner, is portrayed in this volume of short fiction. By trusting the intelligence of the reader, Wiggins enhances the reader's participation as these stories unfold. Some stories use the backdrop of world events, such as the 1991 Gulf War and the 1986 nuclear accident at Chernobyl, while others focus on family sorrows and the struggle to forgive. Despite the fact that the stories were written over an extended period of time, from 1979 to 1990, and deal with a wide variety of scenarios, at the end there is a general thematic relationship that ties them all together: the role that memory plays in human life and behavior, sometimes persisting and sometimes failing.

Each story ends with the date and place where it was written, many of them chronicling the travels and travails of Wiggins's life in exile with Rushdie. These stories are very autobiographical, despite Wiggins's assertion in a 1990 interview that she could not write about their life in hiding for personal and safety reasons.

"Croeso i Gymru" begins with a forceful announcement, the first part of which reads, "We were on the lam in Wales." This sentence perhaps most succinctly sums up Wiggins's feelings from this period (though using different words, she has stated similar ideas during interviews). In addition, when her first-person main character says, "I depend on books for meaning. I depend on them for definition," the reader can believe that the key to Wiggins's emotional survival during this time was, in fact, being able to read and to continue writing.

The strain of the time that Wiggins spent in hiding comes through best in "Croeso i Gymru." There was the worry that people would recognize who she is, for she was allowed to go out (although presumably Rushdie was not). She occupied her time learning Welsh, reading the local, very rural newspapers, and walking among the meadows, inhabited only by sheep and British military personnel out playing war games as Harrier jump jets swooped by overhead. Most of all, however, she and her protectors sit and "wait for one aged psychopath to die."

"Balloons'n Tunes" is an intriguing story about the sorrow of an old man, Carl Tanner, and his interaction with his neighbor, Dolores. After the death of his wife, Tanner realizes how much he misses her and continues to carry on conversations with her as though she were still alive. Dolores, a curious, nosy, but concerned neighbor, is worried and upset by Tanner's babblings. The story centers on their mutual search for meaning in life and for an understanding of each other.

Like many of Wiggins's other short fictional stories, "Balloons'n Tunes" seems rather adroit and sometimes haunting. The story appears to be a reflection of losses suffered in Wiggins's own life, including her two divorces, and her efforts to cope with those losses. Left alone and confronted by an apparently interfering neighbor, Tanner must fill the void in his life left by the reality of losing his wife. At times, his memory plays tricks on him, as he tries to forget her death by continuing to talk with her as though she were present. He has a difficult time trying to understand and accept her death, and the lonely, temporary nature of mortality stares him in the face as those around him, particularly Dolores, perturb his life without understanding him. By taking loved ones for granted when alive, then painfully missing them after their deaths, this story can be interpreted as a literal realization of the title of the book.

Probably the most obviously autobiographical of the *Bet They'll Miss Us When We're Gone* stories, "Grocer's Daughter," was written long before the troubles of 1989, in Martha's Vineyard, in May, 1979. Perhaps it was this rough period that caused Wiggins to remember earlier hurts and hardships. The story interweaves a matter-of-fact narrative with lists and describes Wiggins's father, John, a man whom "life defeated." Wiggins describes him as a man who told her "strange, portenting things: if I ate too much bread, I'd get dandruff." She goes on to flesh out his description with the statement, "He read *Reader's Digest*, *Coronet*, and *Pageant* and didn't believe in evolution."

This story, however, is not all humorous anecdotes; Wiggins's motive in writing was also to achieve a healing in herself, for she says:

There were times I didn't like him. He left abruptly. He left me much unfinished business. . . . I'd like to turn to him today and say, "I love you: too late: I'm sorry: you did the best you could: you were my father: I learned from you: you were an honest man."

Wiggins's writing is at its strongest with these heartfelt remembrances and regrets, for it speaks to the universal feelings that many adult children have upon their parents' deaths. The dedication page for *Bet They'll Miss Us When We're Gone* reads only "remembering my father," but it is this motivation that gives the warmth that infuses the best of Wiggins's work.

OTHER MAJOR WORKS

LONG FICTION: *Babe*, 1975; *Went South*, 1980; *Separate Checks*, 1984; *John Dollar*, 1989; *Eveless Eden*, 1995; *Almost Heaven*, 1998; *Evidence of Things Unseen*, 2003; *The Shadow Catcher*, 2007.

BIBLIOGRAPHY

Field, Michele. "Marianne Wiggins." *Publishers Weekly* 235 (February 7, 1989): 57-58. Written just prior to the uproar over *The Satanic Verses*, this article supplies many biographical details, many of which help to provide background for interpreting Wiggins's work. Also offers a synopsis of Wiggins's writing career, as well as what has motivated her "explicit and frightening" writing.

Garrett, George. "On the Lam in Wales." *The New York Times*, June 30, 1991. A review of *Bet They'll Miss Us When We're Gone* that discusses Wiggins's focus on the persistence and failure of memory, the magic and mystery of language, and the pathetic limits of thinking.

James, Caryn. "Marianne Wiggins and Life on the Run." *The New York Times*, April 9, 1991, p. C13. This brief article is partly a discussion of *Bet They'll Miss Us When We're Gone* and partly a commentary on the reasons why Wiggins believed that it was necessary, ultimately, to leave Rushdie. It discusses Wiggins's feelings while in hiding and how the experience affected her writing, especially by increasing and intensifying its autobiographical nature.

_____. "Wiggins: Author, Feminist, and Wife of Rushdie." *The New York Times*, April 4, 1990, p. C17. Offers biographical details and talks about Wiggins's life in London, her marriage to Salman Rushdie, and her writings in *Herself in Love, and Other Stories*. Written early in Wiggins's exile, it reveals much of Wiggins's character and personality. Most notable about her frame of mind at that time was her determination to stand by Rushdie and not to be cowed by anyone.

Kakutani, Michiko. "Life on the Lam with Rushdie." *The New York Times*, June 14, 1991, p. C23. A review of *Bet They'll Miss Us When We're Gone* that praises three of the stories-- "Angel," "Rex," and "Grocer's Daughter"--and criticizes the rest as being of interest only because of Wiggins's experience as the wife of exiled Salman Rushdie.

Phillips, Andrew. "A Life in Hiding." *Maclean's* 102 (August 21, 1989): 30. This article is most useful for its brief but clear picture of the events that forced Wiggins and Rushdie into hiding. Describes how their exile disrupted her life and career. Maintains that at a time when Wiggins seemed poised on the brink of success, she was forced to withdraw from the limelight, and notes the repercussions that this withdrawal had on her career.

Smiley, Jane. "Vanished Past." A review of *The Shadow Catcher*, by Marianne Wiggins. *Los Angeles Times*, June 3, 2007, p. R1. Smiley, herself a novelist and short-story writer, reviews Wiggins's novel. She describes Wiggins as "one of our most adventuresome and enterprising novelists" who masks these characteristics by narrating her novels in a "simple and friendly" tone.

Zipp, Yvonne. "A Novel Intertwined with the Life Story of *The Shadow Catcher*." Review of *The Shadow Catcher*, by Marianne Wiggins. *The Christian Science Monitor*, July 3, 2007, p. 13. Praises Wiggins's ability to create an innovate structure and interesting plot for this novel and to "conjure up a character in one or two sentences."

*Jo-Ellen Lipman Boon*
*Updated by Alvin K. Benson*

# JOY WILLIAMS

**Born:** Chelmsford, Massachusetts; February 11, 1944

PRINCIPAL SHORT FICTION

*Taking Care: Short Stories,* 1982
*Escapes: Stories,* 1990
*"Craving,"* 1991
*"The Route,"* 1992
*"Marabou,"* 1993
*Honored Guest: Stories,* 2004

OTHER LITERARY FORMS

Although Joy Williams is known mainly for her short fiction, she is also the author of the novels *State of Grace* (1973), *The Changeling* (1978), *Breaking and Entering* (1988), and *The Quick and the Dead* (2000) and nonfiction works *Florida Keys: A History and Guide* (1986) and *Ill Nature: Rants and Reflections on Humanity and Other Animals* (2001). She has also written travel articles for *Esquire* magazine, including "How to Do and Undo Key West" (February, 1996), "Nantucket Now" (September, 1996), "Desert Flower" (January, 1997), and "No Place Like Home" (March, 1997).

ACHIEVEMENTS

Joy Williams has established herself as one of the preeminent practitioners of the short-story form. Along with Raymond Carver, Richard Ford, and a handful of other writers, she has perfected a style and content that accurately render life in late twentieth century America. It is not a pretty picture she paints: In Williams's stories, characters cannot communicate, couples cannot connect, and children are abandoned.

Williams has been the recipient of numerous awards in her career, including a John Simon Guggenheim Memorial Foundation Fellowship in 1974. Her stories have regularly appeared in leading U.S.

literary journals--*Esquire, The New Yorker, Grand Street*--and many have been collected in the annual *The Best American Short Stories* or *Prize Stories: The O. Henry Awards* collections and in other prime anthologies of contemporary American fiction. *Ill Nature* was a finalist for the National Book Critics Circle Award for Criticism. Williams has won the Harold and Mildred Strauss Living Award from the American Academy of Arts and Letters and the 1999 Rea Award for the Short Story.

BIOGRAPHY

Born in 1944, Joy Williams grew up in the small Maine town of Cape Elizabeth, where both her father and her grandfather were Congregational ministers. She holds degrees from Marietta College in Ohio and from the University of Iowa. Married to Rust Hills, the writer and fiction editor at *Esquire*, she has one daughter, Caitlin. She has taught in the writing programs at several leading U.S. universities (including the University of California, Irvine, and the University of Arizona) and has settled into homes in Arizona and Florida.

ANALYSIS

Joy Williams is a short-story writer with a dark vision encased in a clean prose style. While a few of her stories have an experimental, almost surrealistic form, and often a wry, ironic tone, the bulk fall into what can be called the realist mode, minimalist division: Williams deals with American family life in the last third of the twentieth century, focusing on troubles, handicaps, and incompletions. She interests readers in these subjects without divulging all the information that they might ordinarily want or need about the characters and their situations. What further distinguishes her stories is a prose style that is clean but highly metaphorical, for the images and motifs of the stories often carry the meaning more deeply than the action or the exposition.

Hers is not a reassuring portrait of contemporary American life. The families are often dysfunctional, physically as well as psychologically: parents abandon children, by leaving or by dying, and children wander in life without guidance. Alcohol is a cause of the unhappiness as well as its hoped-for cure. In nearly all her stories, love is being sought but is rarely found and nearly as rarely expressed. Characters seem unable to ask the questions that might free them from their unhappiness; the best they can hope for is an escape to some other state, physical or emotional. Disabilities, addictions, dead animals, arguments in restaurants, and car accidents abound in Williams's stories.

Williams's first collection, *Taking Care*, contains stories published in the 1970's and early 1980's in *The New Yorker*, *Partisan Review*, *The Paris Review*, *Esquire*, *Ms.*, and other leading vehicles of contemporary American fiction. These stories show a firmness and subtlety that have marked Williams's style over her entire career (although there is probably more range here than in her second collection). The themes that would mark that career are clearly established in this first collection. While many of the stories are riveting in their subject matter, they leave readers with a sense of hollowness and futility. There are few resolutions in Williams, even early in her career, but there are the tensions, violence, and disconnections that mark most of her stories.

### "TAKING CARE"

In the title story, Jones, a preacher, is "taking care" of two generations: a wife dying of leukemia and a six-month-old baby girl whom his daughter has left him to care for before fleeing to Mexico. Jones baptizes his granddaughter and then brings his wife back from the hospital; in the last line of the story, "Together they enter the shining rooms"--rooms made "shining" by Jones's love and care. This epiphanic ending, however, cannot erase all the abandonment and death. Jones is surely "taking care" of more than his required load in this life, and there is a heaviness, a spiritual sadness, that is expressed appropriately in Williams's flat, terse prose style.

Other stories in *Taking Care* have similar themes and forms. In "Traveling to Pridesup," three sisters in their eighties and nineties, "in a big house in the middle

of Florida," find a baby abandoned in a feed bag on their mailbox. In the journey in their old Mercedes to find someone to help, Lavinia gets them lost, drives hundreds of miles in circles, and finally crashes. In a tragicomic mix reminiscent of Flannery O'Connor, the story ends with a painful revelation, "the recognition that her life and her long, angry journey through it, had been wasteful and deceptive and unnecessary."

"Winter Chemistry" features two students who spy on their teacher every night and inadvertently kill him when they are caught. "Shepherd" concerns a young woman who cannot get over the death of her German shepherd and who will probably lose her boyfriend because of it. ("'We are all asleep and dreaming, you know,'" he tells her in a speech that might apply to characters in other stories in *Taking Care*. "If we could ever actually comprehend our true position, we would not be able to bear it, we would have to find a way out.") In "The Farm," alcohol, infidelities, and the accidental killing of a hitchhiker will destroy the central couple. "Breakfast," too, has many of the stock Williams ingredients: parents who abandon their children, a half-blind dog, and characters who are both alcoholic and lacking direction.

Possibly the only difference in *Taking Care* from Williams's later fiction is that there appears to be more humor in these early stories and more effort by Williams to perfect a wry, ironic style. ("The Yard Boy," for example, is a surreal caricature of a kind of New Age spiritual character.) The other landmarks, however, are present: The style is often flat and cryptic, events and incidents seem to have more a symbolic than a representational quality, and people pass by one another without touching or talking. There is little love in these stories (even in those that are supposedly love stories), but often a violence beneath the surface that is constantly threatening to bubble up and destroy the characters or kill their animals (as in "Preparation for a Collie" or "Woods"). People rarely have names; rather, they are "the woman," "her lover," "the child." Williams writes easily about children, but they wander in an adult world without supervision or love (as in "Train" or "The Excursion"). Williams works in the great American tradition of Sherwood Anderson's *Winesburg, Ohio* (1919), in which characters become what Anderson called "grotesques." Williams writes of grotesques as well, bizarre characters who are lost or losing or obsessive, and whom nothing, apparently, will save.

### ESCAPES

These elements can be found throughout the title story of Williams's second collection, *Escapes*. The narrator, a young girl, describes the time when her alcoholic mother (abandoned by the father) took her to see a magician. The mother, drunk, wanders onto the stage and has to be removed. Layers of escape, both literal and metaphorical, characterize this story: the father's abandonment of his dysfunctional family, the magician's illusions ("Houdini was more than a magician, he was an escape artist"), the mother's addiction to alcohol, and the daughter's dreams of escaping her lot: "I got out of this situation," Lizzie writes in the last line of the story, "but it took me years."

Williams's later short fiction is unique not only for this bleak view of human nature, in which people are shown trapped and searching for some inexpressible transcendence, but also for a prose style that is both less and more than it appears: less because, like other minimalists whom Williams resembles (such as Carver and Ann Beattie), she draws only the outlines of the action and leaves the characters' backgrounds to the reader's imagination and more because Williams manipulates metaphors and motifs in such a way that they carry a heavy weight of meaning in her stories. In "Escapes," for example, the old magician's illusion of sawing a woman in half becomes the vehicle for the story's theme: The alcoholic mother tells her daughter that she witnessed that trick performed by Houdini when she was a child. She wanted to be that lady, "sawed in half, and then made whole again!" Her subsequent intrusion into the show by walking onstage is her attempt to escape by realizing that dream, "to go and come back," but the dream is impossible to realize and therefore self-destructive. The usher escorts mother and daughter out of the theater, assuring the drunken woman that she can "pull [herself] through." She will not, however, succeed in reconstructing herself and her life, and in the end, the reader suspects, the daughter will escape only by abandoning the mother.

The stories in *Escapes* thus seem to work at cross-purposes: While the prose style is clean and uncluttered, the motifs and metaphors lead readers to meanings beneath the surface, to a depth that is full of horror and despair. In the second story, "Rot" (first reprinted in the O. Henry Prize collection of 1988), these concerns and formal characteristics continue. Dwight persuades his wife, who is twenty-five years younger than he is, to allow him to park the vintage Thunderbird he has just bought in their living room. The car is full of rot and rust--a symbol, readers may suspect, of the couple's marriage. The reader learns little about these characters, what they do or where they are headed. Instead, symbolism replaces information: The rusting car was found in a parking lot with its owner dead inside it; now Dwight sits in the car in the living room and looks dead.

The other stories in *Escapes* take a similar approach: "The Skater," which was chosen to appear in the 1985 collection *Best American Short Stories*, presents a family, parents and a daughter, on a tour of East Coast preparatory schools. It slowly becomes apparent that the sickness at the heart of this family is the memory of the daughter--like the skater of the title who glides in and out of the story at several points--who died the previous year; the parents simply want Molly to be away from the sadness of their home.

The young woman in "Lulu" puts an old couple to bed after all three have gotten drunk one morning; she then attempts to drive off with their boa constrictor, apparently searching for love (she wonders, "Why has love eluded me"). In "Health," a twelve-year-old girl is undergoing ultraviolet treatments to help her recover from tuberculosis but is surprised by a man who walks in during one of her tanning sessions, as she lies naked on the couch. The grandmother of "The Blue Men" tries, in part through use of alcohol, to assuage her grief over her dead son, who was executed for murdering a police officer. "The Last Generation," the collection's closing story, depicts a father, numbing his pain over his wife's death through drink and work and neglecting his own children.

Williams's bleak vision is mitigated only by the sureness of her prose and the symbolic poetry of her language. "Bromeliads," in which a young mother abandons her new baby to her parents, becomes the central metaphor of the story's meaning. As the young woman explains, bromeliads are "thick glossy plants with extraordinary flowers. . . . They live on nothing. Just the air and the wind"--a perfect description of the mother herself.

In "White," a couple has moved from Florida to Connecticut to escape the memory of their two babies, who have died. They cannot, however, escape their grief, even in alcohol and evasion. At a party they throw for a departing Episcopal priest, the husband describes a letter that the couple recently has received from the woman's father; after the greeting, the letter contains nothing, "just a page, blank as the day is long." The letter becomes a symbol for the missed communication, the things that are not said and that may in fact be inexpressible, abandonment and death among them.

In the end, readers are left with the bleakness of Williams's stories--despite a minimalist style and a use of metaphor that almost negates that vision. Nevertheless, Williams remains one of the more highly regarded short-fiction writers in modern-day America, often anthologized and the recipient of numerous awards. Along with Carver, Beattie, Ford, and a handful of other contemporaries, she has continued to produce works that are read by university students and the general public alike, and younger writers emulate her polished style.

## HONORED GUEST

The title story of this collection, which was included in *Best American Short Stories 1995*, is a beautiful signature piece for Williams, not only because it deals with the last few months of her ill mother's life but also because it tenaciously explores what she says all art should be about: people's apprehension at the approach of nothingness. To live, the young female protagonist in this story understands as she helplessly watches her mother move inevitably toward death, is to be like an honored guest in a Japanese aboriginal ritual, in which a bear cub is captured and treated royally for some time, until an inevitable day when the villagers drag it out, torture it, and kill it. In what Williams has called an extremely difficult story for her to write, the mother and daughter in "Honored Guest" try to find a way to cope with life's ultimate absurdity by making it the subject of bitter quips and jokes.

Since her first collection, *Taking Care*, was published in 1982, readers seem to have two minds about the stories of Williams. On the one hand, many think she is among the best short-story writers in America, uncannily able to create pearls of revelation with seemingly inconsequential irritants of insight and language. On the other hand, some of her stories grate on the reader's ear and consciousness, with flippant bits of cultural grit. Williams's short stories are an acquired taste, not easy to like on first reading. Lacking discernible plot, sympathetic characters, or easily digestible themes, her previous stories have been described is "quirky," the dictionary definition of which is a sudden sharp twist, a flourish, something unpredictable or unaccountable, a peculiarity that eludes suppression.

Although summaries can never do justice to the stories of Williams, a brief description of some of the stories in *Honored Guest* make it clear that they surely fit these definitions. For example, in "Congress," a woman develops a loving companionship with a lamp made out of four cured deer feet; in "The Visiting Privilege," a woman befriends an older lady in a hospital and after her death takes care of her dog, one of those irritating mechanical things that bark when someone comes near; in "Charity," a woman leaves her husband on the highway to go back to help some people in trouble and cannot escape them; in "Hammer," a sixteen-year-old girl picks up a destitute man at a bus station and brings him home to aggravate her mother, whom she abhors. Although they are often hilarious, these stories are nowhere near as silly as some of them sound. Williams is a master at making readers giggle at ghastly reality. These stories, as Williams has claimed all stories should, will break your heart and make you feel ill at ease. They will also make you laugh at the things people do to cope with what beleaguers them on the way to the inevitable. As Williams once said, a writer "loves the dark . . . cherishes the mystery."

OTHER MAJOR WORKS

LONG FICTION: *State of Grace*, 1973; *The Changeling*, 1978; *Breaking and Entering*, 1988; *The Quick and the Dead*, 2000.

NONFICTION: *Florida Keys: A History and Guide*, 1986; *Ill Nature: Rants and Reflections on Humanity and Other Animals*, 2001.

BIBLIOGRAPHY

Cooper, Rand Richards. "The Dark at the End of the Tunnel." *The New York Times*, January 21, 1990. In this detailed review of *Escapes*, Cooper focuses on the quirky, ominous world the stories create and discusses several stories, arguing that "The Blue Men" and the title story are the strongest.

Fox, Linda A. "Excellent Guide Unlocks the Mysteries of the Keys." *The Toronto Sun*, January 14, 1998, p. 55. A discussion of Williams's travel guide, *The Florida Keys: A History and a Guide*; notes that Williams's book is full of useful information about wildlife, sea life, and local folklore.

Heller, Zoe. "Amazing Moments from the Production Line." *The Independent*, July 21, 1990, p. 28. In this review of *Escapes*, Heller complains that Williams's style has become a mannerism, but singles out "In the Route" as a story that is more interesting than the other formulaic pieces in the collection.

Hills, Rust. Review of *State of Grace*. *Esquire* 80 (July, 1973): 26, 28. Hills recognizes that Williams has a problem with structure but praises her language: "open the novel to virtually any page and you'll instantly see it--a kind of strange phosphorescent style describing disquieting, dark, and funny goings-on. Sentences are brilliant, gorgeous, surprising."

*Kirkus Reviews*. Review of *Escapes*. 57 (November 15, 1989): 1633. This anonymous reviewer recognizes that Williams's "weird, seemingly anesthetized, protagonists are usually in flight: from inexorable fate, from the oppressive past, from reality itself."

Kornblatt, Joyce. "Madness, Murder, and the Surrender of Hope." Review of *Taking Care*. *The Washington Post Book World*, March 21, 1982, p. 4. Noting her similarity to Flannery O'Connor and Joyce Carol Oates, the reviewer here sees the redemptive qualities of Williams's work, for in the "fragile gestures" of these stories, "we glimpse, merely glimpse, an order of being that eschews randomness, that ascribes value, that insists on love in the face of destructiveness."

Malinowski, Sharon. "Joy Williams." In *Contemporary Authors*, edited by Deborah A. Straub. Vol. 22. Detroit: Gale Research, 1988. A good summary of Williams's career, including long passages from reviews of her novels and her short-story collections through 1982. "In Williams's fiction, the ordinary events of daily life are susceptible to bizarre turns of horror and individuals are lost in their private selves, unable to comprehend the forces which shape their lives. Although Williams occasionally alleviates her bleak vision with humor, a sense of hopelessness and despair remains central to her work."

Williams, Joy. "Joy Williams." Interview by Molly McQuade. *Publishers Weekly* 237 (January 26, 1990): 400-401. In this brief but wide-ranging interview Williams talks about her career and her sense of her own writing; words, for example, are intended "to affect the reader in unexpected, mysterious, subterranean ways. The literal surface has to be *very* literal--smooth and exact--yet what makes it strange is what's teeming underneath. Stories should be something other than they appear to be. . . . They should make you uncomfortable."

*David Peck; Mary Hanford Bruce*
*Updated by Charles E. May*

# TENNESSEE WILLIAMS

**Born:** Columbus, Mississippi; March 26, 1911
**Died:** New York, New York; February 25, 1983
**Also known as:** Thomas Lanier Williams

PRINCIPAL SHORT FICTION

*One Arm, and Other Stories,* 1948
*Hard Candy: A Book of Stories,* 1954
*The Knightly Quest: A Novella and Four Short
      Stories,* 1967
*Eight Mortal Ladies Possessed: A Book of Stories,*
      1974
*Collected Stories,* 1985

OTHER LITERARY FORMS

In addition to his three dozen collected and uncollected stories, Tennessee Williams wrote two novels, a book of memoirs, a collection of essays, two volumes of poetry, numerous short plays, a screenplay, and more than twenty full-length dramas. Among the most important of his plays are *The Glass Menagerie* (pr. 1944, pb. 1945), *A Streetcar Named Desire* (pr., pb.1947), *Cat on a Hot Tin Roof* (pr., pb. 1955), and *The Night of the Iguana* (pr., pb. 1961).

ACHIEVEMENTS

Tennessee Williams's most obvious achievements in literature lie in the field of drama, where he is considered by many to be America's greatest playwright, a standing supported by two Pulitzer Prizes, a Commonwealth Award, a Medal of Freedom (presented by President Jimmy Carter), and an election in 1952 to a lifetime membership in the National Institute of Arts and Letters. Williams himself, however, felt that his short fiction contained some of his best writing. Indeed, besides stories appearing in his own collections, Williams published stories in many of America's most prestigious magazines, including *The New Yorker* and *Esquire*, and many have been selected for various anthologies, including three in Martha Foley's *Best American Short Stories* annual anthologies. Williams's short stories and plays alike dramatize the plight of the "fugitive," the sensitive soul punished by a harsh, uncaring world. In the stories, however, readers find specific and frequent voice given to a theme and subject only hinted at in Williams's drama, at least until his later, less memorable, plays: the plight of the homosexual in a bigoted society.

BIOGRAPHY

Descended on his mother's side from a southern minister and on his father's side from Tennessee politicians, Thomas Lanier Williams moved with his family from Mississippi to St. Louis shortly after World War I. He attended the University of Missouri and Washington University, finally graduating from the University of Iowa. After odd jobs in the warehouse of a shoe factory, ushering at a motion-picture theater, and even a stint screenwriting in Hollywood, he turned full-time writer in the early 1940's, encouraged by grants from the Group Theatre and Rockefeller Foundation. Despite purchasing a home in Key West, Florida, in 1950, Williams spent most of the remainder of his life living for short periods in a variety of locales in Europe, the United States, and Mexico. His two Pulitzer Prizes early in his career, plus four Drama Critics Circle Awards, solidified Williams's reputation as a playwright; the quality of his writing declined, however, after the early 1960's, in large part as a result of drug dependency. He died, alone, in a New York City hotel room in 1983.

ANALYSIS

Although during his lifetime Tennessee Williams was commonly held to be without peer among America's--many would say the world's--playwrights, he began his career writing short fiction, with a story entitled "The Vengeance of Nitocris" published in *Weird Tales* in 1928. As late as 1944, when his first theatrical success was in rehearsal, George Jean Nathan reportedly observed that Williams "didn't know how to write drama, that he was really just a short-story writer who didn't understand the theatre." In proportion to the worldwide audience familiar with Williams's dramas, only a handful know more than a story or two, usually from among the ones later transformed into stage plays. Seven of Williams's full-length dramas, in fact, had their genesis in the fiction: *The Glass Menagerie* in "Portrait of a Girl in Glass"; *Summer and Smoke* (pr. 1947, pb. 1948) in "The Yellow Bird"; *Cat on a Hot Tin Roof* in "Three Players of a Summer Game"; *The Night of the Iguana* and *Kingdom of Earth* (pb. 1968) in stories of the same names; *The Milk Train Doesn't Stop Here Anymore* (pr. 1963, revised pb. 1976) in "Man Bring This Up Road"; and *Vieux Carré* (pr. 1977, pb. 1979) in "The Angel in the Alcove" and "Grand."

### "THE NIGHT OF THE IGUANA"

The play *The Night of the Iguana* is sufficiently different from its progenitor to indicate how Williams rethought his material in adapting it to another medium. Both works portray a spinsterish artist, Miss Jelkes; but while Hannah in the play has fought for and achieved inner peace, Edith's harsher name in the story belies her edginess, neurosis, and lack of "interior poise." Having channeled her own "morbid energy" into painting, she discerns in the contrasting "splash of scarlet on snow . . . a flag of her own unsettled components" warring within her. When a servant at the Costa Verde hotel tethers an iguana to the veranda, Edith recoils hysterically from such brutality against "one of God's creatures," taking its suffering as proof of a grotesque "universe . . . designed by the Marquis de Sade."

This picture of cosmic indifference, even malevolence, occurs in a handful of Williams's stories, most notably in "The Malediction," in which the lonely Lucio exists in a meaningless universe verging on the absurd, ruled by a God "Who felt that something was wrong but could not correct it, a man Who sensed the blundering sleep-walk of time and hostilities of chance" and "had been driven to drink." Edith finds God personified in a violent storm "like a giant bird lunging up and down on its terrestrial quarry, a bird

*Tennessee Williams* (AP Photo)

with immense white wings and beak of godlike fury."

Her fellow guests at the hotel are two homosexual writers. Squeamish and yet attracted by the forbidden nature of their relationship, Edith insinuates herself into their company only to become the object of a desperate attack on her "demon of virginity" by the older of the two. Although she has earlier hinted that she always answers, with understanding, cries for help from a fellow sufferer, she ferociously fends off his pathetic advances, metaphorically associated with the predatory "bird of blind white fury." Afterward, however, once the younger man has mercifully cut loose the iguana, Edith feels her own "rope of loneliness had also been severed," and--instead of drawing back in "revulsion" from "the spot of dampness" left on her belly by the older writer's semen--exclaims "Ah, life," evidently having reached through this epiphanic moment a new acceptance and integration of her sexuality. However, unlike Hannah, whose compassionate response to Shannon in the play is for him a saving grace and who can affirm, along with Williams, that "Nothing human disgusts me unless it's unkind, violent," Edith's

inability to answer unselfishly the older man's need-
-the cardinal sin in Williams--may have permanently
maimed him by destroying his self-respect.

Williams does not always capitalize fully on his gift
for writing dialogue in his stories. For all its interest in
light of the later play, the pace of "The Night of the
Iguana" is curiously desultory and enervated, which
might not have been true if the story had been written
from Edith's point of view. Williams does indeed prove
adept at handling first-person narration in several autobiographical tales, whose content seems hardly distin-
guishable at times from the sections of his *Memoirs*
(1975).

### "THE RESEMBLANCE BETWEEN A VIOLIN CASE AND A COFFIN"

Williams can, however, become annoyingly self-
conscious when, in authorial intrusions analogous to
the nonrepresentational techniques that deliberately
destroy the illusion of reality in his dramas, he breaks
the narrative line in a dozen or so stories to interject
comments about himself as writer manipulating his
materials, sometimes apologizing for his awkwardness
in handling the short-story form, or for playing too
freely with chronology or radically shifting tone. At
times these stories provide some notion of Williams's
aesthetic theories and practice, as when, in "Three
Players of a Summer Game," for example, he discusses
the method by which the artist orders experience by a
process that distorts and "yet . . . may be closer than a
literal history could be to the hidden truth of it." These
metafictional asides might indicate his conception of
character portrayal. On that point--while without
qualms at employing clinical details when necessary-
-Williams insists, in "Hard Candy," on the need for "in-
direction" and restraint rather than "a head-on violence
that would disgust and destroy" if he is to remain nonjudgmental and respect the "mystery" at the heart of
character.

An almost identical comment occurs in "The Resemblance Between a Violin Case and a Coffin," part
of a small group of *rites de passage* stories in the Williams canon. The story centers on a love triangle of
sorts as the young narrator faces the destruction of the
"magical intimacy" with his pianist sister as she enters
adolescence--that "dangerous passage" between the

"wild country of childhood" and the "uniform world of
adults"--and turns her attentions toward a fellow musician, Richard Miles. It is as if she has deserted the narrator and "carried a lamp into another room [he] could
not enter." He resents the "radiant" Richard, but also
feels a frightening prepubescent physical attraction for
the older boy. Like many of Williams's adult neurotics
whose libidinous desires rebel against their Puritan re-
pressions, the narrator longs to touch Richard's skin,
yet recoils in shame and guilt from the boy's offer of
his hand as if it were somehow "impure." Seeing
Richard play the violin, however, provides an epiphany
as the narrator "learns the will of life to transcend the
single body" and perceives the connection between
Eros and Thanatos. For the narrator equates the act of
playing the phallic violin with "making love," and the
violin case to "a little black coffin made for a child or
doll." He mourns the loss of youth and innocence and
the birth of the knowledge of sin and death.

Tom, the authorial voice in *The Glass Menagerie*,
confesses to "a poet's weakness for symbols," and one
of Williams's own hallmarks has always been an extensive use of visual stage symbolism-- "the natural
speech of drama." As he remarks in one of his essays, it
can "say a thing more directly and simply and beautifully than it could be said in words"; he employs symbols extensively, however, in only a handful of stories,
although he does rely heavily on figurative language.
In the earlier stories the imagery is ordinarily controlled and striking, as, for example, in this line (reminiscent of Karl Shapiro's "cancer, simple as a flower,
blooms") describing the doctor's tumor from "Three
Players of a Summer Game": "An awful flower grew in
his brain like a fierce geranium that shattered its pot."
In the later tales, however, Williams's diction frequently becomes overwrought and demonstrates some
lack of control, falling into what he criticizes elsewhere
in the same essay as "a parade of images for the sake of
images."

If the mood of "The Resemblance Between a Violin
Case and a Coffin" is tender and elegiac, the tone of a
much later *rite de passage* story, "Completed," is
chilling, but no less haunting and memorable. Miss
Rosemary McCord, a student at Mary, Help a Christian
School, is a withdrawn debutante subjected by

her unsympathetic mother to a pathetic and bizarre coming-out dance. The onset of menstruation has been late in coming for Rosemary, and when it finally does arrive, she is pitifully unprepared for it. Ironically, the fullness of physical development in Rosemary coincides with a death wish; her only "purpose in life is to complete it quick." Her one understanding relative, the reclusive Aunt Ella, deliberately retreats from the external world through morphine; the drug brings her comforting apparitions of the Virgin Mary and tears of peace. Rosemary goes to live with her, aware that she has been taken captive and yet willingly submissive, ready to be calmed through drugs and her own reassuring visions of the Virgin. Her life--apparently the latest of several variations on that of Williams's own sister--is over before it began. Perhaps it is, however, only in such a sheltered, illusory life that this fragile, sensitive girl can exist.

### "SABBATHA AND SOLITUDE"

The other "passage" that threads through Williams's stories is that from life to death, obsessed as he is with what he terms "a truly awful sense of impermanence," with the debilitating effects of time on both physical beauty and one's creative powers, and the sheer tenacity necessary if one is to endure at least spiritually undefeated. In "Sabbatha and Solitude," the aging poetess (undoubtedly semiautobiographical) finds that the process of composition is a trial not unlike the Crucifixion that results only in "a bunch of old repeats," while in the picaresque "Two on a Party," the blond and balding queen and hack screenwriter exist at the mercy of that "worst of all enemies . . . the fork-tailed, cloven-hoofed, pitchfork-bearing devil of Time."

### "COMPLETED"

"Completed" is one of Williams's few later stories--"Happy August the Tenth" is another--that can stand alongside some of his earliest as a fully successful work. Just as there was a noticeable diminution in the power of his later dramas compared with the ones from *The Glass Menagerie* through *The Night of the Iguana*, so, too, each successive volume of short fiction was less impressive than its predecessor. As Williams's vision of the universe darkened and became more private, the once elegiac tone acquired a certain stridency and sharp edge; and as Williams developed a tough,

self-protective shell of laughter as a defense against his detractors, some of the dark humor--what he once called the "jokes of the condemned"--became directed toward the pathetic grotesques who increasingly peopled his works, whereas once there was only compassion.

### "DESIRE AND THE BLACK MASSEUR"

Thus, two of the most representative stories, "One Arm" and "Desire and the Black Masseur," neither of which, significantly, has ever been dramatized, appeared in his first collection. Unquestionably the most macabre of all his tales is "Desire and the Black Masseur," which details the fantastic, almost surreal sadomasochistic relationship between the insecure, sexually repressed Anthony Burns and an unnamed black masseur at a men's bath. Burns, whose name blends that of a Christian saint with the suggestion of consummation by fire--here metaphoric--suffers from an overly acute awareness of his own insignificance, as well as of his separateness and lack of completeness as a human being. Williams views the latter as an inescapable fact of the human condition and proposes three means available to compensate for it: art, violent action, or surrendering oneself to brutal treatment at the hands of others. Burns chooses the third path, submitting himself as if in a dream, finding at the punishing hands of the masseur first pain, then orgasmic pleasure, and ultimately death. Although the masseur thus secures a release from his pent-up hatred of his white oppressors, this tale should not be construed as a social comment reflecting Williams's attitude toward black/white relations, hardly even peripherally a concern in his work, despite his being a southern writer.

Blacks figure importantly in only two other stories. In the ribald "Miss Coynte of Greene," the title character's long-frustrated female eroticism erupts into nymphomania, her pleasure intensified by the dark skin of her sexual partners. In "Mama's Old Stucco House," Williams's gentlest foray into the black/white terrain, the failed artist Jimmy Krenning is cared for physically and emotionally after his own mother's death by the black girl Brinda and her Mama, the latter having always functioned as his surrogate mother.

That "Desire and the Black Masseur" is to be read on levels other than the literal appears clear when Williams places its climax at the end of the Lenten season. The death and devouring of Burns becomes a ritual of expiation, a kind of black mass and perversion of the sacrifice on Calvary, even accomplished in biblical phraseology. Indeed, counterpointed with it is a church service during which a self-proclaimed fundamentalist preacher exhorts his congregation to a frenzy of repentance. What Williams has written, then, is not only a psychological study of man's subconscious desires and an allegory of the division between innocence and evil within all men but also a parable exposing how excessive emphasis on guilt and the need for punishment at the hands of a vengeful God have destroyed the essential New Testament message of love and forgiveness. Burns's strange rite of atonement stands as a forceful indictment of a Puritanism that creates a dark god of hate as a reflection of one's own obsession with evil, which is one of the recurrent emphases in almost all of Williams's important dramas, especially *Suddenly Last Summer* (pr., pb. 1958) and *The Night of the Iguana*.

### "ONE ARM"

Something of the obverse, the possibility for transcending one's knowledge of evil and isolation, occurs in "One Arm," the quintessential--and perhaps the finest--Williams story, in which can be discerned nearly all the central motifs that adumbrate not only his fiction but also his plays. Oliver Winemiller, a former light heavyweight champion who in an accident two years earlier lost an arm, is one of Williams's "fugitive kind," a lonely misfit, cool, impassive, now tasting, like Brick in *Cat on a Hot Tin Roof*, "the charm of the defeated." Since all he possessed was his "Apollo-like beauty," after his physical mutilation he undergoes a psychological and emotional change; feeling that he has lost "the center of his being," he is filled with self-loathing and disgust. He enters on a series of self-destructive sexual encounters, finally committing a murder for which he is sentenced to die.

While in confinement awaiting execution, he receives letters from all over the country from his male lovers, confessing that he had aroused deep feelings in them, that he had effected a "communion" with them that would have been, if he had only recognized it, a

means of "personal integration" and "salvation." If it was not until very late in his dramas that Williams openly treated homosexuality with sympathy, in his stories his unapologetic and compassionate attitude existed from the very first. Oliver's epiphany, that he had been loved, liberates him from his self-imposed insularity; ironically, however, this rebirth makes his approaching death harder to accept. On the eve of his execution, he recognizes that the Lutheran minister who visits him has used religion as an escape from facing his own sexuality, and he desperately hopes that by forcing the minister to come to terms with himself and his "feelings" he can thereby somehow repay his debt to all those who had earlier responded to him with kindness. The minister, however, recognizing a forbidden side of himself and still suffering guilt over his adolescent sexual awakening during a dream of a golden panther, of which Oliver reminds him, refuses to give Oliver a massage and rushes from his cell. Oliver goes to his execution with dignity, gripping the love letters tightly between his things as a protection from aloneness.

The doctors performing the autopsy see in Oliver's body the "nobility" and purity of an "antique sculpture." Williams, however, reminds his readers in the closing line that "death has never been much in the way of completion." Although the work of art is immutable, it is not alive as only the emotionally responsive person can be, for the true artist in William's writing is the person who goes out unselfishly to answer the cry for help of others, and the real work of art is the bond of communion that is formed by that response. Thus "One Arm" incorporates virtually all of Williams's major attitudes, including his somewhat sentimental valuation of the lost and lonely; his romantic glorification of physical beauty and worship of sexuality as a means of transcending aloneness; his castigation of Puritan repression and guilt that render one selfish and judgmental; and his Hawthornian abhorrence of the underdeveloped heart that prevents one from breaking out of the shell of the ego to respond with infinite compassion to all God's misbegotten creatures.

Although Williams's stories, with their frequent rhetorical excesses, their sometimes awkward narrative strategies, and their abrupt shifts in tone, technically do not often approach the purity of form of Oliver's statue, they do as all good fiction must--surprise the reader with their revelations of the human heart and demand that the reader abandon a simplistic perspective and see the varieties of human experience. What in the hands of other writers might seem a too specialized vision, frequently becomes in Williams's work affectingly human and humane.

OTHER MAJOR WORKS

LONG FICTION: *The Roman Spring of Mrs. Stone*, 1950; *Moise and the World of Reason*, 1975.

PLAYS: *Fugitive Kind*, pr. 1937, pb. 2001; *Spring Storm*, wr. 1937, pr., pb. 1999; *Not About Nightingales*, wr. 1939, pr., pb. 1998; *Battle of Angels*, pr. 1940, pb. 1945; *I Rise in Flame, Cried the Phoenix*, wr. 1941, pb. 1951, pr. 1959 (one-act); *This Property Is Condemned*, pb. 1941, pr. 1946 (one-act); *The Parade, or Approaching the End of a Summer*, wr. 1941, pr. 2006; *The Lady of Larkspur Lotion*, pb. 1942 (one-act); *The Glass Menagerie*, pr. 1944, pb. 1945; *You Touched Me*, pr. 1945, pb. 1947 (with Donald Windham); *Twenty-Seven Wagons Full of Cotton*, pb. 1945, pr. 1955 (one-act); *A Streetcar Named Desire*, pr., pb. 1947; *Summer and Smoke*, pr. 1947, pb. 1948; *American Blues*, pb. 1948 (collection); *Five Short Plays*, pb. 1948; *The Long Stay Cut Short: Or, The Unsatisfactory Supper*, pb. 1948 (one-act); *The Rose Tattoo*, pr. 1950, pb. 1951; *Camino Real*, pr., pb. 1953; *Cat on a Hot Tin Roof*, pr., pb. 1955; *Sweet Bird of Youth*, pr. 1956, pb. 1959 (based on *The Enemy: Time*); *Orpheus Descending*, pr. 1957, pb. 1958 (revision of *Battle of Angels*); *Suddenly Last Summer*, pr., pb. 1958; *The Enemy: Time*, pb. 1959; *Period of Adjustment*, pr. 1959, pb. 1960; *The Night of the Iguana*, pr., pb. 1961; *The Milk Train Doesn't Stop Here Anymore*, pr. 1963, revised pb. 1976; *The Eccentricities of a Nightingale*, pr., pb. 1964 (revision of *Summer and Smoke*); *Slapstick Tragedy: "The Mutilated" and "The Gnädiges Fräulein,"* pr. 1966, pb. 1970 (one-acts); *The Two-Character Play*, pr. 1967, pb. 1969; *The Seven Descents of Myrtle*, pr., pb. 1968 (as *Kingdom of Earth*); *In the Bar of a Tokyo Hotel*, pr. 1969, pb. 1970; *Confessional*, pb. 1970; *Dragon Country*, pb. 1970 (collection); *Out Cry*, pr. 1971, pb. 1973 (revision of *The Two-Character Play*); *The Theatre of Tennessee Williams*, pb. 1971-1981 (seven volumes); *Small Craft Warnings*, pr., pb. 1972 (revision of *Confessional*); *The Red Devil Battery Sign*, pr. 1975, pb. 1988; *Vieux Carré*, pr. 1977, pb. 1979; *A Lovely Sunday for Creve Coeur*, pr. 1979, pb. 1980; *Clothes for a Summer Hotel*, pr. 1980; *Something Cloudy, Something Clear*, pr. 1981, pb. 1995; *A House Not Meant to Stand*, pr. 1981, pb. 2008; *The Traveling Companion, and Other Plays*, pb. 2008 (Annette J. Saddik, editor).

SCREENPLAYS: *The Glass Menagerie*, 1950 (with Peter Berneis); *A Streetcar Named Desire*, 1951 (with Oscar Saul); *The Rose Tattoo*, 1955 (with Hal Kanter); *Baby Doll*, 1956; *Suddenly Last Summer*, 1960 (with Gore Vidal); *The Fugitive Kind*, 1960 (with Meade Roberts; based on *Orpheus Descending*); *Stopped Rocking, and Other Screenplays*, 1984.

POETRY: *In the Winter of Cities*, 1956; *Androgyne, Mon Amour*, 1977; *The Collected Poems of Tennessee Williams*, 2002.

NONFICTION: *Memoirs*, 1975; *Where I Live: Selected Essays*, 1978, rev. ed. 2009 (as *New Selected Essays: Where I Live*); *Five O'Clock Angel: Letters of Tennessee Williams to Maria St. Just, 1948-1982*, 1990; *The Selected Letters of Tennessee Williams*, 2000-2004 (two volumes; Albert J. Devlin and Nancy M. Tischler, editors); *Notebooks*, 2006 (Margaret Bradham Thornton, editor).

BIBLIOGRAPHY

Bennett, Consuella. "Death to the Author! Expunging the Authorial Presence from Tennessee Williams's Short Stories." *CLA Journal* 51, no. 1 (September, 2007): 39-60. Bennett applies the critical theories of Roland Barthes to critique Williams's short stories, analyzing them without considering their autobiographical elements.

Bloom, Harold, ed. *Tennessee Williams*. Updated ed. New York: Bloom's Literary Criticism, 2007. Collection of essays that analyze Williams's life and works. Although most of the essays focus on his plays, Nancy M. Tischler's essay, "Romantic Textures in Tennessee Williams's Plays and Short Stories," examines his short fiction.

Falk, Signi Lenea. *Tennessee Williams*. 2d ed. Boston: Twayne, 1978. Though devoting most of her attention to Williams's plays, Falk addresses many of the short stories. Falk's discussions of "One Arm," "Desire and the Black Masseur," and "Portrait of a Girl in Glass" are especially interesting. Contains a useful, though dated, bibliography.

Gelfant, Blanche H., ed. *The Columbia Companion to the Twentieth-Century American Short Story*. New York: Columbia University Press, 2000. Includes a chapter in which Williams's short stories are analyzed.

Gross, Robert F., ed. *Tennessee Williams: A Casebook*. New York: Routledge, 2002. Collection of essays about Williams's works. "The Hungry Women of Tennessee Williams's Fiction," by Michael R. Schiavi, includes some discussion of the short stories, and other references to the stories are listed in the index.

Kolin, Philip C, ed. *The Tennessee Williams Encyclopedia*. Westport, Conn.: Greenwood Press, 2004. A useful guide to Williams and his work containing more than 150 alphabetically arranged entries. References to the short stories are listed in the index.

_____. "Williams's 'Sand.'" *The Explicator* 63, no. 3 (Spring, 2005): 173-176. An analysis of this short story, including discussion of its plot and characters.

Leahey, Joseph R. "John Horne Burns and Tennessee Williams's 'Hard Candy.'" *ANQ* 23, no. 2 (Spring, 2010): 71-75. Examines the connections between Williams's short story "Hard Candy" and Burns's novel *The Gallery*, which depicts the experience of homosexuals during World War II.

Leverich, Lyle. *The Unknown Tennessee Williams*. New York: Crown, 1995. This first volume of a projected two-volume biography traces Williams's life for the first thirty-three years. Draws on previously unpublished letters, journals, and notebooks. Discusses Williams's focus on how society has a destructive influence on sensitive people and his efforts to change the form of drama.

Martin, Robert A., ed. *Critical Essays on Tennessee Williams*. New York: G. K. Hall, 1997. An excellent, accessible collection of criticism of Williams's works.

Murphy, Brenda, ed. *Critical Insights: Tennessee Williams*. Pasadena, Calif.: Salem Press, 2011. Collection of original and reprinted essays providing critical readings of Williams's work. Also includes a biography, a chronology of major events in Williams's life, a complete list of his works, and a bibliography listing resources for further research.

Spoto, Gary. *The Kindness of Strangers: The Life of Tennessee Williams*. Boston: Little, Brown, 1985. Spoto's study is the closest to a definitive biography of Williams, although it provides only passing mention of the short stories. Includes a brief bibliography.

Tharpe, Jac, ed. *Tennessee Williams: A Tribute*. Jackson: University Press of Mississippi, 1977. A collection of fifty-three essays on various aspects of Williams's art. Many of the essays note Williams's short fiction in passing, and four are fully or primarily devoted to the short fiction. Contains a bibliography.

Vannatta, Dennis. *Tennessee Williams: A Study of the Short Fiction*. Boston: Twayne, 1988. The only book-length study of Williams's short fiction. Contains essays by various scholars analyzing Williams's short fiction and a selection of Williams's own letters, essays, and reviews.

Woodhouse, Reed. *Unlimited Embrace: A Canon of Gay Fiction, 1945-1995*. Amherst: University of Massachusetts Press, 1998. Includes a chapter on Williams's gay short stories. Argues that the most astonishing thing about the stories is their lack of special pleading; while they are not graphic, they are not apologetic for their homosexuality. Provides an extended analysis of the story "Hard Candy."

*Thomas P. Adler*
*Updated by Dennis Vannatta*

# WILLIAM CARLOS WILLIAMS

**Born:** Rutherford, New Jersey; September 17, 1883
**Died:** Rutherford, New Jersey; March 4, 1963

## PRINCIPAL SHORT FICTION

*The Knife of the Times, and Other Stories,* 1932
*Life Along the Passaic River,* 1938
*Make Light of It: Collected Stories,* 1950
*The Farmers' Daughters: The Collected Stories of
    William Carlos Williams,* 1961
*The Doctor Stories,* 1984
*The Collected Stories of William Carlos Williams,*
    1996

## OTHER LITERARY FORMS

Best known as a poet, William Carlos Williams nevertheless wrote in a variety of literary forms (some of them defying categorization) including poetry, novels, short stories, prose poetry, essays, autobiography, and plays. *Paterson,* his extended poem published in four separate volumes (1946-1951), with a fifth volume serving as a commentary (1958), is his most famous and enduring work.

## ACHIEVEMENTS

William Carlos Williams received numerous awards, including the Dial Award in 1926, the National Book Award in 1950, the Bollingen Award in 1953, and, posthumously, the Pulitzer Prize for poetry in 1963.

## BIOGRAPHY

After attending public schools in New Jersey, spending time in Europe, and then finishing high school in New York, William Carlos Williams enrolled in the University of Pennsylvania's medical school in 1902. While completing his M.D. there, he met Ezra Pound, Hilda Doolittle (better known as the writer H. D.), and the painter Charles Demuth. In 1910, he began work as a general practitioner in Rutherford, New Jersey; in addition to this practice, from 1925 on he became a pediatrician at Passaic General Hospital. Williams held these positions until several strokes forced him to retire in 1951. His medical and literary careers always coexisted. In 1909, he had his first volume, *Poems,* privately published. As his reputation grew, he traveled to Europe several times and encountered such writers as James Joyce, Gertrude Stein, and Ford Madox Ford. He married Florence Herman in 1912, and they had two sons. Williams died on March 4, 1963, in his beloved Rutherford.

## ANALYSIS

William Carlos Williams was one of the major figures of literary modernism whose peers included Ezra Pound and Wallace Stevens. Highly influenced by the visual arts and the imagist movement, Williams's work was marked by a rejection of metaphysics, characterized by his famous dictum: "No ideas/ But in things." Williams's objective approach to literature is reflected in the coarse realism of his short stories. His prose shares the basic principles of his poetic theory: use of an American idiom, adherence to a locale, communication through specifics, and belief in organic form. The pastiche effects of Williams's poetry and prose had a profound influence on the next generation of American literary modernists, particularly the so-called Objectivist School, which included Louis Zukofsky, George Oppen, Carl Rakosi, and Charles Reznikoff.

M. L. Rosenthal claims that William Carlos Williams's short stories "are often vital evocations of ordinary American reality--its toughness, squalor, pathos, intensities." As such, this short fiction tends to exhibit distinctive characteristics. First, its style is the American idiom, with heavy reliance on dialogue and speech rhythm. Second, Williams inevitably writes of his own locale and stresses the Depression's dramatic effect on ordinary working people. Third, as he shows in his poem "A Sort of a Song," there should be "No ideas/ But in things"; in other words, details should suggest underlying ideas, not vice versa. Fourth, Williams himself is often present, but as a doctor, never as a poet; thus biography and autobiography constitute important plot elements. Last, the author allows plot to develop organically, which affects length (the tales range from one to thirty pages) and structure (the stories may appear diffuse or highly compressed).

Williams published two main short-story anthologies: *The Knife of the Times, and Other Stories* and *Life Along the Passaic River*. In 1950, he collected these and other stories into a single volume called *Make Light of It*; then, in 1961, this was superseded by his complete collected stories entitled *The Farmers' Daughters*. Although these stories may indicate progressive technical sophistication or experimentation, they all treat "the plight of the poor" (as Williams says on several occasions) or the physician's frequently ambiguous role of healing the sick within an infected society.

## "OLD DOC RIVERS"

On the choice of title for his first short-story collection, *The Knife of the Times*, Williams observes "The times--that was the knife that was killing them" (the poor). A typical story is "Old Doc Rivers," which provides a full background on one rural general practitioner. It also contains a strong autobiographical element because the narrator is a younger doctor (apparently Williams). An enormously complex picture emerges of Doc Rivers: efficient, conscientious, humane, yet simultaneously crude, cruel, and addicted to drugs and alcohol. The story builds this portrait by piling up specifics about the physician's personal and professional lives and interweaving case studies among the young doctor-narrator's comments. The narrator is astonished by River's psychological sharpness, intuition for the correct diagnosis, and ability to inspire blind faith in his patients. Like many Williams tales, the reader's moral response is ambiguous, for when sober, Rivers is not a good doctor, yet when drunk or doped, he is at least as good as anyone else. The plot follows a roughly chronological structure which charts Rivers's gradual mental and physical

decline. This story's particular strengths are its narrator's voice, concrete details, re-creation of dialogue, and exploration of the doctor-patient relationship.

## "JEAN BEICKE"

Williams further considers the physician-patient relationship in "Jean Beicke" and "A Face of Stone," representative of his second short-fiction collection, *Life Along the Passaic River*. Told by a pediatrician-narrator (but this time an established, not a beginning, doctor), "Jean Beicke" is set in a children's ward during the Depression and recounts the story of a "scrawny, misshapen, worthless piece of humanity." Although Jean is desperately ill, she wins the hearts of the physicians and nurses by her sheer resilience: "As sick as she was," the narrator marvels, "she took her grub right on time every three hours, a big eight ounce bottle of milk and digested it perfectly." Little Jean's symptoms puzzle the medics, and despite initial improvement, she finally dies. Up to this point, doctors and readers alike have been ignorant of her previous history, but when her mother and aunt visit the dying infant, it is learned that she is the third child of a woman whose husband deserted her. As her aunt says, "It's better off dead-- never was any good anyway." After the autopsy, the doctors discover they have completely misdiagnosed Jean. The storyteller ends the tale like this:

> I called the ear man and he came down at once. A clear miss, he said. I think if we'd gone in there earlier, we'd have saved her.
> For what? said I. Vote the straight Communist ticket. Would it make us any dumber? said the ear man.

Williams thought "Jean Beicke" was "the best short story I ever wrote." One reason is its involved narrator, whose sophisticated social conscience (why cure these Depression babies only to return them to a sick society?) contrasts with the nurses' instinctive (but perhaps naïve) humanitarianism. The story's careful structure takes readers from external details--Jean's misshapen body, tiny face, and pale blue eyes--to internal ones--in the postmortem--and so suggests that beneath society's superficial ills lie fundamental, perhaps incurable, troubles. Once again, Williams shows his skill for catching the speech patterns of ordinary Americans, especially in the monologue of Jean's aunt.

Finally, the author's main achievement is to individualize yet not sentimentalize Jean and to dramatize her life-and-death struggle so that it matters to him--and to the reader.

### "A FACE OF STONE"

In "A Face of Stone," the doctor-narrator becomes the main character. A harried family doctor, he finds himself at the end of a busy morning confronted by a young Jewish couple. The husband, one of "the presuming poor," insists that he examine their baby, while the wife maintains an expressionless, stony face. As the doctor approaches the baby boy, his mother clutches him closer and is extremely reluctant to relinquish him. Frustrated and tired, the doctor is brusque and patronizing. When he eventually looks at the child, he discovers that it is quite healthy. During the winter, the people request a house call, but he refuses to go; then, in the spring, they return and still protest that the child is unwell. Conquering his annoyance at their persistence, the family doctor checks the boy and says that he simply needs to be fed regularly and weaned. Now the physician expects the consultation to finish, but the young Jew asks him to examine his wife. The doctor is by this time exhausted and furious; however, he starts to check this passive, poverty-stricken, physically unattractive woman. Then, almost accidentally, he discovers she is a Polish Jew who has lost her whole family. Immediately, he forgets her ugliness, grasps her intense anxiety for her baby, and realizes the strong bond between wife and husband: "Suddenly I understood his half shameful love for the woman and at the same time the extent of her reliance on him. I was touched." The woman smiles for the first time when the doctor prescribes painkillers for her varicose veins and she senses that she can trust him.

This story effectively dramatizes the shifting reactions between patients and doctors as they try to establish a viable relationship. Often, a physician may exploit his position of power (as this one does at the beginning) and forget that his clients are human. If he does, he turns into Doc Rivers at his worst. The best relationship occurs when both parties move beyond stereotypes to view each other as individuals. Because the doctor narrates the tale, the reader follows his process of discovery, so when he stops stereotyping the couple, the reader does too. Williams once again successfully uses dialogue to convey character interaction. Also, as in "Jean Beicke," he reveals people through detail, such as the woman's ripped dress, bowlegs, and high-heeled, worn-out shoes.

### "THE FARMERS' DAUGHTERS"

Williams composed few notable short stories after *Life Along the Passaic River*, mainly because he diverted his energies into longer projects, such as novels, plays, and *Paterson*. From the early 1940's to the mid-1950's, however, he worked on a long short story which he eventually called "The Farmers' Daughters," and whose title he used for his collected short fiction. The title characters are Helen and Margaret, two southern women who have been, and continue to be, betrayed by their men. Their similar background and experience form the basis of an enduring, unshakable friendship that terminates only with Margaret's death. Technically, this is one of Williams's best stories: It unfolds quickly in a "paragraph technique" as the narrator--once more a doctor--re-creates the women's conversations and letters, then links them chronologically with his own comments. The teller refers to himself in the third person, so that most of the time the story progresses through dialogue. This extract, in which Margaret and the doctor chat, illustrates the strength of using direct, idiomatic speech:

> What's your favorite flower, Margaret?
> Why?
> I just want to know.
> What's yours?
>
> No. Come on--don't be so quick on the trigger so early in the evening. I think I can guess. Petunias! (emphasizing the second syllable.) God knows I've seen enough of them. No. Red roses. Those are really what I love.

Unlike Williams's previous stories, "The Farmers' Daughters" relies on complex character depiction and development rather than on plot or theme.

Most short-story writers merely write, but Williams left behind theoretical as well as practical evidence of his interest in the genre. *A Beginning on the Short Story: Notes* (1950) outlines his basic tenets:

truthfulness, unsentimentality, and simplicity. "The finest short stories," he states, "are those that raise . . . one particular man or woman, from that Gehenna, the newspapers, where at last all men are equal, to the distinction of being an individual." From the herd of humanity, Williams succeeds in individualizing Doc Rivers, little Jean Beicke, the Jewish couple, Margaret, Helen, and all his various doctor-narrators.

## Other major works

LONG FICTION: *The Great American Novel*, 1923; *A Voyage to Pagany*, 1928; *White Mule*, 1937; *In the Money*, 1940; *The Build-Up*, 1952.

PLAYS: *A Dream of Love*, pb. 1948; *Many Loves, and Other Plays*, pb. 1961.

POETRY: *Poems*, 1909; *The Tempers*, 1913; *Al Que Quiere!*, 1917; *Kora in Hell: Improvisations*, 1920; *Sour Grapes*, 1921; *Spring and All*, 1923; *Last Nights of Paris*, 1929 (translation of Philippe Soupault; with Elena Williams); *Collected Poems, 1921-1931*, 1934; *An Early Martyr, and Other Poems*, 1935; *Adam and Eve and the City*, 1936; *The Complete Collected Poems of William Carlos Williams, 1906-1938*, 1938; *The Broken Span*, 1941; *The Wedge*, 1944; *Paterson*, 1946-1958; *The Clouds*, 1948; *Selected Poems*, 1949; *A Beginning on the Short Story: Notes* (1950); *Collected Later Poems*, 1950, 1963; *Collected Earlier Poems*, 1951; *A Dog and the Fever*, 1954 (translation of Pedro Espinosa; with Elena Williams); *The Desert Music, and Other Poems*, 1954; *Journey to Love*, 1955; *Pictures from Brueghel*, 1962; *Selected Poems*, 1985; *The Collected Poems of William Carlos Williams: Volume I, 1909-1939*, 1986; *The Collected Poems of William Carlos Williams: Volume II, 1939-1962*, 1988; *Selected Poems*, 2004 (Robert Pinsky, editor).

NONFICTION: *In the American Grain*, 1925; *A Novelette, and Other Prose*, 1932; *The Autobiography of William Carlos Williams*, 1951; *Selected Essays of William Carlos Williams*, 1954; *The Selected Letters of William Carlos Williams*, 1957; *I Wanted to Write a Poem: The Autobiography of the Works of a Poet*, 1958; *The Embodiment of Knowledge*, 1974; *A Recognizable Image*, 1978; *William Carlos Williams, John Sanford: A Correspondence*, 1984; *William Carlos Williams and James Laughlin: Selected Letters*, 1989;

*Pound/Williams: Selected Letters of Ezra Pound and William Carlos Williams*, 1996 (Hugh Witemeyer, editor); *The Correspondence of William Carlos Williams and Louis Zukofsky*, 2003 (Barry Ahearn, editor); *The Humane Particulars: The Collected Letters of William Carlos Williams and Kenneth Burke*, 2003 (James H. East, editor); *The Letters of William Carlos Williams to Edgar Irving Williams, 1902-1912*, 2009 (Andrew J. Krivak, editor).

TRANSLATIONS: *Last Nights of Paris*, 1929 (of Philippe Soupault; with Raquel Hélène Williams); *A Dog and the Fever*, 1954 (of Francisco de Quevedo; with Raquel Hélène Williams).

MISCELLANEOUS: *The Descent of Winter*, 1928 (includes poetry, prose, and anecdotes); *Imaginations*, 1970 (includes poetry, fiction, and nonfiction).

## Bibliography

Copestake, Ian D., ed. *Rigor of Beauty: Essays in Commemoration of William Carlos Williams*. New York: Peter Lang, 2004. Collection of essays about Williams's work, including discussions of Williams's faith in art, his photography, his poetry, his plays, and his fiction about working-class Americans. Peter Halter's essay examines "The Hidden Artistry of Williams's 'Doctor Stories.'"

Dietrich, R. F. "Connotations of Rape in 'The Use of Force.'" *Studies in Short Fiction* 3 (Summer, 1966): 446-450. Argues that the language of the story suggests a sexual encounter: The wooden spatula is a phallic symbol; the girl's bleeding is a violation; the idea of its being a pleasure to attack her suggests rape. Contends that the sexual connotations suggest the savagery of human nature that lies close to the surface.

Entin, Joseph B. "William Carlos William's Short Fiction and the Bodies of New Immigrants." In *Sensational Modernism: Experimental Fiction and Photography in Thirties America*. Chapel Hill: University of North Carolina Press, 2007. Examines Williams's depiction of the "new immigrants" who lived in the neighborhoods where he worked as a physician. Entin argues that Williams's stories show a "pervasive anxiety" about these immigrants, as well as a sense that they may represent a "truth" that "extends "far beyond the bounds of class, ethnicity, and gender" that separate Williams from them.

Gelfant, Blanche H., ed. *The Columbia Companion to the Twentieth-Century American Short Story*. New York: Columbia University Press, 2000. Includes a chapter in which Williams's short stories are analyzed.

Gish, Robert. *William Carlos Williams: A Study of the Short Fiction*. Boston: Twayne, 1989. A fine single-volume study of Williams's substantial contributions to the short story and the essay.

Kenner, Hugh. *A Homemade World: The American Modernist Writers*. New York: Alfred A. Knopf, 1975. A useful introduction to Williams and his work. Establishes the author's significance within the milieu of his fellow modernist writers.

Paul, Sherman. *The Music of Survival: A Biography of a Poem by William Carlos Williams*. Urbana: University of Illinois Press, 1968. One of the best introductory monographs on Williams's poem "The Desert Music." This volume is useful because it lucidly examines Williams's poetic methods, which he also used in his prose.

Sayre, Henry M. *The Visual Text of William Carlos Williams*. Urbana: University of Illinois Press, 1983. Sayre ably demonstrates the influence that modernist painters and photographers had on Williams's poetry and prose, and he examines the visual effects of the graphic presentation of Williams's poetry on the printed page.

Wagner, Linda W. "Williams' 'The Use of Force': An Expansion." *Studies in Short Fiction* 4 (Summer, 1967): 351-353. Disagrees with the rape interpretation of the story, arguing that nothing could be further from the doctor's intention and that his use of force can be attributed to other reasons.

Whitaker, Thomas R. *William Carlos Williams*. 1964. Rev. ed. Boston: Twayne, 1989. Whitaker's discussion of the short stories in Chapter 6 of this general introduction to Williams's life and art focuses primarily on the stories in *The Knife of the Times*. Whitaker provides a brief discussion of the oral style of these stories and the transformation of their anecdotal core.

*Kathryn Zabelle Derounian*
*Updated by William E. Grim*

# LARRY WOIWODE

**Born:** Carrington, North Dakota; October 30, 1941

PRINCIPAL SHORT FICTION

*The Neumiller Stories,* 1989
*Silent Passengers: Stories,* 1993

OTHER LITERARY FORMS

For the most part, Larry Woiwode (WI-wood-ee) is a writer of fiction, primarily the novel. His several novels, which have received critical acclaim, are closely related to his short stories in style, setting, and characters. He has also written poetry and the nonfiction works *Acts* (1993), *Aristocrat of the West: The Story of Harold Schafer* (2000), *What I Think I Did: A Season of Survival in Two Acts* (2000), *My Dinner with Auden* (2006), and *A Step from Death: A Memoir* (2008).

ACHIEVEMENTS

In 1970, Larry Woiwode received the William Faulkner Foundation First Novel Award and a notable book award from the American Library Association for *What I'm Going to Do, I Think* (1969). He received a John Simon Guggenheim Memorial Foundation Fellowship (1971-1972), and in 1976 his novel *Beyond the Bedroom Wall: A Family Album* (1975) was a finalist for both the National Book Award and the National Book Critics Circle Award and won the award in fiction from the Friends of American Writers. North Dakota State University awarded him an honorary doctorate in 1977; in 1977 and 1978, he received Bush Foundation Fellowships. In 1980 Woiwode won an Ernest Hemingway Foundation Award and that same year received an award in fiction from the American Academy of Arts and Letters.

BIOGRAPHY

Larry Alfred Woiwode was born on October 30, 1941, in Carrington, North Dakota, and grew up in nearby Sykestown. His father, Everett Woiwode, taught high school English, and when Woiwode was ten, his father moved the family to Manito, Illinois. In high school, Woiwode wrote poems for a local newspaper, and while attending the University of Illinois at Urbana-Champaign (1959-1964), he continued his writing, was published often, won some writing prizes, and earned an associate degree in rhetoric. After leaving college, he worked briefly in Florida with a theatrical company before moving to New York, where he began his professional writing career.

According to Woiwode, William Maxwell, an editor for *The New Yorker*, was responsible for shifting his writing from what he calls "postmodernism" to a concern for an authentic voice, one rooted in his past. At Maxwell's urging, he became a freelance writer and published stories and poems in such journals as *The Atlantic Monthly, The New Yorker*, and *Harper's*. Four of those stories formed the nucleus of *What I'm Going to Do, I Think*, his first novel. He spent 1973 and 1974 as writer-in-residence at the University of Wisconsin. *Beyond the Bedroom Wall: A Family Album*, his second novel, features narrative shifts, unconventional, nonliterary material, and many Neumiller characters. It, too, received critical acclaim.

Before he continued the Neumiller saga in *Born Brothers* (1988), he wrote two other books: *Even Tide* (1977), a collection of poems, and *Poppa John* (1981), an atypical Woiwode novel about the plight of an elderly, out-of-work soap opera actor. Both works reflect Woiwode's deepening religious faith. Woiwode, reared as a Roman Catholic, and his wife joined the Orthodox Presbyterian church in 1977, and his writing has continued to focus on religious issues and to employ Christian symbols, allusions, and myths. His novel *Born Brothers* (1988), in fact, is a conscious reworking of the Jacob and Esau story with an overlay of the Cain and Abel tale. After deciding that New York was not the place for family life, Woiwode and his family lived, by his admission, in about ten states before settling on a ranch in North Dakota.

## ANALYSIS

Larry Woiwode has used his life and his North Dakota and Illinois childhood to create a series of fictional autobiographical works, rooted in a narrowly circumscribed region peopled by a family that spans several generations. Like his southern counterparts William Faulkner and Flannery O'Connor, he is a regionalist whose depiction of his characters' values, religion, and family transcends the immediate and topical because his themes--memory, death, guilt, identity--are universal. Even when his characters leave the Midwest, they take those values with them, and the clash of those values with more urban ones is at the root of some of Woiwode's best fiction. That fiction is expressed in a style that encompasses shifting points of view and the inclusion of materials, such as diaries, letters, lists, and prose, creating a sense of a prose photograph, an image caught in time.

### THE NEUMILLER STORIES

Woiwode's short fiction has appeared in a number of magazines, most notably *The New Yorker*, where he received the encouragement and guidance of editor William Maxwell. After the stories' publication, many of them were revised and included in *Beyond the Bedroom Wall: A Family Album*, a long, multigenerational novel that resembles an album, or scrapbook, because it contains lists, diaries, and descriptions of photographs, the last a recurrent motif in his fiction. The sprawling nature of his novel accommodated the altered Neumiller stories, which were reworked again for their appearance in *The Neumiller Stories*.

Although *The Neumiller Stories* is divided into three parts representing three phases of Woiwode's literary career (1964-1967, 1968-1972, and 1982-1989), the collection seems unified in character, setting, and theme. While the stories do not progress sequentially from the first North Dakota Neumillers to the last, there is novellike development, with flashbacks, and the last three stories focus on the latest Neumillers. Moreover,

the collection begins and ends with a male attempting to deal with the death of Alpha Neumiller, who serves as the center of the collection of stories--the date of her death becomes the point from which the time and setting of each story is measured and located.

"Deathless Lovers," the first story, occurs within a year of Alpha's death and concerns a brief conversation between an unnamed boy, probably Jerome, and his grandmother. Unlike the rest of the stories, it is written in the present tense, a literary device Woiwode used in his early stories but soon abandoned because of its limits. In this six-page story, the present tense is workable and appropriate because it suggests the temporary suspension of time, the sense of the snapshot, the moment not to be forgotten. Even though the boy is with his maternal grandmother, his thoughts are of his mother.

Half the story concerns the turbulent relationship between the grandmother and grandfather, which the boy accurately perceives as love because of the "so, so" she croons to her invalid husband. Her love for the boy is not stated but is reflected in her "so, so" assurance to the boy as she takes him in her arms. The smell of her dress is "a smell he will remember in its layers of detail . . . whenever he loves a woman, fears that he'll lose her, and his love becomes so smothering and possessive that she runs from him." The grandmother is the mother, who in turn becomes all women he loves and fears losing, and that fear is encapsulated in his memory as a moment, a smell that will recur throughout his life.

A nine-year-old serves as the first-person narrator of "Beyond the Bedroom Wall," which concerns his perception of the events surrounding Alpha's death. One of Woiwode's literary strengths is his ability to capture a child's thoughts, apprehensions, and sense of isolation. In this story, Jerome's physical isolation in his windowless bedroom mirrors his isolation from the adult world. The "wall" is both physical and emotional. After dreaming about being unable to follow his mother, Jerome wakes to find a "wall" on the wrong side of his bed: "If there was a wall where I was convinced there was none, I couldn't imagine what waited for me in that emptiness where the wall should be." Jerome senses the "emptiness" is his mother's death, which has yet to happen but which will always stay with him.

In both "The Visitation" and "Pheasants," memory is associated, metaphorically and literally, with a photograph. Through a metaphorical photograph, the visit by Jerome's uncles becomes a "visitation" as Conrad, Elling, and Alpha become spirits: "As if he were viewing a photograph that had been snapped of them at that moment, and began receding into his mind . . . retreating like spirits he had taken by surprise." In "Pheasants," Alpha's memory of "her mother's favorite photograph of her, taken when she was a child of five or six" is juxtaposed with her current situation as hopes are juxtaposed to reality. What might have been, symbolized by the attractive neighbor, differs from what is and makes her "capable of doing serious harm to her sons," the physical manifestations of her constricted situation.

"The Beginning of Grief," which ends the first part of Woiwode's book, also uses optical imagery to describe the diminished world in which Martin, Alpha's husband, lives after her death, "imprisoned within the sphere of his eye." Alpha, "at the periphery of every thought," lives on in the gestures and "averted eyes" of their children, who also attempt, with varying degrees of success, to cope with their mother's death. In this story, Woiwode shifts the focus from Jerome to Charles, the second son, whose bad behavior is caused by Alpha's death. Martin, who seems unaware that he, too, is affected by his wife's death, loses control and kicks Charles, but the two are eventually reconciled--not verbally, for both are incapable of expressing their feelings in words, but physically, through reaching out to each other.

The second five stories, written between 1968 and 1972, are more varied, though family history links them together. "The Suitor" recounts Martin's proposal to Alpha in 1939; "Pneumonia," interesting because of a dramatic shift in point of view, concerns their son Charles's narrow escape from death. While "The Old Halvorson Place" is also about Martin, Alpha, and their family, it incorporates not only the Neumiller saga but also a history of the house, which Alpha realizes is not really theirs. As in "Beyond the Bedroom Wall," the house seems alive, throbbing with memories that impinge on the lives and actions of the children. From the start, the attic is off limits to the children, who nevertheless play there, thereby tampering "with the heart of the house." While the rest of the house "was becoming Alpha's," the "heart" of the house is not hers. When Father James Russell, whose family had also lived at the Halvorson Place, appears to tell her about his family's life there, Alpha is defeated: "now the Russells, as well as the Halvorsons, would always occupy a part of their house."

The past also lives on in "Marie," a story told from the perspective of Martin and Alpha's older daughter, who has unconsciously assumed her dead mother's role. Her borrowed identity is threatened by Laura, a widow Martin will soon marry. As she reviews the family situation at the Christmas holidays, Marie turns to the favorite photograph of her mother and prays, "Oh, Mom, come back, come back." She looks at the family album but finds that the "pattern had been lost." Marie wants to preserve the status quo, to keep things the way they are, and to preserve her identity: "I was just starting to find out where I belong in this family." At the end of the story, Marie has so thoroughly identified with her mother that her father's impending marriage is a rejection of her mother and, more significantly, of her.

"Burial," the last of the second five stories, is both a beginning and an end, for it is a flashback containing information about the first North Dakota Neumiller, Otto, and also an account of how Charles, Otto's son, not only buries his father but also comes to terms with the past and closes a chapter of his life. Exhausted and suffering from a hangover, Charles returns to North Dakota to bury his father and make arrangements for his aunt Augustina. After he arrives, he must confront not only his father's dead body, which he prepares for burial, but also the legacy that his father left: a community mistakenly convinced that Otto "owes" them money. In his father's house, he meets his father's "presence": "It was the height of his father. The presence turned a new side in Charles's direction." Only by obeying his father's wishes for burial can the Hamlet-like Charles exorcize his father's ghost and be free.

The last three of *The Neumiller Stories*, written between 1982 and 1989, do form the basis for another of the Neumiller novels. All three involve Charles, Martin, Martin's wife Katherine, Alpha's son, and their life in New York City. Like F. Scott Fitzgerald's protagonist, they are westerners in a corrupt East, where they are "disenfranchised," alienated from others, one another, and themselves. "Firstborn," narrated through Charles's consciousness, depicts him as an egocentric young man who feels trapped into marriage, guilty of the death of his newborn son, and only after the birth of his fourth child "freed into forgiveness" and able to "begin again to see." Charles's forgiveness comes only after his prayer, "Good God, forgive me," and reflects the Christian influence on Woiwode's writing.

"A Brief Fall," which alludes to Katherine's affair, concerns her second pregnancy, but the story is told from her perspective, and the portrait of Charles reveals him as an insecure person using sex to counterbalance his loss of youth. When she meets Robert F. Kennedy, Katherine sees "a picture of the shattering end of his brother, the president, which seemed the end of youth, and of Charles." At the end of the story, however, a waiting Katherine looks in the mirror, another "frame" like the artist's "frame" that incorporates art and perhaps reality, and sees "a new and untraceable geography of weighty beauty."

This upbeat ending is followed by "She," the last of the stories. In it, the first-person narrator is a writer who tells a story within the story itself. Using Estrelaria, an Indian from Guatemala, he returns again to his mother's death: "These incidents began to interconnect . . . because of my mother." At the end of the story, the narrator reflects on the emotional and geographical identification between land, mother, and (the last words of the book) "my wife." Thus, it is the mother's "legacy" that enables Charles to persevere, that allows him to structure experience, and that provides Woiwode with a center for his multigenerational fictional world.

### SILENT PASSENGERS

In *Silent Passengers* Woiwode abandons the Neumillers and focuses on new characters, though they live in familiar Woiwode territory and reenact parent-child relationships and memories. "Confessionals," the only spiritually explicit story, is a first-person account of a person's, probably Woiwode's, conversion from Catholicism to Protestantism, though the narrator uses the Abraham and Isaac story to identify himself as the sacrificial son waiting for the father's redemption. In "Owen's Father," the son's glimpse of his father's fifteen-year-old passport forces him to relive the events surrounding his father's suicide and to move from identifying with his father to discovering his own identity. By comparing the son's insights with the bare-bones newspaper account of the father's death, Woiwode shows the reader how reliving or rethinking the past can free one from that past.

In "Black Winter," a retired and weary professor returns to his family home to manual, rather than intellectual, labor and reexamines his childhood. At the end of the story he is "past the pale of existence," where he discovers, with the aid of a "presence as powerful as his father," that he had "subverted" his childhood by assuming that his father did not care "one whit" what he did. A similar reworking of the past occurs in "Summer Storms," in which the narrator, a writer like Woiwode (in fact, in these stories the traditional distinction between author and narrator seems almost to be obliterated), is reminded of a summer storm that occurred when he was thirteen. Despite a terrible storm, he rides his horse to a birthday party for Siobhan, a flirtatious girl he idolizes. When she discovers that he is the "only damn person here" because of the storm, Siobhan "dismisses" him. However, he comes to realize that her "dismissal" also acknowledges his tenacity and his ability to survive.

Parents in Woiwode's fiction affect their children, but they also learn from them. In "Blindness," Mel's temporary blindness-- a physical infirmity that reminds him of his aging father's limitations-- enables him to see a new world, "the world of his daughter," who now leads him. Similarly, Steiner, the protagonist in "Silent Passengers," is redeemed from his guilt by his injured son, who returns to pet the horse who maimed him. The son, who has a way with "pardon," provides his father with a vision, one of those suspended moments in Woiwode's fiction that promises forgiveness for one of Woiwode's fallen characters.

OTHER MAJOR WORKS

LONG FICTION: *What I'm Going to Do, I Think*, 1969; *Beyond the Bedroom Wall: A Family Album*, 1975; *Poppa John*, 1981; *Born Brothers*, 1988; *Indian Affairs*, 1992.

POETRY: *Poetry North: Five North Dakota Poets*, 1970 (with Richard Lyons, Thomas McGrath, John R. Milton, and Antony Oldknow); *Even Tide*, 1977.

NONFICTION: *Acts*, 1993; *Aristocrat of the West: The Story of Harold Schafer*, 2000; *What I Think I Did: A Season of Survival in Two Acts*, 2000; *My Dinner with Auden*, 2006; *A Step from Death: A Memoir*, 2008.

BIBLIOGRAPHY

Flower, Dean. Review of *The Neumiller Stories*, by Larry Woiwode. *The Hudson Review* 43 (Summer, 1990): 311. Flower's extensive and perceptive review of Woiwode's stories examines the early stories, their alterations in novel form, and their "ungathering," revising, and "unrevising" in *The Neumiller Stories*. For Flower, the stories form a "superb family chronicle," with the three new stories adding new layers to the Neumiller characters. Of particular interest is Flower's comment on the way Woiwode "expands the frame" at the end of the story and leaves his readers with an image that resembles a snapshot, a moment caught in time.

Hansen, Ron. "A Crazy-Making Existence." Review of *A Step from Death: A Memoir*, by Larry Woiwode. *America* 119, no. 4 (August 18, 2008): 26. Hansen's review of Woiwode's memoir provides details about Woiwode's life, including a near-death experience resulting from a "horrific" accident which occurred he was his baling hay.

Moritz, Charles. *Current Biography Yearbook*. New York: H. W. Wilson, 1989. The essay on Woiwode traces his life and literary work to date and reviews critical responses to his novels. For the most part, the novels are discussed in terms of their autobiographical content, especially of the characters, including those who most resemble Woiwode himself. Although it does not contain much criticism about Woiwode's work, this essay is particularly helpful, since it identifies and evaluates the available secondary sources. Includes a bibliography.

Reichard, Mary R., ed. *Encyclopedia of Catholic Literature*. Westport, Conn.: Greenwood Press, 2004. Includes a lengthy essay analyzing the Catholic themes and content of *Beyond the Bedroom Wall*, the novel that was the genesis of *The Neumiller Stories*. Also provides a brief biography of Woiwode, a plot summary, and a discussion of the novel's critical reception.

Siconolfi, Michael T. Review of *The Neumiller Stories*, by Larry Woiwode. *America* 163 (December 1, 1990): 434-435. In this lengthy, informative review, Siconolfi discusses the reworkings of stories as they become parts of novels and then resurface as the short stories in this collection. He maintains that while Woiwode's stories can stand on their own, they also are interrelated "like distant branches of a family tree," an apt comparison since the stories are rooted in family. While Sinconolfi mentions several of the stories, he focuses on Woiwode's gift at working the "nurturing, eternal feminine" and on the novelist's acknowledging of his grandmother's influence.

Tallent, Elizabeth. "Before the Bedroom Wall." Review of *The Neumiller Stories*, by Larry Woiwode. *The New York Times Book Review* (December 17, 1989): 17. Tallent points out that ten of the thirteen stories had appeared before, once in journals and once in revised form, in Woiwode's *Beyond the Bedroom Wall: A Family Album*. In their latest form, the stories seem, to Tallent, to lack some of the immediacy and detail they had in the novel. Her review is of special interest because she notes that Alpha Neumiller's death in childbirth is the pivotal event in the collection and that the collection begins and ends with a boy's, then a man's, projection of Alpha's persona onto another female character.

Woiwode, Larry. Interview by Michele Field. *Publishers Weekly* 234 (August 5, 1988): 67-68. Woiwode discusses his life, his career, and the relationship between biographical fact and fiction.

_____. "An Interview with Larry Woiwode." *Christianity and Literature* 29 (Winter, 1979): 11-18. Woiwode discusses the autobiographical nature of his work, the Jacob/Esau biblical framework of *Born Brothers*, the "mechanics of memory," his religious rebirth, the influence of William Maxwell, and his future writing plans. This frank, informative interview contains a considerable amount of biographical information, most of which is applied to Woiwode's writing, and some perceptive comments about the Christian themes of *Born Brothers*.

_____. "An Interview with Larry Woiwode." Interview by Ed Block, Jr. *Renascence: Essays on Value in Literature* 44 (Fall, 1991): 17-30. Woiwode discusses the writer's task, the importance of his own

family to his work, his current writing projects, his personal life, and his opinion of several young writers.

_____. "The Reforming of a Novelist." Interview by Timothy K. Jones. *Christianity Today* 36 (October 26, 1992): 86-88. In this interview Woiwode discusses his conversion experience, his church service, the role of faith in his writing, and reactions to his books.

*Thomas L. Erskine*

# THOMAS WOLFE

**Born:** Asheville, North Carolina; October 3, 1900
**Died:** Baltimore, Maryland; September 15, 1938

PRINCIPAL SHORT FICTION

*From Death to Morning,* 1935
*The Hills Beyond,* 1941
*The Complete Short Stories of Thomas Wolfe,* 1987

OTHER LITERARY FORMS

While some novelists are failed poets, a tradition that began with Miguel de Cervantes in the early seventeenth century, Thomas Wolfe was a failed playwright. None of his plays was accepted for commercial production. Wolfe is most famous (his fame in the 1930's was international) for his early novels. His first editor unfortunately persuaded him to stay away from the novella or short novel form, and the editor of his posthumous novels essentially pieced them together out of shorter pieces that Wolfe saw as short novels, not as parts of a rambling, protean novel. Hugh Holman's collection of Wolfe's short novels and Richard Kennedy's study of his last editor's stewardship are beginning to establish Wolfe's very real talent for the shorter forms.

The best-known of Wolfe's novels are *Look Homeward, Angel* (1929) and *You Can't Go Home Again* (1940). Wolfe's notebooks are also very informative, not only to scholars but also to young writers interested

in the processes through which a writer refines experience (and Wolfe was more able to do this than his first wave of admirers would admit). It is particularly fascinating to see how the "real" incident that inspired one of the scenes in "Death the Proud Brother" became transformed into that scene.

ACHIEVEMENTS

It can be argued that Thomas Wolfe did not write short stories at all and that his "stories" were only fragments torn from the single great body of his life's work. Even Francis E. Skipp, the editor of *The Complete Short Stories of Thomas Wolfe*, acknowledges that Wolfe or his editors cut and shaped these fragments into discrete units to suit monetary or publishing needs as opportunities presented themselves. Since Wolfe seldom, if ever, seriously applied himself to writing individual stories rather than pieces belonging to the grand epic of his own self-expression, it is unfair to hold him rigorously to the standards of the modern story.

Wolfe's reputation was at one time enormous both at home and abroad. He has often been the writer that young writers read; age and artistic maturity, however, usually dampen that youthful enthusiasm. Although many critics praised his work, a reaction against Wolfe set in even during his lifetime. Among his detractors was Bernard De Voto, who, in a 1936 essay called "Genius Is Not Enough," attacked Wolfe, citing his first two novels as books full of "long, whirling discharges of words, unabsorbed in the novel, unrelated to the proper business of fiction, badly if not altogether unacceptably written. . . ." The controversy continues. Wolfe's real strength, formerly obscured by the hands of his editors, may indeed lie in the novella or short-novel form. Whatever the critical opinion, Wolfe will always have supporters. William Faulkner said,

> My admiration for Wolfe is that . . . he was willing to throw away style, coherence, all the rules of preciseness, to try to put all the experience of the human heart on the head of a pin. . . .

BIOGRAPHY

Thomas Clayton Wolfe was the youngest child of Julia Elizabeth Westall and William Oliver Wolfe, a Pennsylvania mason and stonecutter who went south to find work. One of Wolfe's brothers, Benjamin Harrison Wolfe, died at age eighteen, as does the brother in *Look Homeward, Angel*. Although Wolfe's mother did run a tourist home, The Old Kentucky Home, it is important to remember that his family was very prosperous; one scholar estimates that they were financially in the upper two percent of the town's population. Although this fact does not mean that an affluent adolescent cannot suffer the torments of the damned, it nevertheless somewhat negates the concept of Thomas Wolfe as the poor, suffering, and morbidly sensitive child, which was fashioned by the early members of his literary cult. The Wolfes were German, an unusual ethnic origin in that part of Carolina, where most of the people were Scotch-Irish or English, and they lived in the western, mountain end of North Carolina, which had more in common with east Tennessee, Appalachian Ohio, and mountain Pennsylvania than with eastern North Carolina, the Tidewater of Virginia, or even northern Mississippi (the setting of Faulkner's stories). Both ethnic background and geographic environment are reflected strongly in Wolfe's works.

Wolfe was enrolled at the University of North Carolina at Chapel Hill; at that time it was the university's only campus and was restricted to males during his first two years. He majored in the classics and in English literature, and he began his writing career as a playwright with the Carolina Playmakers. By college age,

Wolfe had achieved his full growth (he was six feet, six inches tall and later, as a slightly older man, weighed two hundred and fifty pounds) and in appearance was a man of epic proportions, as well as epic ambitions. Wolfe went to Harvard University in 1920 to study under George Pierce Baker at the drama workshop; he left Harvard in 1923, after earning an M.A. in English and writing *Welcome to Our City* (pr. 1921, pb. 1970) and *The Mountains* (pr. 1923, pb. only in Germany as *Willkommen in Altamont*, 1962), about a family feud.

From 1924 to 1930 he led a rather unhappy existence as an English instructor at New York University, a private university on Washington Square. He was not able to find a producer for *Welcome to Our City* or *Mannerhouse* (pb. 1948), a play about the Civil War. In 1925, he met Aline Bernstein, and their stormy relationship became the most important one in his short life. Aline Frankau Bernstein was almost twenty years older than Wolfe. When she was still nineteen, she had married a broker, Theodore Bernstein, and became interested in making sets and costumes for her friends in the Neighborhood Playhouse when it was founded in 1915, soon becoming the first woman member of United Scenic Artists. As her biographer says, "without intending to, she rather took the color out of those men at hand." In 1925, she met Wolfe; a relationship developed that Wolfe described as "the met halves of the broken talisman."

In 1926, he went to Europe with Aline and began *Look Homeward, Angel*, with some assistance, both literary and financial, from her. In 1928, after another trip abroad with Aline and a breakup with her, he finished *Look Homeward, Angel*, and Scribner's showed interest in the manuscript. The editor who found Wolfe's gigantic manuscript and who greatly helped him during his early career was Maxwell Perkins. With Perkins's constant help, Wolfe published *Look Homeward, Angel*, which sold fifteen thousand copies and earned for Wolfe about six thousand dollars. Although Wolfe, at this point in his career, wanted to publish two shorter novels, one of which had already been partly set in type, Perkins gave Wolfe what modern scholars conclude was "unfortunate" advice and leadership; he advised him to work on yet another big novel. Upon Perkins's advice, he concentrated on *Of Time and the*

*River: A Legend of Man's Hunger in His Youth* (1935); three years after its publication he died of tuberculosis of the brain, a rare condition that had not immediately been diagnosed. Although he had been working in his last years toward shorter and more controlled stories which used different viewpoint techniques, when he died, Edward C. Aswell at Harper's publishing company gave the public what it wanted: He created the "old" Wolfe by piecing together two more gigantic novels. There is no doubt that Wolfe needed editing and that he placed himself at the mercy of those who edited his works, and the massive amount of material written prior to his death became the basis from which Aswell would create *The Web and the Rock* (1939) and *You Can't Go Home Again* (1940).

### ANALYSIS

Some of Thomas Wolfe's short stories were printed in *The Hills Beyond*, a posthumous volume compiled by Edward C. Aswell after he had published Wolfe's two "novels" of his own creation. The tough-minded old Confederate general of the story "The Dead World Relived" mourns a South ten times as full of frauds after the Civil War as before it; the story is unforgettable and furnishes a much-needed corrective to the myth that southerners in the American literary renaissance of the 1920's and 1930's could hardly wait to start writing about the old colonels.

### "A KINSMAN OF HIS BLOOD"

"A Kinsman of His Blood" is a short, concise, and moving story in its subtly achieved pathos and its nostalgia for what life and history are, rather than for what people might want them to be, and is probably the best story in *The Hills Beyond*. The action takes place entirely in the foreground, and the story is really that of Arthur Pentland, also known from the beginning of the story as Arthur Penn. The viewpoint through which the reader sees Arthur is that of the ubiquitous Eugene Gant; the third character in the story is Eugene's uncle, Bascom Pentland, who appears in *Of Time and the River*. It could be the tale of any three men related to each other; Arthur is the son of Bascom and the only one "who ever visited his father's house; the rest were studiously absent, saw their father only at Christmas or Thanksgiving." Even so, the relation between Bascom and Arthur is "savage and hostile."

*Thomas Wolfe* (Library of Congress)

Arthur is a huge, obese, dirty, disheveled, grubby, distraught man who has trouble speaking clearly and coherently. The reader is told nothing of the history of his problems, or of Eugene's background, and knows only that the conflict is stark, ugly, and dramatic. Some of Arthur's behavior is clearly sociopathic. His table manners are not only embarrassing but also offensive. On one occasion, he tells an anecdote about a Harvard man who climbed into a cage with a gorilla; although the man knew fourteen languages, the gorilla killed him. Arthur's summation of the incident is as frightening as anything in European fiction which tries to depict the mindless, anarchic malevolence of the crazy or the revolutionary.

Arthur decides that his grammar school teacher really loves him; even though the woman ignores his protestations of love, then tries to silence him with rudeness, he persists. He refuses to believe his mother when she tells him the woman does not really care for him, and he storms out "like a creature whipped with furies." Finally, he goes to California to see the woman. Arthur is a pitiful, subnormal, obviously seriously disturbed creature, but frightening in his obesity, his filth, his animal-like inability to understand human beings. The story ends with Eugene, out walking in the rain through the South Boston slums, spotting Arthur as he shuffles along, a bundle of old newspapers under one arm. Eugene, a nice man, is glad to see him and offers to shake his hand. Arthur denies twice that he is Arthur Pentland, then says he is Arthur Penn and screams out in terror, begging Eugene to leave him alone. There is no sentimentality here; this is tragedy, however small and prosaic.

### "NO DOOR"

The only collection of short fiction Wolfe prepared himself and saw through publication was *From Death to Morning*; it contains the stories "No Door" and "Death the Proud Brother."

"No Door" is about a writer and his short acquaintance with "well-kept people who have never been alone in all their life"-- in this case a man who lives in a penthouse near the East River. His home is furnished with several sculptures by Jacob Epstein, rare books and first editions, and a view of Manhattan that displays its "terrific frontal sweep and curtain of starflung towers, now sown with the diamond pollen of a million lights." The writer is told by these people how marvelous it is to live alone with creatures of the slums. Their remarks trigger recollections of the lower depths of stinking, overcrowded, working-class Brooklyn. The writer hangs around, partly amused, partly chagrined, partly in awe of the rich man and his mistress, thinking that *they* may be the ones who will open the door to the life of glamour and ease for which he, as a poor writer, yearns. Even as he hopes, however, he knows it is useless: These creatures are foreign to him. He tells of the agony and senselessness and brutality and sordidness of his existence, and the man and his mistress condescendingly and patronizingly wish his lot were theirs. Finally, at the end of the evening, he returns to Brooklyn and hears two old people discussing the death of a priest, and the story ends on a note of desperation and impotent fury.

The effect of the story depends on the consciousness of the narrator, here appearing in the first person although the reader sees him through the second person, an almost unheard-of viewpoint in English. Wolfe makes his points subtly, the length is a rather modest one for him, his satirical eye is sharp, and the rhetoric meshes with the inner turmoil lying just beneath the surface of conversation. If Wolfe had written more stories like this he might have been one of the giants of the American short story.

### "DEATH THE PROUD BROTHER"

"Death the Proud Brother" is a very long, almost unstructured, twenty-two-thousand-word novella that attempts to present as a unified narrative several unrelated incidents of death and loneliness. Wolfe said of this story, "It represents *important* work to me." The story's thematic unity arises from the narrator's successful unifying of all the incidents within his own consciousness, drawing the world to him, exercising implicit rights of selection, unlike the third-person, omniscient narrators of Wolfe's last novels. This story is a masterpiece in its conjunction of viewpoint and material. Only this viewpoint could master this material, and only disjointed, logically discrete material such as the story presents requires a first-person viewpoint.

There is no plot, but there is some structure. Wolfe describes three violent deaths. The fourth death is that of an old bum on a bench, and it occurs quietly, imperceptibly, anonymously--he is a "cipher." His death, which takes up the bulk of the novella, furnishes Wolfe with a chance to study America. If it is true that everybody talks about America but nobody can find it, then Wolfe came closest in this last movement of the novella, which was his favorite. The story is typically Wolfean in many ways; by the passion and the wise guile of his rhetoric, Wolfe becomes so thoroughly a part of the writing that he, too, becomes a cipher--the transparent narrator. It surely is no accident that the death which moves the narrator so profoundly is the death of an urban Everyman. This is the kind of story, perhaps even the story itself, that caused Faulkner to say that Wolfe had tried to put all of life on the head of a pin.

### OTHER MAJOR WORKS

LONG FICTION: *Look Homeward, Angel*, 1929; *Of Time and the River: A Legend of Man's Hunger in His Youth*, 1935; *The Web and the Rock*, 1939; *You Can't*

*Go Home Again*, 1940; *The Short Novels of Thomas Wolfe*, 1961 (C. Hugh Holman, editor).

PLAY: *The Mountains*, pr. 1921, pb. 1970; *Welcome to Our City*, pr. 1923 (pb. only in Germany as *Willkommen in Altamont*, 1962); *Mannerhouse*, pb. 1948.

POETRY: *The Face of a Nation: Poetical Passages from the Writings of Thomas Wolfe*, 1939; *A Stone, a Leaf, a Door: Poems by Thomas Wolfe*, 1945.

NONFICTION: *The Story of a Novel*, 1936; *Thomas Wolfe's Letters to His Mother*, 1943 (John Skally, editor); *The Portable Thomas Wolfe*, 1946 (Maxwell Geisman, editor); *The Letters of Thomas Wolfe*, 1956 (Elizabeth Nowell, editor); *The Notebooks of Thomas Wolfe*, 1970 (Richard S. Kennedy and Paschal Reeves, editors); *The Thomas Wolfe Reader*, 1982 (C. Hugh Holman, editor); *Beyond Love and Loyalty: The Letters of Thomas Wolfe and Elizabeth Nowell*, 1983 (Kennedy, editor); *My Other Loneliness: Letters of Thomas Wolfe and Aline Bernstein*, 1983 (Suzanne Stutman, editor); *The Autobiography of an American Novelist: Thomas Wolfe*, 1983; *To Loot My Life Clean: The Thomas Wolfe/Maxwell Perkins Correspondence*, 2000 (Matthew J. Bruccoli and Park Bucker, editors); *Windows of the Heart: The Correspondence of Thomas Wolfe and Margaret Roberts*, 2007 (Ted Mitchell, editor); *The Magical Campus: University of North Carolina Writings, 1917-1920*, 2008 (Matthew J. Bruccoli and Aldo P. Magi, editors).

BIBLIOGRAPHY

Bassett, John Earl. *Thomas Wolfe: An Annotated Critical Bibliography*. Lanham, Md.: Scarecrow Press, 1996. A helpful tool for the student of Wolfe. Indexed.

Bentz, Joseph. "The Influence of Modernist Structure in the Short Fiction of Thomas Wolfe." *Studies in Short Fiction* 31 (Spring, 1994): 149-162. Argues that while Wolfe's novels owed much to the nineteenth century novel tradition, his short stories were heavily influenced by the modernism of the 1920's and 1930's. Discusses the nonlinear, open-ended nature of such stories as "No Cure for It" and "The Lost Boy."

Bloom, Harold, ed. *Thomas Wolfe*. New York: Chelsea House, 1987. This collection of critical essays focuses on Wolfe's novels. However, "*The Hills Beyond*: A Folk Novel of America," by Leslie A. Field, analyzes a work of short fiction.

Cash, Wiley. "'The Dark Was Hived with Flesh and Mystery': Thomas Wolfe, the American Adam, and the Polemical Persona of Race." *Thomas Wolfe Review* 30, no. 1/2 (2007): 44-55. Analyzes the depiction of African American characters in Wolfe's fiction, including the novel *Look Homeward, Angel*. Argues that the only fully developed black character in all of Wolf's fiction is Dick Prosser in the short story "The Child by Tiger."

Donald, David Herbert. *Look Homeward: A Life of Thomas Wolfe*. 1987. Reprint. Cambridge, Mass.: Harvard University Press, 2003. Donald's painstakingly thorough examination of the huge volume of Wolfe's papers, including the published and unpublished manuscripts, and of Wolfe criticism has produced a work that, in its scope, depth, and readability, makes it the essential biography, replacing such earlier works as Elizabeth Nowell's *Thomas Wolfe: A Biography* (1960) and Andrew Turnbull's *Thomas Wolfe* (1968). A distinguished historian, Donald is on less solid ground when he ventures into the more literary concerns of interpretation and criticism. The questions surrounding the roles of Wolfe's editors and the legitimacy of the published texts are explored if not resolved. Contains exhaustive notes but no formal bibliography.

Field, Leslie A., ed. *Thomas Wolfe: Three Decades of Criticism*. New York: New York University Press, 1968. This collection contains landmark essays by many of the most important people in the field of Wolfe criticism. These essays discuss the central issues and reveal the range of critical response provoked by Wolfe's work, from its first publication through the mid-1960's.

Idol, John Lane, Jr. *A Thomas Wolfe Companion*. New York: Greenwood Press, 1987. An expression of the resurgence of interest in Wolfe by an unabashed devotee, this handy book is a potpourri of Wolfeana with glossaries of characters and places, genealogical charts of Wolfe's fictional families, a descriptive and "analytic" bibliography of primary works, and an annotated bibliography of secondary materials. Also contains information on the various collections of Wolfe material, the Thomas Wolfe Society, and the *Thomas Wolfe Review*.

Johnston, Carol Ingalls. *Of Time and the Artist: Thomas Wolfe, His Novels, and the Critics*. Columbia, S.C.: Camden House, 1996. Looks at Wolfe's autobiographical fiction and the critical response to it.

McElderry, Bruce R. *Thomas Wolfe*. New York: Twayne, 1964. An excellent basic introduction to Wolfe's life and work, McElderry's study provides lucid analysis well supported by standard critical opinion, including a chapter on the shorter fiction. Contains a useful chronology and annotated select bibliographies of primary and secondary sources.

Meindl, Dieter. "Thomas Wolfe and Germany: Modernism and Anti-Anti-Semitism in 'Dark in the Forest, Strange as Time' and 'I Have a Thing to Tell You.'" *Thomas Wolfe Review* 33, no. 1/2 (2009): 6-23. Analyzes the two short stories "Dark in the Forest, Strange as Time" and "I Have a Thing to Tell You," both of which depict Wolfe's interest in Germany after he realized the evils of Nazism. Describes how both stories feature as a major character a German Jew who will be affected by the rise of Nazism. Discusses the use of symbolism and mystery in the stories and the prophetic nature of their narratives.

Mills, Jerry Leath. "The Dark Side of the Tracks in Thomas Wolfe's 'The Bums at Sunset.'" *Thomas Wolfe Review* 27, no. 1/2 (2003): 14-21. Analyzes the short story "The Bums at Sunset," focusing on Wolfe's use of music in his writing. Mills argues that musical allusion is a thematic device that leads readers to understand the meaning of the story.

Mitchell, Ted, ed. *Thomas Wolfe: An Illustrated Biography*. New York: Pegasus Books, 2006. Features extracts from Wolfe's correspondence, manuscripts, and notebooks that are used to document his career and literary reputation. One of the chapters provides information about *From Death to Morning*.

Phillipson, John S., ed. *Critical Essays on Thomas Wolfe*. Boston: G. K. Hall, 1985. Contains twenty-three essays, most formerly published, written between 1970 and the early 1980's. Arranged by genre, the book contains seven essays on Wolfe's short fiction.

Scotchie, Joseph, and Ralph Roberts. *Thomas Wolfe Revisited*. Alexander, N.C.: Land of the Sky Books, 2001. A study of Wolfe's works, including several short stories.

*John Carr*
*Updated by Douglas Rollins*

# TOBIAS WOLFF

**Born:** Birmingham, Alabama; June 19, 1945

PRINCIPAL SHORT FICTION

*In the Garden of the North American Martyrs,* 1981
*Back in the World,* 1985
*The Stories of Tobias Wolff,* 1988
*The Night in Question,* 1996
*Our Story Begins: New and Selected Stories,* 2008

OTHER LITERARY FORMS

Besides short stories, Tobias Wolff (toh-BI-uhs woolf) has published a novella, *The Barracks Thief* (1984), and a memoir, *This Boy's Life* (1989). He also edited short-story anthologies, including *The Best American Short Stories, 1994* (1994) and *A Doctor's Visit: Short Stories* (1988), which collected those of Anton Chekhov. Wolff published the novel *Old School* in 2003.

ACHIEVEMENTS

The quality of his work has earned for Tobias Wolff much critical respect and numerous literary prizes. He received a Wallace Stegner Fellowship in 1975-1976 to study creative writing at Stanford University, and even before he published his first book, he won creative writing grants from the National Endowment for the Arts (1978, 1985), a Mary Roberts Rinehart grant (1979), and an Arizona Council on the Arts and Humanities fellowship in creative writing (1980). He has also won several O. Henry Awards (1980, 1981, and 1985) and a John Simon Guggenheim Memorial Foundation Fellowship (1982). Wolff's *In the Garden of the North American Martyrs* received the St. Lawrence Award for Fiction (1982), his *The Barracks Thief* (1984) took the PEN/Faulkner Award for Fiction (1985), and he won the Rea Award for short stories (1989). His *This Boy's Life: A Memoir* (1989) won the

*Los Angeles Times* book prize for biography and the Ambassador Book Award of the English-Speaking Union and was a finalist for the National Book Critics Circle Award. *In Pharaoh's Army: Memories of the Lost War* (1994) won *Esquire*-Volvo-Waterstone's Prize for Nonfiction and was a finalist for both the National Book Award (1994) and *The Los Angeles Times* Book Award for biography (1995). He has also received a Whiting Foundation Award (1990), a Lila Wallace-*Reader's Digest* Award (1994), and a Lyndhurst Foundation Award (1994). *Old School* was nominated for a National Books Critics Circle Award for Fiction. He won the 2009 Story Prize for *Our Story Begins*.

BIOGRAPHY

Readers are lucky to have two prime sources that deal with Tobias Jonathan Ansell Wolff's parents and his early life: Wolff's memoir and a recollection of his father entitled *The Duke of Deception: Memories of My Father* (1979), written by Wolff's older brother, the novelist Geoffrey Wolff. Together, these works portray a remarkable family, though Rosemary Loftus, Wolff's mother, wryly observed that, had she known so much was going to be told, she might have watched herself more closely.

The one who bore watching, however, was Wolff's inventive father, a genial Jay Gatsby-like figure who, in pursuit of the good life, forged checks, credentials, and his own identity. He began as Arthur Samuels Wolff, a Jewish doctor's son and boarding-school expellee. Later he emerged as Arthur Saunders Wolff, an Episcopalian and a Yale University graduate. A still later reincarnation was as Saunders Ansell-Wolff III. On the basis of forged credentials, he became an aeronautical engineer and rose to occupy an executive suite. During his time, however, he also occupied a number of jail cells. Still, he showed remarkable creativity in his fabrications, so perhaps it is not surprising that both his sons became writers of fiction. Family life with him was something of a roller coaster, exciting but with many ups and downs. Eventually, this instability led to the family's breakup in 1951: Twelve-year-old Geoffrey remained with the father, while the mother took five-year-old Tobias, who had been born June 19, 1945, in Birmingham, Alabama, one of several locations where the family had chased the American dream. Henceforth reared separately, sometimes a country apart, the two boys were not reunited until Geoffrey's final year at Princeton University.

Meanwhile, Tobias Wolff and his mother lived first in Florida, then in Utah, and finally in the Pacific Northwest, where his mother remarried. The stays in Utah and the Pacific Northwest are recounted in *This Boy's Life*, which covers Wolff's life from the age of ten until he left for Hill School in Pottstown, Pennsylvania (where he faked his references to be accepted). He attended Hill School for a time but did not graduate and ended up joining the military. From 1964 to 1968, Wolff served in the U.S. Army Special Forces and toured Vietnam as an adviser to a South Vietnamese unit, experiences he recounted in his second volume of memoirs, *In Pharaoh's Army*. After this service, deterred by the antiwar movement in the United States, he traveled to England, where he enrolled at Oxford University. He received a B.A., with first-class honors, from Oxford University in 1972.

Returning to the United States, Wolff worked first as a reporter for *The Washington Post*, then at various restaurant jobs in California, and finally entered the Stanford University creative-writing program. He received an M.A. from Stanford in 1978. While at Stanford, he met and became friends with other writers, including Raymond Carver, and taught for a period of time. While pursuing his own writing, Wolff has taught creative writing at Goddard College, Arizona State University, and Syracuse University. In 1975, he married Catherine Dolores Spohn, a teacher and social worker; they had two sons, Michael and Patrick. In 1997, he joined the Humanities faculty at Stanford University, teaching literature and writing.

ANALYSIS

Tobias Wolff is an outstanding contemporary craftsman of the American short story. Working slowly, sometimes taking months and countless drafts, he polishes each story into an entertaining, gemlike work that reads with deceptive ease. He has said, in interviews, that he needs time to get to know his characters but that the finished story no longer holds any surprises for him. For the reader, the result is full of surprises, insights, humor, and other line-by-line rewards, particularly in character portrayal and style. The influences on his work--by his friend Carver and early masters such as Guy de Maupassant, Anton Chekhov, Sherwood Anderson, Ernest Hemingway, and Flannery O'Connor--indicate the company Wolff intends to keep.

No overriding theme, message, or agenda seems to unite Wolff's work--only his interest in people, their quirks, their unpredictability, their strivings and failings, and their predicaments as human beings. Despite their dishonesty and drug use, most of his characters fall within the range of a shaky middle-class respectability or what passes for it in contemporary America. Although most of them do not hope for much, many still have trouble separating their fantasies from reality. Despite their dried-up souls, vague remnants of Judeo-Christian morality still rattle around inside their ribcages, haunting them with the specter of moral choice (Wolff is a Catholic). It is perhaps emblematic that a considerable amount of action in his stories occurs inside automobiles hurtling across the landscape (except when they break down or fly off the road).

Wolff has called his stories autobiographical (just as his memoirs are somewhat fictionalized), but this seems true only in a broad sense. He goes on to say that many of his characters reflect aspects of himself and that he sometimes makes use of actual events. According to Wolff, "The Liar" mirrors himself as a child: The story is about a boy who reacts to his father's death by becoming a pathological liar. A story that appears to make use of an actual event is "The Missing Person," about a priest who, to impress his drinking buddy, fabricates a story about killing a man with his bare hands. Before he knows it, the buddy has spread the news to the nuns. Wolff related a similar story about himself in an *Esquire* magazine article ("Raymond Carver Had

His Cake and Ate It Too," September, 1989), recalling his friend Carver after Carver's death from cancer. In a tale-swapping competition with Carver, known for his bouts with alcohol, Wolff bested his friend by fabricating a story about being addicted to heroin; aghast, Carver repeated the story, and people began regarding Wolff with pity and sorrow.

### IN THE GARDEN OF THE NORTH AMERICAN MARTYRS

Wolff's patented ending is an updated open version of O. Henry's surprise ending, which wrapped things up with a plot twist. Wolff's endings are usually accomplished with a modulation of style, a sudden opening out into revelation, humor, irony, symbolism, or lyricism. Such an ending is illustrated by "Next Door," the first story of *In the Garden of the North American Martyrs*. A quiet couple are scandalized by the goings-on next door, where everybody screams and fights and the husband and wife make love standing up against the refrigerator. To drown out these raucous neighbors, the couple turns up the volume on the television, goes to bed, and watches the film *El Dorado* (1966). Lying next to his wife, the husband becomes sexually aroused, but she is unresponsive. The seemingly uneventful story ends when the husband suddenly imagines how he would rewrite the film--an ambiguous ending that suggests both his desire for some of the lusty, disorderly life next door (and in the film) and the quiet, passionless fate that he is probably doomed to endure.

The next story, "Hunters in the Snow," perhaps Wolff's best, is much more eventful and has an unforgettable ending. The story is set in the wintry fields of the Northwest, where three deer hunters, supposedly old buddies, rib one another and play practical jokes. The ringleader, Kenny, who is driving his old truck, is unmerciful to Frank and especially to Tub. Tub, however, wreaks a terrible revenge when one of Kenny's practical jokes backfires and, through a misunderstanding, Tub shoots him, inflicting a gruesome gut wound. Frank and Tub throw Kenny into the back of the pickup truck and head off over unfamiliar country roads for the hospital fifty miles away. After a while, Frank and Tub become cold from the snow blowing through a hole in the windshield and stop at a tavern for a beer, where they strike up a sympathetic conversation with each other. Leaving the directions to the hospital on the table, they hit the road again. A little farther on, Frank and Tub have to stop at the next tavern for another beer and, this time, a warm meal. Self-absorbed, they continue their discoveries that they have much in common and become real pals. Meanwhile, Kenny is cooling in the back of the truck, and the story ends when they get under way again:

> As the truck twisted through the gentle hills the star went back and forth between Kenny's boots, staying always in his sight. "I'm going to the hospital," Kenny said. But he was wrong. They had taken a different turn a long way back.

The title story, "In the Garden of the North American Martyrs," shows that academics can be just as cruel as hunters (or, in this case, the Iroquois Indians). The story's protagonist is Mary, a mousy historian who has a terrible teaching job at a college in the rainy Northwest. She is invited by her friend Louise--who is a member of the history faculty of a posh college in upstate New York, Iroquois country--to

*Tobias Wolff* (AP Photo/John Todd)

interview for a job opening there. When Mary arrives on campus, she finds that she has been cruelly exploited: The interview was only a setup to fulfill a college requirement that a woman be interviewed for every job opening. As the story ends, Mary changes the topic of her demonstration lecture and--before horrified faculty and students assembled in the college's modernized version of the long house--delivers a grisly account of how the Iroquois "took scalps and practiced cannibalism and slavery" and "tortured their captives."

Two other memorable stories in Wolff's first collection explore the bittersweet possibilities of relationships that never come to fruition. In "Passenger," the strictly behaved protagonist Glen is conned into giving a ride to the aging flower child Bonnie and her dog Sunshine. They become a working unit in the car, like an informal but close-knit family, and the reader sees that they are good for each other but realizes that the relationship probably would not last much longer than the day's journey. That probability is symbolized by a hair-raising incident along the way, when the dog leaps on the driver, Glen, causing the car to go spinning down the wet highway out of control. In "Poaching," a real family gets together again, briefly: A divorced woman visits her former husband and their small son. It is clear that husband and wife should reunite for their own good and the good of the child, but neither will make the first move--even though they sleep together in the same bed. The state of their relationship is symbolized by an old beaver who tries to build his lodge in a pond on the property and is quickly shot.

### BACK IN THE WORLD

The stories in *Back in the World*, Wolff's second collection, are not quite as finished as the ones in his first but include several worth noting. The title is a phrase used by American soldiers in Vietnam to refer to home. Ironically, from Wolff's stories it appears that "back in the world" is also a crazy battle zone. Besides "The Missing Person" and "Our Story Begins," other stories that stand out are "Coming Attractions," "Desert Breakdown, 1968," and "The Rich Brother."

"Coming Attractions," the collection's first story, showcases a precocious teenage girl who is every parent's nightmare. She shoplifts and makes random anonymous phone calls late at night: For example, she calls and wakes the unfortunately named Mr. Love, sixty-one years old, and gets him excited about winning a big contest. First, however, he has to answer the question: "Here's the question, Mr. Love. I lie and steal and sleep around. What do you think about that?" Still, she reveals another side of herself at the end, when she dives to the bottom of an ice-cold swimming pool in the middle of the night and fishes out an abandoned bike for her little brother.

The two other stories feature cars. In "Desert Breakdown, 1968," the car of a young family just back from Germany--a former American soldier, his pregnant German wife, and their first child--breaks down at an isolated service station in the Mojave Desert. The locals do not lift a hand to help, except for a woman who runs the station, and the husband is tempted to abandon his young family there. The story demonstrates that men cannot be depended on, but women are quite capable of taking care of themselves: The German wife beats up one of the local cowboys, and the station operator goes out and shoots rabbits for dinner. In "The Rich Brother," the collection's last story, the lifestyles of two brothers clash. The rich brother drives to a distant religious commune to rescue his young brother, but on the way home, they quarrel, and the rich brother abandons the young one along the roadside. As the story ends, however, the rich brother is having second thoughts, afraid to get home and face the questions of his wife: "Where is he? Where is your brother?"

### THE NIGHT IN QUESTION

The fifteen stories in *The Night in Question* again display Wolff's command of dialogue, expressive detail, and meticulous plotting. The plots frequently turn on situational irony, and the endings show the principal characters suffering unexpectedly because of their behavior. That behavior devolves from self-delusion. The disparity between characters' intentions and the consequences of their actions creates conflict that at times skirts the bizarre but is moving and provocative in the end.

The "Other Miller" illustrates Wolff's use of a surprise ending to reveal the source of self-delusion. Miller, a young soldier, is told that his mother has died. He is delighted because he believes that the authorities have mistaken him for another Miller in his battalion. He plays along to get emergency leave and amuses himself with the sympathy of other soldiers. He never believes his mother has died because she is young and, more important, he is obsessed with punishing her for remarrying after his father's death. His enlistment, in fact, had been meant to punish her. Not until he opens the door to his home does the truth force its way through his childish spite. The only mistake, all along, has been his; his mother now dead, he has punished only himself with his bitter love.

In some stories the ending is foreshadowed, gradually intensifying for the reader the emotional state of the protagonists. "The Life of the Body" concerns an aging preparatory school English teacher. A romantic, he loves the classics and is liberal in applying their themes to modern social problems. The story opens in a bar. Drunk, he makes a pass at a pretty young veterinarian and is beaten up by her boyfriend. The next day, heroically bruised, he does not correct the rumors among his students that he has been mugged by a gang. He tells the truth to a friend and admits his foolishness but continues to pursue the veterinarian, despite her hostility and dangerous boyfriend. As the story ends, she relents slightly, just enough to give him hope for more adventure and romance. However irrational his actions, he deeply craves direct experience.

The title story, "The Night in Question," similarly heightens suspense to depict a complex emotional state with devastating power. Frank and Frances grew up with a violently abusive father. As adults, they seem familiar literary types: Frank has been the wild youth who now has gotten religion; Frances is the long-suffering, practical big sister. In the story, Frank repeats to Frances a sermon he has heard about a man who must choose between saving his beloved son and a passenger train. Frances will have none of the story's pat message about choice and trust in the heavenly Father. It becomes ever clearer as she listens that she is spiritually alive only when she is protecting her brother. In fact, as their names suggest--Frank (Francis) and

Frances--their earthly father's violence has welded them into a single spiritual being. The story makes the psychological concept of codependency potently eerie.

Like Wolff's earlier collections, *The Night in Question* portrays the predicaments of human intercourse vividly and conveys their psychological or philosophical consequence by suggestion. Wolff rarely sermonizes. If he comments at all, he usually comments indirectly, through symbolism or his patented ending. Above all, Wolff is a lover of good stories and is content to tell them and let them stand on their own.

### OUR STORY BEGINS

*Our Story Begins* includes stories from each of Wolff's previous collections of stories, as well as ten new ones. The ten new stories, which originally appeared in such places as *The New Yorker*, *The Atlantic*, and *Playboy*, suggest a man who has accepted himself as a professional writer, who knows he can be well paid for publishing stories in such places, who can be comfortably established in residence at Stanford University, who knows how to exploit the short-story form well, but who does not always challenge himself to go beyond his obvious competency.

For example, "A White Bible" is a conventional story that hooks the reader with pop-fiction suspense, when a young female teacher is kidnapped by a man as she returns to her car after a night drinking with friends. However, the reader's anxiety that the woman is going to be brutally assaulted is defused when the story changes into a thematic tale of cultural conflict. The kidnapper, a Middle Eastern immigrant whose son has been flunked in the woman's class, demands that she not have him expelled. She quickly takes control of the situation, even eliciting an apology from the contrite man.

The weakest story in the new set is "Her Dog," an inconsequential piece about a man whose wife has died and who now cares for her dog, which he ignored when she was alive. Although the theme is potentially significant, Wolff's treatment, in which the reader is privy to the dog's thoughts about how faithful it has always been, is sentimental and a bit banal.

However, there is still some of the old Wolff in these stories. "Awaiting Orders" is a complex story about a gay sergeant who tries to help a woman whose brother, recently sent to Iraq, has neglected his duties to his child. The sergeant's kindness and the woman's tough hillbilly strength create a memorable confrontation. Similarly, "A Mature Student," an encounter between a female ex-soldier and her art professor, an immigrant who betrayed her friends during the Russian invasion of Prague in the 1960's, is a subtle exploration of the nature of cowardice.

In the final story, "Deep Kiss," Wolff returns to his signature theme--the superiority of the imagined life over the real--as a man lives a "submerged life" parallel to his actual existence. It is a theme central to the short story, one that Chekhov explored definitively in his classic "Lady with a Pet Dog," about a man who leads a double life--one in public, full of conventional truth, and another, which "flowed in secret." Wolff's stories, like many great short stories, reflect the secret of the form that Chekhov knew well: "Every individual existence revolves around mystery."

OTHER MAJOR WORKS

LONG FICTION: *Ugly Rumours*, 1975; *The Barracks Thief*, 1984; *Old School*, 2003.

NONFICTION: *This Boy's Life*, 1989; *In Pharaoh's Army: Memories of the Lost War*, 1994.

EDITED TEXTS: *A Doctor's Visit: Short Stories*, 1988 (of Anton Chekhov); *Matters of Life and Death: New American Stories*, 1983; *The Picador Book of Contemporary American Stories*, 1993; *The Best American Short Stories, 1994*, 1994; *The Vintage Book of Contemporary American Short Stories*, 1994; *Best New American Voices*, 2000; *Writers Harvest 3*, 2000.

BIBLIOGRAPHY

Challener, Daniel D. *Stories of Resilience in Childhood: The Narratives of Maya Angelou, Maxine Hong Kingston, Richard Rodriguez, John Edgar Wideman, and Tobias Wolff.* New York: Garland, 1997. Compares the poverty-stricken childhoods of several notable writers, analyzing what led them to overcome early hardship and go on to literary greatness. Includes a bibliography and an index.

Hannah, James. *Tobias Wolff: A Study of the Short Fiction.* Twayne's Studies in Short Fiction 64. New York: Twayne, 1996. A good critical study of the short fiction of Wolff.

Kelly, Colm L. "Affirming the Indeterminable: Deconstruction, Sociology, and Tobias Wolff's 'Say Yes.'" *Mosaic* 32 (March, 1999): 149-166. In response to sociological approaches to literature, argues that stories such as Wolff's are polysemous and therefore not reducible to any single interpretation; provides a deconstructive reading of the story, setting it off against three possible readings derived from current sociological theory, in order to show how the story deconstructs the theories that attempt to explain it.

Livings, Jack. "The Art of Fiction: Tobias Wolff." *The Paris Review* 171 (Fall, 2004): 42-87. Important long interview with Wolff about his career, his writing interests, and his view of the relationship between the writer and his work.

Peters, Joanne M., and Jean W. Ross. "Tobias Wolff (Jonathan Ansell)." In *Contemporary Authors*, edited by Hal May. Vol. 117. Detroit: Gale Research, 1986. Peters gives a brief overview of Wolff's work, but more important is the interview by Ross. In the interview, Wolff talks about his reasons for writing short stories, the writers who have influenced him, his working methods and sources of inspiration, his own reading, and his teaching of creative writing.

Prose, Francine. "The Brothers Wolff." *The New York Times Magazine*, February 5, 1989, p. 22. Prose's fine article, which is also collected in *The New York Times Biographical Service* (February, 1989), introduces the writing of the Wolff brothers, Geoffrey and Tobias. Traces how they grew up apart but eventually became inseparable, even bearing striking resemblances to each other. The article also provides background on their parents, particularly their father.

Wolff, Tobias. "A Forgotten Master: Rescuing the Works of Paul Bowles." *Esquire* 103 (May, 1986): 221-223. Wolff's article not only helps rescue a forgotten master but also provides an index of what Wolff values in writing. He praises Bowles for the mythic quality of his stories, the clarity of his language, his ability to shift moods at will, and his ability to depict a wide range of international characters. He feels that Bowles's pessimism might have contributed to his lack of popularity.

_____. Interview by Nicholas A. Basbanes. *Publishers Weekly* 241 (October 24, 1994): 45-46. A brief biographical sketch and survey of Wolff's career; Wolff discusses his writing habits and his works.

_____. "An Interview with Tobias Wolff." *Contemporary Literature* 31 (Spring, 1990): 1-16. Wolff discusses lying in his story "The Liar" and the nature of "winging it" in his story "In the Garden of the North American Martyrs." Wolff also talks about the fable aspect of his story "The Rich Brother," as well as his fiction about the Vietnam War.

*Harold Branam*
*Updated by Charles E. May*

# RICHARD WRIGHT

**Born:** Roxie, Mississippi; September 4, 1908
**Died:** Paris, France; November 28, 1960

PRINCIPAL SHORT FICTION

*Uncle Tom's Children: Four Novellas,* 1938 (expanded as *Uncle Tom's Children: Five Long Stories*, 1938)
*Eight Men,* 1961

OTHER LITERARY FORMS

Although Richard Wright is best known for his novel *Native Son* (1940), his nonfiction works, such as the two volumes of his autobiography *Black Boy: A Record of Childhood and Youth* (1945) and *American Hunger* (1977) along with books such as *Twelve Million Black Voices* (1941) and *White Man, Listen!* (1957), have proven to be of lasting interest. He developed a Marxist ideology while writing for the Communist *Daily Worker*, which was very influential on his early fiction, notably *Native Son* and *Uncle Tom's Children*, but which culminated in an article, "I Tried to Be a Communist," first published by the *Atlantic Monthly* in 1944. Although he abandoned Marxist ideology, he never abandoned the idea that protest is and should be at the heart of great literature.

ACHIEVEMENTS

Richard Wright is often cited as being the father of the post-World War II African American novel. The works of James Baldwin and Ralph Ellison owe a direct debt to the work of Wright, and his role in inspiring the Black Arts movement of the 1960's is incalculable. In addition, he was one of the first African American novelists of the first half of the twentieth century to capture a truly international audience. Among his many honors were a Guggenheim Fellowship in 1939 and the Spingarn Award from the National Association for the Advancement of Colored People (NAACP) in 1941 for his novel, *Native Son*. This novel, which James Baldwin said was "unquestionably" the "most powerful and celebrated statement we have had yet of what it means to be a Negro in America," along with the first volume of his autobiography and the stories in *Uncle Tom's Children*, constitute Wright's most important lasting contributions to literature. His plots usually deal with how the harrowing experience of racial inequality transforms a person into a rebel--usually violent and usually randomly so. The more subtle achievement of his fiction, however, is the psychological insight it provides into the experience of oppression and rebellion.

BIOGRAPHY

The poverty, racial hatred, and violence that Richard Nathaniel Wright dramatizes in fiction come directly from his own experience as the child of an illiterate Mississippi sharecropper. Richard was six years old when his father was driven off the land and the family moved to a two-room slum tenement in Memphis, Tennessee. The father deserted the family there. Richard's mother, Ella Wright, got a job as a cook, leaving Richard and his younger brother Alan alone in the apartment. When his mother became ill, the brothers were put in an orphanage. An invitation for Ella and the boys to stay with a more prosperous relative in Arkansas ended in panic and flight when white men shot Uncle Hoskins, who had offered the Wrights a home. The family lived for some time with Richard's grandparents, stern Seventh-Day Adventists. In this grim, repressive atmosphere, Richard became increasingly violent and rebellious.

Although he completed his formal education in the ninth grade, the young Richard read widely, especially Stephen Crane, Fyodor Dostoevski, Marcel Proust, T. S. Eliot, and Gertrude Stein. The family eventually migrated to Chicago. Wright joined the Communist Party in 1933, and, in 1937 in New York City, became editor of the *Daily Worker*. The publication of *Uncle Tom's Children, Native Son*, and *Black Boy* brought Wright fame both in the United States and in Europe. In 1945, at the invitation of the French government, Wright went to France and became friends with Jean-Paul Sartre, Simone de Beauvoir, and other existentialists. His next novel, *The Outsider* (1953), has been called the first existential novel by an American writer. Wright traveled widely, lectured in several countries, and wrote journalistic accounts of his experiences in Africa and Spain. He died unexpectedly in Paris of amoebic dysentery, probably contracted in Africa or Indonesia under conditions his friend and biographer Margaret Walker, in *Richard Wright: Daemonic Genius* (1988), believes indicate at least medically questionable decisions, or, possibly, homicide.

### ANALYSIS

"Fire and Cloud" in *Uncle Tom's Children* is perhaps best representative of Richard Wright's early short fiction. It won first prize in the 1938 *Story* magazine contest, which had more than four hundred entries, marking Wright's first triumph with American publishers. Charles K. O'Neill adapted the story for radio after it appeared in *American Scenes*.

### "FIRE AND CLOUD"

Unlike the later works concerning black ghetto experience, "Fire and Cloud" has a pastoral quality, recognizing the strong bond of the southern blacks to the soil and the support they have drawn from religion.

Wright reproduces faithfully the southern black dialect in both conversation and internal meditations. This use of dialect emphasizes the relative lack of sophistication of rural blacks. His protagonist, Reverend Taylor, is representative of the "old Negro," who has withstood centuries of oppression, sustained by hard work on the land and humble faith in a merciful God.

Wright's attitude toward religion, however, is ambivalent. Although he recognizes it as contributing to the quiet nobility of the hero, it also prevents Taylor from taking effective social action when his people are literally starving. The final triumph of Reverend Taylor is that he puts aside the conciliatory attitude that was part of his religious training and becomes a social activist. Instead of turning the other cheek after being humiliated and beaten by white men, he embraces the methods of his Marxist supporters, meeting oppression with mass demonstration. Strength of numbers proves more effective and appropriate for getting relief from the bigoted white establishment than all his piety and loving kindness. Early in the story Taylor exclaims "The good Lawds gonna clean up this ol worl some day! Hes gonna make a new Heaven n a new Earth!" His last words, however, are "Freedom belongs t the strong!"

The situation of the story no doubt reflects Wright's early experience when his sharecropper father was driven off the plantation. Taylor's people are starving because the white people, who own all the land, have prohibited the blacks from raising food on it. No matter how Taylor pleads for relief, the local white officials tell him to wait and see if federal aid may be forthcoming. When two Communist agitators begin pushing Taylor to lead a mass demonstration against the local government, white officials have Taylor kidnapped and beaten, along with several deacons of his church. Instead of intimidating them, this suffering converts them to open confrontation. As the Communists promised, the poor whites join the blacks in the march, which forces the white authorities to release food to those facing starvation.

The story's strength lies in revealing through three dialogues the psychological dilemma of the protagonist as opposing groups demand his support. He resists the Communists initially because their methods employ threat of open war on the whites-- "N tha ain Gawds way!" The agitators say he will be responsible if their demonstration fails through lack of numbers and participants are slaughtered. Conversely, the mayor and chief of police threaten Taylor that they will hold him personally responsible if any of his church members join the march. After a humiliating and futile exchange with these men, Taylor faces his own church deacons, who are themselves divided and look to him for leadership. He knows that one of their number, who is just waiting for a chance to oust him from his church, will run to the mayor and police with any evidence of Taylor's insubordination. In a pathetic attempt to shift the burden of responsibility that threatens to destroy him no matter what he does, he reiterates the stubborn stand he has maintained with all three groups: He will not order the demonstration, but he will march with his people if they choose to demonstrate. The brutal horsewhipping that Taylor endures as a result of this moderate stand convinces him of the futility of trying to placate everybody. The Uncle Tom becomes a rebel.

Critics sometimes deplore the episodes of raw brutality described in graphic detail in Wright's fiction, but violence is the clue here to his message. Behind the white man's paternalistic talk is the persuasion of whip and gun. Only superior force can cope with such an antagonist.

### "THE MAN WHO LIVED UNDERGROUND"

Wright's best piece of short fiction is "The Man Who Lived Underground." Although undoubtedly influenced by Dostoevski's underground man and by Franz Kafka's "K," the plot was based on a prisoner's story from *True Detective* magazine. The first version appeared in 1942 in *Accent* magazine under the subtitle "Two Excerpts from a Novel." This version began with a description of the life of a black servant, but Wright later discarded this opening in favor of the dramatic scene in which an unnamed fugitive hides from the police by descending into a sewer. This approach allowed the story to assume a more universal, symbolic quality. Although racist issues are still significant, the protagonist represents that larger class of all those alienated from their society. Eventually the fugitive's name is revealed as Fred Daniels, but so completely is he absorbed into his Everyman role that he cannot remember

*Richard Wright* (Library of Congress)

his name when he returns to the upper world. His progress through sewers and basements becomes a quest for the meaning of life, parodying classic descents into the underworld and ironically reversing Plato's allegory of the cave.

Although Plato's philosopher attains wisdom by climbing out of the cave where men respond to shadows on the cave wall, Wright's protagonist gains enlightenment because of his underground perspective. What he sees there speaks not to his rational understanding, however, but to his emotions. He moves among symbolic visions that arouse terror and pity--a dead baby floating on the slimy water whose "mouth gaped black in a soundless cry." In a black church service spied on through a crevice in the wall, the devout are singing "Jesus, take me to your home above." He is overwhelmed by a sense of guilt and intuits that there is something obscene about their "singing with the air of the sewer blowing in on them." In a meat locker with carcasses hanging from the ceiling, a butcher is hacking off a piece of meat with a bloody cleaver. When the store proprietor goes home, Fred emerges from the locker and gorges on fresh fruit, but he takes back with him into the sewer the bloody cleaver--why he does not know.

When Fred breaks through a wall into the basement of a motion-picture theater, the analogy to Plato's myth of the cave becomes explicit. He comes up a back stair and sees jerking shadows of a silver screen. The Platonic urge to enlighten the people in the theater, who are bound to a shadow world, merges with messianic images. In a dream he walks on water and saves a baby held up by a drowning woman, but the dream ends in terror and doubt as he loses the baby and his ability to emulate Christ. All is lost and he himself begins to drown.

Terror and pity are not the only emotions that enlarge his sensibilities in this underground odyssey. As he learns the peculiar advantages of his invisibility, he realizes that he can help himself to all kinds of gadgets valued by that shadow world aboveground; he collects them like toys or symbols of an absurd world. He acquires a radio, a light bulb with an extension cord, a typewriter, a gun, and finally, through a chance observation of a safe being opened by combination, rolls of hundred-dollar bills, containers of diamonds, watches, and rings. His motivation for stealing these articles is not greed but sheer hilarious fun at acquiring objects so long denied to persons of his class.

In one of the most striking, surrealist scenes in modern literature, Fred delightedly decorates his cave walls and floor with these tokens of a society that has rejected him. "They were the serious toys of the men who lived in the dead world of sunshine and rain he had left, the world that had condemned him, branded him guilty." He glues hundred-dollar bills on his walls. He winds up all the watches but disdains to set them, for he is beyond time, freed from its tyranny. The watches hang on nails along with the diamond rings. He hangs up the bloody cleaver, too, and the gun. The loose diamonds he dumps in a glittering pile on the muddy floor. Then as he gaily tramps around, he accidentally/on purpose stomps on the pile, scattering the pretty baubles over the floor. Here, indeed, is society's cave of shadows, and only he realizes how absurd it all is.

When the euphoria of these games begins to pall, Fred becomes more philosophical, perceiving the nihilistic implications of his experience.

> Maybe *any*thing's right, he mumbled. Yes, if the world as men had made it was right, then anything else was right, any act a man took to satisfy himself, murder, theft, torture.

In his unlettered, blundering way, he is groping toward Ivan Karamazov's dark meditation: "If there is no God, then all things are permissible." Fred becomes convinced of the reality of human guilt, however, when he witnesses the suicide of the jewelry store's night watchman, who has been blamed for the theft he himself committed. At first, the scene in which police torture the bewildered man to force a confession strikes Fred as hilariously funny, duplicating his own experience. However, when the wretched man shoots himself before Fred can offer him a means of escape, Fred is shocked into a realization of his own guilt.

The protagonist ultimately transcends his nihilism, and like Platonic realism's philosopher who returns to the cave out of compassion for those trapped there, Fred returns to the "dead world of sunshine and rain" to bear witness to the Truth. Like the philosopher who is blinded coming out of the light into cave darkness, Fred seems confused and stupid in the social world aboveground. When he is thrown out of the black church, he tries inarticulately to explain his revelation at the police station where he had been tortured and condemned. The police think he is crazy, but because they now know they accused him unjustly, they find his return embarrassing. Fred euphorically insists that they accompany him into the sewer so that they too can experience the visions that enlightened him. When he shows them his entrance to the world underground, one of the policemen calmly shoots him and the murky waters of the sewer sweep him away.

This ironic story of symbolic death and resurrection is unparalleled in its unique treatment of existential themes. Guilt and alienation lead paradoxically to a tragic sense of human brotherhood, which seems unintelligible to "normal" people. The man who kills Fred Daniels is perhaps the only person who perceives even dimly what Daniels wants to do. "You've got to shoot this kind," he says. "They'd wreck things."

OTHER MAJOR WORKS

LONG FICTION: *Native Son*, 1940; *The Outsider*, 1953; *Savage Holiday*, 1954; *The Long Dream*, 1958; *Lawd Today*, 1963; *A Father's Law*, 2008.

PLAY: *Native Son: The Biography of a Young American*, pr. 1941 (with Paul Green).

POETRY: *Haiku: This Other World*, 1998 (Yoshinobu Hakutani and Robert L. Tener, editors).

NONFICTION: *Twelve Million Black Voices: A Folk History of the Negro in the United States*, 1941 (photographs by Edwin Rosskam); *Black Boy: A Record of Childhood and Youth*, 1945; *Black Power: A Record of Reactions in a Land of Pathos*, 1954; *The Color Curtain*, 1956; *Pagan Spain*, 1957; *White Man, Listen!*, 1957; *American Hunger*, 1977; *Richard Wright Reader*, 1978 (Ellen Wright and Michel Fabre, editors); *Conversations with Richard Wright*, 1993 (Keneth Kinnamon and Fabre, editors).

MISCELLANEOUS: *Works*, 1991 (two volumes).

BIBLIOGRAPHY

Fabre, Michel. *The Unfinished Quest of Richard Wright*. New York: William Morrow, 1973. Although this volume is one of the most important and authoritative biographies available on Wright, readers interested in Wright's life should also consult Margaret Walker's biography.

_____. *The World of Richard Wright*. 1985. Reprint. Jackson: University Press of Mississippi, 2009. A collection of Fabre's essays on Wright. A valuable resource, though not a sustained, full-length study. Contains two chapters on individual short stories by Wright, including the short story "Superstition." Supplemented by an appendix.

Felgar, Robert. *Richard Wright*. Boston: Twayne, 1980. A general biographical and critical source, this work devotes two chapters to Wright's short fiction.

_____. *Student Companion to Richard Wright*. Westport, Conn.: Greenwood Press, 2000. An introductory overview to Wright's life and works, including chapters devoted to the short fiction collections *Uncle Tom's Children* and *Eight Men*.

Gelfant, Blanche H., ed. *The Columbia Companion to the Twentieth-Century American Short Story*. New York: Columbia University Press, 2000. Includes a chapter in which Wright's short stories are analyzed.

Hakutani, Yoshinobu. *Richard Wright and Racial Discourse*. Columbia: University of Missouri Press, 1996. This study of Wright's fiction as racial discourse and the product of diverse cultures devotes one chapter to *Uncle Tom's Children*, focusing primarily on the racial and cultural contexts of "Big Boy Leaves Home."

JanMohamed, Abdul R. *The Death-Bound-Subject: Richard Wright's Archaeology of Death*. Durham, N.C. Duke University Press, 2005. Examines how Wright's works expressed the threat of lynching. Demonstrates how each successive work delved deeper into an investigation of the "death-bound-subject"--the person who must constantly live with the imminent menace of death. JanMohamed devotes one chapter, "*Uncle Tom's Children*: Dialectics of Death," to an analysis of the death-bound-subject theme in this work of short fiction.

Kinnamon, Kenneth, ed. *Critical Essays on Richard Wright's "Native Son."* New York: Twayne, 1997. Divided into sections of reviews, reprinted essays, and new essays. Includes discussions of Wright's handling of race, voice, tone, novelistic structure, the city, and literary influences.

_____. *The Emergence of Richard Wright*. Urbana: University of Illinois Press, 1972. A study of Wright's background and development as a writer, up until the publication of *Native Son*.

_____, ed. *A Richard Wright Bibliography: Fifty Years of Criticism and Commentary: 1933-1982*. Westport, Conn.: Greenwood Press, 1988. A mammoth annotated bibliography, one of the largest annotated bibliographies ever assembled on an American writer, which traces the history of Wright criticism. Invaluable as a research tool.

Rand, William E. "The Structure of the Outsider in the Short Fiction of Richard Wright and F. Scott Fitzgerald." *CLA Journal* 40 (December, 1996): 230-245. Compares the theme, imagery, and form of

Fitzgerald's "The Diamond as Big as the Ritz" with Wright's "The Man Who Lived Underground" in terms of the treatment of the outsider. Argues that both Fitzgerald and Wright saw themselves as out-siders--Wright because of race and Fitzgerald because of economic class.

Rowley, Hazel. *Richard Wright: The Life and Times*. New York: Henry Holt, 2001. Rowley's well-researched biography recounts the facts of Wright's life and reconstructs the times and places in which he lived.

Scofield, Martin. "Charles Chesnutt, Richard Wright, James Baldwin, and the African American Short Story to 1965." In *The Cambridge Introduction to the American Short Story*. New York: Cambridge University Press, 2006. Examines the contributions of the three African American writers to the American short story. Discusses several of Wright's stories from *Eight Men* and *Uncle Tom's Children*.

Tuhkanen, Mikko. "'The Look of the World': Richard Wright on Perspective." In *A Companion to the American Short Story*, edited by Alfred Bendixen and James Nagel. Malden, Mass.: Wiley-Blackwell, 2010. Provides an overview of Wright's short fiction and its place within the development of the American short story.

Walker, Margaret. *Richard Wright: Daemonic Genius*. New York: Warner, 1988. A critically acclaimed study of Wright's life and work written by a friend and fellow novelist. Not a replacement for Michel Fabre's biography but written with the benefit of several more years of scholarship on issues that include the medical controversy over Wright's death. Walker is especially insightful on Wright's early life, and her comments on Wright's short fiction are short but pithy. Includes a useful bibliographic essay.

Wallach, Jennifer Jensen. *Richard Wright: From Black Boy to World Citizen*. Chicago: Ivan R. Dee, 2010. Published on the fiftieth anniversary of Wright's death, Wallach's book relates and celebrates Wright's life from his youth in Mississippi to his development as a writer, his experiences in New York City, and his eventual expatriation in Paris.

Ward, Jerry W., Jr., and Robert J. Butler, eds. *The Richard Wright Encyclopedia*. Westport, Conn.: Greenwood Press, 2008. Alphabetically arranged entries provide information on Wright's life and works, including his short fiction.

*Katherine Snipes*
*Updated by Thomas J. Cassidy*

# PAUL YOON

**Born:** New York, New York; 1980

### PRINCIPAL SHORT FICTION
*Once the Shore,* 2009

### OTHER LITERARY FORMS
Paul Yoon is working on a novel.

### ACHIEVEMENTS
Paul Yoon's story "Once the Shore" was chosen for *Best American Short Stories, 2006.* His story "And We Will Be Here" appeared in *PEN/O. Henry Prize Stories, 2009.* Yoon has been selected as an "emerging writer" by PEN/New England. *Once the Shore* was a *New York Times* Notable Book; it was named a *Los Angeles Times*, *San Francisco Chronicle*, *Publishers Weekly*, and *Minneapolis Star Tribune* Best Book of the Year; it was selected as Best Debut of the Year by National Public Radio. Yoon won the John C. Zacharis First Book Award from *Ploughshares* and was included in the National Book Foundation's *5 Under 35* in 2010.

### BIOGRAPHY
Paul Yoon, of Korean descent, was born in New York City in 1980. He attended Phillips Exeter Academy in Exeter, New Hampshire, and Wesleyan University in Middletown, Connecticut. He settled in Baltimore, Maryland, with fiction writer Laura van den Berg.

### ANALYSIS
Paul Yoon once told an interviewer that for him writing fiction was a love letter to all the books that have stayed with him over the years. He said the power of such books to change his world fuels his own "obsessive desire to enter fictional worlds." Describing his childhood as solitary, with books as his main companions, Yoon is still very much a private man, who shares little of his personal life.

Although he did spend some time at the Ledig House Writers' Colony in upstate New York, against the usual "young writer" stereotype, Yoon did not learn to write in an M.F.A. workshop setting but rather seems to have appeared instantly as a mature writer in 2006, when his first short story, "Once the Shore," was published and chosen for *Best American Short Stories.* Although he had not been to Korea for many years and relied on research in geography and history for his knowledge of Cheju Island, he competently created a complete sense of the culture of the island over a fifty-year period. Although he was only in his late twenties when he wrote the eight stories in his debut collection, he was able to enter the minds and hearts of a sixty-six-year-old "sea woman," who dives for seafood to sell, a older couple who set off to sea to find their missing son, a widow who tries to recapture a romantic vision of her dead husband, and a lonely nine-year-old girl who searches for an image of her dead mother. Yoon is able to participate sympathetically in the lives of characters so different from himself in a seemingly effortless prose style that is never showy or self-conscious, but always stark, evocative, and pure.

### ONCE THE SHORE
Cheju is a volcanic island some sixty miles south of the Korean mainland; it is approximately forty miles long and twenty miles wide-- a place where, as one of Yoon's characters says in this lyrically realistic debut collection of stories, it takes no longer than an hour to get from "here to anywhere." Once a mysterious place of banishment for political dissidents, the island is now a favorite destination for honeymoon couples and tourists and famous for the sea women who dive for shellfish off its shore.

Yoon appropriated Cheju, renamed it Solla, and created a fictional world, in the mode of Sherwood Anderson's *Winesburg, Ohio* (1919), of loneliness and loss. In interviews, Yoon said that although a sense of place is very important to him, when he had finished *Once the Shore* he realized that he had changed everything about the island--geography, events, history--and that the stories were not about Cheju at all. He said that he was most interested in exploring the effect of outside forces invading an isolated environment and changing people's lives on the island, between the military occupation following World War II and its present reincarnation as a visa-free tourist destination. However, historical change and cultural upheaval are not what these stories are about. In spite of the important time span the book encompasses, the book is not a social document or a "story cycle" parading as a sociorealistic "composite novel." Rather, it is a collection of self-sufficient, independent stories about individual lonely lives in the lyrical realistic tradition of Ivan Turgenev.

Four of the stories focus on how women, who have passively grown older on the island, encounter and become involved with visiting men and lonely boys, some of whom they have lost previously and try to recover, some who are forbidden to them by age or nationality. In "Faces to the Fire," a woman who operates a convenience store for tourists and cares for her aging father feels hope for the future when a man with whom she has grown up returns to the island with the intention of staying. Her expectation for a renewed life for herself is dashed when she discovers that her dead mother's jewelry box has been pilfered and that the man has once again left the island.

One of Cheju's famous sea women is the focus of "So They Do Not Hear Us," in which a sixty-six-year-old woman, who began the dangerous dives when she was thirteen, still searches for edible seaweed, mussels, and clams in the waters around the island. Having lost her husband to conscription by the Japanese during the war, she never remarried and takes care of her neighbor's son, who lost his arm to a tiger shark. When she discovers that what she thought were bruises made by bullies are the boy's self-punishment, the two bond, as she tries to teach him to dive for giant sea turtles. Once

again, Yoon's story is more an extended poetic meditation than a linear story, moving slowly and lyrically to the final image of the boy practicing holding his breath in the bathtub, the stub of his arm resting on its edge, as the sea woman inhales deeply and in her imagination joins him.

In "The Woodcarver's Daughter," which takes place two years after the end of World War II, a young woman, who walks with a limp because of a childhood fall, befriends an American interpreter who has come to the island. However, both the woman and the American have secrets. Her injury is the fault of her father, and the American is a deserter. The story ends with him being captured by the American authorities and her slipping her father's woodcarving knife into his pocket as they lead him away, not knowing how he might use it. Although she loses the American, she becomes reconciled with her father.

Chosen for *The PEN/O. Henry Prize Stories* for 2009, "And We Will Be There" focuses on a thirty-four-year-old woman who works for a hospital on the island. When an earthquake destroyed Tokyo, she arrived at an orphanage on the island at the same time as a boy with whom she becomes friends. Ten years later, when the boy leaves the island, the woman moves to a hospital, where she helps care for the wounded men brought there. She becomes obsessively solicitous of one man, thinking he is her missing childhood friend. The story ends when, after hallucinating conversations with a young blind boy, she leaves the hospital with the boy on a bicycle, as he whispers in her ear, "War's ending."

### "ONCE THE SHORE"

The title story, Yoon's first published work, chosen for the 2006 *Best American Short Stories*, transfers from the coast of Hawaii to the coast of Korea the 2001 *Ehime Maru* incident, in which a Japanese fishery school training vessel was sunk by the U.S. nuclear submarine USS *Greeneville*, killing nine Japanese fishermen. Changing the drowned Japanese to Koreans, Yoon tells the story of a twenty-six-year-old waiter at one of the island's resort hotels, whose brother is killed in the accident. Parallel to his experience of loss is the story of an American woman in her sixties visiting the resort, whose husband has been dead only a few months. She tells the waiter the story of how her husband, stationed in the South Pacific during World War II, came to the island on a furlough and carved a heart with their initials in a cave on the island. Although she gradually realized that her husband had lied about this, she wants to locate the cave to somehow find the husband who left her to go to war but did not return the same man. Seeking some reconciliation, too, the waiter is looking for the mythical center of the ocean that his brother had once told him they could find together. When he takes the woman to the caves, he thinks it is possible that this island, his home, is the center of the ocean. After serving her a special communal meal, he takes her into a cave, where with a sharp stone she begins carving on the wall a design that he thinks could be the words of a language "long forgotten." Told in a restrained and lyrical fashion that is both mythic and realistic, "Once the Shore" exhibits the sense of loss and final poetic reconciliation that is a typical pattern for Yoon's stories.

### "AMONG THE WRECKAGE"

Another story about a tragic accident involving the United States is "Among the Wreckage," in which an aging Korean couple lose their forty-year-old fisherman son when American planes drop test bombs on uninhabited islands just after the end of World War II. The old couple set out to search for him on a dilapidated trawler that the father and son once reclaimed and painted. After a cruel encounter with an American patrol boat, they reach the site where the son's boat was destroyed and begin the gruesome task of looking through the debris and human limbs. Casting themselves off from the trawler on a small piece of wood the size of a door, they pull floating bodies closer, lifting the faces out of the water, looking for their son. Once again, Yoon's language is reserved and controlled, as he recounts the tension between the old man and woman that separates them and the horrible quest that unites them.

### "LOOK FOR ME IN THE CAMPHOR TREE"

"Look for Me in the Camphor Tree," the only story told completely from the perspective of a child, is the most fairy-tale-like piece in the book. Since her mother's death a year before, a nine-year-old girl has lived with her father, who decides to sell their farm and sta-

bles, finding them too large for him to manage alone. The lonely child, who feels that leaving the place is like leaving her mother, one day sees a woman in the field, wearing a pale blue dress, similar to the dress the girl's mother wears in a photograph that the girl keeps on her dresser. Later on, when she takes her mother's photograph to show it to the woman, the woman disappears, leaving no indentation or footprints, where she might have walked away. One night, when the child looks out her window, she sees a shadowy shape under the camphor tree that her mother used to sing to the child about, but when she goes to it, she finds it is an old pony from their stables. When she follows it, she falls and cannot move. Later, when the father finds her lying next to the pony, he picks her up and, in the mood of the fairy-tale atmosphere that the story creates, tells her about nighttime and its noises, foxes and maidens, and a woman in a pale blue dress.

### "THE HANGING LANTERNS OF IDO"

The final story in *Once the Shore*, "The Hanging Lanterns of Ido," is the only one that centers on a male protagonist; it is also the most contemporary story, focusing on the island as a favorite tourist destination. The story begins with a routine walk of a comfortable couple who live and work in the tourist industry on the island. When they stop for a meal at a restaurant, the waitress stares at the man as if she knows him and says, "It's you." It is a case of mistaken identity, but later the man is troubled by it, weighing his life against the life he imagines for the other man, wishing he had asked the waitress questions about him.

Because the restaurant where he encountered the waitress was Thai, the man looks up books on Thailand and finds a picture of a hotel in a Thai city, where he thinks he sees part of a figure behind the curtain of an upstairs window--a bare leg, an arm--which he associates with the waitress. This romantic fantasy so obsesses him that it contributes to a sense of alienation from his wife. He looks for the girl, going back to the restaurant, but finds that she has been dismissed for theft. Months later, walking on the boardwalk alone, he sees the waitress again and says to her the same words she earlier spoke to him, "It's you." However, he cannot think of the questions he wanted to ask her, as if the one language that he knew had now failed him.

When he goes home to his wife, they sit alone in their apartment, and he tells her that if she ever goes away, he will remember her face and look for it. "We will be strong. We will be heroic." The man's obsessive fascination with the waitress and the alienation he feels from his wife do not suggest a romantic attraction to the girl or dissatisfaction with his wife. Rather, what he experiences is a poignant sense of "what if" his life had been different. What kind of life would it have been? Like all Yoon's stories, this last one in the collection has the sense of loneliness that Frank O'Connor once attributed to the short story as a form. In their combination of realistic detail and folklore fantasy, Yoon's stories are classic examples of what the short story has always done best since Turgenev discovered the power of lyrical realism.

BIBLIOGRAPHY

Silber, Joan. "Quiet Discomfort." *The New York Times*, April 26, 2009, p. 23. An important review by writer Silber, which praises *Once the Shore*'s spare and beautiful prose. Silber says the beauty of the stories lies in their reserve, their starkness, and their mildness. She argues that the challenge of Yoon's stories is that they feature characters who do not seem to believe in action.

Wyce, Marion. "*Once the Shore*." *Literary Review* 52 (Summer, 2009): 206-208. Wyce argues that the sense of time in Yoon's stories is not strictly linear, for the present is part of everything that has happened before and everything that is yet to happen. Argues that other people are always a mystery in these stories, that Yoon is interested in the way that even the most familiar person ultimately is unknowable and strange.

Yoon, Paul. Interview. *One Story* 58 (June 20, 2005). A long interview with Yoon about the prize-winning story "Once the Shore." He says the most challenging aspect of writing the story was trying to sustain its parallel narratives and to make the real life story of the sinking of the ship, the *Ehime Maru*, believable to the reader.

*Charles E. May*

# RESOURCES

# TERMS AND TECHNIQUES

*Aestheticism:* The European literary movement denied that art needed to have any utilitarian purpose and focused on the slogan "art for art's sake." The movement was predominant in the 1890's and had its roots in France. The doctrines of aestheticism were introduced to England by Walter Pater and can be found in the plays of Oscar Wilde and the short stories of Arthur Symons. In American literature, the ideas underlying the aesthetic movement can be found in the short fiction of Edgar Allan Poe.

*Allegory:* A literary mode in which characters in a narrative personify abstract ideas or qualities and provide a second level of meaning to the work. Two famous examples of allegory are Edmund Spenser's *The Faerie Queene* (1590, 1596) and John Bunyan's *The Pilgrim's Progress from This World to That Which Is to Come,* Part I (1678). Modern examples may be found in Nathaniel Hawthorne's story "The Artist of the Beautiful" and the stories and novels of Franz Kafka.

*Allusion:* A reference to a person or event, either historical or from a literary work, which gives another literary work a wider frame of reference and adds depth to its meaning. For example, Sylvia Townsend Warner's story "Winter in the Air" gains greater suggestiveness from the frequent allusions to William Shakespeare's play *The Winter's Tale* (pr. c. 1610-1611, pb. 1623), and her story "Swans on an Autumn River" is enriched by a number of allusions to the poetry of William Butler Yeats.

*Ambiguity:* Refers to the capacity of language to suggest two or more levels of meaning within a single expression, thus conveying a rich, concentrated effect. Ambiguity has been defined by William Empson in *Seven Types of Ambiguity* (1930) as "any verbal nuance, however, slight, which gives room for alternative reactions to the same piece of language." It has been suggested that because of the short story's highly compressed form, ambiguity may play a more important role in this genre than it does in the novel.

*Anachronism:* An event, person, or thing placed outside--usually earlier than--its proper historical era. William Shakespeare uses anachronism in *King John* (pr. c. 1596-1597, pb. 1623), *Antony and Cleopatra* (pr. c. 1606-1607, pb. 1723), and *Julius Caesar* (pr. c. 1599-1600, pb. 1623). Mark Twain employed anachronism to comic effect in *A Connecticut Yankee in King Arthur's Court* (1889).

*Anecdote:* The short narration of a single interesting incident or event. An anecdote differs from a short story in that it does not have a plot, relates a single episode, and does not range over different times and places.

*Antagonist:* A character in fiction who stands in opposition, or rivalry, to the protagonist. In William Shakespeare's *Hamlet, Prince of Denmark* (pr. c. 1600-1601, pb. 1603), for example, King Claudius is the antagonist of Hamlet.

*Anthology:* A collection of prose or poetry, usually by various writers. Often serves to introduce the work of little-known authors to a wider audience.

*Aphorism:* A short, concise statement that states an opinion, precept, or general truth, such as Alexander Pope's "Hope springs eternal in the human breast."

*Aporia:* An interpretative point in a story that basically cannot be decided, usually as the result of some gap or absence.

*Apostrophe:* A direct address to a person (usually absent), inanimate entity, or abstract quality. Examples are the first line of William Wordsworth's sonnet "London, 1802," "Milton! Thou should'st be living at this hour," and King Lear's speech in William Shakespeare's *King Lear* (pr. c. 1605-1606, pb. 1698), "Blow, winds, and crack your cheeks! rage! blow!"

*Appropriation:* The act of taking over part of a literary theory or approach for one's own ends, for example, male critics using the feminist approach.

*Archetypal theme:* Recurring thematic patterns in literature. Common archetypal themes include death and rebirth (Samuel Taylor Coleridge's *The Rime of the Ancient Mariner*, 1798), paradise-Hades (Coleridge's "Kubla Khan," 1816), the fatal woman (Guy de Maupassant's "Doubtful Happiness"), the earth goddess ("Yanda" by Isaac Bashevis Singer), the scapegoat (D. H. Lawrence's "The Woman Who Rode Away," 1925), and the return to the womb (Flannery O'Connor's "The River," 1953).

*Archetype:* This term was used by psychologist Carl Jung to describe what he called "primordial images," which exist in the "collective unconscious" of humankind and are manifested in myths, religion, literature, and dreams. Now used broadly in literary criticism to refer to character types, motifs, images, symbols, and plot patterns recurring in many different literary forms and works.

*Architectonics:* A term borrowed from architecture to describe the structural qualities, such as unity and balance, of a work of literature. If the architectonics are successful, the work will give the impression of organic unity and balance, like a solidly constructed building in which the total value is more than the sum of the parts.

*Asides:* In drama, short passages generally spoken by one dramatic character in an undertone or directed to the audience, so as not to be heard by other characters on stage.

*Atmosphere:* The mood or tone of a work; it is often associated with setting but can also be established by action or dialogue. The opening paragraphs of Edgar Allan Poe's "The Fall of the House of Usher" (1839) and James Joyce's "Araby" (1914) provide good examples of atmosphere created early in the works and which pervade the remainder of the story.

*Ballad:* Popular ballads are songs or verse that tell dramatic, usually impersonal, tales. Supernatural events, courage, and love are frequent themes, but any experience that appeals to ordinary people is acceptable material. Literary ballads--narrative poems based on popular ballads--have frequently been in vogue in English literature, particularly during the Romantic period. One of the most famous is Samuel Taylor Coleridge's *The Rime of the Ancient Mariner*.

*Black humor:* A general term of modern origin that refers to a form of "sick humor" that is intended to produce laughter out of the morbid and the taboo. Examples are the works of Joseph Heller, Thomas Pynchon, Günter Grass, and Kurt Vonnegut.

*Broadside ballad:* A ballad printed on one side of a large, single sheet of paper and sung to a popular tune. Dating from the sixteenth century in England, the subject of the broadside ballad was a topical event or issue.

*Burlesque:* A work that, by imitating attitudes, styles, institutions, and people, aims to amuse. Burlesque differs from satire in that it aims to ridicule simply for the sake of amusement rather than for political or social change.

*Canon:* The standard or authoritative list of literary works that are widely accepted as outstanding representatives of their period and genre. In recent literary criticism, however, the established canon has come under fierce assault for its alleged culture and gender bias.

*Canonize:* The act of adding a literary work to the list of works that form the primary tradition of a genre or literature in general. For example, a number of stories by female and African American writers previously excluded from the canon of the short story, such as Charlotte Perkins Gilman's "The Yellow Wallpaper" (1892) and Charles Waddell Chesnutt's "The Sheriff's Children (1899)," have recently been canonized.

*Caricature:* A form of writing that focuses on unique qualities of a person and then exaggerates and distorts those qualities in order to ridicule the person and what he or she represents. Contemporary writers, such as Flannery O'Connor, have used caricature for serious and satiric purposes in such stories as "Good Country People" (1955) and "A Good Man Is Hard to Find" (1955).

*Character type:* The term can refer to the convention of using stock characters, such as the *miles gloriosus* (braggart soldier) of Renaissance and Roman comedy, the figure of vice in medieval morality plays, or the clever servant in Elizabethan comedy. It can also describe "flat" characters (the term was coined by E. M. Forster) in fiction who do not grow or change during the course of the narrative and who can be easily classified.

*Chronicle:* The precursors of modern histories, chronicles were written accounts of national or world events. One of the best known is the *Anglo-Saxon Chronicle*, begun in the reign of King Alfred in the late ninth century. Many chronicles were written in Elizabethan times, and these were used by William Shakespeare as source documents for his history plays.

*Classic/Classicism:* A literary stance or value system consciously based on the example of classical Greek and Roman literature. While the term is applied to an enormous diversity of artists it generally denotes a cluster of values, including formal discipline, restrained expression, reverence of tradition, and an objective rather than subjective orientation. Often contrasted to Romanticism.

*Climax:* Similar to crisis, the moment in a work of fiction at which the action reaches a turning point and the plot begins to be resolved. Unlike crisis, this term is also used to refer to the moment in which the reader's emotional involvement with the work reaches its highest point of intensity.

*Comic story:* Encompasses a wide variety of modes and inflections, such as parody, burlesque, satire, irony, and humor. Frequently, the defining quality of comic characters is that they lack self-awareness; the reader tends not to identify with them but perceives them from a detached point of view, more as objects than persons.

*Conceit:* A type of metaphor that makes highly intellectualized comparisons between seemingly disparate things. It is associated with the Metaphysical poets and the Elizabethan sonneteers; examples can also be found in the poetry of Emily Dickinson and T. S. Eliot.

*Conflict:* The struggle that develops between the protagonist and another person, the natural world, society, or some force within the self. In short fiction, the conflict is most often between the protagonist and the self or the human condition.

*Connotation/Denotation:* Denotation is the explicit, formal definition of a word, exclusive of its emotional associations. When a word takes on an additional meaning, other than its denotative one, it achieves connotation. For example, the word "mercenary" denotes a soldier who is paid to fight in an army not of his own region, but connotatively a mercenary is an unprincipled scoundrel who kills for money.

*Conte:* French for tale, a conte was originally a short adventure tale. In the nineteenth century, the term was used to describe a tightly constructed short story. In England, the term is used to describe a work longer than a short story and shorter than a novel.

*Crisis:* A turning point in the plot, at which the opposing forces reach the point that a resolution must take place.

*Criticism:* The study and evaluation of works of literature. Theoretical criticism, as for example in Aristotle's *Peri poētikēs* (c. 334-323 b.c.e.; *Poetics*, 1705), sets out general principles for interpretation. Practical criticism (Samuel Taylor Coleridge's lectures on William Shakespeare, for example) offers interpretations of particular works or authors.

*Deconstruction:* A literary theory, primarily attributed to French critic Jacques Derrida, which has spawned a wide variety of practical applications, the most prominent being the critical tactic of laying bare a text's self-reflexivity, that is, showing how it continually refers to and subverts its own way of meaning.

*Defamiliarization:* A term coined by the Russian Formalists to indicate a process by which the writer makes the reader perceive the concrete uniqueness of an object, event, or idea that has been generalized by routine and habit.

*Dénouement:* Literally, "unknotting"; the conclusion of a drama or fiction, when the plot is unraveled and the mystery solved.

*Detective story:* The "classic" detective story (or "mystery") is a highly formalized and logically structured mode of fiction in which the focus is on a crime solved by a detective through interpretation of evidence and clever reasoning. Many modern practitioners of the genre, however, such as Raymond Chandler, Patricia Highsmith, and Ross Macdonald, have placed less emphasis on the puzzlelike qualities of the detective story and have focused instead on characterization, theme, and other elements of mainstream fiction. The form was first developed in short fiction by Edgar Allan Poe, and has been used by Jorge Luis Borges.

*Deus ex machina:* A Latin term meaning "god out of the machine." In the Greek theater, it referred to the use of a god lowered out of a mechanism onto the stage to untangle the plot or save the hero. The term has come to signify any artificial device for the easy resolution of dramatic difficulties.

*Device:* Any technique used in literature in order to gain a specific effect. The poet uses the device of figurative language, for example, while the novelist may use the devices of foreshadowing, flashback, and so on, in order to create a desired effect.

*Dialogics:* The theory that many different voices are held in suspension without merging into a single authoritative voice. Developed by Russian critic Mikhail Bakhtin.

*Didactic literature:* Literature that seeks to instruct, give guidance, or teach a lesson. Didactic literature normally has a moral, religious, or philosophical purpose, or it will expound a branch of knowledge (as in Vergil's *Georgics*, c. 37-29 b.c.e.; English translation, 1589). It is distinguished from imaginative works, in which the aesthetic product takes precedence over any moral intent.

*Diegesis:* Refers to the hypothetical world of a story, as if it actually existed in real space and time. It is the illusory universe of the story created by its linguistic structure.

*Doggerel:* Strictly speaking, doggerel refers to rough and jerky versification, but the term is more commonly applied to worthless verse that contains monotonous rhyme and rhythm and trivial subject matter.

*Doppelgänger:* A double or counterpart of a person, sometimes endowed with ghostly qualities. A fictional doppelgänger often reflects a suppressed side of a character's personality, as in Fyodor Dostoevski's novella *Dvoynik* (1846; *The Double*, 1917) and the short stories of E. T. A. Hoffmann. Isaac Bashevis Singer and Jorge Luis Borges, among other modern writers, have also employed the doppelgänger with striking effect.

*Dream vision:* An allegorical form common in the Middle Ages, in which the narrator or a character falls asleep and dreams a dream that becomes the actual framed story. Subtle variations of the form have been used by Nathaniel Hawthorne in "Young Goodman Brown" (1835) and by Edgar Allan Poe in "The Pit and the Pendulum" (1842).

*Dualism:* A theory that the universe is explicable in terms of two basic, conflicting entities, such as good and evil, mind and matter, or the physical and the spiritual.

*Eclogue:* In Greek, the term means literally "selection." It is now used to describe a formal pastoral poem. Classical eclogues are constructed around a variety of conventional themes: the singing match, the rustic dialogue, the lament, the love lay, and the eulogy. During the Renaissance, eclogues were employed as veiled satires.

*Écriture Féminine:* French feminist Hélène Cixous argues for a unique female kind of writing, which in its fluidity disrupts the binary oppositions of male-dominated cultural structures.

*Effect:* The total, unified impression, or impact, made upon the reader by a literary work. Every aspect of the work--plot, characterization, style, and so on--is seen to directly contribute to this overall impression.

*Elegy:* A long, rhymed, formal poem whose subject is meditation upon death or a lamentable theme; Alfred, Lord Tennyson's *In Memoriam* (1850) is a well-known example. The pastoral elegy, such as Percy Bysshe Shelley's *Adonais: An Elegy on the Death of John Keats* (1821), uses a pastoral scene to express grief at the loss of a friend or important person.

*Emotive meaning:* The emotion that is commonly associated with a word. In other words, the connotations of a word, not merely what it denotes. Emotive meaning is contrasted with cognitive or descriptive meaning, in which neither emotions nor connotations are involved.

*Epic:* Although this term usually refers to a long narrative poem that presents the exploits of a central figure of high position, the term is also used to designate a long novel that has the style or structure usually associated with an epic. In this sense, for example, Herman Melville's *Moby Dick: Or, The Whale* (1851) and James Joyce's *Ulysses* (1922) may be called epics.

*Epiphany:* The literary application of this religious term was popularized by James Joyce in his book *Stephen Hero* (1944): "By an epiphany he meant a sudden spiritual manifestation, whether in the vulgarity of speech or of gesture or in a memorable phase of the mind itself." Many short stories since Joyce's collection *Dubliners* (1914) have been analyzed as epiphanic stories in which a character or the reader experiences a sudden revelation of meaning.

*Episode:* In Greek tragedy, the segment between two choral odes. Episode now refers to an incident presented as a continuous action. In a work of literature, many discrete episodes are woven together to form a more complex work.

*Epistolary fiction:* A work of fiction in which the narrative is carried forward by means of letters written by the characters. Epistolary novels were a quite popular form in the eighteenth century. Examples include Samuel Richardson's *Pamela: Or, Virtue Rewarded* (1740-1741) and *Clarissa: Or, The History of a Young Lady* (1747-1748). The form has not been much used in the twentieth century.

*Essay:* A brief prose work, usually on a single topic, that expresses the personal point of view of the author. The essay is usually addressed to a general audience and attempts to persuade the reader to accept the author's ideas.

*Essay-sketch tradition:* The first sketches can be traced to the Greek philosopher Theophrastus in 300 *b.c.e.*, whose character sketches influenced seventeenth and eighteenth century writers in England, who developed the form into something close to the idea of character in fiction. The essay has an equally venerable history, and, like the sketch, had an impact on the development of the modern short story.

*Euphony:* Language that creates a harmonious and pleasing effect; the opposite of cacophony, which is a combination of harsh and discordant sounds.

*Exemplum:* A brief anecdote or tale introduced to illustrate a moral point in medieval sermons. By the fourteenth century these exempla had expanded into exemplary narratives. Geoffrey Chaucer's "The Nun's Priest's Tale" and "The Pardoner's Tale" from *The Canterbury Tales* (1387-1400) are exempla.

*Existentialism:* A philosophy and attitude of mind that gained wide currency in religious and artistic thought after the end of World War II. Typical concerns of existential writers are human beings' estrangement from society, their awareness that the world is meaningless, and their recognition that one must turn from external props to the self. The novels of Albert Camus and Franz Kafka provide examples of existentialist beliefs.

*Exposition:* The part or parts of a work of fiction that provide necessary background information. Exposition not only provides the time and place of the action but also introduces readers to the fictive world of the story, acquainting them with the ground rules of the work. In the short story, exposition is usually elliptical.

*Expressionism:* Beginning in German theater at the start of the twentieth century, expressionism became the dominant movement in the decade following World War I. It abandoned realism and relied on a conscious distortion of external reality in order to portray the world as it is "viewed emotionally." The movement spread to fiction and poetry. Expressionism influenced the plays of Eugene O'Neill, Tennessee Williams, and Thornton Wilder and can be found in the novels of Franz Kafka and James Joyce.

*Fable:* One of the oldest narrative forms. Usually takes the form of an analogy in which animals or inanimate objects speak to illustrate a moral lesson. The most famous examples are the fables of Aesop, who used the form orally in 600 B.C.E.

*Fabliau:* A short narrative poem, popular in medieval French literature and during the English Middle Ages. Fabliaux were usually realistic in subject matter, bawdy, and made a point of satirizing the weaknesses and foibles of human beings. Perhaps the most famous are Geoffrey Chaucer's "The Miller's Tale" and "The Reeve's Tale" from *The Canterbury Tales* (1387-1400).

*Fabulation:* A term coined by Robert Scholes and used in contemporary literary criticism to describe novels that are radically experimental in subject matter, style, and form. Like the Magical Realists, fabulators mix realism with fantasy. The works of Thomas Pynchon, John Barth, Donald Barthelme, and William H. Gass provide examples.

*Fairy tale:* A form of folktale in which supernatural events or characters are prominent. Fairy tales usually depict a realm of reality beyond that of the natural world and in which the laws of the natural world are suspended.

*Fantastic:* In his study *Introduction à la littérature fantastique* (1970; *The Fantastic: A Structural Approach to a Literary Genre*, 1973), the critic Tzvetan Todorov defines the fantastic as a genre that lies between the uncanny and the marvelous. Whereas the marvelous presents an event that cannot be explained by the laws of the natural world and the uncanny presents an event that is the result of hallucination or illusion, the fantastic exists as long as the reader cannot decide which of these two applies. Henry James's *The Turn of the Screw* (1898) is an example of the fantastic.

*Figurative language:* Any use of language that departs from the usual or ordinary meaning to gain a poetic or otherwise special effect. Figurative language embodies various figures of speech, such as irony, metaphor, simile, and many others.

*Fin de siècle:* Literally, "end of the century"; refers to the last decade of the nineteenth century, a transitional period in which artists and writers were aware that they were living at the close of a great age and deliberately cultivated a kind of languor, world weariness, and satiety. Associated with the period of aestheticism and the Decadent movement exemplified in the works of Oscar Wilde.

*Flashback:* A scene that depicts an earlier event; it can be presented as a reminiscence by a character in a story, or it can simply be inserted into the narrative.

*Folktale:* A short prose narrative, usually handed down orally, found in all cultures of the world. The term is often used interchangeably with myth, fable, and fairy tale.

*Form:* The organizing principle in a work of literature; the manner in which its elements are put together in relation to its total effect. The term is sometimes used interchangeably with structure and is often contrasted with content: If form is the building, content is what is in the building and what the building is specifically designed to express.

*Frame story:* A story that provides a framework for another story (or stories) told within it. The form is ancient and is used by Geoffrey Chaucer in *The Canterbury Tales* (1387-1400). In modern literature, the technique has been used by Henry James in *The Turn of the Screw* (1898), Joseph Conrad in *Heart of Darkness* (1899, serial; 1902, book), and John Barth in *Lost in the Funhouse* (1968).

*Framework:* When used in connection with a frame story, the framework is the narrative setting, within which other stories are told. The framework may also have a plot of its own. More generally, the framework is similar to structure, referring to the general outline of a work.

*Gendered:* When a work is approached as thematically or stylistically specific to male or female characteristics or concerns, it is said to be "gendered."

*Genre study:* The concept of studying literature by classification and definition of types or kinds, such as tragedy, comedy, epic, lyrical, and pastoral. First introduced by Aristotle in *Poetics*, the genre principle has been an essential concomitant of the basic proposition that literature can be studied scientifically.

*Gothic genre:* A form of fiction developed in the late eighteenth century which focuses on horror and the supernatural. Examples include Matthew Gregory Lewis's *The Monk: A Romance*, (1796 also published as *Ambrosio: Or, The Monk*), Mary Wollstonecraft Shelley's *Frankenstein* (1818), and the short fiction of Edgar Allan Poe. In modern literature, the gothic genre can be found in the fiction of Truman Capote.

*Grotesque:* Characterized by a breakup of the everyday world by mysterious forces, the form differs from fantasy in that the reader is not sure whether to react with humor or horror. Examples include the stories of E. T. A. Hoffmann and Franz Kafka.

*Gynocriticism:* American feminist critic Elaine C. Showalter coined this term for her theory that women read and write differently than men do because of biological and cultural differences.

*Hasidic tale:* Hasidism was a Jewish mystical sect formed in the eighteenth century. The term "Hasidic tale" is used to describe some American short fiction, much of it written in the 1960's, which reflected the spirit of Hasidism, particularly the belief in the immanence of God in all things. Saul Bellow, Philip Roth, and Norman Mailer have been attracted to the genre, as has the Israeli writer Shmuel Yosef Agnon, who won the Nobel Prize in Literature in 1966.

*Hegemony:* Italian critic Antonio Gramsci maintains that capitalists create and sustain an ideology to support their dominance or hegemony over the working class. By maintaining economic and cultural power, capitalists receive the support of the working class, who adopt their values and beliefs, and thus control the ideology or social consciousness that in turn controls individual consciousness.

*Historical criticism:* In contrast to formalist criticism, which treats literary works as self-contained artifacts, historical criticism emphasizes the social and historical context of literature and allows itself to take into consideration the relevant facts and circumstances of the author's life. The method emphasizes the meaning that the work had in its own time rather than interpreting it for the present.

*Hyperbole:* The term is Greek for "overshooting" and refers to the use of gross exaggeration for rhetorical effect, based on the assumption that the reader will not be persuaded of the literal truth of the overstatement. Can be used for serious or comic effect.

*Imagery:* Often defined as the verbal stimulation of sensory perception. Although the word betrays a visual bias, imagery, in fact, calls on all five senses. In its simplest form, imagery re-creates a physical sensation in a clear, literal manner; it becomes more complex when a poet employs metaphor and other figures of speech to re-create experience.

*In medias res:* Latin phrase used by Horace, meaning literally "into the midst of things." It refers to a literary technique of beginning the narrative when the action has already begun. The term is used particularly in connection with the epic, which traditionally begins *in medias res*.

*Initiation story:* A story in which protagonists, usually children or young persons, go through an experience, sometimes painful or disconcerting, that carries them from innocence to some new form of knowledge and maturity. William Faulkner's "The Bear" (1942), Nathaniel Hawthorne's "Young Goodman Brown" (1835), Alice Walker's "To Hell with Dying" (1967), and Robert Penn Warren's "Blackberry Winter" (1946) are examples of the form.

*Interior monologue:* Defined as the speech of a character designed to introduce the reader directly to the character's internal life, the form differs from other monologues in that it attempts to reproduce thought before any logical organization is imposed upon it. An example is Molly Bloom's long interior monologue at the conclusion of James Joyce's *Ulysses* (1922).

*Interpretation:* An analysis of the meaning of a literary work. Interpretation will attempt to explicate the theme, structure, and other components of the work, often focusing on obscure or ambiguous passages.

*Irrealism:* A term often used to refer to modern or postmodern fiction that is presented self-consciously as a fiction or fabulation rather than a mimesis of external reality. The best-known practitioners of irrealism are John Barth, Robert Coover, and Donald Barthelme.

*Lai/Lay:* A song or short narrative poem. The term was first applied to twelfth and thirteenth centuries French poems and to English poems in the fourteenth century that were based on them, including Geoffrey Chaucer's "The Franklin's Tale" (1387-1400). In the nineteenth century, the term was applied to historical ballads, such as Sir Walter Scott's *The Lay of the Last Minstrel* (1805).

*Legend:* A narrative that is handed down from generation to generation, usually associated with a particular place and a specific event. A legend may often have more historical truth than a myth, and the protagonist is usually a person rather than a supernatural being.

*Leitmotif:* From the German, meaning "leading motif." Any repetition--of a word, phrase, situation, or idea--that occurs within a single work or group of related works.

*Literary short story:* A term that was current in American criticism in the 1940's to distinguish the short fiction of Ernest Hemingway, Eudora Welty, Sherwood Anderson, and others from the popular pulp and slick fiction of the day.

*Local color:* Usually refers to a movement in literature, especially in the United States, in the latter part of the nineteenth century. The focus was on the environment, atmosphere, and milieu of a particular region. For example, Mark Twain wrote about the Mississippi region; Sarah Orne Jewett wrote about New England. The term can also be used to refer to any work that represents the characteristics of a particular region.

*Logocentrism:* Jacques Derrida argues that all Western thought is based on the quest for a nonexistent "transcendental signifier," a sort of primal origin that makes ultimate meaning possible. The Western assumption of some ultimate center, that it calls God, reason, truth, or essence, is what Derrida calls Logocentrism.

*Lyric short story:* A form in which the emphasis is on internal changes, moods, and feelings. The lyric story is usually open-ended and depends on the figurative language usually associated with poetry. Examples of lyric stories are the works of Ivan Turgenev, Anton Chekhov, Katherine Mansfield, Sherwood Anderson, Conrad Aiken, and John Updike.

*Lyrical ballad:* The term is preeminently associated with William Wordsworth and Samuel Taylor Coleridge, whose *Lyrical Ballads* (1798), which drew on the ballad tradition, was one of the seminal books of the Romantic age. *Lyrical Ballads* was a revolt against eighteenth century poetic diction; it was an attempt to create a new kind of poetry by using simple language and taking as subject the everyday lives of common folk and the strong emotions they experience.

*Malaprop/Malapropism:* A malapropism occurs when one word is confused with another because the two words have a similar sound. The term is derived from the character Mrs. Malaprop in Richard Brinsley Sheridan's *The Rivals* (1775), who, for example, uses the word "illiterate" when she really means "obliterate" and mistakes "progeny" for "prodigy."

*Märchen:* German fairy tales, as collected in the works of Wilhelm and Jacob Grimm or in the works of nineteenth century writers, such as Novalis and E. T. A. Hoffmann.

*Marginalization:* The process by which an individual or a group is deemed secondary to a dominant group in power and thus denied access to the benefits enjoyed by the dominant group; for example, in the past women were marginalized by men and non-whites were marginalized by whites.

*Medieval romance:* Medieval romances, which originated in twelfth century France, were tales of adventure in which a knight would embark on a perilous quest to win the hand of a lady, perform a service for his king, or seek the Holy Grail. He had to overcome many obstacles, including dragons and other monsters; magic spells and enchantments were prominent, and the romance embodied the chivalric ideals of courage, honor, refined manners, and courtly love. English romances include the anonymous *Sir Gawain and the Green Knight* (fourteenth century) and Sir Thomas Malory's *Le Morte d'Arthur* (1485).

*Memoir:* Usually written by a person prominent in public life, a memoir is the authors' recollections of famous people they have known and great events they have witnessed. Memoir differs from autobiography in that the emphasis in the latter is on the life of the authors.

*Metafiction:* Refers to fiction that manifests a reflexive tendency, such as Vladimir Nabokov's *Pale Fire* (1962), and John Fowles's *The French Lieutenant's Woman* (1969). The emphasis is on the loosening of the work's illusion of reality to expose the reality of its illusion. Such terms as "irrealism," "postmodernist fiction," and "antifiction" are also used to refer to this type of fiction.

*Metaphor:* A figure of speech in which two dissimilar objects are imaginatively identified (rather than merely compared) on the assumption that they share one or more qualities: "She is the rose, the glory of the day" (Edmund Spenser). The term is often used in modern criticism in a wider sense to identify analogies of all kinds in literature, painting, and film.

*Metonymy:* A figure of speech in which an object that is closely related to a word comes to stand for the word itself, such as when one says "the White House" when meaning the "president."

*Minimalist movement:* A school of fiction writing that developed in the late 1970's and early 1980's and that Roland Barthes has characterized as the "less is more school." Minimalism attempts to convey much by saying little, to render contemporary reality in precise, pared-down prose that suggests more than it directly states. Leading minimalist writers are Raymond Carver and Ann Beattie. A character in Beattie's short story "Snow" (in *Where You'll Find Me*, 1986) seems to sum up minimalism: "Any life will seem dramatic if you omit mention of most of it."

*Mise en abîme:* A small story inside a larger narrative that echoes or mirrors the larger narrative, thus containing the larger within the smaller.

*Modern short story:* The modern short story dates from the nineteenth century and is associated with the names of Edgar Allan Poe (who is often credited with inventing the form) and Nathaniel Hawthorne in the United States, Honoré de Balzac in France, and E. T. A. Hoffmann in Germany. In his influential critical writings, Poe defined the short story as being limited to "a certain unique or single effect," to which every detail in the story should contribute.

*Monologue:* Any speech or narrative presented by one person. It can sometimes be used to refer to any lengthy speech, in which one person monopolizes the conversation.

*Moral tract:* A propaganda pamphlet on a political or religious topic, usually distributed free. The term is often associated with the Oxford Movement in nineteenth century England, which was a movement to reform the Church of England.

*Motif:* An incident or situation in a story that serves as the basis of its structure, creating by repetition and variation a patterned recurrence and consequently a general theme. Russian Formalist critics distinguish between bound motifs, which cannot be omitted without disturbing the thematic structure of the story, and unbound motifs, which serve merely to create the illusion of external reality. In this sense, motif is the same as leitmotif.

*Myth:* An anonymous traditional story, often involving supernatural beings or the interaction between gods and human beings and dealing with the basic questions of how the world and human society came to be as they are. Myth is an important term in contemporary literary criticism. Northrop Frye, for example, has said that "the typical forms of myth become the conventions and genres of literature." By this, he means that the genres of comedy, romance, tragedy, and irony (satire) correspond to seasonal myths of spring, summer, autumn, and winter.

*Narrative:* An account in prose or verse of an event or series of events, whether real or imagined.

*Narrative persona:* Persona means literally "mask": It is the self created by the author and through whom the narrative is told. The persona is not to be identified with the author, even when the two may seem to resemble each other. The narrative persona in Lord Byron's *Don Juan* (1819-1824), for example, may express many sentiments of which Byron would have approved, but he is nevertheless a fictional creation who is distinct from the author.

*Narratology:* The theoretical study of narrative structures and ways of meaning. Most all major literary theories have a branch of study known as narratology.

*Narrator:* The character who recounts the narrative. There are many different types of narrators: The first-person narrator is a character in the story and can be recognized by his or her use of "I"; third-person narrators may be limited or omniscient. In the former, the narrator is confined to knowledge of the minds and emotions of one or, at most, a few characters. In the latter, the narrator knows everything, seeing into the minds of all the characters. Rarely, second-person narration may be used. (An example can be found in Edna O'Brien's *A Pagan Place*, 1973.)

*Novel:* A fictional prose form, longer than a short story or novelette. The term embraces a wide range of types, but the novel usually includes a more complicated plot and a wider cast of characters than the short story. The focus is often on the development of individual characterization and the presentation of a social world and a detailed environment.

*Novella, novelette, Novelle, nouvelle:* These terms all refer to the form of fiction that is longer than a short story and shorter than a novel. Novella, the Italian term, is the term usually used to refer to American works in this genre, such as Joseph Conrad's *Heart of Darkness* (1899, serial; 1902, book) and Henry James's *The Turn of the Screw* (1898). *Novelle* is the German term; *nouvelle* the French; "novelette" the British. The term "novel" derived from these terms.

*Objective correlative:* A key concept in modern formalist criticism, coined by T. S. Eliot in *The Sacred Wood* (1920). An objective correlative is a situation, an event, or an object that, when presented or described in a literary work, expresses a particular emotion and serves as a precise formula by which the same emotion can be evoked in the reader.

*Oral tale:* A wide-ranging term that can include everything from gossip to myths, legends, folktale, and jokes. Among the terms used by Saith Thompson to classify oral tales (*The Folktale*, 1951) are märchen, fairy tale, household tale, *conte populaire*, novella, hero tale, local tradition, migratory legend, explanatory tale, humorous anecdote, and merry tale.

*Oral tradition:* Material that is transmitted by word of mouth, often through chants or songs, from generation to generation. Homer's epics, for example, were originally passed down orally and employ formulas to make memorization easier. Often, ballads, folklore, and proverbs are also passed down in this way.

*Oriental tale:* An eighteenth century form made popular by the translations of *Alf layla wa-layla* (fifteenth century; *The Arabian Nights' Entertainments*, 1706-1708) collected during the period. Oriental tales were usually solemn in tone, contained little characterization, and focused on improbable events and supernatural places.

*Other:* By a process of psychological or cultural projection, an individual or a dominant group accuses those of a different race or gender of all the negative qualities they themselves possess and then respond to them as if they were "other" than themselves.

*Oxymoron:* Closely related to paradox, an oxymoron occurs when two words of opposite meaning are placed in juxtaposition, such as "wise fool," "devilish angel," or "loving hate."

*Parable:* A short, simple, and usually allegorical story that teaches a moral lesson. In the West, the most famous parables are those told in the Gospels by Jesus Christ.

*Paradox:* A statement that initially seems to be illogical or self-contradictory yet eventually proves to embody a complex truth. In New Criticism, the term is used to embrace any complexity of language that sustains multiple meanings and deviates from the norms of ordinary language use.

*Parataxis:* The placing of clauses or phrases in a series without the use of coordinating or subordinating terms.

*Parody:* A literary work that imitates or burlesques another work or author for the purpose of ridicule. Twentieth century parodists include E. B. White and James Thurber.

*Periodical essay/sketch:* Informal in tone and style and applied to a wide range of topics, the periodical essay originated in the early eighteenth century. It is associated in particular with Joseph Addison and Sir Richard Steele and their informal periodical, *The Spectator.*

*Personification:* A figure of speech which ascribes human qualities to abstractions or inanimate objects, as in these lines by W. H. Auden: "There's Wrath who has learnt every trick of guerrilla warfare,/ The shamming dead, the night-raid, the feinted retreat." Richard Crashaw's "Hope, thou bold taster of delight" is another example.

*Plot:* The sequence of events in a play or story and how those events are connected in a cause-and-effect relationship. There are a great variety of plot patterns, each of which is designed to create a particular effect.

*Point of view:* The perspective from which a story is presented to the reader. In simplest terms, it refers to whether narration is first person (directly addressed to the reader as if told by one involved in the narrative) or third person (usually a more objective, distanced perspective.)

*Portmanteau words:* The term was coined by Lewis Carroll to describe the creation of a new word by telescoping two existing words. In this way, "furious" and "fuming" can be combined to create "frumious." The works of James Joyce, as well as Carroll's *Through the Looking Glass and What Alice Found There* (1871), provide many examples of portmanteau words.

*Postcolonial:* A literary approach that focuses on English-language texts from countries and cultures formerly colonized or dominated by America, the British Empire, and other European countries. Postcolonialists focus on the literature of such countries as Australia, New Zealand, Africa, and South America, and such cultural groups as African Americans and Native Americans.

*Postmodern:* Although this term is so broad it is interpreted differently by many different critics, it basically refers to a trend by which the literary work calls attention to itself as an artifice rather than a mirror held up to external reality.

*Prosody:* The study of the principles of verse structure. Includes meter, rhyme, and other patterns of sound, such as alliteration, assonance, euphony and onomatopoeia, and stanzaic patterns.

*Protagonist:* Originally, in the Greek drama, the "first actor," who played the leading role. The term has come to signify the most important character in a drama or story. It is not unusual for a work to contain more than one protagonist.

*Pun:* A pun occurs when words that have similar pronunciations have entirely different meanings. The result may be a surprise recognition of an unusual or striking connection, or, more often, a humorously accidental connection.

*Realism:* A literary technique in which the primary convention is to render an illusion of fidelity to external reality. Realism is often identified as the primary method of the novel form; the realist movement in the late nineteenth century coincided with the full development of the novel form.

*Reception theory:* Theorist Hans Robert Jauss argues that since readers from any historical milieu create their own criteria for judging a text, one should examine how a text was received by readers contemporary with it. Since every period creates its own "horizon of expectation," the meaning of a text changes from one period to another.

*Reminiscence:* An account, written or spoken, of remembered events.

*Rhetorical device:* Rhetoric is the art of using words clearly and effectively, in speech or writing, in order to influence or persuade. A rhetorical device is a figure of speech, or a way of using language, employed to this end. It can include such elements as choice of words, rhythms, repetition, apostrophe, invocation, chiasmus, zeugma, antithesis, and the rhetorical question (a question to which no answer is expected).

*Rogue literature:* From Odysseus to William Shakespeare's Autolocus to Huckleberry Finn, the rogue is a common literary type. He is usually a robust and energetic comic or satirical figure whose roguery can be seen as a necessary undermining of the rigid complacency of conventional society. The picaresque novel (*picaro* is Spanish for "rogue"), in which the picaro lives by his wits, is perhaps the most common form of rogue literature.

*Romance:* Originally, any work written in Old French. In the Middle Ages, romances were about knights and their adventures. In modern times, the term has also been used to describe a type of prose fiction in which, unlike the novel, realism plays little part. Prose romances often give expression to the quest for transcendent truths. Examples of the form include Nathaniel Hawthorne's *The Scarlet Letter* (1850) and Herman Melville's *Moby Dick* (1851).

*Romanticism:* A movement of the late eighteenth and nineteenth centuries which exalted individualism over collectivism, revolution over conservatism, innovation over tradition, imagination over reason, and spontaneity over restraint. Romanticism regarded art as self-expression; it strove to heal the cleavage between object and subject and expressed a longing for the infinite in all things. It stressed the innate goodness of human beings and the evils of the institutions that would stultify human creativity.

*Saga:* Originally applied to medieval Icelandic and other Scandinavian stories of heroic exploits and handed down by oral tradition. The term has come to signify any tale of heroic achievement or great adventure.

*Satire:* A form of literature that employs the comedic devices of wit, irony, and exaggeration to expose, ridicule, and condemn human folly, vice, and stupidity. Justifying satire, Alexander Pope wrote that "nothing moves strongly but satire, and those who are ashamed of nothing else are so of being ridiculous."

*Setting:* The circumstances and environment, both temporal and spatial, of a narrative. The term also applies to the physical elements of a theatrical production, such as scenery and properties. Setting is an important element in the creation of atmosphere.

*Shishōsetsu:* Literally translated as "I novel," *shishōsetsu* is a Japanese genre, a form of autobiographical or confessional writing used in novels and short stories. The protagonist and writer are closely identified. The genre originated in the early part of the twentieth century; a good example is *An'ya Koro* (1921-1928; *A Dark Night's Passing*, 1958) by Shiga Naoya.

*Short story:* A concise work of fiction, shorter than a novella, that is usually more concerned with mood, effect, or a single event than with plot or extensive characterization.

*Signifier/Signified:* Linguist Ferdinand de Saussure proposed that all words are signs made up of a "signifier," which is the written mark or the spoken sound of the word, and a "signified," which is the concept for which the mark or sounds stands.

*Simile:* A type of metaphor in which two things are compared. It can usually be recognized by the use of the words "like," "as," "appears," or "seems": "Float like a butterfly, sting like a bee" (Muhammad Ali); "The holy time is quiet as a nun" (William Wordsworth).

*Skaz:* A term used in Russian criticism to describe a narrative technique that presents an oral narrative of a lowbrow speaker.

*Sketch:* A brief narrative form originating in the eighteenth century, derived from the artist's sketch. The focus of a sketch is on a single person, place, or incident; it lacks a developed plot, theme, or characterization.

*Story line:* The story line of a work of fiction differs from the plot. Story line is merely the events that happen; plot is how those events are arranged by the author to suggest a cause-and-effect relationship.

*Stream of consciousness:* A narrative technique used in modern fiction by which an author tries to embody the total range of consciousness of a character, without any authorial comment or explanation. Sensations, thoughts, memories, and associations pour out in an uninterrupted, prerational and prelogical flow. Examples are James Joyce's *Ulysses* (1922), Virginia Woolf's *To the Lighthouse* (1927), and William Faulkner's *The Sound and the Fury* (1929).

*Structuralism:* Structuralism is based on the idea of intrinsic, self-sufficient structures that do not require reference to external elements. A structure is a system of transformations that involves the interplay of laws inherent in the system itself. The structuralist literary critic attempts, by using models derived from modern linguistic theory, to define the structural principles that operate intertextually throughout the whole of literature, as well as principles that operate in genres and in individual works.

*Style:* Style is the manner of expression, or how the writer tells the story. The most appropriate style is that which is perfectly suited to conveying whatever idea, emotion, or other effect that the author wishes to convey. Elements of style include diction, sentence structure, imagery, rhythm, and coherence.

*Subjective/Objective:* Terms used in critical theory. Subjective refers to works that express the ideas and emotions, the values and judgments of the authors, such as William Wordsworth's *The Prelude* (1850). Objective works are those that appear to be free of the personal sentiments of authors, who take a detached view of the events they record.

*Supplement:* A term used by Jacques Derrida to refer to the unstable relationship between the two elements in a set of binary opposites. For example, in the opposition between truth and lies, although Western thought assumes that truth is superior to lies, closer study reveals that so-called lies frequently reveal profound truths.

*Symbolism:* A literary movement encompassing the work of a group of French writers in the latter half of the nineteenth century, a group that included Charles Baudelaire, Stéphane Mallarmé, and Paul Verlaine. According to Symbolism, a mystical correspondence exists between the natural and spiritual worlds.

*Synesthesia:* Synesthesia occurs when one kind of sense experience is described in terms of another. Sounds may be described in terms of colors, and so on. For example, these lines from John Keats's poem "Isabella," "O turn thee to the very tale,/ And taste the music of that vision pale," combine the senses of taste, hearing, and sight. Synesthesia was used especially by the nineteenth century French Symbolists.

*Tale:* A general term for a simple prose or verse narrative. In the context of the short story, a tale is a story in which the emphasis is on the course of the action rather than on the minds of the characters.

*Tall tale:* A humorous tale popular in the American West; the story usually makes use of realistic detail and common speech, but it tells a tale of impossible events that most often focus on a single legendary, superhuman figure, such as Paul Bunyan or David Crockett.

*Technique:* Refers both to the method of procedure in creating an artistic work and to the degree of expertise shown in following the procedure.

*Thematics:* According to Northrop Frye, when a work of fiction is written or interpreted thematically, it becomes an illustrative fable. Murray Krieger defines thematics in *The Tragic Vision* (1960) as "the study of the experiential tensions which, dramatically entangled in the literary work, become an existential reflection of that work's aesthetic complexity."

*Theme:* Loosely defined as what a literary work means, theme is the underlying idea, the abstract concept, that the author is trying to convey: "the search for love," "the growth of wisdom," or some such formulation. The theme of William Butler Yeats's poem "Sailing to Byzantium" (1928), for example, might be interpreted as the failure of the attempt to isolate oneself within the world of art.

*Tone:* Strictly defined, tone is the authors' attitude toward their subject, their persona, themselves, their audience, or their society. The tone of a work may be serious, playful, formal, informal, morose, loving, ironic, and so on; it can be thought of as the dominant mood of a work, and it plays a large part in the total effect.

*Trope:* Literally "turn" or "conversion"; a figure of speech in which a word or phrase is used in a way that deviates from the normal or literal sense.

*Vehicle:* Used with the term "tenor" to understand the two elements of a metaphor. The tenor is the subject of the metaphor, and the vehicle is the image by which the subject is presented. The terms were coined by I. A. Richards. As an example, in T. S. Eliot's line, "The whole earth is our hospital," the tenor is "whole earth" and the vehicle is the "hospital."

*Verisimilitude:* When used in literary criticism, verisimilitude refers to the degree to which a literary work gives the appearance of being true or real, even though the events depicted may in fact be far removed from the actual.

*Vignette:* A sketch, essay, or brief narrative characterized by precision, economy, and grace. The term can also be applied to brief short stories, less than five hundred words long.

*Yarn:* An oral tale or a written transcription of what purports to be an oral tale. The yarn is usually a broadly comic tale, the classic example of which is Mark Twain's "Jim Baker's Bluejay Yarn" (1879). The yarn achieves its comic effect by juxtaposing realistic detail and incredible events; tellers of the tale protest that they are telling the truth; listeners know differently.

*Bryan Aubrey*
*Updated by Charles E. May*

# BIBLIOGRAPHY

Theoretical and Critical Discussions of Short Fiction

Aycock, Wendell M., ed. *The Teller and the Tale: Aspects of the Short Story*. Lubbock: Texas Tech Press, 1982. A collection of papers presented at a scholarly conference focusing on various aspects of short fiction, including its oral roots, the use of silences in the text, and realism versus antirealism.

Bader, A. L. "The Structure of the Modern Short Story." *College English* 7 (1945): 86-92. Counters the charge that the short story lacks narrative structure by contrasting the traditional "plotted" story with the "modern story," which is more suggestive, indirect, and technically patterned.

Baker, Falcon O. "Short Stories for the Millions." *Saturday Review*, December 19, 1953, 7-9, 48-49. Argues that as a result of formalist New Criticism, the short story has begun to ignore entertainment value and the ordinary reader.

Baldeshwiler, Eileen. "The Lyric Short Story: The Sketch of a History." *Studies in Short Fiction* 6 (1969): 443-453. A brief survey of the lyrical (as opposed to the epical) story from Ivan Turgenev to John Updike. The lyric story focuses on internal changes, moods, and feelings, using a variety of structural patterns depending on the "shape of the emotion itself."

Bates, H. E. *The Modern Short Story: A Critical Survey*. Boston: The Writer, 1941, 1972. A history of the major short-story writers and their work since Edgar Allan Poe and Nikolai Gogol. More focus on English and European short-story writers than most histories.

Bayley, John. *The Short Story: Henry James to Elizabeth Bowen*. New York: St. Martin's Press, 1988. A discussion of some of what Bayley calls the "special effects" of the short-story form, particularly its relationship to poetic techniques and devices. Much of the book consists of analyses of significant stories by Henry James, Ernest Hemingway, Rudyard Kipling, Anton Chekhov, D. H. Lawrence, James Joyce, and Elizabeth Bowen.

Benjamin, Walter. "The Storyteller: Reflections on the Words of Nikolai Leskov." Reprinted in *Modern Literary Criticism: 1900-1970*, edited by Lawrence Lipking and A. Walton Litz. New York: Atheneum, 1972. Benjamin claims that the art of storytelling is coming to an end because of the widespread dissemination of information and explanation. The compactness of a story precludes analysis and appeals to readers through the rhythm of the work itself. For the storyteller, the old religious chronicle is secularized into an ambiguous network in which the worldly and the eschatological are interwoven.

Bonheim, Helmut. *The Narrative Modes: Techniques of the Short Story*. Cambridge, England: D. S. Brewer, 1982. A systematic and statistical study of the short-story form, focusing on basic short-story techniques, especially short-story beginnings and endings. Argues that a limited set of techniques is used repeatedly in story endings. Discusses open and closed endings and argues that dynamic modes are more apt to be open, while static ones are more apt to be closed.

Boulanger, Daniel. "On the Short Story." *Michigan Quarterly Review* 26 (Summer, 1987): 510-514. A highly metaphoric and impressionistic study of the form, focusing primarily on the detached nature of the short story. Claims that there is a bit of Pontius Pilate in the short-story writer, for he or she is always removed from the tragic outcome. Points out how there are no class distinctions in the short story and no hierarchy.

Bowen, Elizabeth, ed. *The Faber Book of Modern Short Stories*. London: Faber & Faber, 1936. Bowen suggests that the short story, because it is exempt from the novel's often forced conclusiveness, more often approaches aesthetic and moral truth. She also suggests that the short story, more than the novel, is able to place the individual alone on that "stage which, inwardly, every man is conscious of occupying alone."

Brickell, Herschel. "What Happened to the Short Story?" *The Atlantic Monthly* 188 (September, 1951): 74-76. Argues that many contemporary writers have succeeded in breaking the short story away from its formal frame by drawing it nearer to poetry.

Brown, Suzanne Hunter. "The Chronotope of the Short Story: Time, Character, and Brevity." In *Creative and Critical Approaches to the Short Story*, edited by Noel Harold Kaylor, Jr. Lewiston, N.Y.: Edwin Mellen Press, 1997. A survey and analysis of the frequent critical assumption that short stories deal with characters as eternal essence and that novels deal with characters who change over time. Argues that Mikhail Bakhtin's concept of "chronotrope," a literary work's projection of time and space, will help develop a generic theory of the short story that considers both historical and technical factors.

_____. "Discourse Analysis and the Short Story." In *Short Story Theory at a Crossroads*, edited by Susan Lohafer and Jo Ellyn Clarey. Baton Rouge: Louisiana State University Press, 1989. A helpful analytical survey of the research being conducted by psychologists into the nature of discourse, storyness, and cognitive response to narrative.

Cortázar, Julio. "Some Aspects of the Short Story." *Arizona Quarterly*, Spring, 1982, 5-17. Cortázar, an Argentine writer and notable practitioner of the short story, discusses the invariable elements that give a good short story its particular atmosphere. He compares the novel and the short story to film and the photograph; the short story's most significant element is its subject, the act of choosing a real or imaginary happening that has the mysterious property of illuminating something beyond itself.

Cox, Alisa, ed. *The Short Story*. Newcastle, England: Cambridge Scholars, 2008. A collection of essays that provides a critical international overview of short fiction. Includes A. L. Kennedy's reflections on writing short stories, a discussion of the contemporary short story sequence, an essay pondering a definition of the short story, and analyses of stories by Italo Calvino, Jorge Luis Borges, Anita Desai, Martin Amis, Ray Bradbury, and others.

Dawson, W. J. "The Modern Short Story." *North American Review* 190 (December, 1909): 799-810. Argues that a short story must be complete in itself and consist of a single incident. The finest writing in a short story, Dawson maintains, is that which takes the reader most quickly to the very heart of the matter at hand.

Eichenbaum, Boris. *O. Henry and the Theory of the Short Story*. Translated by I. R. Titunik. Ann Arbor: University of Michigan, 1968. Originally published in 1925, this essay is a good example of the early Russian Formalist approach to fiction through a consideration of genre. Eichenbaum poses a generic distinction between the novel and the short story. Short stories are constructed on the basis of a contradiction, incongruity, error, or contrast and, like the anecdote, build their weight toward the ending.

Eldred, Janet Carey. "Narratives of Socialization: Literacy in the Short Story." *College English* 53 (October, 1991): 686-700. Based on the critical assumption that all fiction historicizes problems of socialization. Argues that the short story is a narrative of arrested socialization that ends with characters between two cultures who find their own speech inadequate but their new language problematic.

Elliott, George P. "A Defense of Fiction." *Hudson Review* 16 (1963): 9-48. Elliott, himself a short-story writer, discusses the four basic impulses that mingle with the storytelling impulse: to dream, to tell what happened, to explain the sense of things, and make a to likeness.

Ermida, Isabel. *The Language of Comic Narratives: Humor Construction in Short Stories*. New York: Mouton de Gruyter, 2008. Analyzes how humor works in short fiction, examining short stories by Dorothy Parker, Graham Greene, Woody Allen, David Lodge, Evelyn Waugh, and other English and American writers.

Farrell, James T. *The League of Frightened Philistines and Other Papers*. New York: Vanguard Press, 1945. Ridicules the short-story handbooks published in the 1920's and 1930's and claims that in many contemporary short stories the revolutionary point of view appears more tacked on than integral to the story.

Ferguson, Suzanne C. "Defining the Short Story: Impressionism and Form." *Modern Fiction Studies* 28 (Spring, 1982): 13-24. Argues that there is no single characteristic or cluster of characteristics that distinguishes the short story from the novel. Suggests that what is called the modern short story is a manifestation of impressionism rather than a discrete genre.

_____. "The Rise of the Short Story in the Hierarchy of Genres." In *Short Story Theory at a Crossroads*, edited by Susan Lohafer and Jo Ellyn Clarey. Baton Rouge: Louisiana State University Press, 1989. A historical and critical survey of the development of the English short story, showing how social factors influenced the rise and fall of the form's prestige.

FitzGerald, Gregory. "The Satiric Short Story: A Definition." *Studies in Short Fiction* 5 (1968): 349-354. Defines the satiric short story as a subgenre that sustains a reductive attack upon its objects and conveys to its readers a significance different from its apparent surface meaning.

Fonlon, Bernard, "The Philosophy, the Science, and the Art of the Short Story, Part II." *Abbia* 34 (1979): 429-438. A discussion of the basic elements of a story, including character and conflict. Lists elements of intensity, detachment, skill, and unity of effect. Primarily presents a set of rules aimed at inexperienced writers.

Friedman, Norman. "Recent Short Story Theories: Problems in Definition." In *Short Story Theory at a Crossroads*, edited by Susan Lohafer and Jo Ellyn Clarey. Baton Rouge: Louisiana State University Press, 1989. A critical review of major short-story critics, including Mary Rohrberger, Charles May, Susan Lohafer, and John Gerlach. Argues against those critics who support a deductive, single-term, mixed category approach to definition of the form. Urges that what is needed is a more inductive approach that follows the principle of suiting the definition to the facts rather than trying to suit the facts to the definition.

_____. "What Makes a Short Story Short?" *Modern Fiction Studies* 4 (1958): 103-117. Makes use of neo-Aristotelian literary theory to determine the issue of the short story's shortness. To deal with the problem, Friedman argues, one must ask the following questions: What is the size of the action? Is the action composed of a speech, a scene, an episode, or a plot? Does the action involve a change? If so, is the change a major one or a minor one?

Gerlach, John. "The Margins of Narrative: The Very Short Story, the Prose Poem, and the Lyric." In *Short Story Theory at a Crossroads*, edited by Susan Lohafer and Jo Ellyn Clarey. Baton Rouge: Louisiana State University Press, 1989. Explores the basic requirements of a story, focusing particularly on two minimalist stories by Enrique Anderson Imbert and Scott Sanders, as well as a short prose poem by W. S. Merwin. Argues that point-- not mere length or fictionality-- is the principal constituent of story.

Gordimer, Nadine. "South Africa." *The Kenyon Review* 30 (1968): 457-461. Gordimer, a Nobel Prize-winning writer, argues that the strongest convention of the novel, its prolonged coherence of tone, is false to the nature of what can be grasped as reality in the modern world. Short-story writers deal with the only thing one can be sure of--the present moment.

Görtschacher, Wolfgang, and Holger Klein, eds. *Tale, Novella, Short Story: Currents in Short Fiction*. Tübingen, Germany: Stauffenburg, 2004. Reprints the papers delivered at the Tenth International Salzburg Conference, which focused on the short fictional forms of the tale, novella, and short story. Among the topics discussed are the influence of English short fiction on historical texts, such as *The Arabian Nights' Entertainments*; theoretical issues, including the aesthetic principles of compactness and brevity; and analyses of contemporary short fiction from Australia, Africa, the United States, Great Britain, and Ireland.

Gullason, Thomas A. "Revelation and Evolution: A Neglected Dimension of the Short Story." *Studies in Short Fiction* 10 (1973): 347-356. Challenges Mark Schorer's distinction between the short story as an "art of moral revelation" and the novel as an "art of moral evolution." Analyzes D. H. Lawrence's "The Horse Dealer's Daughter" and John Steinbeck's "The Chrysanthemums" to show that the short story embodies both revelation and evolution.

_____. "The Short Story: An Underrated Art." *Studies in Short Fiction* 2 (1964): 13-31. Points out the lack of serious criticism of the short story, suggests some of the reasons for this neglect, and concludes with an analysis of Anton Chekhov's "Gooseberries" and Nadine Gordimer's "The Train from Rhodesia" to disprove the charges that the short story is formulaic and lacks life.

Hanson, Clare, ed. Introduction to *Re-reading the Short Story*. New York: St. Martin's Press, 1989. Claims that the short story is a vehicle for different kinds of knowledge, knowledge that may be in some way at odds with the "story" of dominant culture. The formal properties of the short story--disjunction, inconclusiveness, and obliquity--connect with its ideological marginality and with the fact that the form may be used to express something suppressed or repressed in mainstream literature.

_____. *Short Stories and Short Fictions, 1880-1980*. New York: St. Martin's Press, 1985. Argues that during this period, the authority of the teller, usually a first-person "framing" narrator who guaranteed the authenticity of the tale, was questioned by many modernist writers. Argues that the movements from "teller" to indirect free narration, and from "tale" to "text," were part of a more general movement from "discourse" to "image" in the art and literature of the period. Includes chapters on Rudyard Kipling, Saki, W. Somerset Maugham, James Joyce, Virginia Woolf, Katherine Mansfield, Samuel Beckett.

_____. "Things out of Words: Towards a Poetics of Short Fiction." In *Re-reading the Short Story*, edited by Clare Hanson. New York: St. Martin's Press, 1989. Argues that the short story is a more literary form than the novel. Maintains that short stories are framed, an aesthetic device that gives a sense of completeness which allows gaps and absences to remain in the story; thus readers accept a degree of mystery or elision in the short story that they would not accept in the novel.

Hardy, Sarah. "A Poetics of Immediacy: Oral Narrative and the Short Story." *Style* 27 (Fall, 1993): 352-368. Argues that the oral-epic episode clarifies basic characteristics of the short story: It gives the reader a way to understand the density of meaning in the short story and provides a paradigm of the short-story audience as that of a participating community.

Hedberg, Johannes. "What Is a 'Short Story?' and What Is an 'Essay'?" *Moderna Sprak* 74 (1980): 113-120. Reminds readers of the distinction between the Chekhovian story (lack of plot) and the Maupassantian story (anecdotal and therefore commercial). Discusses basic characteristics of the essay and the story; maintains they are similar in that they are both a whole picture in miniature, not merely a detail of a larger picture--a complete work, not an extract.

Hendricks, William O. "Methodology of Narrative Structural Analysis." In *Essays in Semiolinguistics and Verbal Art*. The Hague, Netherlands: Mouton, 1973. Structuralists, in the tradition of Vladimir Propp and Claude Levi-Strauss, usually bypass the actual sentences of a narrative and analyze a synopsis. This essay is a fairly detailed discussion of the methodology of synopsizing (using William Faulkner's "A Rose for Emily" as an example), followed by a brief discussion of the methodology of structural analysis of the resultant synopsis.

Hesse, Douglas. "A Boundary Zone: First-Person Short Stories and Narrative Essays." In *Short Story Theory at a Crossroads*, edited by Susan Lohafer and Jo Ellyn Clarey. Baton Rouge: Louisiana State University Press, 1989. Argues that the precise boundary point between essays and short stories does not exist. Analyzes George Orwell's essay "A Hanging" as a short story and William Carlos Williams's short story "Use of Force" as an essay. Discusses essays and stories that fall in a boundary zone between essay and story.

Hicks, Granville. "The Art of the Short Story." *Saturday Review* 41 (December 20, 1958): 16. Maintains that the focus of the contemporary short story is an emotional experience for the reader rather than character or plot.

Holloway, John. "Identity, Inversion, and Density Elements in Narrative: Three Tales by Chekhov, James, and Lawrence." In *Narrative and Structure: Exploratory Essays*. Cambridge, England. Cambridge University Press, 1979. Holloway looks at stories in which almost nothing happens. He says there is a distinctive kind of narrative episode introduced by an item that is then followed by another item in inverse relationship to the first, which cancels it out and brings the reader back to where he or she started.

Howe, Irving. "Tone in the Short Story." Sewanee Review 57 (Winter, 1949): 141-152. Maintains that because the short story lacks prolonged characterization and a structured plot, it depends mostly on tone to hold it together.

Ibáñez, José R., José Francisco Fernández, and Carmen M. Bretones, eds. *Contemporary Debates on the Short Story*. New York: Peter Lang, 2007. Collection of critical essays about short fiction, some of which are written from the perspectives of globalization and deconstructionism. Includes a discussion of dissent in the modern Irish short story; an overview of short fiction, including a historical overview of the mystery story; and analyses of short fiction by Wyndham Lewis, Henry James, Salman Rushdie, and Judith Ortiz Cofer.

"International Symposium on the Short Story" in *Kenyon Review*. Contributions from short-story writers from all over the world on the nature of the form, its current economic status, its history, and its significance. Part 1, vol. 30, no. 4 (1969): 443-490 features contributions by Christina Stead (England), Herbert Gold (United States), Erih Koš (Yugoslavia), Nadine Gordimer (South Africa), Benedict Kiely (Ireland), Hugh Hood (Canada), and Henrietta Drake-Brockman (Australia); part 2, vol. 31, no. 1 (1969): 58-94 contains comments by William Saroyan (United States), Jun Eto (Japan), Maurice Shadbolt (New Zealand), Chanakya Sen (India), John Wain (England), and Hans Bender (Germany) and "An Agent's View" by James Oliver Brown; part 3, vol. 31, no. 4 (1969): 450-502 features Ana María Matute (Spain), Torborg Nedreaas (Norway), George Garrett (United States), Elizabeth Taylor (England), Ezekiel Mphahlele (South Africa), Elizabeth Harrower (Australia), Mario Picchi (Italy), Junzo Shono (Japan), and Khushwant Singh (India); part 4, vol. 32, no. 1 (1969): 78-108 includes Jack Cope (South Africa), James T. Farrell (United States), Edward Hyams (England), Luigi Barzini (Italy), David Ballantyne (New Zealand), and H. E. Bates (England).

Jarrell, Randall. "Stories." In *The Anchor Book of Stories*. New York: Doubleday, 1958. Jarrell's introduction to this collection focuses on stories as being closer to dream reality than the waking world of everyday life. He argues that there are basically two kinds of stories: stories in which everything is a happening (in which each event is so charged that the narrative threatens to disintegrate into energy), and stories in which nothing happens (in which even the climax may lose its charge and become one more portion of a lyric continuum).

Jouve, Nicole Ward. "Too Short for a Book." In *Rereading the Short Story*, edited by Clare Hanson. New York: St. Martin's Press, 1989. An impressionistic, noncritical essay about story length. Discusses *The Arabian Nights' Entertainments* as an archetypal model standing behind all stories, collections of stories, and storytelling. Makes a case for collections of stories that stand together as organic wholes rather than single individual stories that stand alone.

Lewis, C. S. "On Stories." In *Essays Presented to Charles Williams*. Grand Rapids, Mich.: Wm. B. Eerdmans, 1966. Although stories are series of events, this series, or what is called plot, is only a necessary means to capture something that has no sequence, something more like a state or quality. Thus, the "means" of a story is always at war with its "end"; this very tension, however, constitutes the story's chief resemblance to life: "We grasp at a state and find only a succession of events in which the state is never quite embodied."

Lohafer, Susan. "A Cognitive Approach to Story-Ness." *Short Story* (Spring, 1990), 60-71. A study of what Lohafer calls "preclosure," those points in a story where it could end but does not. Studies the characters of such preclosure sentences--where they appear and what they signal--as part of a more general effort to clarify what constitutes story-ness.

_____. *Coming to Terms with the Short Story*. Baton Rouge: Louisiana State University Press, 1983. A highly suggestive theoretical study of the short story that focuses on the sentence unit of the form as a way of showing how it differs from the novel.

_____. "Interdisciplinary Thoughts on Cognitive Science and Short Fiction Studies." In *The Tales We Tell: Perspectives on the Short Story*, edited by Barbara Lounsberry, et al. Westport, Conn.: Greenwood Press, 1998. A brief summary of psychological approaches to cognitive strategies for reading short fiction. Makes a number of suggestions about the future of short-story criticism based on the cooperation between narrative theorists and cognitive scientists.

_____. "Preclosure and Story Processing." In *Short Story Theory at a Crossroads*, edited by Susan Lohafer and Jo Ellyn Clarey. Baton Rouge: Louisiana State University Press, 1989. Analyzes responses to a story by Kate Chopin in terms of identifying those sentences that could end the story but do not. This essay is a continuation of Lohafer's study of what she has defined as preclosure in short fiction.

_____. "Preclosure in an 'Open' Story." In *Creative and Critical Approaches to the Short Story*, edited by Noel Harold Kaylor, Jr. Lewiston, N.Y.: Edwin Mellen Press, 1997. Presents the results of an experiment in preclosure studies in which 114 students were asked to read Julio Cortázar's story "Orientation of Cats" and report on their understanding of it. Lohafer asks the students to identify points at which the story might have ended, a preclosure procedure which makes them more aware of reading tactics and their inherent sense of story-ness.

_____. *Reading for Storyness: Preclosure Theory, Empirical Poetics, and Culture in the Short Story*. Baltimore: Johns Hopkins University Press, 2003. Lohafer discusses many of the literary theories presented in her previous articles, arguing that "imminent closure" is the defining trait of the short story. She demonstrates her theories by analyzing stories by Kate Chopin, Katherine Mansfield, Julio Cortázar, Raymond Carver, Bobbie Ann Mason, Ann Beattie, and other writers.

_____. "Why the 'Life of Ma Parker' Is Not So Simple: Preclosure in Issue-Bound Stories." *Studies in Short Fiction* 33 (Fall, 1996): 475-486. In this particular experiment with student reaction to preclosure markers in a story by Katherine Mansfield, Lohafer is interested in showing how attention to preclosure encourages readers to temporarily suppress their ready-made concepts and engage their story competence.

March-Russell, Paul. *The Short Story: An Introduction*. Edinburgh: Edinburgh University Press, 2009. Historical overview of short fiction, defining its origins, the concept of the well-made story, the short story cycle, and specific types of stories, such as ghost stories and modernist, postmodernist, minimalist, and postcolonial short fiction.

Marcus, Mordecai. "What Is an Initiation Story?" *The Journal of Aesthetics and Art Criticism* 14 (1960): 221-227. Distinguishes three types of initiation stories: those that lead protagonists only to the threshold of maturity, those that take the protagonists across the threshold of maturity but leave them in a struggle for certainty, and decisive initiation stories that carry protagonists firmly into maturity.

Matthews, Brander. *The Philosophy of the Short-Story*. New York: Longmans, Green, 1901. An expansion of an 1882 article in which Matthews sets himself forth as the first critic since Edgar Allan Poe to discuss the "short-story" (Matthews contributed the hyphen) as a genre. By asserting that the short story must have a vigorous compression, must be original, must be ingenious, must have a touch of fantasy, and so on, Matthews set the stage for the subsequent host of textbook writers on the short story.

Maugham, W. Somerset. "The Short Story." In *Points of View: Five Essays*. Garden City, N.Y.: Doubleday, 1958. As might be expected, Maugham's preference is for the well-made story exemplified by Guy de Maupassant's "The Necklace." Most of the essay, however, deals with biographical material about Anton Chekhov and Katherine Mansfield.

May, Charles E. "Artifice and Artificiality in the Short Story." *Story* 1 (Spring, 1990): 72-82. Discusses the artificial and formalized nature of the endings of short stories, arguing that the short story is the most aesthetic narrative form. Discusses the ending of several representative stories.

_____. "Metaphoric Motivation in Short Fiction: 'In the Beginning Was the Story.' " In *Short Theory at a Crossroads*, edited by Susan Lohafer and Jo Ellyn Clarey. Baton Rouge: Louisiana State University Press, 1989. A discussion of how short fiction moves from the "tale" form to the "short story" form through motivation by metaphor in "The Fall of the House of Usher," "Bartleby the Scrivener," "The Legend of Sleepy Hollow," and "Young Goodman Brown."

_____. "The Nature of Knowledge in Short Fiction." *Studies in Short Fiction* 21 (Fall, 1984): 227-238. A theoretical study of the epistemological bases of short fiction. Argues that the short story originates as a primal mythic mode that develops into a metaphoric mode.

_____. "Obsession and the Short Story." In *Creative and Critical Approaches to the Short Story*, edited by Noel Harold Kaylor, Jr. Lewiston, N.Y.: Edwin Mellen Press, 1997. An examination of the common charge that the short story is unhealthily limited and obsessed. Discusses the origins of the relationship between psychological obsession and aesthetic unity in the stories of Edgar Allan Poe, Nathaniel Hawthorne, and Herman Melville. Attempts to account for this relationship as a generic characteristic of the short story.

_____. "Prolegomenon to a Generic Study of the Short Story." *Studies in Short Fiction* 33 (Fall, 1996): 461-474. Tries to lay the groundwork for a generic theory of the short story in terms of new theories of this genre. Discusses the short story's historical focus on the strange and unexpected and the formal demands made by this thematic focus. Argues for a mixed genre theory of the short story that can account for the form's essential, as well as historically changing, characteristics.

_____. "Reality in the Modern Short Story. *Style* 27 (Fall, 1993): 369-379. Argues that realism in the modern short story from Anton Chekhov to Raymond Carver is not the simple mimesis of the realistic novel but rather the use of highly compressed selective detail configured to metaphorically objectify that which cannot be described directly. The result is a "hyperrealism" in which story is unified by tone and meaning is created by aesthetic pattern.

_____. *The Short Story: The Reality of Artifice*. New York: Routledge, 2002. A historical survey of the short story, tracing its origins in the tales of Geoffrey Chaucer and Giovanni Boccaccio through the nineteenth century and its contemporary renaissance.

_____. *Short Story Theories*. Athens: Ohio University Press, 1976. A collection of twenty previously published essays on the short story as a genre in its own right.

_____. "A Survey of Short Story Criticism in America." *The Minnesota Review*, Spring, 1973, 163-169. An analytical survey of criticism beginning with Edgar Allan Poe and focusing on the short story's underlying vision and characteristic mode of understanding and confronting reality.

_____. "The Unique Effect of the Short Story: A Reconsideration and an Example." *Studies in Short Fiction* 13 (1976): 289-297. An attempt to redefine Edgar Allan Poe's "unique effect" in the short story in terms of mythic perception. Maintains that the short story demands intense compression and focusing because its essential subject is a manifestation of what philosopher Ernst Cassirer calls the "momentary deity." A detailed discussion of Stephen Crane's story "An Episode of War" illustrates the concept.

McSweeney, Kerry. *The Realist Short Story of the Powerful Glimpse: Chekhov to Carver*. Columbia: University of South Carolina Press, 2007. Focuses on the short fiction of five writers--Anton Chekhov, James Joyce, Ernest Hemingway, Flannery O'Connor, and Raymond Carver--to argue that the realist realist short story is a "glimpse--powerful and tightly focused, into a world that the writer must precisely craft and in which the reader must fully invest."

Menikoff, Barry. "The Problematics of Form: History and the Short Story." *Journal of the Short Story in English*, no. 2 (1984): 129-146. After a brief introduction discussing how the short story has been neglected, Menikoff comments briefly on the importance of

Charles E. May's *Short Story Theories* (1976) and then discusses essays on the short story that appeared in *Critical Survey of Short Fiction* (1981) and a special issue of *Modern Fiction Studies* (1982).

Miall, David. "Text and Affect: A Model for Story Understanding." In *Re-reading the Short Story*, edited by Clare Hanson. New York: St. Martin's Press, 1989. A discussion of what readers are doing in emotional terms when they read, using the defamiliarization model of the Russian Formalists. Focuses on three aspects of emotion: self-reference, domain crossing, and anticipation. Basically determines that whereas literary texts constrain response by means of their shared frames and conventions, their affective responses are highly divergent.

Millhauser, Steven. "The Ambition of the Short Story." *The New York Times Book Review*, October 5, 2008, p. 31. Discussion of the short story's essential characteristics and how the form differs from the novel.

Moffett, James. "Telling Stories: Methods of Abstraction in Fiction." *ETC* 21 (1964): 425-50. Charts a sequence covering an "entire range" of ways in which stories can be told, from the most subjective and personal (interior monologue and dramatic monologue) to the most objective and impersonal (anonymous narration). Includes examples of each type.

Moravia, Alberto. "The Short Story and the Novel." In *Man as End: A Defense of Humanism*. Translated by Bernard Wall. New York: Farrar, Straus & Giroux, 1969. Moravia, who wrote many novels and short stories, maintains that the basic difference between the two is that the novel has a bone structure of ideological themes whereas the short story is made up of intuitions of feelings.

Munson, Gorham. "The Recapture of the Storyable." *University Review* 10 (Autumn, 1943): 37-44. Maintains that the best short-story writers are concerned with only three questions: whether they have found a "storyable" incident, how they should cast their characters, and who would best tell their story.

Oates, Joyce Carol. "Beginnings: The Origin and Art of the Short Story." In *The Tales We Tell: Perspectives on the Short Story*, edited by Barbara Lounsberry, et al. Westport, Conn.: Greenwood Press, 1998. Defines the short story as a form that represents an intensification of meaning rather than an expansion of the imagination. Briefly discusses the importance of Edgar Allan Poe's aesthetic and Mark Twain's oral tale to the development of the American short story.

_____. "The Short Story." *Southern Humanities Review* 5 (1971): 213-214. Maintains that the short story is a "dream verbalized," a manifestation of desire; its most interesting aspect is its "mystery."

O'Connor, Frank. *The Lonely Voice: A Study of the Short Story*. 1963. Reprint. Hoboken, N.J.: Melville House, 2004. O'Connor, an accomplished master of the short-story form, presented his observations of the genre in this study. The introductory chapter contains extremely valuable "intuitive" criticism. O'Connor maintains that the basic difference between the novel and the short story is that in the latter readers always find an intense awareness of human loneliness. He believes that the protagonist of the short story is less an individual with whom readers can identify than a "submerged population group," that is, someone outside the social mainstream. The remaining chapters of the book treat this theme in the works of Ivan Turgenev, Anton Chekhov, Guy de Maupassant, Rudyard Kipling, James Joyce, Katherine Mansfield, D. H. Lawrence, A. E. Coppard, Isaac Babel, and Mary Lavin.

O'Faoláin, Seán. *The Short Story*. New York: Devin-Adair, 1951. This book on the technique of the short story claims that technique is the "least part of the business." O'Faoláin illustrates his thesis that personality is the most important element in short fiction by describing the personal struggles of Alphonse Daudet, Anton Chekhov, and Guy de Maupassant. He does his duty to the assigned subject of the book by also discussing the technical problems of convention, subject, construction, and language.

O'Rourke, William. "Morphological Metaphors for the Short Story: Matters of Production, Reproduction, and Consumption." In *Short Story Theory at a Crossroads*, edited by Susan Lohafer and Jo Ellyn Clarey. Baton Rouge: Louisiana State University Press, 1989. Explores a number of analogies drawn from the social and natural sciences to suggest ways of seeing how the short story is different from the novel: The novel has a structure like a vertebrate, whereas the short story is like an animal with an exoskeleton; the novel is a macro form, whereas the short story is a micro form.

Overstreet, Bonaro. "Little Story, What Now?" *Saturday Review of Literature*, 24 (November 22, 1941): 3-5, 25-26. Overstreet argues that as a result of a loss of faith in the old verities of the nineteenth century, the twentieth century short story is concerned with psychological materials, not with the events in the objective world.

Pain, Barry. *The Short Story.* London: Martin Secker, 1916. Pain claims that the primary difference between the short story and the novel is that the short story, because of its dependence on suggestive devices, demands more of the reader's participation.

Palakeel, Thomas. "Third World Short Story as National Allegory?" *Journal of Modern Literature* 20 (Summer, 1996): 97-102. Argues against Frederic Jameson's claim that Third World fictions are always national allegories. Points out that this claim is even more damaging to the short story than to the novel because the short story is the most energetic literary activity in the Third World. He argues that Jameson's theory cripples any non-Western literature that tries to deal with the psychological or spiritual reality of the individual.

Pasco, Allan H. "The Short Story: The Short of It." *Style* 27 (Fall, 1993): 442-451. Suggests a list of qualities of the short story generated by its brevity, such as the assumptions of considerable background on the part of the readers and that readers will absorb and remember all elements of the work. Claims that the short story shuns amplification in favor of inference, that it is usually single rather than multivalent, that it tends toward the general, and that it remains foreign to loosely motivated detail.

Patrick, Walton R. "Poetic Style in the Contemporary Short Story." *College Composition and Communication* (1957): 77-84. Argues that the poetic style appears more consistently in the short story than in the novel because metaphorical dilations are essential to the writer who "strives to pack the utmost meaning into his restricted space."

Penn, W. S. "The Tale as Genre in Short Fiction." *Southern Humanities Review* 15 (Summer, 1981): 231-241. Discusses the genre from the perspective of structure. Primarily uses suggestions made by Jonathan Culler in *Structuralist Poetics* for constructing a poetic persona in the lyric poem, what Culler calls an "enunciative posture," that is, the detectable or intuited moral relation of the implied author to both the world at large and the world he or she creates. Develops two kinds of tales: the radical oral and the exponential oral.

Perry, Bliss. *A Study of Prose Fiction*. Boston: Houghton Mifflin, 1920. Perry claims that the short story differs from the novel by presenting unique and original characters, by focusing on fragments of reality, and by making use of the poetic devices of impressionism and symbolism.

Pickering, Jean. "Time and the Short Story." In *Rereading the Short Story*, edited by Clare Hanson. New York: St. Martin's Press, 1989. Discusses the distinction between the short story as an art of revelation and the novel as an art of evolution. General implications that derive from this distinction are that short-story writers do not need to know all the details of their characters' lives and that the short story is doubly symbolic. Structure, theme, characterization, and language are influenced by the short story's particular relation to time as a moment of revelation.

Poe, Edgar Allan. Review of *Twice-Told Tales*. *Graham's Magazine*, May, 1842. The first critical discussion of the short story, or the "tale" as Poe terms it, to establish the genre as distinct from the novel. Because of its sense of totality, its single effect, and its patterned design, the short story is second only to the lyric in its demands on high genius and in its aesthetic beauty.

Pratt, Mary Louise. "The Short Story: The Long and the Short of It." *Poetics* 10 (1981): 175-194. A theoretical discussion of the form. Presents eight ways that the short story is better understood if its dependence on the novel is understood.

Prince, Gerald. *A Grammar of Stories: An Introduction.* The Hague, Netherlands: Mouton, 1973. An attempt to establish rules to account for the structure of all the syntactical sets that readers intuitively recognize as stories. The model used is Noam Chomsky's theories of generative grammar.

_____. "The Long and the Short of It." *Style* 27 (Fall, 1993): 327-331. Provides a definition of the short story as "an autonomous, short, fictional story written in prose and offered for display." Admits that such a definition has limited usefulness but argues that this is characteristic of generic definitions; maintains that texts belong not to one but to an indefinitely large number of textual families and use an indefinitely large number of clusters of features.

Pritchett, V. S. "Short Stories." *Harper's Bazaar* 87 (July, 1953): 31, 113. In Pritchett's opinion the short story is a hybrid, owing much to the quickness and objectivity of the cinema, much to the poet and the newspaper reporter, and everything to the "restlessness, the alert nerve, the scientific eye and the short breath of contemporary life." He makes an interesting point about the collapse of standards, conventions, and values which has so bewildered the impersonal novelist but has been the making of the story writer.

Reid, Ian. *The Short Story.* London: Methuen, 1977. A brief study that deals with problems of definition, historical development, and related generic forms. Offers a good introduction to the short story as a genre.

Rohrberger, Mary. "Between Shadow and Act: Where Do We Go from Here?" In *Short Story Theory at a Crossroads*, edited by Susan Lohafer and Jo Ellyn Clarey. Baton Rouge: Louisiana State University Press, 1989. A thought-provoking review of a number of modern short-story critics and theorists, largely by way of responding to, and disagreeing with, the strictly scientific and logical approach to definition of the form suggested by Norman Friedman. Also includes a restatement of the view that Rohrberger enunciated in her earlier book on Nathaniel Hawthorne, in which she argued for the essentially romantic nature of the short-story form.

_____. *Hawthorne and the Modern Short Story: A Study in Genre.* The Hague, Netherlands: Mouton, 1966. Attempts a generic definition of the short story as a form that derives from the Romantic metaphysical view that there is more to the world than can be apprehended through the senses. Nathaniel Hawthorne is the touchstone for Rohrberger's definition, which she then applies to twentieth century stories by Eudora Welty, Ernest Hemingway, Sherwood Anderson, William Faulkner, and others.

Ruthrof, Horst. "Bracketed World and Reader Construction in the Modern Short Story." In *The Reader's Construction of Narrative*. London: Routledge & Kegan Paul, 1981. Discusses the "boundary situation" as the basis for the modern short story. In the pure boundary situation, the reader's act of bracketing transforms the presented crisis into the existential experience of the reading act.

Scott, A. O. "A Good Tale Isn't Hard to Find." *The New York Times*, April 5, 2009, p. WK1. Discussion of the remarkable durability of the short story, suggesting that it may be poised for a resurgence at the end of the first decade of the twenty-first century.

Shaw, Valerie. *The Short Story: A Critical Introduction.* London: Longman, 1983. A discussion of the form that primarily focuses on British writers, with one chapter on the transitional figure Robert Louis Stevenson. The rest of book deals with the patterned form to the artless tale form, with chapters on character, setting, and subject matter. Shaw argues that the short story cannot be defined by unity of effect or by a history of its "favorite devices and eminent practitioners."

Siebert, Hilary. "'Outside History': Lyrical Knowledge in the Discourse of the Short Story." In *Creative and Critical Approaches to the Short Story*, edited by Noel Harold Kaylor, Jr. Lewiston, N.Y.: Edwin Mellen Press, 1997. A discussion of how readers of short stories must often shift from expectations of a revealed, discursive meaning typical of prose to a gradually apprehended suggestive meaning typical of lyric poetry.

Stanzel, Franz K. "Textual Power in (Short) Short Story and Poem." In *Modes of Narrative: Approaches to American, Canadian, and British Fiction*, edited by

Reingard M. Vischik and Barbara Korte. Wursburg, Germany: Konigshausen and Neumann, 1990. Argues that the short story and poetry, which at the beginning of the twentieth century were far apart, have come closer together in both form and content. Suggests some of the similarities between the two forms, such as their focusing the reader's attention on beginnings and endings and their insistence on close readings of the structure of each line and sentence.

Stevick, Philip, ed. *Anti-story: An Anthology of Experimental Fiction*. New York: Free Press, 1971. An influential collection of contemporary short fiction with a helpful introduction that characterizes anti-story as against mimesis, reality, event, subject, the middle range of experience, analysis, and meaning.

Stroud, Theodore A. "A Critical Approach to the Short Story." *Journal of General Education* 9 (1956): 91-100. Makes use of American New Criticism to determine the pattern of the short story, that is, why apparently irrelevant episodes are included and why some events are expanded and others excluded.

Suckow, Ruth. "The Short Story." *Saturday Review of Literature* 4 (November 19, 1927): 317-318. Suckow strongly argues that no one can define the short story, for it is an aesthetic method for dealing with diversity and multiplicity.

Sullivan, Walter. "Revelation in the Short Story: A Note of Methodology." In *Vanderbilt Studies in Humanities*, edited by Richard C. Beatty, John Philip Hyatt, and Monroe K. Spears. Vol. 1. Nashville, Tenn.: Vanderbilt University Press, 1951. The fundamental methodological concept of the short story is a change of view from innocence to knowledge. This change can be either "logical" (coming at the end of the story) or "anticipated" (coming near the beginning); it can be either "intraconcatinate" (occurring within the main character) or "extra-concatinate" (occurring within a peripheral character). Thus defined, the short story did not begin until the final years of the nineteenth century.

Summers, Hollis, ed. *Discussions of the Short Story*. Boston: D. C. Heath, 1963. The nine general pieces on the short story include essays by Edgar Allan Poe and A. L. Bader; excerpts from books by Ray B. West, Seán O'Faoláin, and Brander Matthews; a chapter each from Percy Lubbock's *Craft of Fiction* (1954) and Kenneth Payson Kempton's *The Short Story* (1947); and Bret Harte's "The Rise of the Short Story." Also includes seven additional essays on specific short-story writers.

Szávai, János. "Towards a Theory of the Short Story." *Acta Litteraria Academiae Scientiarum Hungariae, Tomus* 24 (1982): 203-224. Discusses the Giovanni Boccaccio model as a genre that gives the illusion of reflecting reality directly and spontaneously, whereas it is actually a complex, structured entity that both retains and enriches the basic structure of the story. The enrichment resides, on the one hand, in the careful preparation of the point and its attachment to a key motif and, on the other hand, in the introduction of a new dimension in addition to the anecdote.

Todorov, Tzvetan. "The Structural Analysis of Literature." In *Structuralism: An Introduction*, edited by David Robey. London: Clarendon Press, 1973. The "figure in the carpet" in Henry James's stories is the quest for an absolute and absent cause. This cause is either a character, an event, or an object; its effect is the story readers are told. Everything in the story owes its existence to this cause, but because it is absent, the reader sets off in quest of it.

Trask, Georgianne, and Charles Burkhart, ed. *Storytellers and Their Art*. New York: Doubleday Anchor, 1963. A valuable collection of comments on the short-story form by practitioners from Anton Chekhov to Truman Capote. Noteworthy in part 1 are "Definitions of the Short Story" and "Short Story vs. Novel."

Trussler, Michael. "The Short Story: Interview with Charles May and Susan Lohafer." *Wascana Review* 33 (Spring, 1998): 14-24. Interview with two well-known theorists of the short story, who discuss reasons for past critical neglect of the form, conditions of the recent renaissance of interest in the form by both critics and general readers, unique generic characteristics of the short story, and current and future trends in the short story and theoretical approaches to it.

_____. "Suspended Narratives: The Short Story and Temporality." *Studies in Short Fiction* 33 (Fall, 1996): 557-577. An analysis of the critical view that the short-story form focuses on atemporality. Synthesizes a number of theories that emphasize short fiction's focus on existential confrontations while refusing to mitigate such experiences with abstraction, context, or continuity.

Wain, John. "Remarks on the Short Story." *Journal of the Short Story in English* 2 (1984): 49-66. Wain, himself a short-story writer, argues that the short story is a form of its own, with its own laws and logic, and that it is a modern form, beginning with Edgar Allan Poe. He observes that the novel is like a painting, whereas the short story is like a drawing, which catches a moment and is satisfying on its own grounds. He says there are perfectly successful short stories and totally unsuccessful ones, and nothing in between.

Welty, Eudora. "The Reading and Writing of Short Stories." *The Atlantic Monthly*, February, 1949, 54-58; March, 1949, 46-49. An impressionistic but suggestive essay in two installments that focuses on the mystery of the story and the fact that one cannot always see the solid outlines of the story because of the atmosphere that it generates.

West, Ray B. "The Modern Short Story and the Highest Forms of Art." *English Journal* 46 (1957): 531-539. Describes how the rise of the short story in the nineteenth century was a result of the shift in narrative view from the "telescopic" (viewing nature and society from the outside) to the "microscopic" (viewing the unseen world of inner motives and impulses).

Wharton, Edith. "Telling a Short Story." In *The Writing of Fiction*. New York: Charles Scribner's Sons, 1925. Wharton maintains that the chief technical difference between the novel and the short story is that the novel focuses on character while the short story focuses on situation, "and it follows that the effect produced by the short story depends almost entirely on its form."

Williams, William Carlos. *A Beginning on the Short Story: Notes*. Yonkers, N.Y.: The Alicat Bookshop Press, 1950. In these notes from a writers' workshop session, Williams makes several interesting, if fragmentary and impressionistic, remarks about the short-story form: The short story, as contrasted with the novel, is a brushstroke instead of a picture. Stressing virtuosity instead of story structure, it is "one single flight of the imagination, complete: up and down." It is best suited to depicting the life of "briefness, brokenness, and heterogeneity."

Winther, Per, Jacob Lothe, and Hans H. Skei, eds. *The Art of Brevity: Excursions in Short Fiction Theory and Analysis*. Columbia: University of South Carolina Press, 2004. Collection of essays, including some written by noted short-story theorists, such as Mary Rohrberger, Charles E. May, Susan Lohafer, and John Gerlach. Some of the essays examine reasons for readers' neglect of short stories. Other essays analyze short fiction by Robert Olen Butler, Chris Offutt, James Joyce, Sarah Orne Jewett, Linda Hogan, Flannery O'Connor, Eudora Welty, William Faulkner, and Herman Melville; Danish short stories from the 1990's; and works by Australian writers.

Wright, Austin. "On Defining the Short Story: The Genre Question." In *Short Story Theory at a Crossroads*, edited by Susan Lohafer and Jo Ellyn Clarey. Baton Rouge: Louisiana State University Press, 1989. Discusses some of the theoretical problems involved in defining the short story as a genre. Argues for the formalist view of a genre definition as a cluster of conventions.

_____. "Recalcitrance in the Short Story." In *Short Story Theory at a Crossroads*, edited by Susan Lohafer and Jo Ellyn Clarey. Baton Rouge: Louisiana State University Press, 1989. A discussion of stories with endings that resist the reader's efforts to assimilate them and to make sense of them as a whole. Such final recalcitrance, Wright claims, is the extreme kind of resistance that the short story has developed to thwart final closure and reduce the complexity of the story to a conceptual understanding.

AMERICAN SHORT FICTION

Adams, Alice. "The American Short Story in the Cybernetic Age." *Journal of the Short Story in English* 17 (Autumn, 1991): 9-22. After summarizing critical condemnation of the short story in the early twentieth century as mechanical and formulaic, Adams argues that the metafictional story of the 1960's and 1970's tries to reclaim the short story from its low-brow mechanistic state by making its formula palpable.

Allen, Walter. *The Short Story in English*. Oxford, England: Clarendon Press, 1981. A historical study of the development of the genre in England and the United States. Primarily a series of biographical discussions of authors and summary discussions of stories. Good for providing a framework for the development of the form.

Bendixen, Alfred, and James Nagel, eds. *A Companion to the American Short Story*. Malden, Mass.: Wiley-Blackwell, 2010. A comprehensive collection of essays surveying the short fiction genre, divided into four parts. Part 1 focuses on the nineteenth century, with discussions of the emergence and development of the American short story, Herman Melville's "Bartleby the Scrivener," and the works of Edgar Allan Poe, Nathaniel Hawthorne, Charles Waddell Chesnutt, Mark Twain, Charlotte Perkins Gilman, Edith Wharton, and the New England local-colorists. Part 2 charts transitional short fiction of the late nineteenth and early twentieth centuries, including essays on the works of Stephen Crane, Kate Chopin, Frank Norris, and Jack London. Part 3 surveys twentieth century short fiction, specifically the works of Ernest Hemingway, William Faulkner, Katherine Anne Porter, Eudora Welty, F. Scott Fitzgerald, Richard Wright, Saul Bellow, John Updike, Raymond Carver, and Denise Chávez. Part 4, "Expansive Considerations," examines American women's short stories; ghost and detective stories; Asian American, Jewish American, and other multiethnic short fiction; and short story cycles.

Bierce, Ambrose. "The Short Story." In *The Collected Works of Ambrose Bierce*. New York: Gordian Press, 1966. Bierce criticizes William Dean Howells and other writers of the realistic school for their prosaic and pedestrian realism, which fails to perceive the mystery of human life.

Boddy, Kasia. *The American Short Story Since 1950*. Edinburgh: Edinburgh University Press, 2010. Analyzes short fiction by Flannery O'Connor, Eudora Welty, J. D. Salinger, John Cheever, Raymond Carver, Lorrie Moore, Grace Paley, and other writers. The introduction provides a history of the American short story up to 1950; the initial chapters discuss major trends in the short fiction of the period, such as minimalism, fabulism, and realism, as well as short-story sequences written between 1950 and 2000.

Bone, Robert, *Down Home: A History of Afro-American Short Fiction from Its Beginnings to the End of the Harlem Renaissance*. New York: Capricorn Books, 1975. Provides a background for the African-American folktale, the Brer Rabbit Tales, and the local-color writers. Devotes a chapter each to Paul Laurence Dunbar, Charles Waddell Chesnutt, Jean Toomer, Langston Hughes, and Arna Bontemps. Also contains a chapter on the Harlem Renaissance, with mention of Zora Neale Hurston and other writers. Shows how the African-American short story is the child of a mixed heritage.

Bostrom, Melissa. *Sex, Race, and Family in Contemporary American Short Stories*. New York: Palgrave Macmillan, 2007. Describes how the market for contemporary short fiction has affected the depiction of sexual power, the relationships of mothers and daughters, and race in many short stories.

Canby, Henry S. *The Short Story in English*. New York: Holt, Rinehart, and Winston, 1909. A classic historical survey of English-language short fiction, from the Middle Ages through the nineteenth century, with discussion of both British and American writers. Canby argues that the Romantic movement gave birth to the modern short story and that Edgar Allan Poe is its first important figure; the rest of the nineteenth century writers applied Poe's theory of single effect to new subjects, primarily the contrasts of civilization in flux

Clarke, John H. "Transition in the American Negro Short Story." *Phylon* 21 (1960): 360-366. A shorter version of this article appears as the introduction to *American Negro Short Stories*, edited by John Henrik Clarke (1966). A brief historical survey of the African American short story from Paul Laurence Dunbar and Charles Waddell Chesnutt at the beginning of the twentieth century, through the Harlem Renaissance of the 1920's, to the emergence of Richard Wright, who marked the end of the double standard for black writers.

Crow, Charles L., ed. *A Companion to the Regional Literatures of America*. New York: Wiley-Blackwell, 2003. A comprehensive study comprising essays arranged in three sections: an introductory survey of theoretical and historical approaches (eleven essays); a middle section on various regional literatures from New England and the South to the Southwest and Hawaii (fourteen essays); and concluding essays on individual Western regionalist writers, including Bret Harte, Mark Twain, Willa Cather, and Wallace Stegner. Nearly all of the pieces discuss their topics in depth and detail.

Curnutt, Kirk. *Wise Economies: Brevity and Storytelling in American Short Stories*. Moscow: University of Idaho Press, 1997. A historical analysis of the short story's development as the structuring of the tension between brevity and storytelling. Shows how stylistic brevity as an evolving aesthetic practice redefined the interpretative demands placed on readers.

Current-Garcia, Eugene. *The American Short Story, Before 1850*. Boston: Twayne, 1985. Focuses on the types of magazine fiction published before 1820. Devotes individual chapters to Washington Irving, Nathaniel Hawthorne, and Edgar Allan Poe. Also includes a chapter on William Gilmore Simms and the frontier humorists, such as George Washington Harris. The shift toward realism described in the last chapter is largely a result of the fiction of Herman Melville.

Current-Garcia, Eugene, and Walter R. Patrick. Introduction to *American Short Stories*. Rev. ed. Chicago: Scott, Foresman, 1964. A historical survey of the American short story through four periods: Romanticism, realism, naturalism, and the modern period of both traditionalists (those who have carried on the tradition of Edgar Allan Poe, Guy de Maupassant, and Henry James) and experimentalists (those who have focused more on the fragmented inner world of the mind).

_____, eds. *What Is the Short Story?* Rev. ed. New York: Scott, Foresman, 1974. Although this volume is primarily a short-story anthology, it contains a generous selection of mostly American criticism on the short story, arranged in chronological order. Contains a four-page general bibliography on the short story.

Del George, Dana. *The Supernatural in Short Fiction of the Americas: The Other World in the New World*. Westport, Conn.: Greenwood Press, 2001. Describes how cultural encounters between European and indigenous societies and between "scientific materialism" and "premodern supernaturalism" resulted in the creation of new narrative forms, including supernatural short fiction.

Fallon, Erin, et al., eds. *A Reader's Companion to the Short Story in English*. Westport, Conn.: Greenwood Press, 2001. Produced under the auspices of the Society for the Study of the Short Story, this collection of essays, aimed at the general reader, provides brief biographies of numerous writers and analyses of their short fiction. Some of the writers examined are Toni Cade Bambara, John Barth, Donald Barthelme, Anne Beattie, Raymond Carver, Sandra Cisneros, Robert Coover, Louise Erdrich, Richard Ford, Ernest J. Gaines, Maxine Hong Kingston, Bernard Malamud, James Alan McPherson, Lorre Moore, Tim O'Brien, Grace Paley, and Amy Tan.

Firchow, Peter E. "The Americaness of the American Short Story." *Journal of the Short Story in English* 10 (Spring, 1988): 45-66. Examines the common claim that the short story is a particularly American art form. Surveys and critiques a number of critics who have debated the issue. Analyzes generic criteria for determining what is a short story, such as self-consciousness and length; concludes that a short story is simply a story that is short and that the American short story is not unique to America but is merely a story that deals with American cultural contexts.

Fusco, Richard. *Maupassant and the American Short Story: The Influence of Form at the Turn of the Century*. University Park: Pennsylvania State University Press, 1994. Argues that Guy de Maupassant's influence on the twentieth century short story rivals that of Anton Chekhov. Discusses seven different short-story forms in Maupassant's stories: linear, ironic coda, surprise-inversion, loop, descending helical, contrast, and sinusoidal. Describes Maupassant's influence on Ambrose Bierce, O. Henry, Kate Chopin, and Henry James.

Geismar, Maxwell. "The American Short Story Today." *Studies on the Left* 4 (Spring, 1964): 21-27. Criticizes J. D. Salinger, Philip Roth, Bernard Malamud, John Updike, and other writers for ignoring the social realities of the time in their short stories.

Gelfant, Blanche H., ed. *The Columbia Companion to the Twentieth-Century American Short Story*. New York: Columbia University Press, 2000. An excellent introductory overview of the genre. Part 1 contains general, thematic essays, such as discussions of the American short story cycle and of short fiction by African Americans, Asian Americans, Chicanos, Latinos, lesbians and gay men writers, Native Americans, and non-English authors. Part 2 features analyses of the works of about one hundred individual writers, from Alice Adams to Anzia Yezierska.

Gerlach, John. *Toward the End: Closure and Structure in the American Short Story*. Tuscaloosa: University of Alabama Press, 1985. A detailed theoretical study of the American short story, focusing particularly on the importance of closure, or the ending of the form; examines a number of stories in some detail in terms of the concept of closure.

Gerould, Katherine Fullerton. "The American Short Story." *Yale Review*, n.s. 13 (July, 1924): 642-663. Urges that the short story be read as critically as the novel. Argues that the short story must be well made and must focus on a significant event that is either truly momentous for the individual character or typical of the lives of many people.

Gullason, Thomas A. "The 'Lesser' Renaissance: The American Short Story in the 1920's." In *The American Short Story: 1900-1945*, edited by Philip Stevick. Boston: Twayne, 1984. A historical survey of some of the major American short-story writers of the 1920's. The essay analyzes briefly some of the best-known stories of Sherwood Anderson, F. Scott Fitzgerald, Ring Lardner, Ernest Hemingway,

Dorothy Parker, Katherine Anne Porter, and William Faulkner.

Howells, William Dean. "Some Anomalies of the Short Story." *North American Review* 173 (September, 1901): 422-432. Claims that when read in a volume, each story requires so much of the reader's attention that he or she becomes exhausted. Argues that a defect of the short story is that it creates no memorable characters.

Huang, Guiyou, ed. *Asian American Short Story Writers: An A-to-Z Guide*. Westport, Conn.: Greenwood Press, 2003. An encyclopedia containing alphabetically arranged entries about forty-nine Asian American authors living in the United States and Canada, including Frank Chin, Bharti Mukherjee, and Toshio Mori. Each entry provides a biography, a discussion of the writer's major works and themes, and a bibliography. Also contains an introductory overview of Asian American short fiction.

Joselyn, Sister Mary. "Edward Joseph O'Brien and the American Short Story." *Studies in Short Fiction* 3 (1965): 1-15. Attempts a synthesis of O'Brien's philosophic and aesthetic attitudes, which may have determined his choices of "best stories" for his annual anthologies. Discusses O'Brien's contribution to the history, theory, and growth of the American short story.

Karrer, Wolfgang, and Barbara Puschmann-Nalenz, eds. *The African American Short Story, 1970-1990: A Collection of Critical Essays*. Trier, Germany: Wissenschaftlicher Verlag Trier, 1993. These essays provide a historical overview of African American short fiction, as well as analyses of stories by Ann Petry, Toni Cade Barbara, Alice Walker, James Alan McPherson, Ntozake Shange, John Edgar Wideman, and other writers.

Kennedy, J. Gerald. "Short Story and the Short Story Sequence, 1865-1914." In *A Companion to American Fiction, 1865-1914*, edited by Robert Paul Lamb and G. R. Thompson. Malden, Mass.: Blackwell, 2005. An overview of the short story in this period, including discussion of works by Kate Chopin, Charles Waddell Chesnutt, Stephen Crane, Mark Twain, Rebecca Harding Davis, and other writers.

Kimbel, Ellen. "The American Short Story: 1900-1920." In *The American Short Story, 1900-1945*, edited by Philip Stevick. Boston: Twayne, 1984. A historical survey of the development of the short story in the first two decades of the twentieth century. Begins with Henry James and writers, such as Edith Wharton and Willa Cather, who were strongly influenced by James's work. Discusses the innovations of Sherwood Anderson and points out how he differs from earlier writers in developing the modern short story.

Kostelanetz, Richard. "Notes on the American Short Story Today." *The Minnesota Review* 5 (1966): 214-221. Argues that contemporary short-story writers focus on extreme rather than typical experiences and tend to emphasize the medium of language itself more than ever before. In a shift that pulls the genre farther away from narrative and pushes it closer to nonlinear forms of poetry, the contemporary short-story writer attempts to depict the workings of the mad mind, to simulate the feel of madness itself.

Leitch, Thomas M. "The Debunking Rhythm of the American Short Story." In *Short Story Theory at a Crossroads*, edited by Susan Lohafer and Jo Ellyn Clarey. Baton Rouge: Louisiana State University Press, 1989. Argues that a particular kind of closure is typical of the American short story. Uses the phrase "debunking rhythm" to characterize the kind of story in which a character realizes the falseness of one kind of knowledge but achieves no new kind of knowledge to take its place.

_____. "The *New Yorker* School." In *Creative and Critical Approaches to the Short Story*, edited by Noel Harold Kaylor, Jr. Lewiston, N.Y.: Edwin Mellen Press, 1997. A brief history of the development of the so-called *New Yorker* story. Charts the rise of the magazine as a powerful force in the development of the modern short story. Argues that, much like the modern short story generally, the *New Yorker* story has defined itself in terms of its departure from its own norms.

Levy, Andrews. *The Culture and Commerce of the American Short Story*. Cambridge, England: Cambridge University Press, 1993. A historical survey showing how the short story became an image of American values through political movements, editorial policies, and changes in education. Devotes chapters to Edgar Allan Poe's efforts to create a magazine that would accommodate his particular kind of story. Summarizes short-story criticism and theory in the late nineteenth and early twentieth centuries. Provides a brief history of creative-writing programs and handbooks.

Marler, Robert F. "From Tale to Short Story: The Emergence of a New Genre in the 1850's." *American Literature: A Journal of Literary History, Criticism, and Bibliography* 46 (1974): 153-169. Using Northrop Frye's distinction between the tale (embodies "stylized figures which expand into psychological archetypes") and the short story (deals with characters who wear their "*personae* or social masks"), Marler surveys the critical condemnation of the tale form and the increasing emphasis on realism in the 1850's. The broad shift is from Edgar Allan Poe's overt romance to Herman Melville's mimetic portrayals, especially in "Bartleby the Scrivener."

O'Brien, Edward J. *The Advance of the American Short Story*. Rev. ed. New York: Dodd, Mead, 1931. A survey of the development of the American short story from Washington Irving to Sherwood Anderson. The focus is on contributions to the form by various authors: Irving's development of the story from the eighteenth century essay, Nathaniel Hawthorne's discovery of the subjective method for psychological fiction, Edgar Allan Poe's formalizing, Bret Harte's caricaturing, Henry James's development of the "central intelligence," and Anderson's freeing the story from O. Henry's formalism.

_____. *The Dance of the Machines: The American Short Story and the Industrial Age*. New York: Macaulay, 1929. Chapter 4 of this polemic against the machinelike standardization of the industrial age describes thirty characteristics that the short story ("the most typical American form") shares with the machine: For example, it is patterned, impersonal, standardized, speeded up, and cheap.

Pache, Walter. "Towards the Modern English Short Story." In *Modes of Narrative: Approaches to American, Canadian, and British Fiction*, edited by

Reingard M. Vischik and Barbara Korte. Wurzburg, Germany: Konigshausen and Neumann, 1990. A study of the relationship between the short fiction of the 1890's and the modern short story. Surveys changes in periodical publishing during the period, analyzes new directions in short-story theory at the turn of the twentieth century, and suggests some of the basic structural patterns of the end-of-nineteenth-century short story.

Pattee, Fred Lewis. *The Development of the American Short Story*. New York: Harper & Row, 1923. The most detailed and historically complete survey of the American short story from Washington Irving to O. Henry. Charts the changes in taste of the short-story reading public and indicates the major contributions to the form of such classic practitioners as Irving, Nathaniel Hawthorne, Edgar Allan Poe, and Bret Harte. Surveys the effect of the "Annuals," the "Ladies' Books," local color, Brander Matthews's *The Philosophy of the Short-Story* (1901), and the writing handbooks.

Peden, William. *The American Short Story: Continuity and Change, 1940-1975*. 2d ed. Boston: Houghton Mifflin, 1975. Includes chapters on publishing and the short story since 1940; the stories of suburbia by John Cheever, John Updike, and others; stories of physical illness and abnormality by James Purdy, Tennessee Williams, Flannery O'Connor, and Joyce Carol Oates; stories by Jewish writers, such as Bernard Malamud, Saul Bellow, J. D. Salinger, Grace Paley, Philip Roth, and Isaac Bashevis Singer; and stories by African American writers, such as Langston Hughes, Richard Wright, Ann Petry, and Toni Cade Bambera.

_____. "The American Short Story During the Twenties." *Studies in Short Fiction* 10 (1973): 367-371. A highly abbreviated account of the causes of the explosion of short stories during the 1920's. Some of the causes discussed are the new freedom from plotted stories, new emphasis on "now-ness," the boom of little magazines, and the influence of cinematic techniques.

_____. *The American Short Story: Front Line in the National Defense of Literature*. Boston: Houghton Mifflin, 1964. A discussion of major trends in the American short story since 1940. The heart of the book consists of a chapter on those writers who focus on everyday life in contemporary society (John Cheever, John O'Hara, Peter Taylor, John Updike, J. F. Powers, and J. D. Salinger) and a chapter on those who are preoccupied with the grotesque, abnormal, and bizarre (Carson McCullers, Flannery O'Connor, James Purdy, Truman Capote, and Tennessee Williams). An additional chapter surveys other short-story subjects, such as the war, minorities, regions, and science fiction.

Price, Kenneth M., and Susan Belasco Smith, eds. *Periodical Literature in Nineteenth-Century America*. Charlottsville: University Press of Virginia, 1995. A collection of essays by various scholars about how the periodical transformed the American literary marketplace between 1830 and 1890. Critics suggest how the development of the periodical as a market for short fiction had a powerful influence on the development of the form as a unique American genre.

Purcell, William M. *The Rhetorical Short Story: Best American Short Stories on War and the Military, 1915-2006*. Lanham, Md.: University Press of America, 2009. Examines more than ninety stories depicting war from World War I through the twenty-first century conflicts in Iraq and Afghanistan. Argues that during this period the perspective of war short fiction has changed from an insular one, stressing the actions of strong, purposeful individuals, to one in which individuals are uncontrollably caught in an "all-determining stream of events."

Rhode, Robert D. *Setting in the American Short Story of Local Color: 1865-1900*. The Hague, Netherlands: Mouton, 1975. A study of the various functions that setting plays in the local-color story of the late nineteenth century, from setting as merely background to setting in relation to character and setting as personification.

Rohrberger, Mary. "The Question of Regionalism: Limitation and Transcendence." In *The American Short Story, 1900-1945*, edited by Philip Stevick. Boston: Twayne, 1984. Focuses on such writers as Ruth Suckow, Jesse Stuart, Langston Hughes, and Jean Toomer. Calls Toomer's *Cane* the most significant work produced by the Harlem Renaissance and compares it with Sherwood Anderson's *Winesburg, Ohio*. Also discusses works by Ellen Glasgow, Sinclair Lewis, James T. Farrell, Erskine Caldwell, John O'Hara, and John Steinbeck.

Ross, Danforth. *The American Short Story*. Minneapolis: University of Minnesota Press, 1961. A sketchy survey that measures American stories since Edgar Allan Poe against Aristotelian criteria of action, unity, tension, and irony. Ends with the Beat writers who rebelled against the Poe-Aristotle tradition by using shock tactics.

Scofield, Martin. *The Cambridge Introduction to the American Short Story*. New York: Cambridge University Press, 2006. A concise and chronological overview of the genre, with some of the chapters focusing on Washington Irving, Nathaniel Hawthorne, Edgar Alan Poe, Herman Melville, Bret Harte, Mark Twain, Stephen Crane, Kate Chopin, Willa Cather, Edith Wharton, O. Henry, Jack London, Ernest Hemingway, F. Scott Fitzgerald, Katherine Anne Porter, Flannery O'Connor, Richard Wright, James Baldwin, and Raymond Carver.

Shivani, Anis. "Whatever Happened to the American Short Story?" *Contemporary Review* 291 (Summer, 2009): 216-225. Based on his analysis of the stories in *The O. Henry Prize Stories 2007* and *Best New American Voices 2008*, Shivani argues that the contemporary short story represents categories of victimization, reflecting America's decadence, insularity, and sad masochism.

Siebert, Hilary. "Did We Both Read the Same Story? Interpreting Cultural Contexts from Oral Discourses with the American Short Story." *Short Story* n.s. 6 (Spring, 1998). The history of the short story is one of many different types of discourses, both oral and written, blending together. The result of this textual tension and diversity is that educated readers may not be familiar with the variety of discourse conventions and thus read the stories incorrectly.

Stevick, Philip, ed. Introduction to *The American Short Story: 1900-1945*. Boston: Twayne, 1984. Stevick's extensive introduction to this collection of essays by various critics is a helpful historical overview of the development of the twentieth century short story. A

good introduction to many of the features of the modern short story and how they came about at the beginning of the twentieth century.

Voss, Arthur. *The American Short Story: A Critical Survey*. Norman: University of Oklahoma Press, 1973. A comprehensive survey of the major short-story writers in American literature. Valuable for an overview of the stories and criticism.

Watson, James G. "The American Short Story: 1930-1945." In *The American Short Story, 1900-1945*, edited by Philip Stevick. Boston: Twayne, 1984. Claims that the period between 1930 and 1945 produced the most prolific outpouring of short fiction in the history of American literature. Focuses on the importance of the little magazines and discusses the contributions of Ernest Hemingway, William Faulkner, and F. Scott Fitzgerald.

Werlock, Abby H. P., ed. *The Facts on File Companion to the American Short Story*. 2d ed. 2 vols. New York: Facts on File, 2010. Alphabetically arranged entries cover numerous aspects of the American short story from the early nineteenth century to the early twenty-first century. The entries include author biographies and bibliographies, plot synopses, character sketches, and analyses of major short stories.

West, Ray B. "The American Short Story." In *The Writer in the Room*. Detroit: Michigan State University Press, 1968. Originally appeared as West's introduction to *American Short Stories* (1959). Contrasts the short story's "microscopic" focus on inner motives with the novel's "telescopic" view of human beings from the outside. The novel is concerned with human beings' attempt to control nature through social institutions; the short story presents the individual's confrontation with nature as an indifferent force.

_____. *The Short Story in America: 1900-1950*. Chicago: Henry Regnery, 1952. Probably the most familiar and most often recommended history of the American short story. Chapter 1, "The American Short Story at Mid-Century," is a short survey of the development of the short story since Washington Irving, Nathaniel Hawthorne, and Edgar Allan Poe. Chapter 4 is devoted completely to Ernest Hemingway and William Faulkner.

Windholz, Anne M. "The American Short Story and Its British Critics: *Athenaeum* Reviews, 1880-1900." *Victorian Periodicals Review* 23 (Winter, 1990): 156-166. Argues that between 1880 and 1900, reviews of British and American short stories in the British journal *Athenaeum* helped establish an aesthetic that dominated critical analysis of the Anglo-American short story. Surveys reviewers' comments on American humor, dialect, and local color, as well as the importance of conciseness and unity of effect in both British and American short stories between 1880 and 1900.

Wright, Austin. *The American Short Story in the Twenties*. Chicago: University of Chicago Press, 1961. Using a canon of 220 stories, one set selected from the 1920's and the other from the period immediately preceding, Wright examines differing themes and techniques to test the usual judgments of what constitutes the "modern short story." The examination concludes by proving that the short story of the 1920's is different from the short story of the earlier period, that of the naturalists.

# TYPES OF SHORT FICTION

## MODERNIST SHORT FICTION

Childs, Peter. *Modernism*. 2d ed. New York: Routledge, 2008. Chronicles the origins of the modernist movement and describes its impact on late nineteenth and early twentieth century literature. Devotes a chapter to the short story.

Goldberg, Michael E. "The Synchronic Series as the Origin of the Modernist Short Story." *Studies in Short Fiction* 33 (Fall, 1996): 515-527. Goldberg suggests that the cumulative power of modernist collections of stories, such as James Joyce's *Dubliners* (1914) and Ernest Hemingway's *In Our Time* (1924, 1925), is modeled after a synchronic series of stories innovated by Sir Arthur Conan Doyle.

Head, Dominic. *The Modernist Short Story*. Cambridge: Cambridge University Press, 1992. An examination of the short story's formal characteristics from a theoretical framework derived from Louis Althusser and Mikhail Bakhtin. Argues that the short story's emphasis on literary artifice lends itself to modernist experimentalism. Illustrates this thesis with chapters on James Joyce, Tobias Woolf, Katherine Mansfield, and Wyndham Lewis.

## POSTMODERN SHORT FICTION

Clark, Miriam Marty. "After Epiphany: American Stories in the Postmodern Age." *Style* 27 (Fall, 1993): 387-394. Argues that contemporary short stories can no longer be read in terms of epiphany. Claims that critics must develop a new reading strategy, shifting from metaphoric ways of meaning to metonymic ones to redefine the short story in its postmodern context.

Ifterkharrudin, Farhat, et al., eds. *Postmodern Approaches to the Short Story*. Westport, Conn.: Praeger, 2003. This volume, created under the auspices of the Society for the Study of the Short Story, analyzes elements of postmodernism in the works of Jorge Luis Borges, Italo Calvino, Katherine Mansfield, Henry James, Janette Turner Hospital, Jean Toomer, Homi K. Bhabba, and other writers.

_____. *The Postmodern Short Story: Forms and Issues*. Westport, Conn.: Praeger, 2003. Created under the auspices of the Society for the Study of the Short Story, this collection of essays demonstrates how postmodernism has altered the styles and themes of short fiction. Includes analyses of the personal essay, the nonfiction short story, Canadian and American postmodern stories, and works of short fiction by Sandra Cisneros, Lelie Marmon Silko, Joyce Carol Oates, Lorrie Moore, Thom Jones, Tom Paine, Denis Johnson, Edmund White, Ernest Hemingway, Richard Ford, Richard Brautigam, and R. R. R. Dhlomo.

## MINIMALIST SHORT FICTION

Bell, Madison Smartt. "Less Is Less: The Dwindling American Short Story." *Harpers*, April, 1986, 64-69. Discusses several collections of short stories by minimalist writers and points out weaknesses, such as lack of plot and trivial themes.

Campbell, Ewing. "How Minimal Is Minimalism?" In *The Tales We Tell: Perspectives on the Short Story*, edited by Barbara Lounsberry et al. Westport, Conn.: Greenwood Press, 1998. A brief, suggestive essay which tries to define minimalist short fiction not in terms of length but in terms of the demands it makes on the reader. Argues that minimalist stories arrange significant details in such a way that the brain must supply missing information.

Hallett, Cynthia J. "Minimalism and the Short Story." *Studies in Short Fiction* 33 (Fall, 1996): 487-495. Defines minimalism, summarizes the negative connotations of the label "minimalist writer," and points out that the minimalist short story makes connections through intricate patterns that reveal meaning under the surface. Analyzes Mary Robison's "Yours" and Amy Hempel's "In a Tub" as exemplary of minimalist short stories.

Herzinger, Kim. "Minimalism as Postmodernism: Some Introductory Notes." *New Orleans Review* 16 (1989) 73-81. A survey of techniques used in minimalist fiction. Discusses what critics have said about minimalism and compares this style of writing to postmodernism.

March-Russell, Paul. "Minimalism/Dirty Realism/Hyperrealism." In *The Short Story: An Introduction*. Edinburgh, Edinburgh University Press, 2009. Gives an informative overview of minimalism and shows how the realism used in minimalism is similar to elements found in postmodern writing.

Sodowsky, Roland. "The Minimalist Short Story: Its Definition, Writers, and (Small) Heyday." *Studies in Short Fiction* 33 (Fall, 1996): 529-540. A historical survey of minimalism's dominance of the short-story marketplace in the late 1970's and early 1980's in the United States. Based on an examination of short stories in such magazines as *The New Yorker*, *The Atlantic Monthly*, *Esquire*, and *Harper's* between 1975 and 1990, Sodowsky isolates and summarizes some of the basic characteristics of the minimalist short story.

### THE HYPERSTORY

Coover, Robert. "Storying in Hyperspace: 'Linkages.'" In *The Tales We Tell: Perspectives on the Short Story*, edited by Barbara Lounsberry et al. Westport, Conn.: Greenwood Press, 1998. A discussion of the future of the short story in computerized hyperspace as a form that is nonsequential, multidirectional, and interactive. Discusses linked short fictional pieces in the past in the Bible, in medieval romances, and by Giovanni Boccaccio, Miguel de Cervantes, and Geoffrey Chaucer.

May, Charles E. "HyperStory: Teaching Short Fiction with Computers." In *The Tales We Tell: Perspectives on the Short Story*, edited by Barbara Lounsberry, et al. Westport, Conn.: Greenwood Press, 1998. Describes HyperStory, a computer program developed by the author, which teaches students how to read short fiction more carefully and thoughtfully. Uses Edgar Allan Poe's "The Cask of Amontillado" as an example; attempts to explain, with the help of student comments, the success of the program.

### MAGICAL REALISM

Benito, Jesús, Ana Ma Manzanas, and Begoña Simal. *Uncertain Mirrors: Magical Realisms in U.S. Ethnic Literatures*. New York: Rodopi, 2009. Examines Magical Realism in comparison to other literary movements, such as postmodernism and postcolonialism, Studies the use of Magical Realism in works by various authors, discussing how these writers represent themselves and their characters.

Bowers, Maggie Ann. *Magic(al) Realism*. London: Routledge, 2004. Serves as a helpful introduction to the Magical Realism movement. Bowers provides an overview of the genre and a close examination of the genre's connections with postcolonialism.

Faris, Wendy B. *Ordinary Enchantments: Magical Realism and the Remystification of Narrative*. Nashville, Tenn.: Vanderbilt University Press, 2004. Faris discusses key components of Magic Realist fiction and explores the work of authors from around the world. Each chapter focuses on a different aspect of Magical Realism, ranging from studies of narrative structure to the representation of women. Examines the importance of the Magical Realism tradition and its greater cultural implications.

Gaylard, Gerald. *After Colonialism: African Postmodernism and Magical Realism*. Johannesburg: Wits University, 2006. Gaylard describes how two genres of fiction--postmodernism and Magical Realism--provide reflections on and responses to colonialism in Africa. He argues that genres such as Magical

Realism, which allow writers freedom and release, provide African writers with a sense of liberty in an era of colonization and assimilation.

Hart, Stephen, and Wen-chin Ouyang, eds. *A Companion to Magical Realism*. Rochester, N.Y.: Tamesis, 2006. Collection of essays providing a close examination of the Magical Realism genre. Essayists trace the genre's history, its common symbols, and the politics of representation in close readings of texts, including works by Gabriel García Márquez, Jorge Luis Borges, and Isabel Allende.

Hegerfeldt, Anne C. *Lies That Tell the Truth: Magic Realism Seen Through Contemporary Fiction in Britain*. New York: Rodopi, 2005. Hegerfeldt discusses the debate over the definition of the genre and gives in-depth analyses of literary techniques employed often in Magical Realism.

Schroeder, Shannin. *Rediscovering Magical Realism in the Americas*. Westport, Conn.: Praeger, 2004. Examines works of Magical Realism in North and South America, paying special attention to North American Magical Realists. Schroeder acknowledges that the genre is often associated primarily or only with Latin and Central American writers and confronts this assumption with discussion of often neglected Magical Realist writers.

Takolander, Maria. *Catching Butterflies: Bringing Magical Realism to Ground*. Bern, Switzerland: Peter Lang, 2007. Takolander, like other scholars of Magical Realism, discusses the debate over how the genre should be defined, as well as its inception and its influence around the world. By examining historical context, Takolander attempts to provide answers to questions about the genre's presence, dominance, and influence in the literary world.

Zamora, Lois Parkinson, and Wendy B. Faris, eds. *Magical Realism: Theory, History, Community*. London: Duke University Press, 1995. Collection of essays about developments in the Magical Realism movement in art, literature, and other media.

### FOLK TALES AND FAIRY TALES

Ashliman, D. L. *Folk and Fairy Tales: A Handbook*. Westport, Conn.: Greenwood Press, 2004. Ashliman provides readers with a history of fairy tales and folktales, examines the definitions of these genres, and explores some examples of each type of tale.

Bettelheim, Bruno. *The Uses of Enchantment: The Meaning and Importance of Fairy Tales*. New York: Alfred A. Knopf, 1977. This book discusses the tradition of and patterns present in fairy tales, then gives extensive analyses of well-known fairy tales, including "Hansel and Gretel," "Little Red Riding Hood," "Snow White," "Goldilocks and the Three Bears," "The Sleeping Beauty," and "Cinderella."

Bottigheimer, Ruth B. *Grimms' Bad Girls and Bold Boys: The Moral and Social Vision of the Tales*. New Haven, Conn.: Yale University Press, 1987. Bottigheimer discusses the fairy-tale tradition, including specific patterns of the characters' speech, the way in which they endure punishment, their struggle for power, and the value systems implicit in these tales.

Georges, Robert A., and Michael Owen Jones. *Folkloristics: An Introduction*. Bloomington: Indiana University Press, 1995. Defines folklore as a historical tradition, focusing on its role in various cultures, in human psychology, and as a historical science.

Jones, Steven Swann. *The Fairy Tale: The Magic Mirror of the Imagination*. New York: Routledge, 2002. Provides a history of the fairy-tale genre, paying special attention to the roles of men and women in fairy tales of the past and describing how those figures influenced more contemporary stories.

Leeming, David Adams, ed. *Storytelling Encyclopedia*. Phoenix, Ariz.: Oryx Press, 1997. Provides a general discussion of the storytelling tradition and a look at a number of countries and their specific cultural contributions to the tradition. In addition, there are brief entries regarding the most popular people and theories related to the oral and written traditions.

Propp, Vladimir. *Morphology of the Folktale*. Edited by Svatava Pirkova-Jakovson, translated by Laurence Scott. Bloomington: Indiana University Research Center, 1958. All formalist and structuralist studies of narrative owe a debt to this pioneering early twentieth century study. Using one hundred fairy tales, Propp defines the genre itself by analyzing the stories according to characteristic actions or functions.

_____. *Theory and History of Folklore*. Minneapolis: University of Minnesota Press, 1984. This collection of Propp's essays expands on his theory of the narrative that he presented in *Morphology of the Folktale*.

Tatar, Maria. *Off with Their Heads: Fairy Tales and the Culture of Childhood*. Princeton, N.J.: Princeton University Press, 1992. Tatar examines how important writers in the fairy-tale tradition revised these stories so as to be more didactic for children. She argues that the typical portrayal of children in fairy tales is problematic, especially given that the contemporary target audience of fairy tales is children.

Thompson, Stith. *The Folktale*. New York: Dryden Press, 1946. Discusses the nature, theories, and form of the folktale and presents a varied collection of international tales. Selected are tales from many categories, such as the complex and the simple tale.

Warner, Marina. *From the Beast to the Blonde: On Fairy Tales and Their Tellers*. New York: Farrar, Straus and Giroux, 1994. Warner studies the characters whose role is the telling of fairy tales and analyzes gender roles, specifically those of women, including the typical portrayals of daughters, mothers, stepmothers, brides, and runaway girls

Zipes, Jack. *Fairy Tale as Myth, Myth as Fairy Tale*. Lexington: University Press of Kentucky, 1994. Examines the history of the fairy tale and its rise as the genre preceding the folktale. Discusses many well-known fairy tales and their role in society.

_____. *Fairy Tales and the Art of Subversion: The Classical Genre for Children and the Process of Civilization*. New York: Routledge, 1991. Zipes focuses on the didactic function of fairy tales, ranging from the work of the Grimm brothers to later fairy tales. He argues that the primary function of fairy tales is to instill morals and lessons in their child readers.

### SCIENCE-FICTION SHORT STORIES

Amis, Kingsley. *New Maps of Hell: A Survey of Science Fiction*. London: Gollancz, 1960. A slightly superficial study by a critic whose relative ignorance of the genre's history is amply compensated by his insights into the distinctive forms and merits of short science fiction.

Ashley, Michael. *The Time Machines: The Story of the Science-Fiction Pulp Magazines from the Beginning to 1950*. Liverpool, England: Liverpool University Press, 2000.

_____. *Transformations: The Story of the Science-Fiction Magazines from 1950 to 1970, the History of the Science-Fiction Magazine*. Liverpool, England: Liverpool University Press, 2005.

_____. *Gateways to Forever: The Story of the Sience-Fiction Magazines from 1970 to 1980, the History of the Science-Fiction Magazine*. Liverpool, England: Liverpool University Press, 2007. A three-volume history of the American and English pulp science-fiction magazines and the types of short stories they published.

Carter, Paul A. *The Creation of Tomorrow: Fifty Years of Magazine Science Fiction*. New York: Columbia University Press, 1977. An intelligent and well-informed history of the genre, which pays more careful attention to short fiction than most other books on the subject.

Clute, John, and Peter Nicholls. *The Encyclopedia of Science Fiction*. London: Orbit, 1993. By far the most comprehensive guide to the genre's history, practitioners, and themes.

Monk, Patricia. *Alien Theory: The Alien as Archetype in the Science Fiction Short Story*. Lanham, Md.: Scarecrow Press, 2006. Examines the use of alien characters in science-fiction short stories, including stories published in pulp magazines and contemporary works of the genre. Argues that the creation of the alien contributes to readers' understanding of their present-day lives and the future potential of their universe.

Scholes, Robert. *Structural Fabulation: An Essay on Fiction of the Future*. Notre Dame, Ind.: University of Notre Dame Press, 1975. Scholes argues that fabular futuristic fictions are more pertinent to present concerns in a fast-changing world than any fiction set in the present-day can be.

### MYSTERY AND DETECTIVE SHORT FICTION

Haining, Peter. *The Classic Era of American Pulp Magazines*. Chicago: Chicago Review Press, 2001. This American edition of a book originally published in

England provides historical, biographical, and literary analyses of pulp stories published in a number of genres. Chapter 3, "The Coming of the Hardboiled Dicks," focuses on the "crime" pulps which published detective stories.

Herbert, Rosemary, ed. *The Oxford Companion to Crime and Mystery Writing*. New York: Oxford University Press, 1999. Essays and brief entries by hundreds of authorities span every conceivable aspect of the genre, making this an invaluable reference work for the student, casual reader, and scholar.

Kayman, Martin A. "The Short Story from Poe to Chesterton." In *The Cambridge Companion to Crime Fiction*, edited by Martin Priestman. Cambridge, England; Cambridge University Press, 2003. This section will be of particular interest to those looking for information about the development of the genre. The work as a whole is a useful reference tool for all genres, eras, styles, and writers of crime fiction in eighteenth, nineteenth, and twentieth century England and America.

Moore, Lewis D. *Cracking the Hard-Boiled Detective: A Critical History from the 1920's to the Present*. Jefferson, N.C.: McFarland, 2006. Traces the development of the private investigator subgenre from the early days of Raymond Chandler and Dashiell Hammett to current practitioners.

Rzepka, Charles J. *Detective Fiction*. Cambridge, England: Polity, 2005. Rzepka's well-written survey of the genre pays particular attention to the development of scientific investigative methods and cultural issues that shaped the genre. Includes specific essays on Edgar Allan Poe, Sir Arthur Conan Doyle, Dorothy Sayers, and Raymond Chandler.

Symons, Julian. *Bloody Murder*. New York: Mysterious Press, 1993. Written by a leading critic and mystery-fiction writer, this is one of the most thorough, balanced, and readable histories and critical analyses of the genre. Although a bit dated now, it remains indispensable both for the fan and for the student of crime fiction.

THE SHORT-STORY CYCLE

Davis, Rocío G. *Transcultural Reinventions: Asian American and Asian Canadian Short-Story Cycles*. Toronto: TSAR, 2001. Examines how Asian American and Asian Canadian writers have adopted the short-story cycle as a means of both self-representation and empowerment. Some of the writers whose works are analyzed include Amy Tan, Rohinton Mistry, Sara Suleri, Garrett Hongo, Terry Watada, Sylvia Watanabe, M. G. Vassanji, and Wayson Choy.

Harde, Roxanne, ed. *Narratives of Community: Women's Short Story Sequences*. Newcastle, England: Cambridge Scholars, 2007. Collection of essays analyzing women's roles in domestic, social, and literary communities and the ways in which women attain their identities in these communities. Some of the writers whose works are examined include Sandra Cisneros, Margaret Laurence, Salwa Bakr, Mary Caponegro, Gloria Naylor, Elizabeth Gaskell, Virginia Woolf, Alice Munro, and Maxine Hong Kingston.

Ingram, Forrest L. "The Dynamics of Short Story Cycles." *New Orleans Review* 2 (1979): 7-12. A historical and critical survey and analysis of short stories that form a single unit, such as James Joyce's *Dubliners* (1914), Ernest Hemingway's *In Our Time* (1924, 1925), and Sherwood Anderson's *Winesburg, Ohio* (1919). Attempts to define some of the basic devices used in such cycles.

Kennedy, J. Gerald, ed. *Modern American Short Story Sequences: Composite Fictions and Fictive Communities*. Cambridge, England: Cambridge University Press, 1995. An anthology of essays by various critics on short-story sequence collections, such as Jean Toomer's *Cane* (1923), Ernest Hemingway's *In Our Time* (1924, 1925), William Faulkner's *Go Down, Moses* (1942), John Updike's *Olinger Stories: A Selection* (1964), Sherwood Anderson's *Winesburg, Ohio* (1919), and several others. Kennedy's introduction provides a brief survey of the short-story cycle, a definition of the cycle, and a discussion of the implications of the short-story sequence.

Kuttainen, Victoria. *Unsettling Stories: Settler Postcolonialism and the Short Story Composite*. Newcastle upon Tyne, England: Cambridge Scholars, 2010. Examines how the interconnected short-story collection has been used to express issues of postcolonialism in

American, Canadian, and Australian literature. Analyzes works by Tim Winton, Margaret Laurence, William Faulkner, Stephen Leacock, Sherwood Anderson, Tim O'Brien, and others to describe how they describe the nature of the colonial settlement experience.

Lynch, Gerald. *The One and the Many: English-Canadian Short Story Cycles*. Toronto: University of Toronto Press, 2001. A literary-historical survey of the Canadian short-story cycle. Lynch examines Stephen Leacock's *Sunshine Sketches of a Little Town* in order to describe how a short-story cycle conveys meaning and the significant function of its concluding story. He then examines six other cycles, including works by Duncan Campbell Scott, Frederick Philip Grove, and Alice Munro.

Lundén, Rolf. *The United Stories of America: Studies in the Short Story Composite*. Amsterdam: Rodopi, 1999. Analyzes short-story cycles, focusing on the authors' strategies for closing these texts and attaining a sense of unity. Some of the authors whose work is examined include Eudora Welty, William Faulkner, Ernest Hemingway, and Sherwood Anderson.

Luscher, Robert M. "The Short Story Sequence: An Open Book." In *Short Story Theory at a Crossroads*, edited by Susan Lohafer and Jo Ellyn Clarey. Baton Rouge: Louisiana State University Press, 1989. Discusses the need for readers of story cycles, such as *Winesburg, Ohio*, to extend their drive to find a pattern to cover a number of individual sequences. Compares story cycles with mere aggregates of stories, as well as with novelistic sequences.

Nagel, James. *The Contemporary American Short-Story Cycle: The Ethnic Resonance of Genre*. Baton Rouge: Louisiana State University Press, 2001. Argues that the concentric plot of the short-story cycle lends itself particularly well to issues of ethnic assimilation. Demonstrates this argument by analyzing short-story cycles by eight authors: Louise Erdrich, Jamaica Kincaid, Susan Minot, Sandra Cisneros, Tim O'Brien, Julia Alvarez, Amy Tan, and Robert Olen Butler.

Pacht, Michelle. *The Subversive Storyteller: The Short Story Cycle and the Politics of Identity in America*. Newcastle upon Tyne, England: Cambridge Scholars, 2009. Analyzes the works of nineteenth and twentieth century American authors to demonstrate how they adapted the short-story cycle so as to convey controversial ideas without alienating readers and publishers. Focuses on short stories by Washington Irving, Nathaniel Hawthorne, Sarah Orne Jewett, Charles Waddell Chesnutt, Willa Cather, Henry James, Ernest Hemingway, William Faulkner, Flannery O'Connor, Raymond Carver, Maxine Hong Kingston, and Louise Erdrich.

SHORT FICTION AND WOMEN

Bande, Usha, and Atma Ram. *Woman in Indian Short Stories: Feminist Perspective*. Jaipur, India: Rawat, 2003. Examines women writers' depiction of the "new woman" in Marathi, Hindi, Punjab, and Indian-English short stories published from the mid-1940's through the late 1990's.

Bloom, Harold, ed. *Caribbean Women Writers*. Philadelphia: Chelsea House, 1997. A thorough examination of contemporary, female Caribbean authors who write in English, including Jean Rhys, Jamaica Kincaid, Beryl Gilroy, and Edwidge Danticat. Includes bibliographical references and an index.

Brown, Julie, ed. *American Women Short Story Writers: A Collection of Critical Essays*. New York: Garland, 2000. Collection of essays that analyze short fiction by nineteenth and twentieth century women writers, ranging from serious works of literature to popular tales about "sob sisters." Some of the writers whose works are examined are Lydia Maria Child, Elizabeth Stoddard, Louisa May Alcott, Ellen Glasgow, Edith Wharton, Eudora Welty, Dorothy Parker, Joyce Carol Oates, and Denise Chávez.

Burgin, Mary. "The 'Feminine' Short Story: Recuperating the Moment." *Style* 27 (Fall, 1993): 380-386. Argues that there is a connection between so-called feminine writing that focuses on isolated moments and the concerns of women who have chosen the short story as a form. Claims that the twentieth century epiphanic short story is a manifestation of women's tradition of temporal writing as opposed to the spatial writing of men.

Daiya, Krishna. *Post-Independence Women Short Story Writers in Indian English*. New Delhi, India: Sarup and Sons, 2006. Provides an overview of the works of women short-story writers, analyzing the themes, characterization, and styles of their stories. Assesses the status of the short-fiction genre and describes the contributions of women's short fiction to the genre and to Indian literature. Some of the writers whose works are analyzed are Shashi Deshpande, Anita Desai, Jhumpa Lahiri, Githa Hariharan, and Ruth Prawer Jhabvala.

Erro-Peralta, Nora, and Caridad Silva-Núñez, eds. *Beyond the Border: A New Age in Latin American Women's Fiction*. Pittsburgh, Pa.: Cleis Press, 1991. Covers works by Latin American female writers. Includes bibliographical references.

Hanson, Clare. "The Lifted Veil: Women and Short Fiction in the 1880's and 1890's." *The Yearbook of English Studies* 26 (1996): 135-142. Argues that British women writers in the early modernist period chose the short story to challenge the existing dominant order. Shows how this challenge is embodied in such stories as Charlotte Mew's "Mark Stafford's Wife" as an encounter, presented in iconic, painterly terms, between a male protagonist and a woman, who is then unveiled.

Harde, Roxanne, ed. *Narratives of Community: Women's Short Story Sequences*. Newcastle, England: Cambridge Scholars, 2007. Collection of essays analyzing women's roles in domestic, social, and literary communities and how they attain their identities in these communities. Some of the writers whose works are examined are Sandra Cisneros, Margaret Laurence, Salwa Bakr, Mary Caponegro, Gloria Naylor, Elizabeth Gaskell, Virginia Woolf, Alice Munro, and Maxine Hong Kingston.

Harrington, Ellen Burton, ed. *Scribbling Women and the Short Story Form: Approaches by American and British Women Writers*. New York: Peter Lang, 2008. Collection of essays providing feminist analyses of short fiction by British and American women, focusing on how this genre "liberated" women writers in the period from 1850 through the late twentieth century. Some of the women writers whose works are analyzed are Rebecca Harding

Davis, Louise May Alcott, Kate Chopin, Katherine Anne Porter, Flannery O'Connor, Cynthia Ozick, and Lydia Davis.

Palumbo-DeSimone, Christine. *Sharing Secrets: Nineteenth-Century Women's Relations in the Short Story*. Madison, N.J.: Fairleigh Dickinson University Press, 2000. Palumbo-DeSimone contradicts the criticism that many short stories by nineteenth century women writers are framed around a "seemingly meaningless incident," arguing that these stories are detailed, meaningful, and intricately designed works of serious fiction.

Partnoy, Alicia, ed. *You Can't Drown the Fire: Latin American Women Writing in Exile*. Pittsburgh, Pa.: Cleis Press, 1988. Covers twentieth century female writers whose works have been translated into English. Includes bibliographical references.

PERSONAL ACCOUNTS BY SHORT-FICTION WRITERS

Allende, Isabel. "The Short Story." *Journal of Modern Literature* 20 (Summer, 1996): 21-28. This personal account of storytelling makes suggestions about the differences between the novel and the short story, the story's demand for believability, the story's focus on change, the story's relationship to dream, and the story as events transformed by poetic truth.

Bailey, Tom, ed. *On Writing Short Stories*. 2d ed. New York: Oxford University Press, 2011. In addition to containing a sampling of some classic short stories, this book also features a section in which short-story writers discuss some basic issues regarding the definition and form of these works. These writers include Francine Prose, who explains what makes a short story, and Andre Dubus, who explores the "habit of writing." Bailey also contributes an essay about character, plot, setting, time, metaphor, and voice in short fiction.

Barth, John. "It's a Short Story." In *Further Fridays: Essays, Lectures, and Other Nonfiction, 1984-1994*. New York: Little, Brown, 1995. A personal account by a "congenital novelist" of his brief love affair with the short story during the writing of *Chimera* (1972) and the stories in *Lost in the Funhouse* (1968).

Blythe, Will, ed. *Why I Write: Thoughts on the Craft of Fiction*. Boston: Little, Brown, 1998. A collection of essays by various authors about writing fiction. The essays most relevant to the short story are those by Joy Williams, who says that writers must cherish the mystery of discovery in the process of writing; Thom Jones, who discusses his passionate engagement in the writing of short stories; and Mary Gaitskill, who calls stories the "rich, unseen under-layer of the most ordinary moments."

Burgess, Anthony. "Anthony Burgess on the Short Story." *Journal of the Short Story in English*, no. 2 (1984): 31-47. Burgess admits that he disdains the short story because he cannot write it. He says that the novel presents an epoch, while the short story presents a revelation. Discusses different types of stories, distinguishing between the literary short story, which is patterned, and the commercial form, which is anecdotal.

Charters, Ann, ed. *The Story and Its Writer: An Introduction to Short Fiction*. 6th ed. Boston: Bedford/St. Martin's, 2003. A collection of classic short stories, with commentaries by their authors and other writers that analyze the works and describe how the stories were written. Includes appendixes chronicling storytelling before the emergence of the short story and the history of the short story.

Gioia, Dana, and R. S. Gwynn, eds. *The Art of the Short Story*. New York: Pearson Longman, 2006. This anthology includes an "author's perspective" from each of its fifty-two authors, in which the writers comment on the aims, context, and workings of their short stories. For example, Sherwood Anderson and Raymond Carver provide advice on the craft of writing; Margaret Atwood discusses Canadian identity; Alice Walker writes about race and gender; and Flannery O'Connor explains the importance of religious grace in her work. Some of the other authors included in the anthology are John Cheever, Albert Camus, F. Scott Fitzgerald, Ernest Hemingway, Anton Chekhov, James Joyce, Jorge Luis Borges, William Faulkner, Chinua Achebe, Ha Jin, Sandra Cisneros, and Gabriel García Márquez.

Iftekharuddin, Farhat, Mary Rohrberger, and Maurice Lee, eds. *Speaking of the Short Story: Interviews with Contemporary Writers*. Jackson: University Press of Mississippi, 1997. Collection of twenty-one interviews with short-story writers, such as Isabel Allende, Rudolfo A. Anaya, Ellen Douglas, Richard Ford, Bharati Mukherjee, and Leslie Marmon Silko, and short story critics, such as Susan Lohafer, Charles E. May, and Mary Rohrberger.

Lee, Maurice A., ed. *Writers on Writing: The Art of the Short Story*. Westport, Conn.: Praeger, 2005. A collection of essays in which short-story writers from around the world discuss their craft and analyze stories and types of short fiction. Some of the contributors include Amiri Baraka, Olive Senior, Jayne Anne Philips, Janette Turner Hospital, Ivan Wolfers, Singapore writer Kirpal Singh, and Ivan Wolfers.

Mandelbaum, Paul, ed. *Twelve Short Stories and Their Making*. New York: Persea Books, 2005. These twelve stories by contemporary writers have been selected to illustrate six elements of the short story: character, plot, point of view, theme, setting, and structure. The book also includes individual interviews with the twelve authors in which they describe their writing processes and the challenges they faced in composing their selected stories. The featured writers include Elizabeth Tallent, Charles Johnson, Allan Gurganus, Ursula K. Le Guin, Jhumpa Lahiri, Sandra Cisneros, and Tobias Wolff.

O'Connor, Flannery. "Writing Short Stories." In *Mystery and Manners*, edited by Sally and Robert Fitzgerald. New York: Farrar, Straus & Giroux, 1969. In this lecture at a southern writers' conference, O'Connor discusses the two qualities necessary for the short story: "sense of manners," which writers get from the texture of their immediate surroundings, and "sense of mystery," which is always the mystery of personality-- "showing how some specific folks *will* do, in spite of everything."

Senior, Olive. "Lessons from the Fruit Stand: Or, Writing for the Listener." *Journal of Modern Literature* 20 (Summer, 1996): 40-44. An account of one writer's development of the short story as a personal engagement between teller and listener. Discusses the relationship between the oral tradition of gossip and folklore and the development of short-story conventions. Claims that the short story is a form based on bits and pieces of human lives for which there is no total picture.

Turchi, Peter, and Andrea Barrett, eds. *The Story Behind the Story: Twenty-six Writers and How They Work*. New York: W. W. Norton, 2004. The stories in this collection were written by faculty members in the writing program at Warren Wilson College, including Antonya Nelson, Margot Livesey, David Shields, C. J. Hribal, Andrea Barrett, Steven Schwartz, and Jim Shepard. Accompanying each story is a brief essay in which the writer describes how his or her story was created.

Wright, Austin. "The Writer Meets the Critic on the Great Novel/Short Story Divide." *Journal of Modern Literature* 20 (Summer, 1996): 13-19. A personal account by a short-story critic and novelist of some of the basic differences between the critical enterprise and the writing of fiction, as well as some of the generic differences between the short story and the novel.

*Charles E. May*
*Updated by Rebecca Kuzins*

# GUIDE TO ONLINE RESOURCES

Web Sites

The following sites were visited by the editors of Salem Press in 2011. Because URLs frequently change, the accuracy of these addresses cannot be guaranteed; however, long-standing sites, such as those of colleges and universities, national organizations, and government agencies, generally maintain links when sites are moved or updated.

## The American Short Story: A Selective Chronology

http://www.iwu.edu/~jplath/sschron.html

This timeline has been compiled by James Plath, a professor and chair of the English department at Illinois Western University, and is part of his Web site, Plath Country. The chronology charts the development of the American short story from 1741 until the present day, listing the publication dates of many important works of short fiction. It also features a bibliography of books about the short story.

## Bibliomania: Short Stories

http://www.bibliomania.com/0/5/frameset.html

Among Bibliomania's more than two thousand texts are short stories written by American and foreign writers, including Mark Twain, O. Henry, Stephen Crane, and Anton Chekhov, as well as James Joyce's story collection *Dubliners*. The stories can be retrieved via lists of titles and authors.

## Books and Writers

http://www.kirjasto.sci.fi/indeksi.htm

A broad, comprehensive, and easy-to-use resource about hundreds of authors throughout the world, extending from 70 b.c.e to the twenty-first century. Books and Writers contains an alphabetical list of authors with links to pages featuring a biography, a list of works, and recommendations for further reading about each author; each writer's page also includes links to related pages in the site. Although brief, the biographical essays provide a solid overview of the authors' careers, their contributions to literature, and their literary influence.

## A Celebration of Women Writers

http://digital.library.upenn.edu/women

An extensive compendium of information about the contributions of women writers throughout history. The "Local Editions by Authors" and "Local Editions by Category" pages enable users to retrieve electronic texts of the works of numerous writers, including Katherine Mansfield, Edith Wharton, and Virginia Woolf. Users can also access biographical and bibliographical information about women writers by browsing the writers' names, countries of origin, ethnicity, and century in which they lived.

## Classic Short Stories

http://www.classicshorts.com

Features the texts of American and British short stories, as well as some stories by Guy de Maupassant, Anton Chekhov, and other European writers. Stories can be accessed via title or author's name.

## Internet Public Library: Native American Authors

http://www.ipl.org/div/natam

Internet Public Library, a Web-based collection of materials, contains this index to resources about Native American literature. An alphabetical list of authors enables users to link to biographies, lists of works, electronic texts, tribal Web sites, and other online resources. The majority of writers are contemporary American

Indian authors, but some historical authors are also featured. Users can also retrieve information via lists of titles and tribes. In addition, the site contains a bibliography of print and online materials about Native American literature.

### The Literary Gothic

http://www.litgothic.com/index_html.html

The Literary Gothic describes itself as a guide to "all things concerned with literary Gothicism," including ghost stories, with the majority of its resources related to literary works written and published from 1764 through 1820. The site defines gothic literature in broad terms, including some authors usually not associated with the genre, such as Joseph Addison and Willa Cather. An alphabetical list of authors and of titles provides links to biographies and other Web-based resources, including electronic texts of many works of gothic literature.

### LiteraryHistory.com

http://www.literaryhistory.com

An excellent source of Web-based academic, scholarly, and critical literature about eighteenth, nineteenth, and twentieth century American and English writers. This site provides numerous pages about specific eras and literary genres, including individual pages for eighteenth, nineteenth, and twentieth century literature and for African American and postcolonial literature. These pages contain alphabetical lists of authors which link to articles, reviews, overviews, excerpts of works, teaching guides, podcast interviews, and other materials.

### Literary Resources on the Net

http://andromeda.rutgers.edu/~jlynch/Lit

Jack Lynch of Rutgers University maintains this extensive collection of links to Internet sites that are useful to academics, including Web sites about a broad range of literary topics. The site is organized chronically, with separate pages for information about classical Greece and Rome, the Middle Ages, the Renaissance, the eighteenth century, Romantic and Victorian eras,

and twentieth century British and Irish literature. There are also separate pages providing links to Web sites about American literature and to women's literature and feminism.

### Literature: What Makes a Good Short Story

http://www.learner.org/interactives/literature

Annenberg Learner.org, a site providing interactive resources for teachers, contains this section describing the elements of short fiction, including plot construction, point of view, character development, setting, and theme. This section also features the text of "A Jury of Her Peers," a short story by Susan Glaspell, in order to illustrate the components of short fiction.

### LitWeb

http://litweb.net

LitWeb provides biographies of more than five hundred world authors throughout history which can be accessed via an alphabetical listing. The pages about each writer contain a list of his or her works, suggestions for further reading, and illustrations. LitWeb also offers information about past and present winners of major literary prizes.

### The Modern Word: The Libyrinth

http://www.themodernword.com/authors.html

The Modern Word provides a great deal of critical information about postmodern writers and contemporary experimental fiction. The core of the site is "The Libyrinth," which lists authors for which there are links to essays and other resources. There are also sections devoted to Samuel Beckett, Jorge Luis Borges, Gabriel García Márquez, James Joyce, Franz Kafka, and Thomas Pynchon.

### Outline of American Literature

http://www.america.gov/publications/books/outline-of-american-literature.html

This page of the America.gov site provides access to *Outline of American Literature*, a historical overview of prose and poetry from colonial times to the present. The ten-chapter book was written by Kathryn

VanSpanckeren, professor of English at the University of Tampa, and was published by the Department of State. This site contains abbreviated versions of each chapter, as well as access to the entire publication in pdf format.

### The Short Story Library at American Literature

http://www.americanliterature.com/sstitleindex.html

A compilation of more than two thousand short stories which can be accessed via alphabetical lists of story titles and authors. Although the majority of the authors are American, the site also features English translations of stories by Anton Chekhov, Guy de Maupassant, and other writers, as well as works by British authors, such as Charles Dickens, Saki, and Rudyard Kipling. The site provides texts of some of the most well-known works of short fiction, including "The Tell-Tale Heart" by Edgar Allan Poe, "Bartleby the Scrivener" by Herman Melville, and "The Lottery" by Shirley Jackson.

### Voice of the Shuttle

http://vos.ucsb.edu

The most complete and authoritative place for online information about literature. Created and maintained by professors and students in the English department at the University of California, Santa Barbara, Voice of the Shuttle is a database with thousands of links to electronic books, academic journals, association Web sites, sites created by university professors, and many, many other resources about the humanities. The "Literature in English" page provides links to separate pages about the literature of the Anglo-Saxon era, Middle Ages, Renaissance and seventeenth century, Restoration and eighteenth century, Romantic age, Victorian age, and modern and contemporary periods in Great Britain and the United States, as well as a page about minority literature. Another page in the site, "Literatures Other than English," offers a gateway to information about the literature of numerous countries and world regions, including Africa, Eastern Europe, Arabic-speaking nations, China, France, and Germany.

### Voices from the Gaps

http://voices.cla.umn.edu

This site from the English department at the University of Minnesota is "dedicated to bringing together marginalized resources and knowledge about women artists of color," including women writers. Users can retrieve information by artists' names or by a range of subjects. The "Short Stories" subject page lists writers of short fiction, such as Edwidge Danticat, Maxine Hong Kingston, Ann Petry, Leslie Marmon Silko, and Helena María Viramontes.

## ELECTRONIC DATABASES

Electronic databases usually do not have their own URLs. Instead, public, college, and university libraries subscribe to these databases, provide links to them on their Web sites, and make them available to library card holders or specified patrons. Readers can check library Web sites or ask reference librarians to check on the databases' availability.

### Bloom's Literary Reference Online

Facts on File publishes this database of thousands of articles by renowned scholar Harold Bloom and other literary critics, examining the lives and works of great writers worldwide. This database also includes information on more than forty-six thousand literary characters, literary topics, themes, movements, and genres, plus video segments about literature. Users can retrieve information by browsing writers' names, titles of works, time periods, genres, or writers' nationalities.

### Literary Reference Center

EBSCO's Literary Reference Center (LRC) is a comprehensive full-text database containing information from reference works, books, literary journals, and other materials. The database's contents include more than 34,000 plot summaries, synopses, and overviews of literary works; almost 100,000 essays and articles of literary criticism; about 180,000 author biographies; more than 683,000 book reviews; and more than 6,200 author interviews. It also contains the entire contents of

Salem Press's MagillOnLiterature Plus. Users can retrieve information by browsing a list of authors' names or titles of literary works; they can also use an advanced search engine to access information by numerous categories, including an author's name, gender, cultural identity, national identity, and the years in which he or she lived, or by literary title, character, locale, genre, and publication date.

## Literary Resource Center

Published by Gale, this comprehensive literary database contains information on the lives and works of more than 135,000 authors from Gale reference sources in all genres, all time periods, and throughout the world. In addition, the database offers more than 75,000 full-text critical essays and reviews from some of Gale's reference publications, including *Short Story Criticism*; more than 11,000 overviews of frequently studied works; and more than 300,000 full-text short stories, poems, and plays. Literary Resource Center also features a literary-historical time line and an encyclopedia of literature.

## MagillOnLiterature Plus

MagillOnLiterature Plus is a comprehensive, integrated literature database produced by Salem Press and available on the EBSCO host platform. The database contains the full-text of Salem's many literature-related reference works, including *Masterplots* (series I and II), *Cyclopedia of World Authors*, *Cyclopedia of Literary Characters*, *Cyclopedia of Literary Places*, and *Critical Surveys of Literature*. Among its contents are critical essays, brief plot summaries, extended character profiles, and detailed setting discussions about works of literature by more than eighty-five hundred short- and long-fiction writers, poets, dramatists, essayists, and philosophers. The database also features biographical essays on more than twenty-five hundred authors, with lists of each author's principal works and current secondary bibliographies.

## NoveList

NoveList is a readers' advisory service produced by EBSCO Publishing. The database provides access to 155,000 titles of both adult and juvenile fiction, including collections of short fiction. Users can type the words "short story" into the search engine and retrieve more than fourteen thousand short-story collections; users can also search by author's name to access titles of books, information about the author, and book reviews.

## Short Story Index

This index, created by the H. W. Wilson Company, features information on more than 76,500 stories from more than 4,000 collections. Users can retrieve information by author, title, keyword, subject, date, source, literary technique, or a combination of these categories. The subject searches provide information about the stories' themes, locales, narratives techniques, and genres.

*Rebecca Kuzins*

# TIMELINE

| | |
|---|---|
| 1789 | American magazines begin to publish short fiction. |
| 1819-1820 | Washington Irving lays the foundation for the American short story in *The Sketch Book of Geoffrey Crayon, Gant,* a collection that includes the tales "Rip van Winkle" and "The Legend of Sleepy Hollow." |
| 1821 | *The Saturday Evening Post* debuts. This magazine will publish numerous short stories aimed at the general public. |
| 1830-1865 | Romantic Period of American short-story writing |
| 1835 | Augustus Baldwin Longstreet, the foremost writer among the Southwest humorists, publishes *Georgia Scenes, Characters, Incidents, Etc. in the First Half Century of the Republic*, a collection of tall tales told in the vernacular speech of the Georgia frontier. |
| 1837 | Nathaniel Hawthorne publishes *Twice-Told Tales*, a short-fiction collection that will be expanded in a second edition five years later. |
| 1840 | Edgar Allan Poe's first short-story collection, *Tales of the Grotesque and Arabesque*, is published. |
| 1844 | Different versions of "The Purloined Letter" by Edgar Allan Poe are published in two magazines. In this and other stories about C. Auguste Dupin, including "The Murders in the Rue Morgue," Poe establishes the conventions of the modern detective story. |
| 1856 | Herman Melville's collection *The Piazza Tales*, which includes "Bartleby the Scrivener" and "Benito Cereno," is published. |
| 1857 | *The Atlantic Monthly* begins publishing and will become an important venue for short fiction. |
| 1865-1900 | Realistic Period of American short-story writing |
| 1865 | Mark Twain's "The Celebrated Jumping Frog of Calaveras County" makes its first appearance in the *New York Saturday Press*. |
| 1868 | *The Overland Monthly* publishes Bret Harte's "The Luck of Roaring Camp." |
| 1875-1900 | A number of American literary magazines and journals begin publishing, creating a demand for short fiction. |
| 1876 | Joel Chandler Harris publishes his first story about an elderly black man. This character, later named Uncle Remus, will be featured in several short-story collections to be published between 1880 and 1905. |

| 1891 | Hamlin Garland publishes *Main-Travelled Roads: Six Mississippi Valley Stories*. The collection is an example of the "local color" literature of the late nineteenth century--works that focus on the dialects, characters, customs, and other elements of a specific region of the United States. Other local-color short-fiction writers include Mary E. Wilkins Freeman and Sarah Orne Jewett of New England; Kate Chopin, George Washington Cable, and Charles W. Chestnutt from the South: and Bret Harte and Mark Twain from the West. |
| --- | --- |
| 1894 | Kate Chopin's *Bayou Folk*, a collection of stories and sketches, is published. |
| 1897 | Stephen Crane produces "The Open Boat," which many critics consider his greatest short story. |
| 1900 | Naturalist writer Jack London publishes his first short-story collection, *The Son of the Wolf*. |
| 1900-1910 | Naturalistic Period of American short-story writing |
| 1901 | Brander Matthews, a Columbia University professor, publishes *The Philosophy of Short Fiction*, the first full-length study of the short story. |
| 1905 | "Paul's Case," a widely anthologized story by Willa Cather, is published in Cather's collection *The Troll Garden*. |
| 1906 | *The Four Million*, one of numerous short-story collections by O. Henry, is published. O. Henry's popular stories will influence the development of magazine fiction and the modern narrative. |
| 1910-1945 | Period of Modernism in American short-story writing |
| 1915 | *The Best American Short Stories* debuts and will continue to be published annually into the twenty-first century. The anthology features the best short stories published that year in American and Canadian magazines. |
| 1919 | *Winesburg, Ohio*, Sherwood Anderson's innovative collection of short stories, is published. |
| 1919 | The O. Henry Awards are established. The award-winning short stories are published each year in a volume entitled *Prize Stories*. In 2009, prize officials will partner with the PEN American Center to present the renamed PEN/O. Henry Award. |
| 1920 | *Flappers and Philosophers*, the first collection of short fiction by F. Scott Fitzgerald, is published. |
| 1923 | *Cane*, Jean Toomer's collection of prose and poetry, is published. |
| 1925 | *The New Yorker* magazine debuts and will become an important venue for the works of short-fiction writers. |
| 1927 | Ernest Hemingway's *Men Without Women*, a collection of short fiction that includes "The Killers," is published. |

| 1934 | Langston Hughes publishes his first short-fiction collection, *The Ways of White Folks*. |
| --- | --- |
| 1938 | Pearl S. Buck wins the Nobel Prize in Literature. The American author's short stories and other works help shape Western readers' perceptions of China. |
| 1941 | Frederic Dannay and Manfred B. Lee, who collectively write under the pseudonym Ellery Queen, establish *Ellery Queen's Mystery Magazine*, which will rejuvenate the detective short story. |
| 1942 | *My World--And Welcome to It!* by James Thurber is published. The collection includes one of his most popular stories, "The Secret Life of Walter Mitty." |
| 1945 | Dashiell Hammett publishes his first collection of detective stories about The Continental Op, a tough San Francisco-based private investigator whose name is never revealed. |
| 1948 | James Michener wins the Pulitzer Prize for *Tales of the South Pacific*. |
| 1948 | Shirley Jackson's short story "The Lottery" is published in *The New Yorker*, eliciting the largest reader response in the history of the magazine to date. |
| 1951 | William Faulkner's *Collected Stories* receives the National Book Award. |
| 1951 | Carson McCullers publishes *The Ballad of the Sad Café*, a collection of novels and short stories. |
| 1953 | Two collections of short fiction by major American writers are published: *The Enormous Radio* by John Cheever and *Nine Stories* by J. D. Salinger. |
| 1955 | Flannery O'Connor, considered to be one of the most important writers of the short story, publishes her first collection of short fiction: *A Good Man Is Hard to Find, and Other Stories*. |
| 1959 | Grace Paley publishes *The Little Disturbances of Man: Stories of Men and Women in Love*. |
| 1959 | *The Magic Barrel* by Bernard Malamud wins the National Book Award. |
| 1960 | Philip Roth wins the National Book Award for *Goodbye Columbus, and Five Short Stories*. |
| 1963-1980 | Confessional Period of American short-story writing |
| 1963 | H. P. Lovecraft publishes his first collection of horror stories, *The Dunwich Horror and Others*. |
| 1964 | Postmodernist writer Donald Barthelme publishes his first short-fiction collection, *Come Back, Dr. Caligari*. |
| 1965 | James Baldwin's short stories are published in *Going to Meet the Man*. |

| 1966 | *The Collected Stories of Katherine Anne Porter* wins both the National Book Award and the Pulitzer Prize. |
| 1970 | Ama Ata Aidoo of Ghana publishes *No Sweetness Here, and Other Stories*, a collection of female portraits offering various images of womanhood. |
| 1970 | *The Collected Stories of Jean Stafford* receives the Pulitzer Prize. |
| 1971 | Tomás Rivera's *. . . y no se lo tragó la tierra/ . . . and the earth did not part* is published in Spanish and will later be published in a bilingual English-Spanish edition. A Chicano classic, the book contains fourteen stories about the life of migrant farmworkers. |
| 1973 | Pushcart Press is established and soon begins publishing annual anthologies of the best short fiction to appear in small literary magazines. |
| 1974 | *Aiiieeeee! An Anthology of Asian American Writers*, a trail-blazing collections for and by Asian Americans, is published. |
| 1978 | Ann Beattie's stories from *The New Yorker* are published in *Secrets and Surprises*. |
| 1980 | American short-story writing enters its Period of Postmodernism |
| 1981 | Raymond Carver, the master of minimalist short fiction, attains critical and popular acclaim with his collection *What We Talk About When We Talk About Love*. Other American minimalist writers of the 1970's and 1980's are Ann Beattie, Tobias Wolff, Mary Robison, Bobbie Ann Mason, and sometimes Richard Ford, Jayne Anne Phillips, and David Leavitt. |
| 1983 | The University of Georgia Press presents the first annual Flannery O'Connor Award for Short Fiction to David Walton for *Evening Out* and Leigh Allison Wilson for *From the Bottom Up*. |
| 1984 | Ellen Gilchrist receives the National Book Award for *Victory over Japan: A Book of Stories*. |
| 1986 | Cynthia Ozick receives the first Rea Award, presented annually to writers who have made a contribution to the short-story form. |
| 1988 | John Updike receives the first annual PEN/Malamud Award for excellence in the "art of the short story." |
| 1989 | Susan Hubbard wins the Grace Paley Prize for Short Fiction for *Walking on Ice*. |
| 1991 | Frederick Busch and Andre Dubus receive the PEN/Malamud Award. |
| 1992 | Eudora Welty receives the PEN/Malamud Award. |
| 1994 | Tillie Olsen receives the Rea Award. |
| 1996 | Joyce Carol Oates receives the PEN/Malamud Award. |
| 1996 | Andrea Barrett receives the National Book Award for *Ship Fever, and Other Stories*. |
| 1997 | Gina Berriault receives the PEN/Faulkner Award for Fiction for *Women in Their Beds: New and Selected Stories*. |

| 1998 | John Edgar Wideman receives the Rea Award. |
|------|--------------------------------------------|
| 1999 | John Updike edits *The Best American Short Stories of the Century*, featuring one of the stories that appeared in each edition of *The Best American Short Stories* from 1915 through 1999. |
| 2003 | Barry Hannah and Maile Meloy receive the PEN/Malamud Award. |
| 2004 | Edwidge Danticat, a Haitian American writer, receives the first Story Prize for *The Dew Breaker*. The prize is presented annually for a collection of outstanding short fiction that is written in English and initially published in the United States. |
| 2004 | Lorrie Moore receives the Rea Award. |
| 2006 | Adam Haslett and Tobias Wolff win the PEN/Malamud Award. |
| 2010 | Sherman Alexie receives the PEN/Faulkner Award for *War Dances*. |
| 2011 | California writer Brando Skyhorse wins the PEN/Hemingway Award for *The Madonnas of Echo Park*, a collection of short stories about Mexican Americans living in a neighborhood near downtown Los Angeles. |

*Rebecca Kuzins*

# MAJOR AWARDS

### THE BEST AMERICAN SHORT STORIES

Published annually since 1915, *The Best American Short Stories* includes the best stories that were published in American or Canadian magazines during the year. Selection for the volume is considered a high honor.

### The Best Short Stories of 1915, and the Yearbook of the American Short Story,
### *edited by* Edward J. O'Brien

Burt, Maxwell Struthers-- "The Water-Hole"
Byrne, Donn-- "The Wake"
Comfort, Will Levington-- "Chautonville"
Dwiggins, W. A.-- "La Derniere Mobilisation"
Dwyer, James Francis-- "The Citizen"
Gregg, Frances-- "Whose Dog?"
Hecht, Ben-- "Life"
Hurst, Fannie-- "T. B."
Johnson, Arthur-- "Mr. Eberdeen's House"
Jordan, Virgil-- "Vengeance Is Mine"
Lyon, Harris Merton-- "The Weaver Who Clad the Summer"
Muilenburg, Walter J.-- "Heart of Youth"
Noyes, Newbold-- "The End of the Path"
O'Brien, Seumas-- "The Whale and the Grasshopper"
O'Reilly, Mary Boyle-- "In Berlin"
Roof, Katharine Metcalf-- "The Waiting Years"
Rosenblatt, Benjamin-- "Zelig"
Singmaster, Elsie-- "The Survivors"
Steele, Wilbur Daniel-- "The Yellow Cat"
Synon, Mary-- "The Bounty-Jumper"

### The Best Short Stories of 1916, and the Yearbook of the American Short Story,
### *edited by* Edward J. O'Brien

Atherton, Gertrude-- "The Sacrificial Altar"
Benefield, Barry-- "Miss Willett"
Booth, Frederick-- "Supers"
Burnet, Dana-- "Fog"
Buzzell, Francis-- "Ma's Pretties"
Cobb, Irvin S.-- "The Great Auk"
Dreiser, Theodore-- "The Lost Phoebe"
Gordon, Armistead C.-- "The Silent Infare"
Greene, Frederick Stuart-- "The Cat of the Cane-Brake"
Hallet, Richard Matthews-- "Making Port"
Hurst, Fannie-- "Ice water, Pl--!"

### The Best Short Stories of 1917, and the Yearbook of the American Short Story,
### *edited by* Edward J. O'Brien

Babcock, Edwina Stanton-- "Excursion"
Beer, Thomas-- "Onnie"
Burt, Maxwell Struthers-- "Cup of Tea"
Buzzell, Francis-- "Lonely Places"
Cobb, Irvin S.-- "Boys Will Be Boys"
Dobie, Charles Caldwell-- "Laughter"
Dwight, H. G.-- "Emperor of Elam"
Ferber, Edna-- "Gay Old Dog"
Gerould, Katharine Fullerton-- "Knight's Move"
Glaspell, Susan-- "Jury of Her Peers"

Greene, Frederick Stuart-- "Bunker Mouse"

Hallet, Richard Matthews-- "Rainbow Pete"

Hurst, Fannie-- "Get Ready the Wreaths"

Johnson, Fanny Kemble-- "Strange Looking Man"

Kline, Burton-- "Caller in the Night"

O'Sullivan, Vincent-- "Interval"

Perry, Lawrence-- "Certain Rich Man"

Pulver, Mary Brecht-- "Path of Glory"

Steele, Wilbur Daniel-- "Ching, Ching, Chinaman"

Synon, Mary-- "None So Blind"

## The Best Short Stories of 1918, and the Yearbook of the American Short Story,
### *edited by* **Edward J. O'Brien**

Abdullah, Achmed-- "A Simple Act of Piety"

Babcock, Edwina Stanton-- "Cruelties"

Brown, Katharine Holland-- "Buster"

Dobie, Charles Caldwell-- "The Open Window"

Dudly, William-- "The Toast to Forty-Five"

Freedley, Mary Mitchell-- "Blind Vision"

Gerould, Gordon Hall-- "Imagination"

Gilbert, George-- "In Maulmain Fever-Ward"

Humphrey, G.-- "The Father's Hand"

Johnson, Arthur-- "The Visit of the Master"

Kline, Burton-- "In the Open Code"

Lewis, Sinclair-- "The Willow Walk"

Moseley, Katharine Prescott-- "The Story Vinton
    Heard at Mallorie"

Rhodes, Harrison-- "Extra Men"

Springer, Fleta Campbell-- "Solitaire"

Steele, Wilbur Daniel-- "The Dark Hour"

Street, Julian-- "The Bird of Serbia"

Venable, Edward C.-- "At Isham's"

Vorse, Mary Heaton-- "De Vilmarte's Luck"

Wood, Frances Gilchrist-- "The White Battalion"

## The Best Short Stories of 1919, and the Yearbook of the American Short Story,
### *edited by* **Edward J. O'Brien**

Alsop, G. F.-- "The Kitchen Gods"

Anderson, Sherwood-- "An Awakening"

Babcock, Edwina Stanton-- "Willum's Vanilla"

Barnes, Djuna-- "A Night Among the Horses"

Bartlett, Frederick Orin-- "Long, Long Ago"

Brownell, Agnes Mary-- "Dishes"

Burt, Maxwell Struthers-- "The Blood-Red One"

Cabell, James Branch-- "The Wedding-Jest"

Fish, Horace-- "The Wrists on the Door"

Glaspell, Susan-- "'Government Goat'"

Goodman, Henry-- "The Stone"

Hallet, Richard Matthews-- "To the Bitter End"

Hergesheimer, Joseph-- "The Meeker Ritual"

Ingersoll, Will E.-- "The Centenarian"

Johnston, Calvin-- "Messengers"

Jones, Howard Mumford-- "Mrs. Drainger's Veil"

La Motte, Ellen N.-- "Under a Wine-Glass"

Lieberman, Elias-- "A Thing of Beauty"

Vorse, Mary Heaton-- "The Other Room"

Yezierska, Anzia-- "'The Fat of the Land'"

## The Best Short Stories of 1920, and the Yearbook of the American Short Story,
### *edited by* **Edward J. O'Brien**

Anderson, Sherwood-- "The Other Woman"

Babcock, Edwina Stanton-- "Gargoyle"

Bercovici, Konrad-- "Ghitza"

Bryner, Edna Clare-- "The Life of Five Points"

Camp, Wadsroth-- "The Signal Tower"

Crew, Helen Oale-- "The Parting Genius"

Gerould, Katharine Fullerton-- "Habakkuk"

Hartman, Lee Foster-- "The Judgment of Vulcan"

Hughes, Rupert-- "The Stick-in-the-Muds"

Mason, Grace Sartwell-- "His Job"

Oppenheim, James-- "The Rending"

Roche, Arthur Somers-- "The Dummy-Chucker"

Sidney, Rose-- "Butterflies"

Springer, Fleta Campbel-- "The Rotter"

Steele, Wilbur Daniel-- "Out of Exile"

Storm, Ethel-- "The Three Telegrams"

Wheelwright, John T.-- "The Roman Bath"

Whitman, Stephen French-- "Amazement"

Williams, Ben Ames-- "Sheener"

Wood, Frances Gilchrist-- "Turkey Red"

### The Best Short Stories of 1921, and the Yearbook of the American Short Story,
#### *edited by* **Edward J. O'Brien**

Anderson, Sherwood-- "Brothers"

Bercovici, Konrad-- "Fanutza"

Burt, Maxwell Struthers-- "Experiment"

Cobb, Irvin S.-- "Darkness"

Colcord, Lincoln-- "An Instrument of the Gods"

Finger, Charles J.-- "The Lizard God"

Frank, Waldo-- "Under the Dome"

Gerould, Katherine Fullerton-- "French Eva"

Glasgow, Ellen-- "The Past"

Glaspell, Susan-- "His Smile"

Hallet, Richard Matthews-- "The Harbor Master"

Hart, Frances Noyes-- "Green Gardens"

Hurst, Fannie-- "She Walks in Beauty"

Komroff, Manuel-- "The Little Master of the Sky"

Mott, Frank Luther-- "The Man with the Good Face"

O'Sullivan, Vincent-- "Master of Fallen Years"

Steele, Wilbur Daniel-- "The Shame Dance"

Thayer, Harriet Maxon-- "Kindred"

Towne, Charles Hanson-- "Shelby"

Vorse, Mary Heaton-- "The Wallow of the Sea"

### The Best Short Stories of 1922, and the Yearbook of the American Short Story,
#### *edited by* **Edward J. O'Brien**

Aiken, Conrad-- "The Dark City"

Anderson, Sherwood-- "I'm a Fool"

Bercovici, Konrad-- "The Death of Murdo"

Boogher, Susan M.-- "An Unknown Warrior"

Booth, Frederick-- "The Helpless Ones"

Bryner, Edna-- "Forest Cover"

Cohen, Rose Gollup-- "Natalka's Portion"

Finger, Charles J.-- "The Shame of Gold"

Fitzgerald, F. Scott-- "Two for a Cent"

Frank, Waldo-- "John the Baptist"

Freedman, David-- "Mendel Marantz: Housewife"

Gerould, Katharine Fullerton-- "Belshazzar's Letter"

Hecht, Ben-- "Winkelburg"

Hergesheimer, Joseph-- "The Token"

Jitro, William-- "The Resurrection and the Life"

Lardner, Ring-- "The Golden Honeymoon"

Oppenheim, James-- "He Laughed at the Gods"

Rosenblatt, Benjamin-- "In the Metropolis"

Steele, Wilbur Daniel-- "From the Other Side of the South"

Wood, Clement-- "The Coffin"

### The Best Short Stories of 1923, and the Yearbook of the American Short Story,
#### *edited by* **Edward J. O'Brien**

Adams, Bill-- "Way for a Sailor"

Anderson, Sherwood-- "The Man's Story"

Babcock, Edwina Stanton-- "Mr. Cardeezer"

Bercovici, Konrad-- "Seed"

Burnet, Dana-- "Beyond the Cross"

Clark, Valma-- "Ignition"

Cobb, Irvin S.-- "The Chocolate Hyena"

Cournos, John-- "The Samovar"

Dreiser, Theodore-- "Reina"

Ferber, Edna-- "Home Girl"

Goodman, Henry-- "The Button"

Hemingway, Ernest-- "My Old Man"

Hurst, Fannie-- "Seven Candle"

Montague, Margaret Prescott-- "The Today Tomorrow"

Stewart, Solon K.-- "The Contract of Corporal Twing"

Stimson, F. J.-- "By Due Process of Law"

Sukow, Ruth-- "Renters"

Toomer, Jean-- "Blood-Burning Moon"

Vorse, Mary Heaton-- "The Promise"

Wilson, Harry Leon-- "Flora and Fauna"

### The Best Short Stories of 1924, and the Yearbook of the American Short Story,
#### *edited by* **Edward J. O'Brien**

Burke, Morgan-- "Champlin"

Cram, Mildred-- "Billy"

Dell, Floyd-- "Phantom Adventure"

Dobie, Charles Caldwell-- "The Cracked Teapot"

Drake, Carlos-- "The Last Dive"

Finger, Charles J.-- "Adventures of Andrew Lang"

## The Best Short Stories of 1924 (*continued*)

Gale, Zona-- "The Biography of Blade"
Greenwald, Tupper-- "Corputt"
Hervey, Harry-- "The Young Men Go Down"
Hess, Leonard L.-- "The Lesser Gift"
Hughes, Rupert-- "Grudges"
Morris, Gouverneur-- "A Postscript to Divorce"
Reese, Lizette Woodworth-- "Forgiveness"
Sergel, Roger-- "Nocturne: A Red Shawl"

Shiffrin, A. B.-- "The Black Laugh"
Suckow, Ruth-- "Four Generations"
Van den Bark, Melvin-- "Two Women and Hog-Back Ridge"
Van Dine, Warren L.-- "The Poet"
Wescott, Glenway-- "In a Thicket"
Wood, Frances Gilchrist-- "Shoes"

## The Best Short Stories of 1925, and the Yearbook of the American Short Story,
### *edited by* **Edward J. O'Brien**

Alexander, Sandra-- "The Gift"
Anderson, Sherwood-- "The Return"
Asch, Nathan-- "Gertude Donovan"
Benefield, Barry-- "Guard of Honor"
Bercovici, Konrad-- "The Beggar of Alcazar"
Cohen, Bella-- "The Laugh"
Dobie, Charles Caldwell-- "The Hands of the Enemy"
Fisher, Rudolph-- "The City of Refuge"
Gerould, Katherine Fullerton-- "An Army with Banners"
Gilkyson, Walter-- "Coward's Castle"

Komroff, Manuel-- "How Does It Feel to Be Free?"
Lardner, Ring-- "Haircut"
Robinson, Robert-- "The Ill Wind"
Scott, Evelyn-- "The Old Lady"
Stanley, May-- "Old Man Ledge"
Steele, Wilber Daniel-- "Six Dollars"
Waldman, Milton-- "The Home Town"
Wescott, Glenway-- "Fire and Water"
Willoughby, Barrett-- "The Devil Drum"
Wylie, Elinor-- "Gideon's Revenge"

## The Best Short Stories of 1926, and the Yearbook of the American Short Story,
### *edited by* **Edward J. O'Brien**

Benefield, Barry-- "Carrie Snyder"
Carver, Ada Jack-- "Maudie"
Corley, Donald-- "The Glass Eye of Throgmorton"
Crowell, Chester T.-- "Take the Stand, Please"
Dingle, A. E.-- "Bound for Rio Grande"
Dudley, Henry Walbridge-- "Query"
Fauset, Arthur Huff-- "Symphonesque"
Gale, Zona-- "Evening"
Greenwald, Tupper-- "Wheels"
Hemingway, Ernest-- "The Undefeated"

Komroff, Manuel-- "The Christian Bite"
Krunich, Milutin-- "Then Christs Fought Hard"
Lardner, Ring-- "Travelogue"
Mason, Grace Sartwell-- "The First Stone"
Meriwether, Susan-- "Grimaldi"
Morris, Ira V.-- "A Tale from the Grave"
Sherwood, Robert E.-- "'Extra! Extra!'"
Steele, Wilbur Daniel-- "Out of the Wind"
Strater, Edward L.-- "The Other Road"
Tracy, Virginia-- "The Giant's Thunder"

## The Best Short Stories of 1927, and the Yearbook of the American Short Story,
### *edited by* **Edward J. O'Brien**

Anderson, Sherwood-- "Another Wife"
Bradford, Roark-- "Child of God"
Brecht, Harold W.-- "Vienna Roast"
Burman, Ben Lucien-- "Minstrels of the Mist"
Finley-Thomas, Elisabeth-- "Mademoiselle"
Hare, Amory-- "Three Lumps of Sugar"
Hemingway, Ernest-- "The Killers"

Hergesheimer, Joseph-- "Trial by Armes"
Heyward, DuBose-- "The Half Pint Flask"
Hopper, James-- "When it Happens"
La Farge, Oliver-- "North Is Black"
Lane, Rose Wilder-- "Yarbwoman"
Le Sueur, Meridel-- "Persephone"
Marquand, J. P.-- "Good Morning, Major"

Saxon, Lyle-- "Cane River"

Sexton, John S.-- "The Pawnshop"

Shay, Frank-- "Little Dombey"

Sullivan, Alan-- "In Portofino"

Weeks, Raymond-- "The Hound-Tuner of Callaway"

Wister, Owen-- "The Right Honorable the Strawberries"

### The Best Short Stories of 1928, and the Yearbook of the American Short Story,
#### *edited by* Edward J. O'Brien

Brennan, Frederick Hazlitt-- "The Guardeen Angel"

Bromfield, Louis-- "The Cat That Lived at the Ritz"

Brush, Katharine-- "Seven Blocks Apart"

Callaghan, Morley-- "A Country Passion"

Canfield, Dorothy-- "At the Sign of the Three Daughters"

Chambers, Maria Cristina-- "John of God, the Water Carrier"

Cobb, Irvin S.-- "No Dam' Yankee"

Connolly, Myles-- "The First of Mr. Blue"

Edmonds, Walter D.-- "The Swamper"

Harris, Eleanor E.-- "Home to Mother's"

Hughes, Llewellyn-- "Lady Wipers--of Ypres"

Hurst, Fannie-- "Give This Little Girl a Hand"

McKenna, Edward L.-- "Battered Armor"

Parker, Dorothy-- "A Telephone Call"

Paul, L.-- "Fences"

Roberts, Elizabeth Madox-- "On the Mountain-Side"

Seaver, Edwin-- "The Jew"

Stevens, James-- "The Romantic Sailor"

Suckow, Ruth-- "Midwestern Primitive"

Ware, Edmund-- "So-Long, Oldtimer"

### The Best Short Stories of 1929, and the Yearbook of the American Short Story,
#### *edited by* Edward J. O'Brien

Addington, Sarah-- "'Hound of Heaven'"

Anderson, Sherwood-- "The Lost Novel"

Beede, Ivan-- "The Country Doctor"

Bercovici, Konrad-- "'There's Money in Poetry'"

Callaghan, Morley-- "Soldier Harmon"

Cather, Willa-- "Double Birthday"

Coates, Grace Stone-- "Wild Plums"

Edmonds, Walter D.-- "Death of Red Peril"

Glover, James Webber-- "First Oboe"

Hall, James Norman-- "Fame for Mr. Beatty"

Herald, Leon Srabian-- "Power of Horizon"

Jenkins, MacGregor-- "Alcantara"

Leech, Margaret-- "Manicure"

McAlmon, Robert-- "Potato Picking"

McCarty, Wilson-- "His Friend the Pig"

McKenna, Edward L.-- "I Have Letters for Marjorie"

Mullen, Robert-- "Light Without Heat"

Patterson, Pernet-- "'Cunjur'"

Wescott, Glenway-- "A Guilty Woman"

Williams, William Carlos-- "The Venus"

### The Best Short Stories of 1930, and the Yearbook of the American Short Story,
#### *edited by* Edward J. O'Brien

Bishop, Ellen-- "Along a Sandy Road"

Bragdon, Clifford-- "Suffer Little Children"

Burnett, Whit-- "Two Men Free"

Callaghan, Morley-- "The Faithful Wife"

Coates, Grace Stone-- "The Way of the Transgressor"

Draper, Edythe Squier-- "The Voice of the Turtle"

Furniss, Ruth Pine-- "Answer"

Gilkyson, Walter-- "Blue Sky"

Gordon, Caroline-- "Summer Dust"

Hahn, Emily-- "Adventure"

Hartwick, Harry-- "Happiness up the River"

Kittredge, Eleanor Hayden-- "September Sailing"

Komroff, Manuel-- "A Red Coat for Night"

Lewis, Janet-- "At the Swamp"

March, William-- "The Little Wife"

Parker, Dorothy-- "The Cradle of Civilization"

Paulding, Gouverneur-- "The White Pidgeon"

Polk, William-- "The Patriot"

Porter, Katherine Anne-- "Theft"

Upson, William Hazlett-- "The Vineyard at Schloss Ramsburg"

### The Best Short Stories of 1931, and the Yearbook of the American Short Story,
*edited by* **Edward J. O'Brien**

Adamic, Louis-- "The Enigma"

Barber, Solon R.-- "The Sound That Frost Makes"

Bessie, Alvah C.-- "Only We Are Barren"

Boyle, Kay-- "Rest Cure"

Bromfield, Louis-- "Tabloid News"

Burnett, Whit-- "A Day in the Country"

Caldwell, Erskine-- "Dorothy"

Callaghan, Morley-- "The Yound Priest"

Edmonds, Walter D.-- "Water Never Hurt a Man"

Faulkner, William-- "That Evening Sun Go Down"

Fitzgerald, F. Scott-- "Babylon Revisited"

Foley, Martha-- "One with Shakespeare"

Gilpatric, Guy-- "The Flaming Chariot"

Gowen, Emmett-- "Fiddlers of Moon Mountain"

Herbst, Josephine-- "I Hear You, Mr. and Mrs. Brown"

Horgan, Paul-- "The Other Side of the Street"

March, William-- "Fifteen from Company K"

Marquis, Don-- "The Other Room"

Milburn, George-- "A Pretty Cute Little Stunt"

Parker, Dorothy-- "Here We Are"

Read, Allen-- "Rhodes Scholar"

Stevens, James-- "The Great Hunter of the Woods"

Upson, William Hazlett-- "The Model House"

Ward, Leo L.-- "The Threshing Ring"

Wilson, Anne Elizabeth-- "The Miracle"

Wimberly, Lowry Charles-- "White Man's Town"

### The Best Short Stories of 1932, and the Yearbook of the American Short Story,
*edited by* **Edward J. O'Brien**

Adams, Bill-- "The Foreigner"

Bessie, Alvah C.-- "Horizon"

Bragdon, Clifford-- "Love's So Many Things"

Brennan, Louis-- "Poisoner in Motley"

Burnett, Wanda-- "Sand"

Burnett, Whit-- "Sherrel"

Caldwell, Erskine-- "Warm River"

Callaghan, Morley-- "The Red Hat"

Caperton, Helena Lefroy-- "The Honest
    Wine Merchant"

Cournos, John-- "The Story of the Stranger"

DeJong, David Cornel-- "So Tall the Corn"

Diefenthaler, Andra-- "Hansel"

Faulkner, William-- "Smoke"

Komroff, Manuel-- "Napoleon's Hat under Glass"

Le Sueur, Meridel-- "Spring Story"

Lockwood, Scammon-- "An Arrival at Carthage"

March, William-- "Mist on the Meadow"

Milburn, George-- "Heel, Toe, and a 1, 2, 3, 4"

Morris, Ira V.-- "The Kimono"

Neagoe, Peter-- "Shepherd of the Lord"

Schnabel, Dudley-- "Load"

Stallings, Laurence-- "Gentlemen in Blue"

Tuting, Bernhard Johann-- "The Family Chronicle"

Villa, José García-- "Untitled Story"

Ward, Leo L.-- "The Quarrel"

### The Best Short Stories of 1933, and the Yearbook of the American Short Story,
*edited by* **Edward J. O'Brien**

Albee, George-- "Fame Takes the J Car"

Bessie, Alvah C.-- "A Little Walk"

Bishop, John Peale-- "Toadstools Are Poison"

Boyd, Albert Truman-- "Elmer"

Burnett, Whit-- "Serenade"

Caldwell, Erskine-- "The First Autumn"

Callaghan, Morley-- "A Sick Call"

Cantwell, Robert-- "The Land of Plenty"

Dobie, Charles Caldwell-- "The Honey Pot"

Edmonds, Walter D.-- "Black Wolf"

Farrell, James T.-- "Helen, I Love You!"

Fitzgerald, F. Scott-- "Crazy Sunday"

Flandrau, Grace-- "What Was Truly Mine"

Foley, Martha-- "Martyr"

Gowen, Emmett-- "Fisherman's Luck"Hale, Nancy--
    "Simple Aveu"

Halper, Albert-- "Going to Market"

Joffe, Eugene-- "In the Park"

Lambertson, Louise-- "Sleet Storm"

Leenhouts, Grant-- "The Facts in the Case"

Milburn, George-- "The Apostate"
Morris, Ira V.-- "The Sampler"
Morris, Lloyd-- "Footnote to a Life"
Porter, Katherine Anne-- "The Cracked
    Looking-Glass"

Reed, Louis-- "Episode at the Pawpaws"
Shumway, Naomi-- "Ike and Us Moons"
Steele, Wilbur Daniel-- "How Beautiful with Shoes"
Thomas, Dorothy-- "The Joybell"
Villa, José García-- "The Fence"

## The Best Short Stories of 1934, and the Yearbook of the American Short Story,
### *edited by* Edward J. O'Brien

Appel, Benjamin-- "Winter Meeting"
Bessie, Alvah C.-- "No Final Word"
Burnett, Whit-- "The Cats Which Cried"
Caldwell, Erskine-- "Horse Thief"
Callaghan, Morley-- "Mr. and Mrs. Fairbanks"
Childs, Marquis W.-- "The Woman on the Shore"
Corle, Edwin-- "Amethyst"
Corning, Howard McKinley-- "Crossroads Woman"
Faulkner, William-- "Beyond"
Fisher, Rudolph-- "Miss Cynthie"
Foley, Martha-- "She Walks in Beauty"
Godin, Alexander-- "My Dead Brother Comes
    to America"
Gordon, Caroline-- "Tom Rivers"
Goryan, Sirak-- "The Broken Wheel"
Hall, James Norman-- "Lord of Marutea"

Hughes, Langston-- "Cora Unashamed"
Joffe, Eugene-- "Siege of Love"
Komroff, Manuel-- "Hamlet's Daughter"
Lineaweaver, John-- "Mother Tanner"
Mamet, Louis-- "The Pension"
March, William-- "This Heavy Load"
Marshall, Alan-- "Death and Transfiguration"
McCleary, Dorothy-- "Winter"
Ryan, Paul-- "The Sacred Thing"
Sabsay, Nahum-- "In a Park"
Sheean, Vincent-- "The Hemlock Tree"
Sherman, Richard-- "Now There Is Peace"
Tate, Allen-- "The Immortal Woman"
Terrell, Upton-- "Money at Home"
Zugsmith, Leane-- "Home Is Where You Hang
    Your Childhood"

## The Best Short Stories of 1935, and the Yearbook of the American Short Story,
### *edited by* Edward J. O'Brien

Appel, Benjamin-- "Outside Yuma"
Benson, Sally-- "The Overcoat"
Brace, Ernest-- "The Party Next Door"
Brown, Carlton-- "Suns That Our Hearts Harden"
Burnett, Whit-- "Division"
Caldwell, Erskine-- "The Cold Winter"
Callaghan, Morley-- "Father and Son"
Cole, Madelene-- "Bus to Biarritz"
Cooke, Charles-- "Triple Jumps"
DeJong, David Cornel-- "Home-Coming"
Faulkner, William-- "Lo!"
Godchaux, Elma-- "Wild Nigger"
Haardt, Sara-- "Little White Girl"
Haines, William Wister-- "Remarks: None"

Hale, Nancy-- "The Double House"
Horgan, Paul-- "A Distant Harbour"
Mamet, Louis-- "Episode from Life"
McCleary, Dorothy-- "Sunday Morning"
McHugh, Vincent-- "Parish of Cockroaches"
Morang, Alfred-- "Frozen Stillness"
Morris, Edita-- "Mrs. Lancaster-Jones"
Saroyan, William-- "Resurrection of a Life"
Seager, Allan-- "This Town and Salamanca"
Sylvester, Harry-- "A Boxer: Old"
Thielen, Benedict-- "Souvenir of Arizona"
White, Max-- "A Pair of Shoes"
Wolfe, Thomas-- "The Sun and the Rain"

### The Best Short Stories of 1936, and the Yearbook of the American Short Story,
#### *edited by* **Edward J. O'Brien**

Burlingame, Roger-- "In the Cage"

Callaghan, Morley-- "The Blue Kimono"

Canfield, Dorothy-- "The Murder on Jefferson Street"

Carr, A. H. Z.-- "The Hunch"

Cooke, Charles-- "Catafalque"

Coombes, Evan-- "The North Wind Doth Blow"

Faulkner, William-- "That Will Be Fine"

Fessier, Michael-- "That's What Happened to Me"

Field, S. S.-- "Torrent of Darkness"

Flannagan, Roy-- "The Doorstop"

Foley, Martha-- "Her Own Sweet Simplicity"

Gilkyson, Walter-- "Enemy Country"

Hall, Elizabeth-- "Two Words Are a Story"

Kelly, Frank K.-- "With Some Gaiety and Laughter"

Kelm, Karlton-- "Tinkle and Family Take a Ride"

Komroff, Manuel-- "That Blowzy Goddess Fame"

Larsen, Erling-- "A Kind of a Sunset"

Le Sueur, Meridel-- "Annuciation"

Maltz, Albert-- "Man on a Road"

McCleary, Dorothy-- "The Shroud"

Porter, Katherine Anne-- "The Grave"

Richmond, Roaldus-- "Thanks for Nothing"

Seager, Allan-- "Fugue for Harmonica"

Slesinger, Tess-- "A Life in the Day of a Writer"

Thomas, Elisabeth Wilkins-- "Traveling Salesman"

Vines, Howell-- "The Mustydines Was Ripe"

Whitehand, Robert-- "American Nocturne"

Williams, Calvin-- "On the Sidewalk"

Wilson, William E.-- "The Lone Pioneer"

Wolfe, Thomas-- "Only the Dead Know Brooklyn"

### The Best Short Stories of 1937, and the Yearbook of the American Short Story,
#### *edited by* **Edward J. O'Brien**

Buckner, Robert-- "The Man Who Won the War"

Burlingame, Roger-- "The Last Equation"

Callaghan, Morley-- "The Voyage Out"

Cooke, Charles-- "Enter Daisy; to Her, Alexandra"

Faulkner, William-- "Fool About a Horse"

Field, S. S.-- "Goodbye to Cap'm John"

Foley, Martha-- "Glory, Glory, Hallelujah!"

Godchaux, Elma-- "Chains"

Halper, Albert-- "The Poet"

Hemingway, Ernest-- "The Snows of Kilimanjaro"

Heth, Edward Harris-- "Homecoming"

Horgan, Paul-- "The Surgeon and the Nun"

Komroff, Manuel-- "The Girl with the Flaxen Hair"

Krantz, David E.-- "Awakening and the Destination"

Kroll, Harry Harrison-- "Second Wife"

Linn, R. H.-- "The Intrigue of Mr. S. Yamamoto"

MacDougall, Ursula-- "Titty's Dead and Tatty Weeps"

March, William-- "Maybe the Sun Will Shine"

McGinnis, Allen-- "Let Nothing You Dismay"

Morris, Edita-- "A Blade of Grass"

Morris, Ira V.-- "Marching Orders"

Porter, Katherine Anne-- "The Old Order"

St. Joseph, Ellis-- "A Passenger to Bali"

Saroyan, William-- "The Crusader"

Stuart, Jesse-- "Hair"

Thielen, Benedict-- "Lieutenant Pearson"

Thompson, Lovell-- "The Iron City"

Wright, Wilson-- "Arrival on a Holiday"

Zugsmith, Leane-- "Room in the World"

### The Best Short Stories of 1938, and the Yearbook of the American Short Story,
#### *edited by* **Edward J. O'Brien**

Ayre, Robert-- "Mr. Sycamore"

Benedict, Libby-- "Blind Man's Buff"

Benét, Stephen Vincent-- "A Tooth for Paul Revere"

Bond, Nelson S.-- "Mr. Mergenthwirker's Lobblies"

Callaghan, Morley-- "The Cheat's Remorse"

Cheever, John-- "The Brothers"

Cherkasski, Vladimir-- "What Hurts Is That I Was in a Hurry"

Cook, Whitfield-- "Dear Mr. Flessheimer"

Creyke, Richard Paulett-- "Niggers Are Such Liars"

Di Donato, Pietro-- "Christ in Concrete"

Fessier, Michael-- "Black Wind and Lightning"

Hannum, Alberta Pierson-- "Turkey Hunt"

Komroff, Manuel-- "The Whole World Is Outside"

Le Sueur, Meridel-- "The Girl"

Ludlow, Don-- "She Always Wanted Shoes"

March, William-- "The Last Meeting"

McCleary, Dorothy-- "Little Bride"

Moll, Elick-- "To Those Who Wait"

Pereda, Prudencio de-- "The Spaniard"

Prokosch, Frederic-- "A Russian Idyll"

Rayner, George Thorp-- "A Real American Fellow"

Roberts, Elizabeth Madox-- "The Haunted Palace"

Schorer, Mark-- "Boy in the Summer Sun"

Seager, Allan-- "Pro Arte"

Steinbeck, John-- "The Chrysanthemums"

Stuart, Jesse-- "Huey, the Engineer"

Swados, Harvey-- "The Amateurs"

Warren, Robert Penn-- "Christmas Gift"

Welty, Eudora-- "Lily Daw and the Three Ladies"

Wolfert, Ira-- "Off the Highway"

## The Best Short Stories of 1939, and the Yearbook of the American Short Story,
### *edited by* Edward J. O'Brien

Beck, Warren-- "The Blue Sash"

Caldwell, Ronald-- "Vision in the Sea"

Callaghan, Morley-- "It Had to Be Done"

Cheever, John-- "Frère Jacques"

Clark, Gean-- "Indian on the Road"

Coates, Robert M.-- "Passing Through"

Cohn, David L.-- "Black Troubadour"

Danielson, Richard Ely-- "Corporal Hardy"

Ellson, Hal-- "The Rat Is a Mouse"

Halper, Albert-- "Prelude"

Horgan, Paul-- "To the Mountains"

Jenison, Madge-- "True Believer"

Komroff, Manuel-- "What Is a Miracle?"

Le Sueur, Meridel-- "Salutation to Spring"

MacDonald, Alan-- "An Arm Upraised"

Maltz, Albert-- "The Happiest Man on Earth"

St. Joseph, Ellis-- "Leviathan"

Saroyan, William-- "Piano"

Schoenstedt, Walter-- "The Girl from the River Barge"

Seager, Allan-- "Berkshire Comedy"

Seide, Michael-- "Bad Boy from Brooklyn"

Stuart, Jesse-- "Eustacia"

Sylvester, Harry-- "The Crazy Guy"

Thielen, Benedict-- "The Thunderstorm"

Warren, Robert Penn-- "How Willie Proudfit
        Came Home"

Welty, Eudora-- "A Curtain of Green"

Werner, Heinz-- "Black Tobias and the Empire"

Wolfert, Ira-- "The Way the Luck Runs"

Wright, Eugene-- "The White Camel"

Wright, Richard-- "Bright and Morning Star"

## The Best Short Stories of 1940, and the Yearbook of the American Short Story,
### *edited by* Edward J. O'Brien

Boyle, Kay-- "Anschluss"

Caldwell, Erskine-- "The People vs. Abe
    Lathan, Colored"

Callaghan, Morley-- "Getting on in the World"

Eisenberg, Frances-- "Roof Sitter"

Farrell, James T.-- "The Fall of Machine Gun McGurk"

Faulkner, William-- "Hand upon the Waters"

Fitzgerald, F. Scott-- "Design in Plaster"

Gordon, Caroline-- "Frankie and Thomas
    and Bud Asbury"

Hemingway, Ernest-- "Under the Ridge"

King, Mary-- "The Honey House"

Komroff, Manuel-- "Death of an Outcast"

Lull, Roderick-- "That Fine Place We Had Last Year"

Lussu, Emilio-- "Your General Does Not Sleep"

McCleary, Dorothy-- "Something Jolly"

Morris, Edita-- "Kullan"

Morris, Ira V.-- "The Beautiful Fire"

Pasinetti, P. M.-- "Family History"

Pereda, Prudencio de-- "The Way Death Comes"

Pooler, James-- "Herself"

Porter, Katherine Anne-- "The Downward
        Path to Wisdom"

### The Best Short Stories of 1940 (*continued*)

Saroyan, William-- "The Presbyterian Choir Singers"
Seide, Michael-- "Words Without Music"
Shaw, Irwin-- "Main Currents of American Thought"
Slocombe, George-- "The Seven Men of Rouen"
Stern, Morton-- "Four Worms Turning"
Storm, Hans Otto-- "The Two Deaths of Kaspar Rausch"

Stuart, Jesse-- "Rich Men"
Sylvester, Harry-- "Beautifully and Bravely"
Thielen, Benedict-- "Night and the Lost Armies"
Welty, Eudora-- "The Hitch-Hikers"
Zara, Louis-- "Resurgam"

### The Best Short Stories of 1941, and the Yearbook of the American Short Story, *edited by* **Martha Foley**

Ashton, E. B.-- "Shadow of a Girl"
Benét, Stephen Vincent-- "All Around the Town"
Caldwell, Erskine-- "Handy"
Callaghan, Morley-- "Big Jules"
Coates, Robert M.-- "The Net"
DeJong, David Cornel-- "Mamma Is a Lady"
Exall, Henry-- "To the Least . . ."
Fante, John-- "A Nun No More"
Faulkner, William-- "Gold Is Not Always"
Garfinkel, Harold-- "'Color Trouble'"
Gizycka, Felicia-- "The Magic Wire"
Herman, Justin-- "Smile for the Man, Dear"
Kees, Weldon-- "The Life of the Mind"
King, Mary-- "The White Bull"
Kober, Arthur-- "Some People Are Just Plumb Crazy"

La Farge, Christopher-- "Scorn and Comfort"
Levin, Meyer-- "The System Was Doomed"
Lull, Roderick-- "Don't Get Me Wrong"
Maltz, Albert-- "Sunday Morning on Twentieth Street"
Neagoe, Peter-- "Ill-Winds from the Wide World"
Saroyan, William-- "The Three Swimmers and the Educated Grocer"
Shaw, Irwin-- "Triumph of Justice"
Shore, Wilma-- "The Butcher"
Stegner, Wallace-- "Goin' to Town"
Stuart, Jesse-- "Love"
Thielen, Benedict-- "The Psychologist"
Weidman, Jerome-- "Houdini"
Weller, George-- "Strip-Tease"
Wright, Richard-- "Almos' a Man"

### The Best American Short Stories, 1942, and the Yearbook of the American Short Story, *edited by* **Martha Foley**

Algren, Nelson-- "Biceps"
Bemelmans, Ludwig-- "The Valet of the Splendide"
Benson, Sally-- "Fifty-One Thirty-Five Kensington: August, 1903"
Boyle, Kay-- "Nothing Ever Breaks Except the Heart"
Bryan, Jack Y.-- "For Each of Us"
Clark, Walter Van Tilburg-- "The Portable Phonograph"
DeJong, David Cornel-- "That Frozen Hour"
Eakin, Boyce-- "Prairies"
Fineman, Morton-- "Tell Him I Waited"
Gibbons, Robert-- "A Loaf of Bread"
Hale, Nancy-- "Those Are as Brothers"
Kantor, MacKinlay-- "That Greek Dog"
Knight, Eric-- "Sam Small's Better Half"
Lavin, Mary-- "At Sallygap"
Medearis, Mary-- "Death of a Country Doctor"
Morris, Edita-- "Caput Mortuum"

O'Hara, Mary-- "My Friend Flicka"
Peattie, Margaret Rhodes-- "The Green Village"
Saroyan, William-- "The Hummingbird That Lived Through Winter"
Schulberg, Budd Wilson-- "The Real Viennese Schmalz"
Seide, Michael-- "Sacrifice of Isaac"
Shaw, Irwin-- "Search Through the Streets of the City"
Stegner, Wallace-- "In the Twilight"
Steinbeck, John-- "How Edith McGillcuddy Met R. L. Stevenson"
Stuart, Jesse-- "The Storm"
Taylor, Peter-- "The Fancy Woman"
Thomas, Dorothy-- "My Pigeon Pair"
Thurber, James-- "You Could Look It Up"
Vatsek, Joan-- "The Bees"
Worthington, Marjorie-- "Hunger"

### The Best American Short Stories, 1943, and the Yearbook of the American Short Story, *edited by* Martha Foley

Baum, Vicki-- "The Healthy Life"

Beck, Warren-- "Boundary Line"

Boyle, Kay-- "Frenchman's Ship"

Cheever, John-- "The Pleasures of Solitude"

D'Agostino, Guido-- "The Dream of Angelo Zara"

Dyer, Murray-- "Samuel Blane"

Faulkner, William-- "The Bear"

Field, Rachel-- "Beginning of Wisdom"

Fisher, Vardis-- "A Partnership with Death"

Flandrau, Grace-- "What Do You See, Dear Enid?"

Gibbons, Robert-- "Time's End"

Gray, Peter-- "Threnody for Stelios"

Hale, Nancy-- "Who Lived and Died Believing"

Horgan, Paul-- "The Peach Stone"

Knight, Laurette MacDuffie-- "The Enchanted"

Laidlaw, Clara-- "The Little Black Boys"

Lavin, Mary-- "Love Is for Lovers"

Morris, Edita-- "Young Man in an Astrakhan Cap"

Saroyan, William-- "Knife-like, Flower-like, Like Nothing at All in the World"

Schwartz, Delmore-- "An Argument in 1934"

Shaw, Irwin-- "Preach on the Dusty Roads"

Shedd, Margaret-- "My Public"

Stegner, Wallace-- "Chip off the Old Block"

Stuart, Alison-- "Death and My Uncle Felix"

Stuart, Jesse-- "Dawn of Remembered Spring"

Sullivan, Richard-- "The Women"

Thurber, James-- "The Catbird Seat"

Treichler, Jessie-- "Homecoming"

Weidman, Jerome-- "Philadelphia Express"

Welty, Eudora-- "Asphodel"

### The Best American Short Stories, 1944, and the Yearbook of the American Short Story, *edited by* Martha Foley

Alexander, Sidney-- "The White Boat"

Barrett, William E.-- "Señor Payroll"

Bellow, Saul-- "Notes of a Dangling Man"

Canfield, Dorothy-- "The Knot Hole"

De Lanux, Eyre-- "The S.S. Libertad"

Eastman, Elizabeth-- "Like a Field Mouse over the Heart"

Eustis, Helen-- "The Good Days and the Bad"

Fifield, William-- "The Fishermen of Patzcuaro"

Fleming, Berry-- "Strike up a Stirring Music"

Hawthorne, Hazel-- "More Like a Coffin"

Houston, Noel-- "A Local Skirmish"

Jackson, Shirley-- "Come Dance with Me in Ireland"

Johnson, Josephine W.-- "The Rented Room"

Kaplan, H. J.-- "The Mohammedans"

McCullers, Carson-- "The Ballad of the Sad Café"

March, William-- "The Female of the Fruit Fly'"

Meighan, Astrid-- "Shoe the Horse and Shoe the Mare"

Mian, Mary-- "Exiles from the Creuse"

Morris, Edita-- "Heart of Marzipan"

Nabokov, Vladimir-- "'That in Aleppo Once . . . '"

Portugal, Ruth-- "Neither Here nor There"

Powers, J. F.-- "Lions, Harts, Leaping Does"

Schmitt, Gladys-- "All Souls'"

Shaw, Irwin-- "The Veterans Reflect"

Stiles, George-- "A Return"

Surmelian, Leon Z.-- "My Russian Cap"

Trilling, Lionel-- "Of This Time, of That Place"

Warner, Elizabeth-- "An Afternoon"

West, Jessamyn-- "The Illumination"

Winters, Emmanuel-- "God's Agents Have Beards"

### The Best American Short Stories, 1945, and the Yearbook of the American Short Story, *edited by* Martha Foley

Algren, Nelson-- "How the Devil Came Down Division Street"

Beck, Warren-- "The First Fish"

Bromfield, Louis-- "Crime Passionnel"

Bulosan, Carlos-- "My Brother Osong's Career in Politics"

### The Best Short Stories of 1945 (*continued*)

Deasy, Mary-- "Harvest"

Fenton, Edward-- "Burial in the Desert"

Fineman, Morton-- "The Light of Morning"

Gerry, Bill-- "Understand What I Mean?"

Gill, Brendan-- "The Test"

Hagopian, Richard-- "'Be Heavy'"

Hahn, Emily-- "It Never Happened"

Hardy, W. G.-- "The Czech Dog"

Johnson, Josephine W.-- "Fever Flower"

McLaughlin, Robert-- "Poor Everybody"

McNulty, John-- "Don't Scrub off These Names"

Miller, Warren-- "The Animal's Fair"

Panetta, George-- "Papa, Mama, and Economics"

Pennell, Joseph Stanley-- "On the Way to Somewhere Else"

Portugal, Ruth-- "Call a Solemn Assembly"

Pratt, Theodore-- "The Owl That Kept Winking"

Rosenfeld, Isaac-- "The Hand That Fed Me"

Rowell, Donna-- "A War Marriage"

Schmitt, Gladys-- "The Mourners"

Shaw, Irwin-- "Gunners' Passage"

Stafford, Jean-- "The Wedding: Beacon Hill"

Tartt, Ruby Pickens-- "Alabama Sketches"

Taylor, Peter-- "Rain in the Heart"

Warren, Robert Penn-- "Cass Mastern's Wedding Ring"

West, Jessamyn-- "First Day Finish"

Zugsmith, Leane-- "This Is a Love Story"

Zukerman, William-- "A Ship to Tarshish"

### The Best American Short Stories, 1946, and the Yearbook of the American Short Story, *edited by* Martha Foley

Angoff, Charles-- "Jerry"

Beck, Warren-- "Out of Line"

Berryman, John-- "The Lovers"

Bradbury, Ray-- "The Big Black and White Game"

Breuer, Bessie-- "Bury Your Own Dead"

Brown, T. K., III-- "The Valley of the Shadow"

Burnett, W. R.-- "The Ivory Tower"

Clark, Walter Van Tilburg-- "The Wind and the Snow of Winter"

Critchell, Laurence-- "Flesh and Blood"

Deasy, Mary-- "A Sense of Danger"

Elkin, Samuel-- "In a Military Manner"

Gottlieb, Elaine-- "The Norm"

Hardwick, Elizabeth-- "The Mysteries of Eleusis"

Johnson, Josephine W.-- "Story Without End"

Lampman, Ben Hur-- "Old Bill Bent to Drink"

Liben, Meyer-- "The Caller"

Liebling, A. J.-- "Run, Run, Run, Run"

Mitchell, W. O.-- "The Owl and the Bens"

Nabokov, Vladimir-- "Time and Ebb"

Petry, Ann-- "Like a Winding Sheet"

Ruml, Wentzle, III-- "For a Beautiful Relationship"

Schmitt, Gladys-- "The King's Daughter"

Stark, Irwin-- "The Bridge"

Stern, James-- "The Woman Who Was Loved"

Still, James-- "Mrs. Razor"

Taylor, Peter-- "The Scout Master"

Trilling, Lionel-- "The Other Margaret"

Weigel, Henrietta-- "Love Affair"

West, Jessamyn-- "The Singing Lesson"

Woods, Glennyth-- "Death in a Cathedral"

### The Best American Short Stories, 1947, and the Yearbook of the American Short Story, *edited by* Martha Foley

Broderick, Francis L.-- "Return by Faith"

Canfield, Dorothy-- "Sex Education"

Capote, Truman-- "The Headless Hawk"

Fontaine, Robert-- "Day of Gold and Darkness"

Gerstley, Adelaide-- "The Man in the Mirror"

Goodwin, John B. L.-- "The Cocoon"

Goss, John Mayo-- "Bird Song"

Griffith, Paul-- "The Horse like September"

Guérard, Albert J.-- "Turista"

Hardwick, Elizabeth-- "The Golden Stallion"

Harris, Ruth McCoy-- "Up the Road a Piece"

Heggen, Thomas-- "Night Watch"

Heth, Edward Harris-- "Under the Ginkgo Trees"

Humphreys, John Richard-- "Michael Finney and the Little Men"
Lincoln, Victoria-- "Down in the Reeds by the River"
Lowry, Robert-- "Little Baseball World"
Martenet, May Davies-- "Father Delacroix"
Mayhall, Jane-- "The Darkness"
Powers, J. F.-- "Prince of Darkness"
Raphaelson, Samson-- "The Greatest Idea in the World"
Schorer, Mark-- "What We Don't Know Hurts Us"

Shaw, Irwin-- "Act of Faith"
Shirley, Sylvia-- "The Red Dress"
Stafford, Jean-- "The Interior Castle"
Stark, Irwin-- "Shock Treatment"
Stegner, Wallace-- "The Women on the Wall"
Tucci, Niccolò-- "The Seige"
Weaver, John D.-- "Bread and Games"
Williams, Lawrence-- "The Hidden Room"
Seager, Allan-- "Game Chickens"

## The Best American Short Stories, 1948, and the Yearbook of the American Short Story, *edited by* **Martha Foley**

Alexander, Sidney-- "Part of the Act"
Bowles, Paul-- "A Distant Episode"
Bradbury, Ray-- "I See You Never"
Canfield, Dorothy-- "The Apprentice"
Cheever, John-- "The Enormous Radio"
Clay, George R.-- "That's My Johnny-Boy"
Clayton, John Bell-- "Visitor from Philadelphia"
Cousins, Margaret-- "A Letter to Mr. Priest"
Fisher, M. F. K.-- "The Hollow Heart"
Garrigan, Philip-- "'Fly, Fly, Little Dove'"
Gellhorn, Martha-- "Miami-New York"
Grennard, Elliott-- "Sparrow's Last Jump"
Gustafson, Ralph-- "The Human Fly"
Hersey, John-- "Why Were You Sent out Here?"
Jeffers, Lance-- "The Dawn Swings In"

Lincoln, Victoria-- "Morning, a Week Before the Crime"
Lowry, Robert-- "The Terror in the Streets"
Lynch, John A.-- "The Burden"
McHugh, Vincent-- "The Search"
Morse, Robert-- "The Professor and the Puli"
Portugal, Ruth-- "The Stupendous Fortune"
Post, Mary Brinker-- "That's the Man"
Root, Waverley-- "Carmencita"
Sharp, Dolph-- "The Tragedy in Jancie Brierman's Life"
Stegner, Wallace-- "Beyond the Glass Mountain"
Sulkin, Sidney-- "The Plan"
Welty, Eudora-- "The Whole World Knows"
White, E. B.-- "The Second Tree from the Corner"

## The Best American Short Stories, 1949, and the Yearbook of the American Short Story, *edited by* **Martha Foley**

Albee, George-- "Mighty, Mighty Pretty"
Biddle, Livingston, Jr.-- "The Vacation"
Bishop, Elizabeth-- "The Farmer's Children"
Bowles, Paul-- "Under the Sky"
Brookhouser, Frank-- "My Father and the Circus"
Deal, Borden-- "Exodus"
Dolokhov, Adele-- "Small Miracle"
Dorrance, Ward-- "The White Hound"
Felsen, Henry Gregor-- "Li Chang's Million"
Gibbons, Robert-- "Departure of Hubbard"
Griffith, Beatrice-- "In the Flow of Time"
Hardwick, Elizabeth-- "Evenings at Home"
Heller, Joseph-- "Castle of Snow"
Herschberger, Ruth-- "A Sound in the Night"

Hunter, Laura-- "Jerry"
Kjelgaard, Jim-- "Of the River and Uncle Pidcock"
Lull, Roderick-- "Footnote to American History"
Mabry, Thomas-- "The Vault"
Macdonald, Agnes-- "Vacia"
Mayhall, Jane-- "The Men"
Morgan, Patrick-- "The Heifer"
Pfeffer, Irving-- "All Prisoners Here"
Rogers, John-- "Episode of a House Remembered"
Salinger, J. D.-- "A Girl I Knew"
Segre, Alfredo-- "Justice Has No Number"
Shapiro, Madelon-- "An Island for My Friends"
Stafford, Jean-- "Children Are Bored on Sunday"
West, Jessamyn-- "Road to the Isles"

### The Best American Short Stories, 1950, and the Yearbook of the American Short Story,
#### *edited by* **Martha Foley**

Angoff, Charles-- "Where Did Yesterday Go?"
Aswell, James-- "Shadow of Evil"
Babb, Sanora-- "The Wild Flower"
Beck, Warren-- "Edge of Doom"
Bellow, Saul-- "A Sermon by Doctor Pep"
Bennett, Peggy-- "Death Under the Hawthornes"
Bowles, Paul-- "Pastor Dowe at Tacaté"
Christopher, Robert-- "Jishin"
Elliott, George P.-- "The NRACP"
Fiedler, Leslie A.-- "The Fear of Innocence"
Gustafson, Ralph-- "The Pigeon"
Hauser, Marianne-- "The Mouse"
Johnson, Josephine W.-- "The Author"
Kaplan, Ralph-- "The Artist"

Karchmer, Sylvan-- "'Hail Brother and Farewell'"
Lamkin, Speed-- "Comes a Day"
Lincoln, Victoria-- "The Glass Wall"
Maier, Howard-- "The World Outside"
McCoy, Esther-- "The Cape"
Newhouse, Edward-- "My Brother's Second Funeral"
Norris, Hoke-- "Take Her Up Tenderly"
Parker, Glidden-- "Bright and Morning"
Putman, Clay-- "The Old Acrobat and the Ruined City"
Rothberg, Abraham-- "Not with Our Fathers"
Stewart, Ramona-- "The Promise"
Still, James-- "A Master Time"
Strong, Joan-- "The Hired Man"
Taylor, Peter-- "A Wife of Nashville"

### The Best American Short Stories, 1951, and the Yearbook of the American Short Story,
#### *edited by* **Martha Foley**, *assisted by* **Joyce F. Hartman**

Angell, Roger-- "Flight Through the Dark"
Asch, Nathan-- "Inland, Western Sea"
Bennett, Peggy-- "A Fugitive from the Mind"
Bolté, Mary-- "The End of the Depression"
Calisher, Hortense-- "In Greenwich There Are Many Gravelled Walks"
Casper, Leonard-- "Sense of Direction"
Cassill, R. V.-- "Larchmoor Is Not the World"
Cheever, John-- "The Season of Divorce"
Downey, Harris-- "The Hunters"
Enright, Elizabeth-- "The Temperate Zone"
Gardon, Ethel Edison-- "The Value of the Dollar"
Goodman, J. Carol-- "The Kingdom of Gordon"
Goyen, William-- "Her Breath upon the Windowpane"
Jackson, Shirley-- "The Summer People"

Johnson, Josephine W.-- "The Mother's Story"
Karmel, Ilona-- "Fru Holm"
La Farge, Oliver-- "Old Century's River"
Lanning, George-- "Old Turkey Neck"
Lewis, Ethel G.-- "Portrait"
Livesay, Dorothy-- "The Glass House"
Macauley, Robie-- "The Wishbone"
Malamud, Bernard-- "The Prison"
Patt, Esther-- "The Butcherbirds"
Powers, J. F.-- "Death of a Favorite"
Rader, Paul-- "The Tabby Cat"
Stafford, Jean-- "The Nemesis"
West, Ray B., Jr.-- "The Last of the Grizzly Bears"
Williams, Tennessee-- "The Resemblance Between a Violin Case and a Coffin"

### The Best American Short Stories, 1952, and the Yearbook of the American Short Story,
#### *edited by* **Martha Foley**, *assisted by* **Joyce F. Hartman**

Berge, Bill-- "That Lovely Green Boat"
Bethel, Laurence-- "The Call"
Bowen, Robert O.-- "The Other River"
Boyle, Kay-- "The Lost"
Bradbury, Ray-- "The Other Foot"
Calisher, Hortense-- "A Wreath for Miss Totten"

Cardozo, Nancy-- "The Unborn Ghosts"
Chaikin, Nancy G.-- "The Climate of the Family"
Chidester, Ann-- "Wood Smoke"
Eaton, Charles Edward-- "The Motion of Forgetfulness Is Slow"
Elliott, George P.-- "Children of Ruth"

Enright, Elizabeth-- "The First Face"
Garner, Hugh-- "The Conversion of Willie Heaps"
Gellhorn, Martha-- "Weekend at Grimsby"
Glen, Emilie-- "Always Good for a Belly Laugh"
Hale, Nancy-- "Brahmin Beachhead"
Horton, Philip-- "What's in a Corner?"
Kuehn, Susan-- "The Searchers"
Rooney, Frank-- "Cyclists' Raid"
Saroyan, William-- "Palo"

Schulberg, Stuart-- "I'm Really Fine"
Stafford, Jean-- "The Healthiest Girl in Town"
Stegner, Wallace-- "The Traveler"
Still, James-- "A Ride on the Short Dog"
Swados, Harvey-- "The Letters"
Van Doren, Mark-- "Nobody Say a Word"
Waldron, Daniel-- "Evensong"
Weston, Christine-- "Loud Sing Cuckoo"
Yamamoto, Hisaye-- "Yoneko's Earthquake"

### The Best American Short Stories, 1953, and the Yearbook of the American Short Story, *edited by* **Martha Foley,** *assisted by* **Joyce F. Hartman**

Agee, James-- "A Mother's Tale"
Ballard, James-- "A Mountain Summer"
Becker, Stephen-- "The Town Mouse"
Carroll, Joseph-- "At Mrs. Farrelly's"
Cassill, R. V.-- "The Life of the Sleeping Beauty"
Coates, Robert M.-- "The Need"
Deasy, Mary-- "Morning Sun"
Downey, Harris-- "Crispin's Way"
Duke, Osborn-- "Struttin' with Some Barbecue"
Elliott, George P.-- "Faq'"
Froscher, Wingate-- "A Death in the Family"
Gregory, Vahan Krikorian-- "Athens, Greece, 1942"
Hall, James B.-- "A Spot in History"
Jackson, Charles Tenney-- "The Bullalo Wallow"
Jackson, Roberts-- "Fly away Home"
Jones, Madison P., Jr.-- "Dog Days"

Marsh, Willard-- "Beachhead in Bohemia"
Marshall, Elizabeth-- "The Hill People"
Noland, Felix-- "The Whipping"
Pendergast, Constance-- "The Picnic"
Purdy, Ken-- "Change of Plan"
Putman, Clay-- "Our Vegetable Love"
Shattuck, Roger-- "Workout on the River"
Shultz, Henry-- "Oreste"
Sultan, Stanley-- "The Fugue of the Fig Tree"
Van Doren, Mark-- "Still, Still So"
Wesely, Donald-- "A Week of Roses"
Weston, Christine-- "The Forest of the Night"
Williams, Tennessee-- "Three Players of a
    Summer Game"
Wincelberg, Simon-- "The Conqueror"

### The Best American Short Stories, 1954, and the Yearbook of the American Short Story, *edited by* **Martha Foley**

Bush, Geoffrey-- "A Great Reckoning in
    a Little Room"
Clay, Richard-- "A Beautiful Night for Orion"
DeMott, Benjamin-- "The Sense That in the
    Scene Delights"
Dorrance, Ward-- "A Stop on the Way to Texas"
Doughty, LeGarde S.-- "The Firebird"
Enright, Elizabeth-- "Apple Seed and Apple Thorn"
Frazee, Steve-- "My Brother Down There"
Gold, Ivan-- "A Change of Air"
Heath, Priscilla-- "Farewell, Sweet Love"
Hebert, Anne-- "The House on the Esplanade"
Holwerda, Frank-- "Char on Raven's Bench"

Jarrell, Randall-- "Gertrude and Sidney"
Jenks, Almet-- "No Way Down"
Loveridge, George-- "The Latter End"
Patton, Frances Gray-- "The Game"
Payne, Robert-- "The Red Mountain"
Robinson, Rosanne Smith-- "The Mango Tree"
Shaw, Irwin-- "In the French Style"
Stafford, Jean-- "The Shorn Lamb"
Taylor, Kressmann-- "The Pale Green Fishes"
Traven, B.-- "The Third Guest"
Weston, Christine-- "The Man in Gray"
Wolfert, Ira-- "The Indomitable Blue"
Yentzen, Vurell-- "The Rock"

## The Best American Short Stories, 1955, and the Yearbook of the American Short Story,
### *edited by* **Martha Foley**

Bowen, Robert O.-- "A Matter of Price"

Cardozo, Nancy-- "The Excursionists"

Chaikin, Nancy G.-- "Bachelor of Arts"

Cheever, John-- "The Country Husband"

Connell, Evan S., Jr.-- "The Fisherman
from Chihuahua"

Coogan, Joe-- "The Decline and Fall of Augie Sheean"

Curley, Daniel-- "The Day of the Equinox"

Eastlake, William-- "Little Joe"

Elliott, George P.-- "Brother Quintillian and
Dick the Chemist"

Hyman, Mac-- "The Hundredth Centennial"

La Farge, Oliver-- "The Resting Place"

Malumud, Bernard-- "The Magic Barrel"

Merril, Judith-- "Dead Center"

Middleton, Elizabeth H.-- "Portrait of My Son
as a Young Man"

Mudrick, Marvin-- "The Professor and the Poet"

Nemerov, Howard-- "Yore"

O'Connor, Flannery-- "A Circle in the Fire"

Shaw, Irwin-- "Tip on a Dead Jockey"

Stegner, Wallace-- "Maiden in a Tower"

Stuart, David-- "Bird Man"

Swados, Harvey-- "Herman's Day"

Van Doren, Mark-- "I Got a Friend"

Vukelich, George-- "The Scale Room"

Welty, Eudora-- "Going to Naples"

## The Best American Short Stories, 1956, and the Yearbook of the American Short Story,
### *edited by* **Martha Foley**

Angell, Roger-- "In an Early Winter"

Brown, Morris-- "The Snow Owl"

Clay, George R.-- "We're All Guests"

Coates, Robert M.-- "In a Foreign City"

Davis, Wesley Ford-- "The Undertow"

Dorrance, Ward-- "The Devil on a Hot Afternoon"

Downey, Harris-- "The Hobo"

Eastlake, William-- "The Quiet Chimneys"

Elliott, George P.-- "Is He Dead?"

Granit, Arthur-- "Free the Canaries from Their Cages!"

Housepian, Marjorie-- "How Levon Dai Was
Surrendered to the Edemuses"

Jackson, Shirley-- "One Ordinary Day, with Peanuts"

Kerouac, Jack-- "The Mexican Girl"

LaMar, Nathaniel-- "Creole Love Song"

Lyons, Augusta Wallace-- "The First Flower"

Molloy, Ruth Branning-- "Twenty Below, at the
End of a Lane"

O'Connor, Flannery-- "The Artificial Nigger"

Roth, Philip-- "The Contest for Aaron Gold"

Shepley, John-- "The Machine"

Weston, Christine-- "Four Annas"

Yellen, Samuel-- "Reginald Pomfret Skelton"

## The Best American Short Stories, 1957, and the Yearbook of the American Short Story,
### *edited by* **Martha Foley**

Algren, Nelson-- "Beasts of the Wild"

Berriault, Gina-- "Around the Dear Ruin"

Betts, Doris-- "The Proud and Virtuous"

Blassingame, Wyatt-- "Man's Courage"

Butler, Frank-- "To the Wilderness I Wander"

Clemons, Walter-- "The Dark Roots of the Rose"

Connell, Evan S., Jr.-- "Arcturus"

Downey, Harris-- "The Song"

Eastlake, William-- "The Unhappy Hunting Grounds"

Hale, Nancy-- "A Summer's Long Dream"

Langdon, John-- "The Blue Serge Suit"

Mabry, Thomas-- "Lula Borrow"

McClintic, Winona-- "A Heart of Furious Fancies"

O'Connor, Flannery-- "Greenleaf"

Olsen, Tillie-- "I Stand Here Ironing"

Robinson, Anthony-- "The Farlow Express"

Robinson, Rosanne Smith-- "The Impossible He"

Smith, John Campbell-- "Run, Run away, Brother"

Weigel, Henrietta-- "Saturday Is a Poor Man's Port"

Woodward, Gordon-- "Escape to the City"

### The Best American Short Stories, 1958, and the Yearbook of the American Short Story, *edited by* **Martha Foley** *and* **David Burnett**

Agee, James-- "The Waiting"

Baldwin, James-- "Sonny's Blues"

Bowles, Paul-- "The Frozen Fields"

Bradbury, Ray-- "The Day It Rained Forever"

Bradshaw, George-- "'The Picture Wouldn't Fit in the Stove'"

Chester, Alfred-- "As I Was Going up the Stair"

Grau, Shirley Ann-- "Hunter's Home"

Hill, Pati-- "Ben"

Macauley, Robie-- "Legend of Two Swimmers"

McCord, Jean-- "Somewhere out of Nowhere"

Nemerov, Howard-- "A Delayed Hearing"

O'Connor, Flannery-- "A View of the Woods"

Ostroff, Anthony-- "La Bataille des Fleurs"

Parker, Dorothy-- "The Banquet of Crow"

Robin, Ralph-- "Mr. Pruitt"

Scoyk, Bob Ban-- "Home from Camp"

Stafford, Jean-- "A Reasonable Facsimile"

Swados, Harvey-- "Joe, the Vanishing American"

Thurman, Richard-- "Not Another Word"

White, Robin-- "House of Many Rooms"

Wright, Richard-- "Big, Black, Good Man"

### The Best American Short Stories, 1959, and the Yearbook of the American Short Story, *edited by* **Martha Foley** *and* **David Burnett**

Berry, John-- "Jawaharlal and the Three Cadavers"

Bingham, Sallie-- "Winter Term"

Butler, Frank-- "Amid a Place of Stone"

Cheever, John-- "The Bella Lingua"

Coates, Robert M.-- "Getaway"

Finney, Charles G.-- "The Iowan's Curse"

Gass, William H.-- "Mrs. Mean"

Geeslin, Hugh, Jr.-- "A Day in the Life of the Boss"

Gold, Herbert-- "Love and Like"

Holwerda, Frank-- "In a Tropical Minor Key"

Malamud, Bernard-- "The Last Mohican"

Nemerov, Howard-- "A Secret Society"

Rosten, Leo-- "The Guy in Ward Four"

Roth, Philip-- "The Conversion of the Jews"

Sayre, Anne-- "A Birthday Present"

Swados, Harvey-- "The Man in the Toolhouse"

Taylor, Peter-- "Venus, Cupid, Folly, and Time"

Updike, John-- "A Gift from the City"

Williams, Thomas-- "The Buck in Trotevale's"

Wilson, Ethel-- "The Window"

### The Best American Short Stories, 1960, and the Yearbook of the American Short Story, *edited by* **Martha Foley** *and* **David Burnett**

Babb, Sanora-- "The Santa Ana"

Ellin, Stanley-- "The Day of the Bullet"

Elliott, George P.-- "Words Words Words"

Fast, Howard-- "The Man Who Looked Like Jesus"

Gallant, Mavis-- "August"

Garrett, George-- "An Evening Performance"

Graves, John-- "The Last Running"

Hall, Lawrence Sargent-- "The Ledge"

Hardwick, Elizabeth-- "The Purchase"

MacDonald, Lachlan-- "The Hunter"

Malamud, Bernard-- "The Maid's Shoes"

Miller, Arthur-- "I Don't Need You Any More"

Nemerov, Howard-- "Unbelievable Characters"

Roberts, Phyllis-- "Hero"

Roth, Philip-- "Defender of the Faith"

Sturgeon, Theodore-- "The Man Who Lost the Sea"

Swados, Harvey-- "A Glance in the Mirror"

Taylor, Peter-- "Who Was Jesse's Friend and Protector?"

Young, Elisabeth Larsh-- "Counterclockwise"

## The Best American Short Stories, 1961, and the Yearbook of the American Short Story,
*edited by* **Martha Foley** *and* **David Burnett**

Baldwin, James-- "This Morning, This Evening, So Soon"

Berry, John-- "The Listener"

Chester, Alfred-- "Berceuse"

Gass, William H.-- "The Love and Sorrow of Henry Pimber"

Gold, Ivan-- "The Nickel Misery of George Washington Carver Brown"

Goyen, William-- "A Tale of Inheritance"

Harris, Mark-- "The Self-Made Brain Surgeon"

Hurlbut, Kaatje-- "The Vestibule"

Jacobs, Theodore-- "A Girl for Walter"

Lavin, Mary-- "The Yellow Beret"

Ludwig, Jack-- "Confusions"

Marsh, Willard-- "Mexican Hayride"

McKelway, St. Clair-- "First Marriage"

Olive, Jeannie-- "Society"

Olsen, Tillie-- "Tell Me a Riddle"

Peden, William-- "Night in Funland"

Pynchon, Thomas-- "Entropy"

Sandmel, Samuel-- "The Colleagues of Mr. Chips"

Taylor, Peter-- "Miss Leonora When Last Seen"

White, Ellington-- "The Perils of Flight"

## The Best American Short Stories, 1962, and the Yearbook of the American Short Story,
*edited by* **Martha Foley** *and* **David Burnett**

Arkin, Frieda-- "The Light of the Sea"

Choy, Wayson S.-- "The Sound of Waves"

Dahlberg, Edward-- "Because I Was Flesh"

Deal, Borden-- "Antaeus"

Elkin, Stanley-- "Criers and Kibbitzers, Kibbitzers and Criers"

Epstein, Seymour-- "Wheat Closed Higher, Cotton Was Mixed"

Garrett, George-- "The Old Army Game"

Gass, William H.-- "The Pedersen Kid"

Gilbert, Sister Mary-- "The Model Chapel"

Hall, Donald-- "A Day on Ragged"

Karmel-Wolfe, Henia-- "The Last Day"

Lavin, Mary-- "In the Middle of the Fields"

Leahy, Jack Thomas-- "Hanging Hair"

Maddow, Ben-- "'To Hell the Rabbis'"

McKenzie, Miriam-- "Déjà vu"

Miller, Arthur-- "The Prophecy"

Myers, E. Lucas-- "The Vindication of Dr. Nestor"

O'Connor, Flannery-- "Everything That Rises Must Converge"

Selz, Thalia-- "The Education of a Queen"

Shaw, Irwin-- "Love on a Dark Street"

Updike, John-- "Pigeon Feathers"

## The Best American Short Stories, 1963, and the Yearbook of the American Short Story,
*edited by* **Martha Foley** *and* **David Burnett**

Andersen, U. S.-- "Turn Ever So Quickly"

Blattner, H. W.-- "Sound of a Drunken Drummer"

Carter, John Stewart-- "The Keyhole Eye"

Cheever, John-- "A Vision of the World"

Dawkins, Cecil-- "A Simple Case"

Dickerson, George-- "Chico"

Dikeman, May-- "The Sound of Young Laughter"

Elkin, Stanley-- "I Look out for Ed Wolfe"

Godfrey, Dave-- "Newfoundland Night"

Gordon, William J. J.-- "The Pures"

Hermann, John-- "Aunt Mary"

Loeser, Katinka-- "Beggarman, Rich Man, or Thief"

McKelway, St. Clair-- "The Fireflies"

Molinaro, Ursule-- "The Insufficient Rope"

Oates, Joyce Carol-- "The Fine White Mist of Winter"

Phelan, R. C.-- "Birds, Clouds, Frogs"

Richler, Mordecai-- "Some Grist for Mervyn's Mill"

Saroyan, William-- "What a World, Said the Bicycle Rider"

Sassoon, Babette-- "The Betrayal"

Shaw, Irwin-- "Noises in the City"

Taylor, Peter-- "At the Drugstore"

Tucci, Niccolò-- "The Desert in the Oasis"

West, Jessamyn-- "The Picnickers"

### The Best American Short Stories, 1964, and the Yearbook of the American Short Story,
*edited by* **Martha Foley** *and* **David Burnett**

Arkin, Frieda-- "The Broomstick on the Porch"
Brown, Richard G.-- "Mr. Iscariot"
Carter, John Stewart-- "To a Tenor Dying Old"
Curley, Daniel-- "A Story of Love, Etc."
Dikeman, May-- "The Woman Across the Street"
Eastlake, William-- "A Long Day's Dying"
Goyen, William-- "Figure over the Town"
Horgan, Paul-- "Black Snowflakes"
Humphrey, William-- "The Pump"
Jackson, Shirley-- "Birthday Party"
Konecky, Edith-- "The Power"
Lolos, Kimon-- "Mule No. 095"
Malamud, Bernard-- "The German Refugee"
McCullers, Carson-- "Sucker"
Moriconi, Virginia-- "Simple Arithmetic"
Oates, Joyce Carol-- "Upon the Sweeping Flood"
Price, Reynolds-- "The Names and Faces of Heroes"
Randal, Vera-- "Waiting for Jim"
Swados, Harvey-- "A Story for Teddy"
Warren, Robert Penn-- "Have You Seen Sukie?"

### The Best American Short Stories, 1965, and the Yearbook of the American Short Story,
*edited by* **Martha Foley**

Amster, L. J.-- "Center of Gravity"
De Paola, Daniel-- "The Returning"
Elkin, Stanley-- "The Transient"
Gilchrist, Jack-- "Opening Day"
Groshong, James W.-- "The Gesture"
Hamer, Martin J.-- "Sarah"
Howard, Maureen-- "Sherry"
Hutter, Donald-- "A Family Man"
Karmel-Wolfe, Henia-- "The Month of His Birthday"
Lavin, Mary-- "Heart of Gold"
Lynds, Dennis-- "A Blue Blonde in the
    Sky over Pennsylvania"
Morton, Frederic-- "The Guest"
Neugeboren, Jay-- "The Application"
Oates, Joyce Carol-- "First Views of the Enemy"
Robinson, Leonard Wallace-- "The Practice of an Art"
Singer, Isaac Bashevis-- "A Sacrifice"
Somerlott, Robert-- "Eskimo Pies"
Spencer, Elizabeth-- "The Visit"
Stafford, Jean-- "The Tea Time of
    Stouthearted Ladies"
Stein, Gerald-- "For I Have Wept"
Taylor, Peter-- "There"
Yu-Hwa, Lee-- "The Last Rite"

### The Best American Short Stories, 1966, and the Yearbook of the American Short Story,
*edited by* **Martha Foley** *and* **David Burnett**

Cady, Jack-- "The Burning"
Dickerson, George-- "A Mussel Named Ecclesiastes"
Downey, Harris-- "The Vicar-General and
    the Wide Night"
Ely, David-- "The Academy"
Faulkner, William-- "Mr. Acarius"
Grau, Shirley Ann-- "The Beach Party"
Hedin, Mary-- "Places We Lost"
Hood, Hugh-- "Getting to Williamstown"
Jackson, Shirley-- "The Bus"
Jacobsen, Josephine-- "On the Island"
Kreisel, Henry-- "The Broken Globe"
Lavin, Mary-- "One Summer"
Leviant, Curt-- "Mourning Call"
Maxwell, William-- "Further Tales About
    Men and Women"
O'Connor, Flannery-- "Parker's Back"
Rothberg, Abraham-- "Pluto Is the Furthest Planet"
Terry, Walter S.-- "The Bottomless Well"
Wakefield, Dan-- "Autumn Full of Apples"
Whitehill, Joseph-- "One Night for Several Samurai"
Wilner, Herbert-- "Dovisch in the Wilderness"

### The Best American Short Stories, 1967, and the Yearbook of the American Short Story,
*edited by* **Martha Foley** *and* **David Burnett**

Ayer, Ethan-- "The Promise of Heat"

Blake, George-- "A Place Not on the Map"

Boyle, Kay-- "The Wild Horses"

Carver, Raymond-- "Will You Please
Be Quiet, Please?"

Francis, H. E.-- "One of the Boys"

Harris, MacDonald-- "Trepleff"

Hazel, Robert-- "White Anglo-Saxon Protestant"

Hunt, Hugh Allyn-- "Acme Rooms and
Sweet Marjorie Russell"

Lee, Lawrence-- "The Heroic Journey"

Miller, Arthur-- "Search for a Future"

Moore, Brian-- "The Apartment Hunter"

Morgan, Berry-- "Andrew"

Oates, Joyce Carol-- "Where Are You Going, Where
Have You Been?"

Radcliffe, Donald-- "Song of the Simidor"

Roth, Henry-- "The Surveyor"

Rubin, David-- "Longing for America"

Stuart, Jesse-- "The Accident"

Sturm, Carol-- "The Kid Who Fractioned"

Travers, Robert-- "The Big Brown Trout"

Wiser, William-- "House of the Blues"

### The Best American Short Stories, 1968, and the Yearbook of the American Short Story,
*edited by* **Martha Foley** *and* **David Burnett**

Baldwin, James-- "Tell Me How Long the
Train's Been Gone"

Bruce, Janet-- "Dried Rose Petals in a Silver Bowl"

Deck, John-- "Greased Samba"

Farrell, James T.-- "An American Student in Paris"

Freitag, George H.-- "An Old Man and His Hat"

Gardner, Herb-- "Who Is Harry Kellerman and Why Is
He Saying Those Terrible Things About Me?"

Gass, William H.-- "In the Heart of the
Heart of the Country"

Gavell, Mary Ladd-- "The Rotifer"

Gropman, Donald-- "The Heart of This or That Man"

Harrison, William-- "The Snooker Shark"

Higgins, Judith-- "The Only People"

Hudson, Helen-- "The Tenant"

Litwak, Leo E.-- "In Shock"

McKenna, Richard-- "The Sons of Martha"

Moseley, William-- "The Preacher and Margery Scott"

Ostrow, Joanna-- "Celtic Twilight"

Parker, Nancy Huddleston-- "Early Morning,
Lonely Ride"

Phillips, John-- "Bleat Blodgette"

Spingarn, Lawrence P.-- "The Ambassador"

Weathers, Winston-- "The Games That We Played"

### The Best American Short Stories, 1969, and the Yearbook of the American Short Story,
*edited by* **Martha Foley** *and* **David Burnett**

Brennan, Maeve-- "The Eldest Child"

Cady, Jack-- "Play Like I'm Sherrif"

Costello, Mark-- "Murphy's Xmas"

Gerald, John Bart-- "Walking Wounded"

Hughes, Mary Gray-- "The Foreigner in the Blood"

Klein, Norma-- "The Boy in the Green Hat"

Lavin, Mary-- "Happiness"

MacLeod, Alistair-- "The Boat"

Madden, David-- "The Day the Flowers Came"

Malamud, Bernard-- "Pictures of Fidelman"

McGregor, Matthew W.-- "Porkchops with Whiskey
and Ice Cream"

McPherson, James Alan-- "Gold Coast"

Milton, John R.-- "The Inheritance of Emmy
One Horse"

Oates, Joyce Carol-- "By the River"

Pansing, Nancy Pelletier-- "The Visitation"

Plath, Sylvia-- "Johnny Panic and the Bible of Dreams"

Rugel, Miriam-- "Paper Poppy"

Shipley, Margaret-- "The Tea Bowl of Ninsei
Nomura"

Singer, Isaac Bashevis-- "The Colony"

Winslow, Joyce Madelon-- "Benjamen Burning"

### The Best American Short Stories, 1970, and the Yearbook of the American Short Story,
*edited by* **Martha Foley** *and* **David Burnett**

Cady, Jack-- "With No Breeze"
Cleaver, Eldridge-- "The Flashlight"
Coover, Robert-- "The Magic Poker"
Davis, Olivia-- "The Other Child"
Dubus, Andre-- "If They Knew Yvonne"
Gerald, John Bart-- "Blood Letting"
Gillespie, Alfred-- "Tonight at Nine Thirty-Six"
Leffland, Ella-- "The Forest"
Matthews, Jack-- "Another Story"
Maxwell, William-- "The Gardens of Mont-Saint-Michel"
Morris, Wright-- "Green Grass, Blue Sky, White House"
Oates, Joyce Carol-- "How I Contemplated the World from the Detroit House of Correction and Began My Life over Again"
Olsen, Paul-- "The Flag Is Down"
Ozick, Cynthia-- "Yiddish in America"
Siegel, Jules-- "In the Land of the Morning Calm, Deja Vu"
Singer, Isaac Bashevis-- "The Key"
Stone, Robert-- "Porque no tiene, porque le falta"
Taylor, Peter-- "Daphne's Lover"
Weisbrod, Rosine-- "The Ninth Cold Day"

### The Best American Short Stories, 1971, and the Yearbook of the American Short Story,
*edited by* **Martha Foley** *and* **David Burnett**

Banks, Russell-- "With Che in New Hampshire"
Bennett, Hal-- "Dotson Gerber Resurrected"
Blake, James-- "The Widow, Bereft"
Cady, Jack-- "I Take Care of Things"
Canzoneri, Robert-- "Barbed Wire"
Drake, Albert-- "The Chicken Which Became a Rat"
Eastlake, William-- "The Dancing Boy"
Harvor, Beth-- "Pain Was My Portion"
Madden, David-- "No Trace"
Mitchell, Don-- "Diesel"
Montgomery, Marion-- "The Decline and Fall of Officer Fergerson"
Morris, Wright-- "Magic"
O'Connor, Philip F.-- "The Gift Bearer"
Olsen, Tillie-- "Requa I"
Prashker, Ivan-- "Shirt Talk"
Rush, Norman-- "In Late Youth"
Santiago, Danny-- "The Somebody"
Strong, Jonathan-- "Xavier Fereira's Unfinished Book: Chapter One"
Tushnet, Leonard-- "The Klausners"
Valgardson, W. D.-- "Bloodflowers"
Woiwode, Larry-- "The Suitor"

### The Best American Short Stories, 1972, and the Yearbook of the American Short Story,
*edited by* **Martha Foley**

Beal, M. F.-- "Gold"
Brautigan, Richard-- "The World War I Los Angeles Airplane"
Cherry, Kelly-- "Convenant"
Gold, Herbert-- "A Death on the East Side"
Greenberg, Joanne-- "The Supremacy of the Hunza"
Heath, Mary-- "The Breadman"
Holmes, Edward M.-- "Drums Again"
Hughes, Mary Gray-- "The Judge"
Jones, Ann-- "In Black and White"
Just, Ward-- "Three Washington Stories"
Kalechofsky, Roberta-- "His Day Out"
Kavaler, Rebecca-- "The Further Adventures of Brunhild"
L'Heureux, John-- "Fox and Swan"
Malony, Ralph-- "Intimacy"
Mandell, Marvin-- "The Aesculapians"
Ozick, Cynthia-- "The Dock-Witch"
Porter, Joe Ashby-- "The Vacation"
Street, Penelope-- "The Magic Apple"
Warren, Robert Penn-- "Meet Me in the Green Glen"
Weesner, Theodore-- "Stealing Cars"
Yglesias, José-- "The Guns in the Closet"

### The Best American Short Stories, 1973, the Yearbook of the American Short Story,
#### *edited by* **Martha Foley**

Barthelme, Donald-- "A City of Churches"
Bromell, Henry-- "The Slightest Distance"
Cheever, John-- "The Jewels of the Cabots"
Clayton, John J.-- "Cambridge Is Sinking!"
Corrington, John William-- "Old Men Dream Dreams, Young Men See Visions"
Davenport, Guy-- "Robot"
Eastlake, William-- "The Death of Sun"
Greenberg, Alvin-- "The Real Meaning of the Faust Legend"
Hayden, Julie-- "In the Words Of"
Higgins, George V.-- "The Habits of Animals: The Progress of the Seasons"

Just, Ward-- "Burns"
Kenary, James S.-- "Going Home"
Knight, Wallace E.-- "The Way We Went"
Lardas, Konstantinos-- "The Broken Wings"
McPherson, James Alan-- "The Silver Bullet"
Malamud, Bernard-- "God's Wrath"
Oates, Joyce Carol-- "Silkie"
Plath, Sylvia-- "Mothers"
Sandberg-Diment, Erik-- "Come away, Oh Human Child"
Shetzline, David-- "Country of the Painted Freaks"
Williams, Tennessee-- "Happy August the Tenth"

### The Best American Short Stories, 1974, and the Yearbook of the American Short Story,
#### *edited by* **Martha Foley**

Boyer, Agnes-- "The Deserter"
Bumpus, Jerry-- "Beginnings"
Clark, Eleanor-- "A Summer in Puerto Rico"
Esslinger-Carr, Pat M.-- "The Party"
Horne, Lewis B.-- "Mansion, Magic, and Miracle"
Ignatow, Rose Graubart-- "Down the American River"
Kumin, Maxine-- "Opening the Door on Sixty-Second Street"
Lavin, Mary-- "Tom"
L'Heureux, John-- "A Family Affair"
Lopate, Phillip-- "The Chamber Music Evening"

Minot, Stephen-- "The Tide and Isaac Bates"
Mitchell, Beverly-- "Letter from Sakaye"
Rothschild, Michael-- "Dog in the Manger"
Sandberg, Peter L.-- "Calloway's Climb"
Saroyan, William-- "Isn't Today the Day?"
Schneider, Philip H.-- "The Gray"
Targan, Barry-- "Old Vemish"
Updike, John-- "Son"
Vivante, Arturo-- "Honeymoon"
Walker, Alice-- "The Revenge of Hannah Kemhuff"

### The Best American Short Stories, 1975, and the Yearbook of the American Short Story,
#### *edited by* **Martha Foley**

Banks, Russell-- "The Lie"
Barthelme, Donald-- "The School"
Brown, Rosellen-- "How to Win"
Bumpus, Jerry-- "Desert Matinee"
Busch, Frederick-- "Bambi Meets the Furies"
Chaikin, Nancy G.-- "Waiting for Astronauts"
Clearman, Mary-- "Paths unto the Dead"
De Jenkins, Lyll Becerra-- "Tyranny"
Dubus, Andre-- "Cadence"
Ford, Jesse Hill-- "Big Boy"
Hoffman, William-- "The Spirit in Me"

Hunter, Evan-- "The Analyst"
Kaser, Paul-- "How Jerem Came Home"
MacLeod, Alistair-- "The Lost Salt Gift of Blood"
McNamara, Eugene-- "The Howard Parker Montcrief Hoax"
Matthews, Jack-- "The Burial"
Price, Reynolds-- "Night and Day at Panacea"
Rothberg, Abraham-- "Polonaise"
Silko, Leslie Marmon-- "Lullaby"
Targan, Barry-- "The Who Lived"
Yglesias, José-- "The American Sickness"

### The Best American Short Stories, 1976, and the Yearbook of the American Short Story,
*edited by* **Martha Foley**

Adams, Alice-- "Roses, Rhododendron"

Battin, M. Pabst-- "Terminal Procedure"

Briskin, Mae Seidman-- "The Boy Who Was Astrid's Mother"

Chaikin, Nancy G.-- "Beautiful, Helpless Animals"

Corrington, John William-- "The Actes and Documents"

Francis, H. E.-- "A Chronicle of Love"

Hagge, John-- "Pontius Pilate"

Just, Ward-- "Dietz at War"

McCluskey, John-- "John Henry's Home"

Minot, Steven-- "Grubbing for Roots"

Nelson, Kent-- "Looking into Nothing"

Ozick, Cynthia-- "A Mercenary"

Price, Reynolds-- "Broad Day"

Rothschild, Michael-- "Wondermonger"

Targan, Barry-- "Surviving Adverse Seasons"

Taylor, Peter-- "The Hand of Emmagene"

Updike, John-- "The Man Who Loved Extinct Mammals"

### The Best American Short Stories, 1977, and the Yearbook of the American Short Story,
*edited by* **Martha Foley**

Busch, Frederick-- "The Trouble with Being Food"

Caldwell, Price-- "Tarzan Meets the Department Head"

Cheever, John-- "Falconer"

Copeland, Ann-- "At Peace"

Corrington, John William-- "Pleadings"

Damon, Philip-- "Growing up in No Time"

Epstein, Leslie-- "The Steinway Quintet"

Garber, Eugene K.-- "The Lover"

Hampl, Patricia-- "Look at a Teacup"

Kerr, Baine-- "Rider"

Matthews, Jack-- "A Questionnaire for Rudolph Gordon"

Minot, Stephen-- "A Passion for History"

Newman, Charles-- "The Woman Who Thought like a Man"

Oates, Joyce Carol-- "Gay"

O'Brien, Tim-- "Going After Cacciato"

Robbins, Tom-- "The Chink and the Clock People"

Saroyan, William-- "A Fresno Fable"

Sayles, John-- "Breed"

Tyler, Anne-- "Your Place Is Empty"

Wilson, William S.-- "Anthropology: What Is Lost in Rotation"

### The Best American Short Stories, 1978: Selected from U.S. and Canadian Magazines, including the Yearbook of the American Short Story,
*edited by* **Ted Solotaroff**, *with* **Shannon Ravenel**

Baumbach, Jonathan-- "The Return of Service"

Bowles, Jane-- "Two Scenes"

Brodkey, Harold-- "Verona: A Young Woman Speaks"

Cullinan, Elizabeth-- "A Good Loser"

Elkin, Stanley-- "The Conventional Wisdom"

Epstein, Leslie-- "Skaters on Wood"

Gardner, John-- "Redemption"

Helprin, Mark-- "The Schreuderspitze"

Kaplan, James-- "In Miami, Last Winter"

Marsh, Peter-- "By the Yellow Lake"

McCarthy, Tim-- "The Windmill Man"

McEwan, Ian-- "Psychopolis"

Oates, Joyce Carol-- "The Translation"

Petesch, Natalie L. M.-- "Main Street Morning"

Rishel, Mary Ann Malinchak-- "Staus"

Schott, Max-- "Murphy Jones: Pearblossom, California"

Schwartz, Lynne Sharon-- "Rough Strife"

Sintetos, L. Hluchan-- "Telling the Bees"

Sorrells, Robert T.-- "The Blacktop Champion of Ickey Honey"

Sorrentino, Gilbert-- "Decades"

Taylor, Peter-- "In the Miro District"

Williams, Joy-- "Bromeliads"

### The Best American Short Stories, 1979: Selected from U.S. and Canadian Magazines,
#### *edited by* Joyce Carol Oates, *with* Shannon Ravenel

Barthelme, Donald-- "The New Music"

Bellow, Saul-- "A Silver Dish"

Bowles, Paul-- "The Eye"

Brown, Rosellen-- "The Wedding Week"

Coffin, Lyn-- "Falling off the Scaffold"

Hedin, Mary-- "The Middle Place"

Hurlbut, Kaatje-- "A Short Walk into Afternoon"

Kumin, Maxine-- "The Missing Person"

LaSalle, Peter-- "Some Manhattan in New England"

McLaughlin, Ruth-- "Seasons"

Malamud, Bernard-- "Home Is the Hero"

Munro, Alice-- "Spelling"

O'Connor, Flannery-- "An Exile in the East"

Phillips, Jayne Anne-- "Something That Happened"

Rubin, Louis D., Jr.-- "Finisterre"

Sanford, Annette-- "Trip in a Summer Dress"

Schwartz, Lynne Sharon-- "Plaisir D'amour"

Singer, Isaac Bashevis-- "A Party in Miami Beach"

Styron, William-- "Shadrach"

Tennenbaum, Silvia-- "A Lingering Death"

Thompson, Jean-- "Paper Covers Rock"

Virgo, Sean-- "Home and Native Land"

Wilner, Herbert-- "The Quarterback Speaks to His God"

Wilson, Robley, Jr.-- "Living Alone"

Yngve, Rolf-- "The Quail"

### The Best American Short Stories, 1980: Selected from U.S. and Canadian Magazines,
#### *edited by* Stanley Elkin, *with* Shannon Ravenel

Barthelme, Donald-- "The Emerald"

Busch, Frederick-- "Long Calls"

Evanier, David-- "The One-Star Jew"

Gallant, Mavis-- "The Remission; Speck's Idea"

Gass, William H.-- "The Old Folks"

Gertler, T.-- "In Case of Survival"

Hardwick, Elizabeth-- "The Faithful"

Heinemann, Larry-- "The First Clean Fact"

Henderson, Robert-- "Into the Wind"

Johnson, Curt-- "Lemon Tree"

Paley, Grace-- "Friends"

Robison, James-- "Home"

Rooke, Leon-- "Mama Tuddi Done Over"

Sayles, John-- "At the Anarchist's Convention"

Singer, Isaasc Bashevis-- "The Safe Deposit"

Stern, Richard-- "Dr. Cahn's Visit"

Targan, Barry-- "The Rags of Time"

Taylor, Peter-- "The Old Forest"

Updike, John-- "Gesturing"

Waksler, Norman-- "Markowitz and the Gypsies"

Weaver, Gordon-- "Hog's Heart"

### The Best American Short Stories, 1981: Selected from U.S. and Canadian Magazines,
#### *edited by* Hortense Calisher, *with* Shannon Ravenel

Abish, Walter-- "The Idea of Switzerland"

Apple, Max-- "Small Island Republics"

Beattie, Ann-- "Winter: 1978"

Coover, Robert-- "A Working Day"

Dethier, Vincent G.-- "The Moth and the Primrose"

Dubus, Andre-- "The Winter Father"

Gallant, Mavis-- "The Assembly"

Hardwick, Elizabeth-- "The Bookseller"

Mason, Bobbie Ann-- "Shiloh"

McElroy, Joseph-- "The Future"

McGrath, Elizabeth-- "Fogbound in Avalon"

Moseley, Amelia-- "The Mountains Where Cithaeron Is"

Munro, Alice-- "Wood"

Oates, Joyce Carol-- "Presque Isle"

Ozick, Cynthia-- "The Shawl"

Rubin, Louis D., Jr.-- "The St. Anthony Chorale"

Stern, Richard-- "Wissler Remembers"

Tallent, Elizabeth-- "Ice"

Updike, John-- "Still of Some Use"

Woiwode, Larry-- "Change"

**The Best American Short Stories, 1982: Selected from U.S. and Canadian Magazines,**
*edited by* **John Gardner,** *with* **Shannon Ravenel**

Baker, Nicholson-- "K. 590"

Baxter, Charles-- "Harmony of the World"

Carver, Raymond-- "Cathedral"

Coggeshall, Rosanne-- "Lamb Says"

Ferry, James-- "Dancing Ducks and Talking Anus"

Freeman, Anne Hobson-- "The Girl Who Was No Kin
   to the Marshalls"

Greenberg, Alvin-- "The Power of Language Is Such
   That Even a Single Word Taken Truly to Heart
   Can Change Everything"

Gupta, Roberta-- "The Cafe de Paris"

Hauptmann, William-- "Good Rockin' Tonight"

Higgins, Joanna-- "The Courtship of Widow Sobcek"

Johnson, Charles-- "Exchange Value"

Licht, Fred-- "Shelter the Pilgrim"

MacMillan, Ian-- "Proud Monster: Sketches"

McLaughlin, Lissa-- "The Continental Heart"

Milton, Edith-- "Coming Over"

Oates, Joyce Carol-- "Theft"

Renwick, Joyce-- "The Dolphin Story"

Robison, Mary-- "Coach"

Rosner, Anne F.-- "Prize Tomatoes"

Smith, R. E.-- "The Gift Horse's Mouth"

**The Best American Short Stories, 1983: Selected from U.S. and Canadian Magazines,**
*edited by* **Anne Tyler,** *with* **Shannon Ravenel**

Barich, Bill-- "Hard to Be Good"

Bly, Carol-- "The Dignity of Life"

Bond, James-- "A Change of Season"

Carver, Raymond-- "Where I'm Calling From"

Chute, Carolyn-- "'Ollie, Oh . . .'"

Colwin, Laurie-- "My Mistress"

Epstein, Joseph-- "The Count and the Princess"

Erdrich, Louise-- "Scales"

Le Guin, Ursula K.-- "The Professor's Houses; Sur"

Mason, Bobbie Ann-- "Graveyard Day"

Morris, Wright-- "Victrola"

Schumacher, Julie-- "Reunion"

Stark, Sharon Sheehe-- "Best Quality Glass Company,
   New York"

Taylor, Robert-- "Colorado"

Thurm, Marian-- "Starlight"

Updike, John-- "Deaths of Distant Friends"

Vanderhaeghe, Guy-- "Reunion"

Vreuls, Diane-- "Beebee"

Woiwode, Larry-- "Firstborn"

**The Best American Short Stories, 1984: Selected from U.S. and Canadian Magazines,**
*edited by* **John Updike,** *with* **Shannon Ravenel (partial contents)**

Abbott, Lee K.-- "The Final Proof of Fate and
   Circumstance"

Bell, Madison Smartt-- "The Naked Lady"

Benedict, Dianne-- "Unknown Feathers"

Bowles, Paul-- "In the Red Room"

Brown, Mary Ward-- "The Cure"

DeMarinis, Rick-- "Gent"

Dubus, Andre-- "A Father's Story"

Gallant, Mavis-- "Lena"

Hood, Mary-- "Inexorable Progress"

Justice, Donald-- "The Artificial Moonlight"

Kirk, Stephen-- "Morrison's Reaction"

Minot, Susan-- "Thorofare"

Morris, Wright-- "Glimpse into Another Country"

Oates, Joyce Carol-- "Nairobi"

Ozick, Cynthia-- "Rosa"

Pei, Lowry-- "The Cold Room"

Penner, Jonathan-- "Things to Be Thrown Away"

Rush, Norman-- "Bruns"

Salter, James-- "Foreign Shores"

Schinto, Jeanne-- "Caddie's Day"

### The Best American Short Stories, 1985: Selected from U.S. and Canadian Magazines,
*edited by* **Gail Godwin**, *with* **Shannon Ravenel**

Banks, Russell-- "Sarah Cole: A Type of Love Story"

Bishop, Michael-- "Dogs' Lives"

Canin, Ethan-- "Emperor of the Air"

Doctorow, E. L. -- "The Leather Man"

Edwards, Margaret-- "Roses"

Flythe, Starkey-- "Walking, Walking"

Francis, H. E.-- "The Sudden Trees"

Jafek, Bev-- "You've Come a Long Way, Mickey Mouse"

L'Heureux, John-- "Clothing"

Meinke, Peter-- "The Piano Tuner"

Morris, Wright-- "Fellow-Creatures"

Mukherjee, Bharati-- "Angela"

Nugent, Beth-- "City of Boys"

Oates, Joyce Carol-- "Raven's Wing"

Rush, Norman-- "Instruments of Seduction"

Sandor, Marjorie-- "The Gittel"

Seabrooke, Deborah-- "Secrets"

Smiley, Jane-- "Lily"

Stark, Sharon Sheehe-- "The Johnstown Polka"

Williams, Joy-- "The Skater"

### The Best American Short Stories, 1986: Selected from U.S. and Canadian Magazines,
*edited by* **Raymond Carver**, *with* **Shannon Ravenel**

Barthelme, Donald-- "Basil from Her Garden"

Baxter, Charles-- "Gryphon"

Beattie, Ann-- "Janus"

Burke, James Lee-- "The Convict"

Canin, Ethan-- "Star Food"

Conroy, Frank-- "Gossip"

Ford, Richard-- "Communist"

Gallagher, Tess-- "Bad Company"

Hempel, Amy-- "Today Will Be a Quiet Day"

Kaplan, David Michael-- "Doe Season"

Lipsky, David-- "Three Thousand Dollars"

McGuane, Thomas-- "Sportsmen"

McIlroy, Christopher-- "All My Relations"

Munro, Alice-- "Monsieur Les Deux Chapeaux"

Neely, Jessica-- "Skin Angels"

Nelson, Kent-- "Invisible Life"

Paley, Grace-- "Telling"

Simpson, Mona-- "Lawns"

Williams, Joy-- "Health"

Wolff, Tobias-- "The Rich Brother"

### The Best American Short Stories, 1987: Selected from U.S. and Canadian Magazines,
*edited by* **Ann Beattie**, *with* **Shannon Ravenel**

Abbott, Lee K.-- "Dreams of Distant Lives"

Baxter, Charles-- "How I Found My Brother"

Bell, Madison Smartt-- "Lie Detector"

Carlson, Ron-- "Milk"

Carver, Raymond-- "Boxes"

Gallant, Mavis-- "Kingdom Come"

Haruf, Kent-- "Private Debts/Public Holdings"

Lombreglia, Ralph-- "Men Under Water"

Miller, Sue-- "Lover of Women"

Mukherjee, Bharati-- "Tenant"

Munro, Alice-- "Circle of Prayer"

Nova, Craig-- "Prince"

O'Brien, Tim-- "Things They Carried"

Sontag, Susan-- "Way We Live Now"

Stern, Daniel-- "Interpretation of Dreams by Sigmund Freud: A Story"

Tallent, Elizabeth-- "Favor"

Taylor, Robert-- "Lady of Spain"

Updike, John-- "Afterlife"

Williams, Joy-- "Blue Men"

Wolff, Tobias-- "Other Miller"

### The Best American Short Stories, 1988: Selected from U.S. and Canadian Magazines,
*edited by* **Mark Helprin,** *with* **Shannon Ravenel**

Bass, Rick-- "Cats and Students, Bubbles and Abysses"

Bausch, Richard-- "Police Dreams"

Blythe, Will-- "Taming Power of the Small"

Carver, Raymond-- "Errand"

Currey, Richard-- "Waiting for Trains"

Erdrich, Louise-- "Snares"

Gallant, Mavis-- "Dede"

Godshalk, C. S.-- "Wonderland"

Goldman, E. S.-- "Way to the Dump"

Honig, Lucy-- "No Friends, All Strangers"

Jen, Gish-- "Water-Faucet Vision"

Johnson, Hilding-- "Victoria"

Kiteley, Brian-- "Still Life with Insects"

Lacy, Robert-- "Natural Father"

Lombreglia, Ralph-- "Inn Essence"

Milton, Edith-- "Entrechat"

Sandor, Marjorie-- "Still Life"

Stone, Robert-- "Helping"

Taylor-Hall, Mary Ann-- "Banana Boats"

Wolff, Tobias-- "Smorgasbord"

### The Best American Short Stories, 1989: Selected from U.S. and Canadian Magazines,
*edited by* **Margaret Atwood,** *with* **Shannon Ravenel**

Baxter, Charles-- "Fenstad's Mother"

Bell, Madison Smartt-- "Customs of the Country"

Boswell, Robert-- "Living to Be a Hundred"

Boyd, Blanche McCrary-- "The Black Hand Girl"

Brown, Larry-- "Kubuku Riders (This Is It)"

Busch, Frederick-- "Ralph the Duck"

Cunningham, Michael-- "White Angel"

DeMarinis, Rick-- "The Flowers of Boredom"

Doerr, Harriet-- "Edie: A Life"

Gallant, Mavis-- "The Concert Party"

Glover, Douglas-- "Why I Decided to Kill Myself and Other Jokes"

Gowdy, Barbara-- "Disneyland"

Hogan, Linda-- "Aunt Moon's Young Man"

Louie, David Wong-- "Displacement"

Mukherjee, Bharati-- "The Management of Grief"

Munro, Alice-- "Meneseteung"

Phillips, Dale Ray-- "What Men Love For

Richard, Mark-- "Strays"

Robinson, Arthur-- "The Boy on the Train"

Sharif, M. T.-- "The Letter Writer"

### The Best American Short Stories, 1990: Selected from U.S. and Canadian Magazines,
*edited by* **Richard Ford,** *with* **Shannon Ravenel**

Allen, Edward-- "River of Toys"

Bausch, Richard-- "The Fireman's Wife"

Bausch, Richard-- "A Kind of Simple, Happy Grace"

Bell, Madison Smartt-- "Finding Natasha"

Godshalk, C. S.-- "The Wizard"

Henley, Patricia-- "The Secret of Cartwheels"

Houston, Pam-- "How to Talk to a Hunter"

Hustvedt, Siri-- "Mr. Morning"

Johnson, Denis-- "Car-Crash While Hitchhiking"

McFarland, Dennis-- "Nothing to Ask For"

Millhauser, Steven-- "Eisenheim the Illusionist"

Moore, Lorrie-- "You're Ugly, Too"

Munro, Alice-- "Differently"

Munro, Alice-- "Wigtime"

Powell, Padgett-- "Typical"

Segal, Lore--The Reverse Bug"

Tallent, Elizabeth-- "Prowler"

Tilghman, Christopher-- "In a Father's Place"

Wickersham, Joan-- "Commuter Marriage"

Williams, Joy-- "The Little Winter"

## The Best American Short Stories, 1991: Selected from U.S. and Canadian Magazines,
### *edited by* **Alice Adams,** *with* **Katrina Kenison**

Bass, Rick-- "Legend of Pig-Eye"

Baxter, Charles-- "The Disappeared"

Bloom, Amy-- "Love Is Not a Pie"

Braverman, Kate-- "Tall Tales from the Mekong Delta"

Butler, Robert Olen-- "The Trip Back"

D'Ambrosio, Charles, Jr.-- "The Point"

Dillon, Millicent-- "Oil and Water"

Doerr, Harriet-- "Another Short Day in La Luz"

Eisenberg, Deborah-- "The Custodian"

Gordon, Mary-- "Separation"

Graver, Elizabeth-- "The Body Shop"

Hustvedt, Siri-- "Houdini"

Iossel, Mikhail-- "Bologoye"

Jauss, David-- "Glossolalia"

Michaels, Leonard-- "Viva la Tropicana"

Moore, Lorrie-- "Willing"

Munro, Alice-- "Friend of My Youth"

Oates, Joyce Carol-- "American, Abroad"

Prose, Francine-- "Dog Stories"

Updike, John-- "A Sandstone Farmhouse"

## The Best American Short Stories, 1992: Selected from U.S. and Canadian Magazines,
### *edited by* **Alice Adams,** *with* **Katrina Kenison**

Adams, Alice-- "The Last Lovely City"

Bass, Rick-- "Days of Heaven"

Beller, Thomas-- "A Different Kind of Imperfection"

Bloom, Amy-- "Silver Water"

Butler, Robert Olen-- "A Good Scent from a Strange Mountain"

Gallant, Mavis-- "Across the Bridge"

Gautreaux, Tim-- "Same Place, Same Things"

Johnson, Denis-- "Emergency"

Jones, Thom-- "The Pugilist at Rest"

Klimasewiski, Marshall N.-- "JunHee"

Moore, Lorrie-- "Community Life"

Munro, Alice-- "Carried Away"

Oates, Joyce Carol-- "Is Laughter Contagious?"

Price, Reynolds-- "The Fare to the Moon"

Smith, Annick-- "It's Come to This"

Tilghman, Christopher-- "The Way People Run"

Wallace, David Foster-- "Forever Overhead"

Wheeler, Kate-- "Under the Roof"

Winthrop, Elizabeth-- "The Golden Darters"

Wolff, Tobias-- "Firelight"

## The Best American Short Stories, 1993: Selected from U.S. and Canadian Magazines,
### *edited by* **Louise Erdrich,** *with* **Katrina Kenison**

Berry, Wendell-- "Pray Without Ceasing"

Dixon, Stephen-- "Man, Woman, and Boy"

Earley, Tony-- "Charlotte"

Edwards, Kim-- "Gold"

Ellison, Harlan-- "The Man Who Rowed Christopher Columbus Ashore"

Fulton, Alice-- "Queen Wintergreen"

Gaitskill, Mary-- "The Girl on the Plane"

Gordon, Mary-- "The Important Houses"

Johnson, Diane-- "Great Barrier Reef"

Jones, Thom-- "I Want to Live!"

Lee, Andrea-- "Winter Barley"

Moore, Lorrie-- "Terrific Mother"

Munro, Alice-- "A Real Life"

Nelson, Antonya-- "Naked Ladies"

Peery, Janet-- "What the Thunder Said"

Power, Susan-- "Red Moccasins"

Scott, Joanna-- "Concerning Mold upon the Skin, Etc."

Shapiro, Jane-- "Poltergeists"

Updike, John-- "Playing with Dynamite"

Woiwode, Larry-- "Silent Passengers"

**The Best American Short Stories, 1994: Selected from U.S. and Canadian Magazines,**
*edited by* **Tobias Wolff,** *with* **Katrina Kenison**

Alexie, Sherman-- "This Is What It Means to Say Phoenix, Arizona"

Anshaw, Carol-- "Hammam"

Butler, Robert Olen-- "Salem"

Chang, Lan Samantha-- "Pipa's Story"

Cummins, Ann-- "Where I Work"

Dark, Alice Elliott-- "In the Gloaming"

Dybek, Stuart-- "We Didn't"

Earley, Tony-- "The Prophet from Jupiter"

Ferrell, Carolyn-- "Proper Library"

Gardiner, John Rolfe-- "The Voyage Out"

Gates, David-- "The Mail Lady"

Hannah, Barry-- "Nicodemus Bluff"

Jones, Thom-- "Cold Snap"

Keeble, John-- "The Chasm"

Krusoe, Nancy-- "Landscape and Dream"

Louis, Laura Glen-- "Fur"

Offutt, Chris-- "Melungeons"

Robinson, Roxana-- "Mr. Sumarsono"

Shepard, Jim-- "Batting Against Castro"

Tilghman, Christopher-- "Things Left Undone"

Wilson, Jonathan-- "From Shanghai"

**The Best American Short Stories, 1995: Selected from U.S. and Canadian Magazines,**
*edited by* **Jane Smiley,** *with* **Katrina Kenison**

Barrett, Andrea-- "The Behavior of the Hawkweeds"

Braverman, Kate-- "Pagan Night"

Cornell, Jennifer C.-- "Undertow"

Cozine, Andrew-- "Hand Jive"

Davies, Peter Ho-- "The Ugliest House in the World"

Delaney, Edward J.-- "The Drownings"

DeLillo, Don-- "The Angel Esmeralda"

Doybyns, Stephen-- "So I Guess You Know What I Told Him"

Falco, Edward-- "The Artist"

Garland, Max-- "Chiromancy "

Gilchrist, Ellen-- "The Stucco House"

Gordon, Jaimy-- "A Night's Work"

Jen, Gish-- "Birthmates"

Jones, Thom-- "Way down Deep in the Jungle"

Kincaid, Jamaica-- "Xuela"

Mandelman, Avner-- "Pity"

Orozco, Daniel-- "Orientation"

Polansky, Steven-- "Leg"

Thon, Melanie Rae-- "First, Body"

Williams, Joy-- "Honored Guest"

**The Best American Short Stories, 1996: Selected from U.S. and Canadian Magazines,**
*edited by* **John Edgar Wideman,** *with* **Katrina Kenison**

Adams, Alice-- "Complicities"

Bass, Rick-- "Fires"

Brown, Jason-- "Driving the Heart"

Butler, Robert Olen-- "Jealous Husband Returns in Form of Parrot"

Chang, Lan Samantha-- "The Eve of the Spirit Festival"

Chaon, Dan-- "Fitting Ends"

Davies, Peter Ho-- "The Silver Screen"

Díaz, Junot-- "Ysrael"

Dixon, Stephen-- "Sleep"

Dybek, Stuart-- "Paper Lantern"

Galyan, Deborah-- "The Incredible Appearing Man"

Gordon, Mary-- "Intertextuality"

Huddle, David-- "Past My Future"

Keesey, Anna-- "Bright Winter"

Kincaid, Jamaica-- "In Roseau"

Lewis, William Henry-- "Shades"

Lychack, William--A Stand of Fables"

Oates, Joyce Carol-- "Ghost Girls"

Patrinos, Angela-- "Sculpture I"

Perabo, Susan-- "Some Say the World"

Schwartz, Lynne Sharon-- "The Trip to Halawa Valley"

Sharma, Akhil-- "If You Sing Like That for Me"

Thompson, Jean-- "All Shall Love Me and Despair"

Thon, Melanie Rae-- "Xmas, Jamaica Plain"

### The Best American Short Stories, 1997: Selected from U.S. and Canadian Magazines, *edited by* **E. Annie Proulx,** *with* **Katrina Kenison**

Bausch, Richard-- "Nobody in Hollywood"

Bender, Karen E.-- "Eternal Love"

Boyle, T. Coraghessan-- "Killing Babies"

Byers, Michael-- "Rites of Passage: Shipmates down Under"

Cliff, Michelle-- "Identifying the Stranger: Transactions"

Cooke, Carolyn-- "Bob Darling"

Davis, Lydia-- "St. Martin"

Díaz, Junot-- "Perceived Social Values: Fiesta, 1980"

Durban, Pam-- "Soon"

Edgerton, Clyde-- "Send Me to the Electric Chair"

Eugenides, Jeffrey-- "Air Mail"

Franzen, Jonathan-- "Chez Lambert"

Gautreaux, Tim-- "Little Frogs in a Ditch"

Hagy, Alyson-- "Search Bay"

Hall, Donald-- "From Willow Temple"

Jin, Ha-- "Manners and Right Behavior: Saboteur"

Michaels, Leonard-- "A Girl with a Monkey"

Ozick, Cynthia-- "Save My Child!"

Spence, June-- "Missing Women"

Stone, Robert-- "Under the Pitons"

Wolff, Tobias-- "Powder"

### The Best American Short Stories, 1998: Selected from U.S. and Canadian Magazines, *edited by* **Garrison Keillor,** *with* **Katrina Kenison**

Adrian, Chris-- "Every Night for a Thousand Years"

Anshaw, Carol-- "Elvis Has Left the Building"

Ballantine, Poe-- "The Blue Devils of Blue River Avenue"

Broyard, Bliss-- "Mr. Sweetly Indecent"

Carter, Emily-- "Glory Goes and Gets Some"

Chetkovich, Kathryn-- "Appetites"

Crain, Matthew-- "Penance"

Gautreaux, Tim-- "Welding with Children"

Kaplan, Hester-- "Would You Know It Wasn't Love"

Larson, Doran-- "Morphine"

Moore, Lorrie-- "People Like That Are the Only People Here"

Nelson, Antonya-- "Unified Front"

Pearlman, Edith-- "Chance"

Powell, Padgett-- "Wayne in Love"

Proulx, Annie-- "The Half-Skinned Steer"

Schoemperlen, Diane-- "Body Language"

Sharma, Akhil-- "Cosmopolitain"

Swann, Maxine-- "Flower Children"

Updike, John-- "My Father on the Verge"

Wolitzer, Meg-- "Tea at the House"

### The Best American Short Stories, 1999: Selected from U.S. and Canadian Magazines, *edited by* **Amy Tan,** *with* **Katrina Kenison**

Bass, Rick-- "The Hermit's Story"

Díaz, Junot-- "The Sun, the Moon, the Stars"

Divakaruni, Chitra-- "Mrs. Dutta Writes a Letter"

Dobyns, Stephen-- "Kansas"

Englander, Nathan-- "The Tumblers"

Gautreaux, Tim-- "The Piano Tuner"

Hardy, Melissa-- "The Uncharted Heart"

Harrar, George-- "The Five Twenty-Two"

Hemon, A.-- "Islands"

Houston, Pam-- "The Best Girlfriend You Never Had"

Jin, Ha-- "In the Kindergarten"

Julavits, Heidi-- "Marry the One Who Gets There First"

Kaplan, Hester-- "Live Life King-Sized"

Kohler, Sheilia-- "Africans"

Lahiri, Jhumpa-- "Interpreter of Maladies"

Moore, Lorrie-- "Real Estate"

Munro, Alice-- "Save the Reaper"

Proulx, Annie-- "The Bunchgrass Edge of the World"

Spencer, James-- "The Robbers of Karnataka"

Upadhyay, Samrat-- "The Good Shopkeeper"

Yarbrough, Steve-- "The Rest of Her Life"

## The Best American Short Stories of the Century, *edited by* John Updike

To compile this volume, Updike selected the best stories that appeared in *The Best American Short Stories* series from 1915 through 1999; the stories are listed in chronological order of their publication in the series.

Rosenblatt, Benjamin-- "Zelig" (1915)

Lerner, Mary-- "Little Selves" (1916)

Glaspell, Susan-- "A Jury of Her Peers" (1917)

Anderson, Sherwood-- "The Other Woman" (1920)

Lardner, Ring-- "The Golden Honeymoon" (1922)

Toomer, Jean-- "Blood-Burning Moon" (1923)

Hemingway, Ernest-- "The Killers" (1927)

Cather, Willa-- "Double Birthday" (1929)

Coates, Grace Stone-- "Wild Plums" (1929)

Porter, Katherine Anne-- "Theft" (1930)

Faulkner, William-- "That Evening Sun Go Down" (1931)

Parker, Dorothy-- "Here We Are" (1931)

Fitzgerald, F. Scott-- " Crazy Sunday" (1933)

Godin, Alexander-- "My Dead Brother Comes to America" (1934)

Saroyan, William-- "Resurrection of a Life" (1935)

Warren, Robert Penn-- "Christmas Gift" (1938)

Wright, Richard-- "Bright and Morning Star" (1939)

Welty, Eudora-- "The Hitch-Hikers" (1940)

Horgan, Paul-- "The Peach Stone" (1943)

Nabokov, Vladimir-- "That in Aleppo Once . . ." (1944)

Stafford, Jean-- "The Interior Castle" (1947)

Gellhorn, Martha-- "Miami-New York" (1948)

White, E. B.-- "The Second Tree from the Corner" (1948)

Bishop, Elizabeth-- "The Farmer's Children" (1949)

Powers, J. F.-- "Death of a Favorite" (1951)

Williams, Tennessee-- "The Resemblance Between a Violin Case and a Coffin" (1951)

Cheever, John-- "The Country Husband" (1955)

O'Connor, Flannery-- "Greenleaf" (1957)

Hall, Lawrence Sargent-- "The Ledge" (1960)

Roth, Philip-- "Defender of the Faith" (1960)

Elkin, Stanley-- "Criers and Kibitzers, Kibitzers and Criers" (1962)

Malamud, Bernard-- "The German Refugee" (1964)

Oates, Joyce Carol-- "Where Are You Going, Where Have You Been?" (1967)

Gavell, Mary Ladd -- "The Rotifer" (1968)

McPherson, James Alan-- "Gold Coast" (1969)

Singer, Isaac Bashevis-- "The Key" (1970)

Barthelme, Donald-- "A City of Churches" (1973)

Brown, Rosellen-- "How to Win" (1975)

Adams, Alice-- "Roses, Rhododendron" (1976)

Brodkey, Harold-- "Verona: A Young Woman Speaks" (1978)

Bellow, Saul-- "A Silver Dish" (1979)

Updike, John-- "Gesturing" (1980)

Ozick, Cynthia-- "The Shawl" (1981)

Carver, Raymond-- "Where I'm Calling From" (1983)

Beattie, Ann-- "Janus" (1986)

Sontag, Susan-- "The Way We Live Now" (1987)

O'Brien, Tim-- "The Things They Carried" (1987)

Munro, Alice-- "Meneseteung" (1989)

Moore, Lorrie-- "You're Ugly, Too" (1990)

Jones, Thom-- "I Want to Live!" (1993)

Dark, Alice Elliott-- "In the Gloaming" (1994)

Ferrell, Carolyn-- "Proper Library" (1994)

Jen, Gish-- "Birthmates" (1995)

Durban, Pam-- "Soon" (1997)

Proulx, Annie-- "The Half-Skinned Steer" (1998)

Houston, Pam-- "The Best Girlfriend You Never Had" (1999)

### The Best American Short Stories, 2000: Selected from U.S. and Canadian Magazines,
### *edited by* **E. L. Doctorow,** *with* **Katrina Kenison**

Becker, Geoffrey-- "Black Elvis"

Bloom, Amy-- "The Story"

Byers, Michael-- "The Beautiful Days"

Carlson, Ron-- "The Ordinary Son"

Carver, Raymond-- "Call if You Need Me"

Davenport, Kiana-- "Bones of the Inner Ear"

Díaz, Junot-- "Nilda"

Englander, Nathan-- "The Gilgul of Park Avenue"

Everett, Percival-- "The Fix"

Gautreaux, Tim-- "Good for the Soul"

Gurganus, Allan-- "He's at the Office"

Hemon, Aleksandar-- "Blind Jozef Pronek"

Hill, Kathleen-- "The Anointed"

Jin, Ha-- "The Bridegroom"

Krysl, Marilyn-- "The Thing Around Them"

Lahiri, Jhumpa-- "The Third and Final Continent"

Mosley, Walter-- "Pet Fly"

Packer, ZZ-- "Brownies"

Pearlman, Edith-- "Allog"

Proulx, Annie-- "People in Hell Just Want a
   Drink of Water"

Sherwood, Frances-- "Basil the Dog"

### The Best American Short Stories, 2001: Selected from U.S. and Canadian Magazines,
### *edited by* **Barbara Kingsolver,** *with* **Katrina Kenison**

Barrett, Andrea-- "Servants of the Map"

Bass, Rick-- "The Fireman"

Davies, Peter Ho-- "Think of England"

Davis, Claire-- "Labors of the Heart"

Graver, Elizabeth-- "The Mourning Door

Jin, Ha-- "After Cowboy Chicken Came to Town"

Lee, Andrea-- "Brothers and Sisters Around the World"

Moody, Rick-- "Boys"

Moss, Barbara Klein-- "Rug Weaver"

Munro, Alice-- "Post and Beam"

Orner, Peter-- "The Raft"

Parvin, Roy-- "Betty Hutton"

Reisman, Nancy-- "Illumination"

Row, Jess--"The Secrets of Bats"

Sanford, Annette-- "Nobody Listens When I Talk"

Shonk, Katherine-- "My Mother's Garden"

Silver, Marisa-- "What I Saw from Where I Stood"

Trevanian-- "The Apple Tree"

Updike, John-- "Personal Archeology"

West, Dorothy-- "My Baby . . ."

### The Best American Short Stories, 2002: Selected from U.S. and Canadian Magazines,
### *edited by* **Sue Miller,** *with* **Katrina Kenison**

Chabon, Michael-- "Along the Frontage Road"

Cooke, Carolyn-- "The Sugar-Tit"

Cummins, Ann-- "The Red Ant House"

Danticat, Edwidge-- "Seven"

Doctorow, E. L.-- "A House on the Plains"

Ford, Richard-- "Puppy"

Hardy, Melissa-- "The Heifer"

Iagnemma, Karl-- "Zilkowski's Theorem"

Lahiri, Jhumpa-- "Nobody's Business"

Lordan, Beth-- "Digging"

Mattison, Alice-- "In Case We're Separated"

McCorkle, Jill-- "Billy Goats"

McNeal, Tom-- "Watermelon Days"

Michaels, Leonard-- "Nachman from Los Angeles"

Miller, Arthur-- "Bulldog"

Mullins, Meg-- "The Rug"

Munro, Alice-- "Family Furnishings"

Sharma, Akhil-- "Surrounded by Sleep"

Shepard, Jim-- "Love and Hydrogen"

Waters, Mary Yukari-- "Aftermath"

### The Best American Short Stories, 2003: Selected from U.S. and Canadian Magazines,
*edited by* **Walter Mosley,** *with* **Katrina Kenison**

Allison, Dorothy-- "Compassion"

Brockmeier, Kevin-- "Space"

Chaon, Dan-- "The Bees"

Cooper, Rand Richards-- "Johnny Hamburger"

Danticat, Edwidge-- "Night Talkers"

Doctorow, E. L.-- "Baby Wilson"

Doerr, Anthony-- "The Shell Collector"

Erdich, Louise-- "Shamengwa"

Harty, Ryan-- "Why the Sky Turns Red When the Sun Goes Down"

Haslett, Adam-- "Devotion"

Krauss, Nicole-- "Future Emergencies"

Packer, ZZ-- "Every Tongue Shall Confess"

Paschal, Dean-- "Moriya"

Phipps, Marilene-- "Marie-Ange's Ginen"

Pomerantz, Sharon-- "Ghost Knife"

Raboteau, Emily Ishem-- "Kavita Through Glass"

Row, Jess-- "Heaven Lake"

Simpson, Mona-- "Coins"

Straight, Susan-- "Mines

Waters, Mary Yukari-- "Rationing"

### The Best American Short Stories, 2004: Selected from U.S. and Canadian Magazines,
*edited by* **Lorrie Moore,** *with* **Katrina Kenison**

Alexie, Sherman-- "What You Pawn I Will Redeem"

Boyle, T. Coraghessan-- "Tooth and Claw"

Brady, Catherine-- "Written in Stone"

Bynum, Sarah Shun-lien-- "Accomplice"

D'Ambrosio, Charles-- "Screenwriter"

Dybek, Stuart-- "Breasts"

Eisenberg, Deborah-- "Some Other, Better Otto"

Fox, Paula-- "Grace"

Freudenberger, Nell-- "The Tutor"

Jones, Edward P.-- "A Rich Man"

Lewis, Trudy-- "Limestone Diner"

McCorkle, Jill-- "Intervention"

McGuane, Thomas-- "Gallatin Canyon"

Munro, Alice-- "Runaway"

Pneuman, Angela-- "All Saints Day"

Proulx, Annie-- "What Kind of Furniture Would Jesus Pick"

Smith, R. T.-- "Docent"

Updike, John-- "The Walk with Elizanne"

Waters, Mary Yukari-- "Mirror Studies"

Wideman, John Edgar-- "What We Cannot Speak About We Must Pass over in Silence"

### The Best American Short Stories, 2005: Selected from U.S. and Canadian Magazines,
*edited by* **Michael Chabon,** *with* **Katrina Kenison**

Bellows, Nathaniel-- "First Four Measures"

Bezmozgis, David-- "Natasha"

Bissell, Tom-- "Death Defier"

D'Ambrosio, Charles-- "The Scheme of Things"

Doctorow, Cory-- "Anda's Game"

Jones, Edward P.-- "Old Boys, Old Girls"

Lehane, Dennis-- "Until Gwen"

Lennon, J. Robert-- "Eight Pieces for the Left Hand"

Link, Kelly-- "Stone Animals"

McGuane, Thomas-- "Old Friends"

Means, David-- "The Secret Goldfish"

Munro, Alice-- "Silence"

Oates, Joyce Carol-- "The Cousins"

Ohlin, Alix-- "Simple Exercises for the Beginning Student"

Perotta, Tom-- "The Smile on Happy Chang's Face"

Pratt, Tom-- "Heart and Boot"

Reddi, Rishi-- "Justice Shiva Ram Murthy"

Saunders, George-- "Bohemians"

Schwartz, Lynn Sharon -- "A Taste of Dust"

Williams, Joy-- "The Girls"

### The Best American Short Stories, 2006: Selected from U.S. and Canadian Magazines, *edited by* **Ann Patchett,** *with* **Katrina Kenison**

Beattie, Ann, with Harry Matthews-- "Mr. Nobody at All"

Bell, Katherine-- "The Casual Car Pool"

Bezmozgis, David-- "A New Gravestone for an Old Grave"

Coover, Robert-- "Grandmother's Nose"

Englander, Nathan-- "How We Avenged the Bums"

Gaitskill, Mary-- "Today I'm Yours"

Hemon, Aleksandar-- "The Conductor"

Li, Yiyun-- "After a Life"

Livings, Jack-- "The Dog"

McGuane, Thomas-- "Cowboy"

Moffett, Kevin-- "Tattooizm"

Munro, Alice-- "The View from Castle Rock"

Pearlman, Edith-- "Self-Reliance"

Percy, Benjamin-- "Refresh, Refresh"

Ryan, Patrick-- "So Much for Artemis"

Slouka, Mark-- "Dominion"

Swann, Maxine-- "Secret"

Tartt, Donna-- "The Ambush"

Woolf, Tobias-- "Awaiting Orders"

Yoon, Paul-- "Once the Shore"

### The Best American Short Stories, 2007: Selected from U.S. and Canadian Magazines, *edited by* **Stephen King,** *with* **Heidi Pitlor**

Auchincloss, Louis-- "Pa's Darling"

Barth, John-- "Toga Party"

Beattie, Ann-- "Solid Wood"

Boyle, T. Coraghessan-- "Balto"

DeVita, Randy-- "Riding the Doghouse"

Epstein, Joseph-- "My Brother Eli"

Gay, William-- "Where Will You Go When Your Skin Cannot Contain You?"

Gordon, Mary-- "Eleanor's Music"

Groff, Lauren-- "L. DeBard and Aliette, a Love Story"

Jensen, Beverly-- "Wake"

Kesey, Roy-- "Wait"

Kim, Stellar-- "Findings and Impressions"

Kyle, Aryn-- "Allegiance"

McAllister, Bruce-- "Boy in Zaquitos"

Munro, Alice-- "Dimension"

Pollack, Eileen-- "Bris"

Russell, Karen-- "St. Lucy's Home for Girls Raised by Wolves"

Russo, Richard-- "Horseman"

Shepard, Jim-- "Sans Farine"

Walbert, Kate-- "Do Something"

### The Best American Short Stories, 2008: Selected from U.S. and Canadian Magazines, *edited by* **Salman Rushdie,** *with* **Heidi Pitlor**

Boyle, T. Coraghessan-- "Admiral"

Brockmeier, Kevin-- "The Year of Silence"

Brown, Karen-- "Galatea"

Chase, Katie-- "Man and Wife"

Evans, Danielle-- "Virgins"

Goodman, Allegra-- "Closely Held"

Homes, A. M.-- "May We Be Forgotten"

Krauss, Nicole-- "From the Desk of Daniel Varsky"

Lethem, Jonathan-- "The King of Sentences"

Makkai, Rebecca-- "The Worst You Ever Feel"

Millhauser, Steven-- "The Wizard of West Orange"

Mueenuddin, Daniyal-- "Nawabdin Electrician"

Munro, Alice-- "Child's Play"

Penkov, Miroslav-- "Buying Lenin"

Russell, Karen-- "Vampires in the Lemon Grove"

Saunders, George-- "Puppy"

Sneed, Christine-- "Quality of Life"

Tice, Bradford-- "Missionaries"

Wisniewski, Mark-- "Straightaway"

Wolff, Tobias-- "Bible"

### The Best American Short Stories, 2009: Selected from U.S. and Canadian Magazines, *edited by* **Alice Sebold,** *with* **Heidi Pitlor**

Alarcón, Daniel-- "The Idiot President"

Bynum, Sarah Shun-lien-- "Yurt"

De Jarnatt, Steve-- "Rubiaux Rising"

Epstein, Joseph-- "Beyond the Pale"

Fulton, Alice-- "A Shadow Table"

Greenfeld, Karl Taro-- "NowTrends"

Henderson, Eleanor-- "The Farms"

Hrbek, Greg-- "Sagittarius"

Johnson, Adam-- "Hurricanes Anonymous"

Lancelotta, Victoria-- "The Anniversary Trip"

Li, Yiyun-- "A Man Like Him"

Makkai, Rebecca-- "The Briefcase"

McCorkle, Jill-- "Magic Words"

Moffett, Kevin-- "One Dog Year"

Powers, Richard-- "Modulation"

Proulx, Annie-- "Them Old Cowboy Songs"

Rash, Ron-- "Into the Gorge"

Rose, Alex-- "Ostracon"

Rutherford, Ethan-- "The Peripatetic Coffin"

Serpell, Namwali-- "Muzungu"

### The Best American Short Stories, 2010: Selected from U.S. and Canadian Magazines, *edited by* **Richard Russo,** *with* **Heidi Pitlor**

Almond, Steve-- "Donkey Greedy, Donkey Gets Punched"

Barton, Marlin-- "Into Silence"

Baxter, Charles-- "The Cousins"

Egan, Jennifer-- "Safari"

Evans, Danielle-- "Someone Ought to Tell Her There's No Place to Go"

Ferris, Joshua-- "The Valetudinarian"

Groff, Lauren-- "Delicate Edible Birds"

Harrison, Wayne-- "Least Resistance"

Lasdun, James-- "The Hollow"

Makkai, Rebecca-- "Painted Ship, Painted Ocean"

Matthews, Brendan-- "My Last Attempt to Explain What Happened to the Lion Tamer"

### Flannery O'Connor Award for Short Fiction

Established in 1983, the University of Georgia Press presents this award to writers for an outstanding collection of short stories or novellas. The prize is named for the esteemed short-story writer and novelist Flannery O'Connor.

1983: David Walton--*Evening Out* and Leigh Allison Wilson--*From the Bottom Up*

1984: François Camoin--*Why Men Are Afraid of Women*, Mary Hood--*How Far She Went*, Susan Neville--*The Invention of Flight*, and Sandra Thompson--*Close-Ups*

1985: David Curley--*Living with Snakes* and Molly Giles--*Rough Translations*

1986: Tony Ardizzone--*The Evening News* and Peter Meinke--*The Piano Tuner*

1987: Salvatore La Puma--*The Boys of Bensonhurst* and Melissa Pritchard--*Spirit Seizures*

1988: Gail Galloway Adams--*The Purchase of Order* and Philip F. Deaver--*Silent Retreats*

1989: Carole L. Glickfeld--*Useful Gifts* and Antonya Nelson--*The Expendables*

1990: Debra Monroe--*The Source of Trouble* and Nancy Zafris--*The People I Know*

1991: Robert Abel--*Ghosts Traps* and T. M. McNally--*Low Flying Aircraft*

1992: Alfred DePew--*The Melancholy of Departure* and Dennis Hathaway--*The Consequences of Desire*

1993: Rita Ciresi--*Mother Rocket* and Dianne Nelson--*A Brief History of Male Nudes in America*

1994: Christopher McIlroy--*All My Relations* and Alyce Miller--*The Nature of Longing*

1995: Carol Lee Lorenzo--*Nervous Dancer* and C. M. Mayo--*Sky over El Nido*

1996: Wendy Brenner--*Large Animals in Everyday Life* and Paul Rawlins--*No Lie Like Love*

1997: Harvey Grossinger--*The Quarry,* Ha Jin--*Under the Red Flag,* and Andy Plattner--*Winter Money*

1998: Frank Soos--*Unified Field Theory*

1999: Mary Clyde--*Survival Rates* and Hester Kaplan--*The Edge of Marriage*

2000: Robert Anderson--*Ice Age* and Darrel Spencer--*Caution, Men in Trees*

2001: Dana Johnson--*Break Any Woman Down* and Bill Roorbach--*Big Bend*

2002: Gina Ochsner--*The Necessary Grace to Fall* and Kellie Wells--*Compression Scars*

2003: Ed Allen--*Ate It Anyway,* Catherine Brady--*Curled in the Bed of Love,* and Eric Shade--*Eyesores*

2004: Gary Fincke--*Sorry I Worried You* and Barbara Sutton--*The Send-Away Girl*

2005: David Crouse--*Copy Cats*

2006: Greg Downs--*Spit Baths* and Randy F. Nelson--*The Imaginary Lives of Mechanical Men*

2007: Peter LaSalle--*Tell Borges If You See Him: Tales of Contemporary Somnambulism,* Anne Panning--*Super America,* and Margot Singer--*The Pale of Settlement*

2008: Andrew Porter--*The Theory of Light and Matter* and Peter Selgin--*Drowning Lessons*

2009: Geoffrey Becker--*Black Elvis* and Lori Ostlund--*The Bigness of the World*

2010: Linda LeGarde Grover--*The Dance Boots* and Jessica Treadway--*Please Come Back To Me*

## Grace Paley Prize for Short Fiction

The Association of Writers and Writing Programs annually presents this award for book-length works of short fiction. It is named for American short-story writer Grace Paley.

1978: Rebecca Kavaler--*The Further Adventure of Brunhild*

1979: Ian MacMillan--*Light and Power*

1980: Eugene Garber--*Metaphysical Tales*

1981: François Camoin--*The End of the World Is Los Angeles*

1982: Alvin Greenberg--*Delta q*

1983: Charles Baxter--*Harmony of the World*

1984: Rod Kessier--*Off in Zimbabwe*

1985: No winner

1986: Jesse Lee Kercheval--*The Dogeater: Stories*

1987: Anne Finge--*Basic Skills*

1988: Roland Sodowsky--*Things We Lose*

1989: Susan Hubbard--*Walking on Ice*

1990: Karen Brennan--*Wild Desire*

1991: Jack Driscoll--*Wanting Only to Be Heard*

1992: Daniel Lyons--*The First Snow*

1993: E. Bumas--*Significance*

1994: A. Manette Ansay--*Read This and Tell Me What It Says*

1995: David Jauss--*Black Maps*

1996: Charlotte Bacon--*A Private State*

1997: Toni Graham--*The Daiquiri Girls*

1998: Bonnie Jo Campbell--*Women and Other Animals*

1999: C. J. Hribal--*The Clouds in Memphis*

2000: Michelle Richmond--*The Girl in the Fall-Away Dress*

2001: Christie Hodgen--*A Jeweler's Eye for Flaw*

2002: Joan Connor--*History Lessons*

2003: Doreen Baingana--*Tropical Fish*

2004: No winner

2005: Nona Caspers--*Heavier than Air*

2006: Karen Brown--*Pins and Needles*

2007: David Vann--*Legend of a Suicide*

2008: Ramola D--*Temporary Lives, and Other Stories*

2009: Christine Sneed--*Portraits of a Few of the People I've Made Cry*

2010: Douglas Light--*Girls in Trouble*

## PEN/Malamud Award

The PEN/Malamud Award and Memorial Reading, awarded annually by the PEN/Faulkner Foundation, recognizes excellence in "the art of the short story."

| | |
|---|---|
| 1988: John Updike | 2000: Ann Beattie and Nathan Englander |
| 1989: Saul Bellow | 2001: Sherman Alexie and Richard Ford |
| 1990: George Garrett | 2002: Junot Díaz and Ursula K. Le Guin |
| 1991: Frederick Busch and Andre Dubus | 2003: Barry Hannah and Maile Meloy |
| 1992: Eudora Welty | 2004: Richard Bausch and Nell Freudenberger |
| 1993: Peter Taylor | 2005: Lorrie Moore |
| 1994: Grace Paley | 2006: Adam Haslett and Tobias Wolff |
| 1995: Stuart Dybek and William Maxwell | 2007: Elizabeth Spencer |
| 1996: Joyce Carol Oates | 2008: Cynthia Ozick and Peter Ho Davies |
| 1997: Alice Munro | 2009: Alistair MacLeod and Amy Hempel |
| 1998: John Barth | 2010: Edward P. Jones and Nam Le |
| 1999: T. Coraghessan Boyle | |

## PEN/O. Henry Award

The O. Henry Awards, published each year in a volume entitled *Prize Stories*, were established in 1919; in 2009, prize officials partnered with the PEN American Center and the prize was renamed the PEN/O. Henry Award. The annual volume of prize-winners features stories written in English that were published in American and Canadian magazines.

### 1919

**First Prize**

Montague, Margaret Prescott-- "England to America"

**Second Prize**

Steele, Wilbur Daniel-- "For They Know Not What They Do"

**Other Selected Stories**

Alsop, Guglielma-- "The Kitchen Gods"

Cabell, James Branch-- "Porcelain Cups"

Derieux, Samuel A.-- "The Trial in Tom Belcher's Store"

Ferber, Edna-- "April Twenty-Fifth as Usual"

Hurst, Fannie-- "Humoresque"

Marshall, Edison-- "The Elephant Remembers"

Post, Melville D.-- "Five Thousand Dollars Reward"

Ravenel, Beatrice-- "The High Cost of Conscience"

Rice, Louise-- "The Lubbeny Kiss"

Springer, Thomas Grant-- "The Blood of the Dragon"

Terhune, Albert Payson-- "On Strike"

Williams, Ben Ames-- "They Grind Exceedingly Small"

Wood, Frances Gilchrist-- "Turkey Red"

### 1920

**First Prize**

Burt, Maxwell Struthers-- "Each in His Generation"

**Second Prize**

Hart, Frances Noyes-- "Contact!"

**Other Selected Stories**

Fitzgerald, F. Scott-- "The Camel's Back"

Forbes, Esther-- "Break-Neck Hill"

Gilpatric, Guy-- "Black Art and Ambrose"

Hartman, Lee Foster-- "The Judgement of Vulcan"

Hull, Alexander-- "The Argosies"

Lewis, O. F.-- "Alma Mater"

Miller, Alice Duer-- "Slow Poison"

Pelley, William Dudley-- "The Face in the Window"

Perry, Lawrence-- "A Matter of Loyalty"

Robbins, L. H.-- "Professor Todd's Used Car"

Rutledge, Maurice-- "The Thing They Loved"

Sidney, Rose-- "Butterflies"

Smith, Gordon Arthur-- "No Flowers"

Steele, Wilbur Daniel-- "Footfalls"

Whitman, Stephen French-- "The Last Room of All"

## 1921

**First Prize**

Marshall, Edison-- "The Heart of Little Shikara"

**Second Prize**

Jackson, Charles Tenney-- "The Man Who Cursed the Lillies"

**Other Selected Stories**

Allen, Maryland-- "The Urge"

Beer, Thomas-- "Mummery"

Chittenden, Gerald-- "The Victim of His Vision"

Cooper, Courtney Ryley, and Lee F. Creagan-- "Martin Gerrity Gets Even"

Cram, Mildred-- "Stranger Things"

Derieux, Samuel A.-- "Comet"

Heerman, Elizabeth Alexander-- "Fifty-Two Weeks for Florette"

Kerr, Sophie-- "Wild Earth"

Kniffin, Harry Anable-- "The Tribute"

Lewis, O. F.-- "The Get-Away"

Mumford, Ethel Watts-- "Aurore"

Robbins, L. H.-- "Mr. Downey Sits Down"

Steele, Wilbur Daniel-- "The Marriage in Kairwan"

Tupper, Tristram-- "Grit"

## 1922

**First Prize**

Cobb, Irvin S.-- "Snake Doctor"

**Second Prize**

Lane, Rose Wilder-- "Innocence"

**Best Short Short**

Buckley, F. R.-- "Gold-Mounted Guns"

**Other Selected Stories**

Alexander, Charles-- "As a Dog Should"

Barrett, Richmond Brooks-- "Art for Art's Sake"

Beer, Thomas-- "Tact"

Bennett, James W.-- "The Kiss of the Accolade"

Derieux, Samuel A.-- "The Sixth Shot"

Horn, R. de S.-- "The Jinx of the Shandon Belle"

Hull, Helen R.-- "His Sacred Family"

Jackson, Charles Tenney-- "The Horse of Hurricane Reef"

Lewis, O. F.-- "Old Peter Takes an Afternoon Off"

Morris, Gouverneur-- "Ig's Amock"

Steele, Wilbur Daniel-- "The Anglo-Saxon"

Terhune, Albert Payson-- "The Writer-Upward"

Vorse, Mary Heaton-- "Twilight of the God"

## 1923

**First Prize**

Smith, Edgar Valentine-- "Prelude"

**Second Prize**

Connell, Richard-- "A Friend of Napoleon"

**Best Short Short**

Folsom, Elizabeth Irons-- "Towers of Fame"

**Other Selected Stories**

Dell, Floyd-- "Phantom Adventure"

Farogoh, Francis Edwards-- "The Distant Street"

Glenn, Isa Urquhart-- "The Wager"

Hopper, James-- "Célestine"

Larsson, Genevieve-- "Witch Mary"

Lemmon, Robert S.-- "The Bamboo Trap"

Mahoney, James-- "The Hat of Eight Reflections"

Mason, Grace Sartwell-- "Home Brew"

Morris, Gouverneur-- "Derrick's Return"

Synon, Mary-- "Shadowed"

Tarkington, Booth-- "The One Hundred Dollar Bill"

Watts, Mary S.-- "Nice Neighbors"

Williams, Jesse Lynch-- "Not Wanted"

## 1924

**First Place**

Irwin, Inez Haynes-- "The Spring Flight"

**Second Place**

Crowell, Chester T.-- "Margaret Blake"

**Best Short Short**

Newman, Frances-- "Rachel and Her Children"

**Other Selected Stories**

Benét, Stephen Vincent-- "Uriah's Son"

Connell, Richard-- "The Most Dangerous Game"

Dobie, Charles Caldwell-- "Horse and Horse"

Mirrielees, Edith R.-- "Professor Boynton Rereads History"

Mosley, Jefferson-- "The Secret at the Crossroads"

Pattullo, George-- "The Tie That Binds"

Singmaster, Elsie-- "The Courier of the Czar"

Smith, Edgar Valentine-- "'Lijah"

Spears, Raymond S.-- "A River Combine-Professional"

Steele, Wilbur Daniel-- "What Do You Mean--Americans?"

Stone, Elinore Cowan-- "One Uses the Handkerchief"

Welles, Harriet-- "Progress"

## 1925

**First Prize**

Street, Julian-- "Mr. Bisbee's Princess"

**Second Prize**

Williams, Wythe-- "Splendid with Swords"

**Best Short Short**

Austin, Mary-- "Papago Wedding"

**Other Selected Stories**

Anderson, Sherwood-- "The Return"

Babcock, Edwina Stanton-- "Dunelight"

Brady, Mariel-- "Peter Projects"

Brecht, Harold W.-- "Two Heroes"

Carver, Ada Jack-- "Redbone"

Eliot, Ethel Cook-- "Maternal"

Hackett, Francis-- "Unshapely Things"

Heyward, DuBose-- "Crown's Bess"

Peterkin, Julia-- "Maum Lou"

Steele, Wilbur Daniel-- "The Man Who Saw Through Heaven" and "Cornelia's Mountain"

Whitlock, Brand-- "The Sofa"

## 1926

**First Prize**

Steele, Wilbur Daniel-- "Bubbles"

**Second Prize**

Anderson, Sherwood-- "Death in the Woods"

**Best Short Short**

Wetjen, Albert Richard-- "Command"

**Other Selected Stories**

Carver, Ada Jack-- "Threeshy"

Detzer, Karl W.-- "The Wreck Job"

Dobie, Charles Caldwell-- "The Thrice Bereft Widow of Hung Gow"-- "Symphonesque"

Goodloe, Abbie Carter-- "Claustrophobia"

Graeve, Oscar-- "A Death on Eighth Avenue"

Jacobs, Marguerite-- "Singing Eagles"

Kelly, Eleanor Mercein-- "Basquerie"

Saxon, Lyle-- "Cane River"

Skinner, Constance Lindsay-- "The Dew on the Fleece"

Tarkington, Booth-- "Stella Crozier"

Vorse, Mary Heaton-- "The Madelaine"

Williams, Ben Ames-- "The Nurse"

## 1927

**First Prize**

Bradford, Roark-- "Child of God"

**Second Prize**

Hemingway, Ernest-- "The Killers"

**Best Short Short**

Bromfield, Louis-- "The Scarlet"

**Other Selected Stories**

Adams, Bill-- "Jukes"

Bellah, James Warner-- "Fear"

Brush, Katherine-- "Night Club"

Carver, Ada Jack-- "Singing Woman"

Chapman, Elizabeth Cobb-- "With Glory and Honor"

Daniels, Roger-- "Bulldog"

Douglas, Marjory Stoneman-- "He Man"

Ellerbe, Alma, and Paul Ellerbe-- "Don Got Over"

Kelly, Eleanor Mercein-- "Monkey Motions"

Sawyer, Ruth-- "Four Dreams of Gram Perkins"

Suckow, Ruth-- "The Little Girl from Town"

Taylor, Ellen Dupois-- "Shades of George Sand"

## 1928

**First Prize**

Duranty, Walter-- "The Parrot"

**Second Prize**

Douglas, Marjory Stoneman-- "The Peculiar Treasure of Kings"

**Best Short Short**

Gale, Zona-- "Bridal Pond"

**Other Selected Stories**

Adams, Bill-- "Home Is the Sailor"

Aldrich, Bess Streeter-- "The Man Who Caught the Weather"

Avery, Stephen Morehouse-- "Never in This World"

Blackman, M. C.-- "Hot Copy"

Bradford, Roark-- "River Witch"

Brown, Cambray-- "Episode in a Machine Age"

Cobb, Irvin S.-- "An Episode at Pintail Lake"

Connell, Richard-- "The Law Beaters"

Hartman, Lee Foster-- "Mr. Smith" (or "Two Minutes to Live")

Johnson, Nunnally-- "The Actor"

Marquis, Don-- "O'Meara, the Mayflower--and Mrs. MacLirr" and "Lightning"

Tarleton, Fiswoode-- "Curtains" (or "Bloody Ground")

Wescott, Glenway-- "Prohibition"

## 1929
**First Prize**
Parker, Dorothy-- "Big Blonde"
**Second Prize**
Howard, Sidney-- "The Homesick Ladies"
**Best Short Short**
Brush, Katherine-- "Him and Her"
**Other Selected Stories**
Anderson, Sherwood-- "Alice"
Benét, Stephen Vincent-- "The King of the Cats"
Bromfield, Louis-- "The Skeleton at the Feast"
Brush, Katherine-- "Speakeasy"
Chapman, Maristan-- "Treat You Clever"
Johnston, Mary-- "Elephants Through the Country"
Leech, Margaret-- "Manicure"
Marquis, Don-- "The Red-Haired Woman"
Norris, Kathleen-- "Sinners"
Patterson, Pernet-- "Buttin' Blood"
Rushfeldt, Elise-- "A Coffin for Anna"
Sanborn, Ruth Burr-- "Professional Pride"
Slade, Caroline-- "Mrs. Sabin"
Steele, Wilbur Daniel-- "The Silver Sword"

## 1930
**First Prize**
Burnett, W. R.-- "Dressing-Up"
John, William H.-- "Neither Jew Nor Greek"
**Second Prize**
Roberts, Elizabeth Madox-- "The Sacrifice of the
    Maidens"
**Best Short Short**
Connelly, Marc-- "Coroner's Inquest"
**Other Selected Stories**
Bradford, Roark-- "Careless Love"
Burt, Katherine Newlin-- "Herself"
Clements, Colin-- "Lobster John's Annie"
Cobb, Irvin S.-- "Faith, Hope and Charity"
Cooper, Courtney Ryley-- "The Elephant Forgets"
DeFord, Miriam Allen-- "The Silver Knight"
Hallet, Richard Matthews-- "Misfortune's Isle"
Held, John, Jr.-- "A Man of the World"
Johnson, Nunnally-- "Mlle. Irene the Great"
March, William-- "The Little Wife"
Overbeck, Alicia O'Reardon-- "Encarnación"

Pelley, William Dudley-- "The Continental Angle"
Peterkin, Julia-- "The Diamond Ring"
Ryerson, Florence-- "Lobster John's Annie"
Steele, Wilbur Daniel-- "Conjuh"
Street, Julian-- "A Matter of Standards"
Thomason, Capt. John W., Jr.-- "Born on an Iceberg"

## 1931
**First Prize**
Steele, Wilbur Daniel-- "Can't Cross Jordan by Myself"
**Second Prize**
Swain, John D.-- "One Head Well Done"
**Third Prize**
Bradley, Mary Hastings-- "The Five-Minute Girl"
**Best Short Short**
La Farge, Oliver-- "Haunted Ground"
**Other Selected Stories**
Beems, Griffith-- "Leaf Unfolding"
Brush, Katharine-- "Good Wednesday"
Chase, Mary Ellen-- "Salesmanship"
Ryerson, Florence, and Colin Clements-- "Useless"
Dobie, Charles Caldwell-- "The False Talisman"
Faulkner, William-- "Thrift"
Hume, Cyril-- "Forrester"
Loomis, Alfred F.-- "Professional Aid"
Luhrs, Marie-- "Mrs. Schwellenbach's Receptions"
March, William-- "Fifteen from Company K"
Rice, Laverne-- "Wings for Janie"
Smith, Edgar Valentine-- "Cock-a-Doodle-Done!"
Tarkington, Booth-- "Cider of Normandy"
Thorne, Crichton Alston-- "Chimney City"

## 1932
**First Prize**
Benét, Stephen Vincent-- "An End to Dreams"
**Second Prize**
Cozzens, James Gould-- "Farewell to Cuba"
**Best Short Short**
Granberry, Edwin-- "A Trip to Czardis"
**Other Selected Stories**
Boone, Jack H.-- "Big Singing"
Boyle, Kay-- "The First Lover"
Brush, Katherine-- "Football Girl"
Canfield, Dorothy-- "Ancestral Home"
Cobb, Irvin S.-- "A Colonel of Kentucky"
Constiner, Merle-- "Big Singing"

Coombes, Evan-- "Kittens Have Fathers"
Edmonds, Walter D.-- "The Cruise of the Cashalot"
Faulkner, William-- "Turn About"
Marquand, J. P.-- "Deep Water"
Tarkington, Booth-- "She Was Right Once"

## 1933
**First Prize**
Rawlings, Marjorie Kinnan-- "Gal Young Un"
**Second Prize**
Buck, Pearl S.-- "The Frill"
**Best Short Short**
Hale, Nancy-- "To the Invader"
**Other Selected Stories**
Adams, Bill-- "The Lubber"
Aiken, Conrad-- "The Impulse"
Arnold, Len-- "Portrait of a Woman"
Caldwell, Erskine-- "Country Full of Swedes"
Fitzgerald, F. Scott-- "Family in the Wind"
Frost, Francis M.-- "The Heart Being Perished"
Haardt, Sarah-- "Absolutely Perfect"
Lane, Rose Wilder-- "Old Maid"
Robinson, Selma-- "The Departure"
Smith, Robert-- "Love Story"
Thomas, Dorothy-- "The Consecrated Coal Scuttle"
Wilde, Hagar-- "Little Brat"

## 1934
**First Prize**
Paul, Louis-- "No More Trouble for Jedwick"
**Second Prize**
Gordon, Caroline-- "Old Red"
**Third Prize**
Saroyan, William-- "The Daring Young Man on the Flying Trapeze"
**Other Selected Stories**
Appel, Benjamin-- "Pigeon Flight"
Buck, Pearl S.-- "Shanghai Scene"
Caldwell, Erskine-- "Maud Island"
Cole, Madelene-- "Bus to Biarritz"
DeFord, Miriam Allen-- "Pride"
Edmonds, Walter D.-- "Honor of the County"
Faulkner, William-- "Wash"
Fisher, Vardis-- "The Scarecrow"
Johnson, Josephine W.-- "Dark"
Sherman, Richard-- "First Flight"

Steinbeck, John-- "The Murder"
Stribling, T. S.-- "Guileford"
Sylvester, Harry-- "A Boxer: Old"
Wexley, John-- "Southern Highway Fifty-one"
Wolfe, Thomas-- "Boom Town"
Zugsmith, Leane-- "King Lear in Evansville"

## 1935
**First Prize**
Boyle, Kay-- "The White Horses of Vienna"
**Second Prize**
Thomas, Dorothy-- "The Home Place"
**Third Prize**
Johnson, Josephine W.-- "John the Six"
**Other Selected Stories**
Algren, Nelson-- "The Brother's House"
Benét, Stephen Vincent-- "The Professor's Punch"
Hamill, Katherine-- "Leora's Father"
Kantor, MacKinlay-- "Silent Grow the Guns"
Mamet, Louis-- "A Writer Interviews a Banker"
Marquis, Don-- "Country Doctor"
McCleary, Dorothy-- "Little Elise"
O'Donnell, E. P.-- "Jesus Knew"
Paul, Louis-- "Lay Me Low!"
Santee, Ross-- "Water"
Saroyan, William-- "Five Ripe Pears"
Shenton, Edward-- "When Spring Brings Back. . ."
Sherman, Richard-- "First Day"
Terrell, Upton-- "Long Distance"
Weidman, Jerome-- "My Father Sits in the Dark"
Wolfe, Thomas-- "Only the Dead Know Brooklyn"

## 1936
**First Prize**
Cozzens, James Gould-- "Total Stranger"
**Second Prize**
Benson, Sally-- "Suite Twenty Forty-nine"
**Best Short Short**
March, William-- "A Sum in Addition"
**Other Selected Stories**
Bessie, Alvah C.-- "A Personal Issue"
Bird, Virginia-- "Havoc Is Circle"
Brace, Ernest-- "Silent Whistle"
Cain, James M.-- "Dead Man"
Coatsworth, Elizabeth-- "The Visit"
Colby, Nathalie-- "Glass Houses"

Driftmier, Lucille-- "For My Sister"
Edmonds, Walter D.-- "Escape from the Mine"
Faulkner, William-- "Lion"
Gale, Zona-- "Crisis"
Godchaux, Elma-- "Chains"
Heth, Edward Harris-- "Big Days Beginning"
Horgan, Paul-- "The Trunk"
Katterjohn, Elsie-- "Teachers"
Knight, Eric-- "The Marne"
Owen, Janet Curren-- "Afternoon of a Young Girl"

## 1937
**First Prize**
Benét, Stephen Vincent-- "The Devil and Daniel Webster"
**Second Prize**
Moll, Elick-- "To Those Who Wait"
**Third Prize**
Coates, Robert M.-- "The Fury"
**Other Selected Stories**
Appel, Benjamin-- "Awroopdedoop!"
Bird, Virginia-- "For Nancy's Sake"
DeJong, David Cornel-- "The Chicory Neighbors"
Hale, Nancy-- "To the North"
Hilton, Charles-- "Gods of Darkness"
Hunt, Hamlen-- "The Saluting Doll"
March, William-- "The Last Meeting"
Martin, Charles-- "Hobogenesis"
McKeon, J. M.-- "The Gladiator"
O'Hara, John-- "My Girls"
Patten, Katherine-- "Man Among Men"
Pereda, Prudencio de-- "The Spaniard"
Seager, Allan-- "Pro Arte"
Still, James-- "Job's Tears"
Stuart, Jesse-- "Whip-Poor-Willie"
Thibault, David-- "A Woman Like Dilsie"
Warren, Robert Penn-- "Christmas Gift"
Weidman, Jerome-- "Thomas Hardy's Meat"

## 1938
**First Prize**
Maltz, Albert-- "The Happiest Man on Earth"
**Second Prize**
Wright, Richard-- "Fire and Cloud"
**Third Prize**
Steinbeck, John-- "The Promise"

**Other Selected Stories**
Benét, Stephen Vincent-- "Johnny Pye and the Fool-Killer"
Bradley, Mary Hastings-- "The Life of the Party"
Caldwell, Erskine-- "Man and Woman"
Daly, Maureen-- "Sixteen"
Fuchs, Daniel-- "The Amazing Mystery at Storick, Dorschi, Pflaumer, Inc."
Hale, Nancy-- "Always Afternoon"
Hunt, Hamlen-- "Only by Chance Are Pioneers Made"
Moll, Elick-- "Memoir of Spring"
Saroyan, William-- "The Summer of the Beautiful White Horse"
Still, James-- "So Large a Thing as Seven"
Whitehand, Robert-- "The Fragile Bud"

## 1939
**First Prize**
Faulkner, William-- "Barn Burning"
**Second Prize**
Still, James-- "Bat Flight"
**Third Prize**
DeJong, David Cornel-- "Calves"
**Other Selected Stories**
Baker, Dorothy-- "Keeley Street Blues"
Boyle, Kay-- "Anschluss"
Brand, Millen-- "The Pump"
Burt, Maxwell Struthers-- "The Fawn"
Caldwell, Erskine-- "The People V. Abe Lathan, Colored"
Cooke, Charles-- "Nothing Can Change It"
Foster, Joseph O'Kane-- "Gideon"
Gordon, Caroline-- "Frankie and Thomas and Bud Asbury"
Shaw, Irwin-- "God on a Friday Night"
St. Joseph, Ellis-- "A Knocking at the Gate"
Thielen, Benedict-- "Silver Virgin"
Welty, Eudora-- "Petrified Man"

## 1940
**First Prize**
Benét, Stephen Vincent-- "Freedom's a Hard-Bought Thing"
**Second Prize**
Lull, Roderick-- "Don't Get Me Wrong"
**Third Prize**
Havill, Edward-- "The Kill"

**Other Selected Stories**

Boyle, Kay-- "Poor Monsieur Panalitus"

Brooks, Roy Patchen-- "Without Hal"

Coates, Robert M.-- "Let's Not Talk About It Now"

Faulkner, William-- "Hand upon the Waters"

Hale, Nancy-- "That Woman"

King, Mary-- "Chicken on the Wind"

Lumpkin, Grace-- "The Treasure"

McCleary, Dorothy-- "Mother's Helper"

Porter, Katherine Anne-- "The Downward Path to Wisdom"

Rawlings, Marjorie Kinnan-- "The Pelican's Shadow"

Robinson, Mabel L.-- "Called For"

Saroyan, William-- "The Three Swimmers and the Educated Grocer"

Tracy, Tom-- "Homecoming"

Wright, Richard-- "Almos' a Man"

## 1941

**First Prize**

Boyle, Kay-- "Defeat"

**Second Prize**

Welty, Eudora-- "A Worn Path"

**Third Prize**

Abbett, Hallie Southgate-- "Eighteenth Summer"

**Best First-Published Story**

Logan, Andy-- "The Visit"

**Other Selected Stories**

Aiken, Conrad-- "Hello, Tib"

Algren, Nelson-- "A Bottle of Milk for Mother (Biceps)"

Benson, Sally-- "Retreat"

Cheever, John-- "I'm Going to Asia"

Clark, Walter Van Tilburg-- "Hook"

DeJong, David Cornel-- "Seven Boys Take a Hill"

Faulkner, William-- "The Old People"

Gallico, Paul-- "The Snow Goose"

Hale, Nancy-- "Those Are as Brothers"

Kunasz, Paul-- "I'd Give It All up for Tahiti"

Maltz, Albert-- "Afternoon in the Jungle"

Morris, Edita-- "Caput Mortum"

O'Hara, Mary-- "My Friend Flicka"

Sheean, Vincent-- "The Conqueror"

Still, James-- "The Proud Walkers"

Thomas, Dorothy-- "My Pigeon Pair"

## 1942

**First Prize**

Welty, Eudora-- "The Wide Net"

**Second Prize**

Stegner, Wallace-- "Two Rivers"

**Third Prize**

Schramm, Wilbur L.-- "Windwagon Smith"

**Best First-Published Story**

Wylie, Jeanne E.-- "A Long Way to Go"

**Other Selected Stories**

Boyle, Kay-- "Their Name Is Macaroni"

Clark, Walter Van Tilburg-- "The Portable Phonograph"

Davis, Robert Gorham-- "An Interval Like This"

DeJong, David Cornel-- "Snow-on-the-Mountain"

Faulkner, William-- "Two Soldiers"

Green, Eleanor-- "The Dear Little Doves"

Hale, Nancy-- "Sunday-1913"

Jaynes, Clare-- "The Coming of Age"

Johnson, Josephine W.-- "Alexander to the Park"

Laing, Alexander-- "The Workmanship Has to be Wasted"

McCullers, Carson-- "The Jockey"

Shuman, John Rogers-- "Yankee Odyssey"

Steinbeck, John-- "How Edith McGillcuddy Met R. L. Stevenson"

Stuart, Alison-- "The Yodeler"

Sullivan, Richard-- "Feathers"

Weidman, Jerome-- "Basket Carry"

Worthington, Marjorie-- "Hunger"

## 1943

**First Prize**

Welty, Eudora-- "Livvie Is Back"

**Second Prize**

Canfield, Dorothy-- "The Knot Hole"

**Third Prize**

Fifield, William-- "The Fisherman of Patzcuaro"

**Best First-Published Story**

Laidlaw, Clara-- "The Little Black Boys"

**Other Selected Stories**

Boyle, Kay-- "The Canals of Mars"

Breuer, Bessie-- "Pigeons en Casserole"

Buck, Pearl S.-- "The Enemy"

Clark, Walter Van Tilburg-- "The Ascent of Ariel
    Goodbody"
Cook, Whitfield-- "The Unfaithful"
Grinnell, Sarah-- "Standby"
Grossberg, Elmer-- "Black Boy's Good Time"
Hale, Nancy-- "Who Lived and Died Believing"
Johnson, Josephine W.-- "The Glass Pigeon"
Lampman, Ben Hur-- "Blinker was a Good Dog"
McCullers, Carson-- "A Tree. A Rock. A Cloud"
Saroyan, William-- "Knife-like, Flower-like, Like
    Nothing at All in the World"
Smith, Margarita G.-- "White for the Living"
Strong, Austin-- "She Shall Have Music"
Stuart, Alison-- "Death and My Uncle Felix"
Thurber, James-- "The Cane in the Corridor"
Von der Goltz, Peggy-- "The Old She 'Gator"
White, William C.-- "Pecos Bill and the Willful
    Coyote"

## 1944
**First Prize**
Shaw, Irwin-- "Walking Wounded"
**Second Prize**
Breuer, Bessie-- "Home Is a Place"
**Third Prize**
Beems, Griffith-- "The Stagecoach"
**Best First-Published Story**
Yerby, Frank G.-- "Health Card"
**Other Selected Stories**
Clark, Walter Van Tilburg-- "The Buck in the Hills"
Eastman, Elizabeth-- "Like a Field Mouse over
    the Heart"
Fineman, Morton-- "Soldier of the Republic"
Fleming, Berry-- "Strike up a Stirring Music"
Hope, Marjorie-- "That's My Brother"
Johnson, Josephine W.-- "Night Flight"
Knight, Ruth Adams-- "What a Darling Little Boy"
Loveridge, George-- "The Fur Coat"
Osborne, Margaret-- "Maine"
Powers, J. F.-- "Lions, Harts, Leaping Does"
Roane, Marianne-- "Quitter"
Schmitt, Gladys-- "All Souls'"
Schorer, Mark-- "Blockbuster"
Stuart, Alison-- "Sunday Liberty"
Weston, Christine-- "Raziya"

Wilcox, Wendall-- "The Pleasures of Travel"
Young, Marguerite-- "Old James"

## 1945
**First Prize**
Clark, Walter Van Tilburg-- "The Wind and the
    Snow of Winter"
**Second Prize**
Shaw, Irwin-- "Gunner's Passage"
**Third Prize**
Lampman, Ben Hur-- "Old Bill Bent to Drink"
**Other Selected Stories**
Breuer, Bessie-- "Bury Your Own Dead"
Critchell, Laurence-- "Flesh and Blood"
Deasy, Mary-- "Long Shadow on the Lawn"
Fenton, Edward-- "Burial in the Desert"
Gerry, Bill-- "Understand What I Mean"
Gordon, Ethel Edison-- "War Front: Louisiana"
Hardwick, Elizabeth-- "The People on the
    Roller Coaster"
Heyert, Murray-- "The New Kid"
Hubbell, Catherine-- "Monday at Six"
Lavin, Mary-- "The Sand Castle"
Martin, Hansford-- "The Thousand-Yard Stare"
Patton, Frances Gray-- "A Piece of Bread"
Portugal, Ruth-- "Call a Solemn Assembly"
Powers, J. F.-- "The Trouble"
Seager, Allan-- "The Conqueror"
Shattuck, Katharine-- "Subway System"
Smith, Louise Reinhardt-- "The Hour of Knowing"
West, Jessamyn-- "Lead Her Like a Pigeon"
Wilson, Michael-- "Come Away Home"

## 1946
**First Prize**
Goss, John Mayo-- "Bird Song"
**Second Prize**
Shedd, Margaret-- "The Innocent Bystander"
**Third Prize**
Ullman, Victor-- "Sometimes You Break Even"
**Best First-Published Story**
Meyer, Cord, Jr.-- "Waves of Darkness"
**Other Selected Stories**
Berryman, John-- "The Imaginary Jew"
Boyle, Kay-- "Winter Night"

Brookhouser, Frank-- "Request for Sherwood Anderson"

Canfield, Dorothy-- "Sex Education"

Capote, Truman-- "Miriam"

Enright, Elizabeth-- "I Forgot Where I Was"

Hardwick, Elizabeth-- "What We Have Missed"

Highsmith, Patricia-- "The Heroine"

Hutchins, M. P.-- "Innocents"

Le Sueur, Meridel-- "Breathe Upon These Slain"

Lytle, Andrew-- "The Guide"

McCleary, Dorothy-- "Not Very Close"

Rawlings, Marjorie Kinnan-- "Black Secret"

Savler, David S.-- "The Beggar"

Shaw, Irwin-- "Act of Faith"

Thielen, Benedict-- "The Empty Sky"

Welty, Eudora-- "A Sketching Trip"

West, Jessamyn-- "The Blackboard"

## 1947

**First Prize**

Clayton, John Bell-- "The White Circle"

**Second Prize**

Burdick, Eugene L.-- "Rest Camp on Maui"

**Third Prize**

Parsons, Elizabeth-- "The Nightingales Sing"

**Best First-Published Story**

Lewis, Robert-- "Little Victor"

**Other Selected Stories**

Bowles, Paul-- "The Echo"

Bradbury, Ray-- "Homecoming"

Breuer, Bessie-- "The Skeleton and the Easter Lily"

Cobb, Jane-- "The Hot Day"

Deasy, Mary-- "The Holiday"

DeJong, David Cornel-- "The Record"

Elder, Walter-- "You Can Wreck It"

Eustis, Helen-- "An American Home"

Govan, Christine Noble-- "Miss Winters and the Wind"

Kuehn, Susan-- "The Rosebush"

Lynch, John A.-- "The Burden"

Powers, J. F.-- "The Valiant Woman"

Shedd, Margaret-- "The Great Fire of 1945"

Shorer, Mark-- "What We Don't Know Hurts Us"

Smith, John Caswell, Jr.-- "Fighter"

Stafford, Jean-- "The Hope Chest"

Thielen, Benedict-- "Old Boy--New Boy"

Welty, Eudora-- "The Whole World Knows"

West, Jessamyn-- "Horace Chooney, M.D."

## 1948

**First Prize**

Capote, Truman-- "Shut a Final Door"

**Second Prize**

Stegner, Wallace-- "Beyond the Glass Mountain"

**Third Prize**

Bradbury, Ray-- "Powerhouse"

**Best First-Published Story**

Grennard, Elliot-- "Sparrow's Last Jump"

**Other Selected Stories**

Brookhouser, Frank-- "She Did Not Cry at All"

Gidney, James B.-- "The Muse and Mr. Parkinson"

Gordon, Caroline-- "The Petrified Woman"

Greene, Mary Frances-- "The Silent Day"

Hartley, Lodwick-- "Mr. Henig's Wall"

Hauser, Marianne-- "The Other Side of the River"

Ingles, James Wesley-- "The Wind Is Blind"

Janeway, Elizabeth-- "Child of God"

La Farge, Christopher-- "The Three Aspects"

Malkin, Richard-- "Pico Never Forgets"

Morse, Robert-- "The Professor and the Puli"

Parsons, Elizabeth-- "Welcome Home"

Shattuck, Katharine-- "The Answer"

Shelton, William R.-- "The Snow Girl"

Sorenson, Virginia-- "The Talking Stick"

Sulkin, Sidney-- "The Plan"

Terrett, Courtenay-- "The Saddle"

Watson, John-- "The Gun on the Table"

West, Ray B., Jr.-- "The Ascent"

## 1949

**First Prize**

Faulkner, William-- "A Courtship"

**Second Prize**

Van Doren, Mark-- "The Watchman"

**Third Prize**

Dorrance, Ward-- "The White Hound"

**Other Selected Stories**

Ashworth, John-- "High Diver"

Bowles, Paul-- "Pastor Dowe at Tacate"

Calisher, Hortense-- "The Middle Drawer"

Coatsworth, Elizabeth-- "Bremen's"

Connell, Evan S., Jr.-- "I'll Take You to Tennessee"

Conrad, Barnaby-- "Cayetano the Perfect"
Cramer, Alice Carver-- "The Boy Next Door"
Downey, Harris-- "The Mulhausen Girls"
Enright, Elizabeth-- "The Trumpeter Swan"
Goss, John Mayo-- "Evening and Morning Prayer"
Jackson, Shirley-- "The Lottery"
Lavin, Mary-- "Single Lady"
Pierce, Phoebe-- "The Season of Miss Maggie Reginald"
Plagemann, Bentz-- "The Best Bread"
Rice, John Andrew-- "You Can Get Just So Much Justice"
Salinger, J. D.-- "Just Before the War with the Eskimos"
Stafford, Jean-- "A Summer Day"
Weaver, John D.-- "Meeting Time"
West, Jessamyn-- "Public Address System"
Wilson, Leon-- "Six Months Is No Long Time"

## 1950
**First Prize**
Stegner, Wallace-- "The Blue-Winged Teal"
**Second Prize**
Leiper, Gudger Bart-- "The Magnolias"
**Third Prize**
Lowry, Robert-- "Be Nice to Mr. Campbell"
**Other Selected Stories**
Algren, Nelson-- "The Captain Is Impaled"
Bennett, Peggy-- "Death Under the Hawthorns"
Berry, John-- "New Shoes"
Boyle, Kay-- "Summer Evening"
Cheever, John-- "Vega"
Chidester, Ann-- "Mrs. Ketting and Clark Gable"
Enright, Elizabeth-- "The Sardillion"
Humphrey, William-- "The Hardy's"
Justice, Donald-- "The Lady"
Kuehn, Susan-- "The Hunt"
Lamkin, Speed-- "Comes a Day"
Newhouse, Edward-- "Seventy Thousand Dollars"
Parsons, Elizabeth-- "Not a Soul Will Come Along"
Putman, Clay-- "The Wounded"
Robinson, Leonard Wallace-- "The Ruin of Soul"
Salinger, J. D.-- "For Esmé--With Love and Squalor"
Switzer, Robert-- "Death of a Prize Fighter"
Taylor, Peter-- "Their Losses"

Van Ness, Lilian-- "Give My Love to Maggie"
Winslow, Anne Goodwin-- "Seasmiles"

## 1951
**First Prize**
Downey, Harris-- "The Hunters"
**Second Prize**
Welty, Eudora-- "The Burning"
**Third Prize**
Capote, Truman-- "The House of Flowers"
**Other Selected Stories**
Casper, Leonard-- "Sense of Direction"
Cheever, John-- "The Pot of Gold"
Connell, Evan S., Jr.-- "I Came from Yonder Mountain"
Culver, Monty-- "Black Water Blues"
Faulkner, William-- "A Name for the City"
Hall, James B.-- "In the Time of Demonstrations"
Hersey, John-- "Peggety's Parcel of Shortcomings"
Kensinger, Faye Riter-- "A Sense of Destination"
La Farge, Oliver-- "Old Century's River"
Love, Peggy Harding-- "The Jersey Heifer"
Macauley, Robie-- "The Invaders"
McCullers, Carson-- "The Sojourner"
Miller, Arthur-- "Monte Saint Angelo"
Patt, Esther-- "The Butcherbirds"
Patterson, Elizabeth Gregg-- "Homecoming"
Phillips, Thomas Hal-- "The Shadow of an Arm"
Rooney, Frank-- "Cyclists' Raid"
Shirley, Sylvia-- "Slow Journey"
Smith, John Campbell-- "Who Too Was a Soldier"
Stafford, Jean-- "A Country Love Story"
Thompson, R. E.-- "It's a Nice Day--Sunday"

## 1954
**First Prize**
Mabry, Thomas-- "The Indian Feather"
**Second Prize**
Putman, Clay-- "The News from Troy"
**Third Prize**
Wilbur, Richard-- "A Game of Catch"
**Other Selected Stories**
Cassill, R. V.-- "The War in the Air"
Clay, Richard-- "Very Sharp for Jagging"
Elliott, George P.-- "A Family Matter"
Gold, Herbert-- "The Witch"
Hall, James B.-- "Estate and Trespass: A Gothic Story"

Harnden, Ruth-- "Rebellion"

Justice, Donald-- "Vineland's Burning"

Lowrey, P. H.-- "Too Young to Have a Gun"

Maxwell, James A.-- "Fighter"

O'Connor, Flannery-- "The Life You Save May Be Your Own"

Rugel, Miriam-- "The Flower"

Stafford, Jean-- "The Shorn Lamb"

Stern, Richard G.-- "The Sorrows of Captain Schreiber"

Walker, Augusta-- "The Day of the Cipher"

Wallace, Robert-- "The Secret Weapon of Joe Smith"

West, Jessamyn-- "Breach of Promise"

Whitmore, Stanford-- "Lost Soldier"

Whittemore, Reed-- "The Stutz and the Tub"

Wilner, Herbert-- "Whistle and the Heroes"

Worthington, Rex-- "A Kind of Scandal"

## 1955

**First Prize**

Stafford, Jean-- "In the Zoo"

**Second Prize**

O'Connor, Flannery-- "A Circle in the Fire"

**Third Prize**

Buechner, Frederick-- "The Tiger"

**Other Selected Stories**

Bingham, Robert-- "The Unpopular Passenger"

Calisher, Hortense-- "A Christmas Carillon"

Cassill, R. V.-- "The Inland Years"

Cheever, John-- "The Five-forty-eight"

Elliott, George P.-- "Miss Cudahy of Stowes Landing"

Enright, Elizabeth-- "The Operator"

Fowler, Mary Dewees-- "Man of Distinction"

Fuchs, Daniel-- "Twilight in Southern California"

Grau, Shirley Ann-- "Joshua"

Graves, John-- "The Green Fly"

Powers, J. F.-- "The Presence of Grace"

Shultz, William Henry-- "The Shirts off Their Backs"

Steele, Max-- "The Wanton Troopers"

Stegner, Wallace-- "The City of the Living"

Wolfert, Ira-- "The Indomitable Blue"

## 1956

**First Prize**

Cheever, John-- "The Country Husband"

**Second Prize**

Buechler, James-- "Pepicelli"

**Third Prize**

Cassill, R. V.-- "The Prize"

**Other Selected Stories**

Bellow, Saul-- "The Gonzaga Manuscripts"

Calisher, Hortense-- "The Night Club in the Woods"

Carr, Archie-- "The Black Beach"

Coates, Robert M.-- "In a Foreign City"

Faulkner, William-- "Race at Morning"

Gold, Herbert-- "A Celebration for Joe"

Macauley, Robie-- "The Chevigny Man"

Nemerov, Howard-- "Tradition"

Stafford, Jean-- "Beatrice Trueblood's Story"

Steinbeck, John-- "The Affair at Seven, Rue de M--- "

Whitehill, Joseph-- "Able Baker"

Yates, Richard-- "The Best of Everything"

## 1957

**First Prize**

O'Connor, Flannery-- "Greenleaf"

**Second Prize**

Gold, Herbert-- "Encounter in Haiti"

**Third Prize**

Elliott, George P.-- "Miracle Play"

**Other Selected Stories**

Blassingame, Wyatt-- "Man's Courage"

Cassill, R. V.-- "When Old Age Shall This Generation Waste"

Cheever, John-- "The Journal of an Old Gent"

Faulkner, William-- "By the People"

Granit, Arthur-- "Free the Canaries from Their Cages!"

Langdon, John-- "The Blue Serge Suit"

Liberman, M. M.-- "Big Buick to the Pyramids"

Marsh, Willard-- "Last Tag"

McCarthy, Mary-- "Yellowstone Park"

Miller, Nolan-- "A New Life"

Rich, Cynthia Marshall-- "My Sister's Marriage"

Settle, Mary Lee-- "The Old Wives' Tale"

Shaw, Irwin-- "Then We Were Three"

Stafford, Jean-- "The Warlock"

Sunwall, Betty-- "Things Changed"

Thurman, Richard Young-- "The Credit Line"

Walter, Eugene-- "I Love You Batty Sisters"

## 1958

**First Prize**

Gellhorn, Martha-- "In Sickness as in Health"

**Second Prize**

Calisher, Hortense-- "What a Thing, to Keep a Wolf in a Cage!"

**Third Prize**

Steiner, George-- "The Deeps of the Sea"

**Other Selected Stories**

Berriault, Gina-- "The Stone Boy"

Blanton, Lowell D.-- "The Long Night"

Brown, T. K., III-- "A Drink of Water"

Clemons, Walter-- "A Summer Shower"

Enright, Elizabeth-- "The Eclipse"

Granat, Robert-- "My Apples"

Hale, Nancy-- "A Slow Boat to China"

Litwak, Leo-- "The Making of a Clock"

Matthiessen, Peter-- "Travelin Man"

Newhouse, Edward-- "The Ambassador"

Shore, Wilma-- "A Cow on the Roof"

Stafford, Jean-- "My Blithe, Sad Bird"

White, Robin-- "First Voice"

Wilner, Herbert-- "The Passion for Silver's Arm"

## 1959

**First Prize**

Taylor, Peter-- "Venus, Cupid, Folly, and Time"

**Second Prize**

Elliott, George P.-- "Among the Dangs"

**Third Prize**

Turner, Thomas C.-- "Something to Explain"

**Other Selected Stories**

Baldwin, James-- "Come Out of the Wilderness"

Buchwald, Emilie Bix-- "The Present"

Cheever, John-- "The Trouble of Marcie Flint"

Currie, Ellen-- "Tib's Eve"

Eastlake, William-- "Flight of the Circle Heart"

Filer, Tom-- "The Last Voyage"

Harris, MacDonald-- "Second Circle"

O'Connor, Flannery-- "A View of the Woods"

Sandburg, Helga-- "Witch Chicken"

Stafford, Jean-- "A Reasonable Facsimile"

Stone, Alma-- "The Bible Salesman"

Williams, Thomas-- "Goose Pond"

## 1960

**First Prize**

Hall, Lawrence Sargent-- "The Ledge"

**Second Prize**

Roth, Philip-- "Defender of the Faith"

**Third Prize**

White, Robin-- "Shower of Ashes"

**Other Selected Stories**

Berkman, Sylvia-- "Ellen Craig"

Berriault, Gina-- "Sublime Child"

Enright, Elizabeth-- "A Gift of Light"

Fowler, Janet-- "A Day for Fishing"

Gold, Herbert-- "Love and Like"

Granat, Robert-- "To Endure"

Henderson, Robert-- "Immortality"

Kentfield, Calvin-- "In the Cauldron"

Ogden, Maurice-- "Freeway to Wherever"

Purdy, James-- "Encore"

Spencer, Elizabeth-- "First Dark"

Swarthout, Glendon-- "A Glass of Blessings"

Ziller, Eugene-- "Sparrows"

## 1961

**First Prize**

Olson, Tillie-- "Tell Me a Riddle"

**Second Prize**

Gold, Ivan-- "The Nickel Misery of George Washington Carver Brown"

**Third Prize**

Price, Reynolds-- "One Sunday in Late July"

**Other Selected Stories**

Burgess, Jackson-- "The Magician"

Currie, Ellen-- "O Lovely Appearance of Death"

Ford, Jesse Hill-- "How the Mountains Are Made"

Krause, Ervin D.-- "The Quick and the Dead"

Ludwig, Jack-- "Thoreau in California"

Miller, Arthur-- "I Don't Need You Any More"

Shaber, David-- "A Nous La Liberté"

Taylor, Peter-- "Heads of Houses"

Updike, John-- "Wife-Wooing"

## 1962

**First Prize**

Porter, Katherine Anne-- "Holiday"

**Second Prize**

Pynchon, Thomas-- "Under the Rose"

**Third Prize**

Cole, Tom-- "Familiar Usage in Leningrad"

**Other Selected Stories**
Adams, Thomas E.-- "Sled"
Deasy, Mary-- "The People with the Charm"
Grau, Shirley Ann-- "Eight O'Clock One Morning"
Graves, John-- "The Aztec Dog"
Howard, Maureen-- "Bridgeport Bus"
Jackson, David-- "The English Gardens"
McKenzie, Miriam-- "Deja Vu"
Price, Reynolds-- "The Warrior Princess Ozimba"
Schoonover, Shirley W.-- "The Star Blanket"
Shaber, David-- "Professorio Collegio"
Updike, John-- "The Doctor's Wife"
Whitbread, Thomas-- "The Rememberer"

## 1963
**First Prize**
O'Connor, Flannery-- "Everything That Rises Must
    Converge"
**Second Prize**
Krause, Ervin D.-- "The Snake"
**Third Prize**
Selz, Thalia-- "The Education of a Queen"
**Other Selected Stories**
Ansell, Helen Essary-- "The Threesome"
Berkman, Sylvia-- "Pontifex"
Cox, James Trammell-- "That Golden Crane"
Douglas, Ellen-- "On the Lake"
Klein, Norma-- "The Burglar"
Maddow, Ben-- "In a Cold Hotel"
McClure, J. G.-- "The Rise of the Proletariat"
Oates, Joyce Carol-- "The Fine White Mist of Winter"
Saroyan, William-- "Gaston"
Southern, Terry-- "The Road Out of Axotle"
West, Jessamyn-- "The Picknickers"

## 1964
**First Prize**
Cheever, John-- "The Embarkment for Cythera"
**Second Prize**
Oates, Joyce Carol-- "Stigmata"
**Third Prize**
Shedd, Margaret-- "The Everlasting Witness"
**Other Selected Stories**
Bingham, Sallie-- "The Banks of the Ohio"
Calisher, Hortense-- "The Scream on Fifty-seventh
    Street"

Lanning, George-- "Something Just for Me"
Malamud, Bernard-- "The Jewbird"
Ross, Lillian-- "Night and Day, Day and Night"
Roth, Philip-- "Novotnoy's Pain"
Sara-- "So I'm Not Lady Chatterly, So Better I Should
    Know It Now"
Schoonover, Shirley W.-- "Old and Country Tale"
Shaw, Irwin-- "The Inhabitants of Venus"
Stacton, David-- "The Metamorphosis of Kenko"
Stegner, Wallace-- "Carrion Spring"
Zorn, George A.-- "Thompson"

## 1965
**First Prize**
O'Connor, Flannery-- "Revelation"
**Second Prize**
Friedman, Sanford-- "Ocean"
**Third Prize**
Humphrey, William-- "The Ballad of Jesse
    Neighbours"
**Other Selected Stories**
Barthelme, Donald-- "Margins"
Beagle, Peter S.-- "Come Lady Death"
Cavanaugh, Arthur-- "What I Wish (Oh, I Wish) I
    Had Said"
Curley, Daniel-- "Love in the Winter"
Ludwig, Jack-- "A Woman of Her Age"
Manoff, Eva-- "Mama and the Spy"
Mayer, Tom-- "Homecoming"
McCarthy, Mary-- "The Hounds of Summer"
McCullers, Carson-- "Sucker"
Miller, Warren-- "Chaos, Disorder, and the Late Show"
Oates, Joyce Carol-- "First Views of the Enemy"
Potter, Nancy A. J.-- "Sunday's Children"
Rooke, Leon-- "If Lost Return to the Swiss Arms"
Taylor, Peter-- "There"
Wolf, Leonard-- "Fifty-Fifty"

## 1966
**First Prize**
Updike, John-- "The Bulgarian Poetess"
**Second Prize**
Howard, Maureen-- "Sherry"
**Third Prize**
Cole, Tom-- "On the Edge of Arcadia"
**Other Selected Stories**

Berriault, Gina-- "The Birthday Party"
Bingham, Sallie-- "Bare Bones"
Davis, Christopher-- "A Man of Affairs"
Ford, Jesse Hill-- "To the Open Water"
Greene, Philip L.-- "One of You Must Be
    Wendell Corey"
Hale, Nancy-- "Sunday Lunch"
McKinley, Georgia-- "The Mighty Distance"
Michaels, Leonard-- "Sticks and Stones"
Petrakis, Harry Mark-- "The Prison"
Randall, Vera-- "Alice Blaine"
Spencer, Elizabeth-- "Ship Island"
Williams, Joy-- "The Roomer"
Zorn, George A.-- "Mr. and Mrs. McGill"

## 1967

**First Prize**

Oates, Joyce Carol-- "In the Region of Ice"

**Second Prize**

Barthelme, Donald-- "See the Moon?"

**Third Prize**

Strong, Jonathan-- "Supperburger"

**Other Selected Stories**

Buechler, James-- "The Second Best Girl"
Finney, Ernest J.-- "The Investigator"
Ford, Jesse Hill-- "The Bitter Bread"
Jacobsen, Josephine-- "On the Island"
Knickerbocker, Conrad-- "Diseases of the Heart"
Kurtz, M. R.-- "Waxing Wroth"
Macauley, Robie-- "Dressed in Shade"
Mudrick, Marvin-- "Cleopatra"
Oliver, Diane-- "Neighbors"
Updike, John-- "Marching Through Boston"
Wheelis, Allen-- "Sea-Girls"
Yates, Richard-- "A Good and Gallant Woman"

## 1968

**First Prize**

Welty, Eudora-- "The Demonstrators"

**Second Prize**

Broner, E. M.-- "The New Nobility"

**Third Prize**

Katz, Shlomo-- "My Redeemer Cometh . . ."

**Other Selected Stories**

Branda, Eldon-- "The Dark Days of Christmas"
Brower, Brock-- "Storm Still"

Franklin, F. K.-- "Nigger Horse"
Gration, Gwen-- "Teacher"
Hale, Nancy-- "The Most Elegant Drawing Room
    in Europe"
Hall, James B.-- "A Kind of Savage"
Harris, Marilyn-- "Icarus Again"
Kentfield, Calvin-- "Near the Line"
Klein, Norma-- "Magic"
Neugeboren, Jay-- "Ebbets Field"
Oates, Joyce Carol-- "Where Are You Going, Where
    Have You Been?"
Stacton, David-- "Little Brother Nun"
Tyner, Paul-- "How You Play the Game"
Updike, John-- "Your Lover Just Called"

## 1969

**First Prize**

Malamud, Bernard-- "Man in the Drawer"

**Second Prize**

Oates, Joyce Carol-- "Accomplished Desires"

**Third Prize**

Barth, John-- "Lost in the Funhouse"

**Other Selected Stories**

Corfman, Eunice Luccock-- "To Be an Athlete"
Engberg, Susan-- "Lambs of God"
Litwak, Leo-- "In Shock"
Maddow, Ben-- "You, Johann Sebastian Bach"
Michaels, Leonard-- "Manikin"
Mountzoures, H. L.-- "The Empire of Things"
Packer, Nancy Huddleston-- "Early Morning,
    Lonely Ride"
Paley, Grace-- "Distance"
Rubin, Michael-- "Service"
Shefner, Evelyn-- "The Invitations"
Steele, Max-- "Color the Daydream Yellow"
Sterling, Thomas-- "Bedlam's Rent"
Taylor, Peter-- "First Heat"
Tyler, Anne-- "The Common Courtesies"

## 1970

**First Prize**

Hemenway, Robert-- "The Girl Who Sang with the
    Beatles"

**Second Prize**

Eastlake, William-- "The Biggest Thing Since Custer"

**Third Prize**

Rindfleisch, Norval-- "A Cliff of Fall"

**Special Award for Continuing Achievement**

Oates, Joyce Carol-- "How I Contemplated the World from the Detroit House of Correction and Began My Life Over Again"

**Other Selected Stories**

Blake, George-- "A Modern Development"

Buchan, Perdita-- "It's Cold out There"

Cole, Tom-- "Saint John of the Hershey Kisses: 1964"

Donahue, H. E. F.-- "Joe College"

Griffith, Patricia Browning-- "Nights at O'Rear's"

Grinstead, David-- "A Day in Operations"

Malamud, Bernard-- "My Son the Murderer"

McPherson, James Alan-- "Of Cabbages and Kings"

Oates, Joyce Carol-- "Unmailed, Unwritten Letters"

Salter, James-- "Am Strande Von Tanger"

Strong, Jonathan-- "Patients"

Updike, John-- "Bech Takes Pot Luck"

Willard, Nancy-- "Theo's Girl"

## 1971

**First Prize**

Hecht, Florence M.-- "Twin Bed Bridge"

**Second Prize**

Cardwell, Guy A.-- "Did You Once See Shelley?"

**Third Prize**

Adams, Alice-- "Gift of Grass"

**Other Selected Stories**

Cleaver, Eldridge-- "The Flashlight"

Greene, Philip L.-- "The Dichotomy"

Harter, Evelyn-- "The Stone Lovers"

Hoagland, Edward-- "The Final Fate of the Alligators"

Inman, Robert-- "I'll Call You"

Jacobsen, Josephine-- "The Jungle of Lord Lion"

Larson, Charles R.-- "Up From Slavery"

Mazor, Julian-- "The Skylark"

Michaels, Leonard-- "Robinson Crusoe Liebowitz"

Minot, Stephen-- "Mars Revisited"

Oates, Joyce Carol-- "The Children"

Parker, Thomas-- "Troop Withdrawal--The Initial Step"

Price, Reynolds-- "Waiting at Dachau"

Taylor, Eleanor Ross-- "Jujitsu"

## 1972

**First Prize**

Batki, John-- "Strange-Dreaming Charlie, Cow-Eyed Charlie"

**Second Prize**

Oates, Joyce Carol-- "Saul Bird Says: Relate! Communicate! Liberate!"

**Third Prize**

Rascoe, Judith-- "Small Sounds and Tilting Shadows"

**Other Selected Stories**

Adams, Alice-- "Ripped Off"

Barthelme, Donald-- "Subpoena"

Brown, Rosellen-- "A Letter to Ismael in the Grave"

Brown, Margery Finn-- "In the Forests of the Riga the Beasts Are Very Wild Indeed"

Eaton, Charles Edward-- "The Case of the Missing Photographs"

Flythe, Starkey, Jr.-- "Point of Conversion"

Gill, Brendan-- "Fat Girl"

Gold, Herbert-- "A Death on the East Side"

Gottlieb, Elaine-- "The Lizard"

Matthews, Jack-- "On the Shore of Chad Creek"

McClatchy, J. D.-- "Allonym"

Salter, James-- "The Destruction of the Goetheanum"

Tyler, Anne-- "With All Flags Flying"

Zelver, Patricia-- "On the Desert"

## 1973

**First Prize**

Oates, Joyce Carol-- "The Dead"

**Second Prize**

Malamud, Bernard-- "Talking Horse"

**Third Prize**

Brown, Rosellen-- "Mainlanders"

**Other Selected Stories**

Adams, Alice-- "The Swastika on Our Door"

Bromell, Henry-- "Photographs"

Carver, Raymond-- "What Is It?"

Cheever, John-- "The Jewels of the Cabots"

Jacobsen, Josephine-- "A Walk with Raschid"

Johnson, Diane-- "An Apple, An Orange"

Johnson, Curt-- "Trespasser"

Malone, John-- "The Fugitives"

Mayhall, Jane-- "The Enemy"

McPherson, James Alan-- "The Silver Bullet"

Rascoe, Judith-- "A Line of Order"
Reid, Randall-- "Detritus"
Shaber, David-- "Scotch Sour"
Sikes, Shirley-- "The Death of Cousin Stanley"
Zelver, Patricia-- "The Flood"

### 1974
**First Prize**
Adler, Renata-- "Brownstone"
**Second Prize**
Henson, Robert-- "Lizzie Borden in the P.M."
**Third Prize**
Adams, Alice-- "Alternatives"
**Other Selected Stories**
Busch, Frederick-- "Is Anyone Left This Time of Year?"
Carver, Raymond-- "Put Yourself in My Shoes"
Clayton, John J.-- "Cambridge Is Sinking!"
Davenport, Guy-- "Robot"
Eastlake, William-- "The Death of Sun"
Fuller, Blair-- "Bakti's Hand"
Gardner, John-- "The Things"
Hemenway, Robert-- "Troy Street"
Hill, Richard-- "Out in the Garage"
Hochstein, Rolaine-- "What Kind of a Man Cuts His Finger Off"
Klein, Norma-- "The Wrong Man"
Leach, Peter-- "The Fish Trap"
McPherson, James Alan-- "The Faithful"
Salter, James-- "Via Negativa"

### 1975
**First Prize**
Brodkey, Harold-- "A Story in an Almost Classical Mode"
Ozick, Cynthia-- "Usurpation (Other People's Stories)"
**Other Selected Stories**
Arensberg, Ann-- "Art History"
Arking, Linda-- "Certain Hard Places"
Banks, Russell-- "With Che at Kitty Hawk"
Bayer, Ann-- "Department Store"
Carver, Raymond-- "Are You a Doctor?"
Disch, Thomas M.-- "Getting into Death"
Doctorow, E. L.-- "Ragtime"
Kotzwinkle, William-- "Swimmer in the Secret Sea"

Maxwell, William-- "Over by the River"
McCorkle, Susannah-- "Ramona by the Sea"
McPherson, James Alan-- "The Story of a Scar"
Schell, Jessie-- "Alvira, Lettie, and Pip"
Shelnutt, Eve-- "Angel"
Updike, John-- "Nakedness"
Zelver, Patricia-- "Norwegians"

### 1976
**First Prize**
Brodkey, Harold-- "His Son in His Arms, in Light, Aloft"
**Second Prize**
Sayles, John-- "I-80 Nebraska, M. 490-M. 205"
**Third Prize**
Adams, Alice-- "Roses, Rhododendrons"
**Special Award for Continuing Achievement**
Updike, John-- "Separating"
**Other Selected Stories**
Berryman, John-- "Wash Far Away"
Brown, Rosellen-- "Why I Quit the Gowanus Liberation Front"
Bumpus, Jerry-- "The Idols of Afternoon"
Corrington, John William-- "The Actes and Monuments"
Davenport, Guy-- "The Richard Nixon Freischutz Rag"
Francis, H. E.-- "A Chronicle of Love"
Goyen, William-- "Bridge of Music, River of Sand"
Griffith, Patricia Browning-- "Dust"
Halley, Anne-- "The Sisterhood"
Helprin, Mark-- "Leaving the Church"
Hudson, Helen-- "The Theft"
Jacobsen, Josephine-- "Nel Bagno"
O'Brien, Tim-- "Night March"
Oates, Joyce Carol-- "Blood-Swollen Landscape"
Sadoff, Ira-- "An Enemy of the People"
Shreve, Anita-- "Past the Island, Drifting"

### 1977
**First Prize**
Hazzard, Shirley-- "A Long Story Short"
Leffland, Ella-- "Last Courtesies"
**Other Selected Stories**
Adams, Alice-- "Flights"
Ballantyne, Sheila-- "Perpetual Care"

Cheever, John-- "The President of the Argentine"
Colwin, Laurie-- "The Lone Pilgrim"
Dixon, Stephen-- "Mac in Love"
Engberg, Susan-- "A Stay by the River"
Fetler, Andrew-- "Shadows on the Water"
Hedin, Mary-- "Ladybug, Fly Away Home"
McCully, Emily Arnold-- "How's Your Vacuum Cleaner Working?"
Minot, Stephen-- "A Passion for History"
Russ, Joanna-- "Autobiography of My Mother"
Sayles, John-- "Breed"
Simmons, Charles-- "Certain Changes"
Summers, Hollis-- "A Hundred Paths"
Theroux, Paul-- "The Autumn Dog"
Zelver, Patricia-- "The Little Pub"

## 1978
**First Prize**
Allen, Woody-- "The Kugelmass Episode"
**Second Prize**
Schorer, Mark-- "A Lamp"
**Third Prize**
Henson, Robert-- "The Upper and the Lower Millstone"
**Other Selected Stories**
Adams, Alice-- "Beautiful Girl"
Apple, Max-- "Paddycake, Paddycake . . . A Memoir"
Brodkey, Harold-- "Verona: A Young Woman Speaks"
Clayton, John J.-- "Bodies Like Mouths"
Engberg, Susan-- "Pastorale"
Fuller, Blair-- "All Right"
Helprin, Mark-- "The Schreuerspitze"
Jacobsen, Josephine-- "Jack Frost"
Leviant, Curt-- "Ladies and Gentlemen, The Original Music of the Hebrew Alphabet"
O'Brien, Tim-- "Speaking of Courage"
Oates, Joyce Carol-- "The Tattoo"
Pearlman, Edith-- "Hanging Fire"
Schaeffer, Susan Fromberg-- "The Exact Nature of Plot"
Schell, Jessie-- "Undeveloped Photographs"
Schevill, James-- "A Hero in the Highway"

## 1979
**First Prize**
Weaver, Gordon-- "Getting Serious"

**Second Prize**
Bromell, Henry-- "Travel Stories"
**Third Prize**
Hecht, Julie-- "I Want You, I Need You, I Love You"
**Other Selected Stories**
Adams, Alice-- "The Girl Across the Room"
Baumbach, Jonathan-- "Passion?"
Caputi, Anthony-- "The Derby Hopeful"
Disch, Thomas M.-- "Xmas"
Gold, Herbert-- "The Smallest Part"
Goldberg, Lester-- "Shy Bearers"
Heller, Steve-- "The Summer Game"
Leaton, Anne-- "The Passion of Marco Z--- "
Molyneux, Thomas W.-- "Visiting the Point"
Oates, Joyce Carol-- "In the Autumn of the Year"
Peterson, Mary-- "Travelling"
Pfeil, Fred-- "The Quality of Light in Maine"
Schwartz, Lynne Sharon-- "Rough Strife"
Smith, Lee-- "Mrs. Darcy Meets the Blue-eyed Stranger at the Beach"
Thomas, Annabel-- "Coon Hunt"
Van Dyke, Henry-- "Du Cote de Chez Britz"
Yates, Richard-- "Oh, Joseph, I'm So Tired"
Zelver, Patricia-- "My Father's Jokes"

## 1980
**First Prize**
Bellow, Saul-- "A Silver Dish"
**Second Prize**
Hallinan, Nancy-- "Woman in a Roman Courtyard"
**Third Prize**
Michaels, Leonard-- "The Men's Club"
**Other Selected Stories**
Adams, Alice-- "Truth or Consequences"
Arensberg, Ann-- "Group Sex"
Beattie, Ann-- "The Cinderella Waltz"
Chasin, Helen-- "Fatal"
Dillon, Millicent-- "All the Pelageyas"
Dubus, Andre-- "The Pitcher"
Dunn, Robert-- "Hopeless Acts Performed Properly, with Grace"
Gertler, T.-- "In Case of Survival"
Godwin, Gail-- "Amanuensis: A Tale of the Creative Life"
Krysl, Marilyn-- "Looking for Mother"

L'Heureux, John-- "The Priest's Wife"

Phillips, Jayne Anne-- "Snow"

Rose, Daniel Asa-- "The Goodbye Present"

Stafford, Jean-- "An Influx of Poets"

Sullivan, Walter-- "Elizabeth"

Taggart, Shirley Ann-- "Ghosts Like Them"

Targan, Barry-- "Old Light"

Taylor, Peter-- "The Old Forest"

Vaughn, Stephanie-- "Sweet Talk"

## 1981

**First Prize**

Ozick, Cynthia-- "The Shawl"

**Other Selected Stories**

Adams, Alice-- "Snow"

Boyle, Kay-- "St. Stephen's Green"

Flowers, Sandra Hollin-- "Hope of Zion"

Goodman, Ivy-- "Baby"

Irving, John-- "Interior Space"

L'Heureux, John-- "Brief Lives in California"

Matthews, Jack-- "The Last Abandonment"

Novick, Marian-- "Advent"

Oates, Joyce Carol-- "Mutilated Woman"

Packer, Nancy Huddleston-- "The Women Who Walk"

Reid, Barbara-- "The Waltz Dream"

Rottenberg, Annette T.-- "The Separation"

Smith, Lee-- "Between the Lines"

Stern, Steve-- "Isaac and the Undertaker's Daughter"

Tabor, James-- "The Runner"

Theroux, Paul-- "World's Fair"

Thomas, Annabel-- "The Photographic Woman"

Walker, Alice-- "The Abortion"

Wetherell, W. D.-- "The Man Who Loved Levittown"

Wolff, Tobias-- "In the Garden of North
    American Martyrs"

## 1982

**First Prize**

Kenney, Susan-- "Facing Front"

**Second Prize**

McElroy, Joseph-- "The Future"

**Third Prize**

Brooks, Ben-- "A Postal Creed"

**Special Award for Continuing Achievement**

Adams, Alice-- "Greyhound People" and "To See You
    Again"

**Other Selected Stories**

Carkeet, David-- "The Greatest Slump of All Time"

Dixon, Stephen-- "Layaways"

Gewertz, Kenneth-- "I Thought of Chatterton, The
    Marvelous Boy"

Goodman, Ivy-- "White Boy"

Holt, T. E.-- "Charybdis"

Johnson, Nora-- "The Jungle of Injustice"

Malone, Michael-- "Fast Love"

O'Brien, Tim-- "The Ghost Soldiers"

Oates, Joyce Carol-- "The Man Whom
    Women Adored"

Smiley, Jane-- "The Pleasure of Her Company"

Taylor, Peter-- "The Gift of the Prodigal"

Trefethen, Florence-- "Infidelities"

Wheeler, Kate-- "La Victoire"

Wolff, Tobias-- "Next Door"

## 1983

**First Prize**

Carver, Raymond-- "A Small, Good Thing"

**Second Prize**

Oates, Joyce Carol-- "My Warsawa"

**Third Prize**

Morris, Wright-- "Victrola"

**Other Selected Stories**

Benedict, Elizabeth-- "Feasting"

Bienen, Leigh Buchanan-- "My Life as a West African
    Gray Parrot"

Faust, Irvin-- "Melanie and the Purple People Eaters"

Gordon, Mary-- "The Only Son of a Doctor"

Jauss, David-- "Shards"

Klass, Perri-- "The Secret Lives of Dieters"

Lloyd, Lynda-- "Poor Boy"

Meinke, Peter-- "The Ponoes"

Norris, Gloria-- "When the Lord Calls"

Plante, David-- "Work"

Schwartz, Steven-- "Slow-Motion"

Spencer, Elizabeth-- "Jeanne-Pierre"

Svendsen, Linda-- "Heartbeat'

Updike, John-- "The City"

Van Wert, William F.-- "Putting & Gardening"

Wetherell, W. D.-- "If a Woodchuck Could
    Chuck Wood"

Whelan, Gloria-- "The Dogs in Renoir's Garden"

## 1984
**First Prize**
Ozick, Cynthia-- "Rosa"
**Other Selected Stories**
Abbott, Lee K.-- "Living Alone in Iota"
Adams, Alice-- "Alaska"
Baumbach, Jonathan-- "The Life and Times of Major Fiction"
Dickinson, Charles-- "Risk"
Fetler, Andrew-- "The Third Count"
Johnson, Willis-- "Prayer for the Dying"
Justice, Donald-- "The Artificial Moonlight"
Klass, Perri-- "Not a Good Girl"
Leavitt, David-- "Counting Months"
Lish, Gordon-- "For Jerome--with Love and Kisses"
Malamud, Bernard-- "The Model"
Menaker, Daniel-- "The Old Left"
Norris, Gloria-- "Revive Us Again"
Norris, Helen-- "The Love Child"
Paley, Grace-- "The Story Hearer"
Pearlman, Edith-- "Conveniences"
Pritchard, Melissa Brown-- "A Private Landscape"
Salter, James-- "Lost Sons"
Tallent, Elizabeth-- "The Evolution of Birds of Paradise"

## 1985
**First Prize**
Dybek, Stuart-- "Hot Ice"
Smiley, Jane-- "Lily"
**Other Selected Stories**
Beattie, Ann-- "In the White Night"
Cameron, Peter-- "Homework"
Erdrich, Louise-- "Saint Marie"
Hamilton, R. C.-- "Da Vinci Is Dead"
Heller, Steve-- "The Crow Woman"
Hochstein, Rolaine-- "She Should Have Died Hereafter"
Jacobsen, Josephine-- "The Mango Community"
Just, Ward-- "About Boston"
Koch, Claude-- "Bread and Butter Questions"
McElroy, Joseph-- "Daughter of the Revolution"
Minot, Susan-- "Lust"
Morris, Wright-- "Glimpse into Another Country"
Norris, Helen-- "The Quarry"

Oates, Joyce Carol-- "The Seasons"
Raymond, Ilene-- "Taking a Chance on Jack"
Updike, John-- "The Other"
Wilson, Eric-- "The Axe, the Axe, the Axe"
Wolff, Tobias-- "Sister"

## 1986
**First Prize**
Walker, Alice-- "Kindred Spirits"
**Special Award for Continuing Achievement**
Oates, Joyce Carol-- "Master Race"
**Other Selected Stories**
Adams, Alice-- "Molly's Dog"
Cameron, Peter-- "Excerpts from Swan Lake"
DiFranco, Anthony-- "The Garden of Redemption"
Dybek, Stuart-- "Pet Milk"
Eisenberg, Deborah-- "Transactions in a Foreign Currency"
Faust, Irvin-- "The Year of the Hot Jock"
Gerber, Merrill Joan-- "I Don't Believe This"
Johnson, Greg-- "Crazy Ladies"
Just, Ward-- "The Costa Brava, 1959"
Kornblatt, Joyce R.-- "Offerings"
L'Heureux, John-- "The Comedian"
Lish, Gordon-- "Resurrection"
Mason, Bobbie Ann-- "Big Bertha Stories"
Meinke, Peter-- "Uncle George and Uncle Stefan"
Norris, Gloria-- "Holding On"
Spencer, Elizabeth-- "The Cousins"
Vaughn, Stephanie-- "Kid MacArthur"
Wilmot, Jeanne-- "Dirt Angel"

## 1987
**First Prize**
Erdrich, Louise-- "Fleur"
Johnson, Joyce-- "The Children's Wing"
**Other Selected Stories**
Adams, Alice-- "Tide Pools"
Barthelme, Donald-- "Basil from Her Garden"
Bausch, Richard-- "What Feels Like the World"
Berriault, Gina-- "The Island of Ven"
Boswell, Robert-- "The Darkness of Love"
Dillon, Millicent-- "Monitor"
Dybek, Stuart-- "Blight"
Home, Lewis-- "Taking Care"
Lavers, Norman-- "Big Dog"

Lott, James-- "The Janeites"
Norris, Helen-- "The Singing Well"
Oates, Joyce Carol-- "Ancient Airs, Voices"
Paley, Grace-- "Midrash on Happiness"
Pitzen, Jim-- "The Village"
Robison, Mary-- "I Get By"
Stern, Daniel-- "The Interpretation of Dreams by
        Sigmund Freud: A Story"
Taylor, Robert, Jr.-- "Lady of Spain"
Wallace, Warren-- "Up Home"

## 1988
**First Prize**
Carver, Raymond-- "Errand"
**Other Selected Stories**
Adams, Alice-- "Ocrakoke Island"
Baumbach, Jonathan-- "The Dinner Party"
Beattie, Ann-- "Honey"
Currey, Richard-- "The Wars of Heaven"
Deaver, Philip F.-- "Arcola Girls"
Dubus, Andre-- "Blessings"
Hazzard, Shirley-- "The Place to Be"
Kohler, Sheila-- "The Mountain"
La Puma, Salvatore-- "The Gangster's Ghost"
LaSalle, Peter-- "Dolphin Dreaming"
Mason, Bobbie Ann-- "Bumblebees"
Neugeboren, Jay-- "Don't Worry About the Kids"
Oates, Joyce Carol-- "Yarrow"
Plant, Richard-- "Cecil Grounded"
Sayles, John-- "The Halfway Diner"
Smiley, Jane-- "Long Distance"
Spencer, Elizabeth-- "The Business Venture"
Updike, John-- "Leaf Season"
Williams, Joy-- "Rot"

## 1989
**First Prize**
Finney, Ernest J.-- "Peacocks"
**Second Prize**
Oates, Joyce Carol-- "House Hunting"
**Third Prize**
Doerr, Harriet-- "Edie: A Life"
**Other Selected Stories**
Adams, Alice-- "After You're Gone"
Bass, Rick-- "The Watch"
Boyle, T. Coraghessan-- "Sinking House"

Casey, John-- "Avid"
Dickinson, Charles-- "Child in the Leaves"
Dillon, Millicent-- "Wrong Stories"
Harrison, Barbara Grizzuti-- "To Be"
Herman, Ellen-- "Unstable Ground"
Lary, Banning K.-- "Death of a Duke"
Minot, Susan-- "Île Séche"
Petroski, Catherine-- "The Hit"
Ross, Jean-- "The Sky Fading Upward to Yellow: A
Footnote to Literary History"
Salter, James-- "American Express"
Sherwook, Frances-- "History"
Simmons, Charles-- "Clandestine Acts"
Starkey, Flythe, Jr.-- "CV Ten"
Wallace, David Foster-- "Here and There"

## 1990
**First Prize**
Litwak, Leo-- "The Eleventh Edition"
**Second Prize**
Matthiessen, Peter-- "Lumumba Lives"
**Third Prize**
Segal, Lore-- "The Reverse Bug"
**Other Selected Stories**
Ackerman, Felicia-- "The Forecasting Game: A Story"
Adams, Alice-- "1940: Fall"
Blaylock, James P.-- "Unidentified Objects"
Boyle, T. Coraghessan-- "The Ape Lady
        in Retirement"
Brinson, Claudia Smith-- "Einstein's Daughter"
Eidus, Janice-- "Vito Loves Geraldine"
Fleming, Bruce-- "The Autobiography of Gertrude Stein"
Gillette, Jane Brown-- "Sins Against Animals"
Greenberg, Joanne-- "Elizabeth Baird"
Jersild, Devon-- "In Which John Imagines His Mind
        as a Pond"
Kaplan, David Michael-- "Stand"
McKnight, Reginald-- "The Kind of Light That Shines
        on Texas"
Oates, Joyce Carol-- "Heat"
Osborn, Carolyn-- "The Grands"
Schumacher, Julie-- "The Private Life of
        Robert Shumann"
Sides, Marilyn-- "The Island of the Mapmaker's Wife"
Steinbach, Meredith-- "In Recent History"

## 1991
**First Prize**

Updike, John-- "A Sandstone Farmhouse"

**Selected Stories**

Adams, Alice-- "Earthquake Damage"

Averill, Thomas Fox-- "During the Twelfth Summer of Elmer D. Peterson"

Baxter, Charles-- "Saul and Patsy Are Pregnant"

Broughton, T. Alan-- "Ashes"

Dillon, Millicent-- "Oil and Water"

Hall, Martha Lacy-- "The Apple-Green Triumph"

Johnson, Wayne-- "Hippies, Indians, Buffalo"

Klass, Perri-- "For Women Everywhere"

Le Guin, Ursula K.-- "Hand, Cup, Shell"

Lear, Patricia-- "Powwow"

Levenberg, Diane-- "The Ilui"

McFarland, Dennis-- "Nothing to Ask For"

Norris, Helen-- "Raisin Faces"

Oates, Joyce Carol-- "The Swimmers"

Stark, Sharon Sheehe-- "Overland"

Sukenick, Ronald-- "Ecco"

Swick, Marly-- "Moscow Nights"

Walker, Charlotte Zoe-- "The Very Pineapple"

Watanabe, Sylvia A.-- "Talking to the Dead"

## 1992
**First Prize**

Ozick, Cynthia-- "Puttermesser Paired"

Updike, John-- "A Sandstone Farmhouse"

**Other Selected Stories**

Adams, Alice-- "The Last Lovely City"

Barnes, Yolanda-- "Red Lipstick"

Braverman, Kate-- "Tall Tales from the Mekong Delta"

Chowder, Ken-- "With Seth in Tana Toraja"

Dillon, Millicent-- "Lost in L.A."

Doerr, Harriet-- "Way Stations"

Herrick, Amy-- "Pinocchio's Nose"

Honig, Lucy-- "English as a Second Language"

Klass, Perri-- "Dedication"

Long, David-- "Blue Spruce"

McNeal, Tom-- "What Happened to Tully"

Meltzer, Daniel-- "People"

Myers, Les-- "The Kite"

Nelson, Kent-- "The Mine from Nicaragua"

Nelson, Antonya-- "The Control Group"

Oates, Joyce Carol-- "Why Don't You Come Live with Me It's Time"

Packer, Ann-- "Babies"

Pomerance, Murray-- "Decor"

Sherwood, Frances-- "Demiurges"

Wagner, Mary Michael-- "Acts of Kindness"

## 1993
**First Prize**

Jones, Thom-- "The Pugilist at Rest"

**Second Prize**

Lee, Andrea-- "Winter Barley"

**Third Prize**

Van Wert, William F.-- "Shaking"

**Other Selected Stories**

Adams, Alice-- "The Islands"

Askew, Rilla-- "The Killing Blanket"

Dixon, Stephen-- "The Rare Muscovite"

Eastman, Charles-- "Yellow Flags"

Egan, Jennifer-- "Puerto Vallerta"

Jacobsen, Josephine-- "The Pier-Glass"

Johnson, Charles-- "Kwoon"

Levenberg, Diane-- "A Modern Love Story"

Moore, Lorrie-- "Charades"

Nelson, Antonya-- "Dirty Words"

Nixon, Cornelia-- "Risk"

Oates, Joyce Carol-- "Goose-Girl"

Poverman, C. E.-- "The Man Who Died"

Richardson, John H.-- "The Pink House"

Schwartz, Steven-- "Madagascar"

Stern, Daniel-- "A Hunger Artist by Franz Kafka: A Story"

Svendsen, Linda-- "The Edger Man"

Van Kirk, John-- "Newark Job"

Weltner, Peter-- "The Greek Head"

Wheeler, Kate-- "Improving My Average"

## 1994
**First Prize**

Baker, Alison-- "Better Be Ready 'Bout Half Past Eight"

**Second Prize**

Gardiner, John Rolfe-- "The Voyage Out"

**Third Place**

Moore, Lorrie-- "Terrific Mother"

**Other Selected Stories**

Bain, Terry-- "Games"
Barton, Marlin-- "Jeremiah's Road"
Bloom, Amy-- "Semper Fidelis"
Cherry, Kelly-- "Not the Phil Donahue Show"
Cox, Elizabeth-- "The Third of July"
Dybek, Stuart-- "We Didn't"
Eidus, Janice-- "Pandora's Box"
Fox, Michael-- "Rise and Shine"
Fremont, Helen-- "Where She Was"
Graver, Elizabeth-- "The Boy Who Fell Forty Feet"
Hester, Katherine L.-- "Labor"
Kennedy, Thomas E.-- "Landing Zone X-Ray"
McLean, David-- "Marine Corps Issue"
Oness, Elizabeth-- "The Oracle"
Ortiz Cofer, Judith-- "Nada"
Richards, Susan Starr-- "The Hanging in the Foaling Barn"
Tannen, Mary-- "Elaine's House"
Trudell, Dennis-- "Gook"

## 1995
**First Prize**
Nixon, Cornelia-- "The Women Come and Go"
**Second Prize**
Clayton, John J.-- "Talking to Charlie"
**Other Selected Stories**
Adams, Alice-- "The Haunted Beach"
Baker, Alison-- "Loving Wanda Beaver"
Baxter, Charles-- "Kiss Away"
Bradford, Robin-- "If This Letter Were a
    Beaded Object"
Byers, Michael-- "Settled on the Cranberry Coast"
Cameron, Peter-- "Departing"
Cooper, Bernard-- "Truth Serum"
Delaney, Edward J.-- "The Drowning"
Eisenberg, Deborah-- "Across the Lake"
Gates, David-- "The Intruder"
Gilchrist, Ellen-- "The Stucco House"
Goodman, Allegra-- "Sarah"
Hardwick, Elizabeth-- "Shot: A New York Story"
Klass, Perri-- "City Sidewalks"
Krieger, Elliot-- "Cantor Pepper"
Oates, Joyce Carol-- "You Petted Me and I Followed
    You Home"
Pierce, Anne Whitney-- "Star Box"
Powell, Padgett-- "Trick or Treat"

Updike, John-- "The Black Room"

## 1996
**First Prize**
King, Stephen-- "The Man in the Black Suit"
**Second Prize**
Sharma, Akhil-- "If You Sing Like That for Me"
**Other Selected Stories**
Adams, Alice-- "His Women"
Baker, Alison-- "Convocation"
Dillen, Frederick G.-- "Alice"
Douglas, Ellen-- "Grant"
Graver, Elizabeth-- "Between"
Hagenston, Becky-- "'Til Death Do Us Part"
Hoffman, William-- "Stones"
Honig, Lucy-- "Citizens Review"
Kriegel, Leonard-- "Players"
Lombreglia, Ralph-- "Somebody Up There Likes Me"
McNally, T. M.-- "Skin Deep"
Menaker, Daniel-- "Influenza"
Mosley, Walter-- "The Thief"
Oates, Joyce Carol-- "Mark of Satan"
Paine, Tom-- "Will You Say Something
    Monsieur Eliot"
Schumacher, Julie-- "Dummies"
Smiley, Jane-- "The Life of the Body"
Wiegand, David-- "Buffalo Safety"

## 1997
**First Prize**
Gordon, Mary-- "City Life"
**Second Prize**
Saunders, George-- "The Falls"
**Third Prize**
Abbott, Lee K.-- "The Talk Talked Between Worms"
**Other Selected Stories**
Barth, John-- "On with the Story"
Bradford, Arthur-- "Catface"
Cooke, Carolyn-- "The TWA Corbies"
Davenport, Kiana-- "The Lipstick Tree"
Dubus, Andre-- "Dancing After Hours"
Eisenberg, Deborah-- "Mermaids"
Gaitskill, Mary-- "Comfort"
Glave, Thomas-- "The Final Inning"
Klam, Matthew-- "The Royal Palms"
MacMillan, Ian-- "The Red House"

Moody, Rick-- "Demonology"
Morgan, Robert-- "The Balm of Gilead Tree"
Munro, Alice-- "The Love of a Good Woman"
Ruff, Patricia Elam-- "The Taxi Ride"
Schaeffer, Susan Fromberg-- "The Old Farmhouse and the Dog-Wife"
Schutt, Christine-- "His Chorus"
Shields, Carol-- "Mirrors"

## 1998
**First Prize**
Moore, Lorrie-- "People Like That Are the Only People Here"
**Second Prize**
Millhauser, Steven-- "The Knife Thrower"
**Third Prize**
Munro, Alice-- "The Children Stay"
**Other Selected Stories**
Bass, Rick-- "The Myths of Bears"
Cooke, Carolyn-- "Eating Dirt"
Davies, Peter Ho-- "Relief"
Erdrich, Louise-- "Satan: Hijacker of a Planet"
Evenson, Brian-- "Two Brothers"
Heuler, Karen-- "Me and My Enemy"
Jones, Thom-- "Tarantula"
MacDonald, D. R.-- "Ashes"
McKnight, Reginald-- "Boot"
Mehta, Suketu-- "Gare du Nord"
Novakovich, Josip-- "Crimson"
Proulx, Annie-- "Brokeback Mountain"
Saunders, George-- "Winky"
Sharma, Akhil-- "Cosmopolitan"
Swann, Maxine-- "Flower Children"
Weltner, Peter-- "Movietone: Detour"
Zancanella, Don-- "The Chimpanzees of Wyoming Territory"

## 1999
**First Prize**
Baida, Peter-- "A Nurse's Story"
**Second Prize**
Holladay, Cary-- "Merry-Go-Sorry"
**Third Prize**
Munro, Alice-- "Save the Reaper"

**Other Selected Stories**
Benedict, Pinckney-- "Miracle Boy"
Boyle, T. Coraghessan-- "The Underground Gardens"
Chabon, Michael-- "Son of the Wolfman"
Cunningham, Michael-- "Mister Brother"
Davenport, Kiana-- "Fork Used in Eating Reverend Baker"
Forbes, Charlotte-- "Sign"
Houston, Pam-- "Cataract"
Lahiri, Jhumpa-- "Interpreter of Maladies"
Potok, Chaim-- "Moon"
Proulx, Annie-- "The Mud Below"
Reilly, Gerald-- "Nixon Under the Bodhi Tree"
Saunders, George-- "Sea Oak"
Schirmer, Robert-- "Burning"
Schwartz, Sheila-- "Afterbirth"
Wallace, David Foster-- "The Depressed Person"
Wetherell, W. D.-- "Watching Girls Play"
Whitty, Julia-- "A Tortoise for the Queen of Tonga"

## 2000
**First Prize**
Wideman, John Edgar-- "Weight"
**Second Prize**
Lordan, Beth-- "The Man with the Lapdog"
**Third Prize**
Gordon, Mary-- "The Deacon"
**Other Selected Stories**
Banks, Russell-- "Plains of Abraham"
Banner, Keith-- "The Smallest People Alive"
Barrett, Andrea-- "Theories of Rain"
Bertles, Jeannette-- "Whileaway"
Biguenet, John-- "Rose"
Budnitz, Judy-- "Flush"
Brockmeier, Kevin-- "These Hands"
Byers, Michael-- "The Beautiful Days"
Carver, Raymond-- "Kindling"
Dark, Alice Elliott-- "Watch the Animals"
Davenport, Kiana-- "Bones of the Inner Ear"
Englander, Nathan-- "The Gilgul of Park Avenue"
Gautreux, Tim-- "Easy Pickings"
Gurganus, Allan-- "He's at the Office"
Lennon, J. Robert-- "The Fool's Proxy"
Pritchard, Melissa-- "Salve Regina"
Walbert, Kate-- "The Gardens of Kyoto"

## 2001

**First Prize**

Swan, Mary-- "The Deep"

**Second Prize**

Chaon, Dan-- "Big Me"

**Third Prize**

Munro, Alice-- "Floating Bridge"

**Other Selected Stories**

Barrett, Andrea-- "Servants of Map"

Benedict, Pinckney-- "Zog 19: A Scientific Romance"

Boyle, T. Coraghessan-- "The Love of My Life"

Carlson, Ron-- "At the Jim Bridger"

Erdrich, Louise-- "Revival Road"

Gay, William-- "The Paperhanger"

Graver, Elizabeth-- "The Mourning Door"

Kalam, Murad-- "Bow Down"

Leebron, Fred G.-- "That Winter"

Nelson, Antonya-- "Female Trouble"

Oates, Joyce Carol-- "The Girl with the Blackened Eye"

Peck, Dale-- "Bliss"

Saunders, George-- "Pastoralia"

Schickler, David-- "The Smoker"

## 2002

**First Prize**

Brockmeier, Kevin-- "The Ceiling"

**Second Prize**

Lewis, Mark Ray-- "Scordatura"

**Third Prize**

Erdrich, Louise-- "The Butcher's Wife"

**Other Selected Stories**

Beattie, Ann-- "The Last Odd Day in L.A."

Danticat, Edwidge-- "Seven"

Divakaruni, Chitra Banerjee-- "The Lives of Strangers"

Doerr, Anthony-- "The Hunter's Wife"

Eisenberg, Deborah-- "Like It or Not"

Ford, Richard-- "Charity"

Gates, David-- "George Lassos Moon"

Homes, A. M.-- "Do Not Disturb"

Leavitt, David-- "Speonk"

Lee, Andrea-- "Anthropology"

Lee, Don-- "The Possible Husband"

Munro, Alice-- "Family Furnishings"

Nolan, Jonathan-- "Memento Mori"

Roorbach, Bill-- "Big Bend"

Schmidt, Heidi Jon-- "Blood Poison"

Wallace, David Foster-- "Good Old Neon"

Waters, Mary Yukari-- "Egg-Face"

## 2003

**Juror Favorites**

Byatt, A. S-- "The Thing in the Forest"

Johnson, Denis-- "Train Dreams"

**Other Selected Stories**

Adichie, Chimamanda Ngozi-- "The American Embassy"

Boyle, T. Coraghessan-- "Swept Away"

Connell, Evan S., Jr.-- "Election Eve"

Desnoyers, Adam-- "Bleed Blue in Indonesia"

Doerr, Anthony-- "The Shell Collector"

Giles, Molly-- "Two Words"

Harleman, Ann-- "Meanwhile"

Johnston, Tim-- "Irish Girl"

Kemper, Marjorie-- "God's Goodness"

Kittredge, William-- "Kissing"

Leff, Robyn Jay-- "Burn Your Maps"

Light, Douglas-- "Three Days. A Month. More"

Morrow, Bradford-- "Lush"

Munro, Alice-- "Fathers"

O'Brien, Tim-- "What Went Wrong"

Pearlman, Edith-- "The Story"

Silber, Joan-- "The High Road"

Trevor, William--Sacred Statues"

**2004** (No prizes awarded)

## 2005

**Juror Favorites**

Alexie, Sherman-- "What You Pawn I Will Redeem"

Jhabvala, Ruth Prawer-- "Refuge in London"

Stuckey-French, French-- "Mudlavia"

**Other Selected Stories**

Berry, Wendell-- "The Hurt Man"

Brockmeier, Kevin-- "The Brief History of the Dead"

Crouse, Timothy-- "Sphinxes"

D'Ambrosio, Charles-- "The High Divide"

Fountain, Ben-- "Fantasy for Eleven Fingers"

Fox, Paula-- "Grace"

Freudenberg, Nell-- "The Tutor"

Hadley, Tessa-- "The Card Trick"

Jones, Edward P.-- "A Rich Man"
Jones, Gail-- "Desolation"
Macy, Caitlin-- "Christie"
Parker, Michael-- "The Golden Era of Heartbreak"
Peck, Dale-- "Dues"
Peebles, Frances de Pontes-- "The Drowned Woman"
Rash, Ron-- "Speckle Trout"
Reisman, Nancy-- "Tea"
Ward, Liza-- "Snowbound"

## 2006
**Juror Favorites**
Eisenberg, Deborah-- "Window"
Jones, Edward P.-- "Old Boys, Old Girls"
Munro, Alice-- "Passion"
**Other Selected Stories**
Brown, Karen-- "Unction"
Clark, George Makana-- "The Center of the World"
Erdrich, Louise-- "The Plague of Doves"
Fox, Paula-- "The Broad Estates of Death"
Kay, Jackie-- "You Go When You Can No
     Longer Stay"
Means, David-- "Saulte Ste. Marie
Morse, David Lawrence-- "Conceived"
Peelle, Lydia-- "Mule Killers"
Reents, Stepahnie-- "Disquisition on Tears"
Schaeffer, Susan Fromberg-- "Wolves"
Svoboda, Terese-- "'80's Lilies"
Thon, Melanie Rae-- "Letters in the Snow . . . "
Trevor, Douglas-- "Girls I Know"
Trevor, William--The Dressmaker's Child"
Vapnyar, Lara-- "Puffed Rice and Meatballs"
Vaswani, Neela-- "The Pelvis Series"
Xu Xi-- "Famine"

## 2007
**Juror Favorites**
Chuculate, Eddie-- "Galveston Bay, 1826"
Trevor, William--The Room"
**Other Selected Stories**
Altschul, Andrew Foster-- "A New Kind of Gravity"
Anapol, Bay-- "A Stone House"
Curtis, Rebecca-- "Summer, with Twins"
Dorfman, Ariel-- "Gringos"
D'Souza, Tony-- "Djamilla"
Dymond, Justine-- "Cherubs"

Ellison, Jan-- "The Company of Men"
Evenson, Brian-- "Mudder Tongue"
Haslett, Adam-- "City Visit"
Kraskikov, Sana-- "Companion"
Lambert, Charles-- "The Scent of Cinnamon"
McCann, Richard-- "The Diarist"
Munro, Alice-- "The View from Castle Rock"
Murphy, Yannick-- "In a Bear's Eye"
Schutt, Christine-- "The Duchess of Albany"
Silbert, Joan-- "War Buddies
Straight, Susan-- "El Ojo de Agua"
Tran, Vu-- "The Gift of Years"

## 2008
**Juror Favorites**
Munro, Alice-- "What Do You Want to Know For?"
Trevor, William--Folie à Deux"
Zentner, Alexi-- "Touch"
**Other Selected Stories**
Cain, Shannon-- "The Necessity of Certain
     Behaviors"
Doerr, Anthony-- "Village 113"
Faber, Michel-- "Bye-Bye Natalia"
Gaitskill, Mary-- "The Little Boy"
Gass, William H.-- "A Little History of Modern Music"
Jin, Ha-- "A Composer and His Parakeets"
Jones, Edward P.-- "Bad Neighbors"
Kohler, Sheila-- "The Transitional Object"
Li, Yiyun-- "Prison"
McDonald, Roger-- "The Bullock Run"
Malouf, David-- "Every Move You Make"
Millhauser, Steven-- "A Change in Fashion"
Olafsson, Olaf-- "On the Lake"
Segal, Lore-- "Other People's Deaths"
Sonnenberg, Brittani-- "Taiping"
Tremain, Rose-- "A Game of Cards"
Tulathimutte, Tony-- "Scenes from the Life of the
     Only Girl in Water Shield, Alaska"

## 2009
**Juror Favorites**
Díaz, Junot-- "Wildwood"
Graham, Joyce-- "An Ordinary Soldier of the Queen"
**Other Selected Stories**
Brown, Karen-- "Isabel's Daughter"
Burnside, John-- "The Bell Ringer"

Dien, Viet-- "Substitutes"
Godimer, Nadine-- "A Beneficiary"
Greer, Andrew Sean-- "Darkness"
Horrocks, Caitlin-- "This Is Not Your City"
Jin, Ha-- "The House Behind a Weeping Cherry"
Lunstrum, Kristen Sundberg-- "The Nursery"
Miller, L. E.-- "Kind"
Morgan, Alistair-- "Icebergs"
Muñoz, Manuel-- "Tell Him About Brother John"
Nash, Roger-- "The Camera and the Cobra"
Sikka, Mohan-- "Uncle Musto Takes a Mistress"
Silver, Marisa-- "The Visitor"
Slate, E. V.-- "Purple Bamboo Park"
Theroux, Paul-- "Twenty-Two Stories"
Troy, Judy-- "The Order of Things"
Yoon, Paul-- "And We Will Be Here"

## 2010
### Juror Awards
Lasdun, John-- "On Death"

Mueenuddi, Daniyal-- "A Spoiled Man"
Trevor, William-- "The Woman of the House"
**Other Selected Stories**
Adichie, Chimamanda Ngozi-- "Stand by Me"
Alarcón, Daniel-- "The Bridge"
Allio, Kirstin-- "Clothed, Female Figure
Bakopoulos, Natalie-- "Fresco, Byzantine"
Berry, Wendell-- "Sheep May Safely Graze"
Bradley, George-- "An East Egg Update"
Cameron, Peter-- "The End of My Life in New York"
Galgut, Damon-- "The Lover"
Munro, Alice-- "Some Women"
Proulx, Annie-- "Them Old Cowboy Songs"
Rash, Ron-- "Into the Gorge"
Row, Jess-- "Sheep May Safely Graze"
Samarasan, Pretta-- "Birth Memorial"
Sanders, Ted-- "Obit"
Segal, Lore-- "Making Good"
Watson, Brad-- "Visitation"
Wideman, John Edgar-- "Microstories"

## Rea Award

Awarded annually since 1986 to living American writers who have made a significant contribution to the short-story form.

1986: Cynthia Ozick
1987: Robert Coover
1988: Donald Barthelme
1989: Tobias Wolff
1990: Joyce Carol Oates
1991: Paul Bowles
1992: Eudora Welty
1993: Grace Paley
1994: Tillie Olsen
1995: Richard Ford
1996: Andre Dubus
1997: Gina Berriault

1998: John Edgar Wideman
1999: Joy Williams
2000: Deborah Eisenberg
2001: Alice Munro
2002: Mavis Gallant
2003: Antonya Nelson
2004: Lorrie Moore
2005: Ann Beattie
2006: John Updike
2007: Stuart Dybek
2008: Amy Hempel
2009: Mary Robison

## Story Prize

Established in 2004, the Story Prize award honors the author of an outstanding collection of short fiction that is written in English and initially published in the United States.

2004: Edwidge Danticat--*The Dew Breaker*
2005: Patrick O'Keefe--*The Hill Road*
2006: Mary Gordon--*The Stories of Mary Gordon*

2007: Jim Shepard--*Like You'd Understand, Anyway*
2008: Tobias Wolff--*Our Story Begins*
2009: Daniyal Mueenuddin--*In Other Rooms, Other Wonders*

## American Literary Awards

The American Academy of Arts and Letters Award of Merit is presented annually, in rotation, to an outstanding writer in one of the following arts: the short story, the novel, poetry, drama, painting, and drama. This list includes all of the short-story winners.

1983: Elizabeth Spencer
1989: Doris Betts
1995: Larry Woiwode

2001: Frederick Busch
2007: Charles Baxter

## National Book Award

Awarded annually since 1950 to books by U.S. citizens "that have contributed most significantly to human awareness, to the vitality of our national culture and to the spirit of excellence." This listing includes only authors who have won this award for works of short fiction.

1951: William Faulkner--*Collected Stories*
1959: Bernard Malamud--*The Magic Barrel*
1960: Philip Roth--*Goodbye, Columbus, and Five Short Stories*
1966: Katherine Anne Porter--*The Collected Stories of Katherine Anne Porter*

1972: Flannery O'Connor--*Flannery O'Connor: The Complete Stories*
1984: Ellen Gilchrist--*Victory over Japan: A Book of Stories*
1996: Andrea Barrett--*Ship Fever, and Other Stories*

## PEN/Faulkner Award for Fiction

Awarded annually since 1981 to the most distinguished work of fiction by an American writer. This listing includes only authors who have won this award for works of short fiction.

1986: Peter Taylor--*The Old Forest, and Other Stories*
1989: James Salter--*Dusk, and Other Stories*
1997: Gina Berriault--*Women in Their Beds: New and Selected Stories*

2004: John Updike--*The Early Stories, 1953-1975*
2010: Sherman Alexie--*War Dances*

## Pulitzer Prize in Letters

Awarded annually since 1917, this award was given for novels only until 1948, but is now given for any work of fiction. This listing includes only authors who have received this award for works of short fiction.

1966: Katherine Ann Porter--*The Collected Stories of Katherine Ann Porter*
1970: Jean Stafford--*The Collected Stories of Jean Stafford*
1978: James Alan McPherson--*Elbow Room*

1979: John Cheever--*The Stories of John Cheever*
1993: Robert Olen Butler--*A Good Scent from a Strange Mountain: Stories*
2000: Jhumpa Lahiri--*Interpreter of Maladies: Stories*

## International Awards

Named in honor of Irish writer Frank O'Connor, the Frank O'Connor International Short Story Award is presented annually for a collection of short stories. The award was inaugurated in 2005.

2005: Yiyun Li--*A Thousand Years of Good Prayers*--China/United States
2006: Haruki Murakami--*Blind Willow, Sleeping Woman*--Japan
2007: Miranda July--*No One Belongs Here More Than You*--United States

2008: Jhumpa Lahiri--*Unaccustomed Earth*--United States
2009: Simon Van Booy--*Love Begins in Winter*--England
2010: Ron Rash--*Burning Bright*--United States

## Franz Kafka Prize

This international prize honors writer Franz Kafka by presenting an award to a writer for lifetime achievement. First presented in 2001, the prize is cosponsored by the Franz Kafka Society and the city of Prague, Czech Republic. This listing cites only the prize-winning authors whose works include short fiction.

2001: Philip Roth--United States
2002: Ivan Klíma--Czech Republic
2003: Péter Nádas--Hungary

2006: Haruki Murakami--Japan
2008: Arnošt Lustig--Czech Republic
2009: Peter Handke--Austria

## Jerusalem Prize for the Freedom of the Individual in Society

The Jerusalem Prize is a biennial literary award presented to writers whose works have dealt with themes of human freedom in society. This listing cites only the prize-winning authors whose works include short fiction.

1965: Max Frisch--Switzerland
1969: Ignazio Silone--Italy
1971: Jorge Luis Borges--Argentina
1973: Eugene Ionesco--Romania/France
1975: Simone de Beauvoir--France
1981: Graham Green--England
1983: V. S. Naipaul--Trinidad and Tobago/England

1985: Milan Kundera--Czech Republic/France
1993: Stefan Heym--Germany
1995: Mario Vargas Llosa--Peru
1999: Don DeLillo--United States
2001: Susan Sontag--United States
2003: Arthur Miller--United States
2009: Haruki Murakami--Japan

## Man Booker International Prize

Established in 2005, this award is presented biennially to a living author of any nationality for fiction published in English or generally available in English translation. The first four winners have all written short fiction.

2005: Ismail Kadaré--Albania
2007: Chinua Achebe--Nigeria

2009: Alice Munro--Canada
2011: Philip Roth--United States

## Neustadt International Prize for Literature

Awarded biennially since 1970, this award, sponsored by the University of Oklahoma, honors writers for a body of work. This listing cites only the prize-winning authors whose works include short fiction.

1970: Giuseppe Ungaretti--Italy
1972: Gabriel García Márquez--Colombia
1976: Elizabeth Bishop--United States
1980: Josef Škvorecký--Czechoslovakia/Canada
1984: Paavo Haavikko--Finland
1986: Max Frisch--Switzerland

1988: Raja Rao--India/United States
1998: Nuruddin Farah--Somalia
2000: David Malouf--Australia
2002: Álvaro Mutis--Colombia
2006: Claribel Alegría--Nicaragua/El Salvador
2008: Patricia Grace--New Zealand

## Nobel Prize in Literature

Awarded annually since 1901, this award is generally regarded as the highest honor that can be bestowed upon an author for his or her total body of literary work. This listing of winners includes only authors whose works include short fiction.

1904: José Echegaray y Eizaguirre--Spain
1905: Henryk Sienkiewicz--Poland
1907: Rudyard Kipling--England
1909: Selma Lagerlöf--Sweden
1910: Paul Heyse--Germany
1912: Gerhart Hauptmann--Germany
1913: Rabindranath Tagore--India
1916: Verner von Heidenstam--Sweden
1917: Henrik Pontoppidan--Denmark
1920: Knut Hamsun--Norway
1921: Anatole France--France
1922: Jacinto Benavente--Spain
1923: William B. Yeats--Ireland
1924: Władysław Reymont--Poland
1925: George Bernard Shaw--Ireland
1926: Grazia Deledda--Italy
1928: Sigrid Undset--Norway
1929: Thomas Mann--Germany
1930: Sinclair Lewis--United States
1932: John Galsworthy--England
1933: Ivan Bunin--Russia

1934: Luigi Pirandello--Italy
1938: Pearl S. Buck--United States
1939: Frans Eemil Sillanpää--Finland
1944: Johannes V. Jensen--Denmark
1946: Hermann Hesse--Switzerland
1947: André Gide--France
1949: William Faulkner--United States
1951: Pär Lagerkvist--Sweden
1954: Ernest Hemingway--United States
1955: Halldór Laxness--Iceland
1957: Albert Camus--France
1958: Boris Pasternak (declined)--Russia
1961: Ivo Andrić--Yugoslavia
1962: John Steinbeck--United States
1964: Jean-Paul Sartre (declined)--France
1965: Mikhail Sholokhov--Russia
1966: Shmuel Yosef Agnon--Israel; Nelly
    Sachs--Sweden
1967: Miguel Angel Asturias--Guatemala
1968: Yasunari Kawabata--Japan
1969: Samuel Beckett--Ireland

1970: Aleksandr Solzhenitsyn--Russia

1972: Heinrich Böll--Germany

1973: Patrick White--Australia

1974: Eyvind Johnson--Sweden

1976: Saul Bellow--United States

1978: Isaac Bashevis Singer--United States

1982: Gabriel García Márquez--Colombia

1983: William Golding--England

1988: Naguib Mahfouz--Egypt

1989: Camilo José Cela--Spain

1991: Nadine Gordimer--South Africa

1994: Kenzaburō Ōe--Japan

1998: José Saramago--Portugal

2000: Gao Xingjian--China

2001: V. S. Naipaul--Trinidad and Tobago/England

2007: Doris Lessing--England

2008: J. M. G. Le Clézio--France/Mauritias

2009: Herta Müller--Germany

2010: Mario Vargas Llosa--Peru

# CHRONOLOGICAL LIST OF WRITERS

This chronology lists authors covered in this subset in order of their dates of birth. This arrangement serves as a supplemental time line for those interested in the development of short fiction over time.

## Born up to 1850

Franklin, Benjamin (January 17, 1706)
Irving, Washington (April 3, 1783)
Longstreet, Augustus Baldwin (September 22, 1790)
Hawthorne, Nathaniel (July 4, 1804)
Simms, William Gilmore (April 17, 1806)
Poe, Edgar Allan (January 19, 1809)
Melville, Herman (August 1, 1819)
Stockton, Frank R. (April 5, 1834)
Twain, Mark (November 30, 1835)
Harte, Bret (August 25, 1836)
Aldrich, Thomas Bailey (November 11, 1836)
Howells, William Dean (March 1, 1837)
Bierce, Ambrose (June 24, 1842)
James, Henry (April 15, 1843)
Cable, George Washington (October 12, 1844)
Harris, Joel Chandler (December 9, 1848)
Jewett, Sarah Orne (September 3, 1849)

## Born 1851-1880

Chopin, Kate (February 8, 1851)
Freeman, Mary E. Wilkins (October 31, 1852)
Chesnutt, Charles Waddell (June 20, 1858)
Gilman, Charlotte Perkins (July 3, 1860)
Garland, Hamlin (September 14, 1860)
Wharton, Edith (January 24, 1862)
Henry, O. (September 11, 1862)
Norris, Frank (March 5, 1870)
Dreiser, Theodore (August 27, 1871)
Crane, Stephen (November 1, 1871)
Dunbar, Paul Laurence (June 27, 1872)
Glasgow, Ellen (April 22, 1873)
Cather, Willa (December 7, 1873)
Stein, Gertrude (February 3, 1874)
London, Jack (January 12, 1876)
Anderson, Sherwood (September 13, 1876)

## Born 1881-1890

Roberts, Elizabeth Madox (October 30, 1881)
Williams, William Carlos (September 17, 1883)
Lardner, Ring (March 6, 1885)
Steele, Wilbur Daniel (March 17, 1886)
Chandler, Raymond (July 23, 1888)
Aiken, Conrad (August 5, 1889)
Porter, Katherine Anne (May 15, 1890)
Lovecraft, H. P. (August 20, 1890)

## Born 1891-1900

Hurston, Zora Neale (January 7, 1891)
Buck, Pearl S. (June 26, 1892)
Cain, James M. (July 1, 1892)
Parker, Dorothy (August 22, 1893)
Hammett, Dashiell (May 27, 1894)
Thurber, James (December 8, 1894)
Toomer, Jean (December 26, 1894)
Gordon, Caroline (October 6, 1895)
Fitzgerald, F. Scott (September 24, 1896)
Faulkner, William (September 25, 1897)
Benét, Stephen Vincent (July 22, 1898)
Nabokov, Vladimir (April 23, 1899)
White, E. B. (July 11, 1899)
Hemingway, Ernest (July 21, 1899)
Wolfe, Thomas (October 3, 1900)

## Born 1901-1905

Wescott, Glenway (April 11, 1901)
Hughes, Langston (February 1, 1902)
Boyle, Kay (February 19, 1902)
Steinbeck, John (February 27, 1902)
West, Jessamyn (July 18, 1902)
Bontemps, Arna (October 13, 1902)
Cozzens, James Gould (August 19, 1903)

Caldwell, Erskine (December 17, 1903)
Perelman, S. J. (February 1, 1904)
Farrell, James T. (February 27, 1904)
Lee, Manfred B. (January 11, 1905)
O'Hara, John (January 31, 1905)
Warren, Robert Penn (April 24, 1905)
Dannay, Frederic (October 20, 1905)

## Born 1906-1910
Still, James (July 16, 1906)
Carr, John Dickson (November 30, 1906)
Heinlein, Robert A. (July 7, 1907)
Stuart, Jesse (August 8, 1907)
Hale, Nancy (May 6, 1908)
Saroyan, William (August 31, 1908)
Wright, Richard (September 4, 1908)
Petry, Ann (October 12, 1908)
Stegner, Wallace (February 18, 1909)
Derleth, August (February 24, 1909)
Algren, Nelson (March 28, 1909)
Welty, Eudora (April 13, 1909)
Himes, Chester (July 29, 1909)
Clark, Walter Van Tilburg (August 3, 1909)
Agee, James (November 27, 1909)
Morris, Wright (January 6, 1910)
Doerr, Harriet (April 8, 1910)
Bowles, Paul (December 30, 1910)

## Born 1911-1915
Williams, Tennessee (March 26, 1911)
Calisher, Hortense (December 20, 1911)
Olsen, Tillie (January 14, 1912)
Cheever, John (May 27, 1912)
McCarthy, Mary (June 21, 1912)
Shaw, Irwin (February 27, 1913)
Weidman, Jerome (April 4, 1913)
Schwartz, Delmore (December 8, 1913)
Ellison, Ralph (March 1, 1914)
Malamud, Bernard (April 26, 1914)
Purdy, James (July 17, 1914)
Hall, Lawrence Sargent (April 23, 1915)
Goyen, William (April 24, 1915)
Bellow, Saul (June 10, 1915)
Stafford, Jean (July 1, 1915)

## Born 1916-1920
Jackson, Shirley (December 14, 1916)
Taylor, Peter (January 8, 1917)
McCullers, Carson (February 19, 1917)
Bowles, Jane (February 22, 1917)
Powers, J. F. (July 8, 1917)
Auchincloss, Louis (September 27, 1917)
Sturgeon, Theodore (February 26, 1918)
Elliott, George P. (June 16, 1918)
Salinger, J. D. (January 1, 1919)
Cassill, R. V. (May 17, 1919)
Asimov, Isaac (January 2, 1920)
Bradbury, Ray (August 22, 1920)

## Born 1921-1925
Highsmith, Patricia (January 19, 1921)
Douglas, Ellen (July 12, 1921)
Spencer, Elizabeth (July 19, 1921)
Vonnegut, Kurt (November 11, 1922)
Paley, Grace (December 11, 1922)
Fox, Paula (April 22, 1923)
Hall, Martha Lacy (August 19, 1923)
Gold, Herbert (March 9, 1924)
Humphrey, William (June 18, 1924)
Gass, William H. (July 30, 1924)
Baldwin, James (August 2, 1924)
Connell, Evan S. (August 17, 1924)
Capote, Truman (September 30, 1924)
O'Connor, Flannery (March 25, 1925)
Salter, James (June 10, 1925)

## Born 1926-1930
Berriault, Gina (January 1, 1926)
Adams, Alice (August 14, 1926)
Knowles, John (September 16, 1926)
Davenport, Guy (November 23, 1927)
Stern, Richard G. (February 25, 1928)
Angelou, Maya (April 4, 1928)
Ozick, Cynthia (April 17, 1928)
Dick, Philip K. (December 16, 1928)
Marshall, Paule (April 9, 1929)
Garrett, George (June 11, 1929)
Grau, Shirley Ann (July 8, 1929)
Le Guin, Ursula K. (October 21, 1929)

Hoch, Edward D. (February 22, 1930)
Friedman, Bruce Jay (April 26, 1930)
Elkin, Stanley (May 11, 1930)
Barth, John (May 27, 1930)
Brodkey, Harold (October 25, 1930)

## Born 1930-1935

Doctorow, E. L. (January 6, 1931)
Barthelme, Donald (April 7, 1931)
Coover, Robert (February 4, 1932)
Updike, John (March 18, 1932)
Betts, Doris (June 4, 1932)
Greenberg, Joanne (September 24, 1932)
Plath, Sylvia (October 27, 1932)
Targan, Barry (November 30, 1932)
Michaels, Leonard (January 2, 1933)
Gaines, Ernest J. (January 15, 1933)
Sontag, Susan (January 16, 1933)
Price, Reynolds (February 1, 1933)
Roth, Philip (March 19, 1933)
Gardner, John (July 21, 1933)
Ellison, Harlan (May 27, 1934)
Berry, Wendell (August 5, 1934)
Baraka, Amiri (October 7, 1934)
Vizenor, Gerald (October 22, 1934)
L'Heureux, John (October 26, 1934)
Brautigan, Richard (January 30, 1935)
Gilchrist, Ellen (February 20, 1935)
Proulx, E. Annie (August 22, 1935)
Allen, Woody (December 1, 1935)
Rivera, Tomás (December 22, 1935)

## Born 1936-1940

Conroy, Frank (January 15, 1936)
Chappell, Fred (May 28, 1936)
Dixon, Stephen (June 6, 1936)
Pearlman, Edith (June 26, 1936)
Dubus, Andre (August 11, 1936)
Burke, James Lee (December 5, 1936)
Major, Clarence (December 31, 1936)
Pynchon, Thomas (May 8, 1937)
Godwin, Gail (June 18, 1937)
Norman, Gurney (July 22, 1937)
Stone, Robert (August 21, 1937)

Harrison, Jim (December 11, 1937)
Carver, Raymond (May 25, 1938)
Oates, Joyce Carol (June 16, 1938)
Schwartz, Lynne Sharon (March 19, 1939)
Bambara, Toni Cade (March 25, 1939)
McGuane, Thomas( December 11, 1939)
Disch, Thomas M. (February 2, 1940)
Banks, Russell (March 28, 1940)
Mason, Bobbie Ann (May 1, 1940)
Kingston, Maxine Hong (October 27, 1940)
Cherry, Kelly (December 21, 1940)

## Born 1941-1945

Wideman, John Edgar (June 14, 1941)
Busch, Frederick (August 1, 1941)
Apple, Max (October 22, 1941)
Tyler, Anne (October 25, 1941)
Woiwode, Larry (October 30, 1941)
Delany, Samuel R. (April 1, 1942)
Dybek, Stuart (April 10, 1942)
Hannah, Barry (April 23, 1942)
Keillor, Garrison (August 7, 1942)
Gay, William (1943)
Ducornet, Rikki (April 19, 1943)
Millhauser, Steven (August 3, 1943)
McPherson, James Alan (September 16, 1943)
Barthelme, Frederick (October 10, 1943)
Shepard, Sam (November 5, 1943)
Miller, Sue (November 29, 1943)
Walker, Alice (February 9, 1944)
Williams, Joy (February 11, 1944)
Ford, Richard (February 16, 1944)
Smith, Lee (November 1, 1944)
Lopez, Barry (January 6, 1945)
Butler, Robert Olen (January 20, 1945)
Jones, Thom (January 26, 1945)
Dorris, Michael (January 30, 1945)
Bausch, Richard (April 18, 1945)
Wolff, Tobias (June 19, 1945)
Eisenberg, Deborah (November 20, 1945)

## Born 1946-1950

Kaplan, David Michael (April 9, 1946)
Tilghman, Christopher (September 5, 1946)

O'Brien, Tim (October 1, 1946)
Robinson, Roxana (November 30, 1946)
Davis, Lydia (1947)
Gates, David (January 8, 1947)
Prose, Francine (April 1, 1947)
Baxter, Charles (May 13, 1947)
Gurganus, Allan (June 11, 1947)
Helprin, Mark (June 28, 1947)
Beattie, Ann (September 8, 1947)
Carlson, Ron (September 15, 1947)
King, Stephen (September 21, 1947)
Abbott, Lee K. (October 17, 1947)
Gautreaux, Tim (October 19, 1947)
Wiggins, Marianne (November 8, 1947)
Hansen, Ron (December 8, 1947)
Silko, Leslie Marmon (March 5, 1948)
Johnson, Charles (April 23, 1948)
Lordan, Beth (December 1, 1948)
Boyle, T. Coraghessan (December 2, 1948)
Robison, Mary (January 14, 1949)
Allison, Dorothy (April 11, 1949)
Kincaid, Jamaica (May 25, 1949)
Johnson, Denis (July 1, 1949)
Russo, Richard (July 15, 1949)
Smiley, Jane (September 26, 1949)
Gordon, Mary (December 8, 1949)
Thompson, Jean (January 3, 1950)
Braverman, Kate (February 5, 1950)
Leegant, Joan (May 1, 1950)
Sayles, John (September 28, 1950)
Jones, Edward P. (October 5, 1950)

## Born 1951-1955

Harjo, Joy (May 9, 1951)
Brown, Larry (July 9, 1951)
Card, Orson Scott (August 24, 1951)
Shacochis, Bob (September 9, 1951)
Hempel, Amy (December 14, 1951)
Mosley, Walter (January 12, 1952)
Tan, Amy (February 19, 1952)
Ortiz Cofer, Judith (February 24, 1952)
Powell, Padgett (April 25, 1952)
Pancake, Breece D'J (June 29, 1952)
Phillips, Jayne Anne (July 19, 1952)

Crone, Moira (August 10, 1952)
Lee, Andrea (January 1, 1953)
Bloom, Amy (June 18, 1953)
Rash, Ron (September 25, 1953)
Boswell, Robert (December 8, 1953)
Nugent, Beth (1954)
Viramontes, Helena María (February 26, 1954)
Erdrich, Louise (June 7, 1954)
Tallent, Elizabeth (August 8, 1954)
Gaitskill, Mary (November 11, 1954)
Cisneros, Sandra (December 20, 1954)
Pollock, Donald Ray (December 23, 1954)
Brady, Catherine (January 1, 1955)
Grisham, John (February 8, 1955)
Kingsolver, Barbara (April 8, 1955)
Barrett, Andrea (July 17, 1955)
Richard, Mark (November 9, 1955)

## Born 1956-1960

Strout, Elizabeth (January 6, 1956)
McKnight, Reginald (February 26, 1956)
Divakaruni, Chitra Banerjee (July 29, 1956)
Minot, Susan (December 7, 1956)
Everett, Percival (December 22, 1956)
Moore, Lorrie (January 13, 1957)
Simpson, Helen (March 2, 1957)
Simpson, Mona (June 14, 1957)
Bell, Madison Smartt (August 1, 1957)
D'Ambrosio, Charles (1958)
Bass, Rick (March 7, 1958)
McCorkle, Jill (July 7, 1958)
Offutt, Chris (August 24, 1958)
Lott, Bret (October 8, 1958)
Saunders, George (December 2, 1958)
Slavin, Julia (1960)
Silver, Marisa (April 23, 1960)
Canin, Ethan (July 19, 1960)
Alyson (August 1, 1960)
Bank, Melissa (October 11, 1960)
Straight, Susan (October 19, 1960)

## Born 1961-1965

Means, David (1961)
Nelson, Antonya (January 6, 1961)

Earley, Tony (June 15, 1961)
Leavitt, David (June 23, 1961)
Walbert, Kate (August 13, 1961)
Moody, Rick (October 18, 1961)
Homes, A. M. (December 18, 1961)
Paine, Tom (c. 1962)
Houston, Pam (1962)
Wallace, David Foster (February 21, 1962)
Chabon, Michael (May 24, 1963)
Lethem, Jonathan (February 19, 1964)
Benedict, Pinckney (April 12, 1964)
Chaon, Dan (June 11, 1964)
Chang, Lan Samantha (1965)
Waters, Mary Yukari (January 1, 1965)
Banner, Keith (April 18, 1965)

**Born 1966-1970**

Reid, Elwood (1966)
Evenson, Brian (August 12, 1966)
Davies, Peter Ho (August 30, 1966)
Broyard, Bliss (September 5, 1966)
Alexie, Sherman (October 7, 1966)
Almond, Steve (October 27, 1966)
Lahiri, Jhumpa (July 11, 1967)
Johnson, Adam (July 12, 1967)

Peck, Dale (July 13, 1967)
Díaz, Junot (December 31, 1968)
Perabo, Susan (January 6, 1969)
Danticat, Edwidge (January 19, 1969)
Brown, Jason (May 30, 1969)
Bender, Aimee (June 28, 1969)
Englander, Nathan (1970)
Lennon, J. Robert (January 1, 1970)
Haslett, Adam (December 24, 1970)

**Born 1971 and Later**

Byers, Michael (1971)
Johnston, Bret Anthony (December 23, 1971)
Meloy, Maile (January 1, 1972)
Bynum, Sarah Shun-Lien (February 14, 1972)
Li, Yiyun (November 4, 1972)
Brockmeier, Kevin (December 6, 1972)
Packer, ZZ (January 12, 1973)
Tower, Wells (April 14, 1973)
Orringer, Julie (June 12, 1973)
Doerr, Anthony (October 27, 1973)
Freudenberger, Nell (April 21, 1975)
Henríquez, Cristina (1978)
Yoon, Paul (1980)

# INDEX

# CATEGORICAL INDEX

## REGIONAL STORIES

## RELIGIOUS STORIES

# SUBJECT INDEX

*All personages whose names appear in* **boldface** *type in this index are the subjects of articles in* Critical Survey of Short Fiction, Fourth Revised Edition.